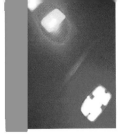

# map pages

KT-474-784

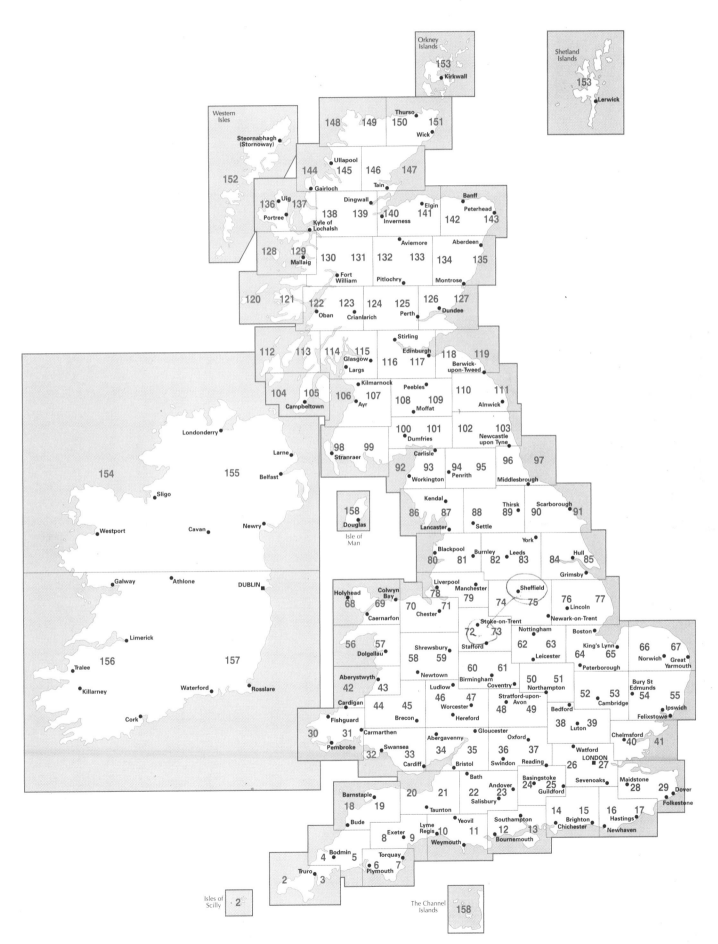

# Road Atlas of the
# British Isles
# 1999

# Helping Members ...that's the job of the AA

TO OUR MEMBERS WE'RE THE 4TH EMERGENCY SERVICE

**AA**

## TO JOIN CALL
## 0800 444 999 Ext 5725

# contents

**9th edition August 1998**
8th edition August 1997
7th edition September 1996
6th edition September 1995
5th edition September 1994
4th edition September 1993
Reprinted October 1993
3rd edition October 1992
Reprinted October 1992
2nd edition September 1987
Reprinted October 1991
1st edition September 1990

© The Automobile Association 1998

Published by AA Publishing (a trading name of Automobile Association Developments Limited, whose registered office is Norfolk House, Priestley Road, Basingstoke, Hampshire RG24 9NY. Registered number 1878835).

Mapping produced by the Cartographic Department of The Automobile Association. This atlas has been compiled and produced from the Automaps database utilising electronic and computer technology.

ISBN 0 7495 1866 9

A CIP catalogue record for this book is available from The British Library.

Printed in Italy by Pizzi, Milan

The contents of this atlas are believed to be correct at the time of the latest revision. However, the publishers cannot be held responsible for loss occasioned to any person acting or refraining from action as a result of any material in this atlas, nor for any errors, omissions or changes in such material. The publishers would welcome information to correct any errors or omissions and to keep this atlas up to date. Please write to the Cartographic Editor, Publishing Division, The Automobile Association, Fanum House, Basing View, Basingstoke, Hampshire RG21 4EA.

Information on National Parks provided by the Countryside Commission for England and the Countryside Council for Wales.

Information on National Scenic Areas in Scotland provided by Scottish Natural Heritage.

Information on Forest Parks provided by the Forestry Commission.

The RSPB sites shown are a selection chosen by the Royal Society for the Protection of Birds.

National Trust properties shown are a selection of those open to the public as indicated in the handbooks of the National Trust and the National Trust for Scotland.

# THE TOURIST'S BRITISH ISLES
## · SYMBOLS ·

*Rochester Castle, in Kent, is a fine example of Norman military architecture.*

WHETHER you are looking to spend an afternoon with the family or want to plan a holiday, knowing exactly where to go and what you can see when you get there can often be a problem. The following pages have been designed to give you an idea of what is on offer wherever you happen to be visiting.

Your needs could be as simple as locating a suitable place to enjoy a picnic, where to launch your boat for a day's sailing or where you can find further information about the area.

Whatever your requirement, some 50 symbols, highlighting over 8,000 features of interest, give you a chance to choose what interests you.

Pages 6 to 48 give a taste of what can be seen and where to find it.

Each place located on the atlas by the use of red symbols, has been chosen because it is open and has reasonable access for the public. Although some places may not be

open to the public, they have been included simply because they are an interesting feature or landmark, waterfall, windmill etc.

The AA is constantly checking and updating these entries in its atlases and other publications to ensure accurate, up-to-date information is given. All the attractions featured in *Days Out in Britain*, published annually by the AA, are highlighted in this atlas by the red symbols. The atlas, however, includes even more places and the information on locations such as country parks, nature reserves, nature trails, RSPB sites and Forest Parks, is supplied by the numerous authorities and national bodies such as the Countryside Commission, the Forestry Commission and many others.

There is a wide range of interests to choose from.

For cultural tastes, museums, art galleries, historic houses, castles, abbeys and cathedrals are featured. A stately home like Stourhead, in Wiltshire, may be more famous for its garden than its house and will therefore be depicted by the red

garden symbol. Others, like Chatsworth in Derbyshire, which are better known for the architectural splendour of the house, even though they are also renowned for their garden features, will be indicated by the red house symbol. Larger, specific garden features, classified as arboreta, are depicted accordingly. Major sporting venues such as athletics stadiums, county cricket grounds and horse racing courses are located by appropriate symbols. It is not possible to indicate league football grounds because of their large numbers and the limitations of the map scale. However, some are shown on the town plans at the back of the atlas where appropriate.

For those who like to participate rather than spectate, outdoor and leisure-type facilities, such as ski slopes, golf courses and coastal launching sites for boats are located.

If you have a particular interest in Ancient Britain, you can choose from the various hill-forts, Roman antiquities and prehistoric monuments which are found throughout the country. Even battle

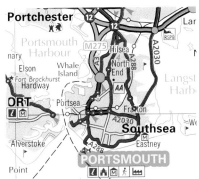

*The places behind Portsmouth's tourist symbols. Left Tourist Information at The Hard. Below left Industrial Interest with restored steam pumping engines at Eastney. Below right The Cathedral. Right HMS Warrior, just one of the city's many Museums.*

sites, where the course of history has often been changed, are shown. Some of these have interpretative centres which help you to relive and understand the events that occurred there.

Animal lovers can visit the major wildlife collections (both mammals and birds), zoos, and aquariums, or see nature in the wild at one of the numerous nature reserves, Forest Parks and RSPB sites. Another option is to follow one of the nature trails through the countryside. The more adventurous can attempt part or all of one of the national trails which traverse some of Britain's most spectacular scenic areas.

Industrial interest covers a wide spectrum from heritage centres and museums to mills, mines and slate caverns. Old railways, many of which served these industries in the past, now delight the public with a taste of the golden days of steam.

Family days out are catered for by the theme parks. The AA has selected eight of these for inclusion on the basis that they provide multi-purpose entertainment and leisure facilities

and have numerous fairground attractions that are unnervingly described as 'white knuckle' rides. Along with the country parks, they make ideal places to spend the whole day rather than just a quick visit.

Picnic sites are selected and inspected by the AA on a regular basis and are easily accessible, being sited on or by A and B roads. Viewpoints are shown if they offer vistas of at least 180 degrees, and many have panoramic 360 degree views.

Other places of interest which are worth visiting but do not fall easily into the categories symbolised are indicated by a small red star alongside their name. There is a great variety of these – waterfalls, water mills, visitor centres and market crosses, among others.

New additions for the 1990s include the National Parks of England and Wales and the National Scenic Areas of Scotland, along with 930 miles of Heritage Coasts along the shores of England and Wales.

When the red symbols are boxed, this indicates the attractions are in

urban areas. Some of these places may seem bare compared to the surrounding countryside. However, it may be that one symbol for a museum covers several museums in the town, but it is not practical to include them all because of space limitations.

Ireland is included in this special tourist section, and places of interest are located in the atlas, but the scale of mapping does not allow a large selection. Nevertheless, all the most important of Ireland's many tourist attractions are clearly marked.

Wherever possible, the red pictorial symbols used in the atlas are based on the Department of Transport's brown tourist signposts, so that the maps correspond with the road signs. In addition to all this information in the special tourist spreads, a month by month calendar on pages 46 and 47 tells you which customs and events occur throughout the year. This can assist you in deciding when to go. Page 48 describes the services offered by Britain's Tourist Information Centres to help you get the most out of your visits

Abbey, cathedral
or priory

Ruined abbey,
cathedral or
priory

Top *Tintern Abbey: majestic roofless ruin beside the River Wye in Gwent.* Above *St David's Cathedral, Dyfed, where the bones of St David lie.*

## Abbeys
## Cathedrals
## Priories

Augustinian, Benedictine, Cistercian and Dominican – the monastic orders which preserved ideals and scholarship after the fall of Rome have left a rich heritage in stone across Britain. Each imposing ruin or active place of worship tells its own story. All evoke a sense of wonder at the faith and industry of the medieval builders and monks. Which of any of them is the loveliest, however, will for ever be a matter of personal preference.

Burnt down in 1174, four years after Becket's murder, the choir of **Canterbury Cathedral** was rebuilt in a manner worthy of the martyr and appears today much as it was in the early 16th century. The 'Altar of the Sword's Point' and a modern cruciform sculpture, dedicated in

1986, mark the site of Becket's martyrdom. The long vistas back to the nave, at a lower level than the choir aisles, show the evolution of Gothic style over three centuries.

The west front of **York**, the largest Gothic church north of the Alps, presents an almost 13th-century 'French' outline, with its glorious façades. The Minster contains the largest single collection of medieval stained glass in England – the West Window painted in 1339 by Master Robert and the East Window, the work of John Thornton of Coventry, between 1405 and 1408. The Pilgrim Window dates from about 1312 and the Bellfounders' Window was given by Richard Tunnoc, buried in the Minster in 1330.

A fire, started by lightning on 9 July 1984, destroyed much of the south transept. Craftsmen, incorporating 20th-century improvements for future safety, restored the medieval beauty of the transept, reopened by the Queen in October 1988.

Embodiment of the spirit of the nation, **Westminster**, the Norman abbey of Edward the Confessor, took on its Gothic appearance after its rebuilding by Henry III. Fortunately, when the 600-year-old Benedictine community was disbanded, the buildings were spared. The Lady Chapel houses the Confessor's shrine, ringed by the tombs of five kings and three queens. In the centre is the Coronation Chair and below the oaken seat the Stone of Scone.

In the Sanctuary beyond the choir every monarch since the Conqueror has been crowned, with the exception of Edward V and Edward VIII. Early Parliaments met in the Chapter House, and the Henry VII Chapel has a superb fan-vaulted roof – the most glorious, some would say, in the country. Near the West Door lies the 'Unknown Warrior', brought back from France after World War I to sleep among the nation's great.

On its rocky promontory dominating the city and a loop in the River Wear, the Norman architecture of **Durham Cathedral** gives an impression, inside as well as out, of overwhelming power. Huge, deeply grooved columns alternating with massive piers support gallery, clerestory and beautiful vault. The Early English Chapel of the Nine Altars is a 13th-century addition, its tall lancet windows paralleled only in the now ruined Fountains Abbey. In the Treasury are evocative relics of the 7th-century St Cuthbert, including his tiny portable altar, his delicate gold pectoral cross and the remains

of his original carved oak coffin.

One of the most delicate of England's cathedrals must be **Salisbury**, built in the 40 years following 1220 of local silver-grey limestone with pointed arches and soaring windows. The spire, at 404 feet (123m), is the tallest in the country. It is such inspired work that it blends perfectly with the rest, though crossing piers of clustered black marble had to be reinforced in the 15th century to support the added 6,500 tons of the spire.

**Wells** is the first cathedral church in the Early English style. Its west front is still, despite Puritan vandalism, one of England's richest displays of 13th-century sculpture. Inside, the most striking feature is the inverted arches, built from 1338 to 1348 to combat subsidence of the tower.

The Norman crypt and transepts of **Winchester Cathedral** survive, the rest being 13th and 14th century. At 556 feet (169m) it is the longest Gothic church in Europe. Saved from demolition in 1652 by a petition of the citizens, it was again saved at the beginning of this century by a diver, William Walker. Working alone, from 1906 to 1912, in pitch dark waters of the marshy foundations, he replaced the rotting 13th-century beech tree raft (on which the cathedral had originally been built) with cement.

Near York are three jewels – Beverley, Selby and Ripon. **Beverley Minster** houses the Percy Tomb, the most splendid of British Decorated funerary monuments. It shares, with St Mary's Church nearby, wonderful misericords and the largest collection of carvings of medieval musical instruments anywhere in the world.

Benedictine **Selby Abbey**, founded in 1069, predates Durham. The west front ranges in style from strength and simplicity to later elegance. The easternmost arches of the nave have distorted spectacularly, due to a high water table. High up above the south side of the choir is a 14th-century window with the arms of the Washington family – the 'Stars and Stripes' motif of the American flag.

**Ripon Cathedral** is built over the tiny 11 by 8 ft (3.4 x 2.4m) Saxon crypt of St Wilfrid's Church, one of the few Saxon structures left in England. The cathedral has a beautiful Early English west front. One woodcarver, working from 1939 to 1945, replaced all the 'idolatrous images' on the choir screen, destroyed by Puritans in 1643.

There are modern cathedrals, too. The new **Coventry Cathedral** appears to grow out of the old St Michael's and the overwhelming impression is of height, light and colour. South-facing angled windows enable sunlight to flood the nave with colour. Dominating the whole cathedral is the huge tapestry designed by Graham Sutherland, *Christ in Glory.*

Liverpool's **Anglican Cathedral** is, in the words of Sir John Betjeman, 'vastness, strength and height no words can describe'. Sir Giles Gilbert Scott designed Britain's largest cathedral in medieval style but on a scale which no medieval builder would have attempted. His memorial is set in the floor of the central space under the tower. He, a Catholic, is buried just outside the West Door.

The **Metropolitan Cathedral of Christ the King** in Liverpool, often irreverently called 'Paddy's Wigwam', stands above the huge crypt of the cathedral which Sir Edwin Lutyens started before the war. Inside the 194ft (59m) circular nave, completed by Sir Frederick Gibberd, every member of the 2,300 congregation has an uninterrupted view of the white marble high altar.

A cathedral conveys 'city status' on a town, however small. Pass through the gatehouse at **St David's,** Dyfed, and the lichen-encrusted purple stone of Wales's greatest church is dramatically revealed. It was restored in Decorated Gothic style after an earthquake in 1248 and the whole building slopes upwards some 14 feet (4m) from west to east – an unnerving first glimpse for the visitor entering at the western end

of the nave. The relics of St David rest in an oak and iron reliquary, hidden at the Reformation and discovered during restoration work in 1866.

**St Asaph Cathedral**, in Clwyd, is on the site of a monastic community founded in AD570. It houses the tomb of Bishop William Morgan, translator of the Bible into Welsh, and the 16th-century Bible itself, which was used at the Investiture of the Prince of Wales in 1969.

Henry VIII's Dissolution left a legacy of ruined religious centres across the country, many of which still survive today in all their shattered glory.

Perhaps one of the most magnificent monastic ruins is **Rievaulx Abbey**, two miles north-west of Helmsley. It was founded in 1131 and is the first Cistercian house in the north of England. The name, pronounced 'Reevo', comes from Rye Vallis or valley of the River Rye, above which it stands, surrounded by wooded hills. Its chief glory is its choir built *c.* 1225. The scale of the buildings gives an idea of the activities and work of the 600 and more monks and lay brothers who lived here in the 13th century.

The Cistercian community of **Fountains Abbey**, near Ripon, became the centre of an enormous enterprise, with fish-farms, forestry,

*Right The ancient kings of Northumbria lie buried near Tynemouth Priory.*
*Below Cistercian Fountains Abbey, now part of the Studley Royal estate.*

iron-workings and, above all, sheep, which funded its building. It was one of the first foundations to be sold by Henry VIII in 1540. In 1768 the Aislabie family bought it as a picturesque addition to their Studley Royal estate.

The condition of the Benedictine **Whitby Abbey** cannot wholly be blamed on King Henry. The gaunt ruins of the clifftop site, chosen by St Hilda in AD657, became the setting for Bram Stoker's *Dracula* and suffered further indignity when they were bombarded by German warships during World War I.

The 7th-century buildings at **Much Wenlock** were destroyed by the Danes and later refounded by Leofric, husband of Lady Godiva. Today's ruins are the remains of the church built in the 1220s by Prior Humbert, whose lodging is one of the finest examples of English domestic architecture from around the 1500s.

*Abbey, cathedral or priory*

*Ruined abbey, cathedral or priory*

Castle

## Castles

Maiden Castle to Balmoral, Mousa Broch to Dover – Britain is rich in castles dating from Bronze to Victorian ages. The very name 'castle', conjuring up visions of power, of menace and later of opulence, has often been affected by builders of lesser dwellings.

Castles begin with the hillforts of the Bronze Age and stone brochs of pre-Christian Scotland, primarily refuges for men and cattle in time of local warfare. The ruins of Norman timber-built motte and bailey castles – a stone keep on a mound, surrounded by a defensive wall – later converted by the Plantagenets to stone fortresses, still dominate many towns, river crossings and strategic points across the country.

These were not solely refuges, but administrative headquarters, stores and living quarters. Even in times of peace they would have been bustling centres of activity; in time of war, life must have been pretty chaotic, with garrisons, stores, cattle and weaponry increased and as many of the local population as

Below *Orford Castle, in Suffolk, has a remarkable 18-sided polygonal keep.* Inset *The Welsh border castle of Goodrich, in the Wye Valley.*

could be squeezed in taking refuge in the bailey. Castles were not designed for passive defence but for vigorous action. They were not safe refuges in which to avoid conflict, but ingeniously contrived to make the enemy fight at a disadvantage – they were meant to be costly to capture – both in time and in lives. Henry II (1154-1189), after the mayhem of Stephen's reign 'took every castle of England into his hands', destroyed about 500 unlicensed castles and founded a line of castle-building kings – Richard, John, Henry III, Edward I and III.

Visiting some of these castles, it needs only a little imagination to bring to life the history of their times. The castles of Edward I (1272-1307) around the coast of North Wales are symbols of the organising ability and engineering skills as well as reminders of the vast expense of castle building in the Middle Ages.

Norman and Plantagenet castles vary to suit the site on which they are built but the first criterion was always that of aggressive defence. Where possible a ditch or moat – dry or flooded – was dug to prevent besiegers tunnelling under the walls. Towers without sharp

corners were less likely to be undermined, and so became the fashion.

From about 1268, the date of **Caerphilly Castle** in Mid Glamorgan, the defenders of the outer curtain wall and its towers would be supported by covering fire from higher inner walls. A formidable array of outworks defends gateways and sluices, further protected by drawbridge and portcullis. Barbicans and towers ensured that attackers were subjected to murderous flanking crossfire before they got anywhere near anything so flammable as a wooden gate.

Caerphilly, at 30 acres the largest castle in Wales, surpassed only by **Dover** and **Windsor**, is sufficiently well preserved to give a vivid idea of the way these defensive ideas worked together. It has wide water defences, in imitation of those which Henry III had built at **Kenilworth** and which Simon de Montfort held so successfully against him. Edward I, on his return from the Crusades, liked what he saw at Caerphilly and began to turn the **Tower of London** into a concentric castle. He also introduced at **Caernarfon** and **Conwy** an idea from his campaigns in Gascony –

Castle

the 'bastide' – an extension of the bailey to enclose a small town in which traders, labourers and craftsmen could live under the protection of the castle.

Edward I's castle building in North Wales is well documented and throws fascinating light on the feudal power and organisation at the King's command. Ditch diggers were recruited from the Fens and marched across by mounted serjeants – to discourage deserters – to dig the canal around **Rhuddlan Castle.**

At **Conwy**, Edward's young Spanish queen, Eleanor, homesick for the courts and fountains of her native Castile, had a small garden and fishpond built in the castle's east barbican. In the hot summer of 1283 a labourer hauled water from the well, to 'water the Queen's new grass'. Here at Conwy it is believed that Eleanor introduced one of our favourite summer flowers – the sweet pea.

At **Caernarfon Castle** where his son, later Edward II, was born on 25 April 1284, Edward sought to bring Arthurian and Welsh legends to life and make the seat of his government in Wales a new imperial Constantinople. Octagonal towers are set in a single curtain wall, banded with red sandstone in imitation of those of the 5th-century Turkish capital. Defended passages within the thickness of the masonry and ingenious triple arrow slits allowed three bowmen a wide angle of fire through only one external opening.

The more settled times of the Tudor dynasty after the Wars of the Roses reduced the military significance of the castle. Gunpowder played no little part in this. Castles continued to be built, but design changed. Henry VIII began a series of symmetrically planned coastal 'artillery forts' from the Thames to Dorset in 1538. **Deal, Walmer** and **Sandgate** are three, but these were garrisoned rather than lived in – the garrisons complaining that 'they stank of gunpowder and dogs'. Comfort and elegance dictated the style of Elizabethan and Jacobean buildings, though many were still castellated and defensible.

The Civil War saw many castles used again as strongpoints. They stood up so well, even to improved 17th-century firepower, that the victorious Parliamentarians decreed that those which had been so vigorously defended should be 'slighted' – demolished so as to make them useless for military purposes. Some of these 'ruins Cromwell knocked about a bit', if not too badly damaged, became the

local prison and the Norman word for the keep – *donjon* – became the English dungeon.

In Scotland, Northumberland, Cumbria and the troubled lands of the Borders, there are over 1,100 'castles' of one sort or another, excluding the baronial houses of the last 200 years. Most are tower houses or 'peles', built in stone, for timber was always short in the region, and usually several storeys high. **Craigievar**, west of Aberdeen, is the masterpiece of this uniquely Scottish style. Seven storeys high with, even today, few windows in its pink granite walls, it must have been a formidable sight for any would-be attacker.

Many peles have been absorbed into later houses. **Traquair House** west of Galashiels, now more 'château' than castle, claims to be the oldest continuously inhabited house in Scotland. Buried within the north-east corner is a pele tower dating back to the reign of Alexander I (1107-24).

**Stirling Castle**, which looked down on Edward II's ignominious defeat at Bannockburn in 1314, was still an earthen and timber construction. The 'Gateway to the Highlands' was transformed under the Stuarts, first into a stone fortress, then into a splendid Renaissance royal palace.

Castles lived on in the romantic imaginations of later centuries. Sir Charles Cavendish, son of Bess of Hardwick, built his mansion at **Bolsover**, Derbyshire, in the 1620s with the turrets, crenellations and medieval fancies so popular with the Elizabethans. As tastes began to rebel against Classical symmetry and long for 'the good old days', mock medieval 'castles' were built

Above *Caernarfon Castle, Gwynedd, built by Edward I to subdue the Welsh.* Right *St Andrews' 13th-century castle overlooks the North Sea.*

and some genuine 14th-century castles, such as **Croft**, in Shropshire, were 'gothicised'.

William Burges built two for the Marquess of Bute, at **Cardiff** and **Castell Coch**, reconstructing the motte and bailey castle the Normans had built at Cardiff within a Roman fort into an extravaganza rivalling the creations of Ludwig of Bavaria – with a medieval tower suite complete with smoking room, Gothic chapel and banqueting hall. At Castell Coch, to the north of Cardiff, Burges transformed the ruins of a keep destroyed in the 15th century into a mock 13th-century retreat. Its conical roofs recall the illustrations in the Duc de Berry's 'Book of Hours' but the thick walls have arrow slits and 'murder holes' and a portcullis and drawbridge which function.

The last such conceit built in Britain was designed by Edwin Lutyens, who in 1901 had made a comfortable home for the publisher of *Country Life* magazine within the ramparts of **Lindisfarne**, off the Northumbrian coast. For 20 years, from 1910, **Castle Drogo**, Lutyen's composite Norman and Tudor 'castle' arose overlooking the River Teigne in Devon, home to the founder of the Home & Colonial Stores and is – to date, at any rate – Britain's 'last castle'.

Historic house

National Trust
properties

## Historic Houses

The Greek historian, Thucydides said 'Men, not walls, make a city'. The same holds true for a house and the human stories of the builders, owners or residents add interest to it, however humble, however grand. Membership of the National Trust and English Heritage – an outlay quickly recouped if you are going to visit even half a dozen properties in a season – will give you a wonderful selection from which to choose, rich in architecture and in treasures, but above all in personalities.

The name 'Mote' at **Ightham Mote** in Kent recalls the 'moot', the council which met here, in the Great Hall, dating from 1340. Three centuries of continuous ownership by the Selby family have left their mark, from Jacobean fireplaces through 17th-century wallpaper to Victorian bedrooms. All told there are 600 years of England's history to be discerned at Ightham.

*Ightham Mote, Kent, is one of the best examples of a medieval manor house.*

Built in 1340 by a Lord Mayor of London, the Great Hall at **Penshurst Place** in Kent is the finest to have survived. Birthplace of the Elizabethan courtier, soldier and poet, Sir Philip Sidney, the house remains in the same family today. Later ranges of building have left it light and airy. The Long Gallery marries house to garden and medieval to Renaissance, a fitting memorial to the man who personified all that was best in the Elizabethan age.

The Elizabethan house Bess of Hardwick built with Sir William Cavendish at **Chatsworth** in Derbyshire has been absorbed into the present house. Chatsworth is the home of the Cavendish family, the Dukes of Devonshire, the first of whom, in the early 1700s, transformed the house into a baroque palace, a second Versailles. Treasures are everywhere – in the Painted Hall, the State Rooms, Sculpture Gallery – works by famous artists, painters and sculptors abound. The Library has over 17,000 volumes, among them those of Henry Cavendish, the 18th-century discoverer of hydrogen. Capability Brown laid out much of the garden, but retained Grillet's 1696 Cascade, the sound of the water varying as it falls over steps of different height. Joseph Paxton, too, worked here, and his Great Conservatory was the forerunner of the Crystal Palace.

**Montacute** in Somerset is one of the least altered of late Elizabethan houses. Begun in the year of the Armada, it expresses the rise to power of an astute lawyer, Edward Phelips. He led the prosecution of Guy Fawkes and became Speaker of the House of Commons. The house, with its mullioned front and statues standing in their lofty niches, is the masterpiece of a local genius, William Arnold. No one, though, who has seen the charming Elizabethan pavilions can ever doubt the delicacy and humour of this Elizabethan mason who has so completely captured his master's wish to display his continuing good fortune.

After a spell in the Tower and a stiff fine, Sir John Thynne retired to his Wiltshire estate at **Longleat**, following his support of the disgraced Lord Protector to Edward VI. He began Longleat in about 1546, and today it is still home to the Thynne family, now the Marquesses of Bath. The Great Hall, with its 16th-century fireplace and hunting scenes, is the least altered part of the house. Sir John broke from the tradition of the Elizabethan 'E-shaped' house and built around two inner courts. The top floor of the house was the library and home of Thomas Ken, Bishop of Bath and Wells, who was given refuge

here when he fell foul of both James II and William and Mary. Lord Bath, an innovator like his ancestor, opened his house to the public in 1949 and in 1966 introduced the 600-acre safari park, a 'drive-through' reserve of giraffes, rhinoceroses, elephants, tigers – and the well-known 'lions of Longleat'.

Bess of Hardwick married four times, each time increasing her fortune. She married Sir William Cavendish when she was 27 and their second son inherited Chatsworth. She left her fourth husband, the Earl of Shrewsbury, for his alleged infatuation with his prisoner, Mary, Queen of Scots. Then, aged 70, she began to build **Hardwick Hall**. The accounts of the building reflect the imperiousness of the owner who, living a hundred yards away in her old hall, strode across to inspect and criticise every day. Her descendants preferred Chatsworth and Hardwick remained, frozen in time, one of the purest examples of 16th-century design and decor in the country, a memorial to the indomitable woman whose portrait stares down from the tapestried wall of the Long Gallery.

Robert Cecil, first Earl of Salisbury, builder of **Hatfield House**, Hertfordshire, was adviser to both Elizabeth I and James I. James suggested that Robert Cecil exchange the house his father, Lord Burghley, had built at Theobalds, for the palace at Hatfield – a 'suggestion' he could scarcely refuse. Between 1607 and 1611, Cecil built himself a vast new house nearby.

Great Halls and Long Galleries were by then going out of fashion, but Hatfield would have lost much had Cecil not been traditionalist enough to include them. His own quarters and the guest wing, however, have smaller rooms. Here conversation and gracious living could flourish. The style of the great house was changing. It was a later Cecil, Marquess of Salisbury, three times Prime Minister to Queen Victoria and amateur scientist, who installed electricity in 1881 and it is reported that 'the naked wires on the Gallery ceiling tended to burst into flame, being extinguished by members of the family who threw cushions a them before returning to their conversation'.

By the time **Petworth** was built, 70 years or so after Hatfield, Long Galleries and Great Halls had gone completely from the English building scene. The house passed by marriage from the Percys to the 'Proud Duke' of Somerset, who began building – using his wife's fortune – in 1688. The name and skill of Grinling Gibbons will always be associated with Petworth. His mastery of limewood carving is complete. The house also

*Historic house*

*National Trust
properties
Scotland*

boasts excellent tracery work by Jonathan Ritson, and the Marble Hall has wonderful carving by John Selden, the Duke's estate carpenter.

Just to the south of Wrexham lies **Erddig**. It was completed by a local mason in 1689 and owned by the Yorke family since 1733, who collected much and threw little away! Subsidence from coal mining almost destroyed the house and restoration began in 1973. The interest of the house is not in its architecture or its treasures, but in the relationship that a local family maintained with their servants. Portraits of master and servant hang in drawing room and servants' hall, many with little poems and descriptions. There are frequent group photographs of the whole staff, enabling us to follow some servants right through their careers. Erddig is one of the few houses to show the public the maids' bedrooms as well as the public rooms. Here, 200 years of the running of a self contained estate come vividly to life.

Soldier turned dramatist on his return to England in 1692, John Vanbrugh came to the notice of Charles Howard, 3rd Earl of Carlisle, perhaps through his popular and bawdy plays. Howard chose this enthusiastic amateur to build him a home fitted to the position of an Earl, and so Castle Howard came about. Vanbrugh was widely helped by one of Sir Christopher Wren's assistants, Nicholas Hawksmoor, who turned Vanbrugh's ideas into working drawings. Castle Howard impresses

but does not overawe, as does their later work at Blenheim. At the heart of the house is the Great Hall, rising 70 feet (21m) through two storeys into the painted dome. It is the most light-hearted but impressive concept of English architecture. Treasures and portraits abound, including one of a stricken Henry VIII, painted by Holbein just after the execution of Catherine Howard, and a portrait of her uncle, Thomas Howard, who escaped the block because the king died on the day of his execution.

The story of **Blenheim Palace** is full of powerful men and women. It was built for John Churchill, Duke of Marlborough. Queen Anne instigated the idea of the palace as a reward for Churchill's victory over the French and Bavarians at the battle of Blenheim. She later quarrelled with Sarah, Duchess of Marlborough, as did Vanbrugh, the architect. Sarah wanted a comfortable country house and Vanbrugh wanted something even greater than Castle Howard. Sir Winston Churchill, born here, became Prime Minister at a time when a man of Marlborough's character was again needed.

William Adam began to build **Mellerstain** in the Scottish borders for George Baillie in 1725 and his son, Robert, finished it in 1770. It is the interiors, by Robert, that are the main attraction, for William was never able to finish the exterior as planned and it lacks a noble central block. The colours Adam used in his decorations make the rooms particularly attractive.

Above *Vanbrugh's spectacular Castle Howard, in North Yorkshire.*
Right *The beautiful Georgian mansion of Mellerstain, in the Borders.*

### The National Trust

Many of the historic houses mentioned on these two pages are in the care of the National Trust of England, Wales and Northern Ireland and the National Trust for Scotland. Apart from maintaining many of Britain's finest buildings the Trust also owns gardens such as the renowned Hidcote Manor Garden near Chipping Campden, ruins such as **Fountains Abbey** in North Yorkshire, tracts of especially scenic shoreline, such as 110 miles of spectacular Cornish coast, follies, windmills, locks and even pubs, of which *The Fleece Inn* at Bretforton, on the edge of the Cotswolds, is a particularly attractive example. The letters 'NT' designate where the Trust owns property or land.

11

Museum or art
gallery

*Concorde 01 is on show at the Imperial
War Museum, Duxford, Cambridgeshire.*

## Museums
## Art Galleries

Among the prized possessions of
the British Museum in its early days
were a landscape painted on a
spider's web, a two-headed chicken,
Chinese shoes, figures of King
William III and Queen Mary carved
out of walnut shells and various
unpleasant-looking things preserved
in spirits and hidden in the
basement in case they might
frighten pregnant women. A far cry
from the British Museum of today
with its Elgin Marbles, Assyrian
winged bulls and the Sutton Hoo
treasure included in its fabulous
array of objects from every corner of
the globe.

The ancestors of today's museums
and art galleries were the collections
of classical sculptures and
antiquities formed during the
Renaissance period by rulers,
wealthy churchmen and merchant
princes like the Medicis of Florence.
They were inspired by the
devouring interest which had
sprung up in ancient Greece and
Rome. With interest also rapidly
developing in science, others
assembled natural history collections
and 'cabinets of curiosities', which
contained animal bones, weapons,
coins, shells, oddly shaped plants or
stones – anything that took the
collector's fancy.

In England the two John
Tradescants, father and son, who
were keen naturalists, plant-hunters
and gardeners to Charles I in the
17th century, formed a substantial
collection, or 'museum' as it was
called: one of its star pieces was a
stuffed dodo. The collection passed
to Elias Ashmole, the antiquary,
herald and pioneer Freemason, who
added to it and passed it on in turn
to Oxford University. Twelve wagon
loads of objects were conveyed to
Oxford, to form the nucleus of the
**Ashmolean Museum**, opened to the
public in 1683 and the oldest
museum in Britain.

The Ashmolean today glories in
its Egyptian mummy cases and
medieval jewellery, its Old Master
paintings and British art, but it still
honours Ashmole's memory and
items from the original Tradescant
collection can be seen, with other
curiosities such as Guy Fawkes's
lantern.

The **British Museum** opened its
doors in London to 'studious and
curious persons' in 1759, the word
'museum' now meaning the
building in which a collection was
kept rather than the collection itself.
It was established by Parliament and
funded by a state lottery to house
the collections of Robert Harley, Earl
of Oxford, and the books and
manuscripts assembled by Sir
Robert Cotton – which included the
Lindisfarne Gospels and two copies
of Magna Carta. Also included was
the astonishing collection of no less
than 79,575 objects put together by
Sir Hans Sloane. A successful
London doctor, Sloane's fanatical
zeal as a collector extended to
classical antiquities, coins, jewels,
fossils, plants, butterflies, zoological
specimens and oddities of every
kind. Those who came to feast their
eyes on these items consisted, as
the Trustees reported in 1784,
'chiefly of Mechanics and persons of
the lower Classes'.

Zeal to improve and educate
'persons of the lower classes' gained
strength in the 19th century,
especially in the heavily populated
towns created by the industrial
revolution, and prompted the
establishment of numerous
museums and art galleries. The
splendid **City Art Gallery** in
Manchester, for example was
opened in 1834 and is today noted
for its superb Victorian and Pre-
Raphaelite paintings. The
**Birmingham Museum and Art
Gallery** was founded in 1867 and
the building it now occupies was
opened in 1885. Approximately a
hundred museums opened in Britain
in the 1870s and '80s.

The Victorian boom in museums
and art galleries was also stimulated
by an ambition to promote scientific
and technological advance and to
improve standards of design. This
was why the **Victoria & Albert
Museum** in London was founded by
the Prince Consort in 1852,
originally as a 'museum of
manufactures', in the wake of the
Great Exhibition of the previous
year.

National and civic pride were also
a factor. The **National Gallery** in

London is now the country's premier collection of Western painting down to 1900 (developments since then are the preserve of the **Tate Gallery**). It was founded in 1824 to emulate the national art galleries already established in Vienna, Paris, Berlin and other European capitals. The government bought 38 paintings to start it off from the collection of a banker, Sir John Julius Angerstein: they included the Rubens *Rape of the Sabine Women*, two Rembrandts and Raphael's *Portrait of Julius II*.

Major museums and galleries generally have two functions and there is often a tension between them. The obvious function is to instruct and entertain the public. The other, carried on out of the public eye, is the advancement of scholarship. An example of this dual role is the **National Museum of Wales** in Cardiff, opened in 1927 (in a building which has leaked ever since). It was founded to inform both the Welsh and the rest of the world about Wales, which it does. However, its own staff and visiting academics also work behind the scenes on collections far too voluminous for public display – 230,000 pressed plant specimens, more than 300,000 fossils, serried multitudes of dead beetles.

The museum is also a good example of the fact that the functions of an institution of this kind today go far beyond the display of objects in showcases. Activities include lectures, the loan of items to schools, and guided family walks with experts from the staff discoursing learnedly along the way.

Museums like this take a wide range of subjects for their province. Others concentrate on specialised areas. There is a museum of Scottish tartans at **Comrie**, for example, of stained glass at **Ely**, of horse racing at **Newmarket**. Military museums concentrate on regiments: the **Durham Light Infantry** in Durham, the **Staffordshire Regiment** in Lichfield, the **Royal Green Jackets** at Winchester. Some museums concentrate on World War II, such as the **German Occupation Museum** in Guernsey. Portsmouth has an unrivalled battery of naval attractions, with the excellent **Royal Naval Museum**, Nelson's flagship HMS *Victory*, the Tudor warship *Mary Rose* and the **Submarine Museum** in Gosport among others.

There are museums which concentrate on a single famous person: **John Bunyan** in Bedford, **Jane Austen** at Chawton, **Captain Cook** in Middlesbrough, **Barbara Hepworth** at St Ives. There are also galleries which preserve a collection formed by a single person or family – the enchanting **Lady Lever Art Gallery** at Port Sunlight, for instance, or the gorgeous **Bowes Museum** at Barnard Castle. Some of the most rewarding preserve a collection accumulated by a business firm: **Colman's Mustard** in Norwich, the **Harvey's Wine Museum** in Bristol, the **Pilkington Glass Museum** in St Helen's, the **Bass Museum of Brewing** at Burton upon Trent, treasures of **Minton** at Stoke-on-Trent, **Wedgwood** at Barlaston, **Royal Crown Derby** in Derby.

There are agricultural museums, costume museums, museums which collect whole buildings, like the **Weald and Downland Museum** in Sussex. So does the sparkling **Welsh Folk Museum** in St Fagans, founded in 1947 and an example of the growing post-war interest in the lives of ordinary people in the past.

The **North of England Open Air Museum** at Beamish in County Durham, which is showered with awards like confetti, re-creates the way of life of working-class people in the North around the turn of the century.

Since the 1950s there has been a second museum boom, on a far greater scale than the first. There were perhaps 700 museums all told in Britain when World War II ended. There are now more than 2,000. A substantial number of these, about a third, are independent institutions, not set up by the government or the local authorities, but by private operators. To survive, they depend on their ability to attract and please paying customers and among them are some of the best museums in the country. The **National Motor Museum** at Beaulieu in Hampshire has more than 250 historic vehicles on show and visitors are carried in moving 'pods' past displays which show how motoring developed in Britain from the late 19th century on and how it may develop in the future. In Shropshire there is the marvellous **Ironbridge Gorge** complex of museums, bringing one of the key sites of the industrial revolution to life. In the old canal docks at Gloucester is the immensely enjoyable and nostalgic **Robert Opie Collection** of packets, wrappers, tins and advertising material, a museum of all our domestic yesterdays.

The best independents have contributed to the general enlivening of museums over the last 20 years. The old, musty institution of yore, full of mournful stuffed birds, prehistoric flint implements and dauntingly uninformative captions, is now a collector's item, if you can find one.

Some of the newest museums and galleries have been encouraged or funded by local authorities bent on developing tourist attractions to bring visitors and money into an area. In Bradford, for example, the **National Museum of Photography, Film and Television** opened in 1983, with the biggest cinema screen in Britain. It has galleries with 'interactive displays', where you can see yourself reading the news on TV!

There are teapots to admire in **Norwich**, trams to ride at **Crich** in Derbyshire, pork pies in **Melton Mowbray** and buns in **Abingdon**, voices in Lincolnshire dialect to listen to on the telephone in **Lincoln**, while the **Town Docks Museum** in Hull echoes to the voices of whales moaning in the deep. Certainly no one could sensibly complain of a lack of variety and interest in Britain's museums and galleries today.

*Museum or art gallery*

Below *The ship's wheel of HMS Warrior on show at Portsmouth.* Bottom *One of the locomotives at the National Railway Museum, in York.*

*Industrial interest*

*Tourist railway or steam centre*

## Industrial Interest
## Tourist Railways
## and Steam Centres

Agriculture, industry and transport are the three principal activities through which successive generations have altered the appearance and character of Britain's landscape. Far back in the Stone Age there were axe factories in the Lake District and men wielding deer antlers as picks were digging shafts 40ft (12m) deep to mine for flint in Norfolk and Sussex. Since then the face of the land has been scarred wherever opportunity offered, by quarrying for building stone and mining for coal, iron ore, copper, lead and tin.

The great majority of Britain's sites of industrial interest today are legacies from the industrial revolution. They date roughly from the 1750s on, when water power and subsequently steam power were harnessed to the mass production of goods in mills and factories. The products were efficiently transported to customers along

*Below Handsome 18th-century Quarry Bank Mill, at Styal in Cheshire. Bottom The splendid iron bridge in Ironbridge in Shropshire.*

improved roads, later by canals and in the 19th century by railways.

Interest in preserving what was left of the old industrial heritage gathered strength after World War II. The term 'industrial archaeology' was coined in about 1950 and since then some exceptionally impressive sites have been rescued from dereliction or threatened destruction.

Perhaps the single most important one is the **Ironbridge Gorge** in Shropshire, where the River Severn cuts its way through steep, wooded hills. Here in the mining village of Coalbrookdale, the Darby dynasty of ironmasters succeeded in 1709 in smelting iron with coke – a fundamental advance in technology which led to the mass production of iron. It was in Coalbrookdale that the great Iron Bridge across the Severn was cast, the first important iron bridge in the world. The bridge is still there and the complex of museums and sites in the area today includes blast furnaces and engines, and a charmingly restored 1890s industrial community at Blists Hill, with a working foundry, a candle mill, other installations and railway exhibits.

The Darby family and other ironmasters pressed on to exploit the use of steam. One of the pioneers was John Wilkinson, known as 'Iron-Mad Wilkinson' because of his passionate advocacy of iron for every conceivable use. He wore an iron hat, was buried in an iron coffin when he died in 1808, and an iron obelist was raised to his memory. It was Wilkinson who patented the method of boring cylinders which made James Watt's steam engine a practical proposition. His ironworks at **Bersham**, near Wrexham in North Wales, is today the centrepiece of an industrial heritage centre. This itself is on an eight-mile trail which traces the industrial history of this area from Roman times to the present day.

Another pioneer was Richard Arkwright, the Lancashire barber turned textile magnate, who built a water-powered cotton mill in the 1770s at **Cromford** in Derbyshire, with model housing for his factory hands. The site is being restored by the Arkwright Society. In Cheshire the National Trust owns **Quarry Bank Mill** at Styal, where another factory town was created round the cotton mill by the Greg family from the 1780s on. The machinery is running again, cotton goods woven in the mill are on sale and visitors can see the huge 85ft (26m) water-wheel, the village and the house where the pauper children lived.

The vast, dinosaur-like wheels and engines of the early industrial age always attract and awe visitors. Lead mining was long an important industry on the northern moors and an enormous wheel is the most striking feature of the **Killhope Lead Mine** in Weardale, County Durham. In Cornwall giant engines were needed to pump water out of the shafts of tin mines driven 2,000ft (610m) deep and sometimes far out under the sea. The ruined engine houses and chimney stacks of abandoned tin mines are a dramatic and melancholy feature of the Cornish landscape. The National Trust preserves two of the engines at **East Pool Mine**, near Camborne. North of St Austell, in the strange white moonscape of china clay heaps, the 19th-century **Wheal Martyn** pit is a museum of the industry.

The titanic 1876 steam engine which pumped Brighton's water up from 160ft (49m) below ground has been restored, with many other engines, at the **British Engineerium** in Hove. Machinery clatters and rattles energetically away at the **Stott Park Bobbin Mill** in Cumbria, now in the care of English Heritage. This bobbin factory built in the 1830s is virtually unchanged. Wheels turn and fan-belts flap alarmingly at **Camden Works** in Bath, in the former brass foundry of J B Bowler. Here the most elementary safety precautions were ignored. The firm also made dubious aerated soft drinks. Nothing was ever thrown away at Bowler's and the whole ramshackle place is a delight.

Scotland is not as rich in industrial sites as it might be, but drinks of quite a different kind can be sampled in a clutch of whisky distilleries in the Dufftown area. There is a 70-mile, eight-distillery Whisky Trail for enthusiasts, who are urged to let someone else do the driving.

Coal mining and ironworking were carried on for centuries on a small scale in the Forest of Dean. One of the eerier experiences in Britain is to make your way down into the echoing tunnels and caverns of the **Clearwell Caves Iron Mine**, which had its heyday between 1850 and 1900.

In Wales, among the mountains of Snowdonia, there are dramatic sites where the hillsides are torn and broken by quarrying for slate, the principal industry of the area for 200 years until quite recently. At the **Llechwedd Slate Caverns** near Blaenau Ffestiniog, visitors are taken deep underground into the tunnels and caverns, and there are demonstrations of the skilled art of slate-splitting. Close by is the **Gloddfa Ganol Slate Mine**, once the biggest in the world. At Llanberis there is a museum of the industry in the workshops of the now-closed **Dinorwic Quarry**.

The country's most dramatic and convincing coal mining museum is in South Wales. This is **Big Pit**, near Blaenafon in Gwent, in a colliery which closed in 1980. You go down almost 300ft (90m) in the cage, wearing your miner's helmet with lamp – which you need – and an ex-miner guides the party through the tunnels.

The application of steam power to transport created the great age of railways in Britain in the 19th and 20th centuries. The landscape was changed for every by the Herculean works involved; the construction of embankments, cuttings and tunnels, the throwing of noble bridges and soaring viaducts across rivers and valleys. The sight of a powerful steam locomotive hammering along the rails at full tilt under a plume of smoke, the screaming of its whistle echoing across country, became part of the right order of things. When steam gave way to diesel and electric power, and much-loved branch lines were closed down in the 1950s and '60s, preservation societies were formed to keep steam lines running or restore them to operation.

Many of the preserved lines go through particularly attractive stretches of country. The **Severn Valley Railway** runs more trains than any other, for 16 miles close to the River Severn between Bridgnorth, Bewdley and Kidderminster. Among its steam warhorses are some fine old Great Western locomotives.

The **Bluebell Railway** in Sussex has five miles of track between Sheffield Park and Horsted Keynes, through woods shining with bluebells in the spring. The **North Yorkshire Moors Railway** steams the 18 miles from Pickering to Grosmont through superlative scenery in the North York Moors National Park and runs a Pullman service regularly. There are gaslit stations on the **Keighley and Worth Valley Railway**, whose headquarters are at Haworth in the Brontë Country. The **Lakeside & Haverthwaite Railway** puffs amicably through the Cumbrian woods to connect with the steamers on Lake Windermere.

In 19th-century England and Scotland the standard gauge of 4ft 8¹/₂in held sway, but elsewhere, especially in mountainous areas, a narrow gauge might be better suited

to the terrain – the **Isle of Man Railway's** 15-mile line from Douglas to Port Erin, has a 3ft gauge. Wales has a special reputation for its 'great little trains', on which the traveller can enjoy the steam, the shining paintwork and polished brass, and extremely spectacular scenery.

The **Vale of Rheidol Railway**, for instance, which opened in 1902, clanks its way along the mountainsides and round sharp bends from Aberystwyth to the famous beauty spot of the Devil's Bridge. The **Ffestiniog Railway**, originally built to haul slate, clambers up into Snowdonia from the harbour of Porthmadog past lakes and waterfalls and into the mountains. Some of its genial, round-faced engines have been making the trip for a hundred years. The **Talyllyn Railway**, which has been running since 1865, travels seven miles inland from Tywyn on Cardigan Bay, with splendid mountain prospects. This was the first railway in Britain to be saved by volunteers from destruction. It set an example many were glad to follow.

*A vintage steam engine on the Brecon Mountain Railway near Merthyr Tydfil.*

Industrial interest

Tourist railway or steam centre

*Garden*

*Arboretum*

## Gardens
## Arboreta

'An Englishman's home is his castle' and round his castle he creates a garden. Despite – or perhaps because of – the vagaries of our climate, the closeness of the Gulf Stream and the collections brought back from all over the world particularly in the 18th and 19th centuries, Britain has a wonderful heritage of gardens and arboreta.

The **Royal Horticultural Society**, inaugurated in 1804, has gardens at **Wisley**, near Woking, **Rosemoor**, in Devon, as well as close affiliations with the College of Horticulture, at **Pershore** and Liverpool University Botanic Garden, at **Ness**, on the Wirral. The RHS has, since 1889, published *'The Garden'*, describing what can be seen, when and where. At all these places, keen gardeners can readily obtain advice and information.

The **Royal Botanic Garden** at Kew was established in 1759, in the reign of George II. Joining the traditional Victorian Palm and Temperate Houses, is Kew's latest feature, the Princess of Wales Conservatory, a

*The gardens at Bodnant, Gwynedd, are among the most beautiful in Britain.*

complex of 10 independently controlled climatic environments, growing a range of plants from desert to tropical forest species.

Since 1965 the National Trust property at **Wakehurst Place**, near Ardingly, has been 'Kew in the country' and it is here that a national seed bank is maintained.

As we become increasingly aware of the fragile nature of our planet's eco-system, plant collections and gene banks are more and more a vital part of horticulture. The National Council for the Conservation of Plants and Gardens has, since 1982, co-ordinated collections such as the magnolias at **Savill Garden**, near Windsor, violas at **Leicester University,** clematis at **Tenbury**, peonies at **Hidcote** and rhododendrons at **Leonardslee, Nymans** and at **Exbury. Abbotsbury,** in Devon, looks after eucalyptus and in scores of smaller gardens, amateurs as well as professionals nurture border plants, primroses, celandines, buddleias and asters. For bigger specimens, arboreta play their part. Seventeen miles of pathways lead through the 500 acres of the Forestry Commission's **Westonbirt Arboretum** in Gloucestershire, where plantings have been

continuous for 150 years. Oak, chestnut, pine and beech shelter more exotic specimens, such as acers and willows, azaleas and rhododendrons.

The **Granada Arboretum**, in Manchester, and the National Trust's **Winkworth Arboretum**, in Surrey, maintain sorbus and malus. Winter-flowering plants such as daphnes, honeysuckle, camellias and viburnum can be seen at the **Hillier Arboretum**, near Romsey, and plants which flourish on chalky soils are the specialty of **Hidcote Manor Garden**, north of Chipping Campden.

Many of the gardens lovingly tended in the past have now been restored. At **New Place,** in Surrey, the Edwardian garden of Gertrude Jekyll was recovered from beneath couch grass and poppies. At East Grinstead, the mullioned windows of 16th-century **Gravetye Manor** now reflect the glory of a Victorian garden created by William Robinson. At **Erddig**, near Wrexham, another 18th-century design has been re-created in the grounds of the National Trust house and **Culpeper Flower Garden** now flourishes at **Leeds Castle**, in Kent, 17th-century home of the Culpeper family. The 18th-century garden at

**Painshill Park** in Surrey was laid out in the 1740s by Charles Hamilton. Sadly decayed, the combination of classical architecture, lake and landscaping is being restored and it may once again rival the garden of Hamilton's friend, Henry Hoare at Stourhead.

Gardens stretch the length and breadth of the British isles. **Inverewe**, in Wester Ross, despite its northern latitude, enjoys frost-free conditions, due to the warm North Atlantic Drift, and **Tresco Abbey Gardens** in the Scilly Isles, created and maintained since 1834 by successive generations of the same family, relishes mild, moist weather. In the 1790s garden of 13th-century **Drum Castle**, near Aberdeen, a collection illustrating the development of roses from the 17th-century has recently been created by the National Trust for Scotland.

The **University Botanic Gardens** at St Andrews, training ground for future professionals, also provide a well laid out and informative garden for the visitor. Its high point is the peat, water and rock complex simulating the natural progression from mountain crag to scree to meadow and bog. The **Royal Botanic Garden**, in Edinburgh, second oldest in the country after Oxford, also has a superb rock garden and, like the new conservatory at Kew, grows the astonishing *Victoria Amazonica* water lily, its huge leaves capable of supporting a small child, but which grow from seed annually.

Across on the west coast are the gardens of **Brodick Castle**, on the Isle of Arran. Sir John Ramsden, then owner of **Muncaster Castle**, in Cumbria, after a visit to Brodick sent his hostess some rhododendrons for her garden – in all 80 tons! In 1953 an expedition to Burma brought back hundreds more plants and yet more varieties, most of which flourish in the mild climate.

At **Belsay**, north of Newcastle, English Heritage has restored the gardens, partly in the quarry used by Charles Monck, a keen member of the Horticultural Society. At **Thorp Perrow**, near Ripon, there is a cherry avenue which is a riot of blossom in May. Several 'autumn bays' provide colour from September to November and there is a rowan avenue, with spring blossom and autumn berries.

John Aislabie, Chancellor of the Exchequer at the time of the South Sea Bubble, retired to his estate at **Studley Royal**, in Yorkshire, albeit under something of a cloud. The garden he designed is a work of true inspiration, anticipating

Stourhead by 40 years. It now incorporates the ready-made 'folly', so essential to Romantic landscaping, acquired when his son purchased the nearby Fountains Abbey.

**Harlow Carr Botanical Garden**, near Harrogate, has been since 1948 the headquarters of the Northern Horticultural Society, working closely with the RHS and offering a similar range of walks, workshops and demonstrations as Wisley. **Newby Hall**, near Ripon, has something to delight the eye all year round, but is best known for its display of roses in early summer and its herbaceous border plants.

At **Eaton Hall**, Eccleston, near Chester, there is an unheated glasshouse 360 feet (110m) long, with camellias which are usually at their best in April. **Bodnant**, near Llandudno, always associated with the Aberconway family, has rhododendrons, azaleas, magnolias and camellias. Here, too, there is a wonderful laburnum walk where, on a sunny day in May, you can walk through a tunnel of glorious yellow blossom. Near Welshpool is **Powis Castle**, once the home of Clive of India. Its terraces are one of the few remaining medieval-style gardens in the country.

**Doddington Hall**, south-west of Lincoln, was built by the Elizabethan architect, Smythson, who designed Longleat and Hardwick Hall. The garden, even as late as 1919, had cattle grazing on the lawns, but now the walled west garden is full of the old-fashioned roses for which Doddington is famous, as well as a profusion of irises.

Near Colchester, **Beth Chatto's Garden** covering 12 acres, has developed into a centre where gardeners can pick up hints on what grows best in hard-baked sandy soil, sour silt or waterlogged clay. At **Sissinghurst**, in Kent, the garden of this Tudor house is a monument to Vita Sackville-West who, in the 1930s, created walks where each of the gardens opening off had its own colour scheme.

In **Sheffield Park**, near East Grinstead, famous for its autumn colours, you can wander away from the lakeside rhododendrons and discover the wonderful collection of conifers. One group of maritime pines is reputed to have been planted by Sir Joseph Banks, a founder of the RHS. David Douglas, after whom the Douglas fir is named, brought Monterey pines here from California and there is a dwarf Siberian pine planted in the 1920s, which has just about reached five feet (one and a half metres) and can thus be highly recommended for the small garden!

The National Trust property at **Kingston Lacy** in Dorset, has a delightful fernery planted with snowdrops for an early effect and the Cedar Walk has carefully recorded plantings by the Duke of Wellington, King Edward VII, the Kaiser and King George V, who planted an oak here to commemorate his Coronation. At **Stourhead**, north of Shaftesbury, lake, bridge, temples and grottoes combine to achieve one of the finest 'landscaped' gardens in the world, the creation of Henry Hoare in the 1740s, a generation before Capability Brown began diverting rivers and moving mountains around many of the great houses of his day.

**Penjerrick**, in Cornwall, was begun in the 1830s and many exotic plants here were grown from seed brought into nearby Falmouth by clipper captains, but rhododendrons remain one of its glories.

Wherever you go, at no matter what season of the year, there are gardens to be enjoyed all over Britain. Provided you do not pick a Bank Holiday weekend, in most cases you will find someone ready to pass on the secret of their success to you.

*Garden*

*Arboretum*

*Hillier Arboretum in Hampshire.*

*Country park*

*The forested slopes at Afan Argoed resemble those in Switzerland.*

## Country Parks

In the 1960s and '70s, increasing affluence, more leisure time, more cars and faster roads combined to bring the open countryside within the reach of far more people. The number of townspeople and suburbanites driving out for a day in the country was growing rapidly and there was a need to accommodate the demand without spoiling the countryside which everyone was eager to enjoy.

In 1966 a government white paper on 'Leisure in the Countryside' suggested the establishment of country parks and the idea was taken up in the Countryside Acts which followed. The two Countryside Commissions, one for England and Wales, the other for Scotland, were given the responsibility for stimulating the creation of country parks, providing advice and grants of taxpayers' money to projects they approved.

Most of the country parks have been set up by local authorities. One of their fundamental functions is to make available country places where visitors know they have a right to be. Opinion polls and studies have shown time and time again that people are held back from enjoying the countryside by an uneasy feeling that they may be trespassing or at least not wanted. A country park is a place where you are welcome. It is also a place where there will be toilets and somewhere to park the car.

There are now more than 200 country parks in Britain, varying considerably in size and character. The larger ones have visitor centres where you will find information about the landscape, the wildlife and often the area's history; wardens or rangers who keep an eye on things and provide help and information when needed; way-marked paths; amusements for children, and refreshments.

Country parks are usually open every day during daylight hours, and in the great majority of them admission is free, though boating, bowls or other special facilities may have to be paid for. Activities vary from one park to another – from riding, fishing, hang-gliding and grass-skiing to orienteering, golfing, boating and sailing.

Some of the earliest country parks were areas which were already heavily visited and where better facilities were needed. An example is **Box Hill**, near Dorking in Surrey, named after the rare wild box trees on the chalk hill. For centuries past people have loved to walk there and admire the views of the Weald. Much of the area is owned by the National Trust and there is a car park, information room and shop.

Another case in point is **Butser Hill**, a much-visited beauty spot on the A3 south of Petersfield where

Hampshire County Council created the **Queen Elizabeth Country Park,** opened by the Queen in 1976. The park covers 1,400 acres of downs, Forestry Commission beechwoods and stands of yew at the western edge of the South Downs Way footpath. There are splendid views from the top of Butser Hill, a nature reserve and waymarked trails, with downland plants and flowers to see, woodpeckers, butterflies and deer. The Ancient Farm Research Project here farms the way Iron Age man did 2,000 years ago and the park has an information centre with an audio-visual programme, a café and a picnic area.

Another heavily visited area is the **Brimham Rocks Country Park** on the moors near Pateley Bridge in North Yorkshire. The rocks, weathered into strange shapes over the centuries, drew sightseers in such numbers that the area was in danger of being badly damaged. It is owned by the National Trust and the threat to the rocks has been brought under control.

Since country parks were intended primarily for town dwellers, they tend to be more numerous close to heavily populated urban areas. They are not thick on the ground in Norfolk and Suffolk, for example, but there is quite a concentration of them in Essex, nearer London. One of these is the attractive **Hatfield Forest Country Park,** near Bishop's Stortford, an area of ancient hunting forest which was only just rescued from the developer's grasp in the 1920s and which is famous for its hornbeams and its nightingales.

Similarly, there are fewer country parks in North and Central Wales than in the former mining and industrial areas of South Wales. One of the biggest and best is **Margam Country Park,** near Port Talbot. Its 850 acres include what were once the stately grounds of the Mansel family's fine house. There are landscaped gardens, a deer park, a handsome orangery which is used for concerts, a theatre, a large maze and boating on the lake, which is also occupied by swans, coots and moorhens. A herd of Glamorgan cattle and an Iron Age hillfort with commanding views over the Bristol Channel add to its enormous appeal. There is an adventure playground, a heronry in the nature reserve and there are skylarks and buzzards. Just outside the park is the ruined church of 12th-century Margam Abbey.

Many other parks have solved the problem of what to do with fine country estates the owners can no longer keep up. **Mount Edgcumbe Country Park,** which looks out over Plymouth Sound, preserves the formal gardens with their statues and fountains laid out for the Edgcumbe family in the 18th century. Stretching for miles along the coast, it boasts follies, woods, a deer park and a fabulous collection of camellias.

Many country parks, by contrast, have contributed to the reclamation of derelict industrial wasteland. East of Sheffield, on the border of Yorkshire and Derbyshire, the **Rother Valley Country Park** has arisen phoenix-like from an area of opencast coal mining, with 350,000 freshly planted trees and no less than three lakes for fishing and watersports. There are footpaths and visitors can hire cycles to ride along the network of bicycle tracks.

The **Strathclyde Country Park** in the south-eastern outskirts of Glasgow was formally opened in 1978. Millions of pounds were spent to take a derelict, stagnant wasteland of exhausted colliery workings and desolate spoil heaps and turn it back into pleasant countryside. The River Clyde was diverted to create a 200-acre loch, trees and shrubs and long stretches of grass were planted, paths were laid out by the loch and picnic areas and car parks provided.

Now the trees have matured. The loch, almost two miles long, is a watersports centre for sailing, canoeing and waterskiing. There is a golf course and sports pitches, an interpretation centre and a nature reserve which attracts wintering whooper swans and other waterfowl. Also inside the park are the remains of a Roman fort and a peculiar 19th-century mausoleum, which was constructed for the Dukes of Hamilton but turned out to have such a noisy echo in the chapel inside that it was impossible to use it.

Country park landscapes vary from the heath and scrub of **Cannock Chase** in Staffordshire to the giant trees in **Sherwood Forest,** the ducal landscape by Capability Brown not far away in **Clumber Park** in Nottinghamshire and on to the deer and rugged rocks of **Bradgate Park** in Leicestershire, with the ruins of the house in which the tragic Lady Jane Grey grew up. On top of **Ham Hill** in Somerset, the grassed-over stone quarries make a wonderful arena for hide-and-seek. On **Berry Head**, south of Torbay in South Devon, towering cliffs command bracing views of the English Channel and the nests of kittiwakes and guillemots. The need to protect the wild orchids and other rare plants here was one reason why the local council bought the land in 1968. Further on along the Channel coast, at the **Lepe Country Park** in Hampshire, you can look across the Solent to the Isle of Wight and idly watch the ships and the black-headed gulls go by.

One question which remains is: are the visitors at country parks enjoying real countryside or a mock-up? Nowadays the Countryside Commission believes that the parks should be treated less as ends in themselves and more as gateways to the true countryside beyond.

*Brimham Rocks, in North Yorkshire,*
*where the rocks form weird shapes.*

Theme park

*The 'Thunder River' rapid-water ride, for all the family, at Thorpe Park.*

## Theme Parks

The British theme park has its spiritual ancestor across the Atlantic. Disneyland, which opened in Anaheim in the southern suburbs of Los Angeles in 1955, combined four basic characteristics. First there was a central theme – the world of Disney cartoons and films. Second, there were illusions, using the latest technology, and visitors experienced a simulated river trip in the African jungle, or thought they were going deep underwater in a submarine, when in fact they were only a few inches beneath the surface. Next, there were 'white knuckle' rides – an exciting roller-coaster, a terrifying helter-skelter and other thrilling fairground rides, again using the latest technology. And last, Disneyland catered for the motor car, the family with children and modern mass tourism, with a parking lot of gargantuan proportions and an ample supply of toilets and places to eat.

The lessons of Disneyland were absorbed and put to use at **Alton Towers**, the 500-acre 'leisure park' in Staffordshire which is now attracting two and a half million visitors a year. Alton Towers employs a staff of 1,400 people during the summer and has six different restaurants, of varying types and price levels, with innumerable kiosks scattered about the grounds selling ice-creams and soft drinks. There is no single central theme, but six 'themed areas', which include Fantasy World, Aqualand and Kiddies Kingdom. Among the 'white knuckle' rides are the gravity-defying Corkscrew Roller-coaster, which lives up to its name, as well as the New Black Hole, the Alton Beast, and the water-based Log Flume

and Grand Canyon Rapids Ride.

There are gentler rides for those of nervous disposition or with small children, with a beautiful carousel, and a mass of indoor attractions and Disney-style parades with bands, floats and performers in life-size animal costumes.

In addition to all this is a wonderful Victorian Gothic ruin and some of the most spectacular gardens in the country, inherited from the Earls of Shrewsbury, whose country seat Alton Towers used to be. The 15th and 16th Earls constructed an enormous pseudo-medieval fantasy palace here, replete with towers and spires, turrets and battlements. A W Pugin himself, the high priest of Victorian Gothic, was called in to preside over the interior decor. Outside, meanwhile, a fortune was spent to lay out a magnificent park and gardens. Lakes and pools were dug out, fed by water brought from a spring two miles off. Terraces, miles of walks, giant stairways and grand glasshouses were built at colossal expense by an army of workmen.

The future Queen Victoria visited Alton in 1832, at the age of 13, and was entertained to luncheon on gold plates. The Chinese-style Pagoda Fountain was built, and shoots a jet of water 70ft (21m) high. A Swiss cottage was erected on the hillside to provide a fine prospect over the grounds while a blind Welsh harper was stationed there to play soothing music. Today it is a restaurant.

In later years it proved impossible to keep the house up and the mansion fell into the condition of picturesque ruin in which visitors see it now. The gardens were properly maintained, however, and are a delight to walk in today.

More 'white knuckle' rides can be found by the adventurous at the **Chessington World of Adventures**, in Surrey. 'This Ride Is Not For The

Faint-Hearted' one sign warns. There is a blood chilling roller-coaster called the Vampire, which zooms along at tree-top height and dives underground. It is set in a 'Transylvania' village which also has a bubble works fantasy ride for children through a simulated fizzy pop factory, and a restaurant wittily named the Black Forest Chateau.

The theme areas at Chessington feature encounters with horrible science fiction monsters, and Calamity Canyon, where there's a Wild West trading post, a shooting gallery and a roller-coaster called the Runaway Mine Train. In the Mystic East area visitors see the Palace of the Nine Dragons, the Giant Buddha and the Cambodian temple of Angkor Wat, and go on a 'dragon river' water ride through a bamboo jungle, where the boat is attacked by a crocodile. In addition, Chessington has a zoo, a circus, a miniature railway, plenty of eating places and live entertainment with bands, dancers, clowns, street performers and 'madcap' characters in costume.

Halfway between Derby and Nottingham may seem an odd place to meet cowboys and shoot-outs, but the Wild West is one of the main themes at the **American Adventure**, near Ilkeston in Derbyshire. Pistol-packing posses career through town, bullets fly and saloon girls squeal as badmen get their come-uppances. There is live entertainment in Lazy Lil's Saloon and jazz on a Mississippi riverboat.

The numerous rides include a double-drop log flume in Thunder Canyon and a charge through the raging torrents of the Great Niagara Rapids. Or you can take a triple-looping roller-coaster called the Missile and blast off to the stars from Space Port USA. There are special attractions to keep small children happy in Pioneer Playland, including a cartoon cinema.

At the **Pleasurewood Hills American Theme Park**, near Lowestoft in Suffolk, southern fried chicken is on the menu, and attractions range from the evil Rattlesnake roller-coaster and the New Tempest, which hangs you upside down 100ft (30m) in the air, to a waterborne voyage to Aladdin's Cave, a land of dinosaurs, fairground big wheels, a spooky haunted castle and shows by performing sea lions and parrots.

In Yorkshire, near Ripon, the **Lightwater Valley Theme Park**, in the 1970s a peaceful pig farm, prides itself on the sheer appalling terror of its 'white knuckle' rides. It opened the longest roller-coaster ride in the world in 1990, at a cost of over £5 million, running close to

1¹/₂ miles (2.4km) with a drop of 158ft (48m) and a top speed of about 60mph. This joined a nightmare ride called The Rat, which runs entirely underground in pitch darkness, 'through smelly sewers alive with the shrieks and shrills of rats' – rated tops for sheer horror by the *Daily Mirror*.

There are calmer pleasures at Lightwater Valley, too – a nine-hole golf course, three boating lakes, an old-fashioned fairground, a miniature railway and a shopping centre. There is skateboarding, a go-kart track, an adventure playground for smaller children and a theatre with live entertainment.

At Charnock Richard in Lancashire, there awaits 'an enchanted day out for the whole family' in 'the magical kingdom' of **Camelot.** The theme here is the world of King Arthur and his heroic knights of the Round Table. Knights in full armour thunder into combat on their chargers in the jousting arena. Jesters and grotesque animal figures wander about. A chilling roller-coaster hurtles into the Tower of Terror, where something unspeakable called the Beast lurks in its dark lair. Guinevere's swan ride negotiates Merlin's magic mountain, the Grail trail crosses a swinging rope bridge and Sir Bedevere's Bridge leads to the enchantments of the Wild Wood.

You can eat at the Round Table Burger Bar, naturally, but altogether Camelot has 28 outlets selling food and drink. It reckons to cook 2¹/₂ miles of sausages every season, as well as 250,000 pounds of dragon burgers and 315,000 pounds of chips.

The 'family leisure park' at **Thorpe Park**, near Chertsey in Surrey, is close to both the M3 and the M25. It opened in 1979 on the site of old gravel workings, which gave it plenty of lakes and pools. Water skiing, windsurfing and other watersports rank high among its pleasures, water barges carry visitors from one area of the park to another and there are river-boat restaurants.

The original theme was Britain's maritime history, but now, with the need to attract repeat visitors, the emphasis has changed. 'White knuckle' rides are not particularly important here and the park concentrates more on entertainments and amusements which families with children aged about four to 14 can all enjoy together. There is live entertainment at two theatres, lots of street entertainment, musicians, clowns and giant sub-Disney animal grotesques, and a large amusement centre with

video games and one-armed bandits. The log flume ride in the Canadian Rockies theme area has a drop of 50ft and there is a fast Space Station Zero ride, but more typical is the complete working farm, which operates as it did in the 1930s. A simulated medieval town square has a double-decker carousel and other attractions include a nature trail, miniature railway, roller skating rink, crazy golf and a cartoon cinema.

All theme parks are geared to a safe, enjoyable family day out, and you pay once, on entry, and get the rides and other attractions thrown in. Alton Towers is the kingpin in terms of visitor figures, but the numbers rung up at the other parks – over a million and a quarter at Thorpe Park and a similar figure at Chessington – suggest that this type of transatlantic family attraction is in Britain to stay.

*The 'Runaway Mine Train' at Chessington World of Adventures.*

Theme Park

*Zoo*

*Wildlife collection – mammals*

*Wildlife collection – birds*

*Aquarium*

## Zoos
## Wildlife Collections
## Aquariums

The oldest picture of an elephant in England is in Exeter Cathedral, a 13th-century wood carving under one of the choir seats. It is quite likely to be a portrait of a real African elephant, the one which was presented to Henry III by the King of France in 1253. Its arrival in England created a sensation and people flocked to see the great beast as it tramped from the port of Sandwich to London.

### Zoos
The century before, Henry I had established a menagerie at Woodstock in Oxfordshire. It was later moved to the Tower of London and survived there until well into the 19th century. The public was let in to see the animals, which in 1609 consisted of 11 lions, two leopards, a jackal, two mountain cats, three eagles and two owls.

Kings and noblemen continued to keep private menageries, but the 19th century saw the creation of public zoological gardens – zoos for short – as part of the same educational and improving impulse responsible for the establishment of so many museums. The first in the field was the **Regent's Park Zoo** in London, laid out by Decimus Burton and opened in 1828 by the recently founded Zoological Society of London. The animals from the Tower were moved here.

Municipal zoos now opened, combining serious study of animals with public instruction and entertainment. In Dublin, for example, the Royal Zoological Society of Ireland opened a zoo in **Phoenix Park** in 1830. It gained a substantial reputation for breeding lions, as **Glasgow Zoo** breeds porcupines and Edinburgh Zoo is famous for its penguins.

### Wildlife Collections
After World War II, a tide of disapproval set in against the old-fashioned 19th-century zoo, which seemed little better than a prison with its cramped cages and unnatural conditions, and against the whole attitude to animals which this type of zoo was felt to represent. The consequence was the modernisation of many zoos and the coming of the safari park and a new style of wildlife collection.
The development of the open-range zoo, where animals roam in large enclosures instead of being penned in cages, had begun in 1931, when the Zoological Society of London opened a country branch at **Whipsnade Park** in Bedfordshire, near Dunstable. Whipsnade covers

*The famous lions of Longleat.*

more than 500 acres, most of the animals live in herds in sizeable paddocks and well over 90 per cent of them were born in the zoo. In the last 30 years many other zoos have moved closer to the open-range system.

Britain's first safari park opened in 1966 at **Longleat** in Wiltshire, the palatial Elizabethan seat of the Marquess of Bath. The prime movers in the enterprise were the Marquess himself and Jimmy Chipperfield, of the well-known circus family, an experienced supplier of wild animals to zoos. The idea was for visitors to drive through the spacious enclosures where the animals roamed: in other words, for a change, the animals would be free and the public confined. The project proved extremely popular.

Lions were the first and have always been the foremost attraction at Longleat, but many other animals can be seen there today – including the country's only white Bengal tiger, as well as white rhinos, camels, giraffes and gorillas. The monkeys enjoy riding on visitors' cars and there are boat trips to see hippos and sea lions. In some areas visitors can leave their cars and stroll about or even have a picnic among the animals. Like other safari parks, Longleat depends on and provides for the motor car and there is plenty of parking with no problem about finding a restaurant or a toilet.

The Duke of Bedford was not far behind in opening a safari park of his own at his stately Bedfordshire mansion of **Woburn**. Jimmy Chipperfield was again involved. But Woburn already had a distinguished history of keeping and breeding wild animals. Père David's deer are named after a French missionary, who saw the only remaining herd of them in the imperial park outside Peking where they were kept in the 19th century. A few animals were grudgingly shipped out to European zoos and

*Flamingoes at Slimbridge Wildfowl Trust*

when the Chinese herd was wiped out, the 16 Père David's deer in Europe were the only ones left. The 11th Duke of Bedford rounded all 16 up in 1894 and settled them in his park at Woburn, where they prospered and multiplied. All the Père David's deer in the world are descended from them, and in 1985 some were sent back to China, to the same park outside Peking.

Woburn also played a part in saving the European bison from extinction. The Père David's deer are still there, and so are the bison, and the **Woburn Wild Animal Kingdom** today is Britain's largest drive-through collection of wild creatures. A ride in aerial cars gives a bird's eye view of the park and there are performing sea lions, and even performing macaws.

A wildlife collection of an entirely different flavour can be enjoyed at **Chillingham**, in Northumberland, where visitors can cautiously inspect the 50-strong herd of wild white cattle. With their wicked, curving horns, they are the nearest thing to prehistoric cattle still in existence. They have been kept in the park at Chillingham for centuries and have never been crossbred.

John Aspinall has set up two Kent

zoo parks: **Howletts**, near Canterbury, famous for breeding gorillas and African elephants, and its sister at **Port Lympne**, near Hythe. Here magnificent Siberian tigers, black rhino and the country's only breeding colony of majestic Barbary lions loll about in aristocratic splendour.

Breeding animals, and especially breeding species which in the wild are threatened with extinction, has become an important function of zoos, safari parks and wildlife collections, and a key justification of their existence. **Chester Zoo**, for example, which ranks second only to London in its tally of visitors and has a wide range of animals in attractive grounds, has successfully bred orang-utans, Madagascan tree boas and rare fruit bats, among other species. **Bristol Zoo**, where the creatures on view range from tigers to tarantulas and penguins to piranhas, counts gorillas and orang-utans, Persian leopards, colobus monkeys and long-tailed macaques among its breeding successes. **Twycross Zoo**, near Atherstone in Warwickshire, a small zoo with a remarkable collection of apes and monkeys, has a notable breeding record and **Marwell**, near Winchester, breeds rare Sumatran tigers and the endangered oryx.

In 1947 there were only 50 breeding pairs of the Hawaiian geese (called nene) left in the world, all of them in Hawaii. The species was saved by successful breeding at the Wildfowl & Wetlands Trust reserve at **Slimbridge** in Gloucestershire, founded by the late Sir Peter Scott. Some of the birds from here were later sent back to Hawaii in the hope of re-establishing them in their native land.

The splendid Slimbridge reserve is on the bank of the River Severn. Other Wildfowl Trust reserves include those at **Arundel** in Sussex, **Washington** in Tyne and Wear, and **Caerlaverock**, near Dumfries in Scotland. At **Stagsden** in Bedfordshire is one of the first specialist bird collections in Britain. The Bird Gardens concentrate on cranes, but there are 150 species or more on view in all. **Birdworld**, near Farnham in Surrey, has a collection ranging from tiny hummingbirds to outsize ostriches, and is successfully breeding Humboldt penguins.

**Aquariums**

The first public aquarium in Britain opened in London in 1853. It was not until a hundred years later that the first massive sea aquariums, or oceanariums, opened in the United States, with huge tanks containing

*The 'Penguin Parade' – the star attraction at Edinburgh Zoo.*

hundreds of fish of different species swimming together. The example has been followed in Britain, for example at the **Sea Life Centre** in Weymouth, which opened in 1983 with the biggest display tank in Europe. Visitors can see dolphins and porpoises, British sharks, octopus and squid and evil-looking conger eels, and fish in drifting droves. There is a special flatfish tank and a tank with a simulated sunken wreck and the marine life that would gather around it. There are also 'touch pools' and plenty of fun for children.

Of the same genre, but on a much more modest scale, is **Anglesey Sea Zoo**, near Brynsiencyn, close to the shore of the Menai Strait, with its tanks of fish, lobsters and crabs from the local waters and 'touch tanks' for the children.

There is plenty of enjoyment and discovery at other sea life centres in seaside towns, like Brighton, Blackpool and Southsea and at Barcaldine in Scotland where young seals can be viewed prior to their release back into the wild. While wildlife is increasingly threatened in the wild, it flourishes in British zoos, safari parks and aquariums.

Nature reserve

RSPB site

**Nature Reserves**
**Nature Trails**
**RSPB Sites**
**Brownsea Island** is a much-treasured Dorset beauty spot, a 500-acre island in Poole Harbour, accessible only by boat. It has an honoured place in the history of the Boy Scouts, as it was here in 1907 that General Baden-Powell held his first scout camp. A succession of wealthy and sometimes eccentric owners preserved the island from contamination by development until, with the death of the last of them in 1961, it passed to the National Trust. It was then a wildly overgrown paradise for red squirrels, the late owner's peacocks, Sika deer, herons and seabirds. The National Trust has protected it ever since and thousands of visitors go there every year to enjoy the beaches, walk the heathland and woodland glades and admire stunning views of the Dorset coast.

A substantial area of the island is sealed off against casual visitors dropping in, though parties are guided round at regular intervals. This is a nature reserve, managed by the Dorset Trust for Nature Conservation, with a heronry, two lakes and a marsh fringed with reeds, where wildfowl congregate in

*A view from a hide overlooking Welney Wildfowl Refuge, in Norfolk.*

safety – terns and oystercatchers, godwits and sandpipers, dunlins and redshanks.

**Nature Reserves**
Unlike a National Park or a country park, a nature reserve is not protected for the sake of human visitors, but for the sake of the wild creatures, birds, insects and rare plants, and the habitats and conditions they need to survive and flourish. Many nature reserves are open to the general public; at others a permit may be needed or access may be limited, but some are closed altogether.

As long ago as 1912 the need to set aside areas in which threatened species could survive was recognised with the founding of the Society for the Promotion of Nature Reserves by the pioneering naturalist Charles Rothschild. When he died the movement lost impetus. After World War II, however, the pressure of expanding population and expanding leisure time bore so heavily on the country's wildlife that something plainly needed to be done. In 1949 the government set up the Nature Conservancy Council (NCC) as its wildlife protection arm, and one of the new body's responsibilities was 'to establish, manage and maintain nature reserves'.

At the same time vigorous county

and local wildlife protection trusts were forming and establishing nature reserves of their own. Charles Rothschild's society re-emerged into the limelight as the national organisation and mouthpiece of these groups, as the Royal Society for Nature Conservation.

Today Britain has more than 2,000 nature reserves, occupying more than half a million acres of land between them. Some are managed by the NCC, but a far larger number are run by the county or local trusts for nature conservation, naturalists' trusts or wildlife trusts. Others are owned and managed by the Forestry Commission, others again by local authorities and conservation bodies.

From a visitor's point of view, nature reserves supply a way of seeing and coming close to the full range of Britain's wildlife and plant life without any danger of trespassing or going where one is not wanted. They can be found on the coast and inland, on high ground and on low, in a great variety of countryside.

At **Caerlaverock**, for instance, on the Solway Firth coast of Scotland, the NCC established a reserve in 1957 on the low-lying saltmarshes among muddy flats and creeks. Multitudes of birds feed and roost there: golden plovers in legions,

Nature reserve

RSPB site

greylag geese, pintail and all manner of ducks and waders. Thousands of barnacle geese fly in from the Arctic every winter, and there are birds of prey, as well as saltmarsh plants in abundance. This is also one of the breeding grounds of the rare and noisy natterjack toad. Visitor access is limited, partly because the flats and creeks are dangerous when the tide sweeps in suddenly. There is also a Wildfowl Trust refuge close by and the romantic pink ruin of Caerlaverock Castle to visit.

By contrast, not so many miles away inland, east of Newton Stewart, the NCC runs the **Cairnsmore of Fleet** nature reserve, largely a trackless waste of peat and heather moorland, bog and mountainside. It is important as the home of the red deer, wild goats and ravens. Access is again restricted.

Similarly, there is a cluster of contrasting nature reserves in the Gower Peninsula of South Wales, which is famed for packing a remarkable variety of scenery into a small area, and for the accompanying wealth of wildlife. At **Cwmllwyd Wood**, west of Swansea, for instance, West Glamorgan County Council has a reserve of oak woods, grassland and marsh, with hides from which to watch snipe and woodcock. At **Oxwich** on the south coast there is an NCC reserve of quite different character in an area of sand dunes, wooded headlands and marshes, explored by nature trails. Keep an eye out for adders on the slopes.

### RSPB Sites

Some of the most rewarding nature reserves in the country belong to the Royal Society for the Protection of Birds (RSPB). Founded in 1889, the RSPB is devoted to the conservation of wild birds. It has built up a portfolio of well over a hundred reserves in which the habitats of breeding and wintering birds and birds of passage are preserved.

Some of the RSPB reserves are as far flung as the **Orkneys** and **Shetlands**, but most of them are more accessible. There is one at **Dungeness** on the Kent coast, where the nuclear power station broods over a desolate landscape of shingle beach, ponds and abandoned gravel workings, and tangled gorse and brambles. But there is plenty of life here – marsh frogs, plants like viper's bugloss, and waterfowl in huge numbers, with many migrating birds making a landfall at this point.

Up in Lancashire, at **Leighton Moss** near Silverdale, the RSPB preserves an area of swamp,

*The 300ft (91m) high cliffs of Marwick Head's RSPB reserve, Orkney.*

shallow meres and scrubland. Here bitterns boom and breed among the reeds and marsh harriers pass by in spring, while below are otters, deer, bats and beautiful wild orchids.

The Forest of Dean is one of the few remaining ancient royal forests left in England. Although commercial forestry plantations have replaced much of the original oak woods, there are still a few areas where magnificent oaks over 150 years old can be found. One of these is at the RSPB **Nagshead Reserve** which covers some of the best remaining oak woodland and has a rich bird community. Summer visitors include wood warblers, redstarts and pied flycatchers as well as the whole range of woodland species including all three species of woodpecker, sparrowhawks, treecreepers and nuthatches.

At **Nene Washes** in Cambridgeshire the RSPB reserve, saved from drainage and ploughing, is an example of a landscape now nearly lost. Once, hay meadows like these – rich in flowers in spring and full of birds in winter – were common; now there are only scattered remnants left. It is ironic that the washes are entirely man-made, created in the 18th century as part of flood control and drainage schemes. Breeding birds here include redshanks, snipe, sedge warblers, yellow wagtails and shovelers. Winter brings Bewick's swans, wigeon, teal and pintails in large numbers.

On the north-west tip of Holy Island, is the RSPB reserve of **South Stack Cliffs**. This reserve consists of two separate areas: the dramatic sea cliffs and heathland of Holyhead Mountain make up the northern part, while the maritime heathland of Penrhosfeilw Common is the

southern section. The most numerous seabirds are guillemots but there are razorbills, puffins and kittiwakes. The reserve is one of the foremost migration watchpoints in North Wales, both for landbirds and seabirds. On most summer days, especially with a westerly wind, Manx shearwaters and gannets may be seen flying past, while in spring and autumn large movements of passerines can be recorded in suitable weather conditions. Hundreds of wheatears and swallows may pass through daily, with smaller numbers of willow and grasshopper warblers, whinchats and ring ouzels. In early winter thousands of starlings, chaffinches and other species pass westward to the warmer climate of Ireland.

One of the RSPB's most celebrated reserves is **Bempton Cliffs** near Goole. These spectacular 445ft chalk cliffs hold the largest breeding colony of seabirds in England. Puffins and guillemots nest here but the most famous of Bempton's seabirds is the gannet, whose colony is the only mainland one in Britain. Seawatching can be exceptionally good, especially in the autumn, when the terns and skuas are moving south. The narrow band between the cliffs and the cliff-top fields is an excellent place for wild flowers.

Though the primary purpose of a reserve is protection, the RSPB welcomes visitors – the general public as well as its own members – in order to encourage public sympathy and support for conservation. Trails and hides are provided to help visitors see as much as possible, while interfering as little as possible with the birds.

### National Trails

Enthusiasm for long distance walking has grown apace in Britain since World War II, as part of a general quickening of appetite for exploring and enjoying the countryside at first hand, away from main roads and crowded tourist spots. The first national long distance walking route, the Pennine Way, was declared open in 1965. Since then many more paths have been established. Ten of them are now classified by the Countryside Commission as 'national trails'. These are continuous routes over substantial distances, which can take a week or more to traverse though, of course, many people enjoy walking for only a few hours or a day or two on part of one of the routes.

The ten national trails in England and Wales are: the Cleveland Way; the North Downs Way; the Offa's Dyke Path; the Peddars Way and Norfolk Coast Path; the Pembrokeshire Coast Path; the Pennine Way; the Ridgeway Path; the South Downs Way; the South

Below *Offa's Dyke Path traces the 8th-century English – Welsh boundary.*
Bottom *The 50 miles of the Peddar's Way, in Norfolk, follow a Roman road.*

*National trail*

West Coast path; and the Wolds Way. Placed end to end, these 10 routes together cover approximately 1,750 miles. Three of them are in the South of England, one is in East Anglia, two are in Wales and the Marches, and three in the North. There are also three more long distance walking routes in Scotland.

The founding father of this whole network was the late Tom Stephenson of the Ramblers' Association, who in 1935 put forward the idea of a continuous public footpath running the whole length of the Pennine Chain to the Cheviots and the Scots Border. It took 30 years during which much opposition had to be overcome, but he lived to see his brainchild brought safely to birth as the Pennine Way.

The **Pennine Way** runs 250 miles up the backbone of England from the High Peak in Derbyshire to the Scottish border. It starts in the Peak District National Park and crosses two other National Parks – the Yorkshire Dales and Northumberland – as well as an Area of Outstanding Natural Beauty in the North Pennines.

You can walk it either way, naturally, but travelling from south to north keeps the weather at the walker's back and the route is usually described in this direction. It starts at Edale in the delectable valley of the River Noe, close to Castleton and its deep, eerie limestone caverns. The Way goes up across the Kinder Scout plateau (there are alternative routes here and elsewhere along the trail) to the aptly named wasteland of Bleaklow. It then passes by Blackstone Edge, with its exceptionally well preserved stretch of Roman road, and across the Calder Valley close to Hebden Bridge, where the rows of millhands' houses cling to the steep hillsides, to the beauty spot of Hardcastle Crags. North from here are the wild moors of the Brontë Country, near Haworth, and the bleak scenery and atmosphere of *Wuthering Heights* at the ruined farmhouse at Withins.

The Way crosses the Craven district to reach the tremendous limestone scenery of the Yorkshire Dales National Park: 'a strange landscape,' as the great fell-walker Wainwright has written, 'almost lunar, in places awesome, in places beautiful, and everywhere fascinating.' From Malham, the beetling gorge of Gordale Scar is a mile or so off the path, which scrambles up the sheer curving cliff of Malham Cove, close to 250ft (76m) high, to the cracked and fissured limestone 'pavement' on top. Malham Tarn is the lake where Charles Kingsley was inspired to

create *The Water Babies*. Further on is the isolated hump of Pen-y-ghent, 2,273ft (693m).

On to Ribblesdale and to Wensleydale, at Hawes, and close to Hardraw Force, where the water tumbles over a 100ft (30m) rock. Further on is Middleton in Teesdale and the Way follows the swirling, rock-strewn Tees to three spectacular waterfalls in succession: Low Force, High Force and Cauldron Snout, where the river boils and rages down the rock ledges for 200ft (61m). At the stupendous horseshoe of High Cup Nick an immense abyss opens, whose sides are sheer for almost 1,000ft (305m).

Northwards again, up the valley of the South Tyne to Hadrian's Wall, getting on for 1,900 years old now, but still swooping athletically over the crags. The Way follows it for nine miles, passing Housesteads, where there are the remains of a substantial Roman fort, with legionary latrines and a museum. Then the route lies on north over heathery moors to Bellingham, across Redesdale and through the forest to the high Cheviots, the lonely open spaces of the Northumberland National Park, and the Border at last, coming to a final grateful halt at Kirk Yetholm.

The **Wolds Way** in the old East Riding of Yorkshire is about as unlike the Pennine Way as two walking routes in the same country could conceivably be. In length, by comparison, the Wolds Way is a mere pygmy of 79 miles all told. It is easy going where the Pennine Way is hard. And instead of daring the wild and lonely places, and scenes of spectacular grandeur, the Wolds Way walker is in placid, pretty country and never far from a small town or a village, a bed, a meal, a drink.

Open since 1982, the Wolds Way begins at Hessle on the north bank of the Humber and runs under the northern end of the mighty Humber Suspension Bridge. Then the route heads north to the Yorkshire Wolds, rounded chalk hills with attractive valleys. The path lies through farming country and woods, over gentle slopes, along farm tracks and roads. A point of special interest is the deserted village of Wharram Percy, north of Thixendale. It was abandoned in Tudor times and only the ruined church is still standing.

From the northern scarp of the Wolds there are fine views across the Vale of Pickering to the North York Moors, and later to the North Sea as the footpath comes to the Victorian seaside resort of Filey. It passes close to Filey Brigg, a mile-long finger of rock protruding into the sea, going on along the cliffs to join the Cleveland Way.

The **Cleveland Way** was the second long distance footpath to be opened, in 1969. It steers its course northwards along the Yorkshire coast by Scarborough and Whitby to Saltburn. There it turns inland and changes course to the south-west, to spend the rest of its energies in the Cleveland Hills and the North York Moors National Park before coming to an end at Helmsley, not far from the haunting ruins of Rievaulx Abbey.

The **Pembrokeshire Coast Path**, 180 miles round Wales's south-western corner, and the **South West Coast Path** both take the walker through heroic coastal scenery of massive sea-beaten cliffs, coves and sandy beaches, lighthouses, vast seaward panoramas and superlative sunsets. The South West Coast Path follows the entire coastline from Minehead on the Bristol Channel in Somerset, along the North Devon shore, all round Cornwall by Land's End and the Lizard, back along the South Devon coast and the Dorset shoreline to finish on the edge of Poole Harbour.

The longest of the Scottish long distance paths is the **Southern Upland Way**, 212 miles clear across the country between Cockburnspath, east of Dunbar on the North Sea shore, and Portpatrick, looking out over the Irish Sea from the Rhinns of Galloway. This is a demanding route over a great variety of Border landscape, and positively dripping in history – passing through the Lammermuirs and the Scott Country, by the austere Jacobite mansion of Traquair, past St Mary's Loch and across the wild country of the Galloway Forest Park.

The 95 miles of the **West Highland Way**, opened in 1980, also make a romantic pilgrimage. The route is by Loch Lomond, across bleak Rannoch Moor and past the grim mountain gates of Glen Coe to Kinlochleven and Fort William, in the shadow of Ben Nevis.

The English and Welsh paths, too, have historic roots. **Offa's Dyke Path**, which is quite heavily trampled in some sections but satisfactorily lonely in others, runs the whole length of the Welsh Marches for 168 miles. From Chepstow on the River Severn it goes up the entrancing Wye Valley and long the edge of the Brecon Beacons National Park, then makes its way through the solitary, eerie Shropshire Hills and over the Clwydian Range to reach the coast of North Wales at Prestatyn. For about one-third of a distance it follows the line of the formidable bank and ditch constructed by Offa, 8th-century King of Mercia, to mark and defend his frontier with the Welsh.

The **North Downs Way**, similarly, 140 miles from Farnham to Dover and Folkestone, in part runs along the traditional medieval pilgrims' route to Canterbury, to the shrine of St Thomas à Becket. The **South Downs Way** runs 106 miles on pre-historic tracks from towering Beachy Head across Sussex and Hampshire to Winchester, commanding on the way wonderful views over the English Channel and across the Sussex Weald. The **Peddars Way**, again, follows an ancient track from the Suffolk border across Norfolk to the coast, and the **Ridgeway Path** across Wiltshire is an immensely ancient route, passing close to the important prehistoric monuments of Avebury, Wayland's Smithy and the White Horse of Uffington. On these timeworn, well-trodden ways, today's walkers tread in the footsteps of travellers of long ago.

*National trail*

*A view from Benbrack Hill, along the Southern Upland Way in Galloway.*

Cave

Prehistoric
monument

Hillfort

Roman antiquity

*Stonehenge is one of the most famous
prehistoric monuments in Europe.*

**Caves
Prehistoric Monuments
Hillforts
Roman Antiquities**

As the last great Ice Age held
Britain in its grip, early man and the
animals he hunted with increasingly
sophisticated stone weapons
followed shifts of climate. Small
family groups took refuge from the
sleet-lashed tundra in many natural
limestone caverns.

**Caves**
**Creswell Crags**, in Derbyshire, one
of the most important Palaeolithic
sites in Britain, has a visitor centre
which illustrates the life they must
have led, both in the main cave and
in nearby **Pin Hole** and **Robin
Hood's Cave**. At **Cheddar Gorge**,
Gough's Cave and Cox's Cave have
displays in a nearby museum. Other
caves worth visiting are the remains
of mine workings for lead and later
for semi-precious fluorspar near
Castleton, Derbyshire – the **Treak
Cliff** and **Speedwell Caverns**, near
Buxton, as well as the **Blue John
Cavern** itself.

**Prehistoric Monuments**
Long after the retreating glaciers
and rising sea levels had submerged
the mud flats to the east of Britain,
agriculturalists arrived from Europe.

By about 5000BC, they had given
the British upland landscape a basic
appearance which was to remain
largely unchanged until the
introduction of intensive farming
methods in the 20th century. But in
that landscape began to appear
burial mounds and much larger
monuments.

Most famous must be
**Stonehenge**, but from **Callanish**, on
the Isle of Lewis, through **Arbor
Low** and the **Nine Ladies**, near
Matlock, to the **Rollright Stones**,
north of Oxford, similar circles have
filled later generations with awe.
Possibly built, like **Castlerigg** in
Cumbria and the **Ring of Brodgar**
on Orkney, in connection with solar
or lunar observation and associated
rituals, the 'alignments' so often
attributed to these circles, and to
groups such as the **Devil's Arrows**,
near Boroughbridge, should be
treated with caution. Stonehenge
pre-dates the Druid cult by 3,000
years and yet, in the Romantic age
and the 19th century was thought to
have been a Druid temple. In
today's 'computer climate' it has
become, for some, an astronomical
calculator.

Orientation to the rising and
setting sun does appear to have
influenced the builders of most of
the megalithic burial mounds in
Britain. One of these, at
**Newgrange**, north of Dublin, a
splendid example of Neolithic

carving in its own right, is so
aligned that the midwinter sunrise
casts a beam directly into the tomb
chamber. Newgrange predates
Stonehenge by a thousand years
and the positions of earth and sun,
of sunrise – midwinter or
midsummer – have changed, but
the east–west alignments remain an
intriguing facet of the study of all
these monuments.

The village of **Avebury**, in
Wiltshire, is set within another huge
stone circle and earthwork rampart.
A museum here displays finds and
explains the way in which rampart
and circle were constructed.

**Stonehenge** has seen many phases
in its construction, from its origins
in 3000BC to its present form, which
dates from around 1800BC. The
sheer manpower involved is
amazing. Four million cubic feet of
chalk were dug out at Avebury,
using antler picks. This and the
hauling on raft and sledge of the
Stonehenge bluestones from the
Preseli Mountains in Wales and the
transport of the 80 huge sarsens
from the Marlborough Downs, tells
us something of the beliefs and
about the organisational ability of
the builders of both monuments.
Illiterate agriculturalists they may
have been – certainly they were
ignorant of the use of iron – and yet
their kings and priests were able to
organise and plan huge civil
engineering projects.

Associated with Stonehenge is the huge circular timber building – **Woodhenge**. It is not difficult to imagine a conical thatched roof supported by timber uprights, their positions now marked by concrete posts. When was it built? Around 2750BC – that at least is known. Why was it built? Who used it? There is no scatter of the usual debris associated with hut circles and their domestic middens, so Woodhenge and the nearby **Durrington Walls** site would seem to have a public and ceremonial function. Perhaps the forest of tree trunk pillars recalled forest groves which had long had religious significance. At Woodhenge a three-year-old child, its skull split, was buried, perhaps as a dedication, at the centre of the complex. When the timbers at last decayed, a memorial stone was placed at the centre of the circle.

**Silbury Hill**, near Avebury, has so far yielded up few of its secrets. Why this 130ft (40m) mound, covering over five acres at its base, was raised is still a mystery. Trenches have been dug, seeking a burial somewhere within, but all these excavations have found is that it was very carefully built. Inside the turf mound is a stepped cone of compacted chalk rubble, each layer being finished with smooth chalk blocks. The steps were later filled with earth except for the topmost one, still visible as a terrace. The fact that the whole of the Stonehenge circle would fit comfortably within this topmost terrace gives an idea of the scale of the mound.

Carbon-14 dating has placed its construction at around 2600BC – and the trenches have told us that it was started in July or August, for right at the core have been found winged ants – but maybe there is a more important burial still to be discovered. Nearby is **West Kennet Long Barrow** and its sarsen façade – burial chamber perhaps, of the chieftains who commanded the building of Avebury.

## Hillforts

The 'Beaker Folk', so called from the distinctive pottery vessels found in their graves, arrived in Britain around 2700BC. They brought with them the Aryan roots of our language and their knowledge of metal working was gradually learnt by the established communities into which they merged. By 1800BC the British climate was deteriorating and tribes vied for workable land. Local chiefs gained power and protected their arable land and pasture from the safety of upland hillforts, which gradually became tribal 'capitals'

rather than merely bolt holes in case of war.

Thousands of these hillforts dot the landscape, and many were inhabited well into the Roman age. **Ingleborough**, just north of the National Park Centre at Clapham, North Yorkshire, is the highest in Britain. Life must have been very hard on this high windswept plateau. Earlier settlers in the area possibly make themselves a warmer home in the cave systems nearby, at **Ingleborough Show Cave** and **Gaping Gill**. One of the largest and most important hill-forts in Britain is **Maiden Castle**. Built initially around 300BC, it finally fell to Vespasian's troops in AD43. Boards around the two-mile perimeter provide much information and the museum in nearby Dorchester displays finds from the site.

Often associated with these hill-forts are the figures carved into the chalk hillsides – horses and giant figures – but only a handful can be said with certainty to be 'pre-historic'. **Uffington White Horse**, between Swindon and Wantage, certainly is. Overlooking the Ridgeway Path, an ancient trade route across the north Berkshire Downs, its disintegrated simplicity resembles the horses – tribal totems, perhaps – which feature on Celtic coinage. The **Cerne Abbas Giant,** north of Dorchester, is probably not more than 1,500 years old, but its club-wielding phallic figure possibly represents Hercules, part of a god-cult which flourished around AD100. The iron Age enclosure above him was used for May Day and fertility ceremonies long after the foundation of the nearby Benedictine priory in the 10th century. **Wilmington Long Man**, near Alfriston, inland from Beachy Head, could well be Romano-British, too.

From 700BC onwards, Celtic settlers brought their language, their chariots and a love of finery, gold and ornaments. Iron swords gave them an ascendancy in battle over the native Britons, who were pushed westwards. Celtic immigrant groups shared a common dialect but their lack of any concept of 'nationhood' left their society an easy prey to the civilising might of Rome.

## Roman Antiquities

The lure of corn, gold, iron, slaves and hunting dogs was enough to make the Romans decide that an invasion of Britannia in the summer of AD43 was worthwhile. By AD70 50 or more towns were linked by a network of roads. *Lex Romana* tamed the unruly land and Latin became yet another rootstock from

which English would eventually spring. Evidence of Roman military occupation is everywhere – from **Hadrian's Wall** and the lighthouse in **Dover Castle**, to the legionary fortress at **Caerleon** in Gwent.

Many of the civilising influences of Rome can still be seen today – an aqueduct which supplied fresh water 12 miles along the Frome Valley to Dorchester, sewers in Lincoln, Colchester and York, and bath houses. The finest of these, at **Bath**, is rivalled by the complex of baths and exercise halls at Viroconium, near **Wroxeter**. Theatres such as those of Verulamium and Caerleon, and the busy shopping centres which developed around the forum or the town gates, attracted people to the towns. Mosaic floors like those at **Aldborough**, in Yorkshire, reflect a very comfortable style of life. This wealth is mirrored, too, by the remains of many Roman villas such as those at Lullingstone, near **Eynsford** in Kent, **Fishbourne** in Sussex and **Chedworth** in Gloucestershire.

*Below* Westbury White Horse, on Bratton Down, Wiltshire.
*Bottom* Housesteads Fort along Hadrian's Wall, in Northumbria.

Cave

Prehistoric monument

Hillfort

Roman antiquity

THE BATTLE OF FLODDEN FIELD
9th September 1513

Above *The site of the Battle of Flodden. Inset A display board at Flodden chronicles the battle which was fought here.* Top right *According to tradition, men watched London's Great Fire from Outwood Mill, Surrey.* Bottom *Porthcurno's Minack open-air theatre.*

Windmill

Other place of
interest

## Battlefields
## Windmills
## Other Places of Interest

Normans and Plantagenets, wars in Scotland and Wales, the Wars of the Roses, the Civil War and the Jacobite risings, have all left the map of Britain dotted with 'crossed swords' symbols. In the 250 years that separate us from Culloden, in 1746, the last battle on British soil, farming, roads and railways, canals and houses have changed the fields on which the history of the nation was written.

### Battlefields

We do not commemorate our battles as lavishly as the Visitor Centres at places such as Waterloo or Gettysburg, but there are still fields where there is something to be seen today. Facilities are available, mainly in the tourist season, for organised groups to be taken round and it is worth telephoning to see whether you can join one.

The Battle of **Hastings**, on 14 October 1066, certainly changed things in England. Stories of the battle are well enough known – Harold's forced march of 250 miles from battle against the Norwegian king at Stamford Bridge, near York, to meet the Norman invaders; the Norman minstrel Taillefer charging

the shield-wall; the hail of arrows harassing the axemen; the final stand of the house-carles around the royal standard of Wessex. All are vividly recalled in an audio-visual presentation in the Tourist Office on the green just opposite the gateway of the Abbey which William founded, its altar traditionally on the spot where Harold fell. Now an English Heritage property, the pathways around and overlooking main sectors of the battlefield are well signposted, with information boards at regular intervals.

In the **Bannockburn** Heritage Centre the full story of the battle of 24 June 1314, is graphically told in an audio-visual entitled *The Forging of a Nation*. On the field itself is preserved the Borestone, where Robert the Bruce raised his banner before this decisive culmination of the Wars of Independence.

From the top of the Durham Cathedral tower the battlefield of **Neville's Cross** can be seen as it was by the monks who gave 'moral support' by singing hymns there in 1346. A leaflet explaining the battle is available from the Tourist Office and a half mile walk from the city brings the visitor to the battlefield itself.

An exhibition is mounted on **Bosworth** battlefield, near Sutton

Cheney, with an audio-visual presentation including scenes from Laurence Olivier's *Richard III*. There is a battlefield trail, with another information centre halfway round at Shenton Station. Here, Richard of Gloucester, uncle of the Princes in the Tower, met his end, having found no one to answer his cry 'My kingdom for a horse!'

At a call from France for help from the 'auld alliance', James IV of Scotland marched into England. On Pipers' Hill, at **Flodden Edge**, is a monument 'To the Brave of both Nations', with the battlefield spread out below. A booklet and map from nearby Coldstream enable you to follow the course of the battle. King Henry VIII had left the old Earl of Surrey, a veteran of Bosworth, to defend the north. Surrey had borrowed the banner of St Cuthbert, obviously a powerful morale raiser, from Durham Cathedral. But it was artillery fire that stung the Scots into premature offensive action, allowing English archers to reach the crest of Pipers' Hill and pour a murderous arrow storm into the massed pikemen below. Flodden was the last major battle won largely by the longbow.

The Castle Inn, in **Edgehill,** was built on the spot where King Charles raised his Standard. There

is a memorial on the field below and a map and guidebook will enable you to follow the course of the fighting. Neither side seemed willing to strike the first blow until a Parliamentary gunner spotted the King on the hill, fired – and missed. Prince Rupert charged – found an ally in the inaptly named Sir Faithful Fortescue, one of the Parliamentary cavalry commanders – and they all dashed the two miles or so to Kineton, where they rested their horses and indulged in a little light looting. Roundhead foot soldiers were about to finish off the exhausted Royalists when they were attacked owing to the opportune return of Prince Rupert and the cavalry. Captain John Smith, of the King's Lifeguard, met a party of Roundheads escorting a Royalist prisoner and the Royal Standard which they had just captured. The prisoner recognised Smith and called to him. Smith charged, killed one Roundhead, wounded another and the other four fled. He was knighted on the spot by the King for recovering the Standard, which had not been in Parliamentary hands above fifteen minutes.

In the village of **Naseby** is a museum with dioramas and a ten minute commentary of different stages of the battle of 14 July 1645.

Should the museum be closed, then try the village shop or the church for the descriptive leaflet and map, which will make the whole encounter more easy to follow.

A drive up the Naseby-Sibbertoft road takes you to a monument marking the position from which Cromwell led his cavalry to win the day and from where there is a good view over the whole battlefield.

Information about the battle of **Worcester**, 3 September 1651, is available from both the Tourist Office and the Civil War Centre at the Commandery. Worcester was the scene of the first and last battles of the war. During the summer, frequent 're-enactments' are staged by several groups, particularly in September.

**Sedgemoor**, the last battle fought on English soil, on 6 July 1685, followed the landing by the Duke of Monmouth, illegitimate son of Charles II, to claim the throne of James II. A stone monument marks the site of the battle, and information can be obtained from the Admiral Blake Museum in Bridgwater.

The Battle of **Culloden**, on the moors outside Inverness, ended the Jacobite Rising in 1746. Bonnie Prince Charlie, with the help of Flora Macdonald, escaped 'over the sea to Skye' and the Stuart cause was swept away. The whole story is graphically told in the visitor centre on the battlefield, which has been restored to its 18th-century appearance, but now dotted with emotive memorial cairns and the Graves of the Clans, on which no heather ever grows.

Since Culloden, we may be thankful that no armies have fought on British soil – only *above* it, in 1940. Aerial bombardment brought the realities of war much closer to the public than did any of the very localised combats of the previous 700 years.

### Windmills
Few things add as much atmosphere to the countryside as a windmill. They have drained marshlands and ground corn since medieval times. One tradition suggests that they were introduced by crusaders returning home from the wars. Whether or not this is true, we know for a fact that they were first built here some eight centuries ago. None of the original structures remain, but some have survived a few hundreds years. Still in working order is **Berney Arms Mill**, in Norfolk, from the top of which there is a splendid view and the working wind pump at **Wicken Fen**, a remnant of the wetlands drained by Dutch engineers, which

became England's first nature reserve, in 1899. **Bourn Mill**, near Cambridge, is a 17th-century 'post mill', the oldest surviving mill in the country. Unlike the conical tower windmills with a rotating cap, here the sails and machinery all turn together, revolving round a central post. A tide mill has stood on the river bank at **Woodbridge** in Suffolk since the 12th century and the present one was working until 1956, when the shaft of the waterwheel broke. Careful restoration has successfully restored it to working condition.

### Other Places of Interest
There is a wide range of other places of interest which are well worth visiting. From waterfalls, wells, bridges and towers to dovecotes, follies, monuments and parks, Britain has something to offer every visitor.

Not far from Land's End, on the cliffs near Porthcurno, is the **Minack Theatre**, carved out of the living rock in the 1930s, with the sea as a backdrop for the stage. North of Tavistock is **Lydford Gorge**, a deep wooded gorge with the lovely White Lady Waterfall at the end of a mile or so walk.

Further along the coast, north-west of Weymouth, the extraordinary Chesil Beach, a 12-mile long pebble bank, shelters the **Abbotsbury Swannery**, where swans were bred for the table by the monks as long ago as the 14th century. Today it is a breeding haven for hundreds of wild mute swans. At St Fagans, to the west of Cardiff, is the **Welsh Folk Museum**, a collection of rural buildings from the 17th century onwards from all over Wales, carefully re-erected in the grounds of St Fagans Castle, an elegant Elizabethan mansion.

Waterfalls abound, but one not to be missed is **Hardraw Force**, north of Hawes, North Yorkshire, a spectacular 90ft (27m) drop into a glen which has been used for brass band contests – a great local tradition – on account of its splendid acoustics. Further north, near Moffat on the A708, is one of Scotland's highest falls, the **Grey Mare's Tail**, where Loch Skeen plunges 200ft (61m) to meet Moffat Water.

Shire horses, Clydesdales and Suffolk Punches have ploughed England's fields – and delivered England's beer – for centuries. In the **National Shire Horse Centre**, at Plymouth, there is stabling dating back to 1772 and three parades a day are staged in summer. Courage Breweries have a **Shire Horse Centre** near Maidenhead, as do Whitbread at their **Hop Farm**, on the B2015, east of Tonbridge.

*Battle site with year*

*Windmill*

*Other place of interest*

31

*Viewpoint*

*Picnic site*

*Agricultural showground*

## Viewpoints
## Picnic Sites
## Agricultural Showgrounds

The **Clee Hills** of Shropshire, in the Welsh Marches, are in a remote and exceptionally attractive area of the country – an official Area of Outstanding Natural Beauty, in fact. They are 'young' hills, geologically, jagged and more impressive than their official height statistics would suggest, and in the past were heavily quarried for coal, building stone, iron and copper. A wealth of folklore still attaches to them, with sinister tales of witches and evil forces. They are also the site of a spectacular viewpoint.

### Viewpoints

The viewpoint is on the A4117, six miles east of Ludlow. In the immediate foreground to the north is the bulk of Titterstone Clee, 1,750ft (533m) with its aerials and radar dishes, and one of the biggest Iron Age hillforts in Britain on its summit. Beyond the hill is the long,

*Below The picnic site at David Marshall Lodge, Aberfoyle.*
*Bottom View of South Stack lighthouse from the viewpoint on Anglesey.*

wooded ridge of Wenlock Edge and to the west beyond Ludlow rise the mountains of Wales.

Viewpoints, as marked in AA Road Atlases, are all easily accessible by car and have a plaque to identify landmarks and places of interest in the area. Each viewpoint has a prospect of at least 180 degrees and some command wider vistas still. The **Cockleroy** viewpoint, two miles south of Linlithgow in the Lothian region of Scotland, has marvellous views over the full 360 degrees. To the east the eye ranges over Edinburgh to the Firth of Forth, to the south-east lie the Pentland Hills, in the west is Glasgow and in the north the outlying bastions of the Highlands.

The viewpoint is in the Beecraigs Country Park, among the Bathgate Hills, with trails through the woodland, a reservoir with hides for watching the numerous waterfowl and a deer farm with a viewing platform. At Linlithgow are the romantic ruins of the palace of the Stuart kings, where Mary, Queen of Scots was born, and the church where she was christened. Not far away is Torphichen Preceptory, once the Scottish base of the crusading order of the Knights of St John of Jerusalem. A little to the south there are superlative views again, from Cairnpaple Hill, where prehistoric men buried their dead over a period of 2,500 years and more.

On the other side of Glasgow, the **Lyle Hill** viewpoint is just outside the former shipbuilding town of Greenock, the birthplace of James Watt, and during World War II the principal Free French naval base. The viewpoint is near the war memorial to those sailors, an anchor surmounted by a Cross of Lorraine. Down below is the Firth of Clyde and its swarming ferries. To the north and north-west lie Holy Loch and the woods and mountains of the Argyll Forest Park on the Cowal Peninsula, with the serrated crests of The Cobbler in the distance. West and south-west are the Isle of Bute, separated from the mainland by the narrow Kyles of Bute, the Isle of Arran rising to Goat Fell and, beyond Arran, the Kintyre Peninsula.

Far away at the other end of the country, in Cornwall, the majestic harbour of Carrick Roads was an important United States Navy base during the war. The viewpoint is on **Pendennis Point**, outside Falmouth, commanding a sweeping prospect of the harbour and out to the English Channel and the Lizard Peninsula. Close at hand is the round keep of Pendennis Castle,

one of the artillery strongpoints built along the coast in Henry VIII's time against attack by the French. Across the water is its other half, St Mawes Castle. These twin fortresses have done their job, and no enemy force has ever attempted to penetrate Carrick Roads.

Another viewpoint with naval connections lies eastward along the coast, on **Portsdown Hill** in Hampshire, a mile north of Cosham. Immediately to the south sprawls Portsmouth, with its historic harbour and the Royal Navy dockyard where Nelson's HMS *Victory* rests in honourable retirement. Birds wheel above the Farlington Marshes at the northern end of Langstone Harbour and the eagle eye pierces 10 miles across the Solent to the Isle of Wight. For visitors who would like something to eat as well as watch, there is a picnic site here.

So there is at the viewpoint at **David Marshall Lodge**, the Forestry Commission visitor centre in the scenic Trossachs area, in the Central region of Scotland, a mile north of Aberfoyle on A821. There are spectacular views here of Ben Lomond, the Highland mountains and the valleys of the Forth.

The haunting beauty of the Trossachs – 'So wondrous wild, the whole might seem the scenery of a fairy dream' – with its lochs, peaks and 'wildering forest' – was praised by Sir Walter Scott in 1810 in his immensely popular poem *The Lady of the Lake.* To add to its romantic attractions, much of the area was Rob Roy country.

Strictly speaking, the Trossachs ('the cross places' in Gaelic) means the narrow belt of land between Loch Katrine and Loch Achray, but the name is more often used broadly for the whole area between Loch Lomond and Callander. Much of it is now in the Forestry Commission's enormous Queen Elizabeth Forest Park. After Scott, tourists began to flock to the area in such numbers that the local landowner, the Duke of Montrose, built the road north from Aberfoyle which is now the A821, or Duke's Road. There are parking places and a picnic site along it, and more along the Forestry Commission's one-way Achray Forest Drive, which leaves the Duke's Road to make its way seven miles through the woods, by Loch Drunkie and Loch Achray. There are more scenic viewpoints here and a waymarked forest walk.

### Picnic Sites

One of the Countryside Commission's achievements has been to stimulate local authorities to

Viewpoint

Picnic site

Agricultural
showground

provide places where motorists could pull off the road to enjoy a picnic. Opinion surveys and studies repeatedly made it clear that many people were deterred from enjoying the countryside by an uneasy fear of trespassing or going where they were not wanted; an official picnic spot is somewhere where you know you are entitled to be. Although most sites have been organised by county councils, many have been provided by the Forestry Commission, others by the National Trust and by private landowners.

Many sites provide a view of attractive scenery or are close to an outstanding attraction. There is one near the ruins of **Mount Grace Priory**, for instance, the medieval Carthusian monastery near Osmotherley in North Yorkshire (where each of the tiny hermit-like cells had running water, incidentally) and there is one close to the **Hardraw Force** waterfall, off the Pennine Way. In Wales there are several with views of **Llyn Clywedog**, near Llanidloes in Powys, a three-mile long reservoir. An old iron mine can also be visited here, and not far away is another picnic site beside the infant River Severn, as it starts its long journey to the sea from the high moors of Plynlimon. There are more looking over **Lake Vyrnwy** in Powys, a beautiful 1880s reservoir with wooded shores and a striking Victorian Gothic tower. In England too, reservoirs make pleasing picnic spots, as at **Rutland Water** in Leicestershire, or **Grafham Water** in Cambridgeshire.

### Agricultural Showgrounds

The 'traditional' English landscape of green fields, hedgerows and narrow lanes was created by the agricultural revolution of the 18th century, which introduced improved farming methods. County agricultural societies were formed to spread knowledge of the new ways and raise standards. They organised annual county shows at which farmers and breeders showed off their achievements and competed against each other. For 200 years and more these agricultural shows have been part of the accustomed round of country life, with their marquees and bands, their displays of the latest farm machinery and equipment, and their classes for heavy horses, cattle and sheep. One of the oldest is the **Royal Bath and West Show**, which can trace its history back to 1777 and draws 100,000 people every year to its permanent showground near Shepton Mallet in Somerset. Before the War, the county shows normally moved around from one

country estate or farmer's fields to another, year by year. After 1945 the cost of staging a show escalated alarmingly. Some shows folded up, some amalgamated and others established permanent showgrounds. The leader in the field was the Yorkshire Agricultural Society, which planted its **Great Yorkshire Show** on a permanent site at Harrogate. The **Royal Highland Show** chose a location at Ingliston, a few miles west of Edinburgh, for its shows.

Other leading shows which have equipped themselves with fixed locations include the **Three Counties** at Great Malvern (the three counties being Herefordshire, Worcestershire and Gloucestershire), the **South of England** at Ardingly in Sussex, the **Royal Cornwall** at Wadebridge, the

*A plaque marking the viewpoint on Sugar Loaf Mountain in Wales.*

**East of England** near Peterborough and the **Royal Welsh** at Builth Wells. The Royal Agricultural Society of England, founded in 1838, held its first show at Oxford the following year. The 'Royal' moved about the country every year until 1963, when it settled at Stoneleigh in Warwickshire, in a permanent home where the **National Agriculture Centre** evolved in the 1970s. The agricultural shows have had heavy weather to come through in recent years, but they have survived, and altogether are estimated to attract about three million visitors a year to share country triumphs and pleasures.

*Horse racing*

*Show jumping and equestrian circuit*

**Horse Racing**
**Show Jumping and**
**Equestrian Circuits**
**Athletics Stadiums**
**Motor Racing Circuits**

Becher's Brook . . . Valentine's . . . the Canal Turn . . . the Chair. The familiar litany of names conjures up **Aintree** on Grand National Day – the jostle at the start, the crash and crackle of horse meeting thorn-and-fir fence, horses and jockeys falling, the clamour of the crowd. The early history of the great race is obscure, but it is usually traced back to the Grand Liverpool Steeplechase of 1839. That race was won by a horse appropriately named Lottery and that was the year the gallant Captain Becher, a well-known gentleman rider of the day, fell into the brook that bears his name. His horse, named Conrad, fell in as well.

**Horse Racing**

A steeplechase as the name implies, did not originally take place on a course at all. A by-product of hunting, it was a wild pell-mell gallop across country over hedges and ditches, towards a distant steeple or other agreed marker. Not

*World famous Derby Day, at Epsom Race Course in Surrey.*

until the 19th century did organised racing over artificial jumps on a set course begin. Racing started at Aintree in 1829, on the course owned by the Earls of Sefton for another 120 years. The course, in a dreary northern suburb of Liverpool, has the most formidable fences in the sport and in 1928 a horse named Tipperary Tim won the Grand National simply by being the only finisher of 42 starters. Far and away the most famous horse associated with Aintree and the National, however, is Red Rum, the only three-time winner (in 1973, 1974 and 1977).

The most prestigious steeplechase course in England is at **Cheltenham**, in a delightful country situation outside the town, at Prestbury Park, under the looming Cotswold bulwark of Cleeve Hill. It is a testing track on heavy clay. The major event of the year is the Cheltenham Gold Cup in March, first held in 1924. The great horse Golden Miller won it five years in succession from 1932 to 1936 (and in 1934 won the Grand National as well). The Champion Hurdle at Cheltenham is the premier hurdle event in the country.

The capital of the flat racing industry is across the other side of the country at **Newmarket**. The

town developed as a racing and breeding centre for 'the sport of kings' under royal patronage. Charles II rode his own horses in races there: hence the name Rowley Mile for one of Newmarket's two courses, from the king's nickname, Old Rowley. In the mid-18th century the aristocratic Jockey Club was founded at Newmarket. It owns the two courses and Newmarket Heath, the open country around the town on which strings of staggeringly valuable racehorses can be seen exercising. It occupies a suitably august red brick building in the centre of the town, and nearby is the highly enjoyable National Horseracing Museum, which opened in 1983.

Two of the five 'classic' races are held at Newmarket: the Two Thousand Guineas, and the One Thousand Guineas for fillies only, inaugurated in 1809 and 1814 respectively. Both are run on the Rowley Mile course, which has a long flat straight, followed by a dip and rise to the finish. Long races cannot easily be seen from the grandstands because the course was laid out long before the days of packed modern race crowds.

The most famous race in the world is run early in June every year at **Epsom.** It is named after the

12th Earl of Derby, though it might easily have been called the Bunbury. Lord Derby and Sir Charles Bunbury tossed a coin in 1780 to decide the name of a new race for three-year-old colts and fillies. As if in compensation, Bunbury's horse Diomed won the first Derby, and Lord Derby had to wait until 1787 to win with Sir Peter Teazle.

The other classic race at Epsom, the Oaks, restricted to fillies, was first run in 1779 and was named after a house which Lord Derby had taken nearby.

W P Frith's well-known painting *Derby Day* gives a vivid impression of the occasion in Victorian times, when it was virtually a public holiday. Huge numbers of people swarmed to enjoy a day out and all the fun of the fair on Epsom Downs. The Derby course is more or less level for the first three-quarters of a mile and then drops to a sharp turn at Tattenham Corner before the run-in.

The last of the classics, in September, is the oldest; the St Leger, which goes all the way back to 1776 and is named after a prominent Yorkshire sportsman of the time. It is run at **Doncaster,** on the Town Moor, the common land outside the town which, as at Epsom, was the natural place for the races.

One of the oldest courses in the country, and one of the oddest, is the Roodee at **Chester,** where there was apparently organised racing in Henry VIII's time. The course has the River Dee on one side with the old city wall on the other and is circular, with almost no straight. At **York,** there was racing on the Knavesmire, common land outside the city, early in the 18th century. Here in August is contested the Gimcrack Stakes, named in honour of a famous grey. The sport's most attractive setting is claimed by **Goodwood,** near Chichester in Sussex, where the course was laid out by the 3rd Duke of Richmond with the first meeting staged in 1801.

The smartest social occasion of the racing year is the **Royal Ascot** meeting in June, attended by the Queen, with a royal procession up the straight in carriages and much media fuss about fashionable hats. Races were first held at Ascot, in Berkshire, in 1711. The King George VI and Queen Elizabeth Diamond Stakes, run in July with the richest prize money in the sport, was inaugurated in 1951 to mark the Festival of Britain.

### Showjumping and Equestrian Circuits
The first show jumping contest on record was held in London in 1869. From 1912 the sport was regularly included in the Olympic Games, but it is only since 1945 that it has attracted strong public and media interest. The popular Horse of the Year show, at **Wembley Arena** in London, dates from 1949. The same year saw the first horse trials at **Badminton,** in Avon, on a testing course laid out in the grounds of his palatial mansion by the Duke of Beaufort. Himself a redoubtable huntsman, the duke was determined to do something about the indifferent showing of the British equestrian team in the 1948 Olympics. The three day event at Badminton in the spring now draws spectators in thousands. In 1984 Lucinda Green won Badminton for a record sixth time, on six different horses. Another stately home course is the one at **Burghley House,** near Stamford, in the grounds of the palace of the Cecils, right-hand men to Elizabeth I and James I. The Marquess of Exeter, a former Olympic athlete, offered a home for a three day event here, first held in 1961. The Burghley Horse Trials in September are now firmly established as a prestigious occasion in the show jumping calendar.

The sport's equivalent of Aintree and Epsom combined is the course at **Hickstead** in Sussex, opened in 1960 at his home by a leading rider, Douglas Bunn, to provide a permanent arena with formidable obstacles. The first British Show Jumping Derby was held there in 1961.

### Athletics Stadiums
Athletics is less well equipped with tracks and grounds than other major sports. The principal arena for international athletics is at the **Crystal Palace** in South London, where a 12,000-seater stadium was opened in 1964. Ten years later, an all-weather track was installed in the town stadium at **Gateshead,** and home-town athlete Brendan Foster set a new 3,000m world record to celebrate. The cross-country course at Gateshead is also well known.

### Motor Racing Circuits
The magic name from the early history of motor racing in England is **Brooklands,** the track near Weybridge in Surrey which, sadly, closed in 1939. Every great figure of the early days raced there and John Cobb set a lap record of 143mph in a Napier-Railton in 1935. Another leading venue was **Donington Park,** near Derby, where Grand Prix events were held in the 1930s. During the war the site was taken over by the Army. Years later the circuit was reopened for racing, in the 1970s. The Motor Museum there has a notable collection of Grand Prix racing cars.

Since 1945 the two major British circuits have been Silverstone and Brands Hatch. **Silverstone**, in Northamptonshire near Towcester, opened in 1948 on a former airfield, hence the name Hangar Straight for part of the course. The British Grand Prix is staged there, but for many years it alternated with Brands Hatch, near Farningham in Kent. It opened for Formula Three racing in 1949 and in 1960 opened the Grand Prix course.

*Athletics stadium*

*Motor racing circuit*

*A rider in the TT races, held every June on the Isle of Man.*

*Golf course*

*County cricket ground*

*National rugby ground*

*A scene at Lord's, the home of Middlesex County Cricket Club.*

**Golf Courses
County Cricket Grounds
National Rugby Grounds
Ski Slopes
Coastal Launching Sites**

Of all the world's great golf courses, the most august is the venerable and venerated Old Course at **St Andrews** in Scotland, where the Victorian clubhouse of the Royal and Ancient Golf Club is the temple and citadel of the game. A links, or seaside course – as all the country's top courses are – the Old Course is four miles in length and so many golfers are keen to play it that it normally opens at six o'clock in the morning. The notorious par 4 17th, or Roadhole, is said to have driven more great golfers to rage and bitter despair than any other golf hole in the world.

**Golf Courses**

Golf was played at St Andrews on the springy turf beside the North Sea as long ago as the 15th century, it seems, and when 22 noblemen and gentlemen founded the Society of St Andrews Golfers in 1754, they described the game as an 'ancient and healthful exercise'. The club was dubbed 'royal' in 1834 by King William IV and became the governing body of the game.

Another illustrious club is the Honourable Company of Edinburgh Golfers, which was founded in 1744 (as the Gentlemen Golfers of Leigh), ten years before the Royal and Ancient. It drew up the first set of rules, which the R and A adopted. The club now has its headquarters at **Muirfield**, a famous championship course on the outskirts of the village of Gullane, east of Edinburgh. It is close to the shore of the Firth of Forth, whose invigorating breezes are claimed to account for the great age which the Edinburgh Golfers commonly attain. The course is known for its meticulously constructed bunkers. Jack Nicklaus won his first British Open at Muirfield in 1966 and Nick Faldo won there in 1987.

There is a clutch of notable courses across on the Ayrshire shore, on hillocky ground on the sandy turf and coarse grass beside the sea. The **Prestwick** club organised the first British Open championship in 1860 and it was played there many times, but after 1925 the course was no longer big enough for the crowds which the event was beginning to attract. Few of them are these days.

**Royal Troon,** just to the north, has holes with names – they start with Seal and to on to Postage Stamp and Rabbit. In the 1973 Open two holes-in-one were scored at Postage Stamp. One was by the veteran American Gene Sarazen and the other by the amateur David Russell, who happened to be respectively the oldest and the youngest players in the field.

There is another group of redoubtable courses in England along the Lancashire coast. **Royal Lytham and St Anne's,** near Blackpool, was in open countryside when the club was founded in 1886, but is now an oasis in a desert of housing estates. Here, the first Ladies Open was played in 1893 and Tony Jacklin had his Open triumph in 1969. Near Southport is another crack course, **Royal Birkdale,** and further south on the tip of the Wirral Peninsula, is **Hoylake,** where the first British Amateur championship was contested in 1885. The demanding course is no longer considered adequate to cope with Open crowds. The Open is still played over the **Royal St George's** course at Sandwich on the Kent coast, one of the toughest in Britain, and the scene of a famous fictitious match in Ian Fleming's *Goldfinger*.

Other courses are celebrated not for the championships fought out over them, but for their associations with heroic figures of the past. The legendary James Braid, five times Open champion, was professional at **Walton Heath** in Surrey for 45 years until he died in 1950 at the age of 80. On his birthday he invariably went out and played the course in as many strokes as his age or less.

His contemporary, the incomparable John Henry Taylor, learned his golf at the **Royal North Devon's** links at Westward Ho!, on the bumpy sandy ground of the Burrows, frequented by horses, cows and sheep as well as golfers.

Speaking of animals on a course, in 1934 the professional at the **St Margaret's at Cliffe** club in Kent killed a cow with his tee shot to the 18th. And in 1975 at **Scunthorpe,** Humberside, a drive at the 14th hole, named the Mallard, hit and killed a mallard duck in flight.

### Cricket Grounds

Cricket, like golf, emerged from the mists of obscurity into the light of history in the 18th century. The most famous ground in the country, and the world, is **Lord's** in the St John's Wood district of London. It takes its name from its original proprietor, a Yorkshireman named Thomas Lord, who came to London in 1787, was instrumental in the founding of the MCC (Marylebone Cricket Club) and opened the St John's Wood ground in 1812. Lord's is also the home of the Middlesex County Cricket Club. The original pavilion, a one-room hut, and the tavern provided by Thomas Lord have been replaced over the years by a Victorian pavilion and modern stands. The grand entrance gates to the ground were specially designed in 1923 as a memorial to W G Grace, the greatest cricketer of his age, and Lord's now has a good museum of cricket.

The other famous London ground is the **Oval,** in Kennington, south of the river. Originally a market garden, and long famed for a fine view of the local gasometers, the ground has been the headquarters of the Surrey county club since its formation in a nearby pub in 1845. Like Lord's, the Oval is a regular Test match arena. The highest innings ever recorded in Test cricket was notched up there in 1938, when England scored 903 for 7 declared, with Len Hutton making 364.

One of cricket's most attractive settings is the county ground at **Worcester,** where the cathedral rises nobly in the background across the Severn. The drawback is that when the river floods, as in 1990, the pitch is covered with tons of thick black mud. Another attractive county cricket arena is the St Lawrence ground at **Canterbury** in Kent. The Canterbury Week cricket festival has been held since 1847.

The ground at **Old Trafford** in the southern suburbs of Manchester has seen many a Test match and many a tussle between the red rose of Lancashire and the white rose of Yorkshire. The principal Yorkshire

ground is at **Headingley,** a couple of miles from the centre of Leeds. Two other grounds regularly used for Test cricket are **Trent Bridge** in Nottingham, where cricket has been played since 1838, and **Edgbaston,** the Warwickshire county ground in Birmingham.

### Rugby Grounds

Rugby's equivalent of Lord's is the 'cabbage patch' at **Twickenham,** a market garden bought by the Rugby Union in 1907. The choice was fiercely criticised for being too far from Piccadilly Circus, but the motor car changed all that and the ground has been developed into a spanking modern arena. For Welsh rugby men, however, the holy of holies of their national game is **Cardiff Arms Park,** beside the River Taff close to the heart of the city, where the stands echo on great occasions to the impassioned sound of Welsh singing. The Cardiff Football Club began to practise on a piece of meadow here beside the river in 1876. Today it is a thoroughly up-to-date arena with

*Above* The clubhouse at St Andrew's. *Right* Skiing in the Cairngorms, one of Scotland's busiest resorts.

two stadiums. The two other home international grounds are Murrayfield in Edinburgh and Lansdowne Road in Dublin.

### Ski Slopes

Increasing affluence since 1945 has brought skiing within the reach of far more people than before, and although all the major ski slopes are abroad, a skiing industry has developed in Scotland. The Highland village of **Aviemore,** a quiet haven for anglers and mountaineers, was transformed into a thriving winter sports resort in the 1960s. There are ski schools and dry-ski slopes, and Aviemore is the

base for the nearby Cairngorms ski area, with its chairlifts and ski tows.

There are cross-country ski trails of varying degrees of difficulty in this area, too. The other main Scottish ski areas are **Glenshee,** south of Braemar on the A93, Britain's highest main road, the **Lecht** area on the A939 near Tomintoul and the **Glencoe** area above the A82, where the road crosses Rannoch Moor.

### Coastal Launching Sites

Sailing has also become more popular. Most of its enthusiasts are weekend sailors, who do not go far from shore, and there are boat launching sites at harbours and marinas all round the coast, from **St Ives** harbour in Cornwall to **Thurso Bay** on the north coast of Scotland. They vary from the broad, sheltered expanses of **Carrick Roads** or **Plymouth Sound** to the flat shingle shore at **Deal** in Kent, close to the historic anchorage of The Downs, or the exposed Suffolk coastline at **Walberswick** or **Southwold.**

*Natural ski slope*

*Artificial ski slope*

*Coastal launching site*

*Heritage Coast*

Above *Looking across Embleton Bay, a view for Dunstanburgh Castle.*
Left *Spectacular rock formation at Elegug stacks, Pembrokeshire.*

### ▌Heritage Coasts

For centuries the white cliffs of Dover have stood as symbols of English nationhood, independence and pride, confronting foes across the Channel with unyielding defiance. It was the sight of the white cliffs which told generations of weary English travellers that they were nearing home. Today, to keep the white cliffs unspoiled, they have to be protected as two four-mile stretches of Heritage Coast, either side of Dover.

### Heritage Coasts

Before World War II, concern was growing about the substantial areas of coastline which had been ruined by commercial development and the threat that what was left would go the same way, disappearing under an ever-rising tide of cliff-top bungalows and caravan sites. The

Coastal Preservation Committee mounted a campaign in the 1930s. During the War, the distinguished geographer J A Steers surveyed the coast for the government, and his work would later be the basis on which Heritage Coasts were chosen.

In 1965 the National Trust, thoroughly alarmed, launched Enterprise Neptune, a campaign to raise money to buy threatened coastline. This campaign continues and the Trust now owns and protects more than one mile in every six along the shoreline of England, Wales and Northern Ireland, including the **Giant's Causeway** on the scenic North Antrim seacoast of Northern Ireland and more than a quarter of the entire coast of **Cornwall.**

In 1970 the Countryside Commission recommended to the government that scenically outstanding stretches of undeveloped coast should be designated as Heritage Coasts and protected against undesirable development. This was duly set in train and by the end of the 1980s there were some 850 miles of Heritage Coast in total, amounting to a little over 30 per cent of the coastline of England and Wales. In Scotland more than 20 stretches of coastline of scenic, ecological or environmental importance have been designated by the Scottish

Development Department as Preferred Conservation Zones.

The Heritage Coasts reflect much of the wide variety of scenery and wildlife of the shores of England and Wales. Atop the sheer chalk cliffs of **Dover**, **Beachy Head** and the **Seven Sisters** orchids grow, and they make good places to watch jackdaws and swallows as well as seabirds. Right across on the other side of the country, the granite **Isles of Scilly** lie 28 miles out to sea off Land's End. In legend the islands are all that is left above the surface of the lost land of Lyonesse, which sank beneath the waves when King Arthur's reign came to an end.

The local environmental trust manages 40 miles of Heritage Coast in the Scillies, where the long Atlantic rollers cream on sandy beaches and rocky coves. The mild climate fosters a wealth of wildlife – snails and worms, sea urchins and anemones in the sand or in rock pools, seaweed trailing and undulating in the waves. Here Manx shearwaters, stormy petrels and puffins breed and there are multitudes of terns and gulls. Marram and sand sedge grow in the dunes, with the dwarf pansy – found only here and in the Channel Islands.

The **Suffolk** Heritage Coast is altogether different. This is an understated shore of low cliffs under enormous skies, and shingle beaches where the sea's melancholy retreating roar rattles the pebbles. The sea has swallowed up stretches of this coast, but contrariwise has constructed the shingle bulk of Orford Ness and the long shingle spit that runs six miles down the North Weir Point. Martello towers stud the shoreline. The country's principal breeding colony of avocets has been established by the RSPB in the reserve at Havergate Island. Further north is the Sizewell nuclear power station and beyond is the RSPB reserve at Minsmere. Here among the marshes and shallow 'scrapes', or lagoons, are more avocets, as well as bitterns, marsh harriers, nightingales and nightjars, all told the largest number of breeding bird species on any British reserve.

Bird sanctuaries are again a feature of the **North Norfolk** Heritage Coast between Holme-next-the-Sea and Weybourne. This is a hauntingly desolate coast and another shifting shoreline, which has left places 'next the sea' – like Holme, Cley and Wells – marooned some distance inland. Along the shore an almost unbroken succession of nature reserves protects the saltmarshes, sand dunes and shingle spits, where mats of sea lavender edge the muddy inlets. Hundreds of species of moths gladden the hearts of entomologists here, and there are birds in millions. Rarities sometimes seen include hoopoes and ospreys. The nature reserve on Scolt Head Island is famous for its nesting terns and there are more at Blakeney Point.

Though it faces the same North Sea, the **North Yorkshire and Cleveland** Heritage Coast is a different matter altogether. Lying north of Scarborough and on either side of Whitby, this is the seaward edge of the North York Moors National Park, a line of high cliffs and bays, dramatic headlands and narrow, wooded ravines. Fishing villages huddle in deep clefts, and this is where the great explorer Captain Cook first learned his seamanship. Geologically it is an area of unusual interest and pieces of jet picked up along the shore are the foundation of the trade in Whitby jet ornaments. At Robin Hood's Bay the village houses crowd above each other on a 1-in-3 gradient.

Further up the same coast is the **North Northumberland** area, where there is a different landscape again, with miles of delectable sandy beaches, many of them owned by the National Trust. There are no titanic cliffs here, but low, rocky headlands thrust into the sea. On one of them sprawls ruined Dunstanburgh Castle, lazily menacing like a lion lying in the sun. Bamburgh Castle looks out seawards to the Farne Islands bird sanctuaries and there are memories here of gallant Grace Darling, the lighthouse keeper's daughter who in 1838 rowed out in a storm to rescue shipwrecked sailors. The tides race in across the gleaming mudflats to cut Lindisfarne off from the mainland.

The only Heritage Coast in Cumbria and Lancashire is the short section round **St Bees Head.** The sheer red sandstone cliffs here command views of the Isle of Man on a clear day and the seabirds wheel and cry – fulmars, herring gulls, black-headed gulls and kittiwakes. Thrift, harebell and wild thyme grow by the cliff path.

**The Great Orme** is another dramatic headland with stark cliffs looming above Llandudno on the North Wales coast. Further south, miles more of formidable cliff scenery have been designated as Heritage Coasts: around the **Lleyn Peninsula**, along the **Pembrokeshire** shore and in **Devon, Cornwall** and **Dorset**.

Heritage Coasts have a great variety of owners, not all of whom are equally conscientious in their stewardship: from the National Trust, the RSPB and other conservation bodies to county councils, local authorities, farmers, private estates and individuals. The Countryside Commission itself gives advice and financial help, but does not own any of the land.

Where a piece of Heritage Coast is owned by an organisation like the National Trust or the RSPB, the public can feel entirely certain there will be proper protection. Matters are not as straightforward along the other Heritage Coasts. Here, each area has a Heritage Coast plan, drawn up by the local authority on Countryside Commission guidelines. The aim is to involve all local interests in a common approach to the management of the area, to conserve it and to encourage locals and visitors to take tender care of it.

**Pollution Free Beaches**
Quite apart from the physical constitution of the coastline, there is concern about polluted beaches. In 1988 one-third of the bathing beaches in England, Wales and Northern Ireland failed to meet EEC standards of cleanliness: sewage levels in the water were too high. This was at least an improvement on 1986, when half the beaches had failed the test. The great majority of bathing beaches in Cornwall, Devon, Dorset, East Anglia, Wales and Northern Ireland were passed as clean. Along the Kent, Sussex and Hampshire shore, in southern Northumberland and especially in the North-West, the situation was not so good.

Large amounts of money are being spent on the problem. The Marine Conservation society publishes *The Good Beach Guide,* which gives lists and details of the country's cleanest beaches. These include most of those which have won a Blue Flag award from the Tidy Britain Group. The Blue Flag winners were mostly town beaches; those which are cleaned every day during the season and where water cleanliness is high. More beaches in Britain are clean than are not, but there is still work to be done.

*Alum Bay, Isle of Wight, whose colourful sands are sold as souvenirs.*

*Heritage Coast*

## National Parks

Wordsworth, in his *Guide to the Lakes* wrote: 'the Lakes are a sort of national property, in which every man has a right and interest who has an eye to perceive and a heart to enjoy'. In the 19th century 'being outdoors' was seen as being good for body and soul.

Earlier this century, on many wild moors shooting took precedence over amenities for walkers. In the Peak District, an area much appreciated by those wishing to escape for a while from nearby large industrial communities, a mass trespass took place on Kinder Scout in 1932 and five men were arrested and imprisoned.

The Standing Committee on National Parks (SCNP) met for the first time on 26 May 1936, the start of an organised effort to protect and to make available to all the wild landscapes of Britain. The Council for National Parks now oversees the 11 National Parks in Britain, which have been set up since the National Parks and Access to the Countryside Act became law in 1949.

Reservoirs, power lines, roads, quarrying, forestry, TV transmitter

*A spectacular view towards Derwent Dale, in the Peak District.*

*National Park*

masts, power boats, caravan sites, even the tourists themselves by eroding footpaths are all potential threats to the preservation of the National Parks. But, provided informed and responsible public opinion and a spirit of co-operation prevail, all these amenities will be available to future generations.

It is fitting that, after the Kinder Scout protest, the **Peak District** should have been established as the first National Park. The Pennine Way was opened on the anniversary of the protest in 1965 and follows the backbone of England from Edale in Derbyshire, across Hadrian's Wall, to Kirk Yetholm, in the Cheviots. Seventeen million people live within a couple of hours' drive of the park and many come to enjoy walking the deep dales of the White Peak or the dramatic moors and peat bogs of the Dark Peak. Fishing, cycling and rock climbing on the gritstone edges have been joined as leisure activities by gliding and hang-gliding. An Iron Age fort on Man Tor overlooks Roman lead workings and the mine near Castleton, where deposits of decorative fluorspar – blue john – have been worked since Roman times. Heather covers one third of the Park and provides food for the red grouse.

Largest of the National Parks, the **Lake District** combines mountain and lake, woodland and farmland. Moving ice shaped these troughs and corries and glacial rubble dammed the valleys, but the underlying rock dictated whether the hills were softly rounded, like Skiddaw, or wildly rugged, like Scafell and Helvellyn. Broad-leaved woodland like the Borrowdale and Witherslack woods, of great interest to conservationists, cover about five per cent of the Park.

The Snowdon massif is the heartland of the **Snowdonia National Park** and Cader Idris is one of the most popular areas. Half a million people reach Snowdon Summit each year and only a quarter of them admit to using the railway! Many fewer visit the Aran Mountains in the south, or the rugged Rhynogydd. Harlech Castle lies on part of the park's 20 or so miles of sweeping sandy coastline, backed by beautiful mountain scenery. For the 'railway buff' there are six narrow-gauge railways to enjoy and to the 5,000 acres of ancient broad-leaved woodland have been added another 5,000, which with commercial forestry, now cover over 10 per cent of the Park.

Two plateaux make up **Dartmoor,** the largest and wildest stretch of open country in southern Britain, rising to over 2,000ft (610m). Covered with

blanket bog and heather moorland, they are divided by the River Dart. Granite tors protrude near the edges, where other rivers have eroded deep valleys. Over a third of the Park is farmland and the high northern moors have been a military training area since the 1870s. The Dartmoor pony – descendant of ponies turned out to graze in the Middle Ages – grazes much of the lower lying heather moorland. There are hundreds of ancient sites – chambered tombs, hillforts and stone circles – in the Park and medieval crosses and waymarks can still be useful to today's traveller.

The **Pembrokeshire Coast National Park**, the smallest of the Parks, hugs the coast and is only three miles wide along most of its length. Steep cliffs display spectacularly folded and twisted rock formations, while sheltered bays invite bathing, and scuba diving. Offshore, islands such as Skomer and Skokholm support huge colonies of seabirds, among them the world's largest concentration of Manx shearwaters and puffins. Inland from the Milford Haven oil terminal, with its facilities for 300,000-ton tankers, is the Daugleddau, a drowned river valley with dense woodlands and in the north, the windswept moorlands of the Preseli Hills, source of the 'bluestones' of Stonehenge.

Though Middlesbrough and York are not far away, the **North York Moors** is a relatively quiet Park. The moors rise sharply from Pickering in the south, Teesside in the north and the Vale of York in the west. The eastern boundary is the sea, with Staithes, home of Captain Cook, and Whitby (outside the Park boundaries), famous for its clifftop Abbey and its jet – a fossilised black amber – so popular with the Victorians. Rievaulx and Rosedale Abbeys are within the Park, as is Mount Grace Priory, the best preserved Carthusian priory in Britain. Evidence of man's occupation of the high moors ranges from the burial mounds of the neolithic farmers who first cleared the land to the giant golf ball-like radar domes of the Fylingdales early warning system.

Nearly half of the **Yorkshire Dales** is farmland, but there is little woodland. Over four centuries the monasteries' sheep walks developed into the start of a road system across the fells, the best known today being the green lane between Kilnsey and Malham. Miles of dry stone walling are a man-made feature of the landscape, as is the Settle–Carlisle railway with its spectacular Ribblehead Viaduct. Public transport facilities being poor, the Dalesrail scheme makes recreational use of this line for walkers, who form the second largest group of visitors, after the touring motorist. As well as a part of the Pennine Way, there are popular areas for walkers and day trippers around Malham Cove and Tarn, with its fascinating limestone pavement 'grikes' – sheltered habitats for lime- and shade-loving plants. Aysgarth Falls, in Wensleydale, attract over half a million visitors a year. There is a 'Bunk House Barns' project, offering basic shelter for walkers in field barns which used to over-winter the dairy cattle.

R D Blackmore's *Lorna Doone* has made **Exmoor** known to many, as has Williamson's *Tarka the Otter.* The heartland, rising to 1,500ft (460m), from Chapman Barrows to Dunkery Beacon is still the windswept haunt of falcon and hawk. The 'hog's back' cliffs along the coast are broken by deep valleys with waterfalls which make protected breeding sites for seabirds. Exmoor is known for its Bronze and Iron Age sites, and a recent aerial survey has added over 2,000 fresh areas to be investigated. The medieval Tarr Steps bridge in the Barle Valley is a popular tourist attraction. With the Quantocks, Exmoor is the last secure habitat in the south of

England for the red deer. The number of Exmoor ponies, adapted to rough grazing and wild winters, is declining, but a small herd has been established to maintain the breed.

Cheviot sheep graze the open moorland which makes up most of the **Northumberland National Park.** Remote from all settlements and mostly above 1,000ft (300m), it is often a harsh environment and must have seemed the end of the world to Roman legionaries from sunny Spain and Italy who manned Hadrian's Wall, part of which runs along the southern edge of the Park. Housesteads fort and Vindolanda have interesting visitor centres and museums. Otterburn and other battles over the 300 years up to the Union of Crowns in 1603 have given rise to many a Border ballad.

The **Brecon Beacons,** four high red sandstone mountain blocks, divide the ancient rocks of mid-Wales from the coalfields and industrialisation further south. From the Black Mountains, near Hay-on-Wye, through the Brecon Beacons and Fforest Fawr, the Park stretches to Black Mountain in the west. Along its southern edge a limestone belt provides a dramatic change in scenery with hundreds of sink-holes and cave systems. The most

spectacular are the Dan-yr-Ogof Caves, on the A4067, at the head of the Tawe valley. The ruins of Carreg Cennen Castle, a 13th-century stronghold on sheer limestone cliffs, lie just off the A40, near Llandeilo.

The **Broads Authority** was rejected together with the Sussex Downs from the twelve candidates in 1949, but was established as a National Park on 1 April 1989. We owe Britain's most famous stretch of inland waterways to the peat-digging activities of our ancestors in the 9th century, which caused flooding in the 14th, and its survival as a recreational area to the strenuous efforts of the Broads Authority, in the 1980s, to halt the environmental degradation. Algae flourished on increased nutrients from effluents and fertilisers, the water 'died', reed cover was lost and the banks became eroded. Much has been done, but care is still needed.

The **New Forest** is the latest area to be granted the status of a National Park, although, as it is administered by the Forestry Commission, the status is not 'real'.

*Hound Tor, an example of Dartmoor's striking landscape.*
Inset *The deep waters of Llyn Cau, from Cader Idris, Gwynedd.*

National Park

**National Scenic Areas (Scotland)**

*National Scenic Area (Scotland)*

Where England and Wales have National Parks, Scotland has National Scenic Areas. There are 40 of them, designated in 1978 by the Countryside Commission for Scotland, established to conserve Scotland's natural beauty and improve public access to and enjoyment of it. Though the Commission's stated policy is not 'to see land in Scotland managed as though it were a museum', the National Scenic Areas are protected from development which would harm their scenic qualities. Between them they cover close to one eighth of the total area of Scotland.

Inevitably, the great majority of these National Scenic Areas lie in the Highlands and Islands, along or north of the Highland Line, the geological fault which separates Highland from Lowland Scotland. It runs diagonally from south-west to north-east clear across the country from the Isle of Arran to Stonehaven on the east coast. North and west of this line Scotland's wilder, more solitary, most spectacular and least spoiled landscapes are to be found. The land to the south and east is far more given to farming and industry, and some of it is heavily populated.

A few of the areas lie south of the Highland Line, however. In the Borders, for instance, the **Eildon and Leaderfoot** area includes the uncannily beautiful Eildon Hills. The Leader Water runs south to join the River Tweed below the three volcanic Eildon peaks, the highest rising to 1,385ft (422m). These

*Looking out to Scarista Bay, from Borve on the west coast of Harris.*

shapely hills are steeped in legend and romance. King Arthur and his gallant knights of the Round Table are said to lie sleeping beneath them, under an enchantment, awaiting the time of their recall to life. It was here that Thomas the Rhymer, the 13th-century poet and prophet, encountered the Queen of Fairyland. Dressed all in green, and very fair, she took him away to her magic realm for seven years and gave him the power to see into the future. Here, below the hills, lies ruined Melrose Abbey, where the heart of Robert the Bruce was buried, and close by is Abbotsford, the house Sir Walter Scott built for himself in the countryside he loved.

Scott's immensely popular poems and novels whetted the appetite of prospective tourists for his native land. The process was helped along by Queen Victoria and Prince Albert, who made themselves a Highland retreat at Balmoral in the 1840s. They loved to go stalking deer in the mountains, picnicking at the remote shielings, or shepherds' huts, and fishing for trout in a lumbering rowing boat on Loch Muick.

The region today is the **Deeside and Lochnagar** National Scenic Area, which is the only one in the Grampian Region. The high granite ridge of Lochnagar, a favourite with climbers, rises to 3,786ft (1,154m) to the south of Braemar, in an area of mountain and forest where the River Dee flows past Balmoral Castle on its way to the North Sea at Aberdeen. Lord Byron wrote rhapsodically of 'the crags that are wild and majestic, the steep frowning slopes of dark Lochnagar'. Ever since Queen Victoria's time,

the Highland Gathering at Braemar has been regularly attended by the royal family and marks the annual apogee of the Highland Games season.

From Deeside westwards, the pass called the Lairg Ghru runs through another National Scenic Area, negotiating the heart of the **Cairngorm Mountains** on its way to Speyside. This is the largest tract of land above 3,000ft (915m) in Britain. Rearing up between Braemar and the valley of the Spey, the lofty granite summits of Ben Macdhui, Braeriach, Cairn Toul and Cairn Gorm itself all clear 4,000ft (1,220m) and are outstripped in height only by Ben Nevis.

The lures of hill walking, rock climbing and wintersports draw visitors here. The Forestry Commission manages an extensive Forest Park and near Loch an Eilein are Scots pines at least 250 years old. A hundred square miles of nature reserve lie to the south of Glen More and includes both Braeriach and Cairn Toul. Arctic and alpine plant rarities grow here, with all sorts of mosses and ferns. Reindeer were reintroduced a few years ago and red deer and wildcat roam the mountainsides. Golden eagles soar above the corries and in the woods capercaillies make popping noises like corks.

Scottish scenery is renowned not only for its breathtaking grandeur, its harmony of sky and mountain and water, but for the romantic and often violent history which seems to cling still to every peak and corrie, every pass and glen. The **Ben Nevis** and **Glen Coe** areas contain both the highest mountain in Britain at 4,408ft (1,344m) and one of the most notorious localities in all Scotland's bloody and tragic past. Ben Nevis, which is more of a hump than a peak, can be climbed fairly easily in good weather, though it will take a good many hours up and down, and there are colossal views from the top on a clear day. In Fort William, down below the mountain, the West Highland Museum illuminates the natural and the human history of the district.

To the south are the peaks which tower above Glen Coe, on an overcast day one of the bleakest and most melancholy places in the British Isles. The celebrated and treacherous massacre of the local Macdonalds by a party of Campbell soldiery occurred on a bitter February night in 1692. The site of the Macdonald settlement and much of the surrounding country is now owned by the National Trust for Scotland, which has a visitor centre in the glen. There is also a folk museum in Glencoe village. Further

*National Scenic Area (Scotland)*

south still, and part of the National Scenic Area, is the brooding wasteland of Rannoch Moor, with its peaty bogs and lochans, vividly described in an episode of Robert Louis Stevenson's *Kidnapped.*

Famed again in song and story are the **Cuillin Hills** of the Isle of Skye, which reach up in savage splendour above dramatic Loch Coruisk. These are black, jagged, precipitous, sinister mountains, the highest peak being Sgurr Alasdair at 3,309ft (1,009m). The Cuillins are an irresistible magnet to rock climbers, but they have an old reputation for treachery – compasses go oddly astray, mists descend suddenly, climbers are lost and cut off. Among marginally safer attractions on Skye are Talisker malt whisky and the MacLeods' ancestral castle at Dunvegan with its singularly daunting dungeon.

There is wonderful mountain and loch scenery again to the north, where six massive ranges rear their peaks to the sky in the National Scenic Area of **Wester Ross.** The sun glitters on Loch Maree and its islands, and the warmth of the North Atlantic Drift fosters a subtropical paradise in the luxuriant gardens at Inverewe, at the head of Loch Ewe. The gardens were created from the 1860s on by Osgood Mackenzie on what was initially barren peat wasteland.

The island of Foula is included in the Shetlands National Scenic Area, and so is Fair Isle, familiar from weather forecasts. In the Orkneys

the island of **Hoy** is protected, with its dramatic isolated 450ft (137m) stack, the Old Man of Hoy. Man-made Orkney attractions include the Stone Age village of Skara Brae and the enormous Stone Age tomb of Maes Howe, as well as the cathedral of St Magnus in Kirkwall.

Though most of the National Scenic Areas protect mountain scenery, one of them is centred on the old town of **Dunkeld** in the Tayside Region, where the River Tay sweeps past the ruined cathedral among its lawns and sheltering trees. There are memorials in the church to a renowned Scottish regiment, the Black Watch, and to the Scottish Horse, a regiment raised by the Duke of Atholl to fight in the Boer War. An attractive walk through the woods by the River Braan leads to a waterfall and an 18th-century folly. Not far away in the opposite direction is the Loch of the Lowes nature reserve, run by the Scottish Wildlife Trust, where visitors who are lucky may see ospreys. *Macbeth's* Birnam Wood is not far away either.

Lying across the Highland Line are the 'bonnie banks' of **Loch Lomond,** 24 miles long and the largest stretch of inland water in Britain. This is another National Scenic Area. The narrow northern end of the loch protrudes into the Highlands between Ben Vorlich and Ben Lomond, both over 3,000ft (915m). The southern end, with its numerous islands, lies in more

Top *The rocks and tumbling waters of the River Dee, in Royal Deeside.* Above *Beinn Alligin's peak, with Upper Loch Torridon in the foreground.*

placid country. The burial place of the outlawed Clan MacGregor is on the island of Inchaillach, which is part of the nature reserve at the lower end of the loch.

To the south-west there is a return to mountain landscape in the National Scenic Area of **North Arran,** among the jagged heights of this island in the Firth of Clyde. The highest is Goat Fell at 2,866ft (874m), which can be climbed from the town of Brodick and offers wonderful views, stretching on a clear day to England, Ireland and the Isle of Man. It is to be hoped that the National Scenic Areas will continue to reward Scots and their visitors for many generations to come.

*Forest Park*

*Forest Drive*

## Forest Parks
## Forest Drives

Long ago, before man began to make his mark, most of the land surface of Britain was thickly covered with trees. Far back in the New Stone Age, 6,000 years ago or more, farmers began to fell and burn the woodlands to make clearings for crops and pasture stock. By the Middle Ages more than 80 per cent of the original woodland cover had been cleared. Little is left today of the tangled Wealden forest through which the defeated English were chased by William the Conqueror's Normans after Hastings, or of the oaks and glades of Sherwood Forest where Robin Hood and his outlaws hunted.

In this century huge new man-made forests have been created by the Forestry Commission, set up in 1919 to repair the ravages of World War I, when no timber was imported. The Commission's principal purpose has always been a commercial one, to grow saleable timber. It planted pine, larch and spruce – fast-growing softwood trees that thrive in poor soil and are ready for harvesting in 25 or 30 years – and it has been fiercely criticised for its regimented ranks of

*This vast, wooded region of Argyll became Scotland's first Forest Park.*

conifers marching monotonously over hill and dale. Increasingly, however, the Commission has recognised the importance of its role as a provider of recreation and its responsibility to the environment.

### Forest Parks

In Scotland, where it is the largest landowner, the Commission began to create Forest Parks in scenically attractive areas. The first of them, set under way as far back as 1935, was the **Argyll Forest Park,** extending over 100 square miles of the Cowal Peninsula in the Strathclyde region. Lying between Loch Fyne and Loch Long, it is mountain country, long dominated by the Campbell clan, who feuded with the local Lamonts. The ruined Campbell hold of Carrick Castle glowers out over Loch Goil and the churchyard of Kilmun on Holy Loch was the traditional burying place of the Campbell chiefs.

Visitors can enjoy driving the forest roads, walking on miles of tracks, pony trekking, fishing, sailing and waterskiing. Deer, wildcats, otters, golden eagles and ravens live here. Near the head of Loch Long are fine peaks, including The Cobbler at 2,891ft (881m) and the pass called 'Rest and be Thankful' on the A83, named from the inscription on a stone seat that used to be there. Close to the

southern end of Loch Eck, Benmore House, weirdly and wonderfully Scots Baronial, was given to the Forestry Commission in 1928. The Younger Botanic Garden here is open to the public and is celebrated for its marvellous azaleas and rhododendrons. A brook runs through Puck's Glen, a narrow cleft among the rocks with rare mosses and ferns.

Further south and more than twice as big in area is the **Galloway Forest Park,** designated in 1943, a wild area of wooded mountains, moorland, lochs and streams lying to the north of Newton Stewart. There are ten peaks above 2,000ft (610m), the highest being Merrick, 2,766ft (843m) near the centre of the park. There is climbing, walking, fishing and swimming to enjoy, and a tremendous richness of wildlife – deer, wild goats, pine martens, wildcats, red squirrels, golden eagles and hen harriers.

There are miles of trails for walkers, but motor roads are few and far between in this part of the world. North of Newton Stewart, Loch Trool, bowered among wooded slopes, has a good forest trail. The main road in the park is the Queen's Drive, or more prosaically the A712, from New Galloway to Newton Stewart. Bruce's Stone marks the place where Robert the Bruce scored an early

victory over the English and the man-made Clatteringshaws Loch is part of a hydro-electric scheme. The Galloway Deer Museum is informative not only about the deer but the park and its wildlife in general. The Raiders' Road Forest Drive turns off to the south and follows an old cattle thieves' route through the woods for 10 miles beside the Black Water of Dee, with bathing places and picnic spots.

The **Glen More Forest Park** is in the National Scenic Area of the Cairngorms. The **Queen Elizabeth Forest Park,** designated in 1953, links two National Scenic Areas, Loch Lomond and the Trossachs. In the Tayside Region there is pony trekking, mountain biking and fishing in the **Tummel Forest Park,** with numerous walks of varying length and degrees of difficulty. Forestry Commission walks are graded as 'Easy', 'Strenuous' or 'Difficult'. There are camp sites, picnic sites and plenty of car parks, with deer, red squirrels and capercaillies to watch. The forest here has mostly been planted since World War II, but a specially enticing attraction is a guided walk through the magically named Black Wood of Rannoch. On the south shore of Loch Rannoch, this is one of the rare remaining fragments of the great Caledonian pine forest, which once stretched for hundreds of miles. The visitor centre for the Forest Park is above Loch Tummel at the Queen's View, where you can stand in the footsteps of Queen Victoria, who admired the prospect in 1866. She also admired the Pass of Killiecrankie, not far away, a wooded gorge and battlefield where the National Trust for Scotland has a visitor centre.

The Forest Park idea spread from Scotland south into England. The **Border Forest Park,** designated in 1955, straddles the high sparse moors on both sides of the Anglo-Scots border, where so many raiding and rustling parties rode about their nefarious business in past centuries. Ruins of pele towers and castles testify to a violent history of feuding and marauding. At the heart of the park lies Kielder Water, a spectacular man-made reservoir seven miles long in the valley of the North Tyne, holding 40 million gallons of water. Ferry boats ply across it in the summer, and it is reached by the 12-mile Kielder Forest Drive from the A68. The drive runs past viewpoints and picnic spots to the Forestry Commission's visitor centre at Kielder Castle. In the remoter areas, you may catch sight of red deer, wild goats, blue hares and red squirrels.

On a much smaller scale is the **Grizedale Forest Park,** occupying a slice of Lake District scenery between Coniston Water and Esthwaite Water, south-west of Hawkshead. There are walks and guided tours, orienteering courses, cycle trails, a disabled trail, and a theatre. A trail bears witness to past industries: bloomeries where iron ore was smelted, charcoal pits, potash pits for soap-making, kilns, a tannery and a blast furnace.

The **North Riding Forest Park** lies north-east of Pickering in the rolling landscape of the North York Moors. Centred on the Dalby Valley, in the Middle Ages it was part of the much larger royal hunting forest of Pickering. A nine-mile forest drive takes the motorist gently through the woodland today, with an ample supply of parking pull-offs and places for a picnic. Leaflets detail forest walks for those who want to stretch their legs. Part of the drive follows the Staindale Beck, which was dammed to create an attractive lake, and there is a walk from here to the strange rock formations called the Bridestones, in a nature reserve run by the National Trust and the Yorkshire Wildlife Trust.

### Forest Drives

Where there is no Forest Park, there is still occasionally a forest drive: as in the **Hamsterley Forest**, the largest area of woodland in County Durham. It covers 5,000 acres west of Bishop Auckland, off the A68. The Forestry Commission bought the estate from the last Surtees owner, a descendant of the famous Victorian sporting novelist R S Surtees. The drive runs for four miles along the Bedburn Beck and the Spurlswood Beck, through

*Right Helpful information at the Visitor Centre in the Borders Forest Park. Below Kielder Forest Drive, between Kielder Castle and Redesdale.*

woodland which sports much pine and fir, spruce and larch. There are no less than 60 varieties of tree here all told, with oak and ash, beech and thorn among them. Red squirrels and roe deer, bats and lizards frequent these woods and there are large numbers of woodpeckers and fungi. There are waymarked walks, though more adventurous visitors can explore wherever they like.

In South Wales, meanwhile, it takes a tough cyclist to manage the splendid **Cwmcarn Forest Drive.** The seven-mile drive starts at an excellent new visitor centre south of Abercarn, near Newport. Higher up are picnic places and barbecue spots with commanding views across country and to the Bristol Channel. Walks lead off at intervals, including one which climbs to the summit. The trees are mostly spruce, larch and pine, but oaks, beeches and rowans temper the conifers.

The drive runs through part of the Forestry Commission's Ebbw Forest, a distant man-made descendant of the ancient forest of Machen, which was eaten away over the centuries by sheep and charcoal burners and finally fell victim to the devouring demand for timber in the South Wales coal mines. So here man has put back something of what he has destroyed.

Forest Park

Forest Drive

# THE TOURIST'S BRITISH ISLES
# ·CALENDAR·

## SPRING

### MARCH

**Whuppity Scoorie**
Lanark, Strathclyde
(March 1)

**Ideal Home Exhibition**
Earls Court, London
(early March to early April)

**Belfast Musical Festival**
Belfast
(March – 3rd week)

**Oxford v Cambridge Boat Race**
Putney to Mortlake,
London
(late March or early April)

### APRIL

**Midgley Pace Egg Play**
Calder Valley, West
Yorkshire
(Good Friday)

**Nutters Dance**
Bacup, Lancashire
(Easter Saturday)

**Easter Parade**
Battersea Park, London
(Easter Monday)

**Harness Horse Parade**
Regent's Park, London
(Easter Monday)

**Hare Pie Scramble and Bottle Kicking**
Hallaton, Leicestershire
(Easter Monday)

**Hocktide Festival**
Hungerford, Berkshire
(Easter Tuesday)

**Northumbria Gathering**
Morpeth, Northumbria
(week after Easter)

**The Grand National**
Aintree, Merseyside
(April – 2nd Saturday)

**Shakespeare's Birthday Celebrations**
Stratford-upon-Avon,
Warwickshire
(April 21)

**Spring Flower Show**
Harrogate, North Yorkshire
(late April)

**Badminton Three Day Event**
Badminton, Avon
(late April or early May)

### MAY

**May Morning Ceremony**
Oxford
(May 1)

**Royal May Day Celebrations**
Knutsford, Cheshire
(May – 1st Saturday)

**Flower Parade**
Spalding, Lincolnshire
(early May)

**Furry Dance**
Helston, Cornwall
(May 8)

**Garland Day**
Abbotsbury, Dorset
(May 13)

**Goat Fell Race**
Isle of Arran, Strathclyde
(May – 2nd or 3rd
Saturday)

**Bath International Festival of the Arts**
Bath, Avon
(late May to early June)

**Chelsea Flower Show**
Royal Hospital, Chelsea,
London
(late May to early June)

**TT Motorcycle Races**
Isle of Man
(late May to early June)

**Arbor Tree Day**
Aston on Clun, Shropshire
(late May)

**Garland Day**
Castleton, Derbyshire
(May 29)

**Dickens Festival**
Rochester, Kent
(late May or early June)

**Royal Bath and West Show**
Shepton Mallet, Somerset
(late May or early June)

**Woolsack Races**
Tetbury, Gloucestershire
(Spring Bank Holiday)

## SUMMER

### JUNE

**The Derby**
Epsom, Surrey
(June – 1st Wednesday)

**Scuttlebrook Wake**
Chipping Campden,
Gloucestershire
(Saturday following Spring
Bank Holiday)

**Appleby Horse Fair**
Appleby, Cumbria
(June – 2nd Tuesday and
Wednesday)

**Trooping the Colour**
Horse Guards Parade,
London
(June – 2nd Saturday)

**Royal Cornwall Show**
Wadebridge, Cornwall
(June – 2nd week)

**Aldeburgh Festival of Music and the Arts**
Aldeburgh, Suffolk
(June – 2nd to 4th
weeks)

**Selkirk Common Riding**
Selkirk, Borders
(mid-June)

**Three Counties Agricultural Show**
Great Malvern, Hereford &
Worcester
(mid-June)

**Stour Music Festival**
Boughton Aluph, Kent
(June – 2nd half)

**Royal Highland Show**
Ingliston, Lothian
(June – 3rd week)

**Royal Ascot Race Meeting**
Ascot, Berkshire
(late June)

**Wimbledon Lawn Tennis Championships**
Wimbledon, London
(late June to early July)

### JULY

**Tynwald Day**
Isle of Man
(July 5)

**Henley Royal Regatta**
Henley on Thames,
Oxfordshire
(July – 1st week)

**Cheltenham International Festival of Music**
Cheltenham,
Gloucestershire
(July – 1st and 3rd weeks)

**British Rose Festival**
Gardens of the Rose,
Chiswell Green,
Hertfordshire
(July – 1st or 2nd week)

**Royal International Agricultural Show**
Stoneleigh, Warwickshire
(early July)

**Great Yorkshire Agricultural Show**
Harrogate, North Yorkshire
(July – 2nd week)

**International Musical Eisteddfod**
Llangollen, Clwyd
(early July)

**Sham Fight**
Scarva, Co Down
(July 13)

**Royal Welsh Show**
Builth Wells, Powys
(July – 3rd week)

**Black Cherry Fair**
Chertsey, Surrey
(July – 3rd Saturday)

**Royal Tournament**
Earls Court, London
(mid-July)

**Buxton International Arts Festival**
Buxton, Derbyshire
(mid-July to early August)

**Tweedmouth Salmon Feast**
Tweedmouth,
Northumberland
(Sunday after July 18)

**Tolpuddle Martyrs Procession**
Tolpuddle, Dorset
(July – 3rd Sunday)

**Durham Miners Gala**
Durham
(July – Saturday of 2nd
week)

**Croagh Patrick Pilgrimage**
Near Westport, Co Mayo
(July–last Sunday)

## AUGUST

**Royal National Eisteddfod**
Varying locations in Wales
(August – 1st week)

**The Burry Man Festival**
Queensferry, Lothian
(August – 2nd Friday)

**Cowes Week**
Cowes, Isle of Wight
(August – 2nd week)

**Puck Fair**
Killorglin, Co Kerry
(August 10–12)

**Marymass Festival**
Irvine, Strathclyde
(August – 2nd or 3rd
weeks)

**Edinburgh International
Festival**
Edinburgh
(August – last three weeks)

**Priddy Sheep Fair**
Priddy, Somerset
(mid-August)

**Grasmere Sports**
Grasmere, Cumbria
(Thursday nearest
August 20)

**Burning of Bartle**
West Witton, North
Yorkshire
(Saturday nearest
August 24)

**Oul' Lammas Fair**
Ballycastle, Co Antrim
(August – last Tuesday)

**Plague Sunday Service**
Eyam, Derbyshire
(August – last Sunday)

**Navy Days**
Plymouth and Portsmouth
(August Bank Holiday)

AUTUMN

## SEPTEMBER

**Ben Nevis Hill Race**
Fort William, Highland
(September – 1st Saturday)

**Braemar Gathering**
Braemar, Grampian
(September – 1st Saturday)

**Hop Hoodening**
Canterbury, Kent
(early September)

**St Giles's Fair**
Oxford
(September – 1st full week)

**Horn Dance**
Abbots Bromley,
Staffordshire
(Monday after 1st Sunday
following September 4)

**Burghley Horse Trials**
Burghley House, Stamford
(early September)

**Blackpool Illuminations**
Blackpool, Lancashire
(early September to early
November)

**International Air Show**
Farnborough, Hampshire
(September – 1st week)

**Clarinbridge Oyster
Festival**
Clarinbridge, Co Galway
(early or mid-September)

**World Carriage Driving
Championships**
Windsor, Berkshire
(September – 3rd week)

**Victorian Festival**
Llandrindod Wells, Powys
(September – 3rd week)

**Great Autumn Flower
Show**
Harrogate, North Yorkshire
(mid-September)

**Dr Johnson's Birthday**
Lichfield, Staffordshire
(on or near September 18)

**Egremont Crab Fair**
Egremont, Cumbria
(Saturday nearest
September 18)

**Barnstaple Old Fair**
Barnstaple, Devon
(September – 3rd week)

**Painswick Church
Clipping**
Painswick, Gloucestershire
(September – 3rd week)

**Dublin Theatre Festival**
Dublin
(late September to early
October)

## OCTOBER

**Nottingham Goose Fair**
Nottingham
(early October)

**Tavistock Goose Fair**
Tavistock, Devon
(October 10)

**Pack Monday Fair**
Sherborne, Dorset
(1st Monday after
October 10)

**Border Shepherds Show**
Alwinton, Northumberland
(October – 2nd week)

**Horse of the Year Show**
Wembley Arena, London
(mid-October)

**Stratford Mop Fair**
Stratford-upon-Avon,
Warwickshire
(mid-October)

**Wexford Opera Festival**
Wexford, Co Wexford
(late October to
mid-November)

## NOVEMBER

**London to Brighton
Veteran Car Run**
Hyde Park Corner, London
(November – 1st Sunday)

**Guy Fawkes Night**
Lewes, East Sussex, and
elsewhere
(November 5)

**Tar-Barrel Rolling**
Ottery St Mary, Devon
(November 5)

**Lord Mayor's Show**
Guildhall to the Strand,
London
(November – 2nd Saturday)

**Belfast Festival at Queen's**
Belfast
(mid to late November)

**Contemporary Music
Festival**
Huddersfield, West
Yorkshire
(late November)

WINTER

## DECEMBER

**Royal Smithfield Show**
London
(early December)

**Festival of Carols and
Lessons**
King's College Chapel,
Cambridge
(December 24)

**Ba' Games**
Kirkwall, Orkney Islands
(December 25 and
January 1)

**Greatham Sword Dance**
Greatham, Cleveland
(December 26)

**Allendale Tar-Barrel
Ceremony**
Allendale, Northumberland
(December 31)

**Fireball Ceremony**
Stonehaven, Grampian
(December 31)

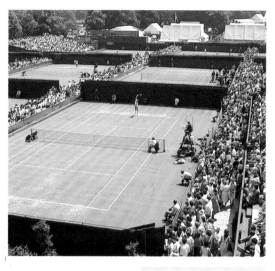

**Flambeaux Procession**
Comrie, Tayside
(December 31)

## JANUARY

**Haxey Hood Game**
Haxey, Humberside
(January 5 or 6)

**Straw Bear Festival**
Whittlesey, Cambridgeshire
(Friday and Saturday
before Plough Monday)

**Plough Stots Service**
Goathland, North
Yorkshire
(Monday after January 6)

**Burning the Clavie**
Burghead, Grampian
(January 11)

**Wassailing the Apple Tree**
Carhampton, Somerset
(January 17)

**Up Helly Aa**
Lerwick, Shetland Islands
(January – last Tuesday)

## FEBRUARY

**Jorvik Viking Festival**
York, North Yorkshire
(February – whole month)

**Pancake Day Race**
Olney, Buckinghamshire
(Shrove Tuesday)

**Shrovetide Football**
Ashbourne, Derbyshire
(Shrove Tuesday)

**Shrovetide Skipping**
Scarborough, North
Yorkshire
(Shrove Tuesday)

*Left Traditional maypole
dancing at Chipping Campden
in Gloucestershire.
Inset A familiar sight in The
Mall, the Household Cavalry.
Above Wimbledon draws the
crowds each summer.
Below May Day celebrations
in Oxford, which were started
in the mid-17th century.*

**Tourist
Information
Centre**

**Tourist
Information
Centre
(Summer only)**

### Tourist Information Centres

With over 800 offices nationwide, Britain's Tourist Information Centres offer a free service, welcoming calls both in person and by phone.

Whatever your query – whether you are looking for something new to do on a Sunday, somewhere to take the family for the day or simply a good place to eat, your local Tourist Information Centre is only too willing to help.

The staff at each centre have details on just about everything within a 50-mile radius and this is backed up by a comprehensive range of brochures, pamphlets and guides both free and for sale.

They can help with excursions and outings, giving you details and route directions to a variety of places, from castles and craft centres to model villages and museums, tell you which bus to catch, the best place for a picnic, or a walk or a scenic drive. They can even advise on which restaurant is likely to provide a high-chair for the baby or which stately home involves a lot of walking about. They also have details of local events: concerts, carnivals, festivals and fêtes and

*Inside the London Tourist Board
Information Centre at Victoria.*

what is on in town in the evenings.

Another invaluable service is to offer on-the-spot help with finding places to stay. Most centres have up-to-date lists of all kinds of holiday accommodation in the area such as hotels, holiday homes and campsites. They can make local reservations for you, if available, or reservations at any other town which has a centre offering this facility, for the same or the following day. A fee or deposit may be payable for these services.

Most of the centres keep regular office hours from 9 to 5, Monday to Friday, but many are also open at weekends or for longer periods, especially in the summer. Some, however, are open from Easter to September only, but you can always refer your enquiries to the nearest all-year-round centre.

Britain's Tourist Information Centres are at your service and are always happy to help, no matter what the query.

---

The following signs indicate where you will find a Tourist Information Centre in a town.

 – directional sign for road traffic

 – sign for pedestrians

 – this sign means a Tourist Information Centre is just a few yards away

# Road Atlas of the
# British Isles
## 1999

# using this atlas

## Route planner (pages VIII–XIII)

Maps to help you plan long journeys, showing principal routes and pin-pointing major towns and cities throughout the country.

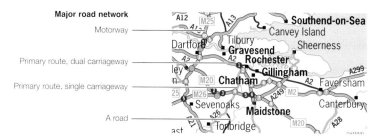

Major road network

Motorway

Primary route, dual carriageway

Primary route, single carriageway

A road

## Motorways – restricted junctions (pages XVI–XVII)

A selection of motorway junctions displayed as clear diagrams to help you pin-point individual restrictions.

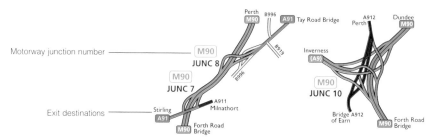

Motorway junction number

Exit destinations

## Road maps (pages 2–158)

Clear, easy-to-read road mapping enables you to plan detailed journeys. A wealth of motoring information including motorways, primary roads, A and B roads, unclassified roads, interchanges and roundabouts, vehicle ferries, the rail network and numerous places of interest.

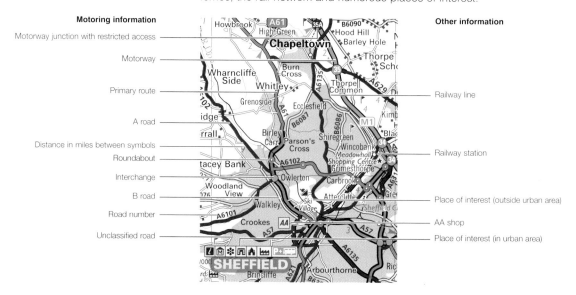

Motoring information

Motorway junction with restricted access

Motorway

Primary route

A road

Distance in miles between symbols

Roundabout

Interchange

B road

Road number

Unclassified road

Other information

Railway line

Railway station

Place of interest (outside urban area)

AA shop

Place of interest (in urban area)

IV

## Town plans (pages 159–231)

84 fully indexed town plans provide you with essential town centre motoring information plus a wide selection of places of interest.

Motoring information

AA-Recommended road

Restricted road

One-way street

Other information

Building of interest

Car park

Shopmobility

Pedestrian only

Public convenience

## District maps (pages 232–243)

Unique planning maps designed to help you navigate through and around major urban areas.

Motoring information

B road, single carriageway

A road, single carriageway

Primary route, dual carriageway

Motorway

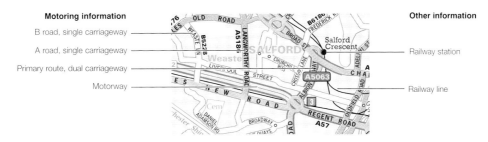

Other information

Railway station

Railway line

## Central London (pages 244–261)

Comprehensive, fully indexed maps of inner London provide a simple guide to finding your way around the city.

Motoring information

Banned turn

Classified road

Restricted road

One-way street

Other information

Underground railway station

Garage parking

Major place of tourist interest

## Ports and airports (pages 264–267)

Plans of major airports and seaports that indicate approach roads and provide you with valuable car-parking information.

Motoring information

Approach road

Other information

Public transport stop

Car park

# how the AA can help you

The AA is Britain's largest motoring organisation, providing accurate and up-to-date information services for all motorists – just give us a call

All 09003 prefixed numbers are charged at 50p per minute at all times (correct at time of going to press)

## Check the traffic before you leave

**Call AA Roadwatch** for the latest reports on traffic hold-ups and roadworks

**Call 09003 401** plus the 3 digits for the relevant area on the map

**London and the South East area**
**401 122** Area within M25
**401 123** Essex, Herts, Beds, Bucks, Oxon, Berks
**401 125** Hants, Surrey, Sussex, Kent
**401 127** M25 and link roads

**National motorway network**
**09003 401 110**

**Continental Roadwatch  09003 401 904**
For traffic conditions to and from ferry ports, ferry news and major European events

## Prepare for the weather

**Call AA Weatherwatch** for the latest weather report followed by a 4-day forecast

**Call 09003 401** plus the 3 digits shown on the relevant area of the map

**Latest national forecast**
**09003 401 130**

**Weather reports for crossing the Channel and for Northern France**
**09003 401 361**

## Travelling abroad

**Just dial 09003** followed by the numbers shown

**Seaports** – how to get there, parking and other essential information
**401 891** Hampshire/Dorset/Kent ports

**The Channel Tunnel  401 362**
Le Shuttle boarding details, terminal facilities, restrictions, passport control, journey times and general travel information

**Airports** – how to get there, parking, air-links and other essential information

**401 935** Birmingham, Edinburgh, Gatwick, Heathrow, Luton, Manchester, Stansted and London City Airport

**Taking your car abroad** – be prepared for different laws, paperwork and driving conditions

**401 866** for the information line and a report on your destination

## Calling on the move

**Mobile Phones** (dial 6 digits only) **401 110**
A special service for VODAFONE or CELLNET users
VODAFONE connects you to the local Roadwatch traffic message
CELLNET connects you to a cellular menu from which you select the appropriate message (Calls cost 50p per minute at all times in addition to your mobile call tariff)

**Vodafone 'Fast Dial'** (dial 4 digits only) **2222**
A special service for VODAFONE users for easy access to AA motoring advice and other travel information (Calls cost 41p per minute at all times. Call charges correct at time of going to press)

## Need expert advice?

Access the expertise of the AA, **call 09003** followed by the numbers shown

**Motoring hints and advice**

| | |
|---|---|
| **401 505** Checks before you start, route planning and motorway driving | **401 509** Motoring for disabled drivers |
| **401 506** Child seats and harnesses | **401 522** Towing: matching the vehicle to the load |
| **401 508** Safe motorway driving | **401 526** Motorway breakdowns |

**Motoring and the law**

| | |
|---|---|
| **401 841** Accidents: reporting to police, exchanging details | **401 852** Wheel clamping |
| **401 847** Drinking and driving: what is the law and penalties? | **401 853** Parking: restrictions and enforcements |
| **401 850** Lights: use in daytime, rear, high-intensity (fog) lights | **401 855** Seat belts |
| **401 851** MoT: who needs one, what is tested, penalties and checks | **401 856** Speed limits in the UK: what is the law? |
| | **401 857** Tyre safety: keeping safe and within the law |

The material contained in these 09003 recorded information services has been researched by the AA. While every effort is made to ensure that it is accurate, no liability can be accepted arising from inaccuracies or omissions. © The Automobile Association 1998

## Useful numbers

**AA The Driving School  0800 60 70 80**
Book your driving lessons anywhere in mainland Britain

**Road User Information Line (Highways Agency)  0345 50 40 30**
For information on motorways and trunk roads, to make a complaint or comment on road conditions or roadworks, for MoT and vehicle licence enquiries

**Trace Service (Greater London only)  0171 747 4747**
Track down your car if it has been towed away

## Exclusive services for AA Members

All 0990 prefixed numbers are charged at BT's National Rate

**AA Hotel Booking Service  0990 05 05 05** (8.30am–7.30pm, Mon–Sat)
Free reservation service for business or leisure travel. Take advantage of the many special offers available at over 8,000 AA-inspected hotels, guest houses, inns and farmhouses in Britain and Ireland

**UK Route Planning  0990 500 600** (24 hours, 7 days a week)
Free personalised itineraries for routes within Great Britain and Ireland

**Special Offers and AA Services  0990 500 600** (24 hours, 7 days a week)
Expert advice and assistance on legal and technical aspects of motoring.
Details of discounts on AA services and other exclusive offers negotiated to help AA members keep the cost of motoring down

**AA Membership Administration 0990 444 444** (8am–8pm, Mon–Fri; 8am–noon, Sat)
All Membership enquiries, including renewal, upgrades and name or address changes

If you are not an AA Member and would like to be – **call 0800 444 999** for details on how to join

## Visit our web site  www.theaa.co.uk

# route planner

Port Nis
(Port of Ness)

A857

Tolsta Head

Steornabhagh
(Stornoway)

Isle of
Lewis

The Minch

A859

Tairbeart
(Tarbert)

Harris

Gairloch

Kinloche

Outer Hebrides

Sound of Harris

Uibhist a Tuath
(North Uist)

Loch nam Madadh
(Lochmaddy)

Uig

A87

Beinn na Faoghla
(Benbecula)

Dunvegan

Portree

A865

Uibhist a Deas
(South Uist)

Kyle of
Lochalsh

Isle
of
Skye

A87

Loch Baghasdail
(Lochboisdale)

Sound of Barra

Rum

Mallaig

Barra

Eigg

A830

Inner Hebrides

Coll

A861

Tobermory

A884

Lochaline

A826

Tiree

Craignure
Isle of Mull

Fionnphort

A849

Oban

A816

Colonsay

In

Lochgilphead

Port
Askaig

Jura

Tarbert

A846

Kennacra

Islay

A83

Port Ellen

A84

Arrar

Brodi

Campbeltown

## Legend

| | |
|---|---|
| ═══ | Motorway |
| ─── | Primary route dual carriageway |
| ─── | Primary route single carriageway |
| ─── | Other A roads |

0   10   20   30 miles

0   10   20   30   40 kilometres

Stromness
Kirkwall
Orkney Islands
John O'Groats
Thurso
A836
Melvich
A9
A882
Tongue
A838
Wick
A894
Altnaharra
A897
A99
Latheron
Helmsdale
Lairg
A839
A835
Ullapool
A837
Bonar Bridge
Tain
Moray Firth
Alness
A832
Cromarty
Dingwall
Achnasheen
Nairn
Elgin
Cullen
Banff
Macduff
Fraserburgh
A98
A95
A96
A940
Forres
A941
Keith
Turriff
Peterhead
Inverness
Aberlour
Huntly
A947
A952
A90
A82
Drumnadrochit
Tomatin
Grantown-on-Spey
Ellon
Oldmeldrum
Invermoriston
A938
Tomintoul
Inverurie
Aviemore
A939
Aberdeen
A887
A87
Kingussie
Newtonmore
Invergarry
A93
Braemar
Ballater
Banchory
Stonehaven
A86
Fort William
A92
Pitlochry
Brechin
Montrose
Aberfeldy
Blairgowrie
Forfar
A827
A826
A94
Coupar Angus
Arbroath
Killin
Tyndrum
Dundee
Carnoustie
A85
Lochearnhead
Crianlarich
Perth
Newport-on-Tay
Crieff
Auchterarder
St Andrews
A91
Cupar
M90
A84
Callander
A915
A917
Tarbet
Kinross
Glenrothes
Dunblane
Buckhaven
M9
Alloa
A977
Stirling
Dunfermline
Kirkcaldy
A811
A815
Firth of Forth
NORTH SEA
A985
M80
Dunbar
Gourock
Dumbarton
Falkirk
Edinburgh
EDINBURGH
A1
Linlithgow
Greenock
Glasgow
Cumbernauld
Musselburgh
M8
M73
Airdrie
A8
A80
Livingston
Dalkeith
Eyemouth
Paisley
GLASGOW
A78
Largs
M77
Motherwell
A71
A702
A68
Berwick-upon-Tweed
A737
A77
East Kilbride
A73
A703
A7
A697
Kilwinning
Strathaven
M74
Lanark
A721
A701
Peebles
Coldstream
A698
Ardrossan
Irvine
Biggar
A72
Galashiels
Firth of Clyde
Kilmarnock
Lesmahagow
Kelso
Wooler
Troon
Prestwick
A76
Selkirk
Ayr
A708
Cumnock
Jedburgh
A70
A74(M)
New Cumnock
Hawick
Alnwick
Maybole
A713
A74
A1068
Amble
Dalmellington
Moffat

Amble
lington

Whitley Bay
Tynemouth
South Shields
NEWCASTLE UPON TYNE
Jarrow
**SUNDERLAND**
Chester-le-Street
A1(M)
A19
pennymoor
**Hartlepool**
Stockton-on-Tees
**Middlesbrough**
A66
lington
A171
Guisborough
Whitby
A172
Stokesley
A169
A171
ch
ner
A684
Northallerton
A19
Scalby
A170
Scarborough
Thirsk
Helmsley
A170
Pickering
Filey
A168
A19
Easingwold
A64
Malton
A165
A61
A1(M)
Bridlington
A59
A166
A614
A165
te
A658
A614
Driffield
York
Wetherby
A64
A19
Market
Weighton A1035
A165
A61
A1
A63
Selby
A1079
A164
Beverley
LEEDS
A163
A614
M62
M62
Hessle
HULL
M1
A645
Goole
A15
Barton-upon-Humber
Wakefield
M18
Thorne
Scunthorpe
Immingham
Barnsley
M180
A18
**Grimsby**
A635
Doncaster
Brigg
Cleethorpes
Rotherham
A159
A46
IELD
Bawtry
A15
A631
Market Rasen
A16
A1031
A1(M)
A57
A631
Gainsborough
A46
Louth
Mablethorpe
Worksop
Retford
A156
A157
A16
A52
M1
A1
Staveley
A619
A57
A158
A52
Chesterfield
A60
A614
Lincoln
Horncastle
A158
Skegness
A619
A15
Mansfield
A617
A52
Alfreton
A17
Sleaford
A6
A38
A6097
Newark-on-Trent
A17
Boston
The Wash
urne
Ilkeston
A6097
A1
A17
A52
DERBY
**NOTTINGHAM**
A52
Grantham
A50
Long Eaton
A52
A606
Spalding
A17
Sheringham
Cromer
ton upon Trent
A453
A607
A15
King's Lynn
A149
A148
North Walsham
A606
Bourne
A151
Hunstanton
A148
Aylsham
de-ch
M1
Melton Mowbray
A1
Dersingham
Fakenham
A1065
A140
A1151
A149
A511
A50
Oakham
Stamford
A16
A16
Wisbech
A10
A1065
Dereham
A47
Norwich
Caister-on-Sea
worth
**LEICESTER**
A606
A47
A1122
Swaffham
A47
A146
A143
Great Yarmouth
Hinckley
Wigston
A47
Peterborough
A134
A11
Attleborough
Lowestoft
M1
Market Harborough
A6003
A43
March
A141
A1065
A143
Bungay
Beccles
AM
M69
A5
A6116
A1(M)
Chatteris
A1066
Diss
Corby
Ely
A1101
Thetford
Southwold
M6
A14
A4304
A43
Kettering
A14
A10
A142
A11
A143
OVENTRY
Rugby
A508
A14
A14
Huntingdon
A14
Bury St Edmunds
A140
A1120
A12
ington Spa
M45
A45
A45
St Neots
A428
Newmarket
A134
Aldeburgh
A425
Daventry
A428
A6
Northampton
Cambridge
Stowmarket
A14
Woodbridge
M40
Towcester
A1198
A421
Biggleswade
A11
A1307
Sudbury
Ipswich
Bedford

### Legend
Motorway
Primary route dual carriageway
Primary route single carriageway
Other A roads

0  10  20  30 miles
0  10  20  30  40 kilometres

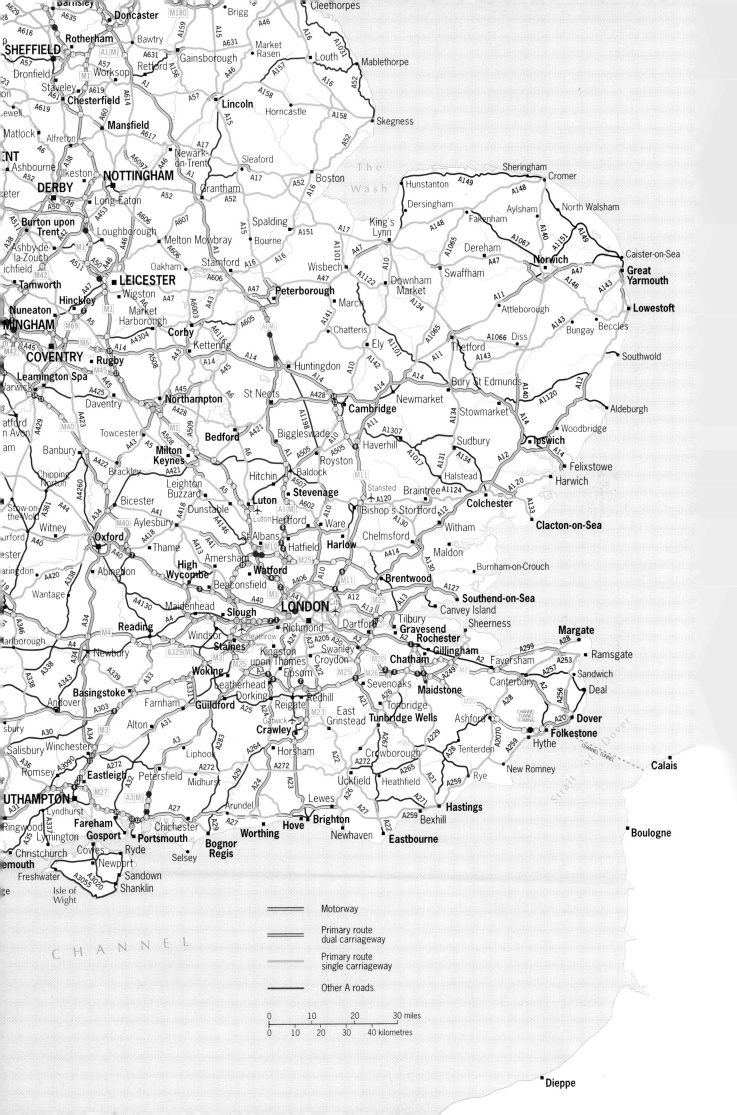

# road signs

## Classes of signs

Our road system has a consistent and comprehensive set of road signs that provide you with information, instructions and warnings.

| Circles order and prohibit | Triangles warn | Rectangles provide information |
|---|---|---|

## Junctions and roundabouts

These signs provide you with important information about the nature of the junction or the roundabout ahead.

| Distance to 'STOP' line ahead | Distance to 'GIVE WAY' line ahead | Give way to traffic on major road | Stop and give way | Crossroads | T-junction | Staggered junction | Roundabout | Mini-roundabout (roundabout circulation) | No through road |
|---|---|---|---|---|---|---|---|---|---|

## Traffic behaviour

Signs which must be obeyed. They indicate the speed or action you are required to take in particular situations.

| No stopping (clearway) | National speed limit applies | Maximum speed | Give priority to vehicles from opposite direction | No overtaking | Motor vehicles prohibited except for access | No entry for vehicular traffic | No U-turns | No right turn | No left turn |
|---|---|---|---|---|---|---|---|---|---|

| Turn left ahead | | Turn left | Vehicles may pass either side to reach same destination | Ahead only | Keep left |
|---|---|---|---|---|---|

## The road ahead

Advance warning of the road layout ahead enables you to plan a safe approach.

| Bend to left | Double bend, first to left | Bend to right | Double bend, first to right | Road hump or series of road humps ahead | Worded warning sign | Dual carriageway ends | Steep hill downwards | Steep hill upwards |
|---|---|---|---|---|---|---|---|---|

| No goods vehicles over maximum gross weight shown (in tonnes) | Axle weight limit (in tonnes) | No vehicles over height shown | Sharp deviation of route | Two-way traffic straight ahead | Traffic merges from left | Traffic merges from right | Road narrows on left | Road narrows on both sides |
|---|---|---|---|---|---|---|---|---|

# Hazards ahead

These signs warn you of potential hazards on the road ahead.

| Hospital ahead with accident and emergency facilities | Pedestrian crossing | Cycle route ahead | Slippery road | Road works | Uneven road | Wild animals | Falling or fallen rocks | Other danger |

| Children | Children going to or from school | School crossing patrol ahead | School crossing patrol | Traffic signals | Hump bridge | Opening or swing bridge ahead | Quayside or river bank |

# On the motorway

These signals are used to warn you of conditions ahead and the lanes affected. They may be located overhead, on the central reservation or over the nearside lane. Drivers must observe the advisory speed limits and should remember that the red circle means a mandatory speed control.

  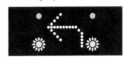 

| Temporary maximum speed limit and information message | Change lane | Leave motorway at next exit | Do not proceed further in this lane |

| Reduced visibility ahead | Lane ahead closed | Temporary maximum speed limit | End of restriction | National speed limits apply | Traffic building up ahead. Reduce speed to a maximum of 60mph to help maintain flow | Traffic getting heavier ahead. Reduce speed to a maximum of 50mph or lower if incidents occur | Traffic improving. Maximum speed increased to 60mph | Traffic is lighter. Flow easier. Return to national speed limits. This will appear for 3 minutes before going blank |

# Motorway diversions

Where the motorway is closed, special signs advise you of the recommended diversion route around the incident.

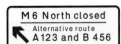      

Symbols showing emergency diversion route
for motorway traffic

# motorways – restricted junctions

Diagrams of selected motorway junctions which have entry
and exit restrictions

XVI

## M1 London–Leeds

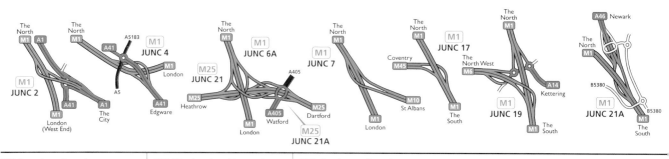

## M1 London–Leeds | M2 Rochester–Faversham | M3 Sunbury–Southampton

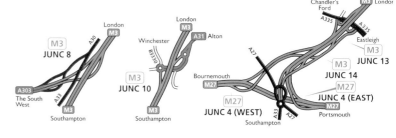

## M4 London–South Wales | M5 Birmingham–Exeter

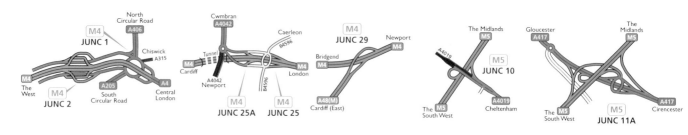

## M5 Birmingham–Exeter | M6 Rugby–Carlisle

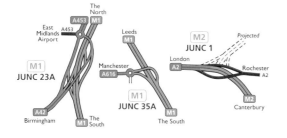

## M6 Rugby–Carlisle | M8 Edinburgh–Bishopton

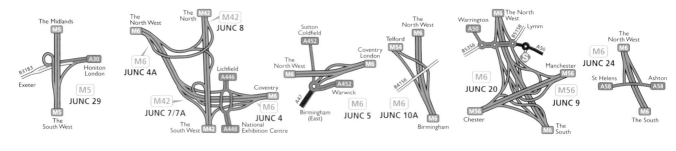

## M8 Edinburgh–Bishopton

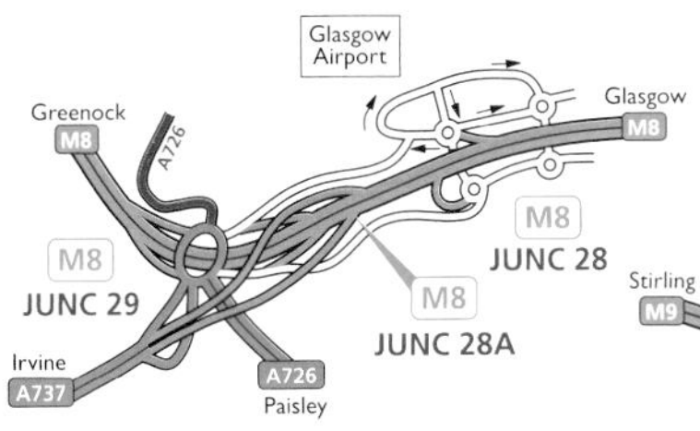

Glasgow Airport

Greenock
M8
A726

M8
JUNC 29

Irvine
A737

A726
Paisley

M8
JUNC 28A

Glasgow
M8

M8
JUNC 28

## M9 Edinburgh–Dunblane

M9
JUNC 8

Stirling
M9

Edinburgh
M9

Forth Road Bridge
(A8000)

Stirling
M9

M9

M876
Glasgow

M9
JUNC 1

M9
Edinburgh

## M11 London–Cambridge

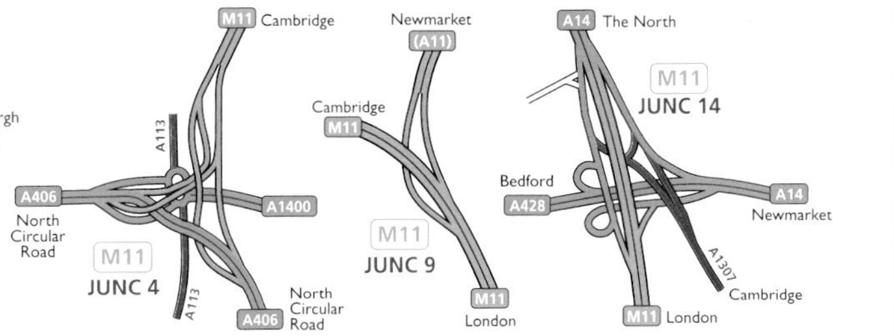

M11 Cambridge

A113

A406
North Circular Road

A1400

M11
JUNC 4

M11
A113

A406
North Circular Road

Newmarket
(A11)

Cambridge
M11

M11
JUNC 9

M11
London

A14 The North

M11
JUNC 14

Bedford
A428

A14
Newmarket

A1307

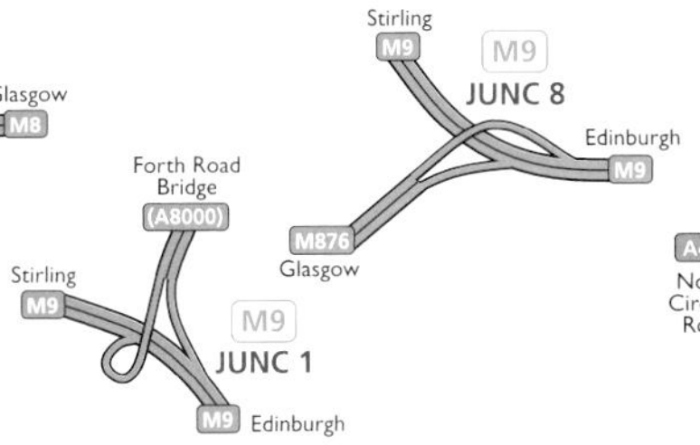

M11 London

Cambridge

## M20 Swanley–Folkestone

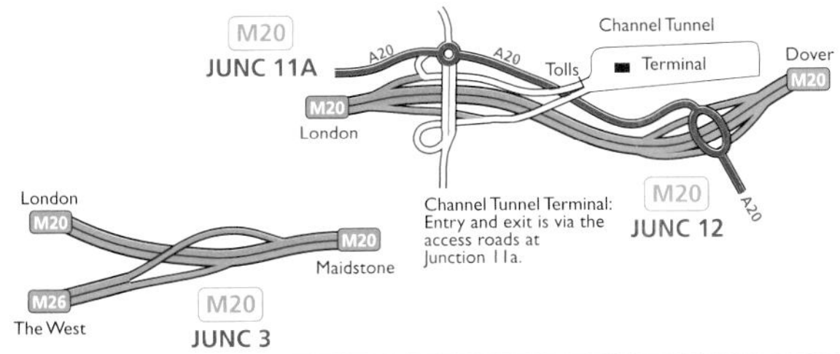

M20
JUNC 11A

A20
London

A20

Channel Tunnel

Terminal

Tolls

Dover
M20

Channel Tunnel Terminal: Entry and exit is via the access roads at Junction 11a.

M20
JUNC 12

A20

London
M20

M20
Maidstone

M26
The West

M20
JUNC 3

## M25 London Orbital

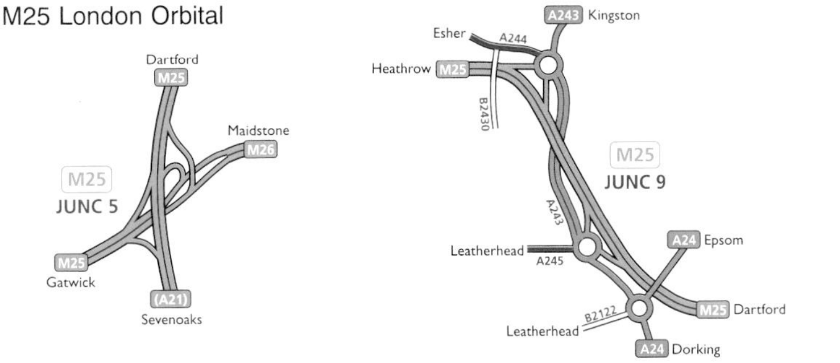

Dartford
M25

Maidstone
M26

M25
JUNC 5

M25
Gatwick

(A21)
Sevenoaks

Esher
A244

A243 Kingston

Heathrow M25

B2430

M25
JUNC 9

A243

Leatherhead
A245

A24 Epsom

Leatherhead
B2122

M25 Dartford

A24 Dorking

## M25 London Orbital

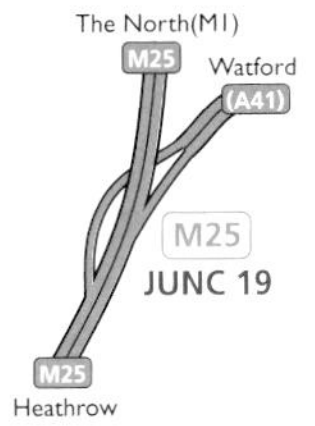

The North(M1)

M25
Watford
A41

M25
JUNC 19

M25
Heathrow

## M27 Cadnam–Portsmouth

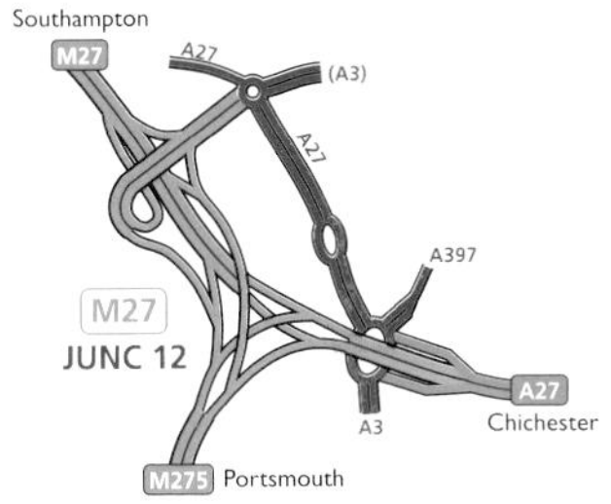

Southampton
M27

A27
(A3)

A27

A397

M27
JUNC 12

A27
Chichester

A3

M275 Portsmouth

## M40 London–Birmingham

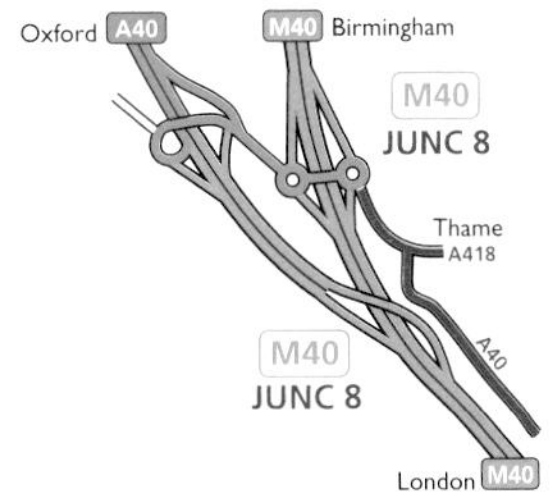

Oxford A40

M40 Birmingham

M40
JUNC 8

Thame
A418

M40
JUNC 8

A40

London M40

## M42 Bromsgrove–Measham

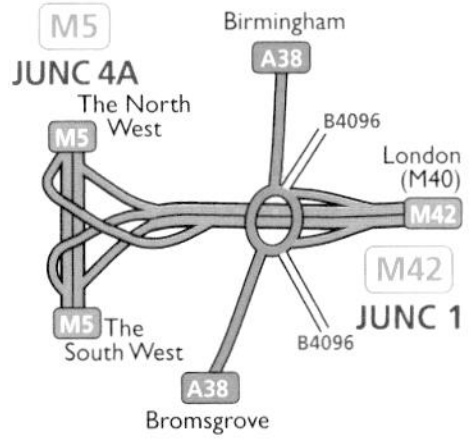

M5
JUNC 4A
The North West

M5

Birmingham
A38

B4096

London (M40)
M42

M5 The South West

B4096

M42
JUNC 1

A38
Bromsgrove

## M56 North Cheshire Motorway

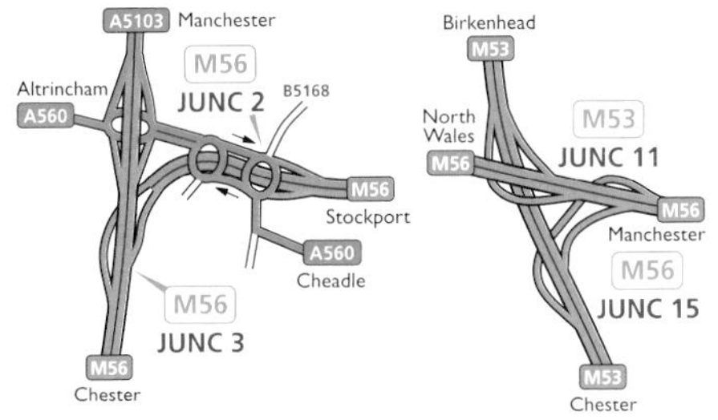

A5103 Manchester

M56
JUNC 2

B5168

Altrincham
A560

Stockport

A560
Cheadle

M56
JUNC 3

M56
Chester

Birkenhead
M53

North Wales
M56

North Wales

M56
JUNC 11

M56
Manchester

M56
JUNC 15

M53
Chester

## M60 Greater Manchester

Preston (M61)
M60

A34 Manchester

M60
JUNC 3

Stockport
M60

M56
JUNC 1

M56

A34
Wilmslow

Manchester A5103

M60

Preston (M61)
M60

Stockport
M60

A5103

M60
JUNC 5

Chester (M56)

(A666) Bolton

M61
JUNC 3

M61

M61

M61
Preston

M61
JUNC 2

M61
JUNC 1

M60
Leeds

M60
JUNC 14

A580
St Helens

Liverpool M60

M60
JUNC 15

A580
Manchester

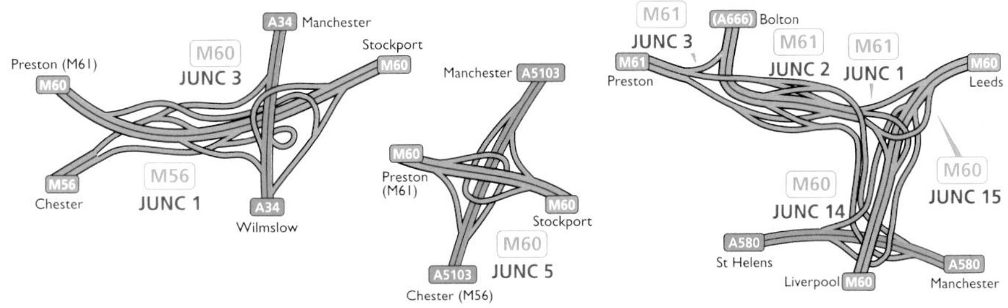

## M60 Greater Manchester

M60
JUNC 16

Bolton
A666

Leeds
M60

M60
Liverpool

A666
Swinton

M60
JUNC 27

A626

M60
Chester (M56)

A560

B6104

A626
Stockport

M60
JUNC 26

Ashton
M60

A6017

M60
JUNC 25

A560
Bredbury

B6104

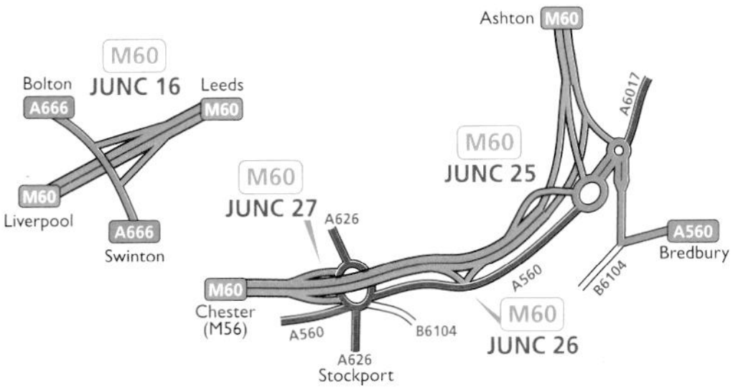

## M62 Liverpool-Humberside

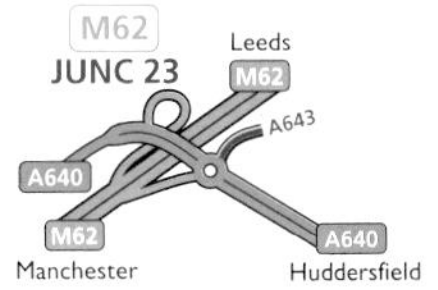

M62
JUNC 23

A640

Leeds
M62

A643

M62
Manchester

A640
Huddersfield

## M73 East of Glasgow

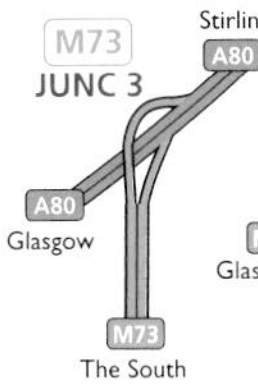

M73
JUNC 3

Stirling
A80

A80
Glasgow

M73
The South

M74
Glasgow (SE)

A74

M73
JUNC 1

A721

M74
JUNC 4

The South

## M74 Glasgow–Gretna

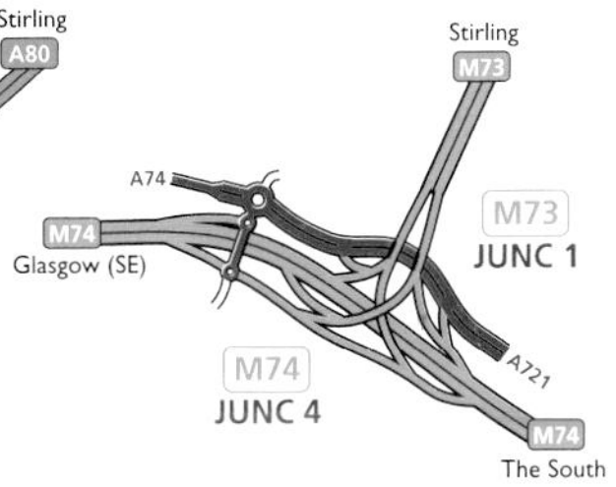

Stirling
M73

## M74, A74(M) Glasgow–Gretna

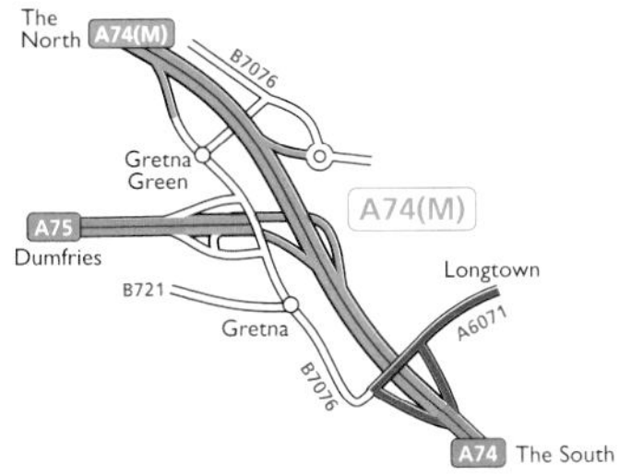

The North
A74(M)

B7076

Gretna Green

A75
Dumfries

B721

Gretna

A74(M)

Longtown

A6071

B7076

A74 The South

## M80 Glasgow–Stirling

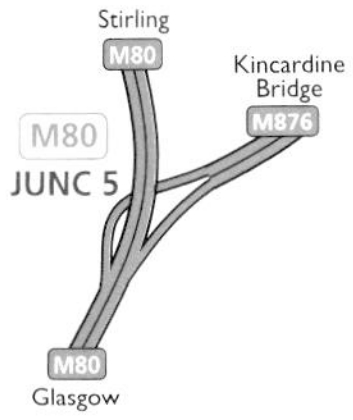

Stirling
M80

Kincardine Bridge
M876

M80
JUNC 5

M80
Glasgow

A91

A911
Milnathort

M90
Forth Road Bridge

## M90 Forth Road Bridge–Perth

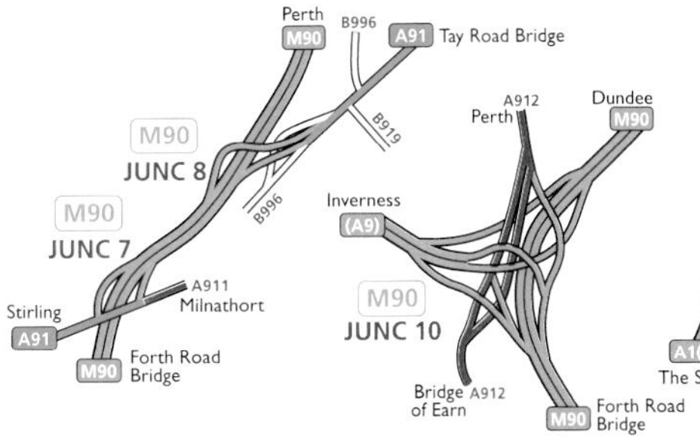

Perth
M90

B996

A91 Tay Road Bridge

M90
JUNC 8

B919

A912 Perth

Dundee
M90

M90
JUNC 7

Stirling

Inverness
(A9)

M90
JUNC 10

Bridge of Earn
A912

Forth Road Bridge
M90

## A1(M) Scotch Corner–Tyneside

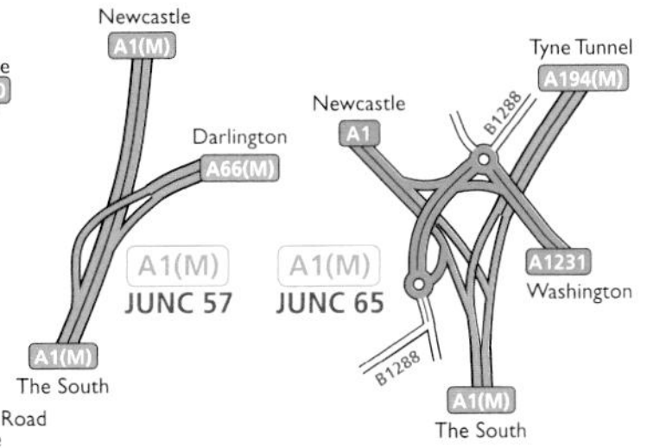

Newcastle
A1(M)

Darlington
A66(M)

Newcastle
A1

A1(M)
JUNC 57

A1(M)
The South

Tyne Tunnel

A194(M)

B1288

A1(M)
JUNC 65

A1231
Washington

B1288

A1(M)
The South

# map symbols

## motoring information

|  |  |
|--------|-------------|
| M4 | Motorway with number |
| 11 | Motorway junction with and without number |
| 3 | Restricted motorway junctions |
| S Fleet | Motorway service area |
| | Motorway and junction under construction |
| A3 | Primary route single/dual carriageway |
| S Oxford | Primary route service area |
| BATH | Primary route destination |
| A1123 | Other A road single/dual carriageway |
| B2070 | B road single/dual carriageway |

|  |  |
|--------|-------------|
| | Unclassified road single/dual carriageway |
| | Roundabout |
| | Interchange |
| | Narrow primary/other A/B road with passing places (Scotland) |
| | Road under construction |
| | Road tunnel |
| | Steep gradient (arrows point downhill) |
| Toll | Road toll |
| 5 | Distance in miles between symbols |

|  |  |
|--------|-------------|
| V | Vehicle ferry – Great Britain |
| BERGEN V | Vehicle ferry – continental |
| ✈ | Airport |
| H | Heliport |
| F | International freight terminal |
| | Boxed symbol indicating towns with permanent Park and Ride schemes |
| | Railway line/in tunnel |
| —○——✕— | Railway station and level crossing |
| ++++++++++ | Tourist railway |

|  |  |
|--------|-------------|
| AA | AA shop |
| ☎ | AA telephone |
| | Urban area and village |
| 628 ▲ | Spot height in metres |
| | River, canal, lake |
| | Sandy beach |
| | County/County Borough/ Council Area boundary |
| | National boundary |
| 85 | Page overlap and number |

## tourist information

|  |  |
|--------|-------------|
| 𝒊 | Tourist Information Centre |
| 𝒊 | Tourist Information Centre (seasonal) |
| ♠ | Abbey, cathedral or priory |
| ⅄ | Ruined abbey, cathedral or priory |
| ♖ | Castle |
| ⌂ | Historic house |
| Ⓜ | Museum or art gallery |
| ⚒ | Industrial interest |
| ✻ | Garden |
| ♣ | Arboretum |
| ♈ | Country park |
| ♇ | Agricultural showground |

|  |  |
|--------|-------------|
| ⛩ | Theme park |
| 🐘 | Zoo |
| 🐃 | Wildlife collection – mammals |
| 🐦 | Wildlife collection – birds |
| 🐟 | Aquarium |
| 🦆 | Nature reserve |
| RSPB | RSPB site |
| ⋯⋯ | Forest drive |
| – – – – | National trail |
| • | Viewpoint |
| ⚑ | Picnic site |
| ⋮ | Hill-fort |

|  |  |
|--------|-------------|
| ♞ | Roman antiquity |
| 🏛 | Prehistoric monument |
| ✕ 1066 | Battle site with year |
| 🚂 | Steam centre (railway) |
| ◉ | Cave |
| ✹ | Windmill |
| ⚑ | Golf course |
| 🏏 | County cricket ground |
| 🏉 | Rugby Union national ground |
| 🏃 | International athletics ground |
| 🏇 | Horse racing |
| 🏇 | Show jumping/equestrian circuit |

|  |  |
|--------|-------------|
| 🏁 | Motor-racing circuit |
| ✈ | Air show venue |
| ⛷ | Ski slope – natural |
| ⛷ | Ski slope – artificial |
| NT | National Trust property |
| NTS | National Trust for Scotland property |
| ★ | Other place of interest |
| ☐ | Boxed symbols indicate attractions within urban areas |
| | National Park (England & Wales) |
| | National Scenic Area (Scotland) |
| | Forest Park |
| | Heritage Coast |

## Ireland (see pages 154–157) For tourist information see opposite page

| | | |
|---|---|---|
| Motorway | National primary route (Republic of Ireland) | Primary route (Northern Ireland) | Road under construction |
| Motorway junction with and without number | National secondary route (Republic of Ireland) | A road (Northern Ireland) | Distance in miles between symbols |
| Restricted motorway junctions | Regional road (Republic of Ireland) | B road (Northern Ireland) | International boundary |

Motorway

Motorway junction with and without number

Restricted motorway junctions

N17 — National primary route (Republic of Ireland)

N54 — National secondary route (Republic of Ireland)

R182 — Regional road (Republic of Ireland)

A4 — Primary route (Northern Ireland)

A21 — A road (Northern Ireland)

B75 — B road (Northern Ireland)

Road under construction

Distance in miles between symbols

International boundary

## district maps (see pages 232–243)

Motorway

Primary route single/dual

Other A road single/dual

B road single/dual

Unclassified road single/dual

Road under construction

Restricted road

Railway line/in tunnel

Railway station

Inner London Regional Transport (LRT) station

Outer London Regional Transport (LRT) station

Railway station/LRT interchange

Light railway/tramway station

Sports stadium

Hospital

Crem — Crematorium

Place of interest

Golf course

AA — AA shop

## Central London (see pages 244–254)

Motorway

Primary route single/dual

Other A road single/dual

B road single/dual

Unclassified road single/dual

Unclassified road wide/narrow

Road under construction

Road tunnel wide/narrow

Restricted road (access only/private)

Footpath

Track

Pedestrian street

Railway line/in tunnel

One-way street

Compulsory turn

Banned turn

Banned turn (restricted periods only)

Ahead only

Mini-roundabout

Barrier

Railway station

London Regional Transport (LRT) station

Docklands Light Railway station

Parking

PO — Post Office

POL — Police station

Steps

† Church

AA — AA shop

i — Tourist Information Centre

i — Tourist Information Centre (seasonal)

**Royal Parks (opening and closing times for traffic)**

Green Park        Constitution Hill: closed Sundays, 08.00–dusk
Hyde Park         Open 05.00–midnight
Regent's Park     Open 07.00–midnight
St James's Park   The Mall: closed Sundays, 08.00–dusk

New traffic regulations in the City of London include security checkpoints and restrict the number of entry and exit points.

**Note:** Oxford Street is closed to through-traffic (except buses & taxis) 07.00–19.00, Monday–Saturday

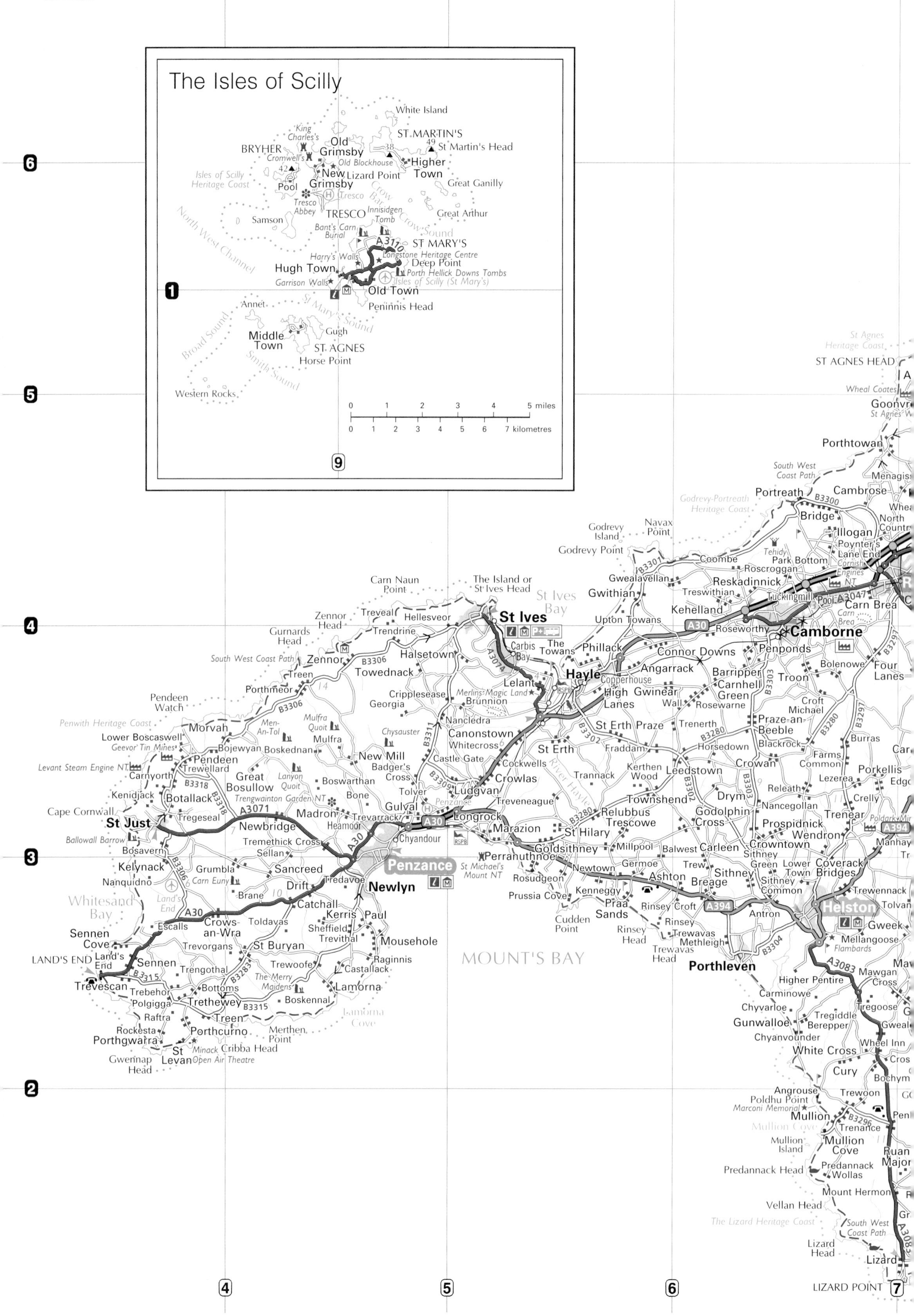

The Isles of Scilly
White Island
King Charles's
Old Grimsby
ST MARTIN'S
BRYHER
Cromwell's
38
49
St Martin's Head
42
Old Blockhouse
Higher Town
Isles of Scilly Heritage Coast
New Grimsby
Lizard Point
Pool
Great Ganilly
Tresco Abbey
Tresco
Crow Bar
North West Channel
Samson
TRESCO
Innisidgen Tomb
Great Arthur
Crow Sound
Bant's Carn Burial
A3110
ST MARY'S
Harry's Walls
Longstone Heritage Centre
Hugh Town
Deep Point
Porth Hellick Downs Tombs
Garrison Walls
Isles of Scilly (St Mary's)
Old Town
Annet
St Mary's Sound
Peninnis Head
Broad Sound
Middle Town
Gugh
ST AGNES
Smith Sound
Horse Point
Western Rocks
0 1 2 3 4 5 miles
0 1 2 3 4 5 6 7 kilometres
9
St Agnes Heritage Coast
ST AGNES HEAD
Wheal Coates
Goonvr
St Agnes
Porthtowan
South West Coast Path
Menagis
Godrevy-Portreath Heritage Coast
Portreath
B3300
Cambrose
Bridge
North Country
Navax Point
Godrevy Island
Illogan
Godrevy Point
Tehidy
Poynter's Lane End
Park Bottom
Cornish Engines NT
B3301
Coombe
Roscroggan
Gwealavellan
Reskadinnick
Carn Naun Point
The Island or St Ives Head
Gwithian
Treswithian
Tuckingmill
Pool
A3047
Carn Brea
St Ives Bay
Kehelland
Carn Brea
Zennor Head
Treveal
Hellesveor
St Ives
Upton Towans
A30
Roseworthy
Camborne
Gurnards Head
Trendrine
Carbis Bay
The Towans
Phillack
Connor Downs
Penponds
South West Coast Path
Zennor
B3306
Halsetown
A3074
Hayle
Angarrack
Barripper
Bolenowe
Four Lanes
Treen
Towednack
Lelant
Copperhouse
Carnhell Green
B3303
Troon
Porthmeor
Cripplesease
Merlins Magic Land
High Lanes
Gwinear
Pendeen Watch
Georgia
Brunnion
Wall
Rosewarne
Croft Michael
B3306
Men-An-Tol
Mulfra Quoit
Nancledra
St Erth Praze
Trenerth
Praze-an-Beeble
B3280
B3297
Penwith Heritage Coast
Morvah
Chysauster
B3311
Canonstown
B3302
B3280
Burras
Lower Boscaswell
Mulfra
Whitecross
St Erth
Fraddam
Horsedown
Blackrock
Geevor Tin Mines
Bojewyan
Boskednan
New Mill
Castle Gate
Farms Common
Car
Pendeen
Trewellard
Badger's Cross
Cockwells
Kerthen Wood
Leedstown
Crowan
Porkellis
Levant Steam Engine NT
Carnyorth
Great Bosullow
Lanyon Quoit
B3309
River Hayle
Trannack
B3302
Lezerea
Edgc
B3318
Boswarthan
Crowlas
B3303
Releath
Kenidjack
Botallack
B3318
Trengwainton Garden NT
Bone
Tolver
Ludgvan
Townshend
Drym
Crelly
Cape Cornwall
A3071
Madron
Gulval
Penzance
Treveneague
Nancegollan
St Just
Tregeseal
Newbridge
Heamoor
Trevarrack
A30
Longrock
B3280
Relubbus
Godolphin Cross
Trenear
Poldark Mine
Ballowall Barrow
Tremethick Cross
A30
Chyandour
Marazion
Trescowe
Prospidnick
A394
Bosavern
Sellan
RSPB
St Hilary
Millpool
Balwest
Carleen
Wendron
Manhay
Kelynack
Grumbla
Sancreed
Perranuthnoe
Goldsithney
Crowntown
Penzance
St Michael's Mount NT
Sithney Green
Lower Town
Coverack Bridges
Nanquidno
Carn Euny
Drift
Tredavoe
Newlyn
Rosudgeon
Newtown
Germoe
Ashton
Trew
Sithney
Sithney Common
Trewennack
Whitesand Bay
Land's End
Brane
Prussia Cove
Kenneggy
Breage
Tolvan
A30
Catchall
Praa Sands
Rinsey Croft
A394
Helston
Sennen Cove
Escalls
Crows-an-Wra
Toldavas
Kerris
Paul
Cudden Point
Rinsey
Antron
Gweek
Sheffield
Mousehole
Rinsey Head
Trewavas
Mellangoose
LAND'S END
Land's End
Trevorgans
Trevithal
Trewavas Head
Methleigh
Flambards
Sennen
St Buryan
Raginnis
MOUNT'S BAY
B3304
Trengothal
Trewoofe
Castallack
Porthleven
A3083
Mawgan Cross
Trevescan
B3315
The Merry Maidens
Lamorna
Higher Pentire
Trebehor
Bottoms
B3283
Carminowe
Polgigga
Trethewey
B3315
Boskennal
Chyvarloe
Tregoose
Raftra
Treen
Lamorna Cove
Tregiddle
Gunwalloe
Berepper
Rockesta
Porthcurno
Merthen Point
Chyanvounder
Porthgwarra
St Levan
Minack Open Air Theatre
Cribba Head
Wheel Inn
Gwennap Head
White Cross
Cury
Bochym
Angrouse
Trewoon
Poldhu Point
Marconi Memorial
Mullion
B3296
Pen
Mullion Cove
Trenance
Mullion Island
Mullion Cove
Ruan Major
Predannack Head
Predannack Wollas
Mount Hermon
Vellan Head
The Lizard Heritage Coast
South West Coast Path
A3083
Lizard Head
Lizard
LIZARD POINT
6
5
4
3
2
1
4
5
6
7

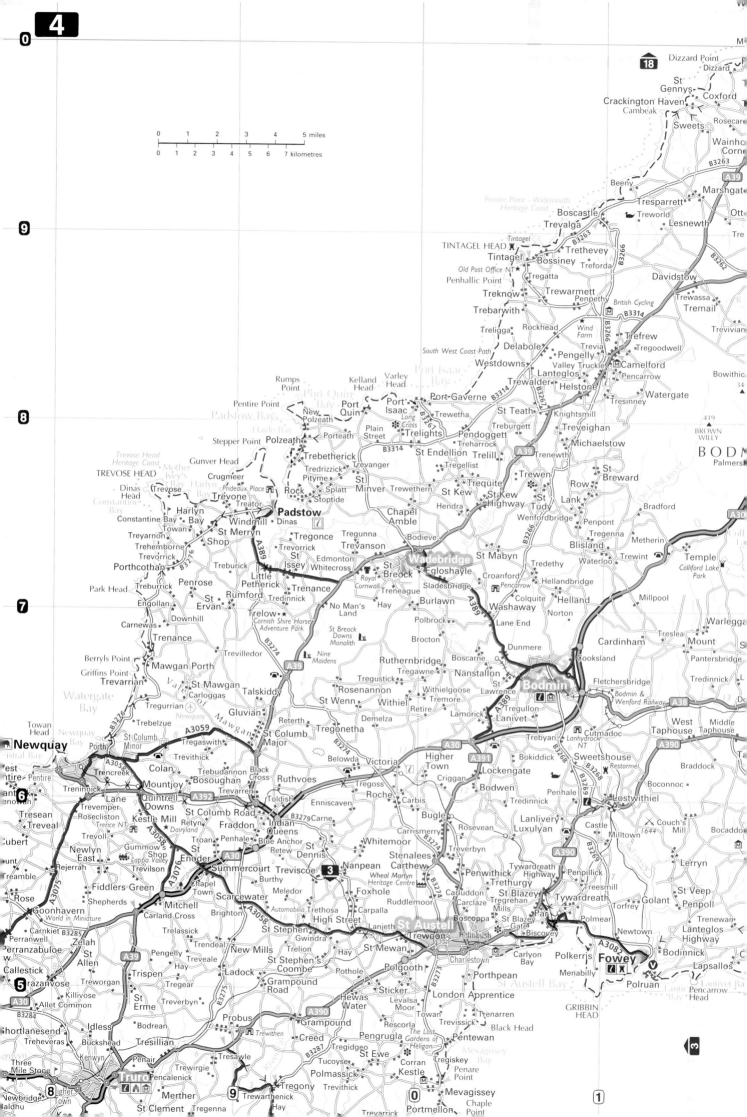

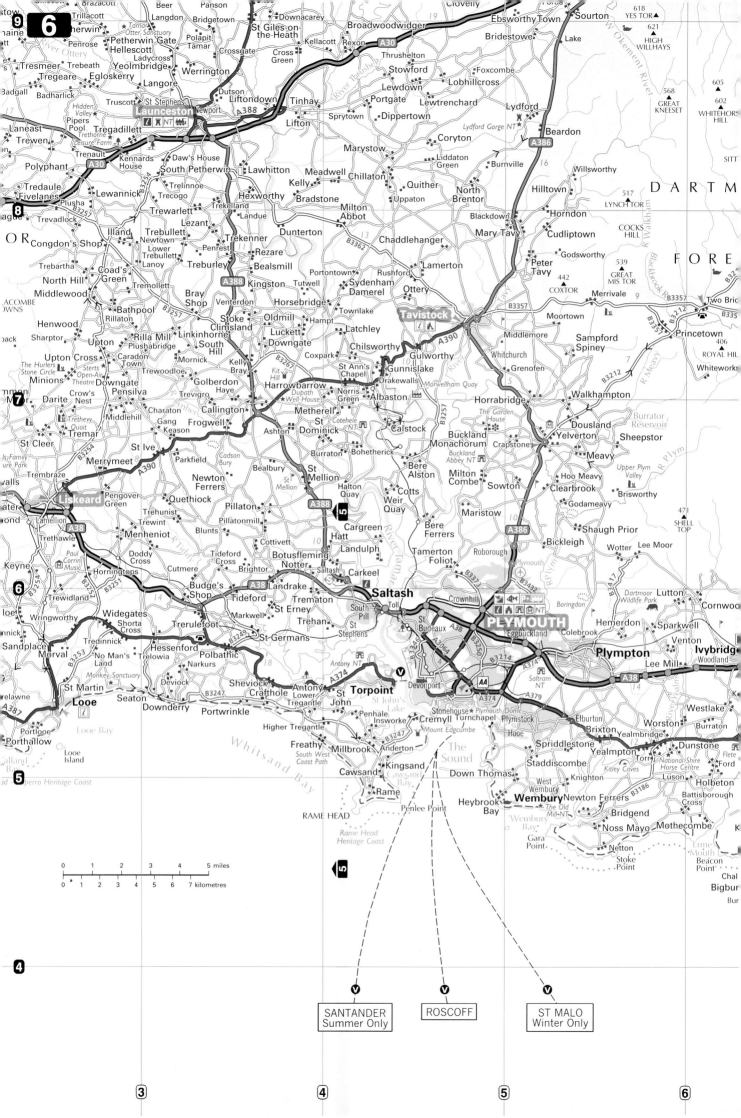

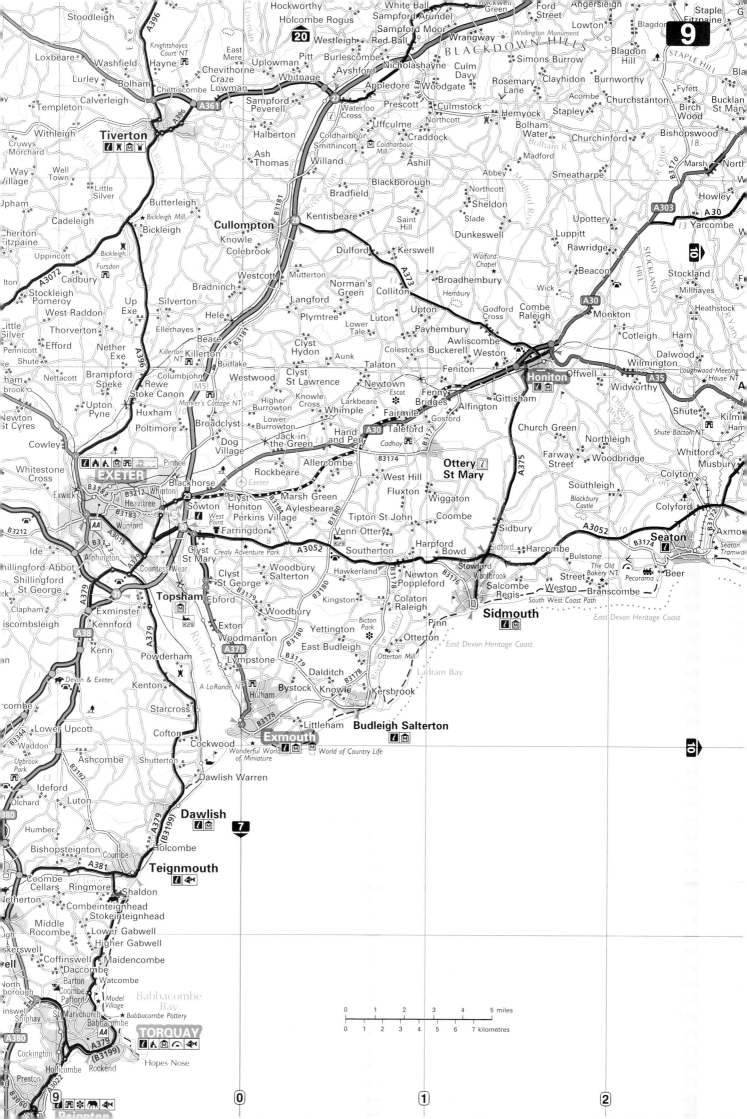

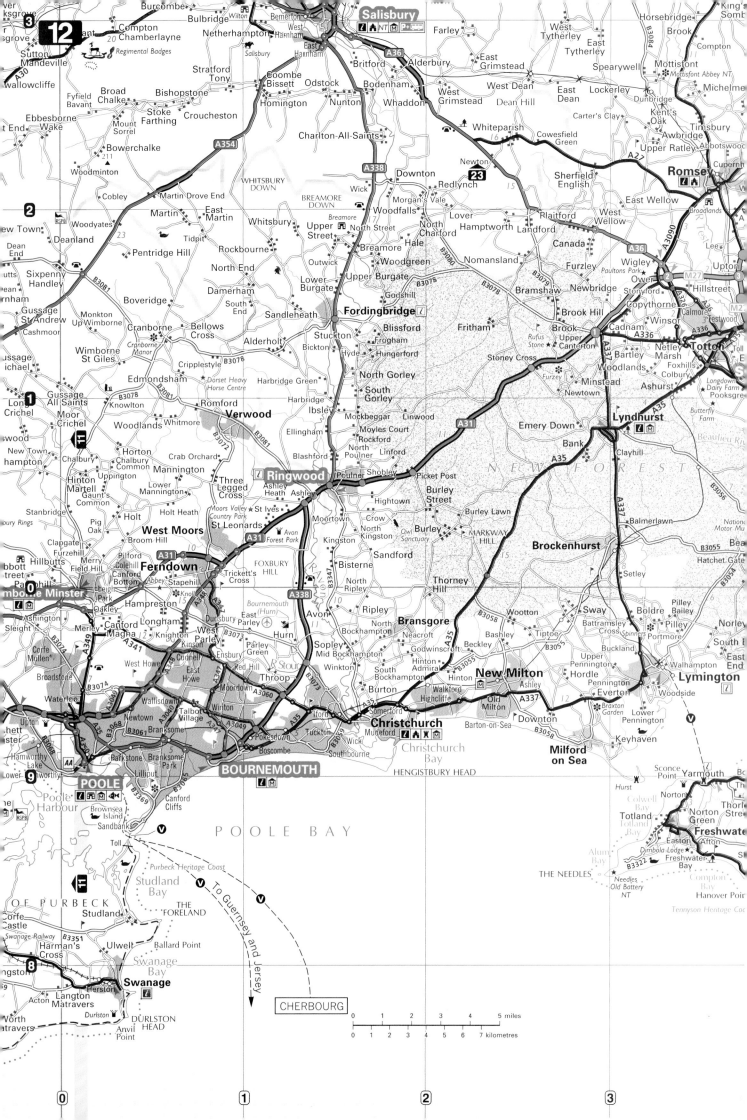

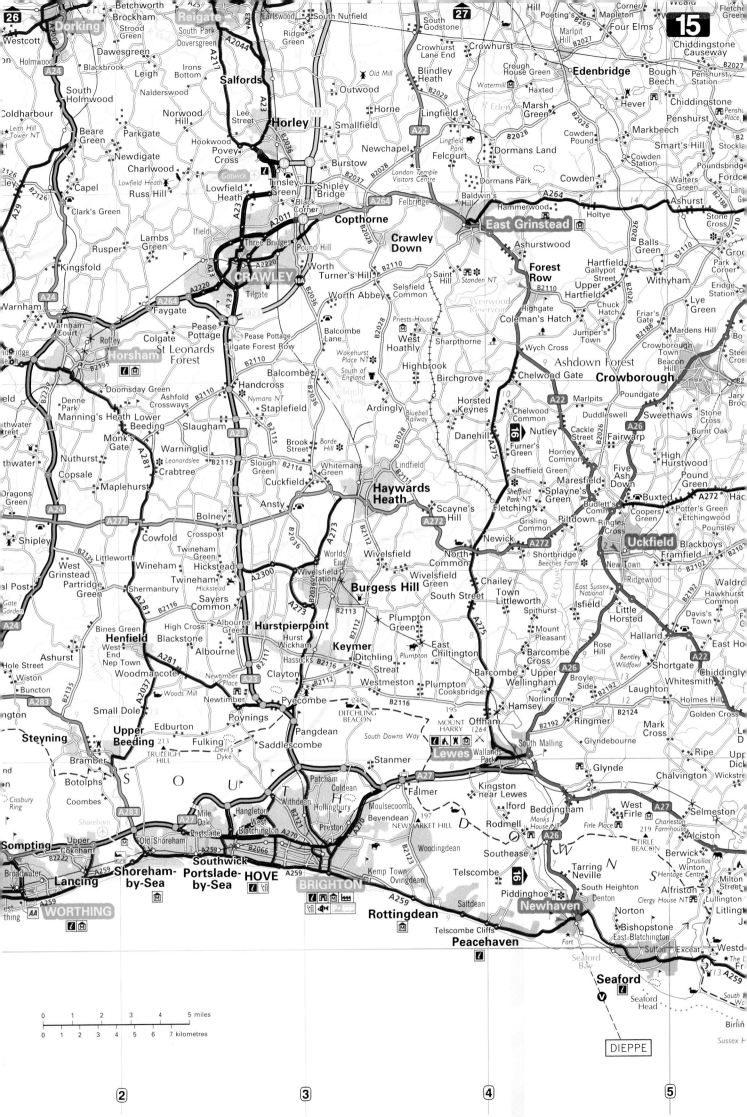

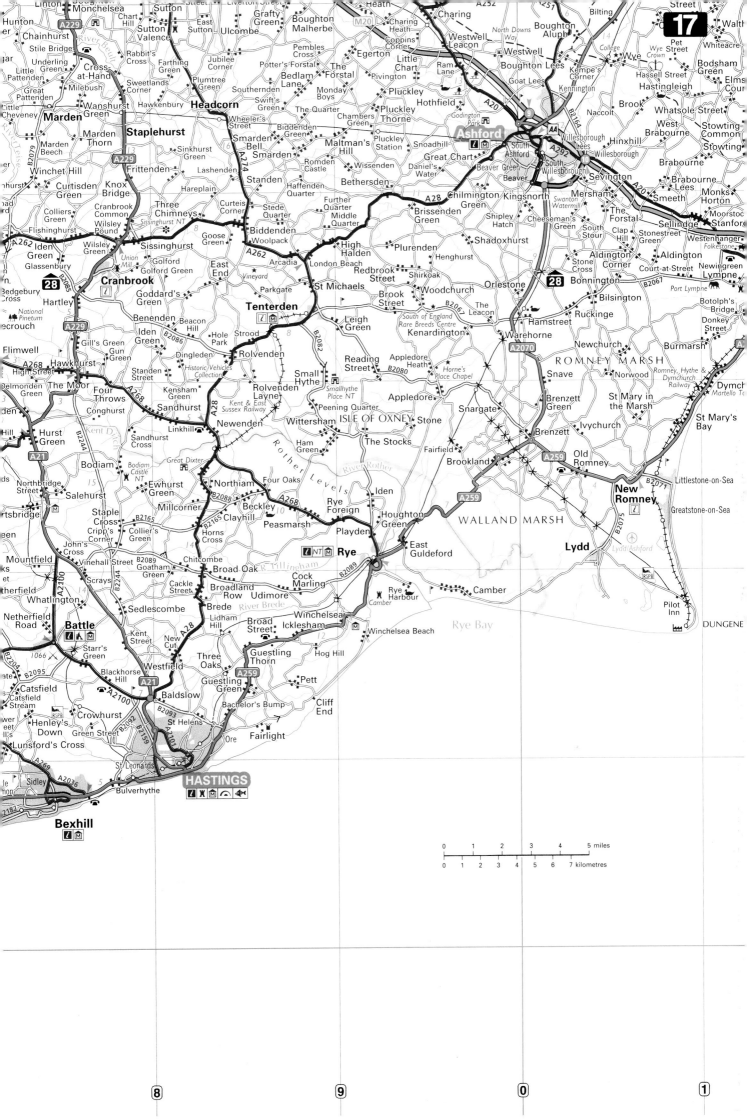

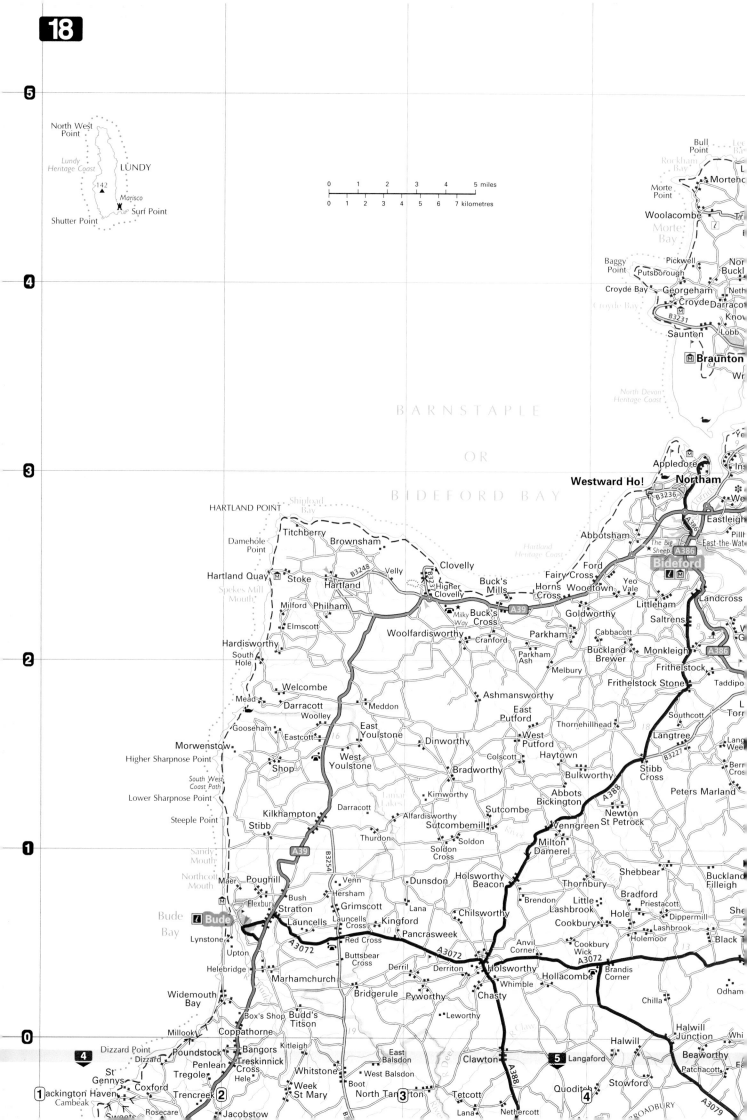

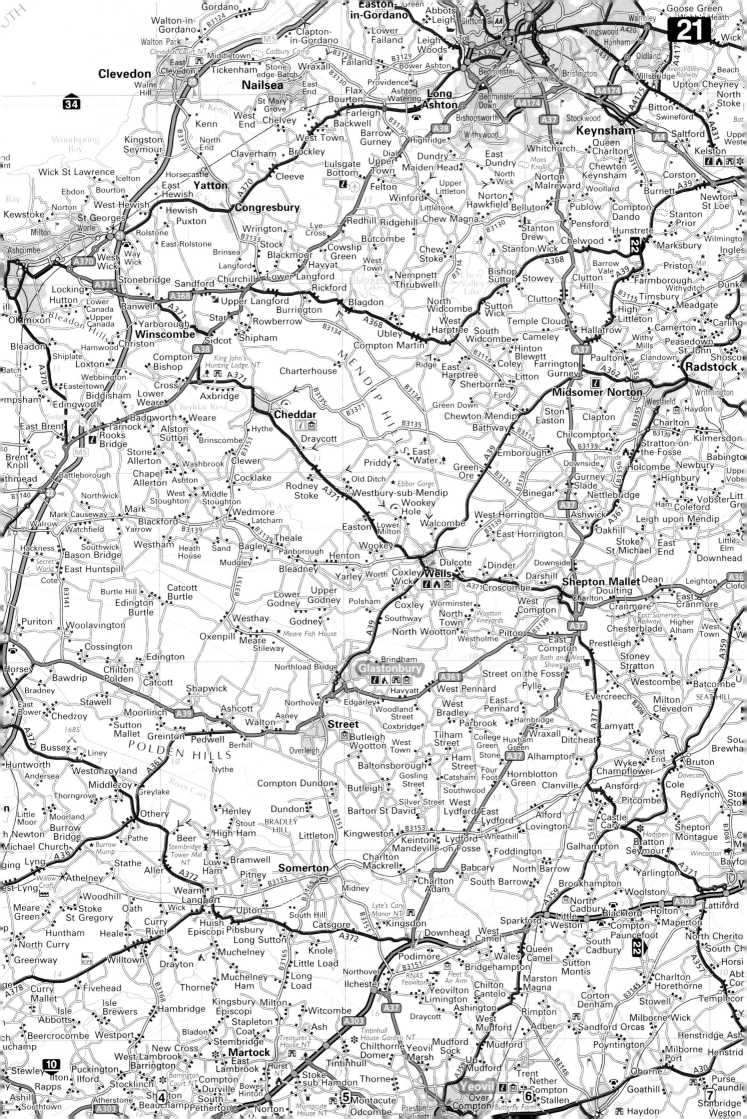

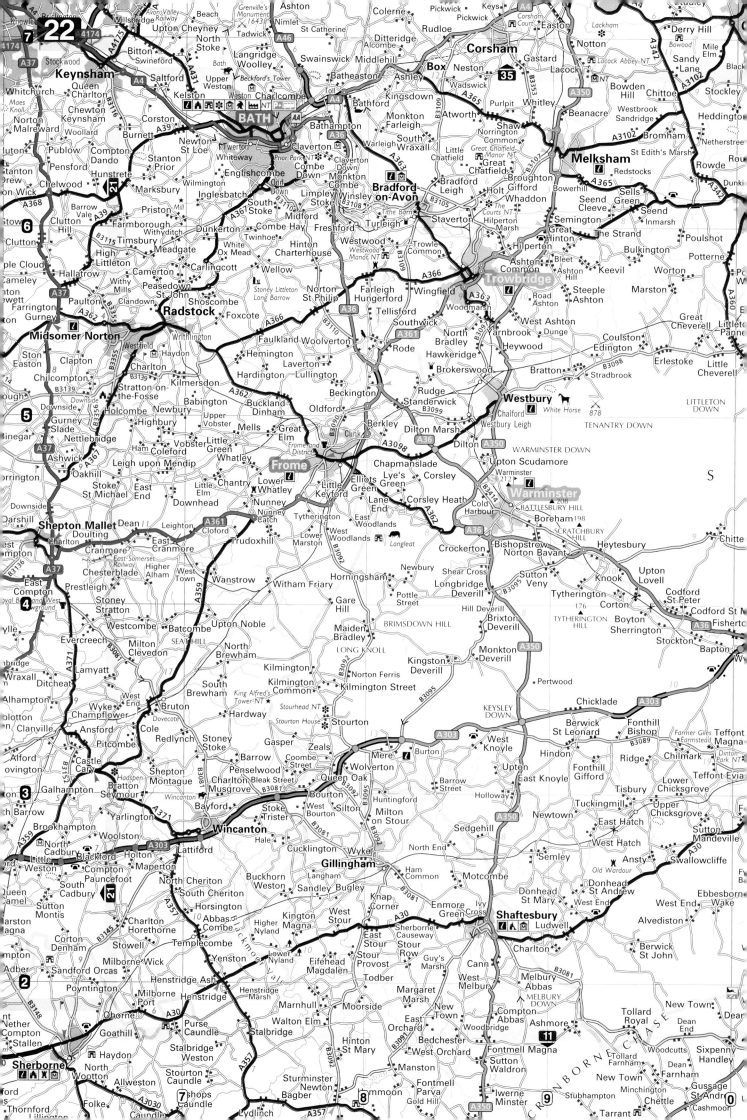

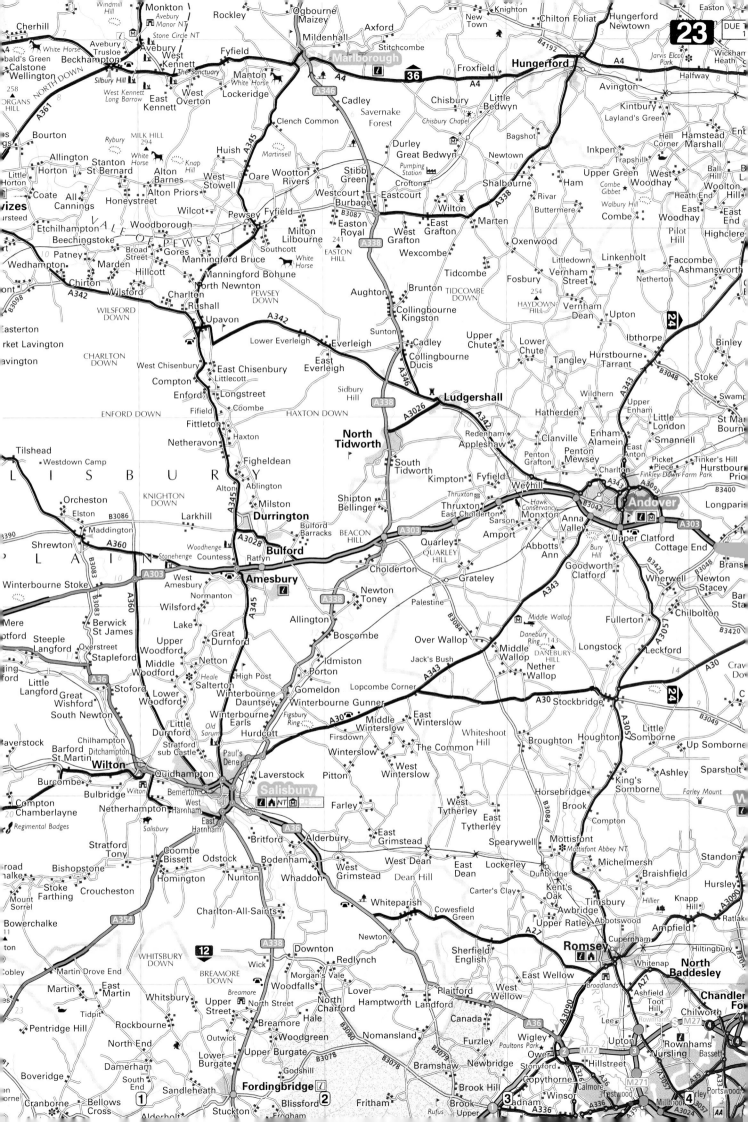

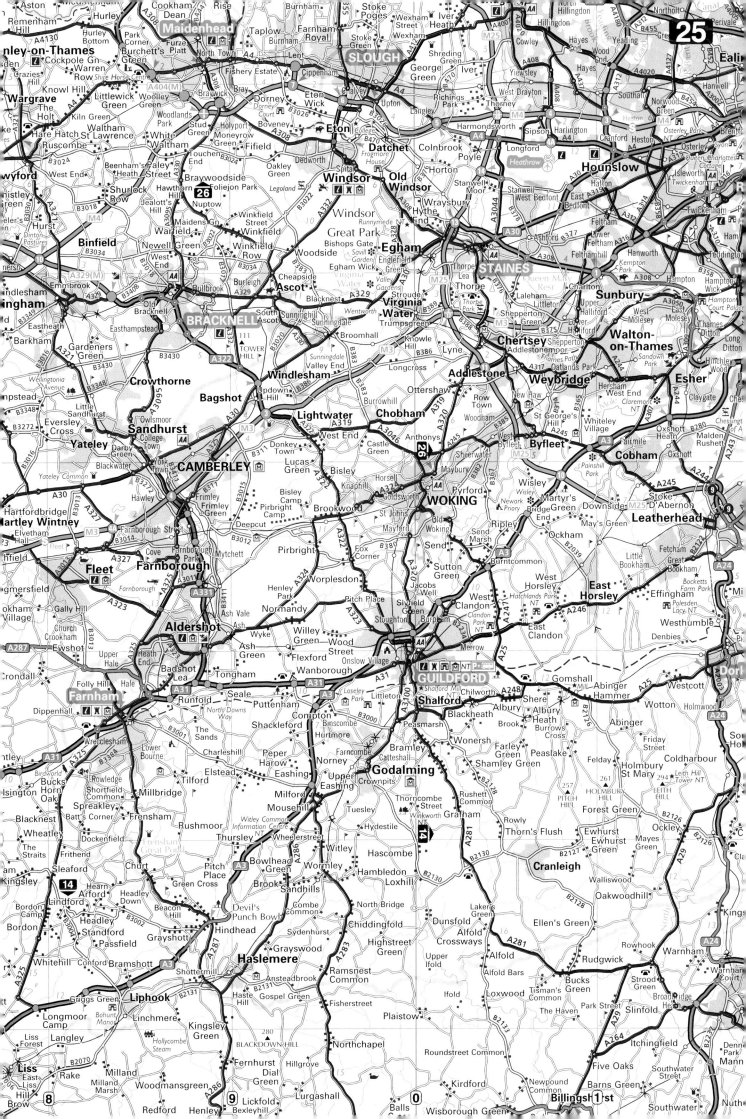

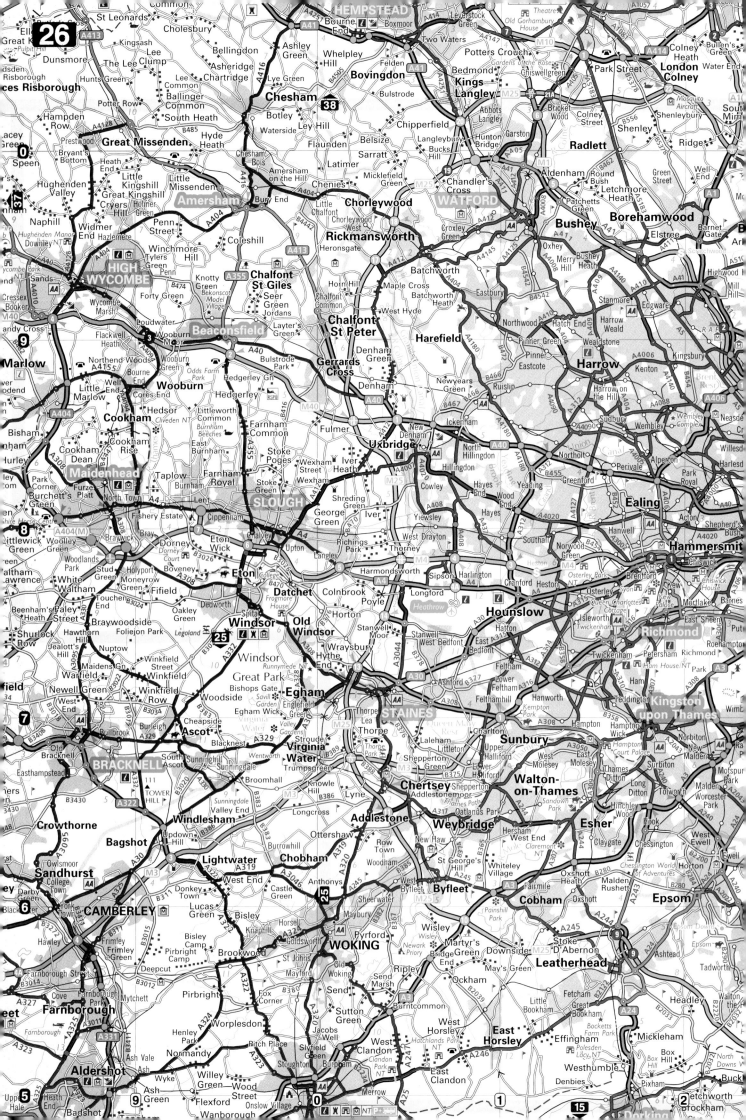

Sea

NORTH FORELAND

Foreness Point

**MARGATE**

Westgate
on Sea  Westbrook  Cliftonville  Northdown  Kingsgate

Minnis
Bay  Birchington  Dent-
de-Lion  Garlinge  Northdown  Reading
Street J

**Herne Bay**

Hampton  Bishopstone  Reculver  Hillborough  Potten
Street  Brooks
End  Salmestone
Grange  St Peter's

**Whitstable**

Whitstable
Bay  Tankerton  Swalecliffe  Greenhill  Eddington  Beltinge  Minnis
Bay  ISLE OF
THANET  Westwood  **Broadstairs**

Seasalter  Chestfield  South
Street  Herne  Broomfield  St Nicholas
at Wade  Acol  Manston  Haine  St
Lawrence  Dumpton
Hereson

Yorkletts  Highstreet  Honey
Hill  Bullockstone  Herne
Common  Boyden
Gate  Sarre  Chislet  Gore
Street  Hoo  Monkton  Way  Durlock  Cliffsend  **Ramsgate**

Dargate  Denstroude  Tyler
Hill  Maypole  Hoath  West
Stourmouth  Plucks Gutter  **Minster**  St Augustine's
Cross  Viking
Ship
'Hugin'  Pegwell  **OOSTENDE**

Hernhill  Staplestreet  **Blean**  Broad
Oak  Calcott  Highstead  Upstreet  East Stourmouth  Pegwell Bay

Dunkirk  Upper
Harbledown  Hales
Place  Westbere  Grove  Westmarsh  Paramour Street  Goldstone  Richborough  Prince's  Sandwich
Bay

uth Street  Harbledown  Rough
Common  Fordwich  Wickhambreaux  Walmestone  Preston
Street  Elmstone  Cop
Street  Hoaden  Weddington  Cooper
Street  Great
Stonar  Royal St George's

ersland  Thanington  **Canterbury**  Old Town Hall  Littlebourne  Seaton  Ickham  Durlock  Guilton  Ash  Great
Stonar  Toll  **Sandwich**

Chartham
Hatch  Bekesbourne
Hill  Shatterling  Wingham  Marshborough  Stone
Cross

Old Wives
Lees  Nackington  Bridge  Bramling  Bekesbourne  Twitham  Staple  Barnsole  Woodnesborough

Chartham  Street End  Lower Hardres  Patrixbourne  Goodnestone  Heronden  Eastry  Worth  Statenborough  Hacklinge  The
Downs

agham  Shalmsford
Street  Bishopsbourne  Adisham  Ratling  Chillenden  Knowlton  Ham  West
Street  Marley  Finglesham

Mountain
Street  Garlinge
Green  Pett
Bottom  Aylesham  Nonington  Easole Street  Betteshanger  Great Mongeham  Marley  Sholden  Northbourne  **Deal**

Petham  Anvil
Green  Kingston  Elmstead  Holt
St  Tilmanstone  Elvington  Lower
Eythorne  Little
Mongeham  Sutton  Ripple

Crundale  Waltham  Upper Hardres
Court  Marley  Derringstone  Barham  Womenswold  Frogham  Eythorne  East
Studdal  Ringwould

Sole
Street  Whiteacre  Bossingham  Woolage
Village  Barfrestone  Shepherdswell  Ashley  Sutton Downs  Martin  Kingsdown

Pet
Crown  Bodsham
Green  Stelling
Minnis  Bladbean  Breach  Woolage
Green  West
Langdon  East Langdon

Hassell Street  North
Leigh  Denton  Wingmore  Coldred  West
Cliffe  St Margaret's
Bay

Hastingleigh  Elmsted
Court  Maxted
Street  Wheelbarrow
Town  Wootton  Geddinge  Lydden  Whitfield  Guston  St Margaret's at Cliffe

Whatsole Street  Sixmile
Cottages  Exted  North Elham  Selsted  Ewell
Minnis  Temple
Ewell  East Langdon  SOUTH FORELAND

West
Braborne  Stowting
Common  Lymbridge
Green  Elham  Swingfield
Minnis  Kearsney  Chilton  River  West
Cliffe  South Foreland
Lighthouse, NT

Brabourne  Rhodes
Minnis  Ottinge  Swingfield
Street  Alkham  Wolverton  Buckland  South Foreland
Heritage Coast

Braborne
Lees  Woodland  Ridge
Row  Densole  St Radigund's  Maxton

Smeeth  Monks
Horton  Newbarn  Lyminge  Upper
Standen  Drellingore  West
Hougham  **DOVER**

Sellindge  Moorstock
Stanford  Postling  Paddlesworth  Lower
Standen  Capel
le-Ferne  Farthingloe  **CALAIS**

Stonestreet
Green  Westenhanger  Etchinghill  Hawkinge  Peene  Satmar  **CALAIS**

Aldington  Newington  Channel
Tunnel
Terminal  Battle of
Britain  East
Wear Bay

Court-at-Street  Newingreen  Brockhill  Cheriton  Morehall  **FOLKESTONE**

Lympne  Pedlinge  Saltwood  Horn
Street  Sandgate

Port Lympne  Botolph's
Bridge  West
Hythe  Seabrook  **BOULOGNE**

Donkey
Street  **Hythe**

Burmarsh  Lympne

Romney, Hythe &
Dymchurch
Railway  Dymchurch  Martello Tower

y in
arsh  St Mary's
Bay

Littlestone-on-Sea

ney  Greatstone-on-Sea

STRAIT OF DOVER

0 1 2 3 4 5 miles

0 1 2 3 4 5 6 7 kilometres

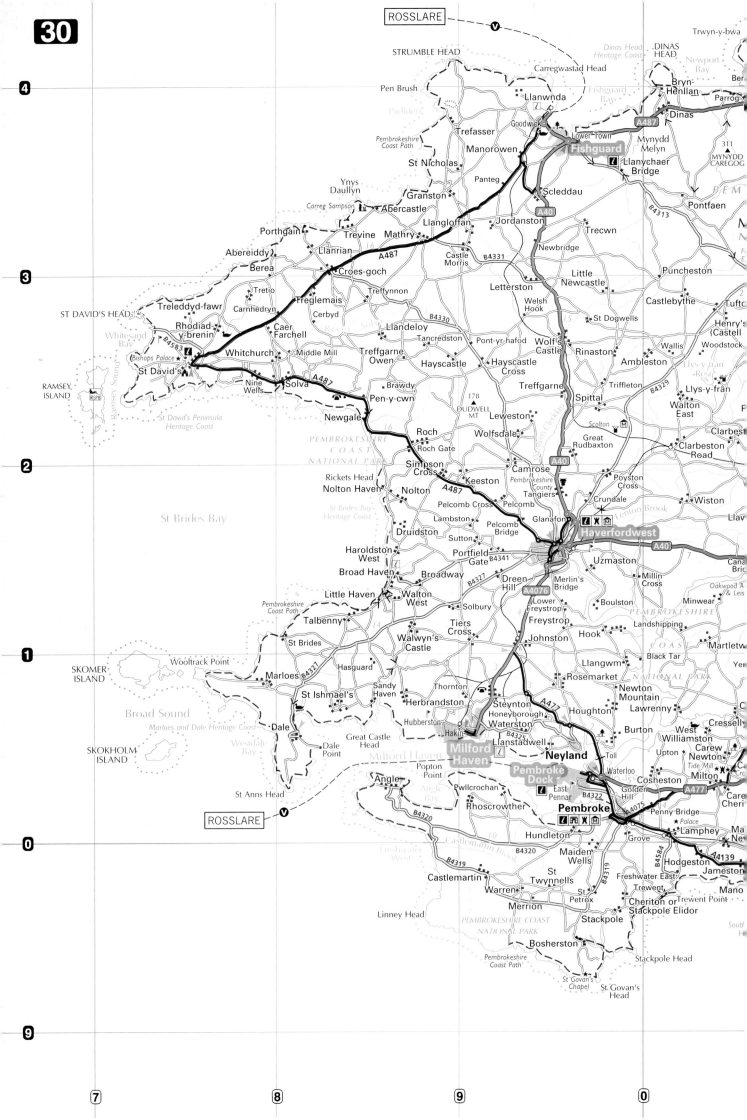

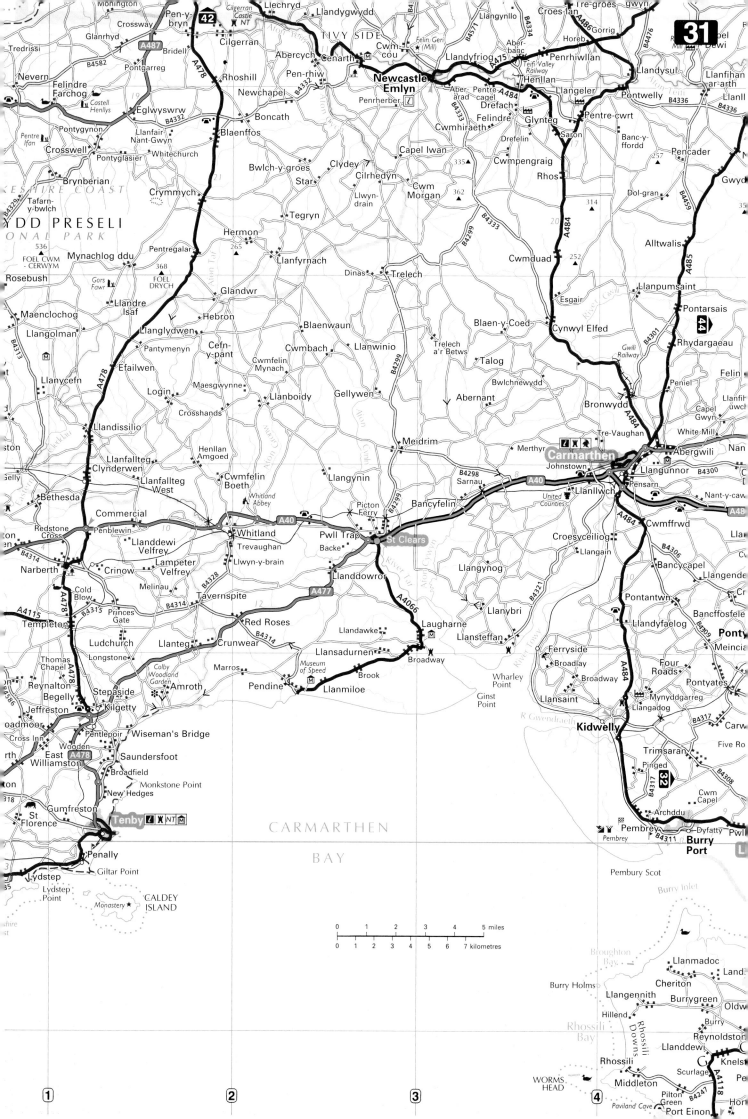

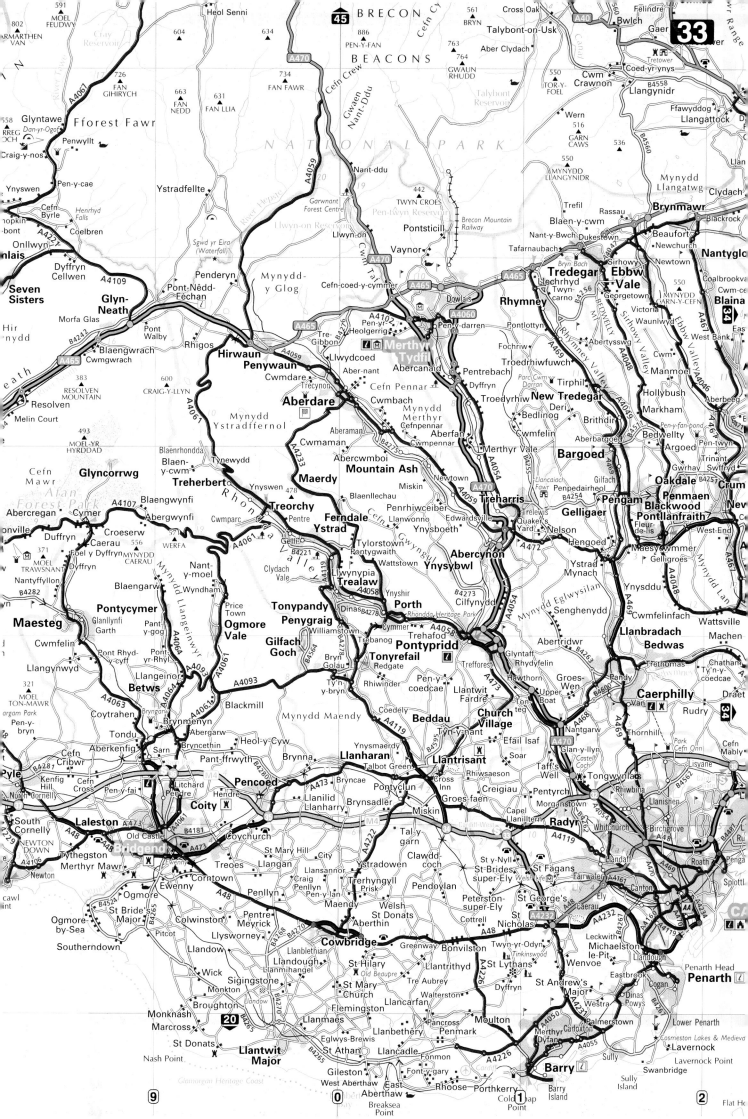

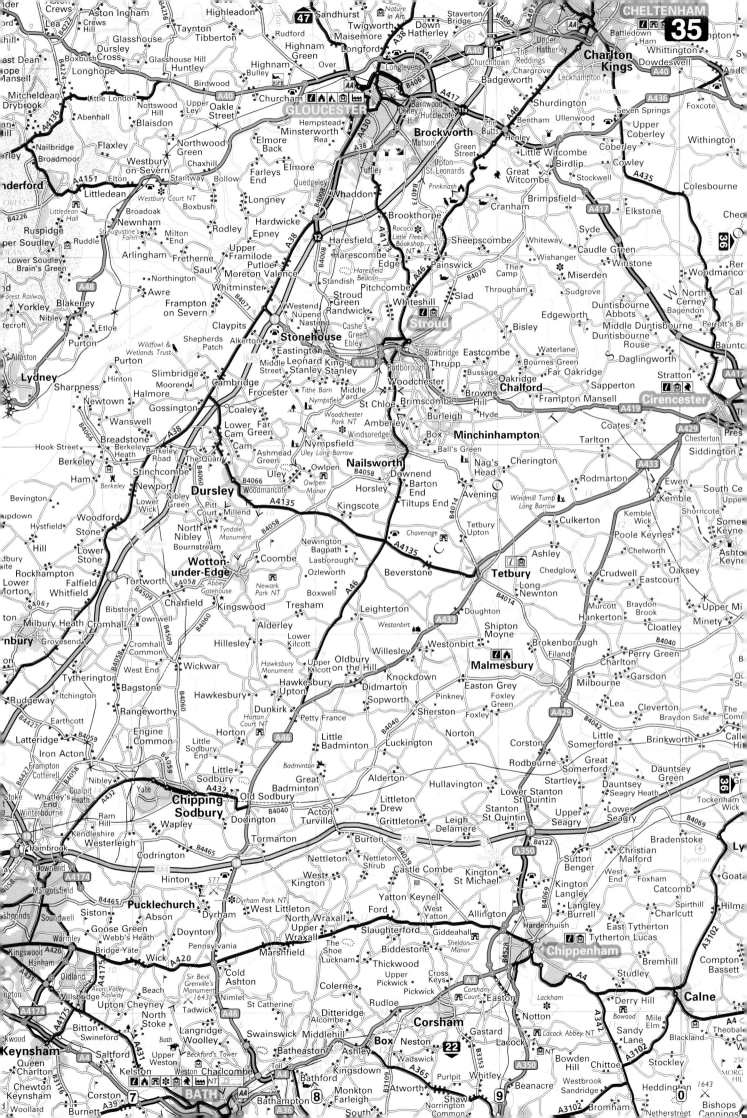

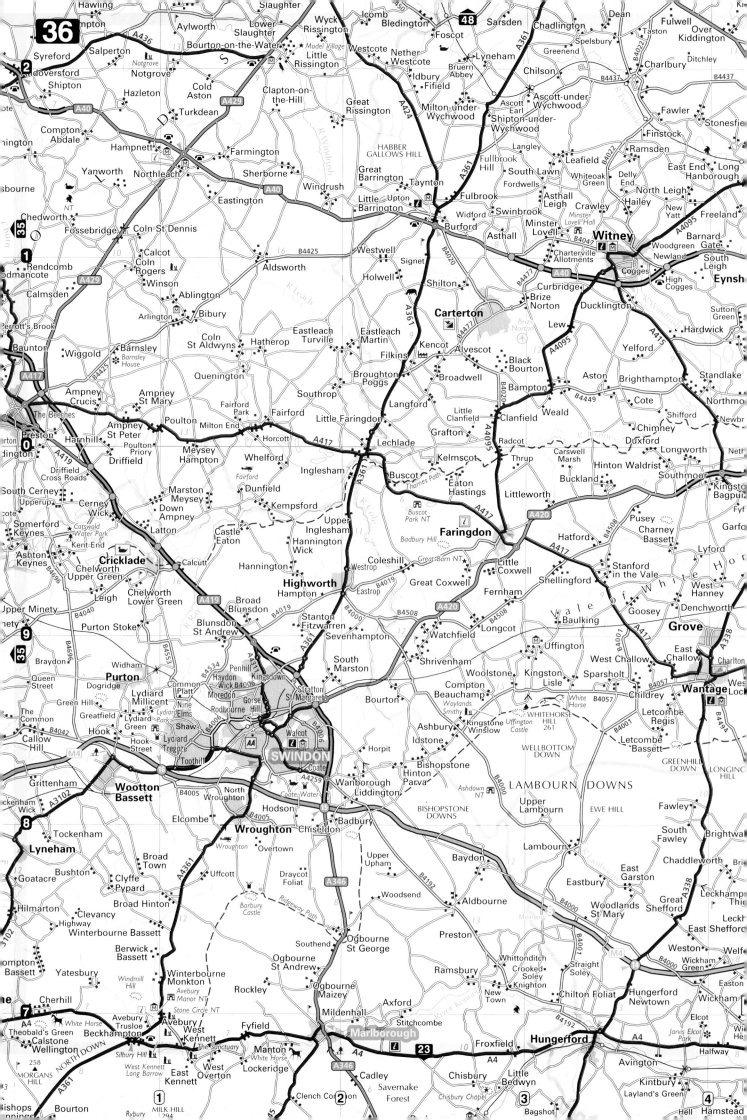

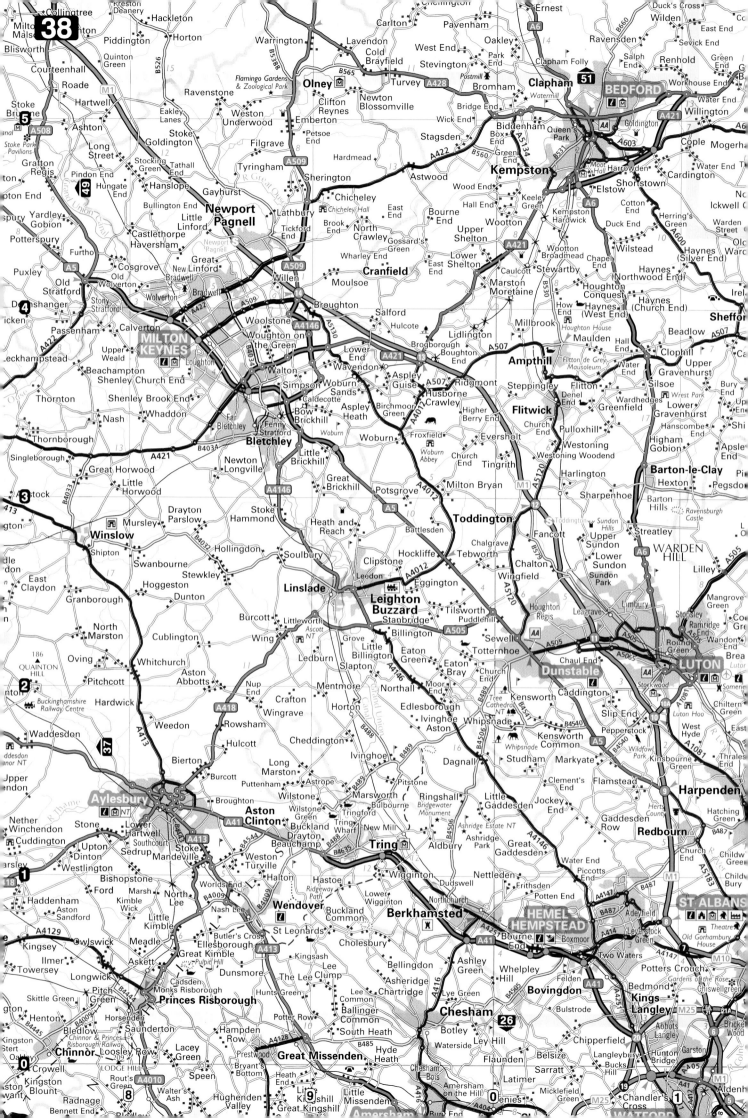

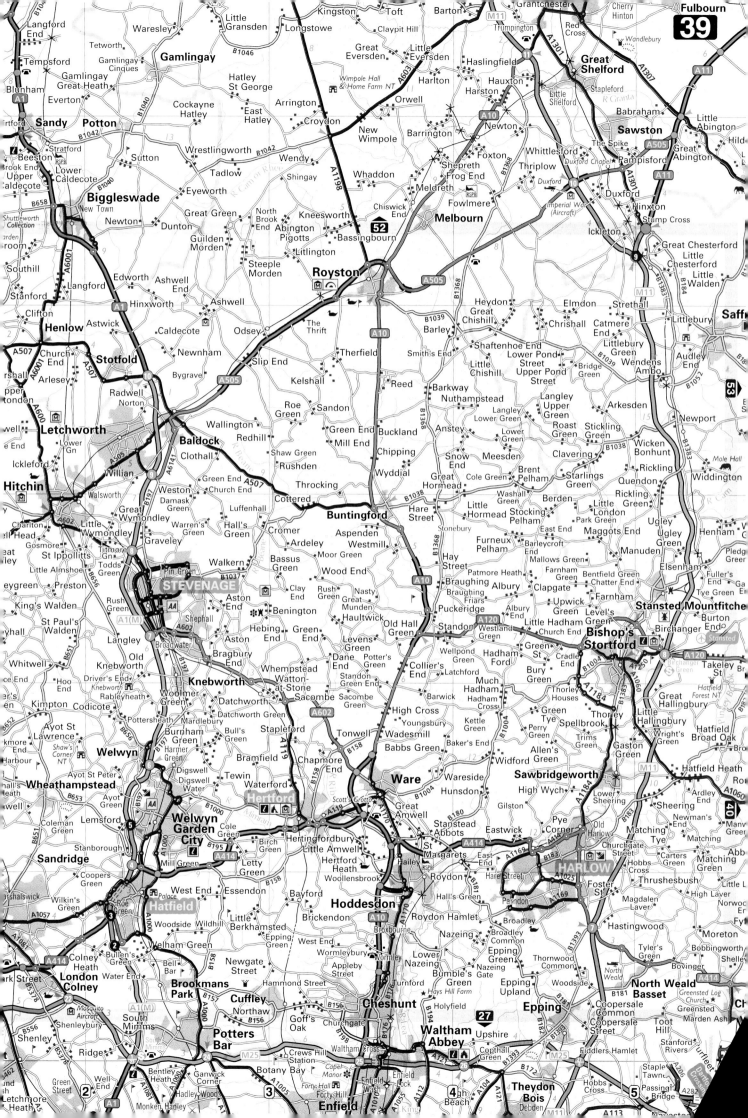

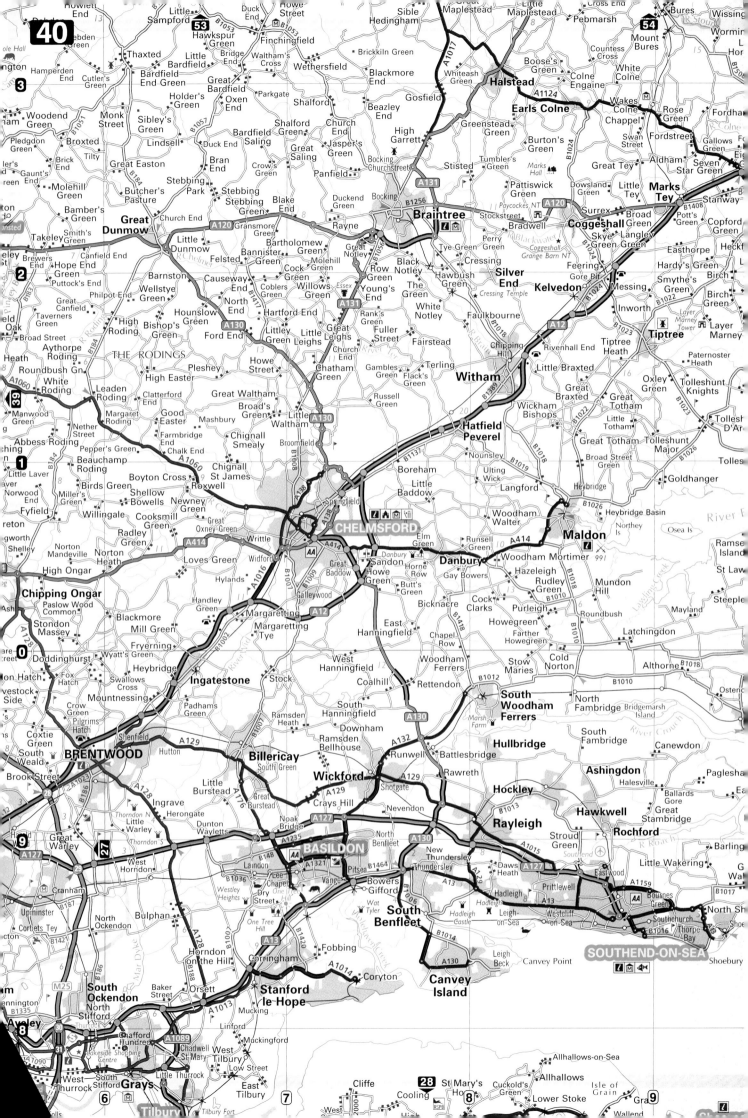

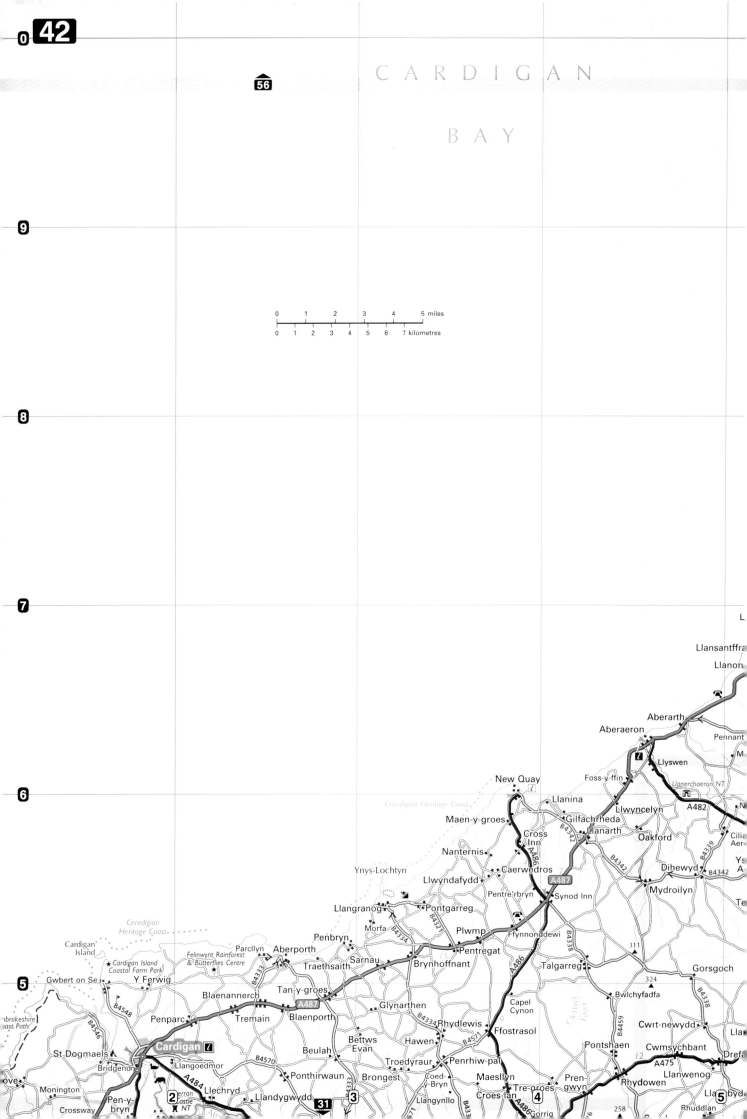

CARDIGAN

BAY

56

0    1    2    3    4    5 miles

0  1  2  3  4  5  6    7 kilometres

9

8

7

L

Llansantffra

Llanon

Aberarth

Aberaeron        Pennant

Llyswen            M

New Quay        Foss-y-ffin        Llanerchaeron NT

6        Ceredigion Heritage Coast        Llanina        Llwyncelyn        A482        N

Maen-y-groes        Gilfachrheda        Cilia
                    Cross        Llanarth        Oakford        Aer
Nanternis        Inn                                Ys
            Caerwedros        Dihewyd        A
Ynys-Lochtyn        Llwyndafydd        Synod Inn        B4342        Mydroilyn
        Pentre'rbryn        A487
Llangranog        Pontgarreg        Te
        Morfa        Plwmp
Penbryn                Ffynnonddewi        311
        Pentregat
Ceredigion                Talgarreg        Gorsgoch
Heritage Coast        Brynhoffnant
Cardigan        Parcllyn        Sarnau        324        Bwlchyfadfa
Island        Aberporth
    Cardigan Island        Felinwynt Rainforest        Traethsaith
    Coastal Farm Park        & Butterflies Centre
5    Y Ferwig                Capel        Cwrt-newydd
Gwbert on Sea                Glynarthen        Cynon
        Blaenannerch        Tan-y-groes                Pontshaen        Cwmsychbant
nbrokeshire                A487        Rhydlewis        Ffostrasol
oast Path        Penparc        Tremain        Blaenporth                Prengwyn        A475        Drefa
        Bettws        Hawen                        Llanwenog
St Dogmaels        Cardigan        Evan                Maesllyn        Rhydowen        Lla
ove        B4570        Beulah        Troedyraur        Penrhiw-pal                        5        Rhuddlan
Monington        Llangoedmor        Ponthirwaun        Brongest        Coed-        Tre-groes        4
Crossway        Pen-y-        Llechryd        Llandygwydd        y-Bryn        Croes-lan        A486        258
        bryn        2        3        Llangynllo        Gorrig

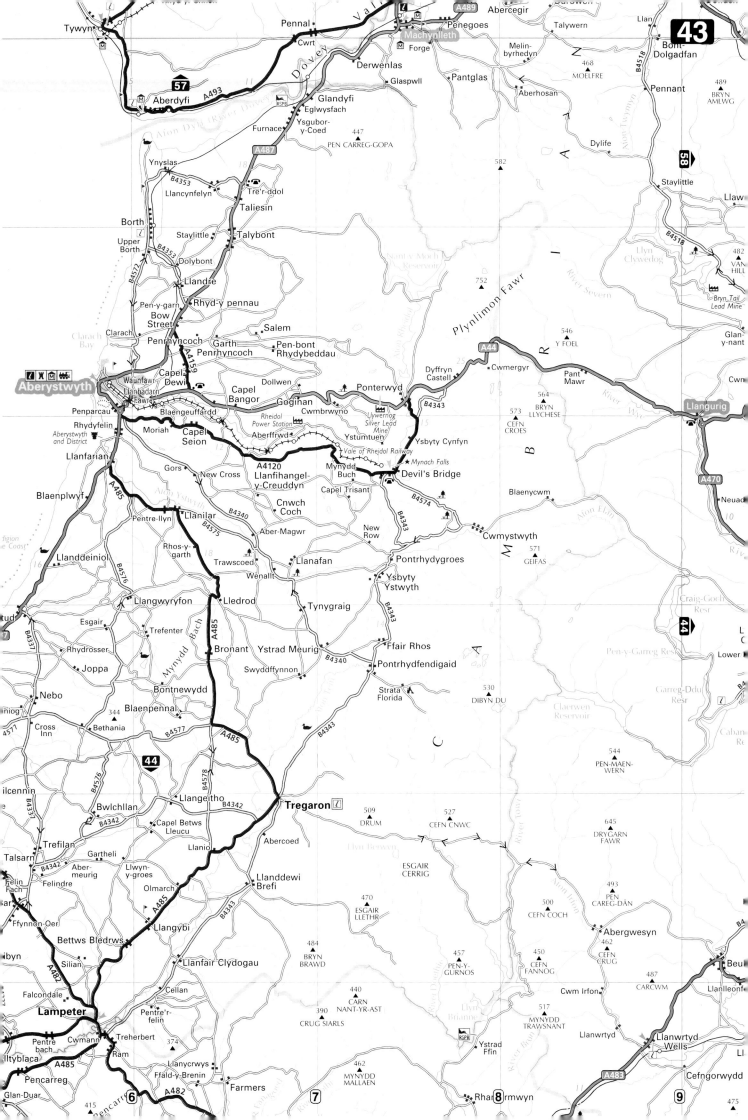

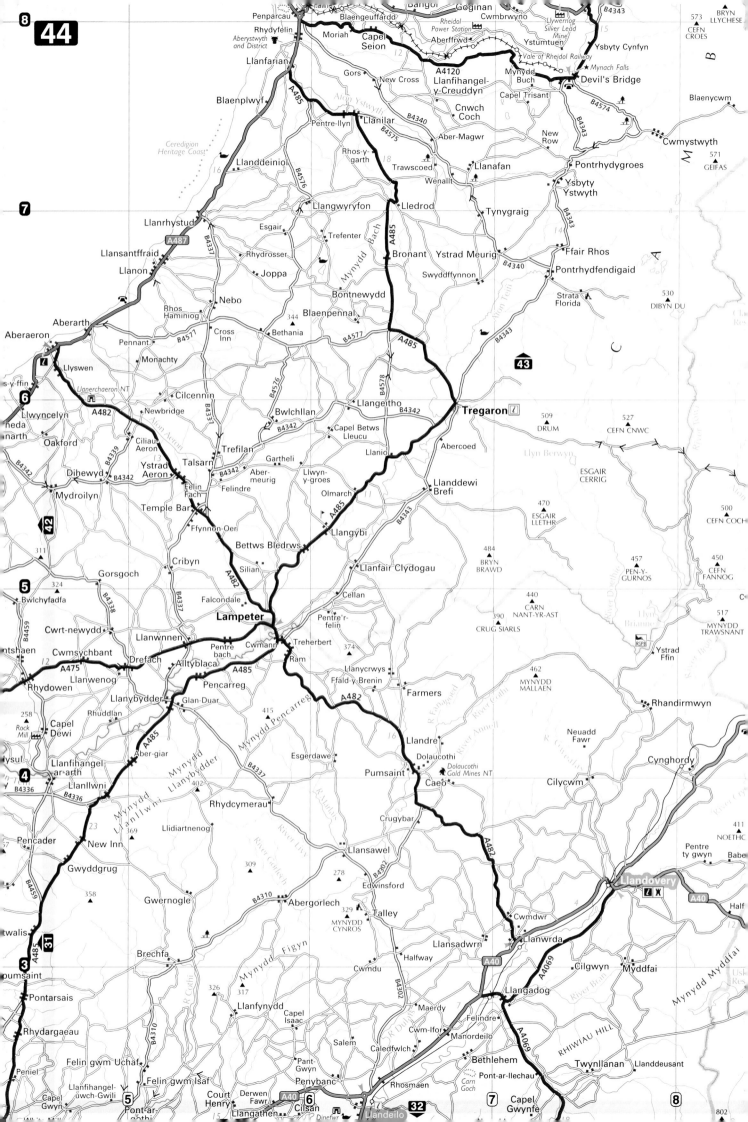

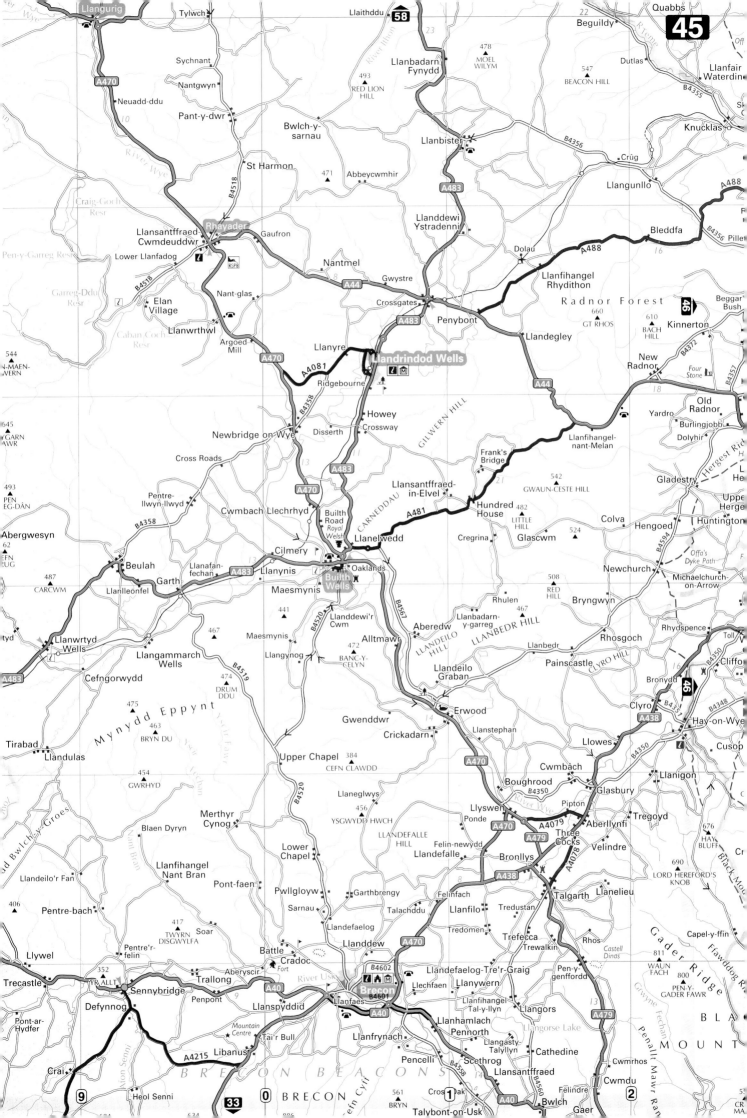

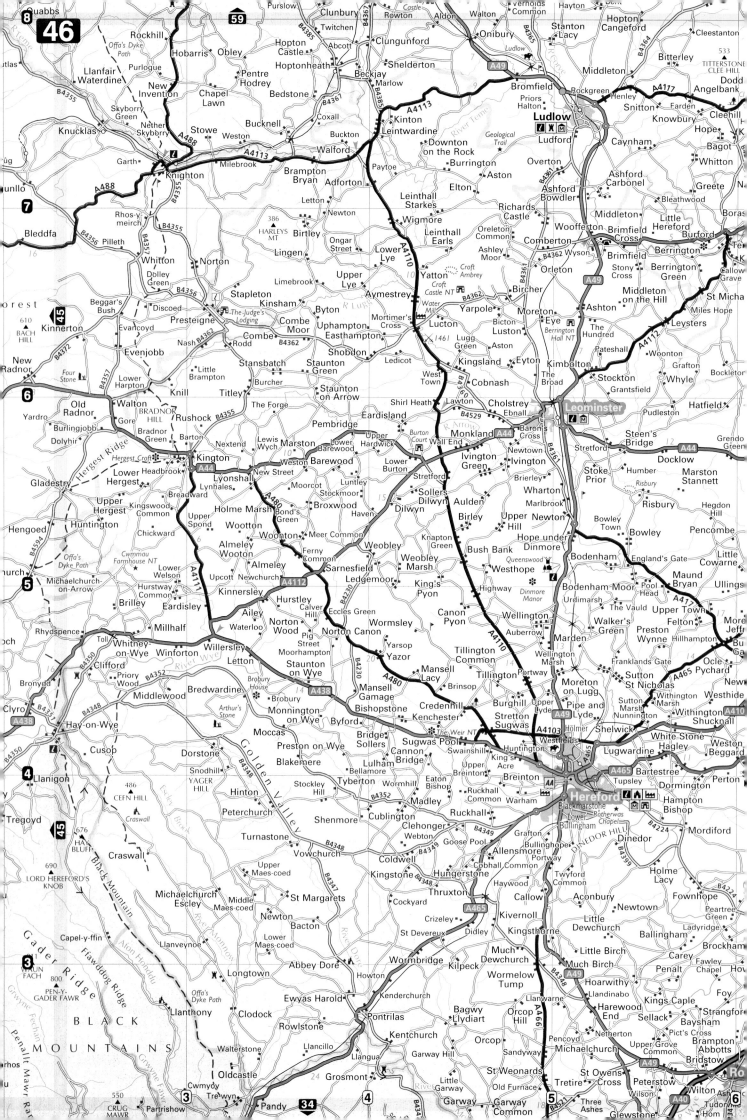

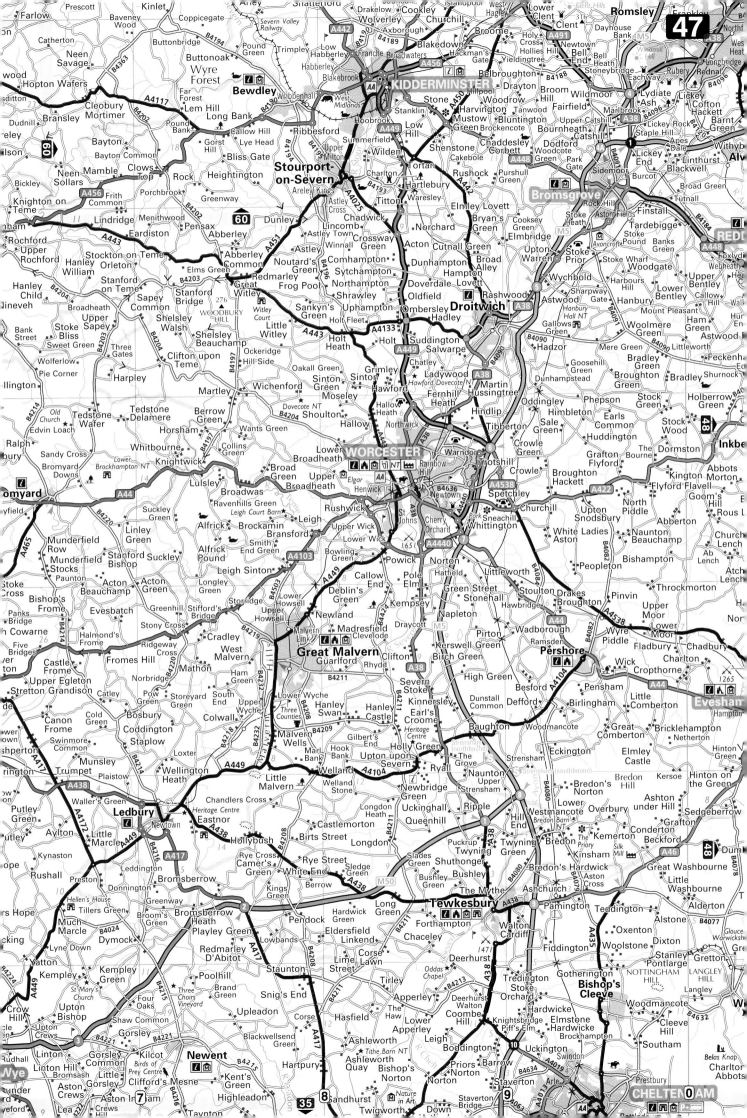

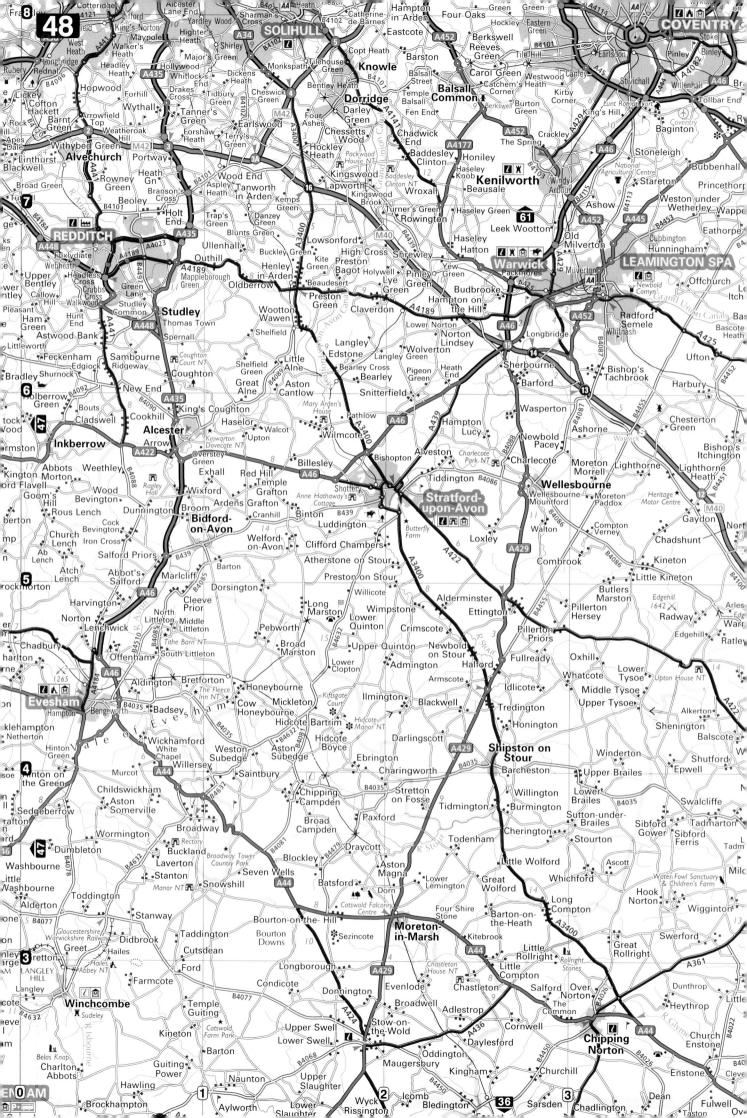

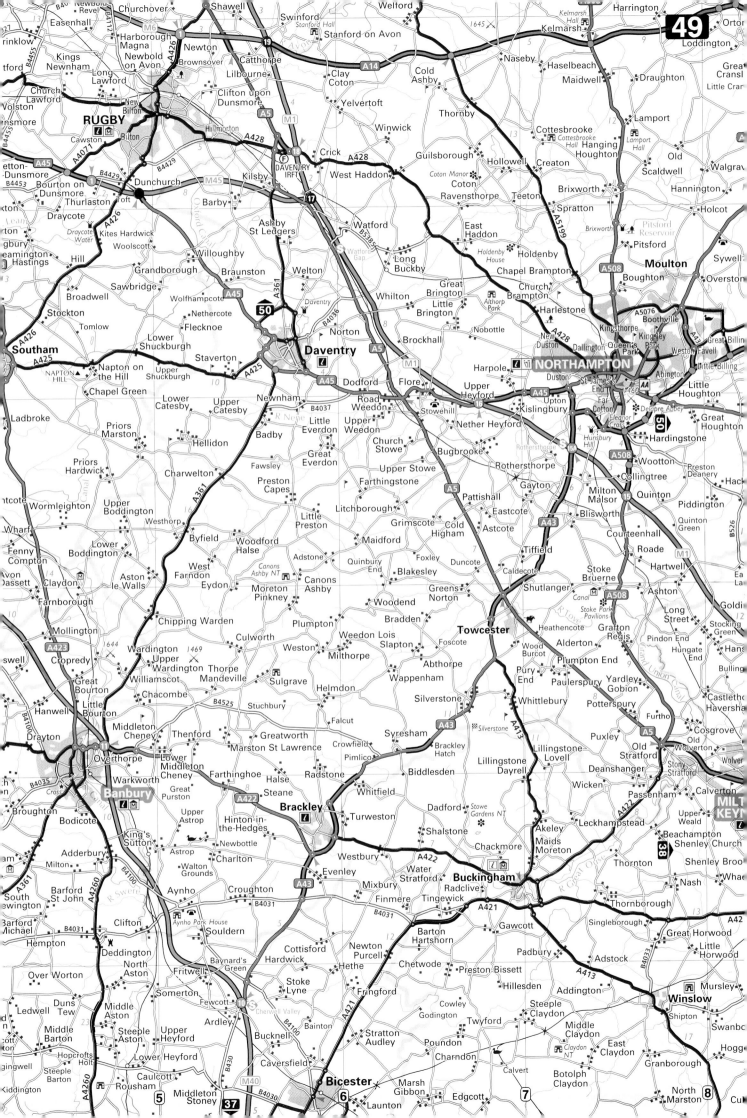

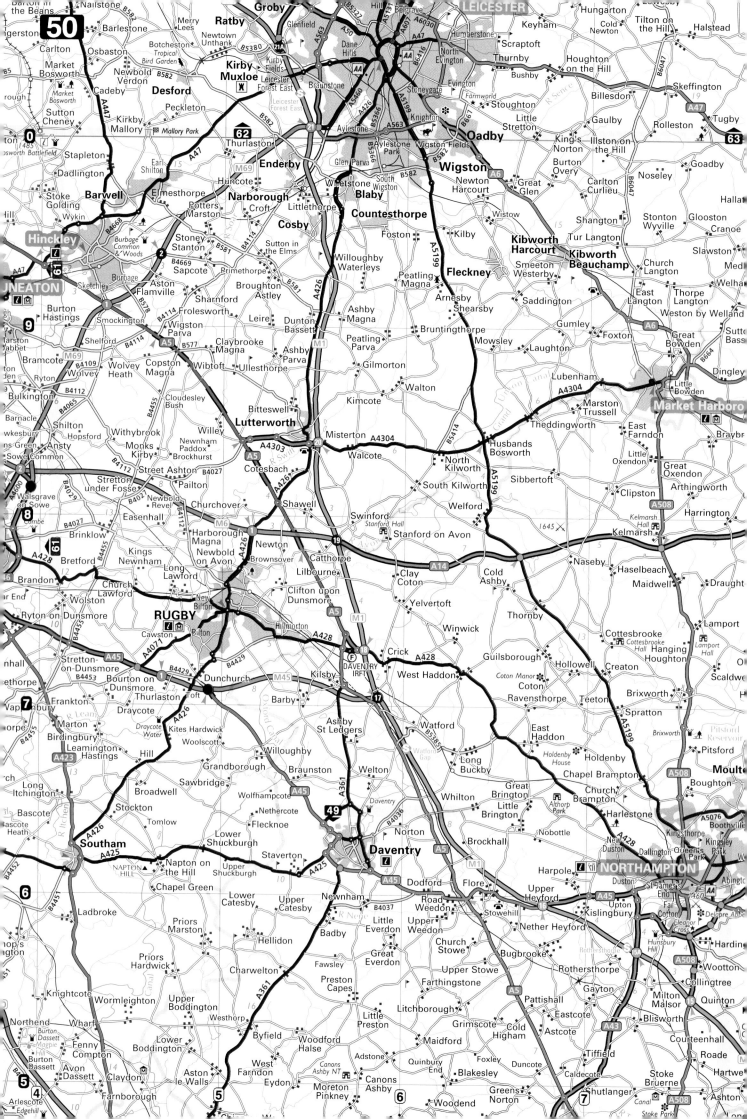

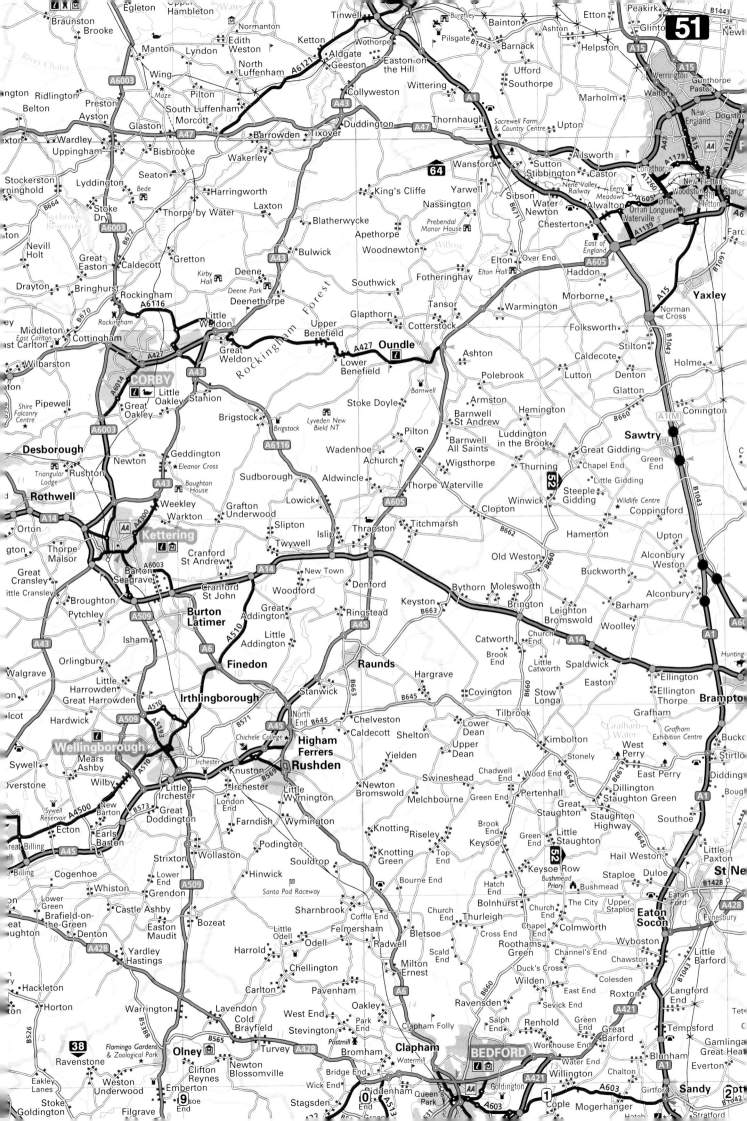

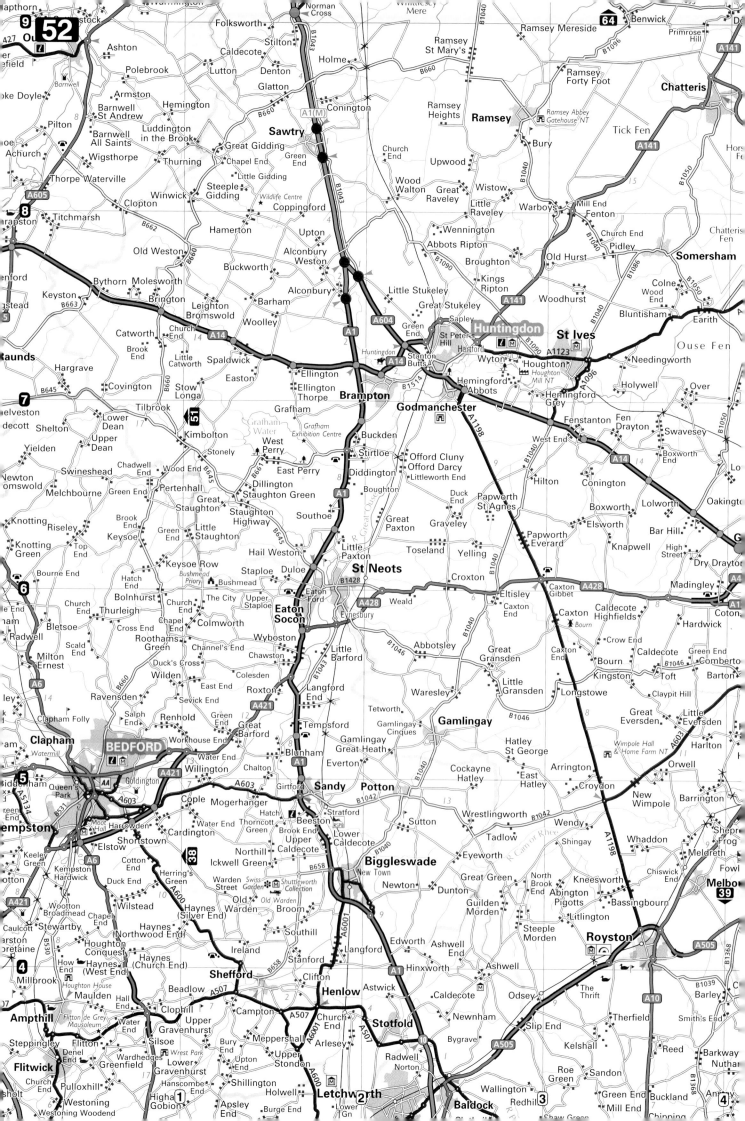

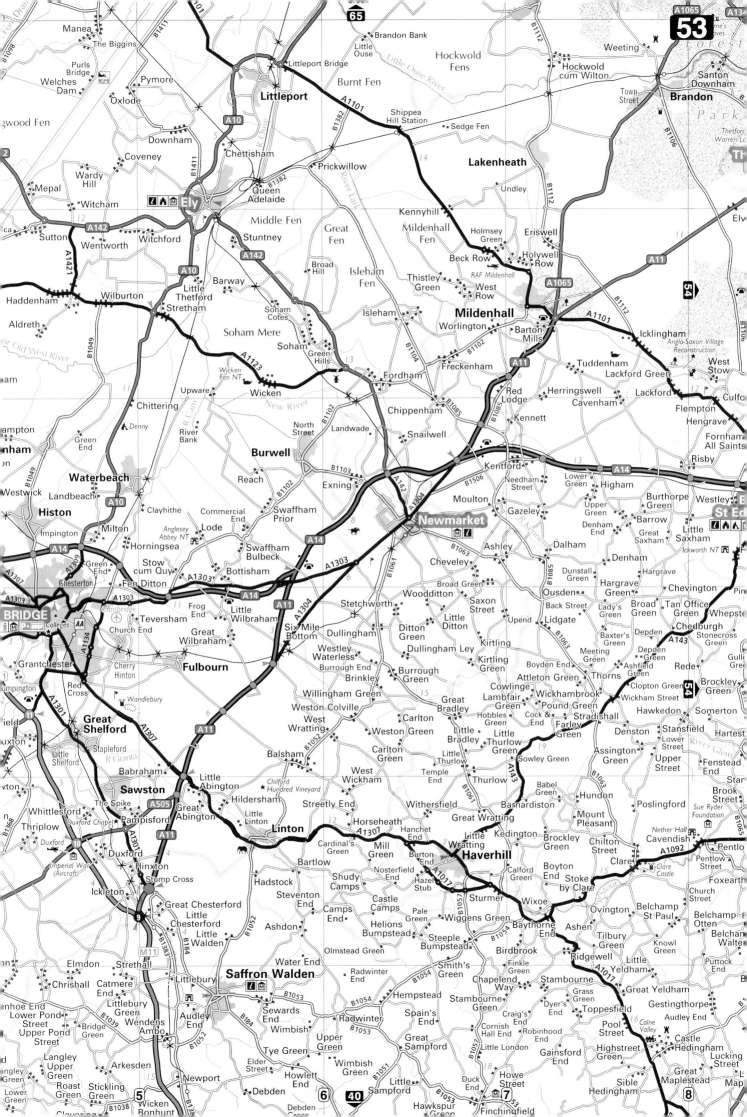

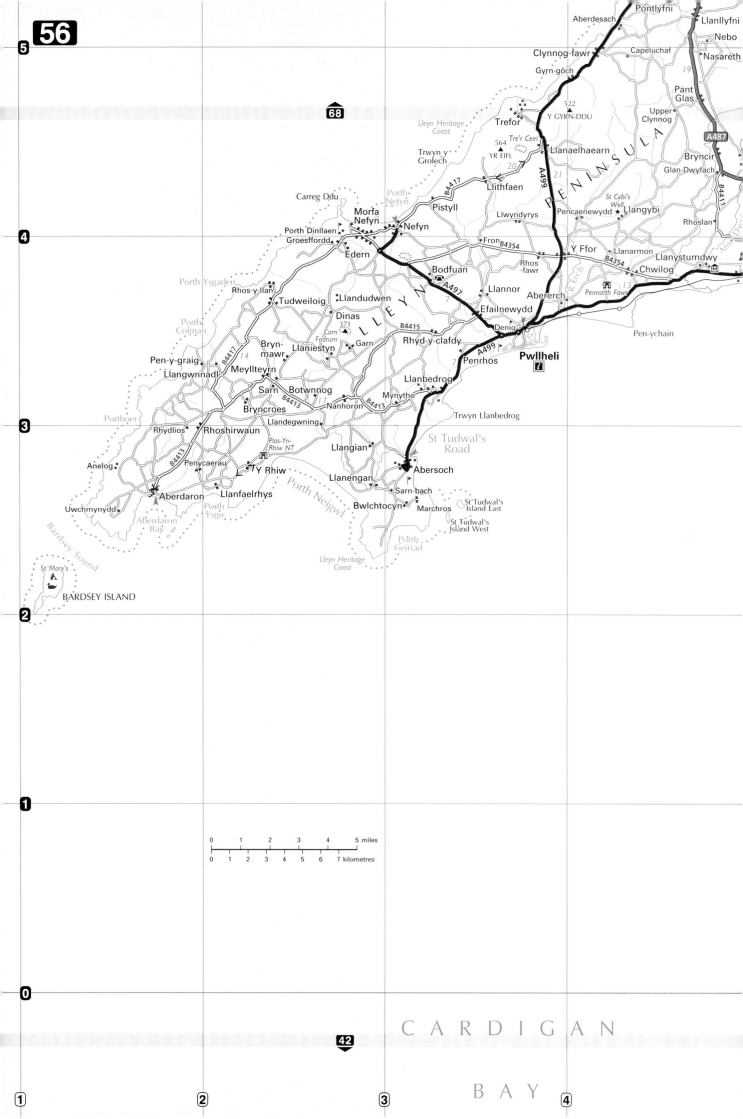

5

68

4

3

2

1

0

**BARDSEY ISLAND**

St Mary's

Bardsey Sound

Uwchmynydd

Aberdaron

Aberdaron Bay

Anelog

Penycaerau

Y Rhiw

Llanfaelrhys

Plas-Yn-Rhiw NT

Porth Ysgo

Porth Neigwl

Llanengan

Llangian

Bwlchtocyn

Sarn-bach

Marchros

St Tudwal's Island West

St Tudwal's Island East

Porth Geiriad

Lleyn Heritage Coast

Rhydlios

Rhoshirwaun

B4413

Sarn

Bryncroes

Botwnnog

Llandegwning

Nanhoron

B4413

Llanbedrog

Trwyn Llanbedrog

St Tudwal's Road

Abersoch

Mynytho

Pen-y-graig

Llangwnnadl

Meyllteyrn

B4417

14

Brynmawr

Llaniestyn

Garn

Carn Fadrum

371

Dinas

Llandudwen

LLEYN

B4415

Rhyd-y-clafdy

Penrhos

7

A499

Denio

Pwllheli

i

Rhos-y-llan

Tudweiloig

Porth Colman

Porth Ysgaden

Porthor

Carreg Ddu

Morfa Nefyn

Porth Dinllaen

Groesffordd

Edern

A497

Bodfuan

7

Llannor

Efailnewydd

Abererch

Y Ffor

B4354

Rhos-fawr

Llanarmon

Pennarth Fawr

13

Chwilog

Llanystumdwy

B4354

M

Afon Dwyfor

Pen-ychain

Nefyn

Pistyll

Porth Nefyn

Trwyn y Grolech

Lleyn Heritage Coast

B4417

Llithfaen

Llwyndyrys

Fron

B4354

564

YR EIFL

Tre'r Ceiri

20

21

A499

Llanaelhaearn

Pencaenewydd

St Cybi's Well

★

Llangybi

Rhoslan

PENINSULA

Trefor

Y GYRN-DDU

522

Gyrn-gôch

Clynnog-fawr

Aberdesach

Pontlyfni

Llanllyfni

Nebo

Nasareth

Capeluchaf

Upper Clynnog

Pant Glas

19

A487

Bryncir

Glan-Dwyfach

B4411

0  1  2  3  4  5 miles

0  1  2  3  4  5  6  7 kilometres

42

C A R D I G A N

B A Y

1    2    3    4

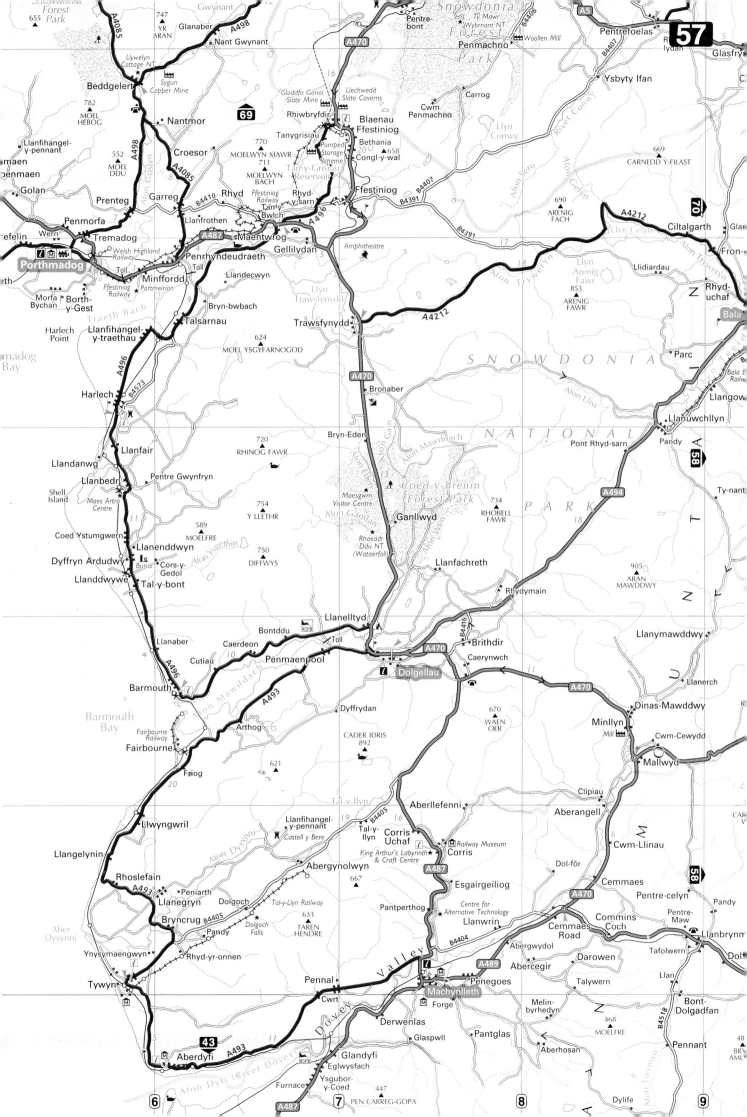

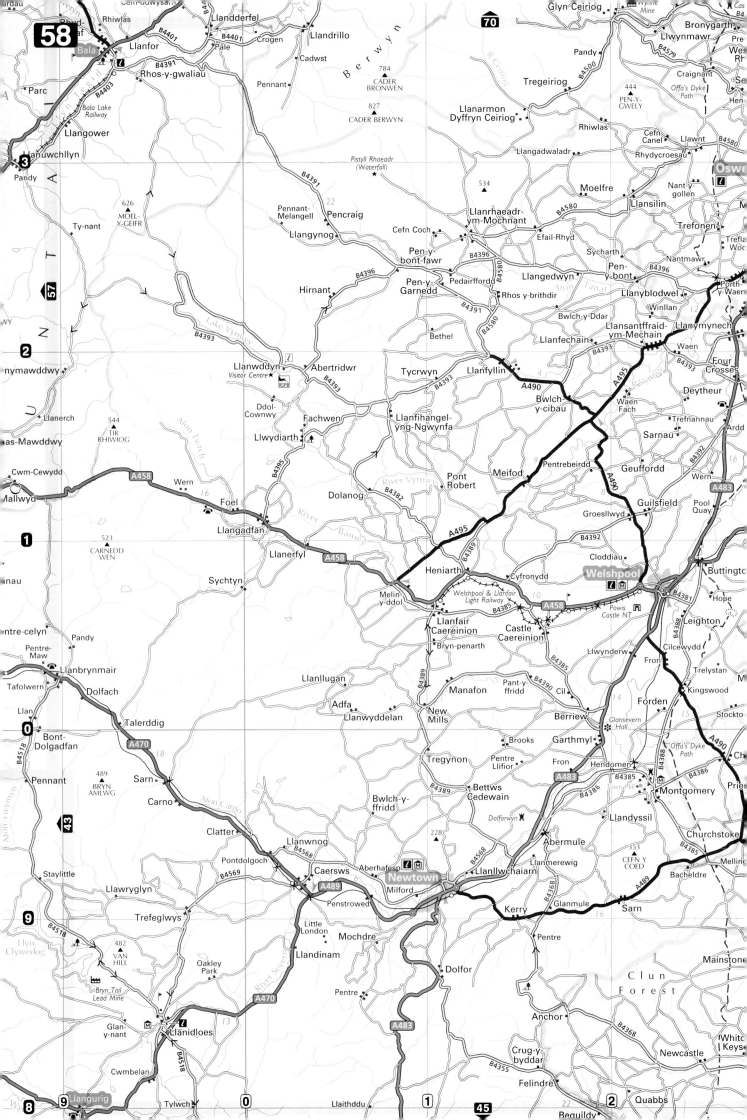

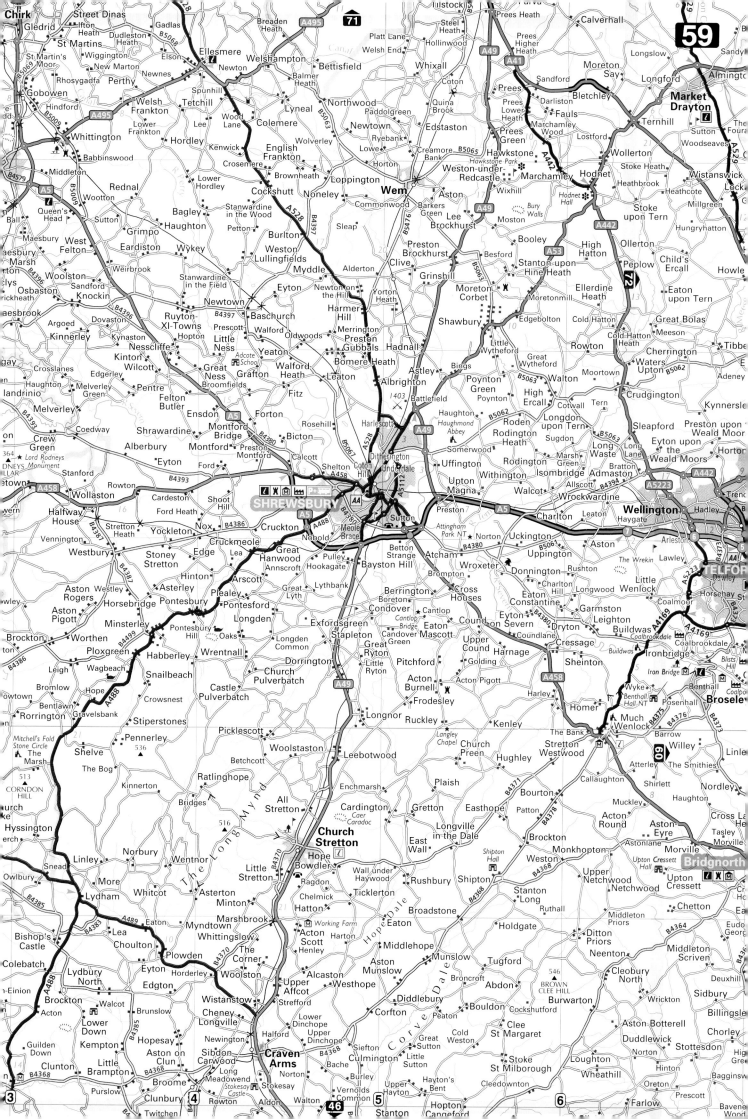

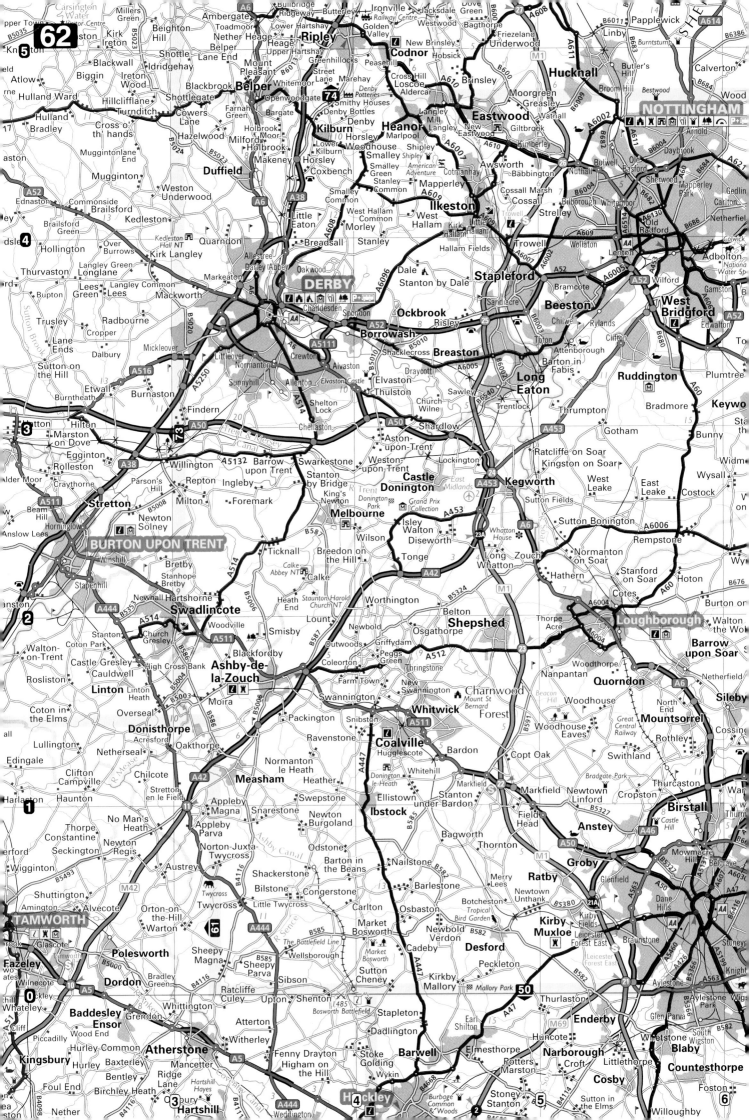

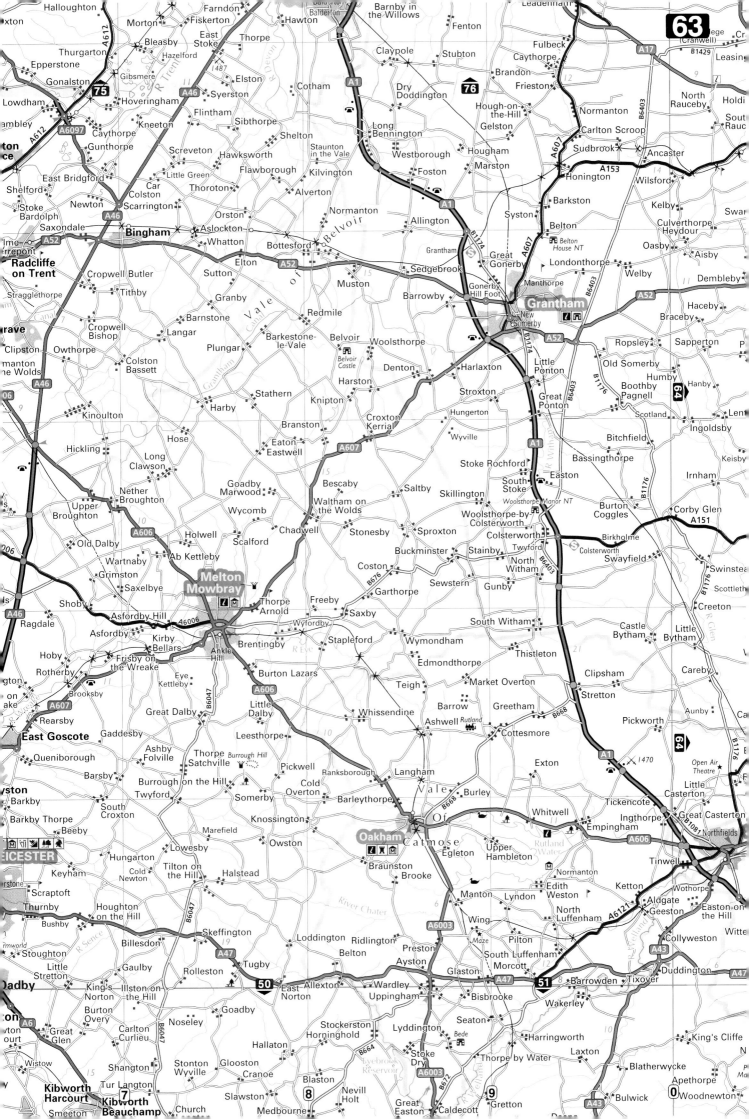

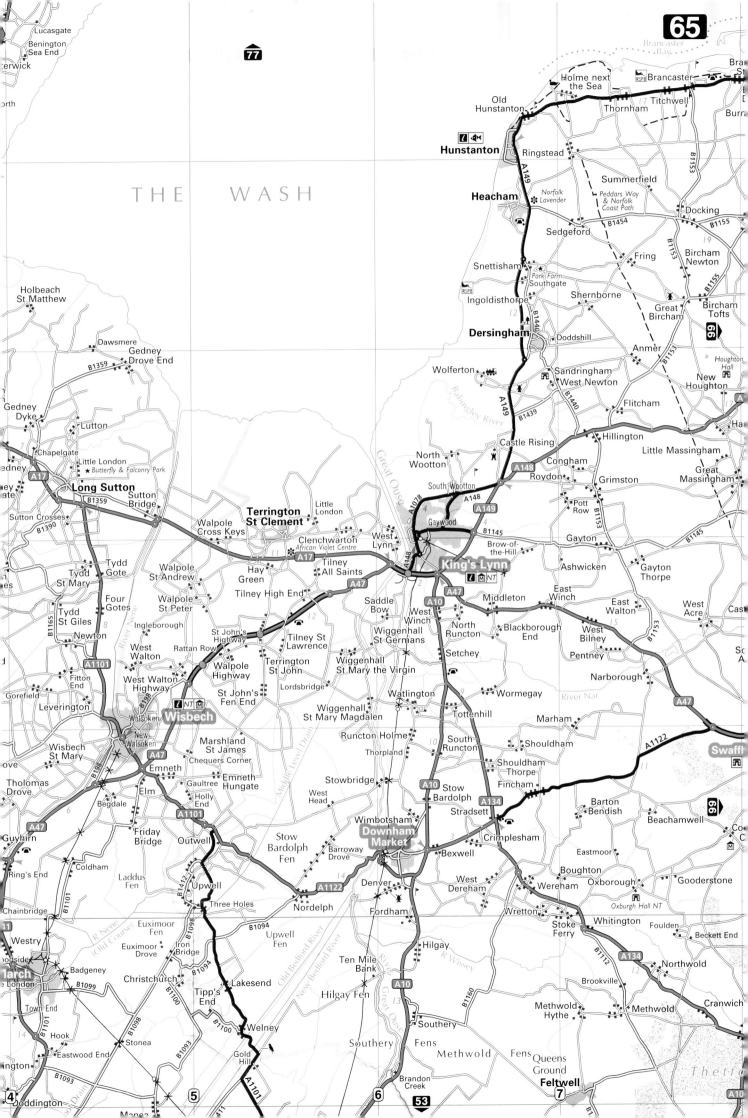

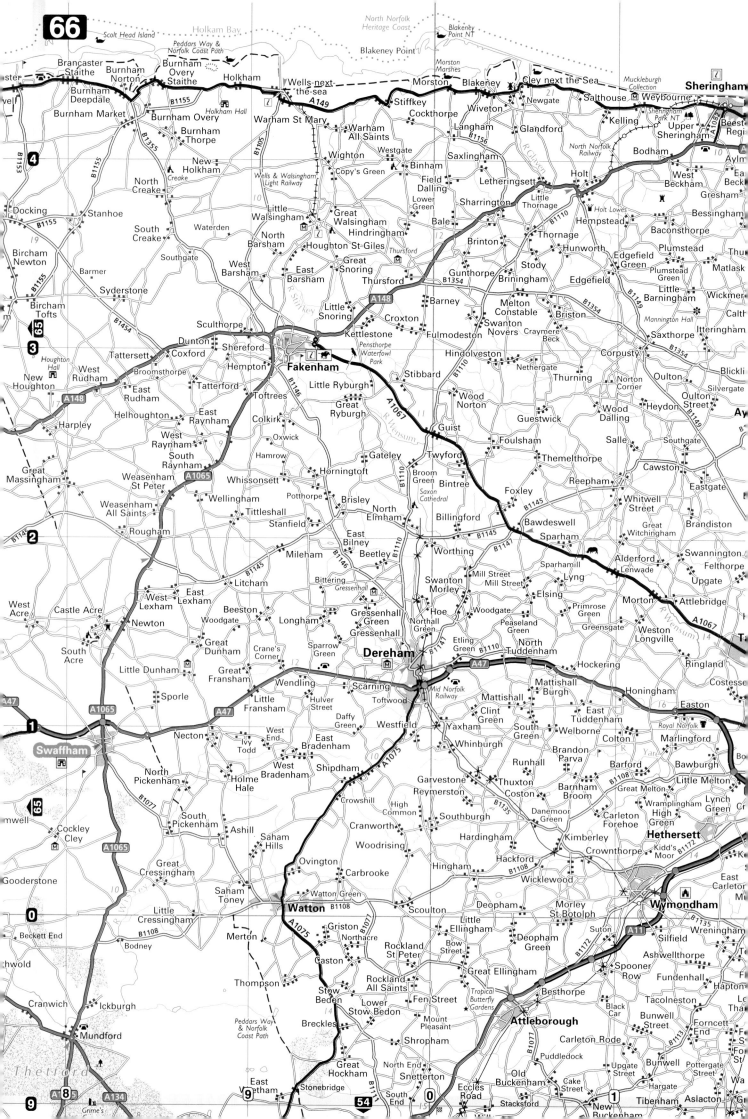

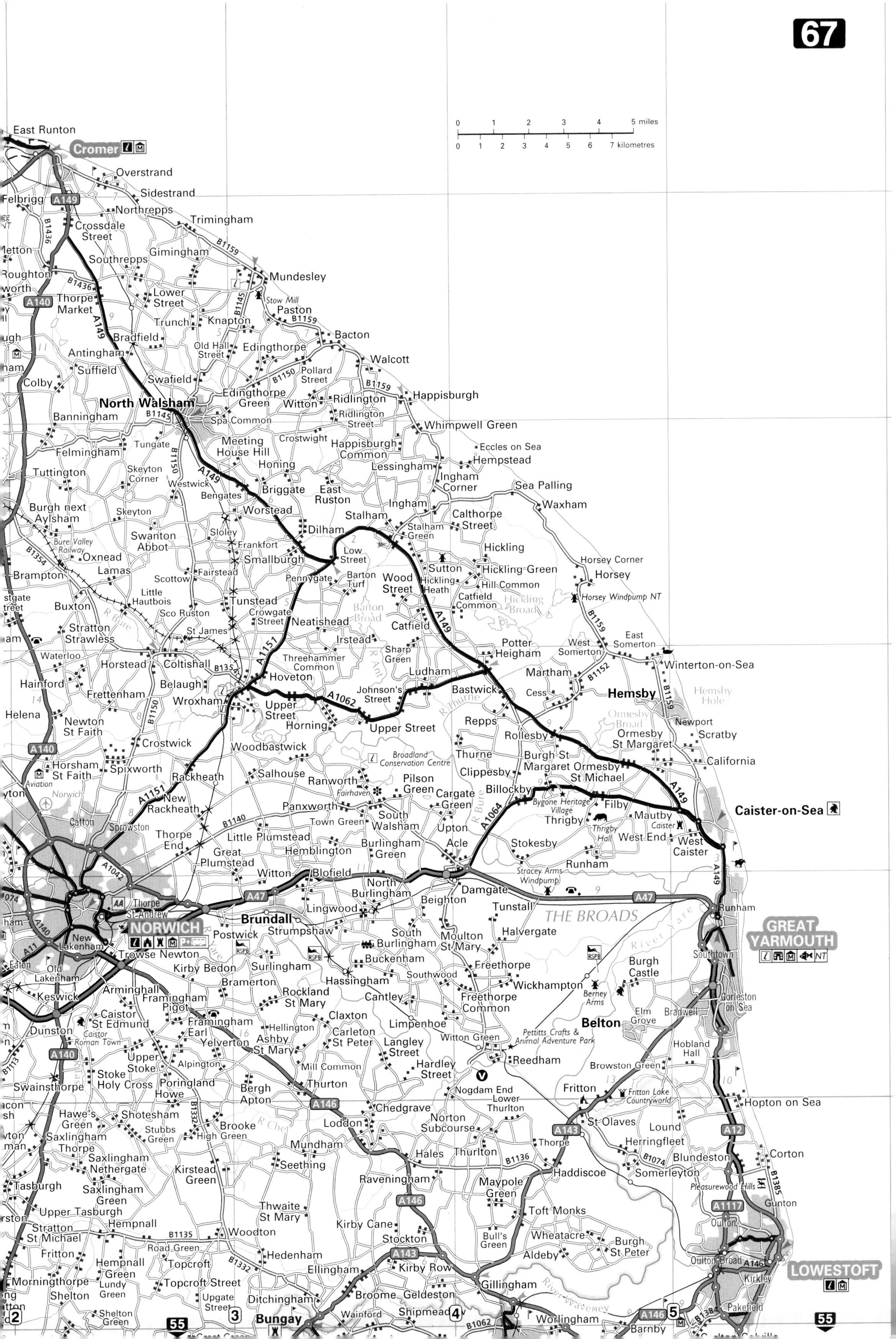

5 miles
0 1 2 3 4 5 miles
0 1 2 3 4 5 6 7 kilometres

East Runton
**Cromer**
Overstrand
Sidestrand
Felbrigg
A149
Northrepps
Trimingham
Crossdale Street
Gimingham
Mundesley
Metton
B1436
Roughton
worth
B1436
Thorpe Market
Lower Street
Stow Mill
Paston
Trunch
Knapton
B1159
Suffield
Bradfield
Old Hall Street
Edingthorpe
Bacton
Antingham
A149
Walcott
Colby
Swafield
Edingthorpe Green
Pollard Street
B1150
B1159
Happisburgh
**North Walsham**
Witton
Ridlington
Whimpwell Green
Banningham
B1145
Spa Common
Ridlington Street
Eccles on Sea
Felmingham
Meeting House Hill
Crostwight
Happisburgh Common
Hempstead
Tungate
Honing
Lessingham
Ingham Corner
Sea Palling
Tuttington
Skeyton Corner
Briggate
East Ruston
Ingham
Waxham
Westwick
Bengates
Worstead
Stalham
Calthorpe Street
Skeyton
B1150
A149
Stalham Green
Hickling
Horsey Corner
Burgh next Aylsham
Sloley
Dilham
Sutton
Hickling Green
Horsey
Swanton Abbot
Frankfort
Low Street
Hickling Heath
Hill Common
Oxnead
Lamas
Scottow
Fairstead
Smallburgh
Barton Turf
Wood Street
Catfield Common
Hickling Broad
Horsey Windpump NT
Brampton
Little Hautbois
Sco Ruston
Tunstead
Pennygate
Barton Broad
Catfield
A149
Stratton Strawless
St James
Crowgate Street
Neatishead
Irstead
Potter Heigham
West Somerton
East Somerton
Buxton
Waterloo
Horstead
Coltishall
Threehammer Common
Sharp Green
Ludham
Bastwick
Martham
B1152
Winterton-on-Sea
Hainford
Belaugh
Hoveton
Johnson's Street
B1159
Hemsby Hole
Frettenham
Wroxham
A1062
Upper Street
Cess
**Hemsby**
Helena
Upper Horning
Upper Street
Repps
Rollesby
Ormesby
Newport
Scratby
Newton St Faith
B1150
Woodbastwick
Thurne
Burgh St Margaret
Ormesby St Margaret
California
Crostwick
Broadland Conservation Centre
Clippesby
St Michael
Horsham St Faith
Spixworth
Salhouse
Ranworth
Pilson Green
Thrigby
A149
Rackheath
Fairhaven
Cargate Green
Billockby
Bygone Heritage Village
Mautby
**Caister-on-Sea**
A1151
New Rackheath
Panxworth
Town Green
South Walsham
Upton
A1064
Filby
Caister
West End
West Caister
Sprowston
Thorpe End
Little Plumstead
Great Plumstead
Burlingham Green
Acle
Stokesby
Thrigby Hall
Runham
Catton
Hemblington
Witton
Blofield
North Burlingham
Damgate
Stracey Arms Windpump
A47
**NORWICH**
A1042
Thorpe St Andrew
Lingwood
Beighton
THE BROADS
Runham
**GREAT YARMOUTH**
New Lakenham
**Brundall**
Postwick
South Burlingham
Moulton St Mary
Tunstall
River Yare
Southtown
Trowse Newton
Strumpshaw
Halvergate
Burgh Castle
Gorleston on Sea
Old Lakenham
Kirby Bedon
Buckenham
Freethorpe
Wickhampton
Berney Arms
Keswick
Bramerton
Surlingham
Southwood
Freethorpe Common
Elm Grove
Bradwell
Arminghall
Rockland St Mary
Cantley
**Belton**
Hobland Hall
Framingham Pigot
Hassingham
Limpenhoe
Pettitts Crafts & Animal Adventure Park
Dunston
Caister St Edmund
Framingham Earl
Claxton
Carleton St Peter
Langley Street
Witton Green
Reedham
Browston Green
Caister Roman Town
Yelverton
Hellington
Ashby St Mary
Mill Common
Hardley Street
Upper Stoke
Alpington
Thurton
Nogdam End
Lower Thurlton
Fritton
Fritton Lake Countryworld
Hopton on Sea
Stoke Holy Cross
Poringland Howe
Bergh Apton
A146
Chedgrave
Norton Subcourse
St Olaves
Lound
Corton
Swainsthorpe
Hawe's Green
Shotesham
Brooke
Loddon
Thorpe
Herringfleet
Blundeston
Hales
Thurlton
A143
B1074
Tasburgh
Saxlingham Thorpe
Stubbs Green
High Green
Mundham
B1136
Haddiscoe
Somerleyton
Gunton
Saxlingham Nethergate
Kirstead Green
Seething
Raveningham
Maypole Green
Pleasurewood Hills
A1117
Saxlingham Green
Upper Tasburgh
Thwaite St Mary
Toft Monks
Oulton
Hempnall
Stratton St Michael
B1135
Woodton
Kirby Cane
Bull's Green
Wheatacre
Burgh St Peter
Oulton Broad
A146
Fritton
Hempnall Green
Topcroft
Stockton
Aldeby
Kirkley
Morningthorpe
Shelton
Lundy Green
Topcroft Street
B1332
Hedenham
A143
Kirby Row
Geldeston
Broome
Ellingham
Ditchingham
Upgate Street
Wainford
Shipmeads
Worlingham
Gillingham
River Waveney
Pakefield
**Bungay**
**LOWESTOFT**

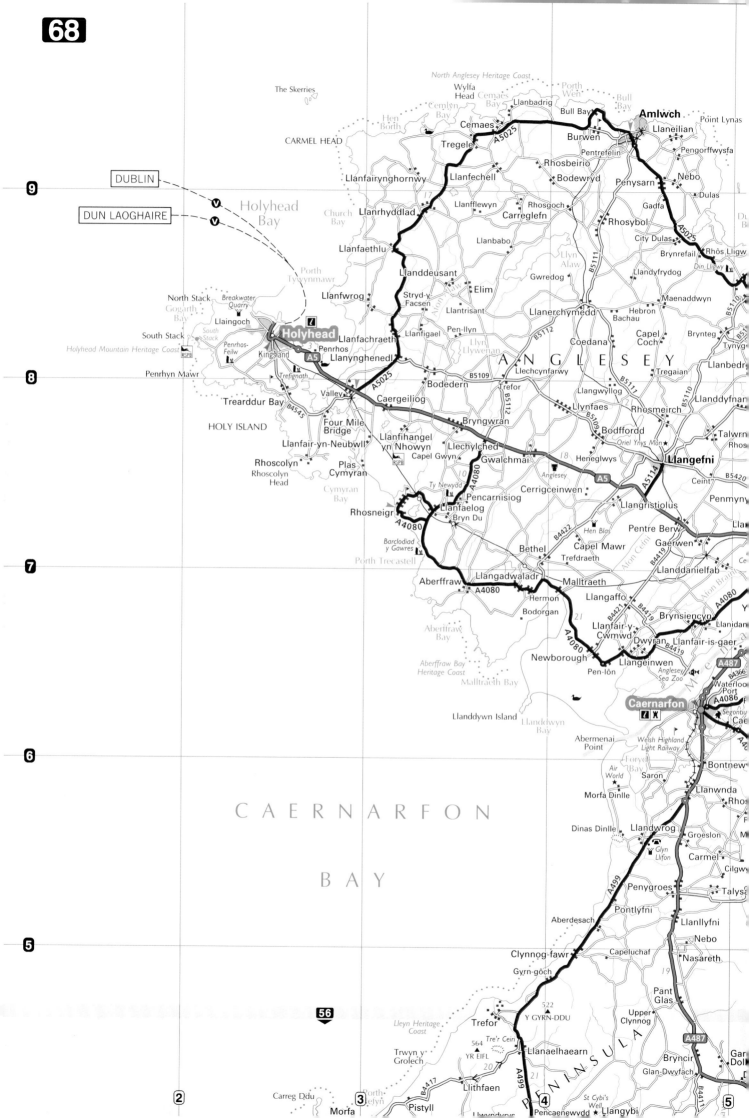

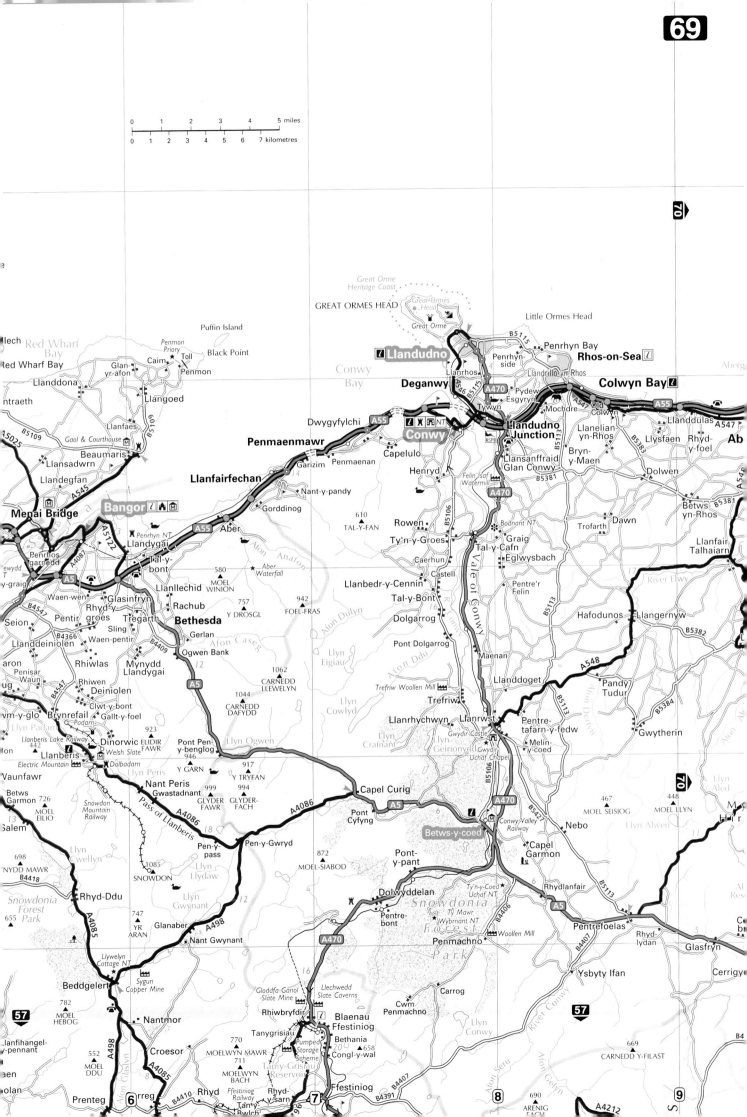

**70**

Great Orme
Heritage Coast
GREAT ORMES HEAD
Great Ormes Head
Great Orme
Little Ormes Head
**Llandudno**
Penrhyn Bay
**Rhos-on-Sea**
Penrhyn-side
Llandrillo-yn-Rhos
Conwy
Bay
**Deganwy**
Pydew
**Colwyn Bay**
Llanrhos
Esgyryn
Mochdre
Tywyn
Old Colwyn
Llanddulas
A547
Dwygyfylchi
**Conwy**
**Llandudno Junction**
Llanelian-yn-Rhos
Llysfaen
Rhyd-y-foel
**Ab**
**Penmaenmawr**
Llansanffraid Glan Conwy
Bryn-y-Maen
Capelulo
RSPB
Garizim
Penmaenan
Henryd
A470
Dolwen
**Llanfairfechan**
Nant-y-pandy
Felin Isaf Watermill
Betws yn-Rhos
Gorddinog
Rowen
B5106
Bodnant NT
Dawn
610
**Aber**
TAL-Y-FAN
Ty'n-y-Groes
Trofarth
Llanfair Talhaiarn
Afon Anaton
Aber
Waterfall
Caerhun
Tal-y-Cafn
Graig
Eglwysbach
River Elwy
Llandygai
580
MOEL WINION
Llanbedr-y-Cennin
Castell
Pentre'r
Felin
Tal-y-bont
**Bangor**
Aber
Penrhyn NT
757
Y DROSGL
942
FOEL-FRAS
Tal-y-Bont
Hafodunos
Llangernyw
**Menai Bridge**
Llanllechid
Rachub
Dolgarrog
B5113
Waen-wen
Glasinfryn
Rhyd-y-
groes
Tregarth
Afon Caseg
Pont Dolgarrog
Seion
Gerlan
**Bethesda**
Afon Dulyn
Vale of Conwy
Llanddeiniolen
Ogwen Bank
Llyn
Eigiau
Maenan
B5382
Pentir
Waen-pentir
12
Trefriw Woollen Mill
Llanddoget
A548
Pandy
Tudur
Rhiwlas
Mynydd Llandygai
1062
CARNEDD LLEWELYN
Trefriw
Gwytherin
Rhiwen
Deinolen
1044
CARNEDD DAFYDD
Llyn
Cowlyd
Llanrhychwyn
**Llanrwst**
Pentre-tafarn-y-fedw
Clwt-y-bont
Gallt-y-foel
923
Llyn Ogwen
Gwydir Castle
Melin-
y-coed
Brynrefail
Padarn
Pont Pen-
y-benglog
Llyn
Geirionydd
Gwydir
Uchaf Chapel
Llanberis Lake Railway
Dinorwic
ELIDIR
FAWR
Welsh Slate
946
Y GARN
Llyn
Crafnant
**Llanberis**
Electric Mountain
Dolbadarn
917
Y TRYFAN
B5106
70
Llyn
Aled
Vaunfawr
Nant Peris
Gwastadnant
994
GLYDER-
FACH
**Capel Curig**
A5
467
MOEL SEISIOG
448
MOEL LLYN
Betws
Garmon
726
MOEL
EILIO
Pass of Llanberis
A4086
GLYDER
FAWR
Pont
Cyfyng
6
Nebo
Salem
18
Pen-y-
pass
Pen-y-Gwryd
**Betws-y-coed**
Conwy Valley Railway
Capel
Garmon
698
NYDD MAWR
Snowdon
Mountain
Railway
1085
SNOWDON
Llyn
Llydaw
872
MOEL-SIABOD
Pont-
y-pant
Rhydlanfair
B5113
**Rhyd-Ddu**
Ty'n-y-Coed
Uchaf NT
A5
Snowdonia
Forest
Llyn
Gwynant
12
**Dolwyddelan**
Pentre-
bont
Wybrnant NT
Pentrefoelas
747
YR
ARAN
Glanaber
A498
Nant Gwynant
A470
Park
Ty Mawr
Woollen Mill
Rhyd-
lydan
Glasfryn
Llywelyn
Cottage NT
**Beddgelert**
Sygun
Copper Mine
Penmachno
Ysbyty Ifan
782
MOEL
HEBOG
Nantmor
Gloddfa Ganol
Slate Mine
Llechwedd
Slate Caverns
Cwm
Penmachno
Carrog
57
**57**
Croesor
A4085
**Rhiwbryfdir**
**Blaenau Ffestiniog**
669
CARNEDD Y-FILAST
Llanfihangel-
y-pennant
552
MOEL
DDU
Tanygrisiau
Pumped
Storage
Scheme
Bethania
Congl-y-wal
770
MOELWYN MAWR
658
Llyn
Conwy
Prenteg
rreg
Rhyd
711
MOELWYN BACH
Tan-y-Grisiau
Reservoir
Ffestiniog
Railway
Rhyd-
y-sarn
**Ffestiniog**
690
ARENIG
A4212
6
7
8
9

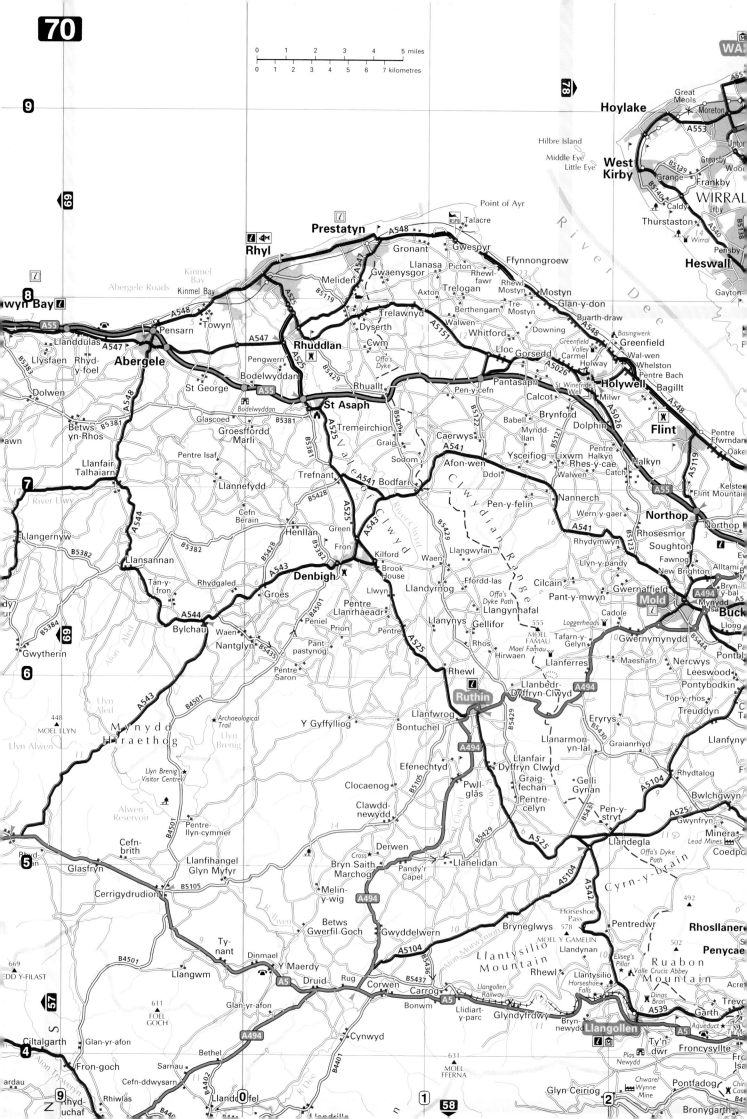

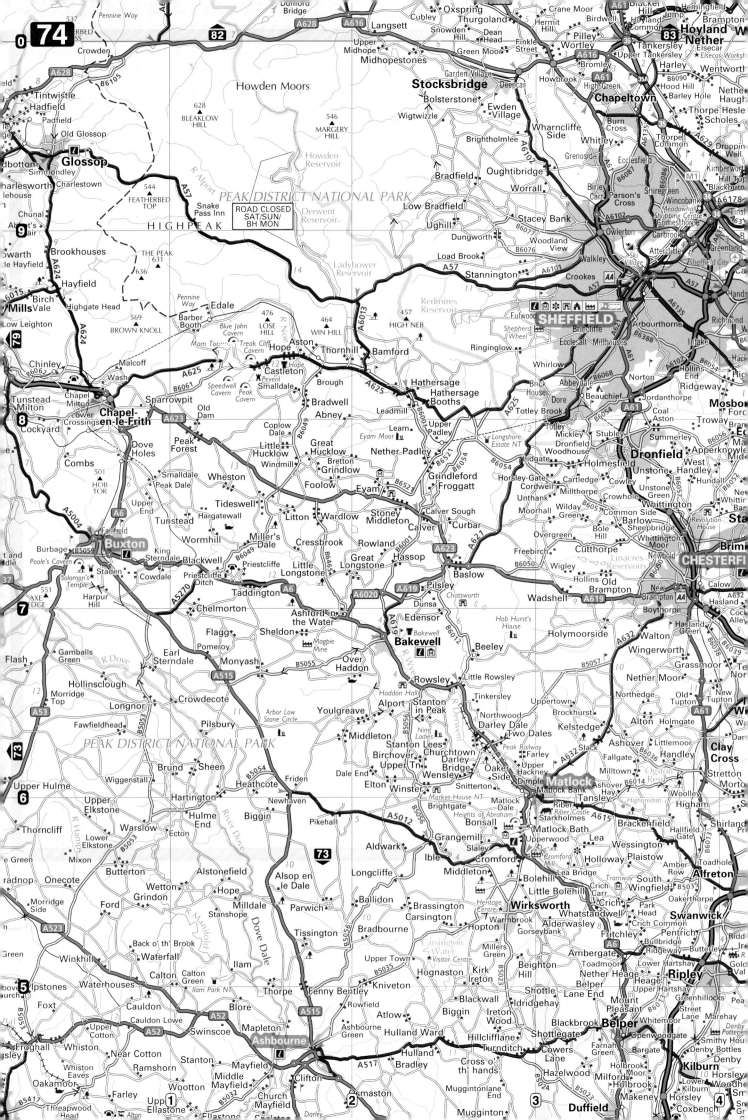

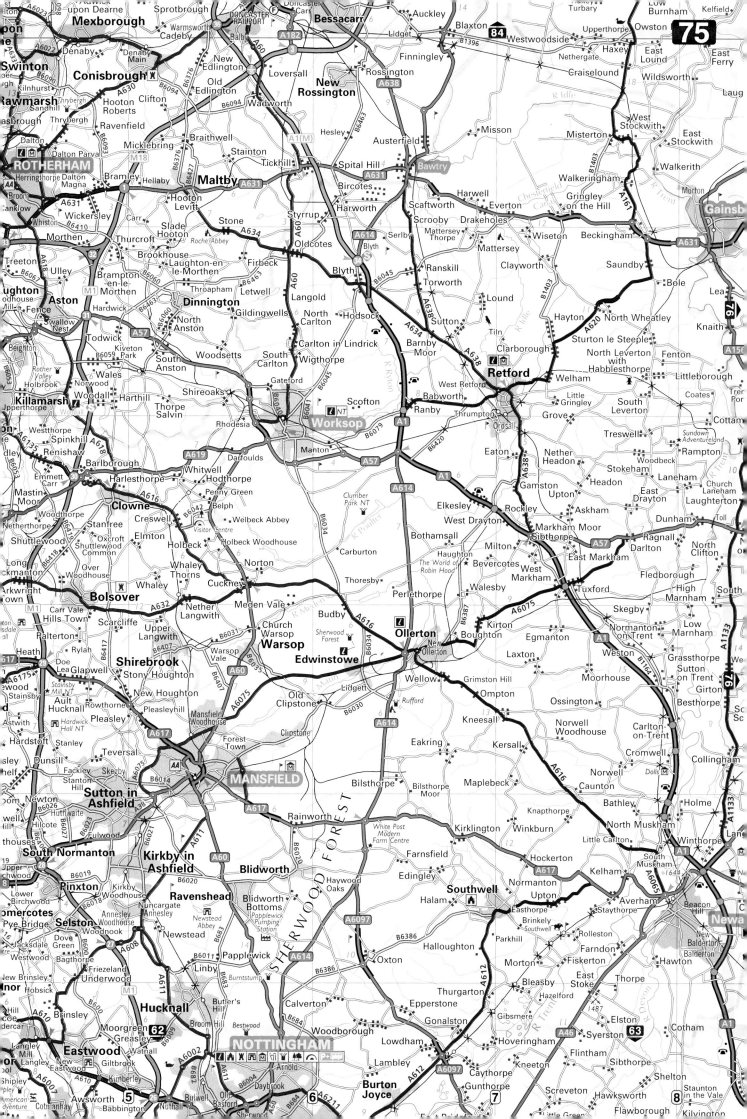

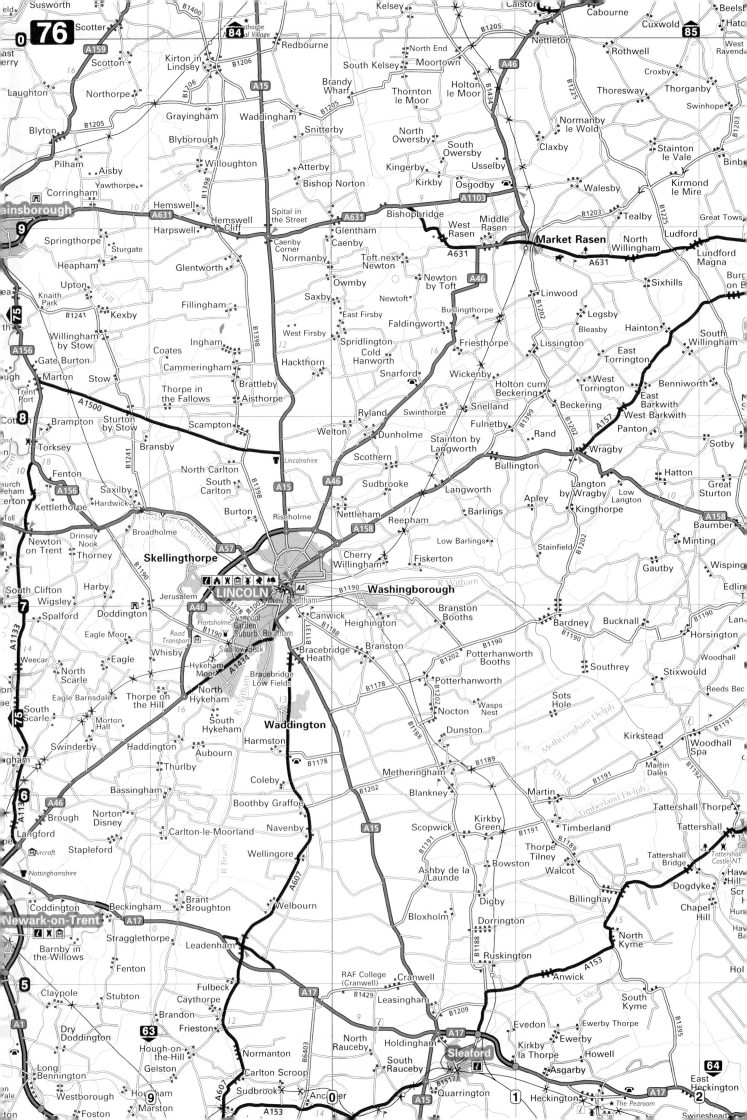

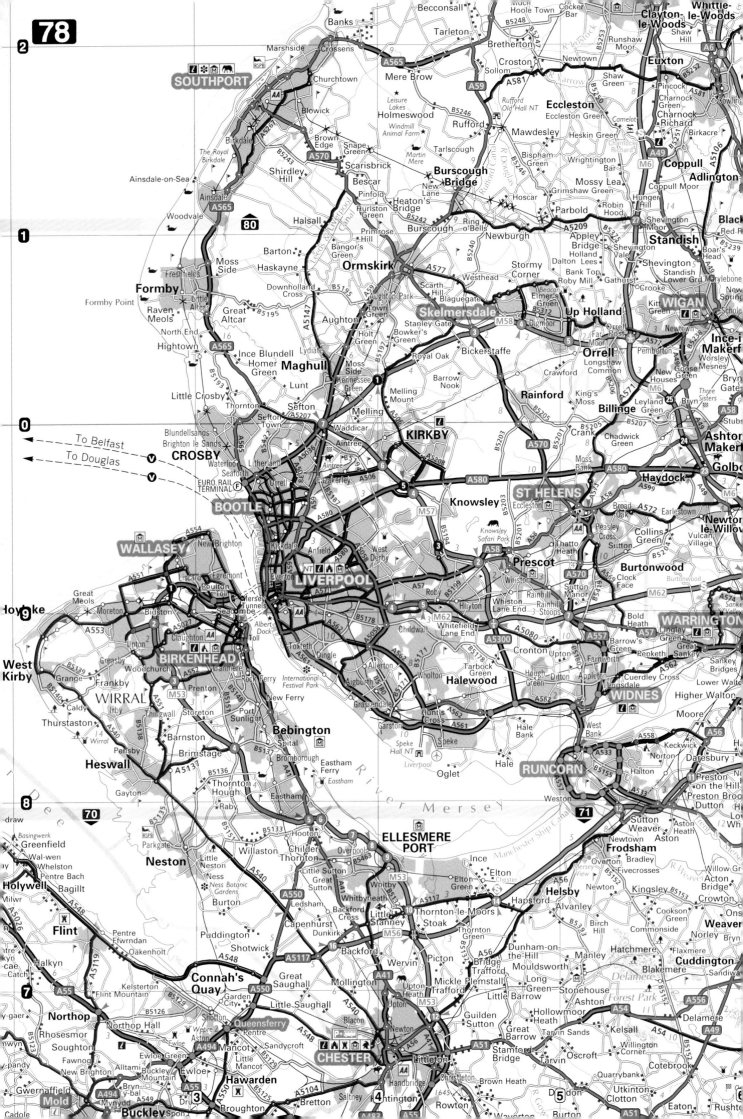

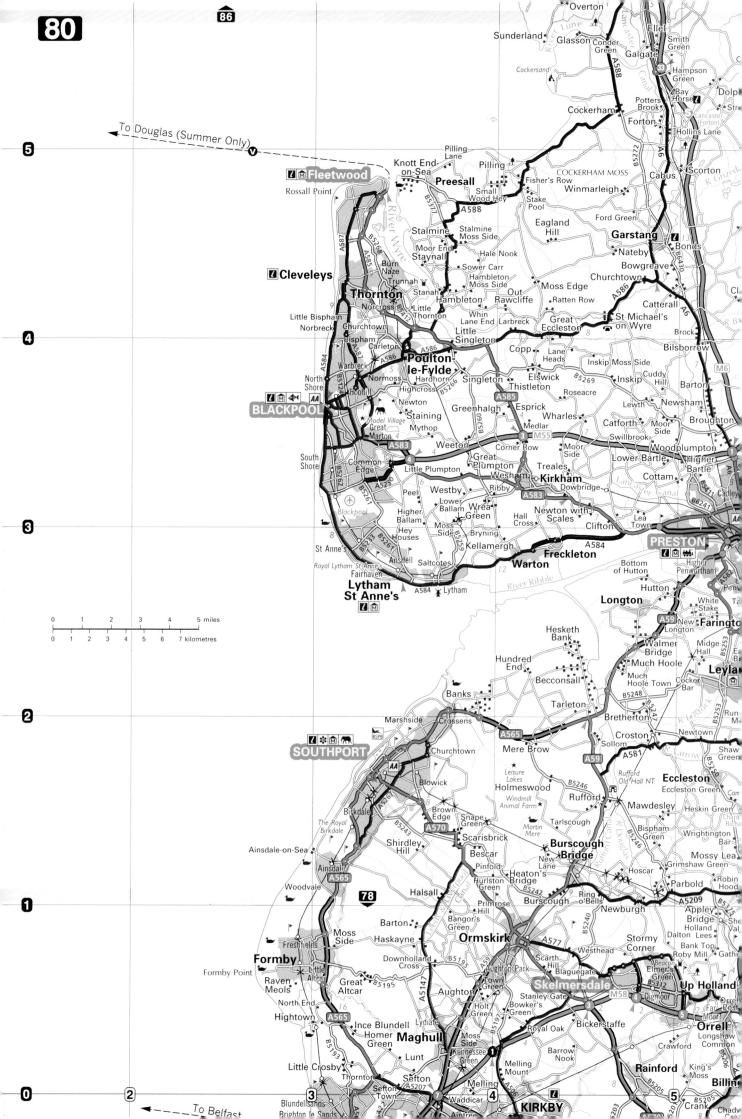

86

To Douglas (Summer Only)

**Fleetwood**
Rossall Point
Knott End-on-Sea
Pilling Lane
Pilling
**Preesall**
Small Wood Hey
Fisher's Row
COCKERHAM MOSS
Cabus
Scorton

Overton
Sunderland
Glasson
Conder Green
Galgate
Smith Green
Hampson Green
Bay Horse
Dolp

Cockerham
Forton
Hollins Lane
A6

Winmarleigh
Ford Green
**Garstang**
Nateby
Bowgreave
Churchtown
Bonds

Cleveleys
Burn Naze
Trunnah
Stalmine
Stalmine Moss Side
Hale Nook
Sower Carr
Moss Edge
Catterall

**Thornton**
Norcross
Little Thornton
Stanah
Hambleton
Moor End
Staynall
Hambleton Moss Side
Out Rawcliffe
Ratten Row
St Michael's on Wyre
Brock

Little Bispham
Norbreck
Churchtown
Bispham
Carleton
Whin Lane End
Larbreck
Great Eccleston
Bilsborrow

Little Singleton
Copp
Lane Heads
Inskip Moss Side

**Poulton-le-Fylde**
Hardhorn
Normoss
Highcross
Singleton
Elswick
Thistleton
Inskip
Cuddy Hill
Barton
Newsham

North Shore
Hoohill
Newton
Staining
Greenhalgh
Roseacre
Lewth
Catforth
Moor Side
Broughton

**BLACKPOOL**
Model Village
Great Marton
Mythop
Weeton
Corner Row
Medlar
Wharles
Swillbrook
Woodplumpton
Lower Bartle
Higher Bartle

South Shore
Common Edge
A583
Little Plumpton
Great Plumpton
Wesham
**Kirkham**
Dowbridge
Cottam

Peel
Westby
Ribby
Lower Ballam
Wrea Green
Newton with Scales
Lea Town
Clifton

Blackpool
Higher Ballam
Hey Houses
Moss Side
Bryning
Kellamergh
Hall Cross
A584
**Freckleton**
**Warton**

St Anne's
Ansdell
Saltcotes
Royal Lytham St Anne's
Fairhaven
Lytham
Bottom of Hutton
Hutton
Higher Penwortham
**PRESTON**

**Lytham St Anne's**
River Ribble
Longton
New Longton
Farington
White Stake
A59

Hesketh Bank
Walmer Bridge
Much Hoole
Midge Hall
Leyland

Hundred End
Becconsall
Much Hoole Town
Cocker Bar
Run

Banks
Tarleton
Bretherton
Croston
Shaw Green
Newtown

Marshside
Crossens
A565
Sollom
A581
A59

**SOUTHPORT**
Churchtown
Mere Brow
Leisure Lakes
Holmeswood
Rufford
Old Hall NT
**Eccleston**
Eccleston Green

Blowick
Windmill Animal Farm
Mawdesley
Heskin Green
Wrightington

Birkdale
Brown Edge
A570
Snape Green
Martin Mere
Bispham Green
Bar

The Royal Birkdale
Shirdley Hill
Scarisbrick
Bescar
Tarlscough
**Burscough Bridge**
Hoscar
Mossy Lea
Parbold

Ainsdale-on-Sea
Ainsdale
A565
Woodvale
Pinfold
New Lane
Heaton's Bridge
Hurlston Green
Grimshaw Green
Robin

78
Halsall
Hillock
Burscough
Ring o'Bells
Newburgh
Appley Bridge

Barton
Bangor's Green
Primrose Hill
A5209

**Formby**
Formby Point
Little Altcar
Moss Side
Haskayne
Downholland Cross
**Ormskirk**
A577
Scarth Hill
Westhead
Holland
Dalton
Bank Top
Roby Mill
Beacon

Raven Meols
Great Altcar
Lydiate
Aughton Park
Blaguegate
Stormy Corner
Elmer's Green
**Up Holland**

North End
Hightown
A565
Holt Green
Aughton
Town Green
**Skelmersdale**
Digmoor
M58
Orrell

Ince Blundell
Homer Green
Stanley Gate
Bowker's Green
Royal Oak
Bickerstaffe
Crawford
Far Moor

**Maghull**
Moss Side
Kennessee Green
Lunt
Melling Mount
Barrow Nook
**Rainford**
King's Moss

Little Crosby
Thornton
Sefton
Waddicar
Melling
**KIRKBY**
Billin

Blundellsands
Brighton le Sands
Sefton Town
Crank

To Belfast

SCALE:
0  1  2  3  4  5 miles
0  1  2  3  4  5  6  7 kilometres

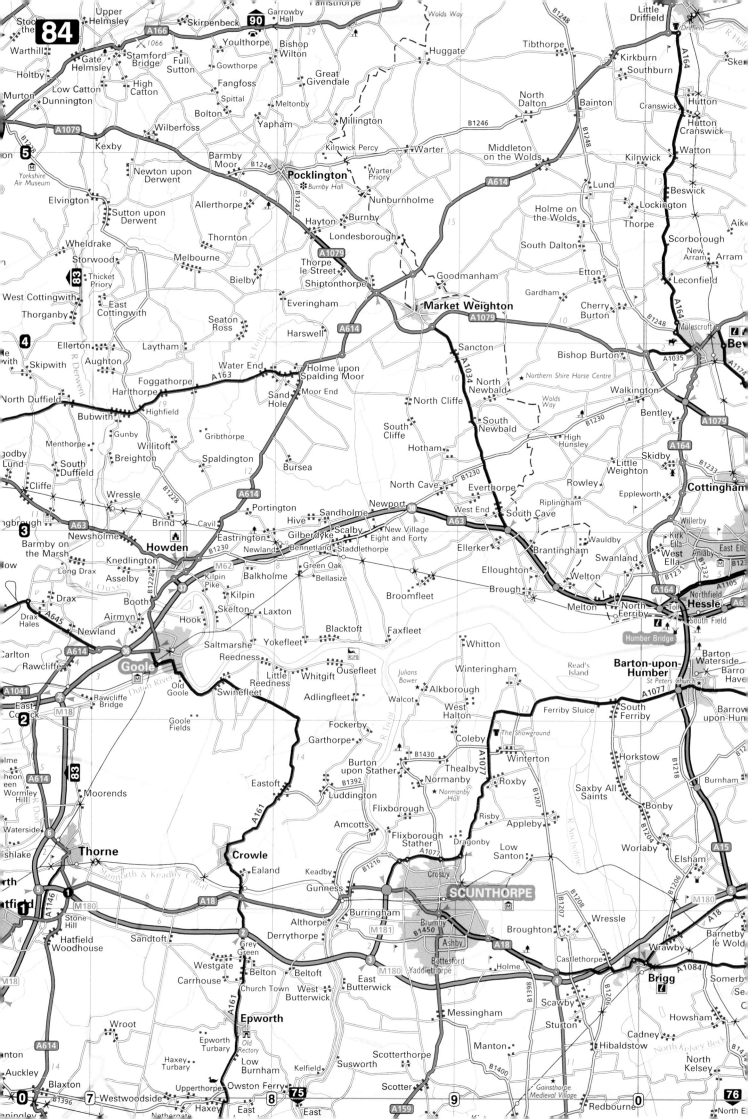

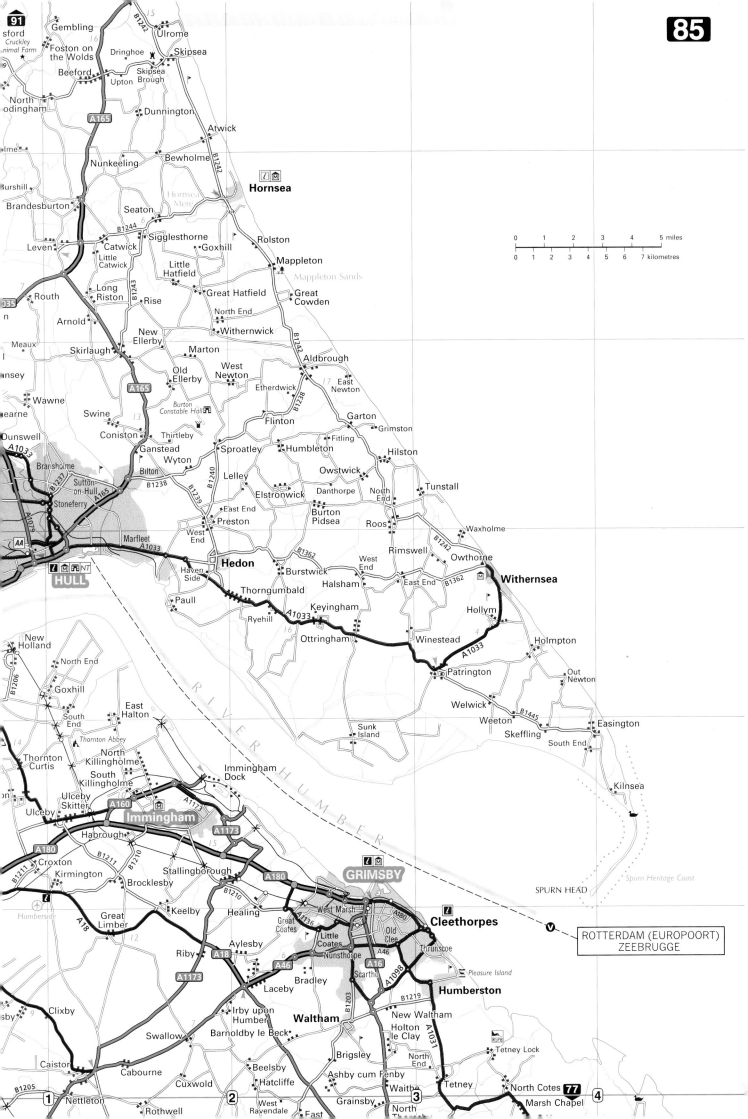

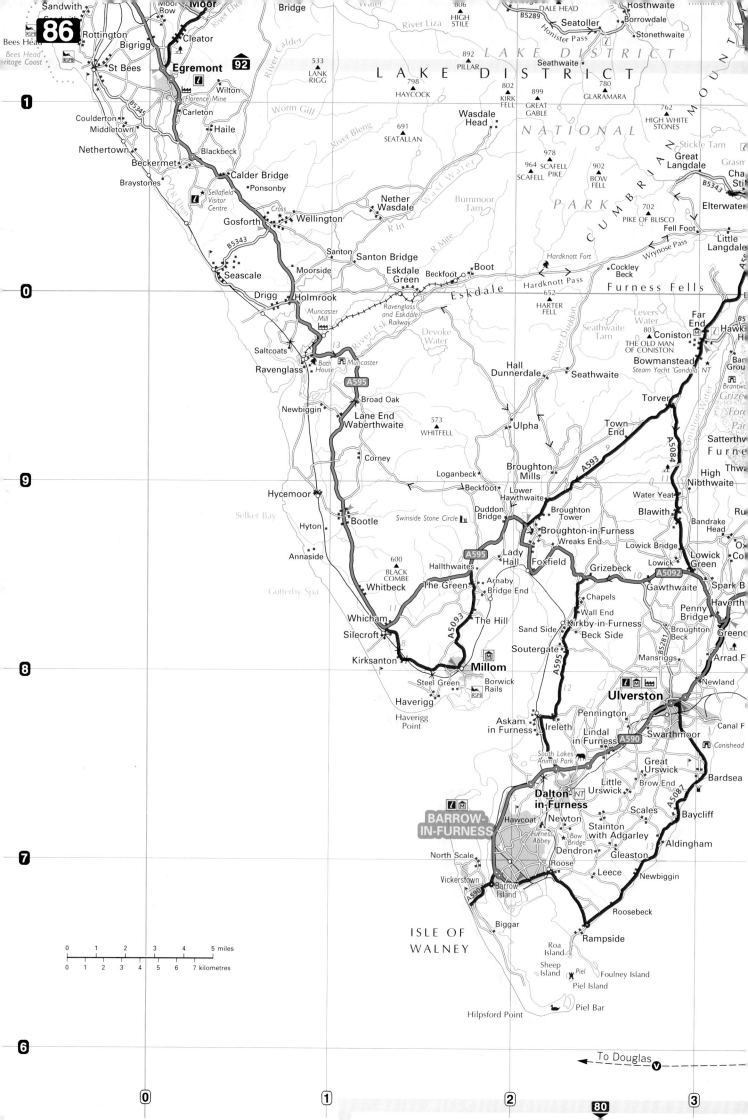

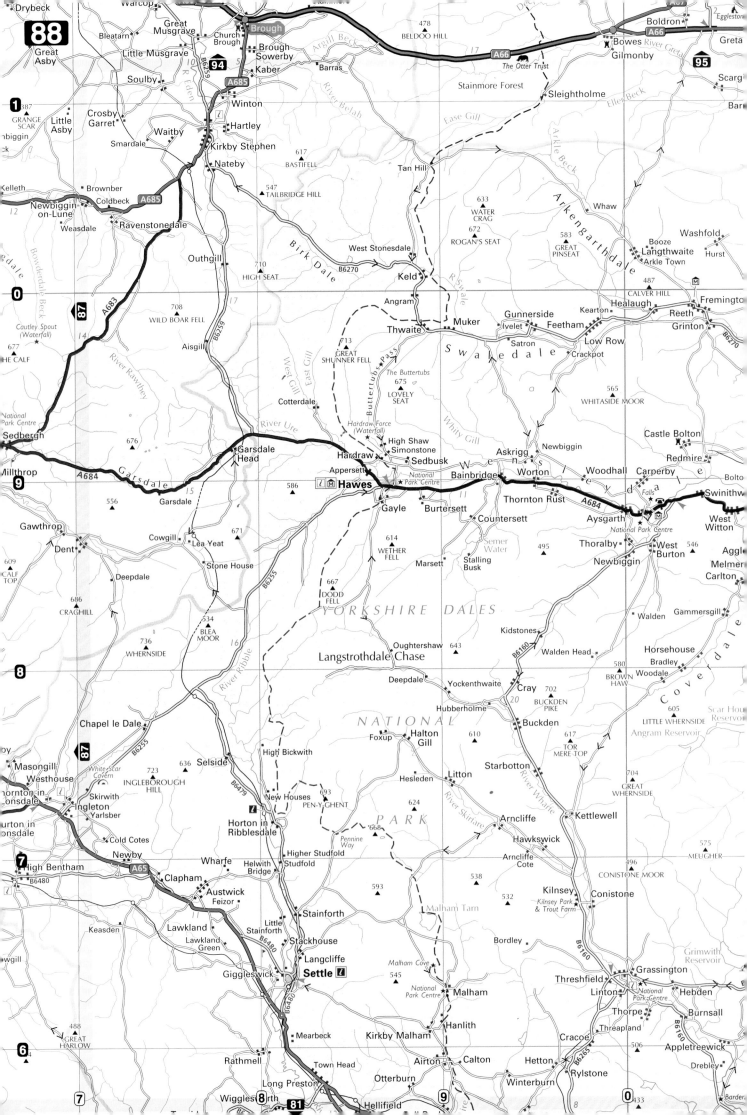

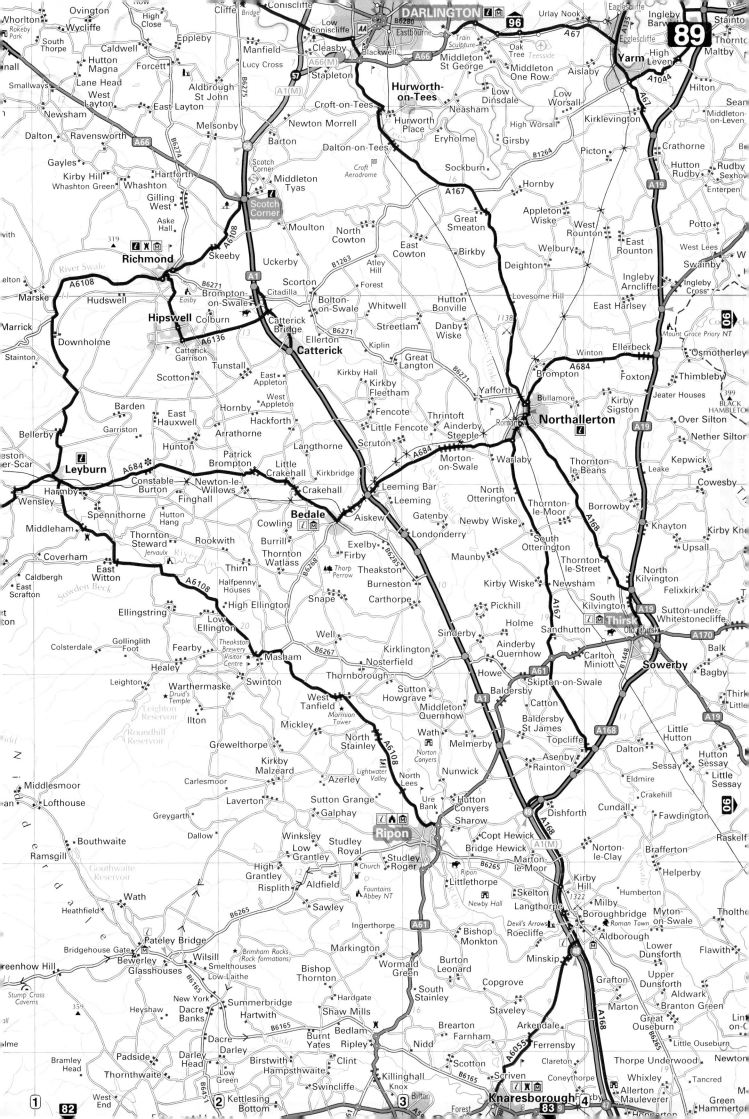

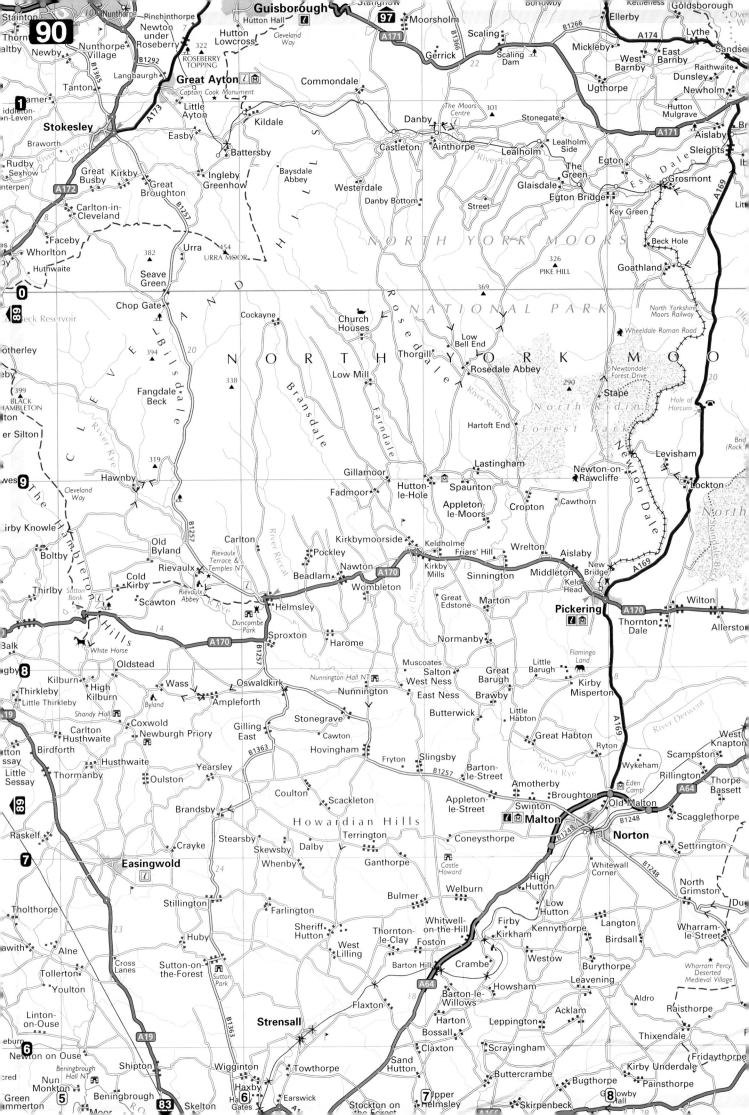

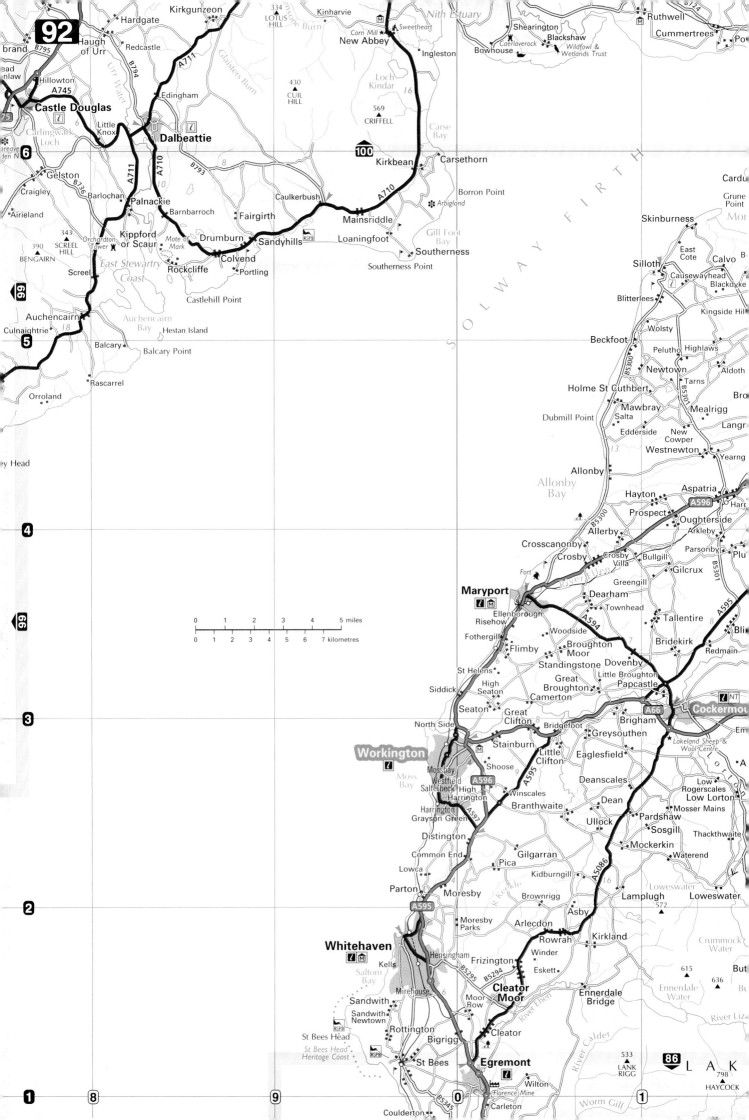

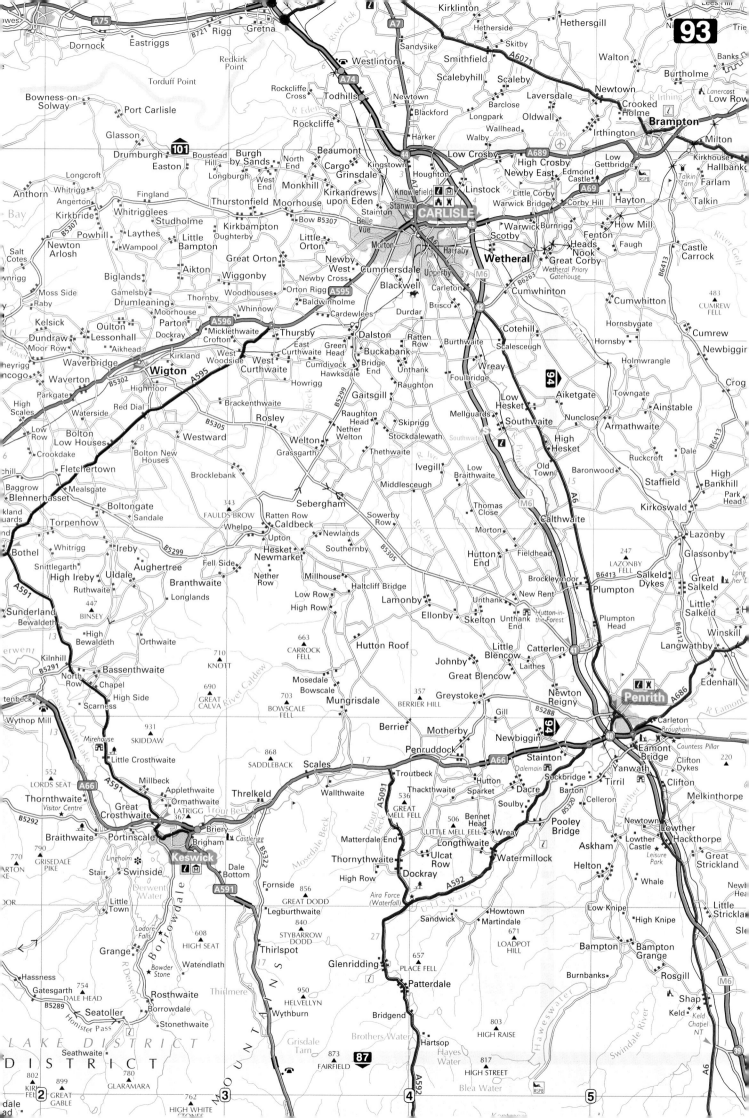

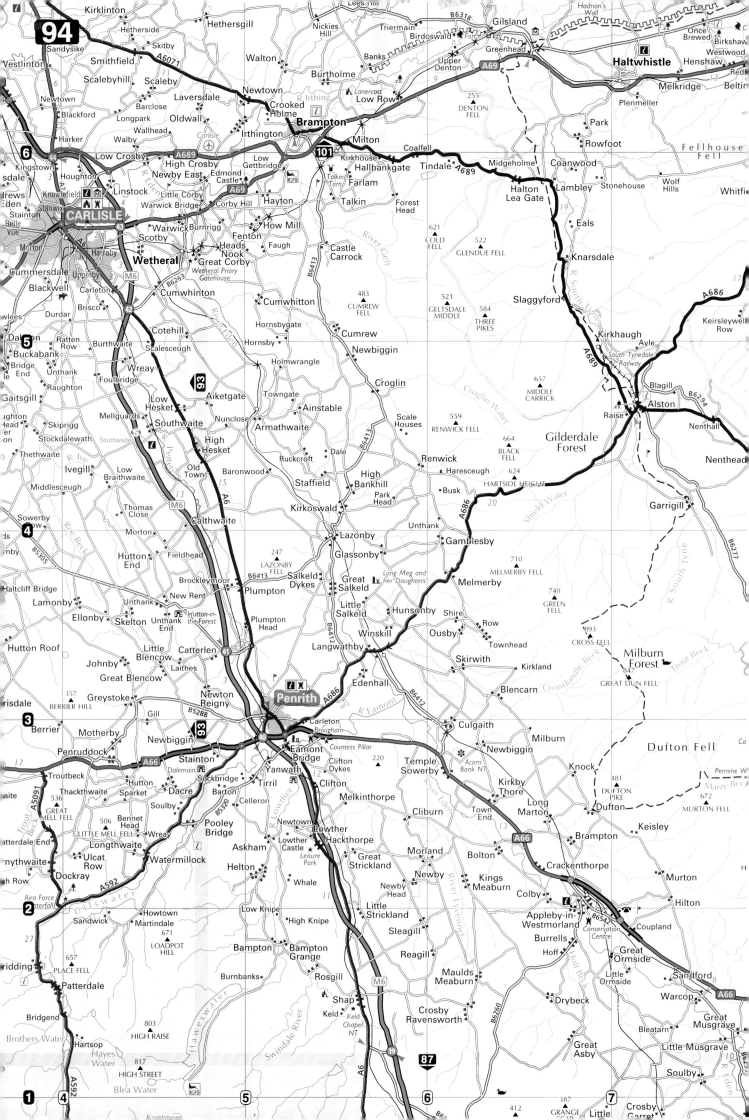

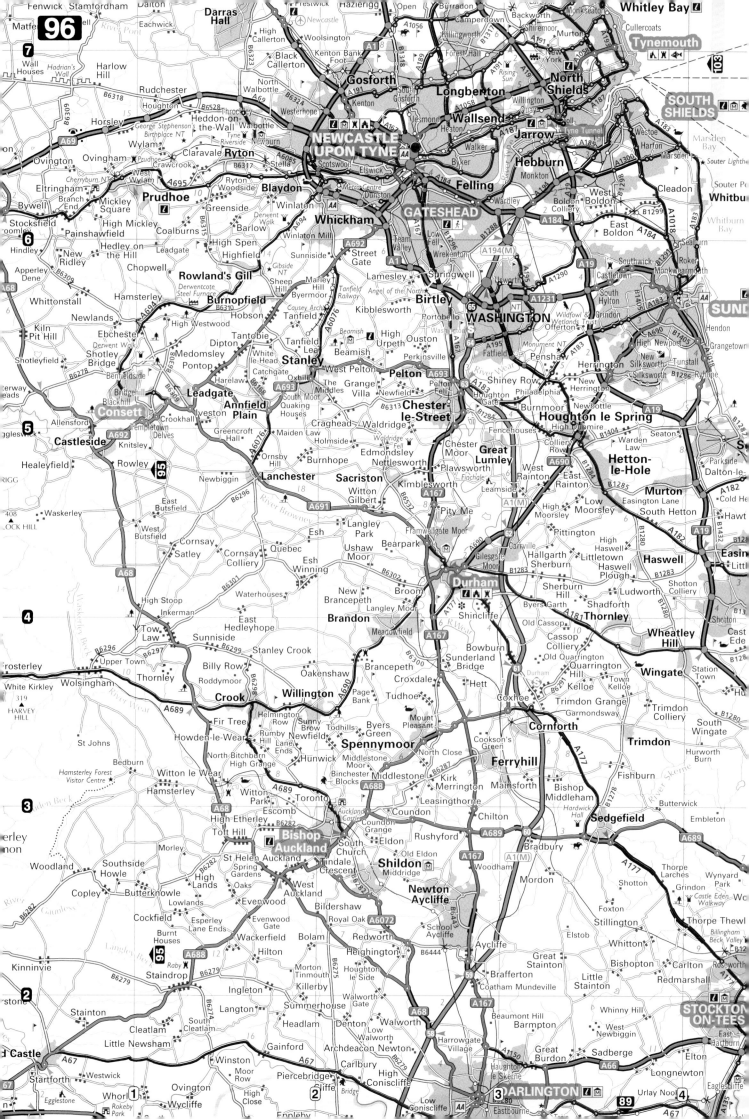

BERGEN
STAVANGER

GÖTEBORG
Summer Only

HAMBURG
Summer Only

AMSTERDAM

...ND

0  1  2  3  4  5 miles

0  1  2  3  4  5  6  7 kilometres

...gton Colliery

...e

...terlee

Blackhall Colliery
Blackhall Rocks

...ackhall
...den

A1086

Hart Station

...ry
...ton

Hart

A179

High
Throston

Historic
Quay

Headland

...lwick

AA

**HARTLEPOOL**

Dalton
Piercy

B1271

Hartlepool Bay

Brierton

Seaton
Carew

B1277

...9

A689

Greatham

Gr.aythorpe

Tees Bay

Newton
Bewley

A178

Hartlepool Power
Station Visitor
Centre

**Billingham**

A1185

Coatham

Warrenby

**Redcar**

Cowpen
Bewley

Seal
Sands

Teesport

Marske-by-
the-Sea

B1275

A1046

Haverton Hill

Port
Clarence

River Tees

A1042

B1269

A1085

A174

Saltburn-by-the-Sea

Toll

A66

Kirkleatham

Yearby

New
Marske

Saltburn Smugglers

A174

New Brotton

Hummersea Scar

North
Ormesby

South Grangetown

Bank

Lazenby

Old Hall

Lackenby

Wilton

Upleatham

B1267

**Brotton**

**Skelton**

Carlin
How

Skinningrove

Street
Houses

Boulby

**MIDDLESBROUGH**

A174

Normanby

Dunsdale

B1269

New
Skelton

North
Skelton

Kilton

Liverton
Mines

Loftus

Dalehouse

Easington

Staithes

Heritage Centre

Teesside Park

AA

Acklam

A172

Ormesby

Tocketts

A173

Boosbeck

Lingdale

Kilton
Thorpe

Port Mulgrave

...naby
...ees

A1032

Marton

Ormesby Hall NT

A171

Margrove
Park

Liverton

Handale

Roxby

Newton
Mulgrave

Runswick

A19

B1380

Stainton

Hemlington

Nunthorpe

Newton

**5**

Pinchinthorpe

**6**

**Guisborough**

Hutton Hall

Stanghow

Borrowby

**90**

Moorsholm

**7**

North Yor
Cleveland

Runswick
Bay

Kettleness

Ellerby

**8**

Göldsborc

B1266

Lythe

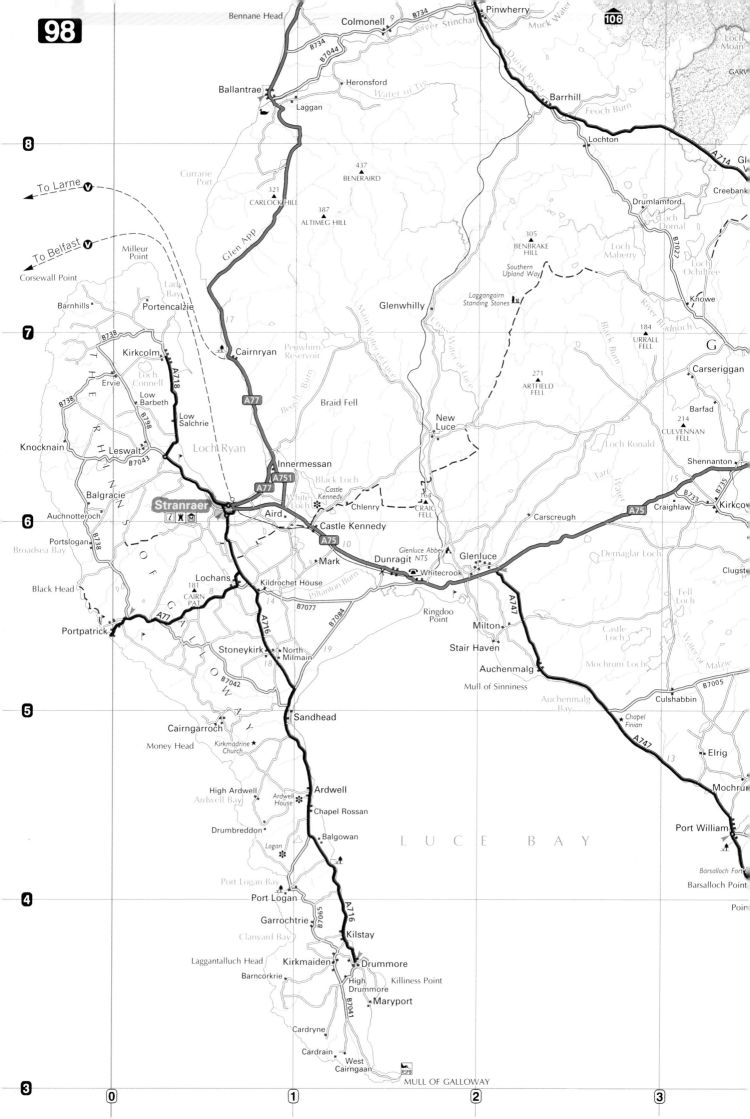

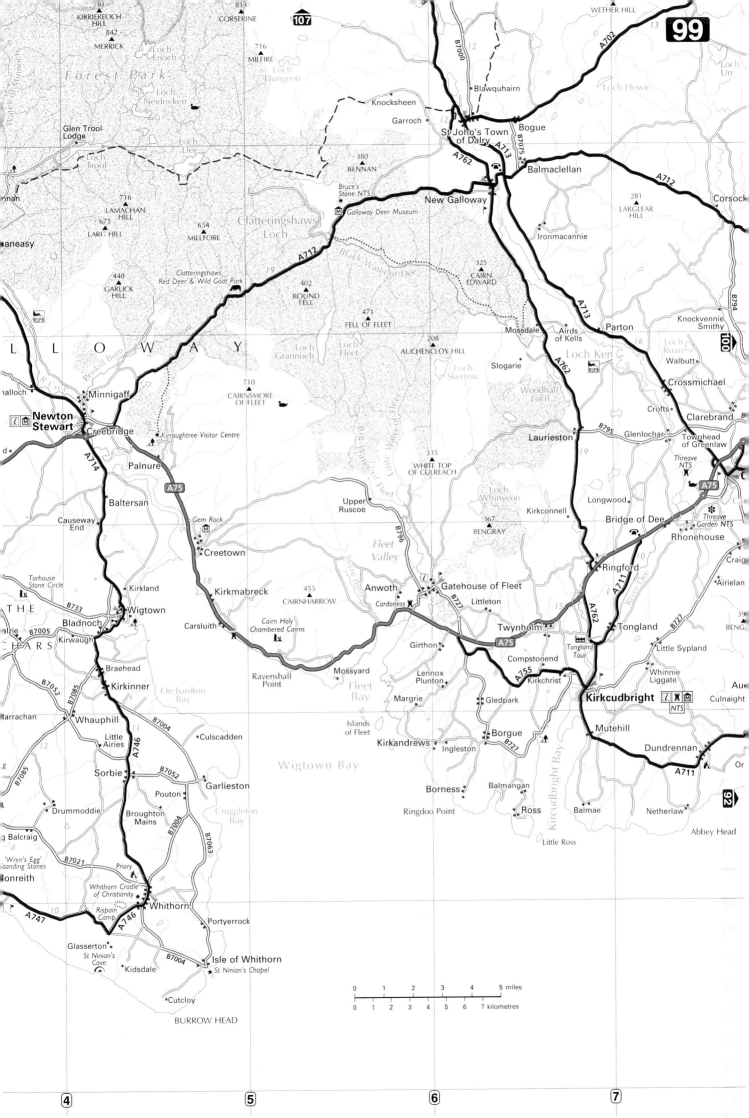

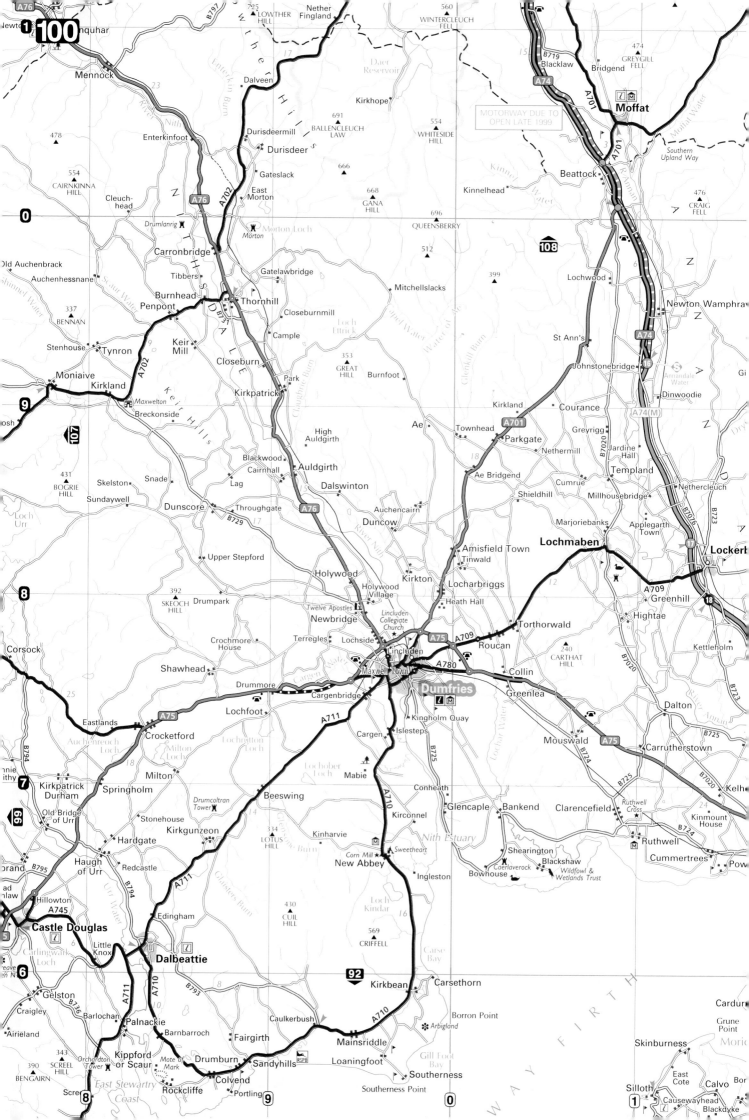

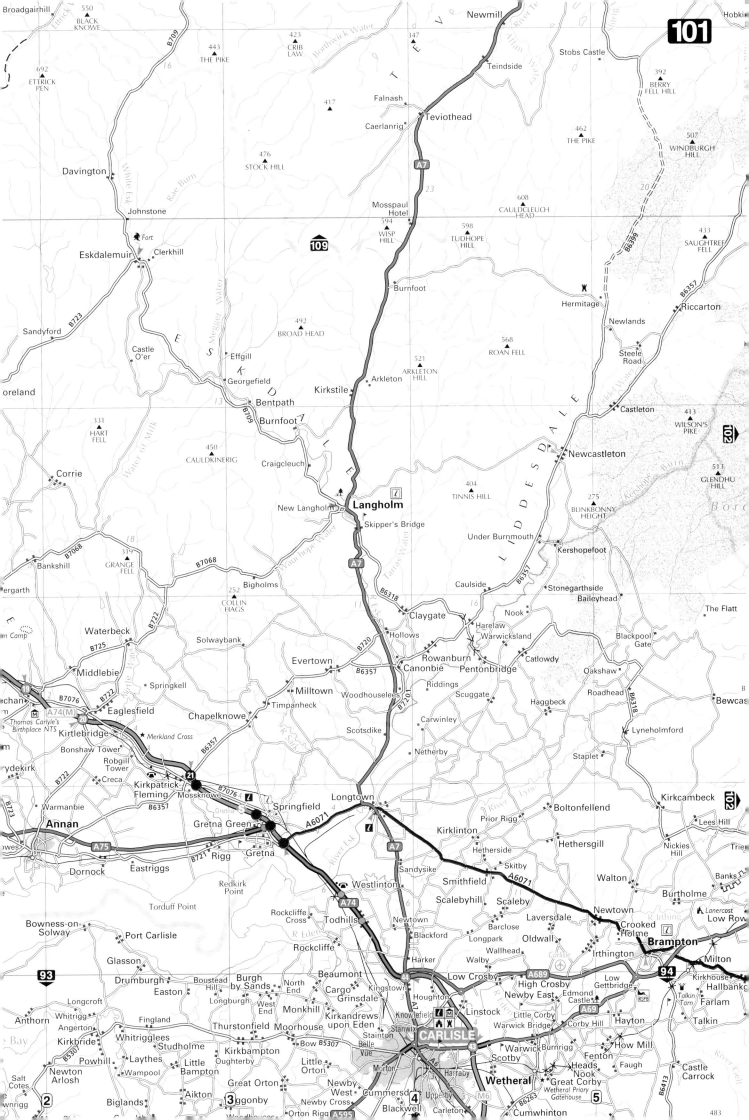

Broadgairhill
550
BLACK KNOWE
B709
443 THE PIKE
423 CRIB LAW
Borthwick Water
Newmill
River Te
347
Hobki

692 ETTRICK PEN
16
Teindside
Stobs Castle
392 BERRY FELL HILL

Davington
417
Falnash
Teviothead
507 WINDBURGH HILL

White Esk
Rae Burn
476 STOCK HILL
Caerlanrig
A7
23
462 THE PIKE

Johnstone
Mosspaul Hotel
594
608 CAULDCLEUCH HEAD
B6399

Eskdalemuir
Fort
Clerkhill
109
WISP HILL
598 TUDHOPE HILL
20

ESK
Megget Water
Effgill
Burnfoot
Hermitage
Newlands
Riccarton
B6357

Sandyford
492 BROAD HEAD
Georgefield
Kirkstile
521 ARKLETON HILL
568 ROAN FELL
Steele Road

oreland
13
Bentpath
Burnfoot
B709
Arkleton
Castleton
413 WILSON'S PIKE

331 HART FELL
Castle O'er
450 CAULDKINERIG
404 TINNIS HILL
275 BLINKBONNY HEIGHT
102

Corrie
Craigcleuch
New Langholm
Langholm
Newcastleton
513 GLENDHU HILL

LIDDESDALE
Bor

Skipper's Bridge
Under Burnmouth
Kershopefoot

Bankshill
B7068
319 GRANGE FELL
18
Bigholms
A7
B6318
Caulside
Stonegarthside
Baileyhead
The Flatt

B7068
252 COLLIN HAGS
Wauchope Water
Tarras Water
Claygate
16
Nook
Roadhead

Waterbeck
Solwaybank
Evertown
Hollows
Harelaw
Warwicksland
Blackpool Gate

B725
B722
Timpanheck
B720
Rowanburn
Catlowdy
Oakshaw

19
B7076
Middlebie
Springkell
Milltown
Canonbie
Pentonbridge
B6318

A74(M)
Eaglesfield
Chapelknowe
Woodhouselees
Riddings
Scuggate
Haggbeck
Roadhead
Bewcas

Thomas Carlyle's Birthplace NTS
20
Kirtlebridge
Merkland Cross
B6357
Scotsdike
Carwinley
Lyneholmford

Bonshaw Tower
B7201
Netherby
Staplet

ydekirk
Robgill Tower
Creca
21
Kirkpatrick Fleming
B7076
Longtown
Boltonfellend
Kirkcambeck
102

B722
Warmanbie
Mossknowe
Springfield
A6071
Prior Rigg
Lees Hill

Annan
Gretna Green
Kirklinton
Hetherside
Hethersgill
Nickies Hill
Trie

A75
B721
Rigg
Gretna
A7
Skitby
A6071
Walton
Burtholme

Dornock
Eastriggs
Redkirk Point
Westlinton
Sandysike
Smithfield
Scaleby
Laversdale
Lanercost
Low Row

Torduff Point
A74
Todhills
Newtown
Scalebyhill
Newtown
Crooked Holme
Brampton

Bowness-on-Solway
Port Carlisle
Rockcliffe Cross
Rockcliffe
Blackford
Longpark
Barclose
Oldwall
Irthington
Milton

93
Glasson
Drumburgh
Harker
Low Crosby
Wallhead
Walby
94
Kirkhouse

Bowstead Hill
Beaumont
Kingstown
High Crosby
Newby East
Low Gettbridge
Hallbank

Anthorn
Whitrigg
North End
Cargo
Grinsdale
Houghton
Linstock
Little Corby
Edmond Castle
Hayton
Farlam

Angerton
Whitrigglees
West End
Monkhill
Kirkandrews upon Eden
Stanwix
Warwick Bridge
Corby Hill
Talkin

Kirkbride
Studholme
Kirkbampton
Bow B5307
CARLISLE
Belle Vue
Warwick
Burnrigg
Scotby
How Mill
Castle Carrock

Powhill
Laythes
Oughterby
Little Bampton
Morton
Harraby
43
Fenton Heads Nook
Faugh
B6413

Salt Cotes
Newton Arlosh
Wampool
Great Orton
Newby West
Newby Cross
A6
M6
Wetheral
Great Corby
Wetheral Priory Gatehouse

2
Biglands
Aikton
3
ggonby
Orton Rigg
4
Upperby
Carleton
Cumwhinton
5

A595

River Laggan

490
BEINN BHEIGEIR

V Port Askaig · Kennacraig

Rudha Liath
Ardtalla

454
BEINN URARAIDH
Loch Uraraidh

Claggain
Bay

Tarbert

A846

B8016

Glenegedale

L a g g a n

Islay
(Port Ellen)

Kintour

Kildalton
Cross

Ardmore
Point

V

Ardaily

GIGHA

B a y

112

346
BEINN SHOLUM

113

Ardminish

Achamore

Eilean
a' Chuirn

Rudha Mòr

Port
Ellen

Port Ellen · Kennacraig

5

165
MAOL BUIDHE

Ardbeg
Lagavulin

A846

Rudha na
Gainmhich

Cara

T H E   O A

Risabus

Laphroaig

Texa

Lower
Killeyan

Kilnaughton Bay

Kinnabus
American
Monument

Loch
Kinnabus

MULL
OF OA

4

Rudha nan Leacan

Glenacardoc
Poi

Gle

Bellochantuy Bay

3

0   1   2   3   4   5 miles

0   1   2   3   4   5   6   7 kilometres

Kil

Machrihanish
Bay

Machrihanish

2

Drumlem

Earadale Point

385
THE
STATE

446
CNOC
MOY

Dalsmeran

Glen Break

1

Strone Glen

BEINN NA LICE
428

Carskey

MULL OF KINTYRE

Borgadelmo

Ballycastle · Ca
(Summer

0

3                    4                    5                    6

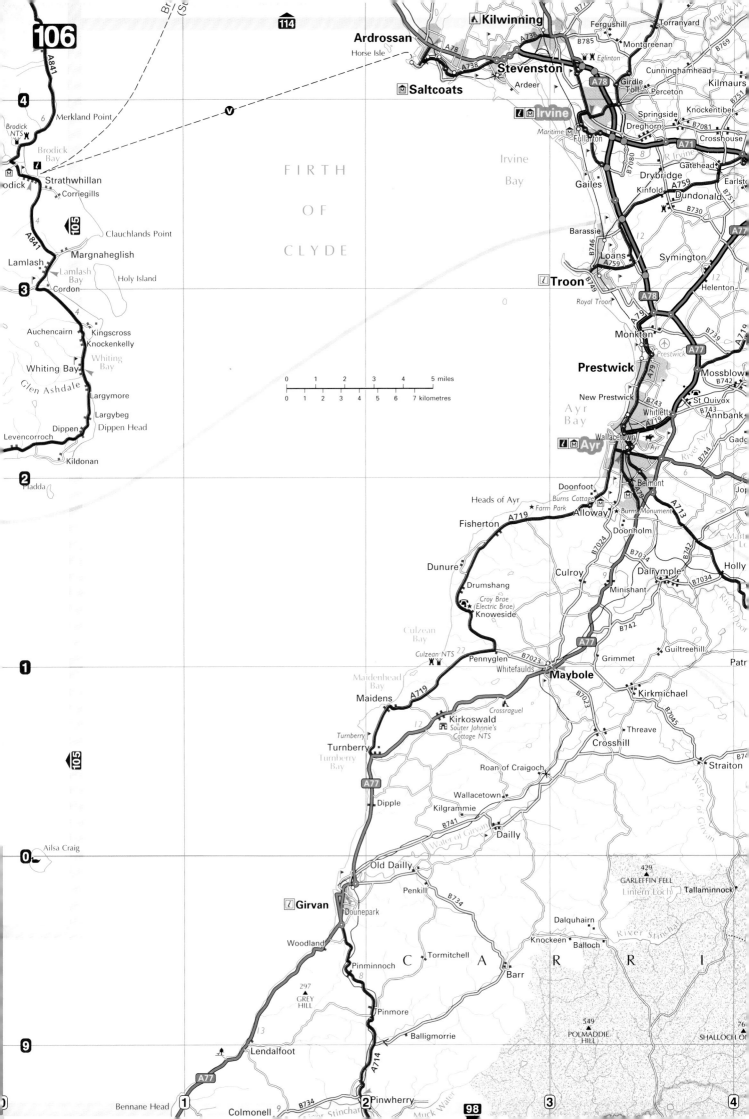

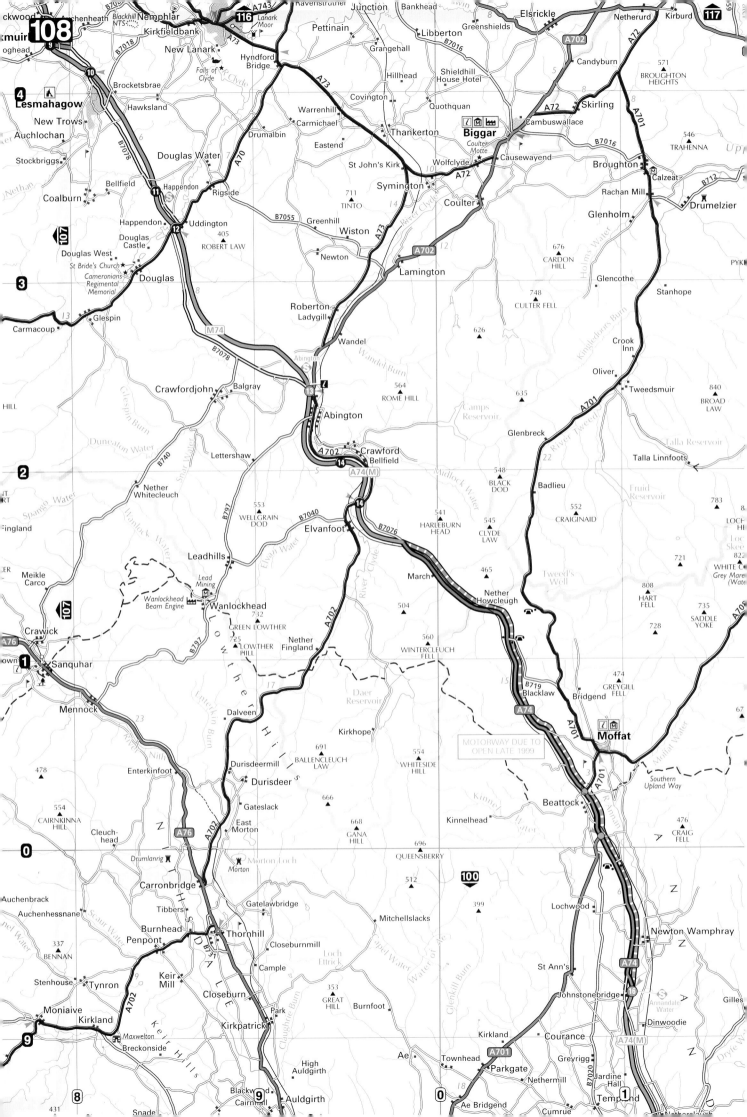

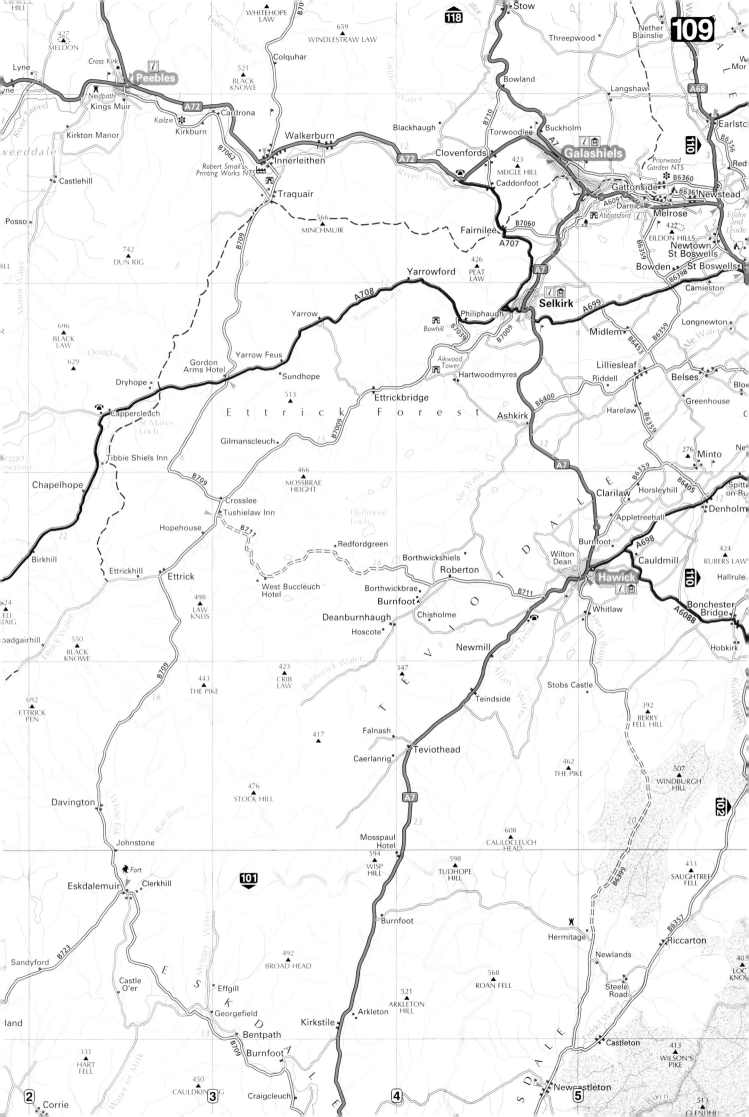

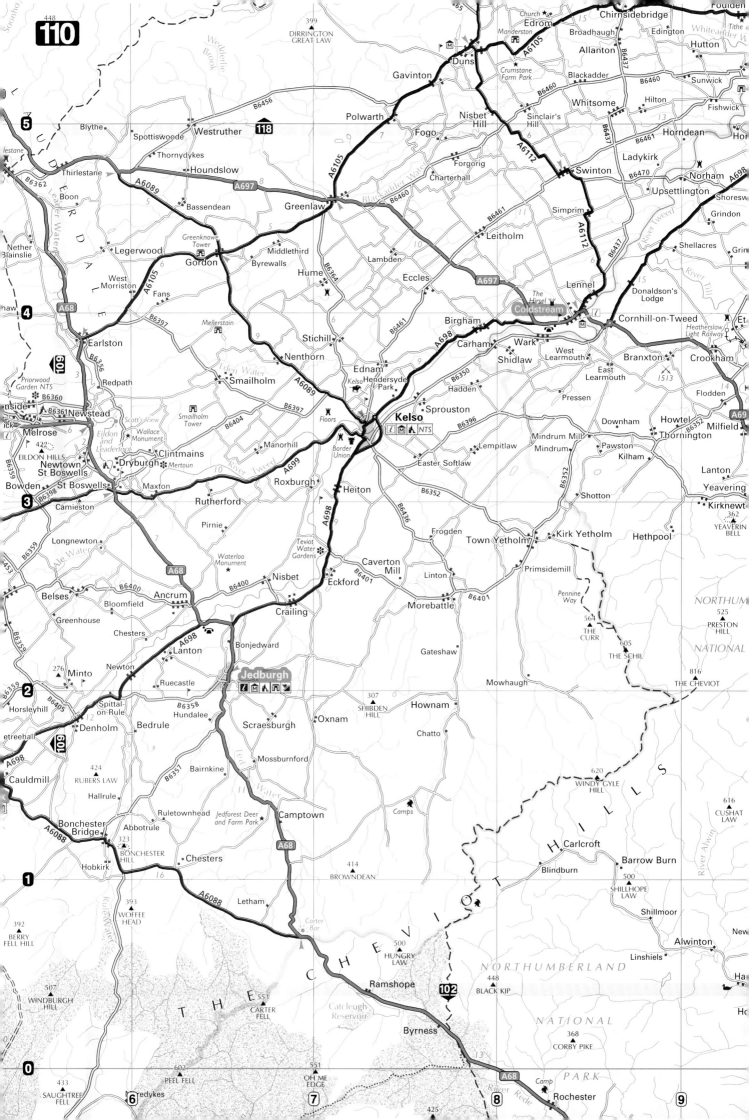

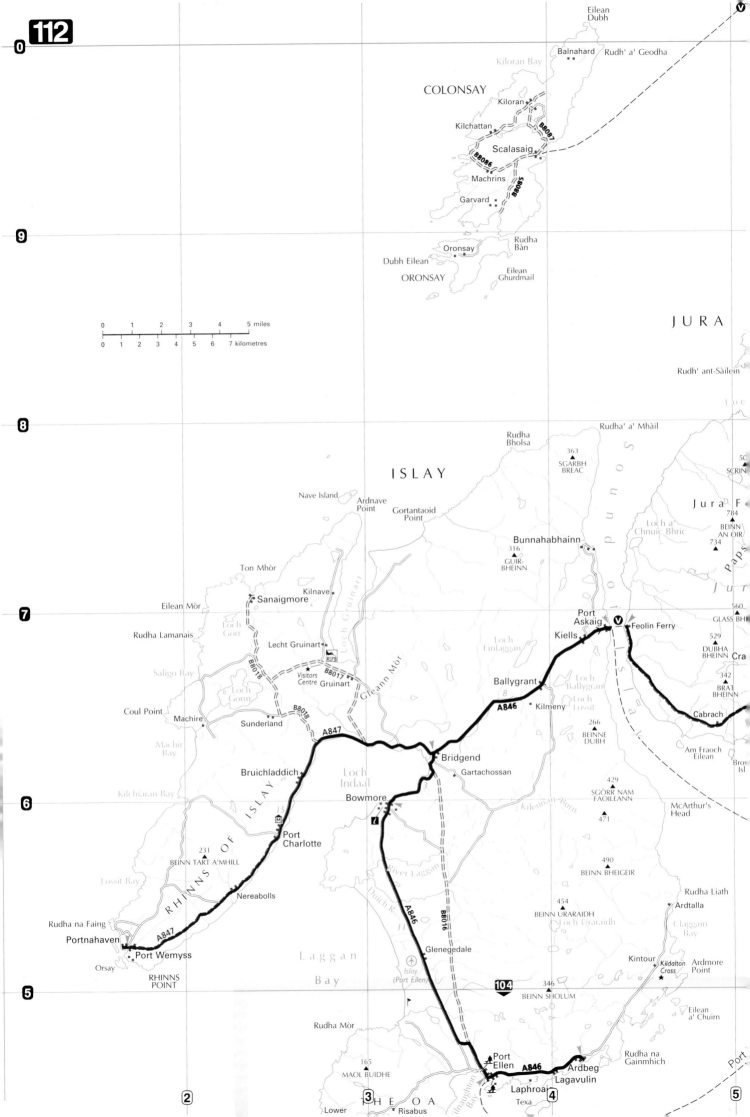

0

9

8

7

6

5

**COLONSAY**

Eilean
Dubh

Balnahard

Rudh' a' Geodha

Kiloran Bay

Kiloran

Kilchattan

B8087

Scalasaig

B8086

Machrins

B8085

Garvard

Rudha
Bàn

Oronsay

Dubh Eilean

**ORONSAY**

Eilean
Ghurdmail

V

J U R A

Rudh' ant-Sàilein

Loc

0    1    2    3    4    5 miles

0  1  2  3  4  5  6  7 kilometres

Rudha
Bholsa

Rudha' a' Mhàil

363
SGARBH
BREAC

5C
SCRIN

**ISLAY**

J u r a  F

784
BEINN
AN OIR

Nave Island

Ardnave
Point

Gortantaoid
Point

Bunnahabhainn

316
GUIR-
BHEINN

Loch a'
Chnuic Bhric

734

Ton Mhòr

Kilnave

Sanaigmore

Eilean Mòr

Rudha Lamanais

Loch
Gorr

Lecht Gruinart

RSPB

B8017
Gruinart

Gleann Mòr

Loch
Finlaggan

Port
Askaig

Kiells

V

Feolin Ferry

560
GLASS BH

529
DUBHA
BHEINN    Cra

Saligo Bay

B8018

Visitors
Centre

Loch
Gorm

Ballygrant

Loch
Ballygrant

A846

Kilmeny

Loch
Lossit

342
BRAT
BHEINN

Cabrach

Coul Point

Machire

Sunderland

B8018

A847

266
BEINNE
DUBH

Am Fraoch
Eilean

Machir
Bay

Bridgend

Gartachossan

429
SGORR NAM
FAOILEANN

Bros
Isl

Kilchiaran Bay

Bruichladdich

Loch
Indaal

Bowmore

Kilennan Burn

McArthur's
Head

471

231
BEINN TART A'MHILL

Port
Charlotte

M

i

490
BEINN BHEIGEIR

Lossit Bay

River Laggan

Rudha Liath

Ardtalla

Nereabolls

Duich R.

A846

B8016

454
BEINN URARAIDH

Loch Uraraidh

Claggan
Bay

Rudha na Faing

Portnahaven

A847

Port Wemyss

Orsay

RHINNS
POINT

L a g g a n

B a y

Glenegedale

Islay
(Port Ellen)

104
BEINN SHOLUM

346

Kintour

Kildalton
Cross

Ardmore
Point

Rudha Mòr

165
MAOL BUIDHE

R H I N N S   O F   I S L A Y

Eilean
a' Chuirn

Port
Ellen

A846

Ardbeg
Lagavulin

Laphroar

Texa

Rudha na
Gainmhich

Port

Lower
Risabus

P H E  O A

2        3        4        5

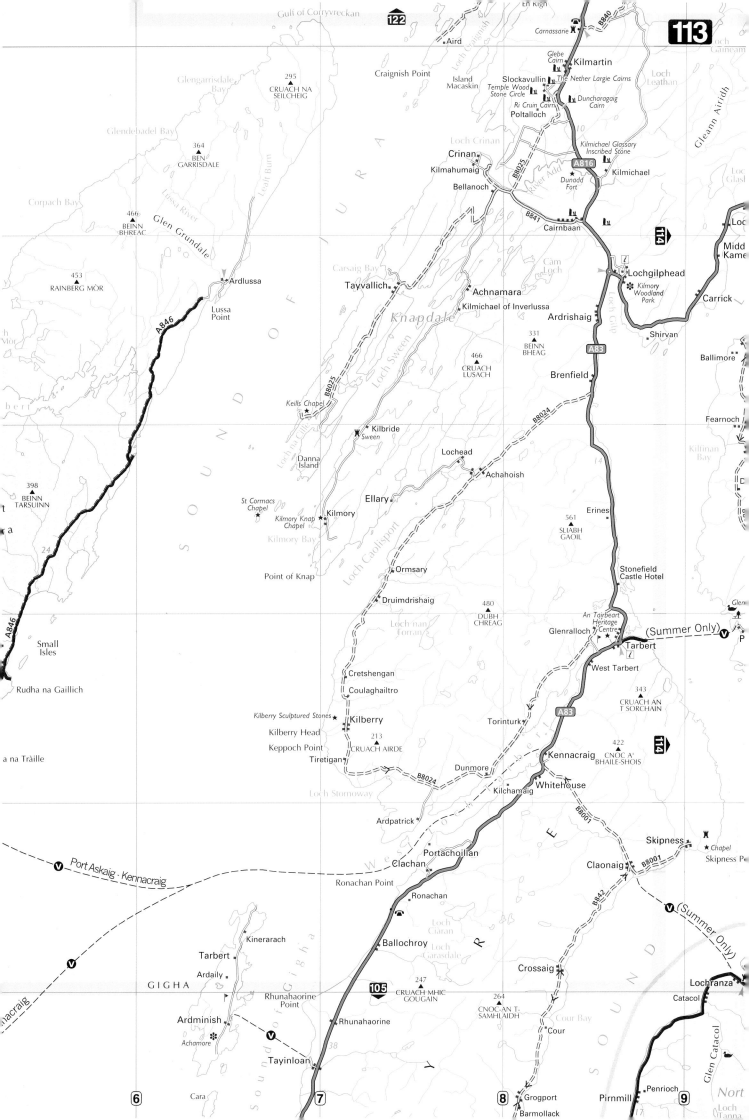

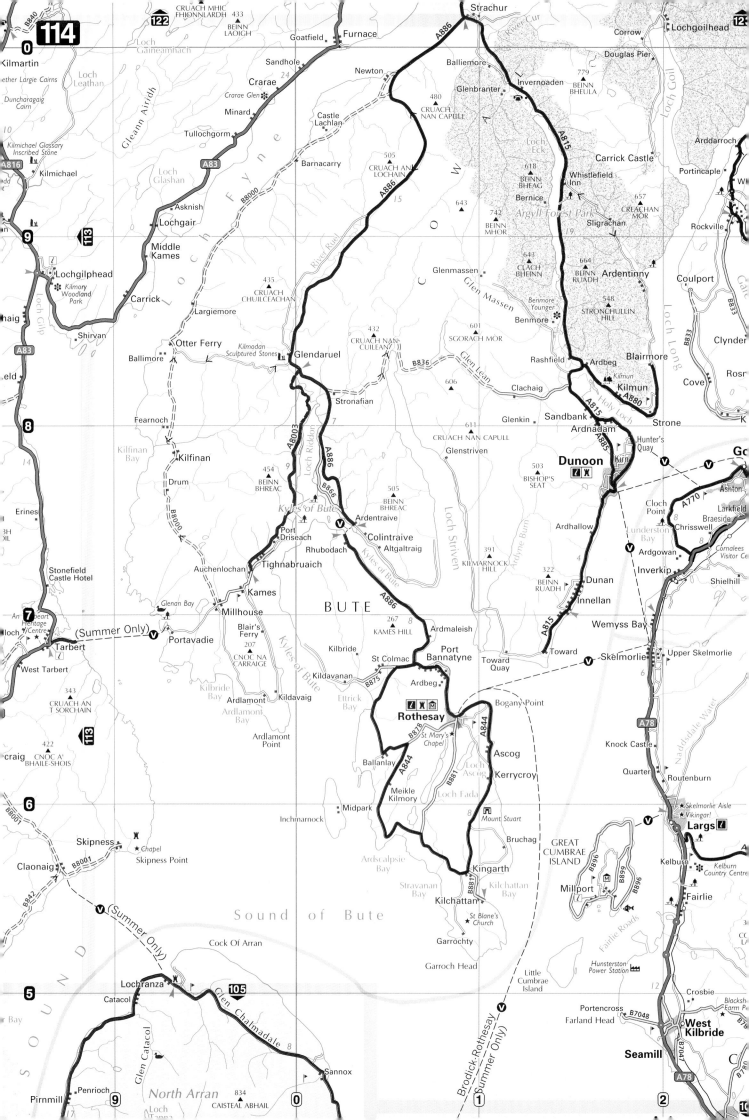

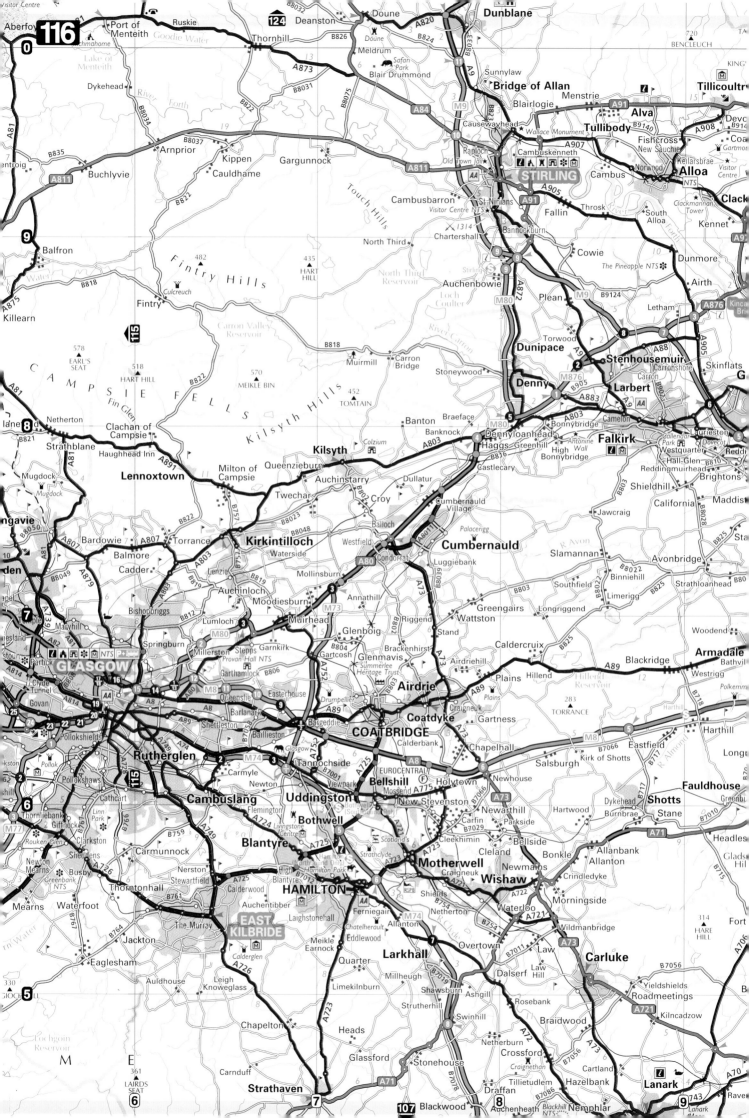

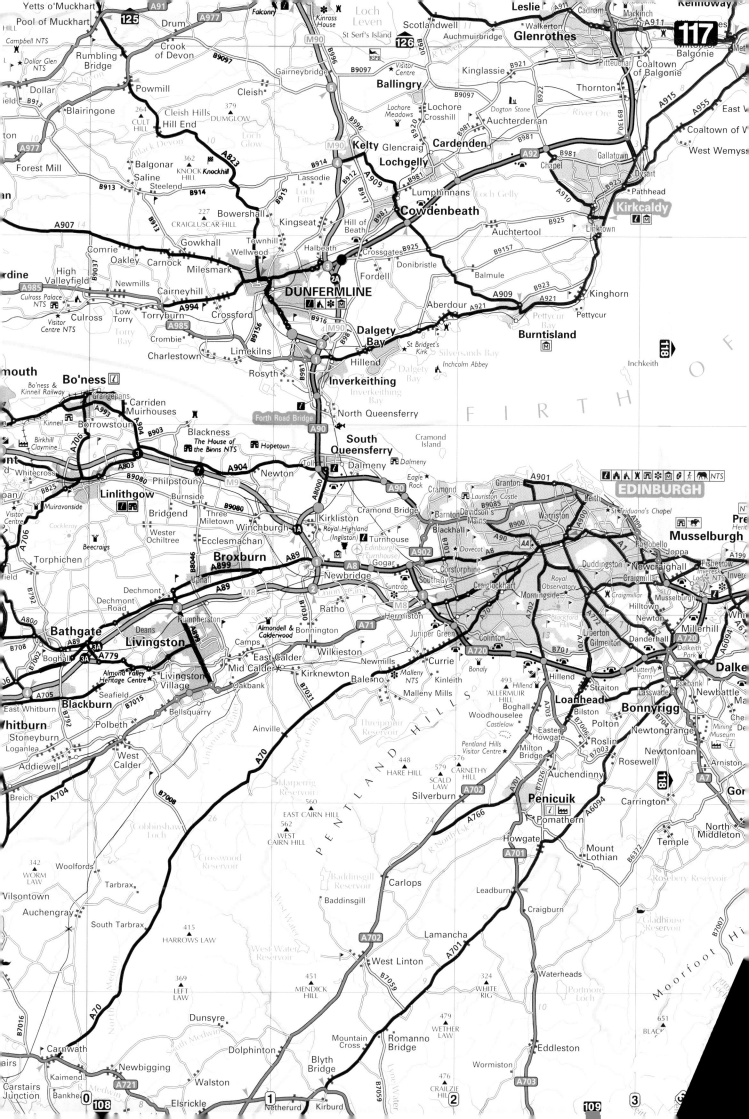

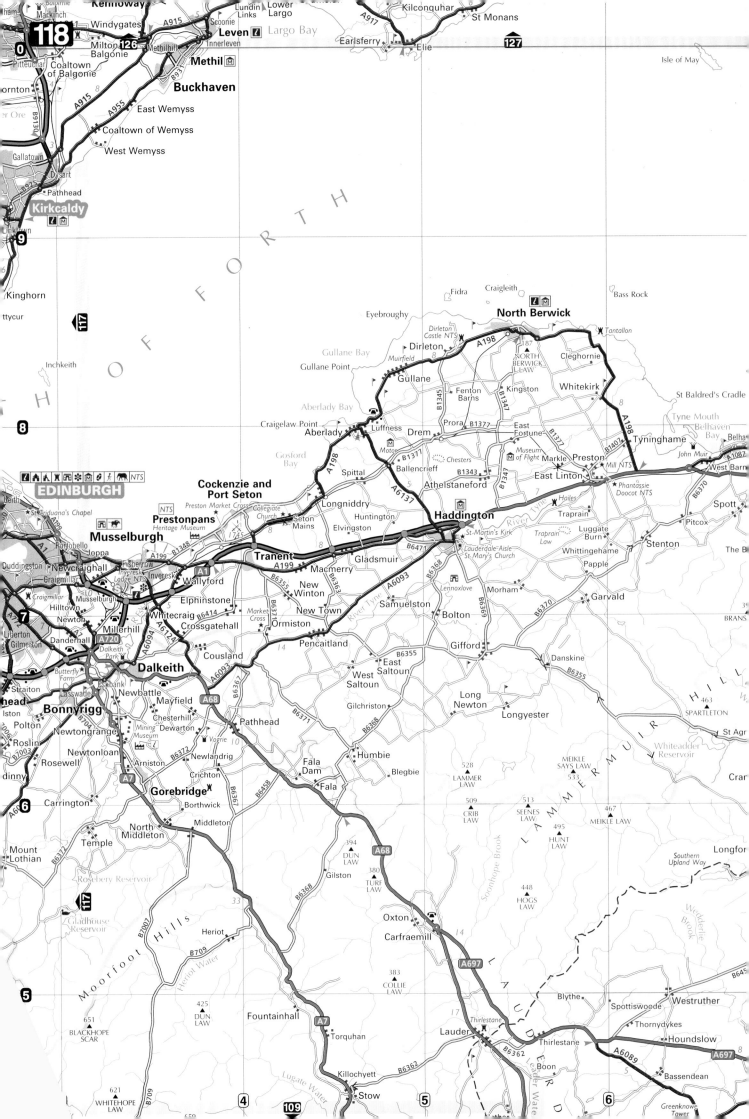

127

0 1 2 3 4 5 miles
0 1 2 3 4 5 6 7 kilometres

nbar 🛈

Broxburn
Barns Ness
1650
East Barns
A1
Chapel Point
Skateraw
Torness Power Station
Thorntonloch
Crowhill
Innerwick
Reed
Point
Dunglass
Collegiate
Church
Cove
Pease
Bay
Siccar
Point
Fast Castle Head
Cockburnspath
319
COCKLAW
HILL
Oldhamstocks
A1107
196
BROWN
RIG
ST ABB'S HEAD
Ecclaw
391
HEART
LAW
Southern
Upland Way
Butterdean
Grantshouse
St Abbs
Coldingham
Coldingham
Bay
Quixwood
Houndwood
Heugh
Head
Cairncross
Eyemouth 🛈 🏛
Abbey St Bathans
262
HORSELEY HILL
B6438
A1107
A1
Edin's
Hall Broch
14
B6438
Reston
Ayton
Burnmouth
Ellemford
325
COCKBURN
LAW
Auchencrow
Whitchester
Marygold
B6355
B6112
Lintlaw
Lamberton
Marshall Meadows Bay
399
RRINGTON
REAT LAW
B6365
Primrosehill
Preston
B6437
B6355
Chirnside
Foulden
1333
North Northumberland Heritage Coast
Cumledge
Church
Manderston
Edrom
15
Chirnsidebridge
Broadhaugh
Edington
Tithe Barn
A6105
Berwick-upon-Tweed
A6105
Gavinton
Duns
Crumstane
Farm Park
Allanton
Hutton
Barracks
Town Ramparts 🛈 🏛
Polwarth
Fogo
Blackadder
B6437
Sunwick
Paxton
B6461
Tweedmouth
Spittal
110
Nisbet
Hill
Sinclair's
Hill
B6460
Whitsome
Hilton
Fishwick
Loanend
Paxton
East
Ord
Huds
Head
Gavinton
7
B6112
Horndean
B6461
Horncliffe
111
Scremerston
Charterhall
Forgorig
Ladykirk
Murton
Unthank
A1
enlaw
A6105
B6460
Simprim
A6112
Swinton
B6470
Norham
A698
Thornton
Cheswick
7
8
9
Upsettlington
Shoreswood
Grindon
West Allerdean
Ancroft
0
B6525
Haggerston
Leitholm
B6461
Shellacres
Felkington
B6354
Goswick

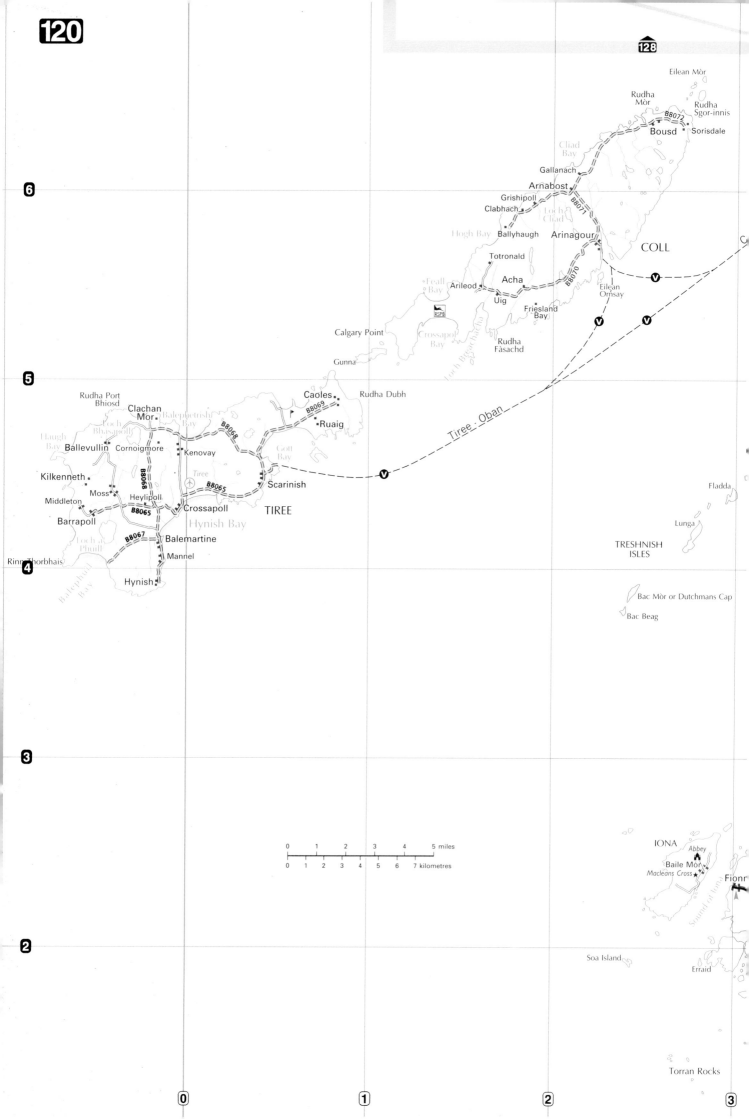

128

**6**

Eilean Mòr

Rudha Mòr

Rudha Sgor-innis

B8072

Bousd  Sorisdale

Cliad Bay

Gallanach

Arnabost

Grishipoll

Clabhach

Loch Cliad

B8071

Hogh Bay  Ballyhaugh  Arinagour  COLL  C

Totronald

Acha

Arileod  B8070

Uig  Eilean Ornsay

RSPB  Friesland Bay

Feall Bay

Calgary Point  Crossapol Bay

Gunna  Rudha Fàsachd

Loch Bgeuchachd

**5**

Rudha Dubh

Caoles

Rudha Port Bhiosd

Clachan Mor  Balephetrish Bay  B8069

B8068  Ruaig

Loch Bhasapoll  Tiree : Oban

Haugh Bay  Ballevullin  Cornoigmore  Kenovay

Gott Bay

Kilkenneth  B8068  Tiree

Moss  Heylipoll  B8065  Scarinish

Middleton  Crossapoll

Barrapoll  B8065  TIREE  V

Rinn Thorbhais  B8067  Balemartine

Loch a' Phuill  Hynish Bay

Mannel

**4**  Balephuil Bay  Hynish

Fladda

Lunga

TRESHNISH ISLES

Bac Mòr or Dutchmans Cap

Bac Beag

**3**

| 0 | 1 | 2 | 3 | 4 | 5 miles |
|---|---|---|---|---|---|

| 0 | 1 | 2 | 3 | 4 | 5 | 6 | 7 kilometres |
|---|---|---|---|---|---|---|---|

IONA

Abbey

Baile Mòr

Macleans Cross  Fionn

**2**

Soa Island

Sound of Iona

Erraid

Torran Rocks

**0**  **1**  **2**  **3**

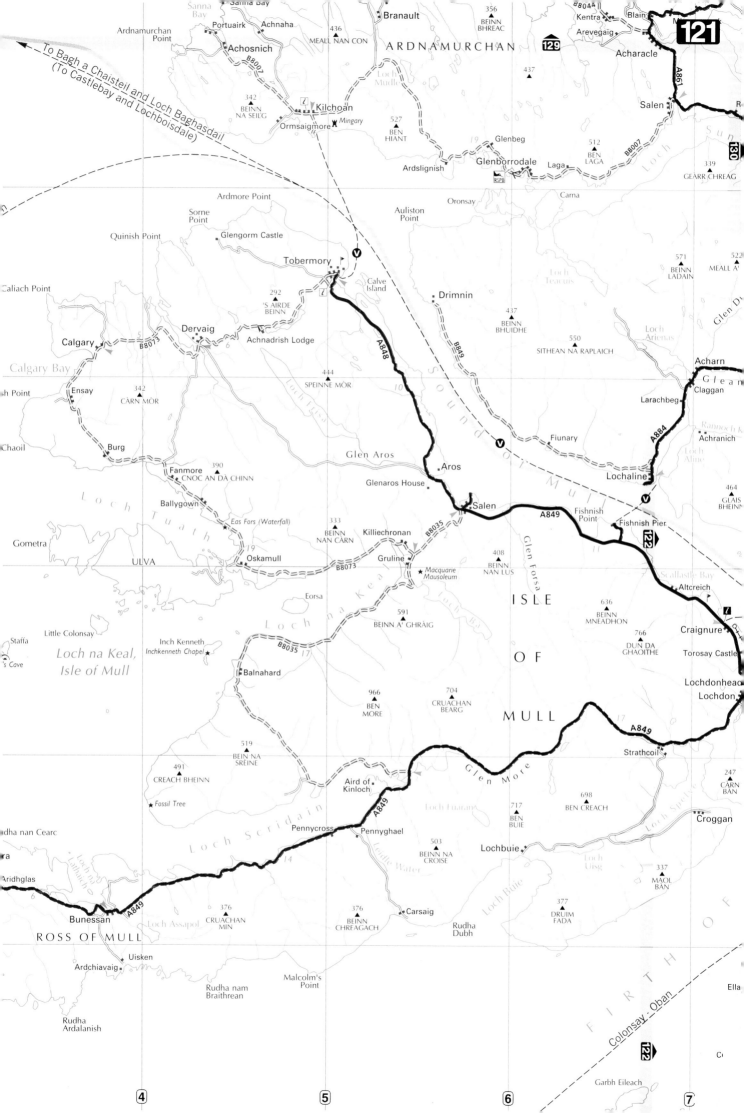

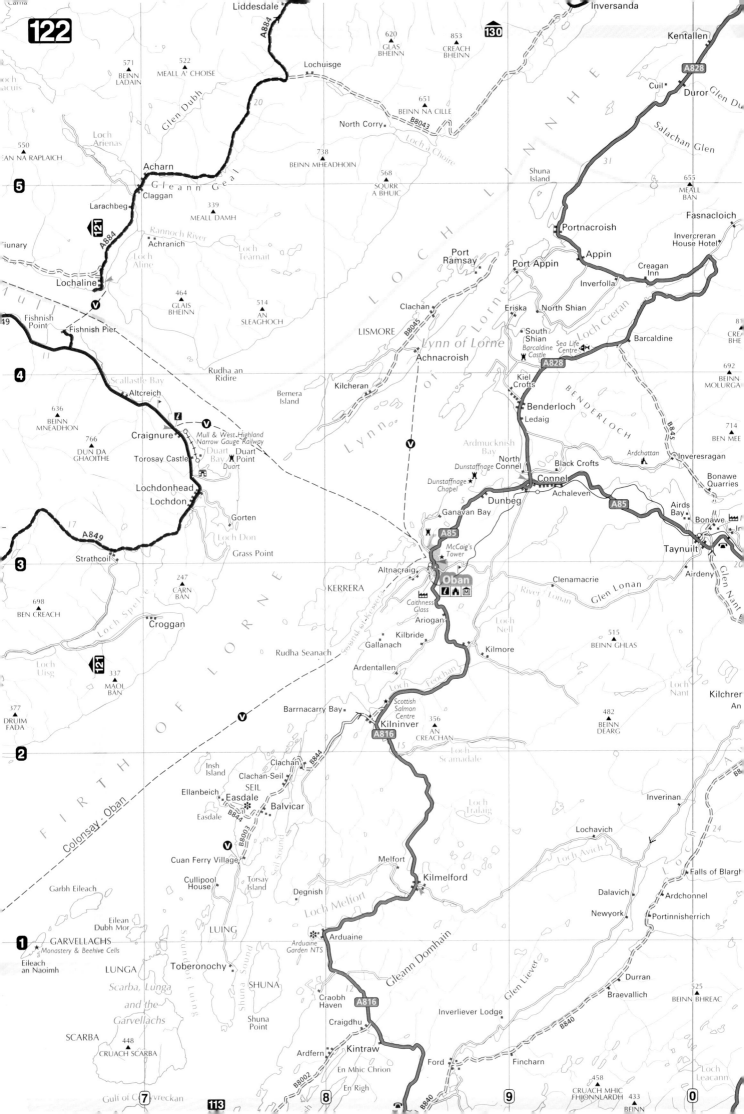

Liddesdale
Inversanda
Kentallen
Cuil
Duror
A828
Glen Du
A884
Lochuisge
130
GLAS BHEINN 620
CREACH BHEINN 853
BEINN LADAIN 571
MEALL A' CHOISE 522
Glen Dubh
651
BEINN NA CILLE
North Corry
B8043
Loch a' Choire
Shuna Island
MEALL BAN 655
FASNACLOICH
550
AN NA RAPLAICH
Loch Arienas
Acharn
BEINN MHEADHOIN 738
Portnacroish
Invercreran House Hotel
**5**
Claggan
Gleann Geal
SQURR A BHUIC 568
Appin
Creagan Inn
339
Larachbeg
MEALL DAMH
Port Ramsay
Inverfolla
121
A884
Achranich
Rannoch River
Loch Tearnait
Port Appin
North Shian
Loch Aline
Clachan
Eriska
iunary
Lochaline
South Shian
Barcaldine
V
LISMORE
B8045
Kiel Crofts
BEINN MOLURGA 692
**4**
Fishnish Point
Fishnish Pier
GLAIS BHEINN 464
AN SLEAGHOCH 514
Kilcheran
Lynn of Lorne
Sea Life Centre
Barcaldine Castle
A828
Benderloch
BENDERLOCH
714 BEN MEE
49
Scallastle Bay
Altcreich
Rudha an Ridire
Bernera Island
Achnacroish
Ledaig
B845
636 BEINN MNEADHON
i
V
Ardmucknish Bay
Ardchattan
Inveresragan
Craignure
Mull & West Highland Narrow Gauge Railway
North Connel
Black Crofts
Bonawe Quarries
766 DUN DA GHAOITHE
Torosay Castle
Duart Bay
Duart Point
Dunstaffnage
Dunstaffnage Chapel
Connel
Achaleven
A85
Airds Bay
Bonawe
Lochdonhead
Duart
5
Dunbeg
Lochdon
Ganavan Bay
Taynuilt
3
Strathcoil
A849
Gorten
Loch Don
Grass Point
McCaig's Tower
Altnacraig
Oban
i
M
Clenamacrie
River Lonan
Glen Lonan
Airdeny
Glen Nant
247 CARN BAN
KERRERA
Caithness Glass
Ariogan
Loch Nell
BEINN GHLAS 515
698 BEN CREACH
Loch Spelve
Croggan
Rudha Seanach
Kilbride
Gallanach
Kilmore
Loch Nant
Kilchren
An
121
337 MAOL BAN
Ardentallen
Loch Feochan
BEINN DEARG 482
Loch Uisg
377 DRUIM FADA
V
Barrnacarry Bay
Scottish Salmon Centre
Kilninver
A816
356 AN CREACHAN
Loch Scamadale
**2**
Insh Island
Clachan
B844
Inverinan
Ellanbeich
Clachan-Seil
SEIL
Loch Tralaig
Easdale
Balvicar
Lochavich
GARVELLACHS
Colonsay - Oban
Easdale
B844
B8003
Loch Avich
Falls of Blargh
V
Cuan Ferry Village
Melfort
Cullipool House
Torsay Island
Degnish
Kilmelford
Dalavich
Ardchonnel
Newyork
Portinnisherrich
**1** GARVELLACHS
Monastery & Beehive Cells
Eileach an Naoimh
Eilean Dubh Mor
LUING
Loch Melfort
Arduaine
Arduaine Garden NTS
Gleann Domhain
Glen Liever
Durran
525 BEINN BHREAC
LUNGA
Scarba, Lunga and the Garvellachs
Toberonochy
SHUNA
Craobh Haven
A816
Inverliever Lodge
B840
Braevallich
SCARBA
448 CRUACH SCARBA
Shuna Point
Craigdhu
Kintraw
Ardfern
B8002
En Mhic Chrion
En Righ
Ford
Fincharn
458 CRUACH MHIC FHIONNLARDH 433
Loch Leacann
Gulf of Corryvreckan
7
113
8
B840
9
0

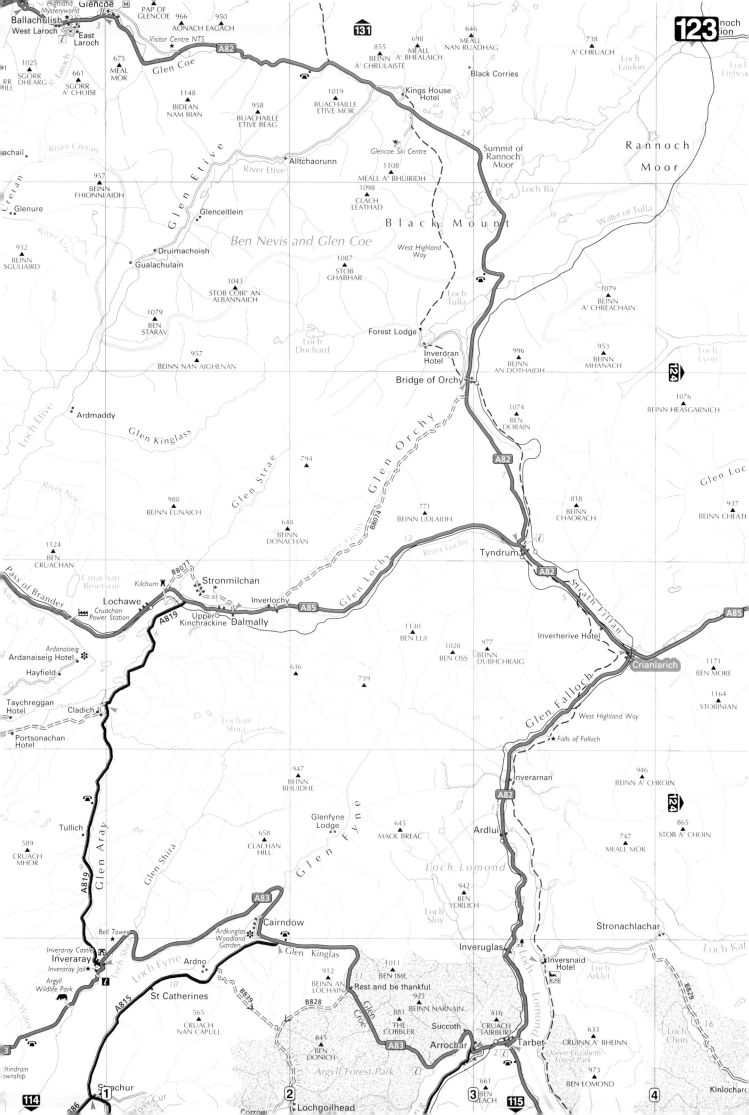

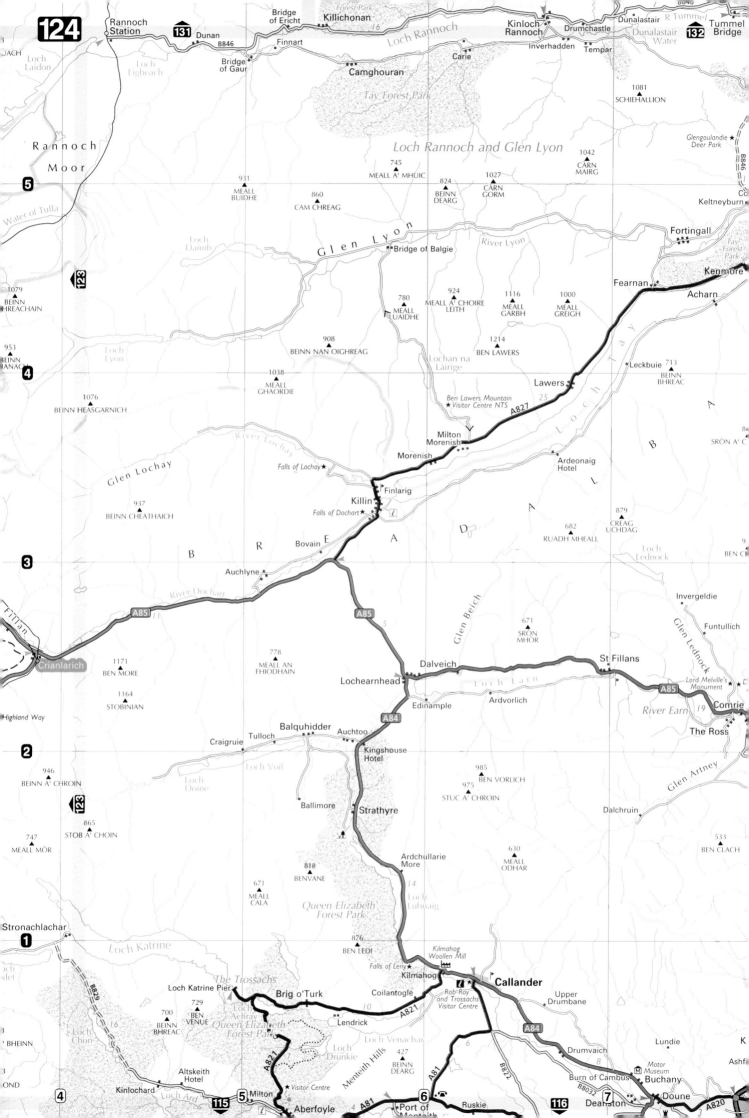

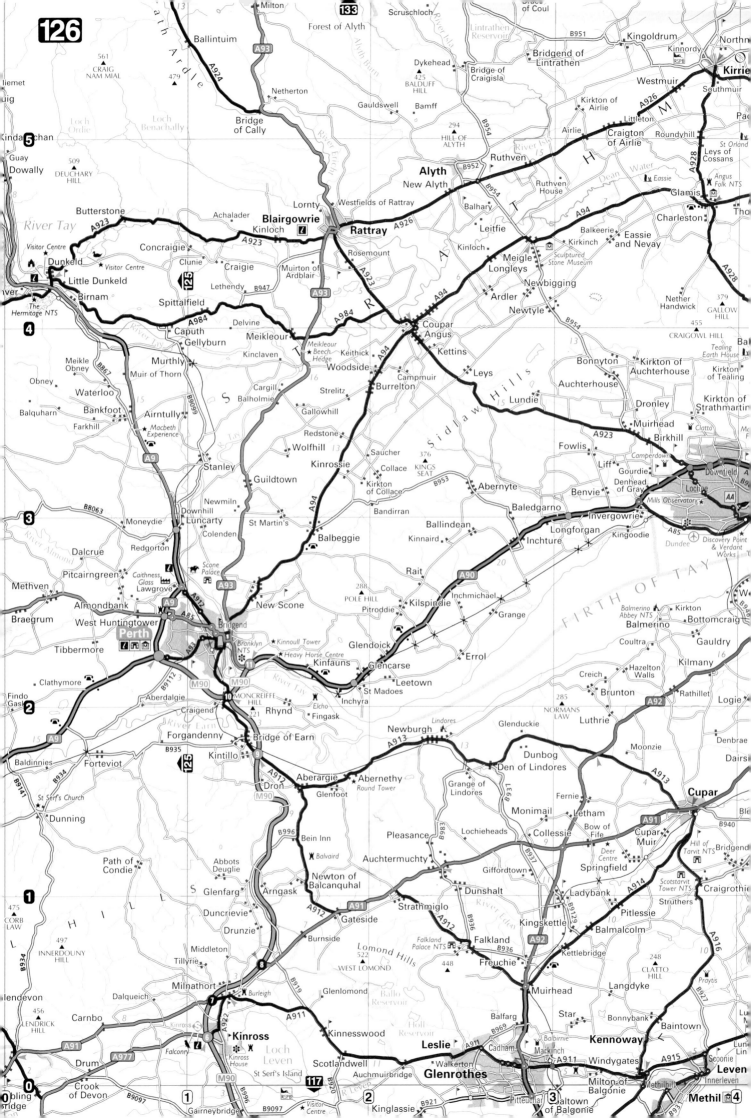

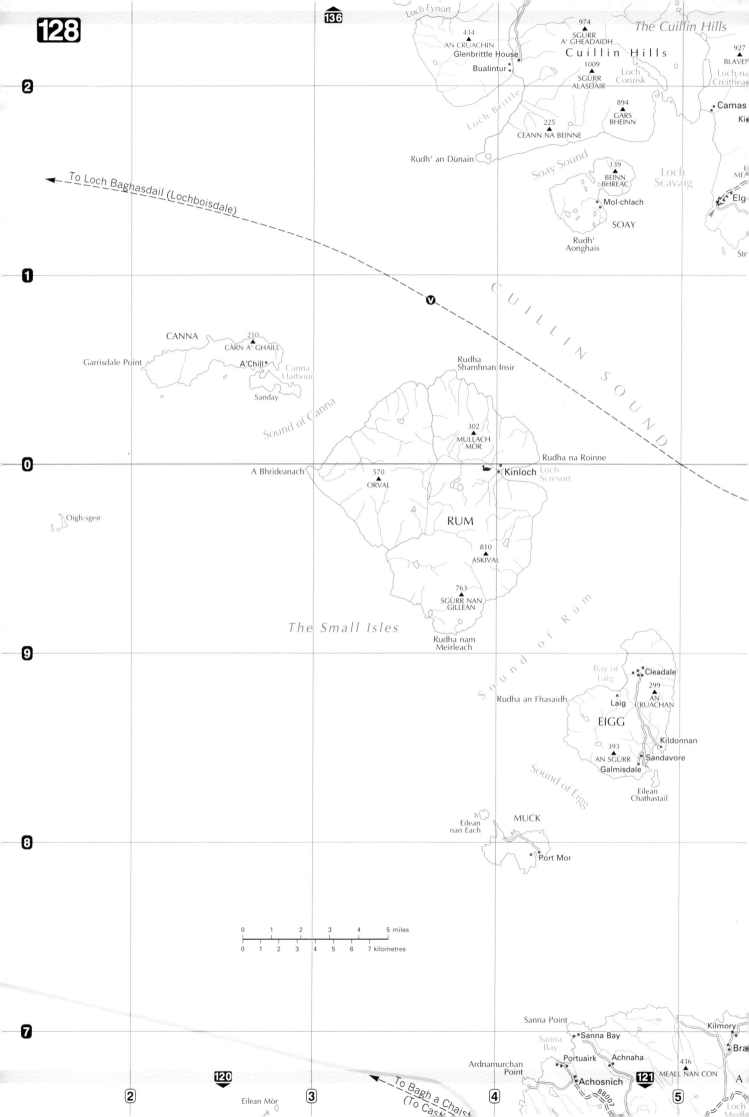

The Cuillin Hills

**2**

974
SGÙRR
A' GHEADAIDH

434
AN CRUACHIN

Glenbrittle House

Cuillin Hills

927
BLAVEN

Bualintur

1009
SGÙRR
ALASDAIR

Loch
Coruisk

Loch na
Crèitheac

894
GARS
BHEINN

Camas

225
CEANN NA BEINNE

Ki

Rudh' an Dùnain

Soay Sound

139
BEINN
BHREAC

Loch
Scavaig

E
MEA

Elg

Mol-chlach

To Loch Baghasdail (Lochboisdale)

SOAY

Rudh'
Aonghais

C U I L L I N   S O U N D

**1**

V

CANNA

210
CÀRN A' GHAILL

A'Chill

Rudha
Shamhnan Insir

Garrisdale Point

Canna
Harbour

Sanday

Sound of Canna

302
MULLACH
MÒR

Rudha na Roinne

**0**

A Bhrideanach

570
ORVAL

Kinloch

Loch
Scresort

Oigh-sgeir

RUM

810
ASKIVAL

Sound of Rum

763
SGÙRR NAN
GILLEAN

The Small Isles

Rudha nam
Meirleach

**9**

Bay of
Laig

Cleadale

299
AN
CRUACHAN

Rudha an Fhasaidh

Laig

EIGG

Kildonnan

393
AN SGÙRR

Sandavore

Galmisdale

Eilean
Chathastail

Sound of Eigg

MUCK

Eilean
nan Each

**8**

Port Mor

| 0 | 1 | 2 | 3 | 4 | 5 miles |
|---|---|---|---|---|---|
| 0 | 1 | 2 | 3 | 4 | 5 | 6 | 7 kilometres |

Sanna Point

**7**

Sanna
Bay

Sanna Bay

Kilmory

Bra

Ardnamurchan
Point

Portuairk

Achnaha

436
MEALL NAN CON

A

Achosnich

To Bagh a Chaisl
(To Cas

B8007

**120**

**121**

**2**

Eilean Mòr

**3**

**4**

**5**

Loch

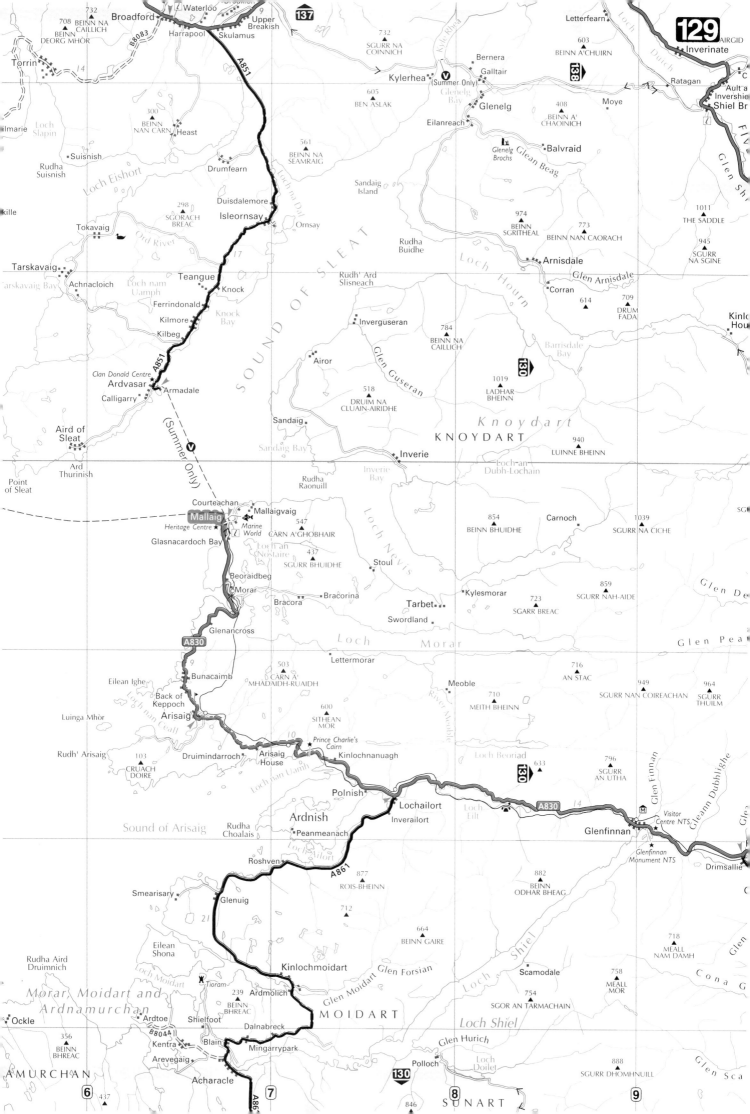

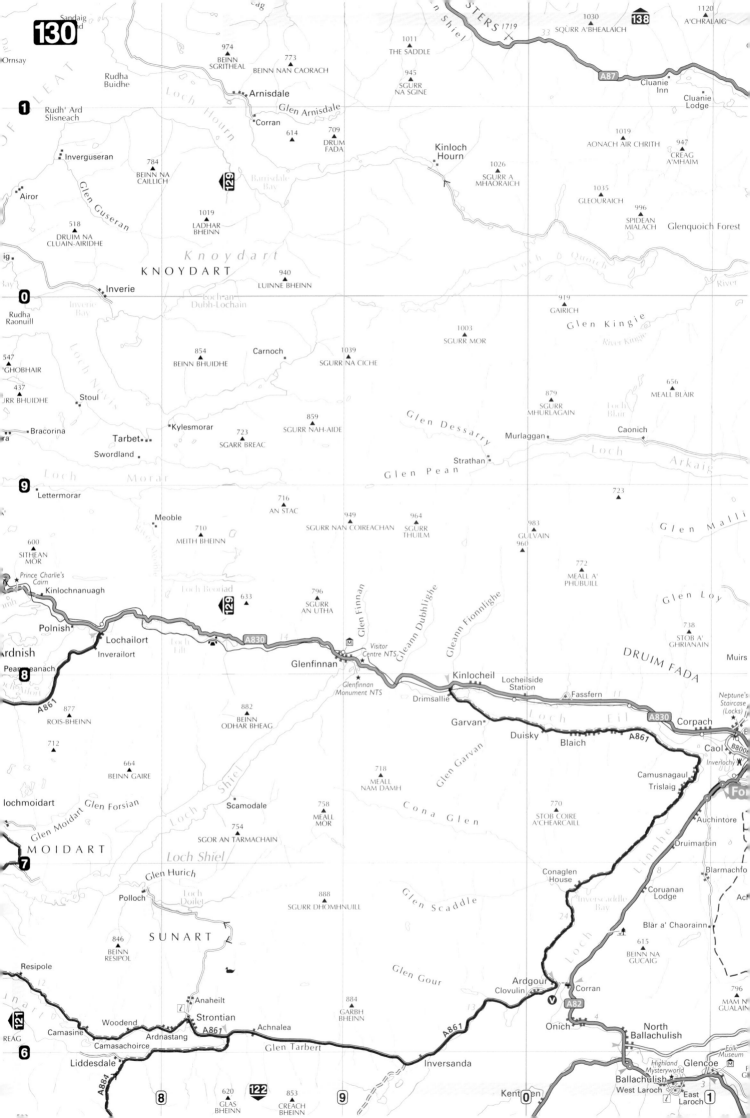

Ornsay

Sandaig

Rudha Buidhe

**1** Rudh' Ard Slisneach

Inverguseran

**0**

Rudha Raonuill

**547** 'GHOBHAIR

**437** URR BHUIDHE

Bracorina

**9** Lettermorar

**600** SITHEAN MOR

Prince Charlie's Cairn

Kinlochnanuagh

Polnish

rdnish

Pean meanach

**8**

A861

**877** ROIS-BHEINN

**712**

lochmoidart

Glen Moidart

Glen Forsian

**M O I D A R T**

**7**

Glen Hurich

Polloch

**121**

REAG

**6**

Resipole

**846** BEINN RESIPOL

Camasine

Woodend

Ardnastang

Camasachoirce

Liddesdale

A884

**8**

LOCH na LEAT

**974** BEINN SGRITHEAL

**773** BEINN NAN CAORACH

Arnisdale

Glen Arnisdale

Corran

**614**

**709** DRUM FADA

**784** BEINN NA CAILLICH

**129**

Barrisdale Bay

Loch Hourn

**518** DRUIM NA CLUAIN-AIRIDHE

Glen Guseran

Airor

ig

**1019** LADHAR BHEINN

*K n o y d a r t*

**K N O Y D A R T**

Inverie

Inverie Bay

Loch nan Dubh-Lochain

**940** LUINNE BHEINN

Stoul

Kylesmorar

Tarbet

Swordland

Loch Morar

Meoble

**710** MEITH BHEINN

River Meoble

Loch Beoraid

**633**

**129**

**796** SGURR AN UTHA

Loch Eilt

A830

**854** BEINN BHUIDHE

Carnoch

**1039** SGURR NA CICHE

**723** SGARR BREAC

**859** SGURR NAH-AIDE

**716** AN STAC

**949** SGURR NAN COIREACHAN

**964** SGURR THUILM

Glen Finnan

Glenfinnan

Glenfinnan Monument NTS

Visitor Centre NTS

Inverailort

Lochailort

**664** BEINN GAIRE

**882** BEINN ODHAR BHEAG

Scamodale

**754** SGOR AN TARMACHAIN

Loch Shiel

Loch Doilet

**888** SGURR DHOMHNUILL

**S U N A R T**

Anaheilt

Strontian

A861

Achnalea

**620** GLAS BHEINN

**122**

**853** CREACH BHEINN

**9**

*O N S T E R S* 1719

**1011** THE SADDLE

**945** SGURR NA SGINE

Kinloch Hourn

**1026** SGURR A MHAORAICH

Glen Kingie

**1003** SGURR MOR

**919** GAIRICH

River Kingie

Glen Dessarry

**879** SGURR MHURLAGAIN

Loch Blair

**656** MEALL BLAIR

Murlaggan

Caonich

Strathan

Glen Pean

Loch Arkaig

**723**

Glen Malli

**983** GULVAIN **960**

**772** MEALL A' PHUBUILL

Gleann Dubhlighe

Gleann Fionnlighe

Kinlocheil

Locheilside Station

Drimsallie

Garvan

Glen Garvan

Duisky

Blaich

Loch Eil

A861

**718** MEALL NAM DAMH

Cona Glen

Glen Scaddle

Conaglen House

**770** STOB COIRE A'CHEARCAILL

Glen Gour

Ardgour

Clovulin

**V**

A82

Onich

Inversanda

Kent llen

**0**

**1030** SQÙRR A'BHEALAICH

**138**

**1120** A'CHRALAIG

A87

Cluanie Inn

Cluanie Lodge

**1019** AONACH AIR CHRITH

**947** CREAG A'MHAIM

**1035** GLEOURAICH

**996** SPIDEAN MIALACH

Glenquoich Forest

Loch Quoich

River

**DRUIM FADA**

Muirs

Glen Loy

**738** STOB A' GHRIANAIN

Neptune's Staircase (Locks)

A830

Corpach

Caol

B800

Inverlochy

Camusnagaul

Trislaig

**For**

Auchintore

Druimarbin

Coruanan Lodge

Loch Linnhe

Blarmachfo

Blàr a' Chaorainn

**615** BEINN NA GUCAIG

Ac

Corran

North Ballachulish

Highland Mysteryworld

Folk Museum

Glencoe

Ballachulish

West Laroch

East Laroch

**796** MAM N GUALAIN

**1**

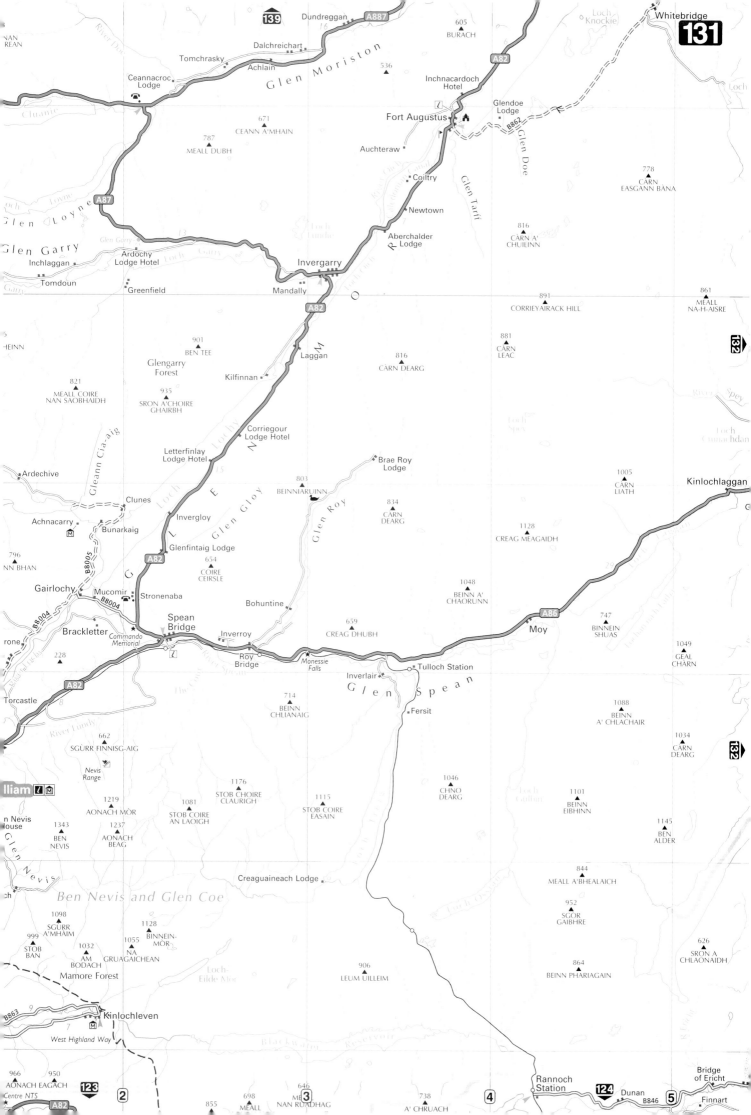

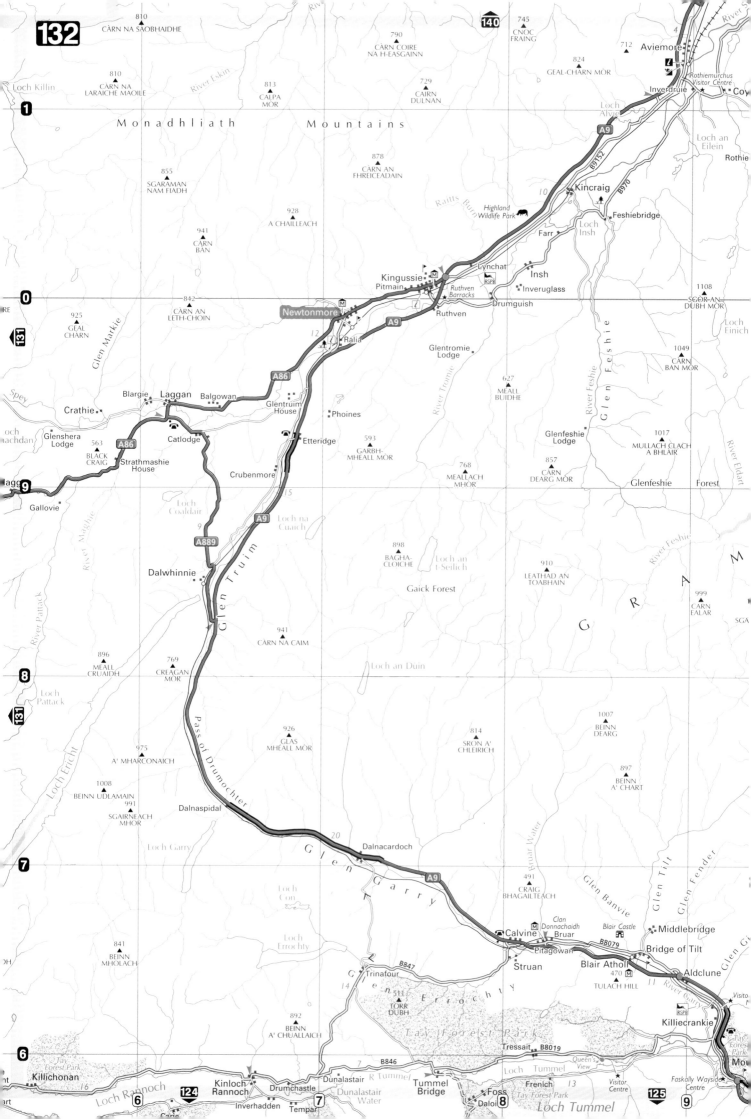

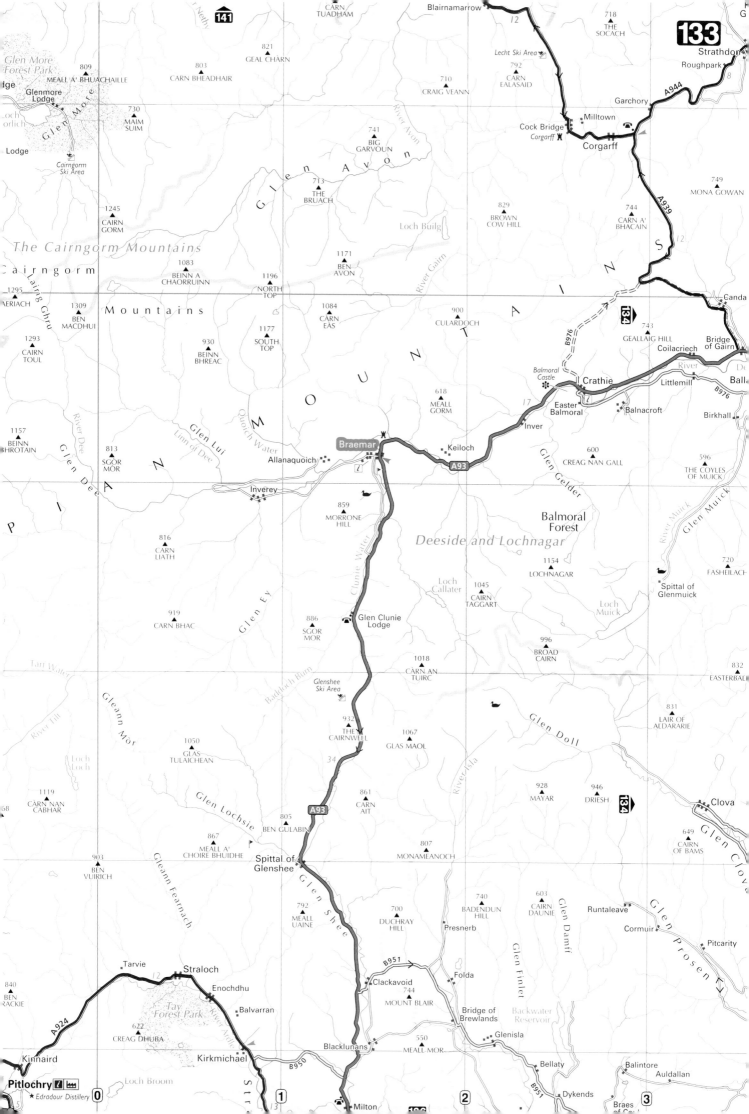

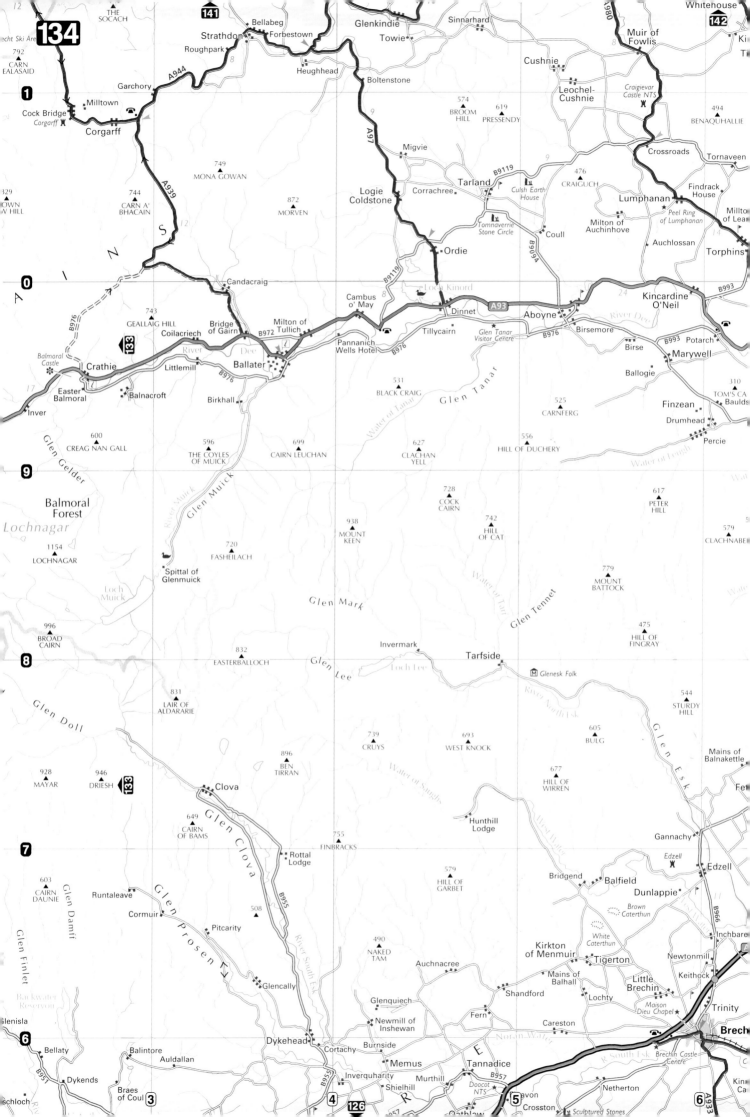

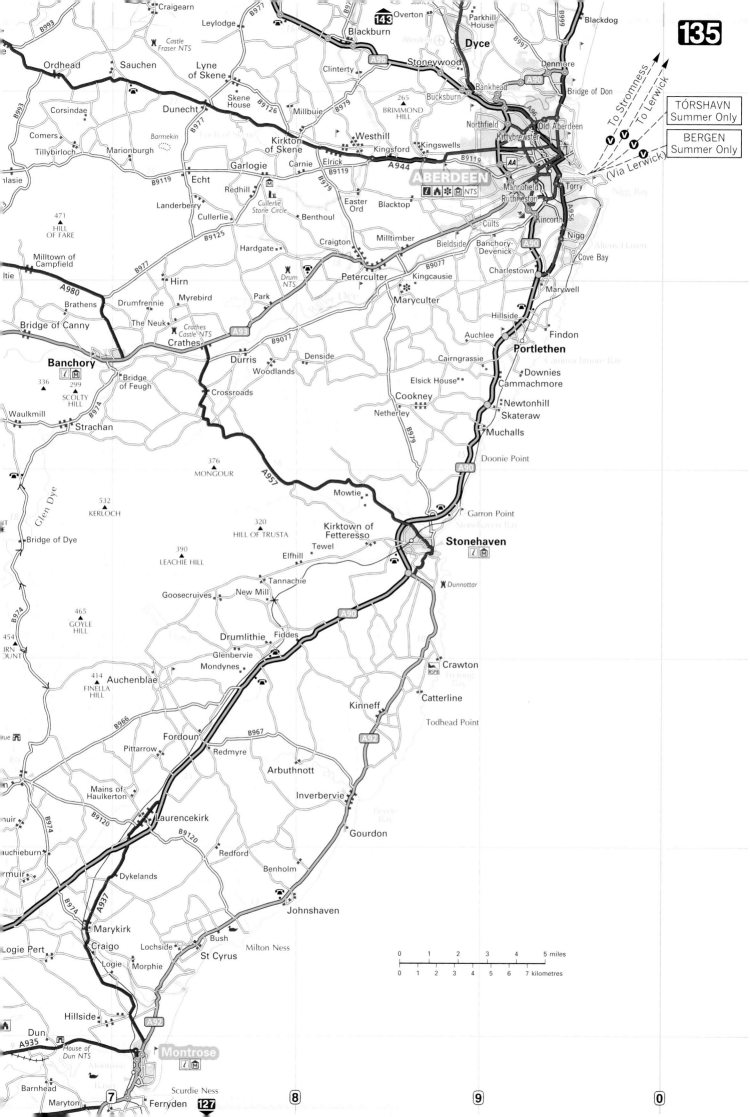

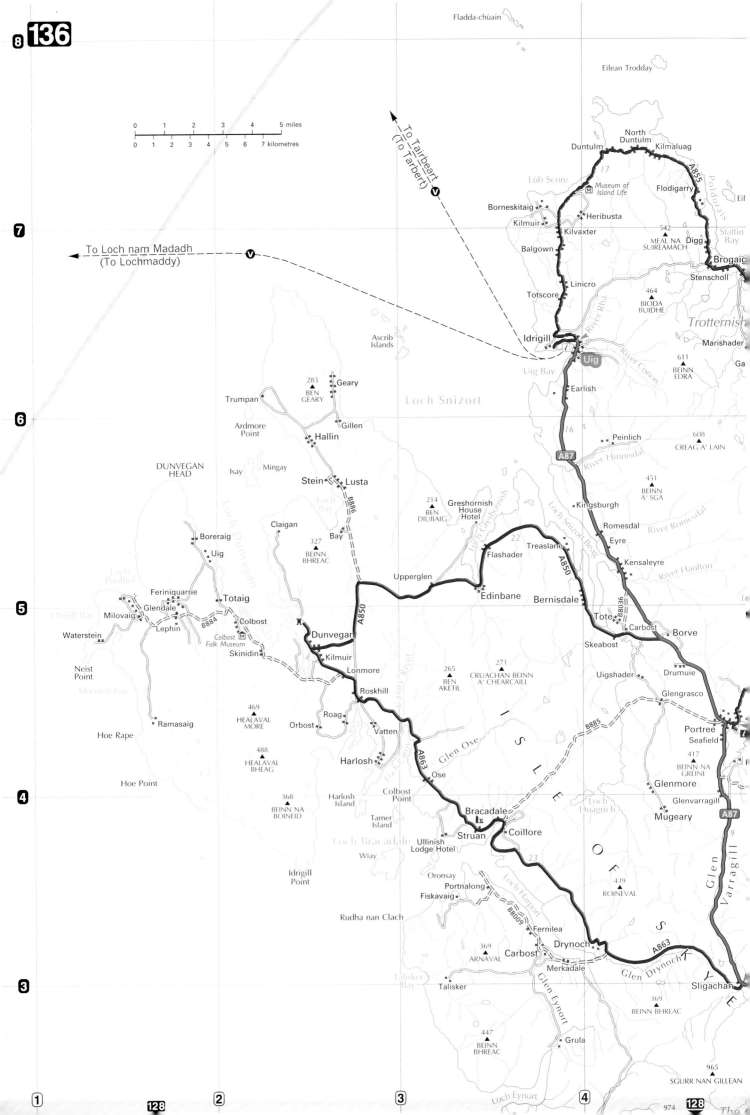

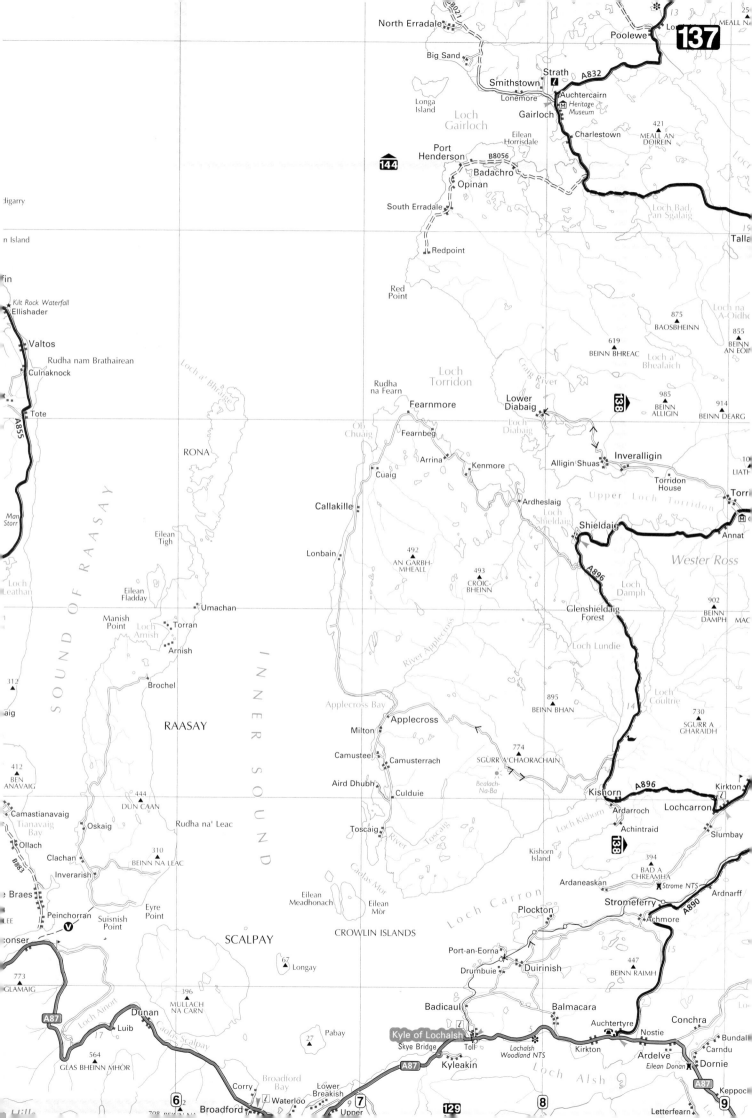

North Erradale

Poolewe

Big Sand

Strath
A832
Smithstown
Lonemore
Auchtercairn
Heritage
Museum
Gairloch

Longa
Island
Loch
Gairloch

Charlestown
421
MEALL AN
DOIREIN

Eilean
Horrisdale

Port
Henderson
B8056
Badachro
Opinan

Loch Bad
an Sgalaig

South Erradale

Talla

Redpoint

Red
Point

875
BAOSBHEINN

Loch na
A-Oidhe

855
BEINN
AN EOII

619
BEINN BHREAC
Loch a'
Bhealaich

Kilt Rock Waterfall
Ellishader

Loch
Torridon

Rudha
na Fearn

985
BEINN
ALLIGIN

914
BEINN DEARG

Lower
Diabaig

Valtos

Rudha nam Brathairean

Culnaknock

Loch a' Bhraige

Fearnmore

Loch
Diabaig

Fearnbeg

Inveralligin

Tote

RONA

Arrina

Kenmore

All.gin Shuas
Torridon
House

Torr

10
LIATH

A855

Cuaig

Upper Loch Torridon

Callakille

Ardheslaig

Loch
Shieldaig

Shieldaig
Annat

Wester Ross

Man
Storr

Eilean
Tigh

Lonbain

492
AN GARBH-
MHEALL

A896

Loch
Damph

902
BEINN
DAMPH
MAC

Loch
Leathan

Eilean
Fladday

493
CROIC-
BHEINN

Glenshieldaig
Forest

SOUND OF RAASAY

Manish
Point
Loch
Arnish

Umachan

Torran

Loch Lundie

730
SGURR A
GHARAIDH

aig

312

Arnish

River Applecross

895
BEINN BHAN

Loch
Coultrie

Brochel

14

RAASAY

Applecross Bay

774
SGURR A'CHAORACHAIN

INNER SOUND

412
BEN
ANAVAIG

444
DUN CAAN

Applecross
Milton

Camusteel
Camusterrach

Bealach-
Na-Ba

Kishorn

A896

Kirkton

Camastianavaig
Tianavaig
Bay

Oskaig

Rudha na' Leac

Aird Dhubh
Culduie

Ardarroch
Lochcarron

Ollach

310
BEINN NA LEAC

Toscaig

River Toscaig

Achintraid

Slumbay

Clachan

Inverarish

Eyre
Point

Eilean
Meadhonach

Eilean
Mòr

CROWLIN ISLANDS

Kishorn
Island

394
BAD A
CHREAMHA

B883

e Braes

LEE

Peinchorran
Suisnish
Point

Caolas Mòr

Ardaneaskan
Strome NTS
Ardnarff

Loch Carron

Plockton

Stromeferry

A890

onser

SCALPAY

67 Longay

Port-an-Eorna

Achmore

773
GLAMAIG

Drumbuie

447
BEINN RAIMH

A87

Loch Ainort

Dunan

Duirinish

Balmacara

Conchra

Luib
17

Pabay

Badicaul

Auchtertyre

Nostie

Bundall

396
MULLACH
NA CARN

27

Kyle of Lochalsh
Skye Bridge
Toll

Ardelve
Carndu

Kirkton
Lochalsh
Woodland NTS

Dornie
Eilean Donan

564
GLAS BHEINN MHÒR

Caolas Scalpay

Kyleakin

5

A87

Keppoc

Corry
Broadford
Bay

Lower
Breakish

Loch Alsh

Waterloo

Upper

Broadford

Letterfearn

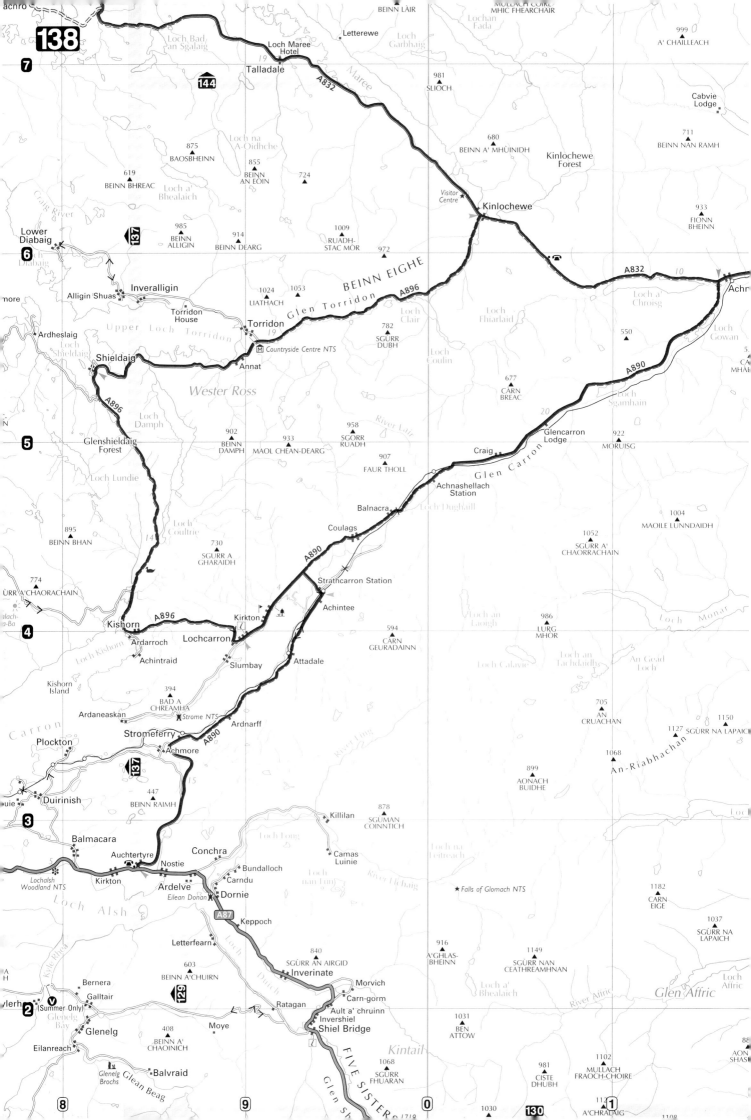

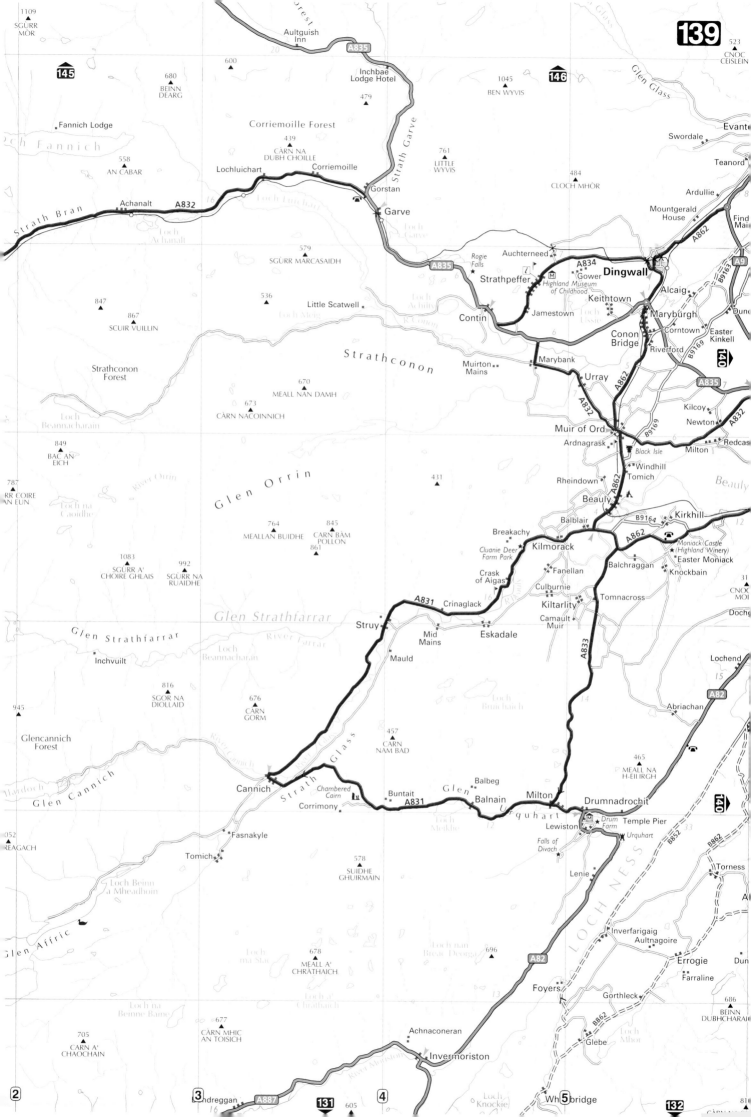

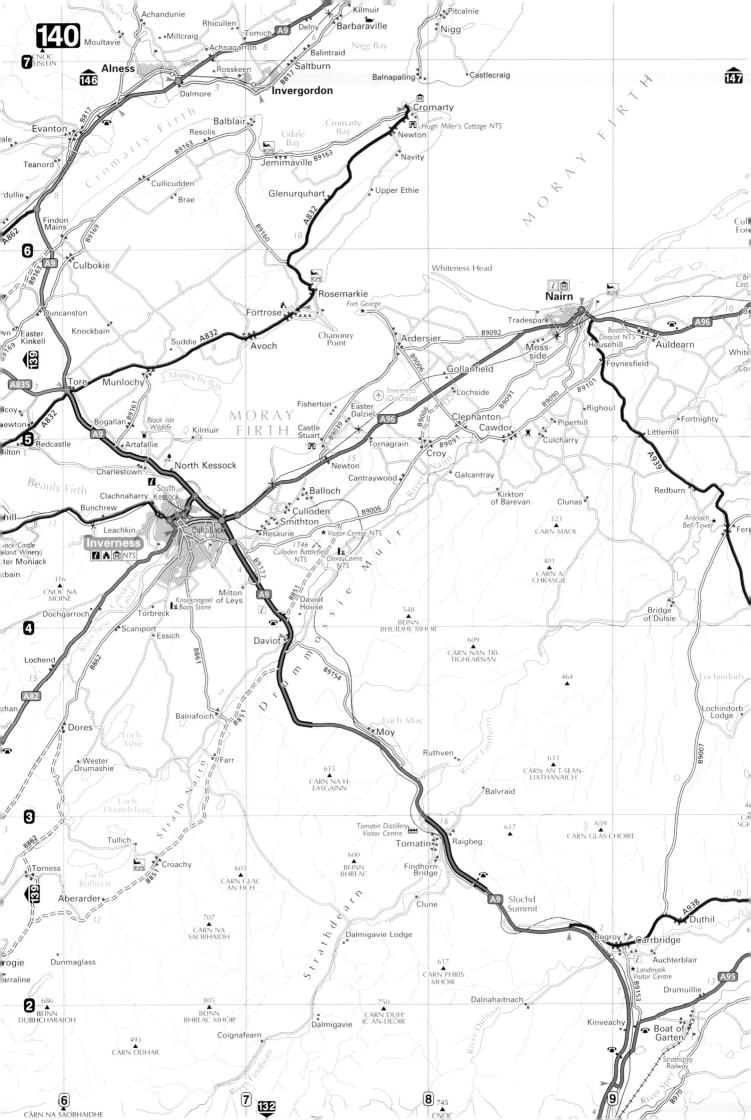

Branderburgh
Stotfield
**Lossiemouth**
B9040
Burnside
Hopeman
Burghead Well
Burghead
Cummingston
Duffus
Kinneddar
B9012
St Peters Kirk & Parish Cross
Roseisle
Duffus
B9013
College of Roseisle
B9012
B9135
B9103
Quarrywood
Stonewells
Kingston on Spey
Tugnet Ice House
Spey Bay
Spey Bay
Burghead Bay
Findhorn
Hempriggs
B9089
Newton
Bishopmill
A941
Spynie Palace
Lochill
Viewfield
Nether Dallachy
Culbin Sands
Findhorn Bay
Kinloss
Coltfield
A96
Alves
New Elgin
**Elgin**
Calcots
Innesmill
Binns Farm
Garmouth
Upper Dallachy
Bogmoor
Kincorth House
East Grange
Grange Hall
Kilbuiack
Linkwood
Linkwood
Urquhart
Lhanbryde
The Lochs
Newton
B9104
Stynie
Auchenhalrig
Bridge of Tynet
Dyke
Sueno's Stone
Muir of Miltonduff
Clackmarras
Longmorn
Orbliston
B9103
Mosstodloch
Baxters Visitor Centre
Crofts of Dipple
Dipple
Fochabers
**142**
Whiterow
**Forres**
Califer
Pluscarden
Barnhill
Fogwatt
Millbuies
Longmorn
B9015
Boghead Farm
264
WHITEASH HILL
Dallas Dhu Distillery
Rafford
B9010
Shougle
A941
Glen of Rothes
262 FINDLAY'S SEAT
Garbity
Inchberry
Ordiequish
A96
Cooperhill
Branchill
Kellas
Dallas
River Lossie
355 PIKEY HILL
Newlands of Dundurcas
Crofts
Cairnty
Sound Muir
Craiglug
250 THIEF'S HILL
Forgie
Rumbach
A940
Logie
371 MILL BUIE
365 CAIRN UISH
Glen Grant Distillery
Rothes
Speyside Way
B9015
Auchroisk
B9103
Upper Mulben
Mulben
Deanshaugh
Tauchers
Rosarie
Dunphail
400 CARN NA CAILLEICHE
369 HUNT HILL
471 BEN AIGAN
372 KNOCKAN
338 HILL OF TOWIE
Glenerney
River Divie
522 CARN KITTY
Arndilly House
Dandaleith
Maggieknockater
B9115
Drumm
Archiestown
B9102
Ringorm
Craigellachie
Glenfiddich Distillery
B9014
Cardhu
Knockando
Speyview
Aberlour
543 LARIG HILL
515
Carron
Glenallachie
Milltown of Edinvillie
Dufftown
Balvenie
Dava
Blacksboat
Marypark
A95
Pitchroy
Glenfarclas Distillery
Dava Moor
548 CARN NA LOINE
Ballindalloch
Ballindalloch
Kirktown of Mortlach
A940
B9102
Bridge of Avon
Delnashaugh Inn
840 BEN RINNES
Glen Rinnes
503
A95
Advie
B9008
Achnastank
Lettoch
Mains of Dalvey
Drumin
B9009
A941
Camerory
Delliefure
Lynn of Shenval
766 CORRYHABBIE HILL
Bridgend
Grantown-on-Spey
Cromdale
B9136
Glenlivet
**142**
Glenbeg
River Spey
Hills of Cromdale
Glenlivet Distillery
571 ROUND HILL
Cabra
Craggan
Speybridge
Strath Avon
Tomnavoulin
Glen Livet
Aldivalloch
Aldunie
A939
459 CARN NA LOINNE
Glen Lochy
Speyside Way
Auchnarrow
629 HILL OF THREE STONES
B970
Nethy Bridge
Lettoch
Bridge of Brown
Clashnoir
787
Badenyon
632 CREAG AN EUNAN
Glen Brown
Bridge of Avon
Tomintoul
Chapeltown
Ladder Hills
Dorback Lodge
River Nethy
**133**
606 CARN TUADHAM
A939
Blairnamarrow
803 CARN MOR
718 THE
656 MOSS HILL
Kirkton of Glenbuchat
Belnacraig
**134**

Portknockie
Findochty
Bow Fiddle Rock
Cullen
Findlater
Sandend Bay
A942
Portessie
**Buckie**
Buckpool
Rathven
Cullen Bay
Sandend
Portsoy
Whitehills
**Banff**
**Macduff**
Ga
Lintmill
Tochieneal
Birkenbog
Inver-boyndie
Silverford
A98
A95
Portgordon
Cairnfield House
Drybridge
Milton
Fordyce
Boyndie
B9139
Duff House
Longmanhill
ether
allachy
Upper
allachy
Broadley
Farnachty
321
BIN OF CULLEN
Deskford
Berryhillock
Windsole
Ord
Ella
Alvah
A97
Gorrachie
A947
Bridge of Tynet
Clochan
Deskford Church
Danshillock
**6**
141
B9016
272
ADDIE HILL
Craibstone
B9018
12
313
LURG HILL
Cornhill
B9025
A95
B9023
B9121
Bad Farm
264
WHITEASH HILL
Braes of Enzie
301
MILLSTONE HILL
Gordonstown
Muirden
Fintry
96
Forgie
Aultmore
Forgieside
Grange Crossroads
Berryhillock
429
KNOCK HILL
Glenbarry
271
WETHER HILL
Lootcherbrae
Aberchirder
Clunie
B9025
**Turriff**
Rumbach
ulben
Newmill
B9017
Bracobrae
Knock
Drumnagorrach
Bridge of Marnoch
Carnousie
Muiresk
Darra
Howe of
en
**5**
osarie
rs
Strath Isla
Strathisla Distillery
Fife Keith
**Keith**
Davoch of Grange
A95
Farmtown
B9022
B9117
Rothiemay
Inverkeithny
Auchininna
Fortrie
Birkenhills
B9024
338
HILL OF TOWIE
365
MEIKLE BALLOCH
Yonder Bognie
Forgue
Carlincraig
Pitglassie
Dykeside
B9014
A96
Newtack
Ruthven
Bogniebrae
B9001
Glendronach Distillery
Drumblair House
B992
Auchterless
A947
B9115
Drummuir
Cairnie
B9022
A97
Balgaveny
B9001
Gou
Invermarkie
A920
Affleck
Drumblade
Gordonstown
Fyvie
Cast
**4**
Haugh of Glass
**Huntly**
A96
Brideswell
Badenscoth
B992
B9001
Rothiebrisbane
Strath Bogie
Thomastown
Ythanwells
Fisherford
Rothienorman
Bridgend
Kirkstile
Newtongarry Croft
Bainshole
St Kather
Culdrain
Gartly
419
WICHACH HILL
466
HILL OF FOUDLAND
Glens of Foudland
Culsalmond
Rothmaise
Newseat
Folla Rule
Cross of Jac
525
Kirkney
440
CRANSMILL HILL
Colpy
21
Tocher
Meikle Wartle
Bridgend
A97
Leith Hall NTS
Largie
B992
Kirkton of Rayne
A920
**3**
564
TAP O' NOTH
Picardy Symbol Stone
Dunnideer
Insch
Old Rayne
A96
Loanhead Stone Circle
Daviot
A941
Kennethmont
B9002
Pitmachie
Hillhead of Durno
Cabrach
Belhinnie
Rhynie
Cottown
Clatt
Duncanstone
Kirkton
B9002
Oyne
Whiteford
Pitcaple
Aldunie
A97
B9002
St Mary's Kirk
Archaeolink
Pittodrie House Hotel
Maiden Stone
141
Leslie
Auchleven
B992
Chapel of Garioch
Brandsbutt Symbol Stone
722
THE BUCK
Knockespock House
484
MIRE OF MIDGATES
Mither Tap
518
493
BENNACHIE
Visitor Centre
East Aquhorthies Stone Circle
Port Elphinstone
Lumsden
475
CORREEN HILLS
Lethenty
Burnhervie
**2**
BRUX HILL
632
CREAG AN EUNAN
Mossat
A944
Tullynessle
Scotsmill
Keig
Pitfichie
Pictillum
Monymusk
Kemnay
B99
Kildrummy
Milltown
Bridge of Alford
Montgarrie
Pitmunie
Cottow
ig
of
Glenbuchat
A97
A980
Haughton House
Alford Valley Railway
Alford
Whitehouse
Craigearn
Leylodge
**4**
Glenkindie
Sinnarhard
**5**
134
A94
**6**
A94
**7**

Troup Head
Crovie
Pennan
Protstonhill
Gamrie
New Aberdour
Cullykhan Bay
Aberdour Bay
Netherbrae
BRACKLAMORE HILL 221
New Byth
Bonnykelly
New Pitsligo
Maryhill
Millbrex
Kirkton
Cottown of Gight
Brownhill
Cairnorrie
Haddo
Methlick
Haddo House NTS
Earlsford
Barthol Chapel
Tulloch
Wedderlairs
Auchedly
Ythanbank
Tarves
Craigdam
Ythsie
Kinharrachie
Altar Tomb of William Forbes
Oldmeldrum
Carnbrogie
Tolquhon
Esslemont
Ellon
Pitmedden Garden NTS
Pitmedden
Logierieve
Kirkton of Bourtie
Whiterashes
Woodland
Pettymuk
Udny Green
Udny Station
Culsh
Housieside
Culterchapel
Nether Crimond
Tillygreig
Straloch
Reisque
Kinmuck
Newmachar
Causeyend
Hatton of Fintray
Whitecairns
Kinmundy
Cothal
Dyce Symbol Stones
Overton
Potterton
Blackdog
Parkhill House

Rosehearty
Pittulie
Sandhaven
Craigiefold
Peathill
Percyhorner
Coburby
Mid Ardlaw
Boyndlie
Memsie
Memsie Cairn
Newburgh
WAUGHTON HILL 234
Strichen
New Leeds
Denhead
Fetterangus
Deer Abbey
Maud
Dunshillock
Blackhill of Clackriach
Old Deer
Aden
Mintlaw
Drymuir
Bulwark
New Deer
Slacks of Cairnbanno
Nethermuir
Stuartfield
Knaven
Kinnadie
Millbreck
Auchnagatt
Clola
Inkhorn
Coldwells
Kinknockie
Blackhill
Arthrath
Muirtack
Birness
Artrochie
Kirkton of Logie Buchan
Foveran
Delfrigs
Balmedie
Belhelvie

Lighthouse
Kinnairds Head
Fraserburgh
Kirktown
Fraserburgh Bay
Cairnbulg
Inverallochy
Whitelinks Bay
St Combs
Rathen
Lonmay
Crofts of Savoch
Crimonmogate
Loch of Strathbeg
Rattray Head
Crimond
Blackhill
Leys
Backfolds
Kirktown
St Fergus
Rora
River Ugie
Inverugie
Longside
Buchanhaven
Peterhead
Inverquhomery
Nether Kinmundy
Hillhead of Cocklaw
Peterhead Bay
Little Dens
Blackhill
Stirling
Buchan Ness
Boddam
Lendrum Terrace
Longhaven
Bullers of Buchan
Hatton
Auchiries
North Haven
Slains
Cruden Bay
Bogbrae
Chapel Hill
Bay of Cruden
Whinnyfold
The Skares
Colliestoun
Kirktown of Slains
Newburgh

A90
A98
A981
A952
A950
A981
A948
B9028
A948
A952
A975
A90
A987
A920
B9000
B9000
A90
A975
A947
A999

0 1 2 3 4 5 miles
0 1 2 3 4 5 6 7 kilometres

**2**

**1**

**0**

**9**

**8**

**7**

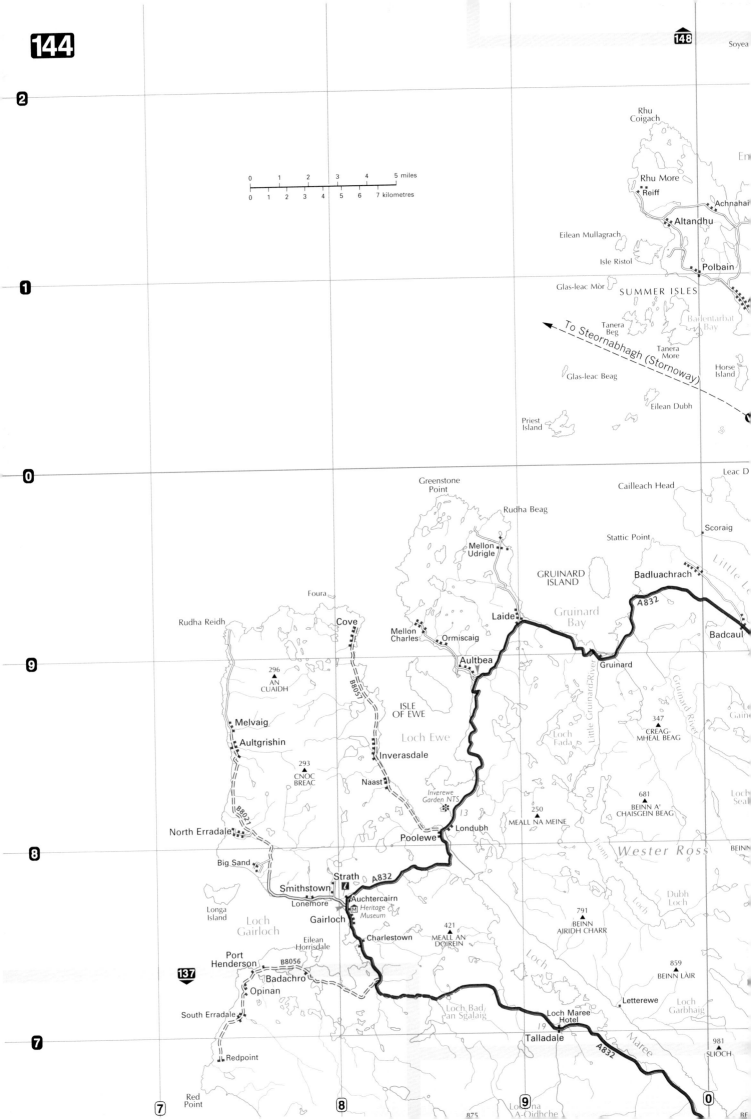

Soyea

Rhu Coigach

Rhu More
Reiff

Achnahai

Altandhu

Polbain

Eilean Mullagrach

Isle Ristol

Glas-leac Mòr

SUMMER ISLES

Badentarbat Bay

To Steornabhagh (Stornoway)

Tanera Beg

Tanera More

Horse Island

Glas-leac Beag

Priest Island

Eilean Dubh

Leac D

Greenstone Point

Cailleach Head

Scoraig

Rudha Beag

Mellon Udrigle

Stattic Point

Little Lo

Badluachrach

GRUINARD ISLAND

Gruinard Bay

A832

Badcaul

Foura

Cove

Mellon Charles

Ormiscaig

Laide

Gruinard

Little Gruinard River

Rudha Reidh

Aultbea

Gruinard River

347 ▲ CREAG-MHEAL BEAG

Le Gaine

296 ▲ AN CUAIDH

B8057

ISLE OF EWE

Loch Ewe

Melvaig

Aultgrishin

293 ▲ CNOC BREAC

Inverasdale

Naast

Inverewe Garden NTS ✿ 13

681 ▲ BEINN A' CHAISGEIN BEAG

Loch Fada

250 ▲ MEALL NA MEINE

Loch Sea

B8021

North Erradale

Londubh

Poolewe

Wester Ross

BEINN

Big Sand

Strath A832

Smithstown

Auchtercairn

Heritage Museum 🏛

791 ▲ BEINN AIRIDH CHARR

Dubh Loch

Longa Island

Lonemore

Loch Gairloch

Gairloch

Charlestown

421 ▲ MEALL AN DOIREIN

859 ▲ BEINN LÀIR

Eilean Horrisdale

Port Henderson

**137**

B8056

Badachro

Opinan

South Erradale

Loch Bad an Sgalaig

Letterewe

Loch Garbhaig

Loch Maree Hotel

Talladale

A832

Maree

981 ▲ SLIOCH

Redpoint

Red Point

875

Loch na A-Oidhche

**7** **8** **9** **0**

RE

0   1   2   3   4   5 miles
0   1   2   3   4   5   6   7 kilometres

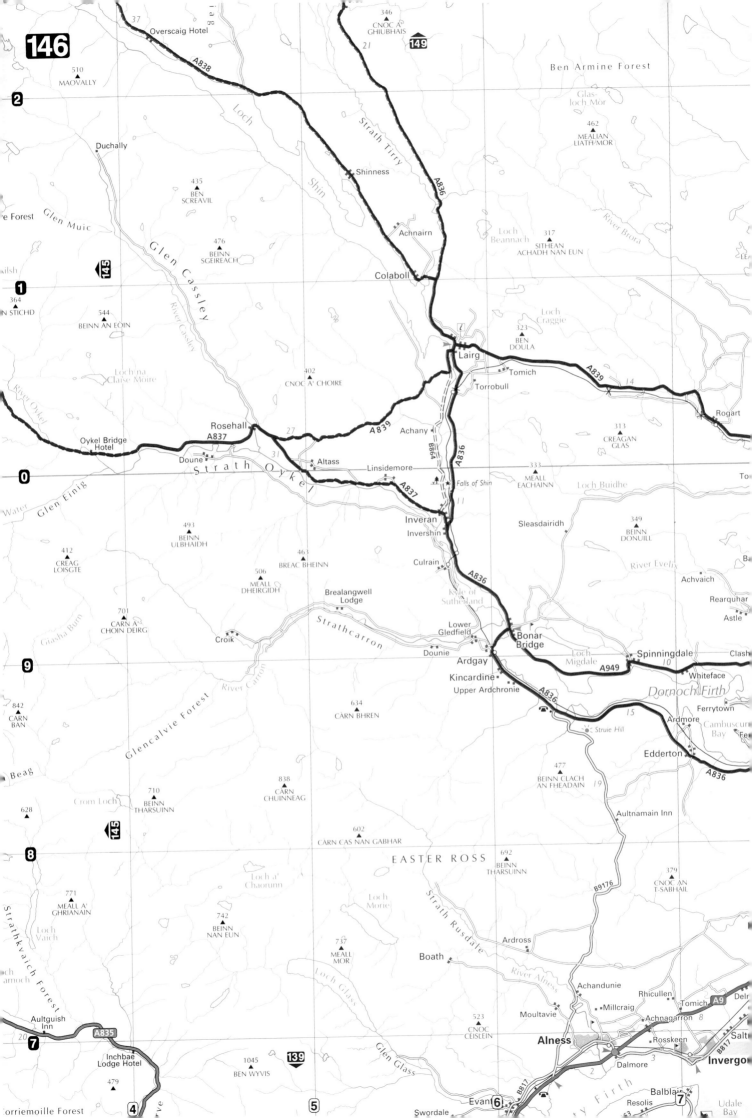

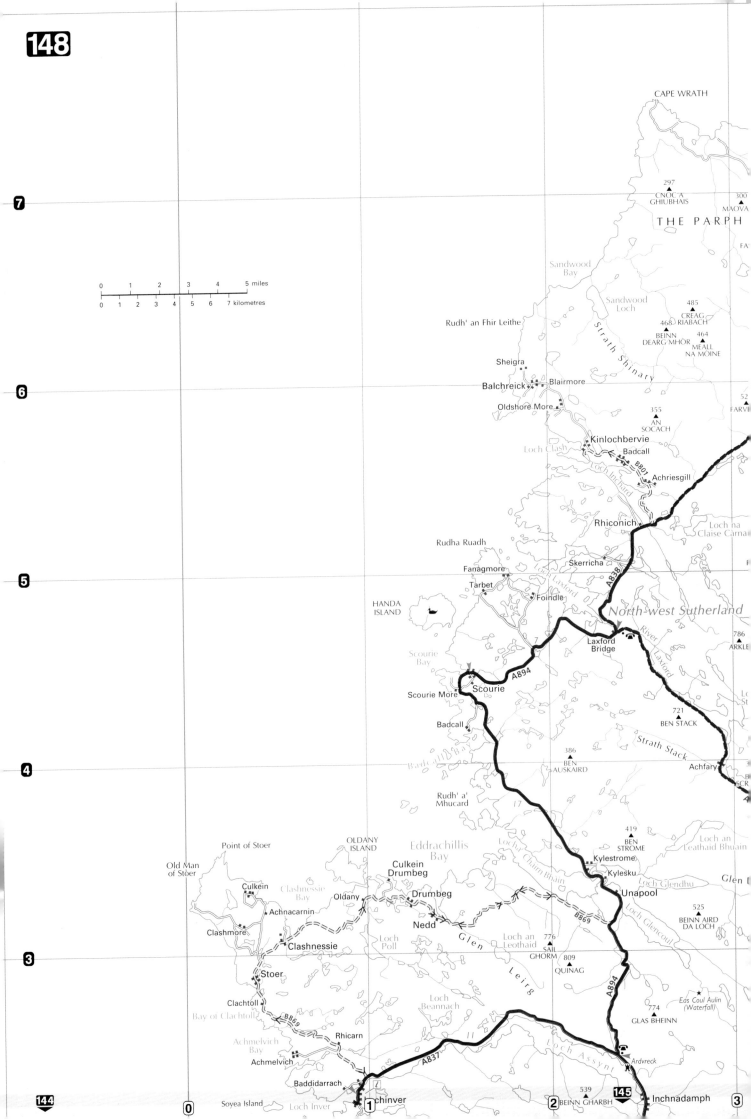

7

6

5

4

3

CAPE WRATH

THE PARPH

297
CNOC A
GHIUBHAIS
300
MAOVA

FA

Sandwood
Bay

485
CREAG
RIABACH
468
BEINN
DEARG MHÒR
464
MEALL
NA MOINE

Sandwood
Loch

Strath Shinary

Rudh' an Fhir Leithe

Sheigra

Balchreick    Blairmore

Oldshore More

355
AN
SOCACH

52
FARVE

Kinlochbervie

Loch Clash    Badcall

B801    Achriesgill

Loch Inchard

Rhiconich    Loch na
Claise Carnai

Rudha Ruadh

Skerricha

A838

Fanagmore

Tarbet    Foindle

Loch Laxford

786
ARKLE

North-west Sutherland

HANDA
ISLAND

Laxford
Bridge

River Laxford

7

Scourie
Bay

A894

Scourie More    Scourie

Badcall

721
BEN STACK

Strath Stack

Achfary
B
SCR

386
BEN
AUSKAIRD

Badcall Bay

Rudh' a'
Mhucard

17

419
BEN
STROME

Loch an
Leathaid Bhuain

Point of Stoer

OLDANY
ISLAND    Eddrachillis
Bay

Loch a' Chuirn Bhàin

Kylestrome

Kylesku    Loch Glendhu    Glen D

Old Man
of Stoer

Culkein
Drumbeg

Culkein    Clashnessie
Bay

Oldany    Drumbeg    Unapool

525
BEINN AIRD
DA LOCH

Achnacarnin

Nedd    Glen    B869

Loch Glencoul

Clashmore

776
SAIL
GHORM

809
QUINAG

Clashnessie

Loch
Poll    Loch an
Leothaid

Leirg

A894

Stoer

Eas Coul Aulin
(Waterfall)

Clachtoll    Loch
Beannach

774
GLAS BHEINN

Bay of Clachtoll    B869

Achmelvich
Bay    Rhicarn    A837    11

Achmelvich    Loch Assynt    Ardvreck

Baddidarrach

Soyea Island    Loch Inver    chinver    539
BEINN GHARBH    Inchnadamph

0    1    2    3    4    5 miles

0    1    2    3    4    5    6    7 kilometres

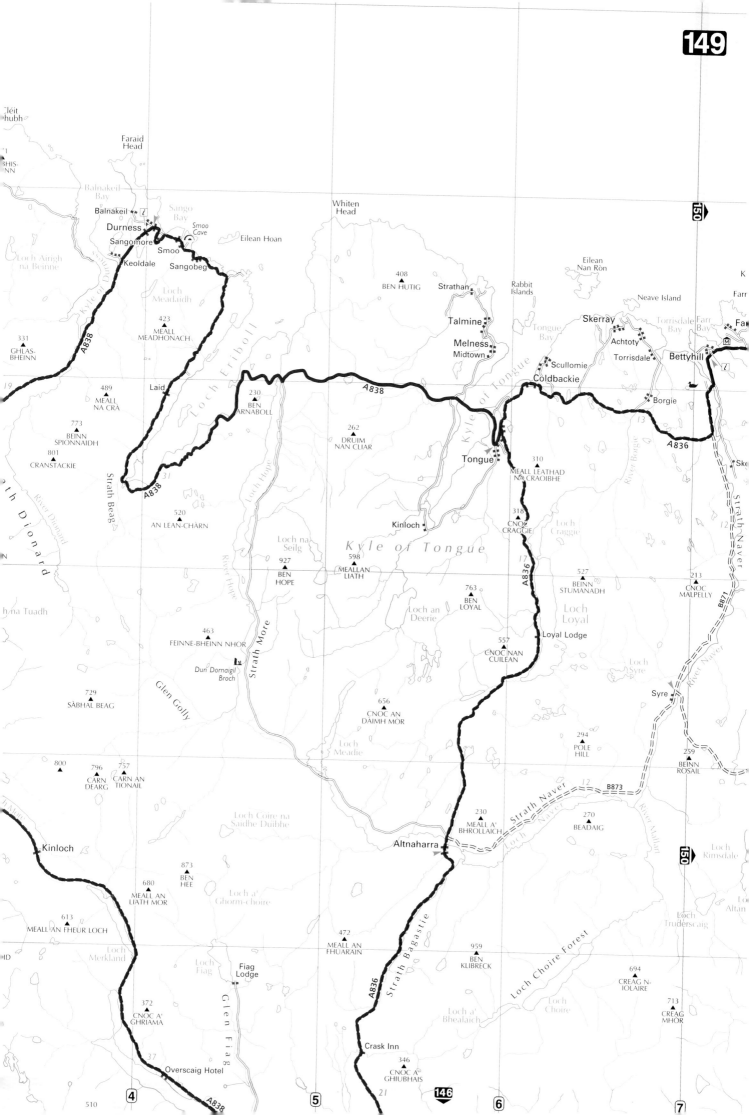

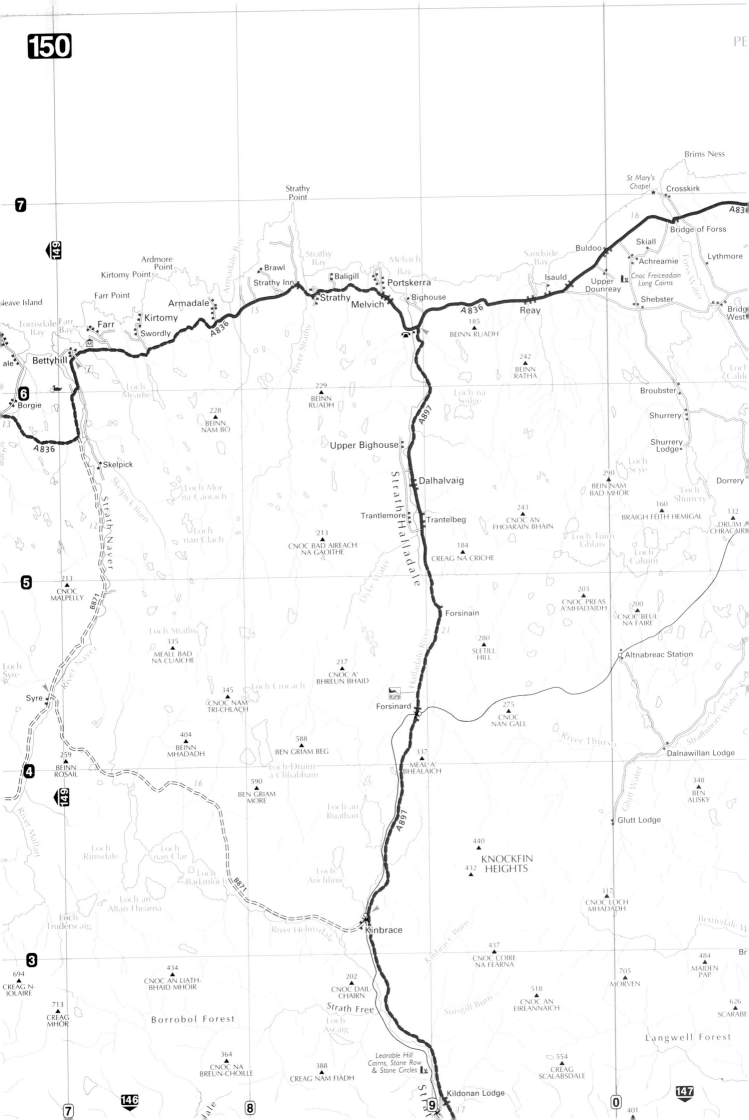

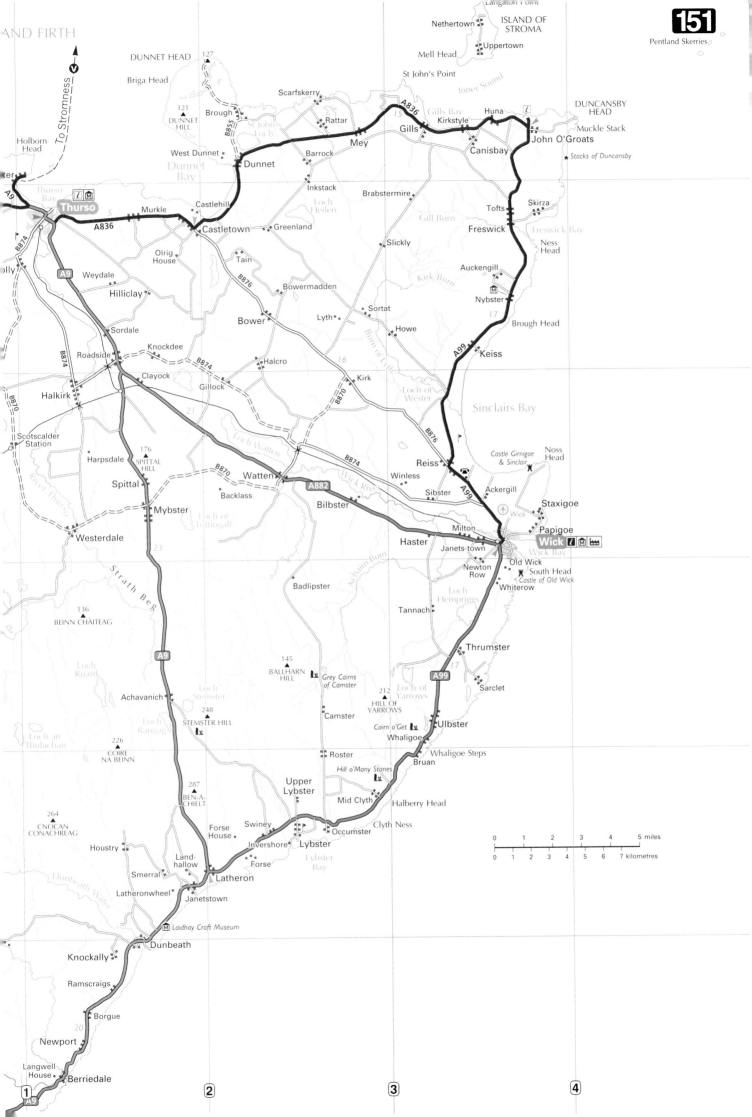

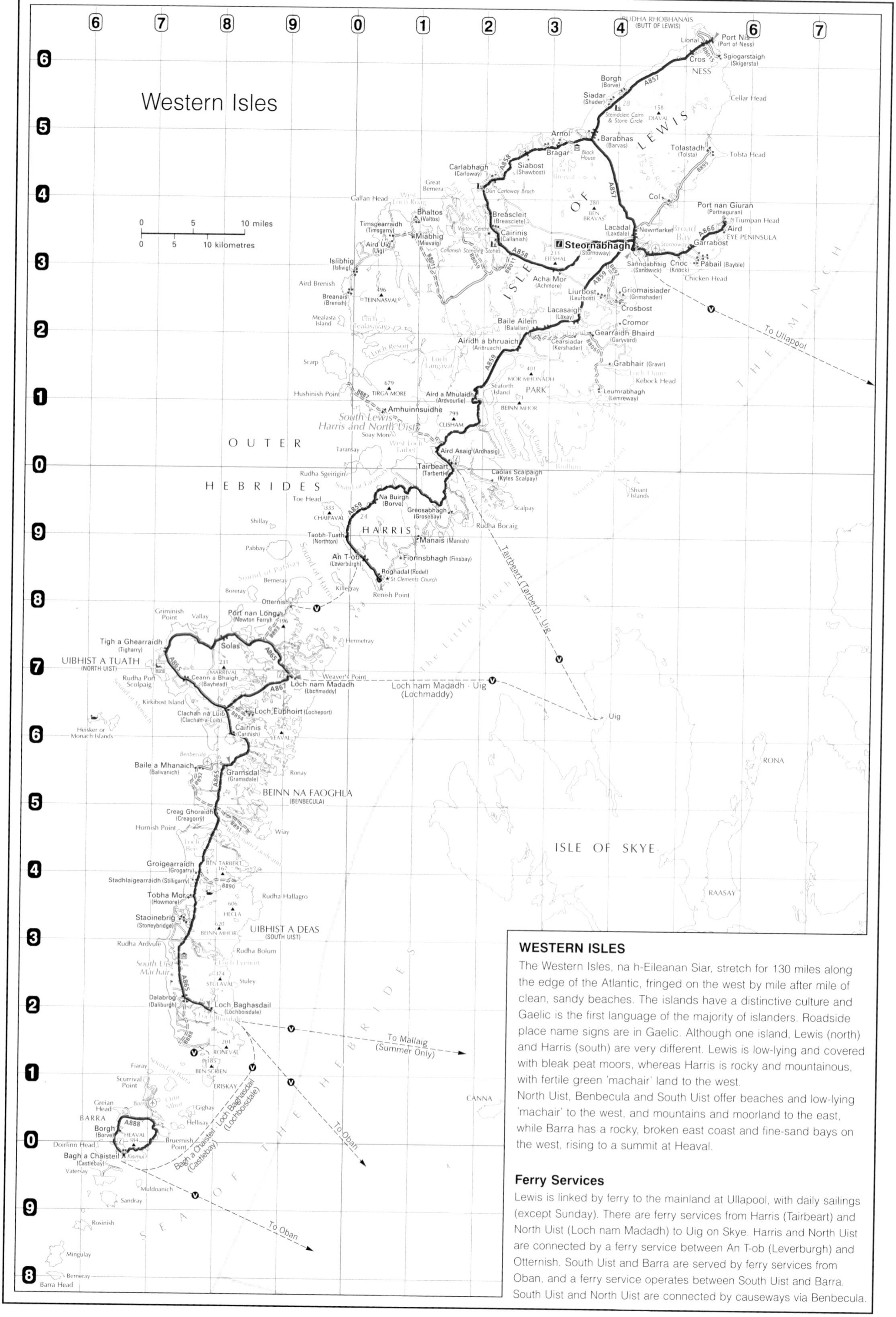

# Western Isles

0     5     10 miles

0     5     10 kilometres

## WESTERN ISLES

The Western Isles, na h-Eileanan Siar, stretch for 130 miles along the edge of the Atlantic, fringed on the west by mile after mile of clean, sandy beaches. The islands have a distinctive culture and Gaelic is the first language of the majority of islanders. Roadside place name signs are in Gaelic. Although one island, Lewis (north) and Harris (south) are very different. Lewis is low-lying and covered with bleak peat moors, whereas Harris is rocky and mountainous, with fertile green 'machair' land to the west.

North Uist, Benbecula and South Uist offer beaches and low-lying 'machair' to the west, and mountains and moorland to the east, while Barra has a rocky, broken east coast and fine-sand bays on the west, rising to a summit at Heaval.

## Ferry Services

Lewis is linked by ferry to the mainland at Ullapool, with daily sailings (except Sunday). There are ferry services from Harris (Tairbeart) and North Uist (Loch nam Madadh) to Uig on Skye. Harris and North Uist are connected by a ferry service between An T-ob (Leverburgh) and Otternish. South Uist and Barra are served by ferry services from Oban, and a ferry service operates between South Uist and Barra. South Uist and North Uist are connected by causeways via Benbecula.

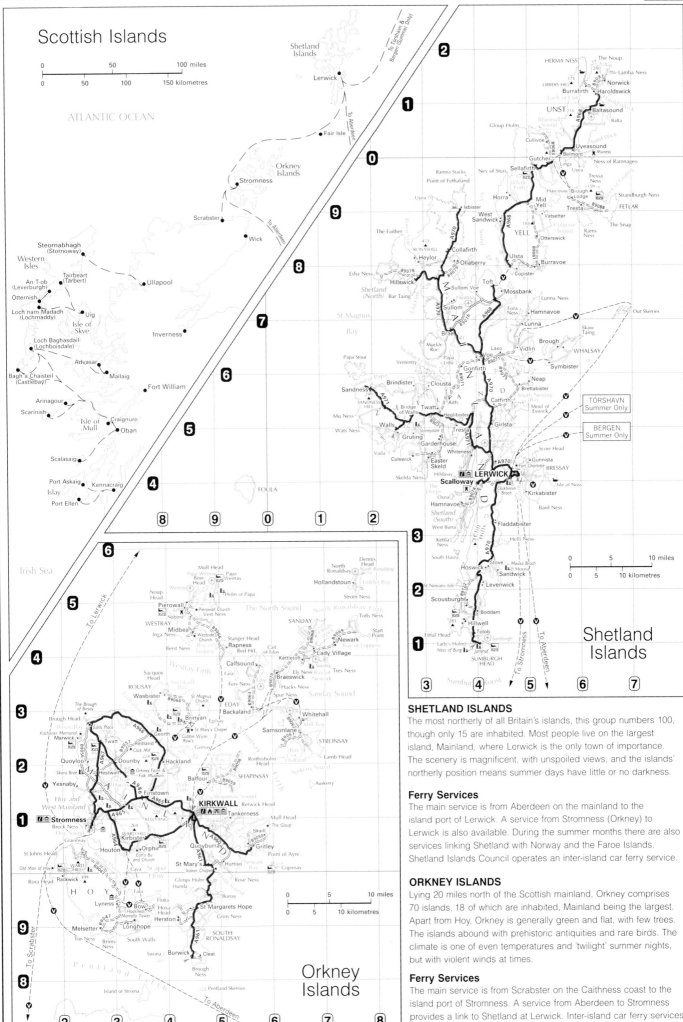

## Scottish Islands

## Shetland Islands

## Orkney Islands

### SHETLAND ISLANDS

The most northerly of all Britain's islands, this group numbers 100, though only 15 are inhabited. Most people live on the largest island, Mainland, where Lerwick is the only town of importance. The scenery is magnificent, with unspoiled views, and the islands' northerly position means summer days have little or no darkness.

#### Ferry Services

The main service is from Aberdeen on the mainland to the island port of Lerwick. A service from Stromness (Orkney) to Lerwick is also available. During the summer months there are also services linking Shetland with Norway and the Faroe Islands. Shetland Islands Council operates an inter-island car ferry service.

### ORKNEY ISLANDS

Lying 20 miles north of the Scottish mainland, Orkney comprises 70 islands, 18 of which are inhabited, Mainland being the largest. Apart from Hoy, Orkney is generally green and flat, with few trees. The islands abound with prehistoric antiquities and rare birds. The climate is one of even temperatures and 'twilight' summer nights, but with violent winds at times.

#### Ferry Services

The main service is from Scrabster on the Caithness coast to the island port of Stromness. A service from Aberdeen to Stromness provides a link to Shetland at Lerwick. Inter-island car ferry services are also operated (advance reservations recommended).

# Ireland

Abbeydorney B3
Abbeyfeale B3
Abbeyleix D3
Adamstown D3
Adare B3
Adrigole B2
Ahascragh C4
Ahoghill E6
Allihies A2
Anascaul A2
Annestown D2
Antrim E6
Ardagh B3
Ardara C6
Ardcath E4
Ardee D5
Ardfert B3
Ardfinnan C3
Ardglass E5
Ardgroom A2
Arklow E3
Arless D3
Armagh E5
Armoy E7
Arthurstown D2
Arvagh D5
Ashbourne E4
Ashford E4
Askeaton B3
Athboy D5
Athenry C4
Athleague C4
Athlone C4
Athy D4
Augher D6
Aughnacloy D6
Aughrim E3
Avoca E3

Bagenalstown D3
(Muine Bheag)
Bailieborough D5
Balbriggan E4
Balla B5
Ballacolla D3
Ballaghaderreen C5
Ballina C3
Ballina B5
Ballinafad C5
Ballinagh D5
Ballinakill D3
Ballinalee C5
Ballinamallard D6
Ballinamore C5
Ballinascarty B2
Ballinasloe C4
Ballindine B5
Ballineen B2
Ballingarry C3
Ballingarry B3
Ballingeary B2
(Béal Átha an
Ghaorfthaidh)
Ballinhassig C2
Ballinlough C5
Ballinrobe B5
Ballinspittle C2
Ballintober C5
Ballintra C6
Ballivor D4
Ballon D3
Ballybaun C4
Ballybay D5
Ballybofey C6
Ballybunion B3
Ballycanew E3
Ballycarry E6
Ballycastle B6
Ballycastle E7
Ballyclare E6
Ballyconneely A4
Ballycotton C2
Ballycumber C4
Ballydehob B1
Ballydesmond B2
Ballyduff C2
Ballyduff B3
Ballyfarnan C5
Ballygalley E6
Ballygar C4
Ballygawley D6
Ballygowan E6
Ballyhaise D5
Ballyhale D3
Ballyhaunis C5
Ballyhean B5
Ballyheige B3
Ballyjamesduff D5
Ballykeeran C4
Ballylanders C3
Ballylongford B3
Ballylooby C3
Ballylynan D3
Ballymahon C4
Ballymakeery B2
Ballymena E6
Ballymoe C5
Ballymoney D7
Ballymore C4
Ballymore Eustace D4
Ballymote C5
Ballynahinch E6
Ballynure E6
Ballyporeen C3
Ballyragget D3
Ballyroan D4
Ballyronan D6
Ballysadare C5
Ballyshannon C6
Ballyvaughan B4
Ballywalter E6
Balrothery E4
Baltimore B1

Baltinglass D3
Banagher C4
Banbridge E6
Bandon B2
Bangor E6
Bangor Erris B5
Bansha C3
Banteer B2
Bantry B2
Beaufort B2
Belcoo C6
Belfast E6
Belgooly C2
Bellaghy D6
Belleek C6
Belmullet B6
(Béal an Mhuirhead)
Belturbet D5
Benburb D6
Bennett's Bridge D3
Beragh D6
Birr C4
Blacklion C6
Blackwater E3
Blarney C2
Blessington D4
Boherbue B2
Borris D3
Borris-in-Ossory C4
Borrisokane C4
Borrisoleigh C3
Boyle C5
Bracknagh D4
Bray E4
Bridgetown D2
Brittas D4
Broadford C3
Broadford B3
Broughshane E6
Bruff C3
Bruree C3
Bunclody D3
Buncrana D7
Bundoran C6
Bunmahon D2
Bunnahowen B6
Bunnyconnellan B5
Burnfort C2
Bushmills D7
Butler's Bridge D5
Buttevant B3

Cadamstown C4
Caherconlish C3
Caherdaniel A2
Cahersiveen A2
Cahir C3
Caledon D6
Callan D3
Caltra C4
Camp A3
Cappagh White C3
Cappamore C3
Cappoquin C2
Carlanstown D5
Carlingford E5
Carlow D3
Carndonagh D7
Carnew D3
Carnlough E7
Carracastle C5
Carrick C6
(An Charraig)
Carrickfergus E6
Carrickmacross D5
Carrickmore D6
Carrick-on-Shannon C5
Carrick-on-Suir D3
Carrigahorig C4
Carrigaline C2
Carrigallen D5
Carriganimmy B2
Carrigans D7
Carrigart C7
(Carraig Airt)
Carrigtohill C2
Carrowkeel D7
Carryduff E6
Cashel C3
Castlebar B5
Castlebellingham E5
Castleblaney D5
Castlebridge D3
Castlecomer D4
Castlederg D6
Castledermot D3
Castleisland B3
Castlemaine B2
Castlemartyr C2
Castleplunket C5
Castlepollard D5
Castlerea C5
Castlerock D7
Castleshane D5
Castletown C4
Castletown
Bearhaven A2
Castletownroche C2
Castletownshend B1
Castlewellan E5
Causeway B3
Cavan D5
Celbridge D4
Charlestown C5
Charleville B3
(Rath Luirc)
Clady D6
Clane D4
Clara C4
Clarecastle B3
Claremorris B5
Clarinbridge B4
Clashmore C2
Claudy D7

Clifden A4
Cliffoney C6
Clogh D3
Cloghan C4
Clogheen C3
Clogher D6
Clohamon D3
Clonakilty B2
Clonard D4
Clonaslee D4
Clonbulloge D4
Clonbur B5
(An Fhairche )
Clondalkin E4
Clones D5
Clonmany D7
Clonmel C3
Clonmellon D5
Clonmore C3
Clonony C4
Clonoulty C3
Clonroche D3
Clontibret D5
Cloondara C5
Cloonlara C3
Clough E6
Cloughjordan C4
Cloyne C2
Coagh D6
Coalisland D6
Cobh C2
Coleraine D7
Collinstown D5
Collon D5
Collooney C5
Comber E6
Cong B5
Conna C2
Cookstown D6
Coole D5
Cooraclare B3
Cootehill D5
Cork C2
Cornamona B4
Corofin B4
Courtmacsherry B2
Courtown Harbour E3
Craigavon E6
Craughwell C4
Creeslough C7
Creggs C5
Croagh B3
Crolly (Croithli) C7
Crookedwood D4
Crookhaven B1
Crookstown B2
Croom B3
Crossakeel D5
Cross Barry B2
Crosshaven C2
Crossmaglen D5
Crossmolina B5
Crumlin E6
Crusheen B4
Culdaff D7
Culleybackey E6
Curracloe D3
Curraghboy C4
Curry C5
Cushendall E7

Daingean D4
Delvin D4
Derrygonnelly C6
Dervock E7
Dingle A2
(An Daingean)
Doagh E6
Donaghadee E6
Donaghmore C3
Donegal C6
Doneraile C2
Doon C4
Doonbeg B3
Douglas C2
Downpatrick E6
Dowra C5
Draperstown D6
Drimoleague B2
Dripsey B2
Drogheda E5
Dromahair C6
Dromara E6
Dromcolliher B3
Dromod C5
Dromore E6
Dromore E6
Dromore West C6
Drum D5
Drumcliff C6
Drumconrath D5
Drumkeeran C5
Drumlish C5
Drumquin D6
Drumshanbo C5
Drumsna C5
Duagh B3
Dublin E4
Duleek E5
Dunboyne D4
Duncormick D2
Dundalk E5
Dunderrow C2
Dundrum E5
Dunfanaghy C7
Dungannon D6
Dungarvan C2
Dungarvan D3
Dungiven D7
Dungloe C7
(An Clochan Liath)
Dungourney C2
Dunkineely C6
Dun Laoghaire E4
Dunlavin D4
Dunleer E5

Dunloy E7
Dunmanway B2
Dunmore E5
Dunmore East D2
Dunmurry E6
Dunshaughlin D4
Durrow D3
Durrus B2
Dysart C4

Easky B6
Edenderry D4
Edgeworthstown D5
Eglinton D7
Elphin C5
Emyvale D6
Enfield D4
Ennis B3
Enniscorthy D3
Enniscrone B6
Enniskean B2
Enniskillen D6
Ennistymon B4
Eyrecourt C4

Farnaght C5
Farranfore B2
Feakle C4
Fenagh C5
Ferbane C4
Fermoy C2
Ferns D3
Fethard D2
Fethard C3
Finnea D5
Fintona D6
Fivemiletown D6
Fontstown D4
Foxford B5
Foynes B3
Freemount B3
Frenchpark C5
Freshford D3
Fuerty C5

Galbally C3
Galway B4
Garrison C6
Garristown E4
Garvagh D7
Geashill C4
Gilford E6
Glandore B1
Glanworth C2
Glaslough D6
Glassan C4
Glenamaddy C5
Glenarm E7
Glenavy E6
Glenbeigh A2
Glencolumbkille C6
(Gleann Cholm
Cille)
Glendalough E4
Glenealy E3
Glengarriff B2
Glenmore D3
Glenties C6
Glin B3
Glinsk B3
(Glinsce)
Golden C3
Goleen B1
Goresbridge D3
Gorey E3
Gort B4
Gortin D6
Gowran D3
Graiguenamanagh
D3
Granard D5
Grange C6
Greyabbey E6

Greystones E4
Gulladuff D6

Hacketstown D3
Headford B4
Herbertstown C3
Hillsborough E6
Hilltown E5
Hospital C3
Holycross C3
Holywood E6
Howth E4

Inch A2
Inchigeelagh B2
Inishannon B2
Irvinestown D6

Johnstown C3

Kanturk B2
Keadue C5
Keady D5
Keel A5
Keenagh C5
Kells E6
Kells D5
Kenmare B2
Kesh C6
Kilbeggan D4
Kilberry D5
Kilbrittain B2
Kilcar C6
(Cill Charthaigh)
Kilcock D4
Kilcolgan B4
Kilconnell C4
Kilcoole E4
Kilcormac C4
Kilcullen D4
Kilcurry E5
Kildare D4
Kildavin D3
Kildorrery C2
Kilfenora B4
Kilgarvan B2
Kilkee B3
Kilkeel E5
Kilkelly C5
Kilkenny D3
Kilkieran B4
Kilkinlea B3
Kill D2
Killadysert B3
Killala B6
Killaloe C3
Killarney B2
Killashee C5
Killeigh D4
Killenaule C3
Killeshandra D5
Killimer B3
Killimor C4
Killiney E4
Killinick D2
Killorglin B2
Killough E5
Killucan D4
Killybegs C6
Killyleagh E6
Kilmacanoge E4
Kilmacrenan C7
Kilmacthomas D2
Kilmaganny D3
Kilmaine B5
Kilmallock C3
Kilmanagh D3
Kilmeadan D3
Kilmeage D4
Kilmeedy B3
Kilmichael B2
Kilmore Quay D2
Kilnaleck D5

Kilrea D7
Kilrush B3
Kilsheelan D3
Kiltealy D3
Kiltegan D3
Kiltimagh B5
Kiltoom C4
Kingscourt D5
Kinlough C6
Kinnegad D4
Kinnitty C4
Kinsale C2
Kinvarra B4
Kircubbin E6
Knock B5
Knockcroghery C4
Knocklofty C3
Knocktopher D3

Lahinch B4
Laragh E4
Larne E6
Lauragh A2
Laurencetown C4
Leap B2
Leenane B5
Leighlinbridge D3
Leitrim C5
Leixlip D4
Lemybrien C2
Letterfrack B5
Letterkenny D7
Lifford D6
Limavady D7
Limerick C3
Lisbellaw D6
Lisburn E6
Liscannor B4
Liscarroll B3
Lisdoonvarna B4
Lismore C2
Lisnaskea D6
Lisryan D5
Listowel B3
Loghill B3
Londonderry D7
Longford C5
Loughbrickland E6
Loughgall D6
Loughglinn C5
Loughrea C4
Louisburgh B5
Lucan D4
Lurgan D6
Lusk E4

Macroom B2
Maghera E5
Maghera D6
Magherafelt D6
Maguiresbridge D6
Malahide E4
Malin D7
Malin More C6
Mallow C2
Manorhamilton C6
Markethill D6
Maynooth D4
Mazetown E6
Middleton D6
Midleton C2
Milford D7
Millstreet B2
Milltown B2
Milltown Malbay B3
Mitchelstown C3
Moate C4
Mohill C5
Monaghan D6
Monasterevin D4
Moneygall C3
Moneymore D6
Monivea C4

Mooncoin D2
Moorfields E6
Mount Bellew C4
Mount Charles C6
Mountmellick D4
Mountrath D4
Mountshannon C4
Moville D7
Moy D6
Moynalty D5
Moyvore C4
Muckross B2
Muff D7
Mullinavat D3
Mullingar D4
Mulrany B5
Myshall D3

Naas D4
Naul E4
Navan D5
Neale B5
Nenagh C3
Newbliss D5
Newbridge D4
(Droichead Nua)
Newcastle E5
Newcastle West B3
Newinn C3
Newmarket B2
Newmarket-on
Fergus B3
Newport C3
Newport B5
New Ross D3
Newry E5
Newtown D3
Newtownabbey E6
Newtownards E6
Newtownbutler D5
Newtownhamilton D5
Newtown-
mountkennedy E4
Newtownstewart D6
Newtown Forbes C5
Nobber D5

Oilgate D3
Oldcastle D5
Omagh D6
Omeath E5
Oola C3
Oranmore B4
Oughterard B4
Ovens B2

Pallas Green C3
Parknasilla A2
Partry B5
Passage East D2
Passage West C2
Patrickswell C3
Paulstown D3
Pettigo D6
Plumbridge D6
Pomeroy D6
Portadown E6
Portaferry E6
Portarlington D4
Portavogie E6
Portglenone E6

Portlaoise D4
Portmarnock E4
Portrane E4
Portroe C3
Portrush D7
Portstewart D7
Portumna C4
Poulgorm Bridge B2
Poyntzpass E6

Raharney D4
Randalstown E6
Rasharkin E7
Rathangan D4
Rathcoole D4
Rathcormack C2
Rathdowney C3
Rathdrum E3
Rathfriland E5
Rathkeale B3
Rathmelton D7
Rathmolyon D4
Rathmore B2
Rathmullan D7
Rathnew E4
Rathowen D5
Rathvilly D3
Ratoath D4
Ray D7
Ring (An Rinn) C2
Ringaskiddy C2
Rockcorry D5
Roosky C5
Rosapenna C7
Rosbercon D3
Roscommon C5
Roscrea C4
Rosslea D5
Ross Carbery B1
Rosscor C6
Rosses Point C5
Rosslare Harbour D2
Rossnowlagh (...)
Rostrevor E5
Roundstone B4
Roundwood E4
Rush E4

St Johnstown D7
Saintfield E6
Sallins D4
Scarriff C4
Scartaglen B2
Scarva E6
Schull B1
Scramoge C5
Seskinore D6
Shanagarry C2
Shanagolden B3
Shannonbridge C4
Shercock D5
Shillelagh D3
Shinrone C4
Shrule B4
Silvermines C3
Sion Mills D6
Sixmilebridge B3
Skerries E4
Skibbereen B1
Slane D5
Sligo C6
Smithborough D6

Sneem A2
Spiddal B4
(An Spideal)
Stewartstown D6
Stonyford D3
Strabane D6
Stradbally D4
Stradone D5
Strandhill C6
Strangford E6
Stranorlar C6
Strokestown C5
Summerhill D4
Swanlinbar C5
Swatragh D6
Swinford B5
Swords E4

Taghmon D3
Tagoat D2
Tahilla A2
Tallaght E4
Tallow C2
Tallowbridge C2
Tandragee E6
Tang C4
Tarbert B3
Templemore C3
Templetouhy C3
Termonfeckin E5
Thomastown D3
Thurles C3
Timahoe D4
Timoleague B2
Tinahely D3
Tipperary C3
Tobercurry C5
Tobermore D6
Toomyvara C3
Toormore B1
Tralee B3
Tramore D2
Trim D4
Tuam B4
Tuamgraney C3
Tulla B3
Tullamore D4
Tullow D3
Tulsk C5
Turlough B5
Tyrellspass D4

Urlingford C3

Virginia D5

Warrenpoint E5
Waterford D2
Watergrasshill C2
Waterville A2
Westport B5
Wexford D3
Whitegate C2
Whitehead E6
Wicklow E4
Woodenbridge E3
Woodford C4

Youghal C2

Aran Island
(An
Donegal Bay
Inishmurray
Grange
Lissadell
Rosses Point
Sligo Bay
Strandhill
Sligo
Ballysadare
Colloney
Glencolumbkille
(Gleann Cholm
Cille)
Folk Museum Carrick
(An Charraig)
Malin
More
Killybeg
SLIEVE LEAGUE 601
Kilcar
(Cill Charthaigh)
St John's Point
Rossan
Point

Erris Head
Downpatrick Head
Belmullet
(Béal an Mhuirhead)
Ballycastle
Easky
Dromore West
Strandhill
Enniscrone
Inishkea North
Killala
Bangor Erris
Bunnahowen
Crossmolina
Ballina
Bunnyconnellan
Inishkea South
Duvillaun More
Achill Head
Keel
SLIEVEMORE
NEPHIN
Foxford
Tobercurry
Curry
Charlestown
Carracastle
Swinford
Achill Island
Mulran
Newport
Turlough
Castlebar
Kiltimagh
Knock
Knock International
Ballaghaderreen
Clare Island
Clew Bay
Westport
CROAGH PATRICK 765
Louisburgh
Ballyhean
Balla
Loughglinn
Castlerea
Inishturk
Caher Island
Partry
Claremorris
Ballyhaunis
Ballinlough
Ballymoe
Inishbofin
Kylemore
Leenane
Ballinrobe
Neale
Kilmaine
Dunmore
Glenamaddy
Inishshark
Letterfrack
Clonbur
(An Fhairche)
Cong
Shrule
Creggs
Clifden
Connemara
National Park
Ballyconneely
Slyne Head
Cornamona
Headford
Tuam
Roundstone
Glinsk
(Glinsce)
Pearse's
Cottage
Oughterard
Aughnanure
Mount Bellew
Caltra
Ballygar

**A**

**B**

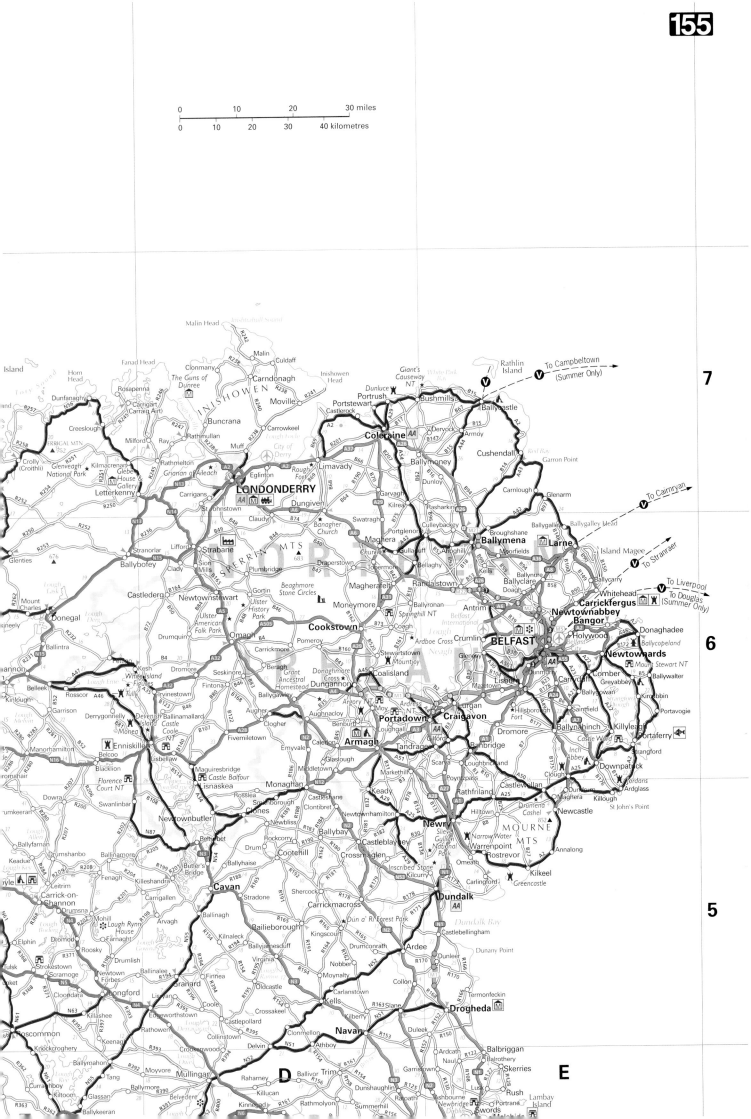

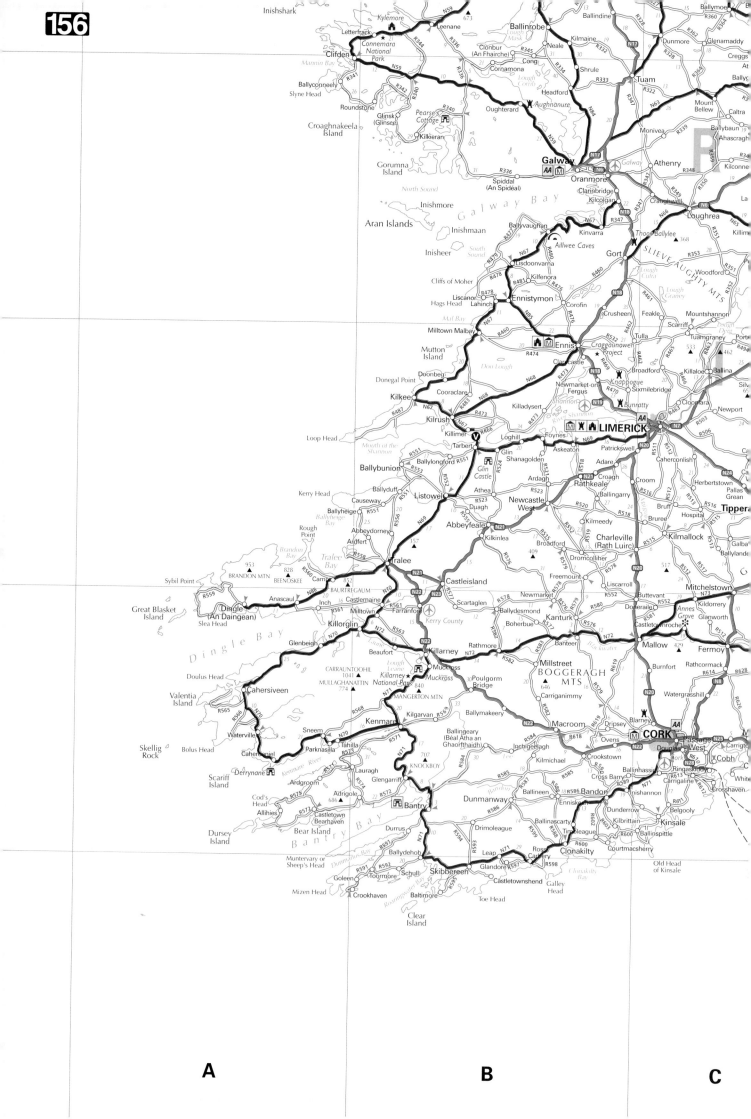

**A**

**B**

**C**

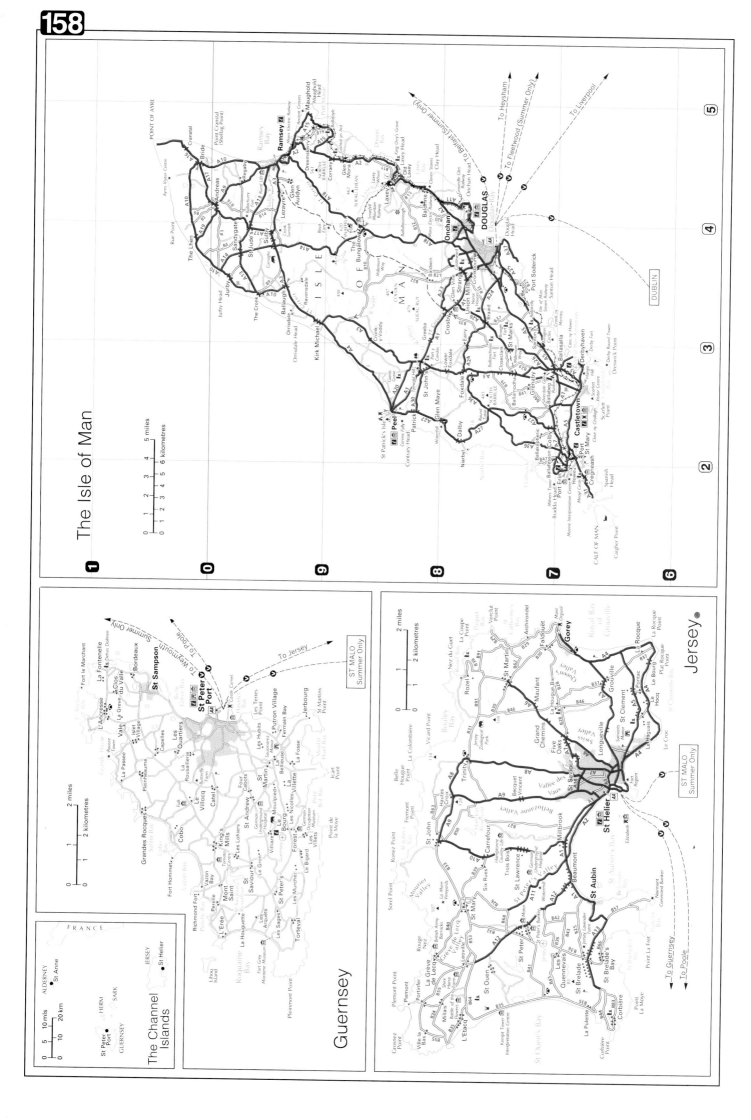

## The Isle of Man

0  1  2  3  4  5 miles

0  1  2  3  4  5  6 kilometres

## The Channel Islands

0    5    10 mls
0    10    20 km

FRANCE

ALDERNEY  • St Anne

HERM
SARK

GUERNSEY
St Peter Port  •

JERSEY  • St Helier

## Guernsey

0    1    2 miles
0    1    2 kilometres

## Jersey

0    1    2 miles
0    1    2 kilometres

# key to town plans

Refer also to page V, 'Using this atlas'

159

## Central London

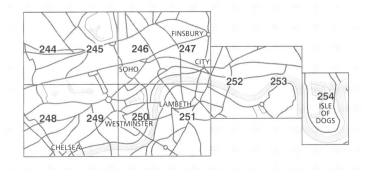

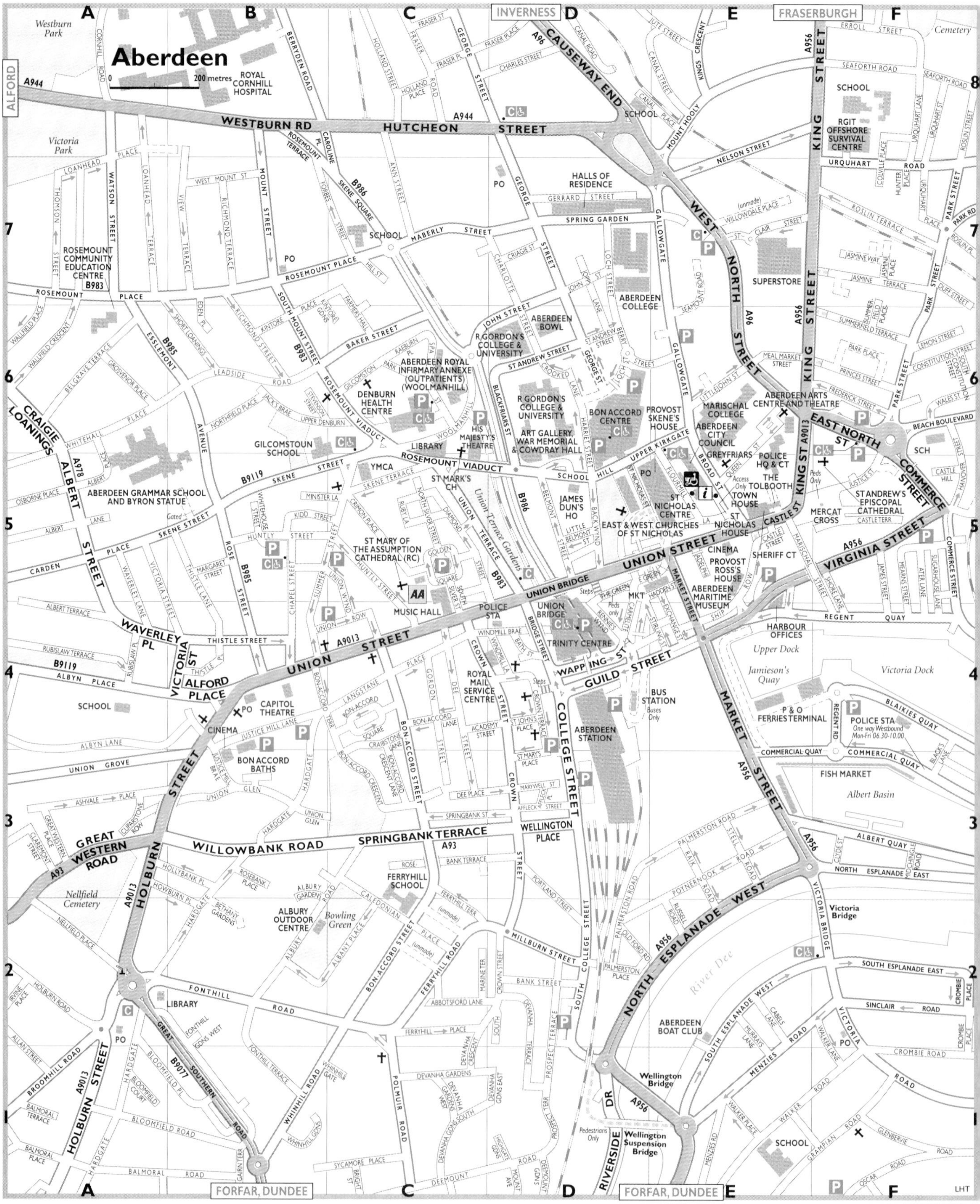

# Aberdeen

INVERNESS
FRASERBURGH
ALFORD
FORFAR, DUNDEE

0    200 metres

Westburn Park
ROYAL CORNHILL HOSPITAL
Victoria Park
ROSEMOUNT COMMUNITY EDUCATION CENTRE
CRAIGIE LOANINGS
ABERDEEN GRAMMAR SCHOOL AND BYRON STATUE
GILCOMSTOUN SCHOOL
DENBURN HEALTH CENTRE
ABERDEEN ROYAL INFIRMARY ANNEXE (OUTPATIENTS) (WOOLMANHILL)
R GORDON'S COLLEGE & UNIVERSITY
ABERDEEN BOWL
ABERDEEN COLLEGE
HALLS OF RESIDENCE
RGIT OFFSHORE SURVIVAL CENTRE
SCHOOL
SUPERSTORE
BON ACCORD CENTRE
PROVOST SKENE'S HOUSE
MARISCHAL COLLEGE
ABERDEEN CITY COUNCIL
GREYFRIARS
ABERDEEN ARTS CENTRE AND THEATRE
POLICE HQ & CT
THE TOLBOOTH
TOWN HOUSE
ST NICHOLAS HOUSE
ST ANDREW'S EPISCOPAL CATHEDRAL
MERCAT CROSS
HIS MAJESTY'S THEATRE
ART GALLERY, WAR MEMORIAL & COWDRAY HALL
LIBRARY
YMCA
ST MARK'S CH
ST MARY OF THE ASSUMPTION CATHEDRAL (RC)
JAMES DUN'S HO
ST NICHOLAS CENTRE
EAST & WEST CHURCHES OF ST NICHOLAS
CINEMA
SHERIFF CT
PROVOST ROSS'S HOUSE
ABERDEEN MARITIME MUSEUM
MUSIC HALL
AA
POLICE STA
UNION BRIDGE
TRINITY CENTRE
WAPPING ST
HARBOUR OFFICES
Upper Dock
Jamieson's Quay
Victoria Dock
CAPITOL THEATRE
CINEMA
BON ACCORD BATHS
ROYAL MAIL SERVICE CENTRE
ABERDEEN STATION
BUS STATION Buses Only
P & O FERRIES TERMINAL
POLICE STA One way Westbound Mon-Fri 06.30-10.00
FISH MARKET
Albert Basin
SCHOOL
FERRYHILL SCHOOL
ALBURY OUTDOOR CENTRE
Bowling Green
WELLINGTON PLACE
Nellfield Cemetery
LIBRARY
Victoria Bridge
ABERDEEN BOAT CLUB
Wellington Bridge
River Dee
Wellington Suspension Bridge
Pedestrians Only
SCHOOL
Cemetery

Streets: WESTBURN RD, HUTCHEON STREET, CAUSEWAY END, WEST NORTH STREET, KING STREET, SEAFORTH ROAD, GALLOWGATE, UNION STREET, GUILD STREET, MARKET STREET, COMMERCE STREET, VIRGINIA STREET, EAST NORTH ST, HOLBURN STREET, GREAT WESTERN ROAD, WILLOWBANK ROAD, SPRINGBANK TERRACE, ALFORD PLACE, WAVERLEY PL, ALBYN PLACE, UNION GROVE, ROSEMOUNT, SKENE STREET, BAKER STREET, MABERLY STREET, SPRING GARDEN, GEORGE STREET, NELSON STREET, URQUHART, ROSLIN TERRACE, PARK ROAD, GREAT SOUTHERN ROAD, RIVERSIDE DR, NORTH ESPLANADE WEST, SOUTH ESPLANADE EAST, CROMBIE ROAD, VICTORIA BRIDGE, ALBERT QUAY, NORTH ESPLANADE EAST, BALMORAL ROAD, POLMUIR ROAD, FERRYHILL ROAD, FONTHILL ROAD, BON-ACCORD STREET, COLLEGE STREET, CROWN STREET

Road numbers: A944, A96, A956, A93, A9013, A978, B983, B985, B986, B9119, B9077, B9119

FORFAR, DUNDEE

LHT

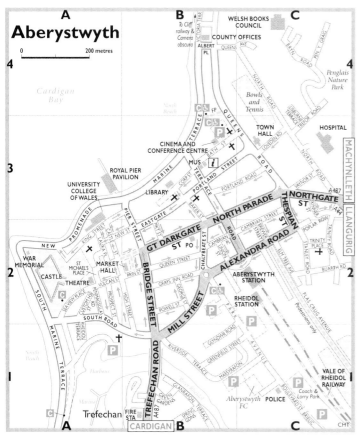

# Aberystwyth

Aberystwyth is found on atlas page **43**, grid reference **5881**

| | | | | | |
|---|---|---|---|---|---|
| Albert Place | B4 | Mill Street | B1-B2 | Trefechan Road | B1 |
| Baker Street | B3 | New Promenade | A2-B3 | Trefor Road | C3-C4 |
| Bath Steet | B3 | New Street | A2-B2 | Trinity Place | C2 |
| Boulevard St Brieuc | C1 | North Parade | B2-C3 | Trinity Road | C2-C3 |
| Brewer Street | C2 | North Road | C3-C4 | Union Street | B2 |
| Bridge Street | B1-B2 | Northgate Street | C3 | Vaynor Street | C3 |
| Bryn Road | C4 | Park Avenue | B2-C1 | Victoria Terrace | B4 |
| Buarth Road | C2 | Pen y Graig | C4 | Vulcan Street | A2 |
| Cambrian Place | B2 | Penmagsglas Road | A2 | | |
| Cambrian Street | C2-C3 | Pier Street | B2-B3 | | |
| Castle Street | A2 | Plas Crug Avenue | C1-C2 | | |
| Chalybeate Street | B2 | Poplar Row | C2-C3 | | |
| Corporation Street | B3 | Portland Road | B3-C3 | | |
| Custom House Street | A2 | Portland Street | B3-C3 | | |
| Eastgate | B2-B3 | Powell Street | B2 | | |
| Elmtree Avenue | C2 | Princess Street | B2 | | |
| George Street | B2 | Prospect Street | A2 | | |
| Glanrafon Terrace | B1 | Queen Street | B2 | | |
| Glyndwr Road | B1 | Queens Avenue | B4-C4 | | |
| Grays Inn Road | B2 | Queens Road | B4-C3 | | |
| Great Darkgate Street | B2 | Rheidol Terrace | A1 | | |
| Green Gardens | B1 | Riverside Terrace | B1 | | |
| Greenfield Street | B1-C1 | St Michael's Place | A2 | | |
| High Street | A2-B2 | Sea View Place | A2 | | |
| King Street | A2-A3 | Skinner Street | C3 | | |
| Laura Place | A2 | South Marine Terrace | A1-A2 | | |
| Lisburne Terrace | C3-C4 | South Road | A2-B1 | | |
| Loveden Road | C3 | Spring Gardens | B1 | | |
| Maesyrafon | B1-C1 | Stanley Road | C2 | | |
| Marine Terrace | B4-B3 | Terrace Road | B3-C2 | | |
| Market Street | B2 | Thespian Street | C2-C3 | | |

161

# Aberdeen

Aberdeen is found on atlas page **135**, grid reference **9306**

**AA shop**
19–20 Golden Square, Aberdeen AB9 1JN C5

| | | | | | |
|---|---|---|---|---|---|
| Abbotsford Lane | C2-D2 | Bon-Accord Crescent | C4-C3 | Spa Street | C6 |
| Academy Street | C4-D4 | Bon-Accord Crescent Lane | C3-C4 | Spring Garden | D7 |
| Adelphi | E5 | Bon-Accord Lane | C4 | Springbank Street | C3-D3 |
| Affleck Place | D3 | Bon-Accord Square | C4 | Springbank Terrace | C3-D3 |
| Affleck Street | D3 | Bon-Accord Street | C2-C3-C4 | Stell Road | E3 |
| Albany Place | B2-C2 | Bon-Accord Terrace | B4-C4 | Stevenson Street | B6 |
| Albert Lane | A5 | Bridge Street | D4 | Stirling Street | D4-E4 |
| Albert Quay | F3-E3 | Bright Street | C1 | Sugar House Lane | F4-F5 |
| Albert Place | A5-A6 | Broad Street | E5-E6 | Summerfield Place | F6-F7 |
| Albert Street | A4-A5 | Broomhill Road | A1-A2 | Summerfield Terrace | F6 |
| Albert Terrace | A4-A5 | Cabels Lane | E2 | Summer Street | B4-B5-C5 |
| Albury Gardens | B2-B3 | Caledonian Place | C3-C2 | Sycamore Place | B1-C1 |
| Albury Road | B2-C3 | Canal Place | D8-E8 | The Green | D4-D5 |
| Albyn Lane | A4-B4 | Canal Road | D8 | Thistle Lane | B5-B4 |
| Albyn Place | A4 | Canal Street | D8-E8 | Thistle Place | B4 |
| Alford Place | B4 | Carden Place | A5 | Thistle Street | B4 |
| Allan Street | A1-A2 | Carmelite Street | D4-D5 | Thomson Street | A7 |
| Ann Street | C7-C8 | Caroline Place | B8-C7 | Union Bridge | D4-D5 |
| Ashvale Place | A3 | Castle Street | E5 | Union Glen | B3 |
| Ater Lane | F4-F5 | Castle Hill | F5 | Union Grove | A3-B3 |
| Back Wynd | D5 | Castle Terrace | F5 | Union Row | B4-C4 |
| Baker Street | C6 | Causewayend | D8 | Union Street | B4-C4-D5-E5 |
| Balmoral Place | A1 | Chapel Street | B5-B4 | Union Terrace | C5-D5 |
| Balmoral Road | A1-B1 | Charles Street | C8-D8 | Union Wynd | B5-C5-C4 |
| Balmoral Terrace | A1 | Charlotte Street | D7-D6 | Upper Denburn | B6-C6 |
| Bank Street | D2 | Claremont Street | A3 | Upper Kirkgate | D5-D6-E6 |
| Bath Street | D4 | Clyde Street | F3 | Urquhart Lane | F7-F8 |
| Beach Boulevard | F6 | College Street | D4-D3 | Urquhart Place | F7 |
| Belgrave Terrace | A6 | Colville Place | F7-F8 | Urquhart Road | F7 |
| Belmont Street | D5 | Commerce Street | F4-F5 | Urquhart Street | F8-F7 |
| Berry Street | D6-E6 | Commercial Quay | E3-F3 | Victoria Bridge | F3-F2 |
| Berryden Road | B8 | Constitution Street | F6 | Victoria Road | F2-F1 |
| Bethany Gardens | B2 | Cornhill Road | A8 | Victoria Street | A5-B4 |
| Blackfriars Street | D5-D6 | Craibstone Lane | C3-C4 | View Terrace | B7-B8 |
| Black's Lane | F3-F4 | Craigie Loanings | A6 | Virginia Street | E5-F5 |
| Blaikies Quay | F4 | Craigie Street | D7 | Wales Street | F6 |
| Bloomfield Court | A1 | Crimon Place | C5 | Walker Lane | F1-F2 |
| Bloomfield Place | A2-A1-B1 | Crombie Place | F2 | Walker Place | E1 |
| Bloomfield Road | A1-B1 | Crombie Road | F1 | Walker Road | E1-F1 |
| Crooked Lane | D6 | Hanover Street | F6-F5 | Wallfield Crescent | A6-A7 |
| Crown Street | C4-D4-D3-D2 | Hardgate | A1-A2-B2-B3-B4 | Wallfield Place | A6-A7 |
| Crown Terrace | D4 | Harriet Street | D5-D6 | Wapping Street | D4 |
| Cuparstone Row | A3 | Highgate Gardens | D1 | Watson Street | A7-A8 |
| Deemount Gardens | D1 | Hill Street | C7 | Waverley Lane | A5-A4 |
| Deemount Road | C1-D1 | Holburn Road | A2 | Waverley Place | A4-B4 |
| Dee Place | C3-D3 | Holburn Street | A1-A2-A3-B3-B4 | Wellington Place | D3 |
| Dee Street | C4-C3 | Holland Place | C8 | West Mount Street | B7 |
| Devanha Crescent | C1-C2-D1 | Holland Street | C8 | West North Street | E7-E6 |
| Devanha Gardens | C1-D1 | Hollybank Place | A3-B3 | Westburn Road | A8-B8 |
| Devanha Gardens East | D1 | Howburn Place | A3-B3-B2 | Whinhill Gardens | B1 |
| Devanha Gardens South | C1 | Hunter Place | F7 | Whinhill Gate | B1-C1 |
| Devanha Gardens West | C1 | Huntly Street | B5-C5-C4 | Whinhill Road | B1-C2 |
| Devanha Terrace | D1-D2 | Hutcheon Street | C8-D8 | Whitehall Place | A5-A6-B6 |
| Diamond Street | C5 | Irvine Place | A2 | Whitehouse Street | B5 |
| Duff Street | F6-F7 | Jack's Brae | B6 | Willowbank Road | A3-B3 |
| East North Street | E6-F6 | James Street | F5-F4 | Willowdale Place | E7 |
| Eden Place | B6-B7 | Jasmine Place | F7 | Windmill Brae | C4-D4 |
| Erroll Street | F8 | Jasmine Terrace | F7 | Windmill Lane | D4 |
| Esslemont Avenue | A6-B6-B5 | Jasmine Way | F7 | Woolmanhill | C6 |
| Exchange Street | E5-E4 | John Street | C6-D6-D7 | | |
| Farmers Hall | C7-C6 | Jopp's Lane | D7-D6 | | |
| Ferryhill Place | C2 | Justice Street | F5 | | |
| Ferryhill Road | C2-D2 | Justice Mill Brae | B3-B4 | | |
| Ferryhill Terrace | C3-C2 | Justice Mill Lane | B3-B4 | | |
| Flourmill Lane | E5-E6 | Jute Street | D8-E8 | | |
| Fonthill Gardens West | B2 | Kidd Street | B5-C5 | | |
| Fonthill Road | A2-B2-C2 | King Street | E5-E6-F7-F8 | | |
| Fonthill Terrace | B1-B2 | Kings Crescent | E8 | | |
| Forbes Street | B7-C7 | Kintore Gardens | B7-B6-C6 | | |
| Fraser Place | C8-D8 | Kintore Place | B6-B7-C7 | | |
| Fraser Road | C8 | Langstane Place | C4 | | |
| Fraser Street | C8 | Leadside Road | B6 | | |
| Frederick Street | F6 | Lemon Street | F6 | | |
| Gairn Terrace | B1 | Little Belmont Street | D5 | | |
| Gallowgate | E7-E6 | Little John Street | E6 | | |
| George Street | C8-D8-D7-D6 | Loanhead Place | A7-A8 | | |
| Gerrard Street | D7 | Loanhead Terrace | A7-A8 | | |
| Gilcomston Park | C6 | Loch Street | D6 | | |
| Glenbervie Road | F1 | Maberly Street | C7-D7 | | |
| Golden Square | C5 | Marischal Street | E5-F5-F4 | | |
| Gordon Street | C4-C3 | Market Street | E5-E4-E3 | | |
| Grampian Road | E1-F1 | Margaret Street | B5 | | |
| Great Southern Road | A2-B1 | Marine Terrace | C2 | | |
| Great Western Place | A3 | Marywell Street | D3 | | |
| Great Western Road | A2-A3 | Meal Market Street | E6 | | |
| Grosvenor Place | A6 | Mearns Street | F5-F4 | | |
| Guild Street | D4-E4 | Menzies Road | E1-E2-F2 | | |
| Hadden Street | E5 | Midchingle Road | F3 | | |
| | | Millburn Street | D2 | | |
| | | Minister Lane | B5-C5 | | |
| | | Mount Avenue | D1 | | |
| | | Mount Hooly | E8 | | |
| | | Mount Street | B7-B8 | | |
| | | Murrays Lane | E1-E2 | | |
| | | Nellfield Place | A2 | | |
| | | Nelson Street | E7-E8 | | |
| | | North Esplanade East | F3 | | |
| | | North Esplanade West | D1-E3 | | |
| | | North Silver Street | C5 | | |
| | | Northfield Place | B6 | | |
| | | Old Ford Road | D2 | | |
| | | Osborne Place | A5 | | |
| | | Oscar Road | F1 | | |
| | | Palmerston Place | D2 | | |
| | | Palmerston Road | D2-D3-E3 | | |
| | | Park Place | F6 | | |
| | | Park Road | F7 | | |
| | | Park Street | F6-F7 | | |
| | | Polmuir Road | C1-C2 | | |
| | | Portland Street | D3-D2 | | |
| | | Poynernook Road | D2-E2-E3 | | |
| | | Princes Street | F6 | | |
| | | Prospect Terrace | D1-D2 | | |
| | | Queen Street | E5-E6 | | |
| | | Raeburn Place | C6 | | |
| | | Raik Road | E3-E2 | | |
| | | Regent Road | F4 | | |
| | | Regent Quay | E4-F4 | | |
| | | Rennies Wynd | D4 | | |
| | | Richmond Street | B6-B7 | | |
| | | Richmond Terrace | B7 | | |
| | | Riverside Drive | D1 | | |
| | | Rose Street | B5-B4 | | |
| | | Rosebank Place | B3 | | |
| | | Rosebank Terrace | C3-D3 | | |
| | | Rosemount Place | A7-B7-C7 | | |
| | | Rosemount Terrace | B8-B7 | | |
| | | Rosemount Viaduct | B6-C5-D5 | | |
| | | Roslin Place | F7 | | |
| | | Roslin Street | F8 | | |
| | | Roslin Terrace | F7 | | |
| | | Rubislaw Place | A4 | | |
| | | Rubislaw Terrace | A4 | | |
| | | Ruby Lane | C5 | | |
| | | Russell Road | E2 | | |
| | | St Andrew Street | D6 | | |
| | | St Clair Street | E7 | | |
| | | St John's Place | D4 | | |
| | | St Mary's Place | D3 | | |
| | | St Nicholas Street | D5-E5 | | |
| | | School Hill | D5 | | |
| | | Seaforth Road | F8 | | |
| | | Seamount Road | E6-E7 | | |
| | | Ship Row | E4-E5 | | |
| | | Shore Lane | F4-F5 | | |
| | | Short Loanings | A7-B6 | | |
| | | Sinclair Road | F2 | | |
| | | Skene Square | B7-C7 | | |
| | | Skene Street | A5-B5-C5 | | |
| | | Skene Terrace | C5 | | |
| | | South College Street | D3-D2-D1 | | |
| | | South Constitution Street | F6 | | |
| | | South Crown Street | D2 | | |
| | | South Esplanade East | F2 | | |
| | | South Esplanade West | E1-E2-F2 | | |
| | | South Mount Street | B7-B6 | | |
| | | South Silver Street | C4-C5 | | |

162

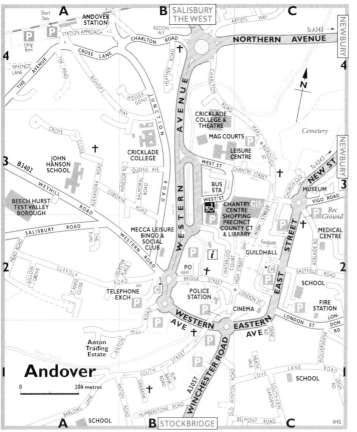

# Andover

Andover is found on atlas page **23**,
grid reference **3645**

| | | | |
|---|---|---|---|
| Adelaide Road | C2-C3 | The Elms | A2 |
| Alexandra Road | A3 | The Pines | A4 |
| Anton Mill Road | A1-B1-B2 | Vigo Road | C3 |
| Anton Road | B1 | Waterloo Court | B2 |
| Artists Way | B4-C4 | Wessex Gardens | B4 |
| Balmoral Road | B3 | Western Avenue | B1-B2-B3 |
| Barlows Lane | A1 | Western Road | A2-B2 |
| Belmont Road | B1-C1 | West Street | B2-B3 |
| Bishop's Way | A4-B4-B3 | Weyhill Road | A3 |
| Bridge Street | B2 | Whynot Lane | A4 |
| Chantry Street | B3-C3 | Winchester Road | B1 |
| Charlton Road | B4-B3-C3 | Windsor Road | B3 |
| Church Close | C3 | Willow Grove | A2 |
| Cross Lane | A4 | Wolversdene Road | C1 |
| Croye Close | A3 | | |
| Dene Road | C1 | | |
| Eastfield Road | C2 | | |
| East Street | C2-C3 | | |
| Eastern Avenue | C1-C2 | | |
| Elmbank Road | B1 | | |
| Heath Vale | C1 | | |
| Heather Drive | B4 | | |
| High Street | B2-C2-C3 | | |
| Humberstone Road | B1 | | |
| Junction Road | B2-B3-B4 | | |
| Leicester Place | B2 | | |
| Leigh Road | C1 | | |
| London Road | C1 | | |
| London Street | C1 | | |
| Love Lane | C1-C2 | | |
| Marlborough Street | C3 | | |
| Mead Road | A2 | | |
| New Street | B1 | | |
| Northern Avenue | B4-C4 | | |
| Oak Bank Road | B1 | | |
| Old Winton Road | B1-C1 | | |
| Osborne Road | A3-B3 | | |
| Queens Avenue | B3 | | |
| Redon Way | B4 | | |
| St Anns Close | A2 | | |
| Salisbury Road | A2 | | |
| South Street | B1-B2 | | |
| Southview Gardens | C1 | | |
| Station Approach | A4 | | |
| Suffolk Road | A2-B2 | | |
| The Avenue | A4 | | |

# Basingstoke

Basingstoke is found on atlas page **24**,
grid reference **6352**

**AA shop**
21–23 Wote Street, Basingstoke RG21 1NE          B2

| | | | |
|---|---|---|---|
| Alencon Link | B3-B4-C3 | New Street | B2 |
| Basing View | C4 | Norn Hill | C4 |
| Beaconsfield Road | B1 | Old Reading Road | C4 |
| Blair Road | A1 | Penrith Road | A2 |
| Bounty Rise | A1 | Provident Way | B4 |
| Bounty Road | A1-B1 | Rayleigh Road | A3 |
| Bramblys Close | A2 | Ringway South | A1-B1-C1 |
| Bramblys Drive | A2 | Rochford Road | A3 |
| Budds Close | A2 | St Mary's Court | C3 |
| Bunnian Place | B4 | Sarum Hill | A2-B2 |
| Burgess Road | A4-B4 | Seal Road | B1-B2 |
| Chapel Hill | A4-B4 | Southend Road | A3 |
| Chequers Road | B2-C3 | Solbys Road | A3 |
| Chester Place | A2 | Soper Grove | B4 |
| Church Square | A2-B2 | Southern Road | B2 |
| Church Street | B2 | Timberlake Road | B3-C3 |
| Churchill Way | A3-B3 | Victoria Street | B2 |
| Churchill Way East | C3 | Vyne Road | B4 |
| Cliddesden Road | B1 | White Hart Lane | C2 |
| Council Road | B1 | Winchcombe Road | A2 |
| Cross Street | B2 | Winchester Road | A1-A2-B2 |
| Crossborough Hill | C1-C2 | Winchester Street | B2 |
| Culver Road | A1 | Worting Road | A3 |
| Devonshire Place | A1-A2 | Wote Street | B2 |
| Eastfield Avenue | C2-C3 | | |
| Eastrop Lane | C2-C3 | | |
| Eastrop Way | C3 | | |
| Elbow Corner | B3 | | |
| Essex Road | A3 | | |
| Fairfields Road | B1 | | |
| Flaxfield Road | A3-B2 | | |
| Frances Road | A2 | | |
| Frescade Crescent | A1 | | |
| Goat Lane | C3 | | |
| Hackwood Road | C1-C2 | | |
| Hamelyn Road | A2 | | |
| Hawkfield Lane | A1 | | |
| Jubilee Road | B1 | | |
| London Road | C2 | | |
| London Street | B2 | | |
| Longcroft Close | A2 | | |
| Mortimer Lane | A3 | | |
| New Road | B2-C2-C3 | | |

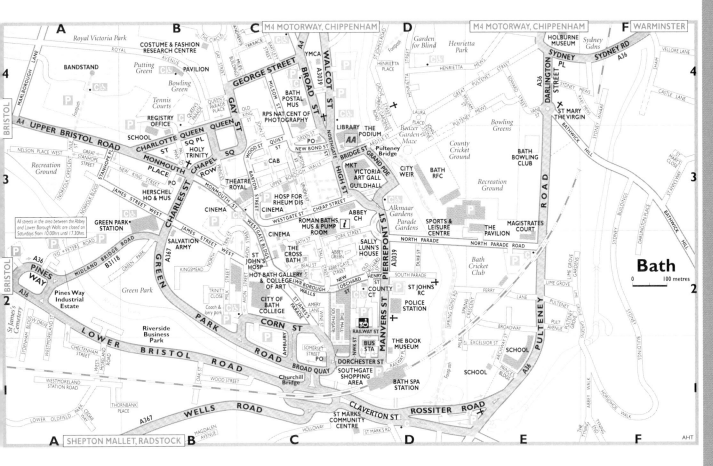

# Bath

Bath is found on atlas page **22**,
grid reference **7464**

**AA shop**
13 Northgate Street, Bath BA1 5AS                    D3

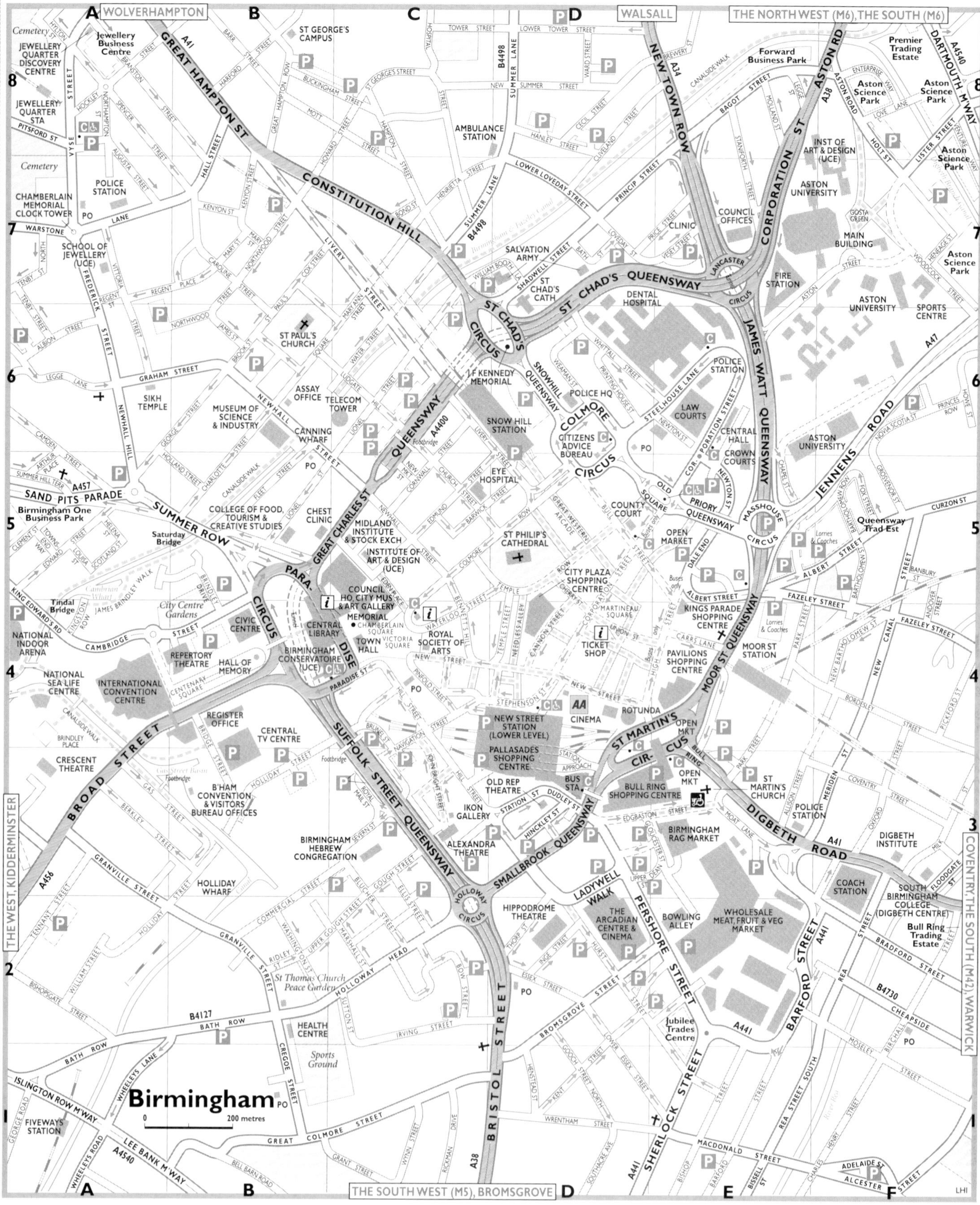

WOLVERHAMPTON · WALSALL · THE NORTH WEST (M6), THE SOUTH (M6)

Cemetery
Jewellery Quarter Discovery Centre
Jewellery Business Centre
Jewellery Quarter Sta
Pitsford St
Cemetery
Chamberlain Memorial Clock Tower
Police Station
Warstone
School of Jewellery (UCE)
Sikh Temple
St Paul's Church
Assay Office
Telecom Tower
Museum of Science & Industry
Canning Wharf
Graham Street
Newhall Hill
Sand Pits Parade
Birmingham One Business Park
Summer Row
Saturday Bridge
College of Food, Tourism & Creative Studies
Chest Clinic
Midland Institute & Stock Exch
Institute of Art & Design (UCE)
Council Ho, City Mus & Art Gallery
Memorial
Chamberlain Square
Town Hall
Victoria Square
Royal Society of Arts
Central Library
Civic Centre
Birmingham Conservatoire (UCE)
City Centre Gardens
Tindal Bridge
Cambrian Wharf
James Brindley Walk
National Indoor Arena
Repertory Theatre
Hall of Memory
Paradise Circus
National Sea Life Centre
International Convention Centre
Centenary Square
Register Office
Central TV Centre
Broad Street
Crescent Theatre
Brindley Place
Canalside Walk
B'ham Convention & Visitors Bureau Offices
Ikon Gallery
Old Rep Theatre
Alexandra Theatre
Birmingham Hebrew Congregation
Holliday Wharf
Suffolk Street Queensway
Holloway Circus
Hippodrome Theatre
The Arcadian Centre & Cinema
St Thomas Church Peace Garden
Health Centre
Sports Ground
Bristol Street
Birmingham
0 — 200 metres
Fiveways Station
Islington Row M'Way
Lee Bank M'Way
A4540
THE SOUTH WEST (M5), BROMSGROVE

Great Hampton St
A41
Constitution Hill
St George's Campus
Ambulance Station
Lower Loveday Street
B4498
J F Kennedy Memorial
Snow Hill Station
Eye Hospital
Queensway
St Chad's Circus
St Chad's Cath
Salvation Army
St Chad's Queensway
New Town Row
Aston Rd
A38
Forward Business Park
Premier Trading Estate
Dartmouth M'Way
Aston Science Park
Inst of Art & Design (UCE)
Aston University
Council Offices
Clinic
Fire Station
Main Building
Aston Science Park
Sports Centre
Aston University
James Watt Queensway
Dental Hospital
Police Station
Police HQ
Law Courts
Corporation St
Colmore Circus
Citizens Advice Bureau
Central Hall
Crown Courts
St Philip's Cathedral
County Court
Old Square
Priory Queensway
Masshouse Circus
Great Western Arcade
City Plaza Shopping Centre
Open Market
Jennens Road
A47
Aston University
Queensway Trad Est
Albert Street
Kings Parade Shopping Centre
Moor St Station
Pavilions Shopping Centre
Dale End
Fazeley Street
New Street Station (Lower Level)
Pallasades Shopping Centre
Cinema
Rotunda
AA
St Martin's Circus
Bull Ring Shopping Centre
St Martin's Church
Bus Sta
Open Mkt
Moat Lane
Digbeth Road
A41
Police Station
Digbeth Institute
Birmingham Rag Market
Ladywell Walk
Pershore Street
Bowling Alley
Wholesale Meat, Fruit & Veg Market
Coach Station
South Birmingham College (Digbeth Centre)
Bull Ring Trading Estate
Smallbrook Queensway
Barford Street
Jubilee Trades Centre
B4730
Cheapside
Sherlock Street
A441
Alcester Street
THE WEST, KIDDERMINSTER
COVENTRY, THE SOUTH (M42), WARWICK

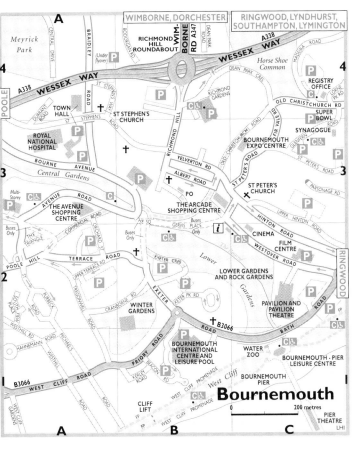

# Bournemouth

Bournemouth is found on atlas page 12,
grid reference 0809

| | | | |
|---|---|---|---|
| Albert Road | B3 | Westhill Road | A1-A2 |
| Avenue Road | A3-B3 | Westover Road | C2 |
| Bath Road | C1-C2 | Wimborne Road | B4 |
| Beacon Road | B1 | Yelverton Road | B3 |
| Bodorgan Road | B4 | | |
| Bourne Avenue | A3-B3 | | |
| Braidley Road | A3-A4 | | |
| Central Drive | A4 | | |
| Commercial Road | A2-A3 | | |
| Cranborne Road | A2-B2 | | |
| Dean Park Crescent | B4-C4 | | |
| Dean Park Road | B4 | | |
| Durrant Road | A4 | | |
| Exeter Crescent | B2 | | |
| Exeter Park Road | B2 | | |
| Exeter Road | B1-B2 | | |
| Fir Vale Road | C3-C4 | | |
| Gervis Place | B2-B3 | | |
| Glenfern Road | C3 | | |
| Hahnemann Road | A1 | | |
| Hinton Road | C2-C3 | | |
| Kerley Road | B1 | | |
| Lorne Park Road | C4 | | |
| Madeira Road | C4 | | |
| Old Christchurch Road | B3-C3-C4 | | |
| Orchard Street | A2-A3 | | |
| Parsonage Road | C3 | | |
| Poole Hill | A2 | | |
| Priory Road | B1-B2 | | |
| Purbeck Road | A2 | | |
| Richmond Gardens | B4 | | |
| Richmond Hill | B3-B4 | | |
| St Michael's Road | A2-A1-B1 | | |
| St Peter's Road | C3 | | |
| St Stephen's Road | A3-A4-B3 | | |
| St Stephen's Way | A4 | | |
| South View Place | A2 | | |
| Terrace Road | A2-B2 | | |
| The Square | B3 | | |
| The Triangle | A2 | | |
| Tregonwell Road | A1-A2 | | |
| Upper Hinton Road | C2-C3 | | |
| Upper Terrace Road | A2 | | |
| Wessex Way | A4-B4-C4 | | |
| West Cliff Gardens | A1 | | |
| West Cliff Road | A1 | | |

**165**

---

# Birmingham

Birmingham is found on atlas page 61,
grid reference 0786

**AA shop**
134 New Street, Birmingham B2 4NP  D4

| | | | | | | | | | |
|---|---|---|---|---|---|---|---|---|---|
| Adelaide Street | F1 | Brook Street | B6 | Edward Street | A5 | Irving Street | C2 | Newton Street | E5-E6 | Temple Row | C5-D5 |
| Albert Street | E5-F5 | Brunel Street | C4 | Ellis Street | C2-C3 | Islington Row Middleway | A1 | Northampton Street | A8-A7 | Temple Street | D4-D5 |
| Albion Street | A6 | Buckingham Street | B8-C8 | Enterprise Way | F8 | James Brindley Walk | A4-A5-B5 | Northwood Street | B6-B7 | Tenby Street | A6-A7 |
| Alcester Street | F1 | Bull Ring | E3-E4 | Essex Street | D2 | James Street | B6 | Nova Scotia Street | F6 | Tenby Street North | A7 |
| Allison Street | E3-F4 | Bull Street | D5-E5 | Fazeley Street | E5-F4 | James Watt Queensway | E5-E6 | Old Square | D5-E5 | Tennant Street | A2-A3 |
| Andover Street | F4-F5 | Cambridge Street | A4-B4 | Fleet Street | B5-B6 | Jennens Road | E5-F5-F6 | Oxford Street | F3-F4 | Thorp Street | D2 |
| Arthur Place | A5 | Camden Street | A6-A5 | Floodgate Street | F3 | John Bright Street | C3 | Paradise Circus | B5-B4 | Tower Street | C8-D8 |
| Aston Road | F8 | Canalside Walk | B3-A3-A4-A5-B5 | Fox Street | F5 | Kent Street | D1-D2 | Paradise Street | B4-C4 | Townsend Way | A5 |
| Aston Street | E6-E7 | Cannon Street | D4 | Frederick Street | A7-A6 | Kenyon Street | B7 | Park Street | E3-E4-E5 | Union Street | D4-E4 |
| Augusta Street | A7-A8 | Caroline Street | B7-B6 | Gas Street | A3-B3 | King Edwards Road | A5-A4 | Pershore Street | D3-D2-E2 | Upper Dean Street | D3-E3 |
| Bagot Street | E8 | Carrs Lane | E4 | George Road | A1 | Kingston Row | A4 | Pickford Street | F4 | Upper Gough Street | B2-C2 |
| Banbury Street | F5 | Cecil Street | D8 | George Street | A5-A6-B6 | Ladywell Walk | D2-D3 | Pinfold Street | C4 | Vesey Street | E7 |
| Barford Street | E1-E2-F2 | Centenary Square | B4 | Gloucester Street | E3 | Lancaster Circus | E7 | Pitsford Street | A8 | Victoria Square | C4 |
| Barr Street | B8 | Chamberlain Square | C4 | Gooch Street North | D1-D2 | Lee Bank Middleway | A1-B1 | Price Street | D7-E7 | Vittoria Street | A6-A7 |
| Bartholomew Row | F5 | Chapel Street | E5 | Gosta Green | F7 | Legge Lane | A6 | Princes Row | F6 | Vyse Street | A7-A8 |
| Bartholomew Street | F4-F5 | Charles Henry Street | E1-F1 | Gough Street | C3 | Legge Street | E8 | Princip Street | D7-E8 | Ward Street | D8 |
| Barwick Street | C5-D5 | Charlotte Street | B5-B6 | Graham Street | A6-B6 | Lionel Street | B5-C6-C7 | Printing House Street | D6 | Warstone Lane | A7-B7 |
| Bath Row | A1-A2-B2 | Cheapside | F2 | Grant Street | B1-C1 | Lister Street | F7-F8 | Priory Queensway | E5 | Washington Street | B2 |
| Bath Street | D7 | Cherry Street | D4-D5 | Granville Street | A3-B2 | Livery Street | B7-C7-C6-D5 | Rea Street | F2-F3 | Water Street | C6 |
| Bell Barn Road | B1 | Church Street | C5-D5 | Great Charles Street Queensway | B5-C5 | Louisa Street | A5 | Rea Street South | E1-F1-F2 | Waterloo Street | C4-D5 |
| Bennett's Hill | C4-C5 | Clement Street | A5 | Great Colmore Street | B1-C1 | Love Lane | F8 | Regent Place | A7-B7 | Weaman Street | D6 |
| Berkley Street | A3-B3 | Cleveland Street | D7-D8-E8 | Great Hampton Row | B8 | Loveday Street | D7 | Regent Street | A7 | Wheeleys Lane | A1-B2 |
| Birchall Street | F1-F2 | Colmore Circus | D5-D6 | Great Hampton Street | A8-B8 | Lower Essex Street | D2-D1-E1 | Rickman Drive | C1 | Wheeleys Road | A1 |
| Bishop Street | E1 | Colmore Row | C5-D5 | Great Western Arcade | D5 | Lower Loveday Street | D7 | Ridley Street | B2 | Whittall Street | D6-E6 |
| Bishopsgate Street | A2 | Commercial Street | B2-B3-C3 | Grosvenor Street | F5 | Lower Tower Street | D8 | Royal Mail Street | C3 | William Booth Lane | C7-D7 |
| Bissell Street | E1 | Constitution Hill | B7-C7 | Hall Street | B7-B8 | Ludgate Hill | B6-C6 | St Chad's Circus | C6-D6-D7 | William Street | A2 |
| Blucher Street | C3-C2 | Cornwall Street | C5-C6 | Hampton Street | C7-C8 | Macdonald Street | E1 | St Chad's Queensway | D6-D7-E7 | Woodcock Street | F7 |
| Bond Street | C7 | Corporation Street | D4-E5-E8 | Hanley Street | D8 | Marshall Street | C2 | St George's Street | C8 | Wrentham Street | D1-E1 |
| Bordesley Street | E4-F4 | Coventry Street | F3 | Harford Street | B8 | Martineau Square | C4 | St Martin's Circus | D3-D4-E4-E3 | Wynn Street | C1 |
| Bow Street | C2 | Cox Street | B7 | Helena Street | A5 | Mary Ann Street | C6-C7 | St Paul's Square | B6-C6-B7 | | |
| Bradford Street | F2 | Cregoe Street | B1-B2 | Heneage Street | F7 | Mary Street | B7 | Sand Pits Parade | A5 | | |
| Branston Street | A8-B8 | Curzon Street | F5 | Henrietta Street | C7 | Masshouse Circus | E5 | Scotland Street | A5 | | |
| Brewery Street | E8 | Dale End | E5 | Henstead Street | D1 | Meriden Street | F3 | Severn Street | C3 | | |
| Bridge Street | B3-B4 | Dartmouth Middleway | F8 | High Street | D4-E4 | Milk Street | F2 | Shadwell Street | D7 | | |
| Brindley Drive | B4-B5 | Digbeth Road | E3-F3 | Hill Street | C3-C4-D3 | Moat Lane | E3 | Sherlock Street | D1-E1-E2 | | |
| Brindley Place | A4 | Dudley Street | D3 | Hinckley Street | D3 | Molland Street | E8 | Smallbrook Queensway | D3 | | |
| Bristol Street | D1-D2-C2 | Eden Place | C5-C4 | Hockley Street | A8-B8 | Moor Street Queensway | E4-E5 | Snowhill Queensway | D6 | | |
| Broad Street | A3-A4-B4 | Edgbaston Street | D3-E3 | Holland Street | A5-B5 | Moseley Street | F1-F2 | Southacre Avenue | D1 | | |
| Bromsgrove Street | D1-D2-E2 | Edmund Street | C5 | Holliday Street | A2-B3-C4 | Mott Street | B8-C8-C7 | Spencer Street | B7-A7-A8 | | |
| | | | | Holloway Circus | C2-C3 | Navigation Street | C3-C4 | Staniforth Street | E8-E7 | | |
| | | | | Holloway Head | B2-C2 | Needless Alley | D4 | Station Approach | D3 | | |
| | | | | Holt Street | F7-F8 | New Bartholomew Street | F4 | Station Street | D3 | | |
| | | | | Hospital Street | C7-C8 | New Canal Street | F4-F5 | Steelhouse Lane | D6-E6 | | |
| | | | | Howard Street | B7-B8-C8 | New Market Street | C5 | Stephenson Street | D4 | | |
| | | | | Howe Street | F6 | New Street | C4-D4 | Suffolk Street Queensway | B4-C3 | | |
| | | | | Hurst Street | D2-E2-E1 | New Summer Street | C8-D8 | Summer Hill Terrace | A5 | | |
| | | | | Hylton Street | A8 | New Town Row | E7-E8 | Summer Lane | C7-D7-D8 | | |
| | | | | Inge Street | D2 | Newhall Hill | A5-A6 | Summer Row | A5-B5 | | |
| | | | | | | Newhall Street | B6-C5 | Sutton Street | C2 | | |

166

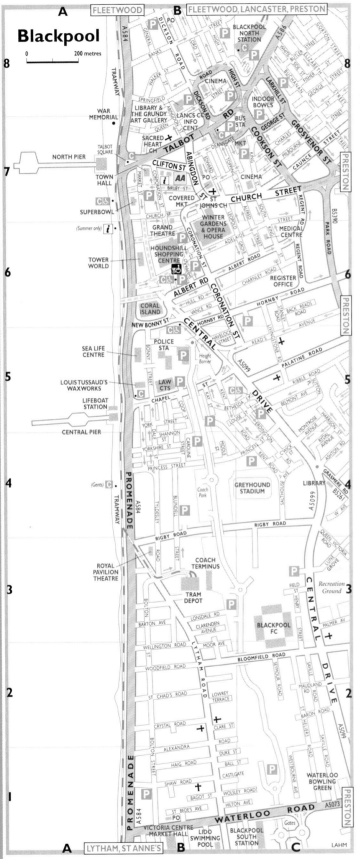

# Blackpool

Blackpool is found on atlas page **80**, grid reference **3036**

**AA shop**
13 Clifton Street, Blackpool FY1 1JD    B7

| | | | |
|---|---|---|---|
| Abingdon Street | B7-B8 | St Chad's Road | B2 |
| Adelaide Street | B6-C7 | St Heliers Road | C1-C2 |
| Albert Road | B6-C6 | Salthouse Avenue | C4 |
| Alexandra Road | B1-B2 | Saville Road | C1-C2 |
| Alfred Street | C6-C7 | Seymour Road | C2 |
| Ashton Road | C4 | Shannon Street | B4-B5 |
| Back Reads Road | C6 | Shaw Road | B1 |
| Bagot Street | B1 | Sheppard Street | B6 |
| Ball Street | B1-C1 | South King Street | C6-C7 |
| Banks Street | B8 | Springfield Road | B8 |
| Baron Road | C2 | Stanley Road | C5-C6 |
| Barton Avenue | B3 | Sutton Place | C5 |
| Belmont Avenue | C5 | Talbot Road | B7-C8 |
| Bethesda Road | B5-C5 | Topping Street | B7-C7 |
| Birley Street | B7 | Tyldesley Road | B3-B4 |
| Bloomfield Road | B2-C3 | Vance Road | B6 |
| Blundell Street | B3-B4 | Walker Street | B8 |
| Bolton Street | B1-B3 | Waterloo Road | B1-C1 |
| Bonny Street | B5 | Wellington Road | B2-B3 |
| Buchanan Street | C7-C8 | Westbourne Avenue | C1 |
| Butler Street | C8 | Whiteside Street | C8 |
| Caroline Street | B4 | Wolsey Road | B1-C1 |
| Castlegate | B1-C1 | Woodfield Road | B2 |
| Caunce Street | C7 | York Street | B5 |
| Central Drive | B6-C1 | Yorkshire Street | B4 |
| Chadwick Street | C4 | | |
| Chapel Street | B5 | | |
| Charles Street | C7-C8 | | |
| Charnley Road | B6-C6 | | |
| Church Street | B7-C8 | | |
| Clarendon Road | B2 | | |
| Clare Street | B2 | | |
| Clifton Street | B7 | | |
| Cocker Street | B8 | | |
| Cookson Street | C7-C8 | | |
| Coop Street | B5 | | |
| Coronation Street | B7-C5 | | |
| Corporation Street | B7 | | |
| Crystal Road | B2 | | |
| Dale Street | B4-B5 | | |
| Deansgate | B7-C8 | | |
| Dickson Road | B7-B8 | | |
| Duke Street | B1 | | |
| Edward Street | B7 | | |
| Elizabeth Street | C8 | | |
| Erdington Road | C4-C5 | | |
| Field Street | C3 | | |
| Fisher Street | C8 | | |
| General Street | B8 | | |
| George Street | C7-C8 | | |
| Gorton Street | C8 | | |
| Grasmere Road | C4 | | |
| Haig Road | B1 | | |
| Harrison Street | C4-C5 | | |
| Havelock Street | B5 | | |
| Henry Street | C2-C3 | | |
| High Street | B8-C8 | | |
| Hilton Avenue | B1-C1 | | |
| Hornby Road | B6-C6 | | |
| Hull Street | B6 | | |
| Kay Street | B5 | | |
| Kent Road | B5-C4 | | |
| Keswick Road | C4 | | |
| King Street | C7 | | |
| Larkhill Street | C8 | | |
| Leamington Road | C7 | | |
| Leopold Grove | B7-C6 | | |
| Livingstone Road | C5-C6 | | |
| Lonsdale Road | B3 | | |
| Lord Street | B8 | | |
| Louise Street | B5-C5 | | |
| Lowrey Terrace | B2 | | |
| Lune Grove | C3 | | |
| Lytham Road | B1-B3 | | |
| Market Street | B7 | | |
| Maudland Road | C2 | | |
| Middle Street | B4 | | |
| Milbourne Street | C7-C8 | | |
| Montrose Avenue | C4-C5 | | |
| Moor Avenue | B2 | | |
| New Bonny Street | B6 | | |
| North Promenade | B6-B8 | | |
| Palatine Road | C5 | | |
| Palmer Avenue | C3 | | |
| Park Road | C5-C7 | | |
| Peter Street | C7 | | |
| Princess Street | B4-C5 | | |
| Promenade | A1-B6 | | |
| Queen Street | B7-B8 | | |
| Queen Victoria Road | C4 | | |
| Read's Avenue | B5-C6 | | |
| Regent Road | C6-C7 | | |
| Ribble Road | C5 | | |
| Rigby Road | B3-C4 | | |
| Rydal Avenue | C4-C5 | | |
| St Bede's Avenue | B1 | | |

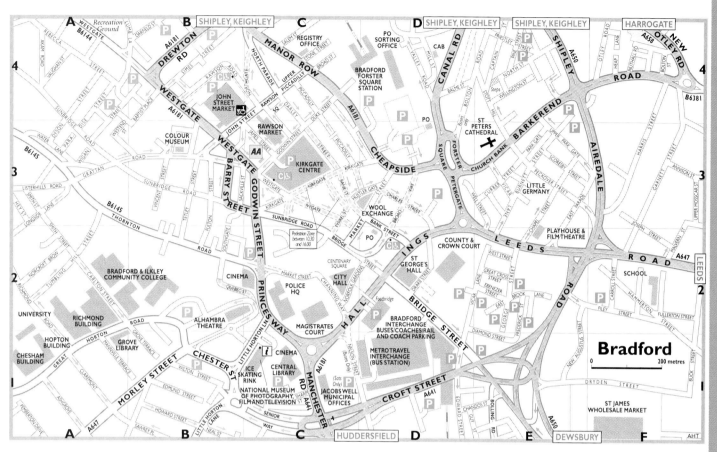

# Bradford

Bradford is found on atlas page **82**,
grid reference **163**2

**AA shop**
101 Godwin Street, Bradford BD1 3PP              C3

| | | | | | | | |
|---|---|---|---|---|---|---|---|
| Akam Road | A4 | East Parade | E2-E3 | Market Street | C2-D3 | Stott Hill | E3-E4 |
| Annison Street | F3 | Ebenezer Street | E2 | Mill Street | D4 | Sunbridge Road | A4-A3-B3-C3 |
| Ashgrove | A1 | Edmund Street | B1 | Morley Street | A1-B1 | Tetley Street | B2-B3 |
| Balme Street | D4 | Edward Street | D1 | Neal Street | B1 | Thornton Road | A3-B2-C2 |
| Bank Street | C3-D2 | Filey Street | E2-F2 | Nelson Street | C1-D1 | Tumbling Hill Street | A2-A3 |
| Baptist Place | B3-B4 | Forster Square | D3 | New Augustus Street | E1-E2 | Tyrrel Street | C2-C3 |
| Barkerend Road | E3-F4 | Frederick Street | E2 | New Otley Road | F4 | Upper Mosscar Street | F3 |
| Barry Street | B3-C3 | Fullerton Street | F2 | Norcroft Brow | A2 | Upper Park Gate | E3 |
| Bolling Road | E1 | Fulton Street | B2-B3 | Norfolk Gardens | C2-D2 | Upper Piccadilly | C4 |
| Bolton Road | D3-E4 | Garnett Street | F2-F4 | North Parade | C4 | Valley Road | D4 |
| Bolton Street | F4 | George Street | E2 | North Street | E4 | Vaughan Street | A4 |
| Bridge Street | C2-E1 | Godwin Street | C2-C3 | Northgate | C4 | Ventnor Street | F3 |
| Broad Street | C4 | Grattan Road | A3-B3 | Nuthall Road | F4 | Vicar Lane | D2-E2-E3 |
| Broad Way | D3 | Great Cross Street | E2 | Otley Road | F4 | Vincent Street | B3 |
| Buck Street | F1-F2 | Great Horton Road | A1-B2 | Paradise Street | A3-A4 | Water Lane | A3 |
| Burnett Street | E3-E4 | Grove Terrace | B1 | Park Gate | E3 | Well Street | D3-E3 |
| Canal Road | D3-D4 | Guy Street | E1 | Peckover Street | E3-F3 | Wellington Street | E4 |
| Captain Street | E4 | Hall Ings | C1-D3 | Pemberton Drive | A1 | West Street | E2 |
| Carlton Street | A2 | Hammerton Street | F1-F2 | Petergate | D3 | Westend Street | A3 |
| Carroll Street | F2 | Harris Street | F3-F4 | Piccadilly | C3-C4 | Westgate | A4-B4-B3-C3 |
| Chandos Street | E1-F1 | Heap Lane | F4 | Pine Street | E4 | Wigan Street | A3-A4-B4 |
| Channing Way | C2 | Hey Street | A3 | Priestley Street | E4 | Wilton Street | B1 |
| Chapel Street | E2-E3 | Holdsworth Street | D4 | Princes Way | C1-C2 | | |
| Charles Street | D3 | Howard Street | B1 | Quebec Street | B2-C2 | | |
| Cheapside | D3 | Hustler Gate | C3-D3 | Rawson Road | B4 | | |
| Chester Street | B1 | Ivegate | C3 | Rawson Square | C4 | | |
| Church Bank | D3-E3 | James Street | C3 | Rebecca Street | A4 | | |
| Claremont | A1 | John Street | B3-C4 | Richmond Road | A1-A2 | | |
| Croft Street | C1-E1 | Joseph Street | F2-F3 | Sackville Street | B3 | | |
| Curber Street | E3 | Kirkgate | C3-D3 | Salem Street | C4 | | |
| Darfield Street | B4 | Leeds Road | D3-F2 | Sawrey Place | B1 | | |
| Darley Street | C3-C4 | Listerhills Road | A3 | Scoresby Street | E3 | | |
| Diamond Street | E1-E2 | Little Horton Lane | C1-C2 | Senior Way | C1 | | |
| Drake Street | D2 | Longside Lane | A2-A3 | Sharpe Street | C1 | | |
| Drewton Road | B4 | Lumb Lane | B4 | Shipley Airedale Road | E2-F3-E4 | | |
| Dryden Street | E1-F1 | Malvern Street | F2-F3 | Simes Street | B4 | | |
| Duke Street | C4 | Manchester Road | C1 | Smith Street | A2-A3 | | |
| Dyson Street | A3-A4 | Mannville Terrace | A1-B1 | Southgate | B2 | | |
| East Brook Lane | E2 | Manor Row | C4 | Stone Street | C4 | | |

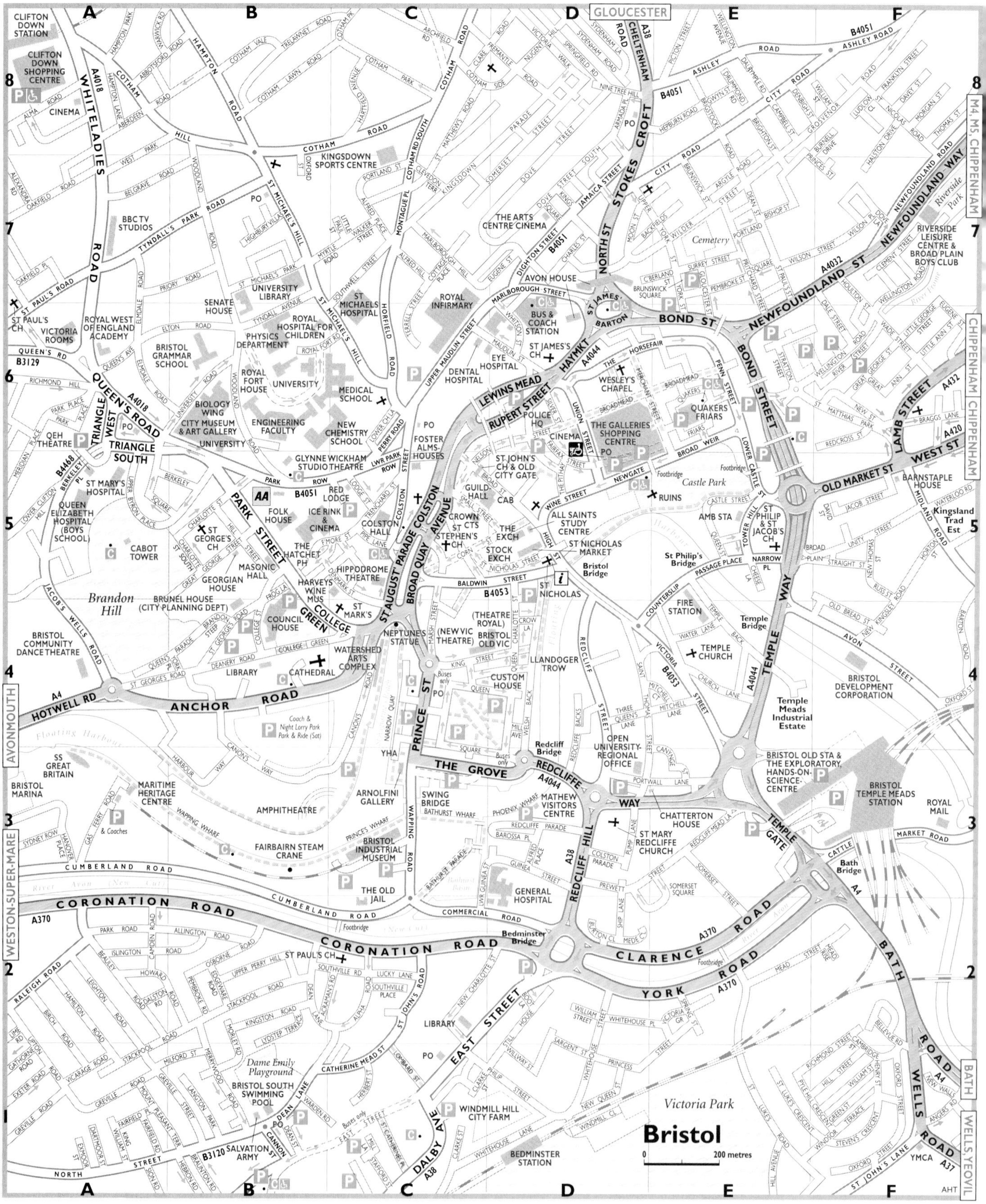
Bristol
200 metres
GLOUCESTER
M4, M5, CHIPPENHAM
CHIPPENHAM
AVONMOUTH
WESTON-SUPER-MARE
BATH
WELLS, YEOVIL
CLIFTON DOWN STATION
CLIFTON DOWN SHOPPING CENTRE
CINEMA
WHITELADIES ROAD
COTHAM HILL
COTHAM ROAD
KINGSDOWN SPORTS CENTRE
BBC TV STUDIOS
TYNDALL'S PARK ROAD
ST MICHAEL'S HILL
THE ARTS CENTRE CINEMA
STOKES CROFT
CHELTENHAM ROAD
ASHLEY ROAD
CITY ROAD
Cemetery
RIVERSIDE LEISURE CENTRE & BROAD PLAIN BOYS CLUB
NEWFOUNDLAND WAY
NEWFOUNDLAND ST
Riverside Park
ST PAUL'S CH
VICTORIA ROOMS
ROYAL WEST OF ENGLAND ACADEMY
SENATE HOUSE
UNIVERSITY LIBRARY
PHYSICS DEPARTMENT
ROYAL HOSPITAL FOR CHILDREN
ST MICHAELS HOSPITAL
ROYAL INFIRMARY
AVON HOUSE
BUS & COACH STATION
BOND ST
BOND STREET
BRISTOL GRAMMAR SCHOOL
ROYAL FORT HOUSE
UNIVERSITY
MEDICAL SCHOOL
DENTAL HOSPITAL
EYE HOSPITAL
ST JAMES'S CH
WESLEY'S CHAPEL
QUAKERS FRIARS
QUEEN'S ROAD
BIOLOGY WING
CITY MUSEUM & ART GALLERY
ENGINEERING FACULTY
NEW CHEMISTRY SCHOOL
FOSTER ALMS HOUSES
POLICE HQ
THE GALLERIES SHOPPING CENTRE
CINEMA
QEH THEATRE
TRIANGLE WEST
TRIANGLE SOUTH
GLYNNE WICKHAM STUDIO THEATRE
ST JOHN'S CH & OLD CITY GATE
Castle Park
RUINS
OLD MARKET ST
WEST ST
LAMB STREET
BARNSTAPLE HOUSE
Kingsland Trad Est
ST MARY'S HOSPITAL
QUEEN ELIZABETH HOSPITAL (BOYS SCHOOL)
CABOT TOWER
PARK STREET
FOLK HOUSE
RED LODGE
ICE RINK & CINEMA
COLSTON HALL
GUILD HALL
CAB
CROWN CTS
ST STEPHEN'S CH
THE EXCH
STOCK EXCH
ALL SAINTS STUDY CENTRE
ST NICHOLAS MARKET
AMB STA
ST PHILIP & ST JACOB'S CH
ST GEORGE'S CH
MASONIC HALL
GEORGIAN HOUSE
THE HATCHET PH
HIPPODROME THEATRE
Bristol Bridge
St Philip's Bridge
Brandon Hill
BRUNEL HOUSE (CITY PLANNING DEPT)
HARVEYS WINE MUS
ST MARK'S
COUNCIL HOUSE
COLLEGE GREEN
ST AUGUST PARADE
BROAD QUAY
COLSTON AVENUE
ST NICHOLAS
BALDWIN STREET
FIRE STATION
Temple Bridge
TEMPLE CHURCH
TEMPLE WAY
BRISTOL COMMUNITY DANCE THEATRE
NEPTUNE'S STATUE
(NEW VIC THEATRE)
(THEATRE ROYAL) BRISTOL OLD VIC
LLANDOGER TROW
CATHEDRAL
LIBRARY
WATERSHED ARTS COMPLEX
CUSTOM HOUSE
BRISTOL DEVELOPMENT CORPORATION
Temple Meads Industrial Estate
HOTWELL RD
ANCHOR ROAD
Floating Harbour
Coach & Night Lorry Park Park & Ride (Sat)
PRINCE ST
SS GREAT BRITAIN
BRISTOL MARINA
YHA
THE GROVE
Redcliff Bridge
REDCLIFFE WAY
OPEN UNIVERSITY-REGIONAL OFFICE
BRISTOL OLD STA & THE EXPLORATORY, HANDS-ON-SCIENCE-CENTRE
BRISTOL TEMPLE MEADS STATION
ROYAL MAIL
MARITIME HERITAGE CENTRE
AMPHITHEATRE
ARNOLFINI GALLERY
SWING BRIDGE
MATHEW VISITORS CENTRE
CHATTERTON HOUSE
ST MARY REDCLIFFE CHURCH
TEMPLE GATE
Bath Bridge
FAIRBAIRN STEAM CRANE
BRISTOL INDUSTRIAL MUSEUM
THE OLD JAIL
GENERAL HOSPITAL
REDCLIFF HILL
SOMERSET SQUARE
CUMBERLAND ROAD
CORONATION ROAD
Bedminster Bridge
CLARENCE ROAD
YORK ROAD
BATH ROAD
ST PAUL'S CH
LIBRARY
EAST STREET
Dame Emily Playground
BRISTOL SOUTH SWIMMING POOL
SALVATION ARMY
WINDMILL HILL CITY FARM
Victoria Park
BEDMINSTER STATION
DALBY AVE
WELLS ROAD
YMCA
NORTH STREET
AHT

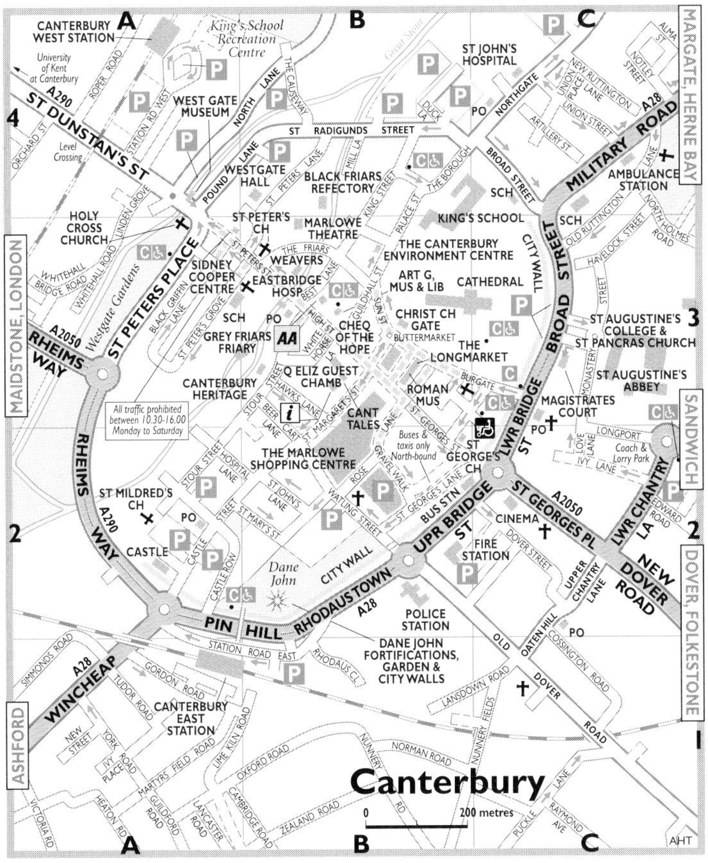


# Canterbury

Canterbury is found on atlas page **29**, grid reference **1457**

### AA shop

13 Best Lane, Canterbury CT1 2JB B3

| | |
|---|---|
| Alma Street | C4 |
| Artillery Street | C4 |
| Beer Cart Lane | C2-B3 |
| Best Lane | B3 |
| Black Griffin Lane | A3 |
| Broad Street | C3 |
| Burgate | B3-C3 |
| Cambridge Road | A1-B1 |
| Cassington Road | C1-C2 |
| Castle Row | A2 |
| Castle Street | A2-B2 |
| Dover Street | C2 |
| Duck Lane | B4 |
| Edward Road | C2 |
| Gordon Road | A1 |
| Gravel Walk | B2 |
| Guildford Road | A1 |
| Guildhall Street | B3 |
| Havelock Street | C3-C4 |
| Hawks Lane | B3 |
| Heath Road | A1 |
| High Street | B3 |
| Hospital Lane | A2-B2 |
| Ivy Lane | C2 |
| Ivy Place | A1 |
| King Street | B3-B4 |
| Lancaster Road | A1 |
| Lansdown Road | B1-C1 |
| Lime Kiln Road | A1-B1 |

| | |
|---|---|
| Linden Grove | A3-A4 |
| Longport | C2 |
| Love Lane | C2 |
| Lower Bridge Street | C2-C3 |
| Lower Chantry Lane | C2 |
| Martyrs Field Road | A1 |
| Mill Lane | B4 |
| Military Road | C4 |
| Monastery Street | C3 |
| New Dover Road | C2 |
| New Ruttington Lane | C4 |
| New Street | A1 |
| Norman Road | B1-C1 |
| North Holmes Road | C3-C4 |
| North Lane | A4-B4 |
| Northgate | C4 |
| Notley Street | C4 |
| Nunnery Fields | B1-C1 |
| Nunnery Road | B1 |
| Oaten Hill | C1-C2 |
| Old Dover Road | B2-C2-C1 |
| Old Ruttington Lane | C3-C4 |
| Orchard Street | A4 |
| Oxford Road | A1-B1 |
| Palace Street | B3-B4 |
| Pin Hill | A2-B2 |
| Pound Lane | A4-B4 |
| Puckle Lane | C1 |
| Raymond Avenue | C1 |

| | |
|---|---|
| Rheims Way | A2-A3 |
| Rhodaus Close | B1 |
| Rhodaus Town | B2 |
| Roper Road | A4 |
| Rose Lane | B2-B3 |
| St Dunstan's Street | A4 |
| St George's Lane | B2-C2 |
| St Georges Place | C2 |
| St Georges Street | B2-B3 |
| St John's Lane | B2 |
| St Margaret's Street | B2-B3 |
| St Mary's Street | A2-B2 |
| St Peter's Grove | A3-B3 |
| St Peters Lane | B3-B4 |
| St Peters Place | A3 |
| St Peters Street | A3-B3 |
| St Radigunds Street | B4 |
| Simmonds Road | A1-A2 |
| Station Road East | A2-A1-B1 |
| Station Road West | A4 |
| Stour Street | A2-B3 |
| Sun Street | B3 |
| The Borough | B4-C4 |
| The Causeway | B4 |
| The Friars | B3 |
| Tudor Road | A1 |
| Union Place | C4 |
| Union Street | C4 |
| Upper Bridge Street | B2-C2 |
| Upper Chantry Lane | C2 |
| Victoria Road | A1 |
| Watling Street | B2 |
| White Horse Lane | B3 |
| Whitehall Road | A3 |
| Whitehall Bridge Road | A3 |
| Wincheap | A1-A2 |
| York Road | A1 |
| Zealand Road | B1 |

# Bristol

Bristol is found on atlas page **34**, grid reference **5972**

### AA shop

Fanum House, 26-32 Park Row, Bristol BS1 5LY B5

| | |
|---|---|
| Abbotsford Road | A8-B8 |
| Aberdeen Road | A8-B8 |
| Acraman's Road | B2-C2 |
| Alexandra Road | A7 |
| Alfred Hill | C7 |
| Alfred Place | C7 |
| Alfred Place | D3 |
| Allington Road | B1-B2 |
| Alma Road | A8 |
| Alpha Road | C2 |
| Anchor Road | A4-B4-C4 |
| Angers Road | F1 |
| Archfield Road | C8 |
| Argyle Road | E7-E8 |
| Armada Place | D8 |
| Ashley Road | E8-F8 |
| Avon Street | E4-F4 |
| Backfields | D7-E7 |
| Baldwin Street | C5-D5 |
| Barossa Place | D3 |
| Barton Road | F4-F5 |
| Bath Road | F1-F2 |
| Bathurst Parade | C3 |
| Beauley Road | A2 |
| Belgrave Road | A7-B7 |
| Bellevue Road | F2 |
| Berkeley Place | A5 |
| Berkeley Square | A5-B5 |
| Birch Road | A1-A2 |
| Bishop Street | E7 |
| Bond Street | D6-E6-E5 |
| Boot Lane | D2 |
| Bragg's Lane | F6 |
| Brandon Steep | B4 |
| Braunton Road | B1 |
| Brighton Street | E8 |
| Brigstocke Road | E7-E8 |
| Broadmead | D6-E6 |
| Broad Plain | E5-F5 |
| Broad Quay | C4-C5 |
| Broad Street | C5-D5 |
| Broad Weir | E5-E6 |
| Brunswick Street | E7 |
| Burnell Drive | E8-F8 |
| Burton Close | D2 |
| Cambridge Street | F1 |
| Camden Road | A2 |
| Campbell Street | E8 |
| Cannon Street | B1 |

| | |
|---|---|
| Canon's Road | C3-C4 |
| Canon's Way | B3-B4 |
| Canynge Street | E3-E4 |
| Castle Street | E5 |
| Catherine Mead Street | B1-C1 |
| Cattle Market Road | F3 |
| Charles Street | D7 |
| Charlotte Street | B5 |
| Charlotte Street South | B5 |
| Cheese Lane | E5 |
| Cheltenham Road | D8 |
| Church Lane | E4 |
| City Road | D7-E7-E8-F8 |
| Clare Road | C8-D8 |
| Clarence Road | D2-E2-E3 |
| Clarke Street | D1 |
| Clement Street | F7 |
| Clevedon Terrace | C7 |
| College Green | B4-C4-B5 |
| College Street | B4 |
| Colston Avenue | C5 |
| Colston Parade | D3 |
| Colston Street | C5-C6 |
| Commercial Road | C2-D2 |
| Corn Street | C5-D5 |
| Coronation Road | A2-B2-C2-D2 |
| Cotham Hill | A8-B8 |
| Cotham Lawn Road | B8-C8 |
| Cotham Park | C8 |
| Cotham Road | B8-C8 |
| Cotham Road South | C7-C8 |
| Cotham Side | C8-D8 |
| Cotham Vale | B8 |
| Cottage Place | C7 |
| Counterslip | D4-E4-E5 |
| Crow Lane | D4 |
| Cumberland Road | A3-B3-B2-C2 |
| Cumberland Street | D7-E7 |
| Dalby Avenue | C1 |
| Dale Street | F6-F7 |
| Dalston Road | A2-B2 |
| Dalyrymple Road | E8 |
| Dartmoor Street | A1 |
| Davey Street | F8 |
| David Street | F5 |
| Deanery Road | B4 |
| Dean Lane | B2 |
| Dean Street | B1 |
| Dean Street | E7 |

| | |
|---|---|
| Denbigh Street | E8 |
| Denmark Street | B5-C5-C4 |
| Dighton Street | D7 |
| Dove Lane | F7 |
| Dove Street | C7-D7-D8 |
| Dove Street South | D7-D8 |
| Drummond Road | E8 |
| East Street | C1-C2-C3-D1 |
| Edgeware Road | B2 |
| Elmdale Road | A7-A6-B6 |
| Elton Road | A6-B6 |
| Eugene Street | C7-D7 |
| Eugene Street | F6-F7 |
| Exeter Road | A1 |
| Exmoor Street | A1 |
| Fairfax Street | D5-D6 |
| Fairfield Place | A1 |
| Fairfield Road | A1 |
| Franklyn Street | F8 |
| Fremantle Road | C8-D8 |
| Frog Lane | B5 |
| Frogmore Street | B5-C5 |
| Gas Ferry Road | A3 |
| Gathorpe Road | A1 |
| Gloucester Street | E7-E6 |
| Great Ann Street | F6 |
| Great George Street | B5 |
| Great George Street | F6 |
| Green Street | F1 |
| Greville Road | A1 |
| Greville Street | A1-B1 |
| Grosvenor Road | E8-F8 |
| Guinea Street | D2-D3 |
| Gwyn Street | E8 |
| Halston Drive | F7-F8 |
| Hamilton Road | A1-A2 |
| Hampton Lane | A8 |
| Hampton Park | A8 |
| Hampton Road | B8 |
| Hanover Place | A3 |
| Harbour Way | A3-B3 |
| Hartfield Avenue | C8 |
| Haymarket | D6 |
| Hebron Road | B1 |
| Henry Street | F1 |
| Hepburn Road | D8-E8 |
| Herbert Street | C1 |
| Highbury Villas | B7 |
| High Street | D5 |
| Hiill Avenue | E1 |
| Hill Street | B5 |
| Hill Street | F1 |
| Horfield Road | C6-C7 |
| Horton Street | F5 |
| Hotwell Road | A3-A4 |
| Houlton Street | F6-F7 |
| Howard Road | A2-B2 |
| Islington Road | A2-B2 |
| Jacob Street | F5 |

| | |
|---|---|
| Jacob's Wells Road | A4-A5 |
| Jamaica Street | D7 |
| Jubilee Street | F5 |
| Kingsdown Parade | C7-C8-D8 |
| Kings Square | D7 |
| King Street | C4-D4 |
| Kingston Road | B2 |
| King William Street | A1 |
| Lamb Street | F5-F6 |
| Langton Park | B1 |
| Leighton Road | A1-A2 |
| Lewins Mead | C6-D6 |
| Lime Road | A2 |
| Little Ann Street | F6 |
| Little George Street | F6-F7 |
| Little Paul Street | C7 |
| Lodge Street | C5 |
| Lombard Street | C1 |
| Lower Castle Street | E5-E6 |
| Lower Church Lane | C6 |
| Lower Clifton Hill | A5 |
| Lower Guinea Street | C2-C3 |
| Lower Maudlin Street | C6-D6 |
| Lower Park Row | C5 |
| Lucky Lane | C2 |
| Ludlow Close | F8 |
| Lydstep Terrace | B2 |
| Marlborough Hill | C7 |
| Marlborough Street | C6-D7 |
| Marsh Street | C4-C5 |
| Mead Rise | F2 |
| Mead Street | E2-F2 |
| Mede Close | D2 |
| Merchant Street | D6-E6 |
| Meridian Place | A5-A6 |
| Merrywood Road | B1-B2 |
| Midland Road | F5 |
| Milford Street | A1-B1 |
| Mill Avenue | D4 |
| Mill Lane | C1 |
| Mitchell Court | E4 |
| Mitchell Lane | E4 |
| Montague Place | C7 |
| Moon Street | D7 |
| Morgan Street | F8 |
| Morley Road | B1-B2 |
| Mount Pleasant Terrace | A1-B1 |
| Murray Street | C1 |
| Myrtle Road | B7-C7 |
| Narrow Place | E5 |
| Narrow Quay | C3-C4 |
| Nelson Street | C5-D6 |
| New Charlotte Street | C2-D2 |
| Newfoundland Road | F7-F8 |
| Newfoundland Street | E6-E7-F7 |
| Newfoundland Way | F7-F8 |
| Newgate | D5 |
| New Kingsley Road | F4-F5 |
| New Queen Street | D1 |
| New Street | F6 |
| New Thomas Street | F5 |
| New Walls | F1 |
| Nine Tree Hill | D8 |
| North Street | A1-B1 |
| North Street | D7 |
| Nugent Hill | D8 |
| Oakfield Place | A7 |
| Oakfield Road | A7 |
| Old Bread Street | F4-F5 |
| Old Market Street | F6 |
| Osborne Road | B2 |
| Oxford Street | F1 |
| Oxford Street | B7 |

| | |
|---|---|
| Oxford Street | F4 |
| Park Place | A6 |
| Park Road | A2 |
| Park Row | B5-C5 |
| Park Street | B5 |
| Passage Place | E5 |
| Pembroke Road | B2 |
| Pembroke Street | E7 |
| Penn Street | E6 |
| Perry Road | C6 |
| Philip Street | C1-D1 |
| Picton Street | E8 |
| Pipe Lane | C5 |
| Portland Square | E7 |
| Portland Street | C7 |
| Portwall Lane | D3-E3 |
| Prewett Street | D3-E3 |
| Prince Street | C3-C4 |
| Princess Street | D1-E1-E2 |
| Princes Street | E8-F7 |
| Priory Road | A7-B7 |
| Pritchard Street | E7-E6 |
| Pump Lane | D3 |
| Pyle Hill Crescent | E1-F1 |
| Quakers Friars | E6 |
| Queen Charlotte Street | D4-D5 |
| Queen's Avenue | A6 |
| Queen's Parade | A4-B4 |
| Queen's Road | A6-B6-B5 |
| Queen Square | C3-C4-D4-D3 |
| Queen Street | E5 |
| Raleigh Road | A2 |
| Redcliff Backs | D3-D4 |
| Redcliffe Parade | D3 |
| Redcliffe Way | D3-D4 |
| Redcliff Hill | D2-D3 |
| Redcliff Mead Lane | E3 |
| Redcliff Street | D3-D4 |
| Redcross Street | F6 |
| Richmond Hill | A6 |
| Richmond Street | E1-F1 |
| River Street | F6 |
| Royal Fort Road | B6-C6 |
| Rupert Street | D6 |
| Russ Street | F5 |
| St Augustine's Parade | C4-C5 |
| St Catherines Place | C1 |
| St George's Road | A4-B4 |
| St James' Barton | D6-D7 |
| St John's Lane | F1 |
| St John's Road | C2 |
| St Luke's Crescent | E1-F1 |
| St Luke's Road | E1-F1-F2 |
| St Matthew's Road | C7-C8 |
| St Matthias Park | E6-F6 |
| St Michael's Hill | B7-B6-C6 |
| St Michael's Park | B7 |
| St Nicholas Road | F8 |
| St Nicholas Street | C5-D5 |
| St Paul's Road | A6-A7 |
| St Paul's Street | E7 |
| St Thomas Street | D3-D4 |
| Sargent Street | D1-D2 |
| Ship Lane | D2-D3 |
| Silver Street | D6 |
| Sion Road | A1 |
| Small Street | C5-D5 |
| Somerset Square | E2-E3 |
| Somerset Street | E3 |
| Southville Place | C2 |
| Southville Road | B2-C2 |
| Southwell Street | C7 |
| Springfield Road | D8 |

| | |
|---|---|
| Spring Street | E2 |
| Stackpool Road | A1-B2 |
| Stafford Street | C1 |
| Steven's Crescent | F1 |
| Stillhouse Lane | D1-D2 |
| Stokes Croft | D7-D8 |
| Straight Street | F5 |
| Stratton Street | E6 |
| Surrey Street | E7 |
| Sydenham Lane | D8 |
| Sydenham Road | D8 |
| Sydney Row | A3 |
| Temple Back | E4-E5 |
| Temple Gate | E3 |
| Temple Way | E4-E5 |
| Terrell Street | C6-C7 |
| The Grove | C3-D3 |
| The Horsefair | D6-E6 |
| The Pithay | D5 |
| Thomas Street | F8 |
| Three Queens Lane | D4 |
| Tower Hill | E5 |
| Trelawney Road | B8-C8 |
| Trenchard Street | C5 |
| Triangle South | A6 |
| Triangle West | A6 |
| Tyndall Avenue | B6-B7 |
| Tyndall's Park Road | A7-B7 |
| Union Street | D5-D6 |
| Unity Street | F5 |
| University Road | A6-B6 |
| Upper Byron Place | A5 |
| Upper Maudlin Street | C6 |
| Upper Perry Hill | B2 |
| Upper York Street | D7-E7 |
| Upton Road | A1-A2 |
| Vicarage Road | A1 |
| Victoria Grove | E2 |
| Victoria Street | D5-D4-E4-E3 |
| Victoria Walk | D8 |
| Wade Street | F6 |
| Walker Street | C7 |
| Wapping Road | C3 |
| Warden Road | C1-D1 |
| Warwick Road | A8 |
| Water Lane | E4 |
| Waterloo Road | F5 |
| Wellington Avenue | E8 |
| Wellington Road | E6-F6-F7 |
| Wells Road | F1 |
| Welsh Back | D4-D5 |
| West Park | A7-A8 |
| West Street | F5-F6 |
| Whitehouse Lane | C1-D1 |
| Whitehouse Place | D2-E2 |
| Whitehouse Street | D1-D2 |
| Whiteladies Road | A6-A7-A8 |
| Whitson Street | D6 |
| Wilder Street | D7-E7 |
| William Street | D2 |
| William Street | E8-F8 |
| William Street | F1 |
| Willway Street | D1 |
| Wilson Place | F7 |
| Wilson Street | E7-F7 |
| Windmill Close | D1 |
| Windsor Terrace | E1-F1 |
| Wine Street | D5 |
| Woodland Road | B5-B6-B7-B8 |
| York Place | B4 |
| York Road | D2-E2-F2 |
| York Street | E6-E7 |

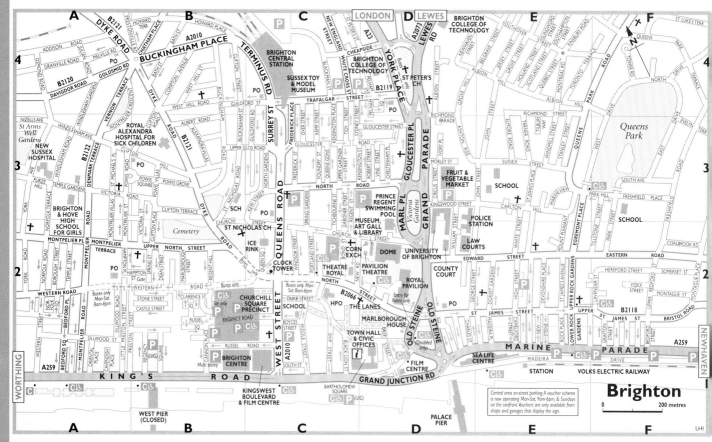

170

# Brighton

Brighton is found on atlas page **15**,
grid reference **3104**

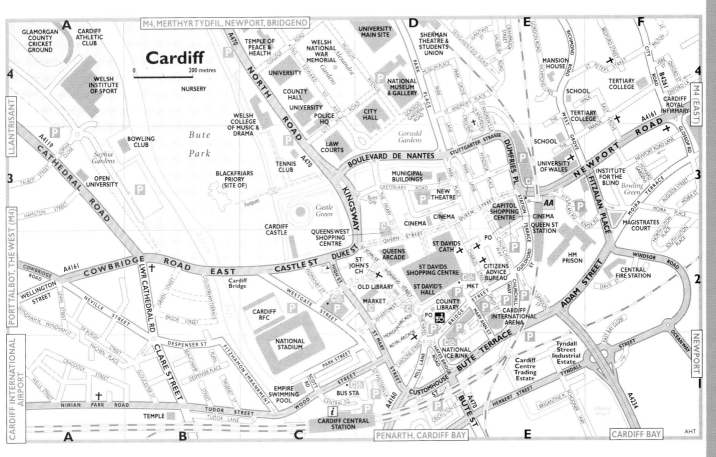

# Cardiff

Cardiff is found on atlas page **33**,
grid reference 1876

## AA shop
Fanum House, 140 Queen Street, Cardiff CF1 1YF          E3

| | | | | | | |
|---|---|---|---|---|---|---|
| Adam Street | E2-F2 | Glossop Road | F3 | Park Lane | D4-D3-E3 | Wood Street | C1-D1 |
| Augusta Street | F3 | Gloucester Street | B1 | Park Place | D4-D3 | Working Street | D2 |
| Bedford Street | F4 | Gordon Road | E4 | Park Street | C1-D1 | Womanby Street | C2 |
| Beauchamp Street | B1 | Gorsedd Gardens Road | D4 | Plantagenet Street | B1-B2 | Wyndham Place | A2 |
| Boulevard de Nantes | C3-D3 | Great Western Lane | D1 | Queen Street | D2-D3-E3 | Wyndham Street | A2-A1 |
| Bridge Street | D1-D2-E2 | Green Street | B2 | Richmond Crescent | E4 | | |
| Brigantine Place | E1 | Greyfrairs Road | D3 | Richmond Road | E4 | | |
| Brook Street | B2 | Guildford Street | E2 | Royal Arcade | D1-D2 | | |
| Bute Street | D1-E1 | Hamilton Street | A3 | St Andrew's Crescent | D3-E4 | | |
| Bute Terrace | D1-E1 | Hayes Bridge Road | D1 | St Andrew's Lane | E3-E4 | | |
| Caroline Street | D1 | Herbert Street | E1 | St Andrew's Place | D4-E4 | | |
| Castle Street | C2 | High Street | C2 | St John Street | D2 | | |
| Cathedral Road | A4-A3-B2 | Howard Gardens | F3 | St Marys Street | D1-D2 | | |
| Central Square | C1 | King Edward VII Avenue | C3-D3 | St Peters Street | E4-F4 | | |
| Charles Street | D3-D2-E2 | Kingsway | C3-D3 | Salisbury Road | E4 | | |
| Churchill Way | E2-E3 | Knox Road | E3-F3 | Sandon Street | E2 | | |
| City Hall Road | C3-C4-D4 | Lewis Street | A2 | Schooner Way | E1 | | |
| City Road | F4 | Llantwit Street | D4-E4 | Scott Road | C1 | | |
| Clare Street | B1 | Lower Cathedral Road | B2 | Senghenydd Road | D4-E4 | | |
| Coldstream Terrace | B2 | Machen Place | A1-B1 | Sophia Close | A3 | | |
| College Road | C4 | Mary Ann Street | E1-E2 | South Luton Place | F2-F3 | | |
| Cowbridge Road | A2 | Mill Lane | D1 | Station Terrace | E2-E3 | | |
| Cowbridge Road East | A2-B2-C2 | Milton Street | F4 | Stuttgarter Strasse | D3-E3 | | |
| Craddock Street | A1-B1 | Morgan Arcade | D1-D2 | The Friary | D3 | | |
| Cranbrook Street | E4 | Moira Place | F3 | The Hayes | D1-D2 | | |
| Crichton Street | D1 | Moira Street | F3 | The Parade | E3-F3-F4 | | |
| Customhouse Street | D1 | Moira Terrace | F2-F3 | The Walk | E3-E4-F4 | | |
| David Street | E2 | Museum Avenue | C4-D4 | Talbot Street | A3 | | |
| Davis Street | F2 | Museum Place | D4 | Tudor Lane | B1-C1 | | |
| De Burgh Street | A1-A2-B1 | Neville Street | A2-B2 | Tudor Street | B1-C1 | | |
| Despenser Place | B1 | Newport Road | E3-F3-F4 | Tyndall Street | E1-F1 | | |
| Despenser Street | B2 | Newport Road Lane | F3 | Vere Street | F4 | | |
| Duke Street | C2-D2 | Ninian Park Road | A1-B1 | Wellington Street | A2 | | |
| Dumfries Place | E3 | North Luton Place | F2-F3 | Wells Street | A1 | | |
| East Bay Close | F1-F2 | North Road | B4-C4-C3 | Westgate Street | C2-D1 | | |
| East Grove | F3 | Ocean Way | F1 | West Grove | E4-E3 | | |
| Fitzalan Place | F2-F3 | Oxford Lane | F4 | Wharton Street | D2 | | |
| Fitzalan Road | E3 | Oxford Street | F4 | Windsor Place | E3 | | |
| Fitzhamon Embankment | B1-C1 | Park Grove | D4 | Windsor Road | F2 | | |

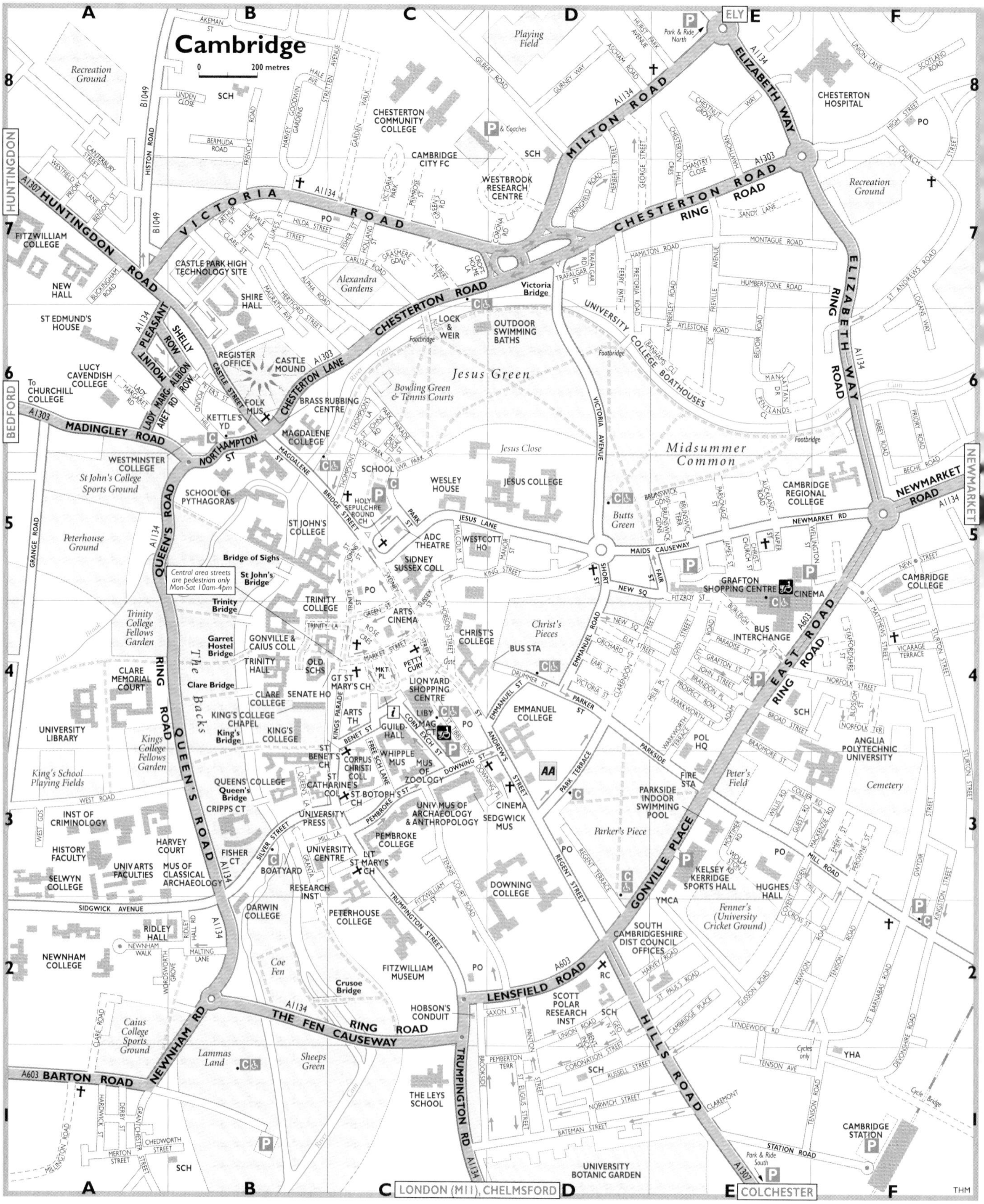

# Cambridge

0    200 metres

Central area streets
are pedestrian only
Mon-Sat 10am-4pm

HUNTINGDON

BEDFORD
To CHURCHILL
COLLEGE

ELY

COLCHESTER

LONDON (M11), CHELMSFORD

NEWMARKET

**Streets and roads**

HUNTINGDON ROAD · MADINGLEY ROAD · VICTORIA ROAD · CHESTERTON ROAD · MILTON ROAD · ELIZABETH WAY · RING ROAD · NEWMARKET ROAD · EAST ROAD · GONVILLE PLACE · HILLS ROAD · LENSFIELD ROAD · THE FEN CAUSEWAY · BARTON ROAD · NEWNHAM RD · QUEEN'S ROAD · GRANGE ROAD · SIDGWICK AVENUE · WEST ROAD · TRUMPINGTON STREET · TRUMPINGTON RD · REGENT STREET · EMMANUEL ROAD · MAIDS CAUSEWAY · PARKSIDE · PARKER STREET · MAGDALENE ST · BRIDGE STREET · ST ANDREW'S STREET · SHELLY ROW · MOUNT PLEASANT · NORTHAMPTON ST · CASTLE STREET · MALTING LANE · MILL ROAD · STATION ROAD

**Places of interest**

FITZWILLIAM COLLEGE · NEW HALL · ST EDMUND'S HOUSE · LUCY CAVENDISH COLLEGE · WESTMINSTER COLLEGE · St John's College Sports Ground · Peterhouse Ground · Trinity College Fellows Garden · CLARE MEMORIAL COURT · UNIVERSITY LIBRARY · King's School Playing Fields · INST OF CRIMINOLOGY · HISTORY FACULTY · UNIV ARTS FACULTIES · SELWYN COLLEGE · MUS OF CLASSICAL ARCHAEOLOGY · NEWNHAM COLLEGE · RIDLEY HALL · DARWIN COLLEGE · Caius College Sports Ground · Lammas Land · Sheeps Green · Coe Fen · Crusoe Bridge · Hobson's Conduit · THE LEYS SCHOOL · FITZWILLIAM MUSEUM · PETERHOUSE COLLEGE · RESEARCH INST · BOATYARD · FISHER CT · UNIVERSITY PRESS · CRIPPS CT · Queen's Bridge · QUEENS' COLLEGE · Clare Bridge · CLARE COLLEGE · TRINITY HALL · GONVILLE & CAIUS COLL · Garret Hostel Bridge · Trinity Bridge · TRINITY COLLEGE · St John's Bridge · ST JOHN'S COLLEGE · Bridge of Sighs · SCHOOL OF PYTHAGORAS · FOLK MUS · KETTLE'S YD · REGISTER OFFICE · CASTLE MOUND · BRASS RUBBING CENTRE · MAGDALENE COLLEGE · HOLY SEPULCHRE ROUND CH · ADC THEATRE · WESTCOTT HO · SIDNEY SUSSEX COLL · ARTS CINEMA · CORPUS CHRISTI COLL · ST CATHARINE'S COL · ST BOTOLPH'S CH · PEMBROKE COLLEGE · UNIV MUS OF ARCHAEOLOGY & ANTHROPOLOGY · SEDGWICK MUS · WHIPPLE MUS · MUS OF ZOOLOGY · CINEMA · DOWNING COLLEGE · Parker's Piece · Peter's Field · Fenner's (University Cricket Ground) · KELSEY KERRIDGE SPORTS HALL · HUGHES HALL · YMCA · SOUTH CAMBRIDGESHIRE DIST COUNCIL OFFICES · SCOTT POLAR RESEARCH INST · UNIVERSITY BOTANIC GARDEN · CAMBRIDGE STATION · YHA · Cemetery · ANGLIA POLYTECHNIC UNIVERSITY · POL HQ · FIRE STA · PARKSIDE INDOOR SWIMMING POOL · BUS INTERCHANGE · BUS STA · GRAFTON SHOPPING CENTRE · CINEMA · CAMBRIDGE COLLEGE · CAMBRIDGE REGIONAL COLLEGE · UNIVERSITY COLLEGE BOATHOUSES · Midsummer Common · Jesus Close · JESUS COLLEGE · Butts Green · WESLEY HOUSE · Bowling Green & Tennis Courts · Jesus Green · OUTDOOR SWIMMING BATHS · LOCK & WEIR · Alexandra Gardens · SHIRE HALL · CASTLE PARK HIGH TECHNOLOGY SITE · WESTBROOK RESEARCH CENTRE · CAMBRIDGE CITY FC · CHESTERTON COMMUNITY COLLEGE · Playing Field · CHESTERTON HOSPITAL · Recreation Ground · Victoria Bridge · Christ's Pieces · Christ's College · GUILDHALL · LION YARD SHOPPING CENTRE · GT ST MARY'S CH · ST MARY'S CH · SENATE HO · OLD SCHS · KING'S COLLEGE · KING'S COLLEGE CHAPEL · King's Bridge · ST BENET'S CH · EMMANUEL COLLEGE · AA · LT ST MARY'S CH · SILVER STREET · PETTY CURY · HARVEY COURT · CHRIST'S COLLEGE

A603 · A1134 · A1303 · A1307 · A1049 · B1049

THM

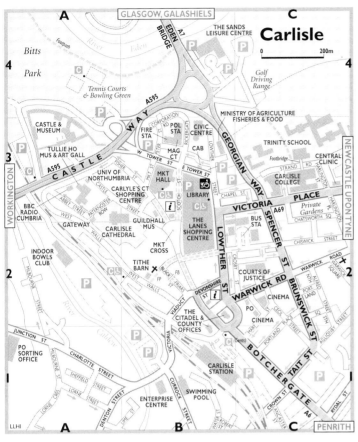

# Carlisle

Carlisle is found on atlas page **93**,
grid reference **3956**

| | | | |
|---|---|---|---|
| Abbey Street | A3 | Tait Street | C1 |
| Aglionby Street | C1-C2 | Victoria Place | B3-C3 |
| Alfred Street North | C2 | Victoria Viaduct | B1-B2 |
| Alfred Street South | C2 | Warwick Road | B2-C2 |
| Blackfriars Street | B2 | Warwick Square | C2 |
| Botchergate | B1-C1 | Water Street | B1 |
| Brunswick Street | C1-C2 | West Tower Street | B3 |
| Castle Street | A3-B3-B2 | West Walls | A3-A2-B2 |
| Castle Way | A3-B3-B4 | | |
| Cecil Street | C1-C2 | | |
| Chapel Street | B3-C3 | | |
| Charlotte Street | A1-B1 | | |
| Chatsworth Square | C3 | | |
| Chiswick Street | C2 | | |
| Corporation Road | B3-B4 | | |
| Crosby Street | B2-C2 | | |
| Crown Street | C1 | | |
| Currock Street | B1 | | |
| Denton Street | A1-B1 | | |
| Devonshire Street | B2 | | |
| East Tower Street | B3 | | |
| Eden Bridge | B4 | | |
| Fisher Street | A3-B3 | | |
| Georgian Way | B3-C3 | | |
| Harlington Place | C2-C3 | | |
| Harlington Street | C3 | | |
| Junction Street | A1 | | |
| Lancaster Street | C1 | | |
| Lime Street | A1-B1 | | |
| Lorne Crescent | A1 | | |
| Lorne Street | A1 | | |
| Lowther Street | B2-B3 | | |
| Market Street | B3 | | |
| Mary Street | C1-C2 | | |
| Milbourne Street | A1-A2 | | |
| Paternoster Row | A3 | | |
| Peter Street | B3 | | |
| Portland Place | C1-C2 | | |
| Portland Square | C2 | | |
| Rickergate | B3 | | |
| Robert Street | B1 | | |
| Rydal Street | C1 | | |
| Scotch Street | B3 | | |
| Sheffield Street | A1 | | |
| Spencer Street | C2-C3 | | |
| Strand Road | C3 | | |

**173**

# Cambridge

Cambridge is found on atlas page **53**,
grid reference **4558**

**AA shop**
Janus House, 46–48 St Andrew's Street, Cambridge CB2 3BH   D3

| | | | | | | | | | |
|---|---|---|---|---|---|---|---|---|---|
| Abbey Road | F5-F6 | Christchurch Street | E5 | Gonville Place | D2-D3-E3 | Linden Close | A8-B8 | Paradise Street | E4 | Searle Street | B7-C7 |
| Adam and Eve Street | E4 | Church Street | F7-F8 | Grafton Street | E4 | Logans Way | F6-F7 | Park Parade | C6 | Shelly Row | A6-B6 |
| Akeman Street | B8 | City Road | E4 | Grange Road | A3-A4-A5-A6 | Lower Park Street | C5-C6 | Park Street | C5 | Short Street | D5 |
| Albert Street | C7 | Clare Road | A1-A2 | Granta Place | B2-B3 | Lyndewode Road | E2 | Park Terrace | D3-D4 | Sidgewick Avenue | A2-B2 |
| Albion Row | B6 | Clare Street | B7 | Grantchester Street | A1 | Mackenzie Road | E3-F3 | Parker Street | D4 | Silver Street | B3-C3 |
| Alpha Road | B7-B6-C6 | Claremont | E1 | Grasmere Gardens | C7 | Madingley Road | A6-B6-B5 | Parkside | E3-D3-D4 | Springfield Road | D7 |
| Arthur Street | B7 | Clarendon Street | D4-E4 | Green Street | C4-C5 | Magdalene Street | B5-B6 | Parsonage Street | E5 | Staffordshire Street | F4 |
| Ascham Road | D8 | Collier Road | E3-F3 | Green's Road | C7 | Magrath Avenue | B7-B6 | Pemberton Terrace | C1-D1 | Station Road | E1-F1 |
| Auckland Road | E5 | Corn Exchange Street | C3-C4 | Gresham Road | E2 | Maids Causeway | D5-E5 | Pembroke Street | C3 | Stretten Avenue | B7-B8-C8 |
| Aylestone Road | D6-E6 | Corona Road | D7 | Guest Road | E3 | Malcolm Street | C5 | Pentlands Close | E6 | Sturton Street | F3-F4-F5 |
| Banhams Close | D6-E6 | Coronation Street | D1-D2 | Gurney Way | D8 | Malting Lane | B2 | Perowne Street | F3 | Sussex Street | C4-C5 |
| Barton Road | A1 | Covent Garden | E2-E3 | Gwydir Street | F2-F3 | Manhattan Drive | E6 | Portugal Street | C6 | Sydney Street | C4-C5 |
| Bateman Street | C1-D1-E1 | Cross Street | E2-F2 | Hale Avenue | B8 | Manor Street | D5 | Pound Hill | B6 | Tenison Avenue | E1 |
| Beche Road | F5-F6 | De Freville Avenue | E6-E7 | Hale Street | B7 | Market Place | C4 | Pretoria Road | D6-D7 | Tenison Road | E1-F1-E2-F2 |
| Belvoir Road | E6-E7 | Derby Street | A1 | Hamilton Road | D7-E7 | Market Street | C4 | Primrose Street | C7 | Tennis Court Road | C3-C2-D2 |
| Benet Street | C4 | Devonshire Road | F1-F2 | Hardwick Street | A1 | Mawson Road | E2-F2-F3 | Priory Road | F5-F6 | The Fen Causeway | B2-C2 |
| Benson Street | A7 | Downing Place | C3-D3 | Harvey Goodwin Gardens | B7-B8 | Melbourne Place | D4-E4 | Priory Street | A7 | Thomson's Lane | C5-C6 |
| Bermuda Road | B8 | Downing Street | C3-D3 | Harvey Road | D2-E2 | Merton Street | A1 | Prospect Row | E4 | Trafalgar Road | D7 |
| Blossom Street | F4 | Drummer Street | D4 | Hawthorn Way | E7-E8 | Mill Lane | B3-C3 | Queen's Lane | B3 | Trafalgar Street | D7 |
| Bradmore Street | E3-E4 | Earl Street | D4 | Herbert Street | D7-D8 | Mill Road | F2-F3-E3 | Queens Road | B2-B4-A4-A5 | Trinity Lane | B4-C4 |
| Brandon Place | E4 | East Road | E3-E4-F4-F5 | Hertford Street | B7-B6-C6 | Mill Street | E3-F3-F2 | Regent Street | D2-D3 | Trinity Street | C4-C5 |
| Brentwick Street | D1-D2 | Eden Street | E4 | High Street | F8 | Millington Road | A1 | Regent Terrace | D2-D3 | Trumpington Street | C2-C3 |
| Bridge Street | B5-C5 | Elizabeth Way | E8-E7-F7-F6-F5 | Hilda Street | B7-C7 | Milton Road | D7-D8-E8 | Ridley Hall Road | B2 | Trumpington Road | C1-C2 |
| Broad Street | E4-F4 | Elm Street | D4-E4 | Hills Road | E1-D2 | Montague Road | E7-F7 | Rose Crescent | C4 | Union Lane | F8 |
| Brookside | C1-C2 | Emery Street | F3 | Histon Road | A7-A8 | Mortimer Road | E3 | Russell Street | D1-E1 | Union Road | D2 |
| Brunswick Gardens | E5 | Emmanuel Road | D4-D5 | Hobson Street | C4-C5 | Mount Pleasant | A6 | St Andrew's Street | D3-D4-C4 | Vicarage Terrace | F4 |
| Brunswick Terrace | E5 | Emmanuel Street | D4 | Holland Street | C7 | Napier Street | E5 | St Andrews Road | F6-F7 | Victoria Avenue | D5-D6-D7 |
| Buckingham Road | A7 | Fair Street | E5 | Humberstone Road | E7-F7 | New Park Street | C5-C6 | St Barnabas Road | F2 | Victoria Park | C7-C8 |
| Burleigh Street | E4-E5 | Ferry Path | D6-D7 | Huntington Road | A7 | New Square | D5-D4 | St Eligius Street | D1 | Victoria Road | A7-B7-C7-D7 |
| Cambridge Place | E2 | Fisher Street | C7 | Hurst Park Avenue | D8-E8 | New Street | F5 | St John's Road | C6 | Victoria Street | D4 |
| Canterbury Street | A7-A8 | Fitzroy Street | E5 | James Street | E5 | Newmarket Road | E5-F5 | St John's Street | C5 | Warkworth Street | E4 |
| Carlyle Road | B7-C7 | Fitzwilliam Street | C2-C3 | Jesus Lane | C5-D5 | Newnham Road | A1-B1-B2 | St Luke's Street | B7 | Warkworth Terrrace | E3-E4 |
| Castle Street | B6 | Free School Lane | C3-C4 | John Street | E4 | Newnham Walk | A2-B2 | St Matthews Street | F4-F5 | Wellington Street | E5-F5 |
| Chantry Close | C7 | French Road | B7-B8 | Kimberley Road | E6-E7 | Norfolk Street | E4-F4 | St Paul's Road | D2-E2 | West Gardens | A3 |
| Chedworth Street | A1-B1 | Garden Walk | C7-C8 | King Street | D5-E5 | Norfolk Terrace | F4 | St Peter's Street | B6 | West Road | A3-B3 |
| Chesterton Hall Crescent | E7-E8 | George IV Street | D2 | Kings Parade | C4 | Northampton Street | B5-B6 | St Tibbs Row | C3-C4 | Westfield Lane | A7 |
| Chesterton Lane | B6-C6 | George Street | D7-D8 | Kingston Street | F2-F3 | Norwich Street | D1-E1 | Sandy Lane | E7 | Willis Road | E3 |
| Chesterton Road | E7-D7-C7-C6 | Gilbert Road | C8-D8 | Lady Margaret Road | A6 | Orchard Street | D4-E4 | Saxon Street | C2-D2 | Wollaston Road | E3 |
| Chestnut Grove | E8 | Glisson Road | E1-E2 | Lenfield Road | C2-D2 | Panton Street | D1-D2 | Scotland Road | F8 | Wordsworth Grove | A2 |

174

# Chester

Chester is found on atlas page **71**,
grid reference **4066**

**AA shop**
63–65 Foregate Street, Chester CH1 1YZ                    D3

| | | | | | | |
|---|---|---|---|---|---|---|
| Abbey Square | C3 | Garden Lane | B4-C4 | Queens Avenue | E3-E4 | Watergate Street | B2-C2 |
| Abbey Street | C3 | George Street | C4 | Queens Drive | E1 | Weaver Street | C2 |
| Albion Street | C1-D1 | Gladstone Avenue | A4 | Queens Park Road | D1-E1 | West Lorne Street | B4 |
| Anne's Way | E1 | Gloucester Street | D4 | Queens Road | E4 | Westminster Road | F4 |
| Bath Street | E2-E3 | Gorse Stacks | C4-D4-D3 | Raymond Street | B4 | Wetherby Close | A4 |
| Beaconsfield Street | E3-F4 | Granville Street | A4-B4 | Russell Street | E3 | Whipcord Lane | A4-B4-B3 |
| Bedward Road | B3 | Grey Friars | B2-C2 | St Anne Street | D4 | York Street | D3 |
| Black Friars | B1-C2 | Grosvenor Park Road | E2-E3 | St George's Crescent | E1 | | |
| Boughton | E3-F3 | Grosvenor Street | C1-C2 | St John Street | D2 | | |
| Bridge Street | C2 | Haydock Close | A4 | St Johns Road | E1 | | |
| Brook Street | D4-E4 | Henry Place | D4 | St Martins Way | B2-B3-B4-C4 | | |
| Bunce Street | B4 | Hoole Lane | F3 | St Oswalds Way | C4-D4-D3-E3 | | |
| Cambrian Road | B4 | Hoole Way | D4 | St Werburgh Street | C2-C3 | | |
| Canal Side | D3-E3 | Hunter Street | B3-C3 | Seaville Street | E3 | | |
| Canal Street | B3-B4-C4 | Kempton Close | A4 | Sedgefield Road | A4 | | |
| Castle Drive | C1 | King Street | B3-C3 | Seller Street | E3 | | |
| Castle Street | C1 | Leadworks Lane | E3 | Shipgate Street | C1 | | |
| Catherine Street | A3-A4-B4 | Lightfoot Street | F4 | Sibell Street | E4 | | |
| Charles Street | D4 | Little St John Street | D2 | Souters Lane | D1-D2 | | |
| Chichester Street | B4-C4 | Lorne Street | B4-C4 | South Crescent Road | E1 | | |
| City Road | E3-E4 | Louise Street | B4 | South View Road | A3-B3 | | |
| City Walls Road | B2-B3 | Love Street | D2-D3 | Stanley Place | B2 | | |
| Commonhall Street | C2 | Lower Bridge Street | C1-C2 | Stanley Street | B2 | | |
| Crewe Street | E4 | Lower Park Road | E1 | Station Road | E4 | | |
| Cross Street | F3-F4 | Lyon Street | D4 | Steam Mill Street | E3 | | |
| Cuppin Street | C1-C2 | Mason Street | C4 | Steele Street | D1 | | |
| Curzon Park North | A1 | Milton Street | D3-D4 | Stuart Place | D4 | | |
| Dee Hills Park | E3-F3 | New Crane Street | B2 | The Groves | D2-E2 | | |
| Dee Lane | E2-E3 | Newgate Street | D2 | Tower Road | A3-B3 | | |
| Delamere Street | C4 | Nicholas Street | C1-C2 | Trafford Street | D4 | | |
| Duke Street | C1-D1 | Nicholas Street Mews | B2 | Union Street | D2-E2 | | |
| Eastgate Street | C2-D2 | Northgate Street | C2-C3 | Upper Northgate Street | C4 | | |
| Edinburgh Way | E1 | Nun's Road | B2-B1-C1 | Vernon Road | A3-A4-B4 | | |
| Egerton Street | D4-E4-E3 | Orchard Street | B4 | Vicars Lane | D2 | | |
| Elizabeth Crescent | E1-F1 | Park Street | D1-D2 | Victoria Crescent | D1-E1 | | |
| Epsom Court | A4 | Pepper Street | C2-D2 | Victoria Road | C4 | | |
| Forest Street | D2-E2 | Phillip Street | F4 | Volunteer Street | D2 | | |
| Francis Street | D4-E4 | Princes Avenue | E3-E4 | Walls Avenue | B2-B3 | | |
| Frodsham Street | D2-D3 | Queen Street | D3 | Water Tower Street | B3-C3 | | |

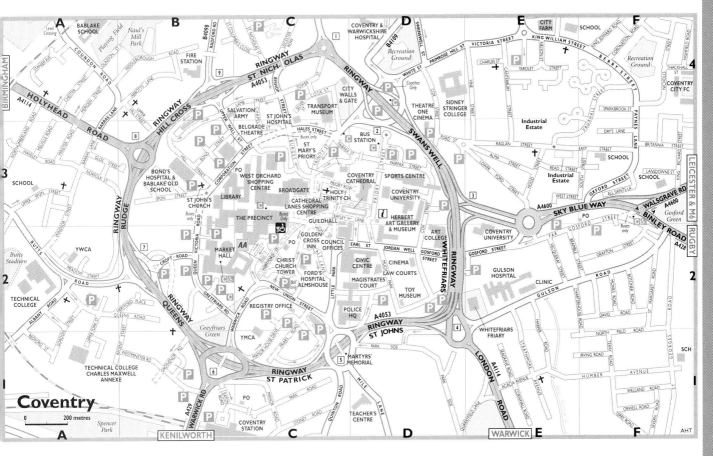

# Coventry

Coventry is found on atlas page **61**,
grid reference **3378**

**AA shop**
39–40 Hertford Street, Coventry CVI ILF      C2

| Street | Grid | Street | Grid | Street | Grid | Street | Grid |
|---|---|---|---|---|---|---|---|
| Abbotts Lane | B4 | Gloucester Street | A3-B3 | Nicholls Street | F4 | Spon Street | B3 |
| Acacia Avenue | E1 | Gordon Street | A1-A2 | Norfolk Street | A3-B3 | Stanier Avenue | A4 |
| Albany Road | A1-A2 | Gosford Street | D2-E2 | Northfield Road | E1-F2 | Stoney Road | C1 |
| All Saints Lane | F3 | Grafton Street | F2 | Northumberland Road | A3-A4 | Stoney Stanton Road | D4 |
| Alma Street | E3 | Greyfriars Road | B2 | Orwell Road | F1 | Strathmore Avenue | E1-E2 |
| Barras Lane | A3-B4 | Grosvenor Road | B1 | Oxford Street | F3 | Swanswell Street | D4 |
| Bayley Lane | C3-D3 | Gulson Road | E2-F2 | Park Road | C1 | Terry Road | F1 |
| Bedford Street | A1-A2 | Hales Street | C3 | Park Side | D1 | Thackhall Street | F4 |
| Berry Street | F4 | Harper Road | E1-E2 | Paynes Lane | F3-F4 | Tower Street | C4 |
| Binley Road | F2-F3 | Hartford Place | B2 | Primrose Hill Street | D4 | Trinity Street | C3 |
| Bishop Street | C3-C4 | Hertford Street | C2 | Priory Row | C3-D3 | Upper Hill Street | B3-B4 |
| Bond Street | B3 | High Street | C2-C3 | Priory Street | D2-D3 | Upper Spon Street | A3 |
| Botoner Road | F2 | Highfield Road | F4 | Quarryfield Lane | D1-E1 | Upper Well Street | B4-C3 |
| Bramble Street | E2-F2 | Hill Street | B3 | Queen Victoria Road | B2-B3 | Upper York Street | A1-A2 |
| Britannia Street | F3 | Holyhead Road | A4-B3 | Queens Road | A2-B2 | Vauxhall Street | E3-F4 |
| Burges | C3 | Hood Street | E3 | Quinton Road | C1 | Vecqueray Street | E2 |
| Butts Road | A3-B2 | Humber Avenue | E1-F1 | Radford Road | B4 | Victoria Street | E4 |
| Canterbury Street | E3-E4 | Irving Road | E1-F1 | Raglan Street | E3 | Vine Street | E3-E4 |
| Charles Street | E4 | Jordan Well | D2 | Read Street | E3 | Walsgrave Road | F3 |
| Chapel Street | C3-C4 | King Edward Road | F4 | Regent Street | A1-B2 | Warwick Road | B1-C2 |
| Charterhouse Road | E1-E2 | King Richard Street | F3-F4 | Ringway Hillcross | B3-B4 | Waveley Road | A3 |
| Chester Street | A4 | King William Street | E4-F4 | Ringway Queens | B1-B2 | Welland Road | F1 |
| Cook Street | C4 | Lamb Street | B3-C4 | Ringway Rudge | B2-B3 | West Street | E3 |
| Cornwall Road | E1 | Lansdowne Street | F3 | Ringway St Johns | D1-D2 | Westminster Road | B1 |
| Coronation Road | F4 | Leicester Row | C4 | Ringway St Nicholas | C4 | White Street | D4 |
| Corporation Street | B3-C3 | Little Park | C2 | Ringway St Patrick | C1 | Windsor Street | A2-A3 |
| Coundon Road | A4-B4 | London Road | D1-E1 | Ringway Swanswell | C4-D3 | Yardley Street | E4 |
| Coundon Street | A4-B4 | Lower Ford Street | E3 | Ringway Whitefriars | D2-D3 | | |
| Cox Street | D2-D4 | Manor Road | B1-C1 | St Columba's Close | B4-C4 | | |
| Croft Road | B2 | Meadow Street | A2 | St Georges Road | F1-F2 | | |
| Charles Street | F1 | Melville Road | A3-A4 | St Margaret Road | F2 | | |
| David Road | F1 | Meriden Street | A4 | St Nicholas Street | C4 | | |
| Days Lane | F3 | Middleborough Road | A4-B4 | Salt Lane | C2 | | |
| Earl Street | C2-D2 | Mile Lane | C1-D1 | Seagrave Road | E1 | | |
| East Street | E3-F3 | Melville Road | A3-A4 | Severn Road | F1 | | |
| Eaton Road | B1 | Minster Road | A3-A4 | Silver Street | C4 | | |
| Fairfax Street | C3-D3 | Monks Road | F2 | Sky Blue Way | E3-F3 | | |
| Far Gosford Street | E2-F3 | Much Park | D2 | South Street | E3-F3 | | |
| Ford Street | D3 | Nelson Street | E4 | Sparkbrook Street | F4 | | |
| Friars Road | C1-C2 | New Union Street | C2 | | | | |

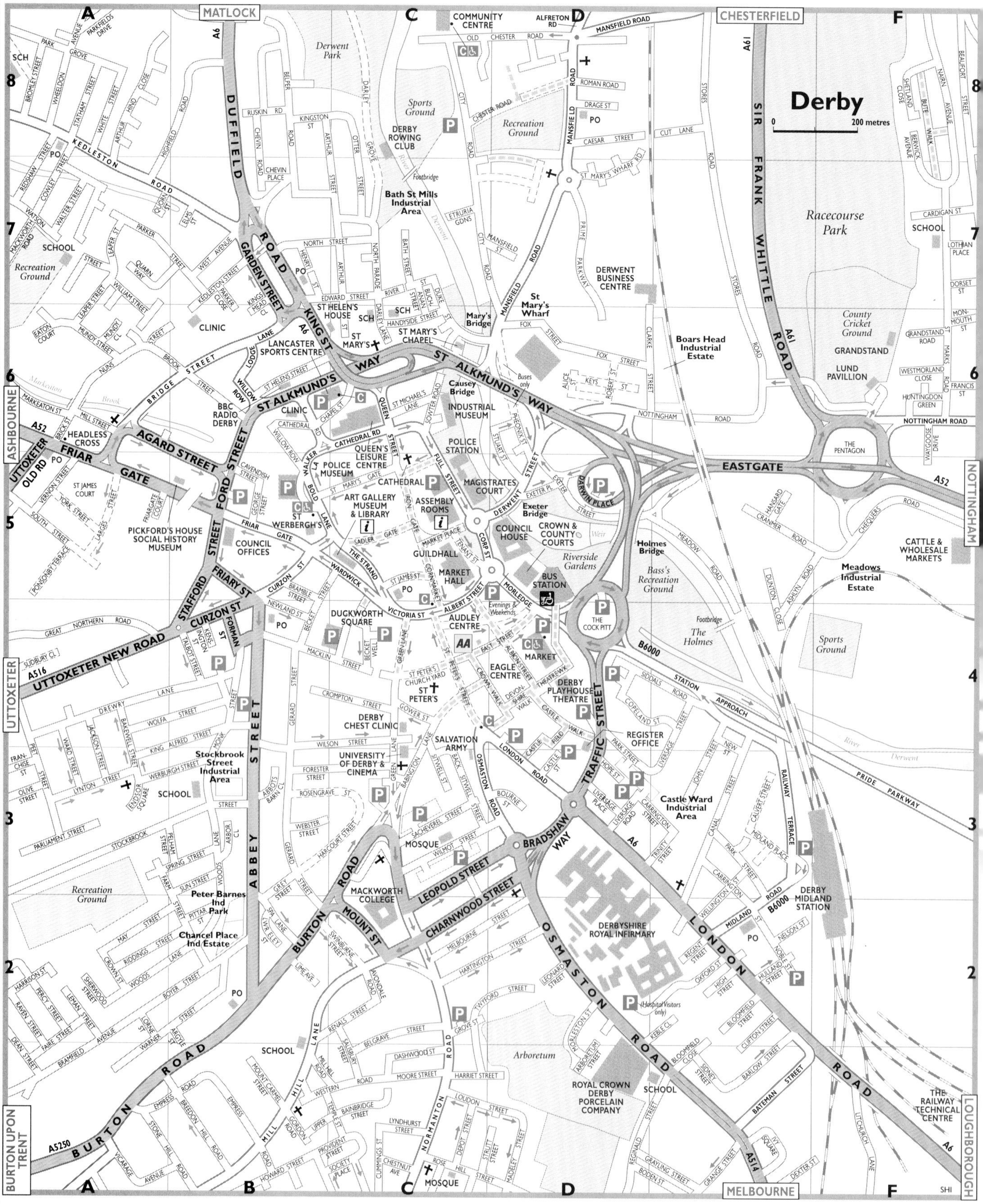

## Derby

0    200 metres

**176**

### Grid references (borders)
A · B · C · D · E · F — 8 · 7 · 6 · 5 · 4 · 3 · 2

### Edge destinations
MATLOCK · CHESTERFIELD · ASHBOURNE · UTTOXETER · NOTTINGHAM · BURTON UPON TRENT · MELBOURNE · LOUGHBOROUGH

### Principal roads
A6 · A61 · A52 · A516 · A5250 · A514 · B6000 · DUFFIELD ROAD · KEDLESTON ROAD · GARDEN STREET · KING STREET · ST ALKMUND'S WAY · FRIAR GATE · AGARD STREET · FORD STREET · STAFFORD STREET · FRIARY STREET · CURZON STREET · UTTOXETER NEW ROAD · UTTOXETER OLD RD · BURTON ROAD · ABBEY STREET · MOUNT STREET · OSMASTON ROAD · TRAFFIC STREET · LONDON ROAD · BRADSHAW WAY · CHARNWOOD STREET · LEOPOLD STREET · MANSFIELD ROAD · SIR FRANK WHITTLE ROAD · NOTTINGHAM ROAD · EASTGATE · PRIDE PARKWAY · ALFRETON RD · CHESTER ROAD · ROMAN ROAD

### Places of interest
Derwent Park · Sports Ground · Recreation Ground · Derby Rowing Club · Bath St Mills Industrial Area · Derwent Business Centre · Boars Head Industrial Estate · Racecourse Park · County Cricket Ground · Grandstand · Lund Pavilion · The Pentagon · St Mary's Wharf · St Mary's Bridge · St Mary's Chapel · Industrial Museum · Causey Bridge · St Helen's House · Lancaster Sports Centre · BBC Radio Derby · Cathedral · Police Museum · Queen's Leisure Centre · Art Gallery Museum & Library · Assembly Rooms · St Werburgh's · Police Station · Magistrates Court · Exeter Bridge · Council House · Crown & County Courts · Riverside Gardens · Bass's Recreation Ground · The Holmes · Holmes Bridge · Headless Cross · Pickford's House Social History Museum · Council Offices · Guildhall · Market Hall · Duckworth Square · Audley Centre · AA · Bus Station · The Cock Pitt · Market · Eagle Centre · St Peter's Church · St Peter's · Derby Chest Clinic · Salvation Army · Derby Playhouse Theatre · Register Office · University of Derby & Cinema · Mackworth College · Derby Midland Station · Castle Ward Industrial Area · Derbyshire Royal Infirmary · Arboretum · Royal Crown Derby Porcelain Company · Meadows Industrial Estate · Cattle & Wholesale Markets · Station Approach · The Railway Technical Centre · Stockbrook Street Industrial Area · Peter Barnes Ind Park · Chancel Place Ind Estate · Recreation Ground · Mosque · Community Centre

### Rivers
River Derwent · Markeaton Brook

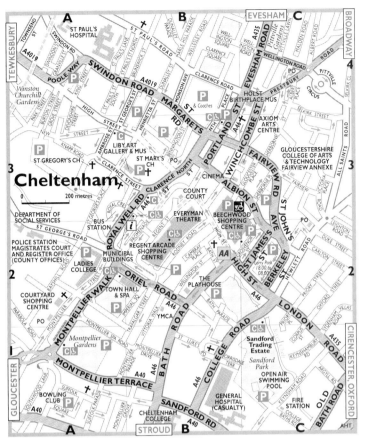

# Cheltenham

Cheltenham is found on atlas page **35**,
grid reference **9422**

**AA shop**
90 High Street, Cheltenham GL50 1EG — B2

| | | | | | | |
|---|---|---|---|---|---|
| Albert Place | C4 | Hewlett Road | C2 | Priory Street | C2 |
| Albert Road | C4 | High Street | A3-A4-B3-C2 | Promenade | B2-B3 |
| Albion Street | B3-C3 | Imperial Square | A2-B2 | Regent Street | B2-B3 |
| All Saints Road | C3-C4 | Keynsham Road | C1 | Rodney Road | B2 |
| Ambrose Street | A3 | Keynshambury Road | C1 | Royal Crescent | A3 |
| Argyll Road | C1 | King Street | A4 | Royal Well Road | A2-B3 |
| Bath Parade | B2 | Knapp Road | A3 | St George's Place | A2-A3 |
| Bath Road | B1-B2 | Leighton Road | C2 | St George's Road | A2-A3 |
| Bath Street | B2 | London Road | C1-C2 | St George's Street | A3-B4 |
| Bayshill Road | A2 | Malden Road | C4 | St John's Avenue | C2-C3 |
| Bennington Street | B3 | Marle Hill Parade | B4 | St Luke's Road | B1 |
| Berkeley Street | C2 | Monson Avenue | B4 | St Margarets Road | B3-B4 |
| Brunswick Street | B4 | Montpellier Drive | B1 | St Paul's Lane | A4-B4 |
| Burton Street | A3-A4 | Montpellier Grove | A1-B1 | St Paul's Road | A4-B4 |
| Cambray Place | B2 | Montpellier Parade | A1-B1 | St Paul's Street South | A4 |
| Carlton Street | C2 | Montpellier Spa Road | A1-A2 | Sandford Road | B1 |
| Clarence Road | B4 | Montpellier Street | A1-A2 | Selkirk Close | C4 |
| Clarence Square | B4 | Montpellier Terrace | A1-B1 | Selkirk Street | C3-C4 |
| Clarence Street | A3-B3 | Montpellier Walk | A1-A2 | Sherborne Place | C3 |
| College Baths Road | C1 | New Street | A3 | Sherborne Street | C3-C4 |
| College Road | B1-C2 | North Place | B3-B4 | Southwood Lane | A1 |
| Corpus Street | C1 | North Street | B3 | Suffolk Parade | A1 |
| Devonshire Street | A3-A4 | Old Bath Road | C1 | Suffolk Square | A1 |
| Duke Street | C2 | Oriel Road | A2-B2 | Swindon Road | A4-B4 |
| Dunalley Parade | B4 | Orrisdale Terrace | B1 | Swindon Street | A4 |
| Dunalley Street | B4 | Oxford Street | C2 | Townsend Street | A4 |
| Evesham Road | C4 | Parabola Road | A1-A2 | Trafalgar Street | B2 |
| Fairview Road | B3-C3 | Park Street | A4 | Victoria Place | C3 |
| Gloucester Place | C3 | Pitville Circus | C4 | Victoria Walk | B1-B2 |
| Granville Street | A4 | Pitville Lawn | C4 | Wellesley Road | B4 |
| Great Norwood Street | A1 | Poole Way | A4 | Wellington Road | C4 |
| Grosvenor Street | C2 | Portland Street | B3-B4 | Wellington Square | B4 |
| Grove Street | A3-A4 | Prestbury Road | C4 | Wellington Street | B2 |
| Henrietta Street | B3-B4 | Priory Place | C2 | Winchcombe Street | B3-C3-C4 |

# Derby

Derby is found on atlas page **62**,
grid reference **3536**

**AA shop**
22 East Street, Derby DE1 2AF — C4

| | | | | | | |
|---|---|---|---|---|---|
| Abbey Street | B2-B3-B4 | Brook Street | A6-B6 | Dean Street | A2-A1 |
| Abbots Barn Close | B3 | Buchanan Street | C6-C7 | Depot Street | C1 |
| Agard Street | A6-B6-B5 | Burton Road | A1-B1-B2-C2-C3 | Derwent Street | D5-D6 |
| Albert Street | C4-C5-D5 | Bute Walk | F8-F7 | Devonshire Walk | D4 |
| Albion Street | D4 | Caesar Street | D8 | Dexter Street | E1-F1 |
| Alfreton Road | D8 | Calvert Street | E3 | Dorset Street | F7 |
| Alice Street | D6 | Canal Street | E3-E4 | Drage Street | D8 |
| Arbor Close | B3 | Cardigan Street | F7 | Drewry Lane | A4-B4 |
| Arboretum Street | D1-D2 | Carrington Street | D3-E3 | Duke Street | C7-C6 |
| Argyle Street | B2 | Castle Field | D3-D4 | Duffield Road | B8-B7 |
| Arthur Hind Close | A7-A8 | Castle Street | D3 | Dunton Close | E5-E4 |
| Arthur Street | B8-C8-C7-C6 | Castle Walk | D4 | Eagle Street | E5 |
| Ashlyn Road | E4-E5-F5 | Cathedral Road | B6-C6 | East Street | C4-D4 |
| Avondale Road | C2 | Cavendish Street | B5 | Eaton Court | A6 |
| Babington Lane | C3-C4 | Chancel Street | B2 | Edward Street | B7-C7 |
| Back Sitwell Street | C3 | Chapel Street | C6 | Elms Street | B7 |
| Bainbridge Street | C1 | Charnwood Street | C2-D2-D3 | Empress Road | A1-B1 |
| Bakewell Street | A4-A3 | Chester Road | C8-D8 | Endsor Square | A3 |
| Barlow Street | E1-E2 | Chequers Road | F5 | Etruria Gardens | C7 |
| Bateman Street | E1 | Chestnut Avenue | C1 | Exeter Place | D5 |
| Bath Street | C7 | Chevin Place | B7 | Exeter Street | D5 |
| Beaufort Street | F8-F7 | Chevin Road | B8-B7 | Faire Street | A1-A2 |
| Becket Street | B4-B5-C5 | City Road | C8-C7-D7-D6 | Farm Street | A3-B3-B2 |
| Becket Well | C4 | Clarke Street | D6-E6 | Ford Street | B5-B6 |
| Belgrave Street | C1-C2 | Clifton Street | E1-E2 | Forester Street | B3-C3 |
| Belper Road | B8-B7 | Copeland Street | D4-E4 | Forman Street | B4 |
| Berwick Avenue | F8-F7 | Corn Market | C5 | Fox Street | D6 |
| Bloomfield Close | E1 | Corporation Street | D5 | Franchise Street | A3 |
| Bloomfield Street | E2 | Cowley Street | A7-A8 | Francis Street | F6 |
| Boden Street | D1-E1 | Cranmer Road | E5-F5 | Friar Gate | A6-A5-B5 |
| Bold Lane | B5-C5 | Crompton Street | B4-C4 | Friargate Court | A5 |
| Bourne Street | D3 | Crown Street | A2 | Friary Street | B5 |
| Boyer Street | A2-B2 | Crown Walk | C4-D4 | Full Street | C6-C5 |
| Bradshaw Way | D3 | Cummings Street | C1 | Garden Street | B6-B7 |
| Bramble Street | B5 | Curzon Street | B4-B5 | George Street | B5 |
| Bramfield Avenue | A1-A2 | Cut Lane | E8 | Gerard Street | B2-B3-B4 |
| Breedon Hill Road | B1 | Darley Grove | C8-C7 | Gordon Road | B1 |
| Brick Street | A6 | Darley Lane | C6-C7 | Gower Street | C4 |
| Bridge Street | A5-A6-B6 | Darwin Place | D5 | Grandstand Road | A6 |
| Bromley Street | A8 | Dashwood Street | C1 | Grange Street | E1 |

| | | | | | | |
|---|---|---|---|---|---|
| Grayling Street | D1-E1 | Hartington Street | C2-D2 | Mount Carmel Street | B1 | Salisbury Street | C1-C2 |
| Great Northern Road | D1-E1 | Henry Street | B7 | Mundy Close | A6 | Sherwood Street | A2 |
| Green Lane | C3-C4 | Highfield Road | A7-A8-B8 | Mundy Street | A6 | Shetland Close | F8 |
| Grey Street | B3 | High Street | E2 | Nairn Avenue | F7-F8 | Siddals Road | D4-E4 |
| Grove Street | C2-D2 | Hope Street | D3 | Nelson Street | E2 | Sidney Street | E1 |
| Handyside Street | C6 | Howard Street | B1 | New Street | E4 | Sir Frank Whittle Road | F6-E6-E8 |
| Hansard Gate | E5 | Hulland Street | E2 | Newland Street | B4 | Sitwell Street | C3 |
| Harcourt Street | B3-C3 | Huntington Green | F6 | Noble Street | C2 | Society Place | C1 |
| Harriet Street | C1-D1 | Iron Gate | C5 | Normanton Road | C1-C2-C3 | South Street | A5 |
| Harrison Street | A2 | Ivy Square | E1 | North Parade | C7 | Sowter Road | C6 |
| | | Jackson Street | A3-A4 | North Street | B7-C7 | Spa Lane | B2 |
| | | John Street | E3-E4 | Nottingham Road | D6-E6-F6 | Spring Street | B3 |
| | | Keble Close | B3 | Nuns Street | A6 | Stafford Street | B4-B5 |
| | | Kedleston Road | A8-A7-B7 | Old Chester Road | C8-D8 | Statham Street | A8 |
| | | Kedleston Street | B7 | Olive Street | A3 | Station Approach | D4-E4 |
| | | Kensington Street | B4 | Osmaston Road | E1-C4 | Stockbrook Street | A2-A3-B3 |
| | | Keys Street | D6 | Otter Street | C7-C8 | Stone Hill Road | A1-B1 |
| | | King Alfred Street | A3-B3-B4 | Oxford Street | E2 | Stores Road | E6-E7-E8 |
| | | Kings Mead Close | B6 | Parker Close | B6-B7 | Strutt Street | D1 |
| | | Kingston Street | B8-C8 | Parker Street | A7-B7 | Stuart Street | D5-D6 |
| | | King Street | B6-C6 | Parkfields Drive | A8 | Sudbury Close | A4 |
| | | Kirk Street | D8 | Park Grove | A8 | Sun Street | B3 |
| | | Larges Street | A5 | Park Street | D4-D3-E3 | Swinburne Street | C2 |
| | | Leaper Street | A6-A7 | Parliament Street | A3 | Talbot Street | B4 |
| | | Leman Street | A4 | Peet Street | A3-A4 | Temple Street | C1 |
| | | Leonard Street | D2 | Pelham Street | B3 | Tenant Street | C5 |
| | | Leopold Street | C2-C3-D3 | Percy Street | A2 | Theatre Walk | D4 |
| | | Lime Avenue | B2-C2 | Phoenix Street | D6 | The Cock Pitt | D4 |
| | | Litchurch Lane | F1 | Pittar Street | B2 | The Pentagon | F5-F6 |
| | | Liversage Place | D3 | Ponsonby Terrace | A5 | The Strand | C5 |
| | | Liversage Road | D3 | Pride Parkway | E4-F3 | Traffic Street | D3-D4 |
| | | Liversage Street | E3-E4 | Prime Parkway | D7 | Trinity Street | E3 |
| | | Lodge Lane | B6 | Provident Street | C1 | Twyford Street | C2-D2 |
| | | London Road | D4-D3-E3-E2-F2-F1 | Quarn Way | A7 | Upper Bainbridge Street | B1-C1 |
| | | Lorne Street | A2 | Quorn Street | A7 | Uttoxeter New Road | A4-B4 |
| | | Lothian Place | F7 | Queen Street | C5-C6 | Uttoxeter Old Road | A5 |
| | | Loudon Street | C1-D1 | Railway Terrace | E3-E4 | Vicarage Avenue | A1-B1 |
| | | Lower Eley Street | B2 | Raven Street | A1-A2 | Victoria Street | C4 |
| | | Lyndhurst Street | C1 | Redshaw Street | A7-A8 | Vernon Street | A5 |
| | | Lynton Street | A3 | Regent Street | E2 | Walter Street | A7 |
| | | Macklin Street | B4-C4 | Reginald Street | D1-E1 | Ward Street | A3-A4 |
| | | Mackworth Road | A7 | Renals Street | B2-C2 | Warner Street | A1-A2-B2 |
| | | Madeley Street | D1 | Riddings Street | A2 | Wardwick | B5-C5-C4 |
| | | Mansfield Road | D6-D7-D8-E8 | River Street | C7 | Watson Street | A7 |
| | | Mansfield Street | C7-D7 | Robert Street | D6 | Waygoose Drive | F5-F6 |
| | | May Street | A2 | Roman Road | D8 | Webster Street | B3-C3 |
| | | Markeaton Street | A6 | Rose Hill Street | C1-D1 | Wellington Street | E2-E3 |
| | | Market Place | C5 | Rosengrave Street | B3-C3 | Werburgh Street | A3-B3 |
| | | Meadow Road | E5 | Ruskin Road | B8 | West Avenue | B7 |
| | | Melbourne Street | C2-D2 | Sacheverel Street | C3 | Western Road | B1-C1 |
| | | Midland Place | E3 | Sadler Gate | C5 | Westmorland Close | F6 |
| | | Midland Road | E2-E3 | St Alkmund's Way | B6-D5 | Wheeldon Avenue | A8 |
| | | Mill Hill Lane | B1-B2-C2 | St Helens Street | B6 | White Street | A8 |
| | | Mill Hill Road | B1-C1 | St James Court | A5 | William Street | A6-A7 |
| | | Mill Street | A6 | St James Street | C5 | Willow Row | B5-B6 |
| | | Monk Street | B3-B4 | St Marks Road | F6-F7 | Wilmot Street | C3-D3 |
| | | Monmouth Street | F6 | St Mary's Gate | B5-C5 | Wilson Street | B3-B4-C4 |
| | | Moore Street | C1 | St Mary's Wharf Road | D7-D8 | Wolfa Street | A4-B4 |
| | | Morledge | D4-D5 | St Michael's Lane | C6 | Woods Lane | A2-B2-B3 |
| | | Morleston Street | D1-D2 | St Peter's Church Yard | C4 | Wood Street | D6 |
| | | Mount Street | C2 | St Peter's Street | C4 | York Street | A5 |

**177**

178

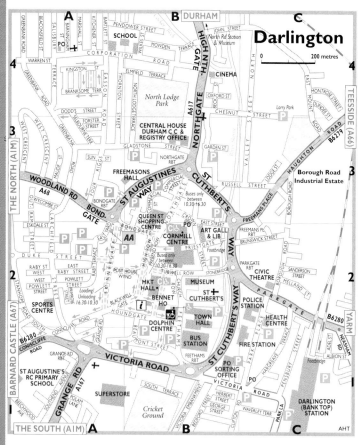

# Darlington

Darlington is found on atlas page **89**,
grid reference **2814**

## AA shop
47 Skinnergate, Darlington DL3 7NR                    A2

| | | | | | | |
|---|---|---|---|---|---|
| Adelaide Street | C1 | High Row | B2 | Thornton Street | A3-A4 |
| Albion Street | C1 | Houndgate | A2-B2 | Tubwell Row | B2 |
| Barningham Street | A4 | John Street | B4-C4 | Valley Street North | C3-C4 |
| Bartlett Street | A4 | Kingston Street | A4 | Victoria Embankment | B1 |
| Beaconsfield Street | A4 | Kitchener Street | A4 | Victoria Road | A1-B1-C1 |
| Beaumont Street | B1-B2 | Larchfield Street | A2-A3 | Warren Street | A4 |
| Beck Street | B4 | Lodge Street | C3 | Waverley Terrace | C1 |
| Bedford Street | B1 | Marshall Street | A4 | West Crescent | A3-A4 |
| Beechwood Avenue | A1 | Maude Street | A3 | West Powlett Street | A2 |
| Blackwell Gate | A2-B2 | Melland Street | C2 | Wilkes Street | B4 |
| Bondgate | A3-A2-B2 | Montrose Street | C4 | Woodland Road | A3 |
| Borough Road | C2-C3 | Mowden Terrace | B4 | Wycombe Street | A3 |
| Branksome Terrace | A4 | Neasham Road | C1 | | |
| Brunswick Street | B2-C2 | North Lodge Terrace | B3-B4 | | |
| Chestnut Street | B4-C4 | Northgate | B2-B3-B4 | | |
| Church Row | B2 | Outram Street | A2-A3 | | |
| Clifton Road | B1-C1 | Oxford Street | B4 | | |
| Commercial Street | B2-B3 | Park Lane | C1 | | |
| Coniscliffe Road | A1-A2 | Park Place | C1-C2 | | |
| Corporation Road | A4-B4 | Parkgate | C2 | | |
| Crown Street | B2-B3 | Pendower Street | A4-B4 | | |
| Dodd's Street | A4 | Pensbury Street | C1-C2 | | |
| Duke Street | A2 | Polam lane | A1 | | |
| Dundee Street | C4 | Post House Wynd | A2-B2 | | |
| Easson Road | A3-A4 | Powlett Street | A2 | | |
| East Mount Road | C3-C4 | Prebend Row | B2 | | |
| East Raby Street | A2 | Priestgate | B2 | | |
| East Street | B2-B3 | Primrose Street | A2 | | |
| Elmfield Terrace | A4-B4 | Raby Street West | A2 | | |
| Eskdale Street | A2 | Raby Terrace | A2 | | |
| Feethams | B1-B2 | Russell Street | B3-C3 | | |
| Forster Street | A3 | Salisbury Terrace | A4 | | |
| Four Riggs | A3 | Salt Yard | A2 | | |
| Freemans Place | C3 | Sanderson Street | C2 | | |
| Garden Street | B3 | Selbourne Terrace | A3-A4 | | |
| George Street | B1 | Skinnergate | A2 | | |
| Gladstone Street | A3-B3 | South Terrace | B1 | | |
| Grange Road | A1-A2 | Southend Avenue | A1 | | |
| Greenbank Road | A3-A4 | St Augustines Way | A3-B3 | | |
| Hargreave Terrace | C1-C2 | St Cuthbert's Way | B1-B2-B3 | | |
| Haughton Road | C3-C4 | Stanhope Road South | A1-A2 | | |
| Herbert Street | B1 | Stonebridge | B2 | | |
| High Northgate | B4 | Sun Street | A3 | | |

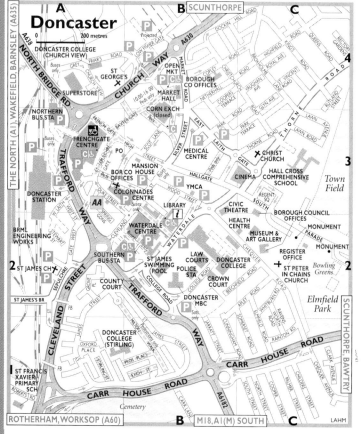

# Doncaster

Doncaster is found on atlas page **83**,
grid reference **5703**

## AA shop
34 Duke Street, Doncaster DN1 3EA                    A3

| | | | |
|---|---|---|---|
| Apley Road | B2-C2 | Park Road | B3-C3-C4 |
| Baxter Gate | A3-B3 | Park Terrace | B3-C3 |
| Beechfield Road | B2-C2 | Prospect Place | B1 |
| Broxholme Lane | C4 | Queens Road | C4 |
| Carr House Road | A1-B1-C1 | Rainton Road | C1 |
| Carr Lane | B1 | Ravensworth Road | C1-C2 |
| Chequer Avenue | C1 | Rectory Gardens | C4 |
| Chequer Road | B2-C2-C1 | Regent Square | C3 |
| Childers Street | C1 | Roberts Road | A1 |
| Christchurch Road | B4-C4-C3 | Royal Avenue | C4 |
| Church View | A4 | Rutland Street | C4 |
| Church Way | A4-B4 | St James's Bridge | A2 |
| Clark Avenue | C1 | St James Street | A1-A2-B2-B1 |
| Cleveland Street | A1-A2-B3 | St Sepulchre Gate | A3 |
| College Road | B2 | St Sepulchre Gate West | A1-A2 |
| Cooper Street | C1 | St Vincent Road | C4 |
| Coopers Terrace | B4 | Scot Lane | B3 |
| Copley Road | B4-C4 | Silver Street | B3 |
| Cunningham Road | B1-C1 | Somerset Road | C1-C2 |
| Dockin Hill Road | B4-C4 | South Parade | C3-C2 |
| Duke Street | A3-B3 | South Street | C1 |
| East Laith Gate | B3-C3 | Spring Gardens | A3-A2 |
| Elmfield Road | C2-C1 | Stewart Street | A2 |
| Exchange Street | B1 | Stirling Street | A1 |
| French Gate | A3 | Thorne Road | C3-C4 |
| Glyn Avenue | C4 | Trafford Way | A3-A2-B2-B1 |
| Grey Friar's Road | A4-B4 | Vaughan Avenue | C4 |
| Grove Place | A2 | Waterdale | B2-B3 |
| Hallgate | B3 | West Laith | A2-A3 |
| High Street | A3-B3 | West Street | A2-A3 |
| Highfield Road | C4 | Whitburn Road | C2 |
| Jarratt Street | B1 | Wood Street | B3 |
| King's Road | C4 | | |
| Lawn Avenue | C3 | | |
| Lawn Road | C3 | | |
| Low Fisher Gate | B4 | | |
| Market Road | B4 | | |
| Milton Walk | A2-B2-B1 | | |
| Netherhall Road | B4-C4 | | |
| North Bridge Road | A4 | | |
| North Street | C1 | | |
| Oxford Place | A1 | | |
| Palmer Street | C1 | | |

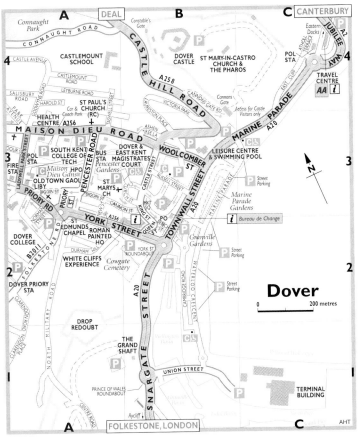

# Dover

Dover is found on atlas page **29**, grid reference **3241**

**AA Port shop**
Eastern Docks Terminal, Dover CT16 1JA — C4

| Street | Grid | Street | Grid |
|---|---|---|---|
| Ashen Tree Lane | B3 | Waterloo Crescent | B2-B1 |
| Atholl Terrace | C4 | Woolcomber Street | B3 |
| Biggin Street | A3 | York Street | A3-B3 |
| Cambridge Road | B2 | | |
| Cannon Street | A3-B3 | | |
| Cannons Gate Road | B4 | | |
| Castle Avenue | A4 | | |
| Castle Hill Road | B4-B3 | | |
| Castle Street | B3 | | |
| Castlemount Road | A4 | | |
| Centre Road | A1 | | |
| Church Street | B3 | | |
| Clarendon Place | A1 | | |
| Clarendon Road | A2-A1 | | |
| Connaught Road | A4 | | |
| Dour Street | A3 | | |
| Durham Hill | A2 | | |
| East Cliff | C4 | | |
| Folkestone Road | A2 | | |
| Godwyne Road | A3-A4 | | |
| Harold Street | A4 | | |
| Jubilee Way | C4 | | |
| King Street | B3 | | |
| Ladywell Park Street | A3 | | |
| Laureston Place | B4-B3 | | |
| Leyburne Road | A4 | | |
| Maison Dieu Road | A3-B3 | | |
| Marine Parade | B2-B3-C4 | | |
| New Street | A3 | | |
| Norman Street | A3 | | |
| North Military Road | A1-A2 | | |
| Park Avenue | A4-A3 | | |
| Pencester Road | A3 | | |
| Priory Road | A3 | | |
| Priory Street | A3 | | |
| Queen Street | B2 | | |
| Russell Street | B3 | | |
| Salisbury Road | A4 | | |
| Snargate Street | B1-B2 | | |
| Taswell Street | A3-A4 | | |
| Townwall Street | B2-B3 | | |
| Union Street | B1 | | |
| Victoria Park | B4 | | |

179

# Dundee

Dundee is found on atlas page **126**, grid reference **4030**

**AA shop**
124 Overgate, Dundee DD1 1DX — B3

| Street | Grid | Street | Grid |
|---|---|---|---|
| Bank Street | B3 | Union Street | B2 |
| Barrack Street | A3-B3 | Victoria Road | B4-C4 |
| Bell Street | A4-B4 | Ward Road | A3 |
| Blackscroft | C4 | West Bell Street | A3-A4 |
| Brown Street | A3 | West Marketgait | A2-A3-A4 |
| Camperdown Street | C3 | Westport | A2 |
| Castle Street | B3-C3 | Whitehall Crescent | B2 |
| Chrichton Street | B2-B3 | Whitehall Street | B2 |
| City Square | B3 | Willison Street | A3-B3 |
| Commercial Street | B3-C3 | | |
| Constable Street | C4 | | |
| Constitution Road | A3-A4 | | |
| Court House Square | A3 | | |
| Cowgate | B4-C4 | | |
| Cross Lane | A2 | | |
| Dens Street | C4 | | |
| Dock Street | C3 | | |
| Dudhope Street | A4-B4 | | |
| East Marketgait | C3-C4 | | |
| Euclid Crescent | B3-B4 | | |
| Exchange Street | C3 | | |
| Gellatly Street | C3 | | |
| Hawkhill | A3 | | |
| Hilltown | B4 | | |
| King Street | C4 | | |
| Laurel Bank | A4 | | |
| Lindsay Street | A3 | | |
| Mary Anne Lane | C3-C4 | | |
| Meadowside | A3-B3-B4 | | |
| Murraygate | B3-B4 | | |
| Nethergate | A2 | | |
| Nethergate High Street | A2-B2-B3 | | |
| North Marketgait | A4-B4-C4 | | |
| Panmure Street | B4 | | |
| Reform Street | B3 | | |
| Riverside Drive | A1-B1 | | |
| Seagate | B3-C3-C4 | | |
| South Marketgait | B2-C2-C3 | | |
| South Tay Street | A2 | | |
| South Ward Road | A3 | | |
| St Andrew's Street | C4 | | |
| St Roque's Lane | C4 | | |
| Trades Lane | C3-C4 | | |

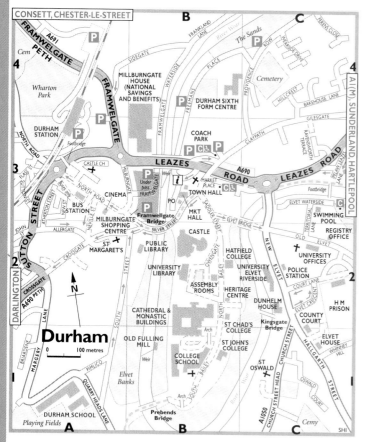

# Durham

Durham is found on atlas page **96**,
grid reference **2742**

| | | | |
|---|---|---|---|
| Allergate | A2 | Sutton Street | A3 |
| Atherton Street | A2-A3 | Territorial Lane | C2-C3 |
| Bakehouse Lane | C4 | Wearside Drive | C4 |
| Briardene | A1 | Whinney Hill | C1 |
| Castle Church | A3 | | |
| Church Street | C1 | | |
| Church Street Head | C1 | | |
| Claypath | B3-C3 | | |
| Court Lane | C2 | | |
| Crossgate | A2 | | |
| Elvet Bridge | B3-C3-C2 | | |
| Elvet Crescent | C2 | | |
| Elvet Waterside | C3 | | |
| Ferens Close | C4 | | |
| Flass Street | A3 | | |
| Framwelgate | A3-A4 | | |
| Framwelgate Peth | A4 | | |
| Framwelgate Waterside | B3-B4 | | |
| Frankland Lane | B4 | | |
| Freemans Place | B3-B4-C4 | | |
| Gilesgate | C3-C4 | | |
| Halgarth Street | C1 | | |
| Hilcrest | C4 | | |
| John Street | A2 | | |
| Leazes Road | B3-C3 | | |
| Margery Lane | A1-A2 | | |
| Milburngate | A3-B3 | | |
| Neville Street | A2-A3 | | |
| New Elvet | C2-C3 | | |
| New Street | A3 | | |
| North Bailey | B1-B2 | | |
| North Road | A3 | | |
| Old Elvet | C2 | | |
| Oswald Court | C1 | | |
| Owengate | B2 | | |
| Pelaw Leazes Lane | C3 | | |
| Pimlico | A1 | | |
| Providence Row | C3-C4 | | |
| Quarry Heads Lane | A1 | | |
| Ravensworth Terrace | C3 | | |
| Saddler Street | B2-B3 | | |
| Sidegate | A4-B4 | | |
| Silver Street | B2-B3 | | |
| South Bailey | B1 | | |
| South Street | A1-A2-B2 | | |
| Sutton Street | A2-A3 | | |

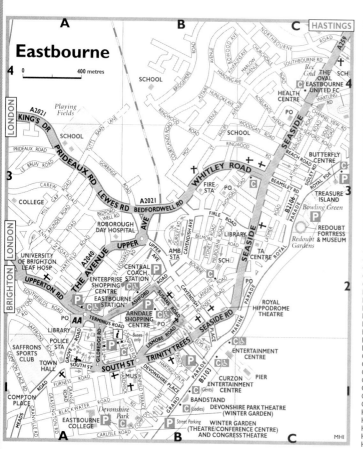

# Eastbourne

Eastbourne is found on atlas page **16**,
grid reference **6199**

### AA shop
2 Terminus Building, Upperton Road, Eastbourne BN21 1BE A2

| | | | |
|---|---|---|---|
| Arundel Road | A2-A3 | Kinfauns Avenue | B4-C4 |
| Ashford Road | A2-B2 | King's Drive | A3-A4 |
| Astaire Avenue | B4 | Langney Road | B2 |
| Avondale Road | B3-C3 | Latimer Road | C2-C3-C4 |
| Beach Road | C3 | Le Brun Road | A3 |
| Beamsley Road | C3 | Lewes Road | A3-B3 |
| Bedfordwell Road | A3-B3 | Lismore Road | B1-B2 |
| Belmore Road | B2-C2 | Marine Parade | B1-B2-C2 |
| Blackwater Road | A1-B1 | Marlow Avenue | C4 |
| Bourne Street | B2 | Meads Road | A1 |
| Bowood Avenue | B4 | Melbourne Road | B2-B3 |
| Bridgemere Road | B4 | Mill Gap Road | A3 |
| Carew Road | A3 | Moy Avenue | B3-B4 |
| Carlisle Road | A1-B1 | Northbourne Road | C4 |
| Cavendish Avenue | B2-B3 | Pevensey Road | B2 |
| Cavendish Place | B1-B2 | Prideaux Road | A3 |
| Channel View Road | C3-C4 | Ringwood Road | B4-B3-C3 |
| Churchdale Road | B4-C4 | Roselands Avenue | C3-C4 |
| Compton Place Road | A1 | Royal Parade | C2-C3 |
| Compton Street | B1 | Saffrons Road | A1-A2 |
| Cornfield Road | B1-B2 | Seaford Road | C3 |
| Cornfield Terrace | B1 | Seaside | C2-C3-C4 |
| Courtlands Road | B3-B4 | Seaside Road | B2 |
| Devonshire Place | B1 | Sidley Road | C3 |
| Dittons Road | A2 | South Street | A1-B1 |
| Dursley Road | B2-B3 | Southbourne Road | C4 |
| Elms Road | B2 | Southfields Road | A2 |
| Enys Road | A2-A3 | St Anne's Road | A2-A3 |
| Fairlight Road | C3-C4 | St Leonards Road | A2-B2 |
| Firle Road | B3-C3 | St Philips Avenue | B3-B4-C4 |
| Furness Road | A1 | Susans Road | B2 |
| Gildredge Road | A1-A2 | Sydney Road | B2-B3 |
| Gorringe Road | A3-B3 | Terminus Road | A2-B2 |
| Grand Parade | B1 | The Avenue | A2 |
| Grange Road | A1 | Trinity Place | B1 |
| Granville Road | A1 | Trinity Trees | B1 |
| Grassington Road | A1 | Tutts Barn Lane | A3-A4-B4 |
| Grove Road | A1-A2 | Upper Avenue | A2-B2-B3 |
| Harding Avenue | B4-C4 | Upperton Road | A2 |
| Hardwick Road | B1 | Wartling Road | C4 |
| Hartfield Road | A2-A3 | Whitley Road | B3-C3 |
| Hartington Place | B1 | Woodgate Road | B4-C4-C3 |
| Hunloke Avenue | B4 | | |

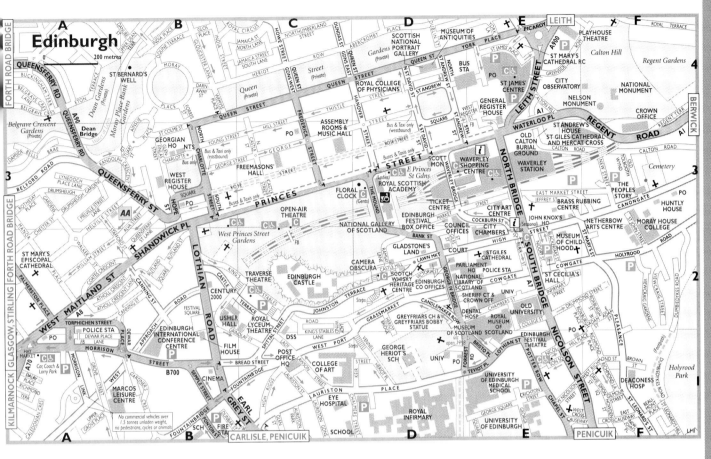

# Edinburgh

Edinburgh is found on atlas page 117,
grid reference 2573

**AA shop**
Fanum House, 18–22 Melville Street, Edinburgh EH3 7PD    A3

| | | | | | | | | |
|---|---|---|---|---|---|---|---|---|
| Abercromby Place | C4-D4 | Davie Street | F1 | High Street | D2-E2-E3 | North Bridge | E3-E2 | St Leonard's Hill | F1 |
| Ainslie Place | B3-B4 | Dewar Place | A1-A2 | Hill Place | E1-F1 | North Castle Street | C3-C4 | St Leonards Street | F2-E3 |
| Alva Street | A2-B3 | Dewar Place Lane | A1 | Hill Street | C3-C4 | North Charlotte Street | B3 | St Mary's Street | F2-E3 |
| Atholl Crescent | A2-B2 | Doune Terrace | B4 | Holyrood Road | F2-F3 | North David Street | D4 | Semple Street | B1 |
| Atholl Crescent Lane | A2-B2 | Drummond Street | E2-F2 | Hope Street | B3 | North St Andrew Street | D4 | Shandwick Place | B2-B3 |
| Bank Street | D2 | Drumsheugh Gardens | A3 | Howden Street | F1 | Northumberland Street | C4 | Simon Square | F1 |
| Beaumont Place | F1 | Dublin Street | D4 | Howe Street | C4 | Old Tolbooth Wynd | F3 | South Bridge | E2 |
| Belford Road | A3 | Dumbiedykes Road | F1-F2 | India Place | B4 | Palmerston Place | A2 | South Charlotte Street | B3 |
| Belgrave Crescent | A4 | Dunbar Street | B1 | India Street | B4 | Picardy Place | E4 | South College Street | E2 |
| Belgrave Crescent Lane | A4 | Dundas Street | C4 | Infirmary Street | E2 | Pleasance | F1-F2 | South David Street | D3-D4 |
| Bells Brae | A3 | Earl Grey Street | B1-C1 | Jamaica Street North Lane | B4-C4 | Ponton Street | B1 | South St Andrew Street | D3-D4 |
| Blackfriars Street | E2 | East Adam Street | F2 | Jamaica Street South Lane | B4-C4 | Potter Row | E1 | Spittal Street | C1-C2 |
| Blair Street | E2 | East Cross Causeway | F1 | Jeffrey Street | E3 | Princes Street | B3-C3-D3-E3 | Stafford Street | A3-A2-B2 |
| Bread Street | B1-C1 | East Market Street | E3-F3 | Johnston Terrace | C2-D2 | Queen Street | B3-B4-C4-D4 | Teviot Place | E1 |
| Bristo Place | E1 | Eton Terrace | A4 | Keir Street | C1-D1 | Queen Street Gardens East | C4 | The Mound | D2-D3 |
| Brown Street | F1 | Forres Street | B4 | King's Stables Road | B2-C2-D2 | Queen Street Gardens West | C4 | Thistle Street | C4-D4 |
| Buckingham Terrace | A4 | Forrest Road | D1 | King's Stables Lane | C2-D2 | Queensferry Road | A3-A4 | Torphichen Street | A2 |
| Caledonian Crescent | A1 | Fountainbridge | B1-C1 | Lady Lawson Street | C1 | Queensferry Street | A3-B3 | Upper Dean Terrace | A4-B4 |
| Calton Hill | E4 | Frederick Street | C3-C4 | Lady Wynd | C2 | Queensferry Street Lane | B2-B3 | Upper Grove Place | A1 |
| Calton Road | E4-E3-F3 | Gardner's Crescent | B1 | Lauriston Gardens | C1 | Ramsay Lane | D2 | Vennel | D1 |
| Candlemaker Row | D2 | George IV Bridge | D2 | Lauriston Park | C1 | Randolph Crescent | A3-B3 | Victoria Street | D2 |
| Canning Street | A2-B2 | George Square | E1 | Lauriston Place | C1-D1 | Regent Road | E4-F4-F3 | Viewcraig Gardens | F2 |
| Canongate | F3 | George Street | B3-C3-D3-D4 | Lauriston Street | C1 | Regent Terrace | F4 | Viewcraig Street | F2 |
| Castle Hill | D2 | Gilmour Street | F1 | Lawn Market | D2 | Richmond Lane | F1 | Walker Street | A2-A3 |
| Castle Street | C3 | Glen Street | C1 | Leith Street | E3-E4 | Richmond Place | F1 | Waterloo Place | E3-E4-F4 |
| Castle Terrace | B2-C2 | Glenfinlas Street | B3 | Lothian Road | B2-B1 | Richmond Terrace | A1 | Waverley Bridge | D3 |
| Chalmers Street | C1-D1 | Gloucester Lane | B4 | Lothian Street | E1 | Rose Street | B3-C3 | Wemyss Place | B4 |
| Chambers Street | D2-E2 | Gloucester Place | B4 | Lynedoch Place Lane | A3 | Rothesay Place | A3 | West Adam Street | F2 |
| Chapel Street | E1-F1 | Grassmarket | D2 | Manor Place | A2-A3 | Roxburgh Place | E2-F2 | West Approach Road | A1-B1-B2 |
| Charlotte Square | B3 | Great Stuart Street | A3-B3 | Market Street | D2-D3-E3 | Roxburgh Street | F2 | West Cross Causeway | E1-F1 |
| Chester Street | A2-A3 | Greenside Row | E4-F4 | Melville Street | A2-A3 | Royal Circus | B4-C4 | West Maitland Street | A1-A2 |
| Clarendon Crescent | A4 | Grindlay Street | B2-B1-C1 | Melville Street Lane | A3 | Royal Terrace | F4 | West Nicolson Street | E1 |
| Coates Crescent | A2-B2 | Grove Street | A1 | Moray Place | B4 | Rutland Square | B2 | West Port | C1-D2 |
| Cowgate | D2-E2-F2 | Hanover Street | C4-D4-D3 | Morrison Link | A1 | Rutland Street | B2 | West Register Street | D4-E4 |
| Cockburn Street | D3-E3-E2 | Haymarket | A1 | Morrison Street | A1-B1 | St Andrew Square | D3-D4 | West Richmond Street | E1-F1 |
| Crichton Street | E1 | Heriot Bridge | D1-D2 | New Street | F3 | St Colme Street | B3 | William Street | A2 |
| Dalry Place | A1 | Heriot Place | D1 | Nicolson Square | E1 | St Giles Street | D2 | York Lane | E4 |
| Damside | A3 | Heriot Row | B4-C4 | Nicolson Street | E1-E2 | St James Place | E4 | York Place | D4-E4 |
| Darnaway Street | B4 | High Riggs | C1 | Niddry Street | E2 | St John Street | F2-F3 | Young Street | B3-C3 |

182

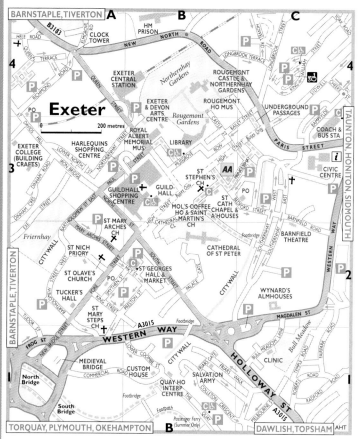

# Exeter

Exeter is found on atlas page **9**,
grid reference **9292**

## AA shop
1–5 Princesshay, Bedford Street, Exeter EX1 1NQ          B3

| | | | |
|---|---|---|---|
| Bailey Street | B3-C3-C4 | Paul Street | A3-B3 |
| Bampfylde Street | C3-C4 | Preston Street | A2-B2 |
| Barnfield Road | C2-C3 | Princesshay | B3-C3 |
| Bartholomew Street East | A2-A3 | Queen Street | A4-B3 |
| Bartholomew Street West | A2 | Queen's Terrace | A4 |
| Bedford Street | B3-C3 | Radford Road | C1 |
| Bull Meadow Lane | C1-C2 | Richmond Road | A4 |
| Castle Street | B3-B4 | Roberts Road | C1 |
| Cathedral Close | B2-B3 | St Davids Hill | A3-A4 |
| Cheek Street | C4 | Sidwell Street | C3-C4 |
| Colleton Crescent | B1-C1 | Smythen Street | A2-B2 |
| Commercial Road | A1-B1 | South Street | B2 |
| Dinham Crescent | A2-A3 | Southernhay East | C2-C3 |
| Dinham Road | A3 | Southernhay West | C2-C3 |
| Elmgrove Road | A4 | Temple Road | C1 |
| Exe Street | A2-A3 | The Quay | B1 |
| Fairpark Road | C1-C2 | Tudor Street | A1-A2 |
| Fore Street | A2-B2 | Western Way | A1-B1 |
| Friars Gate | B1 | Western Way | C2-C3 |
| Friars Walk | B1-C1 | York Road | C4 |
| Frog Street | A1 | | |
| Hele Road | A4 | | |
| High Street | B2-B3-C3 | | |
| Holloway Street | B1-C1 | | |
| Howell Road | C4 | | |
| Iron Bridge | A3 | | |
| King Street | A2-B2 | | |
| King William Street | C4 | | |
| Longbrook Street | C4 | | |
| Longbrook Terrace | B4-C4 | | |
| Lower Coombe Street | B1 | | |
| Lower North Street | A3 | | |
| Magdalen Street | C2 | | |
| Market Street | A2-B2 | | |
| Mary Arches Street | A2 | | |
| Melbourne Street | C1 | | |
| Musgrove Row | B3 | | |
| New Bridge Street | A1-A2 | | |
| New North Road | A4-B4 | | |
| North Street | A3-B3-B2 | | |
| Northernhay Street | A3-B3 | | |
| Palace Gate | B2 | | |
| Paris Street | C3-C4 | | |

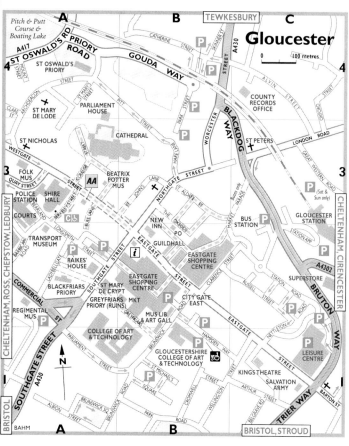

# Gloucester

Gloucester is found on atlas page **35**,
grid reference **8318**

## AA shop
51 Westgate Street, Gloucester GL1 2NW          A3

| | | | |
|---|---|---|---|
| Albion Street | A1 | St Mary's Street | A4 |
| Alvin Street | C3-C4 | St Michael's Square | B1 |
| Archdeacon Street | A3-A4 | St Oswald's Road | A4 |
| Arthur Street | C1 | Skinner Street | B4 |
| Barbican Road | A2 | Southgate Street | A1-B2 |
| Barton Street | C1 | Station Approach | C2 |
| Bearland | A3 | Station Road | C2 |
| Belgrave Road | C1 | The Oxbode | B2-B3 |
| Berkeley Street | A3 | Trier Way | C1 |
| Blackdog Way | B4-C3 | Wellington Street | B1-C1 |
| Brunswick Road | A1-B2 | Westgate Street | A3-B3 |
| Brunswick Square | A1 | Worcester Street | B3-B4 |
| Bruton Way | C1-C3 | | |
| Bull Lane | A2-A3 | | |
| Catherine Street | B4 | | |
| Clare Street | A4 | | |
| Clarence Street | B2-C2 | | |
| College Street | A3 | | |
| Commercial Street | A2 | | |
| Cromwell Street | B1 | | |
| Eastgate Street | B2-C1 | | |
| Gouda Way | A4-B4 | | |
| Great Western Road | C3 | | |
| Greyfriars | A2-B1 | | |
| Hampden Way | B2-C1 | | |
| Hare Lane | B3 | | |
| Ladybellgate | A2 | | |
| London Road | C3 | | |
| Longsmith Street | A2-A3 | | |
| Market Parade | B2-C3 | | |
| Mount Street | A4 | | |
| Nettleton Road | C1-C2 | | |
| Northgate Street | B3 | | |
| Oxford Street | C3-C4 | | |
| Park Road | B1 | | |
| Park Street | B3-B4 | | |
| Parliament Street | A1-B1 | | |
| Pitt Street | A4-B3 | | |
| Priory Road | A4 | | |
| Quay Street | A3 | | |
| Russell Street | B2-C2 | | |
| St Aldate Street | B3 | | |
| St John's Lane | B3 | | |

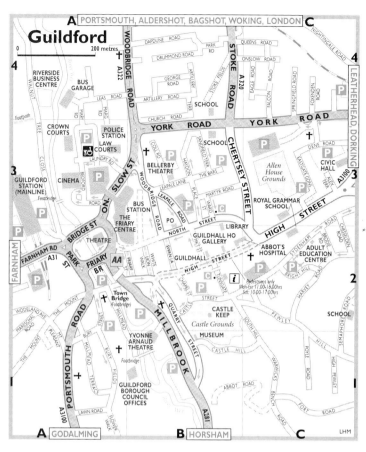

# Guildford

Guildford is found on atlas page **25**,
grid reference **9949**

**AA shop**
22 Friary Street, Guildford GU1 4EH                    A2

| | | | |
|---|---|---|---|
| Abbot Road | B1-C1 | Millmead | A2-B1 |
| Alex Terrace | C3 | Millmead Terrace | A1 |
| Artillery Road | B4 | Mount Pleasant | A1-A2 |
| Artillery Terrace | B4 | Nightingale Road | C4 |
| Bedford Road | A3 | North Street | A2-B3 |
| Bridge Street | A2-A3 | Onslow Road | B4-C4 |
| Bright Hill | C2 | Onslow Street | A3-B4 |
| Brodie Road | C2 | Park Road | B4 |
| Bury Fields | A1 | Park Street | A2 |
| Bury Street | A1-A2 | Pewley Hill | B2-C1 |
| Castle Hill | B1-C1 | Portsmouth Road | A1-A2 |
| Castle Street | B2-C2 | Poyle Road | C1 |
| Chapel Street | B2 | Quarry Street | A2-B1 |
| Chertsey Street | B3-C2 | Queens Road | B4-C4 |
| Chesselden Road | C2-C3 | Sandfield Terrace | B3 |
| Church Road | B3-B4 | Semaphore Road | C1-C2 |
| College Road | B3 | South Hill | B2-C1 |
| Dapdune Road | B4 | Springfield Road | C4 |
| Dene Road | C3 | Stoke Fields | B4 |
| Drummond Road | B4 | Stoke Road | B4 |
| Eagle Road | C4 | Swan Lane | B2 |
| Eastgate Gardens | C3 | Sydenham Road | C2-C3 |
| Falcon Road | C4 | The Bars | B3 |
| Farnham Road | A2 | The Mount | A1-A2 |
| Flower Walk | A1 | Tunsgate | B2 |
| Foxenden Road | C4 | Walnut Tree Close | A2-A4 |
| Friary Bridge | A2 | Ward Street | B3 |
| Friary Street | A2-B2 | Whitelion Walk | B2 |
| George Road | B4 | Wodeland Ave | A2 |
| Harvey Road | C2 | Woodbridge Road | B2-B3-B4-A4 |
| Haydon Place | B3 | York Road | B3-C4 |
| High Pewley | C1 | | |
| High Street | B2-C3 | | |
| Laundry Road | A3 | | |
| Lawn Road | A1 | | |
| Leapale Lane | B3 | | |
| Leapale Road | B3 | | |
| Leas Road | A4 | | |
| Margaret Road | A3-A4 | | |
| Market Street | B2 | | |
| Martyr Road | B3 | | |
| Mary Road | A3-A4 | | |
| Millbrook | A2-B1 | | |

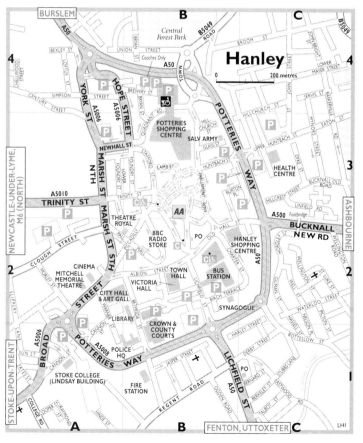

# Hanley

Hanley is found on atlas page **72**,
grid reference **8847**

**AA shop**
32–38 Stafford Street, Hanley ST1 1JP                    B2

| | | | |
|---|---|---|---|
| Albion Street | B2 | Lower Foundry Street | A3 |
| Baskerville Road | C3-C4 | Lower Mayer Street | C4 |
| Berkeley Street | C1 | Marsh Street North | A3 |
| Bernard Street | C1 | Marsh Street South | A2-A3 |
| Bethesda Street | B1-B2 | Mayer Street | B4-C4 |
| Bexley Street | A4 | Morley Street | A2 |
| Birch Terrace | B2-C2 | Mynors Street | C3-C4 |
| Botteslow Street | C1 | Nelson Place | C1-C2 |
| Brewery Street | B4 | Newhall Street | A3-B3 |
| Broad Street | A1-A2 | Ogden Road | B1 |
| Broom Street | B4-C4 | Old Hall Street | B2-C2 |
| Bryan Street | B4 | Pall Mall | A2-B2-B3 |
| Bucknall New Road | C2 | Parliament Row | B3 |
| Bucknall Old Road | C3 | Piccadilly | A2-B2 |
| Burton Place | B3-C3 | Picton Street | C1-C2 |
| Cannon Street | A1-A2 | Potteries Way | A1-B1-C2-B4 |
| Century Street | A3-A4 | Quadrant Road | B3-B4 |
| Charter Street | B2-C2 | Raymond Street | A1 |
| Chellwood Street | A4 | Regent Road | B1 |
| Clough Street | A2 | St John Street | C3-C4 |
| College Road | A1 | St Luke Street | C2 |
| Cooper Street | A1 | Simpson Street | A4 |
| Derby Street | C1 | Slippery Lane | A1-A2 |
| Eastwood Road | C1 | Stafford Street | B3 |
| Eaton Street | C3 | Stubbs Lane | C1 |
| Foundry Street | B3 | Sun Street | A1 |
| Gilman Street | C2 | Talbot Street | C1 |
| Glass Street | B3 | Town Road | B4 |
| Harley Street | B1-C1-C2 | Trinity Street | A3-B3 |
| Hassell Street | C1-C2 | Union Street | A4-B4 |
| Hillchurch Street | B3-C4 | Upper Huntbach Street | C3 |
| Hillcrest Street | C3 | Waterloo Street | C2 |
| Hinde Street | A1 | Well Street | C2 |
| Hope Street | A4-B3-B4 | Wellington Road | C2 |
| Hordley Street | C2 | Wellington Street | C2 |
| Huntbach Street | B3-C3 | Yates Street | A1 |
| Jasper Street | B1 | York Street | A3-A4 |
| Jervis Street | C4 | | |
| John Bright Street | C4 | | |
| Lamb Street | B3 | | |
| Lichfield Street | B1-B2-C1 | | |
| Linfield Road | C3 | | |
| Loftus Street | A4 | | |

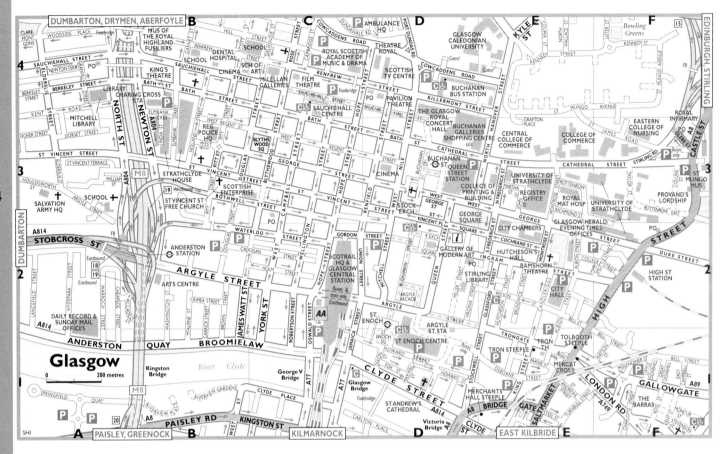

184

# Glasgow

Glasgow is found on atlas page 115,
grid reference 5865

**AA shop**
269 Argyle Street, Glasgow G2 8DW                    C2

| | | | | | | | |
|---|---|---|---|---|---|---|---|
| Albion Street | E1-E2 | Elmbank Crescent | B4 | Maxwell Street | D1 | Scott Street | B4-C4 |
| Anderston Quay | A1-B1 | Elmbank Street | B3-B4 | Mc Alpine Street | B1-B2 | Shuttle Street | F2 |
| Argyle Arcade | D2 | Fox Street | D1 | Miller Street | D2 | South Frederick Street | E2-E3 |
| Argyle Street | B2-C2-D2 | Gallowgate | F1 | Mitchell Street | D2-D3 | Springfield Quay | A1 |
| Bath Street | A4-B4-C4-C3-D3 | Garret Street | B4 | Molendiner Street | F1 | Steel Street | E1 |
| Bell Street | E2-F1 | George Square | D2-D3-E2-E3 | Moncur Street | F1 | Stevenson Street West | F1 |
| Berkeley Place | A4 | George Street | D3-E3-E2-F2 | Montrose Street | E2-E3 | Stirling Road | F3 |
| Berkeley Street | A4-B4 | Glassford Street | E2 | Newton Street | B2-B3-B4 | Stockwell Street | D1-E1 |
| Blythswood Street | B2-B4 | Glebe Street | F3 | North Frederick Street | E3 | Taylor Street | F3 |
| Bothwell Street | A3-C3 | Gordon Street | C2-D2 | North Hanover Street | E3-E4 | Trongate | E1-E2 |
| Bridgegate | D1-E1 | Grafton Place | E3-E4 | North Street | A2-A4 | Turnbull Street | E1 |
| Broomielaw | B1-C1 | Granville Street | A4 | North Wallace Street | E4 | Union Street | C2-D2 |
| Brown Street | B1-B2 | Great Doverhill | F1 | Osborne Street | D1-E1 | Victoria Bridge | D1 |
| Brunswick Street | E2 | High Street | F2-F3 | Oswald Street | C1-C2 | Vincent Place | D2-D3 |
| Buchanan Street | D2-D3 | Hill Street | B4-C4 | Paisley Road | A1-B1 | Virginia Street | D2 |
| Cadogan Street | B2-C2 | Holdsworth Street | A3 | Parnie Street | E1 | Warroch Street | A1-A2 |
| Cambridge Street | C4 | Holland Street | B3-B4 | Piccadilly Street | A2 | Washington Street | B1-B2 |
| Candleriggs | E1-E2 | Holm Street | B3-B4 | Pitt Street | B3-B4 | Waterloo Street | B2-C2 |
| Carlton Place | C1-D1 | Hope Street | C2-C3-C4-D4 | Port Dundas Road | D4 | Watson Street | F1 |
| Carrick Street | B1-B2 | Howard Street | C1-D1 | Queen Street | D2-D3 | Wellington Street | C2-C3-C4 |
| Castle Street | F3-F4 | Hutcheson Street | E2 | Renfield Street | D3-D4 | West Campbell Street | C2-C3-C4 |
| Cathedral Street | D3-F3 | Hydepark Street | A2 | Renfrew Street | B4-C4-D4 | West George Street | B3-C3-D3 |
| Charlotte Street | F1 | India Street | B3-B4 | Richmond Street | E3 | West Nile Street | D3-D4 |
| Cheapside Street | A1-A2 | Ingram Street | D2-E2 | Riverview Gardens | B1 | West Regent Street | B4-B3-C3-D3 |
| Clyde Place | B1 | Jamaica Street | C1-C2 | Riverview Place | B1 | West Street | B1 |
| Clyde Street | C1-D1 | James Watt Street | B1-B2 | Robertson Street | C1-C2 | William Street | A3 |
| Cochrane Street | E2 | John Street | E2-E3 | Rose Street | C4 | Wilson Street | D2-E2 |
| College Street | E2-F2 | Kennedy Street | E4-F4 | Ross Street | F1 | Woodside Place | A4 |
| Collins Street | F3 | Kent Road | A4 | Rottenrow | E3 | York Street | C1-C2 |
| Couper Street | E4 | Kent Street | F1 | Rottenrow East | F3 | | |
| Cowcaddens Road | C4-D4-E4 | Killermont Street | D4-E4 | Royal Exchange Square | D2 | | |
| Crimea Street | B2 | King Street | E1 | St Andrews Street | E3 | | |
| Dixon Street | D1 | Kingston Street | B1-C1 | St Enoch Square | D1 | | |
| Dorset Street | A3 | Kyle Street | E4 | St James Road | E4-E3-F3 | | |
| Douglas Street | B2-B3-C3-C4 | Lancefield Street | A2 | St Mungo Avenue | E4-F4 | | |
| Dover Street | A3 | Lister Street | F4 | St Vincent Street | A3-B3-C3-D3 | | |
| Duke Street | F2 | Little Doverhill | F1 | St Vincent Terrace | A3 | | |
| East Campbell Street | F1 | London Road | E1-F1 | Saltmarket | E1 | | |
| Elderslie Street | A3-A4 | Martha Street | E3 | Sauchiehall Street | A4-B4-C4 | | |

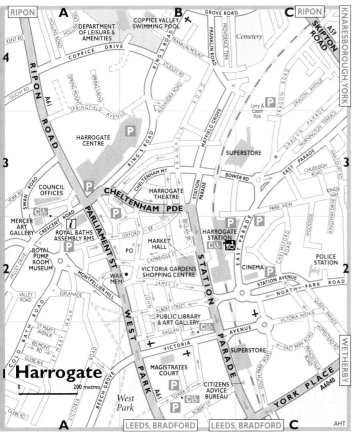

# Harrogate

Harrogate is found on atlas page **82**,
grid reference **3054**

| | | | |
|---|---|---|---|
| Albert Street | B2 | Raglan Street | B1-B2 |
| Alexandra Road | B3-B4 | Ripon Road | A3-A4 |
| Beech Grove | A1-B1 | Robert Street | B1 |
| Belmont Road | A1 | St Mary's Avenue | A1 |
| Beulah Street | B2-B3 | St Mary's Walk | A1-A2 |
| Bower Road | B3-C3 | Skipton Road | C4 |
| Cambridge Street | B2 | South Park Road | C1 |
| Chelmsford Road | C2-C3 | Spring Grove | A4 |
| Cheltenham Mount | B3 | Spring Mount | A4 |
| Cheltenham Parade | A3-B3 | Springfied Avenue | A3-A4-B3-B4 |
| Chudleigh Road | C3 | Station Avenue | C2 |
| Cold Bath Road | A1-A2 | Station Parade | B3-B2-B1-C1 |
| Coppice Drive | A4-B4 | Studley Road | B4 |
| Crescent Road | A2-A3 | Swan Road | A2-A3 |
| Dragon Avenue | C3-C4 | Tower Street | B1 |
| Dragon Parade | C3-C4 | Valley Drive | A2 |
| Dragon Road | C3-C4 | Valley Road | A2 |
| Duchy Road | A4 | Victoria Avenue | B1-C1-C2 |
| East Parade | C2-C3 | Victoria Road | A1-A2 |
| East Park Road | C1-C2 | West Park | B2-B1 |
| Esplanade | A2 | Woodside | C2-C3 |
| Franklin Mount | B4 | York Place | B1-C2 |
| Franklin Road | B3-B4 | York Road | A3 |
| Glebe Avenue | A1 | | |
| Glebe Road | A1 | | |
| Grove Road | B4-C4 | | |
| Harcourt Road | C3 | | |
| Hollins Crescent | A4 | | |
| Hollins Road | A4 | | |
| Homestead Road | C1 | | |
| James Street | B2 | | |
| John Street | B1-B2 | | |
| Kent Road | A4 | | |
| King's Road | A3-B3-B4 | | |
| Kings Way | C3 | | |
| Kingsway Drive | C2-C3 | | |
| Mayfield Grove | B3-B4 | | |
| Montpellier Hill | A2 | | |
| Mornington Terrace | C3-C4 | | |
| North Park Road | C2 | | |
| Oxford Street | A2-B2 | | |
| Park View | B3-C3 | | |
| Parliament Street | A2-A3 | | |
| Princes Villa Road | C1 | | |
| Providence Terrace | B4 | | |
| Queen Parade | C1-C2 | | |

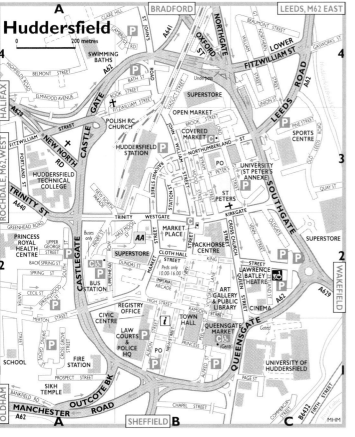

# Huddersfield

Huddersfield is found on atlas page **82**,
grid reference **1416**

**AA shop**
7 Cherry Tree Centre, Market Street, Huddersfield HD1 2ET   B2

| | | | |
|---|---|---|---|
| Albion Street | B1-B2 | Old Leeds Road | C3-C4 |
| Alfred Street | B1 | Oldgate | C2-C3 |
| Back Spring Street | A2 | Outcote Bank | A1-B1 |
| Bankfield Road | A1 | Oxford Street | B4 |
| Bath Street | B4 | Page Street | C1 |
| Beaumont Street | C4 | Peel Street | B1-B2 |
| Belmont Street | A4 | Pine Street | C3 |
| Brook Street | B3 | Portland Street | A3 |
| Byram Street | B3 | Princess Street | B1 |
| Castlegate | B1-A2-B4 | Prospect Street | A1 |
| Cecil Street | A2 | Quay Street | C3 |
| Chapel Street | B1 | Queen Street | C2 |
| Claremont Street | A4 | Queensgate | B1-C2 |
| Cloth Hall Street | B2 | Railway Street | B3 |
| Commercial Street | C1 | Ramsden Street | B2-C2 |
| Cross Church Street | C2 | Rook Street | A4-B4 |
| Cross Grove Street | A1 | St John's Road | B4 |
| Dundas Street | B2 | St Peter's Street | B3-C3 |
| Elmwood Avenue | A4 | South Street | A1-A2 |
| Firth Street | C1 | Southgate | B4-C2 |
| Fitzwilliam Street | A3-B4 | Spring Grove Street | A1 |
| Gasworks Street | C4 | Spring Street | A2 |
| Great Northern Street | C4 | Springwood Street | A2 |
| Greenhead Road | A2 | Station Street | B3 |
| Half Moon Street | B2 | Trinity Street | A3 |
| Henry Street | A2 | Trinity Westgate | A2-B2 |
| High Street | B2 | Union Street | C4 |
| Highfields Road | A4 | Upper George Street | A2 |
| Imperial Arcade | B2 | Upperhead Row | A2 |
| John William Street | B3 | Venn Street | C2-C3 |
| King Street | B2-C2 | Viaduct Street | B4 |
| Kirkgate | B2-C3 | Victoria Lane | B2 |
| Leeds Road | C3-C4 | Water Street | A2-A1 |
| Lord Street | B3-C3 | William Street | B3 |
| Lower Fitzwilliam Street | C4 | Wood Street | B3 |
| Manchester Road | A1-B1 | Zetland Street | C2 |
| Market Street | A2-B2 | | |
| Merton Street | A1-A2 | | |
| New North Parade | A3-B3 | | |
| New North Road | A3-A4 | | |
| New Street | B1-B2 | | |
| Northgate | B4-C4 | | |
| Northumberland Street | B3-C3 | | |

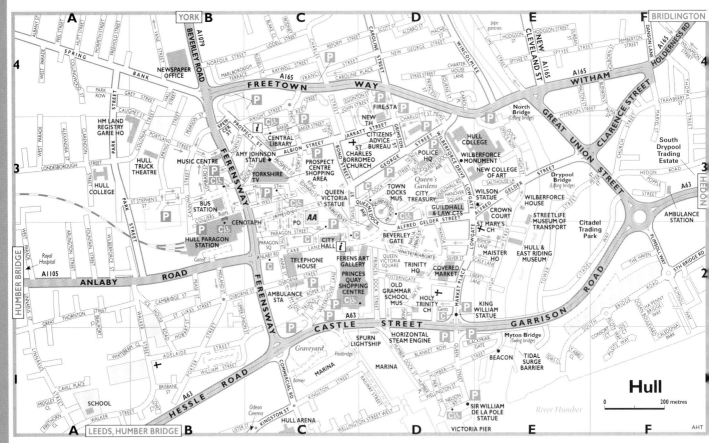

# Hull

Hull is found on atlas page **85**,
grid reference **0829**

**AA shop**
28 Paragon Street, Hull HU1 3NE · C2

| Street | Grid | Street | Grid | Street | Grid | Street | Grid | Street | Grid |
|---|---|---|---|---|---|---|---|---|---|
| Adelaide Street | B1 | Collingwood Street | A4 | Idas Close | E1 | Pease Street | B2 | Strawberry Street | F4 |
| Albion Street | C3 | Colonial Street | B3-B4 | Isis Court | F1-F2 | Peel Street | A4 | Sykes Street | D4 |
| Aldbro Street | D4 | Commercial Road | C1 | Jameson Street | C3 | Pemberton Street | F4 | The Haven | F2 |
| Alexandra Street | A3 | Consort Court | F1 | Jarratt Street | C3-D3 | Percy Street | C3-C4 | Thomas Street | F3-F4 |
| Alfred Gelder Street | D2-D3-E3 | Danson Lane | F4 | John Street | C4-D4 | Pier Street | D1 | Tower Street | E1-E3 |
| Alma Street | F4 | Dock Office Row | E3 | King Edward Street | C2-C3 | Pilots Way | F1-F2 | Trundle Street | C2 |
| Anlaby Road | A2-B2-C2 | Dock Street | C3-D3 | King Street | D2 | Plimsoll Way | F2 | Union Street | C3 |
| Anne Street | C2 | Durban Street | E4 | Kingston Street | C1-D1 | Popple Street | F3 | Upper Union Street | B2-C1 |
| Arlington Street | A2-A3 | Egginton Street | C4-D4 | Liberty Lane | D2-E2 | Porter Street | B1-B2 | Vane Street | B4 |
| Baker Street | C3 | Ferensway | B4-C1 | Liddell Street | C4 | Portland Street | B3 | Walker Street | A1-B2 |
| Beaufort Close | A1-A2 | Firethorn Close | A1 | Lime Street | E4 | Posterngate | D2 | Waterhouse Lane | C2 |
| Beverley Road | B4 | Fountain Street | A2-A3 | Linnaeus Street | A1-A2 | Princes Dock Street | D2 | Wellington Street | D1 |
| Bishop Lane | E2 | Francis Street | C4-D4 | Lister Street | B1-C1 | Princess Street | D4 | Wellington Street West | C1-D2 |
| Blackfriargate | D1-E1 | Freehold Street | A4 | Lombard Street | B3 | Prospect Street | B4-C3 | West Parade | A2-A3-A4 |
| Blake Close | C4 | Freetown Way | B4-E4 | Londesborough Street | A3-B3 | Queen Street | D1 | West Street | C3 |
| Blanket Row | D1 | Garrison Road | D1-F2 | Lovat Close | B1 | Queen's Dock Avenue | D2-D3 | Whitebeam Close | A1-B1 |
| Blenkin Street | F4 | George Street | C3-D4 | Lowgate | D3 | Railway Street | D1 | Whitefriargate | D2 |
| Bond Street | C3 | Great Thornton Street | A1-B2 | Malton Street | E4 | Raywell Street | C4 | Wilberforce Drive | D3-D4 |
| Bourne Street | D4 | Great Union Street | E4-F3 | Manor Street | D2 | Reed Street | C4 | Wilberforce Street | A2 |
| Brisbane Street | B1 | Grey Street | A4-B4 | Market Place | D2 | Reform Street | C4-D4 | William Street | B1 |
| Brook Street | B3-C3 | Grimston Drive | D3 | Marlborough Terrace | B4-C4 | Rodney Close | C4 | Williamson Street | F4 |
| Caledonia Park | F1-F2 | Grimston Street | D3 | Marvel Street | F3-F4 | Roper Street | C2 | Wincolmlee | D4-E4 |
| Cambridge Street | A2 | Guildhall Road | D3 | Midgley Close | A1 | Russell Street | C4 | Witham | E4-F4 |
| Canning Street | B2-B3 | Ha'penny Bridge Way | F2 | Midland Street | B2 | St Abbs Close | E1 | Wright Street | B3-C4 |
| Caroline Place | C4-D4 | Hall Street | B4 | Mill Street | C3 | St Lukes Street | B2 | | |
| Caroline Street | D4 | Hanover Square | D3 | Morpeth Street | A4 | St Peter Street | E3-F3 | | |
| Carr Lane | C2 | Hedon Road | F3 | Myton Street | C2 | St Stephen's Street | A2-B2 | | |
| Carroll Place | D4 | Hessle Road | B1-C1 | Nelson Street | D1 | Salthouse Lane | E3 | | |
| Castle Street | C1-D1 | High Street | E2-E3 | New George Street | D4 | Savile Street | C3 | | |
| Caughey Street | A4-B4 | Hobart Street | B1-B2 | Norfolk Street | B4-C4 | Scale Lane | D2-E2 | | |
| Cavill Place | A1 | Hodgson Street | E4 | North Street | B3 | Scoff Street | D4 | | |
| Charles Street | C3-C4 | Holborn Street | F4 | Ocean Boulevard | F1-F2 | Silver Street | D2 | | |
| Charlotte Street Mews | D3-D4 | Holderness Street | F4 | Osborne Street | B2-C2 | South Bridge Road | E1-F2 | | |
| Charterhouse Lane | D3 | Humber Dock Street | D1 | Paragon Square | C2-C3 | South Street | C2 | | |
| Church Street | F3-F4 | Humber Place | D1 | Paragon Street | C3 | Spencer Street | B3 | | |
| Citadel Way | E2-F3 | Humber Street | D1-E1 | Park Row | A4 | Spring Bank | A4-B4 | | |
| Clarence Street | E4-F4 | Hutt Street | A4 | Park Street | A4-B2 | Spring Street | B3-B4 | | |
| Clarendon Street | A3 | Hyperion Street | E4-F4 | Parliament Street | D2 | Spyvee Street | E4-F4 | | |
| Colliers Street | B3 | Ice House Road | B1-B2 | Pearson Street | B3-B4 | Story Street | C3 | | |

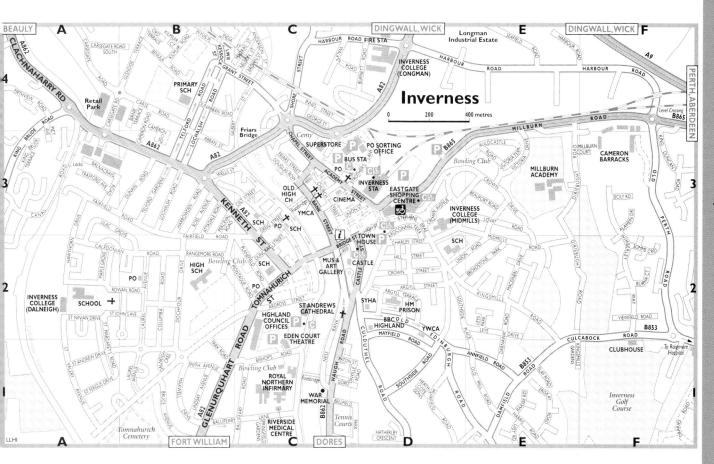

# Inverness

Inverness is found on atlas page **140**,
grid reference **6645**

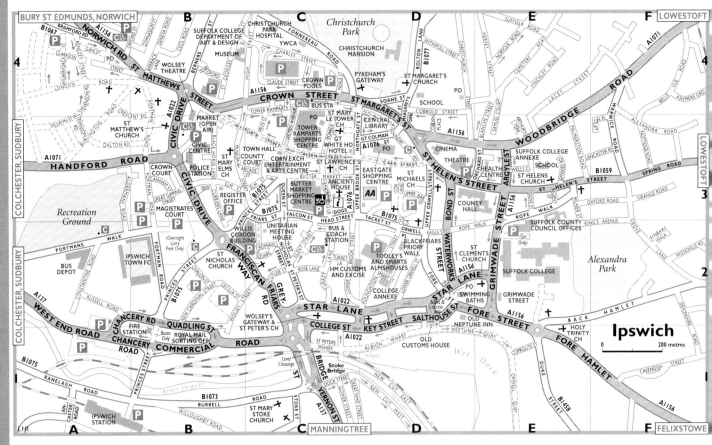

# Ipswich

Ipswich is found on atlas page **54**,
grid reference 1614

**AA shop**
Upper Brook Street, Ipswich IP4 1DU                    D3

| | | | | | | | |
|---|---|---|---|---|---|---|---|
| Albion Wharf | C1-D1 | Coprolite Street | A2 | Key Street | E3-F3 | St Margaret's Street | D4 |
| Aldermans Road | A2-A3 | Cox Lane | E1 | King's Avenue | C1-D2 | St Matthews Street | C4-D3 |
| Alexandra Road | F3-F4 | Crescent Road | D3 | Lacey Street | E2-F3 | St Nicholas Street | B4 |
| Ancaster Road | A1 | Cromwell Square | A4 | Lancaster Road | E3-F4 | St Peter's Street | C2 |
| Arcade Street | B3-C3 | Crown Street | C2 | Lloyds Avenue | E3-F3 | St Peters Wharf | C2 |
| Argyle Street | E3 | Curriers Lane | B4-C4 | London Road | C3-C4 | St Stephen's Lane | C1 |
| Arthur's Terrace | E3 | Cutler Street | B2-B3 | Lower Brook Street | A4-B4 | Salthouse Street | C3 |
| Ashmere Grove | F4 | Dalton Road | C2 | Lower Orwell Street | C2-C3 | Samuel Court | D2 |
| Back Hamlet | E2-F2 | Devonshire Road | A3-B3 | Milner Street | D2 | Silent Street | E3-E4 |
| Barrack Lane | B4 | Dillwyn Street West | A2 | Museum Street | E2-E3 | Smart Street | C2 |
| Bedford Street | B4 | Dock Street | A3-A4 | Providence Street | B3-C3 | Soane Street | D2 |
| Bellevue Road | F3-F4 | Dogs Head Street | C1 | Neale Street | C3-C4 | Spring Road | D4 |
| Benezet Street | A4 | Dove Street | C3 | Neptune Quay | C4 | Star Lane | F3 |
| Berners Street | B4 | Duke Street | E3 | New Cardinal Street | D1-E1 | Stevenson Road | C2-E2 |
| Black Horse Lane | B3 | Eagle Street | E1 | New Cut East | B2 | Stoke Street | A3-A4 |
| Blanche Street | E3-E4 | Elm Street | D2 | New Cut West | C1-D1 | Suffolk Road | C1 |
| Bolton Lane | D4 | Falcon Street | B3-C3 | Norfolk Road | C1-D1 | Tacket Street | E4 |
| Bond Street | D2-D3 | Finbars Walk | C3 | Northgate Street | E4 | Tavern Street | D2-D3 |
| Bramford Road | A4 | Finchley Road | F2 | Norwich Road | C3-D4 | Tower Ramparts | C3 |
| Bridge Street | C1 | Fonnereau Road | E4 | Nottidge Road | A4-B4 | Tower Street | B4-C4 |
| Burlington Road | A3-B4 | Fore Hamlet | C4 | Old Foundry Road | F3 | Turret Lane | C3-C4 |
| Burrell Road | B1-C1 | Fore Street | E1-F1 | Orchard Street | D4-D3 | Upper Bar Street | C2 |
| Butter Market | C3 | Foundation Street | D2-E1 | Orford Street | D3-E3 | Upper Brook Street | D3 |
| Canham Street | B3 | Franciscan Way | D2 | Orwell Place | A4-B4 | Upper Orwell Street | C3 |
| Carr Street | D3 | Friars Street | B2-C2 | Orwell Quay | D2 | Upton Place | D2-D3 |
| Cavendish Street | F1 | Gaye Street | C3 | Oxford Road | E1 | Vernon Street | F3-F4 |
| Cecil Road | B4 | Geneva Road | A4 | Palmerston Road | E3-F3 | Warwick Road | C1 |
| Cecilia Street | B2 | Gower Street | B4 | Portman Road | E3 | Waterworks Street | F3-F4 |
| Cemetery Road | E4 | Grange Road | C1 | Portmans Walk | B2-B4 | Wells Close | D2 |
| Chalon Street | B2 | Great Colman Street | F3 | Princes Street | A2-B2 | West End Road | E3 |
| Chancery Road | B1-A1-A2-B2 | Great Gipping Street | D3 | Quadling Street | A1-C3 | Westgate Street | A1-A2 |
| Charles Street | C4 | Great Whip Street | B3 | Queen Street | B1-B2 | Wilberforce Street | B4-C3 |
| Christchurch Street | D3-D4 | Grey Friars Road | C1-D1 | Ranelagh Road | C3 | Willoughby Road | A4 |
| Civic Drive | B2-B4 | Grimwade Street | C2 | Regent Street | A1 | Withipoll Street | B1 |
| Clarkson Street | A4-B4 | Grove Lane | E2-E3 | Rope Walk | E3 | Wolsey Street | C2 |
| Claude Street | C4 | Gymnasium Street | F2-F3 | Rose Lane | D2-E3 | Woodbridge Road | B1-C2 |
| Cobbold Street | D4 | Handford Road | B4 | Russell Road | C2 | Woodville Road | D3-F4 |
| Cobden Place | D3 | Harvey Street | A3-B3 | St Georges Street | A2 | | |
| College Street | C1-C2 | High Street | E4 | St Helen's Street | B4 | | |
| Commercial Road | B1-C1 | Jefferies Road | B4-C4 | St Margaret's Green | D3-F3 | | |
| Constantine Road | | | | | | | |

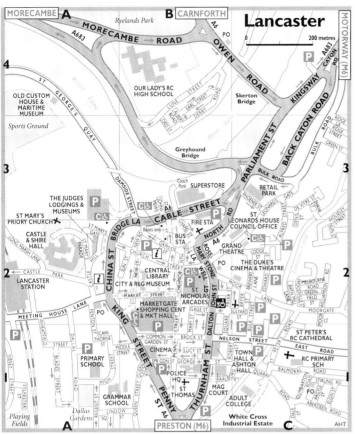

# Lancaster

Lancaster is found on atlas page **87**,
grid reference **4761**

| | | | | | |
|---|---|---|---|---|---|
| Aalborg Place | B1-C1 | Kingsway | C4 | Sun Street | B2 |
| Aberdeen Road | C1 | Lindow Square | A1 | Sylvester Street | A1 |
| Albert Road | B3-B4 | Lindow Street | A1-A2 | Thurnham Street | B1 |
| Alfred Street | C2-C3 | Lodge Street | C2 | Wheatfield Street | A1-A2 |
| Argyle Street | C1 | Long Marsh Lane | A2 | Williamson Road | C2 |
| Back Caton Road | C3-C4 | Lord Street | B3 | Wolseley Street | C2-C3 |
| Balmoral Road | C1 | Lucy Street | B1 | Woodville Street | C2 |
| Bath Mill Lane | C2 | Lune Street | B3-B4 | | |
| Blades Street | A1 | Market Street | A2-B2 | | |
| Brewery Lane | C2 | Mary Street | B1-B2 | | |
| Bridge Lane | A2-B2 | Meeting House Lane | A2 | | |
| Brock Street | B1 | Melbourne Road | C2 | | |
| Bryer Street | C2 | Middle Street | A1-B1 | | |
| Bulk Road | C3-C4 | Moor Close | C1-C2 | | |
| Bulk Street | C1-C2 | Moor Lane | B2-C2 | | |
| Cable Street | B2-B3 | Moorgate | C2 | | |
| Castle Hill | A2 | Morecambe Road | A4-B4 | | |
| Castle Park | A2 | Nelson Street | B1-C1 | | |
| Caton Road | C4 | New Road | B2 | | |
| Cawthorne Street | A1 | New Street | B2 | | |
| Chapel Street | B2 | North Road | B2-B3 | | |
| Cheapside | B2 | Nun Street | C2 | | |
| China Street | A2 | Owen Road | B4-C4 | | |
| Church Street | B2 | Parliament Street | C3-C4 | | |
| Common Garden Street | B1 | Penny Street | B1-B2 | | |
| Dale Street | C1 | Phoenix Street | C3 | | |
| Dallas Road | A1-A2 | Quarry Road | C1 | | |
| Dalton Square | B1-B2 | Queen Square | B1 | | |
| Damside Street | A3-B3-B2 | Queen Street | B1 | | |
| De Vitre Street | C3 | Regent Street | A1 | | |
| Denis Street | C2-C3 | Ridge Lane | C4 | | |
| Derby Road | B3-B4 | Ridge Street | C3 | | |
| Dumbarton Road | C1 | Robert Street | B1 | | |
| Earl Street | B4 | Rosemary Lane | B2 | | |
| East Road | C1 | St George's Quay | A3-A4 | | |
| Edward Street | C2 | St Johns Mews | B3 | | |
| Elgin Street | C1 | St Leonard's Gate | B2-C2-C3 | | |
| Fenton Street | A1-A2 | St Mary's Gate | A2 | | |
| Friar Street | B2 | St Mary's Parade | A2 | | |
| Gage Street | B2 | St Peter's Road | C1-C2 | | |
| George Street | B1 | Shaw Street | C3 | | |
| Great John Street | B2 | Sibsey Street | A1 | | |
| Green Street | C3 | Spring Garden Street | B1 | | |
| Greenfield Street | C2 | Stirling Road | C1 | | |
| High Street | A1 | Stonewell | B2 | | |
| King Street | A2-B2-B1 | Sulyard Street | B2-C2 | | |

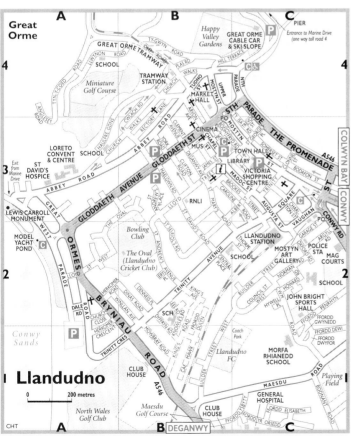

# Llandudno

Llandudno is found on atlas page **69**,
grid reference **7882**

| | | | |
|---|---|---|---|
| Abbey Road | A3-C4 | Hill Terrace | B4-C4 |
| Albert Street | B2-C3 | Howard Road | C2 |
| Anglesey Road | A3-A4 | Hywell Place | C2 |
| Argyll Road | C2 | King's Avenue | B2 |
| Arvon Avenue | B3-B4 | King's Road | B1-B2 |
| Augusta Street | C2-C3 | Knowles Road | B1-B2 |
| Bodafon Street | C3 | Lees Road | B2 |
| Bodnant Road | C1 | Lloyd Street | B3-C3 |
| Brookes Street | B3-C3 | Lloyd Street West | A2 |
| Bryniau Road | A2-B1 | Llwynon Road | A4-B4 |
| Builder Street | C2 | Madoc Street | B3-C3 |
| Builder Street West | B1-C2 | Maelgwn Road | B3 |
| Cae Mawr | B1 | Maesdu Road | B1-C1 |
| Caroline Road | B3-C3 | Mostyn Street | B3-C3 |
| Chapel Street | B3 | Mowbray Road | B1 |
| Charlton Street | C3 | Norman Road | C2 |
| Church Close | A2 | North Parade | C4 |
| Church Walks | A3-B4 | Oxford Road | C2 |
| Clement Avenue | B3 | Plas Road | B4 |
| Clifton Road | B3 | Rectory Lane | B3-B4 |
| Clonnel Street | C3 | St Andrew's Avenue | B2-B3 |
| Conwy Road | C2-C3 | St Andrew's Place | B3 |
| Council Street West | C2 | St David's Road | B2-B3 |
| Cwlach Road | B3-B4 | St George's Place | C3 |
| Cwm Road | C1-C2 | St Mary's Road | B3-C2 |
| Dale Road | A2 | St Seirol's Road | B2-B3 |
| Deganwy Avenue | B3 | Somerset Street | C3 |
| Denness Place | B2 | South Parade | B4-C3 |
| Dinas Road | B2 | The Oval | A2-B3 |
| Dyffryn Road | B1-B2 | The Parade | C3 |
| Eryl Place | B2 | Thorpe Street | C2 |
| Fforde Dewi | C1 | Trevor Street | C2 |
| Fforde Dulyn | B1-B2 | Trinity Avenue | B1-C3 |
| Fforde Dwyfor | C1 | Trinity Crescent | A1-B1 |
| Fforde Elisabeth | C1 | Trinity Square | C3 |
| Fforde Gwynedd | C1 | Tudno Street | B4 |
| Fforde Penrhyn | C1-C2 | Ty-Gwyn Road | B4 |
| Fforde yr Orsedd | C1 | Ty Isa Road | C3-C4 |
| Fforde Ysbyty | B1-C1 | Tyn-y-Coed Road | A4 |
| Garage Street | C2-C3 | Upper Mostyn Street | B4 |
| Gloddaeth Avenue | A2-B3 | Vaughan Street | C2-C3 |
| Gloddaeth Street | B3 | West Parade | A2-A3 |
| Great Ormes Road | A1-A3 | Winllan Avenue | A2-B2 |
| Haulfre Gardens | A3 | York Road | B3 |
| Herkomer Crescent | A1-A2 | | |
| Herkomer Road | A2 | | |

189

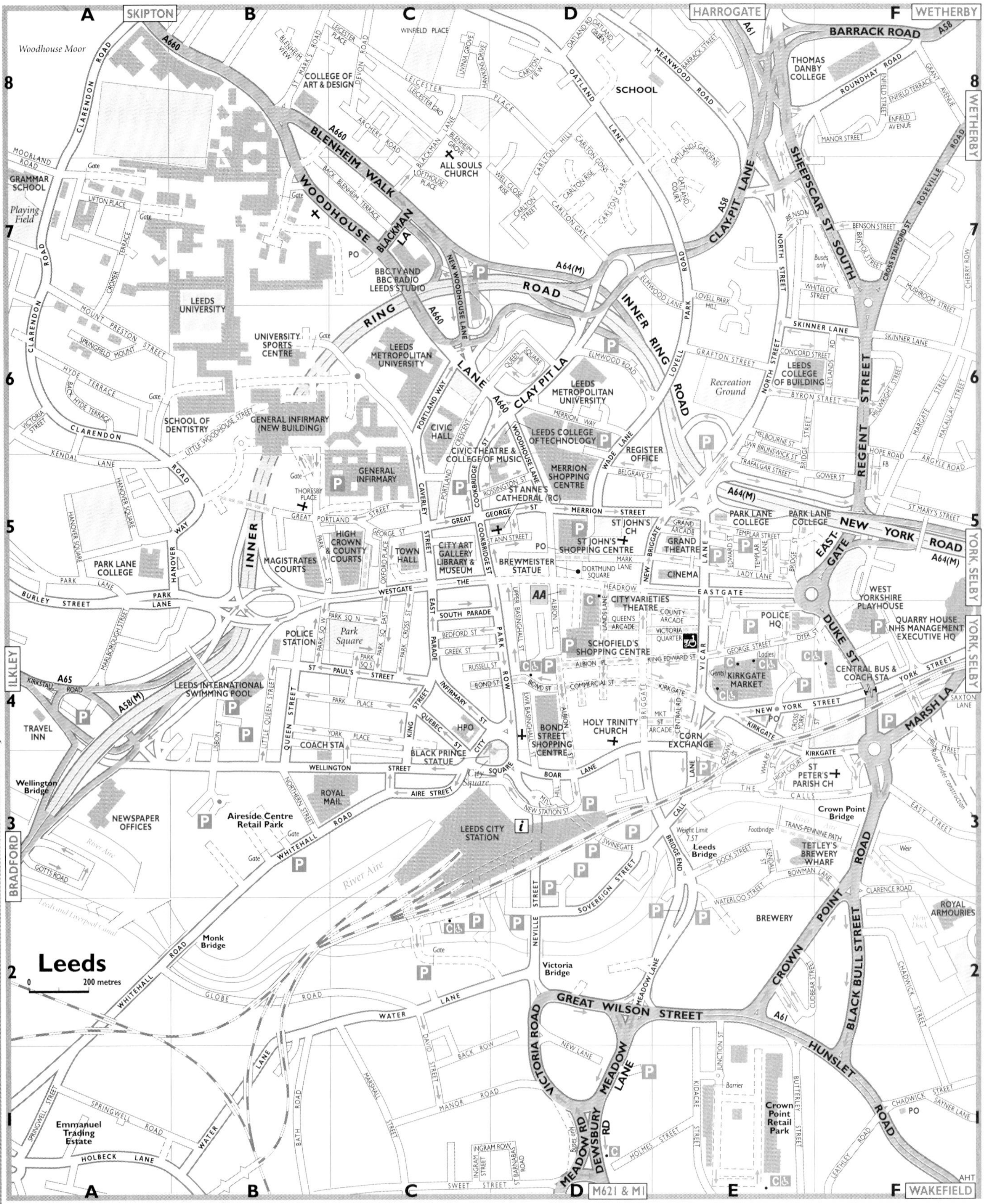

Leeds
0
200 metres
SKIPTON
HARROGATE
WETHERBY
YORK, SELBY
WAKEFIELD
M621 & M1
BRADFORD
ILKLEY
A
B
C
D
E
F
1
2
3
4
5
6
7
8
Woodhouse Moor
CLARENDON ROAD
A660
MOORLAND ROAD
GRAMMAR SCHOOL
Playing Field
LIFTON PLACE
CROMER TERRACE
MOUNT PRESTON STREET
SPRINGFIELD MOUNT
HYDE TERRACE
BACK HYDE TERRACE
VICTORIA STREET
KENDAL LANE
LEEDS UNIVERSITY
UNIVERSITY SPORTS CENTRE
SCHOOL OF DENTISTRY
LITTLE WOODHOUSE STREET
GENERAL INFIRMARY (NEW BUILDING)
GENERAL INFIRMARY
THORESBY PLACE
HANOVER SQUARE
HANOVER WAY
PARK LANE COLLEGE
BURLEY STREET
PARK LANE
MARLBOROUGH STREET
KIRKSTALL ROAD
A65
A58(M)
TRAVEL INN
Wellington Bridge
NEWSPAPER OFFICES
GOTTS ROAD
River Aire
Leeds and Liverpool Canal
COLLEGE OF ART & DESIGN
BLENHEIM WALK
WOODHOUSE LANE
BLACKMAN LA
BLENHEIM VIEW
ST MARK'S ROAD
LEICESTER PLACE
WINFIELD PLACE
DEVON ROAD
ARCHERY ROAD
LEICESTER GRO
BACK BLENHEIM TERRACE
LOFTHOUSE PLACE
ALL SOULS CHURCH
BLENHEIM GROVE
LIVINIA GROVE
HAWKINS DRIVE
CARLTON VIEW
WELL CLOSE RISE
CARLTON HILL
CARLTON GDNS
CARLTON RISE
CARLTON CARR
CARLTON STREET
CARLTON GATE
OATLAND RD
OATLAND COURT
OATLAND GARDENS
OATLAND LANE
SCHOOL
MEANWOOD ROAD
BARRACK STREET
A61
BARRACK ROAD
A58
THOMAS DANBY COLLEGE
ROUNDHAY ROAD
ENFIELD STREET
ENFIELD TERRACE
ENFIELD AVENUE
GRANT AVENUE
MANOR STREET
SHEEPSCAR ST SOUTH
CLAY PIT LANE
ROSEVILLE ROAD
BENSON ST
BENSON STREET
BRISTOL STREET
CROSS STAFFORD ST
CHERRY ROW
MUSHROOM STREET
Buses only
NORTH STREET
WHITELOCK STREET
SKINNER LANE
CONCORD STREET
LEEDS COLLEGE OF BUILDING
LEYLANDS RD
BYRON STREET
MILLWRIGHT STREET
REGENT STREET
Recreation Ground
GRAFTON STREET
LOVELL PARK HILL
LOVELL PARK ROAD
LOVELL ROAD
ELMWOOD LANE
ELMWOOD ROAD
MELBOURNE ST
LWR BRUNSWICK ST
TRAFALGAR STREET
GOWER ST
HOPE ROAD
FB
MARGATE
MACAULAY STREET
ARGYLE ROAD
PO
BBC TV AND BBC RADIO LEEDS STUDIO
NEW WOODHOUSE LANE
A64(M)
RING ROAD
INNER RING ROAD
LEEDS METROPOLITAN UNIVERSITY
PORTLAND WAY
PORTLAND CRESCENT
CIVIC HALL
CIVIC THEATRE & COLLEGE OF MUSIC
COOKRIDGE ST
QUEEN SQUARE
CLAY PIT LA
LEEDS COLLEGE OF TECHNOLOGY
MERRION WAY
MERRION SHOPPING CENTRE
WADE LANE
REGISTER OFFICE
BELGRAVE ST
ROSSINGTON ST
ST ANNE'S CATHEDRAL (RC)
GREAT GEORGE ST
MERRION STREET
ST JOHN'S CH
ST JOHN'S SHOPPING CENTRE
NEW BRIGGATE
GRAND ARCADE
GRAND THEATRE
PARK LANE COLLEGE
NEW YORK ROAD
ST MARY'S STREET
TEMPLAR STREET
TEMPLAR LANE
EDWARD ST
BRIDGE ST
LADY LANE
EASTGATE
INNER
GREAT PORTLAND STREET
GEORGE ST
PARK SQ
HIGH CROWN & COUNTY COURTS
MAGISTRATES COURTS
OXFORD PLACE
TOWN HALL
CAVERLEY STREET
CITY ART GALLERY LIBRARY & MUSEUM
ST ANN STREET
BREWMEISTER STATUE
DORTMUND SQUARE
CINEMA
HEADROW
THE
WESTGATE
AA
CITY VARIETIES THEATRE
COUNTY ARCADE
QUEEN'S ARCADE
VICTORIA QUARTER
SCHOFIELD'S SHOPPING CENTRE
WEST YORKSHIRE PLAYHOUSE
QUARRY HOUSE NHS MANAGEMENT EXECUTIVE HQ
POLICE HQ
DYER ST
GEORGE STREET
DUKE ST
KIRKGATE MARKET
CENTRAL BUS & COACH STA
YORK STREET
SAXTON LANE
MARSH LA
POLICE STATION
Park Square
PARK SQ N
PARK SQ S
PARK SQ W
PARK SQ E
PARK CROSS ST
EAST PARADE
SOUTH PARADE
BEDFORD ST
GREEK ST
ST PAUL'S STREET
UPPER BASINGHALL ST
PARK ROW
ALBION ST
RUSSELL ST
BOND ST
ALBION PL
KING EDWARD ST
COMMERCIAL ST
KIRKGATE
VICAR LANE
LEEDS INTERNATIONAL SWIMMING POOL
LITTLE QUEEN STREET
QUEEN STREET
PARK PLACE
INFIRMARY ST
YORK PLACE
KING ST
QUEBEC ST
HPO
COACH STA
BLACK PRINCE STATUE
CITY SQUARE
City Square
LWR BASINGHALL ST
BOND STREET SHOPPING CENTRE
HOLY TRINITY CHURCH
BRIGGATE
MKT ST ARCADE
CENTRAL RD
CORN EXCHANGE
NEW YORK ST
CROSS YORK ST
WHARF ST
HIGH COURT
ST PETER'S PARISH CH
WELLINGTON STREET
NORTHERN STREET
ROYAL MAIL
AIRE STREET
BOAR LANE
MILL HILL
NEW STATION ST
THE CALLS
Crown Point Bridge
EAST STREET
Road under construction
MILL STREET
Airside Centre Retail Park
WHITEHALL ROAD
Gate
LEEDS CITY STATION
SWINEGATE
Weight Limit 7.5T
Leeds Bridge
BRIDGE END
Footbridge
TRANS-PENNINE PATH
TETLEY'S BREWERY WHARF
DOCK STREET
KENDALL ST
BOWMAN LANE
Weir
CLARENCE ROAD
ROYAL ARMOURIES
New Dock
NEVILLE STREET
SOVEREIGN STREET
WATERLOO STREET
BREWERY
CROWN POINT ROAD
BLACK BULL STREET
Monk Bridge
Victoria Bridge
MEADOW LANE
GLOBE ROAD
WATER LANE
GREAT WILSON STREET
A61
HUNSLET ROAD
CUDBEAR STREET
CHADWICK STREET
VICTORIA ROAD
NEW LANE
DAVID STREET
BACK ROW
MARSHALL STREET
MANOR ROAD
JUNCTION ST
Barrier
KIDACRE STREET
BUTTERLEY STREET
Crown Point Retail Park
CHADWICK STREET
SAYNER LANE
LEATHLEY ROAD
SPRINGWELL STREET
SPRINGWELL ROAD
Emmanuel Trading Estate
HOLBECK LANE
WATER LANE
BATH ROAD
INGRAM ROW
INGRAM STREET
ST BARNABAS ROAD
SWEET STREET
HOLMES STREET
MEADOW RD
DEWSBURY RD
Buses only
AHT

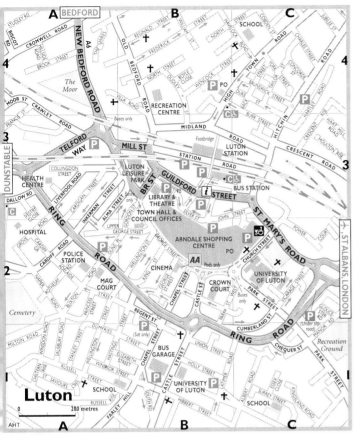

# Luton

Luton is found on atlas page **38**,
grid reference **09**21

**AA shop**
45 George Street, Luton LU1 2AQ                B2

| | | | | | |
|---|---|---|---|---|---|
| Adelaide Street | A2-B2 | Gordon Street | B2-B3 | Silver Street | B3 |
| Albert Road | B1-C1 | Grove Road | A2-A3 | South Road | B1 |
| Alma Street | A2-B3 | Guildford Street | B3-C3 | Stanley Street | A1-A2 |
| Back Street | C4 | Hart Hill Drive | C3 | Station Road | B3-C3 |
| Biscot Road | A4 | Hartley Road | C3-C4 | Strathmore Avenue | C1 |
| Boyle Close | B4 | Hastings Street | A1-B2 | Studley Road | A4 |
| Bridge Street | B3 | Havelock Street | B4-C4 | Surrey Street | C1 |
| Brook Street | A4 | Hibbert Street | B1 | Tavistock Street | B1 |
| Brunswick Street | C4 | High Town Road | B3-C4 | Taylor Street | C4 |
| Burr Street | C3-C4 | Hillside Road | A4 | Telford Way | A3 |
| Buxton Road | A2 | Hitchin Road | C3-C4 | The Shires | A4 |
| Cardiff Grove | A2 | Holly Street | B1 | Union Street | B1 |
| Cardiff Road | A2 | Inkerman Street | A2-A3 | Upper George Street | A2-B2 |
| Cardigan Street | A3 | John Street | B2-C3 | Vestry Close | A3 |
| Castle Street | B1-B2 | Jubilee Street | C4 | Vicarage Street | C2 |
| Chapel Street | B1-B2 | King Street | B2 | Villa Road | A4-B4 |
| Charles Street | C4 | Kingsland Road | C1 | Wellington Street | A1-B2 |
| Chequer Street | C1 | Latimer Road | B1-C1 | Wenlock Street | B4-C4 |
| Chiltern Rise | A1 | Liverpool Road | A3 | William Street | B4 |
| Church Street | B2-C2 | Manor Road | C1-C2 | Windsor Street | A1-B1 |
| Cobden Street | C4 | Meyrick Avenue | A2 | Winsdon Road | A1-A2 |
| Collingdon Street | A3 | Midland Road | D3-C3 | York Street | C4 |
| Concorde Street | C4 | Mill Street | B3 | | |
| Crawley Green Road | C4 | Milton Road | A1 | | |
| Crawley Road | A3-A4 | Moor Street | A4 | | |
| Crescent Rise | C3-C4 | Moulton Rise | C3 | | |
| Crescent Road | C3 | Napier Road | A2 | | |
| Cromwell Road | A4 | New Bedford Street | A4-B3 | | |
| Cumberland Street | C1-C2 | New Town Street | B1-C1 | | |
| Dallow Road | A3 | North Street | B4-C4 | | |
| Dudley Street | B3-B4 | Old Bedford Road | A4-B3 | | |
| Duke Street | C3-C4 | Park Street | C1-C2 | | |
| Dumfries Street | A2-B1 | Park Street West | B2-C2 | | |
| Duns Place | A2-B2 | Power Court | C2 | | |
| Dunstable Road | A4-C2 | Princess Street | A2 | | |
| Elizabeth Street | A1-B1 | Regent Street | B1-B2 | | |
| Essex Close | C1 | Reginald Street | B4 | | |
| Farley Hill | A1-B1 | Rothesay Road | A2 | | |
| Francis Street | A3-A4 | Russell Rise | A1 | | |
| Frederick Street | B4 | Russell Street | A1-B1 | | |
| George Street | B2 | St Mary's Road | C2-C3 | | |
| George Street West | B2 | St Saviours Crescent | A1 | | |
| Gloucester Road | C2 | Salisbury Road | A1-A2 | | |

191

# Leeds

Leeds is found on atlas page **82**,
grid reference **29**32

**AA shop**
95 The Headrow, Leeds LS1 6LU                D5

| | | | | | | | | | | |
|---|---|---|---|---|---|---|---|---|---|---|
| Aire Street | C3 | Chadwick Street | F1-F2 | Grant Avenue | F8 | Lovell Park Road | D6-E6-E7 | Park Cross Street | C4-C5 | The Headrow | C5-D5 |
| Albion Place | D4 | Cherry Row | F6-F7 | Great George Street | C5-D5 | Lower Basinghall Street | D3-D4 | Park Lane | A5-B5 | Thoresby Place | B5 |
| Albion Street | D3-D5 | City Square | C3-C4-D3-D4 | Great Portland Street | B5-C5 | Lower Brunswick Street | E5-E6 | Park Place | B4-C4 | Trafalgar Street | E5 |
| Archery Road | C8 | Clarence Road | F3 | Great Wilson Street | D2-E2 | Macaulay Street | F5-F6 | Park Row | D4 | Upper Basinghall Street | D4-D5 |
| Argyle Road | F5 | Clarendon Road | A8-A7-A6-B5 | Greek Street | C4-D4 | Manor Road | C1-D1 | Park Square East | C4 | Vicar Lane | E4-E5 |
| Back Blenheim Terrace | B7-C7 | Clay-Pit Lane | D6-D7-E7 | Hawkins Drive | C8 | Manor Street | F8 | Park Square North | B4-C4 | Victoria Quarter | D4-E4 |
| Back Hyde Terrace | A6 | Commercial Street | D4 | Hanover Square | A5 | Margate Street | F5-F6 | Park Square South | C4 | Victoria Road | D1-D2 |
| Back Row | C1-D2 | Concord Street | E6-F6 | Hanover Way | B5 | Mark Lane | D5 | Park Square West | B4 | Victoria Street | A6 |
| Barrack Road | F8 | Cookbridge Street | C5-C6 | High Court | E3 | Market Street Arcade | D4-E4 | Park Street | B5 | Wade Lane | D5-D6 |
| Barrack Street | E8 | County Arcade | D4-E4 | Holbeck Lane | A1 | Marlborough Street | A4 | Portland Crescent | C5-C6 | Water Lane | B1-B2-C2-D2 |
| Bath Road | B1-B2 | Cromer Terrace | A6-A7 | Holmes Street | D1-E1 | Marsh Lane | F4 | Portland Way | C6 | Waterloo Street | E2-E3 |
| Bedford Street | C4 | Cross Stamford Street | F6-F7 | Hope Road | F5 | Marshall Street | B1-B2 | Quebec Street | C3-C4 | Well Close Rise | D7 |
| Belgrave Street | D5-E5 | Cross York Street | E4 | Hunslet Road | E2-F1 | Meadow Lane | C1-C2 | Queen's Arcade | D4 | Wellington Street | A3-B3-C3 |
| Benson Street | F7 | Crown Point Road | E2-F2-F3 | Hyde Terrace | A6 | Meadow Road | D1 | Queen Square | D6 | Westgate | C5 |
| Black Bull Street | F1-F2 | Crown Street | E3 | Infirmary Street | C4 | Meanwood Road | D8-E8 | Queen Street | B3-B4 | Wharf Street | E3 |
| Blackman Lane | C7 | Cudbear Street | E2 | Ingram Row | C1-D1 | Melbourne Street | E6 | Regent Street | F5-F6 | Whitehall Road | A1-C3 |
| Blenheim Grove | C8 | David Street | C1-C2 | Ingram Street | C1 | Merrion Street | D5-E5 | Roseville Road | F7-F8 | Whitelock Street | E7-F7 |
| Blenheim View | B8-C8 | Devon Road | C8 | Inner Ring Road | B5-E5 | Merrion Way | D6 | Rossington Street | C5-D5 | Winfield Place | C8 |
| Blenheim Walk | B8-D7 | Dewsbury Road | D1 | Junction Street | E1-E2 | Mill Hill | D3 | Roundhay Road | E8-F8 | Woodhouse Lane | A8-D5 |
| Boar Lane | D3 | Dock Street | E3 | Kelso Road | A7 | Mill Street | F3-F4 | Russell Street | C4-D4 | York Place | B4-C4 |
| Bond Street | C4-D4 | Dortmund Square | D5 | Kendal Lane | A5-A6 | Millwright Street | F6 | St Ann Street | D5 | York Street | F4 |
| Bowman Lane | E3-F3 | Duke Street | F4 | Kendall Street | E3 | Moorland Road | A7 | St Barnabas Road | D1 | | |
| Bridge End | D3 | Dyer Street | E4-F4 | Kidacre Street | E1 | Mount Preston Road | A6-A7 | St Mark's Road | B8 | | |
| Bridge Street | E5-E6 | East Parade | C4-C5 | King Edward Street | D4-E4 | Mushroom Street | F6-F7 | St Mary's Street | F5 | | |
| Briggate | D3-D4 | East Street | F3 | King Street | C3-C4 | Neville Street | D2-D3 | St Paul's Street | B4-C4 | | |
| Bristol Street | F7 | Eastgate | F5 | Kirkgate | E4-E3-F3 | New Briggate | D5-E5 | Saxton Lane | F4 | | |
| Burley Street | A4-A5 | Edward Street | E5 | Kirkstall Road | A4 | New Lane | D1-D2 | Sayner Lane | F1 | | |
| Butterley Street | E1 | Elmwood Lane | D7-E7 | Lands Lane | D4 | New Station Street | D3 | Sheepscar Street South | E7-F7 | | |
| Byron Street | E6-F6 | Elmwood Road | D6 | Leathley Road | F1 | New Woodhouse Lane | C6-C7 | Skinner Lane | E6-F6 | | |
| Call Lane | E3 | Enfield Avenue | F8 | Leicester Grove | C8 | New York Road | E5-F5 | South Parade | C4 | | |
| Carlton Carr | D7 | Enfield Terrace | F8 | Leicester Place | C8-D8 | New York Street | E4-F4 | Sovereign Street | D2-D3 | | |
| Carlton Gate | D7 | Enfield Street | F8 | Leylands Road | F6 | North Street | E6-E7 | Springfield Mount | A6 | | |
| Carlton Gardens | D7-D8 | George Street | C5 | Lifton Place | A7 | Northern Street | B3 | Springwell Road | A1-B1 | | |
| Carlton Hill | D7-D8 | George Street | E4 | Lisbon Street | B3-B4 | Oatland Court | E7 | Springwell Street | A1 | | |
| Carlton Rise | D7 | Globe Road | A2-B2-C2 | Little Queen Street | B3-B4 | Oatland Green | D8 | Sweet Street | C1-D1 | | |
| Carlton Street | D7 | Gotts Road | A3 | Little Woodhouse Street | B5-B6 | Oatland Lane | D7-D8 | Swinegate | D3 | | |
| Carlton View | D8 | Gower Street | E5-F5 | Livinia Grove | C8 | Oatland Road | D8 | Templar Lane | E5 | | |
| Caverley Street | C5-C6 | Grafton Street | E6 | Lofthouse Place | C7 | Oatlands Gardens | E7-E8 | Templar Street | E5 | | |
| Central Road | E4 | Grand Arcade | E5 | Lovell Park Hill | E6-E7 | Oxford Place | C5 | The Calls | E3-F3 | | |

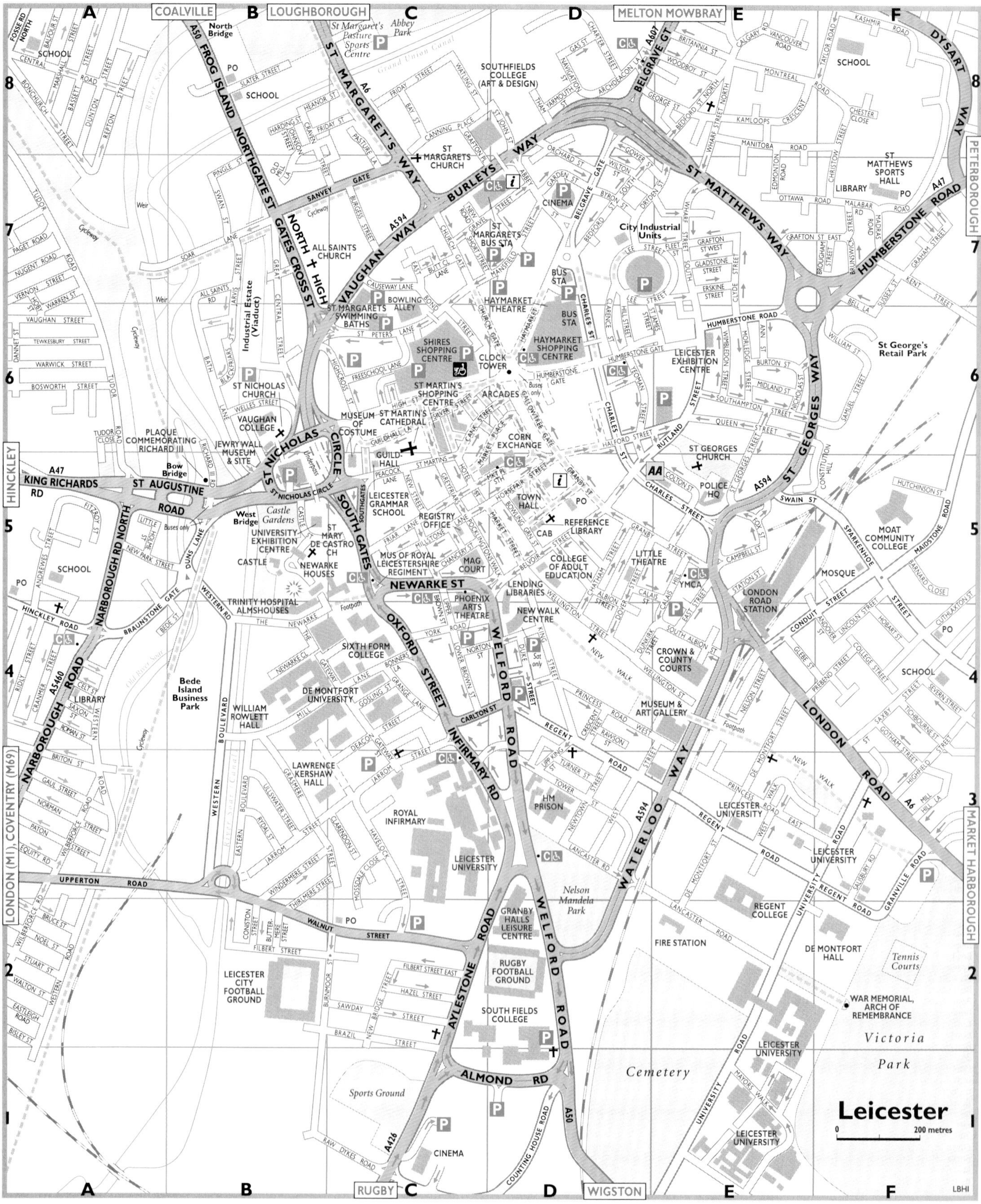

COALVILLE   LOUGHBOROUGH   MELTON MOWBRAY

North Bridge

St Margaret's Pasture Sports Centre

Abbey Park

Grand Union Canal

SCHOOL

FOSSE RD NORTH

SOUTHFIELDS COLLEGE (ART & DESIGN)

St Margarets Church

St Margarets Bus Sta

BURLEYS WAY

ST MARGARET'S WAY

NORTHGATE ST

FROG ISLAND

HIGH CROSS ST

VAUGHAN WAY

All Saints Church

Industrial Estate (Viaduct)

St Margarets Swimming Baths

Bowling Alley

HAYMARKET THEATRE

BUS STA

HAYMARKET SHOPPING CENTRE

City Industrial Units

BELGRAVE GT

ST MATTHEWS WAY

HUMBERSTONE ROAD

St George's Retail Park

St Matthews Sports Hall

LIBRARY

SHIRES SHOPPING CENTRE

CLOCK TOWER

ST MARTIN'S SHOPPING CENTRE

ARCADES

St Nicholas Church

VAUGHAN COLLEGE

MUSEUM OF COSTUME

ST MARTIN'S CATHEDRAL

CORN EXCHANGE

Leicester Exhibition Centre

ST GEORGES WAY

MOAT COMMUNITY COLLEGE

JEWRY WALL MUSEUM & SITE

PLAQUE COMMEMORATING RICHARD III

GUILDHALL

St George's Church

AA

POLICE HQ

HINCKLEY

A47 KING RICHARDS RD

ST AUGUSTINE

ST NICHOLAS CIRCLE

ST NICHOLAS CIRCLE

SOUTHGATES

LEICESTER GRAMMAR SCHOOL

Bow Bridge

West Bridge

Castle Gardens

UNIVERSITY EXHIBITION CENTRE

CASTLE

NEWARKE HOUSES

ST MARY DE CASTRO CH

REGISTRY OFFICE

REFERENCE LIBRARY

TOWN HALL

MAG COURT

CAB

LITTLE THEATRE

YMCA

LONDON ROAD STATION

NARBOROUGH RD NORTH

A5460 NARBOROUGH ROAD

HINCKLEY ROAD

TRINITY HOSPITAL ALMSHOUSES

NEWARKE ST

OXFORD STREET

WELFORD ROAD

PHOENIX ARTS THEATRE

NEW WALK CENTRE

LENDING LIBRARIES

COLLEGE OF ADULT EDUCATION

MUSEUM & ART GALLERY

CROWN & COUNTY COURTS

LONDON WAY

LONDON ROAD

A6

MARKET HARBOROUGH

LIBRARY

Bede Island Business Park

SIXTH FORM COLLEGE

DE MONTFORT UNIVERSITY

WILLIAM ROWLETT HALL

LAWRENCE KERSHAW HALL

ROYAL INFIRMARY

INFIRMARY RD

CARLTON ST

HM PRISON

LEICESTER UNIVERSITY

REGENT ROAD

WATERLOO WAY

A594

Nelson Mandela Park

FIRE STATION

DE MONTFORT HALL

Tennis Courts

LONDON (M1), COVENTRY (M69)

UPPERTON ROAD

WALNUT STREET

AYLESTONE ROAD

WELFORD ROAD

GRANBY HALLS LEISURE CENTRE

RUGBY FOOTBALL GROUND

SOUTH FIELDS COLLEGE

Leicester University

Regent College

De Montfort Hall

WAR MEMORIAL, ARCH OF REMEMBRANCE

Victoria Park

LEICESTER CITY FOOTBALL GROUND

FILBERT STREET

Sports Ground

ALMOND RD

A50

Cemetery

A426

CINEMA

COUNTING HOUSE ROAD

RUGBY   WIGSTON

Leicester University

**Leicester**

0   200 metres

LBHI

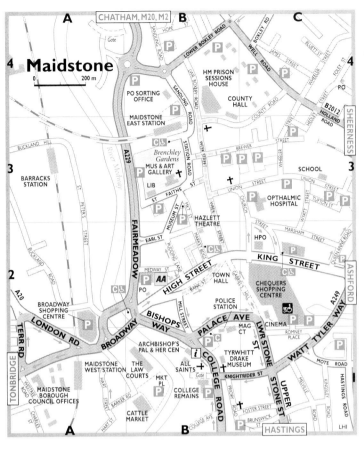

**Maidstone**

## Maidstone

Maidstone is found on atlas page **28**,
grid reference **7555**

**AA shop**
26-27 High Street, Maidstone ME14 1JF      B2

| | | | |
|---|---|---|---|
| Bank Street | B2 | Lower Stone Street | C1-C2 |
| Barker Road | A1-B1 | Market Buildings | B2 |
| Barker Street | A2 | Market Street | B3 |
| Bishops Way | B1-B2 | Marsham Street | C2 |
| Bluett Street | C4 | Medway Street | B2 |
| Boxley Road | C4 | Melville Road | C1 |
| Brewer Street | B3-C3 | Mill Street | B1-B2 |
| Broadway | A1-B2 | Mote Road | C1 |
| Brunswick Street | C1 | Museum Street | B2-B3 |
| Buckland Hill | A3 | Palace Avenue | B1-C2 |
| Buckland Road | A2-A3 | Priory Road | B1 |
| Charles Street | A1 | Pudding Lane | B2 |
| Church Street | C2-C3 | Queen Anne Road | C2 |
| College Avenue | B1 | Romney Place | C1 |
| College Road | B1 | St Faiths Street | B3 |
| County Road | B3-C4 | St Peter's Street | A2-A3 |
| Earl Street | B2 | Sandling Road | B3-B4 |
| Fairmeadow | B2-B4 | Station Road | B3 |
| Foley Street | C4 | Terrace Road | A1-A2 |
| Foster Street | B1-C1 | Tufton Street | C3 |
| Gabriel's Hill | B2-C2 | Union Street | B3-C3 |
| Hart Street | A1 | Upper Stone Street | C1 |
| Hastings Road | C1 | Watt Tyler Way | C1-C2 |
| Hedley Street | C3-C4 | Week Street | B2-B3 |
| High Street | B2 | Well Road | C4 |
| Holland Road | C3-C4 | Westree Road | A1 |
| Hope Street | B4 | Wheeler Street | C3-C4 |
| James Street | C4 | Wyatt Street | C2-C3 |
| Kingsley Road | C1 | | |
| King Street | C3-C4 | | |
| Knightrider Street | B1-C1 | | |
| London Road | A1-A2 | | |
| Lower Boxley Road | B4 | | |

**193**

## Leicester

Leicester is found on atlas page **62**,
grid reference **5804**

**AA shop**
132 Charles Street, Leicester LE1 1NA      E5

| | | | | | |
|---|---|---|---|---|---|
| Abbey Street | D7 | Calais Hill | E4-E5 | Dysart Way | F7-F8 |
| Albion Street | D4-D5 | Calais Street | D5-E5 | East Bond Street | C6-C7 |
| All Saints Road | B6-B7 | Calgary Road | E8 | East Street | E4-E5 |
| Almond Road | C1-D1 | Campbell Street | E5 | Eastern Boulevard | B2-B4 |
| Andrewes Street | A4-A5 | Cank Street | C5-D6 | Eastleigh Road | A2 |
| Ann Street | E6 | Canning Place | C8-D8 | Edmonton Road | E7-E8 |
| Archdeacon Lane | D8 | Carlton Street | C4-D4 | Equity Road | A3 |
| Aylestone Road | C1-D3 | Castle Street | B5-C5 | Erskine Street | E7 |
| Balfour Street | A8 | Causeway Lane | C7 | Filbert Street | B2-C2 |
| Barnard Close | F5 | Celt Street | A4 | Filbert Street East | C2 |
| Bassett Street | A8 | Central Road | A8 | Fitzroy Street | A5 |
| Bath Lane | B5-B6 | Chancery Street | C5 | Fleet Street | E7 |
| Bay Street | C8 | Charles Street | D7-D6-D5-E5 | Fox Street | E5 |
| Bede Street | A4-B4 | Charlton Street | C4-D4 | Freeschool Lane | C6 |
| Bedford Street North | E8 | Charter Street | D8 | Friar Lane | C5 |
| Bedford Street South | D7 | Chatham Street | D4-D5 | Friday Street | B8-C8 |
| Belgrave Gate | D7-D8-E8 | Chester Close | F8 | Frog Island | B8 |
| Bell Lane | F6-F7 | Christow Street | F8 | Gallowtree Gate | D6 |
| Belvoir Street | D5 | Church Gate | C7-C6-D6 | Garden Street | D7 |
| Bisley Street | A1-A2 | Clarence Street | D6-D7 | Gas Street | D8 |
| Blackfriars Street | B6 | Clarendon Street | C3 | Gateway Street | C4-C3 |
| Bonchurch Street | A7-A8 | Clyde Street | E7 | Gaul Street | A3 |
| Bonners Lane | C4 | College Street | F4 | George Street | D8-E8 |
| Bosworth Street | A6 | Colton Street | E5 | Gladstone Street | E7 |
| Bowling Green Street | D5 | Conduit Street | E4-F5 | Glebe Street | E4-F4 |
| Braunstone Gate | A4-B5 | Coniston Street | B2 | Gosling Street | C4 |
| Brazil Street | B2-C1 | Constitution Hill | E5-F5-F6 | Gotham Street | F3-F4 |
| Britannia Street | E8 | Cranmer Street | A4 | Gower Street | D8-E7 |
| Briton Street | A3 | Crescent Street | D4 | Grafton Place | C7-C8 |
| Brougham Street | F7 | Cuthlaxton Street | F4-F5 | Grafton Street East | E7-F7 |
| Bruce Street | A2 | Dannet Street | A6 | Grafton Street West | E7 |
| Brunswick Street | F7 | Deacon Street | C3-C4 | Graham Street | F7 |
| Burgess Street | C7 | De Montfort Street | E2-E3-E4 | Granby Street | D5-E5 |
| Burleys Way | C7-D8 | Dover Street | D4-D5 | Grange Lane | C4 |
| Burnmoor Street | B1-C2 | Dryden Street | D7-E7 | Grasmere Street | B2-B3-C2 |
| Burton Street | E6 | Duke Street | D4 | Gravel Street | C7-D7 |
| Butt Close Lane | C7 | Dunkirk Street | D4-E4 | Great Central Street | B6-B7 |
| Buttermere Street | B2 | Duns Lane | B5 | Greyfriars | C5 |
| Byron Street | D7 | Dunton Street | A8 | Guildhall Lane | C6 |

| | | | | | |
|---|---|---|---|---|---|
| Halford Street | D6-E6 | Newarke Street | C5 | Slater Street | B8 |
| Harding Street | B8 | Newbridge Street | C1-C2 | Soar Lane | A7-B7 |
| Havelock Street | C2-C3 | New Park Street | A5-B5 | South Albion Street | E4 |
| Haymarket | D6-D7 | New Road | C7 | Southampton Street | E6 |
| Hazel Street | C2 | New Street | C5 | Southgates | C5 |
| Heanor Street | B8-C8 | Newtown Street | D3 | Sparkenhoe Street | F4-F5 |
| High Cross Street | C6-B6-B7 | New Walk | D4-E4-E3-F3 | Station Street | E5 |
| Highfield Street | F3-F4 | Nicholas Street | E6 | Stuart Street | A2 |
| High Street | C6-D6 | Noel Street | A2 | Sussex Street | F6-F7 |
| Hinckley Road | A4-A5 | Northgate Street | B7-B8 | Swain Street | E5-F5 |
| Hobart Street | F4 | Norman Street | A3 | Swan Street | B7 |
| Hoby Street | A6-A7 | Norton Street | C4-D4 | The Newarke | B4-C4 |
| Horsefair Street | C5-D5 | Nugent Street | A7 | Taylor Road | F8 |
| Hotel Street | C5 | Old Mill Lane | B7 | Tewkesbury Street | A6 |
| Humberstone Gate | D6-E6 | Orchard Street | D7-D8 | The Gateway | B4-C4 |
| Humberstone Road | E6-F7 | Ottawa Road | E7-F7 | Thames Street | D8 |
| Hutchinson Street | F5 | Oxford Street | C4 | Thirlmere Street | B2-B3 |
| Infirmary Road | C4-D3 | Paget Road | A7 | Tichbourne Street | F4 |
| Jarrom Street | B3-C3-C4 | Pasture Lane | C7-C8 | Tower Street | D3 |
| Jarvis Street | B6-B7 | Paton Street | A3 | Tudor Close | A5 |
| Johnson Street | B8 | Peacock Lane | C5 | Tudor Road | A5-A6-A7 |
| Kamloops Crescent | E8 | Pingle Street | B7 | Turner Street | D3 |
| Kashmir Road | F8-F7 | Pocklingtons Walk | C5-D5 | Ullswater Street | B3 |
| Kent Street | F6-F7 | Prebend Street | E4-F4 | University Road | E1-E2-F3 |
| King Richards Road | A5 | Princess Road East | E3-F3 | Upper King Street | D3 |
| King Street | D4-D5 | Princess Road West | D4-F4 | Upperton Road | A2-B2 |
| Latimer Street | D3-E3-E2 | Queen Street | E6 | Vancouver Road | E8 |
| Lee Street | D7-E7 | Raw Dykes Road | B1-C1 | Vaughan Way | C6-C7 |
| Lincoln Street | F4-F5 | Rawson Street | D4 | Vaughan Street | A6 |
| Little Holme Street | A5 | Regent Road | D4-D3-E3-F3 | Vernon Street | A7 |
| London Road | E4-F3 | Repton Street | A7-A8 | Walnut Street | B2-C2 |
| Lower Brown Street | C4 | Richard III Road | B5-B6 | Walton Street | A2 |
| Madras Road | F7 | Ridley Street | A4 | Warren Street | A6-A7 |
| Maidstone Road | F5-F6 | Roman Street | A4 | Warwick Street | A6 |
| Malabar Road | F7 | Rutland Street | D5-E6 | Waterloo Way | D2-D3-E3-E4 |
| Manitoba Road | E8-F8 | Rydal Street | B3 | Watling Street | C8 |
| Mansfield Street | D7 | St Augustine Road | A5-B5 | Welford Road | D1-D2-D3-D4 |
| Market Place | C5-D6 | St George Street | E5-E6 | Welles Street | B6 |
| Market Place South | C5-C6 | St Georges Way | E5-F5-F6 | Wellington Street | D5-D4-E4 |
| Market Street | D5 | St James Street | E6 | Western Boulevard | B3-B4-B5 |
| Marshall Street | A8 | St John Street | D8 | Western Road | A1-A2-A3-A4-B4 |
| Mayors Walk | E1 | St Margaret's Way | B8-C8-C7 | West Street | D2-D3-E4 |
| Midland Street | E6 | St Martins | C5 | West Walk | E3 |
| Mill Hill Lane | F3 | St Matthews Way | E7 | Wharf Street North | E7-E8 |
| Mill Lane | B4-C4 | St Nicholas Circle | B6-B7-B5-C5 | Wharf Street South | E6-E7 |
| Mill Street | D6-D7 | St Peters Lane | C6 | Wilberforce Road | A1-A2 |
| Millstone Lane | C5 | Salisbury Road | F3 | William Street | F6 |
| Morledge Street | E6 | Samuel Street | F6 | Wilton Street | D7 |
| Montreal Road | E8-F8 | Sanvey Gate | B7-C7 | Wimbledon Street | E6 |
| Mossdale Close | C2-C3 | Sawday Street | C2 | Windermere Street | B3 |
| Narborough Road | A3-A4 | Saxby Street | F4 | Woodboy Street | E8 |
| Narborough Road North | A4-A5 | Saxon Street | A4 | Yeoman Street | D6 |
| Navigation Street | D8 | Severn Street | F4 | York Road | C4 |
| Nelson Street | E4 | Short Street | C7 | | |
| Newarke Close | B4 | Silver Street | C6 | | |

194

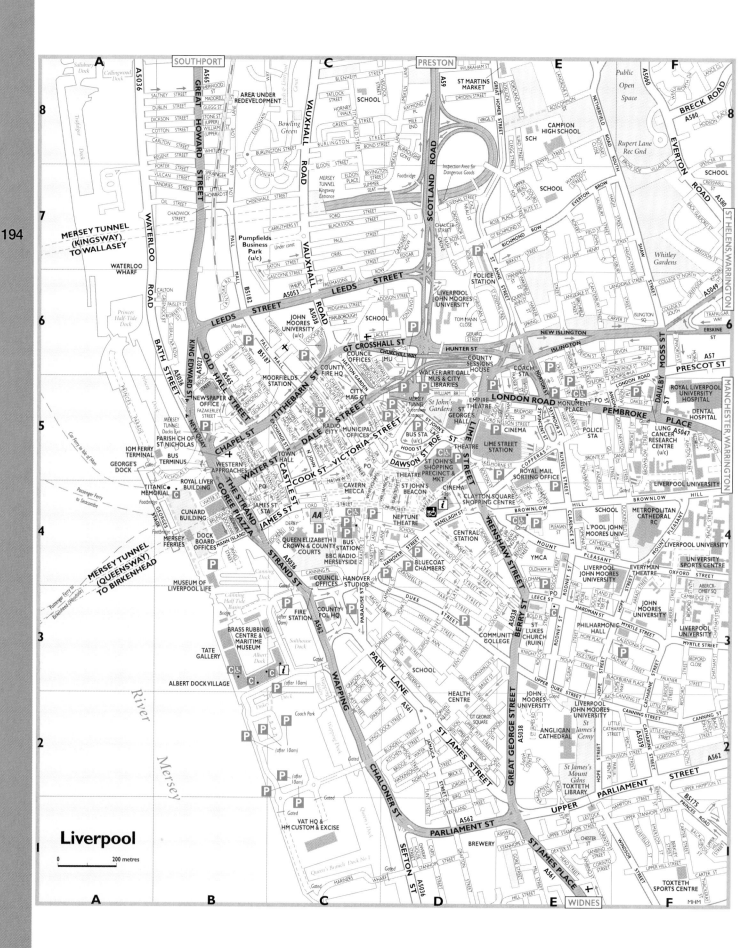

Liverpool

0    200 metres

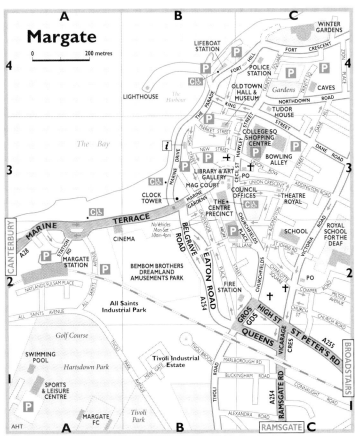

# Margate

Margate is found on atlas page **29**, grid reference **3571**

| | | | | | |
|---|---|---|---|---|---|
| Addington Road | C3 | Fort Crescent | C4 | New Street | B3 |
| Addington Street | C2-C3 | Fort Hill | B4-C4 | Northdown Road | C4 |
| Alexandra Road | B1-C1 | Fulsam Place | A2 | Queens Avenue | C1 |
| All Saints Avenue | A2 | Grosvenor Gardens | C2 | Ramsgate Road | C1 |
| Belgrave Road | B2 | Grosvenor Place | B2-B3 | St Johns Road | C2 |
| Buckingham Road | B1-C1 | Hawley Street | C3-C4 | St Peter's Road | C1 |
| Cecil Street | C3 | High Street | B3-B2-C2 | Station Road | A2 |
| Charlotte Square | C2 | King Street | B4-C4-C3 | The Parade | B4 |
| Churchfields | C2 | Marine Drive | B3 | Tivoli Brooks | B1 |
| Churchfields Place | C2-C3 | Marine Gardens | B3 | Tivoli Park Avenue | A2-A1-B1 |
| Church Road | C2-C1 | Marine Terrace | A2-A3-B3 | Tivoli Road | B1 |
| Church Street | C2 | Market Street | B3-C3 | Trinity Square | C4 |
| Connaught Road | C1 | Marlborough Road | B1-C1 | Union Crescent | C3 |
| Cowper Road | C2 | Mere Gate | B1 | Union Row | C3 |
| Dane Hill | C3-C4 | Mill Lane | B2-C2 | Vicarage Crescent | C1 |
| Dane Road | C3 | Milton Avenue | C2 | Victoria Road | C2-C3 |
| Eaton Road | B1-B2 | Naylands | A2 | Zion Place | C4 |

**195**

# Liverpool

Liverpool is found on atlas page **78**, grid reference **3490**

### AA shop
Lord Street, Derby Square, Liverpool L2 1UF          C4

| | | | | | |
|---|---|---|---|---|---|
| Addison Street | C6-D6 | Brunswick Street | B4 | Covent Garden | B5 |
| Adelaide Place | E8 | Burlington Street | B8-D8 | Craven Street | E5-E6 |
| Ainsworth Street | E4-E5 | Burroughs Gardens | D8 | Cresswell Street | F7 |
| Alfred Mews | E2 | Bute Street | E7 | Cross Hall Street | C5-D5 |
| Anson Place | F5 | Caledonia Street | F3 | Crown Street | F5 |
| Anson Street | E5 | Calton Street | B6 | Cunliffe Place | C5 |
| Argyle Street | C3-D3 | Cambridge Street | F3 | Dale Street | C5-D5 |
| Arrad Street | F3-F4 | Campbell Street | D3-D4 | Dansie Street | E5-F5 |
| Ashton Street | F4-F5 | Canning Place | C4 | Daulby Street | F5 |
| Ashwell Street | E1 | Canning Street | E2-F2 | Dawson Street | D5 |
| Audley Street | E5-E6 | Canterbury Street | E6 | Devon Street | E6-F6 |
| Back Canning Street | F2-F3 | Carlton Street | A8-B8 | Dexter Street | E1 |
| Back Gibson Street | F1 | Carpenters Row | C3 | Dickson Street | A8-B8 |
| Back Guildford Street | F7 | Carruthers Street | B7-C7 | Douro Street | E7 |
| Back Sandon Street | F2 | Carter Street | F1 | Dryden Street | D8 |
| Bailey Street | D2-E3 | Carver Street | E6-F6 | Dublin Street | A8-B8 |
| Baltimore Street | E3-E4 | Caryl Street | D1 | Duckinfield Street | F4 |
| Bath Street | A6-B5 | Castle Street | C4-C5 | Duke Street | C3-E3 |
| Bayhorse Lane | E5-F6 | Catharine Street | F2-F3 | Dwerry House Street | D1 |
| Beckwith Street | C3 | Cathedral Walk | E4 | Earle Street | B5-B6 |
| Bedford Close | F3 | Cazneau Street | D7 | East Street | B4 |
| Bedford Street North | F3-F4 | Chadwick Street | B7 | Eaton Street | B7-C7 |
| Bedford Street South | F2-F3 | Chaloner Street | C2-D1 | Eberle Street | C5 |
| Benson Street | E4 | Chapel Street | B5 | Edgar Street | D7 |
| Berkley Street | F1-F2 | Chatham Street | F3 | Edmund Street | B5 |
| Berry Street | E3 | Chaucer Street | D7 | Egerton Street | F2 |
| Bevington Street | C7-D7 | Cheapside | C5-C6 | Eldon Place | C7 |
| Birchfield Street | E6 | Chester Street | E1 | Eldon Street | C7-C8 |
| Birkett Street | E7 | Chisenhale Street | B7-C7 | Eldonian Way | B8-C8 |
| Bixteth Street | B5-C5 | Christian Street | D6 | Elizabeth Street | F5 |
| Blackburne Place | E3-F3 | Church Street | C4-D4 | Emerson Street | F1 |
| Blackstock Street | C7-D7 | Churchill Way | C6-D6 | Epworth Street | F6 |
| Blair Street | E1 | Clarence Street | E4 | Erskine Street | F6 |
| Blenheim Street | C8-D8 | Clegg Street | E7-E8 | Everton Road | F7-F8 |
| Bluefields Street | F1 | Cockspur Street | C6 | Everton Row | E7 |
| Blundell Street | C2-D2 | College Street North | F6 | Exchange Street East | C5 |
| Bold Place | E3 | College Street South | F6 | Falkner Street | E3-F3 |
| Bold Street | D4-E3 | Colquitt Street | D3-E3 | Fazakerley Street | B5 |
| Bolton Street | D4-D5 | Comus Street | D6-D7 | Fenwick Street | B5-C4 |
| Bond Street | C8-D8 | Constance Street | E6-F6 | Finch Place | F6 |
| Breck Road | F8 | Cook Street | C4-C5 | Fleet Street | D3-D4 |
| Brick Street | D2 | Cookson Street | D2-E2 | Flint Street | D1-D2 |
| Bridgewater Street | D2 | Cooper Street | D4-E4 | Fontenoy Street | D6 |
| Bridport Street | E5 | Copperas Hill | D4-E5 | Ford Street | C7-D7 |
| Bronte Street | E5 | Corinto Street | E1-F1 | Forrest Street | C3-D3 |
| Brook Street | B5 | Corn Hill | C3 | Fox Street | D8-E7 |
| Brow Side | F7-F8 | Cornwall Street | D2 | Fraser Street | E5-E6 |
| Brownlow Hill | D4-F4 | Corwallis Street | D3-E3 | Freemasons Row | C6-D7 |
| Brownlow Street | F4-F5 | Cotton Street | A8-B8 | Gardners Row | D7 |
| | | | | Gascoyne Street | B7-C6 |
| | | | | George Street | B5 |
| | | | | George's Dockway | B4 |
| | | | | Gerard Street | D6 |
| | | | | Gibraltar Row | B6 |
| | | | | Gilbert Street | D3 |
| | | | | Gildart Street | E5-E6 |
| | | | | Gill Street | E5-F5 |
| | | | | Glegg Street | B8 |
| | | | | Gore Street | E1 |
| | | | | Goree Piazza | C4-C5 |
| | | | | Gradwell Street | D3-D4 |

| | | | | | |
|---|---|---|---|---|---|
| Grafton Street | D1 | Matthews Street | C4-C5 | St James Place | E1 |
| Grayson Street | C3 | Midghall Street | C6 | St James Road | E1-E2 |
| Great Crosshall Street | C6-D6 | Mile End | D8 | St James Street | D2-E2 |
| Great George Street | E1-E3 | Mill Street | E1 | St John's Lane | D5 |
| Great Homer Street | D7-D8 | Moira Street | F6 | St Josephs Crescent | D6-E6 |
| Great Howard Street | B6-B8 | Monument Place | E5 | St Nicholas Place | B5 |
| Great Newton Street | F4-F5 | Moorfields | C5 | St Thomas Street | C5-D5 |
| Great Orford Street | F4 | Moss Street | F6 | St Vincent Street | E5 |
| Greek Street | E5 | Mount Pleasant | F4 | Salisbury Street | E7-F6 |
| Green Street | C8-D8 | Mount Pleasant Street | E4-F4 | Saltney Street | A8-B8 |
| Greenland Street | D1-E2 | Mount Street | E3 | Sanbino Street | E1 |
| Greenock Street | B6 | Mulberry Street | F3-F4 | Sandon Street | F2-F3 |
| Greenside | F6 | Myrtle Street | F3 | School Lane | C4-D4 |
| Gregson Street | F7 | Nash Grove | D7 | Scotland Road | D6-D8 |
| Grenville Street South | D3-E2 | Naylor Street | C6-D7 | Seel Street | D4-E3 |
| Grosvenor Street | D7 | Nelson Street | D2 | Sefton Street | D1 |
| Hackins Hey | C5 | Netherfield Road South | E8-F7 | Seymour Street | E5 |
| Haigh Street | E7-F6 | New Bird Street | D1-D2 | Shaw Street | F6-F7 |
| Hampton Street | E1-F2 | New Islington | E6-F6 | Shaws Alley | C3-D2 |
| Hanover Street | C3-D4 | New Quay | B5 | Sherwood Street | B8 |
| Hardman Street | E3 | Newington | E4 | Simpson Street | D2 |
| Harker Street | E6 | Norfolk Street | D2 | Skelthorne Street | D5-E5 |
| Hart Street | E5 | North John Street | C5 | Slater Street | D3-D4 |
| Hatton Garden | C5-C6 | Norton Street | E5-E6 | Soho Street | E7 |
| Hawke Street | E4-E5 | Oakes Street | F5 | South Hunter Street | E3 |
| Head Street | E1 | Oil Street | A7-B7 | South John Street | C4-C5 |
| Henry Street | D3 | Old Hall Street | B5-B6 | Sparling Street | C2-D2-D3 |
| Highfield Street | B6-c6 | Old Leeds Street | B6 | Spencer Street | F8 |
| Hill Street | E1 | Oldham Place | E4 | Spranger Street | B7 |
| Hodson Place | F8 | Oldham Street | E4 | Springfield | E6-E7 |
| Hood Street | D5 | Oriel Street | C7-D7 | Stafford Street | E5-E6 |
| Hope Place | E3 | Ormond Street | B5 | Stanhope Street | D1-E1 |
| Hope Street | E2-F4 | Oxford Street | F4 | Stanley Street | C4-C5 |
| Hopeway | F3 | Paisley Street | B6 | Stone Street | B8 |
| Hornby Walk | C8 | Pall Mall | B7-C5 | Strand Street | B4-C4 |
| Hotham Street | E5 | Paradise Street | C3-C4 | Suffolk Street | D3 |
| Hunter Street | D6 | Park Lane | C3-D2 | Summer Seat | C7-D7 |
| Hurst Street | C2-C3 | Parker Street | D4 | Tabley Street | C2-D3 |
| Huskisson Street | E2-F2 | Parliament Close | E1-D2 | Tarleton Street | D4-D5 |
| Ilford Street | E5 | Parliament Place | F2 | Tatlock Street | C8 |
| Iliad Street | E8 | Parliament Street | D1-E1 | Tempest Hey | C5 |
| Irwell Street | B4 | Parr Street | D3 | Temple Street | C5 |
| Islington | E6 | Paul Street | C7-D7 | Thackeray Street | F1 |
| Islington Square | F6 | Peach Street | F4 | The Strand | B4-B5 |
| Jamaica Street | D1-D2 | Pembroke Place | E5-F5 | Titchfield Street | C7-C8 |
| James Street | B4-C4 | Pembroke Street | F5 | Tithebarn Street | C5-C6 |
| John Street | E7 | Percy Street | F2 | Tom Mann Close | D6 |
| Johnson Street | C5-C6 | Peter's Lane | C4-D4 | Trafalgar Way | F6 |
| Jordan Street | D2 | Philips Street | C6 | Trowbridge Street | E4-E5 |
| Juvenal Street | D7 | Pilgrim Street | E3 | Upper Beau Street | E7 |
| Kempson Street | E6-F6 | Pitt Street | D2-D3 | Upper Duke Street | E2-E3 |
| Kent Street | D3 | Pleasant Street | E4 | Upper Frederick Street | C3-D2-E2 |
| Kinder Street | F6-F7 | Pomonia Street | E4 | Upper Hampton Street | F2 |
| King Edward Street | B5-B6 | Porter Street | A7-B7 | Upper Hill Street | E1 |
| Kings Dock Street | C2-D2 | Portland Place | E8 | Upper Parliament Street | E1-F2 |
| Kitchen Street | D2 | Pownhall Street | C3 | Upper Richmond Street | D7-E7 |
| Knight Street | E3 | Prescot Street | F6 | Upper Stanhope Street | E1-F1 |
| Lace Street | C6-D6 | Prince Edwin Street | E7-E8 | Upper Stone Street | B8 |
| Lance Close | F8 | Princes Parade | A5-A6 | Upper William Street | B8 |
| Langrove Street | E8 | Princes Road | F1-F2 | Vandries Street | A7-B7 |
| Langsdale Street | E6-F6 | Princes Street | C5 | Vauxhall Road | C6-C8 |
| Lanyork Road | B6 | Pudsey Street | D5-E5 | Vernon Street | C5 |
| Leece Street | E3 | Queen Ann Street | E6 | Vescock Street | C8-D8 |
| Leeds Street | B6-D6 | Ranelagh Street | D4 | Victoria Street | C5-D5 |
| Lestock Street | E1 | Raymond Place | D8 | Village Street | F7-F8 |
| Lime Street | D4-D6 | Redcross Street | B4-C4 | Virgil Street | D8 |
| Limekiln Lane | D7-D8 | Regent Street | A8-B8 | Vulcan Street | A7-B7 |
| Little Canning Street | F2 | Renshaw Street | D4-E4 | Wakefield Street | E6 |
| Little Catharine Street | F2 | Rice Street | E3 | Wapping | C2-C3 |
| Little Howard Street | B7 | Richmond Row | D7-E7 | Water Street | B4-B5-C5 |
| Little St Brides Street | F2 | Roberts Street | B6 | Waterloo Road | A6-A8 |
| London Road | D5-E5-F5-F6 | Rodney Street | E3-E4 | Watkinson Street | D2 |
| Lord Nelson Street | D5-E5 | Roe Street | D5 | Watmough Street | E7 |
| Lord Street | C4 | Rokeby Street | E7 | Webster Street | C6-D6 |
| Love Lane | B7-B8 | Roscoe Street | E3-E4 | Wentworth Road | F8 |
| Lower Castle Street | C4-C5 | Roscommon Street | E8 | Whitechapel | C4-D5 |
| Lydia Ann Street | D3 | Rose Hill | D6-D7 | Whitley Street | B8 |
| Maddrell Street | B8 | Rose Place | D7-E7 | Wilbraham Street | D8 |
| Manesty's Lane | C4 | Royal Mail Street | E4-E5 | Wilde Street | E5 |
| Mann Island | B4 | Rumford Street | B5 | William Brown Street | D5 |
| Mansfield Street | E6-E7 | Russell Street | E4-E5 | Williamson Street | D5 |
| Mariners Wharf | C1-D1 | St Andrew Street | E4-E5 | Windsor Street | E1-F1 |
| Marlborough Street | C6 | St Ann Street | D7-E6 | Wood Street | D3-D4 |
| Maryland Street | E4-E3-F3 | St Brides Street | F2-F3 | York Street | D3 |

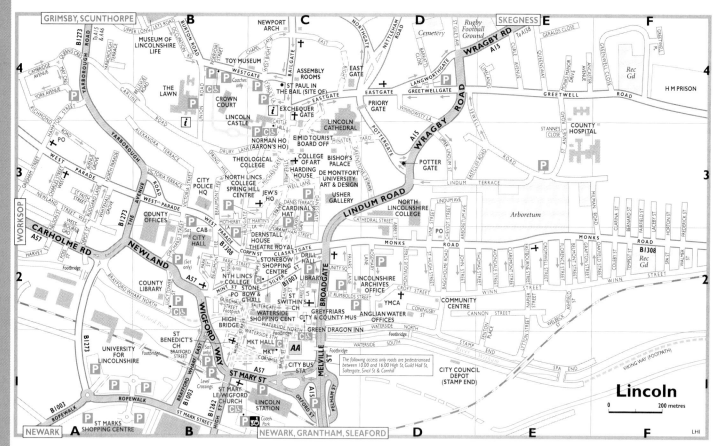

196

# Lincoln

Lincoln is found on atlas page **76**,
grid reference **9771**

**AA shop**
33 Sincil Street, Lincoln LN5 7ET          C1

| | | | | | | | | | |
|---|---|---|---|---|---|---|---|---|---|
| Abbey Street | D2-D3 | Danes Terrace | C3 | Lytton Street | E1-E2 | St Mark Street | B1 | Yarborough Road | A4-B3 |
| Alexandra Terrace | A4-B3 | Danesgate | C2-C3 | May Crescent | A4 | St Martin's Lane | C3 | Yarborough Terrace | A4 |
| Arboretum Avenue | D2-D3 | Depot Street | A2-A3 | Melville Street | D1 | St Mary Street | B1-C1 | York Avenue | A4 |
| Ancaster Way | E4 | Drury Lane | B3-C3 | Michaelgate | C3 | St Pauls Lane | C4 | | |
| Ashfield Street | E2 | Eastbourne Street | E2 | Milman Road | F2-F3 | St Rumbolds Street | C2-D2 | | |
| Ashlin Grove | A3 | East Bight | C4 | Minster Yard | C3-D3 | Saltergate | B2 | | |
| Avondale Street | E2 | Eastcliff Road | D3-E3 | Mint Lane | B2 | Sewell Road | D4-F3 | | |
| Bagholme Road | D2 | Eastgate | C4-D4 | Mint Street | B2 | Silver Street | C2 | | |
| Bailgate | C4 | Fairfield Street | F2-F3 | Monks Manor Drive | E4 | Sincil Street | C1 | | |
| Bank Street | C2 | Fenton Place | E1-E2 | Monks Road | C2-F2 | Spa End | E1-F1 | | |
| Barratts Close | D4 | Flaxengate | C2-C3 | Montague Street | D2 | Spa Street | F2 | | |
| Beaumont Fee | B2-B3 | Florence Street | E2 | Motherby Lane | B3 | Spring Hill | B3 | | |
| Bellevue Road | B4 | Foss Street | A2 | Napier Street | E2 | Stamp End | D1-E1 | | |
| Belmont Street | E2 | Frederick Street | F2-F3 | Nelson Street | A2-A3 | Steep Hill | C3 | | |
| Bernard Street | F2-F3 | Free School Lane | C2 | Nettleham Road | D4 | Tempest Street | F2 | | |
| Brayford Street | B1 | Friars Lane | C2 | Newland | A2-B2 | The Avenue | A2-B3 | | |
| Brayford Wharf East | B1-B2 | Geralds Close | E4 | Newland Street West | A2-A3 | The Strait | C3 | | |
| Brayford Wharf North | A2-B2 | Grafton Street | E2 | Northgate | C4-D4 | Thomas Street | E2 | | |
| Broadgate | C2-C3 | Grantham Street | C2 | North Parade | A3 | Union Road | B3-B4 | | |
| Burton Road | B4 | Greenstone Stairs | C3-D3 | Oakfield Street | F2 | Unity Square | C2 | | |
| Cambridge Avenue | A4 | Greenwell Close | F4 | Occupation Road | B4 | Upper Lindum Street | D3 | | |
| Cannon Street | D2-E2 | Greetwell Place | F4 | Orchard Street | B2-B3 | Upper Long Leys Road | A4-B4 | | |
| Carholme Road | A2-A3 | Greetwell Road | D4-F4 | Oxford Street | C1 | Victoria Street | B3 | | |
| Carline Road | A4-B3 | Greetwellgate | D4 | Park Street | B2-C2 | Victoria Terrace | B3 | | |
| Castle Hill | C3-C4 | Gresham Street | A3 | Pelham Bridge | C1 | Vine Street | D2-D3 | | |
| Cathedral Street | C3-D3 | Guildhall Street | B2 | Pelham Street | C1 | Walmer Street | F2 | | |
| Chapel Lane | B4-C4 | Hampton Street | A3-A4 | Pottergate | D3 | Waterside North | C2-D2 | | |
| Charles Street West | A3 | Harvey Street | A2 | Queens Crescent | A4 | Waterside South | C1-E1 | | |
| Cheviot Street | D2-D3 | High Street | B1-C3 | Queensway | E4 | Welbeck Street | E2 | | |
| Claremont Street | E2 | Horton Street | F2-F3 | Reservoir Street | B4 | Well Lane | C3 | | |
| Clarina Street | F2-F3 | Hungate | B2-B3 | Richmond Road | A4-A3 | West Bight | C4 | | |
| Clasketgate | C2 | John Street | D2 | Ropewalk | A1-B1 | West Parade | A3-B2 | | |
| Coleby Street | F2 | Laceby Street | F2-F3 | Rosemary Lane | D2 | Westbourne Grove | A2-A3 | | |
| Coningsby Street | D2 | Langworthgate | D4 | Rudgard Lane | A3 | Westgate | B4-C4 | | |
| Cornhill | C1 | Limelands | E4 | St Anne's Close | E3 | Whitehall Grove | A3 | | |
| Corporation Street | B2-C2 | Lindum Terrace | D3-E3 | St Anne's Road | E3-E4 | Wigford Way | B1-B2 | | |
| Croft Street | D2 | Lindum Avenue | D3 | St Faith Street | A3 | Winn Street | D2-F2 | | |
| Curle Avenue | E4 | Lindum Road | C2-D3 | St Giles Avenue | D4 | Winnowsty Lane | D3-D4 | | |
| Cromwell Street | E2 | Lucy Tower Street | B2 | St Hugh Street | D2 | Wragby Road | D3-E4 | | |

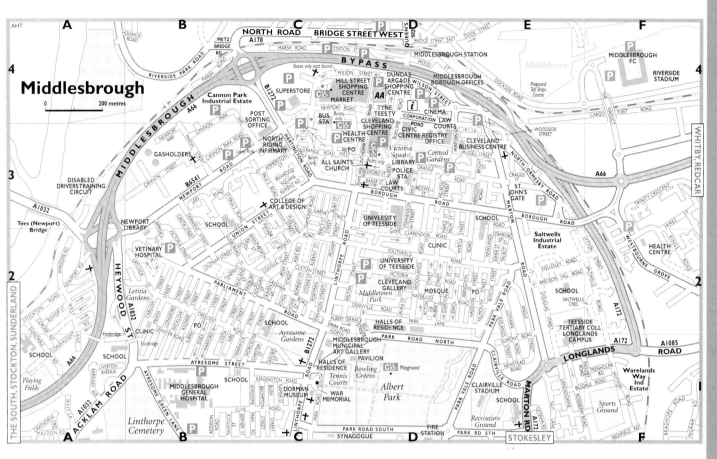

# Middlesbrough

Middlesbrough is found on atlas page **97**,
grid reference **4919**

**AA shop**
17 Corporation Road, Middlesbrough TS11 1LS          D4

| | | | | | | | | | |
|---|---|---|---|---|---|---|---|---|---|
| Abingdon Road | D2-E2 | Cargo Fleet Road | E4-F4 | Gresham Road | C2 | Newport Road | A2-D4 | Tennyson Street | C2 |
| Acklam Road | A1 | Carlow Street | B2 | Greta Street | B2-B3 | Newport Way | B3 | The Viaduct | F3-F4 |
| Acton Street | D2 | Chester Street | C1 | Haddon Street | D2-E2 | Newstead Road | E1 | Trenholme Road | F1 |
| Addison Road | B1 | Clairville Road | E1 | Harford Street | B1-B2 | North Ormesby Road | E3 | Trinity Crescent | F3 |
| Aire Street | B1-B2-C2 | Clarendon Road | D2 | Hartington Road | C3-C4 | North Road | B4-C4 | Union Street | B2-C3 |
| Albany Street | C2 | Clifton Street | C2 | Heywood Street | A1-A2 | Nut Lane | E1 | Victoria Road | C2-D2-E2 |
| Albert Road | D3-D4 | Clive Road | B1-C1 | Highfield Road | F1 | Ottawa Road | E1 | Victoria Street | B2 |
| Albert Terrace | C2-D2 | Colville Street | C2 | Howe Street | C2 | Outram Street | B2 | Warwick Street | B1-C1-C2 |
| Alwent Road | C3 | Connaught Road | A1-A2 | Hutton Road | F1 | Oxford Street | C1 | Waterloo Road | D2-E2 |
| Ammerston Street | C3 | Corder Road | A1-A2 | Ingram Road | F1 | Palm Street | D2-D3 | Watson Street | D3 |
| Angle Street | E1-E2 | Corporation Road | D4 | James Street | F3 | Park Lane | D2 | Wellesley Road | E2-F2 |
| Aske Road | C2 | Costa Street | B1-B2 | Kensington Road | C1 | Park Road | C1 | Wentworth Street | C2 |
| Athol Street | C2 | Craggs Street | C3 | Kildare Street | B1-B2 | Park Road North | C1-E1 | Westbourne Grove | F2-F3 |
| Aubrey Street | D2 | Crathorne Crescent | A1 | King's Road | F2 | Park Road South | C1-D1-E1 | West Lane | A1-A2 |
| Ayresome Green Lane | B1 | Craven Street | C2 | Lamport Street | B2-B3 | Park Vale Road | D1-E1-E2 | Wicklow Street | B1-B2 |
| Ayresome Road | A2 | Crescent Road | B2-C1 | Lansdowne Road | E1 | Parliament Road | B2-C2 | Wilson Street | C4-D4 |
| Ayresome Street | B1-C1 | Derwent Street | B2-B3 | Laura Street | D2 | Pelham Street | C2-C3 | Wilton Street | C2-D2 |
| Baker Street | D3 | Diamond Road | C2-C3 | Laycock Street | B2 | Percy Street | C2-C3 | Wood Street | D4 |
| Barnaby Avenue | A1 | Dockside Road | D4-E4-F4 | Lees Road | B3 | Portman Street | C3 | Woodlands Road | D2-D3 |
| Bedford Street | D3 | Dock Street | D4-E4 | Leinster Road | B1-B2 | Princes Road | C2 | Woodside Street | E3 |
| Belk Street | D1-D2 | Douglas Street | E1-E2 | Linthorpe Road | C1-D4 | Queen's Square | D4 | Worcester Street | C1-C2 |
| Berner Street | C1 | Dunstable Road | A1-A2 | Liverton Avenue | A1 | Riverside Park Road | A4-B4 | Wylam Street | B2-C2 |
| Bilsdale Road | E1-F1 | Egerton Street | D2 | Longford Street | B1-B2 | Romney Street | C2 | | |
| Bishop Street | A2 | Egmont Road | E1 | Longlands Road | E1-F1 | Roscoe Street | E2 | | |
| Borough Road | C3-D3-E3 | Emily Street | D3 | Lothian Road | E1-E2 | Roseberry Road | E1-F1 | | |
| Boswell Street | D3 | Enfield Street | B2 | Lytton Street | E2-F2 | Ruby Street | C3 | | |
| Bow Street | C2 | Errol Street | D2 | Maldon Road | A1 | Russell Street | D3-E3 | | |
| Bradhope Road | F1 | Esher Street | E2 | Manor Street | C2-C3 | St Paul's Road | B3-C3 | | |
| Breckon Hill Road | E2-F2 | Eshwood Square | C3 | Maple Street | D2-D3 | Saltwells Crescent | F2 | | |
| Bridge Street East | D4 | Essex Street | B1-B2 | Marsh Road | B4-C4 | Saltwells Road | F1-F2-E2 | | |
| Bridge Street West | C4-D4 | Falkland Street | B2 | Marsh Street | B3 | Southfield Road | C2-D2-E2 | | |
| Bright Street | E3 | Falmouth Street | E2 | Marton Road | E1-E2-E3-E4 | Stamford Street | E2 | | |
| Brompton Street | C1 | Finsbury Street | C2 | Meath Street | B1-B2 | Station Street | C4-D4 | | |
| Bush Street | C1 | Fleetham Street | C2-C3 | Melrose Street | D3 | Stephenson Street | D2-D3 | | |
| Byelands Street | E1-E2 | Garnet Street | C3 | Metz Bridge Road | B4 | Stockton Road | A2 | | |
| Cadogan Street | C2 | Glebe Road | B2 | Middlesbrough Bypass | A1-F1 | Stowe Street | C2 | | |
| Cannon Park Road | B3 | Grange Road | D3-E3 | Myrtle Street | D2-D3 | Surrey Street | B1-B2 | | |
| Cannon Park Way | B3-B4-C3 | Grange Road West | C3 | Napier Street | C1 | Tavistock Street | B1 | | |
| Cannon Street | B3 | Granville Road | C2-D2 | Newlands Road | E2-E3 | Talbot Street | E2 | | |

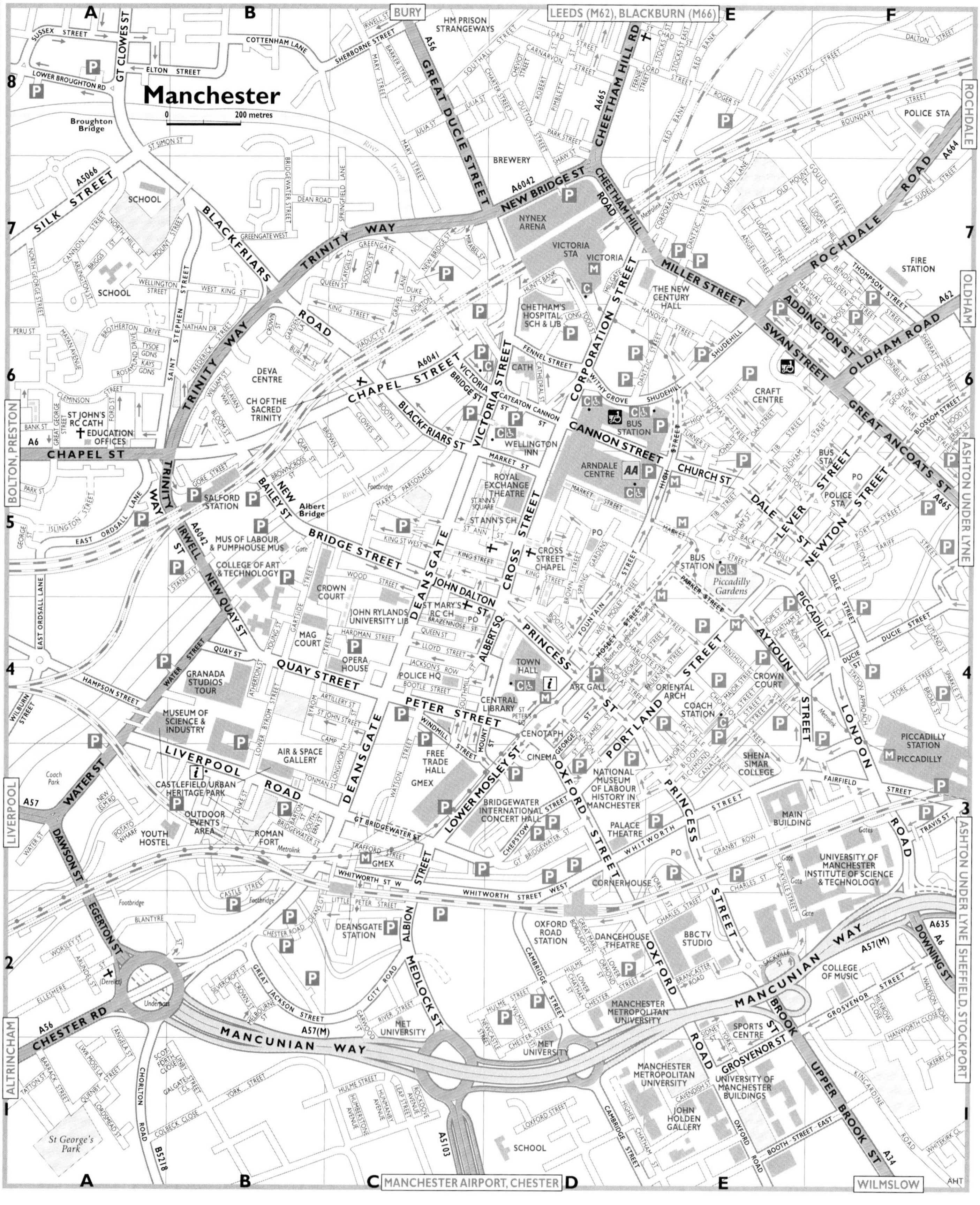

# Manchester

0    200 metres

198

BURY

LEEDS (M62), BLACKBURN (M66)

HM PRISON STRANGEWAYS

MANCHESTER AIRPORT, CHESTER

WILMSLOW

ROCHDALE

OLDHAM

ASHTON UNDER LYNE

ASHTON UNDER LYNE | SHEFFIELD, STOCKPORT

ALTRINCHAM

BOLTON, PRESTON

LIVERPOOL

POLICE STA

FIRE STATION

POLICE STA

NYNEX ARENA

VICTORIA STA

THE NEW CENTURY HALL

CRAFT CENTRE

CHETHAM'S HOSPITAL SCH & LIB

BREWERY

DEVA CENTRE

CH OF THE SACRED TRINITY

ST JOHN'S RC CATH

EDUCATION OFFICES

SALFORD STATION

MUS OF LABOUR & PUMPHOUSE MUS

COLLEGE OF ART & TECHNOLOGY

CROWN COURT

JOHN RYLANDS UNIVERSITY LIB

MAG COURT

OPERA HOUSE

ROYAL EXCHANGE THEATRE

ST ANN'S CH

CROSS STREET CHAPEL

ARNDALE CENTRE

BUS STATION

WELLINGTON INN

POLICE HQ

BOOTLE ST

TOWN HALL

CENTRAL LIBRARY

ART GALL

CENOTAPH

CINEMA

FREE TRADE HALL

GMEX

GRANADA STUDIOS TOUR

MUSEUM OF SCIENCE & INDUSTRY

AIR & SPACE GALLERY

CASTLEFIELD URBAN HERITAGE PARK

OUTDOOR EVENTS AREA

YOUTH HOSTEL

ROMAN FORT

BRIDGEWATER INTERNATIONAL CONCERT HALL

PALACE THEATRE

NATIONAL MUSEUM OF LABOUR HISTORY IN MANCHESTER

CORNERHOUSE

OXFORD ROAD STATION

DANCEHOUSE THEATRE

BBC TV STUDIO

DEANSGATE STATION

COACH STATION

CROWN COURT

SHENA SIMAR COLLEGE

PICCADILLY STATION

MAIN BUILDING

UNIVERSITY OF MANCHESTER INSTITUTE OF SCIENCE & TECHNOLOGY

COLLEGE OF MUSIC

SPORTS CENTRE

MANCHESTER METROPOLITAN UNIVERSITY

UNIVERSITY OF MANCHESTER BUILDINGS

JOHN HOLDEN GALLERY

SCHOOL

St George's Park

Broughton Bridge

Coach Park

St Ann's Square

Piccadilly Gardens

Underpass

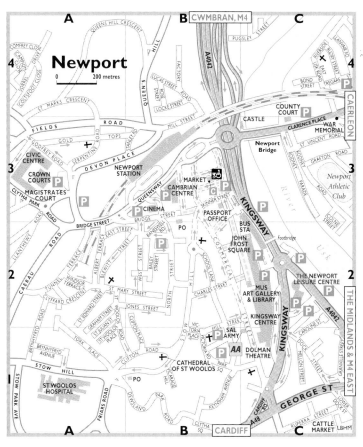

# Newport

Newport is found on atlas page **34**,
grid reference **3188**

**AA shop**
133 Commercial Street, Newport NP9 1LY  C1

| | | | | | | |
|---|---|---|---|---|---|---|
| Albert Terrace | A2 | Fields Road | A3-B3 | Rudry Street | C4 |
| Bailey Street | B2 | Friars Road | A1 | Ruperra Street | C1 |
| Baneswell Road | B2-B3 | George Street | C1 | St Edward Street | A2 |
| Blewitt Street | A2-B2 | Godfrey Road | A3 | St Julian Street | A1-A2 |
| Bond Street | C4 | Gold Tops | A3-B3 | St Marks Crescent | A3-A4 |
| Bridge Street | A2-A3-B2-B3 | Grafton Road | C3 | St Mary Street | A2-B2 |
| Brynhyfryd Avenue | A1 | Graham Street | A1-A2 | St Vincent Road | C3 |
| Brynhyfryd Road | A1-A2 | Granville Street | C1 | St Woolos Place | A1-A2 |
| Caerau Road | A2 | Hill Street | B1-B2-C2 | St Woolos Road | A2-A1-B1 |
| Campion Close | A4 | Jones Street | A2-B2 | School Lane | B2 |
| Cardiff Road | C1 | Keynsham Avenue | B1 | Serpentine Road | A3 |
| Caroline Street | C1-C2 | Kingsway | C1-C2-C3-B3 | Skinner Street | B3 |
| Charles Street | B2 | Llanthewy Road | A2-A3 | Sorrel Drive | A4 |
| Clarence Place | C3-C4 | Llanvair Road | C4 | Stanlet Road | B3 |
| Clifton Place | B2-B1 | Locke Street | B4 | Stow Hill | A1-B1-B2 |
| Clifton Road | A1-B1 | Lower Dock Street | C1 | Stow Park Avenue | A1 |
| Clyffard Crescent | A2 | Lucas Street | B4 | Tregare Street | C4 |
| Clytha Park Road | A3 | Mellon Street | C1 | Tunnel Terrace | A2 |
| Clytha Square | C1 | Mill Street | B3-B4 | Vicarage Hill | B1 |
| Colne Street | C3-C2 | North Street | B2 | Victoria Place | B1 |
| Coltsfoot Close | A4 | Park Square | B1 | Victoria Road | B1 |
| Comfrey Close | A4 | Pugsley Street | B4-C4 | West Street | B2 |
| Commercial Street | B2-C2-C1 | Queen's Hill | B3-B4 | Windsor Terrace | A2 |
| Devon Place | A3-B3 | Queens Hill Crescent | A4-B4 | York Place | A1-A2 |
| Dewsland Park Road | A1-B1 | Queensway | A3-B3 | | |
| Dock Street | C1 | Riverside | C4 | | |
| East Street | A2-B2 | Rodney Parade | C3 | | |
| East Usk Road | C4 | Rodney Road | C3 | | |
| Factory Road | B4 | Rose Street | B4 | | |

**199**

# Manchester

Manchester is found on atlas page **79**,
grid reference **8497**

**AA shop**
St Ann's House, St Ann's Place, Manchester M2 7LP  D5

| | | | | | | | | |
|---|---|---|---|---|---|---|---|---|
| Addington Street | E7-F6 | Brown Street | D4-D5 | Crown Street | B6 | Hanworth Close | F2 | Mount Street | A7-B7 | Sidney Street | E2 |
| Albert Square | C4-D4 | Browncross Street | B5 | Dale Street | E5-F5-F4 | Hardman Street | C4 | Mount Street | C3-C4 | Silk Street | A7 |
| Albion Street | C2-C3 | Bury Street | B6-C6 | Dalton Street | F8 | Henry Street | F5-F6 | Nathan Drive | B6 | Sillavan Way | A7 |
| Angel Street | E6 | Byrom Street | B4-C4 | Dantzic Street | D6-F8 | High Street | E5-E6 | New Bailey Street | B5 | Silvercroft Street | B2 |
| Angela Street | A1-A2 | Cambridge Street | D1-D2 | Dawson Street | A3 | Higher Chatham Street | D1-E1 | New Bridge Street | C7-D7 | Skerry Close | F1 |
| Arlington Street | A7 | Camp Street | B4-C4-C3 | Dean Road | B7-C7 | Hilton Street | E5-F5 | New Elm Road | A3 | Southall Street | C8-D8 |
| Artillery Street | B4-C4 | Canal Street | E3-E4 | Deans Gate | B2 | Hood Street | F6 | New Quay Street | B4-B5 | Southern Street | B3 |
| Arundel Street | A2 | Cannon Street | A7 | Deansgate | C3-C4-C5 | Hope Street | E4 | Newcastle Street | D1-D2 | Southmill Street | C4 |
| Aspin Lane | E7 | Cannon Street | D6-E5 | Dickinson Street | D3-D4 | Hulme Street | C1 | Newton Street | E5-F5 | Sparkle Street | F4 |
| Atherton Street | B4 | Carnarvon Street | D8 | Downing Street | F2 | Hulme Street | C2-D2 | Nicholas Street | D4 | Spring Gardens | D4-D5 |
| Aytoun Street | E4 | Castle Street | B2-B3 | Duke Street | B3 | Humberstone Avenue | C1 | North George Street | A6-A7 | Springfield Lane | C7-C8 |
| Back Piccadilly | E5 | Cateaton Street | D6 | Duke Street | C7 | Humphrey Avenue | C1 | North Hill Street | A7 | Stanley Street | B5 |
| Bank Street | A6 | Cathedral Street | D6 | Ducie Street | F4 | Hunt's Bank | D7 | Norton Street | C6-C7 | Station Approach | F4 |
| Barker Street | C8 | Cavendish Street | E1 | Dutton Street | D7-D8 | Irwell Street | C8 | Oak Street | E6 | Stocks Street | E8 |
| Barrack Street | A1 | Caygill Street | C7 | East Ordsall Lane | A4-A5 | Islington Street | A5 | Old Mount Street | E7 | Stocks Street East | E8 |
| Barton Street | B3 | Chapel Street | A5-B6-C6 | Egerton Street | A2 | Jackson's Row | C4 | Oldham Road | F6-F7 | Store Street | F4 |
| Bendix Street | F6-F7 | Charles Street | E2-E3 | Ellesmere Street | A2 | Jersey Street | F5-F6 | Oldham Street | E5-E6-F6 | Style Street | E7 |
| Blackfriars Road | A7-B7-B6-C6 | Charlotte Street | D4-E4 | Elton Street | A8-B8 | John Dalton Street | C5-D4 | Oxford Street | D3-D2-E2 | Sudell Street | F7-F8 |
| Blackfriars Street | C6 | Charter Street | C8-D8 | Fairfield Street | F3 | John Street | E6 | Park Street | A5 | Sussex Street | A8 |
| Blantyre Street | A2-B2 | Chatham Street | E4 | Faulkner Street | D4-E4 | Julia Street | C8-D8 | Park Street | D8 | Swan Street | E6-F6 |
| Bloom Street | B6 | Chepstow Street | D3 | Fennel Street | D6 | Jutland Street | F4 | Parker Street | E4-E5 | Tariff Street | F5 |
| Bloom Street | E3-E4 | Chester Road | B2 | Fernie Street | D8 | Kays Gardens | A6 | Peru Street | A6 | Tatton Street | A1 |
| Blossom Street | F6 | Chester Road | A1-A2 | Ford Street | A6 | Kincardine Road | F1-F2 | Peter Street | C4-D4 | Thomas Street | E6 |
| Boond Street | C7 | Chester Street | D1-D2-E2 | Fountain Street | D4-D5 | King Street | B6-C6 | Piccadilly | E5-F4 | Thompson Street | F6-F7 |
| Booth Street | C6 | Cheetham Hill Road | D7-D8 | Frederick Street | B6 | King Street | C5-D5 | Pimblett Street | D8 | Tib Street | E5-E6-F6 |
| Booth Street | D4 | Cheviot Street | D8 | Galgate Close | B1 | King Street West | C5 | Port Street | F5 | Todd Street | D6 |
| Booth Street East | E1-F1 | Chorlton Road | A1-A2 | Garden Lane | B6 | Leap Street | C1 | Portland Street | D3-D4-E4 | Tonman Street | B3-C3 |
| Bootle Street | C4 | Chorlton Street | E3-E4 | Gartside Street | B4-B5 | Lever Street | E5-F5-F6 | Potato Wharf | A3 | Trafford Street | C3 |
| Boundary Street | E8-F8 | Church Street | E5 | Garwood Street | C2-C1 | Linby Street | B1 | Princess Street | D4-E3-E2 | Travis Street | F3 |
| Brancaster Road | E2 | City Road | C2 | George Leigh Street | F6 | Little Peter Street | C2 | Quay Street | B4-C4 | Trinity Way | B5-B6-B7-C7 |
| Brazennose Street | C4 | Cleminson Street | A6 | George Street | A5 | Liverpool Road | A4-A3-B3 | Quay Street | B5-B6 | Turner Street | E6 |
| Bridge Street | B5-C5 | Clowes Street | C6 | George Street | D3-D4-E4 | Lloyd Street | C4 | Queen Street | C4 | Tysoe Gardens | A6 |
| Bridgewater Street | B3 | Colbeck Close | A1-B1 | Gore Street | B5 | London Road | F3-F4 | Queen Street | B7-C7 | Upper Brook Street | E1-F1 |
| Bridgewater Street | B7-B8 | Cornell Street | F7 | Gould Street | E8-F7 | Long Millgate | D6-D7 | Quenby Street | A1 | Viaduct Street | C6 |
| Briggs Street | A7 | Corporation Street | D6-D7-E7 | Goulden Street | F6-F7 | Longworth Street | C3-C4 | Red Bank | E7-E8 | Victoria Bridge Street | C6 |
| Broad Street | F4 | Cottenham Lane | B8 | Granby Row | E3 | Lord Street | D8-E8 | Richmond Street | E3-E4 | Victoria Street | C6-D6 |
| Brook Street | E2 | Cross Keys Street | F6-F7 | Gravel Lane | C6-C7 | Lordsmead Street | A1 | River Street | C2 | Wadeson Road | F2 |
| Brotherton Drive | A6 | Cross Street | D5 | Great Ancoats Street | F5-F6 | Lower Broughton Road | A8 | Robert Street | D8 | Water Street | A3-A4-B4 |
| Brown Street | B6-C6-C5 | Crown Street | B2 | Great Bridgewater Street | C3-D3 | Lower Byrom Street | B3-B4 | Roby Street | E4 | Watson Street | C3-C4 |
| | | | | Great Clowes Street | A8 | Lower Camp Street | D2 | Rochdale Road | E7-F7-F8 | Wellington Street | A7-B7 |
| | | | | Great Ducie Street | C8-C7-D7 | Lower Mosley Street | C3-D3 | Rockdove Avenue | C1 | West King Street | B7 |
| | | | | Great George Street | A6 | Lower Moss Lane | A1 | Roger Street | E8 | West Mosley Street | D4-D5 |
| | | | | Great Jackson Street | B2-C2 | Lower Ormond Street | D2 | Rosamund Drive | A6 | Whitekirk Close | F1 |
| | | | | Great Marlborough Street | D2 | Loxford Street | D1 | Sackville Street | E2-E3-E4 | Whitworth Street | D3-E3 |
| | | | | Greengate West | B7 | Ludgate Hill | E7-F7 | St Ann Street | C5-D5 | Whitworth Street West | C3-D3 |
| | | | | Greengate | C7 | Ludgate Street | E7 | St Ann's Square | C5-D5 | Wilburn Street | A4 |
| | | | | Grosvenor Street | E1-F2 | Major Street | E3-E4 | St Chad Street | D8-E8 | William Street | B6 |
| | | | | Hampson Street | A4 | Mancunian Way | B2-F2 | St James Street | D3-D4 | Wilmott Street | D1-D2 |
| | | | | Hanover Street | D7-E6 | Market Street | D5-E5 | St John Street | B4-C4 | Windmill Street | C3-C4 |
| | | | | | | Marshall Street | E7-F7-F6 | St Mary's Parsonage | C5 | Withy Grove | D6 |
| | | | | | | Mary Street | C7-C8 | St Peter's Square | D4 | Wood Street | C5 |
| | | | | | | Mayan Avenue | A6 | St Simon Street | A8-B8 | Worsley Street | A2 |
| | | | | | | Medlock Street | C2 | St Stephen Street | A6-B6 | York Street | B1 |
| | | | | | | Melbourne Street | B2 | Scotforth Close | A1-B1 | York Street | E2-E3 |
| | | | | | | Miller Street | E7 | Sharp Street | E7-F7 | York Street | D5-E4 |
| | | | | | | Milnrow Close | F2 | Shaw Street | D7-D8 | York Street | E1-E2 |
| | | | | | | Minshull Street | E4 | Sherborne Street | B8-C8 | Young Street | B4 |
| | | | | | | Mirabel Street | C7 | Sherratt Street | F6 | | |
| | | | | | | Mosley Street | D4 | Shudehill | D6-E6 | | |

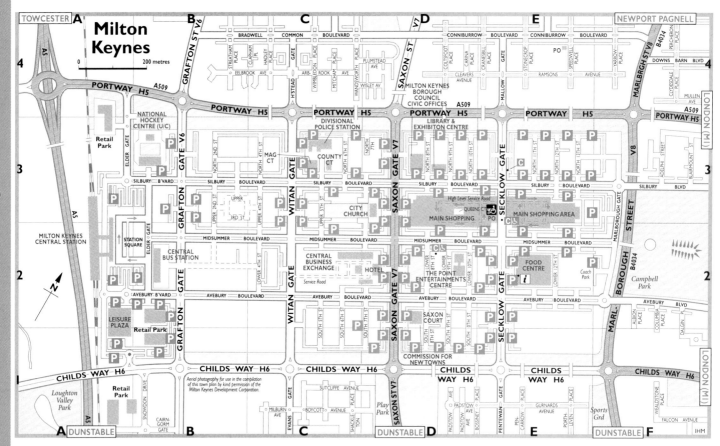

# Milton Keynes

Milton Keynes is found on atlas page **38**,
grid reference **8537**

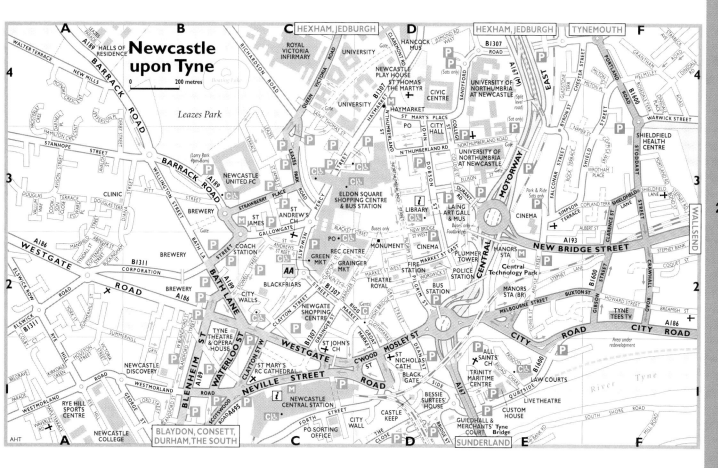

# Newcastle upon Tyne

Newcastle upon Tyne is found on atlas page **103**,
grid reference **2464**

### AA shop

33–35 Whitecross Way, Eldon Centre, Newcastle upon Tyne NE1 7YN   C2

202

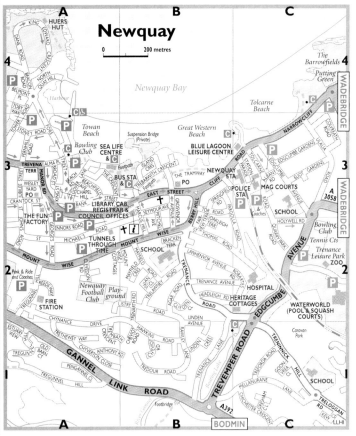

# Newquay

Newquay is found on atlas page **4**,
grid reference **8**1**61**

| Street | Grid | Street | Grid | Street | Grid |
|---|---|---|---|---|---|
| Agar Road | B2 | Linden Crescent | B1 | Trevena Terrace | A3 |
| Albany Road | C3 | Listry Road | A2-B2 | Ulalia Road | C3 |
| Alma Place | A3 | Manor Road | A3 | Vivian Close | B2 |
| Anthony Road | A1-B1 | Marcus Hill | B2-B3 | Wesley Yard | A3 |
| Bank Street | A3-B3 | Mayfield Crescent | B2 | | |
| Beach Road | A3 | Mayfield Road | B2 | | |
| Beachfield Avenue | A3 | Mellanurane Lane | B1-C1 | | |
| Beacon Road | A4 | Mitchell Avenue | B2-B3 | | |
| Belmont Place | A4 | Mount Wise | A2-B2 | | |
| Berry Hill | B2-B3 | Mount Wise Cottages | A2-B2 | | |
| Bracken Terrace | B2 | Narrowcliff | C3-C4 | | |
| Broad Street | A3 | North Quay Hill | A4 | | |
| Chapel Hill | A3 | Oakleigh Terrace | B2 | | |
| Cheviot Road | B1 | Old Barn Court | A1 | | |
| Chichester Crescent | C1 | Pargolla Road | B3-C2 | | |
| Chynance Drive | A1-A2 | Pengannel Close | A1 | | |
| Chyverton Close | A1 | Quarry Park Road | C2 | | |
| Clevedon Road | A2 | Rawley Lane | B1 | | |
| Clifden Close | B2 | Reeds Way | A2 | | |
| Cliff Road | B3-C3 | Robartes Road | C2 | | |
| Colvreath Road | C3 | St George's Road | A2-A3 | | |
| Crantock Street | A3 | St John's Road | A2-A3 | | |
| Dane Road | A4 | St Michael's Road | A2-B2 | | |
| East Street | B3 | St Thomas Road | B2-C2 | | |
| Edgcumbe Avenue | C2-C3 | Seymour Avenue | B3 | | |
| Edgcumbe Gardens | C3 | Springfield Road | B3 | | |
| Eliot Gardens | C3 | Station Parade | C3 | | |
| Ennors Road | A2 | Sydney Road | A3 | | |
| Estuary View | A1 | The Crescent | A3 | | |
| Fairview Terrace | B2-B3 | Toby Way | A4 | | |
| Fernhill Road | A3 | Tolcarne Road | C3 | | |
| Fore Street | A3-A4 | Tor Road | B3 | | |
| Gannel Link Road | A2-A1-B1 | Tower Road | A3-A4 | | |
| Goonvrea Close | C1 | Trebarwith Crescent | B3 | | |
| Gover Lane | A3 | Tredour Road | B1 | | |
| Gresham Close | C1 | Treforda Road | C1 | | |
| Grosvenor Avenue | B2-B3 | Tregunnel Hill | A1-A2 | | |
| Hawkins Road | B1 | Trelawney Road | B2 | | |
| Headleigh Road | B2 | Treloggan Road | C1 | | |
| Holywell Road | C2 | Trembath Crescent | A1-B1 | | |
| Island Crescent | B3 | Trenance Avenue | B2-C2 | | |
| Jubilee Street | A3 | Trenance Lane | B1-B2 | | |
| Kew Close | C1 | Trenance Road | B2-C2 | | |
| King Edward Crescent | A4 | Trenarth Road | B2 | | |
| King Street | A3 | Treninnick Hill | C1 | | |
| Lanhenvor Avenue | B2 | Trethewey Way | A1 | | |
| Linden Avenue | B1-B2 | Trevemper Road | B1-C1 | | |

# Northampton

Northampton is found on atlas page **49**,
grid reference **7**5**60**

**AA shop**
67 Abington Street, Northampton NN1 2BH          C3

| Street | Grid | Street | Grid | Street | Grid |
|---|---|---|---|---|---|
| Abington Square | C3 | Georges Street | A4 | Swan Street | B1-B2 |
| Abington Street | B2-B3-C3 | Gold Street | A2 | The Drappery | A2-B2 |
| Albion Place | B1-B2 | Grafton Street | A4 | The Riding | B2-C2 |
| Alcombe Road | C4 | Great Russell Street | A4 | Tower Street | A3 |
| Alexandra Road | C2-C3 | Greyfriars | A3-B3-C3 | Upper Bath Street | A3 |
| Althorp Street | A3 | Guildhall Road | B1-B2 | Upper Mounts | B3-B4 |
| Angel Street | B2 | Hazelwood Road | C2 | Upper Priory Street | A4 |
| Arundel Street | A4 | Herbert Street | A3 | Victoria Gardens | B1 |
| Ash Street | B4 | Horsemarket | A2-A3 | Victoria Promenade | B1-C1 |
| Bailiff Street | B4 | Horseshoe Street | A1-A2 | Victoria Street | B3-B4 |
| Barrack Road | A4-B4 | Hunter Street | C4 | Wellington Street | B3-C3 |
| Bath Street | A3 | King Street | A2 | William Street | A3 |
| Bedford Road | C1 | Kingswell | A1-A2 | York Road | C2-C3 |
| Bidders Close | B1 | Ladys Lane | A3-B3-C3 | | |
| Billing Road | C2 | Lower Harding Street | A4 | | |
| Bradshaw Street | A2-A3 | Lower Mounts | C3 | | |
| Bridge Street | A1-A2 | Lower Priory Street | A4 | | |
| Broad Street | A3-A4 | Margaret Street | B4 | | |
| Campbell Street | A4-B4 | Market Square | B2 | | |
| Castillian Street | B2 | Mayor Hold | A3 | | |
| Castle Street | A3 | Mercer's Row | B2 | | |
| Cattlemarket Road | B1 | Newland | B3 | | |
| Charles Street | B4-C4 | Oak Street | B4 | | |
| Cheyne Walk | C1-C2 | Overstone Road | C3-C4 | | |
| Church Lane | A3-B3-B4 | Pike Lane | A2-A3 | | |
| Clare Street | C4 | Quorn Way | A4 | | |
| Cloutsham Street | C4 | Regent Street | A4 | | |
| College Street | A2 | Robert Street | B4 | | |
| Commercial Street | A1 | St Andrew's Street | A3-A4 | | |
| Connaught Street | B4 | St Giles Square | B2 | | |
| Cranstoun Street | B4-C4 | St Giles Street | B2-C2 | | |
| Craven Street | B4-C4 | St Giles Terrace | C2-C3 | | |
| Crispin Street | A3 | St James Street | A1 | | |
| Deal Street | B4 | St John's Street | B1 | | |
| Derngate | C1-C2-B2 | St Katherine's Street | A2 | | |
| Duke Street | B4-C4 | St Mary's Street | A2 | | |
| Dunster Street | C3-C4 | St Michael's Road | C3 | | |
| Earl Street | B3-C4 | St Peter's Way | A1 | | |
| Elm Street | B4 | Sheep Street | A3-A4 | | |
| Fetter Street | B1-B2 | Silver Street | A3 | | |
| Foundry Street | A1 | Somerset Street | C4 | | |
| Gas Street | A1 | Spencer Parade | C2 | | |
| George Row | B2 | Spring Gardens | C2 | | |

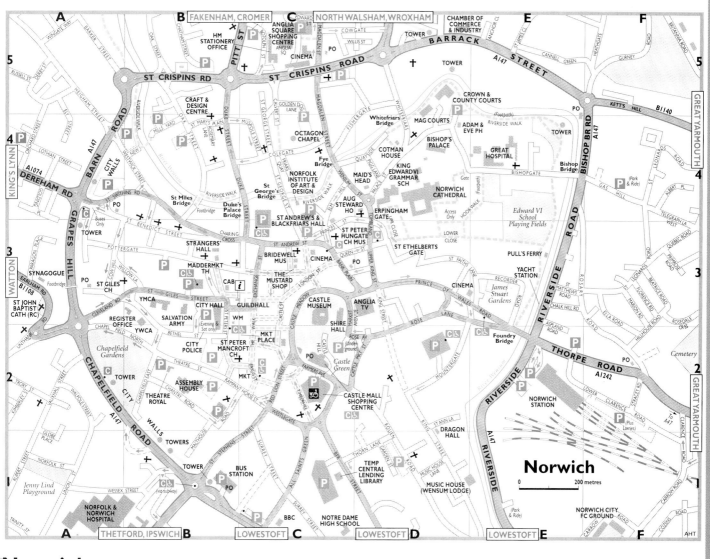

# Norwich

Norwich is found on atlas page **67**,
grid reference **2308**

**AA shop**
Fanum House, 126 Thorpe Road, Norwich NR1 1RL

| | | | | | | | | |
|---|---|---|---|---|---|---|---|---|
| Albert Place | F4 | Chapelfield Road | A2-B2-B1 | Grapes Hill | A3-A4 | Prince of Wales Road | F3 | St Matthews Road | F3-F4 | Wingate Way | C5-D5 |
| All Saints Green | C1 | Charing Cross | B3 | Gurney Road | F5 | Princes Street | D3-E3 | St Peters Street | B4 | | A3-B3 |
| Anchor Close | E5 | Chatham Street | B5 | Heathgate | F5 | Quayside | C3 | St Stephens Street | E3 | | A5 |
| Aspland Road | E2-E3 | Clarence Road | F1-F2 | Heigham Street | A4-A5 | Quebec Road | C4-D4 | St Swithins Road | B2-B3 |
| Barker Street | A5 | Cleveland Road | A3-B3 | Hillhouse Road | F2-F3 | Queen Street | F3 | Stracey Road | B1-C1-C2 |
| Barn Road | A4-A5 | Colegate | B4-C4 | Kett's Hill | F4-F5 | Rampant Horse Street | C3-D3 | Surrey Street | A4-B4-B3 |
| Barrack Street | D5-E5 | Cow Hill | A3 | Kimberley Street | A2 | Recorder Road | B2-C2 | Telegraph Lane West | F2 |
| Beatrice Road | F3 | Cowgate | C5-D5 | King Street | D3-D2-D1-E1 | Red Lion Street | E3 | The Walk | C1-C2 |
| Ber Street | C2-C1-D1 | Cozens Road | F1 | London Street | C3 | Riverside | C2 | Theatre Street | F3-F4 |
| Bethel Street | B2-B3 | Derby Street | A5 | Lothian Street | A4 | Riverside Road | E1-E2 | Thorn Lane | C2-C3 |
| Bishop Road | E4-F4 | Dereham Road | A3 | Lower Clarence Road | E2-F2-F1 | Rosary Road | E2-E3-E4 | Thorpe Road | B2 |
| Bishopgate | E4 | Duke Street | B5-B4-C4-C3 | Magdalen Street | C4-C5 | Rose Avenue | E4-E3-F3-F2 | Timberhill | C1-D1 |
| Botolph Street | C5 | Earlham Road | A3 | Malthouse Road | B1-B2 | Rose Lane | C2-D2 | Tombland | E2-F2 |
| Brigg Street | C2 | Edward Street | C5 | Marion Road | F3 | Rosedale Crescent | D2-D3-E3-E2 | Trinity Street | C2 |
| Britannia Road | F5 | Ella Road | F2-F3 | Market Avenue | C2-C3 | Rosemary Lane | F3 | Trory Street | D3-D4 |
| Calvert Street | C4-C5 | Elm Hill | C3-C4 | Mountergate | D2 | Rouen Road | B4 | Union Street | A1 |
| Cannell Green | E5-F5 | Ely Street | A4-A5 | Music House Lane | D1 | Rupert Street | C2-D2-D1 | Unthank Road | A2 |
| Carrow Road | F1 | Exchange Street | C3 | Muspole Street | B4-C4 | Russell Street | A1-A2 | Upper King Street | A1 |
| Castle Hill | C2 | Farmers Avenue | C2 | New Mills Yard | B4 | St Andrew Street | A5 | Vauxhall Street | A2-A3 |
| Castle Meadow | C2-C3 | Fishergate | C4-D5 | Norfolk Street | A1 | St Ann Lane | C3 | Walpole Street | D3 |
| Castle Street | C3 | Florence Road | F3 | Oak Street | B4-B5 | St Benedict Street | D2 | Wensum Street | A2 |
| Cattle Market Street | C2-D2 | Friars Quay | C4 | Orchard Street | A4-A5 | St Crispins Road | A4-B3 | Wessex Street | A2 |
| Chalk Hill Road | E3 | Garden Street | D1 | Palace Street | D4 | St Faiths Lane | B5-C5-D5 | Westlegate | C4-D4 |
| Chantry Road | B2 | Gas Hill | F4 | Paragon Place | A3 | St George Street | D3-E3 | Westwick Street | A1-B1 |
| Chapel Field North | A2-B2 | Globe Place | A1-A2 | Pigg Lane | D4 | St Giles Street | C3-C4-C5 | Whitefriars | C2 |
| Chapelfield East | B2 | Golden Dog Lane | C5 | Pitt Street | B5-C5 | St James Close | B3 | Willis Street | A4-B4 |
| | | Golding Place | A3-A4 | Pottergate | A3-B3 | St Leonards Road | E5 | Willow Lane | D4-D5 |
| | | | | Primrose Road | | St Mary's Plain | | |

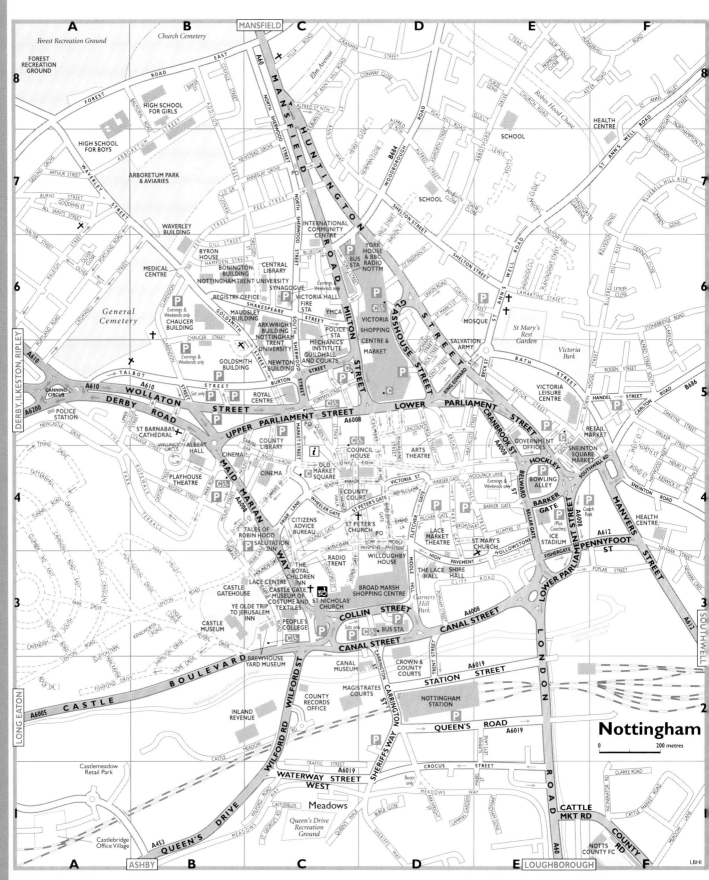

Nottingham

0      200 metres

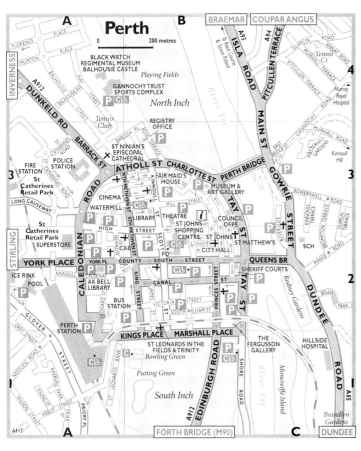

# Perth

Perth is found on atlas page **126**,
grid reference **1123**

| | | | | | |
|---|---|---|---|---|---|
| Abbot Street | A1 | Kings Place | A1-B1 | Tay Street | B1-B3 |
| Annat Road | C4 | Kinnoull Causeway | A2 | Victoria Street | B2 |
| Atholl Street | A3-B3 | Kinnoull Street | B3 | Wilson Street | A1 |
| Balhousie Avenue | A1 | Kinnoull Terrace | C2-C3 | York Place | A2 |
| Balhousie Street | A3-A4 | Leonard Street | A2 | Young Street | A1 |
| Barossa Place | A3-B3 | Long Causeway | A3 | | |
| Barrack Street | A3 | Main Street | C3-C4 | | |
| Bellwood Park | C2 | Manse Road | C2 | | |
| Bowerswell Road | C3 | Marshall Place | B1 | | |
| Brompton Terrace | C2-C3 | Mill Street | B3 | | |
| Caledonian Road | A2-A3 | Muirhall Road | C3 | | |
| Canal Street | B2 | Muirhall Terrace | C4 | | |
| Charlotte Street | B3 | Muirton Place | A4 | | |
| County South Street | A2-B2 | Needless Road | A1 | | |
| Dundee Road | C1-C2 | Newrow | A2 | | |
| Dunkeld Street | A3-A4 | North Methven Street | A3-B3 | | |
| Dupplin Road | C4 | Perth Bridge | B3-C3 | | |
| Dupplin Terrace | C2-C3 | Pitcullen Terrace | C4 | | |
| East Bridge Street | C3 | Potterhill Gardens | C3 | | |
| Edinburgh Road | B1 | Princes Street | B2 | | |
| Florence Place | A4 | Priory Place | A1 | | |
| Friar Street | A1 | Queen's Bridge | C2 | | |
| Gannochy Road | C3-C4 | Raeburn Park | A1 | | |
| Glover Street | A1-A2 | Riverside | C2-C3 | | |
| Gowrie Street | C2-C3 | Rose Terrace | B3 | | |
| Grey Street | A1-A2 | St Catherines Road | A3 | | |
| Hay Street | A3-A4 | St Leonards Bank | A1 | | |
| High Street | A2-B2 | Scott Street | B2 | | |
| Isla Road | B4-C4 | Shore Road | B1 | | |
| James Street | B2 | South Methven Street | B2-B3 | | |
| King Street | B2 | South William Street | B2 | | |

# Nottingham

Nottingham is found on atlas page **62**,
grid reference **5739**

**AA shop**
484 Derby Road, Nottingham NG7 2GT

| | | | | | | | | | |
|---|---|---|---|---|---|---|---|---|---|
| Abbotsford Drive | D6-D7-E7-E8 | Cattle Market Road | E1-F1 | George Street | D4-D5 | London Road | E1-E2-E3 | Plantagenet Street | E6 | Talbot Street | A5-B5 |
| Addison Street | B8-B7-C7 | Cavendish Crescent South | A3 | Gill Street | B6-C6 | Long Row | C4-D4 | Plumptre Street | E4 | Tattershall Drive | A4 |
| Alfred Street North | C8-D8-D7 | Cavendish Road East | A3-A4 | Glasshouse Street | D5-D6 | Low Pavement | D4 | Popham Street | D3 | Teak Close | E8 |
| Alfred Street | D7 | Chapel Bar | B4-C4 | Goldsmith Street | B6-C6-C5 | Lower Parliament Street | D5-E5-E3 | Poplar Street | E3-F3 | Tennis Drive | A4-A5 |
| Alfred Street South | F5-F6 | Chaucer Street | B5-B6 | Goodwin Street | A7 | Lyton Close | F6 | Portland Road | A5-A6-A7 | The Ropewalk | A5-A4-B4 |
| All Saints Street | A7 | Church Road | E8 | Great Freeman Street | D6 | Mabel Street | E1 | Primrose Close | E8 | Thomas Close | E7 |
| Angel Row | C4 | Clarence Street | F5-F6 | Hamilton Drive | B2-B3 | Maid Marian Way | B4-C4-C3 | Queen Street | C4-C5 | Thurland Street | D4-D5 |
| Annesley Grove | B7-C7 | Clarendon Street | B5-B6 | Hampden Street | B6-C6 | Mansfield Grove | B7 | Queen's Drive | B1-C1 | Traffic Street | C1-D1 |
| Arboretum Street | A7-B7-B8 | Clarke Road | F1 | Handel Street | F5 | Mansfield Road | C6-C7-C8 | Queen's Road | D2-E2 | Trent Street | D2-D3 |
| Arkwright Street | D1 | Cliff Road | D3-E3 | Haywood Street | F4-F5 | Manvers Street | F3-F4 | Queen's Walk | C1-D1 | Tulip Avenue | E8 |
| Arthur Street | A7 | Clifton Terrace | A2-A3 | Heathcote Street | D4-D5-E5 | Market Street | C4-C5 | Raleigh Street | A6-A7 | Tunnel Road | A4 |
| Ashforth Street | D7-D8 | Clumber Road East | A3-A4 | Henry Street | F4 | Meadow Lane | F1 | Regent Street | B4 | Union Road | D6 |
| Aster Road | E8-F8 | Clumber Street | D4-D5 | Heskey Close | C7-D7-D8 | Meadows Way | B1-C1-D1-E1 | Rick Street | D5 | Upper College Street | A4-A5 |
| Baker Street | B8 | College Street | A5-B5-B4 | High Pavement | D4-D3-E3 | Middle Hill | D3 | Robin Hood Street | E5-F5-F6 | Upper Eldon Street | F4 |
| Balmoral Road | A8-B8-B7 | Collin Street | C3-D3 | Hockley | E4 | Middle Pavement | D4 | Rock Drive | A2 | Upper Parliament Street | B5-C5 |
| Barker Gate | E4 | Colville Street | B8 | Holles Crescent | A3 | Mount Street | B4-C4 | Roden Street | F5 | Uppingham Gardens | E1 |
| Bath Street | E5 | Conway Close | C8-D8 | Hollowstone | E3-E4 | Newark Crescent | F3 | St Ann's Hill Road | C8 | Victoria Street | D4 |
| Beck Street | E5 | County Road | F1 | Hope Drive | B2-B3 | Newark Street | F3-F4 | St Ann's Valley | F7-F8 | Villa Road | C8 |
| Bellar Gate | E4 | Cranbrook Street | E4-E5 | Hound's Gate | C3-C4 | Newcastle Drive | A4-A5 | St Ann's Way | C7-C8 | Wadhursts Gardens | E7-F7 |
| Belward Street | E4 | Cranmer Street | C8-D8 | Howard Street | D5-D6 | Newstead Grove | B7-C7 | St Ann's Well Road | E6-E7-F7-F8 | Walker Street | F4-F5 |
| Bluebell Hill Rise | F6-F7 | Crocus Street | D1-E1 | Hungerhill Road | E8-F8 | Norman Close | D7 | St George's Road | C1-D1 | Walter Street | A6-A7 |
| Bluecoat Street | C6 | Cromwell Street | A5-A6-B6 | Huntingdon Drive | A4-A3-B3 | North Sherwood Street | C8-C6 | St James Street | B4-C4 | Warser Gate | D4 |
| Bond Street | F4 | Curzon Street | D6-E6 | Huntingdon Street | C7-D6-D5-E5 | North Street | F4 | St James's Terrace | B3-B4 | Wasnidge Close | E6 |
| Bottle Lane | D4 | Dakeyne Street | F5 | Incinerator Road | F1 | Northampton Street | F7-F8 | St Mark's Street | D6 | Waterway Street West | C1-D1 |
| Bridlesmith Gate | D4 | Dane Close | D7-E7 | Instow Rise | E6-E7 | Ogle Drive | B3 | St Mary's Gate | D3-D4 | Watkin Street | D6-D7 |
| Broad Stoney Street | D5-D4-E4 | Dennett Close | F6 | Kelvedon Gardens | F6-F7 | Oliver Close | A6 | St Peter's Gate | C4-D4 | Waverley Street | A8-A7-B7-B6 |
| Broadway | D4-E4 | Derby Road | A5-B5 | Kenilworth Road | B3 | Oliver Street | A6 | Shakespeare Street | B6-C6 | Well Street | D6-D7 |
| Brook Street | E5 | Dreyden Street | C6 | Kent Street | D5 | Oxford Street | B4 | Shelton Street | D7-D6-E6 | West Street | F4-F5 |
| Burge Close | D1 | Ellis Court | E8 | Keswick Street | F4 | Park Drive | A3 | Sheriffs Way | D1-D2 | Westgate Street | F7-F8 |
| Burns Street | A7 | Exchange Walk | C4 | Kilburn Street | C7-C8 | Park Ravine | A2 | Sneinton Road | F4 | Wheeler Gate | C4 |
| Byard Lane | D4 | Fishergate | E3-E4 | King Edward Street | D5-E5 | Park Row | B4 | South Parade | C4-D4 | Wilford Road | C1-C2 |
| Canal Street | C3-D3-E3 | Fishpond Drive | A2-B2 | King Street | C4-C5 | Park Terrace | A4-B4 | South Road | A3 | Wilford Street | C2-C3 |
| Carlton Road | F5 | Fletcher Gate | D4 | Lamartine Street | E6 | Park Valley | A4-B4-B3 | South Sherwood Street | C5-C6 | Wollaton Street | A5-B5-C5 |
| Carrington Street | D2-D3 | Forest Road East | A7-A8-B8-C8 | Lammas Gardens | D1 | Peas Hill Road | D7-D8 | Southampton Street | F7 | Woodborough Road | D7-D8 |
| Castle Boulevard | A2-B2 | Forman Street | C5 | Lenton Road | A2-A3-B3 | Peel Street | B6-B7-C7 | Southwell Road | E4-F4 | Woolpack Lane | D4-E4 |
| Castle Meadow Road | B2-C2 | Friar Lane | C3-C4 | Lewis Close | E7 | Pennyfoot Street | E4-F4 | Stanford Street | C3 | York Street | C6 |
| Castle Road | C3 | Furze Gardens | E8 | Limmen Gardens | F7 | Penrhyn Close | D7 | Station Street | D2-E2 | | |
| Castlefields | C1 | Gedling Grove | A7 | Lincoln Street | D5 | Peveril Drive | B3 | Stonebridge Road | E6-F6 | | |
| Castlegate | C3-C4 | Gedling Street | E4-E5 | Lister Gate | C3 | Pilcher Gate | D4 | Summer Leys Lane | E2 | | |

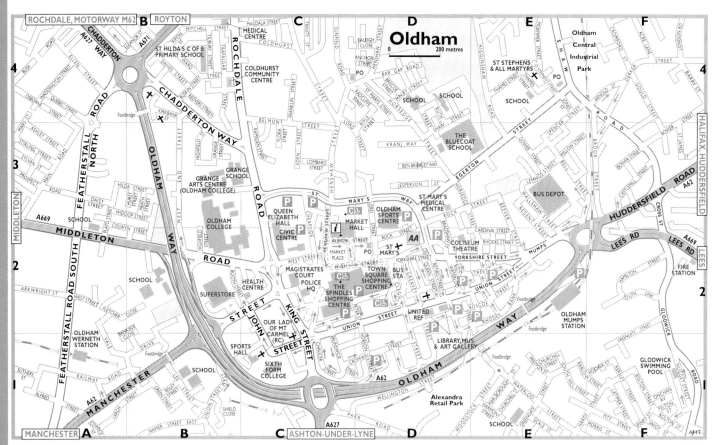

# Oldham

Oldham is found on atlas page **79**,
grid reference **9204**

### AA shop
37 Yorkshire Street, Oldham OL1 3RZ                    D2

| | | | | | | | | | | |
|---|---|---|---|---|---|---|---|---|---|---|
| Acre Lane | F4 | Davies Street | B4 | Kranj Way | D3 | Retiro Street | D2 | West End Street | B2-B3-B4 |
| Albion Street | C2-D2 | Derker Street | F4 | Larch Street | A1-B1 | Rhodes Bank | E2 | West Street | A2 |
| Alfred Street | A1 | Eden Street | C3 | Latimer Street | F1 | Rhodes Street | E2 | West Street | C2 |
| Anchor Street | C4-D4 | Egerton Street | D3-E3-E4 | Lee Street | B1 | Rifle Street | D3-D4 | Widdop Street | A3-B3 |
| Arkwright Street | A2 | Eleanor Street | A4-B4 | Lees Road | F2 | Ripon Street | B4 | Willow Street | E3 |
| Arnold Street | F4 | Ellen Street | A4 | Lemnos Street | E3 | Rochdale Road | B4-B3-C3-C2 | Woodstock Street | D1-E1 |
| Ashley Street | A3-A4 | Featherstall North Road | A3-A4 | Lombard Street | C3 | Rock Street | D2-D3-E3 | Yorkshire Street | D2-E2 |
| Bankside Close | A1-B1-B2 | Featherstall Road South | A1-A2 | London Road | F4 | Roscoe Street | D2-D3 | | |
| Bar Gap Road | D4 | Felton Street | F1 | Lord Street | C4-D3-D2 | Ruskin Street | B4 | | |
| Barlow Street | E1-F1 | Fletcher Close | A2-B2 | Magdala Street | B4-C4 | Ruth Street | D3-D4 | | |
| Barry Street | F4 | Flora Street | C3 | Main Road | A3 | St James Street | F3 | | |
| Beever Street | E2-E3 | Franklin Street | C3 | Malby Street | D4 | St Mary's Way | C3-D3 | | |
| Bell Street | E3 | George Street | C2 | Manchester Street | A1-B1-B2-C2 | St Marys Street | D4 | | |
| Belmont Street | C3-C4 | Glodwick Road | F1-F2 | Marlborough Street | E1 | St Stephen's Street | E4 | | |
| Ben Brierley Way | D3 | Gould Street | F3-F4 | Mars Street | A3-A4 | Savoy Street | F1 | | |
| Bisley Street | B1 | Gower Street | E3 | Middleton Road | A3-A2-B2-C2 | Shaw Road | E4-F4-F3 | | |
| Bolton Street | F1 | Grange Street | B3 | Mitchell Street | B4 | Shaw Street | D3-D4 | | |
| Booth Street | B2-C2 | Greaves Street | D2-D1 | Morris Street | E1-F1 | Shield Close | B1 | | |
| Bow Street | D2-E2 | Green Street | B1 | Mortimer Street | E4 | Sickle Street | E1 | | |
| Bower Street | F3-F4 | Greengate Street | E1-F1-F2 | Mumps | E2 | South Link | F2 | | |
| Bradshaw Street | D2-D3 | Hamilton Street | F2 | Neath Street | B3 | Southill Street | E1-F1 | | |
| Briscoe Street | D4 | Hardy Street | E1-F1 | Nugget Street | F1 | Spencer Street | E3-E4 | | |
| Brook Street | F3-F4 | Harmony Street | E1 | Oldham Way | B4-B1-D1-E2 | Spinks Street | F1 | | |
| Brunswick Street | C1-D1 | Henshaw Street | C2-C3-C4-D4 | Onchan Avenue | F1 | Stirling Street | A3 | | |
| Busk Road | A4 | Higginshaw Road | D4-E4-E3 | Osborne Street | A3-A4 | Sunfield Road | C4 | | |
| Cardinal Street | E2 | High Street | C2-D2 | Park Road | C1-D1 | Suthers Street | A1 | | |
| Castlemill Street | F3 | Highfield Street | B2-B3 | Peter Street | C2-D2 | Sylvan Street | A3 | | |
| Chadderton Way | A4-B4-B3 | Hilda Street | A3-B3 | Pitt Street | E1-F1 | Thames Street | E4 | | |
| Chaucer Street | C1 | Hobson Street | D2-D1 | Plato Street | A2-A3 | Tilbury Street | B4 | | |
| Cheapside Street | C2-C3 | Hooper Street | E1-F1 | Preston Street | E1 | Trafalgar Street | B3-B4 | | |
| Churchill Street | E1 | Horsedge Street | D4-D3-E2 | Prospect Road | A3 | Trinity Street | C4 | | |
| Clegg Street | D2-D1 | Huddersfield Road | F3 | Quebec Street | A4 | Union Street | C1-C2-D2-E2 | | |
| Coldhurst Street | B4-C4 | Hurst Street | A3-B3 | Queen Street | D2 | Union Street West | B1 | | |
| Colwyn Street | A3-A2-B2 | Jesperson Street | D3 | Radcliffe Street | C4-D4 | Vale Drive | A2-A1-B1 | | |
| Coppice Street | A1 | John Street | C2-C1 | Railway Road | A1-B1 | Waddington Street | A4 | | |
| Cromford Street | F4 | Jones Street | E4 | Raleigh Close | C4-D4 | Wallshaw Street | E2-E3 | | |
| Cromwell Street | C1-D1 | Kersley Street | F1 | Ramsden Street | C3 | Ward Street | B4 | | |
| Cross Street | F2-F3 | King Street | C2-C1 | Redvers Street | B4 | Waterloo Street | D2-E1 | | |
| Daisy Street | A3 | Kirkbank Street | B4 | Regent Street | E2-E3 | Wellington Street | C1-D1-D2 | | |

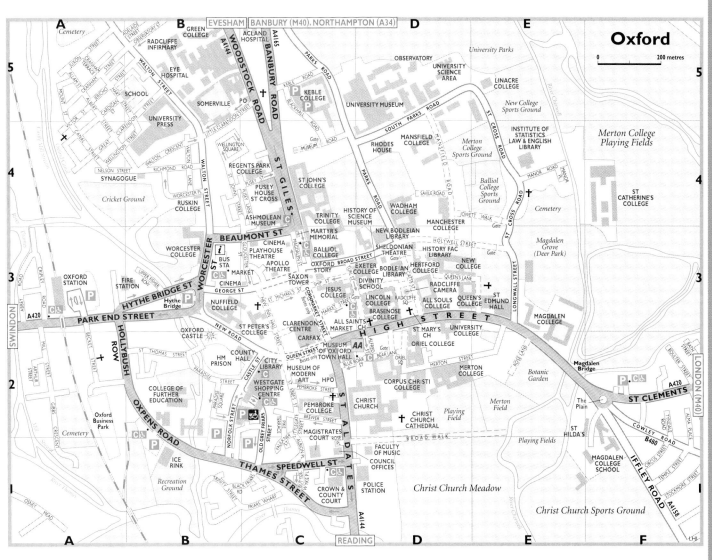

# Oxford

Oxford is found on atlas page **37**,
grid reference **5106**

**AA shop**
133–134 High Street, Oxford OX1 4DN                    C2

| | | | | | | | | |
|---|---|---|---|---|---|---|---|---|
| Abbey Road | A3 | Cowley Road | F1-F2 | Market Street | C3 | Rose Place | C1 | Worcester Place | B4 |
| Adelaide Street | B5 | Cranham Street | A5-B5 | Merton Street | D2-E2 | St Aldates | C1-C2 | Worcester Street | B3 |
| Albert Street | A4-A5 | Cranham Terrace | A5 | Mill Street | A2-A3 | St Clements | F2 | | |
| Albion Place | C1 | Cripley Road | A3 | Mount Street | A5 | St Cross Road | E3-E4-E5 | | |
| Alfred Street | D2 | Faulkner Street | C1-C2 | Museum Road | C4 | St Ebbe's Street | C2 | | |
| Allam Street | A5 | Friars Wharf | C1 | Nelson Street | A4-B4 | St Giles | C4 | | |
| Alma Place | F1-F2 | George Street | B3-C3 | New Inn Hall Street | C2-C3 | St Johns Street | B4-C4 | | |
| Arthur Street | A2 | Gibbs Crescent | A1-A2 | New Road | B3-B2-C2 | St Michael's Street | C3 | | |
| Banbury Road | C4-C5 | Gloucester Street | C3 | Norfolk Street | B1-B2 | St Thomas Street | B2 | | |
| Bath Street | F2 | Great Clarendon Street | A4-B4-B5 | Observatory Street | B5 | Savile Road | D4 | | |
| Bear Lane | D2 | Hart Street | A5-B5 | Old Grey Friars Street | C1-C2 | Ship Street | C3 | | |
| Beaumont Street | B3-C3 | High Street | C2-D3-E3-E2 | Oriel Square | D2 | South Parks Road | D4-D5 | | |
| Becket Street | A2-A3 | Hollybush Row | A3-A2-B2 | Osney Mead | A1 | Speedwell Street | C1 | | |
| Black Friars Road | B1-C1 | Holywell Street | D3-E3 | Oxpens Road | B1-B2 | Stockmore Street | F1 | | |
| Blackhall Road | C4-C5 | Hythe Bridge Street | A3-B3 | Paradise Square | B2 | Temple Street | F1 | | |
| Blue Boar Street | C2-D2 | Iffley Road | F1-F2 | Paradise Street | B2 | Thames Street | B1-C1 | | |
| Boulter Street | F2 | Jericho Street | A5-B5 | Park End Street | A3-B3 | Trinity Street | B1 | | |
| Brewer Street | C2 | Jowett Walk | D4-E4 | Parks Road | C5-C4-D4-D3 | Turl Street | C3-D3 | | |
| Broad Street | C3-D3 | Juxon Street | A5 | Pembroke Street | C2 | Tyndale Road | F2 | | |
| Broad Walk | C1-D1-D2-E2 | Keble Road | C5 | Pike Terrace | C2 | Upper Fisher Row | B3 | | |
| Butterwyke Place | C1 | Little Clarendon Street | B4-B5-C5 | Pusey Lane | C4 | Victor Street | A4-A5 | | |
| Canal Street | A4 | Littlegate Street | C2 | Pusey Street | C4 | Walton Crescent | B4 | | |
| Cardigan Street | A5 | Longwall Street | E3 | Queen Street | C2 | Walton Lane | B4 | | |
| Castle Street | C2 | Magdalen Street | C3 | Queen's Lane | D3-E3 | Walton Street | A5-B5-B4-B3 | | |
| Catte Street | D3 | Manor Place | E4 | Radcliffe Square | D3 | Wellington Square | B4-C4 | | |
| Circus Street | F1 | Manor Road | E4 | Richmond Road | B4 | Wellington Street | A4-B4 | | |
| Cornmarket Street | C2-C3 | Mansfield Road | D4-D5 | Rose Lane | E2 | Woodstock Road | B5-C5-C4 | | |

208

# Peterborough

Peterborough is found on atlas page **64**,
grid reference 1998

**AA shop**
Unit 16 Rivergate Centre, Peterborough PE1 1EL          C3

| | | | | | | | |
|---|---|---|---|---|---|---|---|
| Aldermans Drive | A4 | Fengate | F3 | Midgate | C4-D4 | Thorpe Lea Road | A3-B3 |
| Atkinson Street | E4-F4 | First Drove | F3 | Midland Road | A4-A5 | Thorpe Road | A4-B4 |
| Bishops Road | C3-D3-E4-F3 | Fitzwilliam Street | C5 | Morris Street | E5 | Trinity Street | B3-C3 |
| Boongate | D5-E5-F5 | Flamborough Close | A2 | Nene Street | E4 | Vermont Grove | A3 |
| Bourges Boulevard | C3-B3-B4-B5 | Fletton Avenue | C1-C2 | New Road | D4-D5 | Versen Platz | C3-C2 |
| Bread Street | B1 | Frank Perkins | | North Street | C4-C5 | Vineyard Road | D3-D4 |
| Brewster Avenue | A1 | Parkway | E1-E3-F3-F5 | Northminster Road | C5-D5-D4 | Wake Road | E4 |
| Bridge Street | C3-C4 | Geneva Street | C5 | Oundle Road | A1-B1-C1-C2 | Wellington Street | D5-E5 |
| Bright Street | B5-C5 | George Street | B1-B2 | Palmerston Road | B1 | Wentworth Street | C3 |
| Broadway | C4-C5 | Gladstone Street | B5 | Park Road | C4-C5 | Westgate | B5-B4-C4 |
| Buckle Street | E5 | Glebe Road | C1-D1 | Percival Street | A5 | Wharf Road | A1-A2 |
| Burton Street | E5-F5 | Glenton Street | E4-F4 | Potters Way | E2-E3-F3 | Wheel Yard | C4 |
| Cathedral Square | C4 | Granby Street | D4 | Priestgate | B3-C3 | | |
| Church Street | C5 | Gravel Walk | D3 | Queen Street | C4 | | |
| Church Walk | C5 | Grove Street | B1 | Regency Way | A3 | | |
| Clifton Avenue | A5 | Hadrians Court | D1 | River Lane | A4-B4-B3 | | |
| Cromwell Road | B5 | Harvester Way | F3 | Rivergate | C2-C3 | | |
| Cowgate | B4-C4 | Hereward Street | E4 | Riverside Mead | E1 | | |
| Craig Street | B5-C5 | Holdich Street | A4 | Russell Street | B5-C5 | | |
| Crawthorne Road | D5 | Jubilee Street | B1-B2 | South Street | E4-D4 | | |
| Cross Street | C3-C4 | Kent Road | A4 | St Johns Street | D4-D5 | | |
| De Bec Close | F5 | Kirkwood Close | A3 | St Peters Road | C3 | | |
| Deacon Street | B5 | Lea Gardens | A3-B3 | Stagshaw Drive | D1 | | |
| Dickens Street | D5-E5 | Lincoln Road | C4-C5 | Star Mews | E4-F4-F5 | | |
| East Station Road | C2-D2 | Long Causeway | C4 | Star Road | E4-E5 | | |
| Eastgate | E4 | Manor House Street | C5 | Station Road | B4 | | |
| Exchange Street | C4 | Mayors Walk | B5-A5 | Swain Court | B1 | | |

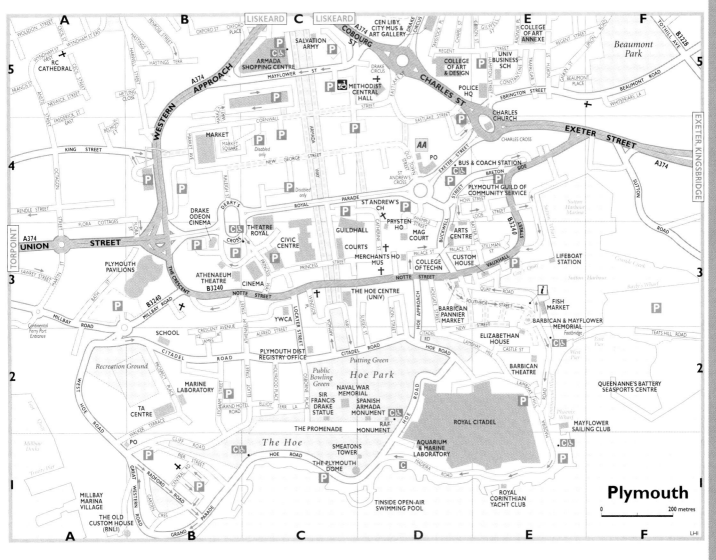

# Plymouth

Plymouth is found on atlas page **6**,
grid reference **4754**

**AA shop**
10 Old Town Street, Plymouth PL1 1DE          D4

| | | | | | | | | | |
|---|---|---|---|---|---|---|---|---|---|
| Alfred Street | C2 | Elliot Street | C2 | Lipson Road | F5 | Radnor Place | E5 | Zion Street | D2-D3 |
| Anstis Street | A4-A5 | Elliot Terrace Lane | C2 | Lockyer Street | C2-C3 | Raleigh Street | B4 | | |
| Armada Way | C2-C3 | Exeter Street | D4-E4-F4 | Looe Street | D4-E4 | Regent Street | D5-E5-F5 | | |
| Athenaeum Street | C2-C3 | Flora Cottages | A3-A4-B4 | Madeira Road | D1-E1-E2 | Rendle Street | A4 | | |
| Bath Street | A3-B3 | Flora Street | B3 | Market Avenue | B4 | Royal Parade | C4-D4 | | |
| Batter Street | D3-E3 | Francis Street | A5 | Market Way | B4-B5 | St James Place | B2 | | |
| Beaumont Place | E5-F5 | Frederick Street East | A4-A5 | Martin Street | A3 | Sawrey Street | A3 | | |
| Beaumont Road | F5 | Garden Crescent | B1 | Mayflower Street | B5-C5-D5 | Southside Street | D3-E3 | | |
| Belmont Street | A4 | Gaskin Street | E5 | Millbay Road | A3-A2-B2 | Stillman Street | E3 | | |
| Breton Side | E4 | Gibbon Street | E5 | Neswick Street | A5 | Sussex Street | D2-D3 | | |
| Buckwell Street | D3-D4 | Gilwell Street | E5 | New George Street | B4-C4-D4 | Sutton Road | F3-F4 | | |
| Castle Street | E2 | Grand Hotel Road | B2-C2 | New Street | D2-E2-E3 | Tavistock Place | D5 | | |
| Catherine Street | D3-D4 | Grand Parade | B1 | North Street | E5 | Teats Hill Road | F2 | | |
| Cecil Street | A5 | Great Western Road | B1 | Notte Street | B3-C3-D3 | The Crescent | B3 | | |
| Central Road | B1 | Hampton Street | E5 | Octagon Street | A3-A4 | Tothill Avenue | F5 | | |
| Chapel Street | D5 | Harwell Street | A5-B5-B4 | Old Town Street | D4 | Trafalgar Street | E5 | | |
| Charles Street | D5 | Hastings Street | B5 | Osborne Place | C2 | Union Street | A3-B3 | | |
| Citadel Road | A2-B2-C2-D2 | Hastings Terrace | B5 | Oxford Place | B5-C5 | Vauxhall Street | E3-E4 | | |
| Cliff Road | B1 | Hetling Close | A5-B5 | Oxford Street | B5 | Walker Terrace | A1-B1-B2 | | |
| Coburg Street | C5-D5 | Hoe Approach | D2-D3 | Palace Street | D3-E3 | West Hoe Road | A2-A1 | | |
| Constantine Street | E5 | Hoe Road | C1-D1-D2 | Penrose Street | B5 | Western Approach | B4-B5-C5 | | |
| Cornwall Street | B4-C4-C5-D5 | Hoegate Street | D2-D3 | Pier Street | B1 | Whimple Street | D3-D4 | | |
| Crescent Avenue | B2-B3 | Holyrood Place | C2 | Princess Street | C3-D3 | Whitefriars Lane | F5 | | |
| Derry's Cross | B3-B4-C4-C3 | How Street | D4-E4 | Princess Way | C3 | Windsor Place | C3 | | |
| Drake Circus | D5 | King Street | A4-B4 | Prospect Place | B2 | Wolsdon Street | A5 | | |
| Eastlake Street | D5-D4 | Lambhay Hill | D2-E2 | Quay Road | D3-E3 | Wyndham Street East | A5 | | |
| Ebrington Street | E5 | Leigham Street | B2 | Radford Road | B1 | Wyndham Street West | A5 | | |

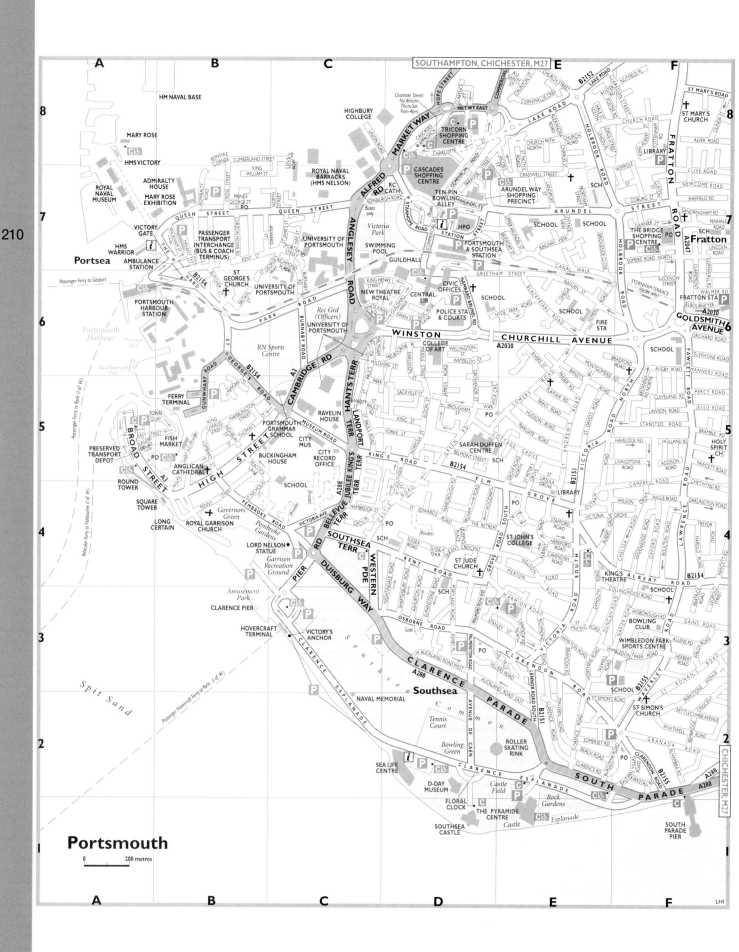

# Portsmouth

0 ___ 200 metres

# Ramsgate

Ramsgate is found on atlas page **29**,
grid reference **3865**

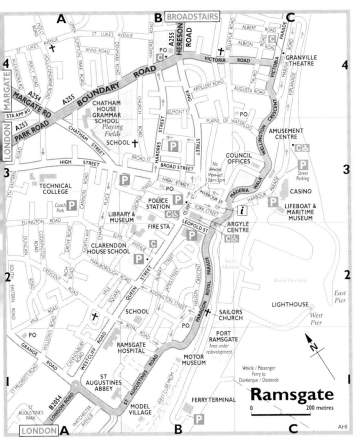

| | | | |
|---|---|---|---|
| Addington Street | B2 | James Street | B2 |
| Albert Road | C4 | King Street | B3-B4 |
| Albert Street | B2 | Leopold Street | B2-B3 |
| Albion Road | B4-C4 | London Road | A1 |
| Alexandra Road | A4 | Madeira Walk | B3-C3 |
| Anns Road | A4 | Margate Road | A4 |
| Artillery Road | B4 | Marina Road | C4 |
| Augusta Road | B4-C4 | Marlborough Road | A2-B2 |
| Bellevue Road | B4 | Nelson Crescent | B2 |
| Belmont Street | B4 | North Avenue | A2 |
| Boundary Road | A4-B4 | Paragon Royal Parade | B1-B2 |
| Broad Street | B3 | Park Road | A3 |
| Cannonbury Road | A1 | Percy Road | A4 |
| Canon Road | A3 | Plains of Waterloo | B3-C3 |
| Chapel Place | A2-A3 | Queen Street | A2-B2-B3 |
| Chatham Street | A3 | Richmond Road | A2 |
| Church Road | B3-B4 | Royal Road | A2-B2-B1 |
| Codrington Road | A2 | St Augustine's Park | A1 |
| Crescent Road | A2 | St Augustines Road | A1-B1 |
| Denmark Road | A4-B4 | St Luke's Avenue | A4-B4 |
| Duncan Road | A2 | St Mildred's Road | A1 |
| Ellington Road | A2-A3 | South Eastern Road | A2-A3 |
| Elms Avenue | A2-B2 | Station Approach Road | A4 |
| Esplanade | C3-C4 | Truro Road | C4 |
| George Street | B3 | Upper Dumpton Park Road | A4 |
| Grange Road | A1 | Vale Road | A1-A2 |
| Grove Road | A2 | Vale Square | A2-B2 |
| Harbour Parade | B3-C3 | Victoria Parade | C4 |
| Harbour Street | B3 | Victoria Road | B4-C4 |
| Hardres Road | B4 | Watchester Avenue | A1 |
| Hardres Street | B3-B4 | Wellington Crescent | C3-C4 |
| Hereson Road | B4 | West Cliff Promenade | B1 |
| High Street | A3-B3 | Westcliff Road | A1-A2 |
| Hollicondane Road | A4 | Willson's Road | A1-A2 |
| Holly Road | A4 | York Street | B3 |

# Portsmouth

Portsmouth is found on atlas page **13**,
grid reference **6400**

**AA shop**
12 London Road, Portsmouth PO1 1NL

| | | | |
|---|---|---|---|
| Addison Road | F5 | Burgoyne Road | E2-F2 |
| Admiralty Road | B7 | Burnaby Road | C6 |
| Albany Road | E4 | Butcher Street | B6-B7 |
| Albert Grove | E4-E5 | Cambridge Road | C5-C6 |
| Albert Road | E4-F4 | Campbell Road | F5 |
| Alec Rose Lane | D6 | Canal Walk | E7 |
| Alexandra Road | E8 | Cascades Approach | D8 |
| Alfred Road | C7-D7 | Castle Road | C4-D4-D5 |
| Alhambra Road | F2 | Cavendish Road | C4 |
| All Saints Street | E8 | Cecil Place | C4 |
| Allens Road | F3 | Charles Street | E7-E8 |
| Alver Road | F8 | Charlotte Street | D8-E8 |
| Anglesey Road | C6-C7 | Chelsea Road | F4 |
| Armory Lane | B5 | Chetwynd Road | F4-F5 |
| Arundel Street | D7-E7-F7 | Church Path North | E8 |
| Ashby Place | D3 | Church Road | E8 |
| Ashurton Road | D3-D4 | Church Street | E8 |
| Auckland Road East | D3-E3-E2 | Claredon Street | F8 |
| Auckland Road West | D3 | Claremont Road | F6-F7 |
| Avenue De Caen | D2 | Clarence Esplanade | C3-F1 |
| Aylward Street | B7-C7 | Clarence Parade | D3-E2 |
| Bailey's Road | E6-E5-F5 | Clarence Road | E2-E3 |
| Beach Road | E2 | Clarence Street | D8 |
| Beatrice Road | F3-F4 | Clarendon Road | D3-E3-E2-F2 |
| Bellevue Terrace | C4 | Cleveland Road | F5 |
| Belmont Street | D5 | Clifton Street | F7 |
| Bembridge Crescent | F2-F3 | Clive Road | F7-F8 |
| Blackfriars Road | E6 | Coburg Street | F7 |
| Bonfire Corner | B8 | Collingwood Road | E4-F4-F3 |
| Boulton Road | F4 | Commercial Road | D7-D8-E8 |
| Bradford Road | E6-F6 | Cornwall Road | F6-F7 |
| Bramble Road | F5 | Cornwallis Crescent | E8 |
| Brandon Road | E3 | Cottage Grove | D5-E5 |
| Bridgeside Close | E7 | Cottage View | E7 |
| Bridport Street | E7 | Crasswell Street | E7 |
| Britain Street | B6 | Cross Street | B7-B8 |
| Britannia Road North | F5-F6 | Cumberland Street | B8-C8 |
| Broad Street | A5-B5-B4 | Curzon Howe Road | B7 |
| Brougham Street | D5 | Darlington Road | F4 |

| | | | |
|---|---|---|---|
| Duisburg Way | C3-C4 | | |
| Duncan Road | E3-F3 | | |
| Earlsdon Street | D6 | | |
| East Street | A5-B5 | | |
| Eastern Villas Road | F2 | | |
| Edinburgh Road | C7-D7 | | |
| Eldon Street | D5 | | |
| Elm Grove | D5-E4 | | |
| Elphinstone Road | D3-D4 | | |
| Exmouth Road | E3-E4 | | |
| Fawcett Road | F5-F6 | | |
| Florence Road | E2 | | |
| Foster Road | E8-F8 | | |
| Fraser Road | E5-E6 | | |
| Fratton Road | F6-F7-F8 | | |
| Gains Road | F3 | | |
| Garnier Street | F7 | | |
| Goldsmith Avenue | F6 | | |
| Goodwood Road | F4 | | |
| Granada Road | F2 | | |
| Great Southsea Street | D4-D5 | | |
| Green Road | D5 | | |
| Greetham Street | D7-E7 | | |
| Grosvenor Street | D5-D6 | | |
| Grove Road North | E5 | | |
| Grove Road South | D4-E4 | | |
| Guildhall Walk | D6 | | |
| Gunwharf Road | B5-B6 | | |
| Hale Street South | E8 | | |
| Hambrook Street | C4-D4 | | |
| Hamilton Road | E3 | | |
| Hampshire Terrace | C5-C6 | | |
| Harold Road | F4 | | |
| Havant Street | B7 | | |
| Havelock Road | F5 | | |
| Hay Street | C7 | | |
| Herbert Road | F3 | | |
| Hereford Road | E4 | | |
| High Street | B4-B5-C5 | | |
| Highbury Street | B5 | | |
| Holbrook Road | F6-F7-E7-E8 | | |
| Holland Road | F5 | | |
| Hope Street | D8 | | |
| Hudson Road | E5 | | |
| Hyde Park Road | D6-E6 | | |
| Inglis Road | F4 | | |
| Isambard Brunel Road | D6 | | |
| Jacob's Street | E8 | | |
| Jessie Road | F5 | | |

| | | | |
|---|---|---|---|
| Jubilee Terrace | C4-C5 | Pain's Road | E5 |
| Kent Road | D4 | Palmerston Road | D3-D4 |
| Kent Street | B7-C7 | Paradise Street | D7-D8-E8 |
| King Albert Street | F8 | Park Road | B6-C6 |
| King Charles Street | B5 | Park Street | C5-D5 |
| King Henry 1 Street | C6-D6 | Parkstone Avenue | F2-F3 |
| King Street | D5 | Peacock Lane | B5 |
| King William Street | B7-C7 | Pelham Road | D4-D5 |
| King's Road | C5-D5 | Pembroke Road | B4-C4 |
| King's Terrace | C5 | Penhale Road | F7 |
| Kirkstall Road | F2 | Penny Street | B4-B5 |
| Lake Road | E8 | Percy Road | F5 |
| Landport Street | C5 | Pier Road | C4 |
| Landport Street | E7 | Playfair Road | E5 |
| Landport Terrace | C5 | Portland Road | D3-D4 |
| Lawrence Road | F4-F5 | Portland Street | C7 |
| Lawson Road | F5 | Prince George Street | B7 |
| Lennox Road North | E3 | Queen Street | B7-C7 |
| Lennox Road South | E2-E3 | Queen's Crescent | D4 |
| Lennox Row | C8 | Queen's Place | D4 |
| Leopold Street | F3-F4 | Raglan Street | E6 |
| Lincoln Road | F7 | Railway View | E7 |
| Livingstone Road | F5 | Richmond Place | C7 |
| Lombard Street | B5 | Richmond Road | E3 |
| Lords Street | E8-F8 | Rivers Street | E6 |
| Lucknow Street | F6 | Rugby Road | F6 |
| Malvern Road | E2-E3 | Sackville Street | D5 |
| Manners Road | F6 | St Andrew's Road | E4-E5-E6 |
| Margate Road | E5 | St David's Road | E5 |
| Market Way | D8 | St Edward's Road | D4 |
| Market Way East | D8 | St Faith's Road | E7-E8 |
| Marmion Road | E3-E4 | St George's Road | B6-B5-C5 |
| Melbourne Place | D6 | St George's Way | B6-B7 |
| Merton Road | E4 | St James's Road | D5-D6 |
| Middle Street | D5-D6 | St Jame's Street | C7 |
| Montgomerie Road | E6-F6 | St Mary's Road | F8 |
| Museum Road | C5 | St Nicholas' Street | B4-C5 |
| Napier Road | F3-F4 | St Paul's Road | C5-C6 |
| Nelson Road | E3-E4 | St Paul's Square | C5 |
| Nettlecombe Avenue | F2 | St Peter's Grove | E4-E5 |
| Newcome Road | F7 | St Ronan's Road | F2-F3 |
| Nightingale Road | D3-D4 | St Simon's Road | E2-F2 |
| Norfolk Street | D5 | St Thomas's Street | B5-C5 |
| North Street | B7-C7 | St Ursula Grove | E5 |
| Northam Street | E7 | St Vincent Road | E3 |
| Nutfield Place | F8 | Sandringham Road | F7 |
| Olinda Street | F8 | Seagers Court | A5 |
| Omega Street | E6 | Selbourne Terrace | F6 |
| Orchard Road | F6 | Shaftesbury Road | D3-D4 |
| Osborne Road | D3 | Sheffield Road | F7 |
| Outram Road | E4-E5 | Somers Road | E5-E6 |
| Oxford Road | F4 | Somers Road North | F7 |

| | |
|---|---|
| Somerset Road | E2-F2 |
| South Parade | E2-F2 |
| Southsea Terrace | C4 |
| Stafford Road | E4 |
| Stanhope Road | D7 |
| Stanley Street | D3-E3 |
| Stansted Road | F5 |
| Station Street | D7 |
| Staunton Road | E8 |
| Sussex Road | D4 |
| Sussex Terrace | D4 |
| Swan Street | D6 |
| Sydenham Terrace | F6 |
| Taswell Road | E3-F3 |
| Telephone Road | F6 |
| The Hard | B6-B7 |
| The Retreat | D4-D5 |
| The Vale | E3 |
| Tottenham Road | F8 |
| Town Quay | A5-B5 |
| Trevor Road | F4 |
| Union Place | E8 |
| Union Road | C8-D8 |
| Upper Arundel Street | E7 |
| Victoria Avenue | C4 |
| Victoria Grove | E4-F4 |
| Victoria Road North | E4-F4-F6 |
| Victoria Road South | E3-E4 |
| Villiers Road | D3-E3 |
| Walmer Road | F6 |
| Waltham Street | C6-D6 |
| Warblington Street | B5 |
| Warwick Crescent | D5-E5 |
| Waterloo Street | D6 |
| Waverley Road | F2-F3-F4 |
| Welch Road | F3 |
| Wellington Street | D6 |
| Western Parade | C3-C4 |
| White Hart Road | B4-B5 |
| White Swan Road | C6-D6 |
| Whitwell Road | F2 |
| Wickham Street | B7 |
| Wilson Grove | F4 |
| Wiltshire Street | C6-D6 |
| Wimbledon Park Road | E3-F3 |
| Wimpole Street | F7-F8 |
| Winston Churchill Avenue | D6-E6 |
| Wisborough Road | F3 |
| Woodpath | D4 |
| Worthing Road | E3 |
| Yarborough Road | D4-D5 |
| Yorke Street | C5-D5 |

212

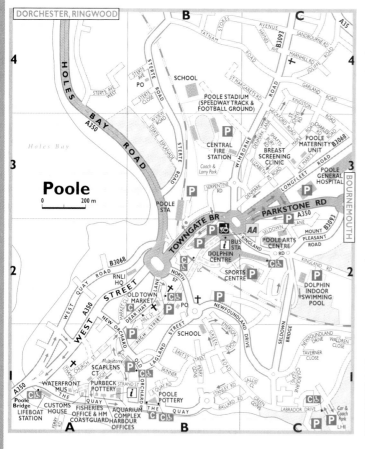

# Poole

Poole is found on atlas page 11,
grid reference 0090

### AA shop
10 Falkland Square, Poole BH15 1ER — B2

| | | | | |
|---|---|---|---|---|
| Ballard Road | B1-C1 | Shaftsbury Road | C3 |
| Charles Road | C3 | Skinner Street | B1 |
| Church Street | A1 | Stanley Road | B1 |
| Colbourne Gardens | C1 | Sterte Avenue | B4 |
| Dear Hay Lane | B2 | Sterte Avenue West | A4 |
| Denmark Lane | C3 | Sterte Close | B4 |
| Denmark Road | C3 | Sterte Esplanade | B3 |
| East Quay Road | B1 | Sterte Road | B4-B3 |
| East Street | B1 | Stokes Avenue | B4-C4 |
| Elizabeth Road | C3 | Strand Street | A1-B1 |
| Emerson Road | B2-B1 | Tatnam Road | B4-C4 |
| Ferry Road | A1 | Taverner Close | C1 |
| Garland Road | C4 | Thames Street | A1 |
| Green Gardens | C1 | The Quay | A1-B1 |
| Green Road | B1 | Towngate Bridge | B2-B3 |
| Haynes Avenue | C4 | Vallis Close | C1 |
| Heckford Road | C3-C4 | Waldren Close | C1 |
| High Street | A1-B1-B2 | West Quay Road | A1-A2-B2 |
| Hill Street | B2 | West Street | A1-A2-B2 |
| Holes Bay Road | A4-B3-B2 | West View Road | B3-B4 |
| Jolliffe Road | C4 | Wimborne Road | B3-C3-C4 |
| Kingland Road | C2 | | |
| Kingston Road | C3-C4 | | |
| Labrador Drive | C1 | | |
| Lagland Street | B1-B2 | | |
| Longfleet Road | C3 | | |
| Maple Road | C3-C4 | | |
| Market Close | A2 | | |
| Marnhill Road | C4 | | |
| Mount Pleasant Road | C2 | | |
| New Orchard | A2-A1 | | |
| Newfoundland Drive | C1 | | |
| North Street | B2 | | |
| Old Orchard | B1 | | |
| Parkstone Road | C3 | | |
| Perry Gardens | B1 | | |
| St Johns Road | C3-C4 | | |
| St Margarets Road | B4-C4 | | |
| St Mary's Road | C3 | | |
| Sandbourne Road | C4 | | |
| Seldown Bridge | C1-C2 | | |
| Seldown Lane | C2 | | |
| Serpentine Road | B3 | | |

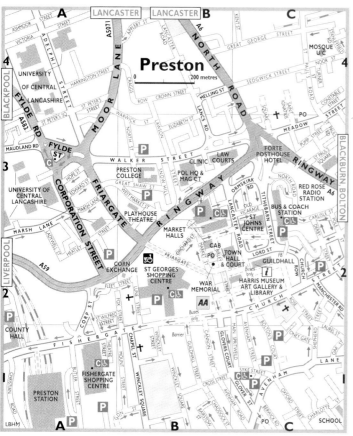

# Preston

Preston is found on atlas page 80,
grid reference 5329

### AA shop
3-4 Cheapside, Preston PR1 2AP — B2

| | | | | | | |
|---|---|---|---|---|---|---|
| Adelphi Street | A3-A4 | Ladywell Street | A2 | Walker Street | A3-B3 |
| Appleby Street | B4 | Lancaster Road | B4-B3-C3-C2 | Warwick Street | A4-B3 |
| Ashmoor Street | A4 | Laurel Street | C1-C2 | West Market Street | B3 |
| Avenham Lane | C1 | Lawson Street | B3-B4 | Winckley Square | B1 |
| Avenham Road | B1-C1 | Lord Street | C2 | Winckley Street | B1 |
| Avenham Street | C1-C2 | Lune Street | B2 | | |
| Bairstow Street | B1 | Main Spritweild | C1-C2 | | |
| Berwick Road | C1 | Manchester Road | C2 | | |
| Birley Street | B2 | Market Street | B2 | | |
| Bolton's Court | C1-C2 | Marsh Lane | A2-A3 | | |
| Butler Street | A1 | Maudland Road | A3 | | |
| Cannon Street | B1-B2 | Meadow Street | C3-C4 | | |
| Carlisle Street | C3 | Melling Street | B4 | | |
| Chaddock Street | B1 | Moor Lane | A3-A4 | | |
| Chapel Street | B1 | Mount Street | B1 | | |
| Charlotte Street | C1 | Noor Street | C4 | | |
| Christian Road | A1 | North Road | B4-C4-C3 | | |
| Church Row | C2 | North Street | B3 | | |
| Church Street | B2-C2 | Oak Street | C1 | | |
| Constable Street | C4 | Old Vicarage | C3 | | |
| Corporation Street | A1-A2-A3 | Orchard Street | B2 | | |
| Craggs Row | B4 | Ormskirk Road | C3 | | |
| Cross Street | B1 | Oxford Street | C1 | | |
| Crown Street | B4 | Pole Street | C2-C3 | | |
| Derby Street | C2 | Pump Street | C3 | | |
| Edward Street | A3 | Ringway | B2-B3-C3 | | |
| Elizabeth Street | B3 | Rose Street | C2 | | |
| Fishergate | A1-B1 | Saint Ignatius Square | C3-C4 | | |
| Fleet Street | A2-B2 | St Paul's Road | C3-C4 | | |
| Fox Street | B1-B2 | St Paul's Square | C3 | | |
| Friargate | A3-B2 | St Peter's Square | A3-A4 | | |
| Fylde Road | A3-A4 | St Peter's Street | A4 | | |
| Fylde Street | A3 | St Wilfred Street | A2 | | |
| Garden Street | B1 | Sedgwick Street | C4 | | |
| Glover Street | C1 | Shepherd Street | C1-C2 | | |
| Glovers Court | B1-B2 | Snow Hill | B3 | | |
| Great George Street | B4-C4 | Stanleyfield Road | C4 | | |
| Great Shaw Street | A3-B3 | Stoney Gate | C1-C2 | | |
| Guildhall Street | B1-B2 | Syke Street | C1 | | |
| Harrington Street | A4 | Theatre Street | A1 | | |
| Heatley Street | A2 | Tithebarn Street | C2-C3 | | |
| Hope Street | A3 | Turner Street | C4 | | |
| Kent Street | C4 | Victoria Street | A4 | | |

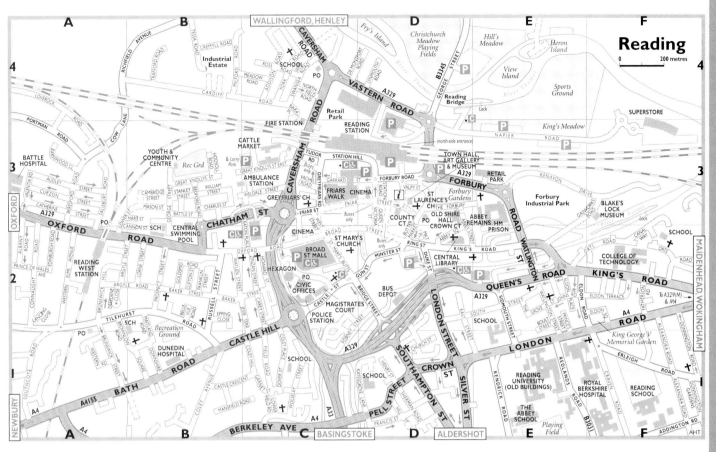

# Reading

Reading is found on atlas page **24**,
grid reference **7173**

214

# Salisbury

Salisbury is found on atlas page **23**,
grid reference **1429**

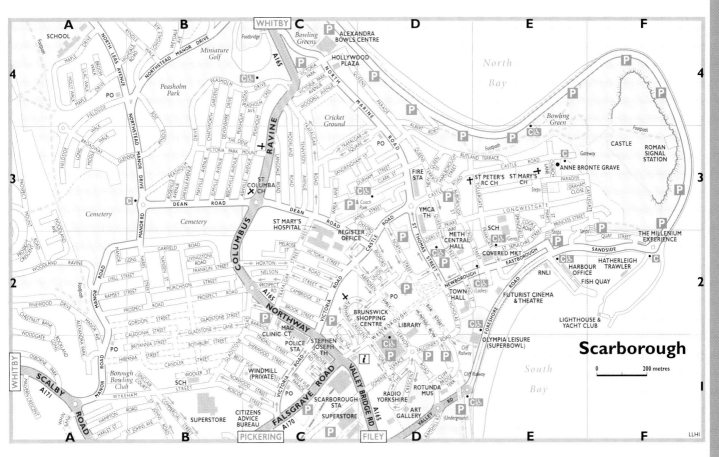

# Scarborough

Scarborough is found on atlas page **91**,
grid reference **0488**

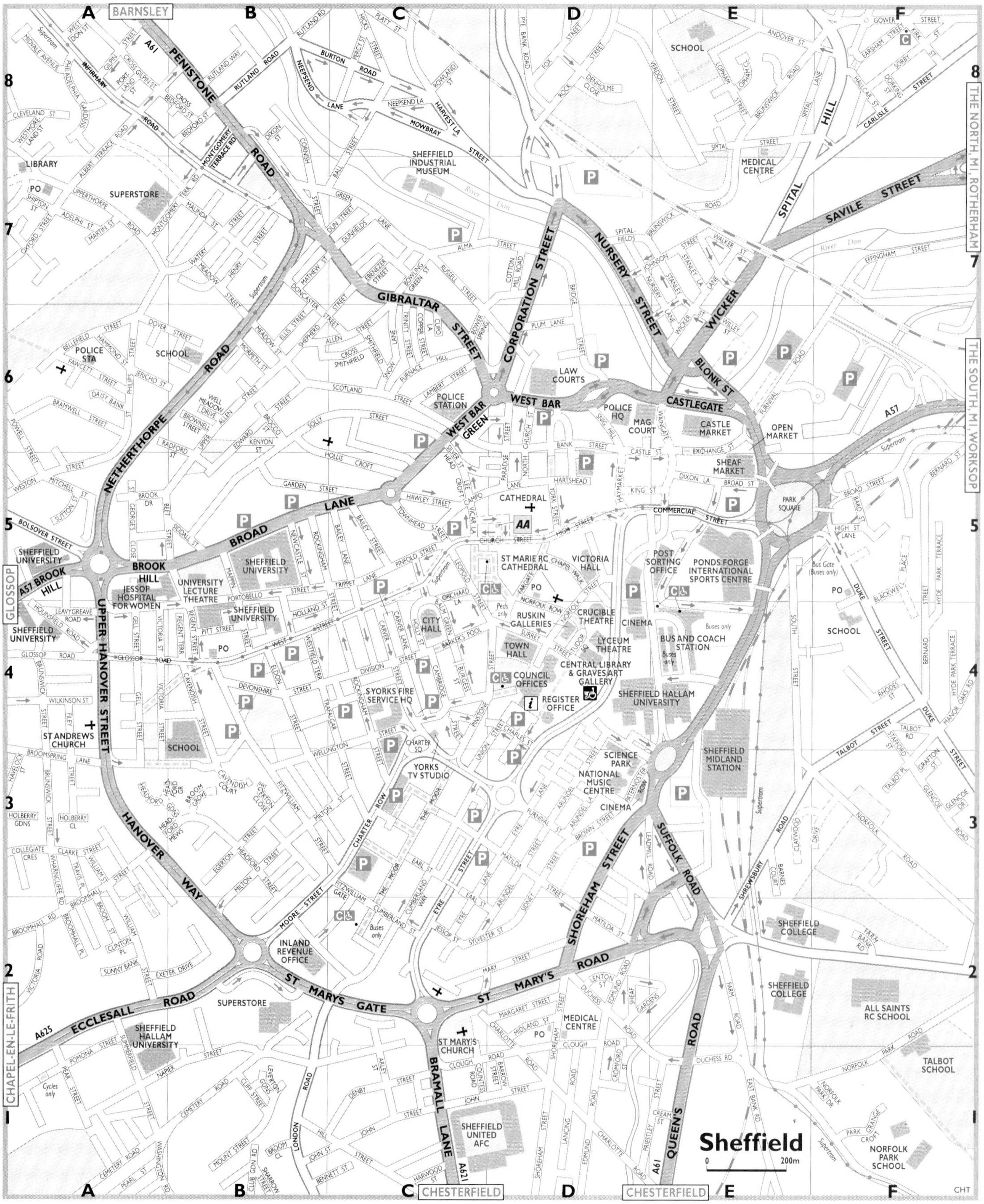

216

# Sheffield

BARNSLEY

THE NORTH, M1, ROTHERHAM

THE SOUTH, M1, WORKSOP

GLOSSOP

CHAPEL-EN-LE-FRITH

CHESTERFIELD

CHESTERFIELD

0        200m

**Sheffield**

CHT

Key streets and places (as labelled on the map):

PENISTONE ROAD · RUTLAND ROAD · NETHERTHORPE ROAD · GIBRALTAR STREET · CORPORATION STREET · NURSERY STREET · WICKER · BLONK ST · CASTLEGATE · SAVILE STREET · SPITAL HILL · BROAD LANE · WEST BAR · WEST BAR GREEN · UPPER HANOVER STREET · HANOVER WAY · BROOK HILL · A57 BROOK HILL · GLOSSOP ROAD · ECCLESALL ROAD · ST MARYS GATE · ST MARY'S ROAD · BRAMALL LANE · SHOREHAM STREET · SUFFOLK ROAD · QUEEN'S ROAD · CHARTER ROW · MOORE STREET · COMMERCIAL STREET · A61 · A57 · A625 · A621

SHEFFIELD INDUSTRIAL MUSEUM · POLICE STA · LIBRARY · SUPERSTORE · PO · SCHOOL · SHEFFIELD UNIVERSITY · UNIVERSITY LECTURE THEATRE · JESSOP HOSPITAL FOR WOMEN · ST ANDREWS CHURCH · LAW COURTS · POLICE STATION · POLICE HQ · MAG COURT · CASTLE MARKET · SHEAF MARKET · OPEN MARKET · EXCHANGE · PARK SQUARE · MEDICAL CENTRE · CATHEDRAL · AA · ST MARIE RC CATHEDRAL · VICTORIA HALL · POST SORTING OFFICE · PONDS FORGE INTERNATIONAL SPORTS CENTRE · RUSKIN GALLERIES · CRUCIBLE THEATRE · CINEMA · BUS AND COACH STATION · CITY HALL · TOWN HALL · LYCEUM THEATRE · S YORKS FIRE SERVICE HQ · COUNCIL OFFICES · CENTRAL LIBRARY & GRAVES ART GALLERY · REGISTER OFFICE · SHEFFIELD HALLAM UNIVERSITY · SCIENCE PARK · NATIONAL MUSIC CENTRE · SHEFFIELD MIDLAND STATION · YORKS TV STUDIO · INLAND REVENUE OFFICE · SHEFFIELD HALLAM UNIVERSITY · SUPERSTORE · ST MARY'S CHURCH · MEDICAL CENTRE · SHEFFIELD UNITED AFC · SHEFFIELD COLLEGE · ALL SAINTS RC SCHOOL · TALBOT SCHOOL · NORFOLK PARK SCHOOL · SCHOOL

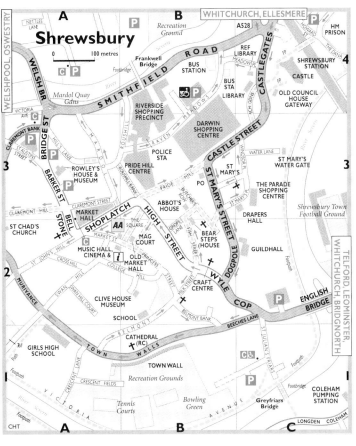

# Shrewsbury

Shrewsbury is found on atlas page **59**,
grid reference **4912**

**AA shop**
8 Market Street, Shrewsbury SY1 1LE — A2

| | | | | | |
|---|---|---|---|---|---|
| Barker Street | A3 | Fish Street | B2-B3 | St John's Hill | A2 |
| Beeches Lane | B1-C2 | Grope Lane | B2-B3 | St Julian's Friars | C1-C2 |
| Belmont | A1-B2 | High Street | B2-B3 | St Mary's Place | B3-C3 |
| Belmont Bank | B2 | Hill's Lane | A3 | St Mary's Street | B2-B3 |
| Bellstone | A2-A3 | Howard Street | C4 | School Gardens | C3-C4 |
| Bridge Street | A3 | Longden Coleham | C1 | Shoplatch | A2-B3 |
| Butcher's Row | B3 | Mardol | A3-A4 | Smithfield Road | A4-C4 |
| Castle Street | B3-C3 | Market Street | A2 | Swan Hill | A2 |
| Castlegates | C4 | Meadow Place | B4-C4 | Swan Hill Court | A2 |
| Claremont Bank | A3 | Milk Street | B2 | The Dana | C4 |
| Claremont Hill | A3 | Murivance | A2 | The Square | B2-B3 |
| Claremont Street | A3 | Nettles Lane | A4 | Town Walls | A2-B1 |
| College Hill | A2-B2 | Pride Hill | B3 | Victoria Avenue | A4 |
| Crescent Fields | A1-B1 | Princess Street | B2 | Water Lane | C3 |
| Crescent Lane | A1 | Raven Meadows | B3-B4 | Welsh Bridge | A4 |
| Cross Hill | A2 | Roushill | A3-B4 | Windsor Place | C3 |
| Dogpole | B2 | Roushill Bank | B3 | Wyle Cop | B2-C2 |
| English Bridge | C2 | St Austins Street | A3 | | |

# Sheffield

Sheffield is found on atlas page **74**,
grid reference **3587**

**AA shop**
5 St James' Row, Sheffield, South Yorks S1 1AY — D5

| | | | | | |
|---|---|---|---|---|---|
| Adelphi Street | A7 | Broomhall Place | A2 | Countess Road | C1 |
| Albert Terrace Road | A7-A8 | Broomhall Road | A2 | Cream Street | E1 |
| Allen Street | B6-C6 | Broomhall Street | A2-A3 | Cromford Street | D1 |
| Alma Street | C7-D7 | Broomspring Lane | A3-A4 | Cross Bedford Street | A8-B8 |
| Andover Street | E8 | Brown Street | D3 | Cross Gilpin Street | A8 |
| Arley Street | C1 | Brownell Street | B6 | Cross Smithfield | B6-C6 |
| Arundel Lane | D3 | Brunswick Road | E7-E8-F8 | Cumberland Street | C2 |
| Arundel Street | C2-D2-D3-D4 | Brunswick Street | A3-A4 | Cumberland Way | C2-C3 |
| Bailey Lane | C5 | Burgess Street | C4 | Cupo Lane | C6 |
| Bailey Street | C5 | Burton Road | B8-C8 | Daisy Bank | A6 |
| Ball Street | C7-C8 | Cambridge Street | C4 | Denby Street | C1 |
| Balm Green | C4-C5 | Campo Lane | C5-D5 | Denholme Close | D8 |
| Bank Street | D6 | Carlisle Street | F7-F8 | Devonshire Street | B4 |
| Bard Street | F5 | Carver Lane | C4 | Division Street | C4 |
| Barker's Pool | C4 | Carver Street | C4 | Dixon Lane | E5 |
| Barnes Court | E3 | Castle Street | D6-E6 | Dixon Street | B8 |
| Barrow Street | D1 | Castlegate | E6 | Doncaster Street | B7-B6-C6 |
| Bedford Street | B8 | Cavendish Court | B3 | Dorking Street | F8 |
| Beet Street | A5-B5 | Cavendish Street | B3-B4 | Dover Street | A6-B6 |
| Bellefield Street | A6 | Cemetery Road | A1-B1 | Duchess Road | D2-D1-E1 |
| Bennett Street | B1-C1 | Chapel Walk | D5 | Duke Street | F3-F4-F5 |
| Bernard Street | F4-F5-F6 | Charles Street | D4 | Dun Street | B7-C7 |
| Blackwell Place | F5 | Charlotte Road | C2-D2-D1-E1 | Dunfields | C7 |
| Blonk Street | E6 | Charter Row | C3 | Earl Street | C3-C2-D2 |
| Bolsover Street | A5 | Charter Square | C3-C4 | Earsham Street | F8 |
| Bower Spring | C6 | Church Street | C5-D5 | East Bank Road | E1 |
| Bowling Green Street | C7 | Clarke Street | A3 | Ebenezer Street | C7 |
| Bramall Lane | C1-C2 | Claywood Drive | E3-F3 | Ecclesall Road | A1-A2-B2 |
| Bramwell Street | A6 | Cleveland Street | A8 | Edmund Road | D1-D2 |
| Bridge Street | D6-D7 | Cliff Street | B1 | Edward Street | B5-B6 |
| Broad Lane | B5-C5 | Clinton Place | A2 | Effingham Street | F7 |
| Broad Street | E5 | Clough Road | C1-D1-D2 | Egerton Close | B3 |
| Broad Street | F5 | Club Garden Road | B1 | Egerton Street | B3 |
| Brocco Street | B6 | Collegiate Crescent | A3 | Eldon Street | B3-B4 |
| Brook Drive | A5 | Commercial Street | D5-E5 | Ellis Street | B6 |
| Brook Hill | A5 | Copper Street | C6 | Exchange Street | E6 |
| Broom Close | B1 | Cornish Street | B7-B8 | Exeter Drive | A2-B2 |
| Broom Grove | B3 | Corporation Street | D6-D7 | Eyre Lane | C2-C3-D3 |
| Broom Street | A2 | Cotton Mill Road | D7 | Eyre Street | C2-C3-D3 |

| | | | | | |
|---|---|---|---|---|---|
| | | | | Fargate | D5 |
| | | | | Farm Bank Road | F2 |
| | | | | Farm Road | E1-E2 |
| | | | | Fawcett Street | A6 |
| | | | | Filey Street | A3-A4 |
| | | | | Fitzwilliam Gate | C2-C3 |
| | | | | Fitzwilliam Street | B4-B3-C3 |
| | | | | Fox Street | D8 |
| | | | | Furnace Hill | C6 |
| | | | | Furnival Road | E6-F6 |
| | | | | Furnival Street | D3 |

| | | | | | |
|---|---|---|---|---|---|
| Garden Street | B5-C5 | Midvale Avenue | A8 | Silver Street Head | C5-C6 |
| Gell Street | A3-A4-A5 | Milton Street | B2-B3-C3 | Smithfield | C6 |
| Gibraltar Street | C6-C7 | Mitchell Street | A5 | Snig Hill | D6 |
| Gilpin Street | A8 | Montgomery Terrace Road A7-B8 | | Snow Lane | C6 |
| Glencoe Drive | F3 | Moore Street | B2-B3-C3 | Solly Street | B5-B6-C6 |
| Glencoe Road | F3 | Morpeth Street | B6 | Sorby Street | F8 |
| Glossop Road | A4-B4 | Mount Street | B1 | South Street | E3-E4-E5 |
| Gower Street | F8 | Mowbray Street | C8-C7-D7 | Spital Hill | E7-E8-F8 |
| Grafton Street | F3 | Napier Street | A1-B1 | Spital Lane | E8-F8 |
| Green Lane | B7-C7 | Neepsend Lane | B8-C8 | Spital Street | E8 |
| Hallcar Street | F8 | Netherthorpe Road A5-A6-B6-B7 | | Spitalfields | D7 |
| Hammond Street | A6 | Newcastle Street | B5 | St George's Close | A5 |
| Hanover Way | A3-B3-B2 | Norfolk Park Drive | F1 | St Mary's Road | C2-D2-E2 |
| Hartshead | D5 | Norfolk Park Road | E1-F1-F2 | St Marys Gate | B2-C2 |
| Harvest Lane | C8 | Norfolk Road | F2-F3 | St Philip's Street | A6 |
| Harwood Street | C1 | Norfolk Row | D4-D5 | Stafford Street | F3-F4 |
| Havelock Street | A3 | Norfolk Street | D4-D5 | Stanley Lane | E7 |
| Hawley Street | C5 | North Church Street | D5-D6 | Stanley Street | E6-E7 |
| Haymarket | D5 | Nursery Lane | D7-E7-E6 | Suffolk Road | E2-E3 |
| Headford Gardens | A3-B3 | Nursery Street | D7-D6-E6 | Summerfield Street | A1-A2 |
| Headford Grove | A3-B3 | Orchard Lane | C5 | Sunny Bank | A2 |
| Headford Mews | A3-B3 | Oxford Street | A7 | Surrey Street | D4 |
| Headford Street | B3 | Paradise Street | D5-D6 | Sutton Street | A5 |
| Henry Street | B7 | Park Grange Croft | F1 | Sylvester Street | C2-D2 |
| Hicks Street | C8 | Park Square | E5-F5 | Talbot Place | F3 |
| High Street | D5 | Paternoster Row | D3 | Talbot Road | F4 |
| High Street Lane | F5 | Pear Street | A1 | Talbot Street | F3-F4 |
| Hill Street | B1-C1 | Pearl Street | A1 | The Moor | C2-C3 |
| Holberry Close | A3 | Penistone Road | A8-B8-B7 | Townhead Street | C5 |
| Holberry Gardens | A3 | Percy Street | C8 | Trafalgar Street | B4-C4-C3 |
| Holland Street | B4 | Philadelphia Gardens | A8 | Travis Place | A3 |
| Hollis Croft | B6-C5 | Pinfold Street | C5 | Trinity Street | C6 |
| Holly Street | C4-C5 | Pinstone Street | C3-C4-D4 | Trippet Lane | C5 |
| Hounsfield Road | A4 | Pitt Street | B4 | Tudor Square | D4 |
| Hyde Park Terrace | F4-F5 | Platt Street | C8 | Union Street | C3-D4 |
| Infirmary Road | A8-B8-B7 | Plum Lane | D6 | Upper Allen Street | B5-B6 |
| Jericho Street | A6 | Pomona Street | A1-A2 | Upper Hanover Street A3-A4-A5 |  |
| Jessop Street | C2 | Portland Street | A8 | Upperthorpe Road | A7 |
| John Street | B1-C1-D1 | Portobello Street | B4-B5 | Verdon Street | D8-E8 |
| Johnson Street | D7-E7 | Powell Street | A5-A6 | Vicar Lane | C5 |
| King Street | D5-E5 | Priestley Street | D1-E1 | Victoria Road | A2 |
| Kirk Street | F8 | Pye Bank Road | D8 | Victoria Street | A3-A4 |
| Lambert Street | C6 | Queen's Road | E1-E2 | Waingate | E6 |
| Lancing Road | D1 | Radford Street | A6-B6 | Walker Street | E7 |
| Leadmill Road | D3-E3 | Regent Street | B4 | Washington Road | A1-B1 |
| Leavygreave Road | A4 | Regent Terrace | B4 | Watery Street | B7 |
| Lee Croft | C5 | Rhodes Street | F4 | Well Meadow Drive | B6 |
| Lenton Street | D2 | Rock Street | D8 | Wellington Street | B3-C4 |
| Leopold Street | C4-C5 | Rockingham Street B5-C5-C4-C3 | | West Bar | D6 |
| Leverton Gardens | B1 | Rowland Street | C8 | West Bar Green | C6 |
| London Road | B1-B2 | Russell Street | C7 | West Don Street | A8 |
| Lopham Close | E8 | Rutland Road | B8 | West Street | B4-C4 |
| Lopham Street | E8 | Rutland Way | B8 | Westfield Terrace | B4 |
| Malinda Street | B7 | Savile Street | E7-F7 | Westmoreland Street | A8 |
| Manor Oaks Road | F4 | Scotland Street | B6-C6 | Weston Street | A5-A6 |
| Mappin Street | B4-B5 | Sharrow Street | B1 | Wharncliffe Road | A2-A3 |
| Margaret Street | D2 | Sheaf Gardens | D2-E2 | Wicker | E6-E7 |
| Martin Street | A7 | Shepherd Street | B6-C6-C7 | Wicker Lane | E6-E7 |
| Mary Street | C2-D2 | Shipton Street | A7 | Wilkinson Street | A4 |
| Mathew Street | B7 | Shoreham Street | D1-D2-D3 | Willey Street | E6 |
| Matilda Street | C3-D3-D2 | Shrewsbury Road | E2-E3 | William Street | A2-A3 |
| Meadow Street | B6-B7 | Siddall Street | B5 | York Street | D5 |
| Midland Street | D2 | Sidney Street | D2-D3 | | |

217

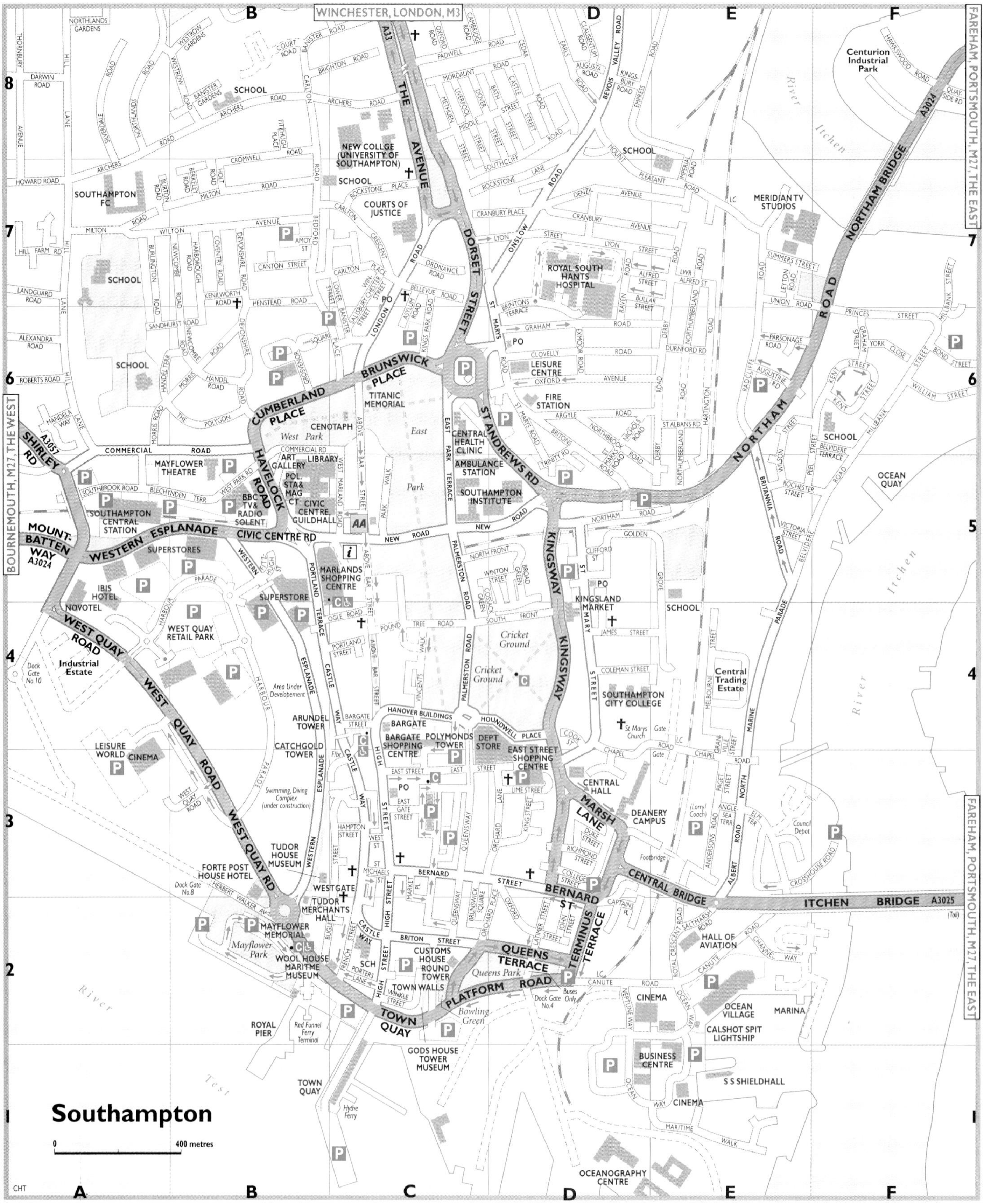

218

# Southampton

WINCHESTER, LONDON, M3

FAREHAM, PORTSMOUTH, M27, THE EAST

BOURNEMOUTH, M27, THE WEST

FAREHAM, PORTSMOUTH, M27, THE EAST

0    400 metres

Centurion Industrial Park

NORTHAM BRIDGE

River Itchen

MERIDIAN TV STUDIOS

SCHOOL

NEW COLLGE (UNIVERSITY OF SOUTHAMPTON)

SCHOOL

SOUTHAMPTON FC

COURTS OF JUSTICE

ROYAL SOUTH HANTS HOSPITAL

LEISURE CENTRE

FIRE STATION

TITANIC MEMORIAL

CUMBERLAND PLACE

BRUNSWICK PLACE

CENOTAPH

West Park

East Park

CENTRAL HEALTH CLINIC

AMBULANCE STATION

SOUTHAMPTON INSTITUTE

ART GALLERY

LIBRARY

MAYFLOWER THEATRE

BBC TV & RADIO SOLENT

SOUTHAMPTON CENTRAL STATION

CIVIC CENTRE RD

CIVIC CENTRE, GUILDHALL

WESTERN ESPLANADE

SUPERSTORES

IBIS HOTEL

NOVOTEL

WEST QUAY ROAD

Industrial Estate

WEST QUAY RETAIL PARK

SUPERSTORE

MARLANDS SHOPPING CENTRE

OCEAN QUAY

KINGSLAND MARKET

SCHOOL

Cricket Ground

Cricket Ground

SOUTHAMPTON CITY COLLEGE

CENTRAL TRADING ESTATE

LEISURE WORLD

CINEMA

ARUNDEL TOWER

CATCHCOLD TOWER

Area Under Developement

Swimming, Diving Complex (under construction)

HANOVER BUILDINGS

BARGATE

BARGATE SHOPPING CENTRE

POLYMONDS TOWER

DEPT STORE

EAST STREET SHOPPING CENTRE

St Marys Church

CENTRAL HALL

DEANERY CAMPUS

MARSH LANE

Council Depot

TUDOR HOUSE MUSEUM

FORTE POST HOUSE HOTEL

WESTGATE

TUDOR MERCHANTS HALL

MAYFLOWER MEMORIAL

Mayflower Park

WOOL HOUSE MARITME MUSEUM

CUSTOMS HOUSE ROUND TOWER

TOWN WALLS

QUEENS TERRACE

Queens Park

CENTRAL BRIDGE

ITCHEN BRIDGE A3025

HALL OF AVIATION

ROYAL PIER

Red Funnel Ferry Terminal

TOWN QUAY

Hythe Ferry

GODS HOUSE TOWER MUSEUM

Bowling Green

PLATFORM ROAD

TERMINUS TERRACE

BERNARD ST

CINEMA

OCEAN VILLAGE

MARINA

CALSHOT SPIT LIGHTSHIP

BUSINESS CENTRE

S S SHIELDHALL

CINEMA

River Test

OCEANOGRAPHY CENTRE

CHT

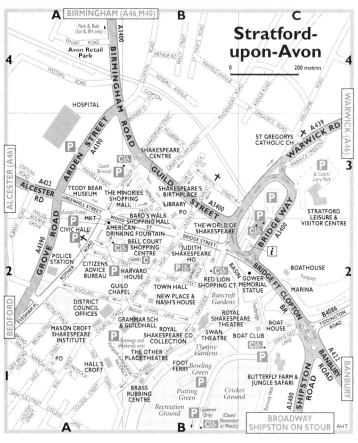

## Stratford-upon-Avon

Stratford-upon-Avon is found on atlas page **48**,
grid reference **2055**

| | | | |
|---|---|---|---|
| Albany Road | A2-A3 | Percy Street | B4 |
| Alcester Road | A3 | Rother Street | A2-A3 |
| Arden Street | A3 | Rowley Crescent | C4 |
| Arthur Road | B4 | St Gregory's Road | C4-C3 |
| Avenue Road | C4 | St Mary's Road | B4 |
| Avonbank Paddock | B1 | Sanctus Street | A1 |
| Banbury Road | C1 | Scholars Lane | A2-B2 |
| Birmingham Road | A4-B3 | Shakespeare Street | B3-B4 |
| Brewery Street | B3-B4 | Sheep Street | B2 |
| Bridge Foot | C2 | Shipston Road | C1 |
| Bridge Street | B2 | Shreeves Walk | B2 |
| Bridge Way | C2-C3 | Southern Lane | A1-B1 |
| Broad Street | A1-A2 | Station Road | A3 |
| Broad Walk | A1 | Swans Nest Lane | C1 |
| Bull Street | A1 | Tiddington Road | C1-C2 |
| Chapel Lane | B2 | Tyler Street | B3 |
| Chapel Street | B2 | Union Street | B2-B3 |
| Chestnut Walk | A1-A2 | Warwick Road | C3 |
| Church Street | A1-A2-B2 | Waterside | B2 |
| Clopton Bridge | C2 | Welcombe Road | C3-C4 |
| Clopton Court | B4 | Wellesbourne Grove | A2-A3 |
| Clopton Road | B4 | Western Road | A4 |
| College Lane | A1 | West Street | A1 |
| College Street | A1 | Wharf Road | A4 |
| Ely Street | A2-B2 | Windsor Street | A3-B3 |
| Evesham Place | A2 | Wood Street | A3-B2 |
| Great William Street | B3 | | |
| Greenhill Street | A3 | | |
| Grove Road | A2-A3 | | |
| Guild Street | B3 | | |
| Henley Street | B2-B3 | | |
| High Street | B2 | | |
| Holtom Street | A1 | | |
| John Street | B3 | | |
| Kendall Avenue | B4 | | |
| Lock Close | B3 | | |
| Maidenhead Road | B3-B4-C4 | | |
| Mansell Street | A3 | | |
| Mayfield Avenue | B4 | | |
| Meer Street | A3-B3 | | |
| Mulberry Street | B3 | | |
| Narrow Lane | A1 | | |
| New Broad Street | A1 | | |
| Old Town | A1 | | |
| Paddock Place | A1 | | |
| Payton Street | B3-C3 | | |

## Southampton

Southampton is found on atlas page **13**,
grid reference **4112**

**AA shop**
126 Above Bar Street, Southampton SO9 1GY          C5

| | | | | | | | |
|---|---|---|---|---|---|---|---|
| Above Bar Street | C4-C5-C6 | Canute Road | D2-E2 | Elm Terrace | E3 | Latimer Street | D2 |
| Albert Road North | E3 | Captains Place | D2 | Empress Road | D8-E8 | Leyton Road | E7 |
| Alexandra Road | A6 | Carlton Crescent | B7-C7 | Exmoor Road | D6 | Lime Street | D3 |
| Alfred Street | D7-E7 | Carlton Place | B7-C7 | Fitzhugh Place | B8 | Liverpool Street | C7-C8 |
| Amoy Street | B7 | Carlton Road | B7-B8 | Fitzhugh Street | B5 | London Road | C6-C7 |
| Andersons Road | E3 | Castle Street | D8 | French Street | C2 | Lower Alfred Street | E7 |
| Anglesea Terrace | E3 | Castle Way | B4-C4-C3-C2 | Golden Grove | D5-E5-E4 | Lower Banister Street | C6-C7 |
| Archers Road | A7-A8-B8-C8 | Cedar Road | B7 | Graham Road | D6-E6 | Lyon Street | C7-D7-E7 |
| Argyle Road | D6-E6 | Central Bridge | D3-E3-E2 | Graham Street | F6 | Mandela Way | A6 |
| Asylum Road | C6-C7 | Channel Way | E2 | Granville Street | E3-E4 | Marine Parade | E3-E4-E5 |
| Augusta Road | D8 | Chapel Road | D3-D4-E4-E3 | Grosvenor Square | B6 | Maritime Walk | E1 |
| Augustine Road | E6 | Civic Centre Road | B5-C5 | Hampton Street | C3 | Market Place | C3 |
| Banister Gardens | B8 | Clausentum Road | D8 | Handel Road | B6 | Marsh Lane | D3 |
| Banister Road | B8-C8 | Clifford Street | D5 | Handel Terrace | A6-B6 | Melbourne Street | E4 |
| Bargate Street | C4 | Clovelly Road | D6-E6 | Hanover Buildings | C4 | Methuen Street | C7-C8 |
| Bath Street | C8-D8 | Coleman Street | D4-E4 | Harborough Road | B7 | Middle Street | C8-D8 |
| Bedford Place | B7-B6-C6 | College Street | D3 | Harbour Parade | A4-B5-B4-B3 | Millbank Street | F6-F7 |
| Bellevue Road | C7 | Commercial Road | A5-A6-B6-C6 | Hartington Road | E5-E6-E7 | Milton Road | A7-B7 |
| Belvidere Road | E5-F5 | Cook Street | D4 | Havelock Road | B5-B6 | Mordaunt Road | C8-D8 |
| Belvidere Terrace | F6 | Cossack Green | C5-D4 | Hawkswood Road | F8 | Morris Road | A6-B6 |
| Berkeley Road | B7 | Court Road | B8 | Henstead Road | B7 | Mount Pleasant Road | D8-D7-E7 |
| Bernard Street | C3-D3 | Coventry Road | B7 | Herbert Walker Avenue | B2-B3 | Mountbatten Way | A5 |
| Bevois Valley Road | D8 | Cranbury Avenue | D7-E7 | High Street | C2-C3-C4 | Neptune Way | D2 |
| Blechynden Terrace | A5-B5 | Cranbury Place | C7-D7 | Hill Farm Road | A7 | New Road | C5-D5 |
| Bond Street | F6 | Cromwell Road | B7-B8 | Hill Lane | A6-A7-A8 | Newcombe Road | B6-B7 |
| Brighton Road | B8-C8 | Crosshouse Road | E3-F3 | Holt Road | B7 | Nichols Road | D6 |
| Brintons Terrace | D6-D7 | Cumberland Place | B6-C6 | Houndwell Place | C4-D4 | North Front | C5-D5 |
| Britannia Road | E5-E6 | Darwin Road | A8 | Howard Road | A7 | Northam Bridge | F7-F8 |
| Briton Street | C2 | Denzil Avenue | D7-E7 | Imperial Road | E7-E8 | Northam Road | D5-E5-E6-F7 |
| Britons Road | D5-D6 | Derby Road | E5-E6-E7 | Itchen Bridge | E2-F2 | Northbrook Road | D5-D6 |
| Broad Green | D5 | Devonshire Road | B6-B7 | James Street | D4-E4 | Northlands Gardens | A8 |
| Brunswick Place | C6 | Dorset Street | C6-C7 | John Street | D2 | Northlands Road | A8 |
| Brunswick Square | C2-C3 | Dover Street | C8-D8 | Kenilworth Road | B7 | Northumberland Road | E5-E6-E7 |
| Bugle Street | B2-C2-C3 | Duke Street | D3 | Kent Street | F6 | Ocean Way | D1-E1-E2 |
| Bullar Street | D7-E7 | Durnford Road | E6 | King Street | D3 | Ogle Road | B4-C4 |
| Burlington Road | A6-A7 | Earls Road | D8 | Kings Park Road | C6-C7 | Onslow Road | D7 |
| Burton Road | A7 | East Gate Street | C3 | Kingsbury Road | D8 | Orchard Lane | D3 |
| Cambridge Road | C8 | East Park Terrace | C5-C6 | Kingsway | D4-D5 | Orchard Place | C2-D2-D3 |
| Canton Street | B7 | East Street | C3-D3 | Landguard Road | A7 | Ordnance Road | C7 |

| | | | |
|---|---|---|---|
| Oxford Avenue | D6-E6 | St Michaels Street | C3 |
| Oxford Road | C8 | Summers Street | E7-F7 |
| Oxford Street | D2-D3 | Terminus Terrace | D2 |
| Padwell Road | C8-D8 | The Avenue | C7-C8 |
| Paget Street | E3 | The Polygon | B6 |
| Palmerston Road | C4-C5 | Thornbury Avenue | A7-A8 |
| Park Walk | C5 | Town Quay | C2 |
| Parsonage Road | E6 | Trinity Road | D5-D6 |
| Peel Street | E5-F6 | Union Road | E7-F7 |
| Platform Road | C2-D2 | Victoria Street | E5 |
| Porters Lane | C2 | Vincents Walk | C4 |
| Portland Street | C4 | West Marland Road | C5 |
| Portland Terrace | B4-B5 | West Park Road | B5 |
| Pound Tree Road | C4 | West Quay Road | A4-B4-B3 |
| Princes Street | F6 | West Street | C3 |
| Quayside Road | F8 | Western Esplanade | A5-B5-B4-B3 |
| Queens Terrace | D2 | Westrow Gardens | B8 |
| Queensway | C2-C3 | Westrow Road | A8-B8 |
| Radcliffe Road | E6-E7 | William Street | F6 |
| Raven Road | D6-D7 | Wilson Street | E5-E6 |
| Richmond Street | D3 | Wilton Avenue | A7-B7 |
| Roberts Road | A6 | Winchester Street | C7 |
| Rochester Street | E5-F5 | Winkle Street | C2 |
| Rockstone Lane | C7-D7 | Winton Street | C5-D5 |
| Rockstone Place | C7 | York Close | F6 |
| Royal Crescent Road | E2 | | |
| Salisbury Street | C6-C7 | | |
| Saltmarsh Road | E2 | | |
| Sandhurst Road | A6-B6 | | |
| Shirley Road | A5-A6 | | |
| Silverdale Road | A8 | | |
| South Front | C4-D4 | | |
| Southbrook Road | A5 | | |
| Southcliff Road | C7-D7-D8 | | |
| St Albans Road | E6 | | |
| St Andrews Road | C6-D6-D5 | | |
| St Marks Road | D5-D6 | | |
| St Mary Street | D3-D4-D5 | | |
| St Marys Road | D5-D6-D7 | | |

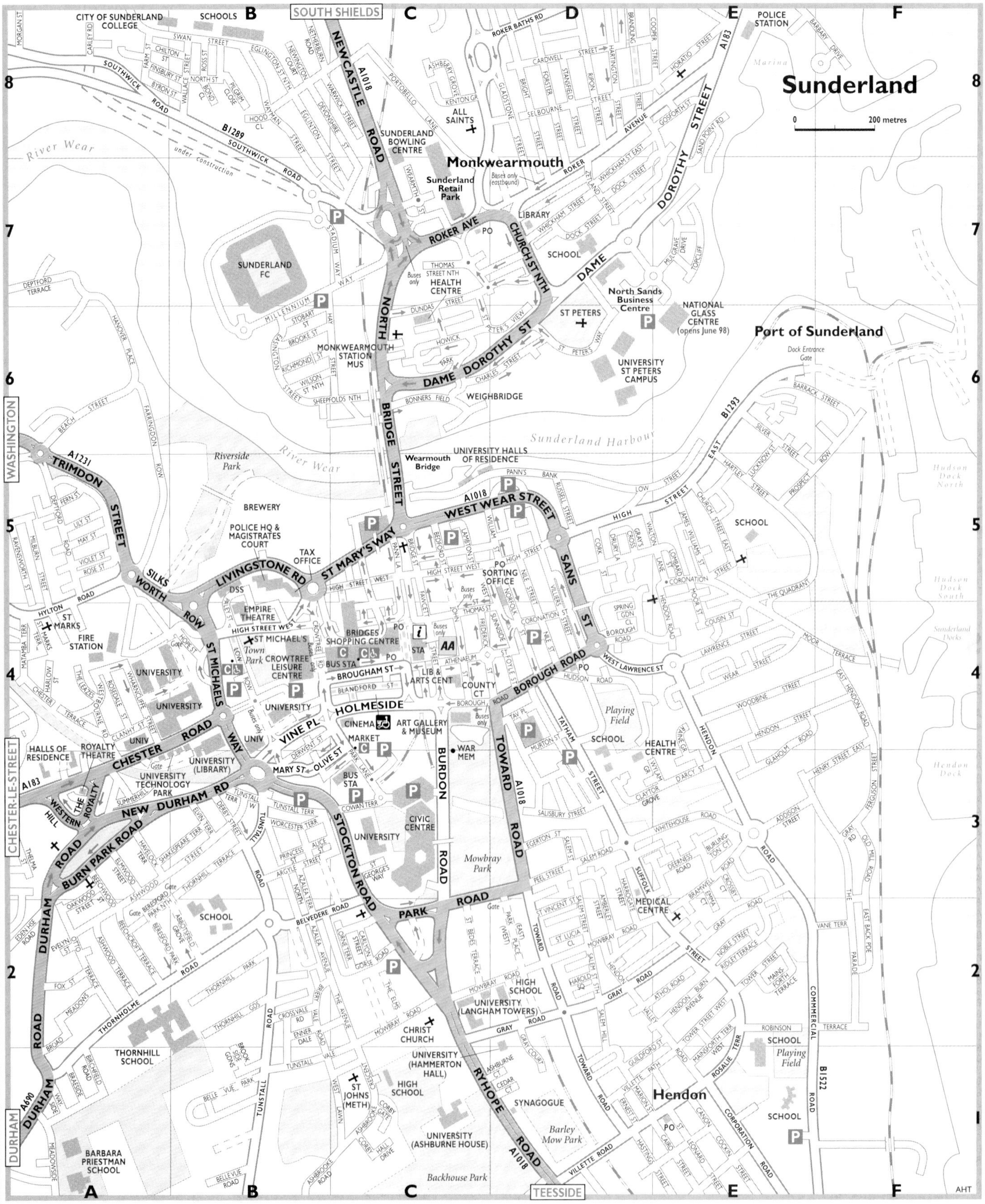

220

**Sunderland**

0    200 metres

SOUTH SHIELDS

CITY OF SUNDERLAND COLLEGE

SCHOOLS

POLICE STATION

Marina

*River Wear*

B1289

SOUTHWICK ROAD

under construction

SUNDERLAND BOWLING CENTRE

ROKER BATHS RD

**Monkwearmouth**

Sunderland Retail Park

Buses only eastbound

LIBRARY

PO

SCHOOL

DAME

DOROTHY STREET

A183

*Deptford Terrace*

SUNDERLAND FC

STADIUM WAY

MILLENNIUM WAY

ROKER AVE

CHURCH ST NTH

THOMAS STREET NTH

HEALTH CENTRE

ST PETERS

North Sands Business Centre

NATIONAL GLASS CENTRE (opens June 98)

**Port of Sunderland**

Dock Entrance Gate

MONKWEARMOUTH STATION MUS

DUNDAS STREET

HOWICK

PETER'S VIEW

UNIVERSITY ST PETERS CAMPUS

DAME DOROTHY ST

CHARLES STREET

SHEEPFOLDS NTH

BONNERS FIELD

WEIGHBRIDGE

*Sunderland Harbour*

BARRACK STREET

*Hudson Dock North*

WASHINGTON

A1231

TRIMDON STREET

*Riverside Park*

*River Wear*

BREWERY

NORTH BRIDGE STREET

Wearmouth Bridge

UNIVERSITY HALLS OF RESIDENCE

PANN'S BANK

B1293

EAST

HARTLEY STREET

SILVER STREET

*Hudson Dock South*

*Sunderland Docks*

SILKSWORTH ROW

POLICE HQ & MAGISTRATES COURT

TAX OFFICE

ST MARY'S WAY

WEST WEAR STREET

SANS ST

HIGH STREET

THE QUADRANT

HYLTON RD

ST MARKS

FIRE STATION

DSS

LIVINGSTONE RD

EMPIRE THEATRE

HIGH STREET WEST

HIGH STREET WEST

SORTING OFFICE

SCHOOL

UNIVERSITY

ST MICHAEL'S

ST MICHAEL'S WAY

Town Park

CROWTREE LEISURE CENTRE

BRIDGES SHOPPING CENTRE

PO

BUS STA

BROUGHAM ST

BLANDFORD ST

LIB & ARTS CENT

COUNTY CT

BOROUGH ROAD

PO

WEST LAWRENCE ST

*Playing Field*

SCHOOL

HEALTH CENTRE

UNIVERSITY

HOLMESIDE

VINE PL

CINEMA

ART GALLERY & MUSEUM

WAR MEM

TOWARD ROAD

HALLS OF RESIDENCE

ROYALTY THEATRE

CHESTER ROAD

UNIVERSITY TECHNOLOGY PARK

UNIVERSITY (LIBRARY)

MARKET

BUS STA

COWAN TERR

CIVIC CENTRE

*Mowbray Park*

CHESTER-LE-STREET

A183

THE ROYALTY

WESTERN HILL

NEW DURHAM RD

NEW DURHAM ROAD

MARY ST

OLIVE ST

BURDON

TUNSTALL

WORCESTER TERR

UNIVERSITY

ST GEORGES WAY

SALISBURY STREET

MEDICAL CENTRE

BURN PARK ROAD

DURHAM ROAD

STOCKTON ROAD

BELVEDERE ROAD

PARK ROAD

HIGH SCHOOL

*Barley Mow Park*

**Hendon**

THORNHILL SCHOOL

THORNHOLME

CHRIST CHURCH

UNIVERSITY (HAMMERTON HALL)

UNIVERSITY (LANGHAM TOWERS)

RHOPE ROAD

A1018

SYNAGOGUE

SCHOOL

ROBINSON TERRACE

SCHOOL

*Playing Field*

B1522

DURHAM

A690

DURHAM ROAD

BARBARA PRIESTMAN SCHOOL

BELLE VUE PARK

ST JOHNS (METH)

HIGH SCHOOL

UNIVERSITY (ASHBURNE HOUSE)

*Backhouse Park*

TEESSIDE

COMMERCIAL ROAD

*Hendon Dock*

AHT

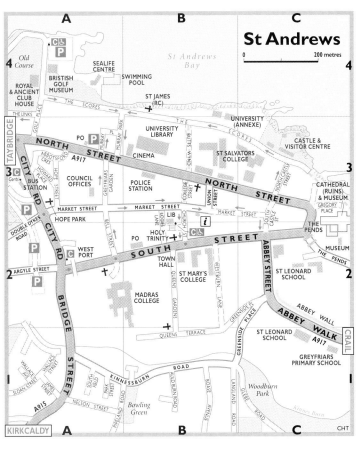

# St Andrews

St Andrews is found on atlas page **127**, grid reference **5116**

| | | | |
|---|---|---|---|
| Abbey Street | C2 | Logies Lane | B2-B3 |
| Abbey Walk | C1-C2 | Market Street | A3-B3-C3 |
| Abbotsford Crescent | A3 | Murray Park | A3-B4 |
| Argyle Street | A2 | Murray Place | A3 |
| Auld Burn Road | B1 | Nelson Street | A1 |
| Bell Street | A2-A3 | North Castle Street | C3 |
| Boase Avenue | B1 | North Street | A3-B3-C3 |
| Bridge Street | A1-A2 | Park Street | A1 |
| Butts Wynd | B3 | Pipeland Road | A1-B1 |
| Church Street | B2-B3 | Queens Gardens | B1-B2 |
| City Road | A2-A3 | Queens Terrace | B1 |
| College Street | B3 | Sloan Street | A1 |
| Double Dykes Road | A2-A3 | South Castle Street | C2-C3 |
| Glebe Road | C1 | South Street | A2-C2 |
| Golf Place | A3-A4 | Southfield | A1 |
| Greenside Place | C1-C2 | The Links | A4 |
| Gregory Place | C3 | The Pends | C2 |
| Greyfriars Gardens | A3 | The Scores | B4-C3 |
| Hope Street | A3 | Union Street | B3 |
| Howard Place | A3 | Wallace Avenue | A1 |
| James Street | A1 | Wallace Street | A1 |
| Kinnessburn Road | A1-B1 | Westburn Lane | B2 |
| Langland Road | B1 | | |

# Sunderland

Sunderland is found on atlas page **96**, grid reference **NZ3957**

**AA shop**
49 Fawett Street, Sunderland SR1 1RR          C4

| | | | | | | | | | | | |
|---|---|---|---|---|---|---|---|---|---|---|---|
| Abbotsfield Grove | B2 | Brougham Street | B4-C4 | Henry Street East | E3-F4 | Park Lane | C3-C4 | Swan Street | A8-B8 |
| Addison Street | E3 | Burdon Road | C2-C4 | High Street | B5-D5 | Park Place West | D2 | Tavistock Place | D4 |
| Alice Street | B3 | Burlington Court | E3 | High Street West | B4-B5-C5 | Park Road | C2-D3 | The Avenue | B2-C2 |
| Amberley Street | D2-D3 | Burn Park Road | A3 | Holmside | C4 | Peel Street | D3 | The Elms | C2 |
| Argyle Street | B3-C3 | Byron Street | A8-B8 | Hood Close | B8 | Pilgrim Close | B8 | The Leazes | A4 |
| Ashberry Grove | C8 | Cairo Street | E1 | Hope Street | A4-B4 | Portobello Lane | C7-C8 | The Parade | E3-F2 |
| Ashbrooke Crescent | C1 | Canon Cockin Street | E1 | Horatio Street | E8 | Princess Street | B3 | The Quadrant | E5 |
| Ashbrooke Road | B1-C1 | Cardwell Street | D8 | Howick Park | C6 | Prospect Row | E5-F6 | The Royalty | A3 |
| Ashburne Court | C1-C2 | Carley Road | A8 | Hudson Street | D4 | Raine Grove | E4 | Thelma Street | A3 |
| Ashwood Street | A2-B3 | Carlyon Street | C2 | Hylton Road | A4-A5 | Ravensworth Street | A4-A5 | Thomas Street North | C7 |
| Ashwood Terrace | A2 | Cedar Court | D1 | James Williams Street | E5 | Richmond Street | B6 | Thornhill Gardens | B2 |
| Athenaeum Street | C4-D4 | Charles Street | C6-D6 | John Street | C4-C5 | Ridley Terrace | E2 | Thornhill Park | B2 |
| Athol Road | D2-E2 | Chester Road | A3-B4 | Kenton Grove | C8 | Ripon Street | D8 | Thornhill Terrace | B3 |
| Azalea Terrace Avenue | B2 | Chester Terrace | A4 | Lambton Street | C5 | Robinson Terrace | E2-F2 | Thornholme Road | A1-B2 |
| Azalea Terrace North | B2-B3 | Chilton Street | A8-B8 | Lawrence Street | E4 | Roker Avenue | C7-E8 | Topcliff | E7 |
| Barbary Drive | E8-F8 | Church Street East | E5 | Lily Street | A5 | Roker Baths Road | D8 | Toward Road | D1-D4 |
| Beach Street | A6 | Clanny Street | A4 | Livingstone Road | B5 | Rosalie Terrace | E1-E2 | Tower Street | B3 |
| Bedford Street | C5 | Clayton Grove | D3-E3 | Lombard Street | E5 | Rose Street | A5 | Tower Street West | E2 |
| Beechcroft Terrace | A2 | Commercial Road | E1-E2 | Lorne Terrace | C2 | Rosedale Street | A4 | Trimdon Street | A5-A6 |
| Beechwood Street | A2-A3 | Cooper Street | E8 | Low Row | B4 | Ross Street | B8 | Tunstall Road | B1-B3 |
| Belle Vue Park | B1 | Corby Gate | C1 | Low Street | D5-E6 | Russell Street | D5 | Tunstall Terrace | B3 |
| Belvedere Road | B2-C3 | Corby Hall Drive | C1 | Lucknow Street | E5-E6 | Ryhope Road | C2-D1 | Tunstall Terrace West | B3 |
| Beresford Park North | A2-B3 | Cork Street | D5 | Mainsforth Terrace | E2 | St Bedes Terrace | C2 | Tunstall Vale | B1-C2 |
| Beresford Road | A2-B2 | Coronation Street | D4-E5 | Mainsforth Terrace West | E1-E2 | St George's Way | C3 | Vane Terrace | F2 |
| Birchfield Road | A1 | Corporation Road | E1 | Marion Street | D1 | St Leonard Street | E1 | Villette Path | D1-E1 |
| Black Road | B7-C7 | Cousin Street | E4 | Mary Street | B3 | St Lucia Close | D2 | Villette Road | D1-E1 |
| Blandford Street | C4 | Cowan Terrace | C3 | Matamba Terrace | A4 | St Marks Terrace | A4 | Villiers Street | D4-D5 |
| Bond Close | B8 | Crossby Court | E3 | May Street | A5 | St Mary's Way | B5-C5 | Vine Place | B3-B4 |
| Bonners Field | C6 | Cross Vale Road | B2 | Meadowside | A1 | St Michael's Way | B3-B4 | Violet Street | A5 |
| Borough Road | C4-E4 | Crowtree Road | B4 | Milburn Street | A5 | St Peter's View | C7-D7 | Wallace Street | B8 |
| Braeside | A1 | D'Arcy Street | E3 | Millennium Way | B6-B7-C7 | St Peter's Way | D6-D7 | Walton Lane | D5-E5 |
| Bramwell Road | E2-E3 | Dame Dorothy Street | D6-E8 | Moor Street | E4-E5 | St Thomas Street | C4-D4 | Warren Street | E6 |
| Brandling Street | D8 | Deerness Road | E3 | Moor Terrace | E4-F4 | St Vincent Street | D2 | Warwick Street | B8-C8 |
| Bridge Street | C5 | Deptford Road | A5 | Morgan Street | A8 | Salem Hill | D2 | Wayman Street | B8-C7 |
| Briery Vale Road | B1-B2 | Deptford Terrace | A7 | Mowbray Road | C2-E2 | Salem Road | D3 | Wayside | A1 |
| Bright Street | D7-D8 | Derby Street | B3 | Mulgrave Drive | E7 | Salem Street | D2-D3 | Wear Street | E4 |
| Broad Meadows | A1-A2 | Derwent Street | B3-C3 | Murton Street | D3-D4 | Salem Street South | D2 | Wearmouth Street | C7 |
| Brooke Street | B6 | Devonshire Street | B8-C7 | Netherburn Road | B8 | Salisbury Street | D3 | West Lawn | B1-C1 |
| Brookside Gardens | B1-B2 | Dock Street | D7-E8 | New Durham Road | A3-B3 | Sand Point Road | E7-E8 | West Lawrence Street | D4-E4 |
| | | Drury Lane | D5 | Newington Court | B8 | Sans Street | D4-D5 | West Sunniside | C5-D4 |
| | | Dundas Street | C6-C7 | Nile Street | D4-D5 | Selbourne Street | D8 | West Wear Street | C5-D5 |
| | | Durham Road | A1-A3 | Noble Street | E2 | Shakespeare Terrace | A3-B3 | Westbourne Road | A3-A4 |
| | | Easington Street | B6 | Norfolk Street | D4-D5 | Sheepfolds North | B6-C6 | Western Hill | A3 |
| | | East Back Poe | F2 | North Bridge Street | C5-C7 | Silksworth Row | A5-B4 | Wharncliffe Street | A4 |
| | | East Barrack Street | D5-F6 | North Street | B8 | Silver Street | E5-E6 | Whickham Street | D7-D8 |
| | | East Hendon Road | F4 | Old Mill Road | F3 | Southwick Road | A8-C7 | Whitehouse Road | D3-E3 |
| | | Eden House Road | A2 | Olive Street | B3-C4 | Spring Garden Close | D4 | Wilson Street North | B6 |
| | | Egerton Street | D3 | Osman Terrace | D3-E3 | Stadium Way | B7-C7 | Woodbine Street | E4-F4 |
| | | Eglinton Street | B8-C7 | Otto Terrace | A2 | Stansfield Street | D7-D8 | Worcester Terrace | B3 |
| | | Eglinton Street North | B8 | Paley Street | B4-B5 | Stobart Street | B6-B7 | Wreath Quay Road | B6-C7 |
| | | Elmwood Street | A3 | Pann's Bank | C5-D5 | Stockton Road | B3-C2 | Wylam Grove | E3 |
| | | Elvin Terrace | B3 | Pann Lane | C5 | Summerhill | A3 | Zetland Street | D7 |
| | | Emma Court | E2-E3 | | | | | | |
| | | Ennerdale | B2 | | | | | | |
| | | Ernest Street | D1 | | | | | | |
| | | Evelyn Street | A2 | | | | | | |
| | | Farm Street | A8 | | | | | | |
| | | Farringdon Row | A5-A6 | | | | | | |
| | | Fawcett Street | C4-C5 | | | | | | |
| | | Ferguson Street | F3 | | | | | | |
| | | Fern Street | A5 | | | | | | |
| | | Finsbury Street | A8-B8 | | | | | | |
| | | Forster Street | D7-D8 | | | | | | |
| | | Fox Street | A2 | | | | | | |
| | | Foyle Street | D4 | | | | | | |
| | | Frederick Street | C4-D4 | | | | | | |
| | | George Street | D5 | | | | | | |
| | | Gladstone Street | D7-D8 | | | | | | |
| | | Glaholm Road | E3-E4 | | | | | | |
| | | Gorse Road | C2 | | | | | | |
| | | Gosforth Street | E8 | | | | | | |
| | | Gray Court | D1-D2 | | | | | | |
| | | Gray Road | C2-E3-F3 | | | | | | |
| | | Grays Cross | D5 | | | | | | |
| | | Guildford Street | D1-E2 | | | | | | |
| | | Gunton Street | B8-C7 | | | | | | |
| | | Hanover Place | A6-A7 | | | | | | |
| | | Harold Square | D2 | | | | | | |
| | | Hartington Street | D8 | | | | | | |
| | | Harlow Street | A4 | | | | | | |
| | | Harrogate Street | D2-D3 | | | | | | |
| | | Hartley Street | E5-E6 | | | | | | |
| | | Hastings Road | D1-E1 | | | | | | |
| | | Havelock Terrace | A3 | | | | | | |
| | | Hay Street | C6-C7 | | | | | | |
| | | Hendon Burn Avenue | D2-E2 | | | | | | |
| | | Hendon Road | E2-E5 | | | | | | |
| | | Hendon Street | E4-F4 | | | | | | |
| | | Hendon Valley Road | D2-E1 | | | | | | |

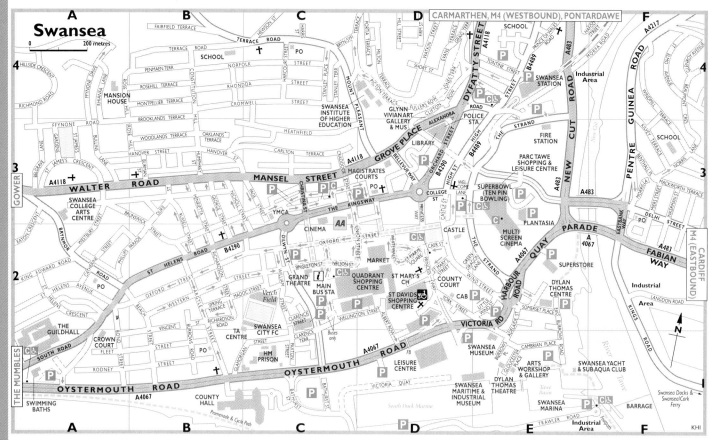

# Swansea

Swansea is found on atlas page **32**,
grid reference **6592**

**AA shop**
20 Union Street, Swansea SA1 3EH                    C3

| | | | | | | |
|---|---|---|---|---|---|---|
| Adelaide Street | E1-E2 | Evans Terrace | D4 | Montpellier Terrace | A4-B4 | Short Street | D4 |

| | | | | |
|---|---|---|---|---|
| Adelaide Street | E1-E2 | Evans Terrace | D4 | Montpellier Terrace | A4-B4 |
| Albert Row | D2-D1 | Fabian Way | F2 | Morfa Road | E4-F4 |
| Alexandra Road | D3-D4-E4 | Fairfield Terrace | B4 | Morris Lane | F3 |
| Argyle Street | B2-B1 | Ffynone Drive | A4-A3 | Mount Pleasant | C4-D3 |
| Bathurst Street | C1 | Ffynone Road | A3 | Nelson Street | C2 |
| Beach Street | A2-B2-B1 | Firm Street | D4 | New Cut Road | E3-E4 |
| Beaumont Crescent | F3-F4 | Fleet Street | A1-B1 | Nicholl Street | B3-C2 |
| Belgrave Lane | A3 | Fullers Row | D4 | Norfolk Street | B4-C4 |
| Bellevue Way | D3 | George Street | B3-B2 | Oaklands Terrace | B3 |
| Benthall Place | F3 | Glamorgan Street | B1-C1 | Orchard Street | D3 |
| Bond Street | A2-A1 | Glenroy Avenue | F4 | Oxford Street | A2-B2-C2-D2 |
| Brooklands Terrace | B3 | Gloucester Place | E1 | Oystermouth Road A1-B1-C1-D1 | |
| Brunswick Street | A3-B3-B2 | Graig Terrace | D4 | Page Street | C3 |
| Bryn-y-mor Road | A3-A2 | Green Dragon Lane | D2-E2 | Paxton Street | C1 |
| Bryn-Syfi Terrace | C4-D4 | Grove Place | D3 | Penmaen Terrace | B4 |
| Bullins Lane | A3 | Hafod Street | F4 | Pentre Guinea Road | F3-F4 |
| Burman Street | B3 | Hanover Street | A3-B3 | Phillips Parade | A2-B2 |
| Burrows Place | E1 | Harbour Road | E2 | Picton Terrace | D4 |
| Burrows Road | B2-B1 | Harcourt Street | C4 | Portia Terrace | D4 |
| Caer Street | D2 | Harris Street | C4 | Prince of Wales Road | E4 |
| Cambrian Place | E1 | Heathfield | B3-C3 | Princess Way | D2-D3 |
| Carlton Terrace | B3-C3 | Henrietta Street | B3-B2 | Quay Parade | E2-F2 |
| Castle Street | D3 | Hewson Street | C4 | Rhianfa Lane | A3-A4 |
| Catherine Street | A2-B2 | High Street | D3-E3-E4 | Rhondda Street | B4-C4 |
| Christina Street | C3 | Hill Street | D4 | Richardson Road | B2 |
| Clarence Street | C2 | Hillside Crescent | A4 | Richardson Street | B2 |
| Clarence Terrace | C1 | Humphrey Street | B3 | Richmond Road | A4 |
| Clifton Row | D3-D4 | Inkerman Street | F2-F3 | Rodney Street | A1-B1 |
| College Street | D3 | Jones Terrace | D4 | Rose Hill | A4-B3 |
| Constitution Hill | B4-B3 | Kilvey Terrace | F3 | Rosehill Terrace | A4-B4 |
| Craddock Street | C3 | King Edward Road | A2 | Russell Street | B3-B2 |
| Cromwell Street | B4-C4 | Kings Road | F2-F1 | St Elmo Avenue | F4 |
| Delhi Street | F3-F2 | Langdon Road | F2 | St Helens Avenue | A2 |
| Dilwyn Street | C2 | Little Wynd Street | E2 | St Helens Crescent | A2 |
| Duke Street | B3 | Mackworth Terrace | F3 | St Helens Road | A1-A2-B2-C2 |
| Dyfatty Street | D4-E4 | Madoc Street | B2-C2 | St James's Crescent | A3 |
| Eastbank Way | F2-F3 | Mansel Street | C3 | St James's Gardens | A3 |
| East Burrows Road | E1-E2 | Miers Street | F2-F3 | St Mary's Square | D2 |
| Eaton Crescent | A2-A3 | Milton Terrace | D4 | St Mary's Street | D2 |

| | |
|---|---|
| Short Street | D4 |
| Singleton Street | C2 |
| Somerset Place | E2 |
| South Road | A1 |
| Spring Terrace | B2 |
| Stanley Place | C4 |
| Stanley Terrace | C4 |
| Terrace Road | B4-C4 |
| The Kingsway | C3-D3 |
| The Strand | E2-D2-D3-E3 |
| Tontine Street | E4 |
| Trawler Road | D1-E1-F1 |
| Union Street | C2-D2 |
| Upper Strand | E4 |
| Victoria Road | D2-E2 |
| Victoria Quay | C1-D1 |
| Vincent Street | A1-B1 |
| Walter Road | A3-B3 |
| Watkin Street | D4 |
| Welcome Lane | D3 |
| Wellington Street | C2-D2 |
| Westbury Street | A2-A3 |
| Western Street | B2-C2 |
| Whitewalls | D2 |
| William Street | C1-C2 |
| Wind Street | D2-E2 |
| Windmill Terrace | F3-F4 |
| Woodlands Terrace | B3 |
| York Street | D2 |

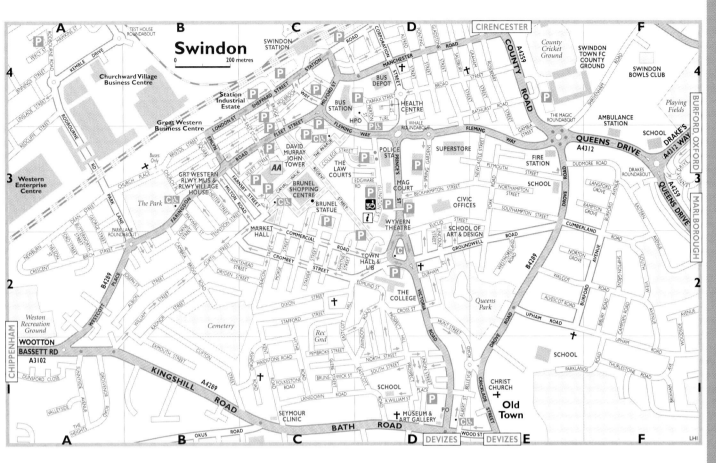

# Swindon

Swindon is found on atlas page **36**,
grid reference **1484**

**AA shop**
22 Canal Walk, Brunel Shopping Centre, Swindon SN1 1LD    C3

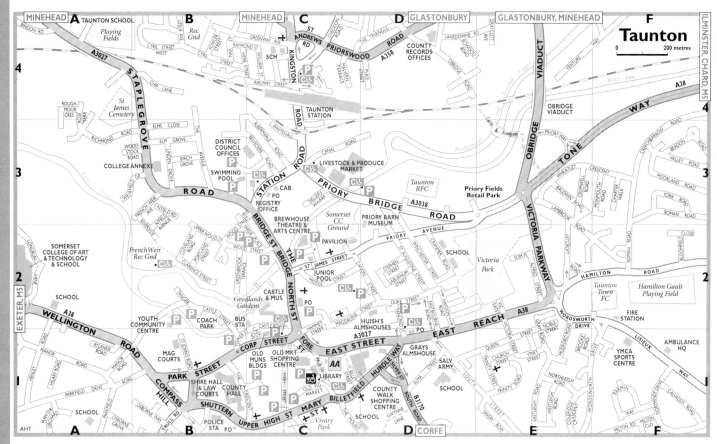

# Taunton

Taunton is found on atlas page **20**,
grid reference **2224**

**AA shop**
6 Cheapside, Taunton TA1 3BR                    C1

| | | | | | | | |
|---|---|---|---|---|---|---|---|
| Albermarle Road | C3-B4-C4 | Eastbourne Road | D2 | Noble Street | E2 | South Street | D1-E1 |
| Alfred Street | E2 | Eastleigh Road | E1 | Normandy Drive | F1 | Staplegrove Road | A4-B4-B3 |
| Alma Street | D1 | Elm Grove | B3 | North Street | C2 | Station Road | C3-C4 |
| Aylands Road | A1 | Elms Close | B3 | Northfield Avenue | B2-B3 | Stephen Street | D2 |
| Baldwin Road | E3 | Fore Street | C2-C1 | Northfield Road | B3 | Tancred Street | D2-D1 |
| Beadon Road | F3 | Fowler Street | B4 | Northleigh Road | E1 | Tangier | B2 |
| Belvedere Road | B3-C3 | French Weir Avenue | B3 | Obridge Road | D4 | The Avenue | B4-B3 |
| Billet Street | C1 | Grays Road | E1-E2 | Obridge Viaduct | E3-E4 | The Bridge | C2 |
| Billetfield | C1-D1 | Greenbrook Terrace | B2 | Old Pig Market | C1 | The Crescent | B1-C1 |
| Bindon Road | A4 | Greenway Avenue | B4-C4 | Osborne Grove | A1-B1 | The Mount | C1 |
| Birch Grove | B3 | Gwynne Lane | D1 | Osborne Way | B1 | The Triangle | C4-D4 |
| Bloomfield Close | F2 | Hamilton Road | E2-F2 | Park Street | B1 | Tone Way | E3-F3-F4 |
| Bowood Road | D4 | Hammet Street | C1-C2 | Parkfield Drive | A1 | Tower Street | B1-C1 |
| Bridge Street | C3-C2 | Henley Road | A1-A2 | Parkfield Road | A1 | Trinity Road | E1 |
| Brooke Road | E1-E2 | Herbert Street | B4-C4 | Parmin Way | F1 | Trinity Street | E1 |
| Calvados Road | F1 | High Street | C1 | Paul Street | C1 | Trull Road | B1 |
| Canal Road | C3-D3 | Hilary Road | A1 | Plais Street | D4 | Upper High Street | B1-C1 |
| Canon Street | C2-D2 | Hurdle Way | D1 | Portland Street | B2 | Upper Wood Street | B3-B2 |
| Castle Bow | C2 | Kingston Road | C4 | Priorswood Road | C4-D4 | Valley Road | F3 |
| Castle Green | C1 | Laburnum Street | D2 | Priory Avenue | D2-D3 | Venture Way | E4-F4 |
| Castle Street | B2-B1 | Lambrook Road | E3-E2-F2 | Priory Bridge Road | C3-D3 | Victoria Gate | E2 |
| Charter Walk | F3 | Lansdowne Road | D4-E4 | Priory Way | E3 | Victoria Parkway | E3-E2 |
| Cheddon Road | C4 | Leslie Avenue | B4 | Queen Street | D1-E1-E2 | Victoria Street | E2-E1 |
| Church Street | E1 | Leycroft Road | E3-E2 | Railway Street | C4 | Viney Street | E1 |
| Clarence Street | B2 | Linden Grove | B3 | Raymond Street | B4-C4 | Weirfield Green | A3-B3 |
| Cleveland Road | B2 | Lisieux Way | F2-F1 | Richmond Road | A3-B3 | Wellington Road | A2-A1-B1 |
| Coleridge Crescent | E1 | Longrun Lane | A2-A3 | Riverside | B3-B2 | Westgate Street | B1 |
| Compass Hill | B1 | Magdalene Street | C2-D2 | Roman Road | F2-F3 | Westleigh Road | E1 |
| Corporation Street | B1-C1 | Malvern Terrace | C4 | Rose Terrace | A3-A4 | Wheatley Crescent | E3-F3 |
| Cranmer Road | D2 | Manor Orchard | A1 | Roughmoor Crescent | A3-A4 | Whitefield | C3 |
| Creechbarrow Road | F3-F4 | Manor Road | A1 | St Andrews Road | C4 | Whitehall | C3 |
| Cromwell Road | E3 | Mary Street | C1 | St Augustine Street | D3-D2 | William Street | D2 |
| Cyril Street | B4 | Max Street | B4 | St James Street | C2 | Winchester Street | D2 |
| Cyril Street West | B4 | Middle Street | C2 | St John's Road | B1 | Wood Street | C2-B2-B3-C3 |
| Deller's Wharf | C3 | Milton Close | F1 | Savery Row | E1 | Woodstock Road | A3-B3 |
| Draycott Avenue | E4 | Milton Road | F1 | Shutter | B1 | Wordsworth Drive | E1-F1-F2-E2 |
| Duke Street | D2 | Monmouth Road | E3-F3 | Silver Street | D1 | Yarde Place | B3-C2 |
| East Reach | D1-D2-E2 | Moorland Road | F3 | Somerset Place | E2 | York Road | F3 |
| East Street | C1-D1 | Mudford Road | E1-E2 | South Road | D1 | | |

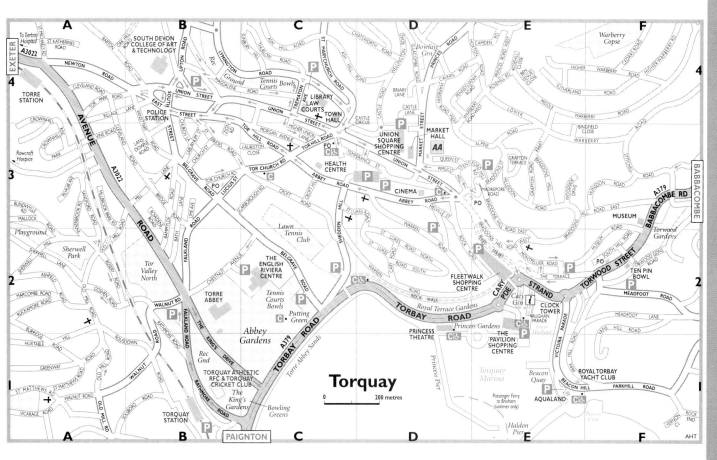

# Torquay

Torquay is found on atlas page **7**,
grid reference **9164**

**AA shop**
8 Market Street, Torquay TQ1 3AQ                    D3

| | | | | | | | |
|---|---|---|---|---|---|---|---|
| Abbey Road | C3-D3 | Ellacombe Road | D4 | Parkhill Road | F1 | Temperance Street | C3-D3 |
| Alpine Road | D3-E3 | Falkland Road | B1-B3 | Pennsylvania Road | D4-E4 | The King's Drive | B2-C1 |
| Ash Hill Road | C4-D4 | Fleet Street | E2-E3 | Pilmuir Avenue | A3 | The Terrace | E2-F2 |
| Ashfield Road | A2 | Goshen Road | A2-B2 | Pimlico Hill | D3 | Thurlow Road | C4 |
| Avenue Road | A4-B2 | Grafton Road | E3 | Princes Road | D4 | Tor Church Road | B3-C3 |
| Babbacombe Road | F2-F3 | Grafton Terrace | E3 | Princes Road West | E4 | Tor Hill Road | B4-C3 |
| Bampfylde Road | B2-B3 | Greenway Road | A1 | Queen Street | D3 | Tor Park Road | A4 |
| Barton Road | A4-B4 | Higher Union Lane | C3 | Rathmore Road | B1-B2 | Torbay Road | C1-E2 |
| Bath Lane | B2-B3 | Higher Warberry Road | E4-F4 | Rillage Lane | A4-B4 | Torwood Close | F2 |
| Beacon Hill | E1-F1 | Hillesdon Road | E3 | Rock End | F1 | Torwood Gardens Road | F2 |
| Belgrave Road | B3-C2 | Hoxton Road | E4 | Rock Road | D3-E2 | Torwood Street | E2-F2 |
| Ben Venue Close | E4 | Hunsdon Road | F3 | Rosery Road | A2 | Trematon Avenue | C4 |
| Bingfield Close | E4 | Huxtable Hill | A1-A2 | Rooklands Avenue | A4 | Union Street | B4-D3 |
| Blindwylle Road | A3 | Innerbrook Road | A2-A3 | Rosehill Road | E4 | Upper Braddons Hill | E3-E4 |
| Braddons Hill Road | D3-E3-E2 | Laburnum Street | B3 | Rosehill Close | E4 | Upton Road | B4 |
| Braddons Hill Road East | E2-E3-F3 | Lansdowne Road | B3 | Rousdown Road | A1-B1 | Vane Hill Road | F1-F2 |
| Braddons Hill Road West | D3-E2 | Lauriston Close | C3 | Rowdens Road | B2-B3 | Vansittart Road | B3-B4 |
| Braddons Street | E3 | Lime Avenue | B3 | Ruckamore Road | A2 | Vaughan Parade | E2 |
| Briary Lane | D4 | Lower Warberry Road | E4-F4 | St Efrides Road | B4-C3 | Vernon Close | F1 |
| Bridge Road | B3 | Lucius Street | B3 | St Katherines Road | A4 | Vicarage Road | A1 |
| Burridge Road | A1-A2 | Lymington Road | B4-C4 | St Lukes Road | C3-D3 | Victoria Parade | E1-E2 |
| Camden Road | E4 | Madrepore Road | D3 | St Lukes Road North | D2 | Vine Road | A3 |
| Cary Parade | E2 | Magdalene Road | B4-C4 | St Lukes Road South | D2 | Walnut Road | A1-B2 |
| Cary Road | D2 | Mallock Road | A2-A3 | St Marychurch Road | C4 | Warberry Road West | D4-E4 |
| Castle Circus | C3 | Marcombe Road | A2 | St Matthews Road | A1 | Warren Road | C2-D2-D3 |
| Castle Lane | D4 | Market Street | D3-D4 | St Michaels Road | A4 | Wellington Road | D4 |
| Castle Road | D3-D4 | Meadfoot Lane | F2 | Sandford Road | A2-A3 | Woodside Drive | E3 |
| Cavern Road | D4-E4 | Meadfoot Road | F2 | Scarborough Road | B3-C3 | Zion Road | B3-B4 |
| Cedars Road | F4 | Melville Street | D3 | Shedden Hill | C2-C3 | | |
| Chatsworth Road | C4-D4 | Middle Warberry Road | E4-F4 | Sherwell Hill | A2 | | |
| Chestnut Avenue | B2-C2 | Mill Lane | B3 | Sherwell Lane | A2 | | |
| Church Lane | B3-B4 | Millbrook Park Road | A3 | Solsboro Road | A1-B1 | | |
| Church Street | B3 | Montpellier Road | E2 | South Hill Road | F2-F3 | | |
| Cleveland Road | A4-B3 | Morgan Avenue | C3 | South Street | B3-B4 | | |
| Croft Hill | C3 | Museum Road | E2-F2 | Stentiford Hill Road | D3-E3 | | |
| Croft Road | C2-C3 | Newton Road | A4 | Stitchill Road | F3-F4 | | |
| Crownhill Park | A3 | Oak Hill Road | A4-B4 | Strand | E2 | | |
| Crownhill Rise | A3-A4 | Old Mill Road | A1-A3 | Sunbury Hill | C4 | | |
| East Street | B4 | Park Hill Road | E1-F2 | Sutherland Road | E4-F4 | | |

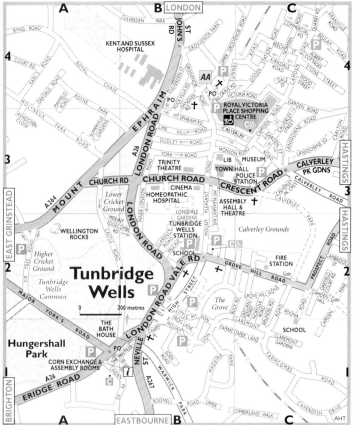

# Tunbridge Wells

Tunbridge Wells is found on atlas page 16,
grid reference 5839

**AA shop**
2 Upper Grosvenor Road, Tunbridge Wells TN1 2EN          B4

| | | | | | | |
|---|---|---|---|---|---|
| Albert Cottages | C4 | Granville Road | C4 | Tunnel Road | B4-C4 |
| Arundel Road | C1-C2 | Grecian Road | C2 | Upper Cumberland Walk | B1-C1 |
| Ashdown Close | A3-A4 | Grosvenor Park | B4 | Upper Grosvenor Road | B4-C4 |
| Beech Street | C4 | Grosvenor Road | B3-B4 | Vale Avenue | B2 |
| Belgrave Road | B4-C4 | Grove Hill Gardens | C2 | Vale Road | B2 |
| Beulah Road | C4 | Grove Hill Road | B2-C2 | Victoria Road | B4-C4 |
| Boyne Park | A4-A3-B3 | Hanover Road | B3-B4 | Warwick Park | B1 |
| Buck Road | B2-C2 | High Street | B2 | Wood Street | C4 |
| Byng Road | A4 | Inner London Road | B2-B3 | York Road | B3 |
| Calverley Park | C2-C3 | Kirkdale Road | C4 | | |
| Calverley Park Crescent | C3 | Lansdowne Road | C3 | | |
| Calverley Park Gardens | C3 | Lansdowne Square | C3 | | |
| Calverley Road | B3-C3 | Lime Hill Road | B3 | | |
| Calverley Street | C3-C4 | Linden Park Road | A1-B1 | | |
| Cambridge Street | C2 | Little Mount Sion | B1-B2 | | |
| Camden Hill | C2 | London Road | A1-B1-B2-B3 | | |
| Camden Park | C1-C2 | Lonsdale Gardens | B2 | | |
| Camden Road | C3-C4 | Madeira Park | B1 | | |
| Carlton Road | C3 | Major York's Road | A1-A2 | | |
| Castle Road | A3-A2-B2-B1 | Mayfield Road | A3-A4 | | |
| Cavendish Drive | C1 | Molyneux Park Road | A3-A4 | | |
| Chapel Place | B1 | Monson Road | B3-C3 | | |
| Church Road | A3-B3 | Mount Edgecombe Road | A2-B2 | | |
| Claremont Gardens | C1 | Mount Ephraim | A2-A3-B3-B4 | | |
| Claremont Road | C1-C2 | Mount Ephraim Road | B3 | | |
| Clarence Road | B2 | Mount Pleasant Avenue | B2-B3 | | |
| Commercial Road | C4 | Mount Pleasant Road | B2-B3 | | |
| Court Road | A4 | Mount Sion | B1 | | |
| Crescent Road | B3-C3 | Neville Street | B1 | | |
| Culverden Park | A4-B4 | Norfolk Road | C1-C2 | | |
| Culverden Street | B4 | Norman Road | C4 | | |
| Dale Street | C4 | Oakdale Road | A4 | | |
| Dudley Road | B3 | Oakfield Court Road | C2 | | |
| Earl's Road | A4 | Poona Road | C2 | | |
| Eden Road | B1 | Prospect Road | C2 | | |
| Eridge Road | A1 | Quarry Road | C4 | | |
| Farmcombe Lane | B1-C1 | Rock Villa Road | B3-B4 | | |
| Farmcombe Road | C1 | Rodmell Road | B1 | | |
| Fir Tree Road | A2 | Royal Chase | A4-B4-B3 | | |
| Frog Lane | B1-B2 | Somerville Gardens | A3 | | |
| Garden Road | C3-C4 | St John's Road | B4 | | |
| Garden Street | C3 | Stone Street | C4 | | |
| Goods Station Road | C4 | The Pantiles | A1-B1 | | |

# Warwick

Warwick is found on atlas page 48,
grid reference 2865

| | | | |
|---|---|---|---|
| Albert Street | A4 | Smith Street | B2-C3 |
| Archery Fields | C1 | Spring Pool | A4 |
| Banbury Road | B2-C1 | Station Avenue | C4 |
| Barn Street | A3 | Station Road | C4 |
| Bartlett Close | C3 | Swan Street | A2 |
| Black Lane | A2 | The Butts | A3-B2 |
| Bowling Green Street | A2 | The Paddocks | C3 |
| Bridge Brooke Close | B1-C1 | Theatre Street | A3 |
| Bridge End | B1-C1 | Victoria Street | A3-A4 |
| Brook Street | A2 | Vine Street | B4 |
| Cape Road | A3-A4 | West Street | A1-A2 |
| Castle Close | A1 | Woodcote Road | C4 |
| Castle Hill | B2 | | |
| Castle Lane | A2-B2 | | |
| Castle Street | A2-B2 | | |
| Cattel Road | A4 | | |
| Chapel Street | B3 | | |
| Cherry Street | C3-C4 | | |
| Church Street | A2 | | |
| Coten End | C3 | | |
| Coventry Road | C3-C4 | | |
| Deerpark Park | A4 | | |
| Edward Street | A3-A4 | | |
| Gerrard Street | B2-B3 | | |
| Guy Street | C3-C4 | | |
| Guys Cliffe Terrace | C4 | | |
| High Street | A2 | | |
| Jury Street | A2-B2 | | |
| Lakin Road | C4 | | |
| Market Place | A3 | | |
| Market Street | A2 | | |
| Mill Street | B2 | | |
| Myton Road | C1 | | |
| New Street | A2-A3 | | |
| Northgate Street | A3 | | |
| Old Square | A3 | | |
| Packmore Street | B4-C4 | | |
| Paradise Street | B4-C4 | | |
| Park Street | A3 | | |
| Priory Road | A3-C3 | | |
| Roe Close | B4 | | |
| St John's Court | C3 | | |
| St Johns | C3 | | |
| St Nicholas Church Street | B2-C3 | | |
| Saltisford | A3-A4 | | |
| Sharpe Close | B4 | | |

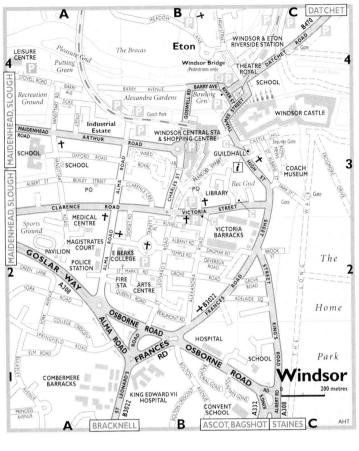

# Windsor

Windsor is found on atlas page **26**, grid reference **9576**

| | | | | |
|---|---|---|---|---|
| Adelaide Square | B2-C2 | Russell Street | B2 |
| Albany Road | B2 | St Albans Street | C3 |
| Albert Road | C1 | St Leonard's Road | A1-B1-B2-B3 |
| Albert Street | A3 | St Mark's Road | A2-B2 |
| Alexandra Road | B1-B2-B3 | Sheet Street | C2-C3 |
| Alma Road | B1-B2-B3 | Springfield Road | A1-A2 |
| Arthur Road | A3-B3 | Stovell Road | A4 |
| Balmoral Gardens | B1 | Temple Road | B2 |
| Barry Avenue | A4-B4 | Thames Street | B3-C4 |
| Beaumont Road | B2 | The Long Walk | C1-C2-C3 |
| Bexley Street | A3 | Trinity Place | B2-B3 |
| Bolton Avenue | B1 | Vansittart Road | A2-A3-A4 |
| Bolton Crescent | B1 | Victoria Street | B3-C3 |
| Brook Street | C2 | Ward Royal | B3 |
| Bulkeley Avenue | A1 | York Avenue | A1-A2 |
| Castle Hill | C3 | York Road | A2 |
| Charles Street | B3 | | |
| Clarence Crescent | B3 | | |
| Clarence Road | A3-B3 | | |
| College Crescent | A1-A2 | | |
| Dagmar Road | B2 | | |
| Datchet Road | C4 | | |
| Devereux Road | B2 | | |
| Dorset Road | B2-B3 | | |
| Duke Street | A3-A4 | | |
| Elm Road | A1 | | |
| Fountain Gardens | B1-C1 | | |
| Frances Road | B1-B2-C2 | | |
| Frogmore Drive | C3 | | |
| Goslar Way | A2 | | |
| Goswell Road | B3-B4 | | |
| Green Lane | A2 | | |
| Grove Road | B2-C2 | | |
| High Street (Eton) | B4 | | |
| High Street (Windsor) | C3 | | |
| King's Road | C1-C2 | | |
| Maidenhead Road | A3 | | |
| Meadow Lane | A4-B4 | | |
| Osborne Road | A2-B2-B1-C1 | | |
| Oxford Road | A3 | | |
| Park Street | C3 | | |
| Peascod Street | B3 | | |
| Princess Avenue | A1 | | |
| Queen's Road | A2-B2 | | |
| River Street | B4 | | |
| Royal Mews | C3 | | |

# Worcester

Worcester is found on atlas page **47**, grid reference **8554**

**AA shop**
Unit 5 Haswell House, St Nicholas Street, Worcester WR1 1UW  B3

| | | | |
|---|---|---|---|
| All Saints Road | A3 | Padmore Street | C3-C4 |
| Angel Place | B3 | Park Street | C1-C2 |
| Angel Row | B3 | Pheasant Street | C3-C4 |
| Angel Street | B3 | Pierpoint Street | B4 |
| Arboretum Road | B4-C4 | Pump Street | B2-C2 |
| Bank Street | B3 | Queen Street | B3-C3 |
| Bath Road | C1 | Sansome Place | B4-C4 |
| Bridge Street | A2-B3 | Sansome Street | B3 |
| Brittania Road | B4 | Sansome Walk | B4 |
| Broad Street | B3 | Severn Street | B1 |
| Castle Street | A4-B4 | Severn Terrace | A4 |
| Charles Street | C2 | Shaw Street | B3 |
| Church Street | B3 | Sidbury | C1 |
| City Walls Road | C1-C2-C3 | South Parade | A2-B2 |
| College Precinct | B1 | Southfield Street | B4-C4 |
| College Street | B1-B2 | Spring Gardens | C2-C3 |
| Copenhagen Street | B2 | St Martin's Gate | C3 |
| Croft Road | A3-A4 | St Nicholas Street | B3 |
| Deans Way | B2-B3 | St Paul's Street | C2-C3 |
| Derby Road | C1 | St Swithun's Street | B3 |
| Dolday | A3 | Taylor's Lane | B4 |
| East Street | C4 | The Butts | A3-B3 |
| Easy Row | A4 | The Cross | B3 |
| Edgar Street | B1-C1 | The Shambles | B2-B3 |
| Farrier Street | B3-B4 | Trinity Street | B3 |
| Foregate | B3 | Union Street | C2 |
| Foregate Street | B3-B4 | Westbury Street | C4 |
| Foundry Street | C2 | Wyld's Lane | C1 |
| Garden Street | C2 | | |
| George Street | C3 | | |
| Grand Stand Road | A3 | | |
| Hamilton Road | C1 | | |
| High Street | B2-B3 | | |
| Infirmary Walk | A4-B4-B3 | | |
| King Street | B1-C1 | | |
| Love's Grove | A4 | | |
| Lowesmoor | C3-C4 | | |
| Lowesmoor Place | C4 | | |
| Lowesmoor Terrace | C4 | | |
| Middle Street | C4 | | |
| New Road | A2 | | |
| New Street | C2-C3 | | |
| North Quay | A2-A3 | | |

227

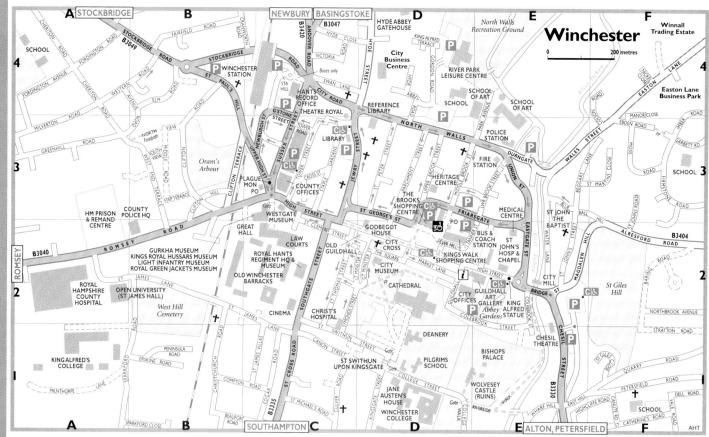

# Winchester

Winchester is found on atlas page **24**,
grid reference **4829**

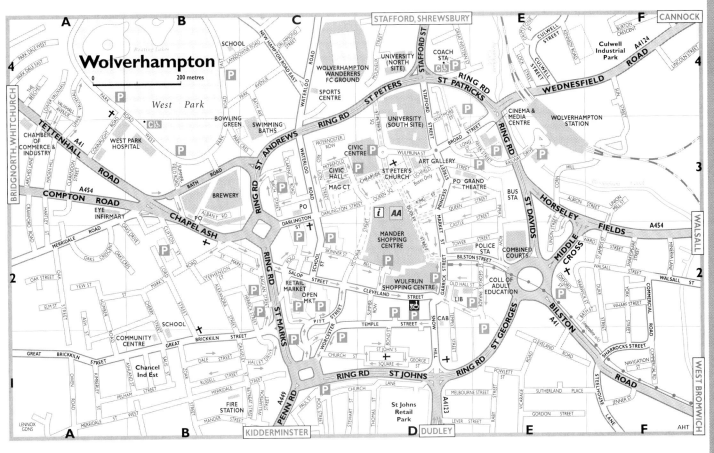

# Wolverhampton

Wolverhampton is found on atlas page **60**,
grid reference **9198**

**AA shop**
19 The Gallery, Mander Centre, Wolverhampton WV1 3NG    D3

| | | | |
|---|---|---|---|
| Albany Road | B3 | Fryer Street | E3 |
| Albion Street | E3-F3 | Garrick Street | D2 |
| Alexandra Street | B1-B2 | George Street | D1 |
| Ash Street | A1-A2 | Gordon Street | E1 |
| Ashland Street | B1 | Gramstone Street | E4 |
| Bath Avenue | C3-C4 | Greasely Street | B1-C1 |
| Bath Road | B3-C3 | Great Brick Kiln Street | A1-B1-C1 |
| Bath Street | E2-F2 | Great Western Street | D4 |
| Bell Street | D2 | Haden Hill | A3 |
| Bilston Road | E2-E1-F1 | Hallet Drive | C1 |
| Bilston Street | D2-E2 | Hartley Street | A2-A3 |
| Birch Street | C3 | Herbert Street | D4 |
| Bond Street | D1 | Herrick Street | C1-C2-B2 |
| Broad Street | D3-E3 | Horseley Fields | E3-E2-F2 |
| Burton Crescent | F4 | Humber Road | A1-A2 |
| Castle Street | D2-D3-C3 | Jenner Street | F1 |
| Chapel Ash | B3-B2 | Kennedy Road | E4 |
| Cheapside | D3 | Kimberley Street | A1 |
| Cherry Street | B1-B2 | King Street | D3 |
| Church Lane | C1-D1 | Laburnum Street | A1-B2 |
| Church Street | C1-D1 | Lansdowne Road | B4-C4 |
| Clarence Road | C3 | Larches Lane | A3 |
| Clarendon Street | A3 | Lennox Gardens | A1 |
| Cleveland Road | E1-F1 | Lever Street | D1-E1 |
| Cleveland Street | C2-D2 | Lichfield Street | D3-E3 |
| Clifton Street | B2-B3 | Lincoln Street | F4 |
| Commercial Road | F1-F2 | Lock Street | E4 |
| Compton Road | A3-B3 | Long Street | D3-E3 |
| Connaught Road | A3-A4 | Lord Street | B1-B2 |
| Corn Hill | E3-F3 | Lower Vauxhall | A4 |
| Crawford Road | A2-A3 | Mander Street | B1-C1 |
| Culwell Street | E4 | Market Street | D2-D3 |
| Dale Street | B1 | Melbourne Street | D1-E1 |
| Darlington Square | C2-C3-D3 | Merridale Road | A2-A3-B3 |
| Drummond Street | C4 | Merridale Street | B1-C1 |
| Dudley Street | D2-D3 | Merridale Street West | A1-B1 |
| Duke Street | F1-F2 | Middle Cross | E2 |
| Elm Street | A2 | Minerva Lane | F2 |
| Fold Street | C2 | Mitrefold | C3 |

| | | | |
|---|---|---|---|
| Molineux Street | D4 | St Georges Parade | E2 |
| Navigation Street | F1 | St James's Street | F2 |
| New Hampton Road East | C4 | St John's Square | D1 |
| Oak Street | A1-A2 | St Mark's Road | A2-B2 |
| Oaks Crescent | A2-B2 | St Marks Street | B2-C2 |
| Oaks Drive | A3-A2-B2 | St Peter's Square | D3-D4 |
| Old Hall Street | D2-E2 | Salisbury Street | B1 |
| Owen Road | A1 | Salop Street | C2 |
| Oxford Street | E2 | School Street | C2 |
| Park Avenue | B4-C4 | Sharrocks Street | F1 |
| Park Crescent | B3-C3 | Shakespeare Street | F2 |
| Park Dale East | A4 | Skinner Street | C2 |
| Park Dale West | A4 | Snow Hill | D1-D2 |
| Park Road East | B3-B4 | Stafford Street | D3-D4 |
| Park Road West | B3-B4-A4 | Steelhouse Lane | F1 |
| Paternoster Row | C3 | Stephenson Street | B2 |
| Paul Street | C1 | Stewart Street | C1 |
| Pelham Street | A1-B1 | Summer Row | D2 |
| Penn Road | C1 | Summerfield Road | B3 |
| Piper's Row | E2-E3 | Sun Street | F3-F4 |
| Pitt Street | C2 | Sutherland Place | E1-F1 |
| Pool Street | C1 | Tempest Street | D1-D2 |
| Powlett Street | E1 | Temple Street | D1-D2-C1-C2 |
| Princess Street | D3 | Tettenhall Road | A4-A3-B3 |
| Queen Street | D3-E3 | The Beeches | A4 |
| Queen Square | D3 | Thomas Street | D1 |
| Raby Street | E1 | Tower Street | D2-E2 |
| Raglan Street | C2 | Union Mill Street | F3 |
| Railway Drive | E3 | Union Street | E2-E3 |
| Red Lion Street | C3 | Upper Vauxhall Avenue | A3-A4 |
| Retreat Street | C1 | Vauxhall Avenue | A4 |
| Ring Road St Andrews | C3 | Vicarage Road | E1 |
| Ring Road St Davids | E2-E3 | Victoria Street | C2-D2-D3 |
| Ring Road St Georges | D1-E1-E2 | Walsall Street | E2-F2 |
| Ring Road St Johns | C1-D1 | Ward Street | E2-F2 |
| Ring Road St Marks | C1-C2 | Warwick Street | E2-F2 |
| Ring Road St Patricks | D4-E4 | Waterloo Road | C3-C4 |
| Ring Road St Peters | C3-C4-D4 | Wednesfield Road | E4-F4 |
| Russell Street | B1 | Wharf Street | F2 |

| | |
|---|---|
| Whitmore Street | D3-D4 |
| Williamson Street | C1 |
| Worcester Street | C1-C2 |
| Wulfruna Street | D3 |
| Yew Street | A2 |
| York Street | F1-F2 |
| Zoar Street | B1 |

**York**

0     200 metres

THIRSK RD · SHIPTON RD · A19 · LEEDS · HARROGATE · MOUNTVALE · A1036 · SELBY · HULL · SCARBOROUGH · HELMSLEY

**Streets and places:**

WATER END · WATER LANE · ABBEY ST · SCHOOL · LUMLEY ROAD · ST LUKES GROVE · SHIPTON STREET · HUDSON ST · SCARBOROUGH TERRACE · NEWBOROUGH TERRACE · WIGGINTON ROAD · B1363

CLIFTON · AVENUE ROAD · AVENUE TERR · BURTON STONE LANE · GROSVENOR ROAD · YORK CITY FOOTBALL CLUB · YORK AND DISTRICT GENERAL HOSPITAL · BOOTHAM PARK HOSPITAL · Footpath

COMPTON STREET · ROBIN GROVE · VIEW · CLIFTON DALE · PETERS WAY · ST PETER'S GROVE · ST OLAVE'S RD · BOOTHAM CRESCENT · GROSVENOR TERRACE · Playing Field

CITY HOSPITAL · WALPOLE STREET · STANLEY STREET · NELSON STREET · ELDON ST · NEVILLE STREET · NEVILLE TERRACE · MARKHAM STREET · MARKHAM CRESCENT · DIAMOND STREET · EMERALD STREET · HAXBY ROAD

HUNTINGTON ROAD · Heworth Golf Course · Greenway · POTTERY LANE · IRWIN AVENUE · DODSWORTH AVENUE · HUNT ROW · HIST GROVE · HAWTHORNE GROVE

GREENCLIFFE DRIVE · WESTMINSTER ROAD · THE AVENUE · ST PETERS SCHOOL · Playing Fields · Footpath · QUEEN ANNE SCHOOL · NORTH PARADE · QUEEN ANNE TERRACE · QUEEN ANNE ROAD

CLIFTON · BOOTHAM · A19 · ST MARY'S · Bowling Green · SYCAMORE TERRACE · SYCAMORE PLACE · LONGFIELD TERRACE · FREDERIC STREET

LOWTHER STREET · UNION TERRACE · CLARENCE ST · PO · TOWNEND STREET · BROOK STREET · GARDEN STREET · GROVES LANE · PENLEY'S GROVE STREET · LOWER EAST DUKE ROW · PARK GROVE · ST JOHN STREET · LORD MAYOR'S WALK

COLLEGE OF RIPON & YORK (HEWORTH CROFT) · HEWORTH GREEN · A1036 · MILL LANE · FIFTH AVENUE · HAWTHORNE STREET · GLEN AVENUE · FABER STREET · HALLFIELD · LAYERTHORPE · MANSFIELD STREET

COLLEGE OF RIPON & YORK ST JOHN · MONKGATE HEALTH CENTRE · SCHOOL · JAGGAR LANE · MONKGATE · FOSS BANK · LITTLE HALLFIELD ROAD · Ebor Industrial Estate

REGISTRY OFFICE · ART GALLERY · KING'S MANOR · ST OLAVE'S CH · ST MARY'S ABBEY · Museum Gardens · YORK CITY COUNCIL OFFS · CENT LIBY & CITY INF BUREAU · YORKSHIRE MUSEUM, BOTANICAL GDNS & TEMPEST ANDERSON HALL · HOSPITIUM · MULTANGULAR TOWER · ST LEONARD'S HOSP · LENDAL TOWER

MINSTER LIBRARY · DE GREY ROOMS · BOOTHAM BAR · TREASURER'S HOUSE · THE ICE HOUSE · MONK BAR · ST WILLIAMS' COLLEGE · YORK MINSTER · Deanery Gdns · Minster Yard · ST MICHAEL LE BELFRY CH · HOLY TRINITY CH · MERCHANT TAYLORS' HALL · ROMAN COLUMN · ROMAN HALL · CITY WALLS · ST CUTHBERT'S CH · BORTHWICK INSTITUTE OF HISTORICAL RESEARCH

GILLYGATE · ST LEONARD'S · MUSEUM ST · MAURICE'S ROAD · ST MAURICE'S RD · JEWBURY · FOSS ISLANDS ROAD

THEATRE ROYAL · DUNCOMBE PL · ASSEMBLY ROOMS · War Memorial Gardens · CITY WAR MEMORIAL · BARKER TOWER · LEEMAN · River Ouse · Footpath · LEEMAN ROAD · PETER ALLEN BUILDING · NATIONAL RAILWAY MUSEUM · YORK MODEL RAILWAY · YORK STATION · PO SORTING OFFICE · HPO · ROMAN BATHS MUS · MANSION HO · GUILDHALL · ST HELEN'S CH · ST MARTIN LE-GRAND CH

NEWGATE OPEN AIR MKT · ALL SAINTS CH PAVMT · THE ARC · THE STONEBOW · SPEN LANE · AMBULANCE STA · DUNCAN ST · PEASHOLME GREEN · ALDWARK · HUNGATE

RED TOWER · NAVIGATION ROAD

RAILWAY WAR MEMORIAL · CHOLERA BURIAL GROUND · BR REGIONAL HQ · CITY WALLS · ALL SAINTS CHURCH · ARTS CENTRE · ST MICHAEL, SPURRIERGATE CH · GRAND OPERA HOUSE · JORVIK VIKING CEN · YORK STORY · COPPERGATE SHOPPING CEN · MERCHANT ADVENTURER'S HALL · ST DENYS CH · ST MARGARET'S CH · WALMGATE

STATION ROAD · STATION AV · STATION RISE · WELLINGTON ROW · ROUGIER ST · TANNER ROW · HUDSON ST · GEORGE ST · MICKLEGATE · ST MARTIN CUM-GREGORY CH · BRIDGE ST · OUSE BRIDGE · CLIFFORD ST · COPPERGATE · PICCADILLY · COOK PLACE

HOLY TRINITY CH · ST MARY'S CH BISHOPHILL JUNIOR · PRIORY SPORTS CENTRE · MICKLEGATE BAR · FRIARGATE MUSEUM · LAW COURTS POL HQ & FIRE STA · REGIMENTAL MUSEUM · CLIFFORD'S TOWER · TYNE TEES TV · ST GEORGE'S CHURCHYARD · PO · JAMES STREET INDUSTRIAL ESTATE · A1079 · LAWRENCE ST · ST LAWRENCE · ELVINGTON TERRACE

QUEEN ST · CINEMA · NUNNERY LANE · THE BAR CONVENT · PRICES LN · BISHOPGATE ST · MUSEUM OF AUTOMATA · BAILE HILL · CASTLE MUSEUM & ASSIZE COURTS · TOWER ST · Skeldergate Bridge · LOCKS · FISHERGATE POSTERN TOWER · FISHERGATE BAR · WALMGATE BAR · CITY WALLS · PARAGON STREET · FISHERGATE · FAWCETT ST · HOPE STREET · LEADMILL LANE · LONG CLOSE LANE · WELLINGTON STREET

BLOSSOM STREET · THE MOUNT · HOLGATE ROAD · A59 · DALTON TERRACE · EAST MOUNT ROAD · MOSS STREET · PARK STREET · SOUTH PARADE · SCHOOL · ST BENEDICT ROAD · BISHOPTHORPE RD · CLEMENTHORPE · HEALTH CENTRE · FLOOD BARRIER · BARBICAN SWIMMING POOL · BARBICAN POOL LEISURE CENTRE · KENT STREET · FEWSTER WAY · ESCRICK STREET · HESLINGTON ROAD · To University

THE MOUNT SCHOOL · MILL MOUNT LANE · DRIFFIELD TERRACE · SCARCROFT ROAD · Bowling Green · NUNTHORPE ROAD · VINE STREET · LOWER EBOR STREET · CARL STREET · CARAVAN SITE · River Ouse · TERRY AVENUE · BLUEBRIDGE LANE · MELBOURNE STREET · MARLBOROUGH GROVE · ST ANNS COURT · ALNE TERRACE · BELLE VUE TER · HORSMAN AVENUE · WINTERSCALE STREET

ST ALBIN'S RD · TRENT HOLME DR · ST JAMES MOUNT · ALBEMARLE ROAD · SCHOOL · CHARLTON STREET · ANNE STREET · FENWICK STREET · RUSSELL STREET · SCOTT STREET · NUNMILL STREET · RICHARDSON STREET · NORFOLK STREET · SOUTHLANDS ROAD · BEWLAY STREET · Rowntree Park · NEW WALK TERRACE · SANDRINGHAM STREET · GRANGEGARTH · GRANGE GARTH · GRANGE STREET · LEVISHAM STREET · HARTOFT STREET · FARNDALE STREET · LEONARD STREET · KENSAL RISE · MAIDA GROVE · EDGEWARE ROAD · Cemetery · FULFORD ROAD · CEMETERY ROAD · A19

LHI

# Great Yarmouth

Great Yarmouth is found on atlas page **67**,
grid reference **5207**

| | | | | | | |
|---|---|---|---|---|---|
| Albemarle Road | C3 | Maygrove Road | B4 | South Market Road | B2 |
| Albion Road | B2-C2 | Middle Market Road | B3 | South Quay | A1 |
| Alderson Road | A4 | Nelson Road Central | B2-B1-C1 | Stonecutters Way | A2 |
| Alexandra Road | B2 | Nelson Road North | B2-B3 | Temple Road | B2-B3 |
| Apsley Road | C1-C2 | North Denes Road | B3-B4 | The Conge | A3 |
| Audley Street | B3 | North Drive | C3-C4 | Theatre Plain | A2-B2 |
| Britannia Road | C2 | North Market Road | B3 | Tolhouse Street | B1 |
| Clarendon Close | B1 | North Quay | A2-A3-A4 | Tottenham Street | B3 |
| Crown Road | B2-C2 | North River Road | A4 | Town Wall Road | A4-B4 |
| Deneside | B1-B2 | Northgate Street | A3-A4 | Trafalgar Road | B2-C2 |
| Dorset Close | B1 | Nottingham Way | A1-B1 | Union Road | B2 |
| East Road | B4 | Orford Close | B1 | Victoria Arcade | A2-B2 |
| Euston Road | C3 | Paget Road | C3 | Victoria Road | B1 |
| Factory Road | B3-B4 | Palgrave Road | A4 | Well Street | B3 |
| Ferrier Road | A4-B4 | Princes Road | C3 | Wellesley Road | C2-C3-C4 |
| Frederick Road | A4-B4 | Priory Gardens | B3 | West Road | B4 |
| Garrison Road | A4 | Priory Plain | A3-B3 | Yarmouth Way | A1-B1-B2 |
| George Street | A3 | Queen Street | A1-A2 | York Road | B1-C1 |
| Greyfriars Way | A1-A2 | Rampart Road | A4 | | |
| Hall Plain | A2 | Regent Road | B2-C2 | | |
| Hall Quay | A2 | Regent Street | A2 | | |
| Howard Street North | A2-A3 | Rodney Road | B1-C1 | | |
| Howard Street South | A2 | Row 106 | A1 | | |
| Jury Street | B3 | Russell Road | C2 | | |
| King Street | A2-B2-B1 | St Francis Way | A2 | | |
| Kitchener Road | A4-B4 | St Georges Road | B2-B1-C1 | | |
| Lancaster Road | B1-C1 | St Nicholas Road | A3-B3 | | |
| Manby Road | B3 | St Peter's Road | B1-C1 | | |
| Marine Parade | C1-C2-C3 | St Peters Plain | B1 | | |
| Market Gates | A2-B2 | Sandown Road | B4-C4 | | |
| Market Place | A2-A3 | Saxon Road | B2 | | |

231

# York

York is found on atlas page **83**,
grid reference **6051**

**AA shop**
6 Church Street, York YO1 2BG  D5

| | | | | | | | |
|---|---|---|---|---|---|---|---|
| Abbey Street | A8 | Cinder Lane | A4 | Fifth Avenue | F6 | Lawrence Street | F3 |
| Agar Street | E6 | Claremont Terrace | C6-C7 | Fishergate | E2-E3 | Layerthorpe | E5-E6-F6 |
| Albemarle Road | A2-A1-B1 | Clarence Street | C6-C7-D7 | Foss Bank | E5-E6 | Leadmill Lane | E3 |
| Aldwark | D5-E5 | Clementhorpe | C2-D2 | Foss Islands Road | E5-F5-F4-F3 | Leake Street | F3 |
| Alne Terrace | F2 | Clifford Street | D3-D4 | Fossgate | D4 | Leeman Road | A5-B5-B4 |
| Amber Street | E8 | Clifton Bootham | A8-A7-B7-B6-C6 | Frederic Street | B5 | Lendal | C5 |
| Anne Street | D1 | Clifton Dale | A8 | Fulford Road | E1-E2 | Levisham Street | E1 |
| Apollo Street | F2 | Colliergate | D4-D5 | Garden Place | E4 | Little Hallfield Road | F5 |
| Avenue Road | A8-B8 | Compton Street | A7-A8 | Garden Street | D7 | Long Close Lane | E3-F3 |
| Avenue Terrace | A8 | Coney Street | C4 | George Hudson Street | C4 | Longfield Terrace | B5-B6 |
| Baile Hill Terrace | C2-C3-D3 | Coppergate | D4 | George Street | E3-E4 | Lord Mayor's Walk | C6-D6 |
| Bar Lane | B3 | Cromwell Road | C3-D3 | Gillygate | C6 | Lower Ebor Street | D2 |
| Barbican Road | E2-F2-F3 | Cygnet Street | C2 | Glen Avenue | F6 | Lower Eldon Street | D7-D8 |
| Belle Vue Street | F2 | Dale Street | B2-B3 | Goodramgate | D5-D6 | Lower Priory Street | C3 |
| Belle Vue Terrace | F2 | Dalton Terrace | A2 | Gordon Street | F2 | Lowpetergate | D5 |
| Bewlay Street | C1-D1 | Davygate | C5-D5 | Grange Street | E1 | Lowther Street | D7-E7 |
| Bishopgate Street | C2-D2-D3 | Deangate | D5 | Grangegarth | E1 | Lowther Terrace | A3 |
| Bishophill Junior | C3 | Dennison Street | E7 | Grape Lane | D5 | Lumley Road | B8 |
| Bishophill Senior | C3 | Dewsbury Terrace | B3-C3 | Greencliffe Drive | A7 | Maida Grove | E1 |
| Bishopthorpe Road | C1-C2 | Diamond Street | E8 | Grosvenor Road | B8-C8 | Mansfield Street | E5 |
| Blake Street | C5 | Dodsworth Avenue | E8-F8-F7 | Grosvenor Terrace | B6-B7-C7-C8 | March Street | D7 |
| Blossom Street | B2-B3 | Driffield Terrace | A1-A2 | Grove View | A7 | Margaret Street | E3 |
| Bluebridge Lane | E2 | Dudley Street | E7 | Hallfield Road | F5-F6 | Market Street | D4 |
| Bootham Crescent | B7-C8 | Duncombe Place | C5 | Hampden Street | C3 | Markham Crescent | D8-D7 |
| Bootham Row | C6 | Dundas Street | E4-E5 | Hartoft Street | E1 | Markham Street | D8 |
| Bootham Terrace | B6 | East Mount Street | B2 | Hawthorne Grove | F6 | Marlborough Grove | E2 |
| Bridge Street | C4 | Edgeware Road | F1 | Hawthorne Street | F6 | Marygate | B5-B6-C6 |
| Brook Street | D7 | Eldon Terrace | D8-E8 | Haxby Street | D7-D8 | Melbourne Street | E2 |
| Brownlow Street | D7-E7-E8 | Elvington Terrace | F3 | Heslington Road | F2 | Micklegate | B3-B4-C4 |
| Buckingham Street | C3 | Emerald Street | E7-E8 | Heworth Green | E6-E7-F7 | Mill Lane | F7 |
| Burton Stone Lane | B7-B8 | Escrick Street | E2 | High Ousegate | D4 | Mill Mount Lane | A2-B2 |
| Cambridge Street | A2-A3 | Faber Street | F6 | Highpetergate | C5-C6 | Millfield Road | C1-C2 |
| Carl Street | D2 | Fairfax Street | C3 | Holgate Road | A2-A3-B3 | Minster Yard | C5-D5 |
| Carmelite Street | E4 | Farndale Street | E1 | Hope Street | E3 | Monkgate | D6-E6 |
| Castlegate | D4 | Fawcett Street | E2-E3 | Horsman Avenue | E2-F2 | Moss Street | B3-B2-C2 |
| Cemetery Road | E1-E2 | Feasegate | D4 | Howard Street | E1 | Mountvale | A1 |
| Charlton Street | C1 | Fenwick Street | C1-D1 | Hudson Street | C8 | Museum Street | C5 |
| Cherry Street | D2 | Fetter Lane | C3-C4 | Hungate | E4 | Navigation Road | E4-F3 |
| Church Street | D5 | Fewster Way | E2 | Huntington Road | E7-E8 | Nelson Street | D8-E8 |
| | | | | Hyrst Grove | F7 | Neville Street | D8 |
| | | | | Irwin Avenue | F7-F8 | Neville Terrace | D8-E8 |
| | | | | Jackson Street | D7-E7 | New Street | C4-C5 |
| | | | | James Street | F3-F4 | New Walk Terrace | E1 |
| | | | | Jewbury | E5 | Newborough Street | C8 |
| | | | | Kensal Rise | E1 | Newton Terrace | C2-C3 |
| | | | | Kent Street | E2 | Norfolk Street | C1-D1 |
| | | | | Kings Staithe | C4-D4-D3 | North Parade | B6 |
| | | | | Knavesmire Road | A1 | North Street | C4 |
| | | | | Kyme Street | C3 | Nunmill Street | C1-C2 |

| | | | | |
|---|---|---|---|---|
| Nunnery Lane | B3-C3-C2 | Shipton Road | A8 |
| Nunthorpe Avenue | B1-B2 | Shipton Street | B8-C8 |
| Nunthorpe Crescent | C1 | Skeldergate | C4-C3-D3 |
| Nunthorpe Grove | C1 | South Parade | B2-B3 |
| Nunthorpe Road | C2 | Southlands Road | C1 |
| Palmer Lane | E4 | Spen Lane | D5-E5 |
| Paragon Street | E3-F3 | Spurriergate | D4 |
| Park Crescent | E7 | Stanley Street | D8 |
| Park Grove | E7-E8 | Station Avenue | B4 |
| Park Street | B2 | Station Rise | B4 |
| Parliament Street | D4 | Station Road | B4-C4-C5 |
| Pavement | D4 | Stonegate | C5-D5 |
| Peasholme Green | E5 | Swann Street | C2-C3 |
| Penley's Grove Street | D7-E7-E6 | Swinegate | D5 |
| Percy's Lane | E4 | Sycamore Place | B6 |
| Peter's Way | A7-B8 | Sycamore Terrace | B5-B6 |
| Piccadilly | D4-E3 | Tanner Row | C4 |
| Portland Street | C6 | Telford Terrace | B1 |
| Pottery Lane | F8 | The Avenue | A7 |
| Prices Lane | C2 | The Crescent | B3 |
| Priory Street | B3-C3 | The Mount | A1-A2-B2 |
| Queen Anne's Road | B6-B7 | The Shambles | D4-D5 |
| Queen Street | B3 | The Stonebow | E4-E5 |
| Railway Terrace | A3 | Thorpe Street | C1-C2 |
| Redeness Street | F5-F6 | Toft Green | B4 |
| Richardson Street | C1-D1 | Tower Street | D3-E3 |
| Rosslyn Street | A7 | Townend Street | D7 |
| Rougier Street | C4 | Trent Holme Drive | A1 |
| Russel Street | C1-C2 | Trinity Lane | C4-C3 |
| St Andrewgate | D5 | Union Terrace | C7-D7 |
| St Anns Court | E2-F2 | Upper Price Road | B2-C2 |
| St Aubyns Place | A1 | Victor Street | C3 |
| St Benedict Road | C2-C3 | Vine Street | C2-D2 |
| St Denys Road | E3-E4 | Walmgate | D4-E4-E3-F3 |
| St James Mount | A1 | Walpole Street | D8-E8 |
| St John's Street | D6-D7 | Water End | A8 |
| St Leonard's | C5-C6 | Water Lane | A8 |
| St Lukes Grove | B8 | Watson Street | A3 |
| St Mary's | B6 | Wellington Row | C4 |
| St Maurice's Road | D6-D5-E5 | Wellington Street | F2-F3 |
| St Olaves Road | B7-B8 | Wentworth Road | B1-B2 |
| St Pauls Terrace | A3 | Westminster Drive | A7 |
| St Peter's Grove | B7 | Wigginton Road | C8-D8-D7 |
| St Saviourgate | D4-D5 | Willis Street | F2-F3 |
| Sandringham Street | E1 | Winterscale Street | E2 |
| Scarborough Terrace | C8 | Wolseley Street | F2 |
| Scarcroft Hill | B1-B2 | | |
| Scarcroft Road | A2-B2-C2 | | |
| Scott Street | C1-C2 | | |

# Manchester district

# Tyne & Wear district

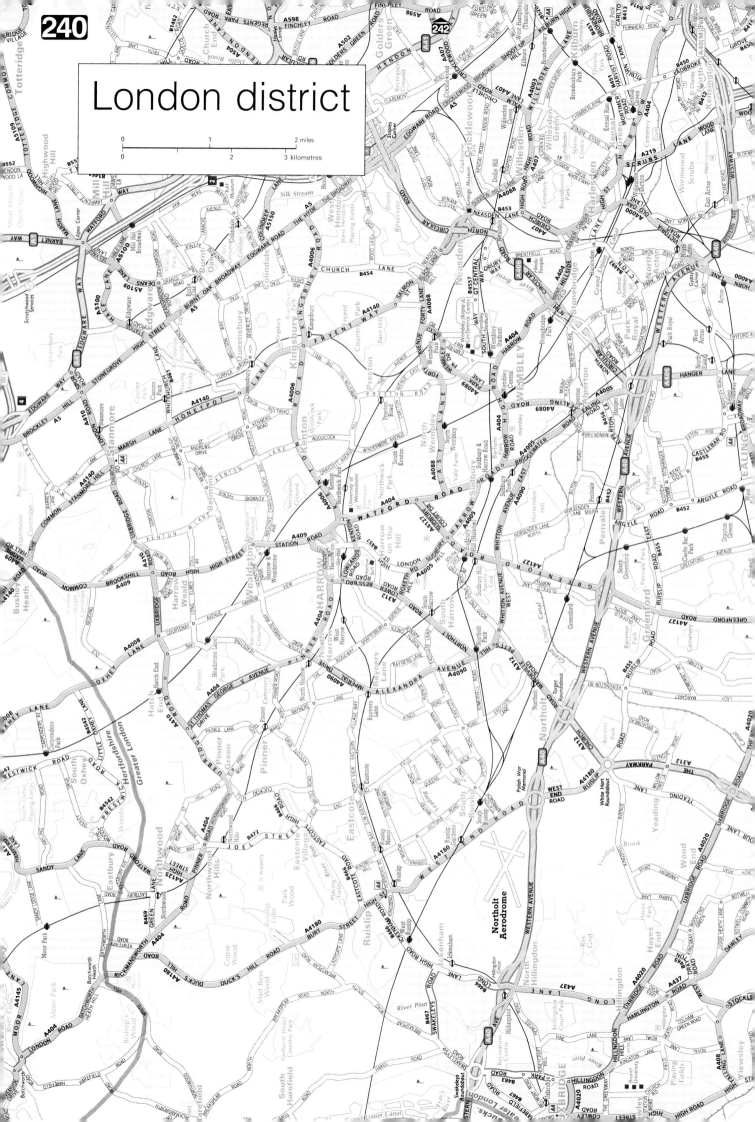

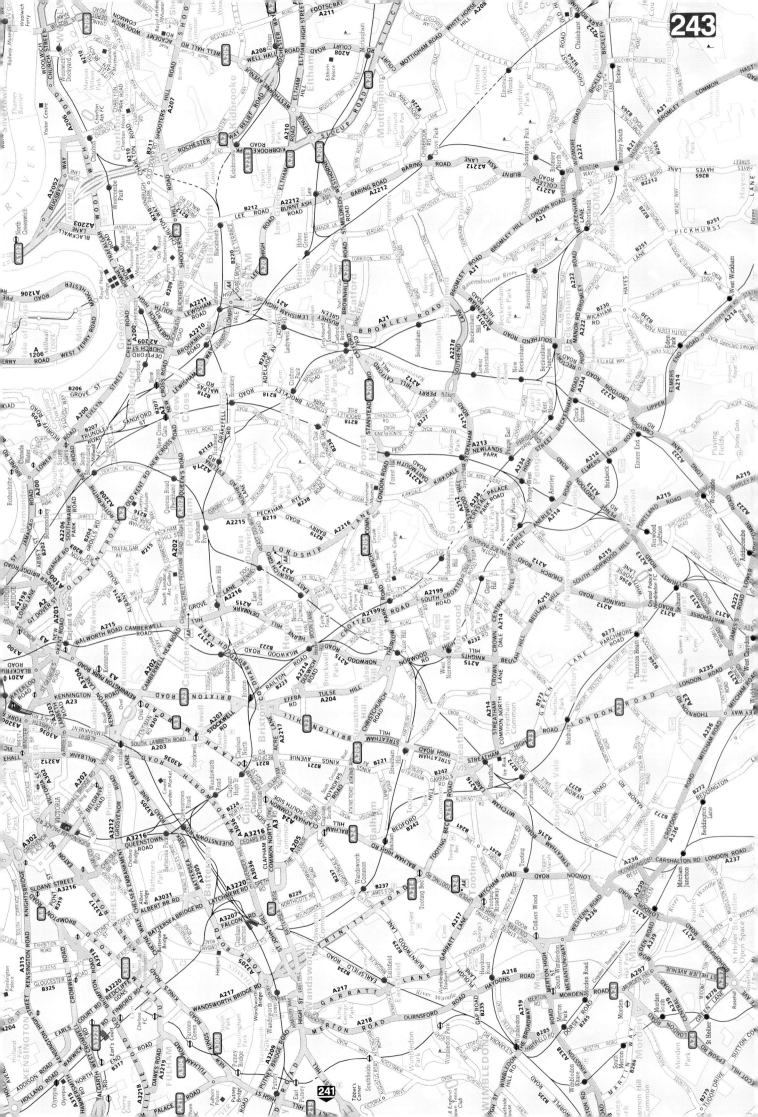

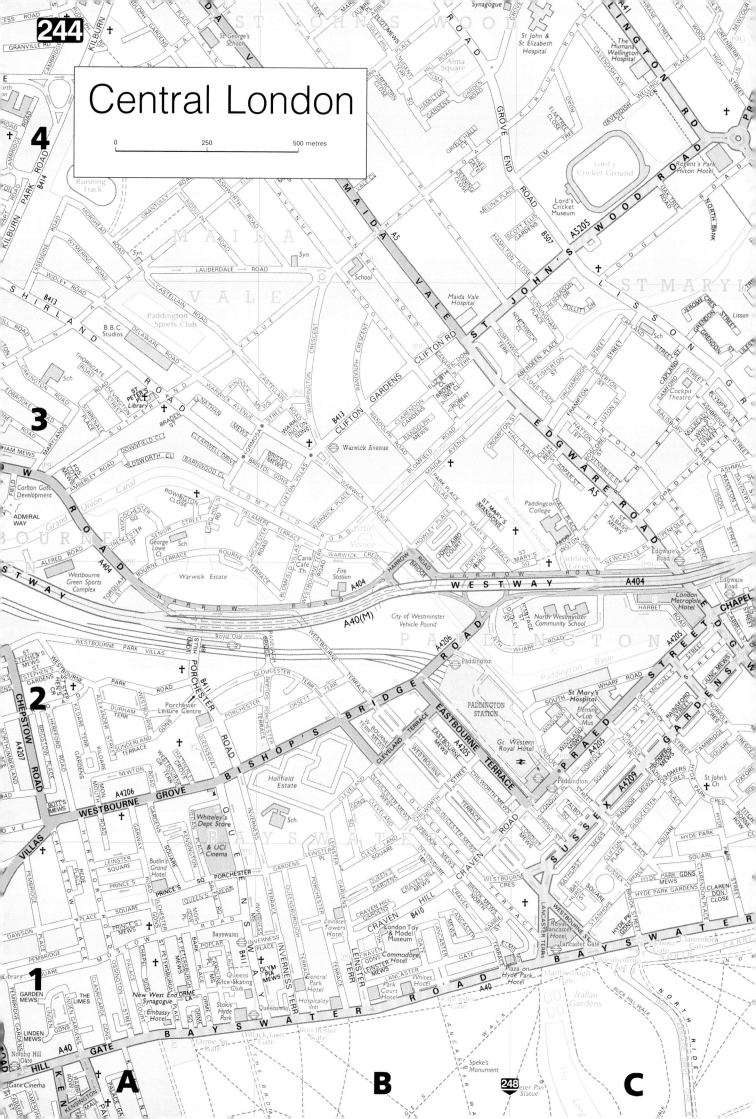

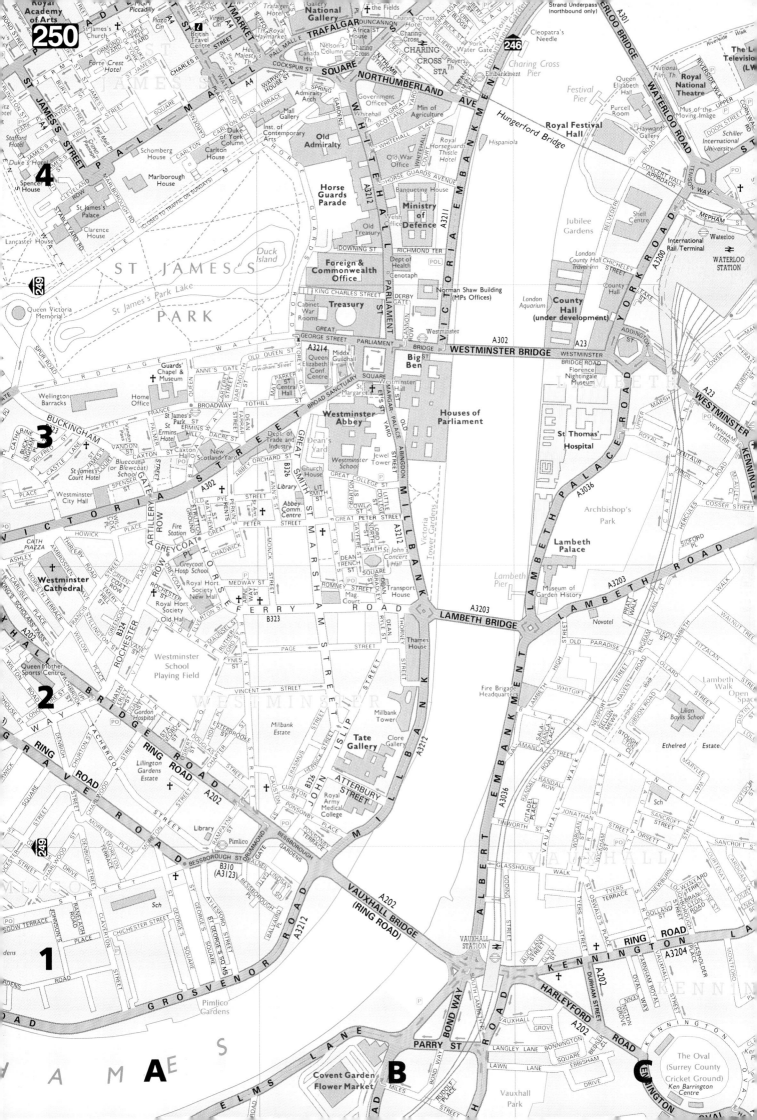

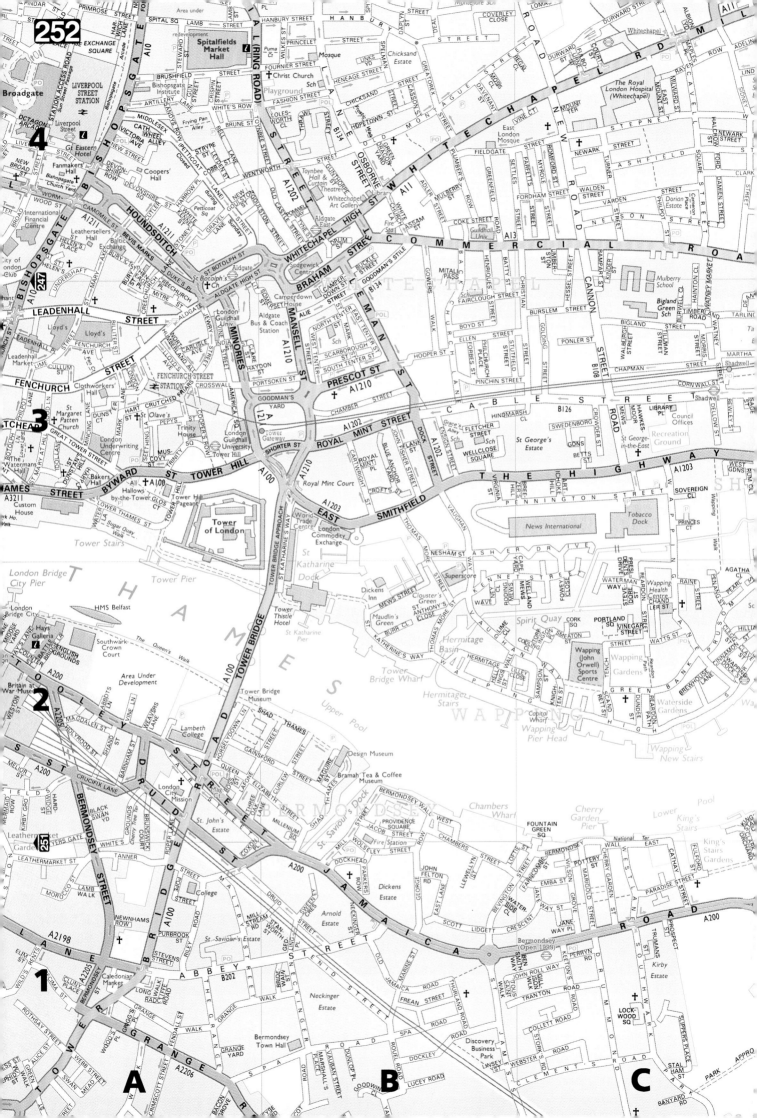

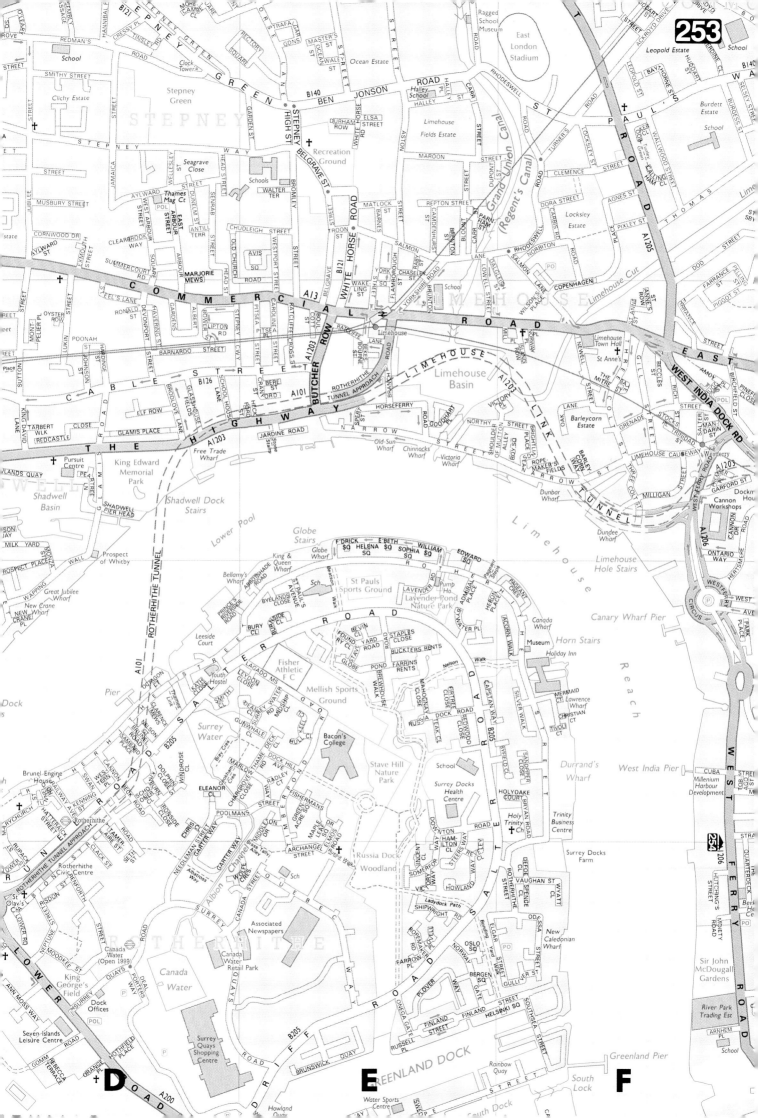

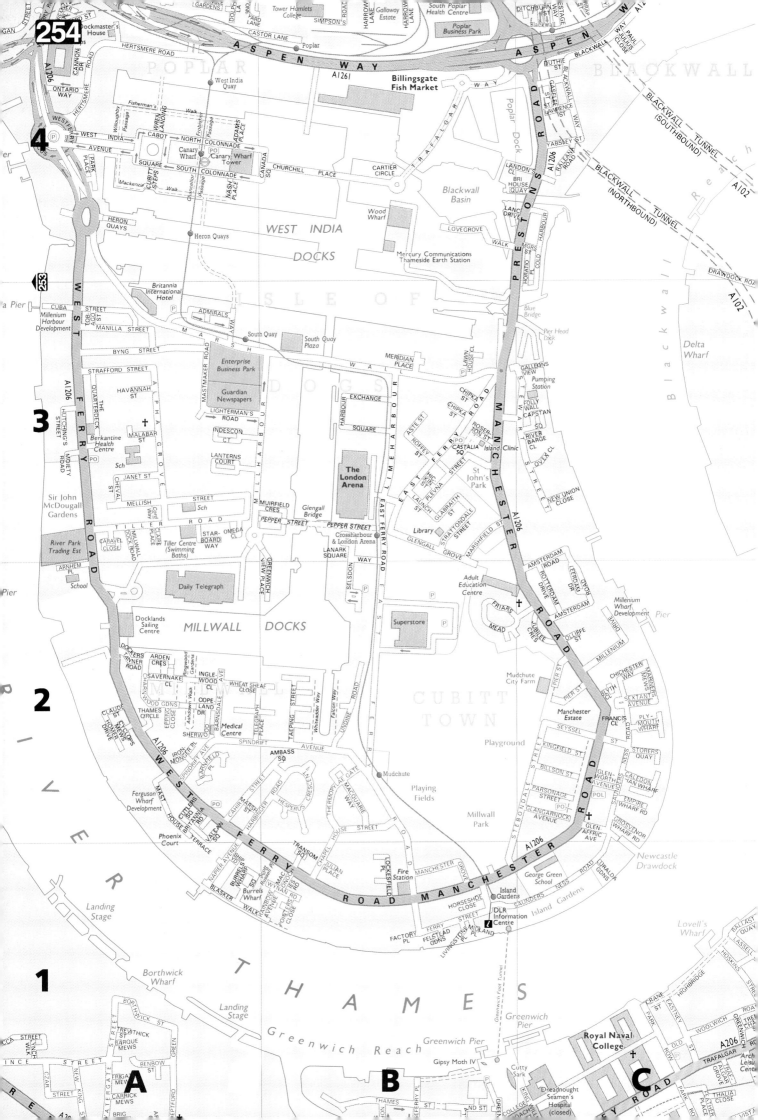

# Central London street index

In the index the street names are listed in alphabetical order and written in full, but may be abbreviated on the map. Postal codes are listed where information is available. Each entry is followed by its map page number in bold type, and an arbitrary letter and grid reference number. For example, for Exhibition Road SW7 **248** C3, turn to page 248. The letter 'C' refers to the grid square located at the bottom of the page; the figure '3' refers to the grid square located at the left-hand side of the page. Exhibition Road is found within the intersecting square. SW7 is the postcode. A proportion of street names and their references are also followed by the name of another street in italics. These entries do not appear on the map due to insufficient space but can be located adjacent to the name of the road in italics.



## A


Abbey Orchard Street *SW1* **250** B3
Abbey Street *SE1* **252** A1
Abbots Gardens *W8* **248** A3
*St Mary's Place*
Abbots Lane *SE1* **252** A2
Abbots Walk *W8* **248** A3
*St Mary's Place*
Abbotshade Road *SE16* **253** E2
Abchurch Lane *EC4* **247** F1
Abercorn Close *NW8* **244** B4
Abercorn Place *NW8* **244** B4
Aberdeen Place *NW8* **244** C3
Aberdour Street *SE1* **251** F2
Abingdon Road *W8* **248** A3
Abingdon Street *SW1* **250** B3
Abingdon Villas *W8* **248** A3
Achilles Way *W1* **249** E4
Ackroyd Drive *E3* **253** F4
Acorn Walk *SE16* **253** F2
Acton Street *WC1* **246** C4
Adam And Eve Court *W1* **245** E1
*Oxford Street*
Adam And Eve Mews *W8* **248** A3
Adam Street *WC2* **246** B1
Adam's Row *W1* **245** E1
Adams Place *E14* **254** A4
Addington Street *SE1* **250** C3
Addle Hill *EC4* **247** E1
Addle Street *EC2* **247** E2
Adelaide Street *WC2* **246** B1
*William IV Street*
Adelina Grove *E1* **252** D4
Adeline Place *WC1* **246** B2
Adelphi Terrace *WC2* **246** B1
*Adams Street*
Adler Street *E1* **252** B4
Admiral Place *SE16* **253** E2
Admiral Way *W9* **244** A3
Admirals Way *E14* **254** A3
Adpar Street *W2* **244** C3
Adrian Mews *SW10* **248** A1
Agar Street *WC2* **246** B1
Agatha Close *E1* **252** C2
Agdon Street *EC1* **247** D3
Agnes Street *E14* **253** F4
Ainstey Street *SE16* **253** D1
*Brunel Road*
Air Street *W1* **246** A1
Alaska Street *SE1* **250** C4
Albany Mews *SE5* **251** E1
Albany Road *SE5* **251** E1
Albany Street *NW1* **245** F4
Albatross Way *SE16* **253** D1
Albemarle Street *W1* **245** F1
Albemarle Way *EC1* **246** C3
*Clerkenwell Road*
Albert Court *SW7* **248** C3
Albert Embankment *SE1* **250** B1
Albert Gardens *E1* **253** D3
Albert Hall Mansions *SW7* **248** C3
Albert Mews *W8* **248** B3
Albert Place *W8* **248** B3
Alberta Street *SE17* **251** D1
Albion Close *W2* **245** D1
Albion Mews *W2* **245** D1
Albion Place *EC1* **247** D3
Albion Street *SE16* **253** D1
Albion Street *W2* **245** D1
Albion Way *EC1* **247** E2
Albion Yard *E1* **252** C4
Aldburgh Mews *W1* **245** E2
*Marylebone Lane*
Aldenham Street *NW1* **246** A4
Aldermanbury *EC2* **247** E2
Aldermanbury Square *EC2* **247** E2
*Aldermanbury*
Alderney Street *SW1* **249** F2
Aldersgate Street *EC1* **247** E3
Aldford Street *W1* **245** E1
Aldgate *EC3* **252** A3
Aldgate High Street *EC3* **252** A3
Aldsworth Close *W9* **244** A3
Aldwych *WC2* **246** C1
Alexander Place *SW7* **248** C2
Alexander Square *SW3* **248** C2
Alexander Street *W2* **244** A2
Alford Place *N1* **247** E4
Alfred Mews *W1* **246** A3
Alfred Place *WC1* **246** A3
Alfred Road *W2* **244** A2
Alice Street *SE1* **251** F3
Alie Street *E1* **252** B3
All Hallows Lane *EC4* **247** F1
All Soul's Place *W1* **245** F2
*Langham Street*
Allen Street *W8* **248** A3
Allington Street *SW1* **249** F3
Allsop Place *NW1* **245** D3
Alma Square *NW8* **244** B4
Alpha Grove *E14* **254** A3
Alpha Place *SW3* **249** D1
Alsace Road *SE17* **251** F1
Alscot Road *SE1* **252** B1
Alvey Street *SE17* **251** F2
Ambassador Square *E14* **254** B2
Ambergate Street *SE17* **251** D1
Amberley Road *W9* **244** A3
Ambrosden Avenue *SW1* **250** A3
Amelia Street *SE17* **251** E2
Amen Corner *EC4* **247** D2
Amen Court *EC4* **247** D2
America Square *EC3* **252** A3
America Street *SE1* **251** E4
Amoy Place *E14* **253** F3
Ampton Place *WC1* **246** C4
Ampton Street *WC1* **246** C4
Amsterdam Road *E14* **254** C2
Amwell Street *EC1* **246** C4
Anderson Street *SW3* **249** D2
Andrew Borde Street *WC2* **246** B2
*Charing Cross Road*
Angel Court *EC2* **247** F2
Angel Court *SW1* **250** A4
*King Street*
Angel Passage *EC4* **247** F1
Angel Place *SE1* **251** E4
Angel Street *EC1* **247** E2
Ann Moss Way *SE16* **253** D1
Ansdell Street *W8* **248** A3
Antill Terrace *E1* **253** D4
Apothecary Street *EC4* **247** D2
*New Bridge Street*
Apple Tree Yard *SW1* **246** A1
Appold Street *EC2* **247** F3
Aquinas Street *SE1* **251** D4
Arbour Square *E1* **253** D4
Archangel Street *SE16* **253** E1
Archer Street *W1* **246** A1
Arden Crescent *E14* **254** A2
Argent Street *SE1* **251** E4
*Loman Street*
Argyle Square *WC1* **246** B4
Argyle Street *WC1* **246** B4
Argyle Walk *WC1* **246** B4
Argyll Road *W8* **248** A3
Argyll Street *W1* **245** F2
Arlington Street *SW1* **249** F4
Arlington Way *EC1* **247** D4
Arne Street *WC2* **246** B2
Arneway Street *SW1* **250** A2
Arnhem Place *E14* **254** A2
Arnside Street *SE17* **251** E1
Arthur Street *EC4* **247** F1
Artichoke Hill *E1* **252** C3
Artillery Lane *E1* **252** A4
Artillery Passage *E1* **252** A4
*Artillery Lane*
Artillery Row *SW1* **250** A3
Artizan Street *E1* **252** A4
*Harrow Place*
Arundel Street *WC2* **246** C1
Ashbridge Street *NW8* **244** C3
Ashburn Gardens *SW7* **248** B2
Ashburn Mews *SW7* **248** B2
Ashburn Place *SW7* **248** B2
Ashby Street *EC1* **247** D4
Ashdown Walk *E14* **254** A2
Asher Drive *E1* **252** B3
Ashfield Street *E1* **252** C4
Ashland Place *W1* **244** E3
Ashley Place *SW1* **249** F3
Ashmill Street *NW1* **244** C3
Ashworth Road *W9* **244** A4
Aske Street *N1* **247** F4
Asolando Drive *SE17* **251** E2
*King & Queen Street*
Aspen Way *E14* **254** B4
Assam Street *E1* **252** B4
Assembly Passage *E1* **253** D4
Aste Street *E14* **254** B3
Astell Street *SW3* **249** D2
Aston Street *E14* **253** E4
Astwood Mews *SW7* **248** B2
Atherstone Mews *SW7* **248** B2
Atterbury Street *SW1* **250** B2
Attneave Street *WC1* **246** C4
Aubrey Place *NW8* **244** B4
Auckland Street *SE11* **250** C1
Augustus Street *NW1* **245** F4
Aulton Place *SE11* **251** D1
Austin Friars *EC2* **247** F2
Austin Friars Square *EC2* **247** F2
*Austin Friars*
Austral Street *SE11* **251** D2
Ave Maria Lane *EC4* **247** E2
Aveline Street *SE11* **250** C1
Avery Row *W1* **245** F1
Avis Square *E1* **253** E4
Avon Place *SE1* **251** E3
Avonmouth Street *SE1* **251** E3
Aybrook Street *W1* **245** E2
Aylesbury Road *SE17* **251** F1
Aylesbury Street *EC1* **247** D3
Aylesford Street *SW1* **250** A1
Aylward Street *E1* **253** D4
Ayres Street *SE1* **251** E4


## B


Babmaes Street *SW1* **250** A4
*Jermyn Street*
Bacchus Walk *N1* **247** F4
Bache's Street *N1* **247** F4
Back Church Lane *E1* **252** B4
Back Hill *EC1* **247** D3
Bacon Grove *SE1* **252** A1
Bainbridge Street *WC1* **246** B2
Baker Street *W1 & NW1* **245** D3
Baker's Mews *W1* **245** E2
Baker's Row *EC1* **247** F3
Baker's Yard *EC1* **247** D3
*Baker's Row*
Bakers Hall Court *EC3* **252** A3
*Harp Lane*
Balcombe Street *NW1* **245** D3
Balderton Street *W1* **245** E1
Baldwin Street *EC1* **247** F4
Baldwin's Gardens *EC1* **246** C3
Balfe Street *N1* **246** B4
Balfour Mews *W1* **245** E1
Balfour Place *W1* **245** E1
Balfour Street *SE17* **251** F2
Ballast Quay *SE10* **254** C1
Balneil Gate *SW1* **250** A1
Baltic Street East *EC1* **247** E3
Baltic Street West *EC1* **247** E3
Balvaird Place *SW1* **250** B2
Bancroft Road *E1* **250** C1
Bank End *SE1* **251** E4
Bankside *SE1* **251** E4
Bankside Jetty *SE1* **247** E1
Banner Street *EC1* **247** E3
Banyard Road *SE16* **252** C1
Barbon Close *WC1* **246** C3
Barge House Street *SE1* **247** D1
Bark Place *W2* **244** A1
Barkston Gardens *SW5* **248** A2
Barleycorn Way *E14* **253** F3
Barlow Place *W1* **245** F1
Barlow Street *SE17* **251** F2
Barnaby Place *SW7* **248** C2
Barnardo Street *E1* **253** D3
Barnby Street *NW1* **246** A4
Barnes Street *E14* **253** E4
Barnfield Place *E14* **254** A2
Barnham Street *SE1* **252** A2
Barnsdale Avenue *E14* **254** A2
Barnwood Close *W9* **244** A3
Baron's Place *SE1* **251** D3
Barque Mews *SE8* **254** A1
Barrett Street *W1* **245** E2
Barrie Street *W2* **244** B1
Barrow Hill Road *NW8* **244** C4
*St Johns Wood High Street*
Barter Street *WC1* **246** B2
Barth Lane *EC2* **247** F2
Bartholomew Close *EC1* **247** E2
Bartholomew Square *EC1* **247** E3
Bartholomew Street *SE1* **251** F2
Barton Street *SW1* **250** B3
Basil Street *SW3* **249** D3
Basinghall Avenue *EC2* **247** E2
Basinghall Street *EC2* **247** E2
Bastwick Street *EC1* **247** E3
Bate Street *E14* **253** F3
Bateman Street *W1* **246** A2
Bateman's Buildings *W1* **246** A2
Bath Court *EC1* **246** C3
*Warner Street*
Bath Place *N1* **247** F4
Bath Street *EC1* **247** E4
Bath Terrace *SE1* **251** E3
Bathurst Mews *W2* **244** C1
Bathurst Street *W2* **244** C1
Battle Bridge Lane *SE1* **251** F4
Batty Street *E1* **252** B4
Bayley Street *WC1* **246** A2
Baylis Road *SE1* **250** C3
Bayswater Road *W2* **244** A1
Baythorne Street *E3* **253** F4
Beaconsfield Road *SE17* **251** F1
Beak Street *W1* **246** A1
Bear Alley *EC4* **247** D2
*Farringdon Street*
Bear Gardens *SE1* **247** E1
Bear Lane *SE1* **251** D4
Bear Street *WC2* **246** B1
*Cranbourn Street*
Beatrice Place *W8* **248** A2
Beauchamp Place *SW3* **249** D3
Beauchamp Street *EC1* **247** D3
*Brooke Street*
Beaufort Gardens *SW3* **249** D3
Beaufort Street *SW3* **248** B1
Beaumont Mews *W1* **245** E2
Beaumont Place *W1* **246** A3
Beaumont Street *W1* **245** E3
Beccles Street *E14* **253** F3
Beckway Street *SE17* **251** F2
Bedale Street *SE1* **251** E3
*Borough High Street*
Bedford Avenue *WC1* **246** B2
Bedford Court *WC2* **246** B1
Bedford Gardens *W8* **248** A4
Bedford Place *WC1* **246** B3
Bedford Row *WC1* **246** C3
Bedford Square *WC1* **246** B2
Bedford Street *WC2* **246** B1
Bedford Way *WC1* **246** B3
Bedfordbury *WC2* **246** B1
Bedser Close *SE11* **250** C1
Beech Street *EC2* **247** E3
Beeston Place *SW1* **249** F3
Bekesbourne Street *E14* **245** E2
*Marylebone Lane*
Bekesbourne Street *E14* **253** E3
Belgrave Mews North *SW1* **249** E3
Belgrave Mews South *SW1* **249** E3
Belgrave Mews West *SW1* **249** E3
Belgrave Place *SW1* **249** E3
Belgrave Road *SW1* **249** F2
Belgrave Square *SW1* **249** E3
Belgrave Street *E1* **253** E3
Belgrove Street *WC1* **246** B4
Bell Lane *E1* **252** A4
Bell Street *NW1* **244** C3
Bell Yard *WC2* **246** C2
Belvedere Buildings *SE1* **251** E3
Belvedere Road *SE1* **250** C4
Ben Jonson Road *E1* **253** E4
Ben Smith Way *SE16* **252** C1
Benbow Street *SE8* **254** A1
Bendall Mews *W1* **245** D3
Bennet's Hill *EC4* **247** E1
*Castle Baynard Street*
Benson Quay *E1* **253** D3
Bentinck Mews *W1* **245** E2
*Marylebone Lane*
Bentinck Street *W1* **245** E2
Bere Street *E1* **253** E3
Bergen Square *SE16* **253** E1
Berkeley Gardens *W8* **248** A4
Berkeley Mews *W1* **245** D2
Berkeley Square *W1* **245** F1
Berkeley Street *W1* **245** F1
Bermondsey Square *SE1* **247** E2
*Long Lane*
Bermondsey Street *SE1* **252** A2
Bermondsey Wall East *SE16* **252** B1
Bermondsey Wall West *SE16* **252** B2
Bernard Street *WC1* **246** B3
Berners Mews *W1* **246** A2
Berners Street *W1* **246** A2
Berry Street *EC1* **247** E3
Berryfield Road *SE17* **251** E1
Berwick Street *W1* **246** A2
Bessborough Gardens *SW1* **250** B2
Bessborough Place *SW1* **250** A1
Bessborough Street *SW1* **250** A1
Betterton Street *WC2* **246** B2
Betts Street *E1* **252** C3
Bevenden Street *N1* **247** F4
Beverston Mews *W1* **245** D2
Bevin Close *SE16* **253** E2
Bevin Way *WC1* **246** C4
Bevington Street *SE16* **252** B1
Bevis Marks *EC3* **252** A4
Bewley Street *E1* **252** C3
Bickenhall Street *W1* **245** D3
Bidborough Street *WC1* **246** B4
Biddulph Road *W9* **244** A4
Bigland Street *E1* **252** C3
Billiter Square *EC3* **252** A3
*Fenchurch Avenue*
Billiter Street *EC3* **252** A3
Billson Street *E14* **254** C2
Bina Gardens *SW5* **248** B2
Bingham Place *W1* **245** E3
Binney Street *W1* **245** E1
Birchfield Street *E14* **253** E3
Birchin Lane *EC3* **247** F1
Bird Street *W1* **245** E2
Birdcage Walk *SW1* **250** A3
Birkenhead Street *WC1* **246** B4
Bishop's Court *EC4* **247** D2
*Old Bailey*
Bishop's Court *WC2* **246** C2
*Chancery Lane*
Bishop's Terrace *SE11* **251** D2
Bishops Bridge Road *W2* **244** B2
Bishopsgate *EC2* **247** F2
Bishopsgate Arcade *EC2* **252** A4
Bishopsgate Churchyard *EC2* **247** F2
Bittern Street *SE1* **251** E3
Black Prince Road *SE1 & SE11* **250** C2
Black Swan Yard *SE1* **252** A2
Blackall Street *EC2* **247** F3
Blackburne's Mews *W1* **245** E1
Blackfriars Bridge *EC4 & SE1* **247** D1
Blackfriars Lane *EC4* **247** D1
Blackfriars Passage *EC4* **247** D1
Blackfriars Road *SE1* **251** D4
Blacklands Terrace *SW3* **249** D2
Blackwall Tunnel *E14 & SE10* **254** C4
Blackwood Street *SE17* **251** F1
Blandford Square *NW1* **245** D3
Blandford Street *W1* **245** F2
Blasker Walk *E14* **254** A1
Bleeding Heart Yard *EC1* **247** D2
*Greville Street*
Blenheim Street *W1* **245** F1
*New Bond Street*
Bletchley Street *N1* **247** E4
Blithfield Street *W8* **248** A3
Blomfield Road *W9* **244** A3
Blomfield Street *EC2* **247** F2
Blomfield Villas *W2* **244** B2
Bloomburg Street *SW1* **249** F2
*Vauxhall Bridge Road*
Bloomfield Place *W1* **245** F1
*Bourdon Street*
Bloomfield Terrace *SW1* **249** E2
Bloomsbury Court *WC1* **246** B2
*High Holborn*
Bloomsbury Place *WC1* **246** B3
*Southampton Row*
Bloomsbury Square *WC1* **246** B2
Bloomsbury Street *WC1* **246** B2
Bloomsbury Way *WC1* **246** B2
Blount Street *E14* **253** E4
Blue Anchor Yard *E1* **252** B3
Blue Ball Yard *SW1* **250** A4
*St James's Street*
Blyth Close *E14* **254** C2
Bolsover Street *W1* **245** F3
Bolt Court *EC4* **247** D2
Bolton Gardens *SW5* **248** A2
Bolton Gardens Mews *SW10* **248** B1
Bolton Street *W1* **249** F4
Boltons Place *SW10* **248** B2
Bond Way *SW8* **250** B1
Bonding Yard Walk *SE16* **253** E1
Bonhill Street *EC2* **247** F3
Bonnington Square *SW8* **250** C1
Booker Close *E14* **253** F4
Boot Street *N1* **247** F4
Booth's Place *W1* **245** F2
*Wells Street*
Boreas Walk *N1* **247** E4
*Nelson Place*
Borough High Street *SE1* **251** E3
Borough Road *SE1* **251** E3
Borrett Close *SE17* **251** E1
Borthwick Street *SE8* **254** A1
Boscobel Place *SW1* **249** E2
Boscobel Street *NW8* **244** C3
Boss Street *SE1* **252** A2
Boston Place *NW1* **244** D3
Boswell Court *WC1* **246** B3
*Boswell Street*
Boswell Street *WC1* **246** B3
Botolph Lane *EC3* **247** F1
Bott's Mews *W2* **244** A2
Boulcott Street *E1* **253** E3
Boundary Lane *SE17* **251** E1
Boundary Road *SE1* **251** D4
Bourdon Street *W1* **245** F1
Bourlet Close *W1* **245** F2
Bourne Street *SW1* **249** E2
Bourne Terrace *W2* **244** A2
Bouverie Street *EC4* **247** D1
Bow Lane *EC4* **247** E1
Bow Street *WC2* **246** B2
Bowden Street *SE11* **251** D1
Bower Street *E1* **253** D3
Bowling Green Lane *EC1* **247** D3
Bowling Green Place *SE1* **251** F4
*Newcomen Street*
Bowling Green Street *SE11* **250** C1
Bowling Green Walk *N1* **247** F4
Boyd Street *E1* **252** B3
Boyfield Street *SE1* **251** D3
Boyle Street *W1* **245** F1
*Savile Row*
Boyson Road *SE17* **251** E1
Brackley Street *EC1* **247** E3
Brad Street *SE1* **251** D4
Braden Street *W9* **244** A3
Bradenham Close *SE17* **251** F1
Braganza Street *SE17* **251** D1
Braham Street *E1* **252** B3
Bramerton Street *SW3* **248** C1
Bramham Gardens *SW5* **248** A2
Branch Road *E14* **253** E3
Brandon Street *SE17* **251** E2
Brangton Road *SE11* **250** C1
Brass Tally Alley *SE16* **253** E1
Bray Crescent *SE16* **253** D2
Bray Place *SW3* **249** D2
Bread Street *EC4* **247** E1
Bream's Buildings *EC* **246** C2
Brechin Place *SW7* **248** B2
Breezer's Hill *E1* **252** C3
Bremner Road *SW7* **248** B3
Brendon Street *W1* **245** D2
Brenton Street *E14* **253** E4
Bressenden Place *SW1* **249** F3
Brettell Street *SE17* **251** F1
Brewer Street *W1* **246** A1
Brewers' Green *SW1* **250** A3
*Caxton Street*
Brewhouse Lane *E1* **252** C2
Brewhouse Walk *SE16* **253** E2
Brick Court *EC4* **246** C2
*Middle Temple Lane*
Brick Street *W1* **249** E4
Bride Lane *EC4* **247** D2
Bridewain Street *SE1* **252** B1
Bridewell Place *EC4* **247** D1
Bridford Mews *W1* **245** F3
Bridge House Quay *E14* **254** C4
Bridge Place *SW1* **249** F2
Bridge Street *SW1* **250** B3
Bridge Yard *SE1* **251** F4
Bridgeport Place *E1* **252** B2
*Kennet Street*
Bridgewater Square *EC2* **247** E3
*Beech Street*
Bridgewater Street *EC2* **247** E3
*Beech Street*
Bridgeway Street *NW1* **246** A2
Bridle Lane *W1* **246** A1
Bridstow Place *W2* **244** A2
Brightlingsea Place *E14* **253** F3
Brill Place *NW1* **246** A4
Briset Street *EC1* **247** D3
Bristol Gardens *W9* **244** A3
Bristol Mews *W9* **244** B3
Britannia Road *E14* **254** A2
Britannia Street *WC1* **246** C4
Britannia Walk *N1* **247** F4
Britten Street *SW3* **248** C1
Britton Street *EC1* **247** D3
Broad Court *WC2* **246** B2
Broad Sanctuary *SW1* **250** B3
Broad Walk *W2* **249** E4
Broadbent Street *W1* **245** F1
Broadley Street *NW8* **244** C4
Broadley Terrace *NW1* **245** D3
Broadstone Place *W1* **245** E2
Broadwall *SE1* **251** D4
Broadway *SW1* **250** A3
Broadwick Street *W1* **246** A1
Brockham Street *SE1* **251** E3
Brodlove Lane *E1* **253** D3
Bromley Street *E1* **253** E4
Brompton Place *SW3* **249** D3
Brompton Road *SW3* **249** D3
Brompton Square *SW3* **248** C3
Bronti Close *SE17* **251** E1
Brook Drive *SE11* **251** D2
Brook Gate *W1* **245** E1
Brook Mews North *W2* **244** B1

256

Dod Street

Harcourt Terrace

Dod Street E14 253 F4
Doddington Grove SE17 251 D1
Doddington Place SE17 251 D1
Dodson Street SE1 251 D3
Dolben Street SE1 251 D4
Dolland Street SE11 250 C1
Dolphin Close SE16 253 D2
Dombey Street WC1 246 C3
Domingo Street EC1 247 E3
Old Street
Dominion Street EC2 247 F2
Donegal Street N1 246 C4
Donne Place SW3 249 D2
Doon Street SE1 250 C4
Dora Street E14 253 F4
Doric Way NW1 246 A4
Dorrington Street EC1 247 D3
Brooke Street
Dorset Close NW1 245 D3
Dorset Mews SW1 249 E3
Dorset Rise EC4 247 D1
Dorset Square NW1 245 D3
Dorset Street W1 245 D2
Doughty Mews WC1 246 C3
Doughty Street WC1 246 C3
Douglas Place SW1 250 A2
Douglas Street
Douglas Street SW1 250 A2
Douro Place W8 248 B3
Dove Mews SW5 248 B2
Dove Walk SW1 249 E2
Dovehouse Street SW3 248 C1
Dover Street W1 245 F1
Dowgate Hill EC4 247 F1
Down Street W1 249 E4
Downfield Close W9 244 A3
Downing Street SW1 250 B4
Downton Road SE16 253 E2
Doyce Street SE1 251 E4
D'Oyley Street SW1 249 E2
Draco Street SE17 251 E1
Drake Street WC1 246 C2
Drawdock Road SE10 254 C4
Draycott Avenue SW3 249 D2
Draycott Place SW3 249 D2
Draycott Terrace SW3 249 D2
Drayson Mews W8 248 A3
Drayton Gardens SW10 248 B1
Druid Street SE1 252 A2
Drum Street E1 252 B4
Drummond Crescent NW1 246 A4
Drummond Gate SW1 250 A1
Drummond Road SE16 252 C1
Drummond Street NW1 245 F3
Drury Lane WC2 246 B2
Dryden Court SE11 251 D2
Duchess Mews W1 245 F2
Duchess Street W1 245 F2
Duchy Street SE1 251 D4
Duck Lane W1 246 A2
Dudley Street W2 244 B2
Dudmaston Mews SW3 248 C2
Dufferin Street EC1 247 E3
Dufour's Place W1 246 A4
Duke Of Wellington Place SW1 249 E3
Duke Of York Street SW1 246 A1
Duke Street W1 245 E2
Duke Street Hill SE1 251 F4
Duke's Lane W8 248 A4
Duke's Place EC3 252 A4
Duke's Road WC1 246 B4
Duke's Yard W1 245 E2
Duke Street
Duncannon Street WC2 246 B1
Dundee Street E1 252 C2
Dundee Wharf E14 253 F3
Dunelm Street E1 253 D4
Dunlop Place SE16 252 B1
Dunraven Street W1 245 E1
Dunstable Mews W1 245 E3
Dunster Court EC3 252 A3
Dunsterville Way SE1 251 F3
Duplex Ride SW1 249 E3
Dupont Street E14 253 E4
Durham House Street WC2 246 B1
Durham Row E1 253 E4
Durham Street SE11 250 C1
Durham Terrace W2 244 A2
Durward Street E1 252 C4
Durweston Street W1 245 D2
Crawford Street
Duthie Street E14 254 C4
Dyott Street WC1 246 B2
Dysart Street EC2 247 F3

# E

Eagle Court EC1 247 D3
Eagle Place SW1 250 A4
Piccadilly
Eagle Street WC2 246 C2
Eardley Crescent SW5 248 A1
Earl Street EC2 247 F3
Earl's Court Gardens SW5 248 A2
Earl's Court Square SW5 248 A1
Earlham Street WC2 246 B2
Earls Court Road W8 248 A2
Earlstoke Street EC1 247 D4
Spencer Street
Earnshaw Street WC2 246 B2
Easley's Mews W1 245 E2
Wigmore Street
East Arbour Street E1 253 D4
East Ferry Road E14 254 B2
East Harding Street EC4 247 D2
East India Dock Wall Road E14 247 D2
East Lane SE16 252 B1
East Mount Street E1 252 C4
East Road N1 247 F4
East Smithfield E1 252 B3
East Street SE17 251 E1
East Tenter Street E1 252 B3
Eastbourne Mews W2 244 B2
Eastbourne Terrace W2 244 B2
Eastcastle Street W1 246 A2
Eastcheap EC3 247 F1
Eastney Street SE10 254 C1
Easton Street WC1 246 C3
Eaton Gate SW1 249 E2
Eaton Mews North SW1 249 E2
Eaton Mews South SW1 249 E2
Eaton Place SW1 249 E2
Eaton Square SW1 249 E2
Eaton Terrace SW1 249 E2
Ebbisham Drive SW8 250 C1
Ebenezer Street N1 247 F4
Ebury Bridge SW1 249 E2
Ebury Bridge Road SW1 249 E1
Ebury Mews SW1 249 E2
Ebury Mews East SW1 249 E2
Ebury Square SW1 249 E2
Ebury Street SW1 249 E2
Eccleston Bridge SW1 249 F2
Eccleston Mews SW1 249 E3
Eccleston Place SW1 249 F2
Eccleston Square SW1 249 F2
Eccleston Square Mews SW1 249 F2
Eccleston Street SW1 249 E2
Edbrooke Road W9 244 A3
Edge Street W8 248 A4
Edgware Road W2 244 C3
Edward Mews NW1 245 F4
Edward Mews W1 245 E2
Edward Square SE16 253 F3
Egerton Crescent SW3 249 D2
Egerton Gardens SW3 248 C2
Egerton Terrace SW3 249 D3
Elba Place SE17 251 E2
Eldon Road W8 248 B3
Eldon Street EC2 247 F2
Eleanor Close SE16 253 D2
Elephant And Castle SE1 251 E2
Elephant Lane SE16 252 C2
Elephant Road SE17 251 E2
Elf Row E1 253 D3
Elgar Street SE16 253 F1
Elgin Avenue W9 244 A3
Elgin Mews North W9 244 A4
Elgin Mews South W9 244 B4
Elia Street N1 247 D4
Elim Street SE1 251 F3
Eliot Mews NW8 244 B4
Elizabeth Bridge SW1 249 F2
Elizabeth Close W9 244 B3
Elizabeth Square SE16 253 E3
Elizabeth Street SW1 249 E2
Ellen Street E1 252 B3
Elliott Road SE9 251 D2
Ellis Street SW1 249 E2
Elm Park Gardens SW10 248 C1
Elm Park Lane SW3 248 B1
Elm Park Road SW3 248 B1
Elm Place SW7 248 C1
Elm Street WC1 246 C3
Elm Tree Close NW8 244 C4
Elm Tree Road NW8 244 C4
Elmfield Way W9 244 A3
Elmos Road SE16 253 E1
Elms Mews W2 244 C1
Elnathan Mews W9 244 A3
Elsa Street E1 253 E4
Elsted Street SE17 251 F2
Elvaston Mews SW7 248 B3
Elvaston Place SW7 248 B3
Elverton Street SW1 250 A2
Ely Place EC1 247 D2
Elystan Place SW3 249 D2
Elystan Street SW3 248 C2
Emba Street SE16 252 C1
Embankment Gardens SW3 249 D1
Embankment Place WC2 250 B4
Emerald Street WC1 246 C3
Emerson Street SE1 251 E4
Emery Hill Street SW1 250 A2
Emery Street SE1 251 D3
Emmett Street E14 253 F3
Emperor's Gate SW7 248 B2
Empire Wharf Road E14 254 C2
Empress Place SW6 248 A1
Empress Street SE17 251 E1
Endell Street WC2 246 B2
Endsleigh Gardens WC1 246 A3
Endsleigh Place WC1 246 A3
Endsleigh Street WC1 246 A3
Enford Street W1 245 D3
English Grounds SE1 252 A2
Enid Street SE16 252 B1
Ennismore Garden Mews SW7 248 C3
Ennismore Gardens SW7 248 C3
Ennismore Mews SW7 248 C3
Ennismore Street SW7 248 C3
Ensign Street E1 252 B3
Ensor Mews SW7 248 B1
Epping Close E14 254 A2
Epworth Street EC2 247 F3
Erasmus Street SW1 250 B2
Errol Street EC1 247 E3
Essendine Road W9 244 A4
Essex Street WC2 246 C1
Esterbrooke Street SW1 250 A2
Ethel Street SE17 251 E2
Europa Place EC1 247 E4
Euston Road NW1 245 F3
Euston Square NW1 246 A4
Euston Street NW1 246 A4
Evelyn Gardens SW7 250 B1
Evelyn Walk N1 247 F4
Evelyn Yard W1 246 A2
Gresse Street
Eversholt Street NW1 246 A4
Ewer Street SE1 251 E4
Exchange Place EC2 252 A4
Exchange Square EC2 252 A4
Exeter Street WC2 246 B1
Exhibition Road SW7 248 C3
Exmouth Market EC1 247 D3
Exmouth Street E1 253 D4
Exon Street SE17 251 F2
Exton Street SE1 250 C4
Eyre Street Hill EC1 247 D3

# F

Factory Place E14 254 B1
Fair Street SE1 252 A2
Fairclough Street E1 252 B3
Falcon Close SE1 251 E4
Falcon Way E14 254 B2
Falconberg Mews W1 246 A2
Sutton Row
Falmouth Road SE1 251 E3
Fann Street EC1 247 E3
Fanshaw Street N1 247 F4
Fareham Street W1 246 B1
Dean Street
Farm Street W1 245 E1
Farmer Street W8 248 A4
Farncombe Street SE16 252 C1
Farnell Mews SW5 248 A1
Farnham Place SE1 251 E4
Farnham Royal SE11 250 C1
Farrance Street E14 253 F3
Farrier Walk SW10 248 B1
Farringdon Lane EC1 247 D3
Farringdon Road EC1 246 C3
Farringdon Street EC4 247 D2
Farrins Rents SE16 253 E2
Farrow Place SE16 253 E1
Farthing Alley SE1 252 B1
Wolseley Street
Farthing Fields E1 252 C2
Raine Street
Fashion Street E1 252 B4
Faunce Street SE17 251 D1
Fawcett Street SW10 248 B1
Feather's Place SE10 254 C1
Featherstone Street EC1 247 F3
Felstead Gardens E14 254 B1
Fen Court EC3 252 A3
Fenchurch Avenue EC3 252 A3
Fenchurch Buildings EC3 247 F1
Fenchurch Street
Fenchurch Place EC3 247 F1
Fenchurch Street
Fenchurch Street EC3 247 F1
Fendall Street SE1 252 A1
Fenning Street SE1 251 F4
St Thomas Street
Fennings Circus W1 246 A2
Fernsbury Street WC1 246 C4
Ferry Street E14 254 B1
Fetter Lane EC4 247 D2
Field Street WC1 246 C4
Fieldgate Street E1 252 B4
Fielding Street SE17 251 E1
Finborough Road SW10 248 A1
Finch Lane EC3 247 F2
Finland Street SE16 253 E1
Finsbury Avenue EC2 247 F2
Finsbury Circus EC2 247 F2
Finsbury Pavement EC2 247 F3
Finsbury Square EC2 247 F3
Finsbury Street EC2 247 F3
First Street SW3 249 D2
Firtree Close SE16 253 E2
Fish Street Hill EC3 247 F1
Fish Wharf EC3 247 F1
Fisher Street WC1 246 C2
Fisherman's Walk E14 254 A4
Fishermans Drive SE16 253 E2
Fisherton Street NW8 244 C3
Fishmongers' Hall Wharf EC4 247 F1
Fitzalan Street SE11 250 C2
Fitzhardinge Street W1 245 E2
Fitzmaurice Place W1 245 F1
Fitzroy Square W1 245 F3
Fitzroy Street W1 245 F3
Flamborough Street E14 253 E3
Flank Street E1 252 B3
Flaxman Terrace WC1 246 B4
Fleet Square WC1 246 C4
Fleet Street EC4 247 D2
Fleming Road SE17 251 D1
Fletcher Street E1 252 B3
Flint Street SE17 251 F2
Flitcroft Street WC2 246 B2
Flood Street SW3 249 D1
Flood Walk SW3 249 D1
Floral Street WC2 246 B1
Flower And Dean Walk E1 252 B4
Thrawl Street
Foley Street W1 245 F2
Folly Wall E14 254 C3
Forbes Street E1 252 B3
Ford Square E1 252 C4
Fordham Street E1 252 C4
Fore Street EC2 247 E2
Fore Street Avenue EC2 247 E2
Formosa Street W9 244 A3
Forset Street W1 245 D2
Forsyth Gardens SE17 251 D1
Fort Street E1 252 A4
Artillery Lane
Fortune Street EC1 247 E3
Foscote Mews W9 244 A3
Foster Lane EC2 247 E2
Foubert's Place W1 245 F1
Foulis Terrace SW7 248 C2
Foundry Close SE16 253 E2
Fountain Green Square SE16 252 C1
Fournier Street E1 252 B4
Fowey Close E1 252 C2
Fox And Knot Street EC1 247 E2
Charterhouse Square
Frampton Street NW8 244 C3
Francis Close E14 254 C2
Francis Street SW1 250 A2
Franklin's Row SW3 249 D1
Frazier Street SE1 250 C3
Frean Street SE16 252 B1
Frederick Close W2 245 D1
Frederick Road SE17 251 E1
Frederick Square SE16 253 E3
Frederick Street WC1 246 C4
Fredericks Row EC1 247 D4
Goswell Road
Fremantle Street SE17 251 F2
French Ordinary Court EC3 252 A3
Hart Street
Friar Street EC4 247 E2
Carter Lane
Friars Mead E14 254 B2
Friday Street EC4 247 E1
Friend Street EC1 247 D4
Frigate Mews SE8 254 A1
Frith Street W1 246 A2
Frobisher Passage E14 254 A4
North Collonade
Frobisher Passage E14 254 A4
Frostic Walk E1 252 B4
Frying Pan Alley E1 252 A4
Fulbourne Street E1 252 C4
Fulford Street SE16 252 C1
Fulham Road SW3,SW6 & SW10 248 C1
Fulwood Place WC1 246 C2
Furnival Street EC4 247 D2
Fynes Street SW1 250 A2

# G

Gabriels Wharf SE1 251 D4
Gaien Place WC1 246 B2
Gainsford Street SE1 252 A2
Galbraith Street E14 254 B3
Galleon Close SE16 253 D2
Kinburn Street
Galleons View E14 254 C3
Galway Street EC1 247 E4
Gambia Street SE1 251 D4
Ganton Street W1 246 A1
Garbutt Place W1 245 E2
Gard Street EC1 247 E4
Garden Mews W2 244 A1
Garden Road NW8 244 B4
Garden Row SE1 251 D3
Garden Street E1 253 E4
Gardeners Lane EC4 247 E1
High Timber Street
Garford Street E14 253 F3
Garlick Hill EC4 247 F1
Garnault Mews EC1 247 D4
Garnet Street E1 252 C3
Garrett Street EC1 247 E3
Garrick Street WC2 246 B1
Garter Way SE16 253 D1
Garway Road W2 244 A2
Gaselee Street E14 254 C4
Gasholder Place SE11 250 C1
Gaspar Close SW5 248 B2
Gaspar Mews SW5 248 B2
Gate Street WC2 246 C2
Gateway SE17 251 E1
Gatliff Road SW1 249 E1
Gaunt Street SE1 251 E3
Gavel Street SE17 251 F2
Gayfere Street SW1 250 B3
Gaywood Street SE1 251 D3
Gaza Street SE17 251 D1
Gedling Place SE1 252 B1
Gee Street EC1 247 E3
Gees Court W1 245 E2
George Mathers Road SE11 251 D2
George Mews NW1 246 A4
George Row SE16 252 B1
George Street W1 245 D2
George Yard EC3 247 F1
George Yard W1 245 E1
Gerald Road SW1 249 E2
Geraldine Street SE11 251 D3
Gerrard Place W1 246 B1
Gerrard Street
Gerrard Street W1 246 A1
Gerridge Street SE1 251 D3
Gibson Road SE11 251 D3
Gilbert Place WC1 246 B2
Gilbert Road SE11 251 D2
Gilbert Street W1 245 E1
Gildea Street W1 245 F2
Gill Street E14 253 F3
Gillingham Street SW1 249 F2
Gillison Walk SE16 252 C1
Gilston Road SW10 248 B1
Giltspur Street EC1 247 D2
Gladstone Street SE1 251 D3
Glamis Place E1 253 D3
Glamis Road E1 253 D3
Glangarnock Avenue E14 254 C2
Glasgow Terrace SW1 249 F1
Glasshill Street SE1 251 E3
Glasshouse Fields E1 253 D3
Glasshouse Street W1 246 A1
Glasshouse Walk SE11 250 B1
Glebe Place SW3 248 C1
Gledhow Gardens SW5 248 B2
Glenaffric Avenue E14 254 C2
Glendower Place SW7 248 C2
Glengall Grove E14 254 B3
Glentworth Street NW1 245 D3
Glenworth Avenue E14 254 C2
Globe Pond Road SE16 253 E2
Globe Street SE1 251 E3
Gloucester Arcade SW7 248 B2
Gloucester Court EC3 252 A3
Gloucester Gate Mews NW1 246 F4
Albany Street
Gloucester Mews W2 244 B2
Gloucester Mews West W2 244 B2
Gloucester Park SW7 248 B2
Gloucester Place NW1 & W1 245 D3
Gloucester Place Mews W1 245 D2
Gloucester Road SW7 248 B3
Gloucester Square W2 244 C2
Gloucester Street SW1 249 F1
Gloucester Terrace W2 244 B2
Gloucester Walk W8 248 A4
Gloucester Way EC1 247 D4
Glyn Street SE11 250 C1
Goat Street SE1 252 A2
Lafone Street
Godfrey Street SW3 249 D2
Goding Street SE11 250 B1
Godliman Street EC4 247 E1
Golden Lane EC1 247 E3
Golden Square W1 246 A1
Golding Street E1 252 C3
Gomm Road SE16 253 D1
Goodge Place W1 246 A2
Goodge Street W1 246 A2
Goodhart Place E14 253 E3
Goodman's Stile E1 252 B4
Goodman's Yard E1 252 B3
Goodwin Close SE16 252 B1
Gophir Lane EC4 247 F1
Bush Lane
Gordon Place W8 248 A4
Gordon Square WC1 246 A3
Gordon Street WC1 246 A3
Gore Street SW7 248 B3
Goring Street E1 252 A4
Bevis Marks
Gosfield Street W1 245 F2
Goslett Yard WC2 246 B2
Goswell Road EC1 247 D4
Gough Square EC4 247 D2
Gough Street WC1 246 C3
Goulston Street E1 252 B4
Gower Place WC1 246 A3
Gower Street WC1 246 A3
Gowers Walk E1 252 B3
Grace's Alley E1 252 B3
Gracechurch Street EC3 247 F1
Graces Mews NW8 244 B4
Grafton Mews W1 245 F3
Grafton Place NW1 246 A4
Grafton Street W1 245 F1
Grafton Way W1 245 A3
Graham Street N1 247 E4
Graham Terrace SW1 249 E2
Granby Terrace NW1 245 F4
Grand Avenue EC1 247 D2
Grand Junction Wharf N1 247 E4
Grange Court WC2 246 C2
Grange Road SE1 252 A1
Grange Walk SE1 252 A1
Grange Yard SE1 252 A1
Grant's Quay Wharf EC3 247 F1
Grantully Road W9 244 A4
Granville Place W1 245 E2
Granville Road NW6 244 A4
Granville Square WC1 246 C4
Granville Street WC1 246 C4
Granville Square
Grape Street WC2 246 B2
Gravel Lane E1 252 A4
Gray Street SE1 251 D3
Gray's Inn Place WC1 246 C2
Gray's Inn Road WC1 246 B4
Great Castle Street W1 245 F2
Great Central Street NW1 245 D3
Great Chapel Street W1 246 A2
Great College Street SW1 245 D1
Seymour Street
Great Cumberland Place W1 245 D2
Great Dover Street SE1 251 F3
Great Eastern Street EC2 247 F3
Great George Street SW1 250 B3
Great Guildford Street SE1 251 E4
Great James Street WC1 246 C3
Great Marlborough Street W1 245 F2
Great Maze Pond SE1 251 F4
Great New Street EC4 247 D2
Great Newport Street WC2 250 C2
Newport Street
Great Ormond Street WC1 246 C3
Great Percy Street WC1 246 C4
Great Peter Street SW1 250 A3
Great Portland Street W1 245 F3
Great Pulteney Street W1 246 A1
Great Queen Street WC2 246 B2
Great Russell Street WC1 246 B2
Great Scotland Yard SW1 250 B4
Great Smith Street SW1 250 B3
Great St Helen's EC3 247 F2
Great St Thomas Apostle EC4 247 E1
Queen Street
Great Suffolk Street SE1 251 E3
Great Sutton Street EC1 247 D3
Great Swan Alley EC2 247 F2
Great Tower Street EC3 252 A3
Great Trinity Lane EC4 247 E1
Garlick Hill
Great Turnstile WC1 246 B2
High Holborn
Great Winchester Street EC2 247 F2
Great Windmill Street W1 246 A1
Greatorex Street E1 252 B4
Greek Street W1 246 B2
Green Bank E1 252 C2
Green Dragon Yard E1 252 B4
Green Street W1 245 E1
Green Walk SE1 251 F3
Green Yard WC1 246 C3
Greenacre Square SE16 253 E2
Greenberry Street NW8 244 C4
Greencoat Place SW1 250 A2
Greencoat Row SW1 250 A2
Greenfield Road E1 252 B4
Greenham Close SE1 251 D3
Greenwell Street W1 245 F3
Greenwich Park Street SE10 254 C1
Greenwich View Place E14 254 C3
Greet Street SE1 251 D4
Gregory Place W8 248 A3
Greig Terrace SE17 251 E1
Grenade Street E14 253 F3
Grendon Street NW8 244 C3
Grenville Place SW7 248 B2
Grenville Street WC1 246 B3
Gresham Street EC2 247 E2
Gresse Street W1 246 A2
Greville Street EC1 247 D2
Greycoat Place SW1 250 A3
Greycoat Street SW1 250 A2
Greystoke Place EC4 247 D2
Fetter Lane
Grigg's Place SE1 252 A1
Groom Place SW1 249 E3
Grosvenor Crescent SW1 249 E3
Grosvenor Crescent Mews SW1 249 E3
Grosvenor Gardens SW1 249 F3
Grosvenor Gate W1 245 E1
Park Lane
Grosvenor Hill W1 245 F1
Grosvenor Place SW1 249 E3
Grosvenor Road SW1 249 F1
Grosvenor Square W1 245 E1
Grosvenor Street W1 245 E1
Grosvenor Wharf Road E14 254 C2
Grove End Road NW8 244 B4
Grove Gardens NW8 245 D4
Grove Hall Court NW8 244 B4
Guildhall Buildings EC2 247 E2
Basinghall Street
Guildhall Yard EC2 247 E2
Guildhouse Street SW1 249 F2
Guilford Place WC1 246 B3
Guilford Street
Guilford Street WC1 246 B3
Guinness Square SE1 251 F2
Gulliver Street SE16 253 F1
Gulston Walk SW3 249 D2
Gun Street E1 252 A4
Gunthorpe Street E1 252 B4
Gunwhale Close SE16 253 E2
Guthrie Street SW3 248 C2
Gutter Lane EC2 247 E2
Guy Street SE1 251 F3
Gwynne Place WC1 246 C4

# H

Haberdasher Street N1 247 F4
Hainton Close E1 252 C3
Halcrow Street E1 252 C4
Half Moon Court EC1 247 E2
Bartholomew Close
Half Moon Street W1 249 F4
Halkin Place SW1 249 E3
Halkin Street SW1 249 E3
Hall Gate NW8 244 B4
Hall Place W2 244 C3
Hall Road NW8 244 B4
Hall Street EC1 247 D4
Hallam Mews W1 245 F3
Hallam Street W1 245 F3
Halley Place E14 253 E4
Halley Street E14 253 E4
Halsey Mews SW3 249 D2
Halsey Street SW3 249 D2
Hamilton Close NW8 244 B4
Hamilton Close SE16 253 E1
Hamilton Gardens NW8 244 B4
Hamilton Place W1 249 E4
Hamilton Square SE1 251 F3
Hamilton Terrace NW8 244 B4
Hammett Street EC3 252 A3
America Square
Hampstead Road NW1 245 F4
Hampton Street SE1 & SE17 251 E2
Hanbury Street E1 252 B4
Handel Street WC1 246 B3
Hankey Place SE1 251 F3
Hannibal Road E1 253 D4
Hanover Place WC2 246 B1
Long Acre
Hanover Square W1 245 F2
Hanover Street W1 245 F2
Hanover Terrace NW1 245 D4
Hanover Terrace Mews NW1 245 D4
Hans Crescent SW1 249 D3
Hans Place SW1 249 D3
Hans Road SW3 249 D3
Hans Street SW1 249 D3
Hanson Street W1 245 F2
Hanway Place W1 246 A2
Hanway Street W1 246 A2
Harbert Road W2 244 C2
Harbinger Road E14 254 A2
Harbour Exchange Square E14 254 B3
Harcourt Street W1 245 D2
Harcourt Terrace SW10 248 B1

257

**258**

259

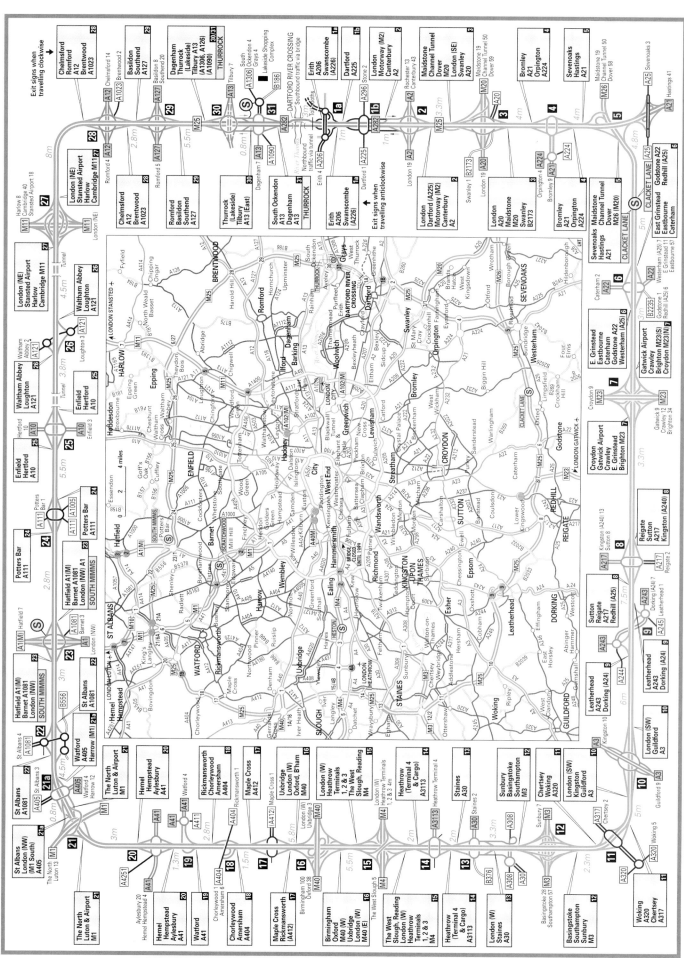

# the Channel Tunnel

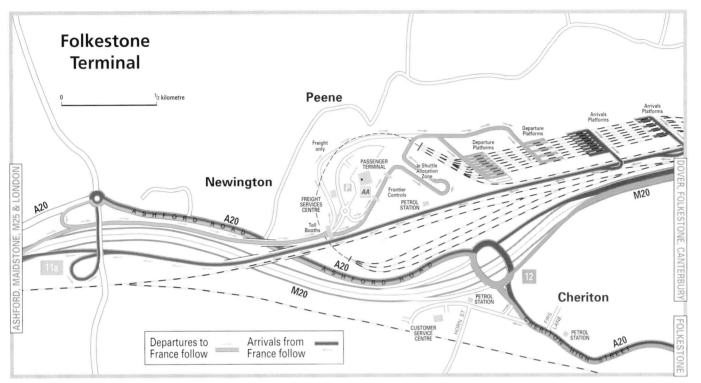

## Services to Europe

Eurotunnel Shuttle Service for cars, cars towing caravans and trailers, motorcycles, coaches and HGV vehicles, runs between terminals at Folkestone and Calais.

It takes just over one hour to travel from the M20 motorway in Kent, via the Channel Tunnel, to the A16 autoroute in France. The service runs 24 hours a day, 365 days of the year. Call Eurotunnel Call Centre (tel: 0990 353535) for the latest ticket and travel information.

Trains run at 15-minute intervals at peak times, with the journey in the tunnel from platform to platform taking just 35 minutes. Travellers pass through British and French frontier controls on departure, saving time on the other side of the Channel. Each terminal has tax-free and duty-free shops, bureaux de change, restaurants and a variety of shops. In Calais, the Cité de l'Europe contains numerous shops and restaurants, hotels and a hypermarket.

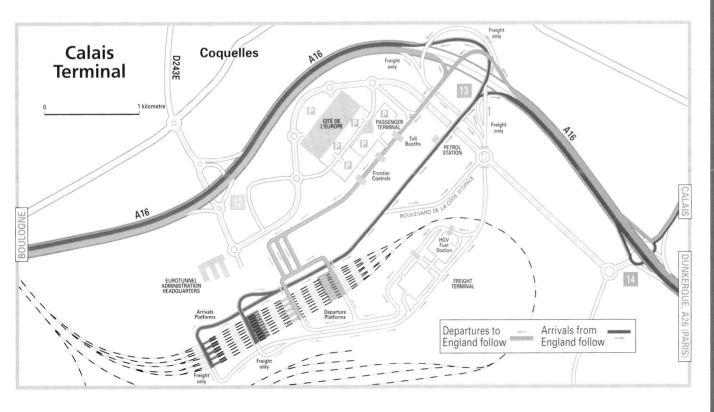

# ports and airports

## London Heathrow Airport – 16 miles west of London

**Telephone:** 0181 759 4321
**Parking:** short-stay, long-stay and business parking is available.
For charge details tel: 0800 844844 or 0345 405000
**Public Transport:** coach, bus, rail and London Underground.
There are several 4-star and 3-star hotels within easy reach of the airport.
Car hire facilities are available.

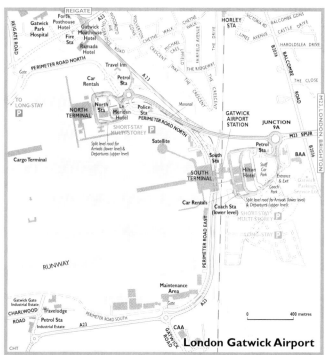

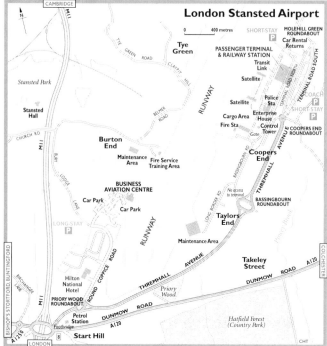

## London Gatwick Airport – 35 miles south of London

**Telephone:** 01293 535353
**Parking:** short and long-stay parking is available at both the North and South terminals.
For charge details tel: 01293 502390 (short-stay) and either 0800 128128 or
0800 626671 (long-stay).
**Public Transport:** coach, bus and rail.
There are several 4-star and 3-star hotels within easy reach of the airport.
Car hire facilities are available.

## London Stansted Airport – 36 miles north-east of London

**Telephone:** 01279 680500
**Parking:** short and long-stay open-air parking is available.
For charge details tel: 01279 681192
**Public Transport:** coach, bus and direct rail link to London on the 'Stansted Skytrain'.
There is one 4-star and one 3-star hotel within easy reach of the airport.
Car hire facilities are available.

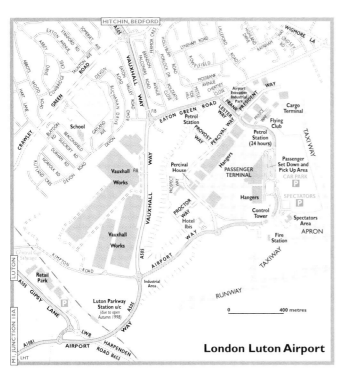

**London Luton Airport**

**London City Airport**

## London Luton Airport – 33 miles north of London

**Telephone:** 01582 405100
**Parking:** short and long-stay open-air parking is available.
**Public Transport:** coach, bus and rail.
There is one 2-star hotel at the airport and several 3-star hotels within easy reach of the airport.
Car hire facilities are available.

## London City Airport – 7 miles east of London

**Telephone:** 0171 646 0000
**Parking:** open-air parking is available.
For charge details tel: 0171 646 0088
**Public Transport:** shuttle-bus service into London. Easy access to the rail network and the London Underground.
There is a 4-star and 2-star hotel within easy reach of the airport.
Car hire facilities are available.

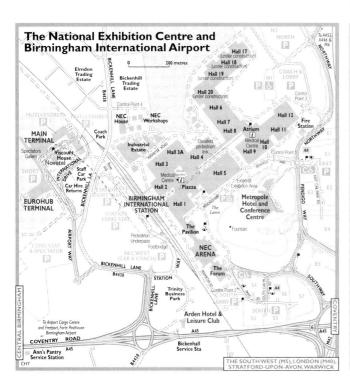

**The National Exhibition Centre and Birmingham International Airport**

**Manchester Airport**

## Birmingham International Airport – 8 miles east of Birmingham

**Telephone:** 0121 767 5511 (Main Terminal), 0121 767 7502 (Eurohub Terminal)
**Parking:** short and long-stay parking is available.
For charge details tel: 0121 767 7861
**Public Transport:** shuttle-bus service to Birmingham International railway station and the NEC.
There are several 3-star hotels within easy reach of the airport.
Car hire facilities are available.

## Manchester Airport – 10 miles south of Manchester

**Telephone:** 0161 489 3000
**Parking:** short and long-stay parking is available.
**Public Transport:** bus, coach and rail. Manchester airport railway station connects with the rail network.
There are several 4-star and 3-star hotels within easy reach of the airport.
Car hire facilities are available.

# major airports

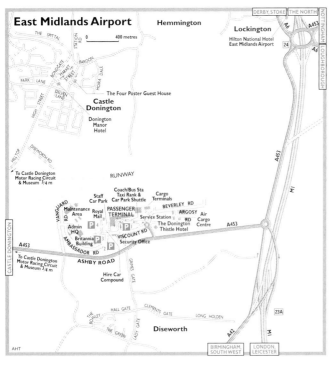

### East Midlands Airport – 15 miles south-west of Nottingham, next to the M1 at junctions 23A and 24

**Telephone:** 01332 852852
**Parking:** short and long-stay parking is available.
For charge details tel: 0800 128128
**Public Transport:** bus and coach services to major towns and cities in the East Midlands.
There is one 4-star and several 3-star hotels within easy reach of the airport.
Car hire facilities are available.

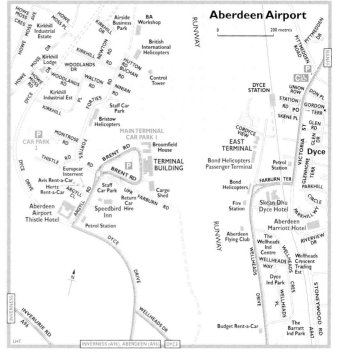

### Aberdeen Airport – 6 miles north-west of Aberdeen

**Telephone:** 01224 722331
**Parking:** open-air parking is available.
For charge details tel: 01224 722331 ext 5142
**Public Transport:** bus to central Aberdeen and Dyce Station.
There are several 4-star and 3-star hotels within easy reach of the airport.
Car hire facilities are available.

### Edinburgh Airport – 7 miles west of Edinburgh

**Telephone:** 0131 333 1000
**Parking:** open-air parking is available.
For charge details tel: 0131 344 3197
**Public Transport:** regular coach services operate between central Edinburgh and Glasgow.
There is one 4-star and several 3-star hotels within easy reach of the airport.
Car hire facilities are available.

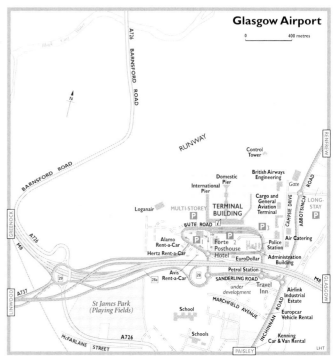

### Glasgow Airport – 8 miles west of Glasgow

**Telephone:** 0141 887 1111
**Parking:** short and long-stay parking is available, mostly open-air.
For charge details tel: 0141 889 2751
**Public Transport:** regular coach services operate between central Glasgow and Edinburgh.
There are several 3-star hotels within easy reach of the airport.
Car hire facilities are available.

266

# major ports

**Dover**

Pay-and-display parking is available at the Dover Eastern Docks and at the Hovercraft Terminal.
**For further information tel:** 01304 240400
Other long-stay parking facilities are available with a collection and delivery service.
**For charge details tel:** 01304 201227

**Harwich International Port**

Open-air parking is available at the terminal.
**For charge details tel:** 01255 242000
Further parking is available 5 miles from Harwich International Port with a collection and delivery service.
**For charge details tel:** 01255 870217

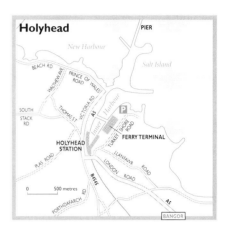

**Holyhead**

Open-air pay-and-display parking is available close to the Ferry Terminal.
**For charge details tel:** 01407 762304 or 606782

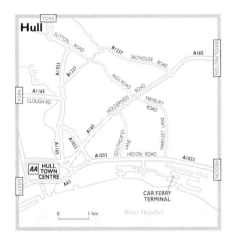

**Hull**

Free open-air parking is available at King George Dock (left at owners' risk).
**Tel:** 01482 795141
Undercover parking is also available.
**For charge details tel:** 01482 781021

**Newhaven**

Open and limited parking is available within the harbour complex.
**For charge details tel:** 01273 514131

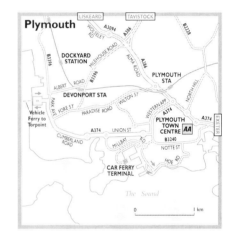

**Plymouth**

Free open-air parking is available outside the terminal building.
**Tel:** 0990 360360 or 01752 252200

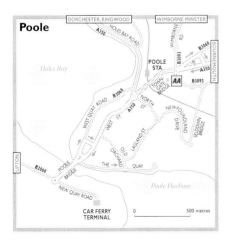

**Poole**

Open-air parking for 600 vehicles is available adjacent to the Ferry Terminal.
**For charge details tel:** 01202 440220

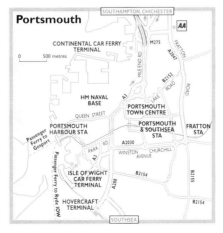

**Portsmouth**

Lock-up parking services are available at Albert Johnson Quay.
**For charge details tel:** 01705 751261
Pay-and-display parking is available opposite the Hovercraft Terminal. Multi-storey parking is also available close to the Isle of Wight Passenger Ferry Terminal.
**For charge details tel:** 01705 823153 or 812071

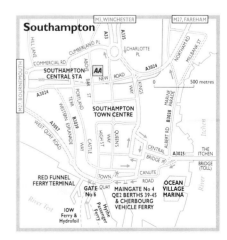

**Southampton**

Covered or fenced compound parking for 1,600 vehicles is available within the Western Docks with a collection and delivery service.
**For charge details tel:** 01703 228001/2/3

# index to place names

## England

| | | |
|---|---|---|
| 5 | *Beds* | **Bedfordshire** |
| 6 | *Berks* | **Berkshire** |
| 10 | *Bristl* | **Bristol** |
| 11 | *Bucks* | **Buckinghamshire** |
| 13 | *Cambs* | **Cambridgeshire** |
| 17 | *Ches* | **Cheshire** |
| 22 | *Cnwll* | **Cornwall** |
| 23 | *Cumb* | **Cumbria** |
| 25 | *Derbys* | **Derbyshire** |
| 26 | *Devon* | **Devon** |
| 27 | *Dorset* | **Dorset** |
| 30 | *Dur* | **Durham** |
| 35 | *E R Yk* | **East Riding of Yorkshire** |
| 36 | *E Susx* | **East Sussex** |
| 37 | *Essex* | **Essex** |
| 41 | *Gloucs* | **Gloucestershire** |
| 42 | *Gt Lon* | **Greater London** |
| 43 | *Gt Man* | **Greater Manchester** |
| 44 | *Guern* | **Guernsey** |
| 46 | *Hants* | **Hampshire** |
| 47 | *Herefs* | **Herefordshire** |
| 48 | *Herts* | **Hertfordshire** |
| 52 | *IOM* | **Isle of Man** |
| 53 | *IOW* | **Isle of Wight** |
| 54 | *IOS* | **Isles of Scilly** |
| 55 | *Jersey* | **Jersey** |
| 56 | *Kent* | **Kent** |
| 57 | *Lancs* | **Lancashire** |
| 58 | *Leics* | **Leicestershire** |
| 59 | *Lincs* | **Lincolnshire** |
| 60 | *Mersyd* | **Merseyside** |
| 67 | *Norfk* | **Norfolk** |
| 70 | *N York* | **North Yorkshire** |
| 71 | *Nhants* | **Northamptonshire** |
| 72 | *Nthumb* | **Northumberland** |
| 73 | *Notts* | **Nottinghamshire** |
| 75 | *Oxon* | **Oxfordshire** |
| 81 | *Rutlnd* | **Rutland** |
| 83 | *Shrops* | **Shropshire** |
| 84 | *Somset* | **Somerset** |
| 87 | *S York* | **South Yorkshire** |
| 88 | *Staffs* | **Staffordshire** |
| 90 | *Suffk* | **Suffolk** |
| 91 | *Surrey* | **Surrey** |
| 94 | *T & W* | **Tyne & Wear** |
| 96 | *Warwks* | **Warwickshire** |
| 100 | *W Mids* | **West Midlands** |
| 101 | *W Susx* | **West Sussex** |
| 102 | *W York* | **West Yorkshire** |
| 103 | *Wilts* | **Wiltshire** |
| 104 | *Worcs* | **Worcestershire** |

## Wales

| | | |
|---|---|---|
| 7 | *Blae G* | **Blaenau Gwent** |
| 9 | *Brdgnd* | **Bridgend** |
| 12 | *Caerph* | **Caerphilly** |
| 14 | *Cardif* | **Cardiff** |
| 15 | *Carmth* | **Carmarthenshire** |
| 16 | *Cerdgn* | **Ceredigion** |
| 21 | *Conwy* | **Conwy** |
| 24 | *Denbgs* | **Denbighshire** |
| 40 | *Flints* | **Flintshire** |
| 45 | *Gwynd* | **Gwynedd** |
| 51 | *IOA* | **Isle of Anglesey** |
| 61 | *Myr Td* | **Merthyr Tydfil** |
| 63 | *Mons* | **Monmouthshire** |
| 65 | *Neath* | **Neath Port Talbot** |
| 66 | *Newpt* | **Newport** |
| 76 | *Pembks* | **Pembrokeshire** |
| 78 | *Powys* | **Powys** |
| 80 | *Rhondd* | **Rhondda Cynon Taff** |
| 92 | *Swans* | **Swansea** |
| 93 | *Torfn* | **Torfaen** |
| 95 | *V Glam* | **Vale of Glamorgan** |
| 105 | *Wrexhm* | **Wrexham** |

## Scotland

| | | |
|---|---|---|
| 1 | *Aber C* | **Aberdeen City** |
| 2 | *Abers* | **Aberdeenshire** |
| 3 | *Angus* | **Angus** |
| 4 | *Ag & B* | **Argyll & Bute** |
| 8 | *Border* | **Borders (Scottish)** |
| 18 | *C Edin* | **City of Edinburgh** |
| 19 | *C Glas* | **City of Glasgow** |
| 20 | *Clacks* | **Clackmannanshire** |
| 28 | *D & G* | **Dumfries & Galloway** |
| 29 | *Dund C* | **Dundee City** |
| 31 | *E Ayrs* | **East Ayrshire** |
| 32 | *E Duns* | **East Dunbartonshire** |
| 33 | *E Loth* | **East Lothian** |
| 34 | *E Rens* | **East Renfrewshire** |
| 38 | *Falk* | **Falkirk** |
| 39 | *Fife* | **Fife** |
| 49 | *Highld* | **Highland** |
| 50 | *Inver* | **Inverclyde** |
| 62 | *Mdloth* | **Midlothian** |
| 64 | *Moray* | **Moray** |
| 68 | *N Ayrs* | **North Ayrshire** |
| 69 | *N Lans* | **North Lanarkshire** |
| 74 | *Ork* | **Orkney Islands** |
| 77 | *P & K* | **Perth & Kinross** |
| 79 | *Rens* | **Renfrewshire** |
| 82 | *Shet* | **Shetland Islands** |
| 85 | *S Ayrs* | **South Ayrshire** |
| 86 | *S Lans* | **South Lanarkshire** |
| 89 | *Stirlg* | **Stirling** |
| 97 | *W Isls* | **Western Isles** |
| 98 | *W Duns* | **West Dunbartonshire** |
| 99 | *W Loth* | **West Lothian** |

Each place name entry in this index is identified by its County, County Borough or Council Area name. These are shown in *italics*.

A list of the abbreviated forms used is shown on the left.

To locate a place name in the atlas turn to the map page indicated in bold type in the index and use the 4-figure grid reference.

For example, **Hythe** *Kent* **29** **1**6**3**4 is found on page 29.

To pin-point our example the first bold figure '**1**' is found along the bottom edge of the page.

The following figure '6' indicates how many imaginary tenths to move east of the line '**1**'.

The next bold figure '**3**' is found up the left-hand side of the page.

The last figure '4' shows how many imaginary tenths to move north of the line '**3**'. You will locate Hythe where these two lines intersect.

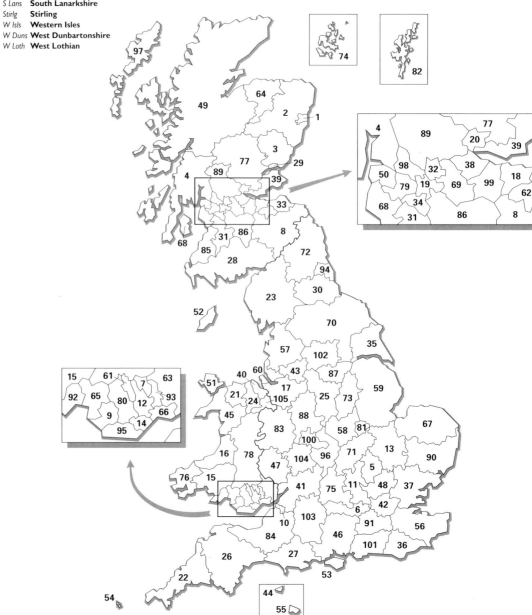

A'Chill Anlaby

# A


A'Chill *Highld* 128 2705
Ab Kettleby *Leics* 63 7223
Ab Lench *Worcs* 47 0151
Abbas Combe *Somset* 22 7022
Abberley *Worcs* 47 7567
Abberley Common *Worcs* 47 7467
Abberton *Essex* 41 0019
Abberton *Worcs* 47 9953
Abberwick *Nthumb* 111 1313
Abbess Roding *Essex* 40 5711
Abbey *Devon* 9 1410
Abbey Dore *Herefd* 46 3830
Abbey Green *Staffs* 72 9757
Abbey Hill *Somset* 10 2718
Abbey St Bathans *Border* 119 7661
Abbey Town *Cumb* 93 1750
Abbey Village *Lancs* 81 6422
Abbey Wood *Gt Lon* 27 4779
Abbeycwmhir *Powys* 45 0571
Abbeydale *S York* 74 3281
Abbeystead *Lancs* 81 5654
Abbot's Chair *Derbys* 74 0290
Abbot's Salford *Warwks* 48 0650
Abbotrule *Border* 110 6113
Abbots Bickington *Devon* 18 3813
Abbots Bromley *Staffs* 73 0724
Abbots Deuglie *P & K* 126 1111
Abbots Langley *Herts* 26 0901
Abbots Leigh *Somset* 34 5474
Abbots Morton *Worcs* 48 0255
Abbots Ripton *Cambs* 52 2377
Abbots Worthy *Hants* 24 4932
Abbotsbury *Dorset* 10 5785
Abbotsham *Devon* 18 4226
Abbotskerswell *Devon* 7 8568
Abbotsleigh *Devon* 7 8048
Abbotsley *Cambs* 52 2256
Abbotstone *Hants* 24 5634
Abbotswood *Hants* 23 3623
Abbott Street *Dorset* 11 9800
Abbotts Ann *Hants* 23 3243
Abcott *Shrops* 46 3978
Abdon *Shrops* 59 5786
Abenhall *Gloucs* 35 6717
Aber *Gwynd* 69 6572
Aber Clydach *Powys* 33 1021
Aber-arad *Carmth* 31 3140
Aber-banc *Cerdgn* 31 3541
Aber-giar *Carmth* 44 5040
Aber-Magwr *Cerdgn* 43 6673
Aber-meurig *Cerdgn* 44 5656
Aber-nant *Rhondd* 33 0103
Aberaeron *Cerdgn* 42 4562
Aberaman *Rhondd* 33 0100
Aberangell *Gwynd* 57 8410
Aberarder *Highld* 140 6225
Aberargie *P & K* 126 1615
Aberarth *Cerdgn* 42 4763
Aberavon *Neath* 32 7489
Aberbargoed *Caerph* 33 1500
Aberbeeg *Blae G* 33 2002
Abercairny *P & K* 125 9222
Abercanaid *Myr Td* 33 0503
Abercarn *Caerph* 33 2194
Abercastle *Pembks* 30 8533
Abercegir *Powys* 57 8001
Aberchalder Lodge *Highld* 131 3403
Aberchirder *Abers* 142 6252
Abercoed *Cerdgn* 44 6757
Abercraf *Powys* 33 8212
Abercregan *Neath* 33 8496
Abercwmboi *Rhondd* 33 0299
Abercych *Pembks* 31 2441
Abercynon *Rhondd* 33 0794
Aberdalgie *P & K* 125 0720
Aberdare *Rhondd* 33 0002
Aberdaron *Gwynd* 56 1726
Aberdeen *Aber C* 135 9306
Aberdesach *Gwynd* 68 4251
Aberdour *Fife* 117 1985
Aberdulais *Neath* 32 7799
Aberdyfi *Gwynd* 43 6196
Aberedw *Powys* 45 0847
Abereiddy *Pembks* 30 7931
Abererch *Gwynd* 56 3936
Aberfan *Myr Td* 33 0700
Aberfeldy *P & K* 125 8549
Aberffraw *IOA* 68 3569
Aberffrwd *Cerdgn* 43 6878
Aberford *W York* 83 4337
Aberfoyle *Stirlg* 115 5200
Abergarw *Brdgnd* 33 9184
Abergarwed *Neath* 33 8102
Abergavenny *Mons* 34 2914
Abergele *Conwy* 70 9477
Abergorlech *Carmth* 44 5833
Abergwesyn *Powys* 45 8552
Abergwili *Carmth* 31 4320
Abergwydol *Powys* 57 7903
Abergwynfi *Neath* 33 8995
Abergwyngregyn *Gwynd* 57 6806
Aberhafesp *Powys* 58 0792
Aberhosan *Powys* 43 8197
Aberkenfig *Brdgnd* 33 8984
Aberlady *E Loth* 118 4679
Aberlemno *Angus* 127 5255
Aberllefenni *Powys* 57 7609
Aberllynfi *Powys* 45 1737
Aberlour *Moray* 141 2642
Abermorddu *Flints* 71 3056
Abermule *Powys* 58 1694
Abernant *Carmth* 31 3323
Abernethy *P & K* 126 1816
Abernyte *P & K* 126 2531
Aberporth *Cerdgn* 42 2651
Abersoch *Gwynd* 56 3127
Abersychan *Torfn* 34 2603
Aberthin *V Glam* 33 0074
Abertillery *Blae G* 33 2104
Abertridwr *Caerph* 33 1289
Abertridwr *Powys* 58 0319
Abertysswg *Caerph* 33 1305
Aberuthven *P & K* 125 9615
Aberyscir *Powys* 45 9929
Aberystwyth *Cerdgn* 43 5881
Abingdon *Oxon* 37 4997
Abinger *Surrey* 14 1145
Abinger Hammer *Surrey* 14 0947
Abington *Nhants* 50 7861
Abington *S Lans* 108 9323
Abington Pigotts *Cambs* 39 3044
Ablington *Gloucs* 36 1007
Ablington *Wilts* 23 1546
Abney *Derbys* 74 1980
Above Church *Staffs* 73 0150
Aboyne *Abers* 134 5298
Abram *Gt Man* 78 6001
Abriachan *Highld* 139 5535
Abridge *Essex* 27 4696
Abson *Gloucs* 35 7074
Abthorpe *Nhants* 49 6446
Aby *Lincs* 77 4078
Acaster Malbis *N York* 83 5845
Acaster Selby *N York* 83 5741
Accott *Devon* 19 6432
Accrington *Lancs* 81 7628
Acha *Ag & B* 120 1854
Acha Mor *W Isls* 152 3029
Achahoish *Ag & B* 113 7877
Achalader *P & K* 126 1245
Achaleven *Ag & B* 122 9233
Achanalt *Highld* 139 2661
Achandunie *Highld* 146 6472
Achany *Highld* 146 5602
Acharacle *Highld* 121 6767
Acharn *Highld* 122 7050
Acharn *P & K* 124 7543
Achavanich *Highld* 151 1842
Achduart *Highld* 145 0403
Achfary *Highld* 148 2939
Achiltibuie *Highld* 144 0208
Achinhoan *Ag & B* 105 7516
Achintee *Highld* 138 9441
Achintraid *Highld* 138 8438
Achlain *Highld* 131 2812
Achmelvich *Highld* 148 0524
Achmore *Highld* 138 8533
Achmore *W Isls* 152 3029
Achnacarnin *Highld* 148 0432
Achnacarry *Highld* 131 1787
Achnacloich *Highld* 129 5908
Achnaconeran *Highld* 139 4118
Achnacroish *Ag & B* 122 8541
Achnadrish Lodge *Ag & B* 121 4652
Achnafauld *P & K* 125 8736
Achnagarron *Highld* 146 6870
Achnaha *Highld* 128 4668
Achnahaird *Highld* 144 0013
Achnairn *Highld* 146 5512
Achnalea *Highld* 130 8561
Achnamara *Ag & B* 113 7887
Achnasheen *Highld* 138 1658
Achnashellach Station *Highld* 138 0048
Achnastank *Moray* 141 2733
Achosnich *Highld* 121 4467
Achranich *Highld* 122 7047
Achreamie *Highld* 150 0166
Achriabhach *Highld* 131 1468
Achriesgill *Highld* 148 2554
Achtoty *Highld* 149 6762
Achurch *Nhants* 51 0283
Achvaich *Highld* 146 7194
Ackergill *Highld* 151 3553
Acklam *N York* 97 4817
Acklam *N York* 90 7861
Ackleton *Shrops* 60 7698
Acklington *Nthumb* 103 2301
Ackton *W York* 83 4121
Ackworth Moor Top *W York* 83 4316
Acle *Norfk* 67 4010
Acock's Green *W Mids* 61 1283
Acol *Kent* 29 3067
Acomb *N York* 83 5651
Acomb *Nthumb* 102 9366
Acombe *Somset* 9 1914
Aconbury *Herefd* 46 5133
Acre *Lancs* 81 7924
Acrefair *Wrexhm* 70 2743
Acresford *Derbys* 61 2913
Acton *Ches* 71 6352
Acton *Dorset* 11 9978
Acton *Gt Lon* 26 2080
Acton *Shrops* 59 3185
Acton *Staffs* 72 8241
Acton *Suffk* 54 8945
Acton *Worcs* 47 8467
Acton Beauchamp *Herefd* 47 6850
Acton Bridge *Ches* 71 5975
Acton Burnell *Shrops* 59 5302
Acton Green *Herefd* 47 6950
Acton Park *Wrexhm* 71 3451
Acton Pigott *Shrops* 59 5402
Acton Round *Shrops* 59 6395
Acton Scott *Shrops* 59 4589
Acton Trussell *Staffs* 72 9318
Acton Turville *Gloucs* 35 8080
Adbaston *Staffs* 72 7627
Adber *Dorset* 21 5920
Adbolton *Notts* 62 5938
Adderbury *Oxon* 49 4735
Adderley *Shrops* 72 6640
Adderstone *Nthumb* 111 1330
Addiewell *W Loth* 117 9962
Addingham *W York* 82 0749
Addington *Bucks* 49 7428
Addington *Gt Lon* 27 3664
Addington *Kent* 28 6559
Addiscombe *Gt Lon* 27 3366
Addlestone *Surrey* 26 0564
Addlestonemoor *Surrey* 26 0565
Addlethorpe *Lincs* 77 5468
Adeney *Shrops* 72 6918
Adeyfield *Herts* 38 0708
Adfa *Powys* 58 0601
Adforton *Herefd* 46 4071
Adisham *Kent* 29 2253
Adlestrop *Gloucs* 48 2426
Adlingfleet *E R Yk* 84 8421
Adlington *Ches* 79 9180
Adlington *Lancs* 81 6013
Admaston *Shrops* 59 6313
Admaston *Staffs* 73 0423
Admington *Warwks* 48 2045
Adsborough *Somset* 20 2729
Adscombe *Somset* 20 1837
Adstock *Bucks* 49 7329
Adstone *Nhants* 49 5951
Adswood *Gt Man* 79 8888
Adversane *W Susx* 14 0723
Advie *Highld* 141 1234
Adwalton *W York* 82 2328
Adwell *Oxon* 37 6999
Adwick Le Street *S York* 83 5308
Adwick upon Dearne *S York* 83 4701
Ae *D & G* 100 9889
Ae Bridgend *D & G* 100 0186
Affetside *Gt Man* 81 7513
Affleck *Abers* 142 5540
Affpuddle *Dorset* 11 8093
Affric Lodge *Highld* 138 1822
Afon-wen *Flints* 70 1371
Afton *Devon* 7 8462
Afton *IOW* 12 3486
Agglethorpe *N York* 89 0885
Aigburth *Mersyd* 78 3886
Aike *E R Yk* 84 0446
Aiketgate *Cumb* 94 4846
Aikhead *Cumb* 93 2349
Aikton *Cumb* 93 2753
Ailby *Lincs* 77 4376
Ailey *Herefd* 46 3348
Ailsworth *Cambs* 64 1198
Ainderby Quernhow *N York* 89 3480
Ainderby Steeple *N York* 89 3392
Aingers Green *Essex* 41 1120
Ainsdale *Mersyd* 80 3112
Ainsdale-on-Sea *Mersyd* 80 2912
Ainstable *Cumb* 94 5246
Ainsworth *Gt Man* 79 7610
Ainthorpe *N York* 90 7007
Aintree *Mersyd* 78 3898
Ainville *W Loth* 117 1063
Aird *Ag & B* 113 7600
Aird *D & G* 98 0960
Aird *W Isls* 152 5635
Aird a Mhulaidh *W Isls* 152 1810
Aird Asaig *W Isls* 152 1202
Aird Dhubh *Highld* 137 7040
Aird of Kinloch *Ag & B* 121 5228
Aird of Sleat *Highld* 129 5900
Aird Uig *W Isls* 152 0533
Airdeny *Ag & B* 122 9929
Airdrie *N Lans* 116 7565
Airdriehill *N Lans* 116 7867
Airds Bay *Ag & B* 122 9932
Airds of Kells *D & G* 99 6770
Airidh a bhruaich *W Isls* 152 2417
Airieland *D & G* 99 7556
Airlie *Angus* 126 3150
Airmyn *E R Yk* 84 7224
Airntully *P & K* 125 0935
Airor *Highld* 129 7205
Airth *Falk* 116 9087
Airton *N York* 88 9059
Aisby *Lincs* 76 8692
Aisby *Lincs* 64 0138
Aisgill *Cumb* 88 7797
Aish *Devon* 7 6960
Aish *Devon* 7 8458
Aisholt *Somset* 20 1935
Aiskew *N York* 89 2788
Aislaby *Dur* 89 4012
Aislaby *N York* 90 8608
Aislaby *N York* 90 7785
Aisthorpe *Lincs* 76 9480
Aith *Shet* 153 3455
Akeld *Nthumb* 111 9529
Akeley *Bucks* 49 7037
Akenham *Suffk* 54 1449
Albaston *Devon* 6 4270
Alberbury *Shrops* 59 3614
Albourne *W Susx* 15 2516
Albourne Green *W Susx* 15 2616
Albrighton *Shrops* 59 4918
Albrighton *Shrops* 60 8004
Alburgh *Norfk* 55 2687
Albury *Herts* 39 4324
Albury *Oxon* 37 6505
Albury *Surrey* 14 0447
Albury End *Herts* 39 4223
Albury Heath *Surrey* 14 0646
Alby Hill *Norfk* 67 1934
Alcaig *Highld* 139 5657
Alcaston *Shrops* 59 4587
Alcester *Warwks* 48 0857
Alcester Lane End *W Mids* 61 0780
Alciston *E Susx* 16 5005
Alcombe *Wilts* 35 8169
Alconbury *Cambs* 52 1875
Alconbury Weston *Cambs* 52 1777
Aldborough *N York* 89 4066
Aldborough *Norfk* 66 1834
Aldbourne *Wilts* 36 2676
Aldbrough *E R Yk* 85 2438
Aldbrough St John *N York* 89 2011
Aldbury *Herts* 38 9612
Aldcliffe *Lancs* 87 4660
Aldclune *P & K* 132 8964
Aldeburgh *Suffk* 55 4656
Aldeby *Norfk* 67 4493
Aldenham *Herts* 26 1498
Alder Moor *Staffs* 73 2226
Alderbury *Wilts* 23 1827
Aldercar *Derbys* 62 4447
Alderford *Norfk* 66 1218
Alderholt *Dorset* 12 1212
Alderley *Gloucs* 35 7690
Alderley Edge *Ches* 79 8478
Aldermans Green *W Mids* 61 3683
Aldermaston *Berks* 24 5965
Alderminster *Warwks* 48 2348
Aldershot *Hants* 25 8650
Alderton *Gloucs* 47 0033
Alderton *Nhants* 49 7446
Alderton *Shrops* 59 4924
Alderton *Suffk* 55 3441
Alderton *Wilts* 35 8482
Alderwasley *Derbys* 73 3053
Aldfield *N York* 89 2669
Aldford *Ches* 71 4159
Aldgate *Rutlnd* 63 9804
Aldham *Essex* 40 9126
Aldham *Suffk* 54 0545
Aldingbourne *W Susx* 14 9205
Aldingham *Cumb* 86 2870
Aldington *Kent* 29 0736
Aldington *Worcs* 48 0644
Aldington Corner *Kent* 29 0636
Aldivalloch *Moray* 141 3526
Aldochlay *Ag & B* 115 3591
Aldon *Shrops* 46 4379
Aldoth *Cumb* 92 1448
Aldreth *Cambs* 53 4473
Aldridge *W Mids* 61 0500
Aldringham *Suffk* 55 4461
Aldro *N York* 90 8162
Aldsworth *Gloucs* 36 1509
Aldsworth *W Susx* 14 7608
Aldunie *Moray* 141 3626
Aldwark *Derbys* 74 2257
Aldwark *N York* 89 4663
Aldwick *W Susx* 14 9198
Aldwincle *Nhants* 51 0081
Aldworth *Berks* 37 5579
Alexandria *W Duns* 115 3979
Aley *Somset* 20 1838
Alfardisworthy *Devon* 18 2911
Alfington *Devon* 9 1197
Alfold *Surrey* 14 0333
Alfold Bars *W Susx* 14 0333
Alfold Crossways *Surrey* 14 0335
Alford *Abers* 142 5715
Alford *Lincs* 77 4575
Alford *Somset* 21 6032
Alfreton *Derbys* 74 4155
Alfrick *Worcs* 47 7453
Alfrick Pound *Worcs* 47 7452
Alfriston *E Susx* 16 5103
Algarkirk *Lincs* 64 2935
Alhampton *Somset* 21 6234
Alkborough *Lincs* 84 8821
Alkerton *Gloucs* 35 7705
Alkerton *Oxon* 48 3743
Alkham *Kent* 29 2542
Alkington *Shrops* 71 5339
Alkmonton *Derbys* 73 1838
All Cannings *Wilts* 23 0661
All Saints South Elmham *Suffk* 55 3482
All Stretton *Shrops* 59 4595
Allaleigh *Devon* 7 8053
Allanaquoich *Abers* 133 1291
Allanbank *N Lans* 116 8458
Allanton *Border* 119 8654
Allanton *N Lans* 116 8457
Allanton *S Lans* 116 7454
Allaston *Gloucs* 35 6304
Allbrook *Hants* 13 4521
Allen End *Warwks* 61 1696
Allen's Green *Herts* 39 4516
Allendale *Nthumb* 95 8355
Allenheads *Nthumb* 95 8645
Allensford *Dur* 95 0750
Allensmore *Herefd* 46 4635
Allenton *Derbys* 62 3732
Aller *Devon* 19 7625
Aller *Somset* 21 4029
Allerby *Cumb* 92 0839
Allercombe *Devon* 9 0494
Allerford *Somset* 20 9046
Allerston *N York* 90 8782
Allerthorpe *E R Yk* 84 7847
Allerton *Mersyd* 78 3987
Allerton *W York* 82 1234
Allerton Bywater *W York* 83 4227
Allerton Mauleverer *N York* 89 4157
Allesley *W Mids* 61 3080
Allestree *Derbys* 62 3439
Allet Common *Cnwll* 3 7948
Allexton *Leics* 51 8100
Allgreave *Ches* 72 9767
Allhallows *Kent* 28 8377
Allhallows-on-Sea *Kent* 40 8478
Alligin Shuas *Highld* 137 8357
Allimore Green *Staffs* 72 8519
Allington *Dorset* 10 4693
Allington *Kent* 28 7557
Allington *Lincs* 63 8540
Allington *Wilts* 35 8975
Allington *Wilts* 23 0663
Allington *Wilts* 23 2039
Allithwaite *Cumb* 87 3876
Alloa *Clacks* 116 8892
Allonby *Cumb* 92 0842
Allostock *Ches* 79 7471
Alloway *S Ayrs* 106 3318
Allowenshay *Somset* 10 3913
Allscott *Shrops* 59 6113
Allscott *Shrops* 60 7396
Alltami *Flints* 70 2665
Alltchaorunn *Highld* 123 1951
Alltmawr *Powys* 45 0746
Alltwalis *Carmth* 31 4431
Alltwen *Neath* 32 7303
Alltyblaca *Cerdgn* 44 5245
Allweston *Dorset* 11 6614
Allwood Green *Suffk* 54 0472
Almeley *Herefd* 46 3351
Almeley Wooton *Herefd* 46 3352
Almer *Dorset* 11 9199
Almholme *S York* 83 5808
Almington *Staffs* 72 7034
Almodington *W Susx* 14 8297
Almondbank *P & K* 125 0625
Almondbury *W York* 82 1614
Almondsbury *Gloucs* 34 6084
Alne *N York* 90 4965
Alnesbourn Priory *Suffk* 55 1940
Alness *Highld* 146 6569
Alnham *Nthumb* 111 9810
Alnmouth *Nthumb* 111 2410
Alnwick *Nthumb* 111 1813
Alperton *Gt Lon* 26 1883
Alphamstone *Essex* 54 8735
Alpheton *Suffk* 54 8750
Alphington *Devon* 9 9190
Alpington *Norfk* 67 2901
Alport *Derbys* 74 2264
Alpraham *Ches* 71 5859
Alresford *Essex* 41 0621
Alrewas *Staffs* 61 1614
Alsager *Ches* 72 7955
Alsagers Bank *Staffs* 72 7948
Alsop en le Dale *Derbys* 73 1554
Alston *Cumb* 94 7146
Alston *Devon* 10 3002
Alston Sutton *Somset* 21 4151
Alstone *Gloucs* 47 9832
Alstone *Somset* 21 3146
Alstone Green *Staffs* 72 8518
Alstonefield *Staffs* 73 1355
Alswear *Devon* 19 7222
Alt *Gt Man* 79 9403
Altandhu *Highld* 144 9812
Altarnun *Cnwll* 5 2281
Altass *Highld* 146 5000
Altcreich *Ag & B* 122 6938
Altgaltraig *Ag & B* 114 0473
Altham *Lancs* 81 7732
Althorne *Essex* 40 9198
Althorpe *Lincs* 84 8309
Altnabreac Station *Highld* 150 0045
Altnacraig *Ag & B* 122 8429
Altnaharra *Highld* 149 5635
Altofts *W York* 83 3823
Alton *Derbys* 74 3664
Alton *Hants* 24 7139
Alton *Staffs* 73 0741
Alton *Wilts* 23 1546
Alton Barnes *Wilts* 23 1062
Alton Pancras *Dorset* 11 7002
Alton Priors *Wilts* 23 1162
Altrincham *Gt Man* 79 7687
Altskeith Hotel *Stirlg* 124 4602
Alva *Clacks* 116 8897
Alvah *Abers* 142 6760
Alvanley *Ches* 71 4974
Alvaston *Derbys* 62 3833
Alvechurch *Worcs* 60 0272
Alvecote *Warwks* 61 2404
Alvediston *Wilts* 22 9723
Alveley *Shrops* 60 7584
Alverdiscott *Devon* 19 5225
Alverstoke *Hants* 13 6098
Alverstone *IOW* 13 5785
Alverthorpe *W York* 82 3121
Alverton *Notts* 63 7942
Alves *Moray* 141 1362
Alvescot *Oxon* 36 2704
Alveston *Gloucs* 35 6388
Alveston *Warwks* 48 2356
Alvingham *Lincs* 77 3691
Alvington *Gloucs* 34 6000
Alwalton *Cambs* 64 1396
Alwinton *Nthumb* 110 9106
Alwoodley *W York* 82 2840
Alwoodley Gates *W York* 82 3140
Alyth *P & K* 126 2448
Amber Hill *Lincs* 76 2346
Amber Row *Derbys* 74 3856
Ambergate *Derbys* 74 3451
Amberley *Gloucs* 35 8501
Amberley *W Susx* 14 0213
Ambirstone *E Susx* 16 5911
Amble *Nthumb* 103 2604
Amblecote *W Mids* 60 8985
Ambler Thorn *W York* 82 0929
Ambleside *Cumb* 87 3704
Ambleston *Pembks* 30 0025
Ambrosden *Oxon* 37 6019
Amcotts *Lincs* 84 8514
America *Cambs* 53 4378
Amersham *Bucks* 26 9597
Amersham on the Hill *Bucks* 26 9798
Amerton *Staffs* 73 9927
Amesbury *Wilts* 23 1541
Amhuinnsuidhe *W Isls* 152 0408
Amington *Staffs* 61 2304
Amisfield Town *D & G* 100 0082
Amlwch *IOA* 68 4492
Ammanford *Carmth* 32 6212
Amotherby *N York* 90 7473
Ampfield *Hants* 13 4023
Ampleforth *N York* 90 5878
Ampney Crucis *Gloucs* 36 0601
Ampney St Mary *Gloucs* 36 0802
Ampney St Peter *Gloucs* 36 0801
Amport *Hants* 23 3044
Ampthill *Beds* 38 0337
Ampton *Suffk* 54 8671
Amroth *Pembks* 31 1608
Amulree *P & K* 125 8936
Amwell *Herts* 39 1613
An T-ob *W Isls* 152 0286
Anaheilt *Highld* 130 8162
Ancaster *Lincs* 63 9843
Anchor *Shrops* 58 1785
Ancroft *Nthumb* 111 9945
Ancrum *Border* 110 6224
Ancton *W Susx* 14 9800
Anderby *Lincs* 77 5275
Andersea *Somset* 21 3333
Andersfield *Somset* 20 2434
Anderson *Dorset* 11 8897
Anderton *Ches* 79 6475
Anderton *Cnwll* 6 4351
Andover *Hants* 23 3645
Andoversford *Gloucs* 35 0219
Andreas *IOM* 158 4199
Anelog *Gwynd* 56 1527
Anerley *Gt Lon* 27 3369
Anfield *Mersyd* 78 3692
Angarrack *Cnwll* 2 5838
Angarrick *Cnwll* 3 7937
Angelbank *Shrops* 46 5776
Angersleigh *Somset* 20 1918
Angerton *Cumb* 93 2257
Angle *Pembks* 30 8603
Angmering *W Susx* 14 0604
Angram *N York* 88 8899
Angram *N York* 83 5248
Angrouse *Cnwll* 2 6619
Anick *Nthumb* 102 9465
Ankerville *Highld* 147 8174
Ankle Hill *Leics* 63 7518
Anlaby *E R Yk* 84 0328

Anmer Avington


Anmer Norfk 65 7429
Anmore Hants 13 6611
Anna Valley Hants 23 3543
Annan D & G 101 1966
Annaside Cumb 86 0986
Annat Ag & B 122 0322
Annat Highld 138 8954
Annathill N Lans 116 7270
Annbank S Ayrs 106 4023
Annesley Notts 75 5053
Annesley Woodhouse Notts 75 4953
Annfield Plain Dur 96 1651
Anniesland C Glas 115 5368
Annitsford T & W 103 2674
Annscroft Shrops 59 4507
Ansdell Lancs 80 3428
Ansford Somset 21 6433
Ansley Warwks 61 3091
Anslow Staffs 73 2125
Anslow Gate Staffs 73 1924
Anslow Lees Staffs 73 2024
Ansteadbrook Surrey 14 9332
Anstey Hants 24 7240
Anstey Herts 39 4033
Anstey Leics 62 5508
Anstruther Fife 127 5703
Ansty W Susx 15 2923
Ansty Warwks 61 4083
Ansty Wilts 22 9526
Ansty Cross Dorset 11 7603
Anthill Common Hants 13 6312
Anthonys Surrey 26 0161
Anthorn Cumb 93 1958
Antingham Norfk 67 2533
Anton's Gowt Lincs 77 3047
Antony Cnwll 5 4054
Antrobus Ches 79 6480
Antron Cnwll 2 6327
Anvil Corner Devon 18 3704
Anvil Green Kent 29 1049
Anwick Lincs 76 1150
Anwoth D & G 99 5856
Aperfield Gt Lon 27 4158
Apes Dale Worcs 60 9972
Apethorpe Nhants 51 0295
Apeton Staffs 72 8518
Apley Lincs 76 1075
Apperknowle Derbys 74 3878
Apperley Gloucs 47 8628
Apperley Bridge W York 82 1937
Apperley Dene Nthumb 95 0558
Appersett N York 88 8690
Appin Ag & B 122 9346
Appleby Lincs 84 9514
Appleby Magna Leics 61 3109
Appleby Parva Leics 61 3008
Appleby Street Herts 39 3304
Appleby-in-Westmorland Cumb 94 6820
Applecross Highld 137 7144
Appledore Devon 18 4630
Appledore Devon 9 0614
Appledore Kent 17 9529
Appledore Heath Kent 17 9530
Appleford Oxon 37 5293
Applegarth Town D & G 100 1084
Applehaigh S York 83 3512
Appleshaw Hants 23 3048
Applethwaite Cumb 93 2625
Appleton Ches 78 5186
Appleton Ches 79 6184
Appleton Oxon 37 4401
Appleton Roebuck N York 83 5542
Appleton Thorn Ches 79 6383
Appleton Wiske N York 89 3804
Appleton-le-Moors N York 90 7387
Appleton-le-Street N York 90 7373
Appletreehall Border 109 5117
Appletreewick N York 88 0560
Appley Somset 20 0721
Appley Bridge Lancs 78 5209
Apse Heath IOW 13 5683
Apsley End Beds 38 1232
Apuldram W Susx 14 8403
Arabella Highld 147 8076
Arbirlot Angus 127 6040
Arboll Highld 147 8781
Arborfield Berks 24 7567
Arborfield Cross Berks 24 7666
Arbourthorne S York 74 3785
Arbroath Angus 127 6441
Arbuthnott Abers 135 8074
Arcadia Kent 28 8836
Archddu Carmth 32 4401
Archdeacon Newton Dur 96 2517
Archencarroch W Duns 115 4182
Archiestown Moray 141 2244
Archirondel Jersey 158 0000
Arclid Green Ches 72 7861
Ardaily Ag & B 104 6450
Ardanaiseig Hotel Ag & B 123 0824
Ardaneaskan Highld 137 8335
Ardarroch Highld 137 8339
Ardbeg Ag & B 104 4146
Ardbeg Ag & B 114 0766
Ardbeg Ag & B 114 1583
Ardcharnich Highld 145 1788
Ardchiavaig Ag & B 121 3818
Ardchonnel Ag & B 122 9812
Ardchullarie More Stirlg 124 5813
Arddarroch Ag & B 114 2494
Arddleen Powys 58 2616
Ardechive Highld 131 1490
Ardeer N Ayrs 106 2740
Ardeley Herts 39 3027
Ardelve Highld 138 8627
Arden Ag & B 115 3684
Ardens Grafton Warwks 48 1154
Ardentallen Ag & B 122 8324
Ardentinny Ag & B 114 1887
Ardentraive Ag & B 114 0374
Ardeonaig Hotel Stirlg 124 6735
Ardersier Highld 140 7855
Ardessie Highld 145 0589
Ardfern Ag & B 122 8004
Ardgay Highld 146 5990
Ardgour Highld 130 0163
Ardgowan Inver 114 2073
Ardhallow Ag & B 114 1674
Ardhasig W Isls 152 1202
Ardheslaig Highld 137 7855
Ardindrean Highld 145 1588
Ardingly W Susx 15 3429
Ardington Oxon 36 4388
Ardington Wick Oxon 36 4389
Ardlamont Ag & B 114 9865
Ardleigh Essex 41 0529
Ardleigh Heath Essex 41 0430
Ardler P & K 126 2642
Ardley Oxon 49 5427
Ardley End Essex 39 5214
Ardlui Ag & B 123 3115
Ardlussa Ag & B 113 6487
Ardmaddy Ag & B 123 0837
Ardmair Highld 145 1097
Ardmaleish Ag & B 114 0768
Ardminish Ag & B 104 6448
Ardmolich Highld 129 7172
Ardmore Ag & B 115 3178
Ardmore Highld 146 7086
Ardnadam Ag & B 114 1780
Ardnagrask Highld 139 5249
Ardnarff Highld 138 8935
Ardnastang Highld 130 8061
Ardno Ag & B 123 1508
Ardochy Lodge Hotel Highld 131 2002
Ardpatrick Ag & B 113 7559
Ardrishaig Ag & B 113 8585
Ardross Highld 146 6174
Ardrossan N Ayrs 106 2342
Ardsley S York 83 3805
Ardsley East W York 82 3025
Ardslignish Highld 121 5661
Ardtalla Ag & B 112 4654
Ardtoe Highld 129 6270
Arduaine Ag & B 122 7910
Ardullie Highld 139 5862
Ardvasar Highld 129 6303
Ardvorlich P & K 124 6322
Ardvourlie W Isls 152 1810
Ardwell D & G 98 1045
Ardwick Gt Man 79 8597
Areley Kings Worcs 60 7970
Arevegaig Highld 129 6568
Arford Hants 14 8236
Argoed Caerph 33 1799
Argoed Shrops 59 3220
Argoed Mill Powys 45 9963
Argos Hill E Susx 16 5728
Aribruach W Isls 152 2417
Aridhglas Ag & B 120 3123
Arileod Ag & B 120 1655
Arinagour Ag & B 120 2257
Ariogan Ag & B 122 8627
Arisaig Highld 129 6586
Arisaig House Highld 129 6984
Arkendale N York 89 3861
Arkesden Essex 39 4834
Arkholme Lancs 87 5871
Arkle Town N York 88 0001
Arkleby Cumb 92 1439
Arkleton D & G 101 3791
Arkley Gt Lon 26 2295
Arksey S York 83 5807
Arkwright Town Derbys 74 4271
Arle Gloucs 47 9223
Arlecdon Cumb 92 0418
Arlescote Warwks 48 3848
Arlesey Beds 39 1936
Arleston Shrops 60 6610
Arley Ches 79 6680
Arley Warwks 61 2890
Arlingham Gloucs 35 7010
Arlington Devon 19 6140
Arlington E Susx 16 5407
Arlington Gloucs 36 1006
Arlington Beccott Devon 19 6241
Armadale Highld 150 7864
Armadale Highld 129 6303
Armadale W Loth 116 9368
Armaside Cumb 92 1527
Armathwaite Cumb 94 5046
Arminghall Norfk 67 2504
Armitage Staffs 73 0715
Armitage Bridge W York 82 1313
Armley W York 82 2833
Armscote Warwks 48 2444
Armshead Staffs 72 9348
Armston Nhants 51 0685
Armthorpe S York 83 6204
Arnabost Ag & B 120 2159
Arnaby Cumb 86 1884
Arncliffe N York 88 9371
Arncliffe Cote N York 88 9470
Arncroach Fife 127 5105
Arndilly House Moray 141 2847
Arne Dorset 11 9788
Arnesby Leics 50 6192
Arnfield Derbys 79 0197
Arngask P & K 126 1410
Arnicle Ag & B 105 7138
Arnisdale Highld 130 8410
Arnish Highld 137 5948
Arniston Mdloth 118 3362
Arnol W Isls 152 3148
Arnold E R Yk 85 1241
Arnold Notts 62 5845
Arnprior Stirlg 116 6194
Arnside Cumb 87 4578
Aros Ag & B 121 5645
Arowry Wrexhm 71 4639
Arrad Foot Cumb 86 3080
Arram E R Yk 84 0344
Arrathorne N York 89 2093
Arreton IOW 13 5386
Arrina Highld 137 7458
Arrington Cambs 52 3250
Arrochar Ag & B 123 2904
Arrow Warwks 48 0856
Arrowfield Top Worcs 61 0374
Arscott Shrops 59 4307
Artafallie Highld 140 6349
Arthington W York 82 2644
Arthingworth Nhants 50 7581
Arthog Gwynd 57 6414
Arthrath Abers 143 9636
Arthursdale W York 83 3737
Artrochie Abers 143 0031
Arundel W Susx 14 0106
Asby Cumb 92 0620
Ascog Ag & B 114 1062
Ascot Berks 25 9268
Ascott Warwks 48 3234
Ascott Earl Oxon 36 3018
Ascott-under-Wychwood Oxon 36 3018
Asenby N York 89 3975
Asfordby Leics 63 7019
Asfordby Hill Leics 63 7219
Asgarby Lincs 64 1145
Asgarby Lincs 77 3366
Ash Devon 19 5208
Ash Devon 7 8349
Ash Dorset 11 8610
Ash Kent 27 6064
Ash Kent 29 2858
Ash Somset 20 2822
Ash Somset 21 4720
Ash Surrey 25 9051
Ash Green Surrey 25 9049
Ash Green Warwks 61 3384
Ash Magna Shrops 71 5739
Ash Mill Devon 19 7823
Ash Parva Shrops 71 5739
Ash Priors Somset 20 1529
Ash Street Suffk 54 0146
Ash Thomas Devon 9 0010
Ash Vale Surrey 25 8951
Ashampstead Berks 37 5676
Ashampstead Green Berks 37 5677
Ashbocking Suffk 54 1754
Ashbocking Green Suffk 54 1854
Ashbourne Derbys 73 1746
Ashbourne Green Derbys 73 1948
Ashbrittle Somset 20 0521
Ashburnham Place E Susx 16 6814
Ashburton Devon 7 7570
Ashbury Devon 5 5098
Ashbury Oxon 36 2685
Ashby Lincs 84 8908
Ashby by Partney Lincs 77 4266
Ashby cum Fenby Lincs 77 2500
Ashby de la Launde Lincs 76 0555
Ashby Folville Leics 63 7012
Ashby Magna Leics 50 5690
Ashby Parva Leics 50 5288
Ashby Puerorum Lincs 77 3271
Ashby St Ledgers Nhants 50 5768
Ashby St Mary Norfk 67 3202
Ashby-de-la-Zouch Leics 62 3516
Ashchurch Gloucs 47 9233
Ashcombe Devon 9 9179
Ashcombe Somset 21 3361
Ashcott Somset 21 4336
Ashdon Essex 53 5842
Ashe Hants 24 5350
Asheldham Essex 41 9701
Ashen Essex 53 7442
Ashendon Bucks 37 7014
Asheridge Bucks 38 9304
Ashfield Hants 12 3619
Ashfield Herefd 46 5923
Ashfield Stirlg 124 7803
Ashfield Suffk 55 2062
Ashfield Green Suffk 53 7655
Ashfield Green Suffk 55 2573
Ashfields Shrops 72 7026
Ashfold Crossways W Susx 15 2328
Ashford Devon 19 5335
Ashford Devon 7 6948
Ashford Kent 28 0142
Ashford Surrey 26 0771
Ashford Bowdler Shrops 46 5170
Ashford Carbonel Shrops 46 5270
Ashford Hill Hants 24 5562
Ashford in the Water Derbys 74 1969
Ashgill S Lans 116 7850
Ashill Devon 9 0811
Ashill Norfk 66 8804
Ashill Somset 10 3217
Ashingdon Essex 40 8693
Ashington Dorset 11 0098
Ashington Nthumb 103 2687
Ashington Somset 21 5621
Ashington W Susx 15 1315
Ashkirk Border 109 4722
Ashlett Hants 13 4603
Ashleworth Gloucs 47 8125
Ashleworth Quay Gloucs 47 8125
Ashley Cambs 53 6961
Ashley Ches 79 7784
Ashley Devon 19 6511
Ashley Dorset 12 1304
Ashley Gloucs 35 9394
Ashley Hants 23 3831
Ashley Hants 12 2595
Ashley Kent 29 3048
Ashley Nhants 50 7990
Ashley Staffs 72 7636
Ashley Wilts 22 8268
Ashley Green Bucks 38 9705
Ashley Heath Dorset 12 1204
Ashley Moor Herefd 46 4767
Ashmansworth Hants 24 4157
Ashmansworthy Devon 18 3418
Ashmead Green Gloucs 35 7699
Ashmill Devon 5 3995
Ashmore Dorset 11 9117
Ashmore Green Berks 24 5069
Ashorne Warwks 48 3057
Ashover Derbys 74 3463
Ashover Hay Derbys 74 3460
Ashow Warwks 61 3170
Ashperton Herefd 47 6441
Ashprington Devon 7 8157
Ashreigney Devon 19 6313
Ashridge Park Herts 38 9912
Ashtead Surrey 26 1857
Ashton Cambs 64 1005
Ashton Ches 71 5069
Ashton Cnwll 2 6028
Ashton Cnwll 5 3868
Ashton Devon 8 8584
Ashton Hants 13 5419
Ashton Herefd 46 5164
Ashton Inver 114 2377
Ashton Nhants 49 7649
Ashton Nhants 51 0588
Ashton Somset 21 4149
Ashton Common Wilts 22 8958
Ashton Hill Wilts 22 9057
Ashton Keynes Wilts 36 0494
Ashton under Hill Worcs 47 9937
Ashton upon Mersey Gt Man 79 7892
Ashton Watering Somset 21 5369
Ashton-in-Makerfield Gt Man 78 5798
Ashton-under-Lyne Gt Man 79 9399
Ashurst Hants 12 3310
Ashurst Kent 16 5138
Ashurst W Susx 15 1715
Ashurstwood W Susx 15 4136
Ashwater Devon 5 3895
Ashwell Herts 39 2639
Ashwell Rutlnd 63 8613
Ashwell Somset 10 3616
Ashwell End Herts 39 2540
Ashwellthorpe Norfk 66 1497
Ashwick Somset 21 6348
Ashwicken Norfk 65 7018
Ashwood Staffs 60 8688
Askam in Furness Cumb 86 2177
Aske Hall N York 89 1703
Askern S York 83 5613
Askerswell Dorset 10 5292
Askett Bucks 38 8105
Askham Cumb 94 5123
Askham Notts 75 7374
Askham Bryan N York 83 5548
Askham Richard N York 83 5347
Asknish Ag & B 114 9391
Askrigg N York 88 9491
Askwith N York 82 1648
Aslackby Lincs 64 0830
Aslacton Norfk 54 1590
Aslockton Notts 63 7440
Asney Somset 21 4636
Aspall Suffk 54 1664
Aspatria Cumb 92 1441
Aspenden Herts 39 3528
Asperton Lincs 64 2637
Aspley Staffs 72 8133
Aspley Guise Beds 38 9335
Aspley Heath Beds 38 9334
Aspley Heath Warwks 61 0970
Aspull Gt Man 78 6108
Aspull Common Gt Man 79 6498
Asselby E R Yk 84 7127
Asserby Lincs 77 4977
Asserby Turn Lincs 77 4777
Assington Suffk 54 9338
Assington Green Suffk 53 7751
Astbury Ches 72 8461
Astcote Nhants 49 6753
Asterby Lincs 77 2679
Asterley Shrops 59 3707
Asterton Shrops 59 3991
Asthall Oxon 36 2811
Asthall Leigh Oxon 36 3013
Astle Highld 146 7391
Astley Gt Man 79 7000
Astley Shrops 59 5218
Astley W York 83 3828
Astley Warwks 61 3189
Astley Worcs 47 7867
Astley Abbots Shrops 60 7096
Astley Bridge Gt Man 81 7111
Astley Cross Worcs 47 8069
Astley Green Gt Man 79 7099
Astley Town Worcs 47 7968
Aston Berks 37 7884
Aston Ches 71 5578
Aston Ches 71 6146
Aston Derbys 74 1783
Aston Flints 71 3067
Aston Herefd 46 4662
Aston Herefd 46 4671
Aston Herts 39 2722
Aston Oxon 36 3403
Aston S York 75 4685
Aston Shrops 59 5328
Aston Shrops 59 6109
Aston Shrops 60 8093
Aston Staffs 72 7541
Aston Staffs 72 8923
Aston Staffs 72 9130
Aston W Mids 61 0888
Aston Abbotts Bucks 38 8420
Aston Botterell Shrops 59 6384
Aston Cantlow Warwks 48 1460
Aston Clinton Bucks 38 8812
Aston Crews Herefd 47 6723
Aston Cross Gloucs 47 9433
Aston End Herts 39 2724
Aston Fields Worcs 47 9669
Aston Flamville Leics 50 4692
Aston Heath Ches 71 5678
Aston Ingham Herefd 47 6823
Aston juxta Mondrum Ches 72 6456
Aston le Walls Nhants 49 4950
Aston Magna Gloucs 48 1935
Aston Munslow Shrops 59 5186
Aston on Clun Shrops 59 3981
Aston Pigott Shrops 59 3305
Aston Rogers Shrops 59 3406
Aston Rowant Oxon 37 7299
Aston Sandford Bucks 37 7507
Aston Somerville Worcs 48 0438
Aston Subedge Gloucs 48 1441
Aston Tirrold Oxon 37 5586
Aston Upthorpe Oxon 37 5586
Aston-Eyre Shrops 59 6594
Aston-upon-Trent Derbys 62 4129
Astonlane Shrops 59 6494
Astrop Nhants 49 5036
Astrope Herts 38 8914
Astwick Beds 39 2138
Astwith Derbys 75 4464
Astwood Bucks 38 9547
Astwood Worcs 47 9365
Astwood Bank Worcs 48 0462
Aswarby Lincs 64 0639
Aswardby Lincs 77 3770
Atch Lench Worcs 48 0350
Atcham Shrops 59 5409
Athelhampton Dorset 11 7694
Athelington Suffk 55 2171
Athelney Somset 21 3428
Athelstaneford E Loth 118 5377
Atherfield Green IOW 13 4679
Atherington Devon 19 5922
Atherington W Susx 14 0000
Atherstone Somset 10 3816
Atherstone Warwks 61 3097
Atherstone on Stour Warwks 48 2051
Atherton Gt Man 79 6703
Atley Hill N York 89 2802
Atlow Derbys 73 2248
Attadale Highld 138 9238
Attenborough Notts 62 5034
Atterby Lincs 76 9792
Attercliffe S York 74 3788
Atterley Shrops 59 6397
Atterton Leics 61 3598
Attleborough Norfk 66 0495
Attleborough Warwks 61 3790
Attlebridge Norfk 66 1216
Attleton Green Suffk 53 7454
Atwick E R Yk 85 1850
Atworth Wilts 22 8565
Auberrow Herefd 46 4947
Aubourn Lincs 76 9262
Auchedly Abers 143 8933
Auchenblae Abers 135 7279
Auchenbowie Stirlg 116 7987
Auchencairn D & G 92 7951
Auchencairn D & G 100 9884
Auchencairn N Ayrs 105 0427
Auchencrow Border 119 8560
Auchendinny Mdloth 117 2561
Auchengray S Lans 117 9954
Auchenhalrig Moray 141 3761
Auchenheath S Lans 108 8043
Auchenhessnane D & G 100 8096
Auchenlochan Ag & B 114 9772
Auchenmade N Ayrs 115 3548
Auchenmalg D & G 98 2352
Auchentibber S Lans 116 6755
Auchentiber N Ayrs 115 3647
Auchentroig Stirlg 115 5493
Auchindrean Highld 145 1980
Auchininna Abers 142 6546
Auchinleck E Ayrs 107 5521
Auchinloch N Lans 116 6570
Auchinstarry N Lans 116 7176
Auchintore Highld 130 0972
Auchiries Abers 143 0737
Auchlee Abers 135 8996
Auchleven Abers 142 6224
Auchlochan S Lans 107 7937
Auchlossan Abers 134 5601
Auchlyne Stirlg 124 5129
Auchmillan E Ayrs 107 5129
Auchmithie Angus 127 6743
Auchmuirbridge Fife 126 2101
Auchnacree Angus 134 4663
Auchnagatt Abers 143 9241
Auchnarrow Moray 141 2023
Auchnotteroch D & G 98 9960
Auchroisk Moray 141 3351
Auchterarder P & K 125 9412
Auchteraw Highld 131 3507
Auchterblair Highld 140 9222
Auchtercairn Highld 144 8077
Auchterderran Fife 117 2195
Auchterhouse Angus 126 3337
Auchterless Abers 142 7141
Auchtermuchty Fife 126 2311
Auchterneed Highld 139 4959
Auchtertool Fife 117 2190
Auchtertyre Highld 138 8427
Auchtoo Stirlg 124 5520
Auckengill Highld 151 3663
Auckley S York 75 6400
Audenshaw Gt Man 79 9197
Audlem Ches 72 6543
Audley Staffs 72 7950
Audley End Essex 39 5337
Audley End Essex 54 8137
Audley End Suffk 54 8553
Audmore Staffs 72 8321
Audnam W Mids 60 8986
Aughertree Cumb 93 2538
Aughton E R Yk 84 7038
Aughton Lancs 78 3905
Aughton Lancs 87 5567
Aughton S York 75 4586
Aughton Wilts 23 2356
Aughton Park Lancs 78 4006
Auldallan Angus 134 3158
Auldearn Highld 140 9255
Aulden Herefd 46 4654
Auldgirth D & G 100 9186
Auldhouse S Lans 116 6250
Ault a' chruinn Highld 138 9420
Ault Hucknall Derbys 75 4665
Aultbea Highld 144 8789
Aultgrishin Highld 144 7485
Aultguish Inn Highld 145 3570
Aultmore Moray 142 4053
Aultnagoire Highld 139 5423
Aultnamain Inn Highld 146 6681
Aunby Lincs 64 0214
Aunk Devon 9 0400
Aunsby Lincs 64 0438
Aust Gloucs 34 5788
Austendike Lincs 64 2821
Austerfield S York 75 6694
Austerlands Gt Man 79 9505
Austhorpe W York 83 3733
Austonley W York 82 1107
Austrey Warwks 61 2906
Austwick N York 88 7668
Authorpe Lincs 77 3980
Authorpe Row Lincs 77 5373
Avebury Wilts 36 1069
Avebury Trusloe Wilts 36 0969
Aveley Essex 27 5680
Avening Gloucs 35 8898
Averham Notts 75 7654
Aveton Gifford Devon 7 6947
Aviemore Highld 132 8913
Avington Berks 23 3767

Avoch Bath Side


Avoch Highld 140 7055
Avon Dorset 12 1498
Avon Dassett Warwks 49 4150
Avonbridge Falk 116 9172
Avonmouth Bristl 34 5178
Avonwick Devon 7 7158
Awbridge Hants 12 3224
Awkley Gloucs 34 5985
Awliscombe Devon 9 1301
Awre Gloucs 35 7008
Awsworth Notts 62 4844
Axborough Worcs 60 8579
Axbridge Somset 21 4354
Axford Hants 24 6043
Axford Wilts 36 2370
Axminster Devon 10 2998
Axmouth Devon 10 2591
Axton Flints 70 1080
Aycliffe Dur 96 2822
Aydon Nthumb 103 0065
Aylburton Gloucs 34 6101
Ayle Cumb 94 7149
Aylesbeare Devon 9 0392
Aylesbury Bucks 38 8213
Aylesby Lincs 85 2007
Aylesford Kent 28 7359
Aylesham Kent 29 2452
Aylestone Leics 50 5700
Aylestone Park Leics 50 5800
Aylmerton Norfk 66 1839
Aylsham Norfk 67 1926
Aylton Gloucs 47 6537
Aylworth Gloucs 36 1021
Aymestrey Herefd 46 4265
Aynho Nhants 49 5133
Ayot Green Herts 39 2214
Ayot St Lawrence Herts 39 1916
Ayot St Peter Herts 39 2115
Ayr S Ayrs 106 3321
Aysgarth N York 88 0088
Ayshford Devon 9 0415
Ayside Cumb 87 3983
Ayston Rutlnd 51 8600
Aythorpe Roding Essex 40 5815
Ayton Border 119 9260
Azerley N York 89 2574


# B


Babbacombe Devon 7 9265
Babbington Notts 62 4943
Babbinswood Shrops 59 3329
Babbs Green Herts 39 3916
Babcary Somset 21 5628
Babel Carmth 44 8235
Babel Green Suffk 53 7348
Babell Flints 70 1573
Babeny Devon 7 6775
Babington Somset 22 7051
Bablock Hythe Oxon 36 4304
Babraham Cambs 53 5150
Babworth Notts 75 6880
Bachau IOA 68 4383
Bache Shrops 59 4681
Bacheldre Powys 58 2492
Bachelor's Bump E Susx 17 8412
Back o' th' Brook Staffs 73 0751
Back of Keppoch Highld 129 6587
Back Street Suffk 53 7458
Backaland Ork 153 5630
Backbarrow Cumb 87 3584
Backe Carmth 31 2615
Backfolds Abers 143 0252
Backford Ches 71 3971
Backford Cross Ches 71 3873
Backies Highld 147 8302
Backlass Highld 151 2053
Backwell Somset 21 4968
Backworth T & W 103 3072
Bacon's End W Mids 61 1888
Baconsthorpe Norfk 66 1236
Bacton Herefd 46 3732
Bacton Norfk 67 3433
Bacton Suffk 54 0567
Bacton Green Suffk 54 0365
Bacup Lancs 81 8622
Badachro Highld 137 7873
Badbury Wilts 36 1980
Badby Nhants 49 5658
Badcall Highld 148 1541
Badcall Highld 148 2455
Badcaul Highld 144 0291
Baddeley Edge Staffs 72 9150
Baddeley Green Staffs 72 9151
Baddesley Clinton Warwks 61 2072
Baddesley Ensor Warwks 61 2798
Baddidarrach Highld 145 0822
Baddinsgill Border 117 1254
Badenscoth Abers 142 6938
Badenyon Abers 141 3319
Badgall Cnwll 5 2486
Badgeney Cambs 65 4397
Badger Shrops 60 7699
Badger's Cross Cnwll 2 4833
Badgers Mount Kent 27 4962
Badgeworth Gloucs 35 9019
Badgworth Somset 21 3952
Badharlick Cnwll 5 2686
Badicaul Highld 137 7529
Badingham Suffk 55 3068
Badlesmere Kent 28 0153
Badlieu Border 108 0518
Badlipster Highld 151 2448
Badluachrach Highld 144 9994
Badninish Highld 147 7594
Badrallach Highld 145 0691
Badsey Worcs 48 0743
Badshot Lea Surrey 25 8648
Badsworth W York 83 4614
Badwell Ash Suffk 54 9868
Badwell Green Suffk 54 0169
Bag Enderby Lincs 77 3571
Bagber Dorset 11 7513
Bagby N York 89 4680
Bagendon Gloucs 35 0106
Bagginswood Shrops 60 6881
Baggrow Cumb 93 1741
Bagh a Chaisteil W Isls 152 6698
Bagham Kent 29 0753
Bagillt Flints 70 2175
Baginton Warwks 61 3474
Baglan Neath 32 7492
Bagley Shrops 59 4027
Bagley Somset 21 4645
Bagley W York 82 2235
Bagmore Hants 24 6544
Bagnall Staffs 72 9250
Bagnor Berks 24 4569
Bagot Shrops 46 5873
Bagshot Surrey 25 9063
Bagshot Wilts 23 3165
Bagstone Gloucs 35 6987
Bagthorpe Notts 75 4651
Bagworth Leics 62 4408
Bagwy Llydiart Herefd 46 4426
Baildon W York 82 1539
Baildon Green W York 82 1439
Baile a Mhanaich W Isls 152 7755
Baile Ailein W Isls 152 2920
Baile Mor Ag & B 120 2824
Bailey Green Hants 13 6627
Baileyhead Cumb 101 5179
Bailiff Bridge W York 82 1425
Baillieston C Glas 116 6764
Bailrigg Lancs 87 4858
Bainbridge N York 88 9390
Bainshole Abers 142 6035
Bainton Cambs 64 0906
Bainton E R Yk 84 9652
Bainton Oxon 49 5827
Baintown Fife 126 3503
Bairnkine Border 110 6515
Baker Street Essex 40 6381
Baker's End Herts 39 3917
Bakewell Derbys 74 2168
Bala Gwynd 58 9235
Balallan W Isls 152 2920
Balbeg Highld 139 4431
Balbeggie P & K 126 1629
Balblair Highld 139 5145
Balblair Highld 140 7066
Balby S York 75 5600
Balcary D & G 92 8149
Balchraggan Highld 139 5343
Balchreick Highld 148 1960
Balcombe W Susx 15 3130
Balcombe Lane W Susx 15 3132
Balcomie Links Fife 127 6209
Baldersby N York 89 3578
Baldersby St James N York 89 3676
Balderstone Gt Man 79 9010
Balderstone Lancs 81 6332
Balderton Notts 75 8151
Baldhu Cnwll 3 7743
Baldinnie Fife 127 4211
Baldinnies P & K 125 0216
Baldock Herts 39 2434
Baldovie Dund C 127 4533
Baldrine IOM 158 4281
Baldslow E Susx 17 8013
Baldwin IOM 158 3581
Baldwin's Gate Staffs 72 7939
Baldwin's Hill Surrey 15 3839
Baldwinholme Cumb 93 3351
Bale Norfk 66 0136
Baledgarno P & K 126 2730
Balemartine Ag & B 120 9841
Balerno C Edin 117 1666
Balfarg Fife 126 2803
Balfield Angus 134 5468
Balfour Ork 153 4716
Balfron Stirlg 115 5489
Balgaveny Abers 142 6540
Balgavies Angus 127 5451
Balgonar Fife 117 0293
Balgowan D & G 98 1142
Balgowan Highld 132 6494
Balgown Highld 136 3868
Balgracie D & G 98 9860
Balgray Angus 126 4038
Balgray S Lans 108 8824
Balham Gt Lon 27 2873
Balhary P & K 126 2646
Balholmie P & K 126 1436
Baligill Highld 150 8565
Balintore Angus 133 2859
Balintore Highld 147 8675
Balintraid Highld 146 7370
Balivanich W Isls 152 7755
Balk N York 89 4780
Balkeerie Angus 126 3244
Balkholme E R Yk 84 7828
Ball Shrops 59 3026
Ball Green Staffs 72 8952
Ball Haye Green Staffs 72 9856
Ball Hill Hants 24 4163
Ball's Green Gloucs 35 8699
Ballabeg IOM 158 2570
Ballachulish Highld 130 0858
Ballafesson IOM 158 2070
Ballakilpheric IOM 158 2271
Ballamodha IOM 158 2773
Ballanlay Ag & B 114 0462
Ballantrae S Ayrs 98 0882
Ballards Gore Essex 40 9092
Ballards Green Warwks 61 2791
Ballasalla IOM 158 2870
Ballater Abers 134 3695
Ballaugh IOM 158 3493
Ballchraggan Highld 147 7675
Ballencrieff E Loth 118 4878
Ballevullin Ag & B 120 9546
Ballidon Derbys 73 2054
Balliekine N Ayrs 105 8739
Balliemore Ag & B 114 1099
Balligmorrie S Ayrs 106 2290
Ballimore Ag & B 114 9283
Ballimore Stirlg 124 5317
Ballindalloch Moray 141 1636
Ballindean P & K 126 2529
Ballingdon Essex 54 8640
Ballinger Common Bucks 38 9103
Ballingham Herefd 46 5731
Ballingry Fife 117 1797
Ballinluig P & K 125 9752
Ballinshoe Angus 126 4153
Ballintuim P & K 126 1055
Balloch Highld 140 7247
Balloch N Lans 116 7374
Balloch P & K 125 8419
Balloch S Ayrs 106 3295
Balloch W Duns 115 3982
Ballochroy Ag & B 113 7352
Ballogie Abers 134 5795
Balls Cross W Susx 14 9826
Balls Green E Susx 16 4936
Ballygown Ag & B 121 4343
Ballygrant Ag & B 112 3966
Ballyhaugh Ag & B 120 1758
Ballymenoch Ag & B 115 3086
Ballymichael N Ayrs 105 9231
Balmacara Highld 137 8028
Balmaclellan D & G 99 6579
Balmae D & G 99 6844
Balmaha Stirlg 115 4290
Balmalcolm Fife 126 3208
Balmangan D & G 99 6445
Balmedie Abers 143 9618
Balmer Heath Shrops 59 4434
Balmerino Fife 126 3524
Balmerlawn Hants 12 3003
Balmore E Duns 115 5973
Balmuchy Highld 147 8678
Balmuir Angus 127 5648
Balmule Fife 117 2088
Balmullo Fife 127 4220
Balnacoil Lodge Highld 147 8011
Balnacra Highld 138 9846
Balnacroft Abers 133 2894
Balnafoich Highld 140 6835
Balnaguard P & K 125 9451
Balnahard Ag & B 121 4534
Balnahard Ag & B 112 4199
Balnain Highld 139 4430
Balnakeil Highld 149 3968
Balnapaling Highld 147 7969
Balne N York 83 5918
Balquharn P & K 125 0235
Balquhidder Stirlg 124 5320
Balsall Common W Mids 61 2376
Balsall Heath W Mids 61 0784
Balsall Street W Mids 61 2276
Balscote Oxon 48 3942
Balsham Cambs 53 5850
Baltasound Shet 153 6208
Balterley Staffs 72 7650
Balterley Green Staffs 72 7650
Balterley Heath Staffs 72 7450
Baltersan D & G 99 4261
Baltonsborough Somset 21 5434
Balvarran P & K 133 0761
Balvicar Ag & B 122 7616
Balvraid Highld 129 8416
Balvraid Highld 140 8231
Balwest Cnwll 2 5930
Bamber Bridge Lancs 81 5625
Bamber's Green Essex 40 5722
Bamburgh Nthumb 111 1734
Bamff P & K 126 2251
Bamford Derbys 74 2083
Bamford Gt Man 81 8612
Bampton Cumb 94 5118
Bampton Devon 20 9522
Bampton Oxon 36 3103
Bampton Grange Cumb 94 5218
Banavie Highld 130 1177
Banbury Oxon 49 4540
Banc-y-ffordd Carmth 31 4037
Bancffosfelem Carmth 32 4811
Banchory Abers 135 6995
Banchory-Devenick Abers 135 9002
Bancycapel Carmth 31 4214
Bancyfelin Carmth 31 3218
Bandirran P & K 126 2030
Bandrake Head Cumb 86 3187
Banff Abers 142 6863
Bangor Gwynd 69 5772
Bangor's Green Lancs 78 3709
Bangor-is-y-coed Wrexhm 71 3845
Bangors Cnwll 18 2099
Bangrove Suffk 54 9372
Banham Norfk 54 0687
Bank Hants 12 2807
Bank Ground Cumb 86 3196
Bank Newton N York 81 9053
Bank Street Worcs 47 6362
Bank Top Lancs 78 5207
Bank Top W York 82 1024
Bankend D & G 100 0268
Bankfoot P & K 125 0635
Bankglen E Ayrs 107 5912
Bankhead Aber C 135 9009
Bankhead S Lans 116 9844
Banknock Falk 116 7779
Banks Cumb 101 5664
Banks Lancs 80 3920
Banks Green Worcs 47 9967
Bankshill D & G 101 1982
Banningham Norfk 67 2129
Bannister Green Essex 40 6920
Bannockburn Stirlg 116 8190
Banstead Surrey 27 2559
Bantham Devon 7 6643
Banton N Lans 116 7480
Banwell Somset 21 3959
Bapchild Kent 28 9263
Bapton Wilts 22 9938
Bar Hill Cambs 52 3863
Barabhas W Isls 152 3649
Barassie S Ayrs 106 3232
Barbaraville Highld 146 7472
Barber Booth Derbys 74 1184
Barber Green Cumb 87 3982
Barbieston S Ayrs 107 4317
Barbon Cumb 87 6282
Barbridge Ches 71 6156
Barbrook Devon 19 7147
Barby Nhants 50 5470
Barcaldine Ag & B 122 9641
Barcheston Warwks 48 2639
Barclose Cumb 101 4462
Barcombe E Susx 15 4114
Barcombe Cross E Susx 15 4115
Barcroft W York 82 0437
Barden N York 89 1493
Barden Park Kent 16 5746
Bardfield End Green Essex 40 6231
Bardfield Saling Essex 40 6826
Bardney Lincs 76 1269
Bardon Leics 62 4412
Bardon Mill Nthumb 102 7764
Bardowie E Duns 115 5873
Bardown E Susx 16 6629
Bardrainney Inver 115 3373
Bardsea Cumb 86 3074
Bardsey W York 83 3643
Bardsley Gt Man 79 9201
Bardwell Suffk 54 9473
Bare Lancs 87 4564
Bareppa Cnwll 3 7729
Barewood Herefd 46 3856
Barfad D & G 98 3266
Barford Norfk 66 1107
Barford Warwks 48 2760
Barford St John Oxon 49 4433
Barford St Martin Wilts 23 0531
Barford St Michael Oxon 49 4332
Barfrestone Kent 29 2650
Bargate Derbys 62 3546
Bargeddie N Lans 116 6964
Bargoed Caerph 33 1599
Bargrennan D & G 98 3577
Barham Cambs 52 1375
Barham Kent 29 2050
Barham Suffk 54 1451
Barholm Lincs 64 0810
Barkby Leics 63 6309
Barkby Thorpe Leics 63 6309
Barkers Green Shrops 59 5228
Barkestone-le-Vale Leics 63 7734
Barkham Berks 25 7766
Barking Gt Lon 27 4484
Barking Suffk 54 0753
Barking Tye Suffk 54 0652
Barkingside Gt Lon 27 4489
Barkisland W York 82 0519
Barkla Shop Cnwll 3 7350
Barkston Lincs 63 9341
Barkston Ash N York 83 4936
Barkway Herts 39 3835
Barlanark C Glas 116 6664
Barlaston Staffs 72 8938
Barlavington W Susx 14 9716
Barlborough Derbys 75 4777
Barlby N York 83 6333
Barlestone Leics 62 4205
Barley Herts 39 4038
Barley Lancs 81 8240
Barley Hole S York 74 3697
Barleycroft End Herts 39 4327
Barleythorpe Rutlnd 63 8409
Barling Essex 40 9389
Barlings Lincs 76 0774
Barlochan D & G 92 8157
Barlow Derbys 74 3474
Barlow N York 83 6428
Barlow T & W 96 1561
Barmby Moor E R Yk 84 7748
Barmby on the Marsh E R Yk 83 6928
Barmer Norfk 66 8133
Barming Heath Kent 28 7255
Barmollack Ag & B 105 8043
Barmouth Gwynd 57 6116
Barmpton Dur 96 3118
Barmston E R Yk 91 1659
Barnaby Green Suffk 55 4780
Barnacarry Ag & B 114 0094
Barnack Cambs 64 0705
Barnacle Warwks 61 3884
Barnard Castle Dur 95 0516
Barnard Gate Oxon 36 4010
Barnardiston Suffk 53 7148
Barnbarroch D & G 92 8456
Barnburgh S York 83 4803
Barnby Suffk 55 4789
Barnby Dun S York 83 6109
Barnby in the Willows Notts 76 8552
Barnby Moor Notts 75 6684
Barncorkrie D & G 98 0935
Barnes Gt Lon 26 2276
Barnes Street Kent 16 6447
Barnet Gt Lon 26 2496
Barnet Gate Gt Lon 26 2195
Barnetby le Wold Lincs 84 0509
Barney Norfk 66 9932
Barnham Suffk 54 8779
Barnham W Susx 14 9503
Barnham Broom Norfk 66 0807
Barnhead Angus 135 6657
Barnhill Ches 71 4854
Barnhill Dund C 127 4731
Barnhill Moray 141 1457
Barnhills D & G 98 9871
Barningham Dur 89 0810
Barningham Suffk 54 9676
Barnoldby le Beck Lincs 85 2303
Barnoldswick Lancs 81 8746
Barns Green W Susx 14 1226
Barnsdale Bar N York 83 5014
Barnsley Gloucs 36 0704
Barnsley S York 83 3406
Barnsley Shrops 60 7592
Barnsole Kent 29 2756
Barnstaple Devon 19 5633
Barnston Essex 40 6419
Barnston Mersyd 78 2783
Barnstone Notts 63 7335
Barnt Green Worcs 60 0173
Barnton C Edin 117 1874
Barnton Ches 71 6375
Barnwell All Saints Nhants 51 0484
Barnwell St Andrew Nhants 51 0584
Barnwood Gloucs 35 8518
Baron's Cross Herefd 46 4758
Barons Wood Devon 8 7003
Baronwood Cumb 94 5143
Barr S Ayrs 106 2794
Barrachan D & G 99 3649
Barrapoll Ag & B 120 9442
Barras Cumb 88 8312
Barrasford Nthumb 102 9173
Barrets Green Ches 71 5859
Barrhead E Rens 115 4958
Barrhill S Ayrs 98 2382
Barrington Cambs 52 3849
Barrington Somset 10 3818
Barripper Cnwll 2 6338
Barrmill N Ayrs 115 3651
Barrnacarry Bay Ag & B 122 8122
Barrock Highld 151 2570
Barrow Gloucs 47 8824
Barrow Lancs 81 7338
Barrow Rutlnd 63 8815
Barrow Shrops 59 6500
Barrow Somset 22 7231
Barrow Suffk 53 7663
Barrow Bridge Gt Man 81 6811
Barrow Burn Nthumb 110 8610
Barrow Gurney Somset 21 5268
Barrow Haven Lincs 84 0622
Barrow Hill Derbys 74 4275
Barrow Island Cumb 86 1968
Barrow Nook Lancs 78 4402
Barrow Street Wilts 22 8330
Barrow upon Soar Leics 62 5717
Barrow upon Trent Derbys 62 3528
Barrow Vale Somset 21 6460
Barrow's Green Ches 78 5287
Barrow's Green Ches 72 6857
Barrow-in-Furness Cumb 86 2068
Barrow-upon-Humber Lincs 84 0620
Barroway Drove Norfk 65 5703
Barrowby Lincs 63 8736
Barrowden Rutlnd 51 9400
Barrowford Lancs 81 8539
Barry Angus 127 5334
Barry V Glam 20 1268
Barry Island V Glam 20 1166
Barsby Leics 63 6911
Barsham Suffk 55 3989
Barston W Mids 61 2078
Bartestree Herefd 46 5640
Barthol Chapel Abers 143 8133
Bartholomew Green Essex 40 7221
Barthomley Ches 72 7652
Bartley Hants 12 3012
Bartley Green W Mids 60 0081
Bartlow Cambs 53 5845
Barton Cambs 52 4055
Barton Ches 71 4454
Barton Cumb 94 4826
Barton Devon 7 9167
Barton Gloucs 48 0925
Barton Herefd 46 2957
Barton Lancs 78 3509
Barton Lancs 80 5137
Barton N York 89 2208
Barton Oxon 37 5507
Barton Warwks 48 1051
Barton Bendish Norfk 65 7105
Barton End Gloucs 35 8498
Barton Green Staffs 73 1717
Barton Hartshorn Bucks 49 6430
Barton Hill N York 90 7064
Barton in Fabis Notts 62 5132
Barton in the Beans Leics 62 3906
Barton Mills Suffk 53 7173
Barton Seagrave Nhants 51 8877
Barton St David Somset 21 5432
Barton Stacey Hants 24 4341
Barton Town Devon 19 6840
Barton Turf Norfk 67 3522
Barton upon Irwell Gt Man 79 7697
Barton Waterside Lincs 84 0222
Barton-le-Clay Beds 38 0830
Barton-le-Street N York 90 7274
Barton-le-Willows N York 90 7163
Barton-on-Sea Hants 12 2393
Barton-on-the-Heath Warwks 48 2532
Barton-under-Needwood Staffs 73 1818
Barton-upon-Humber Lincs 84 0221
Barugh S York 82 3108
Barugh Green S York 82 3107
Barvas W Isls 152 3649
Barway Cambs 53 5575
Barwell Leics 50 4496
Barwick Devon 8 5907
Barwick Herts 39 3819
Barwick Somset 10 5513
Barwick in Elmet W York 83 4037
Baschurch Shrops 59 4221
Bascote Warwks 48 4063
Bascote Heath Warwks 48 3962
Base Green Suffk 54 0163
Basford Green Staffs 72 9851
Bashall Eaves Lancs 81 6943
Bashall Town Lancs 81 7142
Bashley Hants 12 2496
Basildon Berks 37 6078
Basildon Essex 40 7189
Basingstoke Hants 24 6352
Baslow Derbys 74 2572
Bason Bridge Somset 21 3446
Bassaleg Newpt 34 2786
Bassendean Border 110 6245
Bassenthwaite Cumb 93 2332
Bassett Hants 13 4216
Bassingbourn Cambs 39 3343
Bassingfield Notts 62 6137
Bassingham Lincs 76 9060
Bassingthorpe Lincs 63 9628
Bassus Green Herts 39 3025
Basted Kent 27 6055
Baston Lincs 64 1113
Bastwick Norfk 67 4217
Batch Somset 21 3255
Batchworth Herts 26 0694
Batchworth Heath Herts 26 0792
Batcombe Dorset 10 6103
Batcombe Somset 22 6938
Bate Heath Ches 79 6879
Batford Herts 38 1415
Bath Somset 22 7464
Bath Side Essex 41 2532

Brinklow Burnfoot


Brinklow *Warwks* 50 4379
Brinkworth *Wilts* 35 0184
Brinscall *Lancs* 81 6221
Brinscombe *Somset* 21 4251
Brinsea *Somset* 21 4461
Brinsley *Notts* 75 4548
Brinsop *Herefd* 46 4444
Brinsworth *S York* 74 4289
Brinton *Norfk* 66 0335
Brinyan *Ork* 153 4327
Brisco *Cumb* 93 4252
Brisley *Norfk* 66 9421
Brislington *Bristl* 35 6270
Brissenden Green *Kent* 28 9439
Bristol *Bristl* 34 5972
Briston *Norfk* 66 0632
Brisworthy *Devon* 6 5665
Britannia *Lancs* 81 8821
Britford *Wilts* 23 1627
Brithdir *Caerph* 33 1401
Brithdir *Gwynd* 57 7618
British *Torfn* 34 2503
British Legion Village *Kent* 28 7257
Briton Ferry *Neath* 32 7394
Britwell Salome *Oxon* 37 6792
Brixham *Devon* 7 9255
Brixton *Devon* 6 5552
Brixton *Gt Lon* 27 3175
Brixton Deverill *Wilts* 22 8638
Brixworth *Nhants* 50 7470
Brize Norton *Oxon* 36 2907
Broad Alley *Worcs* 47 8867
Broad Blunsdon *Wilts* 36 1491
Broad Campden *Gloucs* 48 1537
Broad Carr *W York* 82 0919
Broad Chalke *Wilts* 23 0325
Broad Clough *Lancs* 81 8623
Broad Ford *Kent* 28 7139
Broad Green *Essex* 40 8823
Broad Green *Suffk* 53 7859
Broad Green *Worcs* 47 7756
Broad Green *Worcs* 60 9970
Broad Haven *Pembks* 30 8613
Broad Hill *Cambs* 53 5976
Broad Hinton *Wilts* 36 1075
Broad Laying *Hants* 24 4362
Broad Marston *Worcs* 48 1446
Broad Meadow *Staffs* 72 8348
Broad Oak *Cumb* 86 1194
Broad Oak *E Susx* 17 8219
Broad Oak *E Susx* 16 6022
Broad Oak *Hants* 24 7551
Broad Oak *Herefd* 34 4821
Broad Oak *Kent* 29 1761
Broad Oak *Mersyd* 78 5395
Broad Road *Suffk* 55 2676
Broad Street *E Susx* 17 8616
Broad Street *Essex* 39 5516
Broad Street *Kent* 28 7672
Broad Street *Kent* 28 8356
Broad Street *Wilts* 23 1059
Broad Street Green *Essex* 40 8509
Broad Town *Wilts* 36 0977
Broad's Green *Essex* 40 6912
Broadbottom *Gt Man* 79 9993
Broadbridge *W Susx* 14 8105
Broadbridge Heath *W Susx* 15 1431
Broadclyst *Devon* 9 9897
Broadfield *Inver* 115 3373
Broadfield *Pembks* 31 1303
Broadford *Highld* 129 6423
Broadford Bridge *W Susx* 14 0921
Broadgairhill *Border* 109 2010
Broadgate *Lincs* 64 3610
Broadgrass Green *Suffk* 54 9663
Broadhaugh *Border* 119 8655
Broadheath *Gt Man* 79 7689
Broadheath *Worcs* 47 6665
Broadhembury *Devon* 9 1004
Broadhempston *Devon* 7 8066
Broadholme *Notts* 76 8874
Broadland Row *E Susx* 17 8319
Broadlay *Carmth* 31 3709
Broadley *Essex* 39 4207
Broadley *Gt Man* 81 8816
Broadley *Moray* 142 3961
Broadley Common *Essex* 39 4207
Broadmayne *Dorset* 11 7286
Broadmere *Hants* 24 6247
Broadmoor *Gloucs* 35 6415
Broadmoor *Pembks* 31 0906
Broadnymett *Devon* 8 7001
Broadoak *Dorset* 10 4396
Broadoak *Gloucs* 35 6912
Broadoak *Wrexhm* 71 3658
Broadstairs *Kent* 29 3967
Broadstone *Dorset* 11 0095
Broadstone *Mons* 34 5102
Broadstone *Shrops* 59 5489
Broadwas *Worcs* 47 7555
Broadwater *Herts* 39 2422
Broadwater *W Susx* 15 1404
Broadwaters *Worcs* 60 8477
Broadway *Carmth* 31 2910
Broadway *Carmth* 31 3808
Broadway *Pembks* 30 8713
Broadway *Somset* 10 3215
Broadway *Suffk* 55 3979
Broadway *Worcs* 48 0937
Broadwell *Gloucs* 34 5811
Broadwell *Gloucs* 48 2027
Broadwell *Oxon* 36 2504
Broadwell *Warwks* 50 4565
Broadwey *Dorset* 11 6683
Broadwindsor *Dorset* 10 4302
Broadwood Kelly *Devon* 8 6106
Broadwoodwidger *Devon* 5 4189
Brobury *Herefd* 46 3444
Brochel *Highld* 137 5846
Brock *Lancs* 80 5140
Brock's Green *Hants* 24 5061
Brockamin *Worcs* 47 7753
Brockbridge *Hants* 13 6118
Brockdish *Norfk* 55 2179
Brockencote *Worcs* 60 8873
Brockenhurst *Hants* 12 3002
Brocketsbrae *S Lans* 108 8239
Brockford Green *Suffk* 54 1265
Brockford Street *Suffk* 54 1167
Brockhall *Nhants* 49 6362
Brockham *Surrey* 15 1949
Brockhampton *Gloucs* 47 9326
Brockhampton *Gloucs* 36 0322
Brockhampton *Hants* 13 7106
Brockhampton *Herefd* 46 5931
Brockhampton Green *Dorset* 11 7106
Brockholes *W York* 82 1510
Brockhurst *Derbys* 74 3364
Brockhurst *Warwks* 50 4683
Brocklebank *Cumb* 93 3042
Brocklesby *Lincs* 85 1311
Brockley *Somset* 21 4666
Brockley *Suffk* 54 8371
Brockley Green *Suffk* 53 7247
Brockley Green *Suffk* 54 8254
Brockleymoor *Cumb* 94 4937
Brockmoor *W Mids* 60 9088
Brockscombe *Devon* 5 4695
Brockton *Shrops* 59 3104
Brockton *Shrops* 60 7103
Brockton *Shrops* 59 3285
Brockton *Shrops* 59 5794
Brockton *Staffs* 72 8131
Brockweir *Gloucs* 34 5401
Brockwood Park *Hants* 13 6226
Brockworth *Gloucs* 35 8916
Brocton *Cnwll* 4 0168
Brocton *Staffs* 72 9619
Brodick *N Ayrs* 105 0135
Brodie *Moray* 140 9757
Brodsworth *S York* 83 5007
Brogaig *Highld* 136 4767
Brogborough *Beds* 38 9638
Broken Cross *Ches* 79 6873
Broken Cross *Ches* 79 8973
Brokenborough *Wilts* 35 9189
Brokerswood *Wilts* 22 8352
Bromborough *Mersyd* 78 3582
Brome *Suffk* 54 1376
Brome Street *Suffk* 54 1576
Bromeswell *Suffk* 55 3050
Bromfield *Cumb* 93 1746
Bromfield *Shrops* 46 4876
Bromham *Beds* 38 0051
Bromham *Wilts* 22 9665
Bromley *Gt Lon* 27 4069
Bromley *S York* 74 3298
Bromley *Shrops* 60 7395
Bromley *W Mids* 60 9088
Bromley Common *Gt Lon* 27 4266
Bromley Cross *Essex* 41 0627
Bromlow *Shrops* 59 3201
Brompton *Kent* 28 7668
Brompton *N York* 89 3796
Brompton *N York* 91 9482
Brompton *Shrops* 59 5408
Brompton Ralph *Somset* 20 0832
Brompton Regis *Somset* 20 9531
Brompton-on-Swale *N York* 89 2199
Bromsash *Herefd* 47 6524
Bromsberrow *Gloucs* 47 7433
Bromsberrow Heath *Gloucs* 47 7333
Bromsgrove *Worcs* 60 9670
Bromstead Heath *Staffs* 72 7917
Bromyard *Herefd* 47 6554
Bromyard Downs *Herefd* 47 6655
Bronaber *Gwynd* 57 7131
Bronant *Cerdgn* 43 6467
Broncroft *Shrops* 59 5486
Brongest *Cerdgn* 42 3245
Bronington *Wrexhm* 71 4839
Bronllys *Powys* 45 1434
Bronwydd *Carmth* 31 4123
Bronydd *Powys* 45 2245
Bronygarth *Shrops* 58 2637
Brook *Carmth* 31 2609
Brook *Hants* 12 2714
Brook *Hants* 23 3429
Brook *IOW* 13 3983
Brook *Kent* 29 0644
Brook *Surrey* 14 9237
Brook *Surrey* 14 0546
Brook End *Beds* 51 0763
Brook End *Beds* 52 1547
Brook End *Bucks* 38 9244
Brook End *Cambs* 51 0773
Brook Hill *Hants* 12 2714
Brook House *Denbgs* 70 0765
Brook Street *Essex* 27 5793
Brook Street *Kent* 17 9333
Brook Street *Suffk* 54 8248
Brook Street *W Susx* 15 3026
Brooke *Norfk* 67 2899
Brooke *Rutlnd* 63 8405
Brookfield *Rens* 115 4164
Brookhampton *Oxon* 37 6098
Brookhampton *Somset* 21 6327
Brookhouse *Lancs* 87 5464
Brookhouse *S York* 75 5188
Brookhouse Green *Ches* 72 8161
Brookhouses *Derbys* 74 0388
Brookland *Kent* 17 9926
Brooklands *Gt Man* 79 7890
Brookmans Park *Herts* 39 2404
Brooks *Powys* 58 1499
Brooks End *Kent* 29 2967
Brooks Green *W Susx* 14 1224
Brooksby *Leics* 63 6715
Brookthorpe *Gloucs* 35 8312
Brookville *Norfk* 65 7396
Brookwood *Surrey* 25 9557
Broom *Beds* 39 1742
Broom *Dur* 96 2441
Broom *S York* 75 4491
Broom *Warwks* 48 0853
Broom Green *Norfk* 66 9823
Broom Hill *Dorset* 12 0302
Broom Hill *Notts* 62 5447
Broom Hill *S York* 83 4102
Broom Hill *Worcs* 60 9175
Broom Street *Kent* 28 0462
Broom's Green *Gloucs* 47 7132
Broome *Norfk* 67 3591
Broome *Shrops* 59 4080
Broome *Worcs* 60 9078
Broome Park *Nthumb* 111 1012
Broomedge *Ches* 79 7085
Broomer's Corner *W Susx* 14 1220
Broomershill *W Susx* 14 0619
Broomfield *Essex* 40 7010
Broomfield *Kent* 28 8452
Broomfield *Kent* 29 1966
Broomfield *Somset* 20 2232
Broomfields *Shrops* 59 4217
Broomfleet *E R Yk* 84 8727
Broomhall *Surrey* 25 9566
Broomhaugh *Nthumb* 103 0261
Broomhill *Nthumb* 103 2401
Broomhill Green *Ches* 71 6247
Broomley *Nthumb* 103 0360
Broomsthorpe *Norfk* 66 8428
Brora *Highld* 147 9103
Broseley *Shrops* 60 6701
Brotherhouse Bar *Lincs* 64 2614
Brotherlee *Dur* 95 9237
Brothertoft *Lincs* 77 2746
Brotherton *N York* 83 4825
Brotton *N York* 97 6819
Broubster *Highld* 150 0359
Brough *Cumb* 95 7914
Brough *Derbys* 74 1882
Brough *E R Yk* 84 9326
Brough *Highld* 151 2273
Brough *Notts* 76 8458
Brough *Shet* 153 5665
Brough Lodge *Shet* 153 5892
Brough Sowerby *Cumb* 95 7912
Broughall *Shrops* 71 5741
Broughton *Border* 108 1136
Broughton *Bucks* 38 8413
Broughton *Bucks* 38 8939
Broughton *Cambs* 52 2878
Broughton *Flints* 71 3363
Broughton *Gt Man* 79 8201
Broughton *Hants* 23 3033
Broughton *Lancs* 80 5234
Broughton *Lincs* 84 9608
Broughton *N York* 82 9451
Broughton *N York* 90 7673
Broughton *Nhants* 51 8375
Broughton *Oxon* 49 4138
Broughton *Staffs* 72 7634
Broughton *V Glam* 33 9270
Broughton Astley *Leics* 50 5292
Broughton Beck *Cumb* 86 2882
Broughton Gifford *Wilts* 22 8763
Broughton Green *Worcs* 47 9561
Broughton Hackett *Worcs* 47 9254
Broughton Mains *D & G* 99 4545
Broughton Mills *Cumb* 86 2290
Broughton Moor *Cumb* 92 0533
Broughton Poggs *Oxon* 36 2303
Broughton Tower *Cumb* 86 2187
Broughton-in-Furness *Cumb* 86 2187
Broughty Ferry *Dund C* 127 4630
Brow End *Cumb* 86 2674
Brow-of-the-Hill *Norfk* 65 6819
Brown Candover *Hants* 24 5739
Brown Edge *Lancs* 80 3614
Brown Edge *Staffs* 72 9053
Brown Heath *Ches* 71 4564
Brown Lees *Staffs* 72 8756
Brown Street *Suffk* 54 0663
Brown's Green *W Mids* 61 0591
Brownber *Cumb* 87 7005
Brownheath *Shrops* 59 4629
Brownhill *Abers* 143 8640
Brownhills *Fife* 127 5215
Brownhills *W Mids* 61 0405
Brownieside *Nthumb* 111 1623
Browninghill Green *Hants* 24 5859
Brownlow Heath *Ches* 72 8360
Brownrigg *Cumb* 92 0420
Brownrigg *Cumb* 92 1652
Browns Hill *Gloucs* 35 8802
Brownsham *Devon* 18 2826
Brownsover *Warwks* 50 5177
Brownston *Devon* 7 6952
Browston Green *Norfk* 67 4901
Broxa *N York* 91 9491
Broxbourne *Herts* 39 3606
Broxburn *E Loth* 119 6977
Broxburn *W Loth* 117 0872
Broxfield *Nthumb* 111 2016
Broxted *Essex* 40 5727
Broxton *Ches* 71 4754
Broxwood *Herefd* 46 3654
Broyle Side *E Susx* 16 4513
Bruan *Highld* 151 3139
Bruar *P & K* 132 8265
Brucefield *Highld* 147 9386
Bruchag *Ag & B* 114 1157
Bruera *Ches* 71 4360
Bruern Abbey *Oxon* 36 2620
Bruichladdich *Ag & B* 112 2661
Bruisyard *Suffk* 55 3266
Bruisyard Street *Suffk* 55 3365
Brumby *Lincs* 84 8909
Brund *Staffs* 74 1061
Brundall *Norfk* 67 3308
Brundish *Suffk* 55 2769
Brundish Street *Suffk* 55 2671
Brunnion *Cnwll* 2 5036
Brunslow *Shrops* 59 3684
Bruntcliffe *W York* 82 2526
Brunthwaite *W York* 82 0546
Bruntingthorpe *Leics* 50 6089
Brunton *Fife* 126 3220
Brunton *Nthumb* 111 2024
Brunton *Wilts* 23 2456
Brushford *Somset* 20 9225
Brushford Barton *Devon* 8 6707
Bruton *Somset* 22 6835
Bryan's Green *Worcs* 47 8868
Bryanston *Dorset* 11 8607
Bryant's Bottom *Bucks* 26 8599
Brydekirk *D & G* 101 1870
Brymbo *Wrexhm* 71 2953
Brympton *Somset* 10 5115
Bryn *Ches* 71 6072
Bryn *Gt Man* 78 5600
Bryn *Neath* 33 8192
Bryn *Shrops* 59 2985
Bryn Du *IOA* 68 3472
Bryn Gates *Lancs* 78 5901
Bryn Golau *Rhondd* 33 0088
Bryn Saith Marchog *Denbgs* 70 0750
Bryn-bwbach *Gwynd* 57 6236
Bryn-coch *Neath* 32 7499
Bryn-Eden *Gwynd* 57 7129
Bryn-Henllan *Pembks* 30 0139
Bryn-mawr *Gwynd* 56 2433
Bryn-newydd *Denbgs* 70 1842
Bryn-penarth *Powys* 58 1004
Bryn-y-bal *Flints* 70 2564
Bryn-y-Maen *Conwy* 69 8376
Bryn-yr-Eos *Wrexhm* 70 2840
Brynaman *Carmth* 32 7114
Brynberian *Pembks* 31 1035
Brynbryddan *Neath* 32 7792
Bryncae *Rhondd* 33 9982
Bryncethin *Brdgnd* 33 9183
Bryncir *Gwynd* 56 4844
Bryncroes *Gwynd* 56 2231
Bryncrug *Gwynd* 57 6103
Bryneglwys *Denbgs* 70 1447
Brynfields *Wrexhm* 71 3044
Brynford *Flints* 70 1774
Bryngwran *IOA* 68 3577
Bryngwyn *Mons* 34 3909
Bryngwyn *Powys* 45 1849
Brynhoffnant *Cerdgn* 42 3351
Bryning *Lancs* 80 4029
Brynithel *Blae G* 33 2101
Brynmawr *Blae G* 33 1911
Brynmenyn *Brdgnd* 33 9084
Brynmill *Swans* 32 6392
Brynna *Rhondd* 33 9883
Brynrefail *Gwynd* 69 5562
Brynrefail *IOA* 68 4886
Brynsadler *Rhondd* 33 0280
Brynsiencyn *IOA* 68 4867
Brynteg *IOA* 68 4982
Bualintur *Highld* 128 4020
Buarth-draw *Flints* 70 1779
Bubbenhall *Warwks* 61 3672
Bubwith *E R Yk* 84 7136
Buchanan Smithy *Stirlg* 115 4689
Buchanhaven *Abers* 143 1247
Buchanty *P & K* 125 9328
Buchany *Stirlg* 124 7102
Buchlyvie *Stirlg* 115 5793
Buck's Cross *Devon* 18 3522
Buck's Mills *Devon* 18 3523
Buckabank *Cumb* 93 3749
Buckden *Cambs* 52 1967
Buckden *N York* 88 9477
Buckenham *Norfk* 67 3505
Buckerell *Devon* 9 1200
Buckfast *Devon* 7 7467
Buckfastleigh *Devon* 7 7366
Buckhaven *Fife* 118 3598
Buckholm *Border* 109 4738
Buckholt *Mons* 34 5016
Buckhorn Weston *Dorset* 22 7524
Buckhurst Hill *Essex* 27 4194
Buckie *Moray* 142 4265
Buckingham *Bucks* 49 6933
Buckland *Bucks* 38 8812
Buckland *Devon* 7 6743
Buckland *Gloucs* 48 0835
Buckland *Hants* 12 3196
Buckland *Herts* 39 3533
Buckland *Kent* 29 3042
Buckland *Oxon* 36 3498
Buckland *Surrey* 26 2150
Buckland Brewer *Devon* 18 4220
Buckland Common *Bucks* 38 9207
Buckland Dinham *Somset* 22 7551
Buckland Filleigh *Devon* 18 4609
Buckland in the Moor *Devon* 7 7273
Buckland Monachorum *Devon* 6 4968
Buckland Newton *Dorset* 11 6805
Buckland Ripers *Dorset* 11 6582
Buckland St Mary *Somset* 10 2613
Buckland-Tout-Saints *Devon* 7 7645
Bucklebury *Berks* 24 5570
Bucklerheads *Angus* 127 4636
Bucklers Hard *Hants* 13 4000
Bucklesham *Suffk* 55 2441
Buckley *Flints* 70 2763
Buckley Green *Warwks* 48 1567
Buckley Mountain *Flints* 70 2765
Bucklow Hill *Ches* 79 7383
Buckminster *Leics* 63 8722
Bucknall *Lincs* 76 1668
Bucknall *Staffs* 72 9047
Bucknell *Oxon* 49 5625
Bucknell *Shrops* 46 3574
Buckpool *Moray* 142 4165
Bucks Green *W Susx* 14 0833
Bucks Hill *Herts* 26 0500
Bucks Horn Oak *Hants* 25 8041
Bucksburn *Aber C* 135 8909
Buckshead *Cnwll* 3 8346
Buckton *E R Yk* 91 1872
Buckton *Herefd* 46 3873
Buckton *Nthumb* 111 0838
Buckworth *Cambs* 52 1476
Budbrooke *Warwks* 48 2665
Budby *Notts* 75 6169
Budd's Titson *Cnwll* 18 2401
Buddileigh *Staffs* 72 7449
Buddon *Angus* 127 5232
Bude *Cnwll* 18 2105
Budge's Shop *Cnwll* 5 3259
Budlake *Devon* 9 9800
Budle *Nthumb* 111 1535
Budleigh Salterton *Devon* 9 0682
Budlett's Common *E Susx* 16 4723
Budock Water *Cnwll* 3 7831
Buerton *Ches* 72 6843
Bugbrooke *Nhants* 49 6757
Bugford *Devon* 7 8350
Buglawton *Ches* 72 8763
Bugle *Cnwll* 4 0158
Bugley *Dorset* 22 7824
Bugthorpe *E R Yk* 90 7757
Buildwas *Shrops* 59 6204
Builth Road *Powys* 45 0353
Builth Wells *Powys* 45 0350
Bulbourne *Herts* 38 9313
Bulbridge *Wilts* 23 0830
Bulby *Lincs* 64 0526
Buldoo *Highld* 150 0067
Bulford *Wilts* 23 1643
Bulford Barracks *Wilts* 23 1843
Bulkeley *Ches* 71 5354
Bulkington *Warwks* 61 3986
Bulkington *Wilts* 22 9458
Bulkworthy *Devon* 18 3914
Bull Bay *IOA* 68 4294
Bull's Green *Herts* 39 2717
Bull's Green *Norfk* 67 4194
Bullamore *N York* 89 3994
Bullbridge *Derbys* 74 3552
Bullbrook *Berks* 25 8869
Bullen's Green *Herts* 39 2105
Bulley *Gloucs* 35 7619
Bullgill *Cumb* 92 0938
Bullinghope *Herefd* 46 5136
Bullington *Hants* 24 4541
Bullington *Lincs* 76 0877
Bullington End *Bucks* 38 8145
Bullockstone *Kent* 29 1665
Bulmer *Essex* 54 8440
Bulmer *N York* 90 6967
Bulmer Tye *Essex* 54 8438
Bulphan *Essex* 40 6385
Bulstone *Devon* 9 1789
Bulstrode *Herts* 26 0302
Bulstrode Park *Bucks* 26 9888
Bulverhythe *E Susx* 17 7708
Bulwark *Abers* 143 9345
Bulwell *Notts* 62 5343
Bulwick *Nhants* 51 9694
Bumble's Green *Essex* 39 4005
Bunacaimb *Highld* 129 6588
Bunarkaig *Highld* 131 1887
Bunbury *Ches* 71 5657
Bunbury Heath *Ches* 71 5558
Bunchrew *Highld* 140 6246
Buncton *W Susx* 15 1413
Bundalloch *Highld* 138 8927
Bunessan *Ag & B* 121 3821
Bungay *Suffk* 55 3389
Bunker's Hill *Lincs* 77 2653
Bunnahabhainn *Ag & B* 112 4173
Bunny *Notts* 62 5829
Buntait *Highld* 139 4030
Buntingford *Herts* 39 3629
Bunwell *Norfk* 66 1292
Bunwell Street *Norfk* 66 1193
Bupton *Derbys* 73 2237
Burbage *Derbys* 74 0472
Burbage *Leics* 50 4492
Burbage *Wilts* 23 2261
Burcher *Herefd* 46 3360
Burchett's Green *Berks* 26 8481
Burchett's Green *E Susx* 16 6631
Burcombe *Wilts* 23 0730
Burcot *Oxon* 37 5695
Burcot *Worcs* 60 9871
Burcote *Shrops* 60 7495
Burcott *Bucks* 38 8415
Burcott *Bucks* 38 8823
Burdale *N York* 90 8762
Bures *Suffk* 54 9034
Burford *Oxon* 36 2512
Burford *Shrops* 46 5868
Burg *Ag & B* 121 3845
Burgates *Hants* 14 7728
Burge End *Herts* 38 1432
Burgess Hill *W Susx* 15 3218
Burgh *Suffk* 55 2351
Burgh by Sands *Cumb* 93 3259
Burgh Castle *Norfk* 67 4805
Burgh Heath *Surrey* 26 2457
Burgh Hill *E Susx* 17 7226
Burgh le Marsh *Lincs* 77 5065
Burgh next Aylsham *Norfk* 67 2125
Burgh on Bain *Lincs* 76 2186
Burgh St Margaret *Norfk* 67 4413
Burgh St Peter *Norfk* 67 4693
Burghclere *Hants* 24 4761
Burghead *Moray* 141 1168
Burghfield *Berks* 24 6668
Burghfield Common *Berks* 24 6566
Burghill *Herefd* 46 4844
Burghwallis *S York* 83 5311
Burham *Kent* 28 7262
Buriton *Hants* 13 7419
Burland *Ches* 71 6153
Burlawn *Cnwll* 4 9970
Burleigh *Berks* 25 9169
Burleigh *Gloucs* 35 8601
Burlescombe *Devon* 9 0716
Burleston *Dorset* 11 7794
Burlestone *Devon* 7 8248
Burley *Hants* 12 2102
Burley *Rutlnd* 63 8810
Burley *Shrops* 59 4881
Burley Gate *Herefd* 46 5947
Burley in Wharfedale *W York* 82 1646
Burley Lawn *Hants* 12 2103
Burley Street *Hants* 12 2004
Burley Wood Head *W York* 82 1544
Burleydam *Ches* 71 6042
Burlingham Green *Norfk* 67 3610
Burlingjobb *Powys* 46 2558
Burlington *Shrops* 60 7711
Burlton *Shrops* 59 4526
Burmarsh *Kent* 17 1032
Burmington *Warwks* 48 2637
Burn *N York* 83 5928
Burn Cross *S York* 74 3496
Burn Naze *Lancs* 80 3443
Burn of Cambus *Stirlg* 124 7102
Burnage *Gt Man* 79 8692
Burnaston *Derbys* 73 2832
Burnbanks *Cumb* 94 5016
Burnbrae *N Lans* 116 8759
Burnby *E R Yk* 84 8346
Burndell *W Susx* 14 9802
Burnden *Gt Man* 79 7207
Burnedge *Gt Man* 79 9110
Burneside *Cumb* 87 5095
Burneston *N York* 89 3084
Burnett *Somset* 22 6665
Burnfoot *Border* 109 4113

Chester-le-Street

Cobley


Chester-le-Street *Dur* 96 2751
Chesterblade *Somset* 22 6641
Chesterfield *Derbys* 74 3871
Chesterfield *Staffs* 61 0905
Chesterhill *Mdloth* 118 3764
Chesters *Border* 110 6022
Chesters *Border* 110 6210
Chesterton *Cambs* 64 1295
Chesterton *Cambs* 53 4660
Chesterton *Gloucs* 35 0100
Chesterton *Oxon* 37 5621
Chesterton *Shrops* 60 7897
Chesterton *Staffs* 72 8349
Chesterton Green *Warwks* 48 3558
Chesterwood *Nthumb* 102 8364
Chestfield *Kent* 29 1365
Chestnut Street *Kent* 28 8763
Cheston *Devon* 7 6858
Cheswardine *Shrops* 72 7130
Cheswell *Shrops* 72 7116
Cheswick *Nthumb* 111 0346
Cheswick Green *W Mids* 61 1376
Chetnole *Dorset* 10 6008
Chettiscombe *Devon* 9 9614
Chettisham *Cambs* 53 5483
Chettle *Dorset* 11 9513
Chetton *Shrops* 60 6690
Chetwode *Bucks* 49 6429
Chetwynd *Shrops* 72 7321
Chetwynd Aston *Shrops* 72 7517
Cheveley *Cambs* 53 6861
Chevening *Kent* 27 4857
Cheverton *IOW* 13 4583
Chevington *Suffk* 53 7859
Chevington Drift *Nthumb* 103 2598
Chevithorne *Devon* 9 9715
Chew Magna *Somset* 21 5763
Chew Moor *Gt Man* 79 6607
Chew Stoke *Somset* 21 5561
Chewton Keynsham *Somset* 21 6566
Chewton Mendip *Somset* 21 5953
Chichacott *Devon* 8 6096
Chicheley *Bucks* 38 9046
Chichester *W Susx* 14 8604
Chickerell *Dorset* 11 6480
Chickering *Suffk* 55 2176
Chicklade *Wilts* 22 9134
Chickward *Herefd* 46 2853
Chidden *Hants* 13 6517
Chiddingfold *Surrey* 14 9635
Chiddingly *E Susx* 16 5414
Chiddingstone *Kent* 16 5045
Chiddingstone Causeway *Kent* 16 5246
Chideock *Dorset* 10 4292
Chidham *W Susx* 14 7903
Chidswell *W York* 82 2623
Chieveley *Berks* 24 4774
Chignall Smealy *Essex* 40 6611
Chignall St James *Essex* 40 6610
Chigwell *Essex* 27 4494
Chigwell Row *Essex* 27 4693
Chilbolton *Hants* 23 3940
Chilcomb *Hants* 24 5028
Chilcombe *Dorset* 10 5291
Chilcompton *Somset* 21 6451
Chilcote *Leics* 61 2811
Child Okeford *Dorset* 11 8312
Child's Ercall *Shrops* 72 6625
Childer Thornton *Ches* 71 3677
Childrey *Oxon* 36 3687
Childswickham *Worcs* 48 0738
Childwall *Mersyd* 78 4189
Childwick Bury *Herts* 38 1410
Childwick Green *Herts* 38 1410
Chilfrome *Dorset* 10 5898
Chilgrove *W Susx* 14 8314
Chilham *Kent* 29 0653
Chilhampton *Wilts* 23 0933
Chilla *Devon* 18 4402
Chillaton *Devon* 5 4381
Chillenden *Kent* 29 2753
Chillerton *IOW* 13 4883
Chillesford *Suffk* 55 3852
Chillingham *Nthumb* 111 0525
Chillington *Devon* 7 7942
Chillington *Somset* 10 3811
Chilmark *Wilts* 22 9732
Chilmington Green *Kent* 28 9840
Chilson *Oxon* 36 3119
Chilsworthy *Cnwll* 5 4172
Chilsworthy *Devon* 18 3206
Chiltern Green *Beds* 38 1319
Chilthorne Domer *Somset* 21 5219
Chilton *Bucks* 37 6811
Chilton *Devon* 9 8604
Chilton *Dur* 96 2829
Chilton *Kent* 29 2743
Chilton *Oxon* 37 4885
Chilton *Suffk* 54 8842
Chilton Candover *Hants* 24 5940
Chilton Cantelo *Somset* 21 5722
Chilton Foliat *Wilts* 36 3170
Chilton Polden *Somset* 21 3740
Chilton Street *Suffk* 53 7546
Chilton Trinity *Somset* 20 2939
Chilwell *Notts* 62 5135
Chilworth *Hants* 13 4018
Chilworth *Surrey* 14 0347
Chimney *Oxon* 36 3501
Chineham *Hants* 24 6555
Chingford *Gt Lon* 27 3894
Chinley *Derbys* 74 0482
Chinnor *Oxon* 37 7501
Chipchase Castle *Nthumb* 102 8775
Chipnall *Shrops* 72 7231
Chippenham *Cambs* 53 6669
Chippenham *Wilts* 35 9173
Chipperfield *Herts* 26 0401
Chipping *Herts* 39 3531
Chipping *Lancs* 81 6243
Chipping Campden *Gloucs* 48 1539
Chipping Hill *Essex* 40 8215
Chipping Norton *Oxon* 48 3127
Chipping Ongar *Essex* 39 5503
Chipping Sodbury *Gloucs* 35 7282
Chipping Warden *Nhants* 49 4948
Chipstable *Somset* 20 0427
Chipstead *Kent* 27 5056
Chipstead *Surrey* 27 2756
Chirbury *Shrops* 58 2698
Chirk *Wrexhm* 58 2837
Chirnside *Border* 119 8756
Chirnsidebridge *Border* 119 8556
Chirton *Wilts* 23 0757
Chisbury *Wilts* 23 2766
Chiselborough *Somset* 10 4614
Chiseldon *Wilts* 36 1880
Chisholme *Border* 109 4112
Chislehampton *Oxon* 37 5999
Chislehurst *Gt Lon* 27 4570
Chislet *Kent* 29 2264
Chisley *W York* 82 0028
Chiswellgreen *Herts* 38 1304
Chiswick *Gt Lon* 26 2078
Chiswick End *Cambs* 52 3745
Chisworth *Derbys* 79 9991
Chitcombe *E Susx* 17 8120
Chithurst *W Susx* 14 8423
Chittering *Cambs* 53 4969
Chitterne *Wilts* 22 9843
Chittlehamholt *Devon* 19 6520
Chittlehampton *Devon* 19 6325
Chittlehampton *Devon* 19 6511
Chittoe *Wilts* 22 9566
Chivelstone *Devon* 7 7838
Chivenor *Devon* 19 5034
Chlenry *D & G* 98 1260
Chobham *Surrey* 25 9762
Cholderton *Wilts* 23 2242
Cholesbury *Bucks* 38 9307
Chollerford *Nthumb* 102 9170
Chollerton *Nthumb* 102 9372
Cholmondeston *Ches* 71 6359
Cholsey *Oxon* 37 5886
Cholstrey *Herefd* 46 4659
Chop Gate *N York* 90 5599
Choppington *Nthumb* 103 2484
Chopwell *T & W* 95 1158
Chorley *Ches* 71 5751
Chorley *Lancs* 81 5817
Chorley *Shrops* 60 6983
Chorley *Staffs* 61 0710
Chorleywood *Herts* 26 0396
Chorleywood West *Herts* 26 0296
Chorlton *Ches* 72 7250
Chorlton Lane *Ches* 71 4547
Chorlton-cum-Hardy *Gt Man* 79 8193
Choulton *Shrops* 59 3788
Chowley *Ches* 71 4756
Chrishall *Essex* 39 4439
Chrisswell *Inver* 114 2274
Christchurch *Cambs* 65 4996
Christchurch *Dorset* 12 1592
Christchurch *Gloucs* 34 5613
Christchurch *Mons* 34 3489
Christian Malford *Wilts* 35 9678
Christleton *Ches* 71 4465
Christmas Common *Oxon* 37 7193
Christon *Somset* 21 3757
Christon Bank *Nthumb* 111 2123
Christow *Devon* 8 8385
Chuck Hatch *E Susx* 16 4733
Chudleigh *Devon* 9 8679
Chudleigh Knighton *Devon* 8 8477
Chulmleigh *Devon* 19 6814
Chunal *Derbys* 74 0390
Church *Lancs* 81 7429
Church Ashton *Shrops* 72 7317
Church Brampton *Nhants* 50 7165
Church Brough *Cumb* 95 7913
Church Broughton *Derbys* 73 2033
Church Crookham *Hants* 25 8051
Church Eaton *Staffs* 72 8417
Church End *Beds* 38 9832
Church End *Beds* 38 9921
Church End *Beds* 38 0334
Church End *Beds* 51 0558
Church End *Beds* 51 1058
Church End *Beds* 39 1937
Church End *Cambs* 51 0873
Church End *Cambs* 52 2082
Church End *Cambs* 52 3278
Church End *Cambs* 53 4857
Church End *Essex* 40 6223
Church End *Essex* 40 7228
Church End *Essex* 40 7316
Church End *Gt Lon* 26 2490
Church End *Hants* 24 6756
Church End *Herts* 38 1011
Church End *Herts* 39 2630
Church End *Herts* 39 4422
Church End *Lincs* 64 2234
Church End *Lincs* 77 4295
Church End *Warwks* 61 2490
Church End *Warwks* 61 2992
Church Enstone *Oxon* 48 3725
Church Fenton *N York* 83 5136
Church Green *Devon* 9 1796
Church Gresley *Derbys* 73 2918
Church Hanborough *Oxon* 36 4213
Church Hill *Ches* 72 6465
Church Hill *Staffs* 60 0011
Church Houses *N York* 90 6697
Church Knowle *Dorset* 11 9481
Church Laneham *Notts* 75 8176
Church Langton *Leics* 50 7293
Church Lawford *Warwks* 50 4576
Church Lawton *Staffs* 72 8255
Church Leigh *Staffs* 73 0235
Church Lench *Worcs* 48 0251
Church Mayfield *Staffs* 73 1544
Church Minshull *Ches* 72 6660
Church Norton *W Susx* 14 8795
Church Preen *Shrops* 59 5498
Church Pulverbatch *Shrops* 59 4303
Church Stowe *Nhants* 49 6357
Church Street *Essex* 53 7943
Church Street *Kent* 28 7174
Church Street *Suffk* 55 4883
Church Stretton *Shrops* 59 4593
Church Town *Lincs* 84 7806
Church Village *Rhondd* 33 0885
Church Warsop *Notts* 75 5668
Church Wilne *Derbys* 62 4431
Churcham *Gloucs* 35 7618
Churchbridge *Staffs* 60 9808
Churchdown *Gloucs* 35 8819
Churchend *Essex* 41 0093
Churchfield *W Mids* 60 0192
Churchgate *Herts* 27 3402
Churchgate Street *Essex* 39 4811
Churchill *Devon* 19 5940
Churchill *Devon* 10 2902
Churchill *Oxon* 48 2824
Churchill *Somset* 21 4459
Churchill *Worcs* 60 8879
Churchill *Worcs* 47 9253
Churchinford *Somset* 9 2112
Churchover *Warwks* 50 5180
Churchstanton *Somset* 9 1914
Churchstoke *Powys* 58 2794
Churchstow *Devon* 7 7145
Churchthorpe *Lincs* 77 3297
Churchtown *Derbys* 74 2662
Churchtown *Devon* 19 6744
Churchtown *Lancs* 80 3240
Churchtown *Lancs* 80 4843
Churchtown *Mersyd* 80 3618
Churnsike Lodge *Nthumb* 102 6677
Churston Ferrers *Devon* 7 9056
Churt *Surrey* 25 8538
Churton *Ches* 71 4156
Churwell *W York* 82 2729
Chwilog *Gwynd* 56 4338
Chyandour *Cnwll* 2 4731
Chyanvounder *Cnwll* 2 6522
Chyeowling *Cnwll* 3 7941
Chyvarloe *Cnwll* 2 6523
Cil *Powys* 58 1701
Cilcain *Flints* 70 1765
Cilcennin *Cerdgn* 44 5260
Cilcewydd *Powys* 58 2204
Cilfrew *Neath* 32 7700
Cilfynydd *Rhondd* 33 0891
Cilgerran *Pembks* 31 1942
Cilgwyn *Carmth* 44 7429
Cilgwyn *Gwynd* 68 4953
Ciliau-Aeron *Cerdgn* 44 5057
Cilmaengwyn *Neath* 32 7405
Cilmery *Powys* 45 0051
Cilrhedyn *Pembks* 31 2834
Cilsan *Carmth* 32 5922
Ciltalgarth *Gwynd* 57 8940
Cilycwm *Carmth* 44 7539
Cimla *Neath* 32 7696
Cinder Hill *W Mids* 60 9294
Cinderford *Gloucs* 35 6514
Cippenham *Berks* 26 9580
Cirencester *Gloucs* 35 0201
Citadilla *N York* 89 2299
City *Gt Lon* 27 3281
City *V Glam* 33 9878
City Dulas *IOA* 68 4687
Clabhach *Ag & B* 120 1858
Clachaig *Ag & B* 114 1181
Clachan *Ag & B* 122 7819
Clachan *Ag & B* 122 8543
Clachan *Ag & B* 113 7556
Clachan *Highld* 137 5436
Clachan Mor *Ag & B* 120 9847
Clachan na Luib *W Isls* 152 8163
Clachan of Campsie *E Duns* 116 6079
Clachan-a-Luib *W Isls* 152 8163
Clachan-Seil *Ag & B* 122 7718
Clachaneasy *D & G* 98 3574
Clachnaharry *Highld* 140 6446
Clachtoll *Highld* 148 0427
Clackavoid *P & K* 133 1463
Clackmannan *Clacks* 116 9191
Clackmarras *Moray* 141 2458
Clacton-on-Sea *Essex* 41 1715
Cladich *Ag & B* 123 0921
Cladswell *Worcs* 48 0558
Claggan *Highld* 122 7049
Claigan *Highld* 136 2354
Clandown *Somset* 22 6855
Clanfield *Hants* 13 6916
Clanfield *Oxon* 36 2801
Clannaborough *Devon* 8 7402
Clanville *Hants* 23 3148
Clanville *Somset* 21 6233
Claonaig *Ag & B* 113 8656
Clap Hill *Kent* 28 0537
Clapgate *Dorset* 11 0102
Clapgate *Herts* 39 4424
Clapham *Beds* 38 0352
Clapham *Devon* 9 8987
Clapham *Gt Lon* 27 2975
Clapham *N York* 88 7469
Clapham *W Susx* 14 0906
Clapham Folly *Beds* 38 0252
Clappersgate *Cumb* 87 3603
Clapton *Somset* 10 4106
Clapton *Somset* 21 6453
Clapton-in-Gordano *Somset* 34 4773
Clapton-on-the-Hill *Gloucs* 36 1617
Clapworthy *Devon* 19 6724
Clarach *Cerdgn* 43 6084
Claravale *T & W* 103 1364
Clarbeston *Pembks* 30 0521
Clarbeston Road *Pembks* 30 0121
Clarborough *Notts* 75 7383
Clare *Suffk* 53 7745
Clarebrand *D & G* 99 7665
Clarencefield *D & G* 100 0968
Clareton *N York* 89 3959
Clarewood *Nthumb* 103 0169
Clarilaw *Border* 109 5218
Clark's Green *Surrey* 15 1739
Clarken Green *Hants* 24 5651
Clarkston *E Rens* 115 5757
Clashmore *Highld* 148 0331
Clashmore *Highld* 146 7489
Clashnessie *Highld* 148 0530
Clashnoir *Moray* 141 2222
Clathy *P & K* 125 9920
Clathymore *P & K* 125 0121
Clatt *Abers* 142 5326
Clatter *Powys* 58 9994
Clatterford End *Essex* 40 6113
Clatworthy *Somset* 20 0531
Claughton *Lancs* 80 5342
Claughton *Lancs* 87 5566
Claughton *Mersyd* 78 3088
Clavelshay *Somset* 20 2531
Claverdon *Warwks* 48 1965
Claverham *Somset* 21 4566
Clavering *Essex* 39 4731
Claverley *Shrops* 60 7993
Claverton *Somset* 22 7864
Claverton Down *Somset* 22 7763
Clawdd-coch *V Glam* 33 0577
Clawdd-newydd *Denbgs* 70 0852
Clawthorpe *Cumb* 87 5377
Clawton *Devon* 18 3599
Claxby *Lincs* 76 1194
Claxby *Lincs* 77 4571
Claxton *N York* 90 6959
Claxton *Norfk* 67 3303
Clay Common *Suffk* 55 4681
Clay Coton *Nhants* 50 5976
Clay Cross *Derbys* 74 3963
Clay End *Herts* 39 3024
Claybrooke Magna *Leics* 50 4988
Claydon *Oxon* 49 4549
Claydon *Suffk* 54 1349
Claygate *D & G* 101 3979
Claygate *Kent* 28 7144
Claygate *Surrey* 26 1563
Claygate Cross *Kent* 27 6155
Clayhall *Gt Lon* 27 4390
Clayhanger *Devon* 20 0222
Clayhanger *W Mids* 61 0404
Clayhidon *Devon* 9 1615
Clayhill *E Susx* 17 8323
Clayhill *Hants* 12 3006
Clayhithe *Cambs* 53 5064
Clayock *Highld* 151 1659
Claypit Hill *Cambs* 52 3554
Claypits *Gloucs* 35 7606
Claypole *Lincs* 76 8449
Claythorpe *Lincs* 77 4178
Clayton *S York* 83 4507
Clayton *W Susx* 15 2914
Clayton *W York* 82 1231
Clayton Green *Lancs* 81 5723
Clayton West *W York* 82 2510
Clayton-le-Moors *Lancs* 81 7530
Clayton-le-Woods *Lancs* 81 5622
Clayworth *Notts* 75 7387
Cleadale *Highld* 128 4789
Cleadon *T & W* 96 3862
Clearbrook *Devon* 6 5265
Clearwell *Gloucs* 34 5608
Clearwell Meend *Gloucs* 34 5808
Cleasby *N York* 89 2512
Cleat *Ork* 153 4584
Cleatlam *Dur* 95 1118
Cleator *Cumb* 92 0113
Cleator Moor *Cumb* 92 0115
Cleckheaton *W York* 82 1825
Clee St Margaret *Shrops* 59 5684
Cleedownton *Shrops* 59 5880
Cleehill *Shrops* 46 5975
Cleekhimin *N Lans* 116 7658
Cleestanton *Shrops* 46 5779
Cleethorpes *Lincs* 85 3008
Cleeton St Mary *Shrops* 46 6178
Cleeve *Oxon* 37 6081
Cleeve *Somset* 21 4666
Cleeve Hill *Gloucs* 47 9827
Cleeve Prior *Worcs* 48 0849
Cleghornie *E Loth* 118 5983
Clehonger *Herefd* 46 4437
Cleish *P & K* 117 0998
Cleland *N Lans* 116 7958
Clement Street *Kent* 27 5370
Clement's End *Beds* 38 0214
Clenamacrie *Ag & B* 122 9228
Clench Common *Wilts* 23 1765
Clenchwarton *Norfk* 65 5920
Clenerty *Abers* 142 7760
Clent *Worcs* 60 9279
Cleobury Mortimer *Shrops* 60 6775
Cleobury North *Shrops* 59 6286
Cleongart *Ag & B* 105 6734
Clephanton *Highld* 140 8150
Clerkhill *D & G* 101 2697
Cleuch-head *D & G* 108 8200
Clevancy *Wilts* 36 0575
Clevedon *Somset* 34 4171
Cleveley *Oxon* 48 3923
Cleveleys *Lancs* 80 3143
Clevelode *Worcs* 47 8347
Cleverton *Wilts* 35 9785
Clewer *Somset* 21 4351
Cley next the Sea *Norfk* 66 0444
Cliburn *Cumb* 94 5824
Cliddesden *Hants* 24 6349
Cliff *Warwks* 61 2197
Cliff End *E Susx* 17 8813
Cliffe *Dur* 96 2115
Cliffe *Kent* 28 7376
Cliffe *Lancs* 81 7333
Cliffe *N York* 83 6631
Cliffe Woods *Kent* 28 7373
Clifford *Herefd* 46 2445
Clifford *W York* 83 4344
Clifford Chambers *Warwks* 48 1952
Clifford's Mesne *Gloucs* 47 7023
Cliffsend *Kent* 29 3464
Clifton *Beds* 39 1639
Clifton *Bristl* 34 5773
Clifton *Cumb* 94 5326
Clifton *Derbys* 73 1644
Clifton *Gt Man* 79 7703
Clifton *Lancs* 80 4630
Clifton *N York* 82 1948
Clifton *N York* 83 5953
Clifton *Notts* 62 5434
Clifton *Nthumb* 103 2082
Clifton *Oxon* 49 4931
Clifton *S York* 75 5296
Clifton *W York* 82 1622
Clifton *Worcs* 47 8446
Clifton Campville *Staffs* 61 2510
Clifton Dykes *Cumb* 44 5427
Clifton Hampden *Oxon* 37 5495
Clifton Reynes *Bucks* 38 9051
Clifton upon Dunsmore *Warwks* 50 5376
Clifton upon Teme *Worcs* 47 7161
Cliftonville *Kent* 29 3771
Climping *W Susx* 14 9902
Clink *Somset* 22 7948
Clint *N York* 89 2659
Clint Green *Norfk* 66 0210
Clinterty *Aber C* 135 8311
Clintmains *Border* 110 6132
Clipiau *Gwynd* 57 8410
Clippesby *Norfk* 67 4214
Clipsham *Rutlnd* 63 9716
Clipston *Nhants* 50 7181
Clipston *Notts* 63 6334
Clipstone *Beds* 38 9426
Clipstone *Notts* 75 5963
Clitheroe *Lancs* 81 7441
Clive *Shrops* 59 5124
Clixby *Lincs* 85 0904
Cloatley *Wilts* 35 9890
Clocaenog *Denbgs* 70 0854
Clochan *Moray* 142 4060
Clochtow *Angus* 127 4852
Clock Face *Mersyd* 78 5291
Cloddiau *Powys* 58 2009
Clodock *Herefd* 46 3227
Cloford *Somset* 22 7244
Clola *Abers* 143 0043
Clophill *Beds* 38 0838
Clopton *Nhants* 51 0680
Clopton *Suffk* 55 2253
Clopton Corner *Suffk* 55 2254
Clopton Green *Suffk* 53 7655
Clopton Green *Suffk* 54 9759
Clos du Valle *Guern* 158 0000
Closeburn *D & G* 100 8992
Closeburnmill *D & G* 100 9094
Closeclark *IOM* 158 2775
Closworth *Somset* 10 5610
Clothall *Herts* 39 2731
Clotton *Ches* 71 5264
Cloudesley Bush *Warwks* 50 4686
Clough *Gt Man* 79 9408
Clough Foot *W York* 81 9123
Clough Head *N York* 82 0918
Cloughton *N York* 91 0194
Cloughton Newlands *N York* 91 0096
Clousta *Shet* 153 3057
Clova *Angus* 134 3273
Clovelly *Devon* 18 3124
Clovenfords *Border* 109 4536
Clovulin *Highld* 130 0063
Clow Bridge *Lancs* 81 8228
Clowne *Derbys* 75 4875
Clows Top *Worcs* 60 7172
Cloy *Wrexhm* 71 3943
Cluanie Inn *Highld* 130 0711
Cluanie Lodge *Highld* 130 0910
Clubworthy *Cnwll* 5 2792
Clugston *D & G* 98 3557
Clun *Shrops* 59 3080
Clunas *Highld* 140 8846
Clunbury *Shrops* 59 3780
Clune *Highld* 140 7925
Clunes *Highld* 131 1988
Clungunford *Shrops* 46 3978
Clunie *Abers* 142 6350
Clunie *P & K* 126 1043
Clunton *Shrops* 59 3381
Clutton *Ches* 71 4654
Clutton *Somset* 21 6259
Clutton Hill *Somset* 21 6359
Clwt-y-bont *Gwynd* 69 5762
Clydach *Mons* 34 2213
Clydach *Swans* 32 6800
Clydach Vale *Rhondd* 33 9792
Clydebank *W Duns* 115 4970
Clydey *Pembks* 31 2535
Clyffe Pypard *Wilts* 36 0777
Clynder *Ag & B* 114 2484
Clynderwen *Carmth* 31 1219
Clyne *Neath* 32 8000
Clynnog-fawr *Gwynd* 68 4149
Clyro *Powys* 45 2143
Clyst Honiton *Devon* 9 9893
Clyst Hydon *Devon* 9 0301
Clyst St George *Devon* 9 9888
Clyst St Lawrence *Devon* 9 0200
Clyst St Mary *Devon* 9 9791
Cnoc *W Isls* 152 4931
Cnwch Coch *Cerdgn* 43 6774
Coad's Green *Cnwll* 5 2976
Coal Aston *Derbys* 74 3679
Coal Pool *W Mids* 60 0199
Coal Street *Suffk* 55 2371
Coalbrookdale *Shrops* 60 6604
Coalbrookvale *Blae G* 33 1909
Coalburn *S Lans* 108 8134
Coalburns *T & W* 96 1260
Coalcleugh *Nthumb* 95 8045
Coaley *Gloucs* 35 7701
Coalfell *Cumb* 94 5959
Coalhill *Essex* 40 7597
Coalmoor *Shrops* 60 6607
Coalpit Heath *Gloucs* 35 6780
Coalpit Hill *Staffs* 72 8253
Coalport *Shrops* 60 6902
Coalsnaughton *Clacks* 116 9195
Coaltown of Balgonie *Fife* 117 2999
Coaltown of Wemyss *Fife* 118 3295
Coalville *Leics* 62 4214
Coanwood *Nthumb* 94 6859
Coat *Somset* 21 4520
Coatbridge *N Lans* 116 7365
Coatdyke *N Lans* 116 7465
Coate *Wilts* 23 0462
Coate *Wilts* 36 1882
Coates *Cambs* 64 3097
Coates *Gloucs* 35 9701
Coates *Lincs* 75 8181
Coates *Lincs* 76 9083
Coates *W Susx* 14 9917
Cotham *N York* 97 5925
Cotham Mundeville *Dur* 96 2820
Cobbaton *Devon* 19 6126
Coberley *Gloucs* 35 9616
Cobhall Common *Herefd* 46 4535
Cobham *Kent* 28 6768
Cobham *Surrey* 26 1060
Coblers Green *Essex* 40 6819
Cobley *Dorset* 12 0220

Cobnash Courteachan


Cobnash Herefd 46 4560
Cobo Guern 158 0000
Cobridge Staffs 72 8747
Coburby Abers 143 9164
Cock & End Suffk 53 7253
Cock Alley Derbys 74 4170
Cock Bank Wrexhm 71 3545
Cock Bevington Warwks 48 0552
Cock Bridge Abers 133 2509
Cock Clarks Essex 40 8102
Cock Green Essex 40 6919
Cock Marling E Susx 17 8718
Cock Street Kent 28 7850
Cockayne N York 90 6198
Cockayne Hatley Beds 52 2649
Cockburnspath Border 119 7770
Cockenzie and Port Seton E Loth 118 4075
Cocker Bar Lancs 80 5022
Cocker Brook Lancs 81 7425
Cockerham Lancs 80 4651
Cockermouth Cumb 92 1230
Cockernhoe Green Herts 38 1223
Cockersdale W York 82 2329
Cockett Swans 32 6394
Cockfield Dur 96 1224
Cockfield Suffk 54 9054
Cockfosters Gt Lon 27 2796
Cocking W Susx 14 8717
Cocking Causeway W Susx 14 8819
Cockington Devon 7 8963
Cocklake Somset 21 4449
Cockle Park Nthumb 103 2091
Cockley Beck Cumb 86 2501
Cockley Cley Norfk 66 7904
Cockpole Green Berks 37 7981
Cocks Cnwll 3 7652
Cockshutford Shrops 59 5885
Cockshutt Shrops 59 4328
Cockthorpe Norfk 66 9842
Cockwells Cnwll 2 5234
Cockwood Devon 9 9780
Cockwood Somset 20 2242
Cockyard Derbys 74 0479
Cockyard Herefd 46 4133
Coddenham Suffk 54 1354
Coddington Ches 71 4555
Coddington Herefd 47 7142
Coddington Notts 76 8354
Codford St Mary Wilts 22 9739
Codford St Peter Wilts 22 9639
Codicote Herts 39 2118
Codmore Hill W Susx 14 0520
Codnor Derbys 74 4149
Codrington Gloucs 35 7278
Codsall Staffs 60 8603
Codsall Wood Staffs 60 8404
Coed Morgan Mons 34 3511
Coed Talon Flints 70 2659
Coed Ystumgwern Gwynd 57 5824
Coed-y-Bryn Cerdgn 42 3545
Coed-y-caerau Newpt 34 3891
Coed-y-paen Mons 34 3398
Coed-yr-ynys Powys 33 1520
Coedana IOA 68 4382
Coedely Rhondd 33 0285
Coedkernew Newpt 34 2783
Coedpoeth Wrexhm 70 2851
Coedway Powys 59 3315
Coelbren Powys 33 8511
Coffinswell Devon 7 8968
Coffle End Beds 51 0159
Cofton Devon 9 9680
Cofton Hackett Worcs 60 0075
Cogan V Glam 33 1771
Cogenhoe Nhants 51 8260
Cogges Oxon 36 3609
Coggeshall Essex 40 8522
Coggin's Mill E Susx 16 5927
Coignafearn Highld 140 7018
Coilacriech Abers 134 3296
Coilantogle Stirlg 124 5907
Coillore Highld 136 3537
Coiltry Highld 131 3506
Coity Brdgnd 33 9281
Col W Isls 152 4739
Colaboll Highld 146 5610
Colan Cnwll 4 8661
Colaton Raleigh Devon 9 0787
Colbost Highld 136 2148
Colburn N York 89 1999
Colbury Hants 12 3410
Colby Cumb 94 6620
Colby IOM 158 2370
Colby Norfk 67 2231
Colchester Essex 41 9925
Cold Ash Berks 24 5169
Cold Ashby Nhants 50 6576
Cold Ashton Gloucs 35 7572
Cold Aston Gloucs 36 1219
Cold Blow Pembks 31 1212
Cold Brayfield Bucks 38 9252
Cold Cotes N York 88 7171
Cold Green Herefd 47 6842
Cold Hanworth Lincs 76 0383
Cold Harbour Herts 38 1415
Cold Harbour Oxon 37 6379
Cold Harbour Wilts 22 8645
Cold Hatton Shrops 59 6221
Cold Hatton Heath Shrops 59 6321
Cold Hesledon Dur 96 4146
Cold Hiendley W York 83 3714
Cold Higham Nhants 49 6653
Cold Kirby N York 90 5384
Cold Newton Leics 63 7106
Cold Northcott Cnwll 5 2086
Cold Norton Essex 40 8500
Cold Overton Leics 63 8010
Cold Weston Shrops 59 5583
Coldbackie Highld 149 6160
Coldbeck Cumb 88 7204
Coldean E Susx 15 3308
Coldeast Devon 7 8174
Colden W York 82 9628
Colden Common Hants 13 4822
Coldfair Green Suffk 55 4360
Coldham Cambs 65 4303
Coldharbour Cnwll 3 7548
Coldharbour Devon 9 0612
Coldharbour Gloucs 34 5503
Coldharbour Surrey 15 1443
Coldingham Border 119 9065
Coldmeece Staffs 72 8532
Coldred Kent 29 2747
Coldridge Devon 8 6907
Coldstream Border 110 8439
Coldwaltham W Susx 14 0216
Coldwell Herefd 46 4235
Coldwells Abers 143 9538
Cole Somset 22 6733
Cole End Warwks 61 2089
Cole Green Herts 39 2811
Cole Green Herts 39 4330
Cole Henley Hants 24 4651
Cole's Cross Devon 7 7746
Colebatch Shrops 59 3187
Colebrook Devon 9 0006
Colebrook Devon 6 5457
Colebrooke Devon 8 7699
Coleby Lincs 84 8919
Coleby Lincs 76 9760
Coleford Devon 8 7701
Coleford Gloucs 34 5710
Coleford Somset 22 6848
Coleford Water Somset 20 1133
Colegate End Norfk 55 1987
Colehill Dorset 12 0201
Coleman Green Herts 39 1812
Coleman's Hatch E Susx 16 4433
Colemere Shrops 59 4332
Colemore Hants 24 7030
Colemore Green Shrops 60 7197
Colenden P & K 126 1029
Coleorton Leics 62 4017
Colerne Wilts 35 8271
Coles Cross Dorset 10 3902
Coles Green Suffk 54 1041
Colesbourne Gloucs 35 0013
Colesden Beds 52 1255
Coleshill Bucks 26 9495
Coleshill Oxon 36 2393
Coleshill Warwks 61 2089
Colestocks Devon 9 0900
Coley Somset 21 5855
Colgate W Susx 15 2332
Colgrain Ag & B 115 3280
Colinsburgh Fife 127 4703
Colinton C Edin 117 2168
Colintraive Ag & B 114 0374
Colkirk Norfk 66 9126
Collace P & K 126 2032
Collafirth Shet 153 3482
Collaton Devon 7 7139
Collaton Devon 7 7952
Collaton St Mary Devon 7 8660
College Green Somset 21 5736
College of Roseisle Moray 141 1466
College Town Berks 25 8560
Collessie Fife 126 2813
Colleton Mills Devon 19 6615
Collier Row Gt Lon 27 5091
Collier Street Kent 28 7145
Collier's End Herts 39 3720
Collier's Green Kent 17 7822
Colliers Green Kent 28 7538
Colliery Row T & W 96 3249
Collieston Abers 143 0328
Collin D & G 100 0276
Collingbourne Ducis Wilts 23 2453
Collingbourne Kingston Wilts 23 2355
Collingham Notts 76 8262
Collingham W York 83 3945
Collington Herefd 47 6460
Collingtree Nhants 49 7555
Collins Green Ches 78 5594
Collins Green Worcs 47 7457
Colliston Angus 127 6045
Colliton Devon 9 0804
Collyweston Nhants 63 9902
Colmonell S Ayrs 98 1485
Colmworth Beds 51 1058
Coln Rogers Gloucs 36 0809
Coln St Aldwyns Gloucs 36 1405
Coln St Dennis Gloucs 36 0810
Colnbrook Berks 26 0277
Colne Cambs 52 3775
Colne Lancs 81 8939
Colne Bridge W York 82 1720
Colne Edge Lancs 81 8841
Colne Engaine Essex 40 8430
Colney Norfk 66 1807
Colney Heath Herts 39 2005
Colney Street Herts 26 1502
Colpy Abers 142 6432
Colquhar Border 109 3341
Colquite Cnwll 4 0570
Colscott Devon 18 3614
Colsterdale N York 89 1381
Colsterworth Lincs 63 9324
Colston Bassett Notts 63 7033
Colt Hill Hants 24 7551
Colt's Hill Kent 16 6443
Coltfield Moray 141 1163
Coltishall Norfk 67 2719
Colton Cumb 86 3185
Colton N York 83 5444
Colton Norfk 66 1009
Colton Staffs 73 0420
Colton W York 83 3732
Columbjohn Devon 9 9699
Colva Powys 45 1952
Colvend D & G 92 8654
Colwall Herefd 47 7542
Colwell Nthumb 102 9575
Colwich Staffs 73 0121
Colwick Notts 62 6140
Colwinston V Glam 33 9375
Colworth W Susx 14 9103
Colwyn Bay Conwy 69 8578
Colyford Devon 10 2592
Colyton Devon 9 2494
Combe Berks 23 3760
Combe Devon 7 7238
Combe Devon 7 8448
Combe Herefd 46 3463
Combe Oxon 36 4116
Combe Almer Dorset 11 9597
Combe Common Surrey 14 9436
Combe Down Somset 22 7662
Combe Fishacre Devon 7 8465
Combe Florey Somset 20 1531
Combe Hay Somset 22 7359
Combe Martin Devon 19 5846
Combe Moor Herefd 46 3663
Combe Raleigh Devon 9 1502
Combe St Nicholas Somset 10 3011
Combeinteignhead Devon 7 9071
Comberbach Ches 79 6477
Comberford Staffs 61 1907
Comberton Cambs 52 3856
Comberton Herefd 46 4968
Combpyne Devon 10 2892
Combridge Staffs 73 0937
Combrook Warwks 48 3051
Combs Derbys 74 0478
Combs Suffk 54 0456
Combs Ford Suffk 54 0457
Combwich Somset 20 2542
Comers Abers 135 6707
Comhampton Worcs 47 8367
Commercial Pembks 31 1416
Commercial End Cambs 53 5563
Commins Coch Powys 57 8402
Common Edge Lancs 80 3232
Common End Cumb 92 0022
Common Moor Cnwll 5 2469
Common Platt Wilts 36 1186
Common Side Derbys 74 3375
Commondale N York 90 6610
Commonside Ches 71 5473
Commonside Derbys 73 2441
Commonwood Shrops 59 4828
Commonwood Wrexhm 71 3753
Compass Somset 20 2934
Compstall Gt Man 79 9690
Compstonend D & G 99 6652
Compton Berks 37 5280
Compton Devon 7 8664
Compton Hants 23 3529
Compton Hants 13 4625
Compton Staffs 60 8284
Compton Surrey 25 9546
Compton W Susx 14 7714
Compton Wilts 23 1351
Compton Abbas Dorset 22 8618
Compton Abdale Gloucs 36 0516
Compton Bassett Wilts 36 0372
Compton Beauchamp Oxon 36 2786
Compton Bishop Somset 21 3955
Compton Chamberlayne Wilts 23 0229
Compton Dando Somset 21 6464
Compton Dundon Somset 21 4932
Compton Durville Somset 10 4117
Compton Greenfield Gloucs 34 5681
Compton Martin Somset 21 5457
Compton Pauncefoot Somset 21 6426
Compton Valence Dorset 10 5993
Compton Verney Warwks 48 3152
Comrie Fife 117 0289
Comrie P & K 124 7722
Conaglen House Highld 130 0268
Conchra Highld 138 8827
Concraigie P & K 125 0944
Conder Green Lancs 80 4556
Conderton Worcs 47 9637
Condicote Gloucs 48 1528
Condorrat N Lans 116 7373
Condover Shrops 59 4905
Coney Hill Gloucs 35 8517
Coney Weston Suffk 54 9578
Coneyhurst Common W Susx 14 1023
Coneysthorpe N York 90 7171
Coneythorpe W York 89 3958
Conford Hants 14 8233
Congdon's Shop Cnwll 5 2878
Congerstone Leics 62 3605
Congham Norfk 65 7123
Conghurst Kent 17 7628
Congl-y-wal Gwynd 57 7044
Congleton Ches 72 8562
Congresbury Somset 21 4363
Congreve Staffs 60 9013
Conheath D & G 100 9969
Conicavel Moray 140 9853
Coningsby Lincs 76 2257
Conington Cambs 52 1885
Conington Cambs 52 3266
Conisbrough S York 75 5098
Conisholme Lincs 77 4095
Coniston Cumb 86 3097
Coniston E R Yk 85 1535
Coniston Cold N York 81 9054
Conistone N York 88 9867
Connah's Quay Flints 71 2969
Connel Ag & B 122 9134
Connel Park E Ayrs 107 6012
Connor Downs Cnwll 2 5939
Conon Bridge Highld 139 5455
Cononley N York 82 9846
Consall Staffs 72 9848
Consett Dur 95 1051
Constable Burton N York 89 1690
Constable Lee Lancs 81 8123
Constantine Cnwll 3 7329
Constantine Bay Cnwll 4 8774
Contin Highld 139 4556
Conwy Conwy 69 7877
Conyer Kent 28 9664
Conyer's Green Suffk 54 8867
Cooden E Susx 17 7107
Cook's Green Essex 41 1818
Cookbury Devon 18 4006
Cookbury Wick Devon 18 3905
Cookham Berks 26 8985
Cookham Dean Berks 26 8685
Cookham Rise Berks 26 8885
Cookhill Warwks 48 0558
Cookley Suffk 55 3475
Cookley Worcs 60 8480
Cookley Green Oxon 37 6990
Cookney Abers 135 8693
Cooks Green Suffk 54 9753
Cooksbridge E Susx 15 4013
Cooksey Green Worcs 47 9069
Cookshill Staffs 72 9443
Cooksland Cnwll 4 0867
Cooksmill Green Essex 40 6306
Cookson Green Ches 71 5774
Cookson's Green Dur 96 2933
Coolham W Susx 14 1122
Cooling Kent 28 7575
Cooling Street Kent 28 7474
Coombe Cnwll 2 6242
Coombe Cnwll 3 8340
Coombe Devon 8 8384
Coombe Devon 7 9373
Coombe Devon 9 1091
Coombe Gloucs 35 7694
Coombe Hants 13 6620
Coombe Wilts 23 1450
Coombe Bissett Wilts 23 1026
Coombe Cellars Devon 7 9072
Coombe Cross Hants 13 6620
Coombe End Somset 20 0329
Coombe Hill Gloucs 47 8826
Coombe Keynes Dorset 11 8484
Coombe Pafford Devon 7 9166
Coombe Street Somset 22 7631
Coombes W Susx 15 1808
Coombeswood W Mids 60 9785
Cooper Street Kent 29 3060
Cooper Turning Gt Man 79 6308
Cooper's Corner Kent 16 4849
Cooperhill Moray 141 9953
Coopers Green E Susx 16 4723
Coopers Green Herts 39 1909
Coopersale Common Essex 27 4702
Coopersale Street Essex 27 4701
Cootham W Susx 14 0714
Cop Street Kent 27 2959
Copdock Suffk 54 1242
Copford Green Essex 40 9222
Copgrove N York 89 3463
Copister Shet 153 4879
Cople Beds 38 1048
Copley Dur 95 0825
Copley Gt Man 79 9798
Copley W York 82 0822
Coplow Dale Derbys 74 1679
Copmanthorpe N York 83 5646
Copmere End Staffs 72 8029
Copp Lancs 80 4239
Coppathorne Cnwll 18 2000
Coppenhall Staffs 72 9019
Coppenhall Moss Ches 72 7058
Copperhouse Cnwll 2 5637
Coppicegate Shrops 60 7379
Coppingford Cambs 52 1679
Coppins Corner Kent 28 9448
Copplestone Devon 8 7702
Coppull Lancs 81 5614
Coppull Moor Lancs 81 5512
Copsale W Susx 15 1724
Copster Green Lancs 81 6733
Copston Magna Warwks 50 4588
Copt Heath W Mids 61 1777
Copt Hewick N York 89 3471
Copt Oak Leics 62 4812
Copthall Green Essex 27 4201
Copthorne Cnwll 5 2692
Copthorne W Susx 15 3139
Copy's Green Norfk 66 9439
Copythorne Hants 12 3014
Coram Street Suffk 54 0042
Corbets Tey Gt Lon 27 5685
Corbiere Jersey 158 0000
Corbridge Nthumb 103 9964
Corby Nhants 51 8988
Corby Glen Lincs 63 0024
Corby Hill Cumb 94 4857
Cordon N Ayrs 105 0230
Cordwell Derbys 74 3176
Coreley Shrops 46 6173
Cores End Bucks 26 9087
Corfe Somset 20 2319
Corfe Castle Dorset 11 9681
Corfe Mullen Dorset 11 9896
Corfton Shrops 59 4985
Corgarff Abers 133 2708
Corhampton Hants 13 6120
Corks Pond Kent 28 6540
Corley Warwks 61 3085
Corley Ash Warwks 61 2986
Corley Moor Warwks 61 2884
Cormuir Angus 134 3066
Cornard Tye Suffk 54 9041
Corndon Devon 8 6985
Corner Row Lancs 80 4134
Corney Cumb 86 1191
Cornforth Dur 96 3134
Cornhill Abers 142 5858
Cornhill-on-Tweed Nthumb 110 8639
Cornholme W York 81 9126
Cornish Hall End Essex 53 6836
Cornoigmore Ag & B 120 9846
Cornriggs Dur 95 8441
Cornsay Dur 96 1443
Cornsay Colliery Dur 96 1643
Corntown Highld 139 5556
Corntown V Glam 33 9177
Cornwell Oxon 48 2727
Cornwood Devon 6 6059
Cornworthy Devon 7 8255
Corpach Highld 130 0976
Corpusty Norfk 66 1129
Corrachree Abers 134 4604
Corran Cnwll 3 9946
Corran Highld 130 8409
Corran Highld 130 0263
Corrany IOM 158 4589
Corrie D & G 101 2086
Corrie N Ayrs 105 0242
Corriecravie N Ayrs 105 9223
Corriegills N Ayrs 105 0335
Corriegour Lodge Hotel Highld 131 2692
Corriemoille Highld 139 3663
Corrimony Highld 139 3730
Corringham Essex 40 7083
Corringham Lincs 76 8691
Corris Gwynd 57 7508
Corris Uchaf Gwynd 57 7408
Corrow Ag & B 114 1800
Corry Highld 137 6424
Cors-y-Gedol Gwynd 57 6022
Corscombe Devon 8 6296
Corscombe Dorset 10 5105
Corse Gloucs 47 7826
Corse Lawn Gloucs 47 8330
Corsham Wilts 35 8770
Corsindae Abers 135 6808
Corsley Wilts 22 8246
Corsley Heath Wilts 22 8245
Corsock D & G 99 7576
Corston Somset 22 6965
Corston Wilts 35 9283
Corstorphine C Edin 117 1972
Cortachy Angus 134 3959
Corton Suffk 67 5497
Corton Wilts 22 9340
Corton Denham Somset 21 6322
Coruanan Lodge Highld 130 0668
Corwen Denbgs 70 0743
Coryates Dorset 10 6285
Coryton Devon 5 4583
Coryton Essex 40 7382
Cosby Leics 50 5495
Coseley W Mids 60 9494
Cosford Shrops 60 8005
Cosgrove Nhants 38 7942
Cosham Hants 13 6505
Cosheston Pembks 30 0003
Coshieville P & K 124 7749
Cossall Notts 62 4842
Cossall Marsh Notts 62 4842
Cossington Leics 62 6013
Cossington Somset 21 3540
Costessey Norfk 66 1711
Costock Notts 62 5726
Coston Leics 63 8422
Coston Norfk 66 0506
Cote Oxon 36 3502
Cote Somset 21 3444
Cotebrook Ches 71 5765
Cotehill Cumb 93 4650
Cotes Cumb 87 4886
Cotes Leics 62 5520
Cotes Staffs 72 8434
Cotes Heath Staffs 72 8334
Cotesbach Leics 50 5382
Cotgrave Notts 63 6435
Cothal Abers 143 8715
Cotham Notts 63 7947
Cothelstone Somset 20 1831
Cotherstone Dur 95 0119
Cothill Oxon 37 4699
Cotleigh Devon 9 2002
Cotmanhay Derbys 62 4543
Coton Cambs 52 4058
Coton Nhants 50 6771
Coton Shrops 59 5334
Coton Staffs 72 8120
Coton Staffs 72 9731
Coton Staffs 61 1804
Coton Clanford Staffs 72 8723
Coton Hayes Staffs 72 9832
Coton Hill Shrops 59 4813
Coton in the Clay Staffs 73 1628
Coton in the Elms Derbys 73 2415
Coton Park Derbys 73 2617
Cott Devon 7 7861
Cottage End Hants 24 4143
Cottam E R Yk 91 9964
Cottam Lancs 80 5032
Cottam Notts 75 8179
Cottenham Cambs 53 4467
Cotterdale N York 88 8393
Cottered Herts 39 3129
Cotteridge W Mids 61 0480
Cotterstock Nhants 51 0490
Cottesbrooke Nhants 50 7173
Cottesmore Rutlnd 63 9013
Cottingham E R Yk 84 0432
Cottingham Nhants 51 8490
Cottingley W York 82 1137
Cottisford Oxon 49 5831
Cottivett Cnwll 5 3662
Cotton Suffk 54 0666
Cotton End Beds 38 0845
Cotton Tree Lancs 81 9039
Cottown Abers 142 5026
Cottown Abers 142 7615
Cottown of Gight Abers 143 8140
Cottrell V Glam 33 0774
Cotts Devon 6 4365
Cotwall Shrops 59 6017
Cotwalton Staffs 72 9234
Couch's Mill Cnwll 4 1459
Coughton Herefd 34 5921
Coughton Warwks 48 0860
Coulaghailtro Ag & B 113 7165
Coulags Highld 138 9645
Coulderton Cumb 86 9808
Coull Abers 134 5102
Coulport Ag & B 114 2187
Coulsdon Gt Lon 27 2959
Coulston Wilts 22 9554
Coulter S Lans 108 0234
Coultershaw Bridge W Susx 14 9719
Coultings Somset 20 2241
Coulton N York 90 6373
Coultra Fife 126 3523
Cound Shrops 59 5505
Coundlane Shrops 59 5705
Coundon Dur 96 2329
Coundon Grange Dur 96 2228
Countersett N York 88 9187
Countess Wilts 23 1542
Countess Cross Essex 40 8631
Countess Wear Devon 9 9489
Countesthorpe Leics 50 5895
Countisbury Devon 19 7449
Coup Green Lancs 81 5927
Coupar Angus P & K 126 2239
Coupland Cumb 94 7118
Coupland Nthumb 110 9330
Cour Ag & B 105 8248
Courance D & G 100 0590
Court Henry Carmth 32 5522
Court-at-Street Kent 17 0935
Courteachan Highld 129 6897

Courteenhall Culross


Courteenhall Nhants 49 7653
Courtsend Essex 41 0293
Courtway Somset 20 2033
Cousland Mdloth 118 3768
Cousley Wood E Susx 16 6533
Cove Ag & B 114 2282
Cove Border 119 7771
Cove Devon 20 9619
Cove Hants 25 8555
Cove Highld 144 8191
Cove Bay Aber C 135 9501
Cove Bottom Suffk 55 4979
Covehithe Suffk 55 5282
Coven Staffs 60 9106
Coven Lawn Staffs 60 9005
Coveney Cambs 53 4882
Covenham St Bartholomew Lincs 77 3394
Covenham St Mary Lincs 77 3394
Coventry W Mids 61 3378
Coverack Cnwll 3 7818
Coverack Bridges Cnwll 2 6630
Coverham N York 89 1086
Covington Cambs 51 0570
Covington S Lans 108 9739
Cow Green Suffk 54 0565
Cow Honeybourne Worcs 48 1143
Cowan Bridge Lancs 87 6376
Cowbeech E Susx 16 6114
Cowbit Lincs 64 2518
Cowbridge V Glam 33 9974
Cowdale Derbys 74 0771
Cowden Kent 16 4640
Cowden Pound Kent 16 4642
Cowden Station Kent 16 4741
Cowdenbeath Fife 117 1691
Cowers Lane Derbys 73 3046
Cowes IOW 13 4996
Cowesby N York 89 4689
Cowesfield Green Wilts 23 2523
Cowfold W Susx 15 2122
Cowgill Cumb 88 7586
Cowhill Gloucs 34 6091
Cowie Stirlg 116 8389
Cowlam E R Yk 91 9665
Cowley Derbys 74 3376
Cowley Devon 9 9095
Cowley Gloucs 35 9614
Cowley Gt Lon 26 0582
Cowley Oxon 37 5304
Cowley Oxon 49 6628
Cowling Lancs 81 5917
Cowling N York 82 9643
Cowling N York 89 2387
Cowlinge Suffk 53 7154
Cowmes W York 82 1815
Cowpe Lancs 81 8320
Cowpen Nthumb 103 2981
Cowpen Bewley Dur 97 4824
Cowplain Hants 13 6810
Cowshill Dur 95 8540
Cowslip Green Somset 21 4861
Cowthorpe N York 83 4252
Cox Common Suffk 55 4082
Coxall Shrops 46 3774
Coxbank Ches 72 6541
Coxbench Derbys 62 3743
Coxbridge Somset 21 5436
Coxford Cnwll 4 1696
Coxford Norfk 66 8529
Coxgreen Staffs 60 8086
Coxheath Kent 28 7451
Coxhoe Dur 96 3136
Coxley Somset 21 5343
Coxley W York 82 2717
Coxley Wick Somset 21 5243
Coxpark Cnwll 5 4072
Coxtie Green Essex 27 5696
Coxwold N York 90 5377
Coychurch Brdgnd 33 9379
Coylton S Ayrs 107 4219
Coylumbridge Highld 132 9111
Coytrahen Brdgnd 33 8885
Crab Orchard Dorset 12 0806
Crabbs Cross Worcs 48 0465
Crabtree W Susx 15 2125
Crabtree Green Wrexhm 71 3344
Crackenthorpe Cumb 94 6622
Crackington Haven Cnwll 4 1496
Crackley Staffs 72 8350
Crackley Warwks 61 2973
Crackleybank Shrops 60 7611
Crackpot N York 88 9796
Cracoe N York 88 9760
Craddock Devon 9 0812
Cradle End Herts 39 4521
Cradley Herefd 47 7347
Cradley W Mids 60 9485
Cradoc Powys 45 0130
Crafthole Cnwll 5 3654
Crafton Bucks 38 8819
Crag Foot Lancs 87 4873
Cragg Hill W York 82 2437
Cragg Vale W York 82 0023
Craggan Highld 141 0226
Craghead Dur 96 2150
Crai Powys 45 8924
Craibstone Moray 142 4959
Craichie Angus 127 5047
Craig Angus 127 6956
Craig Highld 138 0349
Craig Llangiwg Neath 32 7204
Craig Penllyn V Glam 33 9777
Craig's End Essex 53 7137
Craig-y-Duke Neath 32 7002
Craig-y-nos Powys 33 8415
Craigbank E Ayrs 107 5911
Craigburn Border 117 2354
Craigcefnparc Swans 32 6702
Craigcleuch D & G 101 3486
Craigdam Abers 143 8430
Craigdarroch D & G 107 7391
Craigdhu Ag & B 122 8205
Craigearn Abers 142 7214
Craigellachie Moray 141 2844
Craigend P & K 126 1120
Craigend Rens 115 4670
Craigendoran Ag & B 115 3181
Craighlaw D & G 98 3061
Craighouse Ag & B 113 5267
Craigie P & K 126 1143
Craigie S Ayrs 107 4232
Craigiefold Abers 143 9165
Craigley D & G 99 7658
Craiglockhart C Edin 117 2271
Craiglug Moray 141 3355
Craigmillar C Edin 117 3071
Craignant Shrops 58 2535
Craigneston D & G 107 7587
Craigneuk N Lans 116 7765
Craigneuk N Lans 116 7756
Craignure Ag & B 122 7236
Craigo Angus 135 6864
Craigrothie Fife 126 3810
Craigruie Stirlg 124 4920
Craigton Aber C 135 8301
Craigton Angus 127 5138
Craigton E Rens 115 4954
Craigton of Airlie Angus 126 3250
Crail Fife 127 6107
Crailing Border 110 6824
Craiselound Lincs 75 7698
Crakehall N York 89 2489
Crakehill N York 89 4273
Crakemarsh Staffs 73 0936
Crambe N York 90 7364
Cramlington Nthumb 103 2676
Cramond C Edin 117 1976
Cramond Bridge C Edin 117 1775
Cranage Ches 79 7568
Cranberry Staffs 72 8235
Cranborne Dorset 12 0513
Cranbrook Kent 28 7736
Cranbrook Common Kent 28 7838
Crane Moor S York 82 3001
Crane's Corner Norfk 66 9113
Cranfield Beds 38 9542
Cranford Devon 18 3421
Cranford Gt Lon 26 1076
Cranford St Andrew Nhants 51 9277
Cranford St John Nhants 51 9276
Cranham Gloucs 35 8913
Cranham Gt Lon 27 5787
Cranhill Warwks 48 1253
Crank Mersyd 78 5099
Cranleigh Surrey 14 0539
Cranmer Green Suffk 54 0171
Cranmore IOW 13 3990
Cranmore Somset 22 6643
Cranoe Leics 50 7695
Cransford Suffk 55 3164
Cranshaws Border 118 6861
Cranstal IOM 158 4602
Cranswick E R Yk 84 0252
Crantock Cnwll 4 7960
Cranwell Lincs 76 0349
Cranwich Norfk 65 7794
Cranworth Norfk 66 9804
Craobh Haven Ag & B 122 7907
Crapstone Devon 6 5067
Crarae Ag & B 114 9897
Crask Inn Highld 149 5224
Crask of Aigas Highld 139 4642
Craster Nthumb 111 2519
Craswall Herefd 46 2735
Crateford Staffs 60 9009
Cratfield Suffk 55 3175
Crathes Abers 135 7596
Crathie Abers 133 2695
Crathie Highld 132 5793
Crathorne N York 89 4407
Craven Arms Shrops 59 4382
Crawcrook T & W 103 1363
Crawford Lancs 78 4902
Crawford S Lans 108 9520
Crawfordjohn S Lans 108 8823
Crawick D & G 107 7811
Crawley Hants 24 4235
Crawley Oxon 36 3412
Crawley W Susx 15 2636
Crawley Down W Susx 15 3437
Crawley Side Dur 95 9940
Crawshawbooth Lancs 81 8125
Crawton Abers 135 8779
Craxe's Green Essex 40 9419
Cray N York 88 9479
Cray's Pond Oxon 37 6380
Crayford Gt Lon 27 5175
Crayke N York 90 5670
Craymere Beck Norfk 66 0631
Crays Hill Essex 40 7192
Craythorne Staffs 73 2426
Craze Lowman Devon 9 9814
Crazies Hill Oxon 37 7980
Creacombe Devon 18 3219
Creag Ghoraidh W Isls 152 7948
Creagan Inn Ag & B 122 9744
Creagorry W Isls 152 7948
Creaguaineach Lodge Highld 131 3068
Creamore Bank Shrops 59 5130
Creaton Nhants 50 7071
Creca D & G 101 2270
Credenhill Herefd 46 4543
Crediton Devon 8 8300
Creebank D & G 98 3477
Creebridge D & G 99 4165
Creech Heathfield Somset 20 2727
Creech St Michael Somset 20 2725
Creed Cnwll 3 9347
Creedy Park Devon 8 8301
Creekmouth Gt Lon 27 4581
Creeting St Mary Suffk 54 0956
Creeton Lincs 64 0120
Creetown D & G 99 4759
Cregneash IOM 158 1867
Cregrina Powys 45 1252
Creich Fife 126 3221
Creigiau Cardif 33 0781
Crelly Cnwll 2 6732
Cremyll Cnwll 6 4553
Cressage Shrops 59 5904
Cressbrook Derbys 74 1673
Cresselly Pembks 30 0606
Cressex Bucks 26 8492
Cressing Essex 40 7920
Cresswell Nthumb 103 2993
Cresswell Pembks 30 0506
Cresswell Staffs 72 9739
Creswell Derbys 75 5274
Creswell Green Staffs 61 0710
Cretingham Suffk 55 2260
Cretshengan Ag & B 113 7166
Crew Green Powys 59 3215
Crewe Ches 71 4253
Crewe Ches 72 7056
Crewe Green Ches 72 7255
Crewkerne Somset 10 4409
Crews Hill Herefd 35 6722
Crews Hill Station Herts 27 3000
Crewton Derbys 62 3733
Crianlarich Stirlg 123 3825
Cribbs Causeway Gloucs 34 5780
Cribyn Cerdgn 44 5250
Criccieth Gwynd 56 4938
Crich Derbys 74 3454
Crich Carr Derbys 74 3354
Crich Common Derbys 74 3553
Crichton Mdloth 118 3862
Crick Mons 34 4890
Crick Nhants 50 5872
Crickadarn Powys 45 0942
Cricket St Thomas Somset 10 3708
Crickheath Shrops 59 2922
Crickhowell Powys 33 2118
Cricklade Wilts 36 0993
Cricklewood Gt Lon 26 2385
Cridling Stubbs N York 83 5221
Crieff P & K 125 8621
Criggan Cnwll 4 0160
Criggion Powys 59 2915
Crigglestone W York 82 3116
Crimble Gt Man 81 8611
Crimond Abers 143 0556
Crimonmogate Abers 143 0358
Crimplesham Norfk 65 6503
Crimscote Warwks 48 2347
Crinaglack Highld 139 4340
Crinan Ag & B 113 7894
Crindledyke N Lans 116 8356
Cringleford Norfk 67 1905
Cringles N York 82 0448
Crinow Pembks 31 1214
Cripp's Corner E Susx 17 7721
Cripplesease Cnwll 2 5036
Cripplestyle Dorset 12 0812
Crizeley Herefd 46 4532
Croachy Highld 140 6527
Croanford Cnwll 4 0371
Crochmore House D & G 100 8977
Crock Street Somset 10 3213
Crockenhill Kent 27 5067
Crocker End Oxon 37 7086
Crocker's Ash Herefd 34 5316
Crockerhill W Susx 14 9206
Crockernwell Devon 8 7592
Crockerton Wilts 22 8642
Crocketford D & G 100 8372
Crockey Hill N York 83 6246
Crockham Hill Kent 27 4450
Crockhurst Street Kent 16 6245
Crockleford Heath Essex 41 0426
Croes-goch Pembks 30 8330
Croes-lan Cerdgn 42 3844
Croes-y-mwyalch Torfn 34 3092
Croes-y-pant Mons 34 3104
Croeserw Neath 33 8795
Croesor Gwynd 57 6344
Croesyceiliog Carmth 31 4016
Croesyceiliog Torfn 34 3096
Croft Ches 79 6393
Croft Devon 5 5296
Croft Leics 50 5195
Croft Lincs 77 5061
Croft Michael Cnwll 2 6637
Croft-on-Tees Dur 89 2809
Croftamie Stirlg 115 4785
Crofton Cumb 93 3050
Crofton W York 83 3817
Crofton Wilts 23 2562
Crofts D & G 99 7365
Crofts Moray 141 2850
Crofts Bank Gt Man 79 7695
Crofts of Dipple Moray 141 3259
Crofts of Savoch Abers 143 0460
Crofty Swans 32 5294
Crogen Gwynd 58 0036
Croggan Ag & B 122 7027
Croglin Cumb 94 5747
Croik Highld 146 4591
Cromarty Highld 140 7867
Crombie Fife 117 0584
Cromdale Highld 141 0728
Cromer Herts 39 2928
Cromer Norfk 67 2242
Cromford Derbys 73 2956
Cromhall Gloucs 35 6990
Cromhall Common Gloucs 35 6989
Cromor W Isls 152 4021
Crompton Fold Gt Man 79 9409
Cromwell Notts 75 7961
Cronberry E Ayrs 107 6022
Crondall Hants 25 7948
Cronk-y-Voddy IOM 158 3085
Cronkbourne IOM 158 3677
Cronton Mersyd 78 4988
Crook Cumb 87 4695
Crook Dur 96 1635
Crook Inn Border 108 1026
Crook of Devon P & K 117 0400
Crookdake Cumb 93 1943
Crooke Gt Man 78 5507
Crooked End Gloucs 35 6217
Crooked Holme Cumb 101 5161
Crooked Soley Wilts 36 3172
Crookedholm E Ayrs 107 4537
Crookes S York 74 3287
Crookhall Dur 95 1150
Crookham Berks 24 5464
Crookham Nthumb 110 9138
Crookham Village Hants 25 7952
Crooklands Cumb 87 5383
Cropper Derbys 73 2335
Cropredy Oxon 49 4646
Cropston Leics 62 5510
Cropthorne Worcs 47 9945
Cropton N York 90 7589
Cropwell Bishop Notts 63 6835
Cropwell Butler Notts 63 6837
Cros W Isls 152 5061
Crosbie N Ayrs 114 2149
Crosbost W Isls 152 3924
Crosby Cumb 92 0738
Crosby IOM 158 3279
Crosby Lincs 84 8912
Crosby Mersyd 78 3198
Crosby Garret Cumb 88 7209
Crosby Ravensworth Cumb 94 6214
Crosby Villa Cumb 92 0939
Croscombe Somset 21 5944
Crosemere Shrops 59 4329
Crosland Edge W York 82 1012
Crosland Hill W York 82 1114
Cross Somset 21 4154
Cross Ash Mons 34 4019
Cross Coombe Cnwll 3 7251
Cross End Beds 51 0658
Cross End Essex 54 8534
Cross Flatts W York 82 1040
Cross Gates W York 83 3534
Cross Green Devon 5 3888
Cross Green Staffs 60 9105
Cross Green Suffk 54 8353
Cross Green Suffk 54 8955
Cross Green Suffk 54 9852
Cross Hands Carmth 32 5612
Cross Hands Pembks 31 0712
Cross Hill Derbys 74 4148
Cross Hills N York 82 0145
Cross Houses Shrops 59 5307
Cross Houses Shrops 60 6991
Cross in Hand E Susx 16 5521
Cross Inn Cerdgn 42 3957
Cross Inn Cerdgn 43 5464
Cross Inn Pembks 31 1005
Cross Inn Rhondd 33 0582
Cross Keys Ag & B 115 3385
Cross Keys Wilts 35 8771
Cross Lane IOW 13 5089
Cross Lane Head Shrops 60 7195
Cross Lanes Cnwll 2 6921
Cross Lanes Cnwll 3 7642
Cross Lanes N York 90 5364
Cross Lanes Wrexhm 71 3746
Cross o' th' hands Derbys 73 2846
Cross Oak Powys 45 1023
Cross of Jackson Abers 142 7432
Cross Roads Powys 45 9756
Cross Street Suffk 54 1876
Cross Town Ches 79 7578
Cross-at-Hand Kent 28 7846
Crossaig Ag & B 113 8351
Crossapoll Ag & B 120 9943
Crossbush W Susx 14 0306
Crosscanonby Cumb 92 0739
Crossdale Street Norfk 67 2239
Crossens Mersyd 80 3720
Crossford Fife 117 0786
Crossford S Lans 116 8246
Crossgate Cnwll 5 3488
Crossgate Lincs 64 2426
Crossgate Staffs 72 9437
Crossgatehall E Loth 118 3669
Crossgates E Ayrs 115 3744
Crossgates Fife 117 1488
Crossgates N York 91 0284
Crossgates Powys 45 0864
Crossgill Lancs 87 5563
Crosshands Carmth 31 1923
Crosshands E Ayrs 107 4830
Crosshill Fife 117 1796
Crosshill S Ayrs 106 3206
Crosshouse E Ayrs 106 3938
Crosskeys Caerph 34 2292
Crosskirk Highld 150 0369
Crosslands Cumb 87 3489
Crosslanes Shrops 59 3218
Crosslee Border 109 3018
Crosslee Rens 115 4066
Crossley W York 82 2021
Crossmichael D & G 99 7366
Crosspost W Susx 15 2522
Crossroads Abers 134 5607
Crossroads Abers 135 7594
Crosston Angus 127 5256
Crossway Mons 34 4419
Crossway Pembks 31 1542
Crossway Powys 45 0558
Crossway Green Mons 34 5294
Crossway Green Worcs 47 8468
Crossways Dorset 11 7788
Crosswell Pembks 31 1236
Crosthwaite Cumb 87 4391
Croston Lancs 80 4818
Crostwick Norfk 67 2515
Crostwight Norfk 67 3429
Crouch Kent 28 0558
Crouch Kent 27 6155
Crouch End Gt Lon 27 3088
Crouch Hill Dorset 11 7010
Croucheston Wilts 23 0625
Crough House Green Kent 16 4346
Croughton Nhants 49 5433
Crovie Abers 143 8065
Crow Hants 12 1604
Crow Edge S York 82 1804
Crow End Cambs 52 3257
Crow Green Essex 27 5796
Crow Hill Herefd 47 6326
Crow's Green Essex 40 6926
Crow's Nest Cnwll 5 2669
Crowan Cnwll 2 6434
Crowborough E Susx 16 5131
Crowborough Town E Susx 16 5031
Crowcombe Somset 20 1436
Crowdecote Derbys 74 1065
Crowden Derbys 74 0699
Crowden Devon 18 4999
Crowdhill Hants 13 4920
Crowdleham Kent 27 5659
Crowell Oxon 37 7499
Crowfield Nhants 49 6141
Crowfield Suffk 54 1457
Crowfield Green Suffk 54 1458
Crowgate Street Norfk 67 3121
Crowhill E Loth 119 7374
Crowhole Derbys 74 3375
Crowhurst E Susx 17 7512
Crowhurst Surrey 15 3847
Crowhurst Lane End Surrey 15 3747
Crowland Lincs 64 2410
Crowland Suffk 54 0170
Crowlas Cnwll 2 5133
Crowle Lincs 84 7712
Crowle Worcs 47 9256
Crowle Green Worcs 47 9156
Crowmarsh Gifford Oxon 37 6189
Crown Corner Suffk 55 2570
Crownhill Devon 6 4858
Crownpits Surrey 25 9743
Crownthorpe Norfk 66 0803
Crowntown Cnwll 2 6330
Crows-an-Wra Cnwll 2 3927
Crowshill Norfk 66 9506
Crowsnest Shrops 59 3601
Crowthorne Berks 25 8464
Crowton Ches 71 5774
Croxall Staffs 61 1913
Croxby Lincs 76 1898
Croxdale Dur 96 2636
Croxden Staffs 73 0639
Croxley Green Herts 26 0795
Croxton Cambs 52 2460
Croxton Lincs 85 0912
Croxton Norfk 66 9831
Croxton Norfk 54 8786
Croxton Staffs 72 7832
Croxton Green Ches 71 5552
Croxton Kerrial Leics 63 8329
Croxtonbank Staffs 72 7832
Croy Highld 140 7949
Croy N Lans 116 7275
Croyde Devon 18 4439
Croyde Bay Devon 18 4339
Croydon Cambs 52 3149
Croydon Gt Lon 27 3265
Crubenmore Highld 132 6790
Cruckmeole Shrops 59 4309
Cruckton Shrops 59 4310
Cruden Bay Abers 143 0836
Crudgington Shrops 59 6318
Crudwell Wilts 35 9593
Crug Powys 45 1972
Crug-y-byddar Powys 58 1682
Crugmeer Cnwll 4 9076
Crugybar Carmth 44 6537
Crumlin Caerph 33 2197
Crumplehorn Cnwll 5 2051
Crumpsall Gt Man 79 8402
Crundale Kent 29 0749
Crundale Pembks 30 9718
Crunwear Pembks 31 1810
Cruwys Morchard Devon 19 8712
Crux Easton Hants 24 4256
Cruxton Dorset 10 6096
Crwbin Carmth 32 4713
Cryers Hill Bucks 26 8796
Crymmych Pembks 31 1834
Crynant Neath 32 7904
Crystal Palace Gt Lon 27 3371
Cuaig Highld 137 7057
Cuan Ferry Village Ag & B 122 7514
Cubbington Warwks 48 3468
Cubert Cnwll 4 7857
Cubley S York 82 2401
Cublington Bucks 38 8422
Cublington Herefd 46 4038
Cuckfield W Susx 15 3025
Cucklington Somset 22 7527
Cuckney Notts 75 5671
Cuckold's Green Kent 28 8276
Cuckoo Bridge Lincs 64 2020
Cuckoo's Corner Hants 24 7441
Cuckoo's Nest Ches 71 3860
Cuddesdon Oxon 37 5903
Cuddington Bucks 37 7311
Cuddington Ches 71 5971
Cuddington Heath Ches 71 4746
Cuddy Hill Lancs 80 4937
Cudham Gt Lon 27 4459
Cudliptown Devon 5 5279
Cudnell Dorset 12 0696
Cudworth S York 83 3808
Cudworth Somset 10 3810
Cudworth Common S York 83 4007
Cuerden Green Lancs 81 5525
Cuerdley Cross Ches 78 5486
Cufaude Hants 24 6557
Cuffley Herts 39 3003
Cuil Highld 122 9855
Culbokie Highld 140 6059
Culbone Somset 19 8448
Culburnie Highld 139 4941
Culcabock Highld 140 6844
Culcharry Highld 140 8650
Culcheth Ches 79 6694
Culdrain Abers 142 5134
Culduie Highld 137 7140
Culford Suffk 54 8370
Culgaith Cumb 94 6029
Culham Oxon 37 5095
Culkein Highld 148 0333
Culkein Drumbeg Highld 148 1133
Culkerton Gloucs 35 9395
Cullen Moray 142 5167
Cullercoats T & W 103 3570
Cullerlie Abers 135 7603
Cullicudden Highld 140 6463
Cullingworth W York 82 0636
Cullipool House Ag & B 122 7413
Cullivoe Shet 153 5402
Culloden Highld 140 7246
Cullompton Devon 9 0207
Culm Davy Devon 9 1215
Culmington Shrops 59 4982
Culmstock Devon 9 1013
Culnacraig Highld 145 0603
Culnaightrie D & G 92 7750
Culnaknock Highld 137 5162
Culpho Suffk 55 2149
Culrain Highld 146 5794
Culross Fife 117 9886

Culroy Doddington


Culroy S Ayrs 106 3114
Culsalmond Abers 142 6532
Culscadden D & G 99 4748
Culshabbin D & G 98 3051
Culswick Shet 153 2745
Cultercullen Abers 143 9223
Cults Aber C 135 8903
Culverstone Green Kent 27 6362
Culverthorpe Lincs 64 0240
Culworth Nhants 49 5446
Cumbernauld N Lans 116 7674
Cumbernauld Village N Lans 116 7676
Cumberworth Lincs 77 5073
Cumdivock Cumb 93 3448
Cuminestown Abers 143 8050
Cumledge Border 119 7956
Cummersdale Cumb 93 3953
Cummertrees D & G 100 1366
Cummingston Moray 141 1368
Cumnock E Ayrs 107 5620
Cumnor Oxon 37 4504
Cumrew Cumb 94 5550
Cumrue D & G 100 0686
Cumwhinton Cumb 93 4552
Cumwhitton Cumb 94 5052
Cundall N York 89 4272
Cunninghamhead N Ayrs 106 3741
Cupar Fife 126 3714
Cupar Muir Fife 126 3613
Cupernham Hants 23 3622
Curbar Derbys 74 2574
Curbridge Hants 13 5211
Curbridge Oxon 36 3308
Curdridge Hants 13 5213
Curdworth Warwks 61 1792
Curland Somset 10 2717
Curridge Berks 24 4972
Currie C Edin 117 1867
Curry Mallet Somset 21 3221
Curry Rivel Somset 21 3925
Curteis Corner Kent 28 8539
Curtisden Green Kent 28 7440
Curtisknowle Devon 7 7353
Cury Cnwll 2 6721
Cushnie Abers 134 5211
Cushuish Somset 20 1930
Cusop Herefd 46 2441
Cutcloy D & G 99 4534
Cutcombe Somset 20 9339
Cutgate Gt Man 81 8614
Cuthill Highld 147 7587
Cutiau Gwynd 57 6317
Cutler's Green Essex 40 5930
Cutmadoc Cnwll 4 0963
Cutmere Cnwll 5 3260
Cutnall Green Worcs 47 8868
Cutsdean Gloucs 48 0830
Cutsyke W York 83 4224
Cutthorpe Derbys 74 3473
Cuxham Oxon 37 6695
Cuxton Kent 28 7066
Cuxwold Lincs 85 1701
Cwm Blae G 33 1805
Cwm Denbgs 70 0677
Cwm Capel Carmth 32 4502
Cwm Crawnon Powys 33 1419
Cwm Dulais Swans 32 6103
Cwm Irfon Powys 45 8549
Cwm Morgan Carmth 31 2934
Cwm Penmachno Conwy 69 7547
Cwm-bach Carmth 32 4801
Cwm-celyn Blae G 33 2008
Cwm-Cewydd Gwynd 57 8713
Cwm-cou Cerdgn 31 2942
Cwm-Ifor Carmth 44 6625
Cwm-Llinau Powys 57 8408
Cwm-y-glo Carmth 32 5513
Cwm-y-glo Gwynd 69 5562
Cwmafan Neath 32 7791
Cwmaman Rhondd 33 0099
Cwmann Carmth 44 5847
Cwmavon Torfn 34 2706
Cwmbach Carmth 31 2526
Cwmbach Powys 45 1639
Cwmbach Rhondd 33 0201
Cwmbach Llechrhyd Powys 45 0254
Cwmbelan Powys 58 9481
Cwmbran Torfn 34 2994
Cwmbrwyno Cerdgn 43 7180
Cwmcarn Caerph 34 2293
Cwmcarvan Mons 34 4707
Cwmdare Rhondd 33 9803
Cwmdu Carmth 44 6330
Cwmdu Powys 45 1823
Cwmdu Swans 32 6494
Cwmduad Carmth 31 3731
Cwmdwr Carmth 44 7132
Cwmergyr Cerdgn 43 7982
Cwmfelin Brdgnd 33 8589
Cwmfelin Myr Td 33 0901
Cwmfelin Boeth Carmth 31 1919
Cwmfelin Mynach Carmth 31 2224
Cwmfelinfach Caerph 33 1891
Cwmffrwd Carmth 31 4217
Cwmgiedd Powys 32 7911
Cwmgorse Carmth 32 7010
Cwmgwili Carmth 32 5710
Cwmgwrach Neath 33 8604
Cwmhiraeth Carmth 31 3437
Cwmisfael Carmth 32 4915
Cwmllynfell Neath 32 7412
Cwmparc Rhondd 33 9495
Cwmpengraig Carmth 31 3536
Cwmpennar Rhondd 33 0300
Cwmrhos Powys 45 1824
Cwmrhydyceirw Swans 32 6699
Cwmsychbant Cerdgn 44 4746
Cwmtillery Blae G 33 2105
Cwmyoy Mons 46 2923
Cwmystwyth Cerdgn 43 7874
Cwrt Gwynd 32 6800
Cwrt-newydd Cerdgn 44 4947
Cwrt-y-gollen Powys 34 2317
Cyfronydd Powys 58 1408
Cylibebyll Neath 32 7404
Cymer Neath 33 8695
Cymmer Rhondd 33 0290
Cynghordy Carmth 44 8040
Cynheidre Carmth 32 4907
Cynonville Neath 33 8395
Cynwyd Denbgs 70 0541
Cynwyl Elfed Carmth 31 3727


# D


Daccombe Devon 7 9068
Dacre Cumb 93 4526
Dacre N York 89 1960
Dacre Banks N York 89 1962
Daddry Shield Dur 95 8937
Dadford Bucks 49 6638
Dadlington Leics 61 4097
Dafen Carmth 32 5201
Daffy Green Norfk 66 9609
Dagenham Gt Lon 27 5084
Daglingworth Gloucs 35 9905
Dagnall Bucks 38 9916
Dagworth Suffk 54 0361
Dailly S Ayrs 106 2701
Dainton Devon 7 8566
Dairsie Fife 126 4117
Daisy Hill Gt Man 79 6504
Daisy Hill W York 82 2728
Dalabrog W Isls 152 7521
Dalavich Ag & B 122 9612
Dalbeattie D & G 100 8361
Dalbury Derbys 73 2634
Dalby IOM 158 2178
Dalby Lincs 77 4169
Dalby N York 90 6371
Dalcapon P & K 125 9754
Dalchalm Highld 147 9105
Dalchreichart Highld 131 2812
Dalchruin P & K 124 7116
Dalcrue P & K 125 0427
Dalderby Lincs 77 2565
Dalditch Devon 9 0483
Dale Cumb 94 5443
Dale Derbys 62 4338
Dale Pembks 30 8005
Dale Bottom Cumb 93 2921
Dale End Derbys 74 2161
Dale End N York 82 9645
Dale Hill E Susx 16 7030
Dalehouse N York 97 7717
Dalgarven N Ayrs 115 2846
Dalgety Bay Fife 117 1683
Dalgig E Ayrs 107 5512
Dalginross P & K 124 7721
Dalguise P & K 125 9847
Dalhalvaig Highld 150 8954
Dalham Suffk 53 7261
Daliburgh W Isls 152 7521
Dalkeith Mdloth 118 3367
Dallas Moray 141 1252
Dallinghoo Suffk 55 2655
Dallington E Susx 16 6519
Dallington Nhants 49 7362
Dallow N York 89 1971
Dalmally Ag & B 123 1627
Dalmary Stirlg 115 5195
Dalmellington E Ayrs 107 4705
Dalmeny C Edin 117 1477
Dalmigavie Highld 140 7319
Dalmigavie Lodge Highld 140 7523
Dalmore Highld 140 6668
Dalmuir W Duns 115 4871
Dalnabreck Highld 129 7069
Dalnacardoch P & K 132 7270
Dalnahaitnach Highld 140 8519
Dalnaspidal P & K 132 6473
Dalnawillan Lodge Highld 150 0340
Daloist P & K 124 7857
Dalqueich P & K 125 0804
Dalquhairn S Ayrs 106 3296
Dalreavoch Lodge Highld 147 7508
Dalry N Ayrs 115 2949
Dalrymple E Ayrs 106 3514
Dalserf S Lans 116 7950
Dalsmeran Ag & B 104 6413
Dalston Cumb 93 3650
Dalston Gt Lon 27 3384
Dalswinton D & G 100 9385
Dalton Cumb 87 5476
Dalton D & G 100 1173
Dalton Lancs 78 4908
Dalton N York 89 1108
Dalton N York 89 4376
Dalton Nthumb 103 1172
Dalton S York 75 4594
Dalton Magna S York 75 4692
Dalton Parva S York 75 4593
Dalton Piercy Dur 97 4631
Dalton-in-Furness Cumb 86 2274
Dalton-le-Dale Dur 96 4048
Dalton-on-Tees N York 89 2907
Dalveen D & G 108 8806
Dalveich Stirlg 124 6124
Dalwhinnie Highld 132 6384
Dalwood Devon 9 2400
Dam Green Norfk 54 0485
Damask Green Herts 39 2529
Damerham Hants 12 1016
Damgate Norfk 67 4009
Dan-y-Parc Powys 34 2217
Danaway Kent 28 8663
Danbury Essex 40 7805
Danby N York 90 7008
Danby Bottom N York 90 6904
Danby Wiske N York 89 3398
Dandaleith Moray 141 2846
Danderhall Mdloth 117 3069
Dane End Herts 39 3321
Dane Hills Leics 62 5604
Dane Street Kent 28 0552
Danebridge Ches 72 9665
Danegate E Susx 16 5633
Danehill E Susx 15 4027
Danemoor Green Norfk 66 0505
Danesford Shrops 60 7391
Danesmoor Derbys 74 4063
Daniel's Water Kent 28 9541
Danshillock Abers 142 7157
Danskine E Loth 118 5667
Danthorpe E R Yk 85 2532
Danzey Green Warwks 48 1269
Dapple Heath Staffs 73 0425
Darby Green Hants 25 8360
Darcy Lever Gt Man 79 7308
Daren-felen Mons 34 2212
Darenth Kent 27 5671
Daresbury Ches 78 5882
Darfield S York 83 4104
Darfoulds Notts 75 5578
Dargate Kent 29 0861
Darite Cnwll 5 2569
Darland Kent 28 7865
Darland Wrexhm 71 3757
Darlaston Staffs 72 8835
Darlaston W Mids 60 9796
Darlaston Green W Mids 60 9797
Darley N York 89 2059
Darley Abbey Derbys 62 3538
Darley Bridge Derbys 74 2661
Darley Dale Derbys 74 2663
Darley Green Warwks 61 1874
Darley Head N York 89 1959
Darleyhall Herts 38 1422
Darlingscott Warwks 48 2342
Darlington Dur 89 2814
Darliston Shrops 59 5733
Darlton Notts 75 7773
Darnford Staffs 61 1308
Darnick Border 109 5334
Darowen Powys 57 8201
Darra Abers 142 7447
Darracott Cnwll 18 2811
Darracott Devon 18 2317
Darracott Devon 18 4739
Darras Hall Nthumb 103 1570
Darrington W York 83 4820
Darsham Suffk 55 4169
Darshill Somset 21 6144
Dartford Kent 27 5474
Dartington Devon 7 7862
Dartmeet Devon 7 6773
Dartmouth Devon 7 8751
Darton S York 82 3110
Darvel E Ayrs 107 5637
Darwell Hole E Susx 16 6919
Darwen Lancs 81 6922
Datchet Berks 26 9877
Datchworth Herts 39 2619
Datchworth Green Herts 39 2718
Daubhill Gt Man 79 7007
Dauntsey Wilts 35 9782
Dauntsey Green Wilts 35 9981
Dava Highld 141 0038
Davenham Ches 79 6571
Davenport Gt Man 79 9088
Davenport Green Ches 79 8379
Davenport Green Gt Man 79 8086
Daventry Nhants 49 5762
David Street Kent 27 6464
Davidson's Mains C Edin 117 2175
Davidstow Cnwll 4 1587
Davington D & G 109 2302
Davington Hill Kent 28 0161
Daviot Abers 142 7428
Daviot Highld 140 7239
Daviot House Highld 140 7240
Davis's Town E Susx 16 5217
Davoch of Grange Moray 142 4751
Davyhulme Gt Man 79 7595
Daw End W Mids 61 0300
Daw's House Cnwll 5 3182
Dawesgreen Surrey 15 2147
Dawley Shrops 60 6808
Dawlish Devon 9 9576
Dawlish Warren Devon 9 9778
Dawn Conwy 69 8672
Daws Green Somset 20 1921
Daws Heath Essex 40 8188
Dawsmere Lincs 65 4430
Day Green Ches 72 7757
Daybrook Notts 62 5744
Dayhills Staffs 72 9532
Dayhouse Bank Worcs 60 9678
Daylesford Gloucs 48 2425
Ddol Flints 70 1471
Ddol-Cownwy Powys 58 0117
Deal Kent 29 3752
Dean Cumb 92 0725
Dean Devon 19 6245
Dean Devon 19 7048
Dean Devon 7 7364
Dean Dorset 11 9715
Dean Hants 24 4431
Dean Hants 13 5619
Dean Lancs 81 8525
Dean Oxon 36 3422
Dean Somset 22 6743
Dean Bottom Kent 27 5868
Dean Court Oxon 37 4705
Dean End Dorset 11 9717
Dean Head S York 74 2600
Dean Prior Devon 7 7363
Dean Row Ches 79 8781
Dean Street Kent 28 7453
Deanburnhaugh Border 109 3911
Deancombe Devon 7 7264
Deane Gt Man 79 6907
Deane Hants 24 5450
Deanhead W York 82 0415
Deanland Dorset 22 9918
Deanlane End W Susx 13 7412
Deanraw Nthumb 102 8162
Deans W Loth 117 0369
Deanscales Cumb 92 0926
Deanshanger Nhants 49 7639
Deanshaugh Moray 141 3550
Deanston Stirlg 116 7101
Dearham Cumb 92 0736
Dearnley Gt Man 81 9215
Debach Suffk 55 2454
Debden Essex 53 5533
Debden Essex 27 4496
Debden Green Essex 40 5831
Debenham Suffk 54 1763
Deblin's Green Worcs 47 8148
Dechmont W Loth 117 0370
Dechmont Road W Loth 117 0269
Deddington Oxon 49 4631
Dedham Essex 41 0533
Dedham Heath Essex 41 0531
Dedworth Berks 26 9476
Deene Nhants 51 9492
Deenethorpe Nhants 51 9591
Deepcar S York 74 2897
Deepcut Surrey 25 9057
Deepdale Cumb 88 7184
Deepdale N York 88 8979
Deeping Gate Lincs 64 1509
Deeping St James Lincs 64 1609
Deeping St Nicholas Lincs 64 2115
Deerhurst Gloucs 47 8730
Deerhurst Walton Gloucs 47 8828
Deerton Street Kent 28 9762
Defford Worcs 47 9143
Defynnog Powys 45 9227
Deganwy Conwy 69 7779
Degnish Ag & B 122 7812
Deighton N York 89 3801
Deighton N York 83 6244
Deighton W York 82 1519
Deiniolen Gwynd 69 5763
Delabole Cnwll 4 0683
Delamere Ches 71 5668
Delfrigs Abers 143 9620
Dell Quay W Susx 14 8302
Delley Devon 19 5424
Delliefure Highld 141 0730
Delly End Oxon 36 3513
Delmonden Green Kent 17 7330
Delnashaugh Inn Moray 141 1835
Delny Highld 146 7372
Delph Gt Man 82 9807
Delves Dur 95 1149
Delvine P & K 126 1240
Dembleby Lincs 64 0437
Demelza Cnwll 4 9763
Den of Lindores Fife 126 2616
Denaby S York 75 4899
Denaby Main S York 75 4999
Denbies Surrey 26 1450
Denbigh Denbgs 70 0566
Denbrae Fife 126 3818
Denbury Devon 7 8268
Denby Derbys 62 3946
Denby Bottles Derbys 62 3846
Denby Dale W York 82 2208
Denchworth Oxon 36 3891
Dendron Cumb 86 2470
Denel End Beds 38 0335
Denfield P & K 125 9517
Denford Nhants 51 9976
Dengie Essex 41 9802
Denham Bucks 26 0487
Denham Suffk 53 7561
Denham Suffk 55 1974
Denham End Suffk 53 7663
Denham Green Bucks 26 0488
Denham Green Suffk 55 1974
Denhead Abers 143 9952
Denhead Fife 127 4613
Denhead of Gray Dund C 126 3531
Denholm Border 110 5718
Denholme W York 82 0734
Denholme Clough W York 82 0732
Denio Gwynd 56 3635
Denmead Hants 13 6512
Denmore Aber C 135 9411
Denne Park W Susx 15 1628
Dennington Suffk 55 2867
Denny Falk 116 8082
Dennyloanhead Falk 116 8080
Denshaw Gt Man 82 9710
Denside Abers 135 8095
Densole Kent 29 2141
Denston Suffk 53 7652
Denstone Staffs 73 0940
Denstroude Kent 29 1061
Dent Cumb 87 7086
Dent-de-Lion Kent 29 3269
Denton Cambs 52 1587
Denton Dur 96 2118
Denton E Susx 16 4502
Denton Gt Man 79 9295
Denton Kent 28 6673
Denton Kent 29 2147
Denton Lincs 63 8632
Denton N York 82 1448
Denton Nhants 51 8358
Denton Norfk 55 2788
Denton Oxon 37 5902
Denver Norfk 65 6001
Denwick Nthumb 111 2014
Deopham Norfk 66 0400
Deopham Green Norfk 66 0499
Depden Suffk 53 7857
Depden Green Suffk 53 7756
Deptford Gt Lon 27 3777
Deptford Wilts 22 0138
Derby Derbys 62 3536
Derby Devon 19 5633
Derbyhaven IOM 158 2867
Derculich P & K 125 8852
Dereham Norfk 66 9913
Deri Caerph 33 1201
Derril Devon 18 3003
Derringstone Kent 29 2049
Derrington Staffs 72 8922
Derriton Devon 18 3303
Derry Hill Wilts 35 9670
Derrythorpe Lincs 84 8208
Dersingham Norfk 65 6830
Dervaig Ag & B 121 4352
Derwen Denbgs 70 0750
Derwen Fawr Carmth 44 5722
Derwenlas Powys 57 7298
Derwydd Carmth 32 6117
Desborough Nhants 51 8083
Desford Leics 62 4703
Deskford Moray 142 5061
Detchant Nthumb 111 0836
Detling Kent 28 7958
Deuxhill Shrops 60 6987
Devauden Mons 34 4898
Devil's Bridge Cerdgn 43 7376
Deviock Cnwll 5 3155
Devitts Green Warwks 61 2790
Devizes Wilts 22 0061
Devonport Devon 6 4554
Devonside Clacks 116 9196
Devoran Cnwll 3 7939
Dewarton Mdloth 118 3763
Dewlish Dorset 11 7798
Dewsbury W York 82 2421
Dewsbury Moor W York 82 2321
Deytheur Powys 58 2317
Dial Somset 21 5366
Dial Green W Susx 14 9227
Dial Post W Susx 15 1519
Dibberford Dorset 10 4504
Dibden Hants 13 4008
Dibden Purlieu Hants 13 4106
Dickens Heath W Mids 61 1176
Dickleburgh Norfk 54 1682
Didbrook Gloucs 48 0531
Didcot Oxon 37 5290
Diddington Cambs 52 1965
Diddlebury Shrops 59 5085
Didley Herefd 46 4532
Didling W Susx 14 8318
Didmarton Gloucs 35 8287
Didsbury Gt Man 79 8491
Didworthy Devon 7 6862
Digby Lincs 76 0854
Digg Highld 136 4668
Diggle Gt Man 82 0007
Digmoor Lancs 78 4905
Digswell Herts 39 2415
Digswell Water Herts 39 2514
Dihewyd Cerdgn 44 4855
Dilham Norfk 67 3325
Dilhorne Staffs 72 9743
Dillington Cambs 52 1365
Dilston Nthumb 102 9763
Dilton Wilts 22 8548
Dilton Marsh Wilts 22 8449
Dilwyn Herefd 46 4154
Dimple Derbys 74 2960
Dimple Gt Man 81 7015
Dinas Carmth 31 2730
Dinas Cnwll 4 9274
Dinas Gwynd 56 2735
Dinas Pembks 30 0138
Dinas Rhondd 33 0091
Dinas Dinlle Gwynd 68 4356
Dinas Powys V Glam 33 1571
Dinas-Mawddwy Gwynd 57 8515
Dinder Somset 21 5744
Dinedor Herefd 46 5336
Dingestow Mons 34 4510
Dingle Mersyd 78 3687
Dingleden Kent 17 8131
Dingley Nhants 50 7787
Dingwall Highld 139 5458
Dinham Mons 34 4792
Dinmael Conwy 70 0044
Dinnet Abers 134 4598
Dinnington S York 75 5285
Dinnington Somset 10 4012
Dinnington T & W 103 2073
Dinorwic Gwynd 69 5961
Dinton Bucks 37 7610
Dinton Wilts 22 0131
Dinwoodie D & G 100 1190
Dinworthy Devon 18 3015
Dipford Somset 20 2021
Dipley Hants 24 7457
Dippen Ag & B 105 7937
Dippen N Ayrs 105 0422
Dippenhall Surrey 25 8146
Dippermill Devon 18 4406
Dippertown Devon 5 4284
Dipple Moray 141 3258
Dipple S Ayrs 106 2002
Diptford Devon 7 7256
Dipton Dur 96 1554
Diptonmill Nthumb 102 9361
Dirleton E Loth 118 5184
Dirt Pot Nthumb 95 8545
Discoed Powys 46 2764
Diseworth Leics 62 4524
Dishforth N York 89 3873
Disley Ches 79 9784
Diss Norfk 54 1180
Disserth Powys 45 0358
Distington Cumb 92 0023
Ditchampton Wilts 23 0831
Ditchburn Nthumb 111 1320
Ditcheat Somset 21 6236
Ditchingham Norfk 67 3391
Ditchley Oxon 36 3820
Ditchling E Susx 15 3215
Ditherington Shrops 59 5014
Ditteridge Wilts 35 8169
Dittisham Devon 7 8655
Ditton Ches 78 4986
Ditton Kent 28 7158
Ditton Green Cambs 53 6558
Ditton Priors Shrops 59 6089
Dixton Gloucs 47 9830
Dixton Mons 34 5113
Dizzard Cnwll 4 1698
Dobcross Gt Man 82 9906
Dobroyd Castle W York 81 9323
Dobwalls Cnwll 5 2165
Doccombe Devon 8 7786
Dochgarroch Highld 140 6140
Dockenfield Surrey 25 8240
Docker Lancs 87 5774
Docking Norfk 65 7636
Docklow Herefd 46 5657
Dockray Cumb 93 2649
Dockray Cumb 93 3921
Dod's Leigh Staffs 73 0134
Dodbrooke Devon 7 7444
Dodd's Green Ches 71 6043
Doddinghurst Essex 27 5999
Doddington Cambs 52 4090
Doddington Kent 28 9357
Doddington Lincs 76 8970

Doddington Eashing


Doddington Nthumb 111 9932
Doddington Shrops 46 6176
Doddiscombsleigh Devon 8 8586
Doddshill Norfk 65 6930
Doddy Cross Cnwll 5 3062
Dodford Nhants 49 6160
Dodford Worcs 60 9373
Dodington Gloucs 35 7580
Dodington Somset 20 1740
Dodleston Ches 71 3661
Dodscott Devon 19 5419
Dodside E Rens 115 5053
Dodworth S York 82 3105
Dodworth Bottom S York 83 3204
Dodworth Green S York 82 3004
Doe Bank W Mids 61 1197
Doe Lea Derbys 75 4666
Dog Village Devon 9 9896
Dogdyke Lincs 76 2055
Dogley Lane W York 82 1813
Dogmersfield Hants 25 7852
Dogridge Wilts 36 0887
Dogsthorpe Cambs 64 1901
Dol-for Powys 57 8106
Dol-gran Carmth 31 4334
Dolanog Powys 58 0612
Dolau Powys 45 1467
Dolaucothi Carmth 44 6640
Dolbenmaen Gwynd 56 5043
Doley Shrops 72 7429
Dolfach Powys 58 9101
Dolfor Powys 58 1087
Dolgarrog Conwy 69 7767
Dolgellau Gwynd 57 7217
Dolgoch Gwynd 57 6504
Doll Highld 147 8803
Dollar Clacks 117 9698
Dollarfield Clacks 117 9697
Dolley Green Powys 46 2865
Dollwen Cerdgn 43 6881
Dolphin Flints 70 1973
Dolphinholme Lancs 80 5253
Dolphinton S Lans 117 1046
Dolton Devon 19 5712
Dolwen Conwy 69 8874
Dolwyddelan Conwy 69 7352
Dolybont Cerdgn 43 6288
Dolyhir Powys 46 2457
Domgay Powys 58 2818
Donaldson's Lodge Nthumb 110 8741
Doncaster S York 83 5703
Doncaster Carr S York 83 5801
Donhead St Andrew Wilts 22 9124
Donhead St Mary Wilts 22 9024
Donibristle Fife 117 1688
Doniford Somset 20 0842
Donington Lincs 64 2035
Donington on Bain Lincs 76 2382
Donington Southing Lincs 64 2034
Donisthorpe Leics 61 3113
Donkey Street Kent 17 1032
Donkey Town Surrey 25 9360
Donnington Berks 24 4668
Donnington Gloucs 48 1928
Donnington Herefd 47 7034
Donnington Shrops 59 5708
Donnington Shrops 60 7114
Donnington W Susx 14 8501
Donnington Wood Shrops 60 7012
Donyatt Somset 10 3314
Doomsday Green W Susx 15 1929
Doonfoot S Ayrs 106 3219
Doonholm S Ayrs 106 3317
Dorback Lodge Highld 141 0716
Dorchester Dorset 11 6990
Dorchester Oxon 37 5794
Dordon Warwks 61 2500
Dore S York 74 3181
Dores Highld 140 5934
Dorking Surrey 15 1649
Dorking Tye Suffk 54 9236
Dormans Land Surrey 15 4041
Dormans Park Surrey 15 3940
Dormington Herefd 46 5840
Dormston Worcs 47 9857
Dorn Gloucs 48 2034
Dorney Bucks 26 9378
Dornie Highld 138 8826
Dornoch Highld 147 7989
Dornock D & G 101 2366
Dorrery Highld 150 0754
Dorridge W Mids 61 1775
Dorrington Lincs 76 0852
Dorrington Shrops 59 4702
Dorrington Shrops 72 7340
Dorsington Warwks 48 1349
Dorstone Herefd 46 3141
Dorton Bucks 37 6814
Dosthill Staffs 61 2199
Dottery Dorset 10 4595
Doublebois Cnwll 5 1964
Dougarie N Ayrs 105 8837
Doughton Gloucs 35 8791
Douglas IOM 158 3775
Douglas S Lans 108 8330
Douglas and Angus Dund C 127 4233
Douglas Castle S Lans 108 8431
Douglas Pier Ag & B 114 1999
Douglas Water S Lans 108 8736
Douglas West S Lans 108 8231
Douglastown Angus 126 4147
Doulting Somset 21 6443
Dounby Ork 153 2920
Doune Highld 146 4400
Doune Stirlg 116 7201
Dounepark S Ayrs 106 1897
Dounie Highld 146 5690
Dousland Devon 6 5369
Dovaston Shrops 59 3521
Dove Green Notts 75 4652
Dove Holes Derbys 74 0777
Dovenby Cumb 92 0933
Dover Gt Man 78 6000
Dover Kent 29 3241
Dovercourt Essex 41 2431
Doverdale Worcs 47 8666
Doveridge Derbys 73 1133
Doversgreen Surrey 15 2548
Dowally P & K 125 0048
Dowbridge Lancs 80 4331
Dowdeswell Gloucs 35 0019
Dowlais Myr Td 33 0607
Dowland Devon 19 5610
Dowlish Ford Somset 10 3513
Dowlish Wake Somset 10 3712
Down Ampney Gloucs 36 0996
Down Hatherley Gloucs 35 8622
Down St Mary Devon 8 7404
Down Thomas Devon 6 5050
Downacarey Devon 5 3790
Downderry Cnwll 5 3154
Downe Gt Lon 27 4361
Downend Berks 37 4775
Downend Gloucs 35 6577
Downend Gloucs 35 8398
Downend IOW 13 5387
Downfield Dund C 126 3932
Downgate Cnwll 5 2871
Downgate Cnwll 5 3672
Downham Cambs 53 5284
Downham Essex 40 7296
Downham Gt Lon 27 3871
Downham Lancs 81 7844
Downham Nthumb 110 8633
Downham Market Norfk 65 6103
Downhead Somset 21 5625
Downhead Somset 22 6945
Downhill Cnwll 4 8669
Downhill P & K 125 0930
Downholland Cross Lancs 78 3606
Downholme N York 89 1197
Downies Abers 135 9294
Downing Flints 70 1578
Downley Bucks 26 8495
Downside Somset 21 6244
Downside Somset 21 6450
Downside Surrey 26 1057
Downton Hants 12 2693
Downton Wilts 12 1821
Downton on the Rock Herefd 46 4273
Dowsby Lincs 64 1129
Dowsdale Lincs 64 2810
Dowsland Green Essex 40 8724
Doxey Staffs 72 8923
Doxford Nthumb 111 1823
Doynton Gloucs 35 7274
Draethen Caerph 34 2287
Draffan S Lans 116 7945
Dragonby Lincs 84 9014
Dragons Green W Susx 15 1423
Drakeholes Notts 75 7090
Drakelow Worcs 60 8180
Drakemyre N Ayrs 115 2950
Drakes Broughton Worcs 47 9248
Drakes Cross Worcs 61 0876
Drakewalls Cnwll 6 4270
Draughton N York 82 0352
Draughton Nhants 50 7676
Drax N York 83 6726
Drax Hales N York 83 6725
Draycot Foliat Wilts 36 1777
Draycote Warwks 50 4470
Draycott Derbys 62 4433
Draycott Gloucs 48 1835
Draycott Shrops 60 8093
Draycott Somset 21 4751
Draycott Somset 21 5521
Draycott Worcs 47 8548
Draycott in the Clay Staffs 73 1528
Draycott in the Moors Staffs 72 9840
Drayford Devon 19 7813
Draynes Cnwll 5 2169
Drayton Hants 13 6705
Drayton Leics 51 8392
Drayton Lincs 64 2439
Drayton Norfk 66 1813
Drayton Oxon 49 4241
Drayton Oxon 37 4894
Drayton Somset 21 4024
Drayton Worcs 60 9075
Drayton Bassett Staffs 61 1900
Drayton Beauchamp Bucks 38 9011
Drayton Parslow Bucks 38 8328
Drayton St Leonard Oxon 37 5996
Drebley N York 88 0559
Dreemskerry IOM 158 4791
Dreen Hill Pembks 30 9214
Drefach Carmth 31 3538
Drefach Carmth 32 5213
Drefach Cerdgn 44 4945
Drefelin Carmth 31 3637
Dreghorn N Ayrs 106 3538
Drellingore Kent 29 2441
Drem E Loth 118 5079
Dresden Staffs 72 9142
Drewsteignton Devon 8 7391
Driby Lincs 77 3874
Driffield E R Yk 91 0257
Driffield Gloucs 36 0799
Driffield Cross Roads Gloucs 36 0698
Drift Cnwll 2 4328
Drigg Cumb 86 0699
Drighlington W York 82 2228
Drimnin Highld 121 5554
Drimpton Dorset 10 4104
Drimsallie Highld 130 9578
Dringhoe E R Yk 85 1454
Dringhouses N York 83 5849
Drinkstone Suffk 54 9561
Drinkstone Green Suffk 54 9660
Drinsey Nook Notts 76 8773
Drive End Dorset 10 5808
Driver's End Herts 39 2220
Drointon Staffs 73 0226
Droitwich Worcs 47 8963
Dron P & K 126 1416
Dronfield Derbys 74 3578
Dronfield Woodhouse Derbys 74 3378
Drongan E Ayrs 107 4418
Dronley Angus 126 3435
Droop Dorset 11 7508
Dropping Well S York 74 3994
Droxford Hants 13 6018
Droylsden Gt Man 79 9097
Druid Denbgs 70 0443
Druids Heath W Mids 61 0502
Druidston Pembks 30 8616
Druimachoish Highld 123 1246
Druimarbin Highld 130 0770
Druimdrishaig Ag & B 113 7370
Druimindarroch Highld 129 6884
Drum Ag & B 114 9276
Drum P & K 117 0400
Drumalbin S Lans 108 9038
Drumbeg Highld 148 1232
Drumblade Abers 142 5840
Drumblair House Abers 142 6343
Drumbreddon D & G 98 0843
Drumbuie Highld 137 7730
Drumburgh Cumb 93 2659
Drumburn D & G 92 8854
Drumchapel C Glas 115 5270
Drumchastle P & K 132 6858
Drumclog S Lans 107 6438
Drumeldrie Fife 127 4403
Drumelzier Border 108 1334
Drumfearn Highld 129 6716
Drumfrennie Abers 135 7298
Drumguish Highld 132 7900
Drumhead Abers 134 6092
Drumin Moray 141 1830
Drumjohn D & G 107 5297
Drumlamford S Ayrs 98 2876
Drumlasie Abers 135 6405
Drumleaning Cumb 93 2751
Drumlemble Ag & B 104 6619
Drumlithie Abers 135 7880
Drummoddie D & G 99 3845
Drummore D & G 98 1336
Drummore D & G 100 9074
Drummuir Moray 141 3843
Drumnadrochit Highld 139 5030
Drumnagorrach Moray 142 5252
Drumpark D & G 100 8779
Drumrunie Lodge Highld 145 1604
Drumshang S Ayrs 106 2514
Drumuie Highld 136 4546
Drumuillie Highld 140 9420
Drumvaich Stirlg 124 6704
Drunzie P & K 126 1308
Druridge Nthumb 103 2796
Drury Flints 71 2964
Dry Doddington Lincs 63 8546
Dry Drayton Cambs 52 3861
Dry Sandford Oxon 37 4600
Dry Street Essex 40 6986
Drybeck Cumb 94 6615
Drybridge Moray 142 4362
Drybridge N Ayrs 106 3536
Drybrook Gloucs 35 6417
Dryburgh Border 110 5932
Dryhope Border 109 2624
Drym Cnwll 2 6133
Drymen Stirlg 115 4788
Drymuir Abers 143 9046
Drynoch Highld 136 4031
Dryslwyn Carmth 32 5520
Dryton Shrops 59 5905
Dubford Abers 143 7963
Dublin Suffk 54 1669
Duchally Highld 145 3817
Duck End Beds 38 0544
Duck End Cambs 52 2464
Duck End Essex 40 6526
Duck End Essex 53 6833
Duck's Cross Beds 52 1156
Duckend Green Essex 40 7223
Duckington Ches 71 4851
Ducklington Oxon 36 3507
Duddingston C Edin 117 2872
Duddington Nhants 51 9800
Duddlestone Somset 20 2321
Duddleswell E Susx 16 4628
Duddlewick Shrops 59 6583
Duddo Nthumb 110 9342
Duddon Ches 71 5164
Duddon Bridge Cumb 86 1988
Dudleston Shrops 71 3438
Dudleston Heath Shrops 59 3736
Dudley T & W 103 2573
Dudley W Mids 60 9490
Dudley Hill W York 82 1830
Dudley Port W Mids 60 9691
Dudnill Shrops 47 6474
Dudsbury Dorset 12 0798
Dudswell Herts 38 9609
Duffield Derbys 62 3443
Duffryn Neath 33 8495
Dufftown Moray 141 3240
Duffus Moray 141 1668
Dufton Cumb 94 6825
Duggleby N York 90 8767
Duirinish Highld 137 7831
Duisdalemore Highld 129 7013
Duisky Highld 130 0076
Duke Street Suffk 54 0742
Dukestown Blae G 33 1410
Dukinfield Gt Man 79 9397
Dulas IOA 68 4789
Dulcote Somset 21 5644
Dulford Devon 9 0706
Dull P & K 125 8049
Dullatur N Lans 116 7476
Dullingham Cambs 53 6357
Dullingham Ley Cambs 53 6456
Dulnain Bridge Highld 141 9925
Duloe Beds 52 1560
Duloe Cnwll 5 2358
Dulverton Somset 20 9127
Dulwich Gt Lon 27 3373
Dumbarton W Duns 115 3975
Dumbleton Gloucs 47 0135
Dumfries D & G 100 9776
Dumgoyne Stirlg 115 5283
Dummer Hants 24 5846
Dumpton Kent 29 3966
Dun Angus 135 6659
Dunalastair P & K 132 7158
Dunan Ag & B 114 1571
Dunan Highld 137 5828
Dunan P & K 124 4757
Dunaverty Ag & B 105 6807
Dunball Somset 21 3141
Dunbar E Loth 118 6778
Dunbeath Highld 151 1629
Dunbeg Ag & B 122 8833
Dunblane Stirlg 116 7801
Dunbog Fife 126 2817
Dunbridge Hants 23 3226
Duncanston Highld 139 5856
Duncanstone Abers 142 5726
Dunchideock Devon 9 8787
Dunchurch Warwks 50 4871
Duncote Nhants 49 6750
Duncow D & G 100 9683
Duncrievie P & K 126 1309
Duncton W Susx 14 9617
Dundee Dund C 126 4030
Dundon Somset 21 4832
Dundonald S Ayrs 106 3634
Dundonnell Highld 145 0987
Dundraw Cumb 93 2149
Dundreggan Highld 131 3214
Dundrennan D & G 99 7447
Dundry Somset 21 5666
Dunecht Abers 135 7509
Dunfermline Fife 117 0987
Dunfield Gloucs 36 1497
Dunford Bridge S York 82 1502
Dungate Kent 28 9159
Dungavel S Lans 107 6537
Dunge Wilts 22 8954
Dunglass E Loth 119 7671
Dungworth S York 74 2789
Dunham Notts 75 8074
Dunham Town Gt Man 79 7387
Dunham Woodhouses Gt Man 79 7287
Dunham-on-the-Hill Ches 71 4772
Dunhampstead Worcs 47 9160
Dunhampton Worcs 47 8466
Dunholme Lincs 76 0279
Dunino Fife 127 5311
Dunipace Falk 116 8083
Dunk's Green Kent 27 6152
Dunkeld P & K 125 0242
Dunkerton Somset 22 7159
Dunkeswell Devon 9 1407
Dunkeswick W York 82 3047
Dunkirk Ches 71 3872
Dunkirk Gloucs 35 7885
Dunkirk Kent 29 0759
Dunkirk Staffs 72 8152
Dunkirk Wilts 22 9962
Dunlappie Angus 134 5867
Dunley Hants 24 4553
Dunley Worcs 47 7869
Dunlop E Ayrs 115 4049
Dunmaglass Highld 140 5922
Dunmere Cnwll 4 0467
Dunmore Ag & B 113 7961
Dunmore Falk 116 8989
Dunn Street Kent 28 7961
Dunnet Highld 151 2171
Dunnichen Angus 127 5048
Dunning P & K 125 0114
Dunnington E R Yk 85 1551
Dunnington N York 83 6652
Dunnington Warwks 48 0654
Dunnockshaw Lancs 81 8127
Dunoon Ag & B 114 1776
Dunphail Moray 141 0048
Dunragit D & G 98 1557
Duns Border 119 7853
Duns Tew Oxon 49 4528
Dunsa Derbys 74 2470
Dunsby Lincs 64 1026
Dunscar Gt Man 81 7113
Dunscore D & G 100 8684
Dunscroft S York 83 6409
Dunsdale N York 97 6019
Dunsden Green Oxon 37 7377
Dunsdon Devon 18 3008
Dunsfold Surrey 14 0035
Dunsford Devon 8 8189
Dunshalt Fife 126 2410
Dunshillock Abers 143 9848
Dunsill Notts 75 4661
Dunsley N York 90 8511
Dunsley Staffs 60 8583
Dunsmore Bucks 38 8605
Dunsop Bridge Lancs 81 6649
Dunstable Beds 38 0122
Dunstall Staffs 73 1820
Dunstall Common Worcs 47 8843
Dunstall Green Suffk 53 7460
Dunstan Nthumb 111 2419
Dunstan Steads Nthumb 111 2422
Dunster Somset 20 9943
Dunston Lincs 76 0662
Dunston Norfk 67 2202
Dunston Staffs 72 9217
Dunston T & W 96 2362
Dunston Heath Staffs 72 9017
Dunstone Devon 6 5951
Dunstone Devon 7 7175
Dunsville S York 83 6407
Dunswell E R Yk 85 0735
Dunsyre S Lans 117 0748
Dunterton Devon 5 3779
Dunthrop Oxon 48 3528
Duntisbourne Abbots Gloucs 35 9607
Duntisbourne Rouse Gloucs 35 9805
Duntish Dorset 11 6906
Duntocher W Duns 115 4872
Dunton Beds 39 2344
Dunton Bucks 38 8224
Dunton Norfk 66 8830
Dunton Bassett Leics 50 5490
Dunton Green Kent 27 5157
Dunton Wayletts Essex 40 6590
Duntulm Highld 136 4174
Dunure S Ayrs 106 2515
Dunvant Swans 32 5993
Dunvegan Highld 136 2547
Dunwich Suffk 55 4770
Dunwood Staffs 72 9455
Durdar Cumb 93 4051
Durgan Cnwll 3 7727
Durham Dur 96 2742
Durisdeer D & G 108 8903
Durisdeermill D & G 108 8804
Durkar W York 82 3116
Durleigh Somset 20 2736
Durley Hants 13 5116
Durley Wilts 23 2364
Durley Street Hants 13 5217
Durlock Kent 29 2757
Durlock Kent 29 3164
Durlow Common Gloucs 47 6339
Durmgley Angus 127 4250
Durn Gt Man 82 9416
Durness Highld 149 4068
Duror Highld 122 9955
Durran Ag & B 122 9607
Durrington W Susx 14 1105
Durrington Wilts 23 1544
Durris Abers 135 7796
Dursley Gloucs 35 7598
Dursley Cross Gloucs 35 6920
Durston Somset 20 2928
Durweston Dorset 11 8508
Duston Nhants 49 7261
Duthil Highld 140 9324
Dutlas Powys 45 2177
Dutson Cnwll 5 3485
Dutton Ches 71 5779
Duxford Cambs 53 4846
Duxford Oxon 36 3600
Dwygyfylchi Conwy 69 7376
Dwyran IOA 68 4465
Dyce Aber C 135 8812
Dye House Nthumb 95 9358
Dyer's End Essex 53 7238
Dyfatty Carmth 32 4500
Dyffrydan Gwynd 57 6914
Dyffryn Brdgnd 33 8593
Dyffryn Myr Td 33 0603
Dyffryn V Glam 33 0971
Dyffryn Ardudwy Gwynd 57 5823
Dyffryn Castell Cerdgn 43 7782
Dyffryn Cellwen Neath 33 8510
Dyke Lincs 64 1022
Dyke Moray 140 9858
Dykehead Angus 126 2453
Dykehead Angus 134 3859
Dykehead N Lans 116 8759
Dykehead Stirlg 115 5997
Dykelands Abers 135 7068
Dykends Angus 133 2557
Dykeside Abers 142 7243
Dylife Powys 43 8694
Dymchurch Kent 17 1029
Dymock Gloucs 47 7031
Dyrham Gloucs 35 7475
Dysart Fife 117 3093
Dyserth Denbgs 70 0578


# E


Eachway Worcs 60 9876
Eachwick Nthumb 103 1171
Eagland Hill Lancs 80 4345
Eagle Lincs 76 8766
Eagle Barnsdale Lincs 76 8865
Eagle Moor Lincs 76 8868
Eaglescliffe Dur 96 4215
Eaglesfield Cumb 92 0928
Eaglesfield D & G 101 2374
Eaglesham E Rens 115 5751
Eagley Gt Man 81 7112
Eairy IOM 158 2977
Eakley Lanes Bucks 38 8250
Eakring Notts 75 6762
Ealand Lincs 84 7811
Ealing Gt Lon 26 1780
Eals Nthumb 94 6756
Eamont Bridge Cumb 94 5228
Earby Lancs 81 9046
Earcroft Lancs 81 6823
Eardington Shrops 60 7290
Eardisland Herefd 46 4158
Eardisley Herefd 46 3149
Eardiston Shrops 59 3725
Eardiston Worcs 47 6968
Earith Cambs 52 3875
Earl Shilton Leics 50 4697
Earl Soham Suffk 55 2363
Earl Sterndale Derbys 74 0966
Earl Stonham Suffk 54 1059
Earl's Croome Worcs 47 8642
Earl's Down E Susx 16 6419
Earl's Green Suffk 54 0366
Earle Nthumb 111 9826
Earlestown Mersyd 78 5795
Earley Berks 24 7472
Earlham Norfk 67 1908
Earlish Highld 136 3861
Earls Barton Nhants 51 8563
Earls Colne Essex 40 8528
Earls Common Worcs 47 9559
Earlsditton Shrops 47 6275
Earlsdon W Mids 61 3278
Earlsferry Fife 118 4800
Earlsfield Gt Lon 27 2573
Earlsford Abers 143 8334
Earlsheaton W York 82 2621
Earlston Border 110 5738
Earlston E Ayrs 106 4035
Earlswood Surrey 15 2749
Earlswood Warwks 61 1174
Earlswood Common Mons 34 4594
Earnley W Susx 14 8196
Earnshaw Bridge Lancs 80 5222
Earsdon Nthumb 103 1993
Earsdon T & W 103 3272
Earsham Norfk 55 3288
Earswick N York 90 6157
Eartham W Susx 14 9309
Earthcott Gloucs 35 6585
Easby N York 90 5708
Easdale Ag & B 122 7417
Easebourne W Susx 14 9023
Easenhall Warwks 50 4679
Eashing Surrey 25 9443

Easington Elrington


Easington Bucks 37 6810
Easington Dur 96 4143
Easington E R Yk 85 3919
Easington N York 97 7417
Easington Nthumb 111 1234
Easington Oxon 37 6697
Easington Colliery Dur 96 4344
Easington Lane T & W 96 3646
Easingwold N York 90 5269
Easole Street Kent 29 2652
Eassie and Nevay Angus 126 3344
East Aberthaw V Glam 20 0366
East Allington Devon 7 7748
East Anstey Devon 19 8626
East Anton Hants 23 3747
East Appleton N York 89 2395
East Ashey IOW 13 5888
East Ashling W Susx 14 8107
East Aston Hants 24 4445
East Ayton N York 91 9985
East Balsdon Cnwll 5 2898
East Bank Blae G 33 2105
East Barkwith Lincs 76 1681
East Barming Kent 28 7254
East Barnby N York 90 8212
East Barnet Gt Lon 27 2795
East Barns E Loth 119 7176
East Barsham Norfk 66 9133
East Beckham Norfk 66 1639
East Bedfont Gt Lon 26 0873
East Bergholt Suffk 54 0734
East Bierley W York 82 1929
East Bilney Norfk 66 9519
East Blatchington E Susx 16 4800
East Bloxworth Dorset 11 8894
East Boldon T & W 96 3661
East Boldre Hants 12 3700
East Bolton Nthumb 111 1216
East Bower Somset 21 3237
East Bradenham Norfk 66 9308
East Brent Somset 21 3451
East Bridgford Notts 63 6943
East Briscoe Dur 95 9719
East Buckland Devon 19 6831
East Budleigh Devon 9 0684
East Burnham Bucks 26 9584
East Burton Dorset 11 8287
East Butsfield Dur 95 1145
East Butterwick Lincs 84 8306
East Calder W Loth 117 0867
East Carleton Norfk 66 1701
East Carlton Nhants 51 8389
East Carlton W York 82 2143
East Challow Oxon 36 3888
East Charleton Devon 7 7642
East Chelborough Dorset 10 5505
East Chevington Nthumb 103 2699
East Chiltington E Susx 15 3715
East Chinnock Somset 10 4913
East Chisenbury Wilts 23 1452
East Cholderton Hants 23 2945
East Clandon Surrey 26 0651
East Claydon Bucks 49 7325
East Clevedon Somset 34 4171
East Coker Somset 10 5412
East Combe Somset 20 1631
East Compton Somset 21 6141
East Cornworthy Devon 7 8455
East Cote Cumb 92 1255
East Cottingwith E R Yk 84 7042
East Cowes IOW 13 5095
East Cowick E R Yk 83 6620
East Cowton N York 89 3003
East Cramlington Nthumb 103 2776
East Cranmore Somset 22 6743
East Creech Dorset 11 9382
East Curthwaite Cumb 93 3348
East Dean E Susx 16 5598
East Dean Gloucs 35 6520
East Dean Hants 23 2726
East Dean W Susx 14 9012
East Down Devon 19 6041
East Drayton Notts 75 7775
East Dulwich Gt Lon 27 3375
East Dundry Somset 21 5766
East Ella E R Yk 84 0529
East End Beds 38 9642
East End Beds 51 1055
East End Bucks 38 9344
East End E R Yk 85 1931
East End E R Yk 85 2927
East End Essex 39 4210
East End Hants 24 4161
East End Hants 12 3696
East End Herts 39 4527
East End Kent 17 8335
East End Kent 28 9673
East End Oxon 36 3915
East End Somset 34 4770
East End Somset 22 6746
East Everleigh Wilts 23 2053
East Farleigh Kent 28 7353
East Farndon Nhants 50 7184
East Ferry Lincs 75 8199
East Firsby Lincs 76 0085
East Fortune E Loth 118 5479
East Garforth W York 83 4133
East Garston Berks 36 3576
East Ginge Oxon 37 4486
East Goscote Leics 63 6413
East Grafton Wilts 23 2560
East Grange Moray 141 0961
East Green Suffk 55 4065
East Grimstead Wilts 23 2227
East Grinstead W Susx 15 3938
East Guldeford E Susx 17 9321
East Haddon Nhants 50 6668
East Hagbourne Oxon 37 5288
East Halton Lincs 85 1319
East Ham Gt Lon 27 4283
East Hanney Oxon 36 4193
East Hanningfield Essex 40 7701
East Hardwick W York 83 4618
East Harling Norfk 54 9986
East Harlsey N York 89 4299
East Harnham Wilts 23 1428
East Harptree Somset 21 5655
East Hartburn Dur 96 4217
East Hartford Nthumb 103 2679
East Harting W Susx 14 7919
East Hatch Wilts 22 9228
East Hatley Cambs 52 2850
East Hauxwell N York 89 1693
East Haven Angus 127 5836
East Heckington Lincs 64 1944
East Hedleyhope Dur 96 1540
East Helmsdale Highld 147 0315
East Hendred Oxon 37 4588
East Heslerton N York 91 9276
East Hewish Somset 21 4064
East Hoathly E Susx 16 5216
East Holme Dorset 11 8986
East Horrington Somset 21 5846
East Horsley Surrey 26 0952
East Horton Nthumb 111 0330
East Howe Dorset 12 0795
East Huntington N York 83 6155
East Huntspill Somset 21 3445
East Hyde Beds 38 1217
East Ilkerton Devon 19 7147
East Ilsley Berks 37 4980
East Keal Lincs 77 3863
East Kennett Wilts 23 1167
East Keswick W York 83 3644
East Kilbride S Lans 116 6354
East Kimber Devon 5 4998
East Kirkby Lincs 77 3362
East Knighton Dorset 11 8185
East Knowstone Devon 19 8423
East Knoyle Wilts 22 8830
East Kyloe Nthumb 111 0639
East Lambrook Somset 10 4318
East Langdon Kent 29 3346
East Langton Leics 50 7292
East Laroch Highld 130 0858
East Lavant W Susx 14 8608
East Lavington W Susx 14 9416
East Layton N York 89 1609
East Leake Notts 62 5526
East Learmouth Nthumb 110 8637
East Leigh Devon 8 6905
East Leigh Devon 7 6852
East Leigh Devon 7 7657
East Lexham Norfk 66 8517
East Linton E Loth 118 5977
East Liss Hants 14 7827
East Lockinge Oxon 36 4287
East Lound Lincs 75 7899
East Lulworth Dorset 11 8682
East Lutton N York 91 9469
East Lydeard Somset 20 1829
East Lydford Somset 21 5731
East Malling Kent 28 7056
East Malling Heath Kent 28 6955
East Marden W Susx 14 8014
East Markham Notts 75 7373
East Martin Hants 12 0719
East Marton N York 81 9050
East Meon Hants 13 6822
East Mere Devon 9 9916
East Mersea Essex 41 0414
East Molesey Surrey 26 1467
East Morden Dorset 11 9194
East Morton D & G 108 8800
East Morton W York 82 0942
East Ness N York 90 6978
East Newton E R Yk 85 2638
East Norton Leics 50 7800
East Oakley Hants 24 5749
East Ogwell Devon 7 8370
East Orchard Dorset 11 8317
East Ord Nthumb 119 9751
East Panson Devon 5 3692
East Parley Dorset 12 1097
East Peckham Kent 28 6648
East Pennar Pembks 30 9602
East Pennard Somset 21 5937
East Perry Cambs 52 1566
East Portlemouth Devon 7 7538
East Prawle Devon 7 7836
East Preston W Susx 14 0602
East Pulham Dorset 11 7209
East Putford Devon 18 3616
East Quantoxhead Somset 20 1343
East Rainham Kent 28 8267
East Rainton T & W 96 3347
East Ravendale Lincs 76 2399
East Raynham Norfk 66 8825
East Rigton W York 83 3743
East Rolstone Somset 21 3962
East Rounton N York 89 4203
East Rudham Norfk 66 8228
East Runton Norfk 67 1942
East Ruston Norfk 67 3427
East Saltoun E Loth 118 4767
East Scrafton N York 89 0884
East Sheen Gt Lon 26 2075
East Shefford Berks 36 3874
East Sleekburn Nthumb 103 2883
East Somerton Norfk 67 4719
East Stockwith Lincs 75 7894
East Stoke Dorset 11 8686
East Stoke Notts 75 7549
East Stour Dorset 22 8022
East Stourmouth Kent 29 2662
East Stowford Devon 19 6326
East Stratton Hants 24 5440
East Studdal Kent 29 3149
East Sutton Kent 28 8349
East Taphouse Cnwll 4 1863
East Thirston Nthumb 89 1900
East Tilbury Essex 28 6877
East Tisted Hants 24 7032
East Torrington Lincs 76 1483
East Tuddenham Norfk 66 0711
East Tytherley Hants 23 2929
East Tytherton Wilts 35 9674
East Village Devon 8 8405
East Wall Shrops 59 5293
East Walton Norfk 65 7416
East Water Somset 21 5350
East Week Devon 8 6692
East Wellow Hants 12 3020
East Wemyss Fife 118 3497
East Whitburn W Loth 117 9665
East Wickham Gt Lon 27 4677
East Williamston Pembks 31 0904
East Winch Norfk 65 6916
East Winterslow Wilts 23 2434
East Wittering W Susx 14 7997
East Witton N York 89 1486
East Woodburn Nthumb 102 9086
East Woodhay Hants 24 4061
East Woodlands Somset 22 7944
East Worldham Hants 24 7538
East Wretham Norfk 54 9190
East Youlstone Devon 18 2715
East-the-Water Devon 18 4526
Eastbourne Dur 89 3013
Eastbourne E Susx 16 6199
Eastbridge Suffk 55 4566
Eastbrook V Glam 33 1671
Eastburn W York 82 0144
Eastbury Berks 36 3477
Eastbury Herts 26 1092
Eastby N York 82 0154
Eastchurch Kent 28 9871
Eastcombe Gloucs 35 8904
Eastcote Gt Lon 26 1088
Eastcote Nhants 49 6853
Eastcote W Mids 61 1979
Eastcott Cnwll 18 2515
Eastcott Wilts 23 0255
Eastcourt Wilts 35 9792
Eastcourt Wilts 23 2361
Eastdown Devon 7 8249
Eastend Essex 40 9492
Eastend S Lans 108 9537
Easter Balmoral Abers 133 2694
Easter Compton Gloucs 34 5782
Easter Dalziel Highld 140 7550
Easter Howgate Mdloth 117 2463
Easter Kinkell Highld 139 5755
Easter Moniack Highld 139 5543
Easter Ord Abers 135 8304
Easter Pitkierie Fife 127 5606
Easter Skeld Shet 153 3144
Easter Softlaw Border 110 7532
Eastergate W Susx 14 9405
Easterhouse C Glas 116 6865
Eastern Green W Mids 61 2879
Easterton Wilts 23 0254
Eastertown Somset 21 3454
Eastfield N Lans 116 8964
Eastfield N York 91 0484
Eastgate Dur 95 9538
Eastgate Lincs 64 1019
Eastgate Norfk 66 1423
Eastham Mersyd 78 3680
Eastham Ferry Mersyd 78 3681
Easthampstead Berks 25 8667
Easthampton Herefd 46 4063
Eastheath Berks 25 7967
Easthope Shrops 59 5695
Easthorpe Essex 40 9121
Easthorpe Notts 75 7053
Eastington Devon 19 7408
Eastington Gloucs 36 1213
Eastington Gloucs 35 7705
Eastlands D & G 100 8172
Eastleach Martin Gloucs 36 2004
Eastleach Turville Gloucs 36 1905
Eastleigh Devon 18 4827
Eastleigh Hants 13 4519
Eastling Kent 28 9656
Eastmoor Norfk 65 7303
Eastney Hants 13 6698
Eastnor Herefd 47 7237
Eastoft Lincs 84 8016
Easton Berks 24 4172
Easton Cambs 52 1371
Easton Cumb 93 2759
Easton Devon 8 7289
Easton Dorset 11 6971
Easton Hants 24 5132
Easton IOW 12 3486
Easton Lincs 63 9326
Easton Norfk 66 1310
Easton Somset 21 5147
Easton Suffk 55 2858
Easton Wilts 35 8970
Easton Grey Wilts 35 8887
Easton Maudit Nhants 51 8858
Easton on the Hill Nhants 64 0104
Easton Royal Wilts 23 2060
Easton-in-Gordano Somset 34 5175
Eastpeek Devon 5 3494
Eastrea Cambs 64 2997
Eastriggs D & G 101 2466
Eastrington E R Yk 84 7929
Eastrop Wilts 36 2092
Eastry Kent 29 3054
Eastshaw W Susx 14 8724
Eastville Lincs 77 4056
Eastwell Leics 63 7728
Eastwick Herts 39 4311
Eastwood Essex 40 8688
Eastwood Notts 62 4646
Eastwood W York 82 9726
Eastwood End Cambs 65 4292
Eathorpe Warwks 48 3969
Eaton Ches 71 5763
Eaton Ches 72 8765
Eaton Leics 63 7928
Eaton Norfk 67 2006
Eaton Notts 75 7077
Eaton Oxon 37 4403
Eaton Shrops 59 3789
Eaton Shrops 59 5089
Eaton Bishop Herefd 46 4439
Eaton Bray Beds 38 9720
Eaton Constantine Shrops 59 5906
Eaton Ford Beds 52 1759
Eaton Green Beds 38 9621
Eaton Hastings Oxon 36 2598
Eaton Mascott Shrops 59 5305
Eaton Socon Cambs 52 1759
Eaton upon Tern Shrops 72 6523
Eaves Brow Ches 79 6393
Eaves Green W Mids 61 2682
Ebberston N York 91 8982
Ebbesborne Wake Wilts 22 9924
Ebbw Vale Blae G 33 1609
Ebchester Dur 95 1055
Ebdon Somset 21 3664
Ebford Devon 9 9887
Ebley Gloucs 35 8205
Ebnal Ches 71 4948
Ebnall Herefd 46 4758
Ebrington Gloucs 48 1840
Ebsworthy Town Devon 5 5090
Ecchinswell Hants 24 4959
Ecclaw Border 119 7568
Ecclefechan D & G 101 1974
Eccles Border 110 7641
Eccles Gt Man 79 7798
Eccles Kent 28 7360
Eccles Green Herefd 46 3748
Eccles on Sea Norfk 67 4128
Eccles Road Norfk 54 0189
Ecclesall S York 74 3284
Ecclesfield S York 74 3593
Eccleshall Staffs 72 8329
Eccleshill W York 82 1736
Ecclesmachan W Loth 117 0573
Eccleston Ches 71 4162
Eccleston Lancs 80 5217
Eccleston Mersyd 78 4895
Eccleston Green Lancs 80 5216
Echt Abers 135 7405
Eckford Border 110 7026
Eckington Derbys 75 4379
Eckington Worcs 47 9241
Ecton Nhants 51 8263
Ecton Staffs 74 0958
Edale Derbys 74 1285
Edburton W Susx 15 2311
Edderside Cumb 92 1045
Edderton Highld 146 7084
Eddington Kent 29 1867
Eddleston Border 117 2447
Eddlewood S Lans 116 7153
Eden Mount Cumb 87 4077
Eden Park Gt Lon 27 3667
Edenbridge Kent 16 4446
Edenfield Lancs 81 8019
Edenhall Cumb 94 5632
Edenham Lincs 64 0621
Edensor Derbys 74 2469
Edentaggart Ag & B 115 3293
Edenthorpe S York 83 6206
Edern Gwynd 56 2739
Edgarley Somset 21 5238
Edgbaston W Mids 61 0684
Edgcombe Cnwll 2 7133
Edgcott Bucks 37 6722
Edgcott Somset 19 8438
Edge Gloucs 35 8409
Edge Shrops 59 3908
Edge End Gloucs 34 5913
Edge Green Ches 71 4851
Edgebolton Shrops 59 5721
Edgefield Norfk 66 0934
Edgefield Green Norfk 66 0934
Edgefold Gt Man 79 7005
Edgehill Warwks 48 3747
Edgerley Shrops 59 3518
Edgerton W York 82 1317
Edgeside Lancs 81 8322
Edgeworth Gloucs 35 9406
Edgeworthy Devon 19 8413
Edgiock Worcs 48 0461
Edgmond Shrops 72 7119
Edgmond Marsh Shrops 72 7120
Edgton Shrops 59 3885
Edgware Gt Lon 26 1991
Edgworth Lancs 81 7416
Edial Staffs 61 0808
Edinample Stirlg 124 6022
Edinbane Highld 136 3450
Edinburgh C Edin 117 2573
Edingale Staffs 61 2111
Edingham D & G 100 8363
Edingley Notts 75 6655
Edingthorpe Norfk 67 3132
Edingthorpe Green Norfk 67 3031
Edington Border 119 8955
Edington Nthumb 103 1582
Edington Somset 21 3839
Edington Wilts 22 9253
Edington Burtle Somset 21 3943
Edingworth Somset 21 3653
Edith Weston Rutlnd 63 9205
Edithmead Somset 21 3249
Edlesborough Bucks 38 9719
Edlingham Nthumb 111 1109
Edlington Lincs 76 2371
Edmond Castle Cumb 94 4958
Edmondsham Dorset 12 0611
Edmondsley Dur 96 2349
Edmondthorpe Leics 63 8517
Edmonton Cnwll 4 9672
Edmonton Gt Lon 27 3492
Edmundbyers Dur 95 0150
Ednam Border 110 7337
Ednaston Derbys 73 2341
Edradynate P & K 125 8751
Edrom Border 119 8255
Edstaston Shrops 59 5132
Edstone Warwks 48 1861
Edvin Loach Herefd 47 6658
Edwalton Notts 62 5935
Edwardstone Suffk 54 9442
Edwardsville Myr Td 33 0896
Edwinsford Carmth 44 6334
Edwinstowe Notts 75 6266
Edworth Beds 39 2241
Edwyn Ralph Herefd 47 6457
Edzell Angus 134 6068
Efail Isaf Rhondd 33 0884
Efail-fach Neath 32 7895
Efail-Rhyd Powys 58 1626
Efailnewydd Gwynd 56 3535
Efailwen Carmth 31 1325
Efenechtyd Denbgs 70 1155
Effgill D & G 101 3092
Effingham Surrey 26 1153
Efflinch Staffs 73 1816
Efford Devon 9 8901
Egbury Hants 24 4352
Egdean W Susx 14 9920
Egerton Gt Man 81 7014
Egerton Kent 28 9147
Eggbuckland Devon 6 5057
Eggesford Devon 19 6811
Eggington Beds 38 9525
Egginton Derbys 73 2628
Egglescliffe Dur 89 4113
Eggleston Dur 95 9923
Egham Surrey 25 0071
Egham Wick Surrey 25 9870
Eginswell Devon 7 8866
Egleton Rutlnd 63 8707
Eglingham Nthumb 111 1019
Egloshayle Cnwll 4 0072
Egloskerry Cnwll 5 2786
Eglwys Cross Wrexhm 71 4740
Eglwys-Brewis V Glam 20 0068
Eglwysbach Conwy 69 8070
Eglwysfach Cerdgn 43 6996
Eglwyswrw Pembks 31 1438
Egmanton Notts 75 7368
Egremont Cumb 86 0110
Egremont Mersyd 78 3192
Egton N York 90 8006
Egton Bridge N York 90 8004
Eight and Forty E R Yk 84 8529
Eight Ash Green Essex 40 9425
Eilanreach Highld 129 8018
Elan Village Powys 45 9364
Elberton Gloucs 34 6088
Elbridge W Susx 14 9101
Elburton Devon 6 5353
Elcombe Wilts 36 1280
Elcot Berks 36 3969
Elder Street Essex 53 5734
Eldernell Cambs 64 3298
Eldersfield Worcs 47 7931
Elderslie Rens 115 4463
Eldmire N York 89 4274
Eldon Dur 96 2328
Eldwick W York 82 1240
Elfhill Abers 135 8085
Elford Nthumb 111 1831
Elford Staffs 61 1810
Elgin Moray 141 2162
Elgol Highld 128 5213
Elham Kent 29 1744
Elie Fife 118 4900
Elilaw Nthumb 111 9708
Elim IOA 68 3584
Eling Hants 12 3612
Elkesley Notts 75 6975
Elkstone Gloucs 35 9612
Ella Abers 142 6459
Ellanbeich Ag & B 122 7417
Elland W York 82 1120
Elland Lower Edge W York 82 1221
Ellary Ag & B 113 7376
Ellastone Staffs 73 1143
Ellel Lancs 80 4856
Ellemford Border 119 7260
Ellen's Green Surrey 14 0935
Ellenborough Cumb 92 0435
Ellenbrook Gt Man 79 7201
Ellenhall Staffs 72 8426
Ellerbeck N York 89 4396
Ellerby N York 90 7914
Ellerdine Heath Shrops 59 6122
Ellerhayes Devon 9 9702
Elleric Ag & B 123 0448
Ellerker E R Yk 84 9229
Ellers N York 82 0043
Ellerton E R Yk 84 7039
Ellerton N York 89 2598
Ellerton Shrops 72 7125
Ellesborough Bucks 38 8306
Ellesmere Shrops 59 3934
Ellesmere Port Ches 71 4076
Ellicombe Somset 20 9844
Ellingham Hants 12 1408
Ellingham Norfk 67 3592
Ellingham Nthumb 111 1725
Ellingstring N York 89 1783
Ellington Cambs 52 1671
Ellington Nthumb 103 2791
Ellington Thorpe Cambs 52 1670
Elliots Green Somset 22 7945
Ellisfield Hants 24 6446
Ellishader Highld 137 5065
Ellistown Leics 62 4310
Ellon Abers 143 9530
Ellonby Cumb 93 4235
Ellough Suffk 55 4486
Elloughton E R Yk 84 9428
Ellwood Gloucs 34 5908
Elm Cambs 65 4707
Elm Green Essex 40 7705
Elm Grove Norfk 67 4803
Elm Park Gt Lon 27 5385
Elmbridge Worcs 47 9068
Elmdon Essex 39 4639
Elmdon W Mids 61 1783
Elmdon Heath W Mids 61 1680
Elmer W Susx 14 9800
Elmer's Green Lancs 78 5006
Elmers End Gt Lon 27 3668
Elmesthorpe Leics 50 4696
Elmhurst Staffs 61 1112
Elmley Castle Worcs 47 9841
Elmley Lovett Worcs 47 8769
Elmore Gloucs 35 7815
Elmore Back Gloucs 35 7616
Elms Green Worcs 47 7266
Elmscott Devon 18 2321
Elmsett Suffk 54 0546
Elmstead Heath Essex 41 0622
Elmstead Market Essex 41 0624
Elmstead Row Essex 41 0621
Elmsted Court Kent 29 1144
Elmstone Kent 29 2660
Elmstone Hardwicke Gloucs 47 9125
Elmswell E R Yk 91 9958
Elmswell Suffk 54 9964
Elmton Derbys 75 5073
Elphin Highld 145 2111
Elphinstone E Loth 118 3970
Elrick Abers 135 8106
Elrig D & G 98 3247
Elrington Nthumb 102 8563

Elsdon Fieldhead


Elsdon *Nthumb* 102 9393
Elsecar *S York* 74 3899
Elsenham *Essex* 39 5326
Elsfield *Oxon* 37 5410
Elsham *Lincs* 84 0312
Elsick House *Abers* 135 8894
Elsing *Norfk* 66 0516
Elslack *N York* 81 9349
Elson *Hants* 13 6002
Elson *Shrops* 59 3735
Elsrickle *S Lans* 108 0643
Elstead *Surrey* 25 9043
Elsted *W Susx* 14 8119
Elsthorpe *Lincs* 64 0623
Elstob *Dur* 96 3323
Elston *Lancs* 81 5932
Elston *Notts* 63 7647
Elston *Wilts* 23 0644
Elstone *Devon* 19 6716
Elstow *Beds* 38 0546
Elstree *Herts* 26 1795
Elstronwick *E R Yk* 85 2232
Elswick *Lancs* 80 4238
Elswick *T & W* 103 2263
Elsworth *Cambs* 52 3163
Elterwater *Cumb* 86 3204
Eltham *Gt Lon* 27 4274
Eltisley *Cambs* 52 2759
Elton *Cambs* 51 0893
Elton *Ches* 71 4575
Elton *Derbys* 74 2260
Elton *Dur* 96 4017
Elton *Gloucs* 35 7014
Elton *Gt Man* 81 7911
Elton *Herefd* 46 4570
Elton *Notts* 63 7638
Elton Green *Ches* 71 4574
Eltringham *Nthumb* 103 0762
Elvanfoot *S Lans* 108 9517
Elvaston *Derbys* 62 4032
Elveden *Suffk* 54 8280
Elvetham Hall *Hants* 25 7856
Elvingston *E Loth* 118 4674
Elvington *Kent* 29 2750
Elvington *N York* 84 7047
Elwell *Devon* 19 6631
Elwick *Dur* 97 4532
Elwick *Nthumb* 111 1136
Elworth *Ches* 72 7361
Elworthy *Somset* 20 0834
Ely *Cambs* 53 5480
Ely *Cardif* 33 1476
Emberton *Bucks* 38 8849
Embleton *Cumb* 92 1629
Embleton *Dur* 96 4129
Embleton *Nthumb* 111 2322
Embo *Highld* 147 8192
Embo Street *Highld* 147 8091
Emborough *Somset* 21 6151
Embsay *N York* 82 0053
Emery Down *Hants* 12 2808
Emley *W York* 82 2413
Emley Moor *W York* 82 2313
Emmbrook *Berks* 25 8069
Emmer Green *Berks* 37 7276
Emmett Carr *Derbys* 75 4577
Emmington *Oxon* 37 7402
Emneth *Cambs* 65 4807
Emneth Hungate *Norfk* 65 5107
Empingham *Rutlnd* 63 9408
Empshott *Hants* 24 7531
Empshott Green *Hants* 24 7431
Emsworth *Hants* 13 7406
Enborne *Berks* 24 4365
Enborne Row *Hants* 24 4463
Enchmarsh *Shrops* 59 5096
Enderby *Leics* 50 5399
Endmoor *Cumb* 87 5384
Endon *Staffs* 72 9253
Endon Bank *Staffs* 72 9253
Enfield *Gt Lon* 27 3597
Enfield Lock *Gt Lon* 27 3698
Enfield Wash *Gt Lon* 27 3598
Enford *Wilts* 23 1351
Engine Common *Gloucs* 35 6984
England's Gate *Herefd* 46 5451
Englefield *Berks* 24 6272
Englefield Green *Surrey* 25 9971
Englesea-brook *Ches* 72 7551
English Bicknor *Gloucs* 34 5815
English Frankton *Shrops* 59 4529
Englishcombe *Somset* 22 7162
Engollan *Cnwll* 4 8670
Enham-Alamein *Hants* 23 3649
Enmore *Somset* 20 2435
Enmore Green *Dorset* 22 8523
Ennerdale Bridge *Cumb* 92 0615
Enniscaven *Cnwll* 4 9659
Enochdhu *P & K* 133 0662
Ensay *Ag & B* 121 3648
Ensbury *Dorset* 12 0896
Ensdon *Shrops* 59 4017
Ensis *Devon* 19 5626
Enson *Staffs* 72 9328
Enstone *Oxon* 48 3724
Enterkinfoot *D & G* 108 8504
Enterpen *N York* 89 4605
Enville *Staffs* 60 8286
Enys *Cnwll* 3 7836
Epney *Gloucs* 35 7611
Epperstone *Notts* 75 6548
Epping *Essex* 27 4502
Epping Green *Essex* 39 4305
Epping Green *Herts* 39 2906
Epping Upland *Essex* 39 4404
Eppleby *N York* 89 1713
Eppleworth *E R Yk* 84 0131
Epsom *Surrey* 26 2160
Epwell *Oxon* 48 3540
Epworth *Lincs* 84 7803
Epworth Turbary *Lincs* 84 7603
Erbistock *Wrexhm* 71 3541
Erdington *W Mids* 61 1191
Eridge Green *E Susx* 16 5535
Eridge Station *E Susx* 16 5434
Erines *Ag & B* 113 8575
Erisey *Cnwll* 2 7117
Eriska *Ag & B* 122 9043
Eriswell *Suffk* 53 7278
Erith *Gt Lon* 27 5177
Erlestoke *Wilts* 22 9653
Ermington *Devon* 6 6353
Erpingham *Norfk* 67 1931
Erriottwood *Kent* 28 9459
Errogie *Highld* 139 5622
Errol *P & K* 126 2422
Erskine *Rens* 115 4770
Ervie *D & G* 98 0067
Erwarton *Suffk* 55 2234
Erwood *Powys* 45 0942
Eryholme *N York* 89 3208
Eryrys *Denbgs* 70 2057
Escalls *Cnwll* 2 3627
Escomb *Dur* 96 1830
Escott *Somset* 20 0937
Escrick *N York* 83 6242
Esgair *Carmth* 31 3728
Esgair *Cerdgn* 43 5868
Esgairgeiliog *Powys* 57 7606
Esgerdawe *Carmth* 44 6140
Esgyryn *Conwy* 69 8078
Esh *Dur* 96 1944
Esh Winning *Dur* 96 1942
Esher *Surrey* 26 1364
Esholt *W York* 82 1840
Eshott *Nthumb* 103 2097
Eshton *N York* 81 9356
Eskadale *Highld* 139 4540
Eskbank *Mdloth* 118 3266
Eskdale Green *Cumb* 86 1400
Eskdalemuir *D & G* 101 2597
Eskett *Cumb* 92 0516
Eskham *Lincs* 77 3698
Eskholme *S York* 83 6317
Esperley Lane Ends *Dur* 96 1324
Esprick *Lancs* 80 4036
Essendine *Rutlnd* 64 0412
Essendon *Herts* 39 2708
Essich *Highld* 140 6439
Essington *Staffs* 60 9603
Esslemont *Abers* 143 9229
Eston *N York* 97 5418
Etal *Nthumb* 110 9339
Etchilhampton *Wilts* 23 0460
Etchingham *E Susx* 17 7126
Etchinghill *Kent* 29 1639
Etchinghill *Staffs* 73 0218
Etchingwood *E Susx* 16 5022
Etherdwick *E R Yk* 85 2337
Etling Green *Norfk* 66 0113
Etloe *Gloucs* 35 6806
Eton *Berks* 26 9677
Eton Wick *Berks* 26 9478
Etruria *Staffs* 72 8647
Etteridge *Highld* 132 6892
Ettersgill *Dur* 95 8829
Ettiley Heath *Ches* 72 7360
Ettingshall *W Mids* 60 9396
Ettington *Warwks* 48 2749
Etton *Cambs* 64 1406
Etton *E R Yk* 84 9743
Ettrick *Border* 109 2714
Ettrickbridge *Border* 109 3824
Ettrickhill *Border* 109 2514
Etwall *Derbys* 73 2631
Eudon George *Shrops* 60 6888
Euston *Suffk* 54 8979
Euximoor Drove *Cambs* 65 4898
Euxton *Lancs* 81 5519
Evancoyd *Powys* 46 2663
Evanton *Highld* 140 6066
Evedon *Lincs* 76 0947
Evelith *Shrops* 60 7405
Evelix *Highld* 147 7790
Evenjobb *Powys* 46 2662
Evenley *Oxon* 49 5834
Evenlode *Gloucs* 48 2129
Evenwood *Dur* 96 1524
Evenwood Gate *Dur* 96 1624
Evercreech *Somset* 21 6438
Everingham *E R Yk* 84 8042
Everleigh *Wilts* 23 2053
Everley *N York* 91 9788
Eversfield *Devon* 5 4792
Eversholt *Beds* 38 9833
Evershot *Dorset* 10 5704
Eversley *Hants* 25 7762
Eversley Cross *Hants* 25 7961
Everthorpe *E R Yk* 84 9031
Everton *Beds* 52 2051
Everton *Hants* 12 2894
Everton *Mersyd* 78 3491
Everton *Notts* 75 6990
Evertown *D & G* 101 3576
Evesbatch *Herefd* 47 6948
Evesham *Worcs* 48 0344
Evington *Leics* 62 6203
Ewden Village *S York* 74 2796
Ewdness *Shrops* 60 7396
Ewell *Surrey* 26 2262
Ewell Minnis *Kent* 29 2643
Ewelme *Oxon* 37 6491
Ewen *Gloucs* 35 0097
Ewenny *V Glam* 33 9077
Ewerby *Lincs* 76 1247
Ewerby Thorpe *Lincs* 76 1347
Ewesley *Nthumb* 103 0591
Ewhurst *Surrey* 14 0940
Ewhurst Green *E Susx* 17 7924
Ewhurst Green *Surrey* 14 0939
Ewloe *Flints* 71 3066
Ewloe Green *Flints* 71 2966
Ewood *Lancs* 81 6725
Ewood Bridge *Lancs* 81 7920
Eworthy *Devon* 5 4495
Ewshot *Hants* 25 8149
Ewyas Harold *Herefd* 46 3828
Exbourne *Devon* 8 6002
Exbury *Hants* 13 4200
Exceat *E Susx* 16 5199
Exebridge *Somset* 20 9324
Exelby *N York* 89 2987
Exeter *Devon* 9 9292
Exford *Somset* 19 8538
Exfordsgreen *Shrops* 59 4505
Exhall *Warwks* 48 1055
Exhall *Warwks* 61 3485
Exlade Street *Oxon* 37 6581
Exley Head *W York* 82 0440
Exminster *Devon* 9 9487
Exmouth *Devon* 9 0081
Exning *Suffk* 53 6265
Exted *Kent* 29 1744
Exton *Devon* 9 9886
Exton *Hants* 13 6120
Exton *Rutlnd* 63 9211
Exton *Somset* 20 9233
Exwick *Devon* 9 9093
Eyam *Derbys* 74 2176
Eydon *Nhants* 49 5449
Eye *Cambs* 64 2202
Eye *Herefd* 46 4964
Eye *Suffk* 54 1473
Eye Green *Cambs* 64 2303
Eye Kettleby *Leics* 63 7316
Eyemouth *Border* 119 9464
Eyeworth *Beds* 52 2545
Eyhorne Street *Kent* 28 8354
Eyke *Suffk* 55 3151
Eynesbury *Beds* 52 1859
Eynsford *Kent* 27 5465
Eynsham *Oxon* 36 4309
Eype *Dorset* 10 4491
Eyre *Highld* 136 4153
Eythorne *Kent* 29 2849
Eyton *Herefd* 46 4761
Eyton *Shrops* 59 3714
Eyton *Shrops* 59 4422
Eyton *Shrops* 59 3787
Eyton *Wrexhm* 71 3544
Eyton on Severn *Shrops* 59 5806
Eyton upon the
Weald Moors *Shrops* 72 6515


# F


Faccombe *Hants* 23 3857
Faceby *N York* 90 4903
Fachwen *Powys* 58 0316
Facit *Lancs* 81 8819
Fackley *Notts* 75 4761
Faddiley *Ches* 71 5852
Fadmoor *N York* 90 6789
Faerdre *Swans* 32 6901
Fagwyr *Swans* 32 6702
Faifley *W Duns* 115 4973
Failand *Somset* 34 5171
Failford *S Ayrs* 107 4626
Failsworth *Gt Man* 79 8901
Fair Oak *Hants* 13 4918
Fair Oak Green *Hants* 24 6660
Fairbourne *Gwynd* 57 6113
Fairburn *N York* 83 4727
Fairfield *Derbys* 74 0673
Fairfield *Kent* 17 9626
Fairfield *Worcs* 60 9475
Fairford *Gloucs* 36 1501
Fairford Park *Gloucs* 36 1501
Fairgirth *D & G* 92 8756
Fairhaven *Lancs* 80 3227
Fairlie *N Ayrs* 114 2054
Fairlight *E Susx* 17 8511
Fairmile *Devon* 9 0897
Fairmile *Surrey* 26 1161
Fairnilee *Border* 109 4532
Fairoak *Staffs* 72 7632
Fairseat *Kent* 27 6261
Fairstead *Essex* 40 7616
Fairstead *Norfk* 67 2823
Fairwarp *E Susx* 16 4626
Fairwater *Cardif* 33 1477
Fairy Cross *Devon* 18 4024
Fakenham *Norfk* 66 9229
Fakenham Magna *Suffk* 54 9176
Fala *Mdloth* 118 4460
Fala Dam *Mdloth* 118 4361
Falcondale *Cerdgn* 44 5649
Falcut *Nhants* 49 5942
Faldingworth *Lincs* 76 0684
Faldouet *Jersey* 158 0000
Falfield *Gloucs* 35 6893
Falkenham *Suffk* 55 2939
Falkirk *Falk* 116 8880
Falkland *Fife* 126 2507
Fallgate *Derbys* 74 3561
Fallin *Stirlg* 116 8391
Falloden *Nthumb* 111 1922
Fallowfield *Gt Man* 79 8593
Fallowfield *Nthumb* 102 9268
Falls of Blarghour *Ag & B* 122 9913
Falmer *E Susx* 15 3508
Falmouth *Cnwll* 3 8032
Falnash *Border* 109 3905
Falsgrave *N York* 91 0288
Falstone *Nthumb* 102 7287
Fanagmore *Highld* 148 1749
Fancott *Beds* 38 0127
Fanellan *Highld* 139 4942
Fangdale Beck *N York* 90 5694
Fangfoss *E R Yk* 84 7653
Fanmore *Ag & B* 121 4144
Fannich Lodge *Highld* 139 2266
Fans *Border* 110 6140
Far Bletchley *Bucks* 38 8533
Far Cotton *Nhants* 49 7559
Far End *Cumb* 86 3098
Far Forest *Worcs* 60 7275
Far Green *Gloucs* 35 7700
Far Moor *Gt Man* 78 5204
Far Oakridge *Gloucs* 35 9203
Far Sawrey *Cumb* 87 3795
Far Thorpe *Lincs* 77 2674
Farcet *Cambs* 64 2094
Farden *Shrops* 46 5775
Fareham *Hants* 13 5606
Farewell *Staffs* 61 0811
Farforth *Lincs* 77 3178
Faringdon *Oxon* 36 2895
Farington *Lancs* 80 5325
Farkhill *P & K* 125 0435
Farlam *Cumb* 94 5558
Farleigh *Devon* 7 7553
Farleigh *Somset* 21 5069
Farleigh *Surrey* 27 3760
Farleigh Hungerford *Somset* 22 8057
Farleigh Wallop *Hants* 24 6247
Farlesthorpe *Lincs* 77 4774
Farleton *Cumb* 87 5380
Farleton *Lancs* 87 5767
Farley *Derbys* 74 2962
Farley *Staffs* 73 0644
Farley *Wilts* 23 2229
Farley Green *Suffk* 53 7353
Farley Green *Surrey* 14 0545
Farley Hill *Berks* 24 7464
Farleys End *Gloucs* 35 7614
Farlington *N York* 90 6167
Farlow *Shrops* 59 6380
Farm Town *Leics* 62 3916
Farmborough *Somset* 22 6660
Farmbridge End *Essex* 40 6211
Farmcote *Gloucs* 48 0628
Farmcote *Shrops* 60 7791
Farmers *Carmth* 44 6444
Farmington *Gloucs* 36 1315
Farmoor *Oxon* 37 4506
Farms Common *Cnwll* 2 6734
Farmtown *Moray* 142 5051
Farnachty *Moray* 142 4261
Farnah Green *Derbys* 62 3347
Farnborough *Berks* 36 4381
Farnborough *Gt Lon* 27 4464
Farnborough *Hants* 25 8753
Farnborough *Warwks* 49 4349
Farnborough Park *Hants* 25 8755
Farnborough Street *Hants* 25 8756
Farncombe *Surrey* 25 9744
Farndish *Beds* 51 9263
Farndon *Ches* 71 4154
Farndon *Notts* 75 7651
Farnell *Angus* 127 6255
Farnham *Dorset* 11 9515
Farnham *Essex* 39 4724
Farnham *N York* 89 3460
Farnham *Suffk* 55 3660
Farnham *Surrey* 25 8346
Farnham Common *Bucks* 26 9585
Farnham Green *Essex* 39 4625
Farnham Royal *Bucks* 26 9583
Farningham *Kent* 27 5467
Farnley *N York* 82 2148
Farnley *W York* 82 2532
Farnley Tyas *W York* 82 1612
Farnsfield *Notts* 75 6456
Farnworth *Ches* 78 5187
Farnworth *Gt Man* 79 7306
Farr *Highld* 150 7163
Farr *Highld* 140 6833
Farr *Highld* 132 8203
Farraline *Highld* 139 5621
Farringdon *Devon* 9 0191
Farrington Gurney *Somset* 21 6355
Farsley *W York* 82 2135
Farther Howegreen *Essex* 40 8401
Farthing Green *Kent* 28 8146
Farthing Street *Gt Lon* 27 4262
Farthinghoe *Nhants* 49 5339
Farthingloe *Kent* 29 2940
Farthingstone *Nhants* 49 6154
Fartown *W York* 82 1518
Fartown *W York* 82 2233
Farway Street *Devon* 9 1895
Fasnacloich *Ag & B* 122 0247
Fasnakyle *Highld* 139 3128
Fassfern *Highld* 130 0278
Fatfield *T & W* 96 2954
Faugh *Cumb* 94 5154
Fauld *Staffs* 73 1728
Fauldhouse *W Loth* 116 9360
Faulkbourne *Essex* 40 7917
Faulkland *Somset* 22 7354
Fauls *Shrops* 59 5832
Faversham *Kent* 28 0161
Fawdington *N York* 89 4372
Fawdon *Nthumb* 111 0315
Fawfieldhead *Staffs* 74 0763
Fawkham Green *Kent* 27 5865
Fawler *Oxon* 36 3717
Fawley *Berks* 36 3981
Fawley *Bucks* 37 7586
Fawley *Hants* 13 4503
Fawley Chapel *Herefd* 46 5929
Fawnog *Flints* 70 2466
Fawsley *Nhants* 49 5656
Faxfleet *E R Yk* 84 8624
Faygate *W Susx* 15 2134
Fazakerley *Mersyd* 78 3796
Fazeley *Staffs* 61 2001
Fearby *N York* 89 1981
Fearn *Highld* 147 8378
Fearnan *P & K* 124 7244
Fearnbeg *Highld* 137 7359
Fearnhead *Ches* 79 6390
Fearnmore *Highld* 137 7260
Fearnoch *Ag & B* 114 9279
Featherstone *Staffs* 60 9305
Featherstone *W York* 83 4221
Feckenham *Worcs* 47 0162
Feering *Essex* 40 8720
Feetham *N York* 88 9898
Feizor *N York* 88 7867
Felbridge *Surrey* 15 3739
Felbrigg *Norfk* 67 2039
Felcourt *Surrey* 15 3841
Felday *Surrey* 14 1144
Felden *Herts* 38 0404
Felin Fach *Cerdgn* 44 5355
Felin gwm Isaf *Carmth* 44 5023
Felin gwm Uchaf *Carmth* 44 5024
Felin-newydd *Powys* 45 1135
Felindre *Carmth* 32 5521
Felindre *Carmth* 44 7027
Felindre *Carmth* 31 3538
Felindre *Cerdgn* 44 5555
Felindre *Powys* 58 1681
Felindre *Powys* 45 1723
Felindre *Swans* 32 6302
Felindre Farchog *Pembks* 31 1039
Felinfach *Powys* 45 0933
Felinfoel *Carmth* 32 5102
Felixkirk *N York* 89 4684
Felixstowe *Suffk* 55 3034
Felixstowe Ferry *Suffk* 55 3237
Felkington *Nthumb* 110 9444
Felkirk *W York* 83 3812
Fell Foot *Cumb* 86 2903
Fell Lane *W York* 82 0440
Fell Side *Cumb* 93 3037
Felling *T & W* 96 2762
Felmersham *Beds* 51 9957
Felmingham *Norfk* 67 2529
Felpham *W Susx* 14 9499
Felsham *Suffk* 54 9457
Felsted *Essex* 40 6720
Feltham *Gt Lon* 26 1073
Felthamhill *Gt Lon* 26 0971
Felthorpe *Norfk* 66 1618
Felton *Herefd* 46 5748
Felton *Nthumb* 103 1800
Felton *Somset* 21 5265
Felton Butler *Shrops* 59 3917
Feltwell *Norfk* 53 7190
Fen Ditton *Cambs* 53 4860
Fen Drayton *Cambs* 52 3368
Fen End *Lincs* 64 2420
Fen End *W Mids* 61 2274
Fen Street *Norfk* 66 9895
Fen Street *Suffk* 54 1862
Fenay Bridge *W York* 82 1815
Fence *Lancs* 81 8237
Fence *S York* 75 4485
Fencehouses *T & W* 96 3250
Fencote *N York* 89 2893
Fencott *Oxon* 37 5716
Fendike Corner *Lincs* 77 4560
Fenham *Nthumb* 111 0840
Feniscliffe *Lancs* 81 6526
Feniscowles *Lancs* 81 6425
Feniton *Devon* 9 1099
Fenn Green *Shrops* 60 7783
Fenn Street *Kent* 28 7975
Fenny Bentley *Derbys* 73 1749
Fenny Bridges *Devon* 9 1198
Fenny Compton *Warwks* 49 4152
Fenny Drayton *Leics* 61 3596
Fenny Stratford *Bucks* 38 8734
Fenrother *Nthumb* 103 1792
Fenstanton *Cambs* 52 3168
Fenstead End *Suffk* 54 8050
Fenton *Cambs* 52 3279
Fenton *Cumb* 94 5056
Fenton *Lincs* 76 8476
Fenton *Lincs* 76 8751
Fenton *Notts* 75 7982
Fenton *Nthumb* 111 9733
Fenton *Staffs* 72 8944
Fenton Barns *E Loth* 118 5181
Fenwick *E Ayrs* 107 4643
Fenwick *Nthumb* 111 0640
Fenwick *Nthumb* 103 0572
Fenwick *S York* 83 5916
Feock *Cnwll* 3 8238
Feolin Ferry *Ag & B* 112 4469
Fergushill *N Ayrs* 106 3343
Feriniquarrie *Highld* 136 1750
Fermain Bay *Guern* 158 0000
Fern *Angus* 134 4861
Ferndale *Rhondd* 33 9996
Ferndown *Dorset* 12 0700
Ferness *Moray* 140 9645
Fernham *Oxon* 36 2991
Fernhill Heath *Worcs* 47 8759
Fernhurst *W Susx* 14 8928
Fernie *Fife* 126 3115
Ferniegair *S Lans* 116 7354
Fernilea *Highld* 136 3732
Fernilee *Derbys* 79 0178
Ferny Common *Herefd* 46 3651
Ferrensby *N York* 89 3760
Ferriby Sluice *Lincs* 84 9720
Ferrindonald *Highld* 129 6608
Ferring *W Susx* 14 0902
Ferry Point *Highld* 146 7385
Ferrybridge *W York* 83 4824
Ferryden *Angus* 127 7156
Ferryhill *Dur* 96 2832
Ferryside *Carmth* 31 3610
Ferrytown *Highld* 146 7387
Fersfield *Norfk* 54 0683
Fersit *Highld* 131 3577
Feshiebridge *Highld* 132 8504
Fetcham *Surrey* 26 1455
Fetterangus *Abers* 143 9850
Fettercairn *Abers* 135 6573
Fewcott *Oxon* 49 5428
Fewston *N York* 82 1954
Ffair Rhos *Cerdgn* 43 7368
Ffairfach *Carmth* 32 6321
Ffald-y-Brenin *Carmth* 44 6344
Ffawyddog *Powys* 33 2018
Ffestiniog *Gwynd* 57 7042
Ffordd-las *Denbgs* 70 1264
Fforest *Carmth* 32 5704
Fforest *Mons* 34 2820
Fforest Fach *Swans* 32 6295
Fforest Goch *Neath* 32 7401
Ffostrasol *Cerdgn* 42 3747
Ffrith *Flints* 70 2855
Ffynnon-Oer *Cerdgn* 44 5353
Ffynnonddewi *Cerdgn* 42 3852
Ffynnongroew *Flints* 70 1382
Fiag Lodge *Highld* 149 4528
Fickleshole *Surrey* 27 3860
Fiddes *Abers* 135 8080
Fiddington *Gloucs* 47 9231
Fiddington *Somset* 20 2140
Fiddleford *Dorset* 11 8013
Fiddlers Green *Cnwll* 3 8155
Fiddlers Hamlet *Essex* 27 4701
Field *Staffs* 73 0233
Field Broughton *Cumb* 87 3881
Field Dalling *Norfk* 66 0038
Field Head *Leics* 62 4909
Fieldhead *Cumb* 93 4539

Fife Keith
Fyfield Wick


Fife Keith *Moray* 142 4250
Fifehead Magdalen *Dorset* 22 7821
Fifehead Neville *Dorset* 11 7610
Fifehead St Quinton *Dorset* 11 7710
Fifield *Berks* 26 9076
Fifield *Oxon* 36 2418
Fifield *Wilts* 23 1450
Figheldean *Wilts* 23 1547
Filands *Wilts* 35 9388
Filby *Norfk* 67 4613
Filey *N York* 91 1180
Filgrave *Bucks* 38 8648
Filkins *Oxon* 36 2304
Filleigh *Devon* 19 6627
Filleigh *Devon* 19 7410
Fillingham *Lincs* 76 9485
Fillongley *Warwks* 61 2887
Filmore Hill *Hants* 13 6627
Filton *Gloucs* 34 6079
Fimber *E R Yk* 91 8960
Finavon *Angus* 127 4956
Fincham *Norfk* 65 6806
Finchampstead *Berks* 25 7963
Fincharn *Ag & B* 122 9003
Finchdean *Hants* 13 7312
Finchingfield *Essex* 40 6832
Finchley *Gt Lon* 27 2690
Findern *Derbys* 73 3030
Findhorn *Moray* 141 0364
Findhorn Bridge *Highld* 140 8027
Findo Gask *P & K* 125 0019
Findochty *Moray* 142 4667
Findon *Abers* 135 9397
Findon *W Susx* 14 1208
Findon Mains *Highld* 140 6060
Findrack House *Abers* 134 6004
Finedon *Nhants* 51 9172
Fingal Street *Suffk* 55 2169
Fingask *P & K* 126 1619
Fingest *Bucks* 37 7791
Finghall *N York* 89 1889
Fingland *Cumb* 93 2557
Fingland *D & G* 107 7517
Finglesham *Kent* 29 3353
Fingringhoe *Essex* 41 0220
Finkle Green *Essex* 53 7040
Finkle Street *S York* 74 3099
Finlarig *Stirlg* 124 5733
Finmere *Oxon* 49 6332
Finnart *P & K* 124 5157
Finningham *Suffk* 54 0669
Finningley *S York* 75 6799
Finsbay *W Isls* 152 0786
Finstall *Worcs* 60 9770
Finsthwaite *Cumb* 87 3687
Finstock *Oxon* 36 3616
Finstown *Ork* 153 3513
Fintry *Abers* 142 7554
Fintry *Stirlg* 116 6186
Finzean *Abers* 134 5993
Fionnphort *Ag & B* 120 3023
Fionnsbhagh *W Isls* 152 0786
Fir Tree *Dur* 96 1434
Firbank *Cumb* 87 6293
Firbeck *S York* 75 5688
Firby *N York* 89 2686
Firby *N York* 90 7466
Firgrove *Gt Man* 81 9113
Firsby *Lincs* 77 4562
Firsdown *Dorset* 23 2133
Fishbourne *IOW* 13 5592
Fishbourne *W Susx* 14 8304
Fishburn *Dur* 96 3632
Fishcross *Clacks* 116 8995
Fisher *W Susx* 14 8700
Fisher's Pond *Hants* 13 4820
Fisher's Row *Lancs* 80 4148
Fisherford *Abers* 142 6735
Fisherrow *E Loth* 118 3472
Fisherstreet *W Susx* 14 9431
Fisherton *Highld* 140 7451
Fisherton *S Ayrs* 106 2717
Fisherton de la Mere *Wilts* 22 0038
Fisherwick *Staffs* 61 1708
Fishery Estate *Berks* 26 8980
Fishguard *Pembks* 30 9537
Fishlake *S York* 83 6513
Fishleigh *Devon* 8 5405
Fishmere End *Lincs* 64 2837
Fishnish Pier *Ag & B* 121 6542
Fishpond Bottom *Dorset* 10 3698
Fishponds *Bristl* 35 6375
Fishpool *Gt Man* 79 8009
Fishtoft *Lincs* 64 3642
Fishtoft Drove *Lincs* 77 3148
Fishwick *Border* 119 9151
Fishwick *Lancs* 81 5629
Fiskavaig *Highld* 136 3334
Fiskerton *Lincs* 76 0471
Fiskerton *Notts* 75 7351
Fitling *E R Yk* 85 2534
Fittleton *Wilts* 23 1449
Fittleworth *W Susx* 14 0019
Fitton End *Cambs* 65 4313
Fitz *Shrops* 59 4417
Fitzhead *Somset* 20 1228
Fitzroy *Somset* 20 1927
Fitzwilliam *W York* 83 4115
Fiunary *Highld* 121 6246
Five Ash Down *E Susx* 16 4723
Five Ashes *E Susx* 16 5525
Five Bells *Somset* 20 0642
Five Bridges *Herefd* 47 6446
Five Lanes *Mons* 34 4490
Five Oak Green *Kent* 16 6445
Five Oaks *Jersey* 158 0000
Five Oaks *W Susx* 14 0928
Five Roads *Carmth* 32 4805
Five Wents *Kent* 28 8050
Fivecrosses *Ches* 71 5276
Fivehead *Somset* 21 3522
Fivelanes *Cnwll* 5 2280
Flack's Green *Essex* 40 7614
Flackwell Heath *Bucks* 26 8989
Fladbury *Worcs* 47 9946
Fladdabister *Shet* 153 4332
Flagg *Derbys* 74 1368
Flamborough *E R Yk* 91 2270
Flamstead *Herts* 38 0714
Flansham *W Susx* 14 9601
Flanshaw *W York* 82 3020
Flappit Spring *W York* 82 0536
Flasby *N York* 82 9456
Flash *Staffs* 74 0266
Flashader *Highld* 136 3453
Flaunden *Herts* 26 0100
Flawborough *Notts* 63 7842
Flawith *N York* 90 4865
Flax Bourton *Somset* 21 5069
Flaxby *N York* 89 3957
Flaxley *Gloucs* 35 6815
Flaxmere *Ches* 71 5572
Flaxpool *Somset* 20 1435
Flaxton *N York* 90 6762
Fleckney *Leics* 50 6493
Flecknoe *Warwks* 49 5163
Fledborough *Notts* 75 8072
Fleet *Dorset* 10 6380
Fleet *Hants* 13 7201
Fleet *Hants* 25 8053
Fleet *Lincs* 64 3823
Fleet Hargate *Lincs* 65 3925
Fleetend *Hants* 13 5006
Fleetwood *Lancs* 80 3348
Flemingston *V Glam* 20 0169
Flemington *S Lans* 116 6559
Flempton *Suffk* 54 8169
Fletcher Green *Kent* 16 5349
Fletchersbridge *Cnwll* 4 1065
Fletchertown *Cumb* 93 2042
Fletching *E Susx* 16 4223
Fleur-de-lis *Caerph* 33 1696
Flexbury *Cnwll* 18 2107
Flexford *Surrey* 25 9350
Flimby *Cumb* 92 0233
Flimwell *E Susx* 17 7131
Flint *Flints* 70 2472
Flint Mountain *Flints* 70 2470
Flint's Green *W Mids* 61 2680
Flintham *Notts* 63 7445
Flinton *E R Yk* 85 2136
Flishinghurst *Kent* 28 7537
Flitcham *Norfk* 65 7326
Flitton *Beds* 38 0535
Flitwick *Beds* 38 0334
Flixborough *Lincs* 84 8714
Flixborough Stather *Lincs* 84 8614
Flixton *Gt Man* 79 7494
Flixton *N York* 91 0479
Flixton *Suffk* 55 3186
Flockton *W York* 82 2314
Flockton Green *W York* 82 2515
Flodden *Nthumb* 110 9235
Flodigarry *Highld* 136 4671
Flookburgh *Cumb* 87 3675
Flordon *Norfk* 66 1897
Flore *Nhants* 49 6460
Flotterton *Nthumb* 103 9902
Flowers Green *E Susx* 16 6311
Flowton *Suffk* 54 0846
Flushdyke *W York* 82 2820
Flushing *Cnwll* 3 8034
Fluxton *Devon* 9 0893
Flyford Flavell *Worcs* 47 9755
Fobbing *Essex* 40 7183
Fochabers *Moray* 141 3458
Fochriw *Caerph* 33 1005
Fockerby *Lincs* 84 8519
Foddington *Somset* 21 5729
Foel *Powys* 58 9911
Foel y Dyffryn *Brdgnd* 33 8594
Foelgastell *Carmth* 32 5414
Foggathorpe *E R Yk* 84 7537
Fogo *Border* 110 7649
Fogwatt *Moray* 141 2356
Foindle *Highld* 148 1948
Folda *Angus* 133 1963
Fole *Staffs* 73 0437
Foleshill *W Mids* 61 3582
Foliejon Park *Berks* 25 8974
Folke *Dorset* 11 6613
Folkestone *Kent* 29 2336
Folkingham *Lincs* 64 0733
Folkington *E Susx* 16 5603
Folksworth *Cambs* 52 1489
Folkton *N York* 91 0579
Folla Rule *Abers* 142 7332
Follifoot *N York* 83 3452
Folly Gate *Devon* 8 5798
Folly Hill *Surrey* 25 8348
Fonmon *V Glam* 20 0467
Font-y-gary *V Glam* 20 0566
Fonthill Bishop *Wilts* 22 9333
Fonthill Gifford *Wilts* 22 9231
Fontmell Magna *Dorset* 11 8616
Fontmell Parva *Dorset* 11 8214
Fontwell *W Susx* 14 9407
Foolow *Derbys* 74 1976
Foots Cray *Gt Lon* 27 4770
Forbestown *Abers* 134 3513
Forcett *N York* 89 1712
Ford *Ag & B* 122 8603
Ford *Bucks* 37 7709
Ford *Derbys* 74 4080
Ford *Devon* 18 4124
Ford *Devon* 6 6150
Ford *Devon* 7 7940
Ford *Gloucs* 48 0829
Ford *Nthumb* 110 9437
Ford *Shrops* 59 4113
Ford *Somset* 20 0928
Ford *Somset* 21 5953
Ford *Staffs* 73 0653
Ford *W Susx* 14 9903
Ford *Wilts* 35 8475
Ford End *Essex* 40 6716
Ford Green *Lancs* 80 4746
Ford Heath *Shrops* 59 4011
Ford Street *Somset* 20 1518
Ford's Green *Suffk* 54 0666
Forda *Devon* 8 5390
Fordcombe *Kent* 16 5240
Fordell *Fife* 117 1588
Forden *Powys* 58 2201
Forder *Devon* 8 6789
Forder Green *Devon* 7 7967
Fordham *Cambs* 53 6370
Fordham *Essex* 40 9228
Fordham *Norfk* 65 6199
Fordham Heath *Essex* 40 9426
Fordingbridge *Hants* 12 1414
Fordon *E R Yk* 91 0475
Fordoun *Abers* 135 7475
Fordstreet *Essex* 40 9226
Fordton *Devon* 8 8399
Fordwells *Oxon* 36 3013
Fordwich *Kent* 29 1859
Fordyce *Abers* 142 5563
Forebridge *Staffs* 72 9322
Foremark *Derbys* 62 3326
Forest *Guern* 158 0000
Forest *N York* 89 2700
Forest Becks *Lancs* 81 7851
Forest Chapel *Ches* 79 9772
Forest Gate *Gt Lon* 27 4085
Forest Green *Surrey* 14 1241
Forest Hall *Cumb* 87 5401
Forest Hall *T & W* 103 2769
Forest Head *Cumb* 94 5857
Forest Hill *Gt Lon* 27 3672
Forest Hill *Oxon* 37 5807
Forest Lane Head *N York* 83 3356
Forest Lodge *Ag & B* 123 2742
Forest Mill *Clacks* 117 9694
Forest Row *E Susx* 16 4234
Forest Side *IOW* 13 4889
Forest Town *Notts* 75 5662
Forest-in-Teesdale *Dur* 95 8630
Forestburn Gate *Nthumb* 103 0696
Forestside *W Susx* 14 7612
Forfar *Angus* 127 4550
Forgandenny *P & K* 125 0818
Forge *Powys* 57 7699
Forge Hammer *Torfn* 34 2895
Forge Side *Torfn* 34 2408
Forgie *Moray* 141 3854
Forgieside *Moray* 142 4053
Forgorig *Border* 110 7748
Forgue *Abers* 142 6145
Forhill *Worcs* 61 0575
Formby *Mersyd* 78 3006
Forncett End *Norfk* 66 1493
Forncett St Mary *Norfk* 66 1694
Forncett St Peter *Norfk* 66 1693
Fornham All Saints *Suffk* 54 8367
Fornham St Martin *Suffk* 54 8567
Fornside *Cumb* 93 3220
Forres *Moray* 141 0358
Forsbrook *Staffs* 72 9641
Forse *Highld* 151 2234
Forse House *Highld* 151 2135
Forshaw Heath *Warwks* 61 0873
Forsinain *Highld* 150 9148
Forsinard *Highld* 150 8942
Forston *Dorset* 11 6695
Fort Augustus *Highld* 131 3709
Fort Hommet *Guern* 158 0000
Fort le Marchant *Guern* 158 0000
Fort William *Highld* 130 1074
Forteviot *P & K* 125 0517
Forth *S Lans* 116 9453
Forthampton *Gloucs* 47 8532
Fortingall *P & K* 124 7347
Fortnighty *Highld* 140 9350
Forton *Hants* 24 4143
Forton *Lancs* 80 4851
Forton *Shrops* 59 4316
Forton *Somset* 10 3307
Forton *Staffs* 72 7521
Fortrie *Abers* 142 6645
Fortrose *Highld* 140 7256
Fortuneswell *Dorset* 11 6873
Forty Green *Bucks* 26 9291
Forty Hill *Gt Lon* 27 3398
Forward Green *Suffk* 54 1059
Fosbury *Wilts* 23 3157
Foscot *Oxon* 36 2421
Foscote *Nhants* 49 6546
Fosdyke *Lincs* 64 3133
Fosdyke Bridge *Lincs* 64 3232
Foss *P & K* 132 7858
Foss-y-ffin *Cerdgn* 42 4460
Fossebridge *Gloucs* 36 0711
Foster Street *Essex* 39 4809
Fosterhouses *S York* 83 6514
Foston *Derbys* 73 1931
Foston *Leics* 50 6094
Foston *Lincs* 63 8542
Foston *N York* 90 6965
Foston on the Wolds *E R Yk* 85 1055
Fotherby *Lincs* 77 3191
Fothergill *Cumb* 92 0234
Fotheringhay *Nhants* 51 0593
Foul End *Warwks* 61 2494
Foul Mile *E Susx* 16 6215
Foulbridge *Cumb* 93 4248
Foulby *W York* 83 3917
Foulden *Border* 119 9355
Foulden *Norfk* 65 7699
Foulridge *Lancs* 81 8942
Foulsham *Norfk* 66 0324
Fountainhall *Border* 118 4249
Four Ashes *Staffs* 60 9108
Four Ashes *Staffs* 60 8087
Four Ashes *Suffk* 54 0070
Four Ashes *W Mids* 61 1575
Four Cabots *Guern* 158 0000
Four Crosses *Powys* 58 2618
Four Crosses *Staffs* 60 9509
Four Elms *Kent* 16 4648
Four Foot *Somset* 21 5833
Four Forks *Somset* 20 2336
Four Gates *Gt Man* 79 6407
Four Gotes *Cambs* 65 4516
Four Lane End *S York* 82 2702
Four Lane Ends *Ches* 71 5561
Four Lanes *Cnwll* 2 6838
Four Marks *Hants* 24 6735
Four Mile Bridge *IOA* 68 2778
Four Oaks *E Susx* 17 8524
Four Oaks *Gloucs* 47 6928
Four Oaks *W Mids* 61 1098
Four Oaks *W Mids* 61 2480
Four Points *Berks* 37 5579
Four Roads *Carmth* 32 4409
Four Shire Stone *Warwks* 48 2232
Four Throws *Kent* 17 7729
Four Wents *Kent* 27 6251
Fourlanes End *Ches* 72 8059
Fourpenny *Highld* 147 8094
Fourstones *Nthumb* 102 8867
Fovant *Wilts* 22 0028
Foveran *Abers* 143 9723
Fowey *Cnwll* 3 1251
Fowley Common *Ches* 79 6795
Fowlhall *Kent* 28 6946
Fowlis *Angus* 126 3233
Fowlis Wester *P & K* 125 9224
Fowlmere *Cambs* 53 4245
Fownhope *Herefd* 46 5834
Fox Corner *Surrey* 25 9654
Fox Hatch *Essex* 27 5798
Fox Street *Essex* 41 0227
Foxbar *Rens* 115 4561
Foxcombe *Devon* 5 4887
Foxcote *Gloucs* 35 0118
Foxcote *Somset* 22 7155
Foxdale *IOM* 158 2778
Foxearth *Essex* 54 8344
Foxendown *Kent* 27 6466
Foxfield *Cumb* 86 2185
Foxham *Wilts* 35 9777
Foxhills *Hants* 12 3411
Foxhole *Cnwll* 3 9654
Foxhole *Swans* 32 6694
Foxholes *N York* 91 0173
Foxhunt Green *E Susx* 16 5417
Foxley *Nhants* 49 6451
Foxley *Norfk* 66 0422
Foxley *Wilts* 35 8986
Foxley Green *Wilts* 35 8985
Foxlydiate *Worcs* 47 0167
Foxt *Staffs* 73 0348
Foxton *Cambs* 52 4148
Foxton *Dur* 96 3624
Foxton *Leics* 50 7089
Foxton *N York* 89 4296
Foxup *N York* 88 8676
Foxwist Green *Ches* 71 6268
Foxwood *Shrops* 47 6276
Foy *Herefd* 46 5928
Foyers *Highld* 139 4921
Foynesfield *Highld* 140 8953
Fraddam *Cnwll* 2 5834
Fraddon *Cnwll* 4 9158
Fradley *Staffs* 61 1513
Fradswell *Staffs* 73 9931
Fraisthorpe *E R Yk* 91 1561
Framfield *E Susx* 16 4920
Framingham Earl *Norfk* 67 2702
Framingham Pigot *Norfk* 67 2703
Framlingham *Suffk* 55 2863
Frampton *Dorset* 10 6295
Frampton *Lincs* 64 3239
Frampton Cotterell *Gloucs* 35 6682
Frampton Mansell *Gloucs* 35 9202
Frampton on Severn *Gloucs* 35 7407
Frampton West End *Lincs* 64 3041
Framsden *Suffk* 55 1959
Framwellgate Moor *Dur* 96 2644
Frances Green *Lancs* 81 6236
Franche *Worcs* 60 8278
Frandley *Ches* 71 6379
Frank's Bridge *Powys* 45 1156
Frankaborough *Devon* 5 3991
Frankby *Mersyd* 78 2486
Frankfort *Norfk* 67 3024
Franklands Gate *Herefd* 46 5346
Frankley *Worcs* 60 9980
Frankton *Warwks* 50 4270
Frant *E Susx* 16 5835
Fraserburgh *Abers* 143 9966
Frating *Essex* 41 0722
Frating Green *Essex* 41 0823
Fratton *Hants* 13 6500
Freathy *Cnwll* 5 3952
Freckenham *Suffk* 53 6672
Freckleton *Lancs* 80 4329
Freebirch *Derbys* 74 3072
Freeby *Leics* 63 8020
Freefolk *Hants* 24 4848
Freehay *Staffs* 73 0241
Freeland *Oxon* 36 4112
Freethorpe *Norfk* 67 4005
Freethorpe Common *Norfk* 67 4004
Freiston *Lincs* 64 3743
Fremington *Devon* 19 5132
Fremington *N York* 88 0499
French Street *Kent* 27 4552
Frenchay *Gloucs* 35 6377
Frenchbeer *Devon* 8 6785
Frenich *P & K* 132 8258
Frensham *Surrey* 25 8441
Freshfields *Mersyd* 78 2907
Freshford *Somset* 22 7860
Freshwater *IOW* 12 3487
Freshwater Bay *IOW* 12 3485
Freshwater East *Pembks* 30 0198
Fressingfield *Suffk* 55 2677
Freston *Suffk* 54 1638
Freswick *Highld* 151 3667
Fretherne *Gloucs* 35 7210
Frettenham *Norfk* 67 2417
Freuchie *Fife* 126 2806
Freystrop *Pembks* 30 9511
Friar Waddon *Dorset* 11 6486
Friar's Gate *E Susx* 16 4933
Friars' Hill *N York* 90 7485
Friday Bridge *Cambs* 65 4604
Friday Street *E Susx* 16 6203
Friday Street *Suffk* 55 2459
Friday Street *Suffk* 55 3351
Friday Street *Suffk* 55 3760
Friday Street *Surrey* 14 1245
Fridaythorpe *E R Yk* 90 8759
Friden *Derbys* 74 1660
Friendly *W York* 82 0524
Friern Barnet *Gt Lon* 27 2892
Friesland Bay *Ag & B* 120 1954
Friesthorpe *Lincs* 76 0683
Frieston *Lincs* 63 9347
Frieth *Bucks* 37 7990
Friezeland *Notts* 75 4750
Frilford *Oxon* 37 4497
Frilsham *Berks* 24 5473
Frimley *Surrey* 25 8757
Frimley Green *Surrey* 25 8856
Frindsbury *Kent* 28 7469
Fring *Norfk* 65 7334
Fringford *Oxon* 49 6029
Frinsted *Kent* 28 8957
Frinton-on-Sea *Essex* 41 2320
Friockheim *Angus* 127 5949
Friog *Gwynd* 57 6112
Frisby on the Wreake *Leics* 63 6917
Friskney *Lincs* 77 4655
Friskney Eaudike *Lincs* 77 4755
Friston *E Susx* 16 5598
Friston *Suffk* 55 4160
Fritchley *Derbys* 74 3552
Frith Bank *Lincs* 77 3147
Frith Common *Worcs* 47 6969
Fritham *Hants* 12 2314
Frithelstock *Devon* 18 4619
Frithelstock Stone *Devon* 18 4518
Frithend *Hants* 25 8039
Frithsden *Herts* 38 0009
Frithville *Lincs* 77 3150
Frittenden *Kent* 28 8140
Frittiscombe *Devon* 7 8043
Fritton *Norfk* 67 4600
Fritton *Norfk* 67 2293
Fritwell *Oxon* 49 5229
Frizinghall *W York* 82 1435
Frizington *Cumb* 92 0316
Frocester *Gloucs* 35 7803
Frodesley *Shrops* 59 5101
Frodsham *Ches* 71 5177
Frog End *Cambs* 52 3946
Frog End *Cambs* 53 5358
Frog Pool *Worcs* 47 8065
Frogden *Border* 110 7628
Froggatt *Derbys* 74 2476
Froghall *Staffs* 73 0247
Frogham *Hants* 12 1612
Frogham *Kent* 29 2550
Frogmore *Devon* 7 7742
Frognall *Lincs* 64 1610
Frogpool *Cnwll* 3 7540
Frogwell *Cnwll* 5 3468
Frolesworth *Leics* 50 5090
Frome *Somset* 22 7747
Frome St Quintin *Dorset* 10 5902
Frome Whitfield *Dorset* 11 6991
Fromes Hill *Herefd* 47 6846
Fron *Denbgs* 70 0666
Fron *Gwynd* 56 3539
Fron *Gwynd* 68 5054
Fron *Powys* 58 2203
Fron *Powys* 58 1797
Fron Isaf *Wrexhm* 70 2740
Fron-goch *Gwynd* 70 9039
Froncysyllte *Denbgs* 70 2640
Frostenden *Suffk* 55 4781
Frosterley *Dur* 95 0237
Froxfield *Beds* 38 9733
Froxfield *Wilts* 23 2968
Froxfield Green *Hants* 13 7025
Fryern Hill *Hants* 13 4320
Fryerning *Essex* 40 6300
Fryton *N York* 90 6874
Fulbeck *Lincs* 76 9450
Fulbourn *Cambs* 53 5256
Fulbrook *Oxon* 36 2513
Fulflood *Hants* 24 4730
Fulford *N York* 83 6149
Fulford *Somset* 20 2029
Fulford *Staffs* 72 9537
Fulham *Gt Lon* 27 2576
Fulking *W Susx* 15 2411
Full Sutton *E R Yk* 84 7455
Fullaford *Devon* 19 6838
Fullarton *N Ayrs* 106 3238
Fuller Street *Essex* 40 7416
Fuller Street *Kent* 27 5656
Fuller's End *Essex* 39 5325
Fuller's Moor *Ches* 71 4954
Fullerton *Hants* 23 3739
Fulletby *Lincs* 77 2973
Fullready *Warwks* 48 2846
Fullwood *E Ayrs* 115 4450
Fulmer *Bucks* 26 9985
Fulmodeston *Norfk* 66 9930
Fulnetby *Lincs* 76 0979
Fulney *Lincs* 64 2623
Fulstone *W York* 82 1709
Fulstow *Lincs* 77 3297
Fulwell *Oxon* 36 3722
Fulwood *Lancs* 80 5431
Fulwood *Notts* 75 4757
Fulwood *S York* 74 3085
Fulwood *Somset* 20 2120
Fundenhall *Norfk* 66 1596
Funtington *W Susx* 14 8008
Funtley *Hants* 13 5608
Funtullich *P & K* 124 7526
Furley *Devon* 10 2604
Furnace *Ag & B* 114 0200
Furnace *Carmth* 32 5001
Furnace *Cerdgn* 43 6895
Furnace End *Warwks* 61 2491
Furner's Green *E Susx* 15 4126
Furness Vale *Derbys* 79 0083
Furneux Pelham *Herts* 39 4327
Further Quarter *Kent* 28 8939
Furtho *Nhants* 49 7743
Furze Platt *Berks* 26 8782
Furzehill *Devon* 19 7245
Furzehill *Dorset* 11 0101
Furzehills *Lincs* 77 2572
Furzeley Corner *Hants* 13 6510
Furzley *Hants* 12 2816
Fyfett *Somset* 9 2314
Fyfield *Essex* 40 5707
Fyfield *Hants* 23 2946
Fyfield *Oxon* 36 4298
Fyfield *Wilts* 23 1468
Fyfield *Wilts* 23 1760
Fyfield Bavant *Wilts* 22 0125
Fyfield Wick *Oxon* 36 4197

Fylingthorpe Gorey


Fylingthorpe *N York* 91 9404
Fyning *W Susx* 14 8123
Fyvie *Abers* 142 7637


# G


Gabroc Hill *E Ayrs* 115 4550
Gaddesby *Leics* 63 6813
Gaddesden Row *Herts* 38 0512
Gadfa *IOA* 68 4689
Gadgirth *S Ayrs* 106 4022
Gadlas *Shrops* 59 3737
Gaer *Powys* 33 1721
Gaer-llwyd *Mons* 34 4496
Gaerwen *IOA* 68 4871
Gagingwell *Oxon* 48 4025
Gailes *N Ayrs* 106 3235
Gailey *Staffs* 60 9110
Gainford *Dur* 96 1716
Gainsborough *Lincs* 75 8189
Gainsford End *Essex* 53 7235
Gairloch *Highld* 144 8076
Gairlochy *Highld* 131 1784
Gairneybridge *P & K* 117 1398
Gaisby *W York* 82 1536
Gaisgill *Cumb* 87 6305
Gaitsgill *Cumb* 93 3846
Galashiels *Border* 109 4936
Galcantray *Highld* 140 8148
Galgate *Lancs* 80 4855
Galhampton *Somset* 21 6329
Gallanach *Ag & B* 120 2161
Gallanach *Ag & B* 122 8326
Gallantry Bank *Ches* 71 5153
Gallatown *Fife* 117 2994
Galley Common *Warwks* 61 3091
Galleywood *Essex* 40 7003
Gallovie *Highld* 132 5589
Gallowfauld *Angus* 127 4342
Gallowhill *P & K* 126 1635
Gallows Green *Essex* 40 9226
Gallows Green *Worcs* 47 9362
Gallowstree Common *Oxon* 37 6980
Gallt-y-foel *Gwynd* 69 5862
Galltair *Highld* 129 8120
Gally Hill *Hants* 25 8051
Gallypot Street *E Susx* 16 4735
Galmisdale *Highld* 128 4784
Galmpton *Devon* 7 6940
Galmpton *Devon* 7 8856
Galphay *N York* 89 2572
Galston *E Ayrs* 107 5036
Galton *Dorset* 11 7785
Gamballs Green *Staffs* 74 0367
Gambles Green *Essex* 40 7614
Gamblesby *Cumb* 94 6039
Gamelsby *Cumb* 93 2552
Gamesley *Gt Man* 79 0194
Gamlingay *Cambs* 52 2452
Gamlingay Cinques *Cambs* 52 2352
Gamlingay Great Heath *Beds* 52 2151
Gammersgill *N York* 88 0582
Gamrie *Abers* 143 7962
Gamston *Notts* 75 7176
Gamston *Notts* 62 5937
Ganarew *Herefd* 34 5216
Ganavan Bay *Ag & B* 122 8632
Gang *Cnwll* 5 3068
Ganllwyd *Gwynd* 57 7324
Gannachy *Angus* 134 5970
Ganstead *E R Yk* 85 1434
Ganthorpe *N York* 90 6870
Ganton *N York* 91 9977
Ganwick Corner *Herts* 27 2599
Gappah *Devon* 9 8677
Garbity *Moray* 141 3152
Garboldisham *Norfk* 54 0081
Garchory *Abers* 134 3010
Garden City *Flints* 71 3269
Garden Village *Derbys* 74 2698
Gardeners Green *Berks* 25 8266
Gardenstown *Abers* 143 8064
Garderhouse *Shet* 153 3347
Gardham *E R Yk* 84 9542
Gare Hill *Somset* 22 7840
Garelochhead *Ag & B* 114 2491
Garford *Oxon* 36 4296
Garforth *W York* 83 4033
Garforth Bridge *W York* 83 3932
Gargrave *N York* 81 9354
Gargunnock *Stirlg* 116 7094
Garizim *Conwy* 69 6975
Garlic Street *Norfk* 55 2183
Garlieston *D & G* 99 4746
Garlinge *Kent* 29 3369
Garlinge Green *Kent* 29 1152
Garlogie *Abers* 135 7805
Garmond *Abers* 143 8052
Garmondsway *Dur* 96 3434
Garmouth *Moray* 141 3364
Garmston *Shrops* 59 6006
Garn *Gwynd* 56 2834
Garn-Dolbenmaen *Gwynd* 56 4943
Garnant *Carmth* 32 6713
Garnett Bridge *Cumb* 87 5299
Garnkirk *N Lans* 116 6768
Garnswllt *Swans* 32 6209
Garrabost *W Isls* 152 5133
Garrallan *E Ayrs* 107 5418
Garras *Cnwll* 2 7023
Garreg *Gwynd* 57 6141
Garrigill *Cumb* 94 7441
Garriston *N York* 89 1592
Garroch *D & G* 99 5981
Garrochtrie *D & G* 98 1138
Garrochty *Ag & B* 114 0953
Garros *Highld* 136 4962
Garrowby Hall *E R Yk* 90 7957
Garsdale *Cumb* 88 7489
Garsdale Head *Cumb* 88 7891
Garsdon *Wilts* 35 9687
Garshall Green *Staffs* 72 9633
Garsington *Oxon* 37 5802
Garstang *Lancs* 80 4945
Garston *Herts* 26 1100
Garston *Mersyd* 78 4084
Gartachossan *Ag & B* 112 3461
Gartcosh *N Lans* 116 6967
Garth *Brdgnd* 33 8690
Garth *Denbgs* 70 2542
Garth *Mons* 34 3492
Garth *Powys* 45 9549
Garth *Powys* 46 2772
Garth Penrhyncoch *Cerdgn* 43 6484
Garth Row *Cumb* 87 5297
Garthamlock *C Glas* 116 6566
Garthbrengy *Powys* 45 0433
Gartheli *Cerdgn* 44 5856
Garthmyl *Powys* 58 1999
Garthorpe *Leics* 63 8320
Garthorpe *Lincs* 84 8418
Garths *Cumb* 87 5489
Gartly *Abers* 142 5232
Gartmore *Stirlg* 115 5297
Gartness *N Lans* 116 7864
Gartness *Stirlg* 115 5086
Gartocharn *W Duns* 115 4286
Garton *E R Yk* 85 2635
Garton-on-the-Wolds *E R Yk* 91 9759
Gartymore *Highld* 147 0114
Garvald *E Loth* 118 5870
Garvan *Highld* 130 9777
Garvard *Ag & B* 112 3791
Garve *Highld* 139 3961
Garvestone *Norfk* 66 0207
Garvock *Inver* 114 2570
Garway *Herefd* 34 4522
Garway Common *Herefd* 34 4622
Garway Hill *Herefd* 46 4425
Garyvard *W Isls* 152 3619
Gasper *Wilts* 22 7633
Gastard *Wilts* 22 8868
Gasthorpe *Norfk* 54 9781
Gaston Green *Essex* 39 4917
Gatcombe *IOW* 13 4985
Gate Burton *Lincs* 76 8382
Gate Helmsley *N York* 83 6955
Gatebeck *Cumb* 87 5485
Gateford *Notts* 75 5781
Gateforth *N York* 83 5628
Gatehead *E Ayrs* 106 3936
Gatehouse *Nthumb* 102 7889
Gatehouse of Fleet *D & G* 99 5956
Gatelawbridge *D & G* 100 9096
Gateley *Norfk* 66 9624
Gatenby *N York* 89 3287
Gates Heath *Ches* 71 4760
Gatesgarth *Cumb* 93 1915
Gateshaw *Border* 110 7722
Gateshead *T & W* 96 2562
Gateside *Angus* 127 4344
Gateside *E Rens* 115 4858
Gateside *Fife* 126 1809
Gateside *N Ayrs* 115 3653
Gateslack *D & G* 108 8902
Gathurst *Gt Man* 78 5407
Gatley *Gt Man* 79 8488
Gatton *Surrey* 27 2752
Gattonside *Border* 109 5435
Gaufron *Powys* 45 9968
Gaulby *Leics* 50 6900
Gauldry *Fife* 126 3723
Gauldswell *P & K* 126 2151
Gaulkthorn *Lancs* 81 7526
Gaultree *Norfk* 65 4907
Gaunt's Common *Dorset* 12 0205
Gaunt's End *Essex* 39 5525
Gaunton's Bank *Ches* 71 5647
Gautby *Lincs* 76 1772
Gavinton *Border* 119 7652
Gawber *S York* 83 3207
Gawcott *Bucks* 49 6831
Gawsworth *Ches* 79 8969
Gawthorpe *W York* 82 2721
Gawthrop *Cumb* 87 6987
Gawthwaite *Cumb* 86 2784
Gay Bowers *Essex* 40 7904
Gay Street *W Susx* 14 0820
Gaydon *Warwks* 48 3653
Gayhurst *Bucks* 38 8446
Gayle *N York* 88 8688
Gayles *N York* 89 1207
Gayton *Mersyd* 78 2780
Gayton *Nhants* 49 7054
Gayton *Norfk* 65 7219
Gayton *Staffs* 72 9828
Gayton le Marsh *Lincs* 77 4284
Gayton Thorpe *Norfk* 65 7418
Gaywood *Norfk* 65 6320
Gazeley *Suffk* 53 7264
Gear *Cnwll* 3 7224
Gearraidh Bhaird *W Isls* 152 3619
Geary *Highld* 136 2661
Gedding *Suffk* 54 9457
Geddinge *Kent* 29 2346
Geddington *Nhants* 51 8983
Gedling *Notts* 62 6142
Gedney *Lincs* 65 4024
Gedney Broadgate *Lincs* 65 4022
Gedney Drove End *Lincs* 65 4629
Gedney Dyke *Lincs* 65 4126
Gedney Hill *Lincs* 64 3311
Gee Cross *Gt Man* 79 9593
Geeston *Rutlnd* 63 9803
Geldeston *Norfk* 67 3991
Gelli *Rhondd* 33 9794
Gelli *Torfn* 34 2792
Gelli Gynan *Denbgs* 70 1854
Gellifor *Denbgs* 70 1262
Gelligaer *Caerph* 33 1396
Gelligroes *Caerph* 33 1794
Gelligron *Neath* 32 7104
Gellilydan *Gwynd* 57 6839
Gellinudd *Neath* 32 7303
Gelly *Carmth* 31 0819
Gellyburn *P & K* 125 0939
Gellywen *Carmth* 31 2723
Gelston *D & G* 92 7758
Gelston *Lincs* 63 9145
Gembling *E R Yk* 91 1057
Gentleshaw *Staffs* 61 0511
George Green *Bucks* 26 9981
George Nympton *Devon* 19 7023
Georgefield *D & G* 101 2991
Georgeham *Devon* 18 4639
Georgetown *Blae G* 33 1508
Georgia *Cnwll* 2 4836
Georth *Ork* 153 3625
Gerlan *Gwynd* 69 6366
Germansweek *Devon* 5 4394
Germoe *Cnwll* 2 5829
Gerrans *Cnwll* 3 8735
Gerrards Cross *Bucks* 26 0088
Gerrick *N York* 90 7012
Gestingthorpe *Essex* 54 8138
Geuffordd *Powys* 58 2114
Gib Hill *Ches* 79 6478
Gibraltar *Lincs* 77 5558
Gibsmere *Notts* 75 7148
Giddeahall *Wilts* 35 8674
Giddy Green *Dorset* 11 8386
Gidea Park *Gt Lon* 27 5290
Gidleigh *Devon* 8 6788
Giffnock *E Rens* 115 5658
Gifford *E Loth* 118 5368
Giffordtown *Fife* 126 2811
Giggleswick *N York* 88 8063
Gilberdyke *E R Yk* 84 8329
Gilbert Street *Hants* 24 6432
Gilbert's Cross *Staffs* 60 8187
Gilbert's End *Worcs* 47 8342
Gilchriston *E Loth* 118 4865
Gilcrux *Cumb* 92 1138
Gildersome *W York* 82 2429
Gildingwells *S York* 75 5585
Gilesgate Moor *Dur* 96 2942
Gileston *V Glam* 20 0166
Gilfach *Caerph* 33 1598
Gilfach Goch *Brdgnd* 33 9790
Gilfachrheda *Cerdgn* 42 4158
Gilgarran *Cumb* 92 0323
Gill *Cumb* 93 4429
Gill's Green *Kent* 17 7532
Gillamoor *N York* 90 6889
Gillan *Cnwll* 3 7825
Gillen *Highld* 136 2659
Gillesbie *D & G* 100 1691
Gilling East *N York* 90 6176
Gilling West *N York* 89 1805
Gillingham *Dorset* 22 8026
Gillingham *Kent* 28 7768
Gillingham *Norfk* 67 4191
Gillock *Highld* 151 2159
Gillow Heath *Staffs* 72 8858
Gills *Highld* 151 3272
Gilmanscleuch *Border* 109 3321
Gilmerton *C Edin* 117 2868
Gilmerton *P & K* 125 8823
Gilmonby *Dur* 95 9912
Gilmorton *Leics* 50 5787
Gilsland *Nthumb* 102 6366
Gilson *Warwks* 61 1989
Gilstead *W York* 82 1239
Gilston *Herts* 39 4413
Gilston *Mdloth* 118 4456
Giltbrook *Notts* 62 4845
Gilwern *Mons* 34 2414
Gimingham *Norfk* 67 2836
Ginclough *Ches* 79 9576
Gingers Green *E Susx* 16 6212
Gipping *Suffk* 54 0763
Gipsey Bridge *Lincs* 77 2849
Girdle Toll *N Ayrs* 106 3440
Girlington *W York* 82 1334
Girlsta *Shet* 153 4350
Girsby *N York* 89 3508
Girtford *Beds* 52 1649
Girthon *D & G* 99 6053
Girton *Cambs* 53 4262
Girton *Notts* 75 8265
Girvan *S Ayrs* 106 1897
Gisburn *Lancs* 81 8248
Gisleham *Suffk* 55 5188
Gislingham *Suffk* 54 0771
Gissing *Norfk* 54 1485
Gittisham *Devon* 9 1398
Gladestry *Powys* 45 2355
Gladsmuir *E Loth* 118 4573
Glais *Swans* 32 7000
Glaisdale *N York* 90 7705
Glamis *Angus* 126 3846
Glan-Duar *Carmth* 44 5243
Glan-Dwyfach *Gwynd* 56 4843
Glan-rhyd *Powys* 32 7809
Glan-y-don *Flints* 70 1679
Glan-y-llyn *Rhondd* 33 1183
Glan-y-nant *Powys* 58 9384
Glan-yr-afon *Gwynd* 70 9140
Glan-yr-afon *Gwynd* 70 0142
Glan-yr-afon *IOA* 69 6080
Glan-yr-afon *Swans* 32 6305
Glanaber *Gwynd* 69 6351
Glanafon *Pembks* 30 9617
Glanaman *Carmth* 32 6713
Glandford *Norfk* 66 0441
Glandwr *Pembks* 31 1928
Glandyfi *Cerdgn* 43 6996
Glangrwyne *Powys* 34 2416
Glanllynfi *Brdgnd* 33 8690
Glanmule *Powys* 58 1690
Glanrhyd *Pembks* 31 1442
Glanton *Nthumb* 111 0714
Glanton Pike *Nthumb* 111 0514
Glanvilles Wootton *Dorset* 11 6708
Glapthorn *Nhants* 51 0290
Glapwell *Derbys* 75 4766
Glasbury *Powys* 45 1739
Glascoed *Denbgs* 70 9973
Glascoed *Mons* 34 3301
Glascote *Staffs* 61 2203
Glascwm *Powys* 45 1552
Glasfryn *Conwy* 70 9250
Glasgow *C Glas* 115 5865
Glasinfryn *Gwynd* 69 5868
Glasnacardoch Bay *Highld* 129 6795
Glasnakille *Highld* 128 5313
Glaspwll *Powys* 43 7397
Glass Houghton *W York* 83 4324
Glassenbury *Kent* 28 7536
Glasserton *D & G* 99 4237
Glassford *S Lans* 116 7247
Glasshouse *Gloucs* 35 7021
Glasshouse Hill *Gloucs* 35 7020
Glasshouses *N York* 89 1764
Glasson *Cumb* 101 2560
Glasson *Lancs* 80 4456
Glassonby *Cumb* 94 5738
Glasterlaw *Angus* 127 5951
Glaston *Rutlnd* 51 8900
Glastonbury *Somset* 21 5038
Glatton *Cambs* 52 1586
Glazebrook *Ches* 79 6992
Glazebury *Ches* 79 6797
Glazeley *Shrops* 60 7088
Gleadsmoss *Ches* 79 8168
Gleaston *Cumb* 86 2570
Glebe *Highld* 139 5118
Gledhow *W York* 82 3137
Gledpark *D & G* 99 6250
Gledrid *Shrops* 59 3036
Glemsford *Suffk* 54 8348
Glen Auldyn *IOM* 158 4393
Glen Clunie Lodge *Abers* 133 1383
Glen Maye *IOM* 158 2379
Glen Mona *IOM* 158 4588
Glen Nevis House *Highld* 130 1272
Glen Parva *Leics* 50 5798
Glen Trool Lodge *D & G* 99 4080
Glen Vine *IOM* 158 3378
Glenallachie *Highld* 141 2641
Glenancross *Highld* 129 6691
Glenaros House *Ag & B* 121 5544
Glenbarr *Ag & B* 105 6736
Glenbarry *Abers* 142 5554
Glenbeg *Highld* 121 5862
Glenbeg *Highld* 141 0028
Glenbervie *Abers* 135 7680
Glenboig *N Lans* 116 7268
Glenborrodale *Highld* 121 6061
Glenbranter *Ag & B* 114 1197
Glenbreck *Border* 108 0521
Glenbrittle House *Highld* 128 4121
Glenbuck *E Ayrs* 107 7429
Glencally *Angus* 134 3562
Glencaple *D & G* 100 9968
Glencarron Lodge *Highld* 138 0650
Glencarse *P & K* 126 1921
Glenceitlein *Highld* 123 1548
Glencoe *Highld* 130 1058
Glencothe *Border* 108 0829
Glencraig *Fife* 117 1894
Glencrosh *D & G* 107 7689
Glendale *Highld* 136 1749
Glendaruel *Ag & B* 114 9983
Glendevon *P & K* 125 9904
Glendoe Lodge *Highld* 131 4009
Glendoick *P & K* 126 2022
Glenduckie *Fife* 126 2818
Gleneagles *P & K* 125 9208
Gleneagles Hotel *P & K* 125 9111
Glenegedale *Ag & B* 112 3351
Glenelg *Highld* 129 8119
Glenerney *Moray* 141 0146
Glenfarg *P & K* 126 1310
Glenfeshie Lodge *Highld* 132 8493
Glenfield *Leics* 62 5406
Glenfinnan *Highld* 130 9080
Glenfintaig Lodge *Highld* 131 2286
Glenfoot *P & K* 126 1815
Glenfyne Lodge *Ag & B* 123 2215
Glengarnock *N Ayrs* 115 3252
Glengolly *Highld* 151 1065
Glengorm Castle *Ag & B* 121 4457
Glengrasco *Highld* 136 4444
Glenholm *Border* 108 1033
Glenhoul *D & G* 107 6187
Glenisla *Angus* 133 2160
Glenkin *Ag & B* 114 1280
Glenkindie *Abers* 142 4314
Glenlivet *Moray* 141 1929
Glenlochar *D & G* 99 7364
Glenloig *N Ayrs* 105 9435
Glenlomond *P & K* 126 1704
Glenluce *D & G* 98 1957
Glenmassen *Ag & B* 114 1088
Glenmavis *N Lans* 116 7567
Glenmore *Highld* 136 4340
Glenmore Lodge *Highld* 133 9709
Glenquiech *Angus* 134 4261
Glenralloch *Ag & B* 113 8569
Glenridding *Cumb* 93 3817
Glenrothes *Fife* 117 2700
Glenshee *P & K* 125 9834
Glenshera Lodge *Highld* 132 5592
Glenstriven *Ag & B* 114 0878
Glentham *Lincs* 76 0090
Glentromie Lodge *Highld* 132 7897
Glentrool Village *D & G* 98 3578
Glentruim House *Highld* 132 6894
Glentworth *Lincs* 76 9488
Glenuig *Highld* 129 6677
Glenure *Ag & B* 123 0448
Glenurquhart *Highld* 140 7462
Glenvarragill *Highld* 136 4739
Glenwhilly *D & G* 98 1771
Glespin *S Lans* 108 8127
Glewstone *Herefd* 34 5521
Glinton *Cambs* 64 1505
Glooston *Leics* 50 7595
Glororum *Nthumb* 111 1633
Glossop *Derbys* 74 0393
Gloster Hill *Nthumb* 103 2504
Gloucester *Gloucs* 35 8318
Glusburn *N York* 82 0045
Glutt Lodge *Highld* 150 0036
Gluvian *Cnwll* 4 9164
Glympton *Oxon* 36 4221
Glyn Ceiriog *Wrexhm* 70 2038
Glyn-Neath *Neath* 33 8806
Glynarthen *Cerdgn* 42 3148
Glyncorrwg *Neath* 33 8798
Glynde *E Susx* 16 4509
Glyndebourne *E Susx* 16 4510
Glyndyfrdwy *Denbgs* 70 1442
Glyntaff *Rhondd* 33 0889
Glyntawe *Powys* 33 8416
Glynteg *Carmth* 31 3637
Gnosall *Staffs* 72 8220
Gnosall Heath *Staffs* 72 8220
Goadby *Leics* 50 7598
Goadby Marwood *Leics* 63 7726
Goat Lees *Kent* 28 0145
Goatacre *Wilts* 35 0276
Goatfield *Ag & B* 114 0100
Goatham Green *E Susx* 17 8120
Goathill *Dorset* 11 6717
Goathland *N York* 90 8301
Goathurst *Somset* 20 2534
Goathurst Common *Kent* 27 4952
Gobowen *Shrops* 59 3033
Godalming *Surrey* 25 9643
Godameavy *Devon* 6 5364
Goddard's Corner *Suffk* 55 2868
Goddard's Green *Kent* 17 8134
Godford Cross *Devon* 9 1302
Godington *Bucks* 49 6427
Godley *Gt Man* 79 9595
Godmanchester *Cambs* 52 2470
Godmanstone *Dorset* 11 6697
Godmersham *Kent* 28 0550
Godney *Somset* 21 4842
Godolphin Cross *Cnwll* 2 6031
Godre'r-graig *Neath* 32 7506
Godshill *Hants* 12 1715
Godshill *IOW* 13 5281
Godstone *Staffs* 73 0134
Godstone *Surrey* 27 3551
Godsworthy *Devon* 5 5277
Godwinscroft *Hants* 12 1996
Goetre *Mons* 34 3206
Goff's Oak *Herts* 27 3202
Gofilon *Mons* 34 2613
Gogar *C Edin* 117 1672
Goginan *Cerdgn* 43 6881
Golan *Gwynd* 57 5242
Golant *Cnwll* 3 1254
Golberdon *Cnwll* 5 3271
Golborne *Gt Man* 78 6097
Golcar *W York* 82 0915
Gold Hill *Cambs* 65 5392
Gold Hill *Dorset* 11 8213
Goldcliff *Newpt* 34 3683
Golden Cross *E Susx* 16 5312
Golden Green *Kent* 16 6348
Golden Grove *Carmth* 32 5919
Golden Hill *Pembks* 30 9802
Golden Pot *Hants* 24 7143
Golden Valley *Derbys* 74 4251
Goldenhill *Staffs* 72 8553
Golders Green *Gt Lon* 26 2487
Goldfinch Bottom *Berks* 24 5063
Goldhanger *Essex* 40 9008
Golding *Shrops* 59 5403
Goldington *Beds* 38 0750
Golds Green *W Mids* 60 9893
Goldsborough *N York* 90 8314
Goldsborough *N York* 83 3856
Goldsithney *Cnwll* 2 5430
Goldstone *Kent* 29 2961
Goldstone *Shrops* 72 7028
Goldsworth *Surrey* 25 9958
Goldthorpe *S York* 83 4604
Goldworthy *Devon* 18 3922
Golford *Kent* 28 7936
Golford Green *Kent* 28 7936
Gollanfield *Highld* 140 8053
Gollinglith Foot *N York* 89 1481
Golly *Wrexhm* 71 3358
Golsoncott *Somset* 20 0239
Golspie *Highld* 147 8300
Gomeldon *Wilts* 23 1835
Gomersal *W York* 82 2026
Gomshall *Surrey* 14 0847
Gonalston *Notts* 63 6747
Gonerby Hill Foot *Lincs* 63 9037
Gonfirth *Shet* 153 3661
Good Easter *Essex* 40 6212
Gooderstone *Norfk* 65 7602
Goodleigh *Devon* 19 6034
Goodmanham *E R Yk* 84 8843
Goodnestone *Kent* 28 0461
Goodnestone *Kent* 29 2554
Goodrich *Herefd* 34 5719
Goodrington *Devon* 7 8958
Goodshaw *Lancs* 81 8125
Goodshaw Fold *Lancs* 81 8026
Goodstone *Devon* 7 7872
Goodwick *Pembks* 30 9438
Goodworth Clatford *Hants* 23 3642
Goodyers End *Warwks* 61 3385
Goole *E R Yk* 84 7423
Goole Fields *E R Yk* 84 7520
Goom's Hill *Worcs* 47 0154
Goonbell *Cnwll* 3 7249
Goonhavern *Cnwll* 3 7853
Goonvrea *Cnwll* 2 7149
Goose Green *Essex* 41 1327
Goose Green *Essex* 41 1325
Goose Green *Gloucs* 35 6774
Goose Green *Gt Man* 78 5603
Goose Green *Kent* 27 6451
Goose Green *Kent* 28 8437
Goose Green *W Susx* 14 1118
Goose Pool *Herefd* 46 4636
Goosecruives *Abers* 135 7583
Gooseford *Devon* 8 6792
Gooseham *Cnwll* 18 2316
Goosehill Green *Worcs* 47 9361
Goosemoor *Somset* 20 9635
Goosey *Oxon* 36 3591
Goosnargh *Lancs* 81 5536
Goostrey *Ches* 79 7770
Gorddinog *Conwy* 69 6773
Gordon *Border* 110 6443
Gordon Arms Hotel *Border* 109 3025
Gordonstown *Abers* 142 5656
Gordonstown *Abers* 142 7138
Gore *Powys* 46 2558
Gore Pit *Essex* 40 8719
Gore Street *Kent* 29 2765
Gorebridge *Mdloth* 118 3461
Gorefield *Cambs* 65 4112
Gores *Wilts* 23 1158
Gorey *Jersey* 158 0000

Goring Gullane

Goring Oxon 37 6080
Goring Heath Oxon 37 6579
Goring-by-Sea W Susx 14 1102
Gorleston on Sea Norfk 67 5204
Gorrachie Abers 142 7358
Gorran Cnwll 3 9942
Gorran Haven Cnwll 3 0141
Gorran High Lanes Cnwll 3 9843
Gorrig Cerdgn 31 4142
Gors Cerdgn 43 6277
Gorse Hill Wilts 36 1586
Gorsedd Flints 70 1576
Gorseinon Swans 32 5996
Gorseybank Derbys 73 2953
Gorsgoch Cerdgn 44 4850
Gorslas Carmth 32 5713
Gorsley Gloucs 47 6925
Gorsley Common Gloucs 47 6825
Gorst Hill Worcs 60 7373
Gorstage Ches 71 6172
Gorstan Highld 139 3862
Gorstello Ches 71 3562
Gorsty Hill Staffs 73 1028
Gorten Ag & B 122 7432
Gorthleck Highld 139 5420
Gorton Gt Man 79 8896
Gosbeck Suffk 54 1555
Gosberton Lincs 64 2331
Gosberton Clough Lincs 64 1929
Gosfield Essex 40 7829
Gosford Devon 9 1097
Gosforth Cumb 86 0603
Gosforth T & W 103 2368
Gosland Green Ches 71 5758
Gosling Street Somset 21 5433
Gosmore Herts 39 1827
Gospel End Staffs 60 8993
Gospel Green W Susx 14 9431
Gosport Hants 13 6099
Gossard's Green Beds 38 9643
Gossington Gloucs 35 7302
Goswick Nthumb 111 0644
Gotham Notts 62 5330
Gotherington Gloucs 47 9529
Gotton Somset 20 2428
Goudhurst Kent 28 7237
Goulceby Lincs 77 2579
Gourdas Abers 142 7741
Gourdie Angus 126 3532
Gourdon Abers 135 8270
Gourock Inver 114 2477
Govan C Glas 115 5465
Goveton Devon 7 7546
Gowdall E R Yk 83 6222
Gower Highld 139 5058
Gowerton Swans 32 5896
Gowkhall Fife 117 0589
Gowthorpe E R Yk 84 7654
Goxhill E R Yk 85 1844
Goxhill Lincs 85 1021
Grabhair W Isls 152 3915
Graby Lincs 64 0929
Grade Cnwll 2 7114
Gradeley Green Ches 71 5851
Graffham W Susx 14 9217
Grafham Cambs 52 1669
Grafham Surrey 14 0241
Grafton Herefd 46 4936
Grafton N York 89 4163
Grafton Oxon 36 2600
Grafton Shrops 59 4319
Grafton Worcs 46 5761
Grafton Worcs 47 9837
Grafton Flyford Worcs 47 9655
Grafton Regis Nhants 49 7546
Grafton Underwood Nhants 51 9280
Grafty Green Kent 28 8748
Graianrhyd Denbgs 70 2156
Graig Conwy 69 8071
Graig Denbgs 70 0872
Graig-fechan Denbgs 70 1454
Grain Kent 28 8876
Grains Bar Gt Man 79 9608
Grainsby Lincs 77 2799
Grainthorpe Lincs 77 3896
Grampound Cnwll 3 9348
Grampound Road Cnwll 3 9150
Gramsdal W Isls 152 8155
Gramsdale W Isls 152 8155
Granborough Bucks 49 7625
Granby Notts 63 7536
Grand Chemins Jersey 158 0000
Grandborough Warwks 50 4966
Grandes Rocques Guern 158 0000
Grandtully P & K 125 9153
Grange Cumb 93 2517
Grange Kent 28 7968
Grange Mersyd 78 2286
Grange P & K 126 2625
Grange Crossroads Moray 142 4754
Grange Gate Dorset 11 9182
Grange Hall Moray 141 0660
Grange Hill Gt Lon 27 4492
Grange Moor W York 82 2215
Grange of Lindores Fife 126 2516
Grange Villa Dur 96 2352
Grange-over-Sands Cumb 87 4077
Grangehall S Lans 108 9642
Grangemill Derbys 74 2457
Grangemouth Falk 116 9281
Grangepans Falk 117 0181
Grangetown N York 97 5420
Grangetown T & W 96 4154
Gransmoor E R Yk 91 1259
Gransmore Green Essex 40 6922
Granston Pembks 30 8934
Grantchester Cambs 53 4355
Grantham Lincs 63 9135
Granton C Edin 117 2376
Grantown-on-Spey Highld 141 0328
Grantsfield Herefd 46 5260
Grantshouse Border 119 8065
Grappenhall Ches 79 6486
Grasby Lincs 85 0804
Grasmere Cumb 86 3307
Grass Green Essex 53 7338
Grasscroft Gt Man 82 9704
Grassendale Mersyd 78 3985
Grassgarth Cumb 93 3444
Grassington N York 88 0063
Grassmoor Derbys 74 4067
Grassthorpe Notts 75 7967
Grateley Hants 23 2741
Gratwich Staffs 73 0231
Graveley Cambs 52 2563
Graveley Herts 39 2327
Gravelly Hill W Mids 61 1090
Gravelsbank Shrops 59 3300
Graveney Kent 28 0562
Gravesend Kent 28 6574
Gravir W Isls 152 3915
Grayingham Lincs 76 9396
Grayrigg Cumb 87 5796
Grays Essex 27 6177
Grayshott Hants 14 8735
Grayson Green Cumb 92 9925
Grayswood Surrey 14 9134
Graythorpe Dur 97 5227
Grazeley Berks 24 6966
Greasbrough S York 74 4195
Greasby Mersyd 78 2587
Greasley Notts 62 4846
Great Abington Cambs 53 5348
Great Addington Nhants 51 9675
Great Alne Warwks 48 1259
Great Altcar Lancs 78 3305
Great Amwell Herts 39 3712
Great Asby Cumb 94 6713
Great Ashfield Suffk 54 9967
Great Ayton N York 90 5610
Great Baddow Essex 40 7304
Great Badminton Gloucs 35 8082
Great Bardfield Essex 40 6730
Great Barford Beds 52 1351
Great Barr W Mids 61 0495
Great Barrington Gloucs 36 2113
Great Barrow Ches 71 4768
Great Barton Suffk 54 8967
Great Barugh N York 90 7479
Great Bavington Nthumb 102 9880
Great Bealings Suffk 55 2348
Great Bedwyn Wilts 23 2764
Great Bentley Essex 41 1021
Great Billing Nhants 51 8162
Great Bircham Norfk 65 7732
Great Blakenham Suffk 54 1150
Great Blencow Cumb 93 4532
Great Bolas Shrops 72 6421
Great Bookham Surrey 26 1354
Great Bosullow Cnwll 2 4133
Great Bourton Oxon 49 4545
Great Bowden Leics 50 7488
Great Bradley Suffk 53 6753
Great Braxted Essex 40 8614
Great Bricett Suffk 54 0350
Great Brickhill Bucks 38 9030
Great Bridge W Mids 60 9892
Great Bridgeford Staffs 72 8827
Great Brington Nhants 50 6665
Great Bromley Essex 41 0826
Great Broughton Cumb 92 0731
Great Broughton N York 90 5405
Great Budworth Ches 79 6677
Great Burdon Dur 96 3116
Great Burstead Essex 40 6892
Great Busby N York 90 5205
Great Canfield Essex 40 5918
Great Carlton Lincs 77 4085
Great Casterton RutInd 63 0008
Great Chart Kent 28 9841
Great Chatfield Wilts 22 8563
Great Chatwell Staffs 60 7914
Great Chell Staffs 72 8652
Great Chesterford Essex 39 5042
Great Cheverell Wilts 22 9854
Great Chishill Cambs 39 4238
Great Clacton Essex 41 1716
Great Cliffe W York 82 3015
Great Clifton Cumb 92 0429
Great Coates Lincs 85 2309
Great Comberton Worcs 47 9542
Great Comp Kent 27 6356
Great Corby Cumb 93 4754
Great Cornard Suffk 54 8840
Great Cowden E R Yk 85 2342
Great Coxwell Oxon 36 2693
Great Cransley Nhants 51 8376
Great Cressingham Norfk 66 8501
Great Crosthwaite Cumb 93 2524
Great Cubley Derbys 73 1638
Great Dalby Leics 63 7414
Great Doddington Nhants 51 8864
Great Doward Herefd 34 5416
Great Dunham Norfk 66 8714
Great Dunmow Essex 40 6222
Great Durnford Wilts 23 1338
Great Easton Essex 40 6025
Great Easton Leics 51 8492
Great Eccleston Lancs 80 4240
Great Edstone N York 90 7083
Great Ellingham Norfk 66 0196
Great Elm Somset 22 7449
Great Englebourne Devon 7 7756
Great Everdon Nhants 49 5957
Great Eversden Cambs 52 3653
Great Finborough Suffk 54 0158
Great Fransham Norfk 66 8913
Great Gaddesden Herts 38 0211
Great Gidding Cambs 52 1183
Great Givendale E R Yk 84 8153
Great Glemham Suffk 55 3361
Great Glen Leics 50 6597
Great Gonerby Lincs 63 8938
Great Gransden Cambs 52 2655
Great Green Cambs 39 2844
Great Green Norfk 55 2889
Great Green Suffk 54 9155
Great Green Suffk 54 9365
Great Habton N York 90 7576
Great Hale Lincs 64 1442
Great Hallingbury Essex 39 5119
Great Hanwood Shrops 59 4409
Great Harrowden Nhants 51 8770
Great Harwood Lancs 81 7332
Great Haseley Oxon 37 6401
Great Hatfield E R Yk 85 1842
Great Haywood Staffs 73 9922
Great Heck N York 83 5920
Great Henny Essex 54 8637
Great Hinton Wilts 22 9059
Great Hockham Norfk 66 9592
Great Holland Essex 41 2019
Great Horkesley Essex 41 9731
Great Hormead Herts 39 4029
Great Horton W York 82 1431
Great Horwood Bucks 49 7731
Great Houghton Nhants 50 7958
Great Houghton S York 83 4206
Great Hucklow Derbys 74 1777
Great Kelk E R Yk 91 1058
Great Kimble Bucks 38 8205
Great Kingshill Bucks 26 8797
Great Langdale Cumb 86 2906
Great Langton N York 89 2996
Great Leighs Essex 40 7217
Great Limber Lincs 85 1308
Great Linford Bucks 38 8542
Great Livermere Suffk 54 8871
Great Longstone Derbys 74 2071
Great Lumley Dur 96 2949
Great Lyth Shrops 59 4507
Great Malvern Worcs 47 7746
Great Maplestead Essex 54 8034
Great Marton Lancs 80 3235
Great Massingham Norfk 66 7922
Great Melton Norfk 66 1206
Great Meols Mersyd 78 2390
Great Milton Oxon 37 6202
Great Missenden Bucks 26 8901
Great Mitton Lancs 81 7138
Great Mongeham Kent 29 3551
Great Moulton Norfk 54 1690
Great Munden Herts 39 3524
Great Musgrave Cumb 94 7613
Great Ness Shrops 59 3919
Great Notley Essex 40 7421
Great Nurcott Somset 20 9036
Great Oak Mons 34 3810
Great Oakley Essex 41 1927
Great Oakley Nhants 51 8785
Great Offley Herts 38 1427
Great Ormside Cumb 94 7017
Great Orton Cumb 93 3254
Great Ouseburn N York 89 4461
Great Oxendon Nhants 50 7383
Great Oxney Green Essex 40 6606
Great Pattenden Kent 28 7344
Great Paxton Cambs 52 2063
Great Plumpton Lancs 80 3833
Great Plumstead Norfk 67 3010
Great Ponton Lincs 63 9230
Great Potheridge Devon 19 5114
Great Preston W York 83 4029
Great Purston Nhants 49 5139
Great Raveley Cambs 52 2581
Great Rissington Gloucs 36 1917
Great Rollright Oxon 48 3231
Great Rudbaxton Pembks 30 9620
Great Ryburgh Norfk 66 9527
Great Ryle Nthumb 111 0212
Great Ryton Shrops 59 4803
Great Saling Essex 40 6925
Great Salkeld Cumb 94 5536
Great Sampford Essex 53 6435
Great Sankey Ches 78 5688
Great Saredon Staffs 60 9508
Great Saughall Ches 71 3669
Great Saxham Suffk 53 7862
Great Shefford Berks 36 3875
Great Shelford Cambs 53 4651
Great Smeaton N York 89 3404
Great Snoring Norfk 66 9434
Great Somerford Wilts 35 9682
Great Soudley Shrops 72 7229
Great Stainton Dur 96 3322
Great Stambridge Essex 40 8991
Great Staughton Cambs 52 1264
Great Steeping Lincs 77 4364
Great Stoke Bristl 35 6280
Great Stonar Kent 29 3359
Great Strickland Cumb 94 5522
Great Stukeley Cambs 52 2274
Great Sturton Lincs 76 2176
Great Sutton Ches 71 3775
Great Sutton Shrops 59 5183
Great Swinburne Nthumb 102 9375
Great Tew Oxon 48 4028
Great Tey Essex 40 8925
Great Torrington Devon 18 4919
Great Tosson Nthumb 103 0200
Great Totham Essex 40 8611
Great Totham Essex 40 8713
Great Tows Lincs 76 2290
Great Urswick Cumb 86 2674
Great Wakering Essex 40 9487
Great Waldingfield Suffk 54 9144
Great Walsingham Norfk 66 9437
Great Waltham Essex 40 6913
Great Warford Ches 79 8177
Great Warley Essex 27 5890
Great Washbourne Gloucs 47 9834
Great Weeke Devon 8 7187
Great Weldon Nhants 51 9289
Great Welnetham Suffk 54 8759
Great Wenham Suffk 54 0738
Great Whittington Nthumb 103 0070
Great Wigborough Essex 41 9615
Great Wilbraham Cambs 53 5557
Great Wishford Wilts 23 0735
Great Witchingham Norfk 66 1020
Great Witcombe Gloucs 35 9114
Great Witley Worcs 47 7566
Great Wolford Warwks 48 2534
Great Wratting Essex 53 6848
Great Wymondley Herts 39 2128
Great Wyrley Staffs 60 9907
Great Wytheford Shrops 59 5719
Great Yarmouth Norfk 67 5207
Great Yeldham Essex 53 7638
Greatfield Wilts 36 0785
Greatford Lincs 64 0811
Greatgate Staffs 73 0539
Greatham Dur 97 4927
Greatham Hants 14 7730
Greatham W Susx 14 0415
Greatstone-on-Sea Kent 17 0822
Greatworth Nhants 49 5542
Grebby Lincs 77 4368
Greeba IOM 158 3081
Green Denbgs 70 0668
Green Bank Cumb 87 3780
Green Cross Surrey 14 8637
Green Down Somset 21 5753
Green End Beds 38 0147
Green End Beds 51 0864
Green End Beds 51 1063
Green End Beds 52 1252
Green End Cambs 52 2274
Green End Cambs 52 3856
Green End Cambs 53 4668
Green End Cambs 53 4861
Green End Cambs 52 1683
Green End Herts 39 2630
Green End Herts 39 3222
Green End Herts 39 3333
Green End Warwks 61 2686
Green Hammerton N York 83 4556
Green Head Cumb 93 3649
Green Heath Staffs 60 9913
Green Hill Wilts 36 0686
Green Hills Cambs 53 6072
Green Lane Devon 8 7877
Green Lane Warwks 48 0664
Green Moor S York 74 2899
Green Oak E R Yk 84 8127
Green Ore Somset 21 5750
Green Quarter Cumb 87 4603
Green Street E Susx 17 7611
Green Street Gloucs 35 8915
Green Street Herts 39 4521
Green Street Herts 26 1998
Green Street Worcs 47 8749
Green Street Green Gt Lon 27 4563
Green Street Green Kent 27 5870
Green Tye Herts 39 4418
Greenburn W Loth 116 9360
Greencroft Hall Dur 96 1549
Greenend Oxon 36 3221
Greenfield Ag & B 114 2490
Greenfield Beds 38 0534
Greenfield Flints 70 1977
Greenfield Gt Man 82 9904
Greenfield Highld 131 2000
Greenfield Oxon 37 7191
Greenford Gt Lon 26 1482
Greengairs N Lans 116 7870
Greengates W York 82 1937
Greengill Cumb 92 1037
Greenhalgh Lancs 80 4035
Greenham Berks 24 4865
Greenham Somset 20 0820
Greenhaugh Nthumb 102 7987
Greenhead Nthumb 102 6565
Greenheys Gt Man 79 7104
Greenhill D & G 100 1079
Greenhill Falk 116 8279
Greenhill Herefd 47 7248
Greenhill Kent 29 1666
Greenhill S Lans 108 9332
Greenhillocks Derbys 74 4049
Greenhithe Kent 27 5875
Greenholm E Ayrs 107 5437
Greenholme Cumb 87 5905
Greenhouse Border 109 5523
Greenhow Hill N York 89 1164
Greenland Highld 151 2367
Greenland S York 74 3988
Greenlands Bucks 37 7785
Greenlaw Border 110 7146
Greenlea D & G 100 0375
Greenloaning P & K 125 8307
Greenmoor Hill Oxon 37 6481
Greenmount Gt Man 81 7714
Greenock Inver 115 2876
Greenodd Cumb 86 3182
Greens Norton Nhants 49 6649
Greensgate Norfk 66 1015
Greenshields S Lans 108 0243
Greenside T & W 96 1362
Greenside W York 82 1716
Greenstead Essex 41 0125
Greenstead Green Essex 40 8227
Greensted Essex 39 5403
Greenstreet Green Suffk 54 0349
Greenway Gloucs 47 7033
Greenway Somset 21 3124
Greenway V Glam 33 0573
Greenway Worcs 60 7470
Greenwich Gt Lon 27 3877
Greet Gloucs 48 0230
Greete Shrops 46 5770
Greetham Lincs 77 3070
Greetham RutInd 63 9214
Greetland W York 82 0821
Gregson Lane Lancs 81 5926
Greinton Somset 21 4136
Grenaby IOM 158 2672
Grendon Nhants 51 8760
Grendon Warwks 61 2799
Grendon Green Herefd 46 5957
Grendon Underwood Bucks 37 6820
Grenofen Devon 6 4971
Grenoside S York 74 3393
Greosabhagh W Isls 152 1593
Gresford Wrexhm 71 3454
Gresham Norfk 66 1638
Greshornish House Hotel Highld 136 3454
Gressenhall Norfk 66 9615
Gressenhall Green Norfk 66 9616
Gressingham Lancs 87 5769
Gresty Green Ches 72 7053
Greta Bridge Dur 95 0813
Gretna D & G 101 3167
Gretna Green D & G 101 3168
Gretton Gloucs 47 0030
Gretton Nhants 51 8994
Gretton Shrops 59 5195
Grewelthorpe N York 89 2376
Grey Friars Suffk 55 4770
Grey Green Lincs 84 7807
Greygarth N York 89 1872
Greylake Somset 21 3833
Greyrigg D & G 100 0888
Greys Green Oxon 37 7182
Greysouthen Cumb 92 0729
Greystoke Cumb 93 4430
Greystone Angus 127 5343
Greywell Hants 24 7151
Gribb Dorset 10 3703
Gribthorpe E R Yk 84 7635
Griff Warwks 61 3689
Griffithstown Torfn 34 2998
Griffydam Leics 62 4118
Griggs Green Hants 14 8231
Grimeford Village Lancs 81 6112
Grimesthorpe S York 74 3689
Grimethorpe S York 83 4109
Grimley Worcs 47 8360
Grimmet S Ayrs 106 3210
Grimoldby Lincs 77 3988
Grimpo Shrops 59 3526
Grimsargh Lancs 81 5834
Grimsby Lincs 85 2710
Grimscote Nhants 49 6553
Grimscott Cnwll 18 2606
Grimshader W Isls 152 4025
Grimshaw Lancs 81 7024
Grimshaw Green Lancs 80 4912
Grimsthorpe Lincs 64 0422
Grimston E R Yk 85 2735
Grimston Leics 63 6821
Grimston Norfk 65 7222
Grimston Hill Notts 75 6865
Grimstone Dorset 10 6394
Grimstone End Suffk 54 9368
Grinacombe Moor Devon 5 4191
Grindale E R Yk 91 1271
Grindle Shrops 60 7503
Grindleford Derbys 74 2477
Grindleton Lancs 81 7545
Grindley Brook Shrops 71 5242
Grindlow Derbys 74 1877
Grindon Dur 96 3925
Grindon Nthumb 110 9144
Grindon Staffs 73 0854
Grindon T & W 96 3555
Grindon Hill Nthumb 102 8268
Grindonrigg Nthumb 110 9243
Gringley on the Hill Notts 75 7390
Grinsdale Cumb 93 3758
Grinshill Shrops 59 5223
Grinton N York 88 0498
Griomaisiader W Isls 152 4025
Grishipoll Ag & B 120 1859
Grisling Common E Susx 16 4322
Gristhorpe N York 91 0981
Griston Norfk 66 9499
Gritley Ork 153 5504
Grittenham Wilts 36 0382
Grittleton Wilts 35 8580
Grizebeck Cumb 86 2384
Grizedale Cumb 86 3394
Groby Leics 62 5207
Groes Conwy 70 0064
Groes-faen Rhondd 33 0680
Groes-Wen Caerph 33 1286
Groesffordd Gwynd 56 2739
Groesffordd Marli Denbgs 70 0073
Groesllwyd Powys 58 2111
Groeslon Gwynd 68 4755
Groeslon Gwynd 68 5260
Grogarry W Isls 152 7739
Grogport Ag & B 105 8144
Groigearraidh W Isls 152 7739
Gromford Suffk 55 3858
Gronant Flints 70 0983
Groombridge E Susx 16 5337
Grosebay W Isls 152 1593
Grosmont Mons 46 4024
Grosmont N York 90 8305
Groton Suffk 54 9641
Grotton Gt Man 79 9604
Grouville Jersey 158 0000
Grove Bucks 38 9122
Grove Dorset 11 6972
Grove Kent 29 2362
Grove Notts 75 7479
Grove Oxon 36 4090
Grove Pembks 30 9900
Grove Green Kent 28 7856
Grove Park Gt Lon 27 4072
Grove Vale W Mids 61 0394
Grovenhurst Kent 28 7140
Grovesend Gloucs 35 6589
Grovesend Swans 32 5900
Grubb Street Kent 27 5869
Gruinard Highld 144 9489
Gruinart Ag & B 112 2966
Grula Highld 136 3826
Gruline Ag & B 121 5440
Grumbla Cnwll 2 4029
Grundisburgh Suffk 55 2251
Gruting Shet 153 2749
Gualachulain Highld 123 1145
Guanockgate Lincs 64 3710
Guardbridge Fife 127 4518
Guarlford Worcs 47 8145
Guay P & K 125 0049
Guestling Green E Susx 17 8513
Guestling Thorn E Susx 17 8516
Guestwick Norfk 66 0626
Guide Lancs 81 7025
Guide Bridge Gt Man 79 9297
Guide Post Nthumb 103 2585
Guilden Down Shrops 59 3082
Guilden Morden Cambs 39 2744
Guilden Sutton Ches 71 4468
Guildford Surrey 25 9949
Guildstead Kent 28 8262
Guildtown P & K 126 1331
Guilsborough Nhants 50 6772
Guilsfield Powys 58 2211
Guilton Kent 29 2858
Guiltreehill S Ayrs 106 3610
Guineaford Devon 19 5537
Guisborough N York 97 6015
Guiseley W York 82 1942
Guist Norfk 66 0025
Guiting Power Gloucs 48 0924
Gullane E Loth 118 4882

Gulling Green Haslington


Gulling Green Suffk 54 8256
Gulval Cnwll 2 4831
Gulworthy Devon 6 4572
Gumfreston Pembks 31 1001
Gumley Leics 50 6889
Gummow's Shop Cnwll 4 8657
Gun Green Kent 17 7731
Gun Hill E Susx 16 5614
Gun Hill Warwks 61 2889
Gunby E R Yk 84 7035
Gunby Lincs 63 9121
Gunby Lincs 77 4666
Gundleton Hants 24 6133
Gunn Devon 19 6333
Gunnerside N York 88 9598
Gunnerton Nthumb 102 9074
Gunness Lincs 84 8411
Gunnislake Cnwll 6 4371
Gunnista Shet 153 5043
Gunthorpe Cambs 64 1802
Gunthorpe Norfk 66 0134
Gunthorpe Notts 63 6844
Gunton Suffk 67 5395
Gunville IOW 13 4788
Gunwalloe Cnwll 2 6522
Gupworthy Somset 20 9734
Gurnard IOW 13 4795
Gurnett Ches 79 9271
Gurney Slade Somset 21 6249
Gurnos Powys 32 7709
Gushmere Kent 28 0457
Gussage All Saints Dorset 11 0010
Gussage St Andrew Dorset 11 9714
Gussage St Michael Dorset 11 9811
Guston Kent 29 3244
Gutcher Shet 153 5499
Guthrie Angus 127 5650
Guy's Marsh Dorset 22 8420
Guyhirn Cambs 65 4003
Guyhirn Gull Cambs 65 3904
Guyzance Nthumb 103 2103
Gwaenysgor Flints 70 0781
Gwalchmai IOA 68 3876
Gwastadnant Gwynd 69 6157
Gwaun-Cae-Gurwen Carmth 32 6911
Gwbert on Sea Cerdgn 42 1650
Gwealavellan Cnwll 2 6041
Gwealeath Cnwll 2 6922
Gweek Cnwll 2 7026
Gwehelog Mons 34 3804
Gwenddwr Powys 45 0643
Gwendreath Cnwll 3 7217
Gwennap Cnwll 3 7340
Gwenter Cnwll 3 7417
Gwernaffield Flints 70 2065
Gwernesney Mons 34 4101
Gwernogle Carmth 44 5333
Gwernymynydd Flints 70 2162
Gwersyllt Wrexhm 71 3153
Gwespyr Flints 70 1183
Gwindra Cnwll 3 9552
Gwinear Cnwll 2 5937
Gwithian Cnwll 2 5841
Gwredog IOA 68 4085
Gwrhay Caerph 33 1899
Gwyddelwern Denbgs 70 0746
Gwyddgrug Carmth 44 4635
Gwynfryn Wrexhm 70 2552
Gwystre Powys 45 0665
Gwytherin Conwy 69 8761
Gyfelia Wrexhm 71 3245
Gyrn-goch Gwynd 68 4048


# H


Habberley Shrops 59 3903
Habberley Worcs 60 8177
Habergham Lancs 81 8033
Habertoft Lincs 77 5069
Habin W Susx 14 8022
Habrough Lincs 85 1413
Hacconby Lincs 64 1025
Haceby Lincs 64 0236
Hacheston Suffk 55 3059
Hack Green Ches 72 6448
Hackbridge Gt Lon 27 2865
Hackenthorpe S York 74 4183
Hackford Norfk 66 0502
Hackforth N York 89 2492
Hackland Ork 153 3920
Hackleton Nhants 51 8055
Hacklinge Kent 29 3454
Hackman's Gate Worcs 60 8978
Hackness N York 91 9790
Hackness Somset 21 3345
Hackney Gt Lon 27 3484
Hackthorn Lincs 76 9982
Hackthorpe Cumb 94 5423
Hacton Gt Lon 27 5585
Hadden Border 110 7836
Haddenham Bucks 37 7308
Haddenham Cambs 53 4675
Haddington E Loth 118 5173
Haddington Lincs 76 9162
Haddiscoe Norfk 67 4497
Haddo Abers 143 8337
Haddon Cambs 64 1392
Hade Edge W York 82 1404
Hadfield Derbys 74 0296
Hadham Cross Herts 39 4218
Hadham Ford Herts 39 4321
Hadleigh Essex 40 8187
Hadleigh Suffk 54 0242
Hadleigh Heath Suffk 54 9941
Hadley Shrops 60 6711
Hadley Worcs 47 8564
Hadley End Staffs 73 1320
Hadley Wood Gt Lon 27 2698
Hadlow Kent 27 6350
Hadlow Down E Susx 16 5324
Hadnall Shrops 59 5220
Hadstock Essex 53 5644
Hadzor Worcs 47 9162
Haffenden Quarter Kent 28 8840
Hafod-y-bwch Wrexhm 71 3147
Hafod-y-coed Blae G 34 2200
Hafodunos Conwy 69 8666
Hafodyrynys Caerph 34 2298
Haggate Lancs 81 8735
Haggbeck Cumb 101 4773
Haggerston Nthumb 111 0443
Haggington Hill Devon 19 5547
Haggs Falk 116 7879
Hagley Herefd 46 5641
Hagley W Mids 60 9180
Hagmore Green Suffk 54 9539
Hagnaby Lincs 77 3462
Hagnaby Lincs 77 4879
Hagworthingham Lincs 77 3469
Haigh Gt Man 78 6009
Haighton Green Lancs 81 5634
Hail Weston Cambs 52 1662
Haile Cumb 86 0308
Hailes Gloucs 48 0430
Hailey Herts 39 3710
Hailey Oxon 37 6485
Hailey Oxon 36 3512
Hailsham E Susx 16 5909
Hainault Gt Lon 27 4591
Haine Kent 29 3566
Hainford Norfk 67 2218
Hainton Lincs 76 1884
Hainworth W York 82 0638
Haisthorpe E R Yk 91 1264
Hakin Pembks 30 8905
Halam Notts 75 6754
Halbeath Fife 117 1288
Halberton Devon 9 0112
Halcro Highld 151 2360
Hale Ches 78 4782
Hale Cumb 87 5078
Hale Gt Man 79 7786
Hale Hants 12 1818
Hale Somset 22 7427
Hale Surrey 25 8448
Hale Bank Ches 78 4784
Hale Green E Susx 16 5514
Hale Nook Lancs 80 3944
Hale Street Kent 28 6749
Halebarns Gt Man 79 7985
Hales Norfk 67 3797
Hales Staffs 72 7134
Hales Green Derbys 73 1841
Hales Place Kent 29 1459
Halesgate Lincs 64 3226
Halesowen W Mids 60 9683
Halesville Essex 40 9092
Halesworth Suffk 55 3877
Halewood Mersyd 78 4585
Halford Devon 7 8174
Halford Shrops 59 4383
Halford Warwks 48 2645
Halfpenny Cumb 87 5387
Halfpenny Green Staffs 60 8291
Halfpenny Houses N York 89 2284
Halfway Berks 24 4068
Halfway Carmth 44 6430
Halfway Carmth 44 8232
Halfway S York 75 4381
Halfway Bridge W Susx 14 9321
Halfway House Shrops 59 3411
Halfway Houses Kent 28 9372
Halifax W York 82 0925
Halkirk Highld 151 1359
Halkyn Flints 70 2171
Hall E Rens 115 4154
Hall Cliffe W York 82 2918
Hall Cross Lancs 80 4230
Hall Dunnerdale Cumb 86 2195
Hall End Beds 38 0045
Hall End Beds 38 0737
Hall End W Mids 60 0092
Hall Glen Falk 116 8978
Hall Green W Mids 61 1181
Hall's Green Essex 39 4108
Hall's Green Herts 39 2728
Hallam Fields Derbys 62 4739
Halland E Susx 16 4916
Hallaton Leics 50 7896
Hallatrow Somset 21 6357
Hallbankgate Cumb 94 5859
Hallbeck Cumb 87 6288
Hallen Gloucs 34 5580
Hallfield Gate Derbys 74 3958
Hallgarth Dur 96 3243
Hallin Highld 136 2558
Halling Kent 28 7063
Hallington Lincs 77 3085
Hallington Nthumb 102 9875
Halliwell Gt Man 79 6910
Halloughton Notts 75 6951
Hallow Worcs 47 8258
Hallow Heath Worcs 47 8259
Hallrule Border 110 5914
Hallsands Devon 7 8138
Hallthwaites Cumb 86 1885
Halltoft End Lincs 64 3645
Hallworthy Cnwll 4 1787
Hallyne Border 109 1940
Halmer End Staffs 72 7948
Halmond's Frome Herefd 47 6747
Halmore Gloucs 35 7002
Halnaker W Susx 14 9007
Halsall Lancs 78 3710
Halse Nhants 49 5640
Halse Somset 20 1428
Halsetown Cnwll 2 5038
Halsham E R Yk 85 2727
Halsinger Devon 19 5138
Halstead Essex 40 8130
Halstead Kent 27 4861
Halstead Leics 63 7505
Halstock Dorset 10 5308
Halsway Somset 20 1337
Haltcliff Bridge Cumb 93 3636
Haltham Lincs 77 2463
Halton Bucks 38 8710
Halton Ches 78 5481
Halton Lancs 87 5064
Halton Nthumb 103 9967
Halton W York 83 3533
Halton Wrexhm 71 3039
Halton East N York 82 0454
Halton Fenside Lincs 77 4263
Halton Gill N York 88 8776
Halton Green Lancs 87 5165
Halton Holegate Lincs 77 4165
Halton Lea Gate Nthumb 94 6458
Halton Quay Cnwll 5 4165
Halton Shields Nthumb 103 0168
Halton West N York 81 8454
Haltwhistle Nthumb 102 7064
Halvergate Norfk 67 4106
Halwell Devon 7 7753
Halwill Devon 18 4299
Halwill Junction Devon 18 4400
Ham Devon 9 2301
Ham Gloucs 35 9721
Ham Gloucs 35 6898
Ham Gt Lon 26 1772
Ham Kent 29 3254
Ham Somset 20 2825
Ham Somset 22 6748
Ham Wilts 23 3262
Ham Common Dorset 22 8125
Ham Green Herefd 47 7544
Ham Green Kent 28 8468
Ham Green Kent 17 8926
Ham Green Somset 34 5375
Ham Green Worcs 47 0163
Ham Hill Kent 28 6960
Ham Street Somset 21 5534
Hamble-le-Rice Hants 13 4806
Hambleden Bucks 37 7886
Hambledon Hants 13 6414
Hambledon Surrey 25 9638
Hambleton Lancs 80 3742
Hambleton N York 83 5530
Hambleton Moss Side Lancs 80 3842
Hambridge Somset 21 3921
Hambridge Somset 21 5936
Hambrook Gloucs 35 6478
Hambrook W Susx 14 7806
Hameringham Lincs 77 3167
Hamerton Cambs 52 1379
Hamilton S Lans 116 7255
Hamlet Dorset 10 5908
Hamlins E Susx 16 5908
Hammerpot W Susx 14 0605
Hammersmith Gt Lon 26 2378
Hammerwich Staffs 61 0707
Hammerwood E Susx 16 4339
Hammond Street Herts 39 3304
Hammoon Dorset 11 8114
Hamnavoe Shet 153 3735
Hamnavoe Shet 153 4971
Hampden Park E Susx 16 6002
Hampden Row Bucks 26 8501
Hamperden End Essex 40 5730
Hampnett Gloucs 36 0915
Hampole S York 83 5010
Hampreston Dorset 12 0598
Hampsfield Cumb 87 4080
Hampson Green Lancs 80 4954
Hampstead Gt Lon 27 2685
Hampstead Norrey's Berks 37 5276
Hampsthwaite N York 89 2559
Hampt Cnwll 5 3874
Hampton Devon 10 2696
Hampton Gt Lon 26 1369
Hampton Kent 29 1568
Hampton Shrops 60 7486
Hampton Wilts 36 1892
Hampton Worcs 48 0243
Hampton Bishop Herefd 46 5637
Hampton Green Ches 71 5149
Hampton Heath Ches 71 5049
Hampton in Arden W Mids 61 2080
Hampton Loade Shrops 60 7486
Hampton Lovett Worcs 47 8865
Hampton Lucy Warwks 48 2557
Hampton on the Hill Warwks 48 2564
Hampton Poyle Oxon 37 5015
Hampton Wick Gt Lon 26 1769
Hamptworth Wilts 12 2419
Hamrow Norfk 66 9124
Hamsey E Susx 15 4012
Hamsey Green Gt Lon 27 3559
Hamstall Ridware Staffs 73 1019
Hamstead IOW 13 4091
Hamstead W Mids 61 0592
Hamstead Marshall Berks 24 4165
Hamsterley Dur 95 1156
Hamsterley Dur 96 1231
Hamstreet Kent 17 0033
Hamwood Somset 21 3756
Hamworthy Dorset 11 9991
Hanbury Staffs 73 1727
Hanbury Worcs 47 9664
Hanby Lincs 64 0231
Hanchet End Suffk 53 6446
Hanchurch Staffs 72 8441
Hand and Pen Devon 9 0495
Hand Green Ches 71 5460
Handale N York 97 7215
Handbridge Ches 71 4065
Handcross W Susx 15 2629
Handforth Ches 79 8583
Handley Ches 71 4657
Handley Derbys 74 3761
Handley Green Essex 40 6501
Handsacre Staffs 73 0915
Handsworth S York 74 4186
Handsworth W Mids 61 0489
Handy Cross Bucks 26 8590
Hanford Dorset 11 8411
Hanford Staffs 72 8741
Hanging Houghton Nhants 60 7573
Hanging Langford Wilts 23 0337
Hangleton E Susx 15 2607
Hangleton W Susx 14 0803
Hanham Gloucs 35 6472
Hankelow Ches 72 6645
Hankerton Wilts 35 9790
Hankham E Susx 16 6105
Hanley Staffs 72 8847
Hanley Castle Worcs 47 8442
Hanley Child Worcs 47 6565
Hanley Swan Worcs 47 8142
Hanley William Worcs 47 6766
Hanlith N York 88 8961
Hanmer Wrexhm 71 4539
Hannaford Devon 19 6029
Hannah Lincs 77 4979
Hannington Hants 24 5355
Hannington Nhants 51 8170
Hannington Wilts 36 1793
Hannington Wick Wilts 36 1795
Hanscombe End Beds 38 1133
Hanslope Bucks 38 8046
Hanthorpe Lincs 64 0823
Hanwell Gt Lon 26 1579
Hanwell Oxon 49 4343
Hanworth Gt Lon 26 1271
Hanworth Norfk 67 1935
Happendon S Lans 108 8533
Happisburgh Norfk 67 3831
Happisburgh Common Norfk 67 3728
Hapsford Ches 71 4774
Hapton Lancs 81 7931
Hapton Norfk 66 1796
Harberton Devon 7 7758
Harbertonford Devon 7 7856
Harbledown Kent 29 1357
Harborne W Mids 60 0284
Harborough Magna Warwks 50 4879
Harbottle Nthumb 102 9304
Harbourneford Devon 7 7162
Harbours Hill Worcs 47 9565
Harbridge Hants 12 1410
Harbridge Green Hants 12 1410
Harbury Warwks 48 3759
Harby Leics 63 7431
Harby Notts 76 8770
Harcombe Devon 9 8881
Harcombe Devon 9 1590
Harcombe Bottom Devon 10 3395
Harden W Mids 60 0100
Harden W York 82 0838
Hardenhuish Wilts 35 9174
Hardgate Abers 135 7901
Hardgate D & G 100 8167
Hardgate N York 89 2662
Hardgate W Duns 115 5072
Hardham W Susx 14 0317
Hardhorn Lancs 80 3537
Hardingham Norfk 66 0403
Hardingstone Nhants 49 7657
Hardington Somset 22 7452
Hardington Mandeville Somset 10 5111
Hardington Marsh Somset 10 5009
Hardington Moor Somset 10 5112
Hardisworthy Devon 18 2320
Hardley Hants 13 4205
Hardley Street Norfk 67 3701
Hardmead Bucks 38 9347
Hardraw N York 88 8691
Hardsough Lancs 81 7920
Hardstoft Derbys 75 4363
Hardway Hants 13 6001
Hardway Somset 22 7234
Hardwick Bucks 38 8019
Hardwick Cambs 52 3758
Hardwick Lincs 76 8675
Hardwick Nhants 51 8469
Hardwick Norfk 55 2289
Hardwick Oxon 36 3806
Hardwick Oxon 49 5729
Hardwick S York 75 4885
Hardwick W Mids 61 0798
Hardwick Green Worcs 47 8133
Hardwicke Gloucs 35 7912
Hardwicke Gloucs 47 9027
Hardy's Green Essex 40 9320
Hare Croft W York 82 0835
Hare Green Essex 41 1025
Hare Hatch Berks 37 8077
Hare Street Essex 39 4209
Hare Street Essex 27 5300
Hare Street Herts 39 3929
Harebeating E Susx 16 5910
Hareby Lincs 77 3365
Harefield Gt Lon 26 0590
Harehill Derbys 73 1735
Harehills W York 82 3135
Harehope Nthumb 111 0920
Harelaw Border 109 5323
Harelaw D & G 101 4378
Harelaw Dur 96 1652
Hareplain Kent 28 8339
Haresceugh Cumb 94 6042
Harescombe Gloucs 35 8310
Haresfield Gloucs 35 8010
Harestock Hants 24 4631
Harewood W York 83 3245
Harewood End Herefd 46 5227
Harford Devon 6 6359
Hargate Norfk 66 1191
Hargatewall Derbys 74 1175
Hargrave Ches 71 4862
Hargrave Nhants 51 0370
Hargrave Suffk 53 7760
Hargrave Green Suffk 53 7759
Harker Cumb 101 3960
Harkstead Suffk 54 1834
Harlaston Staffs 61 2110
Harlaxton Lincs 63 8832
Harle Syke Lancs 81 8635
Harlech Gwynd 57 5831
Harlescott Shrops 59 4916
Harlesden Gt Lon 26 2183
Harlesthorpe Derbys 75 4976
Harleston Devon 7 7945
Harleston Norfk 55 2483
Harleston Suffk 54 0160
Harlestone Nhants 49 7064
Harley S York 74 3698
Harley Shrops 59 5901
Harlington Beds 38 0330
Harlington Gt Lon 26 0877
Harlington S York 83 4802
Harlosh Highld 136 2841
Harlow Essex 39 4410
Harlow Hill Nthumb 103 0768
Harlthorpe E R Yk 84 7337
Harlton Cambs 52 3852
Harlyn Bay Cnwll 4 8775
Harman's Cross Dorset 11 9880
Harmby N York 89 1289
Harmer Green Herts 39 2515
Harmer Hill Shrops 59 4822
Harmondsworth Gt Lon 26 0577
Harmston Lincs 76 9662
Harnage Shrops 59 5604
Harnham Nthumb 103 0781
Harnhill Gloucs 36 0600
Harold Hill Gt Lon 27 5392
Harold Wood Gt Lon 27 5590
Haroldston West Pembks 30 8615
Haroldswick Shet 153 6312
Harome N York 90 6481
Harpenden Herts 38 1314
Harpford Devon 9 0990
Harpham E R Yk 91 0861
Harpley Norfk 65 7825
Harpley Worcs 47 6861
Harpole Nhants 49 6961
Harpsdale Highld 151 1355
Harpsden Oxon 37 7680
Harpswell Lincs 76 9389
Harpur Hill Derbys 74 0671
Harpurhey Gt Man 79 8501
Harraby Cumb 93 4154
Harracott Devon 19 5527
Harrapool Highld 129 6523
Harrietfield P & K 125 9829
Harrietsham Kent 28 8652
Harringay Gt Lon 27 3188
Harrington Cumb 92 9825
Harrington Lincs 77 3671
Harrington Nhants 50 7780
Harringworth Nhants 51 9197
Harriseahead Staffs 72 8655
Harriston Cumb 92 1541
Harrogate N York 82 3054
Harrold Beds 51 9457
Harrop Dale Gt Man 82 0008
Harrow Gt Lon 26 1588
Harrow Green Suffk 54 8654
Harrow on the Hill Gt Lon 26 1587
Harrow Weald Gt Lon 26 1591
Harrowbarrow Cnwll 5 4070
Harrowden Beds 38 0647
Harrowgate Village Dur 96 2917
Harston Cambs 53 4250
Harston Leics 63 8331
Harswell E R Yk 84 8240
Hart Dur 97 4734
Hart Station Dur 97 4836
Hartburn Nthumb 103 0885
Hartest Suffk 54 8352
Hartfield E Susx 16 4735
Hartford Cambs 52 2572
Hartford Ches 71 6372
Hartford Somset 20 9529
Hartford End Essex 40 6817
Hartfordbridge Hants 25 7757
Hartforth N York 89 1606
Harthill Ches 71 4955
Harthill N Lans 116 9064
Harthill S York 75 4980
Hartington Derbys 74 1260
Hartington Nthumb 103 0288
Hartland Devon 18 2524
Hartland Quay Devon 18 2224
Hartlebury Worcs 60 8471
Hartlepool Dur 97 5032
Hartley Cumb 88 7808
Hartley Kent 27 6066
Hartley Kent 17 7634
Hartley Nthumb 103 3475
Hartley Green Kent 27 6067
Hartley Green Staffs 72 9829
Hartley Wespall Hants 24 6958
Hartley Wintney Hants 24 7656
Hartlip Kent 28 8464
Hartoft End N York 90 7493
Harton N York 90 7061
Harton Shrops 59 4888
Harton T & W 103 3765
Hartpury Gloucs 47 7924
Hartshead W York 82 1822
Hartshead Moor Side W York 82 1625
Hartshill Staffs 72 8546
Hartshill Warwks 61 3194
Hartshorne Derbys 62 3221
Hartside Nthumb 111 9716
Hartsop Cumb 93 4013
Hartswell Somset 20 0827
Hartwell Nhants 38 7850
Hartwith N York 89 2161
Hartwood N Lans 116 8459
Hartwoodmyres Border 109 4324
Harvel Kent 28 6563
Harvington Worcs 60 8775
Harvington Worcs 48 0549
Harwell Notts 75 6891
Harwell Oxon 37 4989
Harwich Essex 41 2531
Harwood Dur 95 8233
Harwood Gt Man 79 7410
Harwood Nthumb 103 0189
Harwood Dale N York 91 9695
Harwood Lee Gt Man 81 7411
Harworth Notts 75 6191
Hasbury W Mids 60 9582
Hascombe Surrey 25 0039
Haselbeach Nhants 50 7177
Haselbury Plucknett Somset 10 4710
Haseley Warwks 48 2367
Haseley Green Warwks 48 2369
Haseley Knob Warwks 61 2371
Haselor Warwks 48 1257
Hasfield Gloucs 47 8227
Hasguard Pembks 30 8509
Haskayne Lancs 78 3508
Hasketon Suffk 55 2450
Hasland Derbys 74 3969
Hasland Green Derbys 74 3968
Haslemere Surrey 14 9032
Haslingden Lancs 81 7823
Haslingden Grane Lancs 81 7522
Haslingfield Cambs 52 4052
Haslington Ches 72 7355

Hassall High Green


Hassall *Ches* 72 7657
Hassall Green *Ches* 72 7858
Hassell Street *Kent* 29 0946
Hassingham *Norfk* 67 3605
Hassness *Cumb* 93 1816
Hassocks *W Susx* 15 3015
Hassop *Derbys* 74 2272
Haste Hill *Surrey* 14 9032
Haster *Highld* 151 3251
Hasthorpe *Lincs* 77 4869
Hastingleigh *Kent* 29 0945
Hastings *E Susx* 17 8209
Hastings *Somset* 10 3116
Hastingwood *Essex* 39 4807
Hastoe *Herts* 38 9209
Haswell *Dur* 96 3743
Haswell Plough *Dur* 96 3742
Hatch *Beds* 52 1547
Hatch Beauchamp *Somset* 20 3020
Hatch End *Beds* 51 0760
Hatch End *Gt Lon* 26 1390
Hatchet Gate *Hants* 12 3701
Hatching Green *Herts* 38 1312
Hatchmere *Ches* 71 5571
Hatcliffe *Lincs* 76 2100
Hatfield *Herefd* 46 5959
Hatfield *Herts* 39 2308
Hatfield *S York* 83 6609
Hatfield *Worcs* 47 8750
Hatfield Broad Oak *Essex* 39 5416
Hatfield Heath *Essex* 39 5215
Hatfield Peverel *Essex* 40 7911
Hatfield Woodhouse *S York* 83 6708
Hatford *Oxon* 36 3395
Hatherden *Hants* 23 3450
Hatherleigh *Devon* 8 5404
Hathern *Leics* 62 5022
Hatherop *Gloucs* 36 1505
Hathersage *Derbys* 74 2381
Hathersage Booths *Derbys* 74 2480
Hatherton *Ches* 72 6847
Hatherton *Staffs* 60 9510
Hatley St George *Cambs* 52 2751
Hatt *Cnwll* 5 4062
Hattersley *Gt Man* 79 9894
Hattingley *Hants* 24 6437
Hatton *Abers* 143 0537
Hatton *Angus* 127 4642
Hatton *Ches* 78 5982
Hatton *Derbys* 73 2130
Hatton *Gt Lon* 26 0975
Hatton *Lincs* 76 1776
Hatton *Shrops* 59 4790
Hatton *Warwks* 48 2367
Hatton Heath *Ches* 71 4561
Hatton of Fintray *Abers* 143 8316
Haugh *E Ayrs* 107 4925
Haugh *Lincs* 77 4175
Haugh *W York* 81 9311
Haugh Head *Nthumb* 111 0026
Haugh of Glass *Moray* 142 4238
Haugh of Urr *D & G* 100 8066
Haugham *Lincs* 77 3381
Haughhead Inn *E Duns* 116 6079
Haughley *Suffk* 54 0262
Haughley Green *Suffk* 54 0264
Haughton *Notts* 75 6872
Haughton *Powys* 59 3018
Haughton *Shrops* 59 3726
Haughton *Shrops* 59 5516
Haughton *Shrops* 60 7408
Haughton *Shrops* 60 6896
Haughton *Staffs* 72 8620
Haughton Green *Gt Man* 79 9393
Haughton le Skerne *Dur* 96 3116
Haughton Moss *Ches* 71 5756
Haultwick *Herts* 39 3323
Haunton *Staffs* 61 2310
Hautes Croix *Jersey* 158 0000
Hauxley *Nthumb* 103 2703
Hauxton *Cambs* 53 4452
Havannah *Ches* 72 8664
Havant *Hants* 13 7106
Haven *Herefd* 46 4054
Haven Bank *Lincs* 76 2352
Haven Side *E R Yk* 85 1827
Havenstreet *IOW* 13 5690
Havercroft *W York* 83 3913
Haverfordwest *Pembks* 30 9515
Haverhill *Suffk* 53 6745
Haverigg *Cumb* 86 1578
Havering-atte-Bower *Essex* 27 5193
Haversham *Bucks* 38 8242
Haverthwaite *Cumb* 87 3483
Haverton Hill *Dur* 97 4822
Havyat *Somset* 21 4761
Havyatt *Somset* 21 5338
Hawarden *Flints* 71 3165
Hawbridge *Worcs* 47 9049
Hawbush Green *Essex* 40 7820
Hawcoat *Cumb* 86 2071
Hawe's Green *Norfk* 67 2399
Hawen *Cerdgn* 42 3446
Hawes *N York* 88 8789
Hawford *Worcs* 47 8460
Hawick *Border* 109 5014
Hawk Green *Gt Man* 79 9687
Hawkchurch *Devon* 10 3400
Hawkedon *Suffk* 53 7953
Hawkenbury *Kent* 28 8045
Hawkeridge *Wilts* 22 8653
Hawkerland *Devon* 9 0588
Hawkes End *W Mids* 61 2982
Hawkesbury *Gloucs* 35 7686
Hawkesbury *Warwks* 61 3784
Hawkesbury Upton *Gloucs* 35 7786
Hawkhill *Nthumb* 111 2212
Hawkhurst *Kent* 17 7530
Hawkhurst Common *E Susx* 16 5217
Hawkinge *Kent* 29 2139
Hawkley *Hants* 24 7429
Hawkridge *Somset* 19 8630
Hawksdale *Cumb* 93 3648
Hawkshaw *Gt Man* 81 7615
Hawkshead *Cumb* 87 3598
Hawkshead Hill *Cumb* 86 3398
Hawksland *S Lans* 108 8439
Hawkspur Green *Essex* 40 6532
Hawkstone *Shrops* 59 5830
Hawkswick *N York* 88 9570
Hawksworth *Notts* 63 7543
Hawksworth *W York* 82 1641
Hawkwell *Essex* 40 8591
Hawkwell *Nthumb* 103 0771
Hawley *Hants* 25 8657
Hawley *Kent* 27 5471
Hawling *Gloucs* 36 0622
Hawnby *N York* 90 5489
Haworth *W York* 82 0337
Hawstead *Suffk* 54 8559
Hawstead Green *Suffk* 54 8658
Hawthorn *Dur* 96 4145
Hawthorn *Hants* 24 6733
Hawthorn *Rhondd* 33 0987
Hawthorn Hill *Berks* 25 8773
Hawthorn Hill *Lincs* 76 2155
Hawthorpe *Lincs* 64 0427
Hawton *Notts* 75 7851
Haxby *N York* 90 6058
Haxby Gates *N York* 83 6056
Haxey *Lincs* 75 7799
Haxey Turbary *Lincs* 84 7501
Haxted *Surrey* 16 4245
Haxton *Wilts* 23 1449
Hay *Cnwll* 3 8651
Hay *Cnwll* 3 9243
Hay *Cnwll* 3 9552
Hay *Cnwll* 4 9770
Hay Green *Norfk* 65 5418
Hay Street *Herts* 39 3926
Hay-on-Wye *Powys* 45 2342
Haydock *Mersyd* 78 5697
Haydon *Dorset* 11 6715
Haydon *Somset* 20 2523
Haydon *Somset* 22 6853
Haydon Bridge *Nthumb* 102 8464
Haydon Wick *Wilts* 36 1387
Haye *Cnwll* 5 3570
Hayes *Gt Lon* 26 0980
Hayes *Gt Lon* 27 4066
Hayes End *Gt Lon* 26 0882
Hayfield *Ag & B* 123 0723
Hayfield *Derbys* 74 0386
Haygate *Shrops* 59 6410
Hayhillock *Angus* 127 5242
Hayle *Cnwll* 2 5537
Hayley Green *W Mids* 60 9582
Haymoor Green *Ches* 72 6850
Hayne *Devon* 9 9515
Hayne *Devon* 8 7685
Haynes (Church End) *Beds* 38 0740
Haynes (Northwood End) *Beds* 38 0941
Haynes (Silver End) *Beds* 38 1042
Haynes (West End) *Beds* 38 0640
Hayscastle *Pembks* 30 8925
Hayscastle Cross *Pembks* 30 9125
Haysden *Kent* 16 5745
Hayton *Cumb* 92 1041
Hayton *Cumb* 94 5157
Hayton *E R Yk* 84 8245
Hayton *Notts* 75 7284
Hayton's Bent *Shrops* 59 5280
Haytor Vale *Devon* 8 7777
Haytown *Devon* 18 3814
Haywards Heath *W Susx* 15 3324
Haywood *Herefd* 46 4834
Haywood *S York* 83 5812
Haywood Oaks *Notts* 75 6055
Hazards Green *E Susx* 16 6812
Hazel Grove *Gt Man* 79 9287
Hazel Street *Kent* 28 6939
Hazel Stub *Suffk* 53 6544
Hazelbank *S Lans* 116 8345
Hazelbury Bryan *Dorset* 11 7408
Hazeleigh *Essex* 40 8203
Hazeley *Hants* 24 7458
Hazelford *Notts* 75 7249
Hazelhurst *Gt Man* 79 9600
Hazelslade *Staffs* 60 0212
Hazelton Walls *Fife* 126 3322
Hazelwood *Derbys* 62 3245
Hazlemere *Bucks* 26 8895
Hazlerigg *T & W* 103 2372
Hazles *Staffs* 73 0047
Hazleton *Gloucs* 36 0718
Heacham *Norfk* 65 6737
Headbourne Worthy *Hants* 24 4832
Headbrook *Herefd* 46 2854
Headcorn *Kent* 28 8344
Headingley *W York* 82 2836
Headington *Oxon* 37 5407
Headlam *Dur* 96 1818
Headland *Dur* 97 5234
Headless Cross *Worcs* 48 0365
Headlesscross *N Lans* 116 9158
Headley *Hants* 24 5162
Headley *Hants* 14 8236
Headley *Surrey* 26 2054
Headley Down *Hants* 14 8336
Headley Heath *Worcs* 61 0676
Headon *Notts* 75 7476
Heads *S Lans* 116 7247
Heads Nook *Cumb* 94 5054
Heage *Derbys* 74 3750
Healaugh *N York* 88 0199
Healaugh *N York* 83 5047
Heald Green *Gt Man* 79 8485
Heale *Devon* 19 6446
Heale *Somset* 20 2420
Heale *Somset* 21 3825
Healey *Lancs* 81 8816
Healey *N York* 89 1780
Healey *Nthumb* 95 0158
Healey *W York* 82 2719
Healeyfield *Dur* 95 0648
Healing *Lincs* 85 2110
Heamoor *Cnwll* 2 4631
Heanor *Derbys* 62 4346
Heanton Punchardon *Devon* 19 5035
Heapey *Lancs* 81 5920
Heapham *Lincs* 76 8788
Hearn *Hants* 14 8337
Hearts Delight *Kent* 28 8862
Heasley Mill *Devon* 19 7332
Heast *Highld* 129 6417
Heath *Derbys* 75 4567
Heath *W York* 83 3520
Heath and Reach *Beds* 38 9228
Heath Common *W Susx* 14 0915
Heath End *Bucks* 26 8898
Heath End *Hants* 24 4161
Heath End *Hants* 24 5862
Heath End *Leics* 62 3621
Heath End *Surrey* 25 8549
Heath End *Warwks* 48 2360
Heath Green *Worcs* 61 0771
Heath Hall *D & G* 100 9979
Heath Hayes *Staffs* 60 0110
Heath Hill *Shrops* 60 7613
Heath House *Somset* 21 4146
Heath Town *W Mids* 60 9399
Heathbrook *Shrops* 59 6228
Heathcote *Derbys* 74 1460
Heathcote *Shrops* 72 6528
Heathencote *Nhants* 49 7147
Heather *Leics* 62 3910
Heathfield *Devon* 8 8376
Heathfield *E Susx* 16 5821
Heathfield *N York* 89 1367
Heathfield *Somset* 20 1626
Heathstock *Devon* 9 2402
Heathton *Shrops* 60 8192
Heatley *Gt Man* 79 7088
Heatley *Staffs* 73 0626
Heaton *Gt Man* 79 6909
Heaton *Lancs* 87 4460
Heaton *Staffs* 72 9562
Heaton *T & W* 103 2666
Heaton *W York* 82 1335
Heaton Chapel *Gt Man* 79 8891
Heaton Mersey *Gt Man* 79 8690
Heaton Norris *Gt Man* 79 8890
Heaton's Bridge *Lancs* 80 4011
Heaverham *Kent* 27 5758
Heaviley *Gt Man* 79 9088
Heavitree *Devon* 9 9492
Hebburn *T & W* 103 3164
Hebden *N York* 88 0263
Hebden Bridge *W York* 82 9927
Hebden Green *Ches* 71 6365
Hebing End *Herts* 39 3122
Hebron *Carmth* 31 1827
Hebron *IOA* 68 4584
Hebron *Nthumb* 103 1989
Heckfield *Hants* 24 7260
Heckfield Green *Suffk* 54 1875
Heckfordbridge *Essex* 40 9421
Heckington *Lincs* 64 1444
Heckmondwike *W York* 82 1824
Heddington *Wilts* 22 9966
Heddon-on-the-Wall *Nthumb* 103 1366
Hedenham *Norfk* 67 3193
Hedge End *Hants* 13 4912
Hedgerley *Bucks* 26 9687
Hedgerley Green *Bucks* 26 9787
Hedging *Somset* 20 3029
Hedley on the Hill *Nthumb* 95 0759
Hednesford *Staffs* 60 9912
Hedon *E R Yk* 85 1928
Hedsor *Bucks* 26 9086
Hegdon Hill *Herefd* 46 5853
Heglibister *Shet* 153 3851
Heighington *Dur* 96 2422
Heighington *Lincs* 76 0269
Heightington *Worcs* 60 7671
Heiton *Border* 110 7130
Hele *Cnwll* 5 2198
Hele *Devon* 19 5347
Hele *Devon* 9 9902
Hele *Devon* 7 7470
Hele *Somset* 20 1824
Hele Lane *Devon* 19 7910
Helebridge *Cnwll* 18 2103
Helensburgh *Ag & B* 115 2982
Helenton *S Ayrs* 106 3830
Helford *Cnwll* 3 7526
Helford Passage *Cnwll* 3 7626
Helhoughton *Norfk* 66 8626
Helions Bumpstead *Essex* 53 6541
Hell Corner *Berks* 23 3864
Hellaby *S York* 75 5092
Helland *Cnwll* 4 0771
Hellandbridge *Cnwll* 4 0671
Hellescott *Cnwll* 5 2888
Hellesdon *Norfk* 67 2010
Hellesveor *Cnwll* 2 5040
Hellidon *Nhants* 49 5158
Hellifield *N York* 81 8556
Hellingly *E Susx* 16 5812
Hellington *Norfk* 67 3103
Helm *Nthumb* 103 1896
Helmdon *Nhants* 49 5943
Helme *W York* 82 0912
Helmingham *Suffk* 54 1857
Helmington Row *Dur* 96 1835
Helmsdale *Highld* 147 0315
Helmshore *Lancs* 81 7821
Helmsley *N York* 90 6183
Helperby *N York* 89 4469
Helperthorpe *N York* 91 9570
Helpringham *Lincs* 64 1440
Helpston *Cambs* 64 1205
Helsby *Ches* 71 4975
Helsey *Lincs* 77 5172
Helston *Cnwll* 2 6527
Helstone *Cnwll* 4 0881
Helton *Cumb* 94 5021
Helwith *N York* 88 0702
Helwith Bridge *N York* 88 8069
Hemblington *Norfk* 67 3411
Hemel Hempstead *Herts* 38 0507
Hemerdon *Devon* 6 5657
Hemingbrough *N York* 83 6730
Hemingby *Lincs* 76 2374
Hemingfield *S York* 83 3801
Hemingford Abbots *Cambs* 52 2871
Hemingford Grey *Cambs* 52 2970
Hemingstone *Suffk* 54 1454
Hemington *Nhants* 51 0985
Hemington *Somset* 22 7253
Hemley *Suffk* 55 2842
Hemlington *N York* 90 5014
Hemp Green *Suffk* 55 3769
Hempholme *E R Yk* 85 0850
Hempnall *Norfk* 67 2494
Hempnall Green *Norfk* 67 2493
Hempriggs *Moray* 141 1063
Hempstead *Essex* 53 6338
Hempstead *Gloucs* 35 8116
Hempstead *Kent* 28 7964
Hempstead *Norfk* 66 1037
Hempstead *Norfk* 67 4028
Hempton *Norfk* 66 9129
Hempton *Oxon* 49 4431
Hemsby *Norfk* 67 4917
Hemswell *Lincs* 76 9290
Hemswell Cliff *Lincs* 76 9489
Hemsworth *W York* 83 4213
Hemyock *Devon* 9 1313
Henbury *Bristl* 34 5678
Henbury *Ches* 79 8773
Hendersyde Park *Border* 110 7435
Hendham *Devon* 7 7450
Hendomen *Powys* 58 2197
Hendon *Gt Lon* 26 2389
Hendon *T & W* 96 4055
Hendra *Cnwll* 3 7237
Hendra *Cnwll* 4 0275
Hendre *Brdgnd* 33 9381
Hendre *Mons* 34 4614
Hendy *Carmth* 32 5803
Heneglwys *IOA* 68 4276
Henfield *W Susx* 15 2115
Henford *Devon* 5 3794
Henghurst *Kent* 28 9536
Hengoed *Caerph* 33 1594
Hengoed *Powys* 45 2253
Hengoed *Shrops* 58 2833
Hengrave *Suffk* 54 8268
Henham *Essex* 39 5428
Henhurst *Kent* 28 6669
Heniarth *Powys* 58 1208
Henlade *Somset* 20 2623
Henley *Dorset* 11 6904
Henley *Gloucs* 35 9016
Henley *Shrops* 59 4588
Henley *Shrops* 46 5476
Henley *Somset* 21 4232
Henley *Suffk* 54 1551
Henley *W Susx* 14 8925
Henley Green *W Mids* 61 3681
Henley Park *Surrey* 25 9352
Henley Street *Kent* 28 6667
Henley's Down *E Susx* 17 7312
Henley-in-Arden *Warwks* 48 1566
Henley-on-Thames *Oxon* 37 7682
Henllan *Cerdgn* 31 3540
Henllan *Denbgs* 70 0268
Henllan Amgoed *Carmth* 31 1819
Henllys *Torfn* 34 2691
Henlow *Beds* 39 1738
Hennock *Devon* 8 8381
Henny Street *Essex* 54 8738
Henry's Moat
(Castell Hendre) *Pembks* 30 0427
Henryd *Conwy* 69 7774
Hensall *N York* 83 5923
Henshaw *Nthumb* 102 7664
Hensingham *Cumb* 92 9816
Henstead *Suffk* 55 4885
Hensting *Hants* 13 4922
Henstridge *Somset* 22 7219
Henstridge Ash *Somset* 22 7220
Henstridge Marsh *Somset* 22 7320
Henton *Oxon* 37 7602
Henton *Somset* 21 4945
Henwick *Worcs* 47 8355
Henwood *Cnwll* 5 2673
Heol Senni *Powys* 45 9223
Heol-las *Swans* 32 6998
Heol-y-Cyw *Brdgnd* 33 9484
Hepburn *Nthumb* 111 0624
Hepple *Nthumb* 103 9901
Hepscott *Nthumb* 103 2284
Heptonstall *W York* 82 9828
Hepworth *Suffk* 54 9874
Hepworth *W York* 82 1606
Herbrandston *Pembks* 30 8707
Hereford *Herefd* 46 5139
Hereson *Kent* 29 3865
Heribusta *Highld* 136 3970
Heriot *Border* 118 3953
Hermiston *C Edin* 117 1870
Hermit Hill *S York* 74 3200
Hermitage *Berks* 24 5072
Hermitage *Border* 101 5095
Hermitage *Dorset* 11 6506
Hermitage *Hants* 13 7505
Hermon *IOA* 68 3968
Hermon *Pembks* 31 2031
Herne *Kent* 29 1865
Herne Bay *Kent* 29 1768
Herne Common *Kent* 29 1765
Herne Hill *Gt Lon* 27 3274
Herne Pound *Kent* 28 6654
Herner *Devon* 19 5826
Hernhill *Kent* 29 0660
Herodsfoot *Cnwll* 5 2160
Heronden *Kent* 29 2954
Herongate *Essex* 40 6291
Heronsford *S Ayrs* 98 1283
Heronsgate *Herts* 26 0294
Herriard *Hants* 24 6646
Herring's Green *Beds* 38 0844
Herringfleet *Suffk* 67 4797
Herringswell *Suffk* 53 7270
Herringthorpe *S York* 75 4492
Herrington *T & W* 96 3453
Hersden *Kent* 29 2062
Hersham *Cnwll* 18 2507
Hersham *Surrey* 26 1164
Herstmonceux *E Susx* 16 6312
Herston *Dorset* 11 0178
Herston *Ork* 153 4191
Hertford *Herts* 39 3212
Hertford Heath *Herts* 39 3510
Hertingfordbury *Herts* 39 3012
Hesket Newmarket *Cumb* 93 3438
Hesketh Bank *Lancs* 80 4423
Hesketh Lane *Lancs* 81 6141
Heskin Green *Lancs* 80 5315
Hesleden *Dur* 96 4438
Hesleden *N York* 88 8874
Hesley *S York* 75 6194
Hesleyside *Nthumb* 102 8183
Heslington *N York* 83 6250
Hessay *N York* 83 5253
Hessenford *Cnwll* 5 3057
Hessett *Suffk* 54 9361
Hessle *E R Yk* 84 0326
Hessle *W York* 83 4317
Hest Bank *Lancs* 87 4666
Hestley Green *Suffk* 54 1567
Heston *Gt Lon* 26 1277
Hestwall *Ork* 153 2618
Heswall *Mersyd* 78 2681
Hethe *Oxon* 49 5929
Hethersett *Norfk* 66 1404
Hethersgill *Cumb* 101 4767
Hetherside *Cumb* 101 4366
Hetherson Green *Ches* 71 5250
Hethpool *Nthumb* 110 8928
Hett *Dur* 96 2836
Hetton *N York* 88 9658
Hetton Steads *Nthumb* 111 0335
Hetton-le-Hole *T & W* 96 3547
Heugh *Nthumb* 103 0873
Heugh Head *Border* 119 8762
Heughhead *Abers* 134 3811
Heveningham *Suffk* 55 3372
Hever *Kent* 16 4745
Heversham *Cumb* 87 4983
Hevingham *Norfk* 67 1921
Hewas Water *Cnwll* 3 9649
Hewelsfield *Gloucs* 34 5602
Hewenden *W York* 82 0736
Hewish *Somset* 21 4064
Hewish *Somset* 10 4208
Hewood *Dorset* 10 3502
Hexham *Nthumb* 102 9364
Hextable *Kent* 27 5170
Hexthorpe *S York* 83 5602
Hexton *Herts* 38 1030
Hexworthy *Cnwll* 5 3581
Hexworthy *Devon* 7 6572
Hey *Lancs* 81 8843
Hey Houses *Lancs* 80 3429
Heybridge *Essex* 40 8508
Heybridge *Essex* 40 6398
Heybridge Basin *Essex* 40 8707
Heybrook Bay *Devon* 6 4949
Heydon *Cambs* 39 4339
Heydon *Norfk* 66 1127
Heydour *Lincs* 63 0039
Heyhead *Gt Man* 79 8285
Heylipoll *Ag & B* 120 9743
Heylor *Shet* 153 2980
Heyrod *Gt Man* 79 9799
Heysham *Lancs* 87 4160
Heyshaw *N York* 89 1761
Heyshott *W Susx* 14 8917
Heyside *Gt Man* 79 9307
Heytesbury *Wilts* 22 9242
Heythrop *Oxon* 48 3527
Heywood *Gt Man* 81 8510
Heywood *Wilts* 22 8753
Hibaldstow *Lincs* 84 9702
Hickleton *S York* 83 4805
Hickling *Norfk* 67 4124
Hickling *Notts* 63 6928
Hickling Green *Norfk* 67 4123
Hickling Heath *Norfk* 67 4022
Hickmans Green *Kent* 29 0658
Hicks Forstal *Kent* 29 1863
Hickstead *W Susx* 15 2620
Hidcote Bartrim *Gloucs* 48 1742
Hidcote Boyce *Gloucs* 48 1742
High Ackworth *W York* 83 4417
High Angerton *Nthumb* 103 0985
High Ardwell *D & G* 98 0745
High Auldgirth *D & G* 100 9187
High Bankhill *Cumb* 94 5542
High Beach *Essex* 27 4198
High Bentham *N York* 87 6669
High Bewaldeth *Cumb* 93 2234
High Bickington *Devon* 19 6020
High Bickwith *N York* 88 8076
High Biggins *Cumb* 87 6078
High Blantyre *S Lans* 116 6756
High Bonnybridge *Falk* 116 8379
High Borrans *Cumb* 87 4300
High Bradley *N York* 82 0049
High Bray *Devon* 19 6934
High Brooms *Kent* 16 5941
High Bullen *Devon* 19 5320
High Buston *Nthumb* 111 2308
High Callerton *Nthumb* 103 1670
High Casterton *Cumb* 87 6278
High Catton *E R Yk* 84 7153
High Close *N York* 96 1715
High Cogges *Oxon* 36 3709
High Common *Norfk* 66 9905
High Coniscliffe *Dur* 96 2215
High Crosby *Cumb* 93 4559
High Cross *Cnwll* 3 7429
High Cross *E Ayrs* 115 4046
High Cross *Hants* 13 7126
High Cross *Herts* 39 3618
High Cross *W Susx* 15 2417
High Cross *Warwks* 48 2067
High Cross Bank *Derbys* 73 2817
High Drummore *D & G* 98 1235
High Dubmire *T & W* 96 3249
High Easter *Essex* 40 6214
High Eggborough *N York* 83 5721
High Ellington *N York* 89 2083
High Ercall *Shrops* 59 5917
High Etherley *Dur* 96 1728
High Ferry *Lincs* 77 3549
High Flats *W York* 82 2107
High Garrett *Essex* 40 7727
High Grange *Dur* 96 1731
High Grantley *N York* 89 2369
High Green *Cumb* 87 4103
High Green *Norfk* 66 1305
High Green *Norfk* 54 1689
High Green *Norfk* 67 2898
High Green *S York* 74 3397
High Green *Shrops* 60 7083
High Green *Suffk* 54 8560

# J

# K

Little Badminton Llanllechid


Little Badminton Gloucs 35 8084
Little Bampton Cumb 93 2755
Little Bardfield Essex 40 6531
Little Barford Beds 52 1756
Little Barningham Norfk 66 1333
Little Barrington Gloucs 36 2012
Little Barrow Ches 71 4769
Little Barugh N York 90 7679
Little Bavington Nthumb 102 9878
Little Bayton Warwks 61 3585
Little Bealings Suffk 55 2247
Little Bedwyn Wilts 23 2866
Little Bentley Essex 41 1125
Little Berkhamsted Herts 39 2907
Little Billing Nhants 51 8061
Little Billington Beds 38 9322
Little Birch Herefd 46 5130
Little Bispham Lancs 80 3141
Little Blakenham Suffk 54 1048
Little Blencow Cumb 93 4532
Little Bloxwich W Mids 60 0003
Little Bognor W Susx 14 0020
Little Bolehill Derbys 73 2954
Little Bollington Ches 79 7286
Little Bookham Surrey 26 1254
Little Bourton Oxon 49 4544
Little Bowden Leics 50 7487
Little Bradley Suffk 53 6852
Little Brampton Herefd 46 3061
Little Brampton Shrops 59 3681
Little Braxted Essex 40 8314
Little Brechin Angus 134 5862
Little Brickhill Bucks 38 9132
Little Bridgeford Staffs 72 8727
Little Brington Nhants 49 6663
Little Bromley Essex 41 0928
Little Broughton Cumb 92 0731
Little Budworth Ches 71 5965
Little Burstead Essex 40 6692
Little Bytham Lincs 64 0118
Little Carlton Lincs 77 3985
Little Carlton Notts 75 7757
Little Casterton Rutlnd 64 0109
Little Catwick E R Yk 85 1244
Little Catworth Cambs 51 1072
Little Cawthorpe Lincs 77 3583
Little Chalfont Bucks 26 9997
Little Charlinch Somset 20 2437
Little Chart Kent 28 9446
Little Chatfield Wilts 22 8563
Little Chesterford Essex 39 5141
Little Cheveney Kent 28 7243
Little Cheverell Wilts 22 9953
Little Chishill Cambs 39 4137
Little Clacton Essex 41 1618
Little Clanfield Oxon 36 2701
Little Clifton Cumb 92 0528
Little Coates Lincs 85 2408
Little Comberton Worcs 47 9643
Little Common E Susx 17 7107
Little Comp Kent 27 6356
Little Compton Warwks 48 2630
Little Corby Cumb 93 4757
Little Cornard Suffk 54 9039
Little Cowarne Herefd 46 6051
Little Coxwell Oxon 36 2893
Little Crakehall N York 89 2390
Little Cransley Nhants 51 8376
Little Cressingham Norfk 66 8700
Little Crosby Mersyd 78 3201
Little Crosthwaite Cumb 93 2327
Little Cubley Derbys 73 1537
Little Dalby Leics 63 7714
Little Dens Abers 143 0643
Little Dewchurch Herefd 46 5231
Little Ditton Cambs 53 6658
Little Doward Herefd 34 5416
Little Driffield E R Yk 91 0058
Little Dunham Norfk 66 8612
Little Dunkeld P & K 125 0342
Little Dunmow Essex 40 6521
Little Durnford Wilts 23 1234
Little Eaton Derbys 62 3641
Little Ellingham Norfk 66 0099
Little Elm Somset 22 7146
Little Everdon Nhants 49 5957
Little Eversden Cambs 52 3753
Little Faringdon S York 36 2201
Little Fencote N York 89 2893
Little Fenton N York 83 5235
Little Fransham Norfk 66 9011
Little Gaddesden Herts 38 9913
Little Garway Herefd 46 4424
Little Gidding Cambs 52 1282
Little Glemham Suffk 55 3458
Little Gorsley Herefd 47 6924
Little Gransden Cambs 52 2755
Little Green Notts 63 7243
Little Green Somset 22 7248
Little Grimsby Lincs 77 3291
Little Gringley Notts 75 7380
Little Habton N York 90 7477
Little Hadham Herts 39 4322
Little Hale Lincs 64 1441
Little Hallam Derbys 62 4640
Little Hallingbury Essex 39 5017
Little Hanford Dorset 11 8411
Little Harrowden Nhants 51 8771
Little Hartlip Kent 28 8464
Little Haseley Oxon 37 6400
Little Hatfield E R Yk 85 1743
Little Hautbois Norfk 67 2521
Little Haven Pembks 30 8512
Little Hay Staffs 61 1102
Little Hayfield Derbys 74 0388
Little Haywood Staffs 73 0021
Little Heath Berks 24 6573
Little Heath Staffs 72 8917
Little Heath W Mids 61 3482
Little Hereford Herefd 46 5568
Little Hermitage Kent 28 7170
Little Horkesley Essex 40 9532
Little Hormead Herts 39 4028
Little Horsted E Susx 16 4718
Little Horton W York 82 1531
Little Horton Wilts 23 0462
Little Horwood Bucks 38 7930
Little Houghton Nhants 51 8059
Little Houghton S York 83 4205
Little Hucklow Derbys 74 1678
Little Hulton Gt Man 79 7203
Little Hungerford Berks 24 5173
Little Hutton N York 89 4576
Little Ingestre Staffs 72 9824
Little Irchester Nhants 51 9066
Little Kelk E R Yk 91 0959
Little Keyford Somset 22 7746
Little Kimble Bucks 38 8207
Little Kineton Warwks 48 3350
Little Kingshill Bucks 26 8999
Little Knox D & G 100 8060
Little Langdale Cumb 86 3103
Little Langford Wilts 23 0436
Little Lashbrook Devon 18 4007
Little Laver Essex 39 5409
Little Leigh Ches 71 6175
Little Leighs Essex 40 7117
Little Lever Gt Man 79 7507
Little Linford Bucks 38 8444
Little Linton Cambs 53 5547
Little Load Somset 21 4724
Little London Bucks 37 6412
Little London Cambs 65 4196
Little London E Susx 16 5620
Little London Essex 39 4729
Little London Essex 53 6835
Little London Gloucs 35 7018
Little London Hants 23 3749
Little London Hants 24 6259
Little London Lincs 64 2321
Little London Lincs 77 3374
Little London Lincs 65 4323
Little London Norfk 65 5621
Little London Powys 58 0488
Little London W York 82 2039
Little Longstone Derbys 74 1871
Little Madeley Staffs 72 7745
Little Malvern Worcs 47 7640
Little Mancot Flints 71 3266
Little Maplestead Essex 54 8234
Little Marcle Herefd 47 6736
Little Marland Devon 18 5012
Little Marlow Bucks 26 8787
Little Massingham Norfk 65 7824
Little Melton Norfk 66 1607
Little Mill Mons 34 3203
Little Milton Oxon 37 6100
Little Missenden Bucks 26 9299
Little Mongeham Kent 29 3351
Little Moor Somset 21 3232
Little Musgrave Cumb 94 7612
Little Ness Shrops 59 4019
Little Neston Ches 71 2976
Little Newcastle Pembks 30 9829
Little Newsham Dur 96 1217
Little Norton Somset 10 4715
Little Norton Staffs 60 0207
Little Oakley Essex 41 2129
Little Oakley Nhants 51 8985
Little Odell Beds 51 9557
Little Offley Herts 38 1328
Little Onn Staffs 72 8315
Little Ormside Cumb 94 7016
Little Orton Cumb 93 3555
Little Ouse Cambs 53 6288
Little Ouseburn N York 89 4460
Little Oxendon Nhants 50 7283
Little Packington Warwks 61 2184
Little Pattenden Kent 28 7445
Little Paxton Cambs 52 1862
Little Petherick Cnwll 4 9172
Little Plumpton Lancs 80 3832
Little Plumstead Norfk 67 3112
Little Ponton Lincs 63 9232
Little Posbrook Hants 13 5304
Little Potheridge Devon 19 5214
Little Preston Nhants 49 5854
Little Preston W York 83 3930
Little Raveley Cambs 52 2579
Little Reedness E R Yk 84 8022
Little Ribston N York 83 3853
Little Rissington Gloucs 36 1819
Little Rollright Oxon 48 2930
Little Rowsley Derbys 74 2566
Little Ryburgh Norfk 66 9628
Little Ryle Nthumb 111 0111
Little Ryton Shrops 59 4803
Little Salkeld Cumb 94 5636
Little Sampford Essex 40 6533
Little Sandhurst Berks 25 8262
Little Saredon Staffs 60 9407
Little Saughall Ches 71 3768
Little Saxham Suffk 54 8063
Little Scatwell Highld 139 3856
Little Sessay N York 89 4674
Little Shelford Cambs 53 4551
Little Silver Devon 9 8601
Little Silver Devon 9 9109
Little Singleton Lancs 80 3739
Little Skipwith N York 83 6538
Little Smeaton N York 83 5216
Little Snoring Norfk 66 9532
Little Sodbury Gloucs 35 7582
Little Sodbury End Gloucs 35 7483
Little Somborne Hants 23 3832
Little Somerford Wilts 35 9684
Little Soudley Shrops 72 7128
Little Stainforth N York 88 8166
Little Stainton Dur 96 3420
Little Stanney Ches 71 4174
Little Staughton Beds 51 1062
Little Steeping Lincs 77 4362
Little Stonham Suffk 54 1160
Little Stretton Leics 50 6600
Little Stretton Shrops 59 4491
Little Strickland Cumb 94 5619
Little Stukeley Cambs 52 2175
Little Sugnall Staffs 72 8031
Little Sutton Ches 71 3776
Little Sutton Shrops 59 5182
Little Swinburne Nthumb 102 9477
Little Sypland D & G 99 7253
Little Tew Oxon 48 3828
Little Tey Essex 40 8923
Little Thetford Cambs 53 5376
Little Thirkleby N York 89 4778
Little Thornage Norfk 66 0538
Little Thornton Lancs 80 3541
Little Thorpe Dur 96 4242
Little Thurlow Suffk 53 6751
Little Thurlow Green Suffk 53 6851
Little Thurrock Essex 27 6277
Little Torrington Devon 18 4916
Little Totham Essex 40 8811
Little Town Ches 79 6494
Little Town Cumb 93 2319
Little Town Lancs 81 6635
Little Twycross Leics 62 3405
Little Urswick Cumb 86 2673
Little Wakering Essex 40 9388
Little Walden Essex 39 5441
Little Waldingfield Suffk 54 9245
Little Walsingham Norfk 66 9337
Little Waltham Essex 40 7012
Little Warley Essex 40 6090
Little Washbourne Gloucs 47 9833
Little Weighton E R Yk 84 9833
Little Weldon Nhants 51 9289
Little Welnetham Suffk 54 8859
Little Welton Lincs 77 3087
Little Wenham Suffk 54 0839
Little Wenlock Shrops 59 6406
Little Weston Somset 21 6225
Little Whitefield IOW 13 5889
Little Whittington Nthumb 102 9869
Little Wilbraham Cambs 53 5458
Little Witcombe Gloucs 35 9115
Little Witley Worcs 47 7863
Little Wittenham Oxon 37 5693
Little Wolford Warwks 48 2635
Little Woodcote Surrey 27 2861
Little Wratting Suffk 53 6847
Little Wymington Beds 51 9565
Little Wymondley Herts 39 2127
Little Wyrley Staffs 60 0105
Little Wytheford Shrops 59 5619
Little Yeldham Essex 53 7839
Littlebeck N York 90 8804
Littleborough Devon 19 8210
Littleborough Gt Man 81 9316
Littleborough Notts 75 8282
Littlebourne Kent 29 2057
Littlebredy Dorset 10 5889
Littlebury Essex 39 5139
Littlebury Green Essex 39 4838
Littlecott Wilts 23 1352
Littledean Gloucs 35 6713
Littledown Hants 23 3457
Littleham Devon 18 4323
Littleham Devon 9 0381
Littlehampton W Susx 14 0201
Littleharle Tower Nthumb 103 0183
Littlehempston Devon 7 8162
Littlehoughton Nthumb 111 2216
Littlemill Abers 134 3295
Littlemill Highld 140 9150
Littlemoor Derbys 74 3663
Littlemore Oxon 37 5302
Littleover Derbys 62 3334
Littleport Cambs 53 5686
Littleport Bridge Cambs 53 5787
Littler Ches 71 6366
Littlestone-on-Sea Kent 17 0824
Littlethorpe Leics 50 5496
Littlethorpe N York 89 3269
Littleton Angus 126 3350
Littleton Ches 71 4466
Littleton D & G 99 6355
Littleton Dorset 11 8904
Littleton Hants 24 4532
Littleton Somset 21 4930
Littleton Somset 21 5563
Littleton Surrey 25 9847
Littleton Surrey 26 0668
Littleton Drew Wilts 35 8380
Littleton Pannell Wilts 22 0053
Littleton-on-Severn Gloucs 34 5989
Littletown Dur 96 3343
Littletown IOW 13 5390
Littlewick Green Berks 37 8379
Littlewindsor Dorset 10 4304
Littlewood Staffs 60 9807
Littleworth Bucks 38 8823
Littleworth Oxon 36 3197
Littleworth Staffs 72 9323
Littleworth Staffs 60 0111
Littleworth W Susx 15 1920
Littleworth Worcs 47 8850
Littleworth Worcs 47 9962
Littleworth Common Bucks 26 9386
Littleworth End Cambs 52 2266
Littley Green Essex 40 6917
Litton Derbys 74 1675
Litton N York 88 9074
Litton Somset 21 5954
Litton Cheney Dorset 10 5490
Liurbost W Isls 152 3725
Liverpool Mersyd 78 3490
Liversedge W York 82 1923
Liverton Devon 7 8075
Liverton N York 97 7115
Liverton Mines N York 97 7117
Liverton Street Kent 28 8750
Livingston W Loth 117 0668
Livingston Village W Loth 117 0366
Lixton Devon 7 6950
Lixwm Flints 70 1671
Lizard Cnwll 2 7012
Llaingoch IOA 68 2382
Llaithddu Powys 58 0680
Llan Powys 57 8800
Llan-y-pwll Wrexhm 71 3752
Llanaber Gwynd 57 6018
Llanaelhaearn Gwynd 56 3844
Llanafan Cerdgn 43 6872
Llanafan-fechan Powys 45 9750
Llanallgo IOA 68 5085
Llanarmon Gwynd 56 4239
Llanarmon
Dyffryn Ceiriog Wrexhm 58 1532
Llanarmon-yn-Ial Denbgs 70 1956
Llanarth Cerdgn 42 4257
Llanarth Mons 34 3710
Llanarthne Carmth 32 5320
Llanasa Flints 70 1081
Llanbabo IOA 68 3787
Llanbadarn Fawr Cerdgn 43 6081
Llanbadarn Fynydd Powys 45 0977
Llanbadarn-y-garreg Powys 45 1148
Llanbadoc Mons 34 3799
Llanbadrig IOA 68 3794
Llanbeder Newpt 34 3890
Llanbedr Gwynd 57 5826
Llanbedr Powys 45 1446
Llanbedr Powys 34 2320
Llanbedr-Dyffryn-
Clwyd Denbgs 70 1459
Llanbedr-y-Cennin Conwy 69 7669
Llanbedrgoch IOA 68 5180
Llanbedrog Gwynd 56 3231
Llanberis Gwynd 69 5760
Llanbethery V Glam 20 0369
Llanbister Powys 45 1173
Llanblethian V Glam 33 9873
Llanboidy Carmth 31 2123
Llanbradach Caerph 33 1490
Llanbrynmair Powys 57 8902
Llancadle V Glam 20 0368
Llancarfan V Glam 33 0470
Llancayo Mons 34 3603
Llancillo Herefd 46 3625
Llancloudy Herefd 34 4921
Llancynfelyn Cerdgn 43 6492
Llandaff Cardif 33 1577
Llandanwg Gwynd 57 5728
Llandawke Carmth 31 2811
Llanddaniel Fab IOA 68 4970
Llanddarog Carmth 32 5016
Llanddeiniol Cerdgn 43 5571
Llanddeiniolen Gwynd 69 5465
Llandderfel Gwynd 58 9837
Llanddeusant Carmth 44 7724
Llanddeusant IOA 68 3485
Llanddew Powys 45 0530
Llanddewi Swans 32 4588
Llanddewi Brefi Cerdgn 44 6655
Llanddewi Rhydderch Mons 34 3512
Llanddewi Velfrey Pembks 31 1415
Llanddewi Ystradenni Powys 45 1068
Llanddewi'r Cwm Powys 45 0348
Llanddoget Conwy 69 8063
Llanddona IOA 69 5779
Llanddowror Carmth 31 2514
Llanddulas Conwy 70 9178
Llanddwywe Gwynd 57 5822
Llanddyfnan IOA 68 5078
Llandecwyn Gwynd 57 6337
Llandefaelog Powys 45 0332
Llandefaelog-Trer-Graig Powys 45 1229
Llandefalle Powys 45 1035
Llandegfan IOA 69 5674
Llandegla Denbgs 70 2051
Llandegley Powys 45 1463
Llandegveth Mons 34 3395
Llandegwning Gwynd 56 2629
Llandeilo Carmth 32 6222
Llandeilo Graban Powys 45 0944
Llandeilo'r Fan Powys 45 8934
Llandeloy Pembks 30 8626
Llandenny Mons 34 4104
Llandevaud Newpt 34 4090
Llandevenny Mons 34 4186
Llandinabo Herefd 46 5128
Llandinam Powys 58 0288
Llandissilio Pembks 31 1221
Llandogo Mons 34 5203
Llandough V Glam 33 9972
Llandough V Glam 33 1673
Llandovery Carmth 44 7634
Llandow V Glam 33 9473
Llandre Carmth 44 6741
Llandre Cerdgn 43 6286
Llandre Isaf Pembks 31 1328
Llandrillo Denbgs 58 0337
Llandrillo-yn-Rhos Conwy 69 8380
Llandrindod Wells Powys 45 0561
Llandrinio Powys 58 2817
Llandudno Conwy 69 7882
Llandudno Junction Conwy 69 7977
Llandudwen Gwynd 56 2736
Llandulas Powys 45 8841
Llandwrog Gwynd 68 4555
Llandybie Carmth 32 6115
Llandyfaelog Carmth 31 4111
Llandyfan Carmth 32 6417
Llandyfriog Cerdgn 31 3341
Llandyfrydog IOA 68 4485
Llandygai Gwynd 69 5971
Llandygwydd Cerdgn 31 2443
Llandynan Denbgs 70 1845
Llandyrnog Denbgs 70 1065
Llandyssil Powys 58 1995
Llandysul Cerdgn 31 4140
Llanedeyrn Cardif 33 2181
Llanedi Carmth 32 5806
Llaneglwys Powys 45 0538
Llanegryn Gwynd 57 6005
Llanegwad Carmth 32 5221
Llaneilian IOA 68 4692
Llanelian-yn-Rhos Conwy 69 8676
Llanelidan Denbgs 70 1150
Llanelieu Powys 45 1834
Llanellen Mons 34 3010
Llanelli Carmth 32 5000
Llanelltyd Gwynd 57 7119
Llanelly Mons 34 2314
Llanelwedd Powys 45 0451
Llanenddwyn Gwynd 57 5823
Llanengan Gwynd 56 2926
Llanerch Gwynd 56 8816
Llanerch Powys 59 3093
Llanerchymedd IOA 68 4184
Llanerfyl Powys 58 0309
Llanfachraeth IOA 68 3182
Llanfachreth Gwynd 57 7522
Llanfaelog IOA 68 3373
Llanfaelrhys Gwynd 56 2026
Llanfaenor Mons 34 4317
Llanfaes IOA 69 6077
Llanfaes Powys 45 0328
Llanfaethlu IOA 68 3186
Llanfair Gwynd 57 5728
Llanfair Caereinion Powys 58 1006
Llanfair Clydogau Cerdgn 44 6251
Llanfair Dyffryn Clwyd Denbgs 70 1355
Llanfair Kilgeddin Mons 34 3506
Llanfair P G IOA 68 5271
Llanfair Talhaiarn Conwy 70 9270
Llanfair Waterdine Shrops 45 2376
Llanfair-is-gaer Gwynd 68 5065
Llanfair-Nant-Gwyn Pembks 31 1637
Llanfair-y-Cwmwd IOA 68 4466
Llanfair-yn-Neubwll IOA 68 3076
Llanfairfechan Conwy 69 6874
Llanfairynghornwy IOA 68 3290
Llanfallteg Carmth 31 1520
Llanfallteg West Carmth 31 1419
Llanfarian Cerdgn 43 5877
Llanfechain Powys 58 1920
Llanfechell IOA 68 3791
Llanferres Denbgs 70 1860
Llanfflewyn IOA 68 3588
Llanfigael IOA 68 3282
Llanfihangel Glyn Myfyr Conwy 70 9849
Llanfihangel Nant Bran Powys 45 9434
Llanfihangel Rhydithon Powys 45 1566
Llanfihangel Rogiet Mons 34 4587
Llanfihangel Tal-y-llyn Powys 45 1128
Llanfihangel yn Nhowyn IOA 68 3277
Llanfihangel-ar-Arth Carmth 31 4540
Llanfihangel-nant-Melan Powys 45 1758
Llanfihangel-uwch-Gwili Carmth 32 4922
Llanfihangel-y-Creuddyn Cerdgn 43 6675
Llanfihangel-y-pennant Gwynd 57 5244
Llanfihangel-y-pennant Gwynd 57 6708
Llanfihangel-y-traethau Gwynd 57 5934
Llanfihangel-yng-Ngwynfa Powys 58 0816
Llanfilo Powys 45 1132
Llanfoist Mons 34 2813
Llanfor Gwynd 58 9336
Llanfrechfa Torfn 34 3293
Llanfrothen Gwynd 57 6241
Llanfrynach Powys 45 0725
Llanfwrog Denbgs 70 1157
Llanfwrog IOA 68 3084
Llanfyllin Powys 58 1419
Llanfynydd Carmth 44 5527
Llanfynydd Flints 70 2856
Llanfyrnach Pembks 31 2231
Llangadfan Powys 58 0110
Llangadog Carmth 31 4207
Llangadog Carmth 44 7028
Llangadwaladr IOA 68 3869
Llangadwaladr Powys 58 1830
Llangaffo IOA 68 4468
Llangain Carmth 31 3815
Llangammarch Wells Powys 45 9346
Llangan V Glam 33 9577
Llangarron Herefd 34 5220
Llangasty-Talyllyn Powys 45 1326
Llangathen Carmth 32 5822
Llangattock Powys 33 2117
Llangattock Lingoed Mons 34 3620
Llangattock-Vibon-Avel Mons 34 4515
Llangedwyn Powys 58 1824
Llangefni IOA 68 4675
Llangeinor Brdgnd 33 9187
Llangeinwen IOA 68 4465
Llangeitho Cerdgn 44 6259
Llangeler Carmth 31 3739
Llangelynin Gwynd 57 5707
Llangendeirne Carmth 32 4513
Llangennech Carmth 32 5601
Llangennith Swans 31 4291
Llangenny Powys 34 2417
Llangernyw Conwy 69 8767
Llangian Gwynd 56 2928
Llangiwg Neath 32 7205
Llangloffan Pembks 30 9032
Llanglydwen Carmth 31 1826
Llangoed IOA 69 6079
Llangoedmor Cerdgn 42 2046
Llangollen Denbgs 70 2141
Llangolman Pembks 31 1127
Llangors Powys 45 1327
Llangovan Mons 34 4505
Llangower Gwynd 58 9032
Llangranog Cerdgn 42 3154
Llangristiolus IOA 68 4373
Llangrove Herefd 34 5219
Llangua Mons 46 3925
Llangunllo Powys 45 2171
Llangunnor Carmth 31 4320
Llangurig Powys 43 9079
Llangwm Conwy 70 9644
Llangwm Mons 34 4299
Llangwm Pembks 30 9909
Llangwm-isaf Mons 34 4300
Llangwnnadl Gwynd 56 2033
Llangwyfan Denbgs 70 1166
Llangwyllog IOA 68 4379
Llangwyryfon Cerdgn 43 5970
Llangybi Cerdgn 44 6053
Llangybi Gwynd 56 4341
Llangybi Mons 34 3796
Llangyfelach Swans 32 6498
Llangynhafal Denbgs 70 1263
Llangynidr Powys 33 1519
Llangynin Carmth 31 2519
Llangynllo Cerdgn 42 3544
Llangynog Carmth 31 3314
Llangynog Powys 58 0526
Llangynog Powys 45 0145
Llangynwyd Brdgnd 33 8588
Llanhamlach Powys 45 0926
Llanharan Rhondd 33 0083
Llanharry Rhondd 33 0080
Llanhennock Mons 34 3592
Llanhilleth Blae G 33 2100
Llanidan IOA 68 4966
Llanidloes Powys 58 9584
Llaniestyn Gwynd 56 2733
Llanigon Powys 45 2139
Llanilar Cerdgn 43 6275
Llanilid Rhondd 33 9781
Llanina Cerdgn 42 4059
Llanio Cerdgn 44 6457
Llanishen Cardif 33 1781
Llanishen Mons 34 4703
Llanllechid Gwynd 69 6268

Lower Sheering Marton


Lower Sheering *Essex* 39 4914
Lower Shelton *Beds* 38 9942
Lower Shiplake *Oxon* 37 7679
Lower Shuckburgh *Warwks* 49 4862
Lower Slaughter *Gloucs* 36 1622
Lower Soothill *W York* 82 2523
Lower Soudley *Gloucs* 35 6609
Lower Standen *Kent* 29 2340
Lower Stanton St Quintin *Wilts* 35 9180
Lower Stoke *Kent* 28 8375
Lower Stone *Gloucs* 35 6794
Lower Stonnall *Staffs* 61 0803
Lower Stow Bedon *Norfk* 66 9694
Lower Street *Dorset* 11 8399
Lower Street *E Susx* 16 7012
Lower Street *Norfk* 67 2635
Lower Street *Suffk* 53 7852
Lower Street *Suffk* 54 1052
Lower Stretton *Ches* 79 6281
Lower Stroud *Dorset* 10 4598
Lower Sundon *Beds* 38 0526
Lower Swanwick *Hants* 13 4909
Lower Swell *Gloucs* 48 1725
Lower Tadmarton *Oxon* 48 4036
Lower Tale *Devon* 9 0601
Lower Tean *Staffs* 73 0138
Lower Thurlton *Norfk* 67 4299
Lower Town *Cnwll* 2 6528
Lower Town *Devon* 7 7172
Lower Town *Herefd* 47 6342
Lower Town *Pembks* 30 9637
Lower Trebullett *Cnwll* 5 3277
Lower Tregantle *Cnwll* 5 3953
Lower Treluswell *Cnwll* 3 7735
Lower Tysoe *Warwks* 48 3445
Lower Ufford *Suffk* 55 2952
Lower Upcott *Devon* 9 8880
Lower Upham *Hants* 13 5219
Lower Upnor *Kent* 28 7571
Lower Vexford *Somset* 20 1135
Lower Walton *Ches* 78 6086
Lower Waterston *Dorset* 11 7395
Lower Weare *Somset* 21 4053
Lower Welson *Herefd* 46 2950
Lower Westmancote *Worcs* 47 9337
Lower Whatcombe *Dorset* 11 8401
Lower Whatley *Somset* 22 7447
Lower Whitley *Ches* 71 6179
Lower Wick *Gloucs* 35 7096
Lower Wick *Worcs* 47 8352
Lower Wield *Hants* 24 6340
Lower Wigginton *Herts* 38 9409
Lower Willingdon *E Susx* 16 5803
Lower Withington *Ches* 79 8169
Lower Woodend *Bucks* 37 8187
Lower Woodford *Wilts* 23 1235
Lower Wraxhall *Dorset* 10 5700
Lower Wyche *Worcs* 47 7743
Lower Wyke *W York* 82 1525
Lowerhouse *Lancs* 81 8032
Lowesby *Leics* 63 7207
Lowestoft *Suffk* 67 5493
Loweswater *Cumb* 92 1421
Lowfield Heath *W Susx* 15 2739
Lowgill *Cumb* 87 6297
Lowgill *Lancs* 87 6564
Lowick *Cumb* 86 2885
Lowick *Nhants* 51 9881
Lowick *Nthumb* 111 0139
Lowick Bridge *Cumb* 86 2986
Lowick Green *Cumb* 86 2985
Lowlands *Dur* 96 1325
Lowlands *Torfn* 34 2996
Lowsonford *Warwks* 48 1868
Lowther *Cumb* 94 5323
Lowther Castle *Cumb* 94 5223
Lowthorpe *E R Yk* 91 0860
Lowton *Devon* 8 6604
Lowton *Gt Man* 78 6197
Lowton *Somset* 20 1918
Lowton Common *Gt Man* 79 6397
Lowton St Mary's *Gt Man* 79 6397
Loxbeare *Devon* 9 9116
Loxhill *Surrey* 25 0038
Loxhore *Devon* 19 6138
Loxhore Cott *Devon* 19 6138
Loxley *Warwks* 48 2553
Loxley Green *Staffs* 73 0630
Loxter *Herefd* 47 7140
Loxton *Somset* 21 3755
Loxwood *W Susx* 14 0331
Loyal Lodge *Highld* 149 6146
Lubenham *Leics* 50 7087
Lucas Green *Surrey* 25 9460
Lucasgate *Lincs* 77 4147
Luccombe *Somset* 20 9243
Luccombe Village *IOW* 13 5879
Lucker *Nthumb* 111 1530
Luckett *Cnwll* 5 3873
Lucking Street *Essex* 54 8134
Luckington *Wilts* 35 8383
Lucknam *Wilts* 35 8272
Luckwell Bridge *Somset* 20 9038
Lucott *Somset* 19 8645
Lucton *Herefd* 46 4364
Lucy Cross *N York* 89 2112
Ludborough *Lincs* 77 2995
Ludbrook *Devon* 7 6654
Ludchurch *Pembks* 31 1411
Luddenden *W York* 82 0426
Luddenden Foot *W York* 82 0325
Luddenham Court *Kent* 28 9963
Luddesdown *Kent* 28 6666
Luddington *Lincs* 84 8316
Luddington *Warwks* 48 1652
Luddington in the Brook *Nhants* 51 1083
Ludford *Lincs* 76 1989
Ludford *Shrops* 46 5174
Ludgershall *Bucks* 37 6517
Ludgershall *Wilts* 23 2650
Ludgvan *Cnwll* 2 5033
Ludham *Norfk* 67 3818
Ludlow *Shrops* 46 5175
Ludney *Somset* 10 3812
Ludwell *Wilts* 22 9122
Ludworth *Dur* 96 3641
Luffenhall *Herts* 39 2928
Luffincott *Devon* 5 3394
Luffness *E Loth* 118 4780
Lugar *E Ayrs* 107 5921
Lugg Green *Herefd* 46 4462
Luggate Burn *E Loth* 118 5974
Luggiebank *N Lans* 116 7672
Lugsdale *Ches* 78 5285
Lugton *E Ayrs* 115 4152
Lugwardine *Herefd* 46 5540
Luib *Highld* 137 5627
Lulham *Herefd* 46 4141
Lullington *Derbys* 61 2412
Lullington *E Susx* 16 5202
Lullington *Somset* 22 7851
Lulsgate Bottom *Somset* 21 5165
Lulsley *Worcs* 47 7455
Lulworth Camp *Dorset* 11 8381
Lumb *Lancs* 81 8324
Lumb *W York* 82 0221
Lumbutts *W York* 82 9523
Lumby *N York* 83 4830
Lumloch *E Duns* 116 6370
Lumphanan *Abers* 134 5804
Lumphinnans *Fife* 117 1792
Lumsden *Abers* 142 4722
Lunan *Angus* 127 6851
Lunanhead *Angus* 127 4752
Luncarty *P & K* 125 0929
Lund *E R Yk* 84 9647
Lund *N York* 83 6532
Lundford Magna *Lincs* 76 1989
Lundie *Angus* 126 2836
Lundie *Stirlg* 124 7304
Lundin Links *Fife* 126 4002
Lundin Mill *Fife* 126 4102
Lundy Green *Norfk* 67 2392
Lunna *Shet* 153 4869
Lunsford *Kent* 28 6959
Lunsford's Cross *E Susx* 17 7210
Lunt *Mersyd* 78 3402
Luntley *Herefd* 46 3955
Luppitt *Devon* 9 1606
Lupridge *Devon* 7 7153
Lupset *W York* 82 3119
Lupton *Cumb* 87 5581
Lurgashall *W Susx* 14 9326
Lurley *Devon* 9 9215
Lusby *Lincs* 77 3467
Luscombe *Devon* 7 7957
Luson *Devon* 6 6050
Luss *Ag & B* 115 3692
Lusta *Highld* 136 2656
Lustleigh *Devon* 8 7881
Luston *Herefd* 46 4863
Luthermuir *Abers* 135 6568
Luthrie *Fife* 126 3319
Lutley *Worcs* 60 9382
Luton *Beds* 38 0921
Luton *Devon* 9 0802
Luton *Devon* 9 9076
Luton *Kent* 28 7766
Lutterworth *Leics* 50 5484
Lutton *Devon* 6 5959
Lutton *Devon* 7 6961
Lutton *Dorset* 11 8980
Lutton *Lincs* 65 4325
Lutton *Nhants* 52 1187
Luxborough *Somset* 20 9738
Luxulyan *Cnwll* 4 0558
Luzley *Gt Man* 79 9600
Lybster *Highld* 151 2435
Lydbury North *Shrops* 59 3486
Lydcott *Devon* 19 6936
Lydd *Kent* 17 0420
Lydden *Kent* 29 2645
Lydden *Kent* 29 3567
Lyddington *Rutlnd* 51 8797
Lyde Green *Hants* 24 7057
Lydeard St Lawrence *Somset* 20 1332
Lydford *Devon* 5 5185
Lydford on Fosse *Somset* 21 5630
Lydgate *Gt Man* 82 9516
Lydgate *W York* 81 9225
Lydham *Shrops* 59 3391
Lydiard Green *Wilts* 36 0885
Lydiard Millicent *Wilts* 36 0986
Lydiard Tregoze *Wilts* 36 1085
Lydiate *Mersyd* 78 3604
Lydiate Ash *Worcs* 60 9775
Lydlinch *Dorset* 11 7413
Lydney *Gloucs* 35 6303
Lydstep *Pembks* 31 0898
Lye *W Mids* 60 9284
Lye Cross *Somset* 21 4962
Lye Green *Bucks* 38 9703
Lye Green *E Susx* 16 5134
Lye Green *Warwks* 48 1965
Lye Head *Worcs* 60 7573
Lye's Green *Wilts* 22 8146
Lyford *Oxon* 36 3994
Lymbridge Green *Kent* 29 1244
Lyme Regis *Dorset* 10 3492
Lyminge *Kent* 29 1641
Lymington *Hants* 12 3295
Lyminster *W Susx* 14 0204
Lymm *Ches* 79 6887
Lympne *Kent* 17 1135
Lympsham *Somset* 21 3354
Lympstone *Devon* 9 9984
Lynbridge *Devon* 19 7248
Lynch *Somset* 20 9047
Lynch Green *Norfk* 66 1505
Lynchat *Highld* 132 7801
Lyndhurst *Hants* 12 3008
Lyndon *Rutlnd* 63 9004
Lyndon Green *W Mids* 61 1485
Lyne *Border* 109 2041
Lyne *Surrey* 26 0166
Lyne Down *Herefd* 47 6431
Lyne of Skene *Abers* 135 7610
Lyneal *Shrops* 59 4433
Lyneham *Devon* 8 8579
Lyneham *Oxon* 36 2720
Lyneham *Wilts* 35 0278
Lyneholmford *Cumb* 101 5172
Lynemouth *Nthumb* 103 2991
Lyness *Ork* 153 3094
Lyng *Norfk* 66 0617
Lyng *Somset* 21 3329
Lynhales *Herefd* 46 3255
Lynmouth *Devon* 19 7249
Lynn *Shrops* 72 7815
Lynn *Staffs* 61 0704
Lynn of Shenval *Moray* 141 2129
Lynsted *Kent* 28 9460
Lynstone *Cnwll* 18 2005
Lynton *Devon* 19 7249
Lyon's Gate *Dorset* 11 6505
Lyonshall *Herefd* 46 3355
Lytchett Matravers *Dorset* 11 9495
Lytchett Minster *Dorset* 11 9693
Lyth *Highld* 151 2762
Lytham *Lancs* 80 3627
Lytham St Anne's *Lancs* 80 3427
Lythbank *Shrops* 59 4607
Lythe *N York* 90 8413
Lythmore *Highld* 150 0566


# M


Mabe Burnthouse *Cnwll* 3 7634
Mabie *D & G* 100 9570
Mablethorpe *Lincs* 77 5085
Macclesfield *Ches* 79 9173
Macduff *Abers* 142 7064
Macharioch *Ag & B* 105 7309
Machen *Caerph* 33 2189
Machire *Ag & B* 112 2164
Machrie *N Ayrs* 105 8934
Machrihanish *Ag & B* 104 6320
Machrins *Ag & B* 112 3693
Machynlleth *Powys* 57 7400
Machynys *Carmth* 32 5198
Mackworth *Derbys* 62 3137
Macmerry *E Loth* 118 4372
Maddaford *Devon* 8 5494
Madderty *P & K* 125 9522
Maddington *Wilts* 23 0744
Maddiston *Falk* 116 9476
Madehurst *W Susx* 14 9810
Madeley *Shrops* 60 6904
Madeley *Staffs* 72 7744
Madeley Heath *Staffs* 72 7845
Madford *Devon* 9 1411
Madingley *Cambs* 52 3960
Madley *Herefd* 46 4238
Madresfield *Worcs* 47 8047
Madron *Cnwll* 2 4531
Maen-y-groes *Cerdgn* 42 3858
Maenaddwyn *IOA* 68 4684
Maenan *Conwy* 69 7965
Maenclochog *Pembks* 31 0827
Maendy *V Glam* 33 0076
Maenporth *Cnwll* 3 7829
Maentwrog *Gwynd* 57 6640
Maer *Cnwll* 18 2008
Maer *Staffs* 72 7938
Maerdy *Carmth* 44 6527
Maerdy *Rhondd* 33 9798
Maes-glas *Newpt* 34 2985
Maesbrook *Shrops* 59 3021
Maesbury *Shrops* 59 3026
Maesbury Marsh *Shrops* 59 3125
Maesgwynne *Carmth* 31 2024
Maeshafn *Denbgs* 70 2061
Maesllyn *Cerdgn* 42 3644
Maesmynis *Powys* 45 0146
Maesmynis *Powys* 45 0350
Maesteg *Brdgnd* 33 8590
Maesybont *Carmth* 32 5616
Maesycwmmer *Caerph* 33 1594
Magdalen Laver *Essex* 39 5108
Maggieknockater *Moray* 141 3145
Maggots End *Essex* 39 4827
Magham Down *E Susx* 16 6011
Maghull *Mersyd* 78 3703
Magor *Mons* 34 4286
Maiden Bradley *Wilts* 22 8038
Maiden Head *Somset* 21 5666
Maiden Law *Dur* 96 1749
Maiden Newton *Dorset* 10 5997
Maiden Wells *Pembks* 30 9799
Maidencombe *Devon* 7 9268
Maidenhayne *Devon* 10 2795
Maidenhead *Berks* 26 8980
Maidens *S Ayrs* 106 2107
Maidens Green *Berks* 25 8972
Maidenwell *Lincs* 77 3179
Maidford *Nhants* 49 6052
Maids Moreton *Bucks* 49 7035
Maidstone *Kent* 28 7555
Maidwell *Nhants* 50 7476
Maindee *Newpt* 34 3288
Mains of Balhall *Angus* 134 5163
Mains of Balnakettle *Abers* 134 6274
Mains of Dalvey *Highld* 141 1132
Mains of Haulkerton *Abers* 135 7172
Mainsforth *Dur* 96 3131
Mainsriddle *D & G* 92 9456
Mainstone *Shrops* 58 2787
Maisemore *Gloucs* 35 8121
Major's Green *Worcs* 61 1077
Makeney *Derbys* 62 3544
Malborough *Devon* 7 7139
Malcoff *Derbys* 74 0782
Malden *Surrey* 26 2166
Malden Rushett *Gt Lon* 26 1761
Maldon *Essex* 40 8506
Malham *N York* 88 9063
Mallaig *Highld* 129 6796
Mallaigvaig *Highld* 129 6897
Malleny Mills *C Edin* 117 1665
Mallows Green *Essex* 39 4726
Malltraeth *IOA* 68 4068
Mallwyd *Gwynd* 57 8612
Malmesbury *Wilts* 35 9387
Malmsmead *Somset* 19 7947
Malpas *Ches* 71 4847
Malpas *Cnwll* 3 8442
Malpas *Newpt* 34 3090
Maltby *Lincs* 77 3183
Maltby *N York* 89 4613
Maltby *S York* 75 5392
Maltby le Marsh *Lincs* 77 4681
Malting Green *Essex* 41 9720
Maltman's Hill *Kent* 28 9043
Malton *N York* 90 7871
Malvern Link *Worcs* 47 7947
Malvern Wells *Worcs* 47 7742
Malzie *D & G* 99 3754
Mamble *Worcs* 60 6871
Mamhilad *Mons* 34 3003
Manaccan *Cnwll* 3 7624
Manafon *Powys* 58 1102
Manais *W Isls* 152 1089
Manaton *Devon* 8 7581
Manby *Lincs* 77 3986
Mancetter *Warwks* 61 3296
Manchester *Gt Man* 79 8497
Mancot *Flints* 71 3167
Mandally *Highld* 131 2900
Manea *Cambs* 53 4789
Maney *W Mids* 61 1195
Manfield *N York* 89 2113
Mangerton *Dorset* 10 4995
Mangotsfield *Gloucs* 35 6676
Mangrove Green *Herts* 38 1224
Manhay *Cnwll* 2 6930
Manish *W Isls* 152 1089
Mankinholes *W York* 82 9523
Manley *Ches* 71 5071
Manmoel *Caerph* 33 1803
Mannel *Ag & B* 120 9840
Manning's Heath *W Susx* 15 2028
Manningford Bohune *Wilts* 23 1357
Manningford Bruce *Wilts* 23 1358
Manningham *W York* 82 1435
Mannington *Dorset* 12 0605
Manningtree *Essex* 41 1031
Mannofield *Aber C* 135 9104
Manor Park *Gt Lon* 27 4285
Manorbier *Pembks* 30 0697
Manorbier Newton *Pembks* 30 0400
Manordeilo *Carmth* 44 6726
Manorhill *Border* 110 6632
Manorowen *Pembks* 30 9336
Mansell Gamage *Herefd* 46 3944
Mansell Lacy *Herefd* 46 4245
Mansergh *Cumb* 87 6082
Mansfield *E Ayrs* 107 6214
Mansfield *Notts* 75 5361
Mansfield Woodhouse *Notts* 75 5363
Mansriggs *Cumb* 86 2980
Manston *Dorset* 11 8115
Manston *Kent* 29 3466
Manston *W York* 83 3634
Manswood *Dorset* 11 9708
Manthorpe *Lincs* 63 9137
Manthorpe *Lincs* 64 0715
Manton *Lincs* 84 9302
Manton *Notts* 75 6078
Manton *Rutlnd* 63 8704
Manton *Wilts* 23 1768
Manuden *Essex* 39 4926
Manwood Green *Essex* 39 5412
Maperton *Somset* 22 6726
Maple Cross *Herts* 26 0393
Maplebeck *Notts* 75 7060
Mapledurham *Oxon* 37 6776
Mapledurwell *Hants* 24 6851
Maplehurst *W Susx* 15 1824
Maplescombe *Kent* 27 5664
Mapleton *Derbys* 73 1647
Mapleton *Kent* 16 4649
Mapperley *Derbys* 62 4342
Mapperley Park *Notts* 62 5842
Mapperton *Dorset* 10 5099
Mappleborough Green *Warwks* 48 0866
Mappleton *E R Yk* 85 2243
Mapplewell *S York* 83 3210
Mappowder *Dorset* 11 7306
Marazanvose *Cnwll* 3 7950
Marazion *Cnwll* 2 5130
Marbury *Ches* 71 5645
March *Cambs* 65 4196
March *S Lans* 108 9914
Marcham *Oxon* 37 4596
Marchamley *Shrops* 59 5929
Marchamley Wood *Shrops* 59 5831
Marchington *Staffs* 73 1330
Marchington Woodlands *Staffs* 73 1128
Marchros *Gwynd* 56 3125
Marchwiel *Wrexhm* 71 3547
Marchwood *Hants* 12 3810
Marcross *V Glam* 20 9269
Marden *Herefd* 46 5146
Marden *Kent* 28 7444
Marden *Wilts* 23 0857
Marden Ash *Essex* 27 5502
Marden Beech *Kent* 28 7442
Marden Thorn *Kent* 28 7642
Mardens Hill *E Susx* 16 5032
Mardlebury *Herts* 39 2618
Mardy *Mons* 34 3015
Marefield *Leics* 63 7407
Mareham le Fen *Lincs* 77 2761
Mareham on the Hill *Lincs* 77 2867
Marehay *Derbys* 62 3947
Marehill *W Susx* 14 0618
Maresfield *E Susx* 16 4624
Marfleet *E R Yk* 85 1429
Marford *Wrexhm* 71 3556
Margam *Neath* 32 7887
Margaret Marsh *Dorset* 22 8218
Margaret Roding *Essex* 40 5912
Margaretting *Essex* 40 6701
Margaretting Tye *Essex* 40 6800
Margate *Kent* 29 3571
Margnaheglish *N Ayrs* 105 0332
Margrie *D & G* 99 5950
Margrove Park *N York* 97 6515
Marham *Norfk* 65 7009
Marhamchurch *Cnwll* 18 2203
Marholm *Cambs* 64 1401
Marian-glas *IOA* 68 5084
Mariansleigh *Devon* 19 7422
Marine Town *Kent* 28 9274
Marionburgh *Abers* 135 7006
Marishader *Highld* 136 4963
Maristow *Devon* 6 4764
Marjoriebanks *D & G* 100 0883
Mark *D & G* 98 1157
Mark *Somset* 21 3847
Mark Causeway *Somset* 21 3547
Mark Cross *E Susx* 16 5010
Mark Cross *E Susx* 16 5831
Mark's Corner *IOW* 13 4692
Markbeech *Kent* 16 4742
Markby *Lincs* 77 4878
Markeaton *Derbys* 62 3237
Market Bosworth *Leics* 62 4002
Market Deeping *Lincs* 64 1310
Market Drayton *Shrops* 72 6734
Market Harborough *Leics* 50 7387
Market Lavington *Wilts* 22 0154
Market Overton *Rutlnd* 63 8816
Market Rasen *Lincs* 76 1089
Market Stainton *Lincs* 76 2279
Market Weighton *E R Yk* 84 8741
Market Weston *Suffk* 54 9877
Markfield *Leics* 62 4809
Markham *Caerph* 33 1601
Markham Moor *Notts* 75 7173
Markinch *Fife* 126 2901
Markington *N York* 89 2865
Markle *E Loth* 118 5777
Marks Tey *Essex* 40 9023
Marksbury *Somset* 22 6662
Markwell *Cnwll* 5 3758
Markyate *Herts* 38 0616
Marl Bank *Worcs* 47 7840
Marlborough *Wilts* 23 1868
Marlbrook *Herefd* 46 5154
Marlbrook *Worcs* 60 9774
Marlcliff *Warwks* 48 0950
Marldon *Devon* 7 8663
Marle Green *E Susx* 16 5816
Marlesford *Suffk* 55 3258
Marley *Kent* 29 1850
Marley *Kent* 29 3353
Marley Green *Ches* 71 5845
Marley Hill *T & W* 96 2058
Marlingford *Norfk* 66 1309
Marloes *Pembks* 30 7908
Marlow *Bucks* 26 8486
Marlow *Herefd* 46 4076
Marlpit Hill *Kent* 16 4347
Marlpits *E Susx* 16 4528
Marlpits *E Susx* 16 7013
Marlpool *Derbys* 62 4345
Marnhull *Dorset* 22 7818
Marple *Gt Man* 79 9588
Marple Bridge *Gt Man* 79 9688
Marr *S York* 83 5105
Marrick *N York* 88 0798
Marros *Carmth* 31 2008
Marsden *T & W* 103 3964
Marsden *W York* 82 0411
Marsden Height *Lancs* 81 8636
Marsett *N York* 88 9085
Marsh *Bucks* 38 8109
Marsh *Devon* 10 2510
Marsh *W York* 82 0235
Marsh Baldon *Oxon* 37 5699
Marsh Chapel *Lincs* 77 3599
Marsh Gibbon *Bucks* 37 6422
Marsh Green *Devon* 9 0493
Marsh Green *Kent* 16 4344
Marsh Green *Shrops* 59 6014
Marsh Green *Staffs* 72 8858
Marsh Lane *Derbys* 74 4079
Marsh Lane *Gloucs* 34 5807
Marsh Street *Somset* 20 9944
Marshall's Heath *Herts* 39 1614
Marshalswick *Herts* 39 1608
Marsham *Norfk* 67 1923
Marshborough *Kent* 29 3057
Marshbrook *Shrops* 59 4489
Marshfield *Gloucs* 35 7873
Marshfield *Newpt* 34 2582
Marshgate *Cnwll* 4 1592
Marshland Green *Gt Man* 79 6899
Marshland St James *Norfk* 65 5209
Marshside *Mersyd* 80 3619
Marshwood *Dorset* 10 3899
Marske *N York* 89 1000
Marske-by-the-Sea *N York* 97 6322
Marston *Ches* 79 6775
Marston *Herefd* 46 3557
Marston *Lincs* 63 8943
Marston *Oxon* 37 5208
Marston *Staffs* 60 8313
Marston *Staffs* 72 9227
Marston *Warwks* 61 2094
Marston *Wilts* 22 9656
Marston Green *W Mids* 61 1785
Marston Jabbet *Warwks* 61 3788
Marston Magna *Somset* 21 5922
Marston Meysey *Wilts* 36 1297
Marston Montgomery *Derbys* 73 1337
Marston Moretaine *Beds* 38 9941
Marston on Dove *Derbys* 73 2329
Marston St Lawrence *Nhants* 49 5341
Marston Stannett *Herefd* 46 5655
Marston Trussell *Nhants* 50 6985
Marstow *Herefd* 34 5518
Marsworth *Bucks* 38 9114
Marten *Wilts* 23 2860
Marthall *Ches* 79 7975
Martham *Norfk* 67 4518
Martin *Hants* 12 0619
Martin *Kent* 29 3447
Martin *Lincs* 76 1259
Martin *Lincs* 77 2466
Martin Dales *Lincs* 76 1762
Martin Drove End *Hants* 12 0520
Martin Hussingtree *Worcs* 47 8860
Martindale *Cumb* 93 4319
Martinhoe *Devon* 19 6648
Martinscroft *Ches* 79 6589
Martinstown *Dorset* 11 6489
Martlesham *Suffk* 55 2547
Martletwy *Pembks* 30 0310
Martley *Worcs* 47 7560
Martock *Somset* 21 4619
Marton *Ches* 71 6267
Marton *Ches* 79 8568

Milton Street
Neatham

Milton Street E Susx 16 5304
Milton-under-Wychwood Oxon 36 2618
Milverton Somset 20 1225
Milverton Warwks 48 3166
Milwich Staffs 72 9632
Milwr Flints 70 1974
Minard Ag & B 114 9796
Minchington Dorset 11 9614
Minchinhampton Gloucs 35 8700
Mindrum Nthumb 110 8432
Mindrum Mill Nthumb 110 8533
Minehead Somset 20 9646
Minera Wrexhm 70 2751
Minety Wilts 36 0290
Minffordd Gwynd 57 5938
Mingarrypark Highld 129 6869
Miningsby Lincs 77 3264
Minions Cnwll 5 2671
Minishant S Ayrs 106 3314
Minllyn Gwynd 57 8514
Minnigaff D & G 99 4166
Minnis Bay Kent 29 2869
Minnonie Abers 142 7760
Minskip N York 89 3864
Minstead Hants 12 2811
Minsted W Susx 14 8520
Minster Kent 28 9573
Minster Kent 29 3064
Minster Lovell Oxon 36 3111
Minsteracres Nthumb 95 0156
Minsterley Shrops 59 3705
Minsterworth Gloucs 35 7817
Minterne Magna Dorset 11 6504
Minterne Parva Dorset 11 6603
Minting Lincs 76 1873
Mintlaw Abers 143 9948
Minto Border 109 5620
Minton Shrops 59 4390
Minwear Pembks 30 0413
Minworth W Mids 61 1691
Mirehouse Cumb 92 9715
Mirfield W York 82 2019
Miserden Gloucs 35 9308
Miskin Rhondd 33 0480
Miskin Rhondd 33 0498
Misson Notts 75 6895
Misterton Leics 50 5583
Misterton Notts 75 7694
Misterton Somset 10 4508
Mistley Essex 41 1231
Mistley Heath Essex 41 1230
Mitcham Gt Lon 27 2768
Mitchel Troy Mons 34 4910
Mitcheldean Gloucs 35 6618
Mitchell Cnwll 3 8554
Mitchellslacks D & G 100 9696
Mitford Nthumb 103 1786
Mithian Cnwll 3 7450
Mitton Staffs 72 8815
Mixbury Oxon 49 6033
Mixenden W York 82 0629
Mixon Staffs 74 0457
Moats Tye Suffk 54 0455
Mobberley Ches 79 7879
Mobberley Staffs 73 0041
Moccas Herefd 46 3542
Mochdre Conwy 69 8278
Mochdre Powys 58 0788
Mochrum D & G 98 3446
Mockbeggar Hants 12 1609
Mockbeggar Kent 28 7146
Mockerkin Cumb 92 0923
Modbury Devon 7 6651
Moddershall Staffs 72 9236
Moel Tryfan Gwynd 68 5156
Moelfre IOA 68 5186
Moelfre Powys 58 1828
Moffat D & G 108 0805
Mogerhanger Beds 52 1449
Moira Leics 62 3115
Mol-chlach Highld 128 4513
Molash Kent 28 0251
Mold Flints 70 2363
Moldgreen W York 82 1516
Molehill Green Essex 40 5624
Molehill Green Essex 40 7120
Molescroft E R Yk 84 0140
Molesden Nthumb 103 1484
Molesworth Cambs 51 0775
Molland Devon 19 8028
Mollington Ches 71 3870
Mollington Oxon 49 4447
Mollinsburn N Lans 116 7171
Monachty Cerdgn 44 5061
Monday Boys Kent 28 9045
Mondynes Abers 135 7779
Monewden Suffk 55 2358
Moneydie P & K 125 0629
Moneyrow Green Berks 26 8977
Moniaive D & G 107 7890
Monifieth Angus 127 4932
Monikie Angus 127 4938
Monimail Fife 126 2914
Monington Pembks 42 1344
Monk Bretton S York 83 3607
Monk Fryston N York 83 5029
Monk Sherborne Hants 24 6056
Monk Soham Suffk 55 2165
Monk Soham Green Suffk 55 2066
Monk Street Essex 40 6128
Monk's Gate W Susx 15 2027
Monken Hadley Gt Lon 26 2497
Monkhide Herefd 46 6144
Monkhill Cumb 93 3458
Monkhopton Shrops 59 6293
Monkland Herefd 46 4557
Monkleigh Devon 18 4520
Monknash V Glam 33 9170
Monkokehampton Devon 8 5805
Monks Eleigh Suffk 54 9647
Monks Heath Ches 79 8474
Monks Horton Kent 29 1139
Monks Kirby Warwks 50 4683
Monks Risborough Bucks 38 8104
Monkseaton T & W 103 3472
Monksilver Somset 20 0737
Monkspath W Mids 61 1376
Monksthorpe Lincs 77 4465
Monkswood Mons 34 3402
Monkton Devon 9 1803
Monkton Kent 29 2964
Monkton S Ayrs 106 3527
Monkton T & W 103 3363
Monkton V Glam 33 9270
Monkton Combe Somset 22 7762
Monkton Deverill Wilts 22 8537
Monkton Farleigh Wilts 22 8065
Monkton Heathfield Somset 20 2526
Monkton Up Wimborne Dorset 11 0113
Monkton Wyld Dorset 10 3396
Monkwearmouth T & W 96 3958
Monkwood Hants 24 6630
Monmore Green W Mids 60 9297
Monmouth Mons 34 5012
Monnington on Wye Herefd 46 3743
Monreith D & G 98 3541
Mont Saint Guern 158 0000
Montacute Somset 10 4916
Montcliffe Gt Man 81 6611
Montford Shrops 59 4114
Montford Bridge Shrops 59 4215
Montgarrie Abers 142 5717
Montgarswood E Ayrs 107 5227
Montgomery Powys 58 2296
Montgreenan N Ayrs 106 3343
Monton Gt Man 79 7699
Montrose Angus 135 7157
Monxton Hants 23 3144
Monyash Derbys 74 1566
Monymusk Abers 142 6815
Monzie P & K 125 8725
Moodiesburn N Lans 116 6970
Moonzie Fife 126 3317
Moor Allerton W York 82 3038
Moor Crichel Dorset 11 9908
Moor End Beds 38 9719
Moor End Devon 19 6609
Moor End E R Yk 84 8137
Moor End Lancs 80 3744
Moor End N York 83 6038
Moor End W York 82 0528
Moor Green Herts 39 3226
Moor Head W York 82 2329
Moor Monkton N York 83 5156
Moor Row Cumb 92 0014
Moor Row Cumb 93 2149
Moor Row Dur 96 1515
Moor Side Lancs 80 4935
Moor Side Lancs 80 4334
Moor Side Lincs 77 2557
Moor Street Kent 28 8265
Moor Street W Mids 60 9982
Moorbath Dorset 10 4395
Moorby Lincs 77 2964
Moorcot Herefd 46 3555
Moordown Dorset 12 0994
Moore Ches 78 5784
Moorend Gloucs 35 7303
Moorends S York 83 6915
Moorgreen Hants 13 4815
Moorgreen Notts 62 4847
Moorhall Derbys 74 3074
Moorhampton Herefd 46 3746
Moorhead W York 82 1337
Moorhouse Cumb 93 2551
Moorhouse Cumb 93 3356
Moorhouse Notts 75 7566
Moorhouse W York 83 4810
Moorhouse Bank Surrey 27 4353
Moorland Somset 21 3332
Moorlinch Somset 21 3936
Moorsholm N York 90 6814
Moorside Cumb 86 0701
Moorside Dorset 22 7919
Moorside Gt Man 79 9407
Moorside W York 82 2436
Moorstock Kent 29 1038
Moorswater Cnwll 5 2364
Moorthorpe W York 83 4611
Moortown Devon 6 5274
Moortown Hants 12 1503
Moortown IOW 13 4283
Moortown Lincs 76 0798
Moortown Shrops 59 6118
Moortown W York 82 2939
Morangie Highld 147 7683
Morar Highld 129 6793
Morborne Cambs 64 1391
Morchard Bishop Devon 8 7707
Morcombelake Dorset 10 4094
Morcott Rutlnd 51 9200
Morda Shrops 58 2827
Morden Dorset 11 9195
Morden Gt Lon 27 2666
Mordiford Herefd 46 5737
Mordon Dur 96 3226
More Shrops 59 3491
Morebath Devon 20 9525
Morebattle Border 110 7724
Morecambe Lancs 87 4364
Moredon Wilts 36 1487
Morefield Highld 145 1195
Morehall Kent 29 2136
Moreleigh Devon 7 7652
Morenish P & K 124 6035
Moresby Cumb 92 9921
Moresby Parks Cumb 92 9919
Morestead Hants 13 5025
Moreton Dorset 11 8089
Moreton Essex 39 5307
Moreton Herefd 46 5064
Moreton Mersyd 78 2689
Moreton Oxon 37 6904
Moreton Staffs 72 7817
Moreton Staffs 73 1429
Moreton Corbet Shrops 59 5623
Moreton Jeffries Herefd 46 6048
Moreton Morrell Warwks 48 3155
Moreton on Lugg Herefd 46 5045
Moreton Paddox Warwks 48 3154
Moreton Pinkney Nhants 49 5749
Moreton Say Shrops 59 6334
Moreton Valence Gloucs 35 7809
Moreton-in-Marsh Gloucs 48 2032
Moretonhampstead Devon 8 7586
Moretonmill Shrops 59 5723
Morfa Cerdgn 42 3053
Morfa Bychan Gwynd 57 5437
Morfa Dinlle Gwynd 68 4358
Morfa Glas Neath 33 8606
Morfa Nefyn Gwynd 56 2840
Morgan's Vale Wilts 12 1920
Morganstown Cardif 33 1281
Morham E Loth 118 5571
Moriah Cerdgn 43 6279
Morland Cumb 94 6022
Morley Ches 79 8282
Morley Derbys 62 3940
Morley Dur 96 1227
Morley W York 82 2627
Morley Green Ches 79 8281
Morley St Botolph Norfk 66 0799
Mornick Cnwll 5 3272
Morningside C Edin 117 2470
Morningside N Lans 116 8355
Morningthorpe Norfk 67 2192
Morpeth Nthumb 103 1986
Morphie Abers 135 7164
Morrey Staffs 73 1218
Morridge Side Staffs 73 0254
Morridge Top Staffs 74 0365
Morriston Swans 32 6697
Morston Norfk 66 0043
Mortehoe Devon 18 4545
Morthen S York 75 4788
Mortimer Berks 24 6564
Mortimer Common Berks 24 6565
Mortimer West End Hants 24 6363
Mortimer's Cross Herefd 46 4263
Mortlake Gt Lon 26 2075
Morton Cumb 93 3854
Morton Cumb 93 4539
Morton Derbys 74 4060
Morton IOW 13 6085
Morton Lincs 75 8091
Morton Lincs 64 0923
Morton Norfk 66 1216
Morton Notts 75 7251
Morton Shrops 59 2924
Morton Hall Lincs 76 8863
Morton Tinmouth Dur 96 1821
Morton-on-Swale N York 89 3291
Morvah Cnwll 2 4035
Morval Cnwll 5 2556
Morvich Highld 138 9621
Morville Shrops 60 6794
Morville Heath Shrops 60 6893
Morwenstow Cnwll 18 2015
Mosborough S York 74 4281
Moscow E Ayrs 107 4840
Mose Shrops 60 7590
Mosedale Cumb 93 3532
Moseley W Mids 60 9498
Moseley W Mids 61 0783
Moseley Worcs 47 8159
Moses Gate Gt Man 79 7306
Moss Ag & B 120 9544
Moss S York 83 5914
Moss Wrexhm 71 3053
Moss Bank Mersyd 78 5197
Moss Edge Lancs 80 4243
Moss End Ches 79 6778
Moss Side Cumb 93 1952
Moss Side Lancs 80 3730
Moss Side Mersyd 78 3802
Moss Side Mersyd 78 3107
Moss-side Highld 140 8555
Mossat Abers 142 4719
Mossbank Shet 153 4575
Mossbay Cumb 92 9927
Mossblown S Ayrs 106 4024
Mossbrow Gt Man 79 7089
Mossburnford Border 110 6616
Mossdale D & G 99 6670
Mossdale E Ayrs 107 4904
Mossend N Lans 116 7460
Mosser Mains Cumb 92 1125
Mossgiel E Ayrs 107 4828
Mossknowe D & G 101 2769
Mossley Ches 72 8861
Mossley Gt Man 82 9701
Mosspaul Hotel Border 109 3999
Mosstodloch Moray 141 3259
Mossy Lea Lancs 80 5312
Mossyard D & G 99 5451
Mosterton Dorset 10 4505
Moston Gt Man 79 8701
Moston Shrops 59 5626
Moston Green Ches 72 7261
Mostyn Flints 70 1580
Motcombe Dorset 22 8525
Mothecombe Devon 6 6047
Motherby Cumb 93 4228
Motherwell N Lans 116 7457
Motspur Park Gt Lon 26 2267
Mottingham Gt Lon 27 4272
Mottisfont Hants 23 3226
Mottistone IOW 13 4083
Mottram in Longdendale Gt Man 79 9995
Mottram St Andrew Ches 79 8778
Mouilpied Guern 158 0000
Mouldsworth Ches 71 5071
Moulin P & K 132 9459
Moulsecoomb E Susx 15 3307
Moulsford Oxon 37 5883
Moulsoe Bucks 38 9141
Moultavie Highld 146 6371
Moulton Ches 79 6569
Moulton Lincs 64 3023
Moulton N York 89 2303
Moulton Nhants 50 7866
Moulton Suffk 53 6964
Moulton V Glam 33 0770
Moulton Chapel Lincs 64 2918
Moulton Seas End Lincs 64 3227
Moulton St Mary Norfk 67 3907
Mount Cnwll 3 7856
Mount Cnwll 4 1468
Mount W York 82 0917
Mount Ambrose Cnwll 2 7043
Mount Bures Essex 40 9032
Mount Hawke Cnwll 2 7147
Mount Hermon Cnwll 2 6915
Mount Lothian Mdloth 117 2757
Mount Pleasant Ches 72 8456
Mount Pleasant Derbys 74 3448
Mount Pleasant Dur 96 2634
Mount Pleasant E Susx 16 4216
Mount Pleasant Norfk 66 9994
Mount Pleasant Suffk 53 7347
Mount Pleasant Worcs 47 0064
Mount Sorrel Wilts 23 0324
Mount Tabor W York 82 0527
Mountain W York 82 0930
Mountain Ash Rhondd 33 0499
Mountain Cross Border 117 1547
Mountain Street Kent 29 0652
Mountfield E Susx 17 7320
Mountgerald House Highld 139 5661
Mountjoy Cnwll 4 8760
Mountnessing Essex 40 6297
Mounton Mons 34 5193
Mountsorrel Leics 62 5814
Mousehill Surrey 25 9441
Mousehole Cnwll 2 4626
Mouswald D & G 100 0672
Mow Cop Ches 72 8557
Mowhaugh Border 110 8120
Mowmacre Hill Leics 62 5807
Mowsley Leics 50 6489
Mowtie Abers 135 8388
Moy Highld 140 7634
Moy Highld 131 4282
Moye Highld 138 8818
Moyles Court Hants 12 1608
Moylgrove Pembks 42 1144
Muasdale Ag & B 105 6840
Much Birch Herefd 46 5030
Much Cowarne Herefd 46 6147
Much Dewchurch Herefd 46 4831
Much Hadham Herts 39 4219
Much Hoole Lancs 80 4723
Much Hoole Town Lancs 80 4722
Much Marcle Herefd 47 6532
Much Wenlock Shrops 59 6299
Muchalls Abers 135 9092
Muchelney Somset 21 4224
Muchelney Ham Somset 21 4423
Muchlarnick Cnwll 5 2156
Mucking Essex 40 6881
Muckingford Essex 40 6779
Muckleford Dorset 10 6393
Mucklestone Staffs 72 7237
Muckley Shrops 59 6495
Muckton Lincs 77 3781
Mucomir Highld 131 1884
Mud Row Kent 28 0072
Muddiford Devon 19 5638
Muddles Green E Susx 16 5413
Mudeford Dorset 12 1892
Mudford Somset 21 5719
Mudford Sock Somset 21 5519
Mudgley Somset 21 4545
Mugdock Stirlg 115 5577
Mugeary Highld 136 4439
Mugginton Derbys 73 2842
Muggintonlane End Derbys 73 2844
Muggleswick Dur 95 0449
Muir of Fowlis Abers 134 5612
Muir of Miltonduff Moray 141 1859
Muir of Ord Highld 139 5250
Muir of Thorn P & K 125 0637
Muirden Abers 142 7054
Muirdrum Angus 127 5637
Muiresk Abers 142 6948
Muirhead Angus 126 3434
Muirhead Fife 126 2805
Muirhead N Lans 116 6869
Muirhouses Falk 117 0180
Muirkirk E Ayrs 107 6927
Muirmill Stirlg 116 7283
Muirshearlich Highld 131 1380
Muirtack Abers 143 9937
Muirton P & K 125 9211
Muirton Mains Highld 139 4553
Muirton of Ardblair P & K 126 1643
Muker N York 88 9097
Mulbarton Norfk 67 1901
Mulben Moray 141 3550
Mulfra Cnwll 2 4534
Mullacott Cross Devon 19 5144
Mullion Cnwll 2 6719
Mullion Cove Cnwll 2 6617
Mumby Lincs 77 5174
Munderfield Row Herefd 47 6451
Munderfield Stocks Herefd 47 6550
Mundesley Norfk 67 3136
Mundford Norfk 66 8093
Mundham Norfk 67 3397
Mundon Hill Essex 40 8602
Mungrisdale Cumb 93 3630
Munlochy Highld 140 6453
Munnoch N Ayrs 114 2548
Munsley Herefd 47 6640
Munslow Shrops 59 5287
Murchington Devon 8 6888
Murcot Worcs 48 0640
Murcott Oxon 37 5815
Murcott Wilts 35 9591
Murkle Highld 151 1668
Murlaggan Highld 130 0192
Murrell Green Hants 24 7455
Murroes Angus 127 4635
Murrow Cambs 64 3707
Mursley Bucks 38 8128
Murston Kent 28 9264
Murthill Angus 134 4657
Murthly P & K 126 1038
Murton Cumb 94 7221
Murton Dur 96 3847
Murton N York 83 6452
Murton Nthumb 111 9748
Murton T & W 103 3270
Musbury Devon 10 2794
Muscoates N York 90 6879
Musselburgh E Loth 118 3472
Muston Leics 63 8237
Muston N York 91 0979
Mustow Green Worcs 60 8774
Muswell Hill Gt Lon 27 2889
Mutehill D & G 99 6848
Mutford Suffk 55 4888
Muthill P & K 125 8717
Mutterton Devon 9 0205
Muxton Shrops 60 7114
Mybster Highld 151 1652
Myddfai Carmth 44 7730
Myddle Shrops 59 4623
Mydroilyn Cerdgn 42 4555
Mylor Cnwll 3 8135
Mylor Bridge Cnwll 3 8036
Mynachlog ddu Pembks 31 1430
Myndd-llan Flints 70 1572
Myndtown Shrops 59 3989
Mynydd Buch Cerdgn 43 7276
Mynydd Isa Flints 70 2563
Mynydd Llandygai Gwynd 69 6065
Mynydd-bach Mons 34 4894
Mynydd-Bach Swans 32 6597
Mynyddgarreg Carmth 31 4208
Mynytho Gwynd 56 3031
Myrebird Abers 135 7398
Myredykes Border 102 5998
Mytchett Surrey 25 8855
Mytholm W York 82 9827
Mytholmroyd W York 82 0126
Mythop Lancs 80 3634
Myton-on-Swale N York 89 4366

# N

Na Buirgh W Isls 152 0394
Naast Highld 144 8283
Nab's Head Lancs 81 6229
Naburn N York 83 5945
Naccolt Kent 28 0544
Nackington Kent 29 1554
Nacton Suffk 55 2240
Nafferton E R Yk 91 0559
Nag's Head Gloucs 35 8898
Nailbridge Gloucs 35 6415
Nailsbourne Somset 20 2128
Nailsea Somset 34 4770
Nailstone Leics 62 4106
Nailsworth Gloucs 35 8499
Nairn Highld 140 8856
Nalderswood Surrey 15 2445
Nancegollan Cnwll 2 6332
Nancledra Cnwll 2 4936
Nanhoron Gwynd 56 2731
Nannerch Flints 70 1669
Nanpantan Leics 62 5017
Nanpean Cnwll 3 9556
Nanquidno Cnwll 2 3629
Nanstallon Cnwll 4 0367
Nant Gwynant Gwynd 69 6350
Nant Peris Gwynd 69 6058
Nant-ddu Powys 33 0014
Nant-glas Powys 45 9965
Nant-y-Bwch Blae G 33 1210
Nant-y-caws Carmth 32 4518
Nant-y-derry Mons 34 3306
Nant-y-gollen Shrops 58 2428
Nant-y-moel Brdgnd 33 9392
Nant-y-pandy Conwy 69 6973
Nanternis Cerdgn 42 3756
Nantgaredig Carmth 32 4921
Nantgarw Rhondd 33 1285
Nantglyn Denbgs 70 0061
Nantgwyn Powys 45 9776
Nantlle Gwynd 68 5153
Nantmawr Shrops 58 2524
Nantmel Powys 45 0366
Nantmor Gwynd 57 6046
Nantwich Ches 72 6552
Nantyffyllon Brdgnd 33 8492
Nantyglo Blae G 33 1910
Naphill Bucks 26 8496
Napleton Worcs 47 8648
Nappa N York 81 8553
Napton on the Hill Warwks 49 4661
Narberth Pembks 31 1015
Narborough Leics 50 5497
Narborough Norfk 65 7412
Narkurs Cnwll 5 3255
Nasareth Gwynd 68 4749
Naseby Nhants 50 6978
Nash Bucks 38 7833
Nash Gt Lon 27 4063
Nash Herefd 46 3062
Nash Newpt 34 3483
Nash Shrops 46 6071
Nash End Worcs 60 7781
Nash Lee Bucks 38 8408
Nash Street Kent 27 6469
Nash's Green Hants 24 6745
Nassington Nhants 51 0696
Nastend Gloucs 35 7906
Nasty Herts 39 3524
Nateby Cumb 88 7706
Nateby Lancs 80 4644
Natland Cumb 87 5289
Naughton Suffk 54 0249
Naunton Gloucs 48 1123
Naunton Worcs 47 8739
Naunton Beauchamp Worcs 47 9652
Navenby Lincs 76 9858
Navestock Essex 27 5397
Navestock Side Essex 27 5697
Navidale House Hotel Highld 147 0316
Navity Highld 140 7864
Nawton N York 90 6584
Nayland Suffk 54 9734
Nazeing Essex 39 4106
Nazeing Gate Essex 39 4105
Neacroft Hants 12 1896
Neal's Green Warwks 61 3384
Neap Shet 153 5058
Near Cotton Staffs 73 0646
Near Sawrey Cumb 87 3795
Neasden Gt Lon 26 2185
Neasham Dur 89 3210
Neath Neath 32 7597
Neatham Hants 24 7440

Neatishead Nigg

Neatishead Norfk 67 3420
Nebo Cerdgn 43 5465
Nebo Conwy 69 8355
Nebo Gwynd 68 4850
Nebo IOA 68 4690
Necton Norfk 66 8709
Nedd Highld 148 1331
Nedderton Nthumb 103 2382
Nedging Suffk 54 9948
Nedging Tye Suffk 54 0149
Needham Norfk 55 2281
Needham Market Suffk 54 0855
Needham Street Suffk 53 7265
Needingworth Cambs 52 3472
Neen Savage Shrops 60 6777
Neen Sollars Shrops 60 6672
Neenton Shrops 59 6387
Nefyn Gwynd 56 3040
Neilston E Rens 115 4857
Nelson Caerph 33 1195
Nelson Lancs 81 8638
Nemphlar S Lans 116 8544
Nempnett Thrubwell Somset 21 5260
Nenthall Cumb 94 7545
Nenthead Cumb 94 7743
Nenthorn Border 110 6837
Neopardy Devon 8 7999
Nep Town W Susx 15 2115
Nercwys Flints 70 2360
Nereabolls Ag & B 112 2255
Nerston S Lans 116 6456
Nesbit Nthumb 111 9833
Nesfield N York 82 0949
Ness Ches 71 3076
Nesscliffe Shrops 59 3819
Neston Ches 71 2977
Neston Wilts 22 8668
Netchwood Shrops 59 6291
Nether Alderley Ches 79 8476
Nether Blainslie Border 109 5443
Nether Broughton Notts 63 6925
Nether Cerne Dorset 11 6798
Nether Compton Dorset 10 5917
Nether Crimond Abers 143 8222
Nether Dallachy Moray 141 3563
Nether Exe Devon 9 9300
Nether Fingland S Lans 108 9310
Nether Handley Derbys 74 4176
Nether Handwick Angus 126 3641
Nether Haugh S York 74 4196
Nether Headon Notts 75 7477
Nether Heage Derbys 74 3650
Nether Heyford Nhants 49 6658
Nether Howcleugh S Lans 108 0212
Nether Kellet Lancs 87 5068
Nether Kinmundy Abers 143 0543
Nether Langwith Notts 75 5370
Nether Moor Derbys 74 3866
Nether Padley Derbys 74 2478
Nether Poppleton N York 83 5654
Nether Row Cumb 93 3237
Nether Silton N York 89 4592
Nether Skyborry Shrops 46 2873
Nether Stowey Somset 20 1939
Nether Street Essex 40 5812
Nether Wallop Hants 23 3036
Nether Wasdale Cumb 86 1204
Nether Welton Cumb 93 3545
Nether Westcote Gloucs 36 2220
Nether Whitacre Warwks 61 2392
Nether Whitecleuch S Lans 108 8319
Nether Winchendon Bucks 37 7312
Netheravon Wilts 23 1448
Netherbrae Abers 143 7959
Netherburn S Lans 116 7947
Netherbury Dorset 10 4799
Netherby Cumb 101 3971
Netherby N York 83 3346
Nethercleuch D & G 100 1186
Nethercote Warwks 49 5164
Nethercott Devon 18 4839
Nethercott Devon 5 3596
Netherend Gloucs 34 5900
Netherfield E Susx 16 7019
Netherfield Leics 62 5816
Netherfield Notts 62 6140
Netherfield Road E Susx 17 7417
Nethergate Lincs 75 7599
Nethergate Norfk 66 0529
Netherhampton Wilts 23 1029
Netherhay Dorset 10 4105
Netherland Green Staffs 73 1030
Netherlaw D & G 99 7444
Netherley Abers 135 8593
Nethermill D & G 100 0487
Nethermuir Abers 143 9044
Netheroyd Hill W York 82 1419
Netherplace E Rens 115 5255
Netherseal Derbys 61 2812
Netherstreet Wilts 22 9864
Netherthong W York 82 1309
Netherthorpe Derbys 75 4474
Netherton Angus 134 5457
Netherton Devon 7 8971
Netherton Hants 23 3757
Netherton Herefd 46 5226
Netherton N Lans 116 7854
Netherton Nthumb 111 9807
Netherton Oxon 36 4199
Netherton P & K 126 1452
Netherton Shrops 60 7382
Netherton Stirlg 115 5579
Netherton W Mids 60 9488
Netherton W York 82 1213
Netherton W York 82 2816
Netherton Worcs 47 9941
Nethertown Cumb 86 9907
Nethertown Highld 151 3578
Nethertown Lancs 81 7236
Nethertown Staffs 73 1017
Netherurd Border 117 1144
Netherwitton Nthumb 103 0990
Nethy Bridge Highld 141 0020
Netley Hants 13 4508
Netley Marsh Hants 12 3313
Nettacott Devon 9 8999
Nettlebed Oxon 37 6986
Nettlebridge Somset 21 6448
Nettlecombe Dorset 10 5195
Nettlecombe IOW 13 5278
Nettleden Herts 38 0110
Nettleham Lincs 76 0075
Nettlestead Kent 28 6852
Nettlestead Green Kent 28 6850
Nettlestone IOW 13 6290
Nettlesworth Dur 96 2547
Nettleton Lincs 76 1100
Nettleton Wilts 35 8278
Nettleton Shrub Wilts 35 8277
Netton Devon 6 5546
Netton Wilts 23 1336
Neuadd Carmth 32 7021
Neuadd Fawr Carmth 44 7441
Neuadd-ddu Powys 45 9175
Nevendon Essex 40 7591
Nevern Pembks 31 0840
Nevill Holt Leics 51 8193
New Abbey D & G 100 9666
New Aberdour Abers 143 8863
New Addington Gt Lon 27 3763
New Alresford Hants 24 5832
New Alyth P & K 126 2447
New Arram E R Yk 84 0344
New Ash Green Kent 27 6065
New Balderton Notts 75 8152
New Barn Kent 27 6169
New Barnet Gt Lon 27 2695
New Barton Nhants 51 8564
New Bewick Nthumb 111 0620
New Bilton Warwks 50 4875
New Bolingbroke Lincs 77 3057
New Boultham Lincs 76 9670
New Bradwell Bucks 38 8341
New Brampton Derbys 74 3771
New Brancepeth Dur 96 2241
New Bridge N York 90 8085
New Brighton Flints 70 2565
New Brighton Mersyd 78 3093
New Brinsley Notts 75 4550
New Brotton N York 97 6920
New Broughton Wrexhm 71 3151
New Buckenham Norfk 54 0890
New Bury Gt Man 79 7304
New Byth Abers 143 8254
New Costessey Norfk 66 1810
New Cowper Cumb 92 1245
New Crofton W York 83 3817
New Cross Cerdgn 43 6376
New Cross Gt Lon 27 3676
New Cross Somset 21 4119
New Cumnock E Ayrs 107 6213
New Cut E Susx 17 8115
New Deer Abers 143 8847
New Delaval Nthumb 103 2979
New Delph Gt Man 82 9907
New Denham Bucks 26 0484
New Duston Nhants 49 7162
New Earswick N York 83 6155
New Eastwood Notts 62 4646
New Edlington S York 75 5398
New Elgin Moray 141 2261
New Ellerby E R Yk 85 1639
New Eltham Gt Lon 27 4472
New End Worcs 48 0560
New England Cambs 64 1801
New Farnley W York 82 2531
New Ferry Mersyd 78 3385
New Fletton Cambs 64 1997
New Fryston W York 83 4526
New Galloway D & G 99 6377
New Gilston Fife 127 4208
New Grimsby IOS 2 8815
New Hartley Nthumb 103 3076
New Haw Surrey 26 0563
New Hedges Pembks 31 1202
New Herrington T & W 96 3352
New Holkham Norfk 66 8839
New Holland Lincs 85 0823
New Houghton Derbys 75 4965
New Houghton Norfk 66 7927
New Houses Gt Man 78 5502
New Houses N York 88 8073
New Hutton Cumb 87 5691
New Hythe Kent 28 7159
New Inn Carmth 44 4736
New Inn Torfn 34 3099
New Invention Shrops 46 2976
New Lakenham Norfk 67 2307
New Lanark S Lans 108 8842
New Lane Lancs 80 4212
New Lane End Ches 79 6394
New Langholm D & G 101 3684
New Leake Lincs 77 4057
New Leeds Abers 143 9954
New Longton Lancs 80 5025
New Luce D & G 98 1764
New Malden Gt Lon 26 2168
New Marske N York 97 6121
New Marston Oxon 37 5207
New Marton Shrops 59 3334
New Mill Abers 135 7883
New Mill Cnwll 2 4534
New Mill Herts 38 9212
New Mill W York 82 1609
New Mills Cnwll 3 8952
New Mills Derbys 79 0085
New Mills Powys 58 0901
New Milton Hants 12 2495
New Mistley Essex 41 1131
New Moat Pembks 30 0625
New Ollerton Notts 75 6667
New Oscott W Mids 61 0994
New Pitsligo Abers 143 8855
New Polzeath Cnwll 4 9379
New Prestwick S Ayrs 106 3424
New Quay Cerdgn 42 3959
New Quay Essex 41 0223
New Rackheath Norfk 67 2812
New Radnor Powys 45 2161
New Rent Cumb 93 4536
New Ridley Nthumb 95 0559
New Road Side N York 82 9743
New Romney Kent 17 0624
New Rossington S York 75 6198
New Row Cerdgn 43 7273
New Row Lancs 81 6438
New Sauchie Clacks 116 8994
New Scone P & K 126 1326
New Sharlston W York 83 3819
New Shoreston Nthumb 111 1932
New Silksworth T & W 96 3853
New Skelton N York 97 6618
New Somerby Lincs 63 9235
New Spilsby Lincs 77 4165
New Springs Gt Man 78 5906
New Stevenston N Lans 116 7659
New Street Herefd 46 3356
New Swannington Leics 62 4215
New Thundersley Essex 40 7789
New Town Beds 52 1945
New Town Dorset 22 8318
New Town Dorset 11 9515
New Town Dorset 11 9907
New Town Dorset 22 9918
New Town E Loth 118 4470
New Town E Susx 16 4720
New Town Nhants 51 9677
New Town Somset 10 2712
New Town Wilts 36 2871
New Tredegar Caerph 33 1403
New Trows S Lans 108 8038
New Tupton Derbys 74 3966
New Village E R Yk 84 8530
New Walsoken Cambs 65 4609
New Waltham Lincs 85 2804
New Whittington Derbys 74 3975
New Wimpole Cambs 52 3549
New Winton E Loth 118 4271
New Yatt Oxon 36 3713
New York Lincs 77 2455
New York N York 89 1963
New York T & W 103 3270
Newall W York 82 1946
Newark Cambs 64 2100
Newark Ork 153 7142
Newark-on-Trent Notts 75 7953
Newarthill N Lans 116 7859
Newbarn Kent 29 1540
Newbattle Mdloth 118 3365
Newbie D & G 101 1764
Newbiggin Cumb 93 4729
Newbiggin Cumb 94 5549
Newbiggin Cumb 94 6228
Newbiggin Cumb 86 0994
Newbiggin Cumb 86 2669
Newbiggin Dur 95 9127
Newbiggin Dur 96 1447
Newbiggin N York 88 9591
Newbiggin N York 88 0086
Newbiggin-by-the-Sea Nthumb 103 3087
Newbiggin-on-Lune Cumb 87 7005
Newbigging Angus 126 2841
Newbigging Angus 127 4237
Newbigging Angus 127 4936
Newbigging Angus 127 4936
Newbigging S Lans 117 0145
Newbold Derbys 74 3672
Newbold Leics 62 4019
Newbold on Avon Warwks 50 4877
Newbold on Stour Warwks 48 2446
Newbold Pacey Warwks 48 2957
Newbold Revel Warwks 50 4580
Newbold Verdon Leics 62 4403
Newborough Cambs 64 2005
Newborough IOA 68 4265
Newborough Staffs 73 1325
Newbottle Nhants 49 5236
Newbottle T & W 96 3351
Newbourne Suffk 55 2743
Newbridge C Edin 117 1272
Newbridge Caerph 33 2097
Newbridge Cerdgn 44 5059
Newbridge Cnwll 2 4231
Newbridge Cnwll 3 7944
Newbridge D & G 100 9479
Newbridge Hants 12 2915
Newbridge IOW 13 4187
Newbridge Oxon 36 4001
Newbridge Pembks 30 9431
Newbridge Wrexhm 70 2841
Newbridge Green Worcs 47 8439
Newbridge on Wye Powys 45 0158
Newbridge-on-Usk Mons 34 3894
Newbrough Nthumb 102 8767
Newbuildings Devon 8 7903
Newburgh Abers 143 9659
Newburgh Abers 143 9925
Newburgh Fife 126 2318
Newburgh Lancs 78 4810
Newburgh Priory N York 90 5476
Newburn T & W 103 1665
Newbury Berks 24 4766
Newbury Somset 22 6949
Newbury Wilts 22 8241
Newby Cumb 94 5921
Newby Lancs 81 8146
Newby N York 90 5012
Newby N York 88 7269
Newby N York 91 0190
Newby Bridge Cumb 87 3686
Newby Cross Cumb 93 3653
Newby East Cumb 93 4758
Newby Head Cumb 94 5821
Newby West Cumb 93 3753
Newby Wiske N York 89 3687
Newcastle Mons 34 4417
Newcastle Shrops 58 2582
Newcastle Emlyn Carmth 31 3040
Newcastle upon Tyne T & W 103 2464
Newcastle-under-Lyme Staffs 72 8445
Newcastleton Border 101 4887
Newchapel Pembks 31 2239
Newchapel Staffs 72 8654
Newchapel Surrey 15 3641
Newchurch Blae G 33 1710
Newchurch Herefd 46 3550
Newchurch IOW 13 5685
Newchurch Kent 17 0531
Newchurch Mons 34 4597
Newchurch Powys 45 2150
Newchurch Staffs 73 1423
Newchurch in Pendle Lancs 81 8239
Newcraighall C Edin 118 3272
Newdigate Surrey 15 1942
Newell Green Berks 25 8770
Newenden Kent 17 8327
Newent Gloucs 47 7225
Newfield Dur 96 2033
Newfield Dur 96 2452
Newfield Highld 147 7877
Newfound Hants 24 5851
Newgale Pembks 30 8522
Newgate Norfk 66 0443
Newgate Street Herts 39 3005
Newhall Ches 71 6145
Newhall Derbys 73 2820
Newham Nthumb 111 1728
Newhaven Derbys 74 1660
Newhaven E Susx 16 4401
Newhey Gt Man 82 9411
Newholm N York 90 8610
Newhouse N Lans 116 7961
Newick E Susx 15 4121
Newingreen Kent 29 1236
Newington Kent 28 8564
Newington Kent 29 1837
Newington Oxon 37 6096
Newington Shrops 59 4283
Newington Bagpath Gloucs 35 8194
Newland Cumb 86 3079
Newland E R Yk 84 8029
Newland E R Yk 84 0631
Newland Gloucs 34 5509
Newland N York 83 6824
Newland Oxon 36 3609
Newland Somset 19 8238
Newland Worcs 47 7948
Newlandrig Mdloth 118 3762
Newlands Border 101 5094
Newlands Cumb 93 3439
Newlands Nthumb 95 0855
Newlands of Dundurcas Moray 141 2951
Newlyn Cnwll 2 4628
Newlyn East Cnwll 3 8256
Newmachar Abers 143 8919
Newmains N Lans 116 8256
Newman's End Essex 39 5112
Newman's Green Suffk 54 8843
Newmarket Suffk 53 6463
Newmarket W Isls 152 4235
Newmill Border 109 4510
Newmill Moray 142 4352
Newmill of Inshewan Angus 134 4260
Newmillerdam W York 83 3215
Newmills C Edin 117 1667
Newmills Fife 117 0186
Newmills Mons 34 5107
Newmiln P & K 126 1230
Newmilns E Ayrs 107 5337
Newnes Shrops 59 3834
Newney Green Essex 40 6507
Newnham Gloucs 35 6911
Newnham Hants 24 7053
Newnham Herts 39 2437
Newnham Kent 28 9557
Newnham Nhants 49 5859
Newnham Worcs 47 6469
Newnham Paddox Warwks 50 4983
Newport Cnwll 5 3285
Newport Devon 19 5632
Newport Dorset 11 8895
Newport E R Yk 84 8530
Newport Essex 39 5234
Newport Gloucs 35 7097
Newport Highld 151 1324
Newport IOW 13 5089
Newport Newpt 34 3188
Newport Norfk 67 5017
Newport Pembks 30 0539
Newport Shrops 72 7419
Newport Pagnell Bucks 38 8743
Newport-on-Tay Fife 127 4228
Newpound Common W Susx 14 0627
Newquay Cnwll 4 8161
Newsam Green W York 83 3630
Newsbank Ches 72 8366
Newseat Abers 142 7032
Newsham Lancs 80 5136
Newsham N York 89 1010
Newsham N York 89 3784
Newsham Nthumb 103 3080
Newsholme E R Yk 84 7129
Newsholme Lancs 81 8451
Newstead Border 109 5634
Newstead Notts 75 5152
Newstead Nthumb 111 1527
Newtack Moray 142 4446
Newthorpe N York 83 4632
Newtimber W Susx 15 2613
Newtoft Lincs 76 0486
Newton Ag & B 114 0498
Newton Beds 39 2344
Newton Border 110 6020
Newton Brdgnd 33 8377
Newton Cambs 65 4314
Newton Cambs 53 4349
Newton Cardif 34 2378
Newton Ches 71 4167
Newton Ches 71 5059
Newton Ches 71 5375
Newton Cumb 86 2271
Newton Derbys 75 4459
Newton Herefd 46 3432
Newton Herefd 46 3769
Newton Herefd 46 5153
Newton Highld 139 5850
Newton Highld 140 7448
Newton Highld 140 7866
Newton Lancs 80 3436
Newton Lancs 87 5974
Newton Lancs 81 6950
Newton Lincs 64 0436
Newton Mdloth 118 3169
Newton Moray 141 1663
Newton Moray 141 3362
Newton N York 90 8872
Newton Nhants 51 8883
Newton Norfk 66 8315
Newton Notts 63 6841
Newton Nthumb 110 9406
Newton Nthumb 103 0364
Newton S Lans 116 6760
Newton S Lans 108 9331
Newton Shrops 59 4234
Newton Somset 20 1038
Newton Staffs 73 0325
Newton Suffk 54 9240
Newton W Loth 117 0977
Newton W Mids 61 0393
Newton W York 83 4527
Newton Warwks 50 5378
Newton Wilts 23 2322
Newton Abbot Devon 7 8571
Newton Arlosh Cumb 93 2055
Newton Aycliffe Dur 96 2724
Newton Bewley Dur 97 4626
Newton Blossomville Bucks 38 9251
Newton Bromswold Beds 51 9966
Newton Burgoland Leics 62 3708
Newton by Toft Lincs 76 0487
Newton Ferrers Cnwll 5 3466
Newton Ferrers Devon 6 5548
Newton Ferry W Isls 152 8978
Newton Flotman Norfk 67 2198
Newton Green Mons 34 5191
Newton Harcourt Leics 50 6497
Newton Heath Gt Man 79 8700
Newton Hill W York 83 3222
Newton Kyme N York 83 4644
Newton Longville Bucks 38 8431
Newton Mearns E Rens 115 5355
Newton Morrell N York 89 2309
Newton Mountain Pembks 30 9808
Newton Mulgrave N York 97 7815
Newton of Balcanquhal P & K 126 1610
Newton on Ouse N York 90 5159
Newton on the Hill Shrops 59 4823
Newton on Trent Lincs 76 8373
Newton Poppleford Devon 9 0889
Newton Purcell Oxon 49 6230
Newton Regis Warwks 61 2707
Newton Reigny Cumb 93 4731
Newton Row Highld 151 3449
Newton Solney Derbys 73 2825
Newton St Cyres Devon 9 8898
Newton St Faith Norfk 67 2217
Newton St Loe Somset 22 7064
Newton St Petrock Devon 18 4112
Newton Stacey Hants 24 4140
Newton Stewart D & G 99 4065
Newton Toney Wilts 23 2140
Newton Tracey Devon 19 5226
Newton under Roseberry N York 90 5713
Newton Underwood Nthumb 103 1486
Newton upon Derwent E R Yk 84 7149
Newton Valence Hants 24 7232
Newton Wamphray D & G 100 1195
Newton with Scales Lancs 80 4530
Newton-by-the-Sea Nthumb 111 2325
Newton-le-Willows Mersyd 78 5995
Newton-le-Willows N York 89 2189
Newton-on-Rawcliffe N York 90 8090
Newton-on-the-Moor Nthumb 111 1705
Newtongarry Croft Abers 142 5735
Newtongrange Mdloth 118 3364
Newtonhill Abers 135 9193
Newtonloan Mdloth 118 3362
Newtonmill Angus 134 6064
Newtonmore Highld 132 7098
Newtown Blae G 33 1709
Newtown Ches 71 6247
Newtown Ches 72 9060
Newtown Ches 71 5278
Newtown Cnwll 2 5729
Newtown Cnwll 3 7423
Newtown Cnwll 3 1052
Newtown Cnwll 5 2978
Newtown Cumb 92 1048
Newtown Cumb 101 5062
Newtown Cumb 94 5224
Newtown Cumb 101 3862
Newtown D & G 107 7710
Newtown Derbys 79 9984
Newtown Devon 9 0699
Newtown Devon 19 7625
Newtown Dorset 10 4802
Newtown Dorset 12 0393
Newtown Gloucs 35 6702
Newtown Gt Man 78 5604
Newtown Hants 12 2710
Newtown Hants 24 4763
Newtown Hants 13 6013
Newtown Herefd 46 4757
Newtown Herefd 46 5333
Newtown Herefd 46 6145
Newtown Herefd 47 7037
Newtown Highld 131 3504
Newtown IOW 13 4290
Newtown Lancs 80 5118
Newtown Nthumb 111 9631
Newtown Nthumb 103 0300
Newtown Nthumb 103 0425
Newtown Powys 58 1091
Newtown Rhondd 33 0598
Newtown Shrops 59 4222
Newtown Shrops 59 4731
Newtown Staffs 60 9904
Newtown Wilts 22 9129
Newtown Wilts 23 2963
Newtown Worcs 47 8755
Newtown Worcs 60 9478
Newtown Linford Leics 62 5209
Newtown of Beltrees Rens 115 3758
Newtown St Boswells Border 110 5732
Newtown Unthank Leics 62 4904
Newtyle Angus 126 2941
Newyears Green Gt Lon 26 0788
Newyork Ag & B 122 9611
Nextend Herefd 46 3357
Neyland Pembks 30 9605
Niarbyl IOM 158 2177
Nibley Gloucs 35 6606
Nibley Gloucs 35 6982
Nibley Green Gloucs 35 7396
Nicholashayne Devon 9 1016
Nicholaston Swans 32 5288
Nickies Hill Cumb 101 5367
Nidd N York 89 3060
Nigg Aber C 135 9402
Nigg Highld 147 8071

Nightcott Old Harlow


Nightcott *Somset* 19 8925
Nimlet *Somset* 35 7470
Nine Elms *Wilts* 36 1085
Nine Wells *Pembks* 30 7924
Ninebanks *Nthumb* 94 7853
Nineveh *Worcs* 47 6265
Ninfield *E Susx* 16 7012
Ningwood *IOW* 13 3989
Nisbet *Border* 110 6725
Nisbet Hill *Border* 119 7950
Niton *IOW* 13 5076
Nitshill *C Glas* 115 5260
No Man's Heath *Ches* 71 5148
No Man's Heath *Warwks* 61 2808
No Man's Land *Cnwll* 4 9470
No Man's Land *Cnwll* 5 2756
Noah's Ark *Kent* 27 5557
Noak Bridge *Essex* 40 6990
Noak Hill *Essex* 27 5494
Noblethorpe *W York* 82 2805
Nobold *Shrops* 59 4710
Nobottle *Nhants* 49 6763
Nocton *Lincs* 76 0564
Nogdam End *Norfk* 67 3900
Noke *Oxon* 37 5413
Nolton *Pembks* 30 8618
Nolton Haven *Pembks* 30 8618
Nomansland *Devon* 19 8313
Nomansland *Wilts* 12 2517
Noneley *Shrops* 59 4828
Nonington *Kent* 29 2552
Nook *Cumb* 101 4679
Nook *Cumb* 87 5481
Norbiton *Gt Lon* 26 1969
Norbreck *Lancs* 80 3140
Norbridge *Herefd* 47 7144
Norbury *Ches* 71 5547
Norbury *Derbys* 73 1241
Norbury *Gt Lon* 27 3069
Norbury *Shrops* 59 3692
Norbury *Staffs* 72 7823
Norbury Common *Ches* 71 5548
Norbury Junction *Staffs* 72 7923
Norchard *Worcs* 47 8568
Norcott Brook *Ches* 78 6080
Norcross *Lancs* 80 3341
Nordelph *Norfk* 65 5501
Norden *Gt Man* 81 8614
Nordley *Shrops* 60 6996
Norham *Nthumb* 110 9047
Norland Town *W York* 82 0622
Norley *Ches* 71 5772
Norleywood *Hants* 12 3597
Norlington *E Susx* 16 4413
Norman Cross *Cambs* 52 1690
Norman's Bay *E Susx* 16 6805
Norman's Green *Devon* 9 0503
Normanby *Lincs* 84 8816
Normanby *Lincs* 76 9988
Normanby *N York* 97 5418
Normanby *N York* 90 7381
Normanby le Wold *Lincs* 76 1295
Normandy *Surrey* 25 9351
Normanton *Derbys* 62 3433
Normanton *Leics* 63 8140
Normanton *Lincs* 63 9446
Normanton *Notts* 75 7054
Normanton *Rutlnd* 63 9305
Normanton *W York* 83 3822
Normanton *Wilts* 23 1340
Normanton le Heath *Leics* 62 3712
Normanton on Soar *Notts* 62 5122
Normanton on the Wolds *Notts* 62 6232
Normanton on Trent *Notts* 75 7868
Normoss *Lancs* 80 3437
Norney *Surrey* 25 9444
Norrington Common *Wilts* 22 8864
Norris Green *Cnwll* 5 4169
Norristhorpe *W York* 82 2123
North Anston *S York* 75 5184
North Aston *Oxon* 49 4828
North Baddesley *Hants* 13 3920
North Ballachulish *Highld* 130 0560
North Barrow *Somset* 21 6129
North Barsham *Norfk* 66 9135
North Benfleet *Essex* 40 7588
North Bersted *W Susx* 14 9201
North Berwick *E Loth* 118 5485
North Bitchburn *Dur* 96 1732
North Blyth *Nthumb* 103 3082
North Boarhunt *Hants* 13 6010
North Bockhampton *Hants* 12 1797
North Bovey *Devon* 8 7484
North Bradley *Wilts* 22 8555
North Brentor *Devon* 5 4881
North Brewham *Somset* 22 7236
North Bridge *Surrey* 14 9636
North Brook End *Cambs* 39 2944
North Buckland *Devon* 18 4840
North Burlingham *Norfk* 67 3609
North Cadbury *Somset* 21 6327
North Carlton *Lincs* 76 9477
North Carlton *Notts* 75 5984
North Cave *E R Yk* 84 8932
North Cerney *Gloucs* 35 0107
North Charford *Hants* 12 1919
North Charlton *Nthumb* 111 1622
North Cheam *Gt Lon* 26 2365
North Cheriton *Somset* 22 6925
North Chideock *Dorset* 10 4294
North Cliffe *E R Yk* 84 8736
North Clifton *Notts* 75 8272
North Close *Dur* 96 2532
North Cockerington *Lincs* 77 3790
North Common *E Susx* 15 3921
North Connel *Ag & B* 122 9034
North Cornelly *Brdgnd* 33 8181
North Corner *Cnwll* 3 7818
North Corry *Highld* 122 8353
North Cotes *Lincs* 77 3400
North Country *Cnwll* 2 6943
North Cove *Suffk* 55 4689
North Cowton *N York* 89 2803
North Crawley *Bucks* 38 9244
North Cray *Gt Lon* 27 4872
North Creake *Norfk* 66 8538
North Curry *Somset* 21 3125
North Dalton *E R Yk* 84 9351
North Deighton *N York* 83 3951
North Duffield *N York* 83 6837
North Duntulm *Highld* 136 4274
North Elham *Kent* 29 1844
North Elkington *Lincs* 77 2890
North Elmham *Norfk* 66 9820
North Elmsall *W York* 83 4712
North End *Cumb* 93 3259
North End *Dorset* 22 8427
North End *E R Yk* 85 1941
North End *E R Yk* 85 2831
North End *Essex* 40 6618
North End *Hants* 12 1016
North End *Hants* 24 5828
North End *Hants* 13 6502
North End *Leics* 62 5715
North End *Lincs* 85 1022
North End *Lincs* 85 3101
North End *Lincs* 76 0499
North End *Lincs* 64 2341
North End *Lincs* 77 4289
North End *Mersyd* 78 3004
North End *Nhants* 51 9668
North End *Norfk* 66 9992
North End *Nthumb* 103 1301
North End *Somset* 21 4266
North End *W Susx* 14 9703
North End *W Susx* 14 1109
North Erradale *Highld* 144 7480
North Evington *Leics* 62 6204
North Fambridge *Essex* 40 8597
North Ferriby *E R Yk* 84 9826
North Frodingham *E R Yk* 85 1053
North Gorley *Hants* 12 1611
North Green *Norfk* 55 2288
North Green *Suffk* 55 3162
North Green *Suffk* 55 3966
North Grimston *N York* 90 8467
North Halling *Kent* 28 7065
North Hayling *Hants* 13 7303
North Hazelrigg *Nthumb* 111 0533
North Heasley *Devon* 19 7333
North Heath *W Susx* 14 0621
North Hele *Somset* 20 0323
North Hill *Cnwll* 5 2776
North Hillingdon *Gt Lon* 26 0784
North Hinksey *Oxon* 37 4905
North Huish *Devon* 7 7156
North Hykeham *Lincs* 76 9465
North Kelsey *Lincs* 84 0401
North Kessock *Highld* 140 6548
North Killingholme *Lincs* 85 1417
North Kilvington *N York* 89 4285
North Kilworth *Leics* 50 6183
North Kingston *Hants* 12 1603
North Kyme *Lincs* 76 1552
North Landing *E R Yk* 91 2471
North Lee *Bucks* 38 8308
North Lees *N York* 89 2973
North Leigh *Kent* 29 1347
North Leigh *Oxon* 36 3813
North Leverton with Habblesthorpe *Notts* 75 7882
North Littleton *Worcs* 48 0847
North Lopham *Norfk* 54 0382
North Luffenham *Rutlnd* 63 9303
North Marden *W Susx* 14 8016
North Marston *Bucks* 37 7722
North Middleton *Mdloth* 118 3559
North Middleton *Nthumb* 111 9924
North Milmain *D & G* 98 0852
North Molton *Devon* 19 7329
North Moreton *Oxon* 37 5689
North Mundham *W Susx* 14 8702
North Muskham *Notts* 75 7958
North Newbald *E R Yk* 84 9136
North Newington *Oxon* 49 4240
North Newnton *Wilts* 23 1257
North Newton *Somset* 20 3031
North Nibley *Gloucs* 35 7495
North Oakley *Hants* 24 5354
North Ockendon *Gt Lon* 27 5985
North Ormesby *N York* 97 5119
North Ormsby *Lincs* 77 2893
North Otterington *N York* 89 3689
North Owersby *Lincs* 76 0594
North Perrott *Somset* 10 4709
North Petherton *Somset* 20 2833
North Petherwin *Cnwll* 5 2789
North Pickenham *Norfk* 66 8606
North Piddle *Worcs* 47 9654
North Pool *Devon* 7 7741
North Poorton *Dorset* 10 5298
North Poulner *Hants* 12 1606
North Quarme *Somset* 20 9236
North Queensferry *C Edin* 117 1380
North Radworthy *Devon* 19 7534
North Rauceby *Lincs* 76 0246
North Reston *Lincs* 77 3883
North Rigton *N York* 82 2749
North Ripley *Hants* 12 1699
North Rode *Ches* 72 8866
North Row *Cumb* 93 2232
North Runcton *Norfk* 65 6416
North Scale *Cumb* 86 1869
North Scarle *Lincs* 76 8466
North Seaton *Nthumb* 103 2986
North Seaton Colliery *Nthumb* 103 2986
North Shian *Ag & B* 122 9143
North Shields *T & W* 103 3568
North Shoebury *Essex* 40 9286
North Shore *Lancs* 80 3037
North Side *Cambs* 64 2799
North Side *Cumb* 92 9929
North Skelton *N York* 97 6718
North Somercotes *Lincs* 77 4296
North Stainley *N York* 89 2876
North Stainmore *Cumb* 95 8314
North Stifford *Essex* 40 6080
North Stoke *Oxon* 37 6186
North Stoke *Somset* 35 7069
North Stoke *W Susx* 14 0110
North Street *Berks* 24 6371
North Street *Cambs* 53 5868
North Street *Hants* 12 1518
North Street *Hants* 24 6433
North Street *Kent* 28 8174
North Street *Kent* 28 0157
North Sunderland *Nthumb* 111 2131
North Tamerton *Cnwll* 5 3197
North Tawton *Devon* 8 6601
North Third *Stirlg* 116 7589
North Thoresby *Lincs* 77 2998
North Tidworth *Wilts* 23 2349
North Town *Berks* 26 8882
North Town *Devon* 19 5109
North Town *Somset* 21 5642
North Tuddenham *Norfk* 66 0314
North Walbottle *T & W* 103 1767
North Walsham *Norfk* 67 2830
North Waltham *Hants* 24 5646
North Warnborough *Hants* 24 7351
North Weald Basset *Essex* 39 4904
North Wheatley *Notts* 75 7585
North Whilborough *Devon* 7 8766
North Wick *Somset* 21 5865
North Widcombe *Somset* 21 5758
North Willingham *Lincs* 76 1688
North Wingfield *Derbys* 74 4065
North Witham *Lincs* 63 9221
North Wootton *Dorset* 11 6514
North Wootton *Norfk* 65 6424
North Wootton *Somset* 21 5641
North Wraxall *Wilts* 35 8175
North Wroughton *Wilts* 36 1481
Northacre *Norfk* 66 9598
Northall *Bucks* 38 9520
Northall Green *Norfk* 66 9914
Northallerton *N York* 89 3694
Northam *Devon* 18 4529
Northam *Hants* 13 4312
Northampton *Nhants* 49 7560
Northampton *Worcs* 47 8365
Northaw *Herts* 27 2702
Northay *Somset* 10 2811
Northborough *Cambs* 64 1507
Northbourne *Kent* 29 3352
Northbridge Street *E Susx* 17 7324
Northbrook *Hants* 24 5139
Northbrook *Oxon* 37 4922
Northchapel *W Susx* 14 9529
Northchurch *Herts* 38 9708
Northcott *Devon* 9 0912
Northcott *Devon* 9 1209
Northcott *Devon* 5 3392
Northcourt *Oxon* 37 4998
Northdown *Kent* 29 3770
Northedge *Derbys* 74 3665
Northend *Bucks* 37 7392
Northend *Warwks* 48 3952
Northend Woods *Bucks* 26 9089
Northenden *Gt Man* 79 8289
Northfield *Aber C* 135 9008
Northfield *E R Yk* 84 0326
Northfield *W Mids* 60 0279
Northfields *Lincs* 64 0208
Northfleet *Kent* 27 6374
Northiam *E Susx* 17 8324
Northill *Beds* 52 1446
Northington *Gloucs* 35 7008
Northington *Hants* 24 5637
Northlands *Lincs* 77 3453
Northleach *Gloucs* 36 1114
Northleigh *Devon* 19 6034
Northleigh *Devon* 9 1995
Northlew *Devon* 19 5099
Northload Bridge *Somset* 21 4939
Northmoor *Oxon* 36 4202
Northmoor *Somset* 20 9028
Northmuir *Angus* 126 3854
Northney *Hants* 13 7303
Northolt *Gt Lon* 26 1384
Northop *Flints* 70 2468
Northop Hall *Flints* 70 2667
Northorpe *Lincs* 76 8997
Northorpe *Lincs* 64 0917
Northorpe *Lincs* 64 2036
Northorpe *W York* 82 2221
Northover *Somset* 21 4838
Northover *Somset* 21 5223
Northowram *W York* 82 1126
Northport *Dorset* 11 9288
Northrepps *Norfk* 67 2439
Northton *W Isls* 152 9989
Northway *Somset* 20 1329
Northway *Swans* 32 5889
Northwich *Ches* 79 6673
Northwick *Gloucs* 34 5686
Northwick *Somset* 21 3548
Northwick *Worcs* 47 8458
Northwold *Norfk* 65 7597
Northwood *Derbys* 74 2664
Northwood *Gt Lon* 26 0990
Northwood *IOW* 13 4992
Northwood *Shrops* 59 4633
Northwood *Staffs* 72 8949
Northwood Green *Gloucs* 35 7216
Norton *Ches* 78 5581
Norton *Cnwll* 4 0869
Norton *Dur* 96 4421
Norton *E Susx* 16 4701
Norton *Gloucs* 47 8524
Norton *Herts* 39 2334
Norton *IOW* 12 3488
Norton *Mons* 34 4420
Norton *N York* 90 7971
Norton *Nhants* 49 5963
Norton *Notts* 75 5771
Norton *Powys* 46 3067
Norton *S York* 83 5415
Norton *S York* 74 3681
Norton *Shrops* 59 5609
Norton *Shrops* 60 7200
Norton *Shrops* 59 4681
Norton *Shrops* 59 6382
Norton *Somset* 21 3463
Norton *Suffk* 54 9565
Norton *Swans* 32 6188
Norton *W Susx* 14 9206
Norton *Wilts* 35 8884
Norton *Worcs* 47 8751
Norton *Worcs* 48 0447
Norton Bavant *Wilts* 22 9043
Norton Bridge *Staffs* 72 8630
Norton Canes *Staffs* 60 0107
Norton Canon *Herefd* 46 3847
Norton Corner *Norfk* 66 0928
Norton Disney *Lincs* 76 8859
Norton Ferris *Wilts* 22 7936
Norton Fitzwarren *Somset* 20 1925
Norton Green *IOW* 12 3488
Norton Green *Staffs* 60 0107
Norton Hawkfield *Somset* 21 5964
Norton Heath *Essex* 40 6004
Norton in Hales *Shrops* 72 7038
Norton in the Moors *Staffs* 72 8951
Norton Lindsey *Warwks* 48 2263
Norton Little Green *Suffk* 54 9766
Norton Malreward *Somset* 21 6064
Norton Mandeville *Essex* 40 5804
Norton St Philip *Somset* 22 7755
Norton sub Hamdon *Somset* 10 4615
Norton Subcourse *Norfk* 67 4198
Norton Wood *Herefd* 46 3648
Norton-Juxta-Twycross *Leics* 61 3207
Norton-le-Clay *N York* 89 4071
Norwell *Notts* 75 7761
Norwell Woodhouse *Notts* 75 7362
Norwich *Norfk* 67 2308
Norwick *Shet* 153 6414
Norwood *Clacks* 116 8793
Norwood *Kent* 17 0530
Norwood *S York* 75 4681
Norwood End *Essex* 40 5608
Norwood Green *Gt Lon* 26 1378
Norwood Green *W York* 82 1326
Norwood Hill *Surrey* 15 2343
Norwoodside *Cambs* 65 4197
Noseley *Leics* 50 7398
Noss Mayo *Devon* 6 5547
Nosterfield *N York* 89 2780
Nosterfield End *Cambs* 53 6344
Nostie *Highld* 138 8527
Notgrove *Gloucs* 36 1020
Nottage *Brdgnd* 33 8177
Notter *Cnwll* 5 3960
Nottingham *Notts* 62 5739
Nottington *Dorset* 11 6682
Notton *W York* 83 3413
Notton *Wilts* 35 9169
Nottswood Hill *Gloucs* 35 7018
Nounsley *Essex* 40 7910
Noutard's Green *Worcs* 47 8066
Nowton *Suffk* 54 8660
Nox *Shrops* 59 4110
Nuffield *Oxon* 37 6687
Nun Monkton *N York* 90 5057
Nunburnholme *E R Yk* 84 8447
Nuncargate *Notts* 75 5054
Nunclose *Cumb* 94 4945
Nuneaton *Warwks* 61 3691
Nuneham Courtenay *Oxon* 37 5599
Nunhead *Gt Lon* 27 3475
Nunkeeling *E R Yk* 85 1449
Nunney *Somset* 22 7345
Nunney Catch *Somset* 22 7344
Nunnington *Herefd* 46 5543
Nunnington *N York* 90 6679
Nunnykirk *Nthumb* 103 0793
Nunsthorpe *Lincs* 85 2607
Nunthorpe *N York* 83 6050
Nunthorpe *N York* 97 5314
Nunthorpe Village *N York* 90 5413
Nunton *Wilts* 23 1526
Nunwick *N York* 89 3274
Nunwick *Nthumb* 102 8774
Nup End *Bucks* 38 8619
Nupdown *Gloucs* 35 6395
Nupend *Gloucs* 35 7806
Nuptow *Berks* 25 8873
Nursling *Hants* 12 3716
Nursted *Hants* 13 7521
Nursteed *Wilts* 23 0260
Nurton *Staffs* 60 8399
Nutbourne *W Susx* 14 7705
Nutbourne *W Susx* 14 0718
Nutfield *Surrey* 27 3050
Nuthall *Notts* 62 5243
Nuthampstead *Herts* 39 4034
Nuthurst *W Susx* 15 1925
Nutley *E Susx* 16 4427
Nutley *Hants* 24 6044
Nuttal Lane *Gt Man* 81 7915
Nutwell *S York* 83 6304
Nybster *Highld* 151 3663
Nyetimber *W Susx* 14 8998
Nyewood *W Susx* 14 8021
Nymet Rowland *Devon* 19 7108
Nymet Tracey *Devon* 8 7200
Nympsfield *Gloucs* 35 8000
Nynehead *Somset* 20 1422
Nythe *Somset* 21 4234
Nyton *W Susx* 14 9305


# O


Oad Street *Kent* 28 8762
Oadby *Leics* 50 6200
Oak Cross *Devon* 8 5399
Oak Tree *Dur* 89 3613
Oakall Green *Worcs* 47 8161
Oakamoor *Staffs* 73 0444
Oakbank *W Loth* 117 0766
Oakdale *Caerph* 33 1898
Oake *Somset* 20 1525
Oaken *Staffs* 60 8602
Oakenclough *Lancs* 80 5447
Oakengates *Shrops* 60 7010
Oakenholt *Flints* 70 2571
Oakenshaw *Dur* 96 1937
Oakenshaw *W York* 82 1727
Oaker Side *Derbys* 74 2760
Oakerthorpe *Derbys* 74 3854
Oakford *Cerdgn* 42 4558
Oakford *Devon* 20 9121
Oakfordbridge *Devon* 20 9122
Oakgrove *Ches* 79 9169
Oakham *Rutlnd* 63 8608
Oakhanger *Ches* 72 7754
Oakhanger *Hants* 14 7635
Oakhill *Somset* 21 6347
Oakhurst *Kent* 27 5550
Oakington *Cambs* 52 4164
Oaklands *Powys* 45 0450
Oakle Street *Gloucs* 35 7517
Oakley *Beds* 51 0153
Oakley *Bucks* 37 6412
Oakley *Dorset* 11 0198
Oakley *Fife* 117 0289
Oakley *Hants* 24 5650
Oakley *Oxon* 37 7500
Oakley *Suffk* 54 1677
Oakley Green *Berks* 26 9276
Oakley Park *Powys* 58 9886
Oakridge *Gloucs* 35 9103
Oaks *Dur* 96 1525
Oaks *Lancs* 81 6733
Oaks *Shrops* 59 4204
Oaks Green *Derbys* 73 1533
Oaksey *Wilts* 35 9993
Oakshaw *Cumb* 101 5176
Oakshott *Hants* 13 7427
Oakthorpe *Leics* 61 3212
Oakwood *Derbys* 62 3738
Oakwood *Nthumb* 102 9465
Oakwoodhill *Surrey* 15 1337
Oakworth *W York* 82 0338
Oare *Kent* 28 0063
Oare *Somset* 19 7947
Oare *Wilts* 23 1563
Oasby *Lincs* 63 0039
Oath *Somset* 21 3827
Oathlaw *Angus* 127 4756
Oatlands Park *Surrey* 26 0865
Oban *Ag & B* 122 8629
Obley *Shrops* 46 3377
Obney *P & K* 125 0237
Oborne *Dorset* 11 6518
Obthorpe *Lincs* 64 0914
Occold *Suffk* 54 1570
Occumster *Highld* 151 2635
Ochiltree *E Ayrs* 107 5021
Ockbrook *Derbys* 62 4235
Ocker Hill *W Mids* 60 9793
Ockeridge *Worcs* 47 7762
Ockham *Surrey* 26 0756
Ockle *Highld* 129 5570
Ockley *Surrey* 15 1440
Ocle Pychard *Herefd* 46 5945
Octon *E R Yk* 91 0369
Odcombe *Somset* 10 5015
Odd Down *Somset* 22 7462
Oddingley *Worcs* 47 9159
Oddington *Gloucs* 48 2225
Oddington *Oxon* 37 5515
Odell *Beds* 51 9657
Odham *Devon* 18 4703
Odiham *Hants* 24 7451
Odsal *W York* 82 1529
Odsey *Herts* 39 2938
Odstock *Wilts* 23 1426
Odstone *Leics* 62 3907
Offchurch *Warwks* 48 3565
Offenham *Worcs* 48 0546
Offerton *T & W* 96 3455
Offham *E Susx* 15 4012
Offham *Kent* 28 6557
Offham *W Susx* 14 0208
Offleymarsh *Shrops* 72 7829
Offord Cluny *Cambs* 52 2267
Offord Darcy *Cambs* 52 2266
Offton *Suffk* 54 0649
Offwell *Devon* 9 1999
Ogbourne Maizey *Wilts* 36 1871
Ogbourne St Andrew *Wilts* 36 1872
Ogbourne St George *Wilts* 36 2074
Ogden *W York* 82 0730
Ogle *Nthumb* 103 1378
Oglet *Mersyd* 78 4481
Ogmore *V Glam* 33 8876
Ogmore Vale *Brdgnd* 33 9390
Ogmore-by-Sea *V Glam* 33 8675
Ogwen Bank *Gwynd* 69 6265
Okeford Fitzpaine *Dorset* 11 8010
Okehampton *Devon* 8 5995
Olchard *Devon* 9 8777
Old *Nhants* 50 7872
Old Aberdeen *Aber C* 135 9407
Old Alresford *Hants* 24 5834
Old Auchenbrack *D & G* 107 7597
Old Basford *Notts* 62 5543
Old Basing *Hants* 24 6652
Old Bewick *Nthumb* 111 0621
Old Bolingbroke *Lincs* 77 3565
Old Bracknell *Berks* 25 8668
Old Bramhope *W York* 82 2343
Old Brampton *Derbys* 74 3371
Old Bridge of Urr *D & G* 100 7767
Old Buckenham *Norfk* 66 0691
Old Burghclere *Hants* 24 4657
Old Byland *N York* 90 5585
Old Cassop *Dur* 96 3339
Old Castle *Brdgnd* 33 9079
Old Church Stoke *Powys* 58 2894
Old Clee *Lincs* 85 2808
Old Cleeve *Somset* 20 0441
Old Clipstone *Notts* 75 6064
Old Colwyn *Conwy* 69 8678
Old Dailly *S Ayrs* 106 2299
Old Dalby *Leics* 63 6723
Old Dam *Derbys* 74 1179
Old Deer *Abers* 143 9747
Old Ditch *Somset* 21 5049
Old Edlington *S York* 75 5397
Old Eldon *Dur* 96 2427
Old Ellerby *E R Yk* 85 1637
Old Felixstowe *Suffk* 55 3135
Old Fletton *Cambs* 64 1997
Old Forge *Herefd* 34 5518
Old Furnace *Herefd* 46 4923
Old Glossop *Derbys* 74 0494
Old Goole *E R Yk* 84 7422
Old Grimsby *IOS* 2 8915
Old Hall Green *Herts* 39 3722
Old Hall Street *Norfk* 67 3033
Old Harlow *Essex* 39 4711

Old Heath Peel


Old Heath *Essex* 41 0122
Old Hill *W Mids* 60 9586
Old Hunstanton *Norfk* 65 6842
Old Hurst *Cambs* 52 3077
Old Hutton *Cumb* 87 5688
Old Kea *Cnwll* 3 8441
Old Kilpatrick *W Duns* 115 4672
Old Knebworth *Herts* 39 2320
Old Lakenham *Norfk* 67 2205
Old Langho *Lancs* 81 7035
Old Laxey *IOM* 158 4483
Old Leake *Lincs* 77 4050
Old Malton *N York* 90 7972
Old Micklefield *W York* 83 4433
Old Milton *Hants* 12 2394
Old Milverton *Warwks* 48 2967
Old Newton *Suffk* 54 0562
Old Quarrington *Dur* 96 3237
Old Radford *Notts* 62 5540
Old Radnor *Powys* 46 2558
Old Rayne *Abers* 142 6728
Old Romney *Kent* 17 0325
Old Shoreham *W Susx* 15 2006
Old Soar *Kent* 27 6254
Old Sodbury *Gloucs* 35 7581
Old Somerby *Lincs* 63 9633
Old Stratford *Nhants* 49 7741
Old Swinford *W Mids* 60 9083
Old Tebay *Cumb* 87 6105
Old Thirsk *N York* 89 4382
Old Town *Cumb* 93 4743
Old Town *Cumb* 87 5982
Old Town *E Susx* 16 5999
Old Town *IOS* 2 9110
Old Town *Nthumb* 102 8891
Old Town *W York* 82 0028
Old Trafford *Gt Man* 79 8196
Old Tupton *Derbys* 74 3865
Old Warden *Beds* 38 1343
Old Weston *Cambs* 51 0977
Old Wick *Highld* 151 3649
Old Windsor *Berks* 25 9874
Old Wives Lees *Kent* 29 0754
Old Woking *Surrey* 26 0157
Old Wolverton *Bucks* 38 8041
Oldany *Highld* 148 0932
Oldberrow *Warwks* 48 1265
Oldburry *Kent* 27 5956
Oldbury *Shrops* 60 7192
Oldbury *W Mids* 60 9888
Oldbury *Warwks* 61 3194
Oldbury Naite *Gloucs* 35 6293
Oldbury on the Hill *Gloucs* 35 8188
Oldbury-on-Severn *Gloucs* 34 6092
Oldcastle *Mons* 46 3224
Oldcastle Heath *Ches* 71 4745
Oldcotes *Notts* 75 5888
Oldfield *W York* 82 0037
Oldfield *Worcs* 47 8464
Oldford *Somset* 22 7850
Oldhall Green *Suffk* 54 8956
Oldham *Gt Man* 79 9204
Oldhamstocks *E Loth* 119 7470
Oldland *Gloucs* 35 6771
Oldmeldrum *Abers* 143 8127
Oldmill *Cnwll* 5 3673
Oldmixon *Somset* 21 3358
Oldridge *Devon* 8 8296
Oldshore More *Highld* 148 2058
Oldstead *N York* 90 5379
Oldwall *Cumb* 101 4761
Oldwalls *Swans* 32 4891
Oldways End *Somset* 19 8724
Oldwoods *Shrops* 59 4520
Olive Green *Staffs* 73 1118
Oliver *Border* 108 0924
Oliver's Battery *Hants* 13 4527
Ollaberry *Shet* 153 3680
Ollach *Highld* 137 5137
Ollerton *Ches* 79 7776
Ollerton *Notts* 75 6567
Ollerton *Shrops* 72 6425
Olmarch *Cerdgn* 44 6255
Olmstead Green *Cambs* 53 6341
Olney *Bucks* 38 8951
Olrig House *Highld* 151 1866
Olton *W Mids* 61 1382
Olveston *Gloucs* 34 6086
Ombersley *Worcs* 47 8463
Ompton *Notts* 75 6865
Once Brewed *Nthumb* 102 7466
Onchan *IOM* 158 3978
Onecote *Staffs* 73 0455
Onehouse *Suffk* 54 0159
Onen *Mons* 34 4314
Ongar Street *Herefd* 46 3967
Onibury *Shrops* 46 4579
Onich *Highld* 130 0261
Onllwyn *Neath* 33 8410
Onneley *Staffs* 72 7542
Onslow Village *Surrey* 25 9849
Onston *Ches* 71 5873
Openwoodgate *Derbys* 62 3647
Opinan *Highld* 137 7472
Orbliston *Moray* 141 3057
Orbost *Highld* 136 2543
Orby *Lincs* 77 4967
Orchard Portman *Somset* 20 2421
Orcheston *Wilts* 23 0545
Orcop *Herefd* 46 4726
Orcop Hill *Herefd* 46 4727
Ord *Abers* 142 6258
Ordhead *Abers* 135 6610
Ordie *Abers* 134 4501
Ordiequish *Moray* 141 3357
Ordley *Nthumb* 95 9459
Ordsall *Notts* 75 7079
Ore *E Susx* 17 8311
Oreleton Common *Herefd* 46 4768
Oreton *Shrops* 59 6580
Orford *Ches* 78 6190
Orford *Suffk* 55 4250
Organford *Dorset* 11 9392
Orgreave *Staffs* 73 1415
Orlestone *Kent* 17 0034
Orleton *Herefd* 46 4967
Orleton *Worcs* 47 7067
Orlingbury *Nhants* 51 8572
Ormathwaite *Cumb* 93 2625
Ormesby *N York* 97 5317
Ormesby St Margaret *Norfk* 67 4914
Ormesby St Michael *Norfk* 67 4714
Ormiscaig *Highld* 144 8590
Ormiston *E Loth* 118 4169
Ormsaigmore *Highld* 121 4763
Ormsary *Ag & B* 113 7472
Ormskirk *Lancs* 78 4108
Ornsby Hill *Dur* 96 1648
Oronsay *Ag & B* 112 3588
Orphir *Ork* 153 3404
Orpington *Gt Lon* 27 4666
Orrell *Gt Man* 78 5303
Orrell *Mersyd* 78 3496
Orrell Post *Gt Man* 78 5305
Orrisdale *IOM* 158 3292
Orroland *D & G* 92 7746
Orsett *Essex* 40 6482
Orslow *Staffs* 72 8015
Orston *Notts* 63 7740
Orthwaite *Cumb* 93 2534
Ortner *Lancs* 80 5354
Orton *Cumb* 87 6208
Orton *Nhants* 51 8079
Orton *Staffs* 60 8795
Orton Longueville *Cambs* 64 1796
Orton Rigg *Cumb* 93 3352
Orton Waterville *Cambs* 64 1595
Orton-on-the-Hill *Leics* 61 3003
Orwell *Cambs* 52 3650
Osbaldeston *Lancs* 81 6431
Osbaldeston Green *Lancs* 81 6432
Osbaldwick *N York* 83 6251
Osbaston *Leics* 62 4204
Osbaston *Shrops* 59 3222
Osborne *IOW* 13 5194
Osbournby *Lincs* 64 0638
Oscroft *Ches* 71 5067
Ose *Highld* 136 3140
Osgathorpe *Leics* 62 4319
Osgodby *Lincs* 76 0792
Osgodby *N York* 83 6433
Osgodby *N York* 91 0584
Oskaig *Highld* 137 5438
Oskamull *Ag & B* 121 4540
Osmaston *Derbys* 73 1943
Osmington *Dorset* 11 7283
Osmington Mills *Dorset* 11 7381
Osmondthorpe *W York* 83 3333
Osmotherley *N York* 89 4596
Osney *Oxon* 37 4906
Ospringe *Kent* 28 0060
Ossett *W York* 82 2720
Ossington *Notts* 75 7564
Ostend *Essex* 40 9397
Osterley *Gt Lon* 26 1577
Oswaldkirk *N York* 90 6278
Oswaldtwistle *Lancs* 81 7327
Oswestry *Shrops* 59 2929
Otford *Kent* 27 5359
Otham *Kent* 28 7953
Otham Hole *Kent* 28 8052
Othery *Somset* 21 3831
Otley *Suffk* 55 2055
Otley *W York* 82 2045
Otley Green *Suffk* 55 2156
Otter Ferry *Ag & B* 114 9384
Otterbourne *Hants* 13 4522
Otterburn *N York* 88 8857
Otterburn *Nthumb* 102 8893
Otterham *Cnwll* 4 1690
Otterham Quay *Kent* 28 8366
Otterhampton *Somset* 20 2443
Otternish *W Isls* 152 9079
Ottershaw *Surrey* 26 0263
Otterswick *Shet* 153 5285
Otterton *Devon* 9 0684
Otterwood *Hants* 13 4102
Ottery *Devon* 6 4475
Ottery St Mary *Devon* 9 1095
Ottinge *Kent* 29 1642
Ottringham *E R Yk* 85 2624
Oughterby *Cumb* 93 2955
Oughtershaw *N York* 88 8780
Oughterside *Cumb* 92 1140
Oughtibridge *S York* 74 3093
Oughtrington *Ches* 79 6987
Oulston *N York* 90 5474
Oulton *Cumb* 93 2450
Oulton *Norfk* 66 1328
Oulton *Staffs* 72 7822
Oulton *Staffs* 72 9035
Oulton *Suffk* 67 5294
Oulton *W York* 83 3628
Oulton Broad *Suffk* 67 5192
Oulton Street *Norfk* 66 1527
Oundle *Nhants* 51 0388
Ounsdale *Staffs* 60 8693
Ousby *Cumb* 94 6134
Ousden *Suffk* 53 7459
Ousefleet *E R Yk* 84 8323
Ouston *Dur* 96 2554
Out Elmstead *Kent* 29 2050
Out Newton *E R Yk* 85 3821
Out Rawcliffe *Lancs* 80 4041
Outchester *Nthumb* 111 1433
Outgate *Cumb* 87 3599
Outhgill *Cumb* 88 7801
Outhill *Warwks* 48 1066
Outlands *Staffs* 72 7630
Outlane *W York* 82 0817
Outwell *Norfk* 65 5103
Outwick *Hants* 12 1417
Outwood *Surrey* 15 3145
Outwood *W York* 83 3323
Outwood Gate *Gt Man* 79 7805
Outwoods *Leics* 62 4018
Outwoods *Staffs* 72 7817
Outwoods *Warwks* 61 2484
Ouzlewell Green *W York* 83 3326
Ovenden *W York* 82 0827
Over *Cambs* 52 3770
Over *Ches* 71 6365
Over *Gloucs* 35 8119
Over *Gloucs* 34 5882
Over Burrows *Derbys* 73 2639
Over Compton *Dorset* 10 5816
Over End *Cambs* 51 0893
Over Green *Warwks* 61 1694
Over Haddon *Derbys* 74 2066
Over Kellet *Lancs* 87 5169
Over Kiddington *Oxon* 36 4021
Over Monnow *Mons* 34 5012
Over Norton *Oxon* 48 3128
Over Peover *Ches* 79 7873
Over Silton *N York* 89 4493
Over Stowey *Somset* 20 1838
Over Stratton *Somset* 10 4315
Over Tabley *Ches* 79 7279
Over Wallop *Hants* 23 2838
Over Whitacre *Warwks* 61 2590
Over Woodhouse *Derbys* 75 4671
Over Worton *Oxon* 49 4329
Overbury *Worcs* 47 9537
Overcombe *Dorset* 11 6982
Overgreen *Derbys* 74 3273
Overleigh *Somset* 21 4835
Overley *Staffs* 73 1515
Overpool *Ches* 71 3877
Overscaig Hotel *Highld* 149 4123
Overseal *Derbys* 73 2915
Oversland *Kent* 28 0557
Overstey Green *Warwks* 48 0957
Overstone *Nhants* 50 7966
Overstrand *Norfk* 67 2440
Overstreet *Wilts* 23 0637
Overthorpe *Nhants* 49 4840
Overton *Aber C* 143 8714
Overton *Ches* 71 5277
Overton *Hants* 24 5149
Overton *Lancs* 87 4358
Overton *N York* 83 5555
Overton *Shrops* 46 5072
Overton *Swans* 32 4685
Overton *W York* 82 2516
Overton *Wrexhm* 71 3741
Overton Bridge *Wrexhm* 71 3542
Overton Green *Ches* 72 8060
Overtown *Lancs* 87 6275
Overtown *N Lans* 116 8053
Overtown *W York* 83 3516
Overtown *Wilts* 36 1579
Overy *Oxon* 37 5893
Oving *Bucks* 37 7821
Oving *W Susx* 14 9004
Ovingdean *E Susx* 15 3503
Ovingham *Nthumb* 103 0863
Ovington *Dur* 89 1314
Ovington *Essex* 53 7642
Ovington *Hants* 24 5631
Ovington *Norfk* 66 9202
Ovington *Nthumb* 103 0663
Ower *Hants* 12 3216
Ower *Hants* 13 4702
Owermoigne *Dorset* 11 7685
Owl's Green *Suffk* 55 2869
Owlbury *Shrops* 59 3191
Owlerton *S York* 74 3389
Owlpen *Gloucs* 35 7998
Owlsmoor *Berks* 25 8462
Owlswick *Bucks* 37 7806
Owmby *Lincs* 85 0704
Owmby *Lincs* 76 0087
Owslebury *Hants* 13 5123
Owston *Leics* 63 7707
Owston *S York* 83 5511
Owston Ferry *Lincs* 75 8000
Owstwick *E R Yk* 85 2732
Owthorne *E R Yk* 85 3328
Owthorpe *Notts* 63 6733
Oxborough *Norfk* 65 7401
Oxbridge *Dorset* 10 4797
Oxcombe *Lincs* 77 3177
Oxcroft *Derbys* 75 4873
Oxen End *Essex* 40 6629
Oxen Park *Cumb* 86 3187
Oxenholme *Cumb* 87 5389
Oxenhope *W York* 82 0334
Oxenpill *Somset* 21 4441
Oxenton *Gloucs* 47 9531
Oxenwood *Wilts* 23 3058
Oxford *Oxon* 37 5106
Oxhey *Herts* 26 1295
Oxhill *Dur* 96 1852
Oxhill *Warwks* 48 3146
Oxley *W Mids* 60 9001
Oxley Green *Essex* 40 9014
Oxley's Green *E Susx* 16 6921
Oxlode *Cambs* 53 4886
Oxnam *Border* 110 6918
Oxnead *Norfk* 67 2224
Oxshott *Surrey* 26 1460
Oxshott Heath *Surrey* 26 1361
Oxspring *S York* 82 2601
Oxted *Surrey* 27 3852
Oxton *Border* 118 4953
Oxton *N York* 83 5042
Oxton *Notts* 75 6351
Oxwich *Swans* 32 4986
Oxwich Green *Swans* 32 4985
Oxwick *Norfk* 66 9125
Oykel Bridge Hotel *Highld* 145 3801
Oyne *Abers* 142 6725
Oystermouth *Swans* 32 6187
Ozleworth *Gloucs* 35 7993


# P


Pabail *W Isls* 152 5231
Packers Hill *Dorset* 11 7110
Packington *Leics* 62 3614
Packmoor *Staffs* 72 8654
Packmores *Warwks* 48 2866
Padanaram *Angus* 127 4251
Padbury *Bucks* 49 7230
Paddington *Ches* 79 6389
Paddington *Gt Lon* 27 2681
Paddlesworth *Kent* 28 6862
Paddlesworth *Kent* 29 1939
Paddock Wood *Kent* 28 6744
Paddolgreen *Shrops* 59 5032
Padeswood *Flints* 70 2762
Padfield *Derbys* 74 0296
Padgate *Ches* 79 6389
Padhams Green *Essex* 40 6497
Padiham *Lancs* 81 7933
Padside *N York* 89 1659
Padstow *Cnwll* 4 9175
Padworth *Berks* 24 6166
Page Bank *Dur* 96 2335
Pagham *W Susx* 14 8897
Paglesham *Essex* 40 9293
Paignton *Devon* 7 8860
Pailton *Warwks* 50 4781
Paine's Cross *E Susx* 16 6223
Painleyhill *Staffs* 73 0333
Painscastle *Powys* 45 1646
Painshawfield *Nthumb* 103 0560
Painsthorpe *E R Yk* 90 8158
Painswick *Gloucs* 35 8609
Painter's Forstal *Kent* 28 9958
Paisley *Rens* 115 4864
Pakefield *Suffk* 55 5390
Pakenham *Suffk* 54 9267
Pale *Gwynd* 58 9836
Pale Green *Essex* 53 6542
Palestine *Hants* 23 2640
Paley Street *Berks* 26 8776
Palfrey *W Mids* 60 0196
Palgrave *Suffk* 54 1178
Pallington *Dorset* 11 7891
Palmers Green *Gt Lon* 27 3192
Palmersbridge *Cnwll* 5 1977
Palmerston *E Ayrs* 107 5019
Palmerstown *V Glam* 20 1369
Palnackie *D & G* 92 8157
Palnure *D & G* 99 4563
Palterton *Derbys* 75 4768
Pamber End *Hants* 24 6158
Pamber Green *Hants* 24 6159
Pamber Heath *Hants* 24 6162
Pamington *Gloucs* 47 9433
Pamphill *Dorset* 11 9900
Pampisford *Cambs* 53 4948
Panborough *Somset* 21 4745
Panbride *Angus* 127 5635
Pancrasweek *Devon* 18 2905
Pancross *V Glam* 20 0469
Pandy *Caerph* 33 1587
Pandy *Gwynd* 57 6202
Pandy *Gwynd* 57 8729
Pandy *Mons* 34 3322
Pandy *Powys* 58 9004
Pandy *Wrexhm* 58 1935
Pandy Tudur *Conwy* 69 8564
Pandy'r Capel *Denbgs* 70 0850
Panfield *Essex* 40 7325
Pangbourne *Berks* 37 6376
Pangdean *W Susx* 15 2911
Panks Bridge *Herefd* 47 6248
Pannal *N York* 82 3051
Pannal Ash *N York* 82 2953
Pannanich Wells Hotel *Abers* 134 4097
Pant *Shrops* 58 2722
Pant Glas *Gwynd* 68 4747
Pant Mawr *Powys* 43 8482
Pant-ffrwyth *Brdgnd* 33 9483
Pant-Gwyn *Carmth* 44 5925
Pant-lasau *Swans* 32 6600
Pant-pastynog *Denbgs* 70 0461
Pant-y-dwr *Powys* 45 9874
Pant-y-ffridd *Powys* 58 1502
Pant-y-gog *Brdgnd* 33 9090
Pant-y-mwyn *Flints* 70 1964
Pantasaph *Flints* 70 1675
Panteg *Pembks* 30 9234
Pantersbridge *Cnwll* 4 1667
Pantglas *Powys* 43 7797
Panton *Lincs* 76 1778
Pantperthog *Gwynd* 57 7404
Pantyffynnon *Carmth* 32 6210
Pantygaseg *Torfn* 34 2599
Pantymenyn *Carmth* 31 1426
Panxworth *Norfk* 67 3513
Papcastle *Cumb* 92 1031
Papigoe *Highld* 151 3851
Papple *E Loth* 118 5972
Papplewick *Notts* 75 5451
Papworth Everard *Cambs* 52 2862
Papworth St Agnes *Cambs* 52 2664
Par *Cnwll* 3 0753
Paramour Street *Kent* 29 2961
Parbold *Lancs* 80 4911
Parbrook *Somset* 21 5736
Parbrook *W Susx* 14 0825
Parc *Gwynd* 57 8834
Parc Seymour *Newpt* 34 4091
Parcllyn *Cerdgn* 42 2451
Pardshaw *Cumb* 92 0924
Parham *Suffk* 55 3060
Park *Abers* 135 7898
Park *D & G* 100 9091
Park *Nthumb* 102 6861
Park Bottom *Cnwll* 2 6642
Park Bridge *Gt Man* 79 9402
Park Corner *Berks* 26 8582
Park Corner *E Susx* 16 5336
Park Corner *Oxon* 37 6988
Park End *Beds* 38 9952
Park End *Nthumb* 102 8675
Park End *Staffs* 72 7851
Park Gate *Hants* 13 5108
Park Gate *W York* 82 1841
Park Gate *Worcs* 60 9371
Park Green *Essex* 39 4628
Park Green *Suffk* 54 1364
Park Head *Cumb* 94 5841
Park Head *Derbys* 74 3654
Park Hill *Gloucs* 34 5799
Park Royal *Gt Lon* 26 1982
Park Street *Herts* 39 1404
Park Street *W Susx* 14 1131
Parkend *Gloucs* 34 6108
Parkers Green *Kent* 16 6148
Parkeston *Essex* 41 2332
Parkeston Quay *Essex* 41 2332
Parkfield *Cnwll* 5 3167
Parkgate *Ches* 70 2878
Parkgate *Cumb* 93 2146
Parkgate *D & G* 100 0288
Parkgate *E Susx* 17 7214
Parkgate *Essex* 40 6829
Parkgate *Kent* 27 5064
Parkgate *Kent* 17 8534
Parkgate *Surrey* 15 2043
Parkhall *W Duns* 115 4871
Parkham *Devon* 18 3921
Parkham Ash *Devon* 18 3620
Parkhill *Notts* 75 6952
Parkhill House *Abers* 143 8914
Parkhouse *Mons* 34 5003
Parkmill *Swans* 32 5489
Parkside *Dur* 96 4248
Parkside *N Lans* 116 8058
Parkside *Wrexhm* 71 3855
Parkstone *Dorset* 12 0391
Parley Green *Dorset* 12 1097
Parlington *W York* 83 4235
Parmoor *Bucks* 37 7989
Parndon *Essex* 39 4308
Parr Bridge *Gt Man* 79 7001
Parracombe *Devon* 19 6745
Parrog *Pembks* 30 0539
Parson Drove *Cambs* 64 3708
Parson's Cross *S York* 74 3492
Parson's Heath *Essex* 41 0226
Parson's Hill *Derbys* 73 2926
Parsonby *Cumb* 92 1438
Partick *C Glas* 115 5467
Partington *Gt Man* 79 7191
Partney *Lincs* 77 4068
Parton *Cumb* 93 2750
Parton *Cumb* 92 9820
Parton *D & G* 99 6970
Partridge Green *W Susx* 15 1919
Partrishow *Powys* 34 2722
Parwich *Derbys* 73 1854
Paslow Wood Common *Essex* 27 5802
Passenham *Nhants* 38 7839
Passfield *Hants* 14 8234
Passingford Bridge *Essex* 27 5097
Paston *Cambs* 64 1802
Paston *Norfk* 67 3234
Pasturefields *Staffs* 73 9924
Patchacott *Devon* 5 4798
Patcham *E Susx* 15 3008
Patchets Green *Herts* 26 1497
Patching *W Susx* 14 0806
Patchole *Devon* 19 6142
Patchway *Gloucs* 34 6082
Pateley Bridge *N York* 89 1565
Paternoster Heath *Essex* 40 9115
Pateshall *Herefd* 46 5262
Path of Condie *P & K* 125 0711
Pathe *Somset* 21 3730
Pathhead *Fife* 117 2992
Pathhead *Mdloth* 118 3964
Pathlow *Warwks* 48 1758
Patmore Heath *Herts* 39 4425
Patna *E Ayrs* 106 4110
Patney *Wilts* 23 0758
Patrick *IOM* 158 2482
Patrick Brompton *N York* 89 2190
Patricroft *Gt Man* 79 7597
Patrington *E R Yk* 85 3122
Patrixbourne *Kent* 29 1855
Patterdale *Cumb* 93 3915
Pattingham *Staffs* 60 8299
Pattishall *Nhants* 49 6754
Pattiswick Green *Essex* 40 8124
Patton *Shrops* 59 5895
Paul *Cnwll* 2 4627
Paul's Dene *Wilts* 23 1432
Paulerspury *Bucks* 49 7145
Paull *E R Yk* 85 1626
Paulton *Somset* 21 6556
Paunton *Herefd* 47 6650
Pauperhaugh *Nthumb* 103 1099
Pave Lane *Shrops* 72 7616
Pavenham *Beds* 51 9955
Pawlett *Somset* 20 2942
Pawston *Nthumb* 110 8532
Paxford *Gloucs* 48 1837
Paxton *Border* 119 9353
Payden Street *Kent* 28 9254
Payhembury *Devon* 9 0901
Paythorne *Lancs* 81 8251
Paytoe *Herefd* 46 4171
Peacehaven *E Susx* 15 4101
Peak Dale *Derbys* 74 0976
Peak Forest *Derbys* 74 1179
Peak Hill *Lincs* 64 2615
Peakirk *Cambs* 64 1606
Peanmeanach *Highld* 129 7180
Pearson's Green *Kent* 28 6943
Peartree Green *Herefd* 46 5932
Pease Pottage *W Susx* 15 2633
Peasedown St John *Somset* 22 7057
Peasehill *Derbys* 74 4049
Peaseland Green *Norfk* 66 0516
Peasemore *Berks* 37 4577
Peasenhall *Suffk* 55 3569
Peaslake *Surrey* 14 0844
Peasley Cross *Mersyd* 78 5294
Peasmarsh *E Susx* 17 8822
Peasmarsh *Somset* 10 3312
Peasmarsh *Surrey* 25 9946
Peat Inn *Fife* 127 4509
Peathill *Abers* 143 9366
Peatling Magna *Leics* 50 5992
Peatling Parva *Leics* 50 5889
Peaton *Shrops* 59 5385
Pebmarsh *Essex* 40 8533
Pebworth *Worcs* 48 1347
Pecket Well *W York* 82 9929
Peckforton *Ches* 71 5356
Peckham *Gt Lon* 27 3476
Peckleton *Leics* 62 4701
Pedairffordd *Powys* 58 1124
Pedlinge *Kent* 17 1335
Pedmore *W Mids* 60 9182
Pedwell *Somset* 21 4236
Peebles *Border* 109 2540
Peel *IOM* 158 2483
Peel *Lancs* 80 3531

Peel Common Polglass


Peel Common Hants 13 5703
Peene Kent 29 1837
Peening Quarter Kent 17 8828
Peggs Green Leics 62 4117
Pegsdon Beds 38 1130
Pegswood Nthumb 103 2287
Pegwell Kent 29 3664
Peinchorran Highld 137 5233
Peinlich Highld 136 4158
Pelcomb Pembks 30 9218
Pelcomb Bridge Pembks 30 9317
Pelcomb Cross Pembks 30 9218
Peldon Essex 41 9816
Pell Green E Susx 16 6432
Pelsall W Mids 60 0203
Pelsall Wood W Mids 60 0204
Pelton Dur 96 2553
Pelton Fell Dur 96 2551
Pelutho Cumb 92 1249
Pelynt Cnwll 5 2055
Pemberton Carmth 32 5300
Pemberton Gt Man 78 5503
Pembles Cross Kent 28 8947
Pembrey Carmth 31 4301
Pembridge Herefd 46 3958
Pembroke Pembks 30 9801
Pembroke Dock Pembks 30 9603
Pembury Kent 16 6240
Pen Rhiwfawr Neath 32 7410
Pen-bont Rhydybeddau Cerdgn 43 6783
Pen-ffordd Pembks 31 0722
Pen-groes-oped Mons 34 3106
Pen-llyn IOA 68 3582
Pen-lon IOA 68 4365
Pen-rhiw Pembks 31 2440
Pen-twyn Caerph 33 2000
Pen-twyn Mons 34 5209
Pen-twyn Torfn 34 2603
Pen-y-bont Powys 58 2123
Pen-y-bont-fawr Powys 58 0824
Pen-y-bryn Neath 33 8384
Pen-y-bryn Pembks 31 1742
Pen-y-cae Powys 33 8413
Pen-y-cae-mawr Mons 34 4195
Pen-y-cefn Flints 70 1175
Pen-y-clawdd Mons 34 4507
Pen-y-coedcae Rhondd 33 0587
Pen-y-cwn Pembks 30 8523
Pen-y-darren Myr Td 33 0506
Pen-y-fai Brdgnd 33 8981
Pen-y-felin Flints 70 1569
Pen-y-garn Cerdgn 43 6285
Pen-y-Garnedd Powys 58 1023
Pen-y-genffordd Powys 45 1729
Pen-y-graig Gwynd 56 2033
Pen-y-Gwryd Gwynd 69 6655
Pen-y-lan V Glam 33 9976
Pen-y-pass Gwynd 69 6455
Pen-y-stryt Denbgs 70 1952
Pen-yr-Heol Mons 34 4311
Pen-yr-Heolgerrig Myr Td 33 0306
Penair Cnwll 3 8445
Penallt Mons 34 5210
Penally Pembks 31 1199
Penalt Herefd 46 5629
Penare Cnwll 3 9940
Penarth V Glam 33 1871
Penblewin Pembks 31 1216
Penbryn Cerdgn 42 2951
Pencader Carmth 31 4436
Pencaenewydd Gwynd 56 4040
Pencaitland E Loth 118 4468
Pencalenick Cnwll 3 8545
Pencarnisiog IOA 68 3573
Pencarreg Carmth 44 5445
Pencarrow Cnwll 4 1082
Pencelli Powys 45 0925
Penclawdd Swans 32 5495
Pencoed Brdgnd 33 9581
Pencombe Herefd 46 5952
Pencoyd Herefd 46 5126
Pencraig Herefd 34 5620
Pencraig Powys 58 0426
Pendeen Cnwll 2 3834
Penderyn Rhondd 33 9408
Pendine Carmth 31 2208
Pendlebury Gt Man 79 7802
Pendleton Lancs 81 7539
Pendock Worcs 47 7832
Pendoggett Cnwll 4 0279
Pendomer Somset 10 5210
Pendoylan V Glam 33 0576
Pendre Brdgnd 33 9181
Penegoes Powys 57 7600
Penelewey Cnwll 3 8140
Pengam Caerph 33 1597
Pengam Cardif 33 2177
Penge Gt Lon 27 3570
Pengelly Cnwll 3 8551
Pengelly Cnwll 4 0783
Pengorffwysfa IOA 68 4692
Pengover Green Cnwll 5 2765
Penhale Cnwll 2 6918
Penhale Cnwll 4 9057
Penhale Cnwll 4 0860
Penhale Cnwll 5 4153
Penhallow Cnwll 3 7651
Penhalurick Cnwll 2 7038
Penhalvean Cnwll 2 7038
Penhill Wilts 36 1588
Penhow Newpt 34 4290
Penhurst E Susx 16 6916
Peniarth Gwynd 57 6105
Penicuik Mdloth 117 2359
Peniel Carmth 31 4324
Peniel Denbgs 70 0362
Penifiler Highld 136 4841
Peninver Ag & B 105 7524
Penisar Waun Gwynd 69 5563
Penistone S York 82 2403
Penjerrick Cnwll 3 7730
Penkelly Cnwll 4 1854
Penketh Ches 78 5587
Penkill S Ayrs 106 2398
Penkridge Staffs 60 9213
Penlean Cnwll 5 2098
Penley Wrexhm 71 4040
Penllergaer Swans 32 6198
Penllyn V Glam 33 9775
Penmachno Conwy 69 7950
Penmaen Caerph 33 1897
Penmaen Swans 32 5288
Penmaenan Conwy 69 7175
Penmaenmawr Conwy 69 7276
Penmaenpool Gwynd 57 6918
Penmark V Glam 20 0568
Penmon IOA 69 6280
Penmorfa Gwynd 57 5540
Penmynydd IOA 68 5074
Penn Bucks 26 9193
Penn W Mids 60 8895
Penn Street Bucks 26 9295
Pennal Gwynd 57 6900
Pennan Abers 143 8465
Pennant Cerdgn 42 5163
Pennant Denbgs 58 0234
Pennant Powys 43 8897
Pennant-Melangell Powys 58 0226
Pennard Swans 32 5688
Pennerley Shrops 59 3599
Pennicott Devon 9 8701
Pennington Cumb 86 2677
Pennington Hants 12 3195
Pennington Green Gt Man 79 6206
Pennorth Powys 45 1125
Pennsylvania Gloucs 35 7473
Penny Bridge Cumb 86 3083
Penny Bridge Pembks 30 0001
Penny Green Notts 75 5475
Penny Hill Lincs 64 3526
Pennycross Ag & B 121 5025
Pennygate Norfk 67 3423
Pennyghael Ag & B 121 5125
Pennyglen S Ayrs 106 2710
Pennymoor Devon 19 8611
Penparc Cerdgn 42 2047
Penparcau Cerdgn 43 5980
Penpedairheol Caerph 33 1497
Penpedairheol Mons 34 3303
Penperlleni Mons 34 3204
Penpethy Cnwll 4 0886
Penpillick Cnwll 3 0856
Penpol Cnwll 3 8139
Penpoll Cnwll 3 1454
Penponds Cnwll 2 6339
Penpont Cnwll 4 0874
Penpont D & G 100 8494
Penpont Powys 45 9728
Penquit Devon 7 6454
Penrest Cnwll 5 3377
Penrherber Carmth 31 2938
Penrhiw-pal Cerdgn 42 3445
Penrhiwceiber Rhondd 33 0597
Penrhiwllan Cerdgn 31 3641
Penrhos Gwynd 56 3433
Penrhos IOA 68 2781
Penrhos Mons 34 4111
Penrhos Powys 32 8011
Penrhos garnedd Gwynd 69 5670
Penrhyn Bay Conwy 69 8281
Penrhyn-side Conwy 69 8181
Penrhyncoch Cerdgn 43 6384
Penrhyndeudraeth Gwynd 57 6139
Penrice Swans 32 4987
Penrioch N Ayrs 105 8744
Penrith Cumb 94 5130
Penrose Cnwll 4 8770
Penrose Cnwll 5 2589
Penruddock Cumb 93 4227
Penryn Cnwll 3 7834
Pensarn Carmth 31 4119
Pensarn Conwy 70 9578
Pensax Worcs 47 7269
Pensby Mersyd 78 2782
Penselwood Somset 22 7531
Pensford Somset 21 6263
Pensham Worcs 47 9444
Penshaw T & W 96 3253
Penshurst Kent 16 5243
Penshurst Station Kent 16 5246
Pensilva Cnwll 5 2970
Pensnett W Mids 60 9189
Penstone Devon 8 7700
Penstrowed Powys 58 0691
Pentewan Cnwll 3 0147
Pentir Gwynd 69 5766
Pentire Cnwll 4 7961
Pentlepoir Pembks 31 1105
Pentlow Essex 54 8146
Pentlow Street Essex 54 8245
Pentney Norfk 65 7214
Penton Grafton Hants 23 3247
Penton Mewsey Hants 23 3247
Pentonbridge Cumb 101 4476
Pentraeth IOA 68 5278
Pentre Denbgs 70 0862
Pentre Flints 71 3267
Pentre Mons 34 3106
Pentre Powys 58 0685
Pentre Powys 58 1589
Pentre Powys 58 2792
Pentre Rhondd 33 9696
Pentre Shrops 59 3617
Pentre Wrexhm 70 2840
Pentre Bach Cerdgn 44 5547
Pentre Bach Flints 70 2175
Pentre Berw IOA 68 4772
Pentre Ffwrndan Flints 70 2572
Pentre Gwynfryn Gwynd 57 5927
Pentre Halkyn Flints 70 2072
Pentre Hodrey Shrops 46 3277
Pentre Isaf Conwy 70 9871
Pentre Llanrhaeadr Denbgs 70 0863
Pentre Llifior Powys 58 1598
Pentre Meyrick V Glam 33 9675
Pentre Saron Denbgs 70 0260
Pentre ty gwyn Carmth 44 8135
Pentre'r Felin Conwy 69 8069
Pentre'r-felin Cerdgn 44 6148
Pentre'r-felin Powys 45 9230
Pentre'rbryn Cerdgn 42 3954
Pentre-bach Powys 45 9132
Pentre-bont Conwy 69 7351
Pentre-cagel Cerdgn 31 3340
Pentre-celyn Denbgs 70 1453
Pentre-celyn Powys 57 8905
Pentre-chwyth Swans 32 6794
Pentre-clawdd Shrops 59 2931
Pentre-cwrt Carmth 31 3838
Pentre-dwr Swans 32 6995
Pentre-Gwenlais Carmth 32 6016
Pentre-llwyn-llwyd Powys 45 9654
Pentre-llyn Cerdgn 43 6175
Pentre-llyn-cymmer Conwy 70 9752
Pentre-Maw Powys 57 8803
Pentre-piod Torfn 34 2601
Pentre-poeth Newpt 34 2686
Pentre-tafarn-y-fedw Conwy 69 8162
Pentrebach Myr Td 33 0604
Pentrebeirdd Powys 58 1813
Pentredwr Denbgs 70 1946
Pentrefelin Gwynd 57 5239
Pentrefelin IOA 68 4392
Pentrefoelas Conwy 69 8751
Pentregalar Pembks 31 1831
Pentregat Cerdgn 42 3551
Pentrich Derbys 74 3852
Pentridge Hill Dorset 12 0317
Pentyrch Cardif 33 1081
Penwithick Cnwll 3 0256
Penwood Hants 24 4461
Penwyllt Powys 33 8515
Penybanc Carmth 44 6123
Penybont Powys 45 1164
Penycae Wrexhm 70 2745
Penycaerau Gwynd 56 1927
Penyffordd Flints 71 3061
Penygraig Rhondd 33 0090
Penygroes Carmth 32 5813
Penygroes Gwynd 68 4752
Penysarn IOA 68 4590
Penywaun Rhondd 33 9804
Penywern Neath 32 7609
Penzance Cnwll 2 4730
Peopleton Worcs 47 9350
Peover Heath Ches 79 7973
Peper Harow Surrey 25 9344
Peplow Shrops 59 6224
Pepper's Green Essex 40 6110
Peppershill Oxon 37 6709
Pepperstock Beds 38 0817
Perceton N Ayrs 106 3540
Percie Abers 134 5992
Percyhorner Abers 143 9665
Perelle Guern 158 0000
Periton Somset 20 9545
Perivale Gt Lon 26 1682
Perkins Village Devon 9 0291
Perkinsville Dur 96 2553
Perlethorpe Notts 75 6470
Perran Wharf Cnwll 3 7738
Perranarworthal Cnwll 3 7738
Perranporth Cnwll 3 7554
Perranuthnoe Cnwll 2 5329
Perranwell Cnwll 3 7739
Perranwell Cnwll 3 7752
Perranzabuloe Cnwll 3 7752
Perrott's Brook Gloucs 35 0106
Perry W Mids 61 0792
Perry Barr W Mids 61 0791
Perry Green Essex 40 8022
Perry Green Herts 39 4317
Perry Green Wilts 35 9689
Perry Street Somset 10 3305
Pershall Staffs 72 8129
Pershore Worcs 47 9446
Pertenhall Beds 51 0865
Perth P & K 126 1123
Perthy Shrops 59 3633
Perton Herefd 46 5940
Perton Staffs 60 8699
Pertwood Wilts 22 8936
Pet Street Kent 29 0846
Peter Tavy Devon 5 5177
Peter's Green Herts 38 1419
Peterborough Cambs 64 1998
Peterchurch Herefd 46 3438
Peterculter Aber C 135 8300
Peterhead Abers 143 1246
Peterlee Dur 96 4241
Peters Marland Devon 18 4713
Petersfield Hants 13 7423
Petersham Gt Lon 26 1873
Peterston-super-Ely V Glam 33 0876
Peterstone Wentlooge Newpt 34 2679
Peterstow Herefd 46 5624
Petham Kent 29 1251
Petherwin Gate Cnwll 5 2889
Petrockstow Devon 19 5109
Petsoe End Bucks 38 8949
Pett E Susx 17 8714
Pett Bottom Kent 29 1552
Pettaugh Suffk 54 1659
Petterden Angus 127 4240
Pettinain S Lans 108 9543
Pettistree Suffk 55 3055
Petton Devon 20 0124
Petton Shrops 59 4326
Petts Wood Gt Lon 27 4567
Petty France Gloucs 35 7885
Pettycur Fife 117 2686
Pettymuk Abers 143 9023
Petworth W Susx 14 9721
Pevensey E Susx 16 6405
Pevensey Bay E Susx 16 6504
Pewsey Wilts 23 1660
Pheasant's Hill Bucks 37 7887
Phepson Worcs 47 9459
Philadelphia T & W 96 3352
Philham Devon 18 2522
Philiphaugh Border 109 4327
Phillack Cnwll 2 5638
Philleigh Cnwll 3 8639
Philpot End Essex 40 6118
Philpstoun W Loth 117 0577
Phocle Green Herefd 47 6326
Phoenix Green Hants 24 7555
Phoines Highld 132 7093
Pibsbury Somset 21 4426
Pica Cumb 92 0222
Piccadilly Warwks 61 2398
Piccotts End Herts 38 0409
Pickburn S York 83 5107
Pickering N York 90 7984
Picket Piece Hants 23 3947
Picket Post Hants 12 1906
Pickford W Mids 61 2881
Pickford Green W Mids 61 2781
Pickhill N York 89 3483
Picklescott Shrops 59 4399
Pickmere Ches 79 6977
Pickney Somset 20 1929
Pickstock Shrops 72 7223
Pickup Bank Lancs 81 7122
Pickwell Devon 18 4540
Pickwell Leics 63 7811
Pickwick Wilts 35 8670
Pickworth Lincs 63 9913
Pickworth Lincs 64 0433
Pict's Cross Herefd 46 5526
Pictillum Abers 142 7317
Picton Ches 71 4371
Picton Flints 70 1182
Picton N York 89 4107
Picton Ferry Carmth 31 2717
Piddinghoe E Susx 16 4303
Piddington Bucks 37 8094
Piddington Nhants 51 8054
Piddington Oxon 37 6317
Piddlehinton Dorset 11 7197
Piddletrenthide Dorset 11 7099
Pidley Cambs 52 3377
Pie Corner Herefd 47 6461
Piercebridge Dur 96 2115
Pierowall Ork 153 4348
Piff's Elm Gloucs 47 9026
Pig Oak Dorset 12 0202
Pig Street Herefd 46 3647
Pigdon Nthumb 103 1588
Pigeon Green Warwks 48 2260
Pikehall Derbys 74 1959
Pilford Dorset 12 0301
Pilgrims Hatch Essex 27 5895
Pilham Lincs 76 8693
Pill Somset 34 5275
Pillaton Cnwll 5 3664
Pillatonmill Cnwll 5 3663
Pillerton Hersey Warwks 48 2948
Pillerton Priors Warwks 48 2947
Pilleth Powys 46 2667
Pilley Hants 12 3298
Pilley S York 74 3300
Pilley Bailey Hants 12 3398
Pillgwenlly Newpt 34 3186
Pillhead Devon 18 4726
Pilling Lancs 80 4048
Pilling Lane Lancs 80 3749
Pilning Gloucs 34 5684
Pilot Inn Kent 17 0818
Pilsbury Derbys 74 1163
Pilsdon Dorset 10 4199
Pilsgate Cambs 64 0605
Pilsley Derbys 74 2371
Pilsley Derbys 74 4262
Pilson Green Norfk 67 3713
Piltdown E Susx 16 4422
Pilton Devon 19 5534
Pilton Nhants 51 0284
Pilton Rutlnd 63 9102
Pilton Somset 21 5941
Pilton Green Swans 32 4487
Pimlico Lancs 81 7443
Pimlico Nhants 49 6140
Pimperne Dorset 11 9009
Pin Green Herts 39 2525
Pinchbeck Lincs 64 2425
Pinchbeck Bars Lincs 64 1925
Pinchbeck West Lincs 64 2024
Pincheon Green S York 83 6517
Pinchinthorpe N York 90 5714
Pincock Lancs 80 5417
Pindon End Bucks 38 7847
Pinfold Lancs 80 3811
Pinford End Suffk 54 8459
Pinged Carmth 31 4203
Pingewood Berks 24 6969
Pinhoe Devon 9 9694
Pinkett's Booth W Mids 61 2781
Pinkney Wilts 35 8686
Pinley W Mids 61 3577
Pinley Green Warwks 48 2066
Pinmill Suffk 55 2037
Pinminnoch S Ayrs 106 1993
Pinmore S Ayrs 106 2091
Pinn Devon 9 1086
Pinner Gt Lon 26 1289
Pinner Green Gt Lon 26 1289
Pinsley Green Ches 71 5846
Pinvin Worcs 47 9549
Pinwherry S Ayrs 98 2086
Pinxton Derbys 75 4554
Pipe and Lyde Herefd 46 5043
Pipe Gate Shrops 72 7340
Pipehill Staffs 61 0907
Piperhill Highld 140 8650
Pipers Pool Cnwll 5 2584
Pipewell Nhants 51 8485
Pippacott Devon 19 5237
Pippin Street Lancs 81 5924
Pipton Powys 45 1637
Pirbright Surrey 25 9455
Pirbright Camp Surrey 25 9356
Pirnie Border 110 6528
Pirnmill N Ayrs 105 8744
Pirton Herts 38 1431
Pirton Worcs 47 8847
Pishill Oxon 37 7389
Pistyll Gwynd 56 3241
Pitagowan P & K 132 8165
Pitblae Abers 143 9864
Pitcairngreen P & K 125 0627
Pitcalnie Highld 147 8072
Pitcaple Abers 142 7225
Pitcarity Angus 134 3365
Pitch Green Bucks 37 7703
Pitch Place Surrey 25 8839
Pitch Place Surrey 25 9852
Pitchcombe Gloucs 35 8508
Pitchcott Bucks 37 7720
Pitcher Row Lincs 64 2933
Pitchford Shrops 59 5303
Pitchroy Moray 141 1738
Pitcombe Somset 22 6732
Pitcot V Glam 33 8974
Pitcox E Loth 118 6475
Pitfichie Abers 142 6716
Pitglassie Abers 142 6943
Pitgrudy Highld 147 7991
Pitkennedy Angus 127 5454
Pitlessie Fife 126 3309
Pitlochry P & K 132 9458
Pitmachie Abers 142 6728
Pitmain Highld 132 7400
Pitmedden Abers 143 8827
Pitmuies Angus 127 5649
Pitmunie Abers 142 6614
Pitney Somset 21 4528
Pitroddie P & K 126 2125
Pitscottie Fife 126 4112
Pitsea Essex 40 7488
Pitses Gt Man 79 9403
Pitsford Nhants 50 7567
Pitstone Bucks 38 9415
Pitt Devon 9 0316
Pitt Hants 24 4528
Pitt Court Gloucs 35 7496
Pitt's Wood Kent 16 6149
Pittarrow Abers 135 7274
Pittenweem Fife 127 5502
Pitteuchar Fife 117 2899
Pittington Dur 96 3244
Pittodrie House Hotel Abers 142 6924
Pitton Wilts 23 2131
Pittulie Abers 143 9567
Pity Me Dur 96 2645
Pityme Cnwll 4 9576
Pivington Kent 28 9146
Pixey Green Suffk 55 2475
Pixham Surrey 26 1750
Plain Street Cnwll 4 9778
Plains N Lans 116 7966
Plaish Shrops 59 5296
Plaistow Derbys 74 3456
Plaistow Gt Lon 27 4082
Plaistow Herefd 47 6939
Plaistow W Susx 14 0030
Plaitford Hants 12 2719
Plank Lane Gt Man 79 6399
Plas Cymyran IOA 68 2975
Plastow Green Hants 24 5361
Platt Kent 27 6257
Platt Bridge Gt Man 78 6002
Platt Lane Shrops 59 5136
Platts Heath Kent 28 8750
Plawsworth Dur 96 2647
Plaxtol Kent 27 6053
Play Hatch Oxon 37 7376
Playden E Susx 17 9221
Playford Suffk 55 2147
Playing Place Cnwll 3 8141
Playley Green Gloucs 47 7631
Plealey Shrops 59 4206
Plean Stirlg 116 8386
Pleasance Fife 126 2312
Pleasington Lancs 81 6426
Pleasley Derbys 75 5064
Pleasleyhill Notts 75 5064
Pleck Dorset 11 7010
Pledgdon Green Essex 40 5626
Pledwick W York 83 3316
Pleinheaume Guern 158 0000
Plemont Jersey 158 0000
Plemstall Ches 71 4570
Plenmeller Nthumb 102 7163
Pleshey Essex 40 6614
Plockton Highld 137 8033
Plowden Shrops 59 3887
Ploxgreen Shrops 59 3604
Pluckley Kent 28 9245
Pluckley Station Kent 28 9243
Pluckley Thorne Kent 28 9244
Plucks Gutter Kent 29 2663
Plumbland Cumb 92 1539
Plumgarths Cumb 87 4994
Plumley Ches 79 7274
Plumpton Cumb 94 4937
Plumpton E Susx 15 3613
Plumpton Nhants 49 5948
Plumpton End Nhants 49 7245
Plumpton Green E Susx 15 3616
Plumpton Head Cumb 94 5035
Plumstead Gt Lon 27 4478
Plumstead Norfk 66 1334
Plumstead Green Norfk 66 1235
Plumtree Notts 62 6132
Plumtree Green Kent 28 8245
Plungar Leics 63 7634
Plurenden Kent 28 9337
Plush Dorset 11 7102
Plusha Cnwll 5 2580
Plushabridge Cnwll 5 3072
Plwmp Cerdgn 42 3652
Plymouth Devon 6 4754
Plympton Devon 6 5456
Plymstock Devon 6 5152
Plymtree Devon 9 0502
Pockley N York 90 6385
Pocklington E R Yk 84 8048
Pode Hole Lincs 64 2121
Podimore Somset 21 5424
Podington Beds 51 9462
Podmore Staffs 72 7835
Point Clear Essex 41 1015
Pointon Lincs 64 1131
Pokesdown Dorset 12 1292
Polapit Tamar Cnwll 5 3389
Polbain Highld 144 9910
Polbathic Cnwll 5 3456
Polbeth W Loth 117 0264
Polbrock Cnwll 4 0169
Pole Elm Worcs 47 8450
Pole Moor W York 82 0615
Polebrook Nhants 51 0686
Polegate E Susx 16 5804
Polelane Ends Ches 79 6479
Polesworth Warwks 61 2602
Polgigga Cnwll 2 3723
Polglass Highld 144 0307

Polgooth Radlett


Polgooth Cnwll 3 9950
Polgown D & G 107 7103
Poling W Susx 14 0404
Poling Corner W Susx 14 0405
Polkerris Cnwll 3 0952
Pollard Street Norfk 67 3332
Pollington E R Yk 83 6119
Polloch Highld 129 7668
Pollokshaws C Glas 115 5661
Pollokshields C Glas 115 5763
Polmassick Cnwll 3 9745
Polmear Cnwll 3 0853
Polmont Falk 116 9378
Polnish Highld 129 7582
Polperro Cnwll 5 2051
Polruan Cnwll 3 1250
Polsham Somset 21 5142
Polstead Suffk 54 9938
Polstead Heath Suffk 54 9940
Poltalloch Ag & B 113 8196
Poltescoe Cnwll 3 7215
Poltimore Devon 9 9696
Polton Mdloth 117 2864
Polwarth Border 119 7450
Polyphant Cnwll 5 2682
Polzeath Cnwll 4 9378
Pomathorn Mdloth 117 2459
Pomeroy Derbys 74 1267
Ponde Powys 45 1037
Ponders End Gt Lon 27 3596
Pondersbridge Cambs 64 2692
Ponsanooth Cnwll 3 7537
Ponsonby Cumb 86 0505
Ponsongath Cnwll 3 7518
Ponsworthy Devon 7 7073
Pont Cyfyng Conwy 69 7357
Pont Dolgarrog Conwy 69 7766
Pont Morlais Carmth 32 5307
Pont Pen-y-benglog Gwynd 69 6560
Pont Rhyd-sarn Gwynd 57 8528
Pont Rhyd-y-cyff Brdgnd 33 8788
Pont Robert Powys 58 1012
Pont Walby Neath 33 8906
Pont-ar-gothi Carmth 32 5021
Pont-ar-Hydfer Powys 45 8627
Pont-ar-llechau Carmth 44 7224
Pont-Ebbw Newpt 34 2985
Pont-faen Powys 45 9934
Pont-Nedd-Fechan Neath 33 9007
Pont-rhyd-y-fen Neath 32 7994
Pont-rug Gwynd 68 5162
Pont-y-blew Wrexhm 71 3138
Pont-y-pant Conwy 69 7554
Pont-yr-hafod Pembks 30 9026
Pont-yr-Rhyl Brdgnd 33 9089
Pontac Jersey 158 0000
Pontamman Carmth 32 6312
Pontantwn Carmth 32 4412
Pontardawe Neath 32 7204
Pontarddulais Swans 32 5903
Pontarsais Carmth 31 4428
Pontblyddyn Flints 70 2760
Pontdolgoch Powys 58 0193
Pontefract W York 83 4521
Ponteland Nthumb 103 1672
Ponterwyd Cerdgn 43 7481
Pontesbury Shrops 59 3906
Pontesbury Hill Shrops 59 3905
Pontesford Shrops 59 4106
Pontfadog Wrexhm 70 2338
Pontfaen Pembks 30 0234
Pontgarreg Cerdgn 42 3353
Pontgarreg Pembks 31 1441
Ponthenry Carmth 32 4709
Ponthir Torfn 34 3292
Ponthirwaun Cerdgn 42 2645
Pontllanfraith Caerph 33 1895
Pontlliw Swans 32 6199
Pontlottyn Caerph 33 1106
Pontlyfni Gwynd 68 4352
Pontnewydd Torfn 34 2896
Pontnewynydd Torfn 34 2701
Pontop Dur 96 1453
Pontrhydfendigaid Cerdgn 43 7366
Pontrhydygroes Cerdgn 43 7472
Pontrhydyrun Torfn 34 2997
Pontrilas Herefd 46 3927
Ponts Green E Susx 16 6715
Pontshaen Cerdgn 42 4446
Pontshill Herefd 35 6421
Pontsticill Powys 33 0511
Pontwelly Carmth 31 4140
Pontyates Carmth 32 4708
Pontyberem Carmth 32 5010
Pontybodkin Flints 70 2759
Pontyclun Rhondd 33 0381
Pontycymer Brdgnd 33 9091
Pontyglasier Pembks 31 1436
Pontygwaith Rhondd 33 0094
Pontygynon Pembks 31 1237
Pontymoel Torfn 34 2900
Pontypool Torfn 34 2800
Pontypool Road Torfn 34 3099
Pontypridd Rhondd 33 0789
Pontywaun Caerph 34 2292
Pooksgreen Hants 12 3710
Pool Cnwll 2 6641
Pool IOS 2 8714
Pool W York 82 2445
Pool Head Herefd 46 5550
Pool of Muckhart Clacks 117 0000
Pool Quay Powys 58 2511
Pool Street Essex 53 7636
Poole Dorset 11 0090
Poole Keynes Gloucs 35 9995
Poolewe Highld 144 8580
Pooley Bridge Cumb 93 4724
Pooley Street Norfk 54 0581
Poolfold Staffs 72 8959
Poolhill Gloucs 47 7229
Pooting's Kent 16 4549
Popham Hants 24 5543
Poplar Gt Lon 27 3780
Poplar Street Suffk 55 4465
Porchbrook Worcs 60 7270
Porchfield IOW 13 4491
Poringland Norfk 67 2701
Porkellis Cnwll 2 6933
Porlock Somset 19 8846
Porlock Weir Somset 19 8647
Port Appin Ag & B 122 9045
Port Askaig Ag & B 112 4369
Port Bannatyne Ag & B 114 0767
Port Carlisle Cumb 101 2461
Port Charlotte Ag & B 112 2558
Port Clarence Dur 97 4921
Port Driseach Ag & B 114 9973
Port Einon Swans 32 4685
Port Ellen Ag & B 104 3645
Port Elphinstone Abers 142 7720
Port Erin IOM 158 1969
Port Gaverne Cnwll 4 0080
Port Glasgow Inver 115 3274
Port Henderson Highld 137 7573
Port Isaac Cnwll 4 9980
Port Logan D & G 98 0940
Port Mor Highld 128 4279
Port Mulgrave N York 97 7917
Port nan Giuran W Isls 152 5537
Port nan Long W Isls 152 8978
Port Nis W Isls 152 5363
Port of Menteith Stirlg 115 5801
Port of Ness W Isls 152 5363
Port Quin Cnwll 4 9780
Port Ramsay Ag & B 122 8845
Port Soderick IOM 158 3472
Port St Mary IOM 158 2067
Port Sunlight Mersyd 78 3384
Port Talbot Neath 32 7689
Port Tennant Swans 32 6893
Port Wemyss Ag & B 112 1651
Port William D & G 98 3343
Port-an-Eorna Highld 137 7732
Portachoillan Ag & B 113 7557
Portavadie Ag & B 114 9369
Portbury Somset 34 5075
Portchester Hants 13 6105
Porteath Cnwll 4 9679
Portencalzie D & G 98 0171
Portencross N Ayrs 114 1748
Portesham Dorset 10 6085
Portessie Moray 142 4366
Portfield Gate Pembks 30 9215
Portgate Devon 5 4285
Portgordon Moray 142 3964
Portgower Highld 147 0013
Porth Cnwll 4 8362
Porth Rhondd 33 0291
Porth Dinllaen Gwynd 56 2740
Porth Navas Cnwll 3 7527
Porth-y-Waen Shrops 58 2623
Porthallow Cnwll 3 7923
Porthallow Cnwll 5 2251
Porthcawl Brdgnd 33 8177
Porthcothan Cnwll 4 8672
Porthcurno Cnwll 2 3822
Porthgain Pembks 30 8132
Porthgwarra Cnwll 2 3721
Porthill Staffs 72 8448
Porthkea Cnwll 3 8242
Porthkerry V Glam 20 0866
Porthleven Cnwll 2 6225
Porthmadog Gwynd 57 5638
Porthmeor Cnwll 2 4337
Portholland Cnwll 3 9541
Porthoustock Cnwll 3 8021
Porthpean Cnwll 3 0250
Porthtowan Cnwll 2 6947
Porthwgan Wrexhm 71 3846
Porthyrhyd Carmth 32 5215
Portincaple Ag & B 114 2393
Portinfer Jersey 158 0000
Portington E R Yk 84 7831
Portinnisherrich Ag & B 122 9711
Portinscale Cumb 93 2523
Portishead Somset 34 4675
Portknockie Moray 142 4868
Portlethen Abers 135 9196
Portling D & G 92 8753
Portloe Cnwll 3 9339
Portlooe Cnwll 5 2452
Portmahomack Highld 147 9184
Portmellon Cnwll 3 0144
Portmore Hants 12 3397
Portnacroish Ag & B 122 9247
Portnaguran W Isls 152 5537
Portnahaven Ag & B 112 1652
Portnalong Highld 136 3434
Portobello C Edin 117 3073
Portobello T & W 96 2856
Portobello W Mids 60 9598
Porton Wilts 23 1836
Portontown Devon 5 4176
Portpatrick D & G 98 9954
Portreath Cnwll 2 6545
Portree Highld 136 4843
Portscatho Cnwll 3 8735
Portsea Hants 13 6300
Portskerra Highld 150 8765
Portskewett Mons 34 4988
Portslade E Susx 15 2506
Portslade-by-Sea E Susx 15 2605
Portslogan D & G 98 9858
Portsmouth Hants 13 6400
Portsmouth W York 81 9026
Portsonachan Hotel Ag & B 123 0420
Portsoy Abers 142 5866
Portswood Hants 13 4214
Portuairk Highld 128 4368
Portway Herefd 46 4844
Portway Herefd 46 4935
Portway W Mids 60 9787
Portway Worcs 61 0872
Portwrinkle Cnwll 5 3553
Portyerrock D & G 99 4738
Posbury Devon 8 8197
Posenhall Shrops 59 6501
Poslingford Suffk 53 7648
Posso Border 109 2033
Post Green Dorset 11 9593
Postbridge Devon 8 6579
Postcombe Oxon 37 7000
Postling Kent 29 1439
Postwick Norfk 67 2907
Potarch Abers 134 6097
Pothole Cnwll 3 9750
Potsgrove Beds 38 9530
Pott Row Norfk 65 7022
Pott Shrigley Ches 79 9479
Pott's Green Essex 40 9122
Potten End Herts 38 0109
Potten Street Kent 29 2567
Potter Brompton N York 91 9777
Potter Heigham Norfk 67 4119
Potter Row Bucks 26 9002
Potter Somersal Derbys 73 1335
Potter's Cross Staffs 60 8484
Potter's Forstal Kent 28 8946
Potter's Green E Susx 16 5023
Potter's Green Herts 39 3520
Pottergate Street Norfk 66 1591
Potterhanworth Lincs 76 0566
Potterhanworth Booths Lincs 76 0767
Potterne Wilts 22 9958
Potterne Wick Wilts 22 9957
Potters Bar Herts 26 2401
Potters Brook Lancs 80 4852
Potters Crouch Herts 38 1105
Potters Green W Mids 61 3782
Potters Marston Leics 50 4996
Pottersheath Herts 39 2318
Potterspury Nhants 49 7543
Potterton Abers 143 9415
Potterton W York 83 4038
Potthorpe Norfk 66 9422
Pottle Street Wilts 22 8140
Potto N York 89 4703
Potton Beds 52 2249
Poughill Cnwll 18 2207
Poughill Devon 19 8508
Poulner Hants 12 1606
Poulshot Wilts 22 9659
Poulston Devon 7 7754
Poulton Gloucs 36 0901
Poulton Mersyd 78 3091
Poulton Priory Gloucs 36 0900
Poulton-le-Fylde Lancs 80 3439
Pound Bank Worcs 60 7374
Pound Green E Susx 16 5123
Pound Green Suffk 53 7153
Pound Green Worcs 60 7578
Pound Hill W Susx 15 2937
Pound Street Hants 24 4561
Poundffald Swans 32 5694
Poundgate E Susx 16 4928
Poundon Bucks 49 6425
Poundsbridge Kent 16 5341
Poundsgate Devon 7 7072
Poundstock Cnwll 18 2099
Pounsley E Susx 16 5221
Pouton D & G 99 4645
Povey Cross Surrey 15 2642
Pow Green Herefd 47 7144
Powburn Nthumb 111 0616
Powderham Devon 9 9684
Powerstock Dorset 10 5196
Powfoot D & G 100 1465
Powhill Cumb 93 2355
Powick Worcs 47 8351
Powmill P & K 117 0297
Poxwell Dorset 11 7384
Poyle Surrey 26 0376
Poynings W Susx 15 2611
Poynter's Lane End Cnwll 2 6743
Poyntington Dorset 21 6520
Poynton Ches 79 9283
Poynton Shrops 59 5617
Poynton Green Shrops 59 5618
Poys Street Suffk 55 3570
Poyston Cross Pembks 30 9819
Poystreet Green Suffk 54 9758
Praa Sands Cnwll 2 5828
Pratt's Bottom Gt Lon 27 4762
Praze-an-Beeble Cnwll 2 6335
Predannack Wollas Cnwll 2 6616
Prees Shrops 59 5533
Prees Green Shrops 59 5531
Prees Heath Shrops 71 5538
Prees Higher Heath Shrops 59 5635
Prees Lower Heath Shrops 59 5732
Preesall Lancs 80 3647
Preesgweene Shrops 59 2936
Pren-gwyn Cerdgn 42 4244
Prendwick Nthumb 111 0012
Prenteg Gwynd 57 5841
Prenton Mersyd 78 3086
Prescot Mersyd 78 4692
Prescott Devon 9 0814
Prescott Shrops 59 4220
Prescott Shrops 60 6681
Presnerb Angus 133 1866
Pressen Nthumb 110 8335
Prestatyn Denbgs 70 0682
Prestbury Ches 79 8976
Prestbury Gloucs 47 9723
Presteigne Powys 46 3164
Prestleigh Somset 21 6340
Prestolee Gt Man 79 7505
Preston Border 119 7957
Preston Devon 7 7451
Preston Devon 7 8574
Preston Devon 7 8962
Preston Dorset 11 7083
Preston E Loth 118 5977
Preston E R Yk 85 1830
Preston E Susx 15 3106
Preston Gloucs 47 6834
Preston Gloucs 36 0400
Preston Herts 39 1824
Preston Kent 28 0260
Preston Kent 29 2460
Preston Lancs 80 5329
Preston Nthumb 111 1825
Preston Rutlnd 63 8602
Preston Shrops 59 5211
Preston Somset 20 0935
Preston Suffk 54 9450
Preston Wilts 36 2774
Preston Bagot Warwks 48 1765
Preston Bissett Bucks 49 6529
Preston Bowyer Somset 20 1326
Preston Brockhurst Shrops 59 5324
Preston Brook Ches 78 5680
Preston Candover Hants 24 6041
Preston Capes Nhants 49 5754
Preston Crowmarsh Oxon 37 6190
Preston Deanery Nhants 50 7855
Preston Green Warwks 48 1665
Preston Gubbals Shrops 59 4919
Preston Montford Shrops 59 4314
Preston on Stour Warwks 48 2049
Preston on Tees Dur 96 4315
Preston on the Hill Ches 78 5780
Preston on Wye Herefd 46 3841
Preston Patrick Cumb 87 5483
Preston Plucknett Somset 10 5316
Preston Street Kent 29 2561
Preston upon the Weald Moors Shrops 72 6815
Preston Wynne Herefd 46 5546
Preston-under-Scar N York 88 0691
Prestonpans E Loth 118 3874
Prestwich Gt Man 79 8104
Prestwick Nthumb 103 1872
Prestwick S Ayrs 106 3525
Prestwood Bucks 26 8700
Prestwood Staffs 60 8786
Price Town Brdgnd 33 9391
Prickwillow Cambs 53 5982
Priddy Somset 21 5250
Priest Hutton Lancs 87 5273
Priestacott Devon 18 4206
Priestcliffe Derbys 74 1471
Priestcliffe Ditch Derbys 74 1371
Priestend Bucks 37 6905
Priestland E Ayrs 107 5737
Priestley Green W York 82 1326
Priestweston Shrops 59 2997
Priestwood Green Kent 28 6564
Primethorpe Leics 50 5293
Primrose Green Norfk 66 0716
Primrose Hill Cambs 52 3889
Primrose Hill Derbys 75 4358
Primrose Hill Lancs 78 3809
Primrose Hill W Mids 60 9487
Primrosehill Border 119 7857
Primsidemill Border 110 8126
Princes Gate Pembks 31 1312
Princes Risborough Bucks 38 8003
Princethorpe Warwks 61 4070
Princetown Devon 6 5873
Prinsted W Susx 14 7605
Prion Denbgs 70 0562
Prior Rigg Cumb 101 4568
Priors Halton Shrops 46 4975
Priors Hardwick Warwks 49 4756
Priors Marston Warwks 49 4957
Priors Norton Gloucs 47 8624
Priory Wood Herefd 46 2645
Prisk V Glam 33 0176
Priston Somset 22 6960
Pristow Green Norfk 54 1388
Prittlewell Essex 40 8687
Privett Hants 13 6727
Prixford Devon 19 5536
Probus Cnwll 3 8947
Prora E Loth 118 5279
Prospect Cumb 92 1140
Prospidnick Cnwll 2 6431
Protstonhill Abers 143 8163
Providence Somset 34 5370
Prudhoe Nthumb 103 0962
Prussia Cove Cnwll 2 5528
Publow Somset 21 6264
Puckeridge Herts 39 3823
Puckington Somset 10 3718
Pucklechurch Gloucs 35 6976
Puckrup Gloucs 47 8836
Puddinglake Ches 79 7269
Puddington Ches 71 3273
Puddington Devon 19 8310
Puddledock Norfk 66 0592
Puddlehill Herts 38 0023
Puddletown Dorset 11 7594
Pudleston Herefd 46 5659
Pudsey W York 82 2232
Pulborough W Susx 14 0418
Puleston Shrops 72 7322
Pulford Ches 71 3758
Pulham Dorset 11 7008
Pulham Market Norfk 55 1986
Pulham St Mary Norfk 55 2085
Pullens Green Gloucs 34 6192
Pulley Shrops 59 4709
Pulloxhill Beds 38 0634
Pumpherston W Loth 117 0669
Pumsaint Carmth 44 6540
Puncheston Pembks 30 0129
Puncknowle Dorset 10 5388
Punnett's Town E Susx 16 6220
Purbrook Hants 13 6707
Purbrook Park Hants 13 6707
Purfleet Essex 27 5578
Puriton Somset 21 3241
Purleigh Essex 40 8402
Purley Berks 37 6675
Purley Gt Lon 27 3161
Purlogue Shrops 46 2877
Purlpit Wilts 22 8766
Purls Bridge Cambs 53 4786
Purse Caundle Dorset 11 6917
Purshull Green Worcs 60 8971
Purslow Shrops 59 3680
Purston Jaglin W York 83 4319
Purtington Somset 10 3908
Purton Gloucs 35 6904
Purton Gloucs 35 6705
Purton Wilts 36 0987
Purton Stoke Wilts 36 0990
Pury End Nhants 49 7145
Pusey Oxon 36 3596
Putley Herefd 47 6337
Putley Green Herefd 47 6437
Putloe Gloucs 35 7709
Putney Gt Lon 26 2374
Putron Village Guern 158 0000
Putsborough Devon 18 4440
Puttenham Herts 38 8814
Puttenham Surrey 25 9247
Puttock End Essex 54 8040
Puttock's End Essex 40 5719
Putton Dorset 11 6480
Puxley Nhants 49 7542
Puxton Somset 21 4063
Pwll Carmth 32 4801
Pwll Trap Carmth 31 2616
Pwll-du Mons 34 2411
Pwll-glas Denbgs 70 1154
Pwll-y-glaw Neath 32 7993
Pwllcrochan Pembks 30 9202
Pwllgloyw Powys 45 0333
Pwllheli Gwynd 56 3735
Pwllmeyric Mons 34 5292
Pydew Conwy 69 8079
Pye Bridge Derbys 75 4452
Pye Corner Herts 39 4412
Pye Corner Newpt 34 3485
Pye Green Staffs 60 9813
Pyecombe W Susx 15 2813
Pyle Brdgnd 33 8282
Pyleigh Somset 20 1330
Pylle Somset 21 6038
Pymore Cambs 53 4986
Pymore Dorset 10 4694
Pyrford Surrey 26 0358
Pyrton Oxon 37 6896
Pytchley Nhants 51 8574
Pyworthy Devon 18 3102


# Q


Quabbs Shrops 58 2180
Quadring Lincs 64 2233
Quadring Eaudike Lincs 64 2433
Quainton Bucks 37 7420
Quaker's Yard Myr Td 33 0995
Quaking Houses Dur 96 1850
Quarley Hants 23 2743
Quarndon Derbys 62 3340
Quarr Hill IOW 13 5792
Quarrier's Homes Inver 115 3666
Quarrington Lincs 64 0544
Quarrington Hill Dur 96 3337
Quarry Bank W Mids 60 9386
Quarrybank Ches 71 5465
Quarrywood Moray 141 1763
Quarter N Ayrs 114 1961
Quarter S Lans 116 7251
Quatford Shrops 60 7391
Quatt Shrops 60 7588
Quebec Dur 96 1743
Quedgeley Gloucs 35 8014
Queen Adelaide Cambs 53 5681
Queen Camel Somset 21 5924
Queen Charlton Somset 21 6367
Queen Dart Devon 19 8316
Queen Oak Dorset 22 7831
Queen Street Kent 28 6845
Queen Street Wilts 35 0287
Queen's Bower IOW 13 5684
Queen's Head Shrops 59 3327
Queen's Park Beds 38 0349
Queen's Park Nhants 49 7562
Queenborough Kent 28 9172
Queenhill Worcs 47 8537
Queensbury W York 82 1030
Queensferry Flints 71 3168
Queenslie C Glas 116 6565
Queenzieburn N Lans 116 6977
Quendon Essex 39 5130
Queniborough Leics 63 6412
Quenington Gloucs 36 1404
Quernmore Lancs 87 5160
Quernmore Park Hall Lancs 87 5162
Queslett W Mids 61 0695
Quethiock Cnwll 5 3164
Quick's Green Berks 37 5876
Quidenham Norfk 54 0287
Quidhampton Hants 24 5150
Quidhampton Wilts 23 1030
Quina Brook Shrops 59 5232
Quinbury End Nhants 49 6250
Quinton Nhants 49 7754
Quinton W Mids 60 9984
Quinton Green Nhants 50 7853
Quintrell Downs Cnwll 4 8460
Quither Devon 5 4481
Quixhall Staffs 73 1041
Quixwood Border 119 7863
Quoditch Devon 5 4097
Quorndon Leics 62 5616
Quothquan S Lans 108 9939
Quoyburray Ork 153 5005
Quoyloo Ork 153 2420


# R


Rabbit's Cross Kent 28 7847
Rableyheath Herts 39 2319
Raby Cumb 93 1951
Raby Mersyd 71 3179
Rachan Mill Border 108 1134
Rachub Gwynd 69 6267
Rackenford Devon 19 8518
Rackham W Susx 14 0413
Rackheath Norfk 67 2814
Rackwick Ork 153 2099
Radbourne Derbys 73 2836
Radcliffe Gt Man 79 7806
Radcliffe Nthumb 103 2602
Radcliffe on Trent Notts 63 6439
Radclive Bucks 49 6734
Radcot Oxon 36 2899
Raddington Somset 20 0225
Radernie Fife 127 4609
Radford Semele Warwks 48 3464
Radlett Somset 20 2038
Radlett Herts 26 1600

Rodmarton St Wenn


Rodmarton *Gloucs* 35 9498
Rodmell *E Susx* 15 4106
Rodmersham *Kent* 28 9261
Rodmersham Green *Kent* 28 9161
Rodney Stoke *Somset* 21 4849
Rodsley *Derbys* 73 2040
Rodway *Somset* 20 2540
Roe Cross *Gt Man* 79 9896
Roe Green *Gt Man* 79 7501
Roe Green *Herts* 39 2107
Roe Green *Herts* 39 3133
Roecliffe *N York* 89 3765
Roehampton *Gt Lon* 26 2273
Roffey *W Susx* 15 1932
Rogart *Highld* 146 7202
Rogate *W Susx* 14 8023
Roger Ground *Cumb* 87 3597
Rogerstone *Newpt* 34 2787
Roghadal *W Isls* 152 0483
Rogiet *Mons* 34 4587
Roke *Oxon* 37 6293
Roker *T & W* 96 4058
Rollesby *Norfk* 67 4416
Rolleston *Leics* 50 7300
Rolleston *Notts* 75 7452
Rolleston *Staffs* 73 2327
Rolston *E R Yk* 85 2144
Rolstone *Somset* 21 3962
Rolvenden *Kent* 17 8431
Rolvenden Layne *Kent* 17 8530
Romaldkirk *Dur* 95 9922
Romanby *N York* 89 3693
Romanno Bridge *Border* 117 1647
Romansleigh *Devon* 19 7220
Romden Castle *Kent* 28 8941
Romesdal *Highld* 136 4053
Romford *Dorset* 12 0709
Romford *Gt Lon* 27 5188
Romiley *Gt Man* 79 9490
Romney Street *Kent* 27 5561
Romsey *Hants* 12 3521
Romsley *Shrops* 60 7883
Romsley *Worcs* 60 9680
Ronachan *Ag & B* 113 7454
Rookhope *Dur* 95 9342
Rookley *IOW* 13 5084
Rookley Green *IOW* 13 5083
Rooks Bridge *Somset* 21 3652
Rooks Nest *Somset* 20 0933
Rookwith *N York* 89 2086
Roos *E R Yk* 85 2830
Roose *Cumb* 86 2269
Roosebeck *Cumb* 86 2567
Roothams Green *Beds* 51 0957
Ropley *Hants* 24 6431
Ropley Dean *Hants* 24 6232
Ropley Soke *Hants* 24 6533
Ropsley *Lincs* 63 9933
Rora *Abers* 143 0650
Rorrington *Shrops* 59 3000
Rosarie *Moray* 141 3850
Roscroggan *Cnwll* 2 6542
Rose *Cnwll* 3 7754
Rose Ash *Devon* 19 7921
Rose Green *Essex* 40 9028
Rose Green *Suffk* 54 9337
Rose Green *Suffk* 54 9744
Rose Green *W Susx* 14 9099
Rose Hill *E Susx* 16 4516
Rose Hill *Lancs* 81 8231
Roseacre *Lancs* 80 4336
Rosebank *S Lans* 116 8049
Rosebush *Pembks* 31 0729
Rosecare *Cnwll* 4 1695
Rosecliston *Cnwll* 4 8159
Rosedale Abbey *N York* 90 7296
Roseden *Nthumb* 111 0321
Rosehall *Highld* 146 4702
Rosehearty *Abers* 143 9267
Rosehill *Shrops* 59 4715
Roseisle *Moray* 141 1466
Roselands *E Susx* 16 6200
Rosemarket *Pembks* 30 9508
Rosemarkie *Highld* 140 7357
Rosemary Lane *Devon* 9 1514
Rosemount *P & K* 126 1843
Rosenannon *Cnwll* 4 9566
Rosenithon *Cnwll* 3 8021
Roser's Cross *E Susx* 16 5420
Rosevean *Cnwll* 4 0258
Rosevine *Cnwll* 3 8736
Rosewarne *Cnwll* 2 6036
Rosewell *Mdloth* 117 2862
Roseworth *Dur* 96 4221
Roseworthy *Cnwll* 2 6139
Rosgill *Cumb* 94 5316
Roshven *Highld* 129 7078
Roskhill *Highld* 136 2744
Roskorwell *Cnwll* 3 7923
Roskrow *Cnwll* 3 7635
Rosley *Cumb* 93 3245
Roslin *Mdloth* 117 2763
Rosliston *Derbys* 73 2416
Rosneath *Ag & B* 114 2583
Ross *D & G* 99 6444
Ross *Nthumb* 111 1337
Ross-on-Wye *Herefd* 46 5923
Rossett *Wrexhm* 71 3657
Rossett Green *N York* 82 2952
Rossington *S York* 75 6298
Rosskeen *Highld* 146 6869
Rossland *Rens* 115 4370
Roster *Highld* 151 2639
Rostherne *Ches* 79 7483
Rosthwaite *Cumb* 93 2514
Roston *Derbys* 73 1340
Rosudgeon *Cnwll* 2 5529
Rosyth *Fife* 117 1082
Rothbury *Nthumb* 103 0501
Rotherby *Leics* 63 6716
Rotherfield *E Susx* 16 5529
Rotherfield Greys *Oxon* 37 7282
Rotherfield Peppard *Oxon* 37 7182
Rotherham *S York* 75 4392
Rothersthorpe *Nhants* 49 7156
Rotherwick *Hants* 24 7156
Rothes *Moray* 141 2749
Rothesay *Ag & B* 114 0864
Rothiebrisbane *Abers* 142 7437
Rothiemay *Moray* 142 5548
Rothiemurchus Lodge *Highld* 133 9407
Rothienorman *Abers* 142 7235
Rothley *Leics* 62 5812
Rothley *Nthumb* 103 0488
Rothmaise *Abers* 142 6832
Rothwell *Lincs* 76 1499
Rothwell *Nhants* 51 8181
Rothwell *W York* 83 3428
Rothwell Haigh *W York* 83 3328
Rotsea *E R Yk* 84 0651
Rottal Lodge *Angus* 134 3769
Rottingdean *E Susx* 15 3602
Rottington *Cumb* 92 9613
Roucan *D & G* 100 0277
Roud *IOW* 13 5180
Rough Close *Staffs* 72 9239
Rough Common *Kent* 29 1259
Rougham *Norfk* 66 8320
Rougham Green *Suffk* 54 9061
Roughlee *Lancs* 81 8440
Roughley *W Mids* 61 1399
Roughpark *Abers* 134 3412
Roughton *Lincs* 77 2464
Roughton *Norfk* 67 2136
Roughton *Shrops* 60 7594
Roughway *Kent* 27 6153
Round Bush *Herts* 26 1498
Round Green *Beds* 38 1022
Round Street *Kent* 28 6568
Roundbush *Essex* 40 8501
Roundbush Green *Essex* 40 5814
Roundham *Somset* 10 4209
Roundhay *W York* 83 3337
Rounds Green *W Mids* 60 9889
Roundstreet Common *W Susx* 14 0528
Roundway *Wilts* 22 0163
Roundyhill *Angus* 126 3750
Rous Lench *Worcs* 47 0153
Rousdon *Devon* 10 2991
Rousham *Oxon* 49 4724
Rout's Green *Bucks* 37 7898
Routenbeck *Cumb* 93 1930
Routenburn *N Ayrs* 114 1961
Routh *E R Yk* 85 0942
Row *Cnwll* 4 0976
Row *Cumb* 94 6234
Row *Cumb* 87 4589
Row Ash *Hants* 13 5413
Row Green *Essex* 40 7420
Row Town *Surrey* 26 0363
Rowanburn *D & G* 101 4177
Rowardennan Hotel *Stirlg* 115 3698
Rowardennan Lodge *Stirlg* 115 3598
Rowarth *Derbys* 79 0189
Rowberrow *Somset* 21 4558
Rowborough *IOW* 13 4684
Rowde *Wilts* 22 9762
Rowden *Devon* 8 6499
Rowen *Conwy* 69 7671
Rowfield *Derbys* 73 1948
Rowfoot *Nthumb* 102 6860
Rowford *Somset* 20 2327
Rowhedge *Essex* 41 0221
Rowhook *W Susx* 14 1234
Rowington *Warwks* 48 2069
Rowland *Derbys* 74 2172
Rowland's Castle *Hants* 13 7310
Rowland's Gill *T & W* 96 1658
Rowledge *Surrey* 25 8243
Rowley *Dur* 95 0848
Rowley *E R Yk* 84 9732
Rowley *Shrops* 59 3006
Rowley Green *W Mids* 61 3483
Rowley Hill *W York* 82 1914
Rowley Regis *W Mids* 60 9787
Rowlstone *Herefd* 46 3727
Rowly *Surrey* 14 0440
Rowner *Hants* 13 5801
Rowney Green *Worcs* 61 0471
Rownhams *Hants* 12 3817
Rowrah *Cumb* 92 0518
Rows of Trees *Ches* 79 8379
Rowsham *Bucks* 38 8417
Rowsley *Derbys* 74 2565
Rowstock *Oxon* 37 4789
Rowston *Lincs* 76 0856
Rowthorne *Derbys* 75 4764
Rowton *Ches* 71 4464
Rowton *Shrops* 59 3612
Rowton *Shrops* 59 6119
Rowton *Shrops* 59 4180
Roxburgh *Border* 110 6930
Roxby *Lincs* 84 9116
Roxby *N York* 97 7616
Roxton *Beds* 52 1554
Roxwell *Essex* 40 6408
Roy Bridge *Highld* 131 2681
Royal Oak *Dur* 96 2023
Royal Oak *Lancs* 78 4103
Royal's Green *Ches* 71 6242
Roydhouse *W York* 82 2112
Roydon *Essex* 39 4010
Roydon *Norfk* 65 7023
Roydon *Norfk* 54 1080
Roydon Hamlet *Essex* 39 4107
Royston *Herts* 39 3540
Royston *S York* 83 3611
Royton *Gt Man* 79 9107
Rozel *Jersey* 158 0000
Ruabon *Wrexhm* 71 3043
Ruaig *Ag & B* 120 0747
Ruan High Lanes *Cnwll* 3 9039
Ruan Lanihorne *Cnwll* 3 8942
Ruan Major *Cnwll* 2 7016
Ruan Minor *Cnwll* 2 7115
Ruardean *Gloucs* 35 6217
Ruardean Hill *Gloucs* 35 6317
Ruardean Woodside *Gloucs* 35 6216
Rubery *Worcs* 60 9977
Ruckcroft *Cumb* 94 5344
Ruckhall *Herefd* 46 4637
Ruckhall Common *Herefd* 46 4539
Ruckinge *Kent* 17 0233
Ruckland *Lincs* 77 3378
Ruckley *Shrops* 59 5300
Rudby *N York* 89 4706
Rudchester *Nthumb* 103 1167
Ruddington *Notts* 62 5732
Ruddle *Gloucs* 35 6811
Ruddlemoor *Cnwll* 3 0054
Rudford *Gloucs* 35 7721
Rudge *Somset* 22 8251
Rudgeway *Gloucs* 35 6386
Rudgwick *W Susx* 14 0834
Rudhall *Herefd* 47 6225
Rudheath *Ches* 79 6772
Rudley Green *Essex* 40 8303
Rudloe *Wilts* 35 8470
Rudry *Caerph* 33 2086
Rudston *E R Yk* 91 0967
Rudyard *Staffs* 72 9557
Ruecastle *Border* 110 6120
Rufford *Lancs* 80 4615
Rufforth *N York* 83 5251
Rug *Denbgs* 70 0543
Rugby *Warwks* 50 5075
Rugeley *Staffs* 73 0418
Ruggaton *Devon* 19 5545
Ruishton *Somset* 20 2625
Ruislip *Gt Lon* 26 0987
Ruletownhead *Border* 110 6113
Rumbach *Moray* 141 3852
Rumbling Bridge *P & K* 117 0199
Rumburgh *Suffk* 55 3481
Rumby Hill *Dur* 96 1634
Rumford *Cnwll* 4 8970
Rumford *Falk* 116 9377
Rumney *Cardif* 33 2178
Rumwell *Somset* 20 1923
Runcorn *Ches* 78 5182
Runcton *W Susx* 14 8802
Runcton Holme *Norfk* 65 6109
Runfold *Surrey* 25 8647
Runhall *Norfk* 66 0507
Runham *Norfk* 67 4610
Runham *Norfk* 67 5108
Runnington *Somset* 20 1221
Runsell Green *Essex* 40 7905
Runshaw Moor *Lancs* 80 5319
Runswick *N York* 97 8016
Runtaleave *Angus* 133 2867
Runwell *Essex* 40 7594
Ruscombe *Berks* 37 7976
Rush Green *Ches* 79 6987
Rush Green *Essex* 41 1515
Rush Green *Gt Lon* 27 5187
Rush Green *Herts* 39 2123
Rush Green *Herts* 39 3325
Rushall *Herefd* 47 6435
Rushall *Norfk* 55 1982
Rushall *W Mids* 60 0200
Rushall *Wilts* 23 1255
Rushbrooke *Suffk* 54 8961
Rushbury *Shrops* 59 5191
Rushden *Herts* 39 3031
Rushden *Nhants* 51 9566
Rushenden *Kent* 28 9071
Rusher's Cross *E Susx* 16 6028
Rushett Common *Surrey* 14 0242
Rushford *Devon* 5 4576
Rushford *Norfk* 54 9281
Rushlake Green *E Susx* 16 6218
Rushmere *Suffk* 55 4986
Rushmere St Andrew *Suffk* 55 1946
Rushmoor *Surrey* 25 8740
Rushock *Herefd* 46 3058
Rushock *Worcs* 60 8871
Rusholme *Gt Man* 79 8594
Rushton *Ches* 71 5863
Rushton *Nhants* 51 8482
Rushton *Shrops* 59 6008
Rushton Spencer *Staffs* 72 9362
Rushwick *Worcs* 47 8254
Rushyford *Dur* 96 2728
Ruskie *Stirlg* 116 6200
Ruskington *Lincs* 76 0851
Rusland *Cumb* 87 3488
Rusper *W Susx* 15 2037
Ruspidge *Gloucs* 35 6611
Russ Hill *Surrey* 15 2240
Russel's Green *Suffk* 55 2572
Russell Green *Essex* 40 7413
Russell's Green *E Susx* 16 7011
Russell's Water *Oxon* 37 7089
Rusthall *Kent* 16 5639
Rustington *W Susx* 14 0402
Ruston *N York* 91 9583
Ruston Parva *E R Yk* 91 0661
Ruswarp *N York* 90 8809
Ruthall *Shrops* 59 5990
Rutherford *Border* 110 6430
Rutherglen *S Lans* 116 6161
Ruthernbridge *Cnwll* 4 0166
Ruthin *Denbgs* 70 1258
Ruthrieston *Aber C* 135 9204
Ruthven *Abers* 142 5046
Ruthven *Angus* 126 2848
Ruthven *Highld* 140 8132
Ruthven *Highld* 132 7699
Ruthven House *Angus* 126 3047
Ruthvoes *Cnwll* 4 9260
Ruthwaite *Cumb* 93 2336
Ruthwell *D & G* 100 0967
Ruxley Corner *Gt Lon* 27 4770
Ruxton Green *Herefd* 34 5419
Ruyton-XI-Towns *Shrops* 59 3922
Ryal *Nthumb* 103 0174
Ryall *Dorset* 10 4095
Ryall *Worcs* 47 8640
Ryarsh *Kent* 28 6660
Rycote *Oxon* 37 6705
Rydal *Cumb* 87 3606
Ryde *IOW* 13 5992
Rye *E Susx* 17 9220
Rye Cross *Worcs* 47 7735
Rye Foreign *E Susx* 17 8922
Rye Harbour *E Susx* 17 9319
Rye Street *Worcs* 47 7835
Ryebank *Shrops* 59 5131
Ryeford *Herefd* 35 6322
Ryehill *E R Yk* 85 2225
Ryeish Green *Nhants* 24 7267
Ryhall *Rutlnd* 64 0310
Ryhill *W York* 83 3814
Ryhope *T & W* 96 4152
Rylah *Derbys* 75 4667
Ryland *Lincs* 76 0179
Rylands *Notts* 62 5335
Rylstone *N York* 88 9658
Ryme Intrinseca *Dorset* 10 5810
Ryther *N York* 83 5539
Ryton *N York* 90 7975
Ryton *Shrops* 60 7602
Ryton *T & W* 103 1564
Ryton *Warwks* 61 4086
Ryton Woodside *T & W* 96 1462
Ryton-on-Dunsmore *Warwks* 61 3874

# S

Sabden *Lancs* 81 7837
Sabine's Green *Essex* 27 5496
Sacombe *Herts* 39 3319
Sacombe Green *Herts* 39 3419
Sacriston *Dur* 96 2447
Sadberge *Dur* 96 3416
Saddell *Ag & B* 105 7832
Saddington *Leics* 50 6691
Saddle Bow *Norfk* 65 6015
Saddlescombe *W Susx* 15 2711
Sadgill *Cumb* 87 4805
Saffron Walden *Essex* 39 5438
Sageston *Pembks* 30 0503
Saham Hills *Norfk* 66 9003
Saham Toney *Norfk* 66 8901
Saighton *Ches* 71 4462
St Abbs *Border* 119 9167
St Agnes *Border* 118 6763
St Agnes *Cnwll* 2 7150
St Albans *Herts* 38 1407
St Allen *Cnwll* 3 8250
St Andrew *Guern* 158 0000
St Andrew's Major *V Glam* 33 1371
St Andrews *Fife* 127 5116
St Andrews Well *Dorset* 10 4793
St Ann's *D & G* 100 0793
St Ann's Chapel *Cnwll* 5 4170
St Ann's Chapel *Devon* 7 6647
St Anne's *Lancs* 80 3228
St Anthony *Cnwll* 3 7825
St Anthony's Hill *E Susx* 16 6201
St Arvans *Mons* 34 5296
St Asaph *Denbgs* 70 0374
St Athan *V Glam* 20 0167
St Aubin *Jersey* 158 0000
St Austell *Cnwll* 3 0152
St Bees *Cumb* 86 9711
St Blazey *Cnwll* 3 0654
St Blazey Gate *Cnwll* 3 0653
St Boswells *Border* 110 5930
St Brelade *Jersey* 158 0000
St Brelade's Bay *Jersey* 158 0000
St Breock *Cnwll* 4 9771
St Breward *Cnwll* 4 0977
St Briavels *Gloucs* 34 5604
St Bride's Major *V Glam* 33 8974
St Brides *Pembks* 30 8010
St Brides Netherwent *Mons* 34 4289
St Brides super-Ely *V Glam* 33 0977
St Brides Wentlooge *Newpt* 34 2982
St Budeaux *Devon* 6 4558
St Buryan *Cnwll* 2 4025
St Catherine *Somset* 35 7769
St Catherines *Ag & B* 123 1207
St Chloe *Gloucs* 35 8401
St Clears *Carmth* 31 2816
St Cleer *Cnwll* 5 2468
St Clement *Cnwll* 3 8543
St Clement *Jersey* 158 0000
St Clether *Cnwll* 5 2084
St Colmac *Ag & B* 114 0467
St Columb Major *Cnwll* 4 9163
St Columb Minor *Cnwll* 4 8362
St Columb Road *Cnwll* 4 9159
St Combs *Abers* 143 0563
St Cross South Elmham *Suffk* 55 2984
St Cyrus *Abers* 135 7464
St David's *P & K* 125 9420
St David's *Pembks* 30 7525
St Day *Cnwll* 3 7242
St Decumans *Somset* 20 0642
St Dennis *Cnwll* 4 9557
St Devereux *Herefd* 46 4431
St Dogmaels *Cerdgn* 42 1645
St Dogwells *Pembks* 30 9727
St Dominick *Cnwll* 5 4067
St Donats *V Glam* 20 9368
St Edith's Marsh *Wilts* 22 9764
St Endellion *Cnwll* 4 9978
St Enoder *Cnwll* 3 8956
St Erme *Cnwll* 3 8449
St Erney *Cnwll* 5 3759
St Erth *Cnwll* 2 5535
St Erth Praze *Cnwll* 2 5735
St Ervan *Cnwll* 4 8970
St Ewe *Cnwll* 3 9746
St Fagans *Cardif* 33 1277
St Fergus *Abers* 143 0952
St Fillans *P & K* 124 6924
St Florence *Pembks* 31 0801
St Gennys *Cnwll* 4 1497
St George *Conwy* 70 9775
St George's *V Glam* 33 1076
St George's Hill *Surrey* 26 0862
St Georges *Somset* 21 3762
St Germans *Cnwll* 5 3657
St Giles in the Wood *Devon* 19 5319
St Giles-on-the-Heath *Cnwll* 5 3690
St Gluvia's *Cnwll* 3 7834
St Harmon *Powys* 45 9872
St Helen Auckland *Dur* 96 1826
St Helena *Norfk* 66 1816
St Helens *Cumb* 92 0232
St Helens *E Susx* 17 8212
St Helens *IOW* 13 6289
St Helens *Mersyd* 78 5195
St Helier *Gt Lon* 27 2567
St Helier *Jersey* 158 0000
St Hilary *Cnwll* 2 5431
St Hilary *V Glam* 33 0173
St Hill *Devon* 9 0908
St Hill *W Susx* 15 3835
St Illtyd *Blae G* 34 2201
St Ippollitts *Herts* 39 1927
St Ishmael's *Pembks* 30 8307
St Issey *Cnwll* 4 9271
St Ive *Cnwll* 5 3167
St Ives *Cambs* 52 3171
St Ives *Cnwll* 2 5140
St Ives *Dorset* 12 1204
St James *Norfk* 67 2720
St James South Elmham *Suffk* 55 3281
St James's End *Nhants* 49 7460
St John *Cnwll* 5 4053
St John *Jersey* 158 0000
St John's *IOM* 158 2781
St John's Chapel *Devon* 19 5329
St John's Chapel *Dur* 95 8837
St John's Fen End *Norfk* 65 5312
St John's Highway *Norfk* 65 5214
St John's Kirk *S Lans* 108 9836
St John's Town of Dalry *D & G* 99 6281
St John's Wood *Gt Lon* 27 2683
St Johns *Dur* 95 0633
St Johns *Kent* 27 5356
St Johns *Surrey* 25 9857
St Johns *Worcs* 47 8454
St Jude's *IOM* 158 3996
St Just *Cnwll* 2 3731
St Just Lane *Cnwll* 3 8535
St Just-in-Roseland *Cnwll* 3 8435
St Katherines *Abers* 142 7834
St Keverne *Cnwll* 3 7921
St Kew *Cnwll* 4 0276
St Kew Highway *Cnwll* 4 0375
St Keyne *Cnwll* 5 2461
St Lawrence *Cnwll* 4 0466
St Lawrence *Essex* 41 9604
St Lawrence *IOW* 13 5376
St Lawrence *Jersey* 158 0000
St Lawrence *Kent* 29 3665
St Leonard's Street *Kent* 28 6756
St Leonards *Bucks* 38 9007
St Leonards *Dorset* 12 1103
St Leonards *E Susx* 17 8009
St Levan *Cnwll* 2 3822
St Lythans *V Glam* 33 1072
St Mabyn *Cnwll* 4 0473
St Madoes *P & K* 126 1921
St Margaret South Elmham *Suffk* 55 3183
St Margaret's at Cliffe *Kent* 29 3544
St Margarets *Herefd* 46 3533
St Margarets *Herts* 39 3811
St Margarets Hope *Ork* 153 4493
St Marks *IOM* 158 2974
St Martin *Cnwll* 5 2555
St Martin *Guern* 158 0000
St Martin *Jersey* 158 0000
St Martin's *P & K* 126 1530
St Martin's Green *Cnwll* 3 7323
St Martin's Moor *Shrops* 59 3135
St Martins *Shrops* 59 3236
St Mary *Jersey* 158 0000
St Mary Bourne *Hants* 24 4250
St Mary Church *V Glam* 33 0071
St Mary Cray *Gt Lon* 27 4768
St Mary Hill *V Glam* 33 9678
St Mary in the Marsh *Kent* 17 0627
St Mary's *Ork* 153 4701
St Mary's Bay *Kent* 17 0827
St Mary's Grove *Somset* 21 4669
St Mary's Hoo *Kent* 28 8076
St Marychurch *Devon* 7 9166
St Maughans *Mons* 34 4617
St Maughans Green *Mons* 34 4717
St Mawes *Cnwll* 3 8433
St Mawgan *Cnwll* 4 8765
St Mellion *Cnwll* 5 3965
St Mellons *Cardif* 34 2281
St Merryn *Cnwll* 4 8874
St Mewan *Cnwll* 3 9951
St Michael Caerhays *Cnwll* 3 9642
St Michael Church *Somset* 20 3030
St Michael Penkevil *Cnwll* 3 8541
St Michael South Elmham *Suffk* 55 3483
St Michael's on Wyre *Lancs* 80 4641
St Michaels *Kent* 17 8835
St Michaels *Worcs* 46 5865
St Minver *Cnwll* 4 9677
St Monans *Fife* 127 5201
St Neot *Cnwll* 4 1868
St Neots *Cambs* 52 1860
St Nicholas *Pembks* 30 9035
St Nicholas *V Glam* 33 0974
St Nicholas at Wade *Kent* 29 2666
St Ninians *Stirlg* 116 7991
St Olaves *Norfk* 67 4599
St Osyth *Essex* 41 1215
St Ouen *Jersey* 158 0000
St Owens Cross *Herefd* 46 5324
St Paul's Walden *Herts* 39 1922
St Pauls Cray *Gt Lon* 27 4768
St Peter *Jersey* 158 0000
St Peter Port *Guern* 158 0000
St Peter's *Guern* 158 0000
St Peter's *Kent* 29 3868
St Peter's Hill *Cambs* 52 2372
St Petrox *Pembks* 30 9797
St Pinnock *Cnwll* 5 2063
St Quivox *S Ayrs* 106 3723
St Ruan *Cnwll* 2 7115
St Sampson *Guern* 158 0000
St Saviour *Guern* 158 0000
St Saviour *Jersey* 158 0000
St Stephen *Cnwll* 3 9453
St Stephen's Coombe *Cnwll* 3 9451
St Stephens *Cnwll* 5 3285
St Stephens *Cnwll* 5 4158
St Teath *Cnwll* 4 0680
St Tudy *Cnwll* 4 0676
St Twynnells *Pembks* 30 9597
St Veep *Cnwll* 3 1455
St Vigeans *Angus* 127 6443
St Wenn *Cnwll* 4 9664

Sheffield Bottom
Soberton Heath

Sheffield Bottom Berks 24 6469
Sheffield Green E Susx 15 4125
Shefford Beds 38 1439
Sheigra Highld 148 1860
Sheinton Shrops 59 6003
Shelderton Shrops 46 4077
Sheldon Derbys 74 1768
Sheldon Devon 9 1208
Sheldon W Mids 61 1584
Sheldwich Kent 28 0156
Sheldwich Lees Kent 28 0156
Shelf W York 82 1228
Shelfanger Norfk 54 1083
Shelfield W Mids 61 0302
Shelfield Warwks 48 1263
Shelfield Green Warwks 48 1261
Shelford Notts 63 6642
Shelford Warwks 50 4288
Shellacres Border 110 8943
Shelley Essex 39 5505
Shelley Suffk 54 0238
Shelley W York 82 2011
Shelley Far Bank W York 82 2010
Shellingford Oxon 36 3193
Shellow Bowells Essex 40 6007
Shelsley Beauchamp Worcs 47 7363
Shelsley Walsh Worcs 47 7263
Shelton Beds 51 0368
Shelton Norfk 67 2291
Shelton Notts 63 7844
Shelton Shrops 59 4613
Shelton Green Norfk 55 2390
Shelton Lock Derbys 62 3730
Shelton Under Harley Staffs 72 8139
Shelve Shrops 59 3399
Shelwick Herefd 46 5242
Shenfield Essex 40 6095
Shenington Oxon 48 3742
Shenley Herts 26 1008
Shenley Brook End Bucks 38 8335
Shenley Church End Bucks 38 8336
Shenleybury Herts 26 1801
Shenmore Herefd 46 3937
Shennanton D & G 98 3363
Shenstone Staffs 61 1004
Shenstone Worcs 60 8673
Shenstone Woodend Staffs 61 1101
Shenton Leics 61 3800
Shepeau Stow Lincs 64 3012
Shephall Herts 39 2623
Shepherd's Bush Gt Lon 26 2380
Shepherd's Green Oxon 37 7183
Shepherds Cnwll 3 8154
Shepherds Patch Gloucs 35 7304
Shepherdswell Kent 29 2647
Shepley W York 82 1909
Shepperdine Gloucs 35 6295
Shepperton Surrey 26 0766
Shepperton Green Surrey 26 0767
Shepreth Cambs 52 3947
Shepshed Leics 62 4819
Shepton Beauchamp Somset 10 4017
Shepton Mallet Somset 21 6143
Shepton Montague Somset 22 6831
Shepway Kent 28 7753
Sheraton Dur 96 4435
Sherborne Dorset 10 6316
Sherborne Gloucs 36 1614
Sherborne Somset 21 5855
Sherborne Causeway Dorset 22 8323
Sherborne St John Hants 24 6255
Sherbourne Warwks 48 2661
Sherburn Dur 96 3142
Sherburn N York 91 9576
Sherburn Hill Dur 96 3342
Sherburn in Elmet N York 83 4933
Shere Surrey 14 0747
Shereford Norfk 66 8829
Sherfield English Hants 23 2922
Sherfield on Loddon Hants 24 6858
Sherfin Lancs 81 7925
Sherford Devon 7 7844
Sherford Dorset 11 9193
Sheriff Hutton N York 90 6566
Sheriffhales Shrops 60 7512
Sheringham Norfk 66 1543
Sherington Bucks 38 8846
Shermanbury W Susx 15 2019
Shernborne Norfk 65 7132
Sherrington Wilts 22 9639
Sherston Wilts 35 8586
Sherwood Notts 62 5643
Shettleston C Glas 116 6464
Shevington Gt Man 78 5408
Shevington Moor Gt Man 78 5410
Shevington Vale Gt Man 78 5309
Sheviock Cnwll 5 3755
Shibden Head W York 82 0928
Shide IOW 13 5088
Shidlaw Nthumb 110 8037
Shiel Bridge Highld 138 9318
Shieldaig Highld 137 8154
Shieldhill D & G 100 0385
Shieldhill Falk 116 8976
Shieldhill House Hotel S Lans 108 0040
Shields N Lans 116 7755
Shielfoot Highld 129 6670
Shielhill Angus 134 4257
Shielhill Inver 114 2472
Shifford Oxon 36 3701
Shifnal Shrops 60 7407
Shilbottle Nthumb 111 1908
Shildon Dur 96 2226
Shillford E Rens 115 4556
Shillingford Devon 20 9824
Shillingford Oxon 37 5992
Shillingford Abbot Devon 9 9088
Shillingford St George Devon 9 9087
Shillingstone Dorset 11 8211
Shillington Beds 38 1234
Shillmoor Nthumb 110 8807
Shilton Oxon 36 2608
Shilton Warwks 61 4084
Shilvinghampton Dorset 10 6284
Shimpling Norfk 54 1583
Shimpling Suffk 54 8651
Shimpling Street Suffk 54 8753
Shincliffe Dur 96 2940
Shiney Row T & W 96 3252
Shinfield Berks 24 7368
Shingay Cambs 52 3046
Shingle Street Suffk 55 3642
Shinnersbridge Devon 7 7862
Shinness Highld 146 5215
Shipbourne Kent 27 5952
Shipbrookhill Ches 79 6771
Shipdham Norfk 66 9507
Shipham Somset 21 4457
Shiphay Devon 7 8965
Shiplake Oxon 37 7678
Shiplake Row Oxon 37 7478
Shiplate Somset 21 3556
Shipley Derbys 62 4444
Shipley Shrops 60 8095
Shipley W Susx 15 1421
Shipley W York 82 1537
Shipley Bridge Surrey 15 3040
Shipley Hatch Kent 28 0038
Shipmeadow Suffk 55 3790
Shippea Hill Station Cambs 53 6484
Shippon Oxon 37 4898
Shipston on Stour Warwks 48 2540
Shipton Bucks 49 7727
Shipton Gloucs 36 0318
Shipton N York 90 5558
Shipton Shrops 59 5692
Shipton Bellinger Hants 23 2345
Shipton Gorge Dorset 10 4991
Shipton Green W Susx 14 8099
Shipton Moyne Gloucs 35 8989
Shipton-on-Cherwell Oxon 37 4716
Shipton-under-Wychwood Oxon 36 2817
Shiptonthorpe E R Yk 84 8543
Shirburn Oxon 37 6995
Shirdley Hill Lancs 80 3612
Shire Cumb 94 6135
Shire Oak W Mids 61 0504
Shirebrook Derbys 75 5267
Shiregreen S York 74 3691
Shirehampton Bristl 34 5376
Shiremoor T & W 103 3171
Shirenewton Mons 34 4793
Shireoaks Notts 75 5580
Shirkoak Kent 17 9435
Shirl Heath Herefd 46 4359
Shirland Derbys 74 4058
Shirlett Shrops 59 6497
Shirley Derbys 73 2141
Shirley Gt Lon 27 3565
Shirley Hants 13 4014
Shirley W Mids 61 1278
Shirrell Heath Hants 13 5714
Shirvan Ag & B 113 8784
Shirwell Devon 19 6037
Shirwell Cross Devon 19 5936
Shiskine N Ayrs 105 9129
Shittlehope Dur 95 0039
Shobdon Herefd 46 4062
Shobley Hants 12 1806
Shobrooke Devon 9 8601
Shoby Leics 63 6820
Shocklach Ches 71 4349
Shocklach Green Ches 71 4349
Shoeburyness Essex 40 9385
Sholden Kent 29 3552
Sholing Hants 13 4511
Shoose Cumb 92 0127
Shoot Hill Shrops 59 4112
Shop Cnwll 18 2214
Shop Cnwll 4 8773
Shop Street Suffk 55 2268
Shopwyke W Susx 14 8805
Shore Gt Man 81 9216
Shoreditch Gt Lon 27 3382
Shoreditch Somset 20 2422
Shoreham Kent 27 5161
Shoreham-by-Sea W Susx 15 2105
Shoreswood Nthumb 110 9446
Shorley Hants 13 5726
Shorncote Gloucs 35 0296
Shorne Kent 28 6971
Shorne Ridgeway Kent 28 6970
Short Heath W Mids 60 9700
Short Heath W Mids 61 0992
Shorta Cross Cnwll 5 2857
Shortbridge E Susx 16 4521
Shortfield Common Surrey 25 8442
Shortgate E Susx 16 4915
Shortheath Hants 14 7636
Shortlanesend Cnwll 3 8047
Shortstown Beds 38 0747
Shorwell IOW 13 4583
Shoscombe Somset 22 7156
Shotesham Norfk 67 2499
Shotgate Essex 40 7592
Shotley Suffk 55 2335
Shotley Bridge Dur 95 0953
Shotley Gate Suffk 41 2433
Shotley Street Suffk 55 2335
Shotleyfield Nthumb 95 0553
Shottenden Kent 28 0454
Shottermill Surrey 14 8832
Shottery Warwks 48 1854
Shotteswell Warwks 49 4245
Shottisham Suffk 55 3244
Shottle Derbys 74 3149
Shottlegate Derbys 62 3147
Shotton Dur 96 3625
Shotton Dur 96 4139
Shotton Flints 71 3168
Shotton Nthumb 110 8430
Shotton Nthumb 103 2277
Shotton Colliery Dur 96 3941
Shotts N Lans 116 8759
Shotwick Ches 71 3371
Shougle Moray 141 2155
Shouldham Norfk 65 6709
Shouldham Thorpe Norfk 65 6607
Shoulton Worcs 47 8159
Shover's Green E Susx 16 6530
Shraleybrook Staffs 72 7849
Shrawardine Shrops 59 3915
Shrawley Worcs 47 8065
Shreding Green Bucks 26 0280
Shrewley Warwks 48 2167
Shrewsbury Shrops 59 4912
Shrewton Wilts 23 0743
Shripney W Susx 14 9302
Shrivenham Oxon 36 2389
Shropham Norfk 66 9893
Shrub End Essex 41 9723
Shucknall Herefd 46 5842
Shudy Camps Cambs 53 6244
Shurdington Gloucs 35 9218
Shurlock Row Berks 25 8374
Shurnock Worcs 48 0360
Shurrery Highld 150 0458
Shurrery Lodge Highld 150 0456
Shurton Somset 20 2044
Shustoke Warwks 61 2290
Shut Heath Staffs 72 8621
Shute Devon 9 8900
Shute Devon 10 2597
Shutford Oxon 48 3840
Shuthonger Gloucs 47 8935
Shutlanger Nhants 49 7249
Shutt Green Staffs 60 8709
Shutterton Devon 9 9679
Shuttington Warwks 61 2505
Shuttlewood Derbys 75 4673
Shuttlewood Common Derbys 75 4773
Shuttleworth Lancs 81 8017
Siabost W Isls 152 2646
Siadar W Isls 152 3854
Sibbertoft Nhants 50 6882
Sibdon Carwood Shrops 59 4183
Sibford Ferris Oxon 48 3537
Sibford Gower Oxon 48 3537
Sible Hedingham Essex 53 7734
Sibley's Green Essex 40 6128
Siblyback Cnwll 5 2372
Sibsey Lincs 77 3550
Sibsey Fenside Lincs 77 3452
Sibson Cambs 51 0997
Sibson Leics 61 3500
Sibster Highld 151 3253
Sibthorpe Notts 75 7273
Sibthorpe Notts 63 7645
Sibton Suffk 55 3669
Sicklesmere Suffk 54 8760
Sicklinghall N York 83 3648
Sid Cop S York 83 3809
Sidbrook Somset 20 2527
Sidbury Devon 9 1391
Sidbury Shrops 60 6885
Sidcot Somset 21 4257
Sidcup Gt Lon 27 4672
Siddick Cumb 92 0031
Siddington Ches 79 8470
Siddington Gloucs 36 0399
Sidemoor Worcs 60 9571
Sidestrand Norfk 67 2539
Sidford Devon 9 1390
Sidlesham W Susx 14 8599
Sidlesham Common W Susx 14 8599
Sidley E Susx 17 7408
Sidmouth Devon 9 1287
Siefton Shrops 59 4883
Sigford Devon 7 7773
Sigglesthorne E R Yk 85 1545
Sigingstone V Glam 33 9771
Signet Oxon 36 2410
Silchester Hants 24 6261
Sileby Leics 62 6015
Silecroft Cumb 86 1381
Silfield Norfk 66 1299
Silian Cerdgn 44 5751
Silk Willoughby Lincs 64 0542
Silkstead Hants 13 4424
Silkstone S York 82 2805
Silkstone Common S York 82 2904
Silksworth T & W 96 3752
Silloth Cumb 92 1153
Silpho N York 91 9692
Silsden W York 82 0446
Silsoe Beds 38 0835
Silton Dorset 22 7829
Silver End Essex 40 8119
Silver Street Kent 28 8760
Silver Street Somset 21 5432
Silverburn Mdloth 117 2060
Silverdale Lancs 87 4674
Silverdale Staffs 72 8146
Silverdale Green Lancs 87 4674
Silverford Abers 142 7763
Silvergate Norfk 66 1727
Silverlace Green Suffk 55 3160
Silverley's Green Suffk 55 2976
Silverstone Nhants 49 6743
Silverton Devon 9 9502
Silverwell Cnwll 3 7448
Silvington Shrops 47 6279
Simmondley Derbys 74 0293
Simonburn Nthumb 102 8773
Simons Burrow Devon 9 1416
Simonsbath Somset 19 7739
Simonstone Lancs 81 7734
Simonstone N York 88 8791
Simprim Border 110 8445
Simpson Bucks 38 8836
Simpson Cross Pembks 30 8919
Sinclair's Hill Border 119 8150
Sinclairston E Ayrs 107 4716
Sinderby N York 89 3482
Sinderhope Nthumb 95 8451
Sinderland Green Gt Man 79 7389
Sindlesham Berks 25 7769
Single Street Gt Lon 27 4359
Singleborough Bucks 49 7631
Singleton Lancs 80 3838
Singleton W Susx 14 8713
Singlewell Kent 28 6570
Sinkhurst Green Kent 28 8142
Sinnarhard Abers 134 4713
Sinnington N York 90 7485
Sinton Worcs 47 8160
Sinton Green Worcs 47 8160
Sipson Gt Lon 26 0777
Sirhowy Blae G 33 1410
Sissinghurst Kent 28 7937
Siston Gloucs 35 6875
Sitcott Devon 5 3691
Sithney Cnwll 2 6328
Sithney Common Cnwll 2 6428
Sithney Green Cnwll 2 6429
Sittingbourne Kent 28 9063
Six Ashes Staffs 60 7988
Six Bells Blae G 34 2202
Six Mile Bottom Cambs 53 5756
Six Rues Jersey 158 0000
Sixhills Lincs 76 1787
Sixmile Cottages Kent 29 1344
Sixpenny Handley Dorset 11 9917
Sizewell Suffk 55 4762
Skaill Ork 153 5806
Skares E Ayrs 107 5317
Skateraw Abers 135 9193
Skateraw E Loth 119 7375
Skeabost Highld 136 4148
Skeeby N York 89 1902
Skeffington Leics 63 7402
Skeffling E R Yk 85 3719
Skegby Notts 75 4961
Skegby Notts 75 7869
Skegness Lincs 77 5663
Skelbo Highld 147 7895
Skelbo Street Highld 147 7994
Skelbrooke S York 83 5012
Skeldyke Lincs 64 3337
Skellingthorpe Lincs 76 9272
Skellorm Green Ches 79 9281
Skellow S York 83 5310
Skelmanthorpe W York 82 2310
Skelmersdale Lancs 78 4606
Skelmorlie N Ayrs 114 1967
Skelpick Highld 150 7256
Skelston D & G 100 8285
Skelton Cumb 93 4335
Skelton E R Yk 84 7625
Skelton N York 89 0900
Skelton N York 97 6618
Skelton N York 89 3668
Skelton N York 83 5756
Skelwith Bridge Cumb 87 3403
Skendleby Lincs 77 4369
Skene House Abers 135 7610
Skenfrith Mons 34 4520
Skerne E R Yk 84 0455
Skerray Highld 149 6563
Skerricha Highld 148 2350
Skerton Lancs 87 4763
Sketchley Leics 50 4292
Sketty Swans 32 6292
Skewen Neath 32 7296
Skewsby N York 90 6270
Skeyton Norfk 67 2425
Skeyton Corner Norfk 67 2527
Skiall Highld 150 0267
Skidbrooke Lincs 77 4393
Skidbrooke North End Lincs 77 4395
Skidby E R Yk 84 0133
Skigersta W Isls 152 5461
Skilgate Somset 20 9827
Skillington Lincs 63 8925
Skinburness Cumb 92 1256
Skinflats Falk 116 9082
Skinidin Highld 136 2247
Skinners Green Berks 24 4465
Skinningrove N York 97 7119
Skipness Ag & B 114 9057
Skipper's Bridge Cumb 101 3783
Skiprigg Cumb 93 3945
Skipsea E R Yk 85 1654
Skipsea Brough E R Yk 85 1454
Skipton N York 82 9851
Skipton-on-Swale N York 89 3679
Skipwith N York 83 6638
Skirlaugh E R Yk 85 1439
Skirling Border 108 0739
Skirmett Bucks 37 7790
Skirpenbeck E R Yk 84 7456
Skirwith Cumb 94 6132
Skirwith N York 87 7073
Skirza Highld 151 3868
Skitby Cumb 101 4465
Skittle Green Bucks 37 7703
Skulamus Highld 129 6622
Skyborry Green Shrops 46 2674
Skye Green Essex 40 8722
Skye of Curr Highld 141 9924
Skyreholme N York 88 0660
Slack Derbys 74 3362
Slack W York 82 9728
Slack Head Cumb 87 4978
Slack Side W York 82 1430
Slackcote Gt Man 82 9709
Slackholme End Lincs 77 5370
Slacks of Cairnbanno Abers 143 8445
Slad Gloucs 35 8707
Slade Devon 19 5046
Slade Devon 9 1108
Slade Somset 19 8327
Slade End Oxon 37 5990
Slade Green Kent 27 5276
Slade Heath Staffs 60 9106
Slade Hooton S York 75 5288
Slades Green Worcs 47 8134
Sladesbridge Cnwll 4 0171
Slaggyford Nthumb 94 6752
Slaid Hill W York 83 3240
Slaidburn Lancs 81 7152
Slaithwaite W York 82 0813
Slaley Derbys 74 2757
Slaley Nthumb 95 9657
Slamannan Falk 116 8572
Slapton Bucks 38 9320
Slapton Devon 7 8245
Slapton Nhants 49 6446
Slattocks Gt Man 79 8808
Slaugham W Susx 15 2528
Slaughterford Wilts 35 8473
Slawston Leics 50 7894
Sleaford Hants 25 8038
Sleaford Lincs 64 0645
Sleagill Cumb 94 5919
Sleap Shrops 59 4826
Sleapford Shrops 59 6315
Sleasdairidh Highld 146 6496
Sledge Green Worcs 47 8134
Sledmere E R Yk 91 9364
Sleight Dorset 11 9898
Sleightholme Dur 88 9510
Sleights N York 90 8607
Slepe Dorset 11 9293
Slickly Highld 151 2966
Sliddery N Ayrs 105 9323
Sligachan Highld 136 4829
Sligrachan Ag & B 114 1791
Slimbridge Gloucs 35 7303
Slindon Staffs 72 8232
Slindon W Susx 14 9608
Slinfold W Susx 14 1131
Sling Gwynd 69 6066
Slingsby N York 90 6974
Slip End Beds 38 0718
Slip End Herts 39 2837
Slipton Nhants 51 9579
Slitting Mill Staffs 73 0217
Slockavullin Ag & B 113 8297
Slogarie D & G 99 6568
Sloley Norfk 67 2924
Sloncombe Devon 8 7386
Sloothby Lincs 77 4970
Slough Berks 26 9879
Slough Green Somset 20 2719
Slough Green W Susx 15 2826
Slumbay Highld 138 8938
Slyfield Green Surrey 25 9952
Slyne Lancs 87 4765
Smailholm Border 110 6436
Small Dole W Susx 15 2112
Small Heath W Mids 61 1085
Small Hythe Kent 17 8930
Small Wood Hey Lancs 80 3948
Smallbridge Gt Man 81 9115
Smallbrook Devon 9 8698
Smallbrook Gloucs 34 5900
Smallburgh Norfk 67 3324
Smalldale Derbys 74 0977
Smalldale Derbys 74 1781
Smalley Derbys 62 4044
Smalley Common Derbys 62 4042
Smalley Green Derbys 62 4043
Smallfield Surrey 15 3143
Smallridge Devon 10 3001
Smallthorne Staffs 72 8850
Smallways N York 89 1111
Smallwood Ches 72 8060
Smallworth Norfk 54 0080
Smannell Hants 23 3749
Smardale Cumb 88 7308
Smarden Kent 28 8742
Smarden Bell Kent 28 8742
Smart's Hill Kent 16 5242
Smeafield Nthumb 111 0937
Smearisary Highld 129 6476
Smeatharpe Devon 9 1910
Smeeth Kent 29 0739
Smeeton Westerby Leics 50 6892
Smelthouses N York 89 1964
Smerral Highld 151 1733
Smestow Staffs 60 8591
Smethwick W Mids 60 0287
Smethwick Green Ches 72 8063
Smisby Derbys 62 3418
Smith End Green Worcs 47 7752
Smith Green Lancs 80 4955
Smith's End Herts 39 4037
Smith's Green Essex 40 5721
Smith's Green Essex 53 6640
Smitheclose IOW 13 5391
Smithfield Cumb 101 4465
Smithies S York 83 3508
Smithincott Devon 9 0611
Smithstown Highld 144 7977
Smithton Highld 140 7145
Smithy Bridge Gt Man 81 9215
Smithy Green Ches 79 7474
Smithy Green Gt Man 79 8785
Smithy Houses Derbys 62 3846
Smockington Leics 50 4589
Smoo Highld 149 4167
Smythe's Green Essex 40 9218
Snade D & G 100 8485
Snailbeach Shrops 59 3702
Snailwell Cambs 53 6467
Snainton N York 91 9282
Snaith E R Yk 83 6422
Snake Pass Inn Derbys 74 1190
Snape N York 89 2684
Snape Suffk 55 3959
Snape Green Mersyd 80 3813
Snape Street Suffk 55 3958
Snaresbrook Gt Lon 27 4089
Snarestone Leics 62 3409
Snarford Lincs 76 0482
Snargate Kent 17 9928
Snave Kent 17 0129
Sneachill Worcs 47 9053
Snead Powys 59 3192
Sneath Common Norfk 54 1689
Sneaton N York 91 8907
Sneatonthorpe N York 91 9006
Snelland Lincs 76 0780
Snelson Ches 79 8074
Snelston Derbys 73 1543
Snetterton Norfk 66 9991
Snettisham Norfk 65 6834
Snibston Leics 62 4114
Snig's End Gloucs 47 7828
Snitter Nthumb 103 0203
Snitterby Lincs 76 9894
Snitterfield Warwks 48 2159
Snitterton Derbys 74 2760
Snittlegarth Cumb 93 2138
Snitton Shrops 46 5575
Snoadhill Kent 28 9442
Snodhill Herefd 46 3240
Snodland Kent 28 7061
Snoll Hatch Kent 28 6648
Snow End Herts 39 4032
Snow Street Norfk 54 0981
Snowden Hill S York 74 2600
Snowshill Gloucs 48 0933
Soake Hants 13 6611
Soar Cardif 33 0983
Soar Devon 7 7037
Soar Powys 45 9731
Soberton Hants 13 6116
Soberton Heath Hants 13 6014

Tovil Uckerby


Tovil *Kent* 28 7554
Tow Law *Dur* 95 1138
Towan *Cnwll* 4 8774
Towan *Cnwll* 3 0148
Toward *Ag & B* 114 1368
Toward Quay *Ag & B* 114 1167
Towcester *Nhants* 49 6948
Towednack *Cnwll* 2 4838
Towersey *Oxon* 37 7305
Towie *Abers* 134 4312
Town End *Cambs* 65 4195
Town End *Cumb* 86 2692
Town End *Cumb* 87 3406
Town End *Cumb* 94 6325
Town End *Cumb* 87 3687
Town End *Cumb* 87 4483
Town Green *Lancs* 78 4005
Town Green *Norfk* 67 3612
Town Head *Cumb* 87 4103
Town Head *N York* 88 8258
Town Head *N York* 82 1748
Town Kelloe *Dur* 96 3536
Town Lane *Gt Man* 79 6999
Town Littleworth *E Susx* 15 4117
Town of Lowdon *Mersyd* 78 6196
Town Row *E Susx* 16 5630
Town Street *Suffk* 53 7785
Town Yetholm *Border* 110 8128
Townend *W Duns* 115 3976
Towngate *Cumb* 94 5246
Towngate *Lincs* 64 1310
Townhead *Cumb* 92 0735
Townhead *Cumb* 94 6334
Townhead *D & G* 100 0088
Townhead *S York* 82 1602
Townhead of Greenlaw *D & G* 99 7464
Townhill *Fife* 117 1089
Townlake *Devon* 5 4074
Towns End *Hants* 24 5659
Townsend *Somset* 10 3614
Townshend *Cnwll* 2 5932
Townwell *Gloucs* 35 7090
Towthorpe *E R Yk* 91 8962
Towthorpe *N York* 90 6258
Towton *N York* 83 4839
Towyn *Conwy* 70 9779
Toxteth *Mersyd* 78 3588
Toy's Hill *Kent* 27 4651
Toynton All Saints *Lincs* 77 3963
Toynton Fen Side *Lincs* 77 3961
Toynton St Peter *Lincs* 77 4063
Trabboch *E Ayrs* 107 4421
Trabbochburn *E Ayrs* 107 4621
Traboe *Cnwll* 3 7421
Tracebridge *Somset* 20 0621
Tradespark *Highld* 140 8656
Traethsaith *Cerdgn* 42 2851
Trafford Park *Gt Man* 79 7896
Trallong *Powys* 45 9629
Tranent *E Loth* 118 4072
Tranmere *Mersyd* 78 3187
Trannack *Cnwll* 2 5633
Trantelbeg *Highld* 150 8952
Trantlemore *Highld* 150 8953
Tranwell *Nthumb* 103 1883
Trap's Green *Warwks* 48 1069
Trapp *Carmth* 32 6518
Traprain *E Loth* 118 5975
Trapshill *Berks* 23 3763
Traquair *Border* 109 3334
Trash Green *Berks* 24 6569
Traveller's Rest *Devon* 19 6127
Trawden *Lancs* 81 9138
Trawscoed *Cerdgn* 43 6672
Trawsfynydd *Gwynd* 57 7035
Tre Aubrey *V Glam* 33 0372
Tre'r-ddol *Cerdgn* 43 6692
Tre-gagle *Mons* 34 5207
Tre-Gibbon *Rhondd* 33 9905
Tre-groes *Cerdgn* 42 4044
Tre-Mostyn *Flints* 70 1479
Tre-Vaughan *Carmth* 31 3921
Tre-wyn *Mons* 34 3222
Trealaw *Rhondd* 33 0092
Treales *Lancs* 80 4332
Treamble *Cnwll* 3 7856
Trearddur Bay *IOA* 68 2579
Treaslane *Highld* 136 3953
Treator *Cnwll* 4 9075
Trebanog *Rhondd* 33 0190
Trebanos *Neath* 32 7103
Trebartha *Cnwll* 5 2677
Trebarvah *Cnwll* 2 7130
Trebarwith *Cnwll* 4 0586
Trebeath *Cnwll* 5 2587
Trebehor *Cnwll* 2 3724
Trebelzue *Cnwll* 4 8464
Trebetherick *Cnwll* 4 9378
Treborough *Somset* 20 0136
Trebudannon *Cnwll* 4 8961
Trebullett *Cnwll* 5 3278
Treburgett *Cnwll* 4 0579
Treburick *Cnwll* 4 8971
Treburley *Cnwll* 5 3577
Treburrick *Cnwll* 4 8670
Trebyan *Cnwll* 4 0763
Trecastle *Powys* 45 8829
Trecogo *Cnwll* 5 3080
Trecott *Devon* 8 6300
Trecwn *Pembks* 30 9632
Trecynon *Rhondd* 33 9903
Tredaule *Cnwll* 5 2381
Tredavoe *Cnwll* 2 4528
Tredegar *Blae G* 33 1408
Tredethy *Cnwll* 4 0672
Tredington *Gloucs* 47 9029
Tredington *Warwks* 48 2543
Tredinnick *Cnwll* 4 9270
Tredinnick *Cnwll* 4 0459
Tredinnick *Cnwll* 4 1666
Tredinnick *Cnwll* 5 2357
Tredinnick *Cnwll* 5 2957
Tredomen *Powys* 45 1231
Tredrissi *Pembks* 31 0742
Tredrizzick *Cnwll* 4 9577
Tredunhock *Mons* 34 3794
Tredustan *Powys* 45 1332
Treen *Cnwll* 2 4337
Treen *Cnwll* 2 3923
Treesmill *Cnwll* 3 0855
Treeton *S York* 75 4387
Trefasser *Pembks* 30 8938
Trefdraeth *IOA* 68 4170
Trefecca *Powys* 45 1431
Trefeglwys *Powys* 58 9690
Trefenter *Cerdgn* 43 6068
Treffgarne *Pembks* 30 9523
Treffgarne Owen *Pembks* 30 8625
Trefforest *Rhondd* 33 0888
Treffynnon *Pembks* 30 8528
Trefil *Blae G* 33 1212
Trefilan *Cerdgn* 44 5456
Treflach Wood *Shrops* 58 2625
Trefnannau *Powys* 58 2316
Trefnant *Denbgs* 70 0570
Trefonen *Shrops* 58 2526
Trefor *Gwynd* 56 3746
Trefor *IOA* 68 3780
Treforda *Cnwll* 4 0988
Trefrew *Cnwll* 4 1084
Trefriw *Conwy* 69 7863
Tregadillett *Cnwll* 5 2983
Tregaian *IOA* 68 4580
Tregare *Mons* 34 4110
Tregarne *Cnwll* 3 7823
Tregaron *Cerdgn* 44 6759
Tregarth *Gwynd* 69 6067
Tregaswith *Cnwll* 4 8962
Tregatta *Cnwll* 4 0587
Tregawne *Cnwll* 4 0066
Tregear *Cnwll* 3 8650
Tregeare *Cnwll* 5 2486
Tregeiriog *Wrexhm* 58 1733
Tregele *IOA* 68 3592
Tregellist *Cnwll* 4 0177
Tregenna *Cnwll* 3 8743
Tregenna *Cnwll* 4 0973
Tregeseal *Cnwll* 2 3731
Tregew *Cnwll* 3 8034
Tregidden *Cnwll* 3 7523
Tregiddle *Cnwll* 2 6723
Tregidgeo *Cnwll* 3 9647
Tregiskey *Cnwll* 3 0146
Treglemais *Pembks* 30 8229
Tregole *Cnwll* 5 1998
Tregolls *Cnwll* 3 7335
Tregonce *Cnwll* 4 9373
Tregonetha *Cnwll* 4 9563
Tregony *Cnwll* 3 9244
Tregoodwell *Cnwll* 4 1183
Tregoose *Cnwll* 2 6823
Tregoss *Cnwll* 4 9660
Tregowris *Cnwll* 3 7722
Tregoyd *Powys* 45 1937
Tregrehan Mills *Cnwll* 3 0453
Tregullon *Cnwll* 4 0664
Tregunna *Cnwll* 4 9673
Tregunnon *Cnwll* 5 2283
Tregurrian *Cnwll* 4 8565
Tregustick *Cnwll* 4 9866
Tregynon *Powys* 58 0998
Trehafod *Rhondd* 33 0490
Trehan *Cnwll* 5 4058
Treharris *Myr Td* 33 0996
Treharrock *Cnwll* 4 0178
Trehemborne *Cnwll* 4 8773
Treherbert *Carmth* 44 5847
Treherbert *Rhondd* 33 9498
Treheveras *Cnwll* 3 8046
Trehunist *Cnwll* 5 3263
Trekelland *Cnwll* 5 3480
Trekenner *Cnwll* 5 3478
Treknow *Cnwll* 4 0586
Trelan *Cnwll* 3 7418
Trelash *Cnwll* 4 1890
Trelassick *Cnwll* 3 8752
Trelawne *Cnwll* 5 2154
Trelawnyd *Flints* 70 0979
Treleague *Cnwll* 3 7821
Treleaver *Cnwll* 3 7716
Trelech *Carmth* 31 2830
Trelech a'r Betws *Carmth* 31 3026
Treleddyd-fawr *Pembks* 30 7528
Trelew *Cnwll* 3 8135
Trelewis *Myr Td* 33 1096
Treligga *Cnwll* 4 0484
Trelights *Cnwll* 4 9979
Trelill *Cnwll* 4 0478
Trelinnoe *Cnwll* 5 3181
Trelion *Cnwll* 3 9252
Trelissick *Cnwll* 3 8339
Trelleck *Mons* 34 5005
Trelleck Grange *Mons* 34 4901
Trelogan *Flints* 70 1180
Trelonk *Cnwll* 3 8941
Trelow *Cnwll* 4 9269
Trelowarren *Cnwll* 2 7124
Trelowia *Cnwll* 5 2956
Treluggan *Cnwll* 3 8838
Trelystan *Powys* 58 2503
Tremadog *Gwynd* 57 5640
Tremail *Cnwll* 4 1686
Tremain *Cerdgn* 42 2348
Tremaine *Cnwll* 5 2389
Tremar *Cnwll* 5 2568
Trematon *Cnwll* 5 3959
Trembraze *Cnwll* 5 2565
Tremeirchion *Denbgs* 70 0873
Tremethick Cross *Cnwll* 2 4430
Tremollett *Cnwll* 5 2975
Tremore *Cnwll* 4 0164
Trenance *Cnwll* 3 8022
Trenance *Cnwll* 4 8568
Trenance *Cnwll* 4 9270
Trenance *Cnwll* 2 6718
Trenarren *Cnwll* 3 0348
Trenault *Cnwll* 5 2683
Trench *Shrops* 60 6912
Trench Green *Oxon* 37 6877
Trencreek *Cnwll* 4 8260
Trencreek *Cnwll* 4 1896
Trendeal *Cnwll* 3 8952
Trendrine *Cnwll* 2 4739
Treneague *Cnwll* 4 9871
Trenear *Cnwll* 2 6731
Treneglos *Cnwll* 5 2088
Trenerth *Cnwll* 2 6035
Trenewan *Cnwll* 4 1753
Trenewth *Cnwll* 4 0778
Trengothal *Cnwll* 2 3724
Trengune *Cnwll* 4 1893
Treninnick *Cnwll* 4 8160
Trenowah *Cnwll* 4 7959
Trenoweth *Cnwll* 3 7533
Trent *Dorset* 10 5918
Trent Port *Lincs* 76 8381
Trent Vale *Staffs* 72 8643
Trentham *Staffs* 72 8740
Trentishoe *Devon* 19 6448
Trentlock *Derbys* 62 4831
Treoes *V Glam* 33 9478
Treorchy *Rhondd* 33 9597
Trequite *Cnwll* 4 0377
Trerhyngyll *V Glam* 33 0077
Trerulefoot *Cnwll* 5 3358
Tresahor *Cnwll* 3 7431
Tresawle *Cnwll* 3 8846
Trescott *Staffs* 60 8597
Trescowe *Cnwll* 2 5731
Tresean *Cnwll* 4 7858
Tresham *Gloucs* 35 7991
Tresillian *Cnwll* 3 8646
Tresinney *Cnwll* 4 1081
Treskinnick Cross *Cnwll* 5 2098
Treslea *Cnwll* 4 1368
Tresmeer *Cnwll* 5 2387
Tresparrett *Cnwll* 4 1491
Tressait *P & K* 132 8160
Tresta *Shet* 153 3650
Tresta *Shet* 153 6090
Treswell *Notts* 75 7879
Treswithian *Cnwll* 2 6241
Trethawle *Cnwll* 5 2662
Trethevey *Cnwll* 4 0789
Trethewey *Cnwll* 2 3823
Trethomas *Caerph* 33 1888
Trethosa *Cnwll* 3 9454
Trethurgy *Cnwll* 3 0355
Tretio *Pembks* 30 7829
Tretire *Herefd* 46 5123
Tretower *Powys* 33 1821
Treuddyn *Flints* 70 2557
Trevadlock *Cnwll* 5 2679
Trevague *Cnwll* 5 2379
Trevalga *Cnwll* 4 0890
Trevalyn *Wrexhm* 71 3856
Trevanger *Cnwll* 4 9677
Trevanson *Cnwll* 4 9773
Trevarrack *Cnwll* 2 4731
Trevarren *Cnwll* 4 9160
Trevarrian *Cnwll* 4 8566
Trevarrick *Cnwll* 3 9843
Trevarth *Cnwll* 3 7240
Trevaughan *Carmth* 31 2015
Treveal *Cnwll* 2 4740
Treveal *Cnwll* 4 7858
Treveale *Cnwll* 3 8751
Treveighan *Cnwll* 4 0779
Trevellas Downs *Cnwll* 3 7452
Trevelmond *Cnwll* 5 2063
Trevemper *Cnwll* 4 8159
Treveneague *Cnwll* 2 5432
Treveor *Cnwll* 3 9841
Treverbyn *Cnwll* 3 8849
Treverbyn *Cnwll* 4 0157
Treverva *Cnwll* 3 7531
Trevescan *Cnwll* 2 3524
Trevethin *Torfn* 34 2801
Trevia *Cnwll* 4 0983
Trevigro *Cnwll* 5 3369
Trevilla *Cnwll* 3 8239
Trevilledor *Cnwll* 4 8867
Trevilson *Cnwll* 3 8455
Trevine *Pembks* 30 8432
Treviscoe *Cnwll* 3 9455
Treviskey *Cnwll* 3 9340
Trevissick *Cnwll* 3 0248
Trevithal *Cnwll* 2 4626
Trevithick *Cnwll* 4 8862
Trevithick *Cnwll* 3 9645
Trevivian *Cnwll* 4 1785
Trevoll *Cnwll* 4 8358
Trevone *Cnwll* 4 8975
Trevor *Denbgs* 70 2742
Trevorgans *Cnwll* 2 4025
Trevorrick *Cnwll* 4 8672
Trevorrick *Cnwll* 4 9273
Trevose *Cnwll* 4 8675
Trew *Cnwll* 2 6129
Trewalder *Cnwll* 4 0782
Trewalkin *Powys* 45 1531
Trewarlett *Cnwll* 5 3380
Trewarmett *Cnwll* 4 0686
Trewarthenick *Cnwll* 3 9044
Trewassa *Cnwll* 4 1486
Trewavas *Cnwll* 2 5926
Treween *Cnwll* 5 2182
Trewellard *Cnwll* 2 3733
Trewen *Cnwll* 5 2583
Trewen *Cnwll* 4 0577
Trewennack *Cnwll* 2 6728
Trewent *Pembks* 30 0197
Trewern *Powys* 58 2811
Trewetha *Cnwll* 4 0080
Trewethern *Cnwll* 4 0076
Trewidland *Cnwll* 5 2559
Trewillis *Cnwll* 3 7717
Trewince *Cnwll* 3 8633
Trewint *Cnwll* 4 1072
Trewint *Cnwll* 5 2180
Trewint *Cnwll* 5 2963
Trewirgie *Cnwll* 3 8845
Trewithian *Cnwll* 3 8737
Trewoodloe *Cnwll* 5 3271
Trewoofe *Cnwll* 2 4425
Trewoon *Cnwll* 2 6819
Trewoon *Cnwll* 3 9952
Treworgan *Cnwll* 3 8349
Treworlas *Cnwll* 3 8938
Treworld *Cnwll* 4 1190
Treworthal *Cnwll* 3 8839
Treyarnon *Cnwll* 4 8673
Treyford *W Susx* 14 8218
Triangle *W York* 82 0422
Trickett's Cross *Dorset* 12 0800
Triermain *Cumb* 102 5966
Triffleton *Pembks* 30 9724
Trillacott *Cnwll* 5 2689
Trimdon *Dur* 96 3634
Trimdon Colliery *Dur* 96 3735
Trimdon Grange *Dur* 96 3635
Trimingham *Norfk* 67 2838
Trimley *Suffk* 55 2737
Trimley Heath *Suffk* 55 2738
Trimley Lower Street *Suffk* 55 2636
Trimpley *Worcs* 60 7978
Trims Green *Herts* 39 4717
Trimsaran *Carmth* 32 4504
Trimstone *Devon* 19 5043
Trinafour *P & K* 132 7264
Trinant *Caerph* 33 2099
Tring *Herts* 38 9211
Tring Wharf *Herts* 38 9212
Tringford *Herts* 38 9113
Trinity *Angus* 134 6061
Trinity *Jersey* 158 0000
Trinity Gask *P & K* 125 9618
Triscombe *Somset* 20 9237
Triscombe *Somset* 20 1535
Trislaig *Highld* 130 0874
Trispen *Cnwll* 3 8450
Tritlington *Nthumb* 103 2092
Troan *Cnwll* 4 8957
Trochry *P & K* 125 9740
Troedrhiwfuwch *Caerph* 33 1204
Troedyraur *Cerdgn* 42 3245
Troedyrhiw *Myr Td* 33 0702
Trofarth *Conwy* 69 8571
Trois Bois *Jersey* 158 0000
Troon *Cnwll* 2 6638
Troon *S Ayrs* 106 3230
Troston *Suffk* 54 8972
Troswell *Cnwll* 5 2592
Trotshill *Worcs* 47 8855
Trottiscliffe *Kent* 27 6460
Trotton *W Susx* 14 8322
Trough Gate *Lancs* 81 8821
Troughend *Nthumb* 102 8692
Troutbeck *Cumb* 93 3927
Troutbeck *Cumb* 87 4002
Troutbeck Bridge *Cumb* 87 4000
Troway *Derbys* 74 3879
Trowbridge *Wilts* 22 8558
Trowell *Notts* 62 4839
Trowle Common *Wilts* 22 8458
Trowse Newton *Norfk* 67 2406
Troy *W York* 82 2439
Trudoxhill *Somset* 22 7443
Trull *Somset* 20 2122
Trumfleet *S York* 83 6011
Trumpan *Highld* 136 2261
Trumpet *Herefd* 47 6539
Trumpington *Cambs* 53 4454
Trumpsgreen *Surrey* 25 9967
Trunch *Norfk* 67 2834
Trunnah *Lancs* 80 3442
Truro *Cnwll* 3 8244
Truscott *Cnwll* 5 2985
Trusham *Devon* 8 8582
Trusley *Derbys* 73 2535
Trusthorpe *Lincs* 77 5183
Trysull *Staffs* 60 8594
Tubney *Oxon* 36 4399
Tuckenhay *Devon* 7 8156
Tuckhill *Shrops* 60 7888
Tuckingmill *Cnwll* 2 6540
Tuckingmill *Wilts* 22 9329
Tuckton *Dorset* 12 1492
Tucoyse *Cnwll* 3 9645
Tuddenham *Suffk* 53 7371
Tuddenham *Suffk* 55 1948
Tudeley *Kent* 16 6245
Tudhoe *Dur* 96 2535
Tudorville *Herefd* 46 5922
Tudweiloig *Gwynd* 56 2436
Tuesley *Surrey* 25 9642
Tuffley *Gloucs* 35 8314
Tufton *Hants* 24 4546
Tufton *Pembks* 30 0428
Tugby *Leics* 63 7601
Tugford *Shrops* 59 5587
Tughall *Nthumb* 111 2126
Tullibody *Clacks* 116 8595
Tullich *Ag & B* 123 0815
Tullich *Highld* 140 6328
Tullich *Highld* 147 8576
Tulliemet *P & K* 125 0052
Tulloch *Abers* 143 8031
Tulloch *Stirlg* 124 5120
Tulloch Station *Highld* 131 3580
Tullochgorm *Ag & B* 114 9695
Tullybeagles Lodge *P & K* 125 0136
Tullynessle *Abers* 142 5519
Tulse Hill *Gt Lon* 27 3172
Tumble *Carmth* 32 5411
Tumbler's Green *Essex* 40 8025
Tumby *Lincs* 76 2359
Tumby Woodside *Lincs* 77 2757
Tummel Bridge *P & K* 132 7659
Tunbridge Wells *Kent* 16 5839
Tundergarth *D & G* 101 1780
Tungate *Norfk* 67 2629
Tunstall *E R Yk* 85 3031
Tunstall *Kent* 28 8961
Tunstall *Lancs* 87 6073
Tunstall *N York* 89 2196
Tunstall *Norfk* 67 4107
Tunstall *Staffs* 72 7727
Tunstall *Staffs* 72 8651
Tunstall *Suffk* 55 3655
Tunstall *T & W* 96 3953
Tunstead *Derbys* 74 1074
Tunstead *Norfk* 67 2921
Tunstead Milton *Derbys* 79 0180
Tunworth *Hants* 24 6748
Tupsley *Herefd* 46 5340
Tur Langton *Leics* 50 7194
Turgis Green *Hants* 24 6959
Turkdean *Gloucs* 36 1017
Turleigh *Wilts* 22 8060
Turleygreen *Shrops* 60 7685
Turn *Lancs* 81 8118
Turnastone *Herefd* 46 3536
Turnberry *S Ayrs* 106 2005
Turnchapel *Devon* 6 4953
Turnditch *Derbys* 73 2946
Turner Green *Lancs* 81 6030
Turner's Green *E Susx* 16 6319
Turner's Green *Warwks* 48 1969
Turner's Hill *W Susx* 15 3435
Turners Puddle *Dorset* 11 8393
Turnford *Herts* 39 3604
Turnhouse *C Edin* 117 1674
Turnworth *Dorset* 11 8207
Turriff *Abers* 142 7250
Turton Bottoms *Gt Man* 81 7315
Turves *Cambs* 64 3396
Turvey *Beds* 38 9452
Turville *Bucks* 37 7691
Turville Heath *Bucks* 37 7490
Turweston *Bucks* 49 6037
Tushielaw Inn *Border* 109 3017
Tushingham cum Grindley *Ches* 71 5246
Tutbury *Staffs* 73 2128
Tutnall *Worcs* 60 9970
Tutshill *Gloucs* 34 5494
Tuttington *Norfk* 67 2227
Tutwell *Cnwll* 5 3875
Tuxford *Notts* 75 7471
Twatt *Ork* 153 2724
Twatt *Shet* 153 3253
Twechar *E Duns* 116 6975
Tweedmouth *Nthumb* 119 9952
Tweedsmuir *Border* 108 1024
Twelve Oaks *E Susx* 16 6820
Twelveheads *Cnwll* 3 7542
Twemlow Green *Ches* 79 7868
Twenty *Lincs* 64 1520
Twerton *Somset* 22 7264
Twickenham *Gt Lon* 26 1673
Twigworth *Gloucs* 35 8422
Twineham *W Susx* 15 2519
Twineham Green *W Susx* 15 2520
Twinhoe *Somset* 22 7559
Twinstead *Essex* 54 8636
Twiss Green *Ches* 79 6595
Twitchen *Devon* 19 7930
Twitchen *Shrops* 46 3779
Twitham *Kent* 29 2656
Two Bridges *Devon* 6 6174
Two Dales *Derbys* 74 2763
Two Gates *Staffs* 61 2101
Two Mile Oak Cross *Devon* 7 8468
Two Pots *Devon* 19 5344
Two Waters *Herts* 38 0505
Twycross *Leics* 62 3304
Twyford *Berks* 37 7976
Twyford *Bucks* 49 6626
Twyford *Hants* 13 4824
Twyford *Leics* 63 7210
Twyford *Lincs* 63 9323
Twyford *Norfk* 66 0123
Twyford Common *Herefd* 46 5135
Twyn-carno *Caerph* 33 1108
Twyn-y-Sheriff *Mons* 34 4005
Twyn-yr-Odyn *V Glam* 33 1173
Twynholm *D & G* 99 6654
Twyning *Gloucs* 47 8936
Twyning Green *Gloucs* 47 9036
Twynllanan *Carmth* 44 7524
Twywell *Nhants* 51 9578
Ty'n-dwr *Denbgs* 70 2341
Ty'n-y-bryn *Rhondd* 33 0087
Ty'n-y-coedcae *Caerph* 33 1988
Ty'n-y-Groes *Conwy* 69 7771
Ty-nant *Conwy* 70 9944
Ty-nant *Gwynd* 58 9026
Tyberton *Herefd* 46 3839
Tyburn *W Mids* 61 1391
Tycroes *Carmth* 32 6010
Tycrwyn *Powys* 58 1018
Tydd Gote *Lincs* 65 4518
Tydd St Giles *Cambs* 65 4216
Tydd St Mary *Lincs* 65 4418
Tye *Hants* 13 7302
Tye Green *Essex* 39 5424
Tye Green *Essex* 53 5935
Tye Green *Essex* 40 7821
Tyersal *W York* 82 1932
Tyldesley *Gt Man* 79 6802
Tyler Hill *Kent* 29 1461
Tyler's Green *Essex* 39 5005
Tylers Green *Bucks* 26 9093
Tylers Green *Surrey* 27 3552
Tylorstown *Rhondd* 33 0095
Tylwch *Powys* 58 9780
Tyn-y-nant *Rhondd* 33 0685
Tyndrum *Stirlg* 123 3230
Tyneham *Dorset* 11 8880
Tynemouth *T & W* 103 3669
Tynewydd *Rhondd* 33 9398
Tyninghame *E Loth* 118 6179
Tynron *D & G* 100 8093
Tynygongl *IOA* 68 5082
Tynygraig *Cerdgn* 43 6969
Tyringham *Bucks* 38 8547
Tyseley *W Mids* 61 1184
Tythegston *Brdgnd* 33 8578
Tytherington *Ches* 79 9175
Tytherington *Gloucs* 35 6688
Tytherington *Somset* 22 7644
Tytherington *Wilts* 22 9141
Tytherleigh *Devon* 10 3103
Tytherton Lucas *Wilts* 35 9474
Tywardreath *Cnwll* 3 0854
Tywardreath Highway *Cnwll* 3 0755
Tywyn *Conwy* 69 7878
Tywyn *Gwynd* 57 5800


# U


Ubbeston Green *Suffk* 55 3271
Ubley *Somset* 21 5258
Uckerby *N York* 89 2402

# Y

# Z

# mileage chart

The distances between towns on the mileage chart are given to the nearest mile, and are measured along the normal AA-recommended routes. It should be noted that AA-recommended routes do not necessarily follow the shortest distance between places but are based on the quickest travelling time, making maximum use of motorways and dual carriageways.

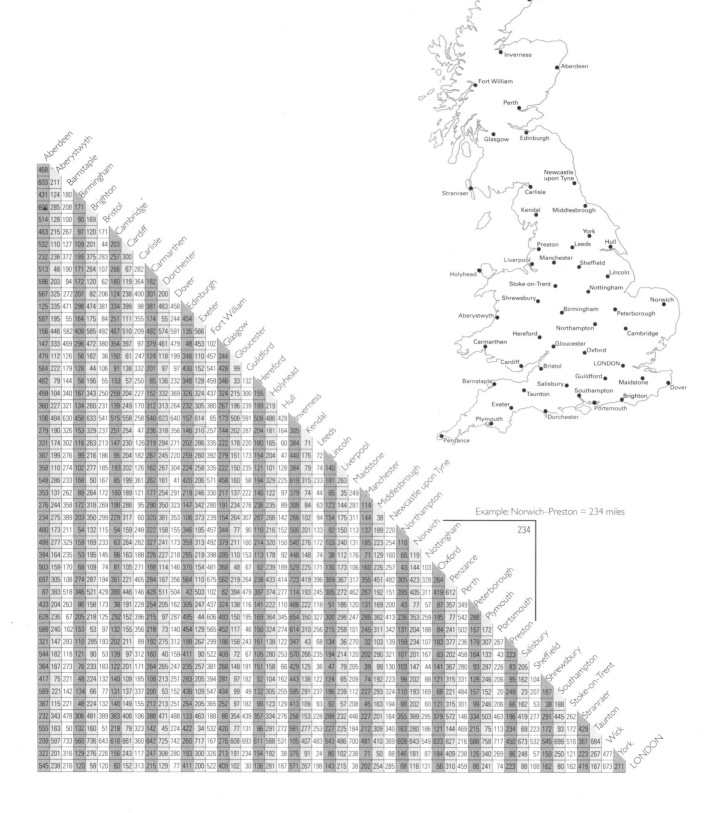

Example: Norwich–Preston = 234 miles

Mileage chart (distances in miles). Cities in diagonal order:
Aberdeen, Aberystwyth, Barnstaple, Birmingham, Brighton, Bristol, Cambridge, Cardiff, Carlisle, Carmarthen, Dorchester, Dover, Edinburgh, Exeter, Fort William, Glasgow, Gloucester, Guildford, Hereford, Holyhead, Hull, Inverness, Kendal, Leeds, Lincoln, Liverpool, Maidstone, Manchester, Middlesbrough, Newcastle upon Tyne, Northampton, Norwich, Nottingham, Oxford, Penzance, Perth, Peterborough, Plymouth, Portsmouth, Preston, Salisbury, Sheffield, Shrewsbury, Southampton, Stoke-on-Trent, Stranraer, Taunton, Wick, York, LONDON

```
Aberdeen            468
Aberystwyth         603 211
Barnstaple          431 124 180
Birmingham          696 285 208 171
Brighton            514 128 100  90 169
Bristol             463 215 267  97 120 171
Cambridge           532 110 127 109 201  44 203
Cardiff             232 236 372 199 375 283 257 300
Carlisle            513  48 190 171 264 107 266  67 282
Carmarthen          596 203  94 172 120  62 180 119 364 182
Dorchester          587 325 272 207  82 206 124 238 400 301 200
Dover               125 335 471 298 474 381 334 399  98 381 463 458
Edinburgh           587 195  55 164 175  84 251 111 355 174  55 244 454
Exeter              156 446 582 409 585 492 467 510 209 492 574 591 135 566
Fort William        147 333 469 296 472 380 354 397  97 379 461 479  48 453 102
Glasgow             479 112 126  56 162  36 150  61 247 124 118 199 346 110 457 344
Gloucester          564 222 179 128  44 106  91 138 332 201  97  97 430 152 541 428  99
Guildford           482  79 144  58 196  55 153  57 250  85 136 232 348 128 459 346  33 132
Hereford            459 104 340 167 343 250 259 204 227 152 332 369 326 324 437 324 215 300 155
Holyhead            360 227 321 134 260 231 139 249 170 312 313 264 232 305 380 267 196 239 199 219
Hull                106 494 630 458 633 541 515 558 258 540 623 640 157 614  65 173 506 591 508 486 428
Inverness           279 190 326 153 329 237 251 254  47 236 318 356 146 310 257 144 202 287 204 181 164 305
Kendal              331 174 302 116 263 213 147 230 126 219 294 271 202 286 335 222 178 220 180 165  60 384  71
Leeds               387 199 276  99 216 186  95 204 182 267 245 220 259 260 392 279 151 173 154 204  47 440 176  72
Lincoln             358 110 274 102 277 185 193 202 126 162 267 304 224 258 335 222 150 235 121 101 128 384  79  74 140
Liverpool           548 286 233 168  50 167  85 199 361 262 161  41 420 206 571 458 160  58 194 329 225 619 315 233 181 263
Maidstone           353 131 262  89 264 172 160 189 121 177 254 291 219 246 330 217 137 222 140 122  97 379  74  44  85  35 249
Manchester          276 244 358 172 318 269 198 286  95 290 350 323 147 342 280 191 234 276 236 235  89 308  84  63 123 144 281 114
Middlesbrough       234 275 389 203 350 299 229 317  60 320 381 353 106 373 239 154 264 307 267 266 142 266  92 154 175 311 144  38
Newcastle upon Tyne 480 173 211  54 132 115  54 159 248 222 158 155 346 195 457 344  77  90 110 216 206 512 206 201 133  97 150 113 137 189 220
Northampton         488 277 329 159 169 233  63 264 282 327 241 173 359 313 492 379 211 160 214 320 150 540 276 172 103 240 131 185 223 254 116
Norwich             394 164 235  53 195 145  86 163 188 226 227 218 265 219 398 285 110 153 113 178  92 446 148  74  38 112 176  71 129 160  66 119
Nottingham          503 159 170  68 109  74  81 105 271 168 114 146 370 154 481 368  48  67  82 239 189 529 225 171 130 173 106 160 226 257  43 144 103
Oxford              697 305 108 274 287 194 361 221 465 284 167 356 564 110 675 562 219 264 238 433 414 723 419 396 369 367 317 355 451 482 305 423 328 264
Penzance             87 383 518 346 521 429 380 446 146 428 511 504  42 503 102  62 394 479 397 374 277 114 193 245 305 272 462 267 192 151 395 405 311 419 612
Perth               433 204 263  86 158 173  38 191 228 254 205 162 305 247 437 324 138 116 141 222 110 486 222 118  51 186 120 131 169 200  43  77  57  87 357 349
Peterborough        628 236  67 205 218 125 292 152 396 215  97 287 495  44 606 493 150 195 169 364 345 654 350 327 300 298 247 286 382 413 236 353 259 195  77 542 288
Plymouth            588 240 162 153  53  97 132 155 356 218  73 140 454 129 565 452 117  46 134  68 134 256 215 258 101 245 311 342 131 204 188  84 241 502 157 172
Portsmouth          321 147 283 110 285 193 202 211  89 192 275 312 188 267 299 186 158 243 161 138 122 347  43  68 134 377 236 179 307 267
Preston             544 182 118 121  90  53 139  97 312 160  40 159 411  90 522 409  72  67 105 280 253 570 266 235 194 214 120 202 290 321 107 201 167  63 202 458 164 133  43 223
Salisbury           364 167 273  76 233 183 122 201 171 264 265 247 235 257 381 268 148 191 151 158  66 429 125  36  47  79 205  39  99 130 103 147  44 141 367 267  93 297 226  83 205
Sheffield           417  75 221  48 224 132 140 109 185 108 213 251 283 205 394 281  97 182  52 104 162 443 138 122 124  65 209  74 192 223  98 202  88 121 315 331 129 246 206  95 162 104
Shrewsbury          569 221 142 134  66  77 131 137 337 200  53 152 436 109 547 434  99  49 132 305 255 595 291 237 196 239 112 227 293 324 110 193 169  66 221 484 157 152  20 248  23 207 187
Southampton         387 115 221  48 224 132 140 149 155 212 213 251 254 205 365 252  97 182  99 123 129 413 109  93  92  57 208  45 163 194  98 202  60 121 315 301  90 246 206  66 162  53  38 188
Stoke-on-Trent      232 343 478 306 481 389 363 406 106 388 471 488 133 463 188  86 354 439 357 334 276 288 153 228 288 232 446 227 201 164 355 389 295 379 572 146 334 503 463 196 419 277 291 445 262
Stranraer           555 163  50 132 160  51 218  79 323 142  45 224 422  34 532 420  77 131  96 291 272 581 277 253 227 225 184 212 309 340 163 280 186 121 144 469 215  75 113 234  69 223 172  93 172 429
Taunton             208 597 733 560 736 643 618 661 360 642 725 742 260 717 167 276 608 693 611 588 531 105 407 483 543 486 700 481 410 369 609 643 549 633 827 216 588 717 450 673 532 545 699 516 361 684
Wick                322 201 316 129 276 226 156 243 117 247 308 280 193 300 326 213 191 234 194 192  38 375  91  24  80 102 238  71  50  88 146 181  87 184 409 238 126 340 269  96 248  57 150 250 121 223 267 477
York                545 238 216 120  59 120  60 152 313 215 129  77 411 200 522 409 102  30 136 281 187 571 267 143 215  38 220 254 285  68 116 131  56 310 459  86 241  74 223  88 168 162  80 162 419 167 673 211
LONDON
```